Electronic Devices and Circuits

Electronic Devices and Circuits

Anil K. Maini
Director
Laser Science and Technology Centre
Defence Research and Development Organization
New Delhi

Varsha Agrawal
Scientist
Laser Science and Technology Centre
Defence Research and Development Organization
New Delhi

Electronic Devices and Circuits

Other Wiley Editorial Offices:
John Wiley & Sons, Inc. 111 River Street, Hoboken, NJ 07030, USA
Wiley-VCH Verlag GmbH, Pappellaee 3, D-69469 Weinheim, Germany
John Wiley & Sons Australia Ltd, 42 McDougall Street, Milton, Queensland 4064, Australia
John Wiley & Sons (Asia) Pte Ltd, 2 Clementi Loop #02-01, Jin Xing Distripark, Singapore 129809
John Wiley & Sons Canada Ltd, 22 Worcester Road, Etobicoke, Ontario, Canada, M9W 1L1

First Edition: 2009
ISBN: 978-81-265-1895-1
www.wileyindia.com
Reprint Edition: 2011

Printed by: Ar-Emm-International

Dedicated to my brother, Shri Sunil Maini
For his unconditional love and support

– Anil K. Maini

Dedicated to my father, Shri Subhash Chandra Agrawal
Thank you for being as special as you are

– Varsha Agrawal

Preface

Electronic Devices and Circuits is one of the important subjects in a course in Electronics and Communication, Instrumentation and Control, Computer Science and Information Technology and Electrical Engineering disciplines. It is so because it is essential to understanding the operational basics and design of linear integrated circuits, digital electronics devices and electronic circuits and to some extent instrumentation also. It is therefore essential for students and engineers to understand electronic devices and circuits and also the building blocks of electronics configured around them.

Electronic Devices and Circuits is a complete book that provides comprehensive coverage of different topics of analog electronics related to electronics devices including discrete devices as well as integrated circuits and electronic circuits. Choice of topics is based on what is taught in prominent Indian and International universities at undergraduate and graduate levels. Each chapter in the book, whether it is related to operational fundamentals or applications, is amply illustrated with diagrams and design examples. Each chapter includes a comprehensive self-evaluation exercise comprising multiple-choice questions (with answers) and other type of objective-type questions (with answers). Unlike most of the books in print on the subject that are either too brief, lacking in illustrated examples and examination-oriented study material, or too voluminous, containing lot of redundant material, the book has been written keeping in mind the topics taught in the subject at undergraduate and graduate levels. The book should also be of interest to practicing engineers and scientists who wish to update their knowledge on the subject.

The book is divided in 17 chapters covering six major topics, which include *Semiconductor Devices* (Chapters 1 to 7), *Small Signal Amplifiers and their low and high frequency response* (Chapters 8 and 9), *Large Signal Amplifiers* (Chapters 10), *Negative Feedback* (Chapter 11), *Oscillators and Wave-Shaping Circuits* (Chapters 12 and 13), *Power Supplies: Linear and Switched Mode* (Chapters 14 and 15) and *Opamp Fundamentals and Applications* (Chapters 16 and 17). The contents of each of the 17 chapters are briefly described in the following paragraphs.

The first seven chapters cover the fundamentals of the semiconductor devices. These include semiconductor diodes, bipolar junction transistors (BJT), field effect transistors (FET), unijunction transistors (UJT) and thyristors and optoelectronic devices. The pattern followed in these chapters is that each device is first introduced by explaining its internal behavior which is then followed up by a discussion on its characteristics and equivalent circuit. Application circuits and design-related information such as package types, lead identification of the devices are also discussed at length in these chapters. Special efforts have been made to give the students a perfect blend of theoretical as well as practical information related to the semiconductor devices.

The first chapter gives a basic introduction to semiconductors to set a platform for understanding the principle of operation of the semiconductor devices discussed in the following six chapters. Semiconductor diode is the most fundamental semiconductor device and is in focus in Chapter 2 of the book. Topics covered include construction of semiconductor diode, its principle of operation, different types of diodes, their application circuits and design-related information including lead identification, testing methods and package types. Different types of diodes discussed in the chapter include PN junction diode, breakdown diodes, varactor diodes, Schottky diodes, power diodes, photodiodes and LEDs. Bipolar junction transistors are discussed in Chapters 3 and 4. Chapter 3 covers the fundamentals of BJT operation highlighting the three BJT configurations, namely, the common-emitter, common-base and common-collector configurations and their input and output characteristics. Lead identification, testing methods and package styles of transistors are also discussed in the chapter. The various transistor biasing configuration circuits are discussed in Chapter 4. These include fixed-bias, self-bias, voltage-divider bias, collector-to-base bias and other miscellaneous configurations.

The focus of chapter 5 is on FETs. The topics covered include construction of FETs, types – junction FETs (JFETs), metal oxide semiconductor FETs (MOSFETs), complementary metal oxide semiconductor (CMOS), vertical metal oxide semiconductor (VMOS) and dual-gate MOSFETs, characteristics, biasing configurations, application circuits and an introduction to insulated gate bipolar transistors (IGBT). Chapter 6 talks about UJTs and devices belonging to the thyristor family including PNPN diode, silicon-controlled rectifier (SCR), DIAC and TRIAC. Optoelectronic devices including photodiodes, phototransistors, photoFETs, photoSCRs, thermal detectors, pyroelectric detectors, LEDs and different types of displays are discussed in Chapter 7. Detailed coverage of the UJTs, thyristors and optoelectronic devices is a major highlight of the book as these are topics which are very important and yet are seldom covered in details in books on the subject. The concepts underlying the different fundamental topics of the semiconductor devices in first seven chapters have been amply illustrated with large number of solved examples to help students have a firm understanding about the functioning of these devices, which is critical to comprehend the advanced topics covered in the subsequent chapters.

After covering the semiconductor devices in Chapters 1 to 7, focus in the following chapters shifts to the analysis and design of electronic circuits and subsystems including amplifiers, oscillators, multivibrators, power supplies and operational amplifiers. The approach followed is to first introduce the circuit on a descriptive basis so as to have a conceptual understanding of its behavior and then follow it up with its mathematical analysis to have quantitative information on its functioning. Chapters 8 and 9 focus on detailed discussion on the design and frequency response of small signal amplifiers configured around BJTs and FETs. Topics covered in these chapters include small signal h-parameter model of BJTs, analysis of BJT amplifiers using h-parameter model, small signal model of FETs, analysis of FET amplifiers and low and high frequency response of these amplifiers. Effect of cascading different amplifier stages is also discussed in detail in these chapters. Chapter 10 covers in detail the operational fundamentals and different classes of large signal or power amplifiers. Design of different types of Class A, B, AB, C and D amplifiers is deliberated in the chapter. The concept of negative feedback in amplifiers, types of feedback networks including series–series feedback, series–shunt feedback, shunt–series feedback and shunt–shunt feedback and their properties are covered in Chapter 11. Following the discussion of negative feedback in Chapter 11, the underlying concepts of positive feedback and oscillator circuits are discussed in Chapter 12. Topics covered include Barkhausen criterion of oscillators, types of oscillators including RC oscillators (RC phase shift, Bubba, Wein Bridge and Quadrature oscillators), LC oscillators (Armstrong, Colpitts, Clapp and Hartley oscillators) and crystal oscillators and frequency stability criterion in oscillators. Chapter 13 discusses another class of positive feedback circuits referred to as multivibrators. The chapter also focuses on design and analysis of simple *R-C*, *R-L* and diode-based circuits including passive low-pass and high-pass filters, diode-based clippers and clampers and so on.

Chapters 14 and 15 are devoted to power supplies. Discussion begins with classification of power supplies into two major categories, namely, linear power supplies and switched mode power supplies and the comparison between the two. Chapter 14 focuses on linear power supplies while the switched mode power supplies are covered in Chapter 15. Different constituents of linear power supply including transformers, filters and regulators are covered in detail in Chapter 14 as regards their operational fundamentals and design concepts. Different types of filter circuits discussed in the chapter include capacitor, inductor, LC and CLC filters and different types of regulators include emitter-follower, series-pass and shunt regulators. Important power supply parameters are also discussed in the chapter. Switched mode power supplies, different types of switching converters including flyback, forward and push–pull converters and switching regulators including buck, boost and buck-boost regulators are covered in Chapter 15. Detailed discussion on power supplies is another highlight of the book.

The last two chapters of the book, that is, Chapters 16 and 17 cover a very important and versatile device – operational amplifier. Chapter 16 covers the fundamental topics of operational amplifiers including their internal architecture, important parameters and types. As a natural follow-up of the chapter, the concluding chapter, that is Chapter 17, highlights the innumerable applications of operational amplifiers including use of operational amplifiers to configure different amplifier circuits, filters, integrators, differentiators, clippers, clampers, comparators and so on.

The motivation to write this book and the selection of topics to be covered were driven mainly by the absence of a textbook which covers all topics of electronics devices and circuits taught at undergraduate and graduate levels. As the authors, we have made an honest attempt to cover the subject in entirety by including comprehensive treatment of all topics on the subject of electronics devices and circuits. Considerable thought has been given to the presentation of the text so as to facilitate the use of the book as self-study material. The effort is to give the undergraduate and graduate students of Electronics and Communication, Instrumentation, Computer science, IT and Electrical engineering a comprehensive yet concise must read textbook on Electronic Devices and Circuits.

Anil K. Maini

Varsha Agrawal

Contents

Preface VII

1 Introduction to Semiconductor Physics 1

1.1 Insulators, Conductors and Semiconductors 1
Insulators 1
Conductors 2
Semiconductors 2

1.2 Semiconductor Types 4
Intrinsic Semiconductors 4
N-Type Extrinsic Semiconductors 10
P-Type Extrinsic Semiconductors 14

1.3 Law of Mass Action 18

1.4 Drift and Diffusion Carriers 20

1.5 Hall Effect 21
Key Terms 22
Objective-Type Exercises 22
Review Questions 23
Problems 24
Answers 24

2 Semiconductor Diodes 25

2.1 P–N Junction 25
Forward-Bias Condition 27
Reverse-Bias Condition 27

2.2 Ideal Diode 28

2.3 Practical Diode 29

2.4 V–I Characteristics of a Diode 29

2.5 Temperature Dependence of the V–I Characteristics 30

2.6 Diode Specifications 31

2.7 Diode Resistance 33
Static Resistance 34
Dynamic Resistance 35
Average AC Resistance 36

2.8 Diode Junction Capacitance 37
Transition Capacitance 38
Diffusion Capacitance 38

2.9 Diode Equivalent Circuits 38

2.10 Load-Line Analysis of a Diode Circuit 43
DC Applied Voltage 43
AC Applied Voltage 44

2.11 Breakdown Diodes 48
Avalanche Diodes 49
Zener Diodes 49

2.12 Varactor Diodes 50

2.13 Tunnel Diodes 51

2.14 Schottky Diodes 53
2.15 Point-Contact Diodes and Power Diodes 54
Point-Contact Diodes 54
Power Diodes 54
2.16 Light-Emitting Diodes 54
2.17 Photodiodes 56
2.18 Connecting Diodes in Series and in Parallel 56
Diodes in Series 56
Diodes in Parallel 57
2.19 Diode Numbers and Lead Identification 58
2.20 Diode Testing 59
Key Terms 60
Objective-Type Exercises 61
Review Questions 62
Problems 63
Answers 65

3 Bipolar Junction Transistors 69
3.1 Bipolar Junction Transistor versus Vacuum Triode 70
3.2 Transistor Construction and Types 70
NPN Transistor 70
PNP Transistor 70
3.3 Transistor Operation 71
3.4 Common-Base Configuration 73
Input Characteristics 73
Output Characteristics 75
3.5 Common-Emitter Configuration 78
Input Characteristics 78
Output Characteristics 79
3.6 Common-Collector Configuration 83
Input Characteristics 83
Output Characteristics 83
3.7 Ebers–Moll Model of Transistors 86
3.8 Transistor Specifications and Maximum Ratings 87
3.9 Lead Identification 89
3.10 Transistor Testing 92
3.11 Phototransistors 94
3.12 Power Transistors 94
3.13 Transistor Construction Techniques 96
Point-Contact Transistors 96
Grown-Junction Type Transistors 96
Alloy-Junction Transistors 97
Diffusion Transistors 97
Epitaxial Transistors 98
Annular Transistors 98
Key Terms 98

	Objective-Type Exercises	98
	Review Questions	101
	Problems	101
	Answers	102
4	**Transistor Biasing and Thermal Stabilization**	**103**
4.1	Operating Point	103
4.2	Common-Emitter Configuration	105
	Fixed-Bias Circuit	105
	Emitter-Bias or Self-Bias Configuration	110
	Voltage-Divider-Bias with Emitter-Bias Configuration	115
	Collector-to-Base-Bias Configuration	124
4.3	Common-Base Circuit	128
4.4	Common-Collector Circuit	130
4.5	Bias Stabilization	132
	Stability Factor	133
	Stability Factor ($S_{I_{CO}}$)	134
	Stability Factor ($S_{V_{BE}}$)	136
	Stability Factor (S_β)	138
4.6	Bias Compensation	144
	Diode Compensation for Base–Emitter Voltage (V_{BE})	144
	Diode Compensation for Leakage Current (I_{CO})	145
	Thermistor Compensation	146
4.7	Thermal Runaway	146
	Operating-Point Considerations in Thermal Runaway	148
4.8	Transistor Switch	152
	Transistor Switching Delays	153
	Key Terms	157
	Objective-Type Exercises	157
	Review Questions	158
	Problems	159
	Answers	161
5	**Field Effect Transistors**	**165**
5.1	Bipolar Junction Transistors versus Field Effect Transistors	165
5.2	Junction Field Effect Transistors	166
	Construction and Principle of Operation	166
	Characteristic Curves	167
	Effect of Temperature on JFET Parameters	170
5.3	Metal Oxide Field Effect Transistors	171
	Depletion MOSFETs	171
	Enhancement MOSFETs	173
5.4	FET Parameters and Specifications	178
	Characteristic Parameters	178
	FET Datasheet Specifications	180
5.5	Differences between JFETs and MOSFETs	182
5.6	Handling MOSFETs	182

5.7 Biasing JFETs 183
Common-Source Configuration 183
Common-Drain Configuration 190
Common-Gate Configuration 192
5.8 Biasing MOSFETs 192
Depletion MOSFETs 192
Enhancement MOSFETs 194
5.9 FET Applications 200
5.10 Testing FETs 203
5.11 Dual-Gate MOSFET 204
5.12 VMOS Devices 205
5.13 CMOS Devices 206
5.14 Insulated Gate Bipolar Transistors (IGBTs) 207
Key Terms 209
Objective-Type Exercises 210
Review Questions 212
Problems 213
Answers 214

6 UJTs and Thyristors 215
6.1 Unijunction Transistor 215
Construction 216
Operational Principle 217
Current-Controllable Device 218
UJT Relaxation Oscillator Circuit 218
6.2 PNPN Diode 220
PNPN Diode Material 222
PNPN Diode Characteristics 222
PNPN Diode as Relaxation Oscillator 224
Rate Effect 226
6.3 Silicon-Controlled Rectifier 227
V–I Characteristics 228
Gate-Triggering Characteristics 228
6.4 DIAC and TRIAC 229
6.5 Thyristor Parameters 230
Repetitive Peak Reverse Voltage 231
Non-Repetitive Peak Reverse Voltage 231
Repetitive Peak OFF-State Voltage 232
Break-Over Voltage 232
Critical Rate of Rise of ON-State Current 232
Critical Rate of Rise of OFF-State Voltage 232
Holding Current and Holding Voltage 232
Latching Current 233
Amperes Squared Seconds (I^2t) Rating 233
6.6 Thyristors as Current-Controllable Devices 233
6.7 Thyristors in Series 234

6.8	Thyristors in Parallel	234
6.9	Applications of Thyristors	235
	SCR as Pulse Generator	235
	SCR as Bistable Multivibrator	236
	Half-Wave Controlled Rectifier	236
	Full-Wave Controlled Rectifier	236
	TRIAC-Based AC Power Control	238
	SCR-Based Crowbar Protection	238
6.10	Gate Turn-OFF Thyristors	241
6.11	Programmable Unijunction Transistor	241
	Key Terms	243
	Objective-Type Exercises	243
	Review Questions	246
	Problems	246
	Answers	248
7	**Optoelectronic Devices**	**249**
7.1	Optoelectronic Devices	250
	Classification	250
	Radiometric and Photometric Units	250
7.2	Photosensors	252
	Characteristic Parameters	252
7.3	Photoconductors	255
	Application Circuits	255
7.4	Photodiodes	259
	Photodiode Types	259
	V–I Characteristics of a Photodiode	262
	Photodiode Application Circuits	263
	Solar Cells	264
7.5	Phototransistors	268
	Phototransistor Application Circuits	269
7.6	PhotoFET, PhotoSCR and PhotoTRIAC	270
	PhotoFET	271
	PhotoSCR	271
	PhotoTRIAC	272
7.7	Photoemissive Sensors	273
	Vacuum Photodiodes	273
	Photomultiplier Tubes	273
	Image Intensifiers	274
7.8	Thermal Sensors	275
	Thermocouple and Thermopile	275
	Bolometers	276
	Pyroelectric Sensors	276
7.9	Displays	278
	Display Characteristics	278
	Types of Displays	278

7.10 Light-Emitting Diodes 279
LED Characteristic Curves 280
LED Parameters 280
LED Drive Circuits 281
7.11 Liquid Crystal Displays 284
Construction of an LCD 284
Driving an LCD 285
LCD Response Time 287
Liquid Crystal Display Types 287
Advantages and Disadvantages 288
7.12 Cathode Ray Tube Displays 288
Advantages and Disadvantages 289
7.13 Emerging Display Technologies 289
Organic Light-Emitting Diodes (OLEDs) 290
Digital Light Processing (DLP) Technology 290
Plasma Display Panels (PDP) 290
Field Emission Displays (FEDs) 290
Electronic Ink Displays 290
7.14 Optocouplers 291
Optocoupler Parameters 291
Optocoupler Application Circuits 293
Key Terms 297
Objective-Type Exercises 298
Review Questions 299
Problems 300
Answers 301

8 Small Signal Analysis of Amplifiers 303
8.1 Amplifier Bandwidth: General Frequency Considerations 303
8.2 Hybrid h-Parameter Model for an Amplifier 305
Determination of h-Parameters 306
8.3 Transistor Hybrid Model 307
h-Parameter Model for the Common-Emitter Configuration 307
Relationships between h-Parameters of Different Transistor Configurations 309
Graphical Determination of h-Parameters 312
8.4 Analysis of a Transistor Amplifier using Complete h-Parameter Model 314
8.5 Analysis of Transistor Amplifier Configurations using Simplified h-Parameter Model 320
Common-Emitter Configuration 320
Emitter–Follower Configuration 323
Common-Base Configuration 325
8.6 Small-Signal Analysis of FET Amplifiers 328
Common-Source FET Amplifier 329
Common-Drain FET Amplifier 330
8.7 Cascading Amplifiers 333
BJT Cascade Amplifier 334
FET Cascade Amplifier 337

8.8 Darlington Amplifiers 338
8.9 Cascode Amplifiers 343
8.10 Low-Frequency Response of Amplifiers 344
Low-Frequency Response of BJT Amplifiers 345
Low-Frequency Response of FET Amplifiers 347
8.11 Low-Frequency Response of Cascaded Amplifier Stages 350
Key Terms 351
Objective-Type Exercises 351
Review Questions 353
Problems 353
Answers 355

9 High-Frequency Response of Small Signal Amplifiers 357
9.1 High-Frequency Model for the Common-Emitter Transistor Amplifier 357
Hybrid-Π Conductances 358
Hybrid-Π Capacitances 361
Variation of Hybrid-Π Parameters 361
9.2 Common-Emitter Short-Circuit Current Gain 362
β Cut-Off Frequency 363
Gain-Bandwidth Product 364
α Cut-Off Frequency 364
9.3 Miller's Theorem 366
9.4 Common-Emitter Current Gain with Resistive Load 370
9.5 High-Frequency Response of Common-Collector Transistor Amplifier 371
9.6 High-Frequency Response of an FET Amplifier 374
Common-Source Amplifier at High Frequencies 374
Common-Drain Amplifier at High Frequencies 377
9.7 High-Frequency Response of Cascaded Amplifier Stages 378
9.8 Amplifier Rise Time and Sag 381
Rise Time 381
Tilt or Sag 381
Key Terms 382
Objective-Type Exercises 382
Review Questions 383
Problems 384
Answers 384

10 Large Signal Amplifiers 385
10.1 Large Signal Amplifiers 386
Classification 386
Large Signal Amplifier Characteristics 389
10.2 Class A Amplifiers 393
Class A Amplifier with Direct-Coupled Resistive Load 393
Transformer-Coupled Class A Amplifiers 397
Class A Push–Pull Amplifiers 403

10.3 Class B Amplifiers 405
Transformer-Coupled Push–Pull Class B Amplifier 406
Complementary-Symmetry Push–Pull Class B Amplifier 410
Quasi-Complementary Push–Pull Class B Amplifier 410
10.4 Class AB Amplifiers 413
10.5 Class C Amplifiers 413
10.6 Class D Amplifiers 414
10.7 Thermal Management of Power Transistors 417
Key Terms 418
Objective-Type Exercises 419
Review Questions 421
Problems 421
Answers 422

11 Feedback Amplifiers 423
11.1 Classification of Amplifiers 423
11.2 Amplifier with Negative Feedback 425
Effect of Negative Feedback on Gain 426
11.3 Advantages of Negative Feedback 429
Desensitivity (or Stability) of Gain 430
Effect on Bandwidth 430
Effect on Non-Linear Distortion 431
Effect on Noise 431
Effect on Input Resistance 432
Effect on Output Resistance 432
11.4 Feedback Topologies 434
11.5 Voltage-Series (Series–Shunt) Feedback 434
11.6 Voltage-Shunt (Shunt–Shunt) Feedback 440
11.7 Current-Series (Series–Series) Feedback 443
11.8 Current-Shunt (Shunt–Series) Feedback 448
Key Terms 452
Objective-Type Exercises 452
Review Questions 454
Problems 455
Answers 456

12 Sinusoidal Oscillators 457
12.1 Classification of Oscillators 457
12.2 Conditions for Oscillations: Barkhausen Criterion 458
Initiation of Oscillations 459
12.3 Types of Oscillators 460
RC Oscillators 460
LC Oscillators 460
Crystal Oscillators 460
12.4 RC Phase Shift Oscillator 461
12.5 Buffered RC Phase Shift Oscillator 465
12.6 Bubba Oscillator 467

12.7 Quadrature Oscillator 468
12.8 Twin-T Oscillator 469
12.9 Wien Bridge Oscillator 471
Distortion in Wien Bridge Oscillator 473
12.10 LC Oscillators 479
12.11 Armstrong Oscillator 479
12.12 Hartley Oscillator 481
12.13 Colpitt Oscillator 483
12.14 Clapp Oscillator 484
12.15 Crystal Oscillator 488
AC Equivalent Circuit of a Quartz Crystal 489
Extremely High Frequency Stability 490
Crystal Oscillator Circuits 490
12.16 Voltage-Controlled Oscillators 493
12.17 Frequency Stability 494
Frequency Stability Criterion 494
Key Terms 495
Objective-Type Exercises 496
Review Questions 498
Problems 499
Answers 501

13 Wave-Shaping Circuits 503
13.1 Basic RC Low-Pass Circuit 503
Step Input 504
Pulse Input 505
13.2 RC Low-Pass Circuit as Integrator 505
13.3 Basic RC High-Pass Circuit 509
13.4 RC High-Pass Circuit as Differentiator 511
13.5 Basic RL Circuit as Integrator 512
13.6 Basic RL Circuit as Differentiator 513
13.7 Diode Clipper Circuits 514
13.8 Diode Clamper Circuits 520
Negative Clamper 520
Positive Clamper 522
13.9 Multivibrators 527
Bistable Multivibrator 527
Schmitt Trigger 529
Monostable Multivibrator 530
Astable Multivibrator 531
13.10 Integrated Circuit (IC) Multivibrators 535
Digital IC-Based Monostable Multivibrators 535
Timer IC-Based Multivibrators 535
Key Terms 543
Objective-Type Exercises 543
Review Questions 544

	Problems	545
	Answers	546
14	**Linear Power Supplies**	**547**
14.1	Constituents of a Linear Power Supply	547
14.2	Designing Mains Transformer	548
14.3	Rectifier Circuits	550
	Characteristic Parameters	550
	Half-Wave Rectifier	552
	Full-Wave Rectifier	553
	Bridge Rectifier	555
14.4	Filters	558
	Inductor Filter	558
	Capacitor Filter	559
	LC Filter	561
	CLC Filter (π-Filter)	563
14.5	Linear Regulators	565
	Emitter–Follower Regulator	565
	Series-Pass Regulator	566
	Current Limiting	568
	Shunt Regulator	571
14.6	Linear IC Voltage Regulators	576
	General-Purpose Precision Linear Voltage Regulator	576
	Three-Terminal Regulators	577
	Boosting Current Delivery Capability	579
14.7	Regulated Power Supply Parameters	582
	Load Regulation	582
	Line Regulation	582
	Output Impedance	582
	Ripple Rejection Factor	582
	Key Terms	584
	Objective-Type Exercises	585
	Review Questions	587
	Problems	588
	Answers	590
15	**Switched Mode Power Supplies**	**591**
15.1	Switched Mode Power Supplies	591
	Linear versus Switched Mode Power Supplies	592
	Different Types of SMPS	592
15.2	Flyback Converters	593
	Self-Oscillating Flyback DC-to-DC Converter	593
	Externally Driven Flyback DC-to-DC Converter	594
	Discontinuous and Continuous Operational Modes	597
	Design Procedure for Externally Driven Flyback DC-to-DC Converter	599

15.3	Forward Converter	604
15.4	Push–Pull Converter	605
	Design Procedure for Push–Pull DC-to-DC Converter	608
15.5	Switching Regulators	613
	Buck Regulator	613
	Boost Regulator	615
	Inverting Regulator	616
	Three-Terminal Switching Regulators	617
15.6	Connecting Power Converters in Series	618
15.7	Connecting Power Converters in Parallel	618
	Key Terms	621
	Objective-Type Exercises	621
	Review Questions	624
	Problems	624
	Answers	625
16	**Introduction to Operational Amplifiers**	**627**
16.1	Operational Amplifier	627
16.2	Inside of the Opamp	628
	Differential Amplifier Input Stage	629
16.3	Ideal Opamp versus Practical Opamp	634
16.4	Performance Parameters	636
	Bandwidth	636
	Slew Rate	638
	Open-Loop Gain	638
	Common Mode Rejection Ratio	639
	Power Supply Rejection Ratio	639
	Input Impedance	641
	Output Impedance	641
	Settling Time	641
	Offsets and Offset Drifts	642
16.5	Types of Opamps	643
	General-Purpose Opamps	644
	High-Speed Opamps	644
	Precision Opamps	644
	Power Opamps	644
	Opamps Comparators	644
	Norton Opamps	645
	Instrumentation Opamps	645
	Isolation Opamps	646
	Key Terms	647
	Objective-Type Exercises	648
	Review Questions	649
	Problems	649
	Answers	650

17 **Operational Amplifier Application Circuits** 651

17.1 Inverting Amplifier 652

Design Information 653

17.2 Non-Inverting Amplifier 654

Design Information 654

17.3 Voltage Follower 655

17.4 Summing Amplifier 659

17.5 Difference Amplifier 661

17.6 Averager 662

17.7 Integrator 663

17.8 Differentiator 664

17.9 Rectifier Circuits 667

17.10 Clipper Circuits 668

17.11 Clamper Circuits 669

17.12 Peak Detector Circuit 670

17.13 Absolute Value Circuit 671

17.14 Comparator 672

Opamp Comparator 674

Comparator with Hysteresis 674

Window Comparator 676

17.15 Active Filters 680

First-Order Filters 680

Second-Order Filters 681

17.16 Phase Shifters 685

17.17 Instrumentation Amplifier 687

17.18 Non-Linear Amplifier 689

17.19 Relaxation Oscillator 690

17.20 Current-To-Voltage Converter 691

17.21 Voltage-To-Current Converter 692

17.22 Sine Wave Oscillators 694

Key Terms 694

Objective-Type Exercises 694

Review Questions 696

Problems 697

Answers 699

Index 701

CHAPTER 1

Introduction to Semiconductor Physics

Learning Objectives

After completing this chapter, you will learn the following:

- Classification of materials as insulators, conductors and semiconductors.
- Difference between intrinsic and extrinsic semiconductors.
- Difference between P-type and N-type semiconductors.
- Current density and Fermi level in a semiconductor.
- Mass action law.
- Hall effect.

This chapter covers the fundamental topics of semiconductor physics of relevance to understanding operational basics of semiconductor devices such as diodes, bipolar junction transistors (BJTs) transistors, field effect transistors (FETs) and so on covered in the latter chapters of the book. This chapter begins with a brief discussion on insulators, conductors and semiconductors and then focuses mainly on the semiconductors. The topics covered include intrinsic and extrinsic semiconductors, carrier charge densities in a semiconductor, mass action law and Hall effect. The chapter is amply illustrated with a large number of solved examples.

1.1 Insulators, Conductors and Semiconductors

Materials, in general, can be classified as insulators, conductors and semiconductors depending upon their conductivity levels. Insulators are materials that offer a large resistance to the flow of current through them. Conductors are materials that support flow of current through them when an external voltage is applied across them. In other words, insulators are materials that offer very poor conductivity while conductors have high conductivity levels. Semiconductors, on the other hand, have conductivity levels somewhere between the extremes of an insulator and a conductor. In the following paragraphs, these three types of materials are discussed in detail.

Insulators

As mentioned above, insulators are materials that offer a large resistance to the flow of current through them. The typical resistivity level of an insulator is of the order of 10^{10} to 10^{12} Ω cm. Therefore, the application of voltage across the insulator results in negligible flow of current. If one looks at the atomic structure of insulators, one finds that they have seven to eight valence electrons. (The electrons in the valence shell, that is, the outermost shell, are referred to as the valence electrons.) Valence electrons are tightly bound to

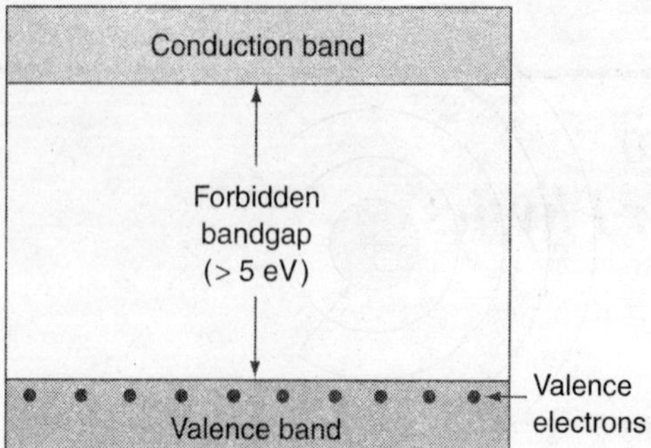

Figure 1.1 Energy band diagram of an insulator.

the atom, so there are no free electrons that can move through the material. Some of the popular insulator materials are mica, glass, quartz, etc.

The energy-band structure of an insulator is shown in Figure 1.1. Band structure of a material defines the band of energy levels that an electron can occupy. Valence band is the range of electron energy where the electrons remain bonded to the atom and do not contribute to the electric current. It is the highest range of electron energies where the electrons are present at absolute zero temperature (0 K). Conduction band is the range of electron energies, higher than the valence band, sufficient to make the electrons free to accelerate under the influence of an external applied electric field resulting in the flow of electric current.

The energy band between the valence band and the conduction band is the forbidden bandgap. As is clear from Figure 1.1, there is a large forbidden bandgap of greater than 5 eV between the valence and the conduction energy bands of an insulator. As an example, the bandgap of diamond is approximately equal to 5.5 eV. Owing to this large forbidden bandgap, there are very few electrons in the conduction band and hence the conductivity of an insulator is poor. Even an increase in temperature or in energy of the applied electric field is insufficient to transfer the electrons from the valence band to the conduction band.

Conductors

Conductors are materials that offer very little resistance to the flow of current through them, that is, they support a generous flow of current when an external electric field is applied across their terminals. Resistivity level of conductors is of the order of 10^{-4} to 10^{-6} Ω cm. Generally, conductors have three or less than three valence electrons. These electrons are loosely bound and are free to move through the material. Metals such as copper, aluminum, gold and silver are good conductors. Figure 1.2(a) shows the atomic structure of copper. Copper has one valence electron and hence is a good conductor. Figure 1.2(b) shows the energy band structure of a conductor. The valence and conduction bands overlap and there is no energy gap for the electrons to overcome in order to move from the valence band to the conduction band. This implies that there are free electrons in the conduction band even at absolute zero temperature (0 K). Therefore, when an external electric field is applied there is a large flow of current through the conductor.

Semiconductors

Semiconductors are materials that have conductivity levels somewhere between the extremes of a conductor and an insulator. The resistivity level of semiconductors is in the range of 10 to 10^4 Ω cm. Two of the most commonly used semiconductor materials are silicon (Si) and germanium (Ge). Silicon has 14 orbiting electrons and germanium has 32 orbiting electrons as shown in Figures 1.3(a) and (b), respectively. As is evident from the figure, both silicon and germanium have four valence electrons. Materials having three and five

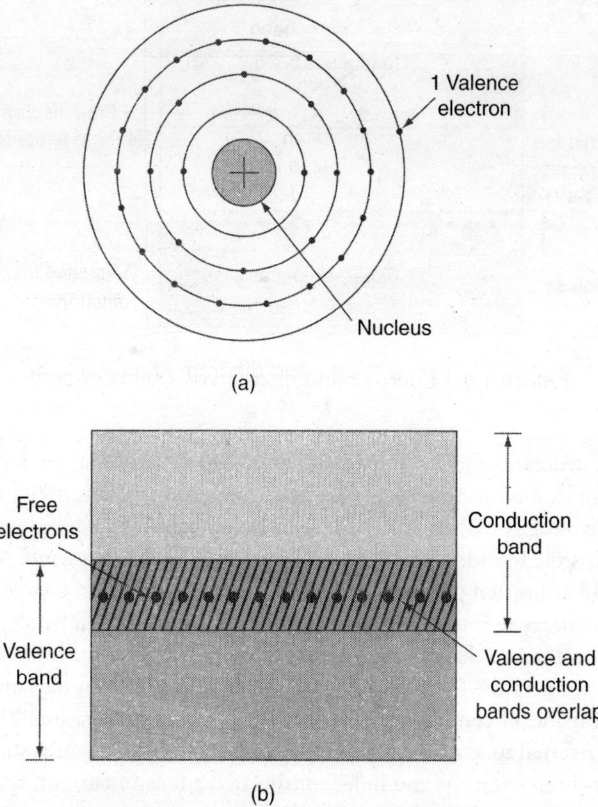

Figure 1.2 (a) Atomic structure of a conductor (copper); (b) energy band diagram of a conductor.

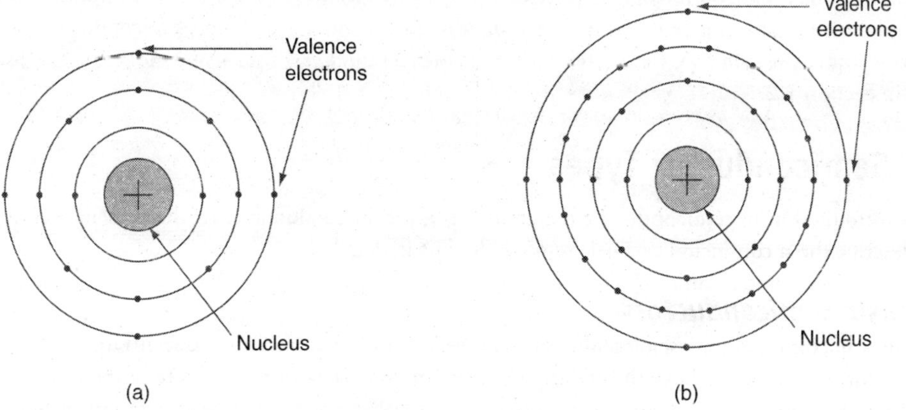

Figure 1.3 (a) Atomic structure of silicon; (b) atomic structure of germanium.

valence electrons combine with each other to form semiconductors. Examples of such semiconductors are gallium arsenide (GaAs) and indium phosphide (InP). The valence electrons in a semiconductor are not free to move as they are in a metal and are trapped in bonds between adjacent atoms.

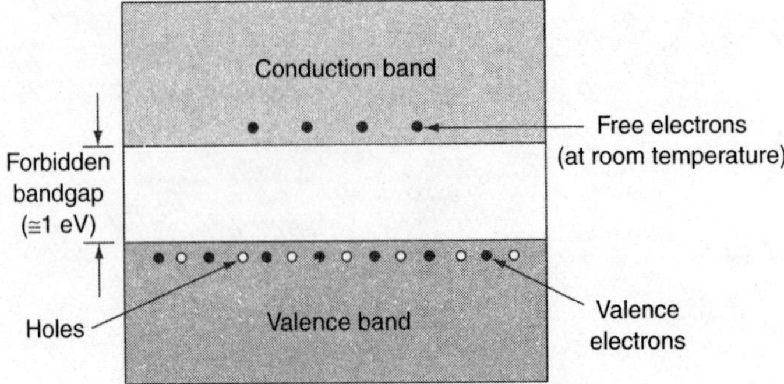

Figure 1.4 | Energy band diagram of a semiconductor.

A look at the band structure of semiconductors (Figure 1.4) suggests that the forbidden bandgap is of the order of 1 eV. For example, the bandgap energy for Si, Ge and GaAs is 1.21, 0.785 and 1.42 eV, respectively, at absolute zero temperature (0 K). At 0 K and at low temperatures, valence band electrons do not have sufficient energy to cross the forbidden bandgap and reach the conduction band. Thus, semiconductors act as insulators at 0 K and at low temperatures. As the temperature increases, a large number of valence electrons acquire sufficient energy to leave the valence band, cross the forbidden bandgap and reach the conduction band. These are now the free electrons as they can move freely under the influence of an external applied electric field. At room temperature (300 K), there are sufficient electrons in the conduction band and hence the semiconductor is capable of conducting some current at room temperature. The absence of an electron in the valence band is referred to as a hole and is represented by a small circle as shown in Figure 1.4. In the case of semiconductors both electrons and holes constitute the flow of current, whereas in the case of conductors, the current is due to the flow of electrons only.

In the discussion above, it is assumed that there are no external atoms added to the parent semiconductor material. Such semiconductors are referred to as *intrinsic semiconductors*. Certain impurity atoms when added to the intrinsic semiconductor materials increase their conductivity. Such semiconductors, with added impurity atoms, are called *extrinsic semiconductors*. Intrinsic and extrinsic semiconductors are discussed in detail in Section 1.2.

1.2 Semiconductor Types

An introduction to semiconductor materials was given in Section 1.1. In the present section, we will describe the intrinsic and extrinsic semiconductors in detail.

Intrinsic Semiconductors

Intrinsic semiconductors are semiconductors with very low level of impurity concentration. They are essentially as pure as can be available through modern technology. The purity levels are of the order of 1 part in 10 billion. Conduction in intrinsic semiconductors is either due to thermal excitation or due to crystal defects. Si and Ge are the two most important semiconductors used. Other examples include GaAs, indium antimonide (InSb) and so on.

Structure

Let us consider the case of silicon. Silicon has 14 orbiting electrons. The innermost shell can hold two electrons, the middle shell eight electrons and the outermost shell four electrons. Therefore, silicon has four valence electrons and is referred to as a tetravalent atom. These four electrons are shared by four neighboring atoms in the crystal. It is the sharing of these four electrons of an atom with their respective neighboring atoms that constitutes a total of eight electrons in its valence shell. This bonding of atoms due to sharing of electrons is called covalent bonding. Figure 1.5(a) shows the crystal structure of silicon at

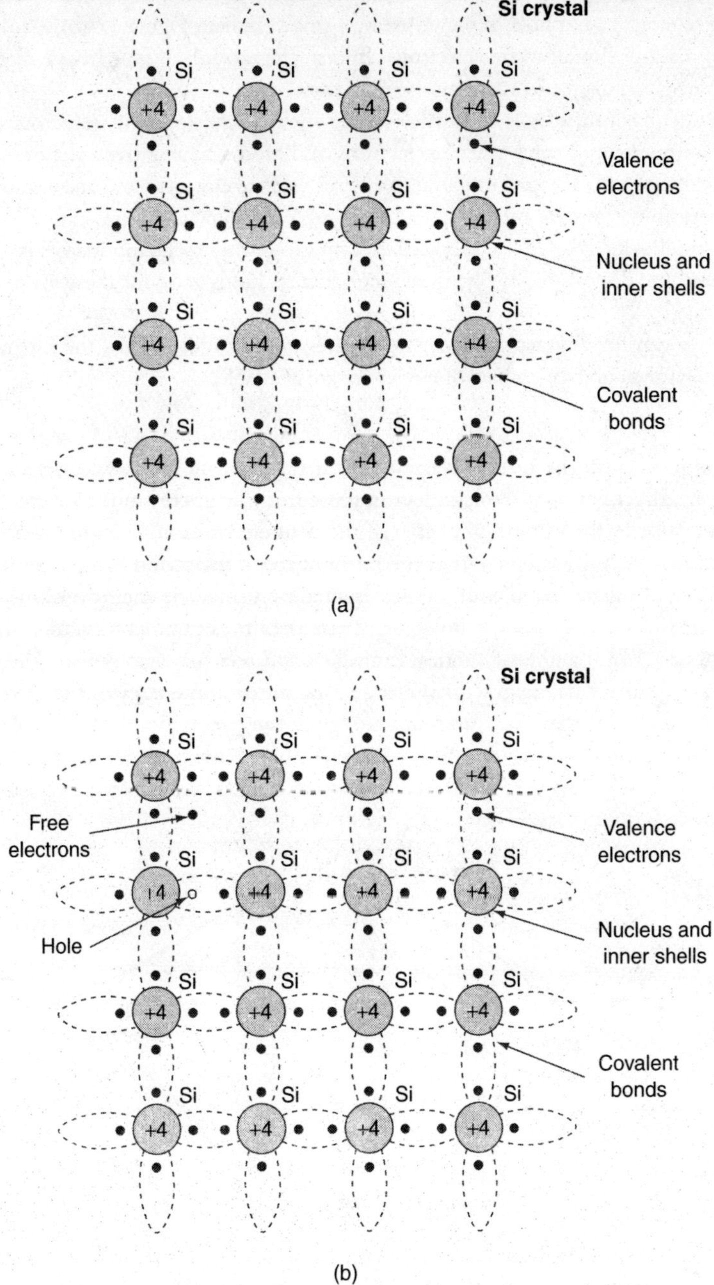

Figure 1.5 Crystal structure of silicon at (a) absolute zero temperature and (b) room temperature.

absolute zero temperature (0 K). Owing to the covalent bonding, the valence electrons are tightly bound to the nucleus and hence the crystal has poor conductivity at low temperatures of the order of 0 K.

At room temperature, the thermal energy is sufficient enough to break some of the covalent bonds as shown in Figure 1.5(b). The electrons are raised to the conduction band and are referred to as free electrons that are available for conduction. The absence of electron in the covalent bond means that the atom now has a positive charge referred to as a hole [represented by a small circle in Figure 1.5(b)]. Holes serve as a carrier of electricity in a manner similar to free electrons. In fact, the motion of hole in one direction is equivalent to the motion of negative charge in the opposite direction.

Germanium also has four electrons in the valence shell. Intrinsic semiconductors are also formed by combination of atoms having three valence electrons and atoms having five valence electrons. Examples include GaAs and InSb. In GaAs, gallium atom has three valence electrons and arsenic atom has five valence electrons. Other combinations are also possible, for example mercury, cadmium and tellurium bond to form mercury cadmium telluride (HgCdTe). Detailed description of these semiconductors is outside the scope of the book. However, the discussion for silicon semiconductors holds good for these intrinsic semiconductors also.

In a nutshell, it can be said that at low temperatures of the order of 0 K, the intrinsic semiconductor behaves as an insulator as no free carriers of electricity are available.

Types

Intrinsic semiconductors can be further classified as *direct bandgap semiconductors* and *indirect bandgap semiconductors*. In a direct bandgap semiconductor, the maximum energy of the valence band occurs at the same momentum value as the minimum energy of the conduction band [Figure 1.6(a)]. Thus, in a direct bandgap semiconductor, electrons present at the minimum of conduction band combine with holes present at the maximum of valence band while conserving momentum. The energy released due to recombination is emitted in the form of photon of light. Therefore, these semiconductors are used in making light-emitting diodes (LED) and laser diodes. Examples of direct bandgap semiconductors include GaAs and HgCdTe. In an indirect bandgap semiconductor, the maximum energy of the valence band occurs at a different momentum value than the minimum energy of the conduction band [Figure 1.6(b)]. Hence, a direct transition across the bandgap does not conserve momentum and does not emit photons of light. Instead, the energy in this case is released in the form of heat. Silicon and germanium are examples of indirect bandgap semiconductors.

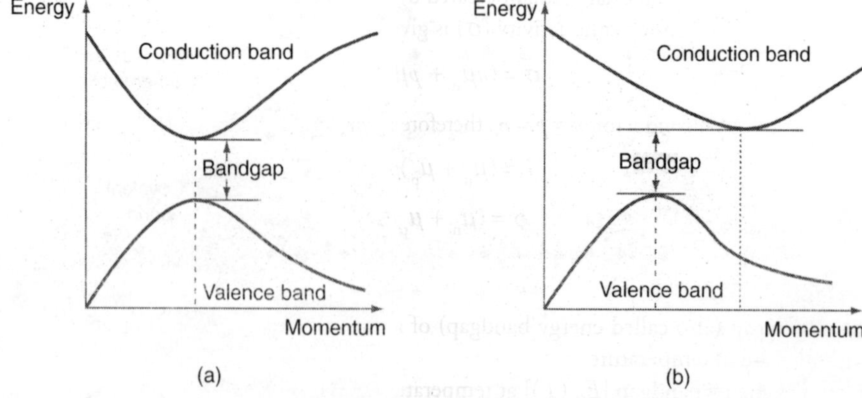

Figure 1.6 (a) Direct bandgap intrinsic semiconductor; (b) indirect bandgap intrinsic semiconductor.

Charge Concentration

In an intrinsic semiconductor, the number of holes is equal to the number of electrons. Hole and electron pairs are generated by thermal agitation and disappear due to recombination. Therefore, in an intrinsic semiconductor

$$n = p = n_{\mathrm{i}} \tag{1.1}$$

where n is the electron concentration (number of electrons/cm^3), p is the hole concentration (number of holes/cm^3) and n_{i} is the intrinsic concentration.

The value of n_{i} is given by

$$n_{\mathrm{i}}^2 = AT^3 \exp(-E_{\mathrm{G0}}/kT) \tag{1.2}$$

where T is the temperature in Kelvin, E_{G0} is the energy gap at 0 K, k is the Boltzmann constant in eV/K and A is a constant. It is clear from Eq. (1.2) that the intrinsic concentration n_{i} increases with increase in temperature.

Electrical Properties

A semiconductor is a bipolar device, that is, both electrons and holes contribute to the flow of current. It may be mentioned here that metals are unipolar devices, that is, only electrons act as current carriers. In a semiconductor there are two different mechanisms of current flow, namely, the "electron flow in the conduction band" and the "hole flow in the valence band". When an external electric field is applied, the free electron may either contribute to the current by drifting through the crystal or combine with a hole in the valence band. The first component constitutes the electron flow in the conduction band. When an electron combines with a hole, it leaves a hole in its initial position. This hole may now be filled by an electron from another covalent bond creating a hole in its position and the process continues. This results in the motion of holes in the valence band in the direction opposite to the direction of motion of electrons.

The mathematical expression for the current density in any material is given by

$$J = (n\mu_{\mathrm{n}} + p\mu_{\mathrm{p}})q\varepsilon \tag{1.3}$$

where J is the current density in A/cm^2, n is the electron concentration (number of electrons/cm^3), p is the hole concentration (number of holes/cm^3), μ_{n} is the mobility of an electron in the material in cm^2/Vs, μ_{p} is the mobility of a hole in the material in cm^2/Vs, q is the charge of an electron (1.6×10^{-19} C) and ε is the applied electric field in V/cm.

This current is due to the potential gradient created by the applied electric field and is referred to as drift current density. The expression for conductivity (σ) is given by

$$\sigma = (n\mu_{\mathrm{n}} + p\mu_{\mathrm{p}})q \tag{1.4}$$

Since in an intrinsic semiconductor, $n = p = n_{\mathrm{i}}$, therefore from Eqs. (1.3) and (1.4), respectively, we obtain

$$J = (\mu_{\mathrm{n}} + \mu_{\mathrm{p}})n_{\mathrm{i}}q\varepsilon \tag{1.5}$$

$$\sigma = (\mu_{\mathrm{n}} + \mu_{\mathrm{p}})n_{\mathrm{i}}q \tag{1.6}$$

Energy Bandgap

The forbidden bandgap (also called energy bandgap) of a semiconductor depends on its temperature and decreases with increase in temperature.

For silicon, the energy bandgap [$E_{\mathrm{G}}(T)$] at temperature T (K) is given by

$$E_{\mathrm{G}}(T) = 1.21 - 3.60 \times 10^{-4}T \tag{1.7}$$

and for germanium it is given by

$$E_G(T) = 0.785 - 2.23 \times 10^{-4}T \tag{1.8}$$

where T is the temperature in Kelvin. At room temperature (taken as 300 K), the bandgap for silicon and germanium are 1.1 and 0.72 eV, respectively.

Fermi Level

The probability that an energy level in a semiconductor is occupied by an electron is given by

$$f(E) = \frac{1}{1 + \exp[(E - E_F)/kT]} \tag{1.9}$$

where $f(E)$ is the Fermi–Dirac probability function (i.e., probability of finding an electron in the energy state E), k is the Boltzmann constant (8.642×10^{-5} eV/K), T is the temperature in Kelvin and E_F is the Fermi level in eV.

Fermi level represents the energy state with 50% probability of being filled by an electron if no forbidden energy bandgap exists. In an intrinsic semiconductor at absolute zero temperature, the probability of finding an electron in the valence band is 100% and the probability of finding the electron in the conduction band is 0%. The Fermi level in an intrinsic semiconductor at absolute zero temperature lies at the center of the forbidden bandgap [Figure 1.7(a)].

As the temperature increases, some of the electrons are excited to higher energy levels. They leave the valence band and jump to the conduction band. Thus, the probability of finding an electron in the valence band decreases and the probability of finding an electron in the conduction band increases [Figure 1.7(b)]. The Fermi level remains at the center of the forbidden bandgap.

EXAMPLE 1.1 *Find the electrical conductivity and resistivity of copper, given that density of copper is 8.96 g/cm³, atomic weight is 63.546 and mobility of electron in copper is 43 cm²/Vs.*

Solution

1. The concentration of atoms in any material is given by

$$\text{Atom concentration} = \frac{6.023 \times 10^{23} \times \text{Density of material}}{\text{Atomic weight}}$$

2. $$\text{Atom concentration in copper} = \frac{6.023 \times 10^{23} \times 8.96}{63.546}$$
$$= 0.849 \times 10^{23} \text{ atoms/cm}^3$$

3. Since each copper atom contributes one free electron, therefore the concentration of free electrons in copper is 0.849×10^{23}.

4. In metals, only electrons contribute to the flow of current. Therefore the conductivity of a metal is given by $\sigma = n\mu_n q$.

   So, the conductivity of copper $= 0.849 \times 10^{23} \times 43 \times 1.6 \times 10^{-19}$
   $= 58.4 \times 10^4\ (\Omega\ \text{cm})^{-1}$

5. $\text{Resistivity} = \dfrac{1}{\text{Conductivity}}$

$$\text{Resistivity of copper} = 1/[58.4 \times 10^4\ (\Omega\ \text{cm})^{-1}]$$
$$= 0.017 \times 10^{-4}\ \Omega\ \text{cm}$$
$$= 17 \times 10^{-9}\ \Omega\ \text{m}$$
$$= 17\ \text{n}\Omega\ \text{m}$$

Answer: The conductivity and resistivity of copper are $58.4 \times 10^4\ (\Omega\ \text{cm})^{-1}$ and 17 nΩ m, respectively.

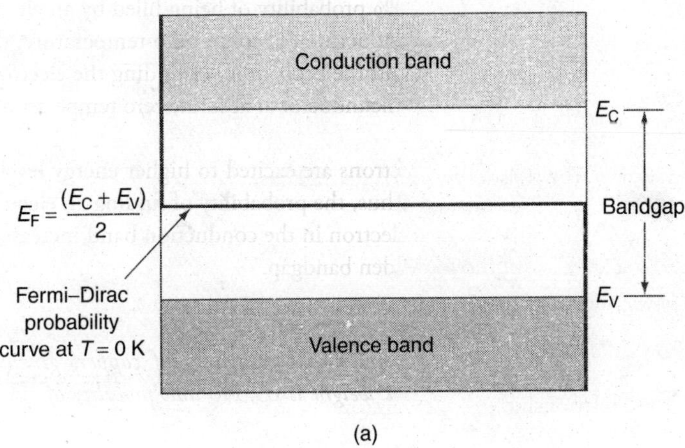

(a)

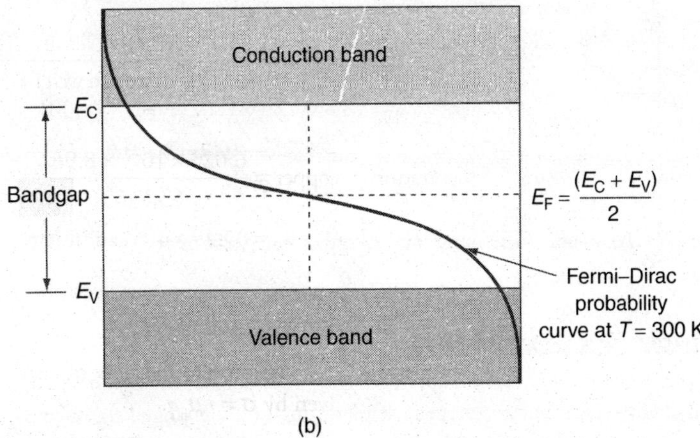

(b)

Figure 1.7 Fermi–Dirac probability function of an intrinsic semiconductor (a) at absolute zero temperature and (b) at 300 K.

EXAMPLE 1.2 *Find the resistivity of intrinsic silicon at 300 K, given that the intrinsic concentration of silicon is 1.5×10^{10} atoms/cm^3 and the mobility of electrons and holes is 1300 cm^2/Vs and 500 cm^2/Vs, respectively. Charge of an electron can be assumed to be 1.6×10^{-19} C.*

Solution

1. The value of conductivity of an intrinsic semiconductor is given by

$$\sigma = (\mu_n + \mu_p) \times n_i q$$

Therefore, conductivity of intrinsic Si is given by

$$(1300 + 500) \times 1.5 \times 10^{10} \times 1.6 \times 10^{-19} = 4.32 \times 10^{-6}\ (\Omega\ \text{cm})^{-1}$$

2. Resistivity of intrinsic Si is

$$\begin{aligned}\text{Resistivity} &= \frac{1}{\text{Conductivity}} \\ &= \frac{1}{4.32 \times 10^{-6}\ (\Omega\ \text{cm})^{-1}} \\ &= 231.481\ \text{k}\Omega\ \text{cm}\end{aligned}$$

Answer: The resistivity is 231.481 kΩ cm.

EXAMPLE 1.3 *Calculate the bandgap energy of germanium (Ge) at 300 K.*

Solution

1. The variation of the bandgap energy of germanium with temperature is given by the relationship

$$E_G(T) = 0.785 - (2.23 \times 10^{-4} \times T)$$

where T is the temperature in Kelvin.

2. Therefore at $T = 300$ K,

$$\begin{aligned}E_G(T) &= 0.785 - (2.23 \times 10^{-4} \times 300) \\ &= 0.785 - 0.0669 \\ &= 0.7181\ \text{eV}\end{aligned}$$

Answer: The bandgap energy of germanium at 300 K is 0.7181 eV.

N-Type Extrinsic Semiconductors

Intrinsic semiconductors have very limited applications as they conduct a very small amount of current. However, the electrical characteristics of an intrinsic semiconductor are changed significantly by adding impurity atoms to the pure semiconductor material. The impurities added are of the order of 1 part in 10^5 parts to 1 part in 10^8 parts. However, this small alteration results in a large change in the semiconductor material properties. For example, the conductivity is increased about 1000 times. This process of adding impurities is called doping and the resultant semiconductor is called an extrinsic semiconductor. If the added impurity is a pentavalent atom, then the resultant semiconductor is called an N-type semiconductor; and if the impurity added is trivalent in nature, then it is called a P-type semiconductor. N-type semiconductors are discussed in this sub-section, while the P-type semiconductors are covered in the next sub-section.

An N-type semiconductor material is created by adding approximately 1 part in 10^8 parts of pentavalent impurities to the intrinsic semiconductor material. Pentavalent atoms are those atoms that have five valence electrons. Some examples of pentavalent atoms are phosphorus, antimony, arsenic, etc. Pentavalent impurity atoms are called the donor atoms. Figure 1.8 shows the crystal structure of an N-type semiconductor material where four of the five electrons of the pentavalent impurity atom (antimony) form covalent bonds with four intrinsic semiconductor atoms; the fifth electron is loosely bound to the pentavalent atom, is relatively free to move within the crystal and is referred to as the free electron. The energy required to detach this fifth electron from the atom is very small, of the order of 0.01 eV for germanium and 0.05 eV for silicon.

The effect of doping creates a discrete energy level called donor energy level in the forbidden bandgap with energy level (E_D) slightly less than the conduction band (Figure 1.9). The difference between the energy

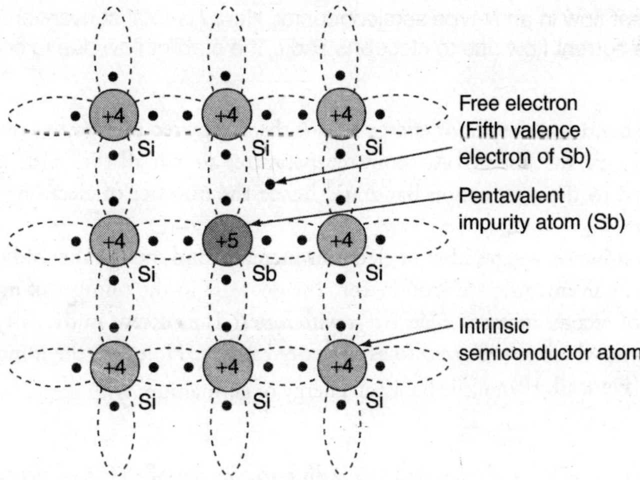

Figure 1.8 Crystal structure of an N-type semiconductor.

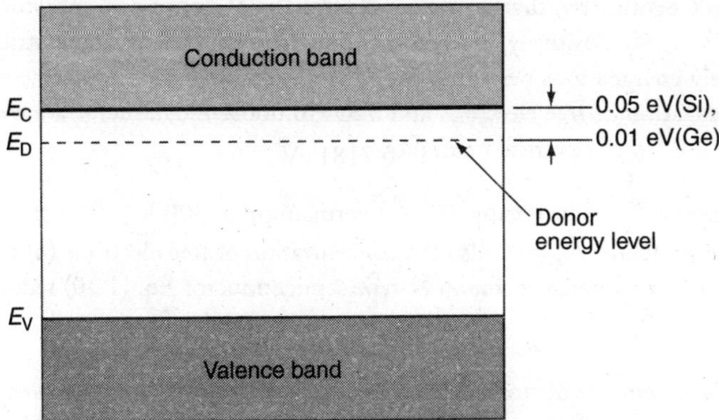

Figure 1.9 Energy band diagram of an N-type semiconductor.

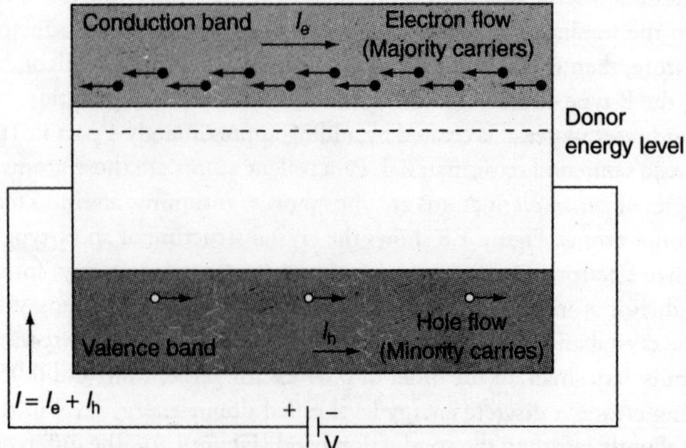

Figure 1.10 Current flow in an N-type semiconductor. Here I is total conventional current flow, I_e the current flow due to electrons and I_h the current flow due to holes.

levels of the conduction band and the donor energy level is the energy required to free the electron (0.01 eV for germanium and 0.05 eV for silicon). At room temperature, almost all the "fifth" electrons from the donor material are raised to the conduction band and hence the number of electrons in the conduction band increases significantly.

In an N-type semiconductor, the number of electrons increases and the number of holes decreases compared to those available in an intrinsic semiconductor. The decrease in the number of holes is attributed to the increase in the rate of recombination of electrons with holes. The current in the N-type semiconductor is dominated by electrons, which are referred to as majority carriers. Holes are the minority carriers in the N-type semiconductor (Figure 1.10).

Electrical Properties

Semiconductor materials are electrically neutral. According to the law of electrical neutrality, in an electrically neutral material the magnitude of positive charge concentration is equal to that of negative charge concentration. Let us consider a semiconductor that has N_D donor atoms per cubic centimeter and N_A acceptor atoms per cubic centimeter, that is, the concentrations of donor and acceptor atoms are N_D and N_A, respectively. Therefore, N_D positively charged ions per cubic centimeter are contributed by the donor atoms and N_A negatively charged ions per cubic centimeter are contributed by the acceptor atoms. Let us assume that the concentration of free electrons and holes in the semiconductor are n and p, respectively. Therefore according to the law of electrical neutrality,

$$N_D + p = N_A + n \tag{1.10}$$

For an N-type semiconductor $N_A = 0$. Also the concentration of free electrons (n) is much greater than the concentration of holes (p). Therefore, for an N-type semiconductor Eq. (1.10) reduces to

$$n \cong N_D \tag{1.11}$$

Hence, for an N-type semiconductor, the free electron concentration is approximately equal to the concentration of donor atoms and vice versa. Therefore, the current density in an N-type semiconductor is given by

$$J \cong N_D \mu_n q \varepsilon \tag{1.12}$$

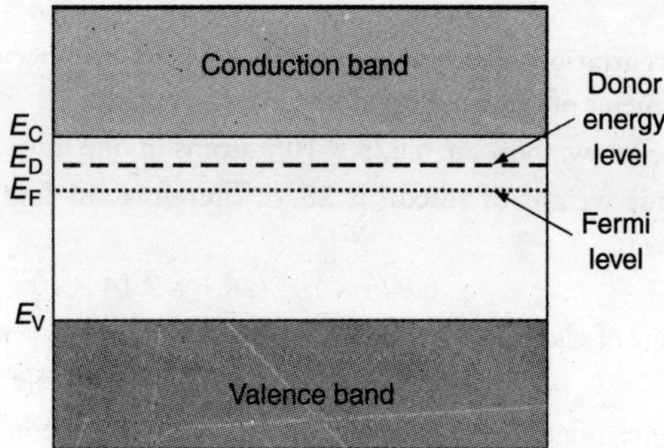

Figure 1.11 Fermi level in an N-type semiconductor.

where μ_n is the mobility of free electrons in the semiconductor (cm^2/Vs) and ε the applied electric field (V/cm). The expression for conductivity in an N-type semiconductor is

$$\sigma \cong N_D \mu_n q \tag{1.13}$$

Fermi Level

The expression for Fermi–Dirac probability function for an extrinsic semiconductor is same as that for the intrinsic semiconductor. The only change that occurs is in the Fermi level. The Fermi level (Figure 1.11) in an N-type semiconductor is raised and is closer to the conduction band as there is a significant increase in the number of electrons in the conduction band and there are fewer holes in the valence band. As the temperature increases, more electron–hole pairs are generated and the Fermi level shifts toward the center of the forbidden energy bandgap.

The Fermi level is given by

$$E_F = E_C - kT \ln\left(\frac{N_C}{N_D}\right) \tag{1.14}$$

where E_C is the energy at the bottom of the conduction band, k the Boltzmann constant in eV/K (8.642×10^{-5} eV/K), T the temperature in Kelvin, N_C the density of states in the conduction band, which is constant for a material at a given temperature, and N_D the donor atom concentration (number of atoms/cm^3).

The value of N_C is given by

$$N_C = 2\left(\frac{2\pi m_n kTq}{h^2}\right)^{3/2}$$

where m_n is the effective mass of an electron, T the temperature in Kelvin, h the Plank's constant and q the electronic charge (1.6×10^{-19} C).

EXAMPLE 1.4 *A pentavalent impurity is added to an intrinsic silicon semiconductor with 1 part in 10^8 parts. Find the concentration of donor atoms and the resistivity of the semiconductor. Also find the Fermi level of the semiconductor. It is given that atomic weight of silicon is 28.1, density is 2.33 g/cm^3, Avogadro's number is 6.023×10^{23}, effective mass of an electron is $1.08 \times$ mass of an electron, mass of the electron is 9.11×10^{-31} kg, mobility of electron is 1300 cm^2/Vs, Boltzmann constant is 8.642×10^{-5} eV/K, Plank's constant is 6.626×10^{-34} Js and temperature is 300 K.*

Solution

1. Concentration of donor atoms refers to the number of donor atoms per cubic centimeter of the semiconductor material.
2. As we know, there are 6.023×10^{23} atoms in one mole of an element.
3. Atomic weight of silicon is 28.1. Therefore, in 1 g of silicon the number of atoms is
$$6.023 \times 10^{23}/28.1 = 2.14 \times 10^{22}$$
4. Density of silicon is 2.33 g/cm^3. Therefore, the number of atoms of silicon in 1 cm^3 is
$$2.33 \times 2.14 \times 10^{22} = 4.986 \times 10^{22}$$
5. It is given that there is one dopant atom per 10^8 silicon atoms. Therefore, the dopant concentration is
$$4.986 \times 10^{22}/1 \times 10^8 = 4.986 \times 10^{14} \text{ atoms/cm}^3$$
6. The conductivity of an N-type semiconductor is given by $\sigma \cong N_D \mu_n q$. That is conductivity is
$$4.986 \times 10^{14} \times 1300 \times 1.6 \times 10^{-19} = 0.103\ (\Omega \text{ cm})^{-1}$$
7. Therefore, resistivity is 1/conductivity, that is
$$1/0.103 = 9.642\ \Omega \text{ cm}$$
8. The expression for Fermi level in an N-type semiconductor is given by
$$E_F = E_C - kT \ln\left(\frac{N_C}{N_D}\right)$$
9. $$N_C = 2\left(\frac{2\pi m_n kTq}{h^2}\right)^{3/2}$$
$$= 2\left(\frac{2 \times 3.14 \times 1.08 \times 9.11 \times 10^{-31} \times 8.642 \times 10^{-5} \times 300 \times 1.6 \times 10^{-19}}{(6.626 \times 10^{-34})^2}\right)^{3/2}$$
$$= 2.8 \times 10^{25} \text{ atoms/m}^3$$
$$= 2.8 \times 10^{19} \text{ atoms/cm}^3$$

Therefore,
$$E_F = E_C - 8.642 \times 10^{-5} \times 300 \ln\left(\frac{2.8 \times 10^{19}}{4.986 \times 10^{14}}\right)$$
$$= E_C - 0.284 \text{ eV}$$
10. Thus, the Fermi level is 0.284 eV below the conduction band.

Answer: The concentration of dopant atoms is 4.986×10^{14} atoms/cm^3, resistivity is 9.642 Ω cm and the Fermi level is 0.284 eV below the conduction band.

P-Type Extrinsic Semiconductors

A P-type semiconductor is created by adding approximately 1 part in 10^5 parts of trivalent impurity to the intrinsic semiconductor. Trivalent atoms have three electrons in their valence shell and are called acceptor atoms in the context of semiconductor devices. Examples of trivalent impurities include boron (B), indium (In) and gallium (Ga). As there are three electrons in the valence shell of these trivalent impurity atoms, only three covalent bonds can be formed with the neighboring intrinsic semiconductor atoms and a vacancy exists in the fourth bond as shown in Figure 1.12. This vacancy is referred to as the hole and is represented by a small circle. The hole is ready to accept an electron from the neighboring atom, thereby creating a hole in the neighboring atom. This hole in turn is ready to accept an electron, thereby creating another hole. In this way, the hole moves through the crystal.

The effect of doping creates a discrete energy level called acceptor level in the forbidden bandgap with energy level (E_A) just above the valence band (Figure 1.13). The difference between the energy levels of the acceptor band (E_A) and the valence band (E_V) is the energy required by an electron to leave the valence band and occupy the acceptor band, thereby leaving a hole in the valence band. This difference ($E_A - E_V$) is of the order of 0.08 eV for silicon and 0.01 eV for germanium. Since very small energy is required for the electron to leave the valence band and occupy the acceptor energy level, large number of electrons jump to the acceptor energy level resulting in a large number of holes in the valence band.

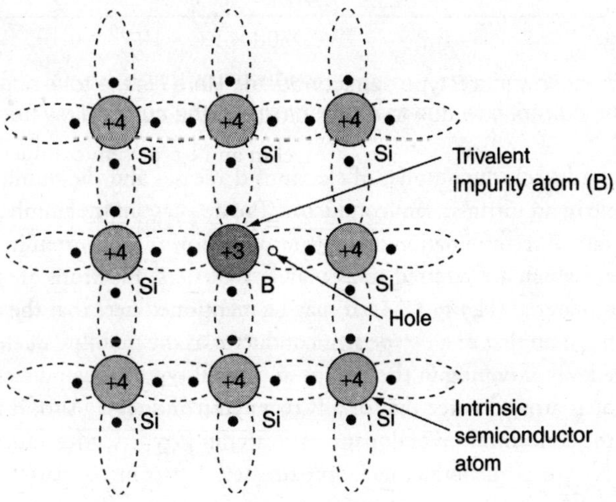

Figure 1.12 | Crystal structure of a P-type semiconductor.

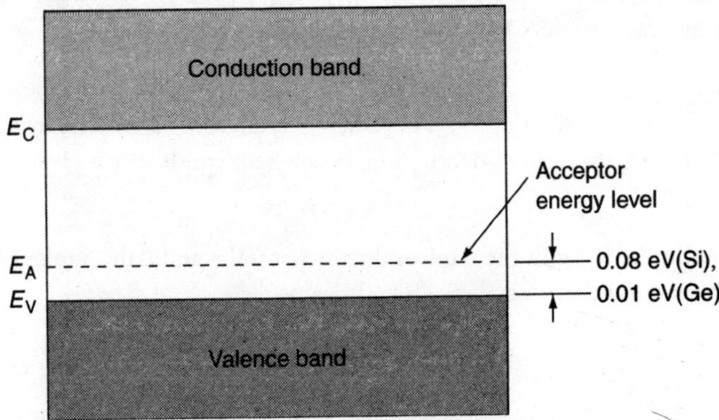

Figure 1.13 | Energy band diagram of a P-type semiconductor.

Figure 1.14 Current flow in a P-type semiconductor. Here I is the total conventional current flow, I_e the current flow due to electrons and I_h the current flow due to holes.

In a P-type semiconductor, the number of electrons decreases and the number of holes increases compared to those available in an intrinsic semiconductor. The decrease in the number of electrons is attributed to the increase in the rate of recombination of electrons with holes. The current in the P-type semiconductor is dominated by holes, which are referred to as majority carriers. Electrons are the minority carriers in a P-type semiconductor material (Figure 1.14). It may be mentioned here that the conductivity of an N-type semiconductor is higher than that of a P-type semiconductor as the mobility of electrons is greater than that of holes. For the same level of doping in the N-type and the P-type semiconductors, the conductivity of an N-type semiconductor is around twice that of a P-type semiconductor. Also, it may be noted in practical semiconductors that the concentration of dopants is greater in P-type semiconductors (approximately 1 part in 10^5 parts) than in N-type semiconductors (approximately 1 part in 10^8 parts).

Electrical Properties

For a P-type semiconductor, $N_D = 0$. Also the concentration of free electrons (n) is much less than the concentration of holes (p). Therefore, for a P-type semiconductor, the hole concentration is approximately equal to the acceptor atom concentration, that is,

$$p \cong N_A \tag{1.15}$$

Alternatively, the number of holes in a P-type semiconductor is approximately equal to the number of acceptor atoms. Therefore, the current density in a P-type semiconductor is given by

$$J \cong N_A \mu_p q \varepsilon \tag{1.16}$$

where μ_p is the mobility of holes in the semiconductor (cm^2/Vs) and ε the applied electric field (V/cm).

The expression for conductivity is

$$\sigma \cong N_A \mu_p q \tag{1.17}$$

Fermi Level

As mentioned before, the Fermi–Dirac probability function for an extrinsic semiconductor is same as that for an intrinsic semiconductor. The only change that occurs is the change in the Fermi level. The Fermi level

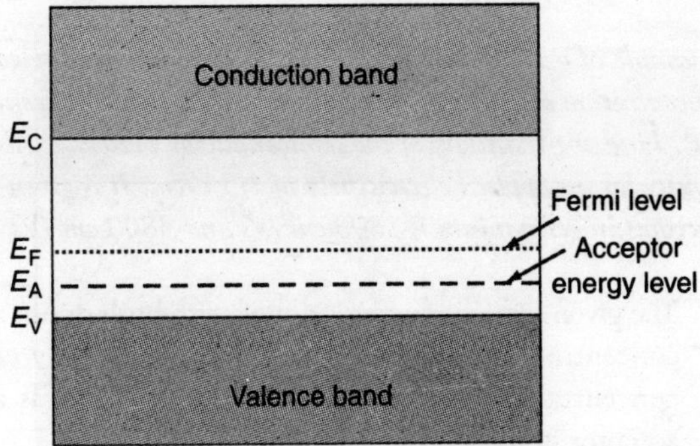

Figure 1.15 | Fermi level in a P-type semiconductor.

in a P-type semiconductor (Figure 1.15) is lower than that of an intrinsic semiconductor and is closer to the valence band; this is because there is a significant increase in the number of holes in the valence band and decrease in the number of electrons in the conduction band. As the temperature increases, more electron-hole pairs are generated and the Fermi level shifts toward the center of the energy gap.

The Fermi level can be derived using the expression

$$E_F = E_V + kT \ln\left(\frac{N_V}{N_A}\right) \tag{1.18}$$

where E_V is the energy at the top of the valence band, N_V the density of states in the valence band, which is constant for a material at a given temperature, N_A the acceptor atom concentration (number of atoms/cm^3) and T the temperature in Kelvin.

The value of N_V can be calculated using

$$N_V = 2\left(\frac{2\pi m_p kTq}{h^2}\right)^{3/2}$$

where m_p is the effective mass of a hole, h the Plank's constant, T the temperature in Kelvin, q the electronic charge (1.6×10^{-19} C) and k the Boltzmann constant in eV/K (= 8.642×10^{-5} eV/K).

EXAMPLE 1.5 *Find the concentration of holes in a P-type silicon at 300 K if its conductivity is 1 (Ω cm)$^{-1}$, given that the mobility of holes in silicon is 500 cm^2/Vs.*

Solution

1. For a P-type semiconductor, the expression for conductivity is $\sigma = N_A \mu_p q$.
2. Therefore, $N_A = 1/(500 \times 1.6 \times 10^{-19})$
   $= 1/(8 \times 10^{-17})$
   $= 1.25 \times 10^{16}$ atoms/cm^3
3. In a P-type semiconductor, hole concentration $\cong N_A$. Therefore, hole concentration = 1.25×10^{16} holes/cm^3.

Answer: The concentration of holes is 1.25×10^{16} holes/cm^3.

EXAMPLE 1.6 *A sample of germanium is doped with both donor and acceptor impurities with donor concentration of 10^{14} donor atoms/cm^3 and acceptor concentration of 10^{15} acceptor atoms/cm^3. Find the resistivity of the semiconductor material. Also find the conduction current density for an applied electric field of 1.5 V/cm. It is given that the mobility of holes and electrons in germanium is 1800 cm^2/Vs and 3800 cm^2/Vs, respectively.*

Solution

1. The given semiconductor is doped with both donor and acceptor impurities. The concentration of free electrons is approximately equal to the donor impurity concentration and the concentration of holes is approximately equal to the acceptor impurity concentration.
2. Therefore, the concentration of free electrons (n) = 10^{14} and the concentration of holes (p) = 10^{15}. The conductivity is

$$\sigma = (n\mu_{\text{n}} + p\mu_{\text{p}}) \times q$$
$$= (10^{14} \times 3800 + 10^{15} \times 1800) \times 1.6 \times 10^{-19}$$
$$= 0.3488\ (\Omega\ \text{cm})^{-1}$$

3. Now resistivity is given by

$$\text{Resistivity} = \frac{1}{\text{Conductivity}}$$
$$= \frac{1}{0.3488}$$
$$= 2.867\ \Omega\ \text{cm}$$

4. Current density in a semiconductor is given by

$$J = \sigma\varepsilon$$
$$J = 0.3488 \times 1.5\ \text{A/cm}^2$$
$$= 0.5232\ \text{A/cm}^2$$

Answer: The value of resistivity is 2.867 Ω cm and the current density is 0.5232 A/cm^2.

1.3 Law of Mass Action

As discussed in the previous section, in an N-type semiconductor electrons are the majority carriers and holes are the minority carriers. For the P-type semiconductor, holes are the majority carriers and electrons are the minority carriers. The concentration of holes and electrons in a semiconductor is governed by the law of mass action. According to the law of mass action, the product of free electron concentration and hole concentration in any semiconductor is constant and is given by

$$np = n_{\text{i}}^2 \tag{1.19}$$

where n is the free electron concentration (negatively charged carriers), p the hole concentration (positively charged carriers) and n_{i} the intrinsic concentration. Therefore, the product of concentration of negative and positive charge carriers in a semiconductor is independent of the type and amount of doping and is equal to the square of the intrinsic concentration. Hence, in an N-type semiconductor as the number of electrons increases the number of holes decreases and in a P-type semiconductor as the number of holes increases the number of electrons decreases.

For an N-type semiconductor,

$$n \cong N_D$$

Therefore,

$$p \cong \frac{n_i^2}{N_D} \tag{1.20}$$

For a P-type semiconductor,

$$p \cong N_A$$

Therefore,

$$n \cong \frac{n_i^2}{N_A} \tag{1.21}$$

EXAMPLE 1.7 *For the semiconductor in Example 1.5, find the concentration of electrons. Also, determine the ratio of holes to the free electrons. It is given that the intrinsic concentration of silicon is 1.5×10^{10}.*

Solution

1. As found out in Example 1.5, the concentration of holes is 1.25×10^{16} holes/cm^3.
2. Using the mass action law, the concentration of free electrons is given by

$$n = \frac{n_i^2}{p} = \frac{(1.5 \times 10^{10})^2}{1.25 \times 10^{16}} = 18000$$

3. The concentration of free electrons is 18000 electrons/cm^3, which is much less than the concentration of holes.
4. $$\frac{\text{Number of holes}}{\text{Number of free electrons}} = \frac{1.25 \times 10^{16}}{18000} = 6.95 \times 10^{11}$$

Answer: The number of electrons is 18000 electrons/cm^3 and the ratio of holes to electrons is 6.95×10^{11}.

1.4 Drift and Diffusion Carriers

The current in a semiconductor is the sum of the drift current and the diffusion current as opposed to a conductor where the current flow is only due to the drift phenomenon. As discussed in Section 1.2, drift current is due to the potential gradient in the semiconductor and is given by the expression

$$J = (n\mu_n + p\mu_p)q\varepsilon \tag{1.22}$$

where J is the current density in A/cm^2, n the free electron concentration in the material (number of free electrons/cm^3), p the hole concentration in the material (number of holes/cm^3), μ_n the mobility of an electron in the material (cm^2/Vs), μ_p the mobility of a hole in the material (cm^2/Vs), q the charge of an electron (1.6×10^{-19} C) and ε the applied electric field (V/cm).

The drift current density due to holes is given by

$$J_p = p\mu_p q\varepsilon \tag{1.23}$$

The drift current density due to electrons is given by

$$J_n = n\mu_n q\varepsilon \tag{1.24}$$

Diffusion current is caused by the concentration gradient in the semiconductor, that is, when there is non-uniform concentration of charge particles in a semiconductor.

The hole diffusion current density is given by the expression

$$J_p = -qD_p \frac{dp}{dx} \tag{1.25}$$

where D_p is the diffusion constant of holes in cm^2/s and dp/dx the variation in hole concentration with distance x (it is positive when the hole concentration increases with distance and is negative when the hole concentration decreases with distance).

Similarly, the electron diffusion current density is

$$J_n = qD_n \frac{dn}{dx} \tag{1.26}$$

where D_n is the diffusion constant of electrons in cm^2/s and dn/dx is the variation of electron concentration with distance x (it is positive when the concentration of electrons increases with distance and is negative if the concentration of electrons decreases with distance).

The diffusion constant of a carrier is related to its mobility and is given by

$$\frac{D_p}{\mu_p} = \frac{D_n}{\mu_n} = V_T \tag{1.27}$$

where V_T is the volt equivalent of temperature, and is equal to kT (k is the Boltzmann constant in eV/K and T is the temperature in Kelvin). The total current is the sum of the diffusion and drift currents. The total hole current density is given by the expression

$$J_p = p\mu_p q\varepsilon - qD_p \frac{dp}{dx} \tag{1.28}$$

The total electron current density is given by the expression

$$J_n = n\mu_n q\varepsilon + qD_n \frac{dn}{dx} \tag{1.29}$$

1.5 Hall Effect

Hall effect is the phenomenon by which a potential difference is created on the opposite sides of a conductor placed in a magnetic field, with the current flowing in perpendicular direction to the magnetic field. The potential created is perpendicular to the direction of both the magnetic field and the current. In other words, if a conductor or a semiconductor carrying current (I) is placed in a transverse magnetic field (B) as shown in Figure 1.16, an electric field (ε) is induced in a direction perpendicular to both B and I. Edwin Hall discovered this effect in the year 1879.

If the current (I) is in the positive X direction and the transverse magnetic field B is in the positive Z direction, a force will be exerted on the current carriers in the negative Y direction. Thus, the carriers will accumulate on the side B as shown in Figure 1.16. For a P-type semiconductor, the holes will accumulate on side B and thus side B will be more positive than side A. Similarly for N-type semiconductors and conductors, electrons will accumulate on side B; and thus side A will be more positive than side B. The magnitude of the voltage will depend on the carrier concentration. Thus, Hall effect can be used to determine the carrier concentration and also whether the semiconductor is a P-type or an N-type semiconductor.

The Hall voltage (V_H) is given by

$$V_H = \frac{BIR_H}{d} \tag{1.30}$$

where B is the magnetic field in Tesla, I the current in amperes, R_H the Hall coefficient and d the width of the conductor or semiconductor in the direction of the magnetic field in meters.

For conductors the value of Hall coefficient R_H is given by

$$R_H = \frac{1}{nq} \tag{1.31}$$

where n is the electron concentration and q the electron charge.

For semiconductors with both positive and negative carriers the value of Hall coefficient R_H is given by

$$R_H = \frac{n\mu_n^2 - p\mu_p^2}{q(n\mu_n + p\mu_p)^2} \tag{1.32}$$

where μ_n is the electron mobility, μ_p the hole mobility, n the electron concentration, p the hole concentration and q the electron charge.

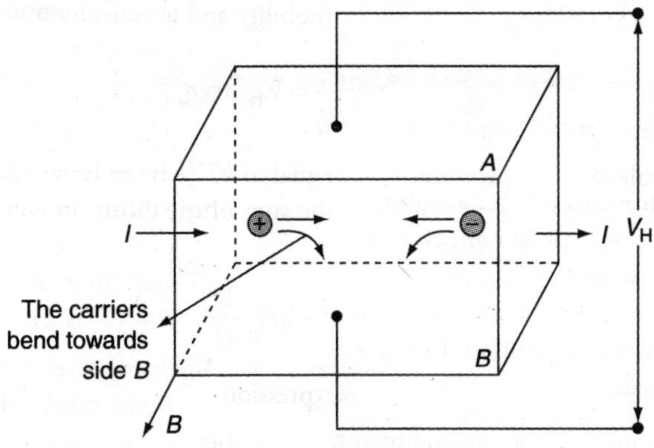

Figure 1.16 Hall effect.

Hall effect is used in design of instruments such as magnetic field meter, Hall-effect multiplier, etc. Magnetic field meters are used to measure the magnetic field. Hall-effect multipliers give an output proportional to the product of two signals. Here, *I* and *B* are made proportional to the two signals.

KEY TERMS

Band structure	Extrinsic semiconductor	Law of mass action
Conduction band	Fermi level	N-type semiconductor
Conductor	Forbidden bandgap	P-type semiconductor
Diffusion current	Hall effect	Semiconductor
Doping	Insulator	Valence band
Drift current	Intrinsic semiconductor	

OBJECTIVE-TYPE EXERCISES

Multiple-Choice Questions

1. Doping of semiconductor is
   a. the process of purifying semiconductor materials.
   b. the process of adding certain impurities to the semiconductor material in controlled amounts.
   c. the process of converting semiconductor material into some form of active device such as FET, UJT, etc.
   d. one of the steps used in fabrication of ICs.

2. Referring to energy level diagram of semiconductor materials, the width of forbidden bandgap is about
   a. 10 eV.
   b. 100 eV.
   c. 1 eV.
   d. 0.1 eV.

3. The forbidden bandgap of the semiconductor material
   a. increases with increase in temperature.
   b. decreases with increase in temperature.
   c. does not vary with temperature.
   d. can increase or decrease with increase in temperature depending upon the semiconductor material.

4. One of the following is not a semiconductor.
   a. Gallium arsenide
   b. Indium
   c. Germanium
   d. Silicon

5. One of the following statements justifies the extensive use of semiconductor materials.
   a. It is because of their low forbidden bandgap.
   b. It is because of their resistance value, which lies between that of a good conductor and an insulator.
   c. It is because of ease of fabrication of semiconductor material into practical active and passive devices.
   d. It is because of the fact they exhibit some wide ranging characteristics when certain specified impurities are added to them in controlled amounts.

6. Which of the following statements is false?
   a. The resistivity of the semiconductor is of the order of 10^{-3} Ω cm.
   b. Silicon and germanium are semiconductors.
   c. Indium is an acceptor impurity.
   d. Arsenic is a donor impurity.

7. The Fermi level of an intrinsic semiconductor is
   a. in the center of the forbidden bandgap.
   b. in the valence band.
   c. in the conduction band.

d. anywhere in the valence, conduction, forbidden bandgap.

8. According to the law of mass action:
   a. The product of free electron concentration and hole concentration in an extrinsic semiconductor is equal to the intrinsic concentration in an intrinsic semiconductor.
   b. The product of free electron concentration and hole concentration in an extrinsic semiconductor is equal to the square of the intrinsic concentration in an intrinsic semiconductor.
   c. The product of free electron concentration and hole concentration in an extrinsic semiconductor is equal to the square root of the intrinsic concentration in an intrinsic semiconductor.
   d. None of these.
9. Which of the following statements is true?
   a. An N-type semiconductor has excess of electrons and hence has a net negative charge.
   b. A P-type semiconductor has excess of holes and hence has a net positive charge.
   c. An N-type semiconductor has excess of electrons and a P-type semiconductor has excess of holes but both of them are neutral.
   d. None of these.
10. According to Hall effect, the Hall voltage is proportional to
   a. the product of B and I.
   b. inverse of the product of B and I.
   c. I only.
   d. B only.

   (where B is the magnetic field and I the current.)

State whether True or False

1. Conductivity of silicon is less than that of germanium at room temperature (300 K).
2. As the temperature increases, the Fermi level of both N-type and P-type semiconductor materials moves toward the center of the forbidden bandgap.
3. For the same level of doping, the conductivity of an N-type semiconductor is same as that of a P-type semiconductor.
4. Under thermal equilibrium conditions, the product of concentration of free electrons and concentration of holes is constant, and is independent of the amount of doping by donor and acceptor impurities.
5. Ratio of majority to minority carriers in an intrinsic semiconductor is very large.

REVIEW QUESTIONS

1. What is a semiconductor material? How does it differ from a conductor and an insulator?
2. Differentiate between
   a. N-type and P-type semiconductors
   b. Extrinsic and intrinsic semiconductors
   c. Drift and diffusion currents
   d. Insulators, conductors and semiconductors
3. Give reasons for the following:
   a. Why the conductivity of intrinsic semiconductors increases with increase in temperature?
   b. Extrinsic semiconductors are used invariably in all applications in contrast to intrinsic semiconductors.
   c. Why are direct bandgap semiconductors used in making light-emitting diodes (LED) and laser diodes?
   d. The Fermi level of an N-type semiconductor is near the conduction band whereas that of a P-type semiconductor is near the valence band?
4. What is Fermi level? Explain how does the Fermi level of a semiconductor change with doping?
5. "*An N-type semiconductor has excess of electrons whereas a P-type semiconductor has excess of holes.*" Comment.

6. "*An N-type semiconductor has excess of electrons and a P-type semiconductor has excess of holes.*" Does that mean N-type materials have a net negative charge and P-type materials a net positive charge? Comment.
7. What is the law of mass action and what does it imply?
8. Explain the following terms:
   a. Majority carriers
   b. Minority carriers
   c. Drift current
   d. Diffusion current
9. What is Hall effect? State any two applications.
10. "*An intrinsic semiconductor behaves like an insulator at absolute zero temperature.*" Comment.

PROBLEMS

1. Find the conductivity and resistivity of the silver metal. (Given that density of silver is 19.3 g/cm^3, atomic weight is 196.96, mobility of electron in silver is 47 cm^2/Vs.)
2. Find the energy bandgap of silicon at 1000 K.
3. An N-type germanium semiconductor has donor concentration of 10^{14} atoms/cm^3. Find the conductivity of the material. What is the concentration of acceptor impurities required to achieve the same conductivity level in a P-type semiconductor? (Given that the mobility of holes and electrons in germanium is 1800 cm^2/Vs and 3800 cm^2/Vs, respectively.)
4. Find the Fermi energy level of an N-type silicon semiconductor having donor concentration of 10^{14} atoms/cm^3. How would the Fermi level change if the donor concentration were changed to 10^{16} atoms/cm^3? (Given that the effective mass of an electron is 1.08 × mass of an electron, mass of the electron is 9.11×10^{-31} kg, Boltzmann constant is 8.642×10^{-5} eV/K, Plank's constant is 6.626×10^{-34} Js and temperature is 300 K.)
5. By what amount would the Fermi level for the N-type silicon semiconductor having donor concentration of 10^{14} atoms/cm^3 shift for a temperature change from 300 K to 500 K. (Given that the effective mass of an electron is 9.84×10^{-31} kg, Boltzmann constant is 8.642×10^{-5} eV/K, Plank's constant is 6.626×10^{-34} Js.)

ANSWERS

Multiple-Choice Questions

1. (b)
2. (c)
3. (b)
4. (b)
5. (d)
6. (a)
7. (a)
8. (b)
9. (c)
10. (a)

State whether True or False

1. True
2. True
3. False
4. True
5. False

Problems

1. 44.38×10^4 (Ω cm)$^{-1}$, 22.53 nΩ m
2. 0.85 eV
3. 0.0608 (Ω cm)$^{-1}$, 2.11×10^{14} atoms/cm^3
4. 0.325 eV below the conduction band, 0.205 eV below the conduction band
5. 0.25 eV toward the center of the forbidden energy bandgap

CHAPTER 2

Semiconductor Diodes

Learning Objectives

After completing this chapter, you will learn the following:

- Basics of diode construction and operation.
- Diode V–I characteristics.
- Diode parameters and their significance.
- Different diode packages and lead identification.
- How to test a diode.
- Different types of diodes.
- Connecting diodes in series and parallel.

Diodes are the simplest of all the semiconductor devices. They are used in a variety of applications including communication systems, radio, TV, computers, power supplies and so on. The focus in this chapter is on semiconductor diodes. The topics covered include fundamental topics such as diode construction and operation, characteristic curves, diode parameters and diode equivalent circuits. A brief description of different types of diodes – including varactor diodes, tunnel diodes, Schottky diodes, power diodes, light-emitting diodes (LEDs) and photodiodes – and their working principle is given. Also, topics of practical interest such as diode packages and lead identification, connection of diodes in series and parallel and diode testing are covered. The concepts are explained with the help of a large number of solved examples.

2.1 P–N Junction

A semiconductor diode is a polarity-sensitive two-terminal device comprising a P–N junction formed between a P-type semiconductor material and an N-type semiconductor material [Figure 2.1(a)]. As discussed in Chapter 1, the N-type semiconductor is formed by introducing pentavalent dopant impurity atoms while the P-type semiconductor is formed by introducing trivalent dopant impurity atoms into the intrinsic semiconductor material. Also, in an N-type semiconductor, electrons are the majority carriers and holes are the minority carriers, whereas in a P-type semiconductor, holes are the majority carriers and electrons are the minority carriers. The P–N junction is formed by introducing the donor impurities on one side and acceptor impurities on the other side of a single crystal of a semiconductor. Figure 2.1(b) shows the circuit symbol of a P–N junction diode. The arrow is associated with the P-region and the vertical line with the N-region. The P- and N-regions are referred to as the anode and the cathode, respectively. Silicon and germanium are the most commonly used materials for fabricating semiconductor diodes.

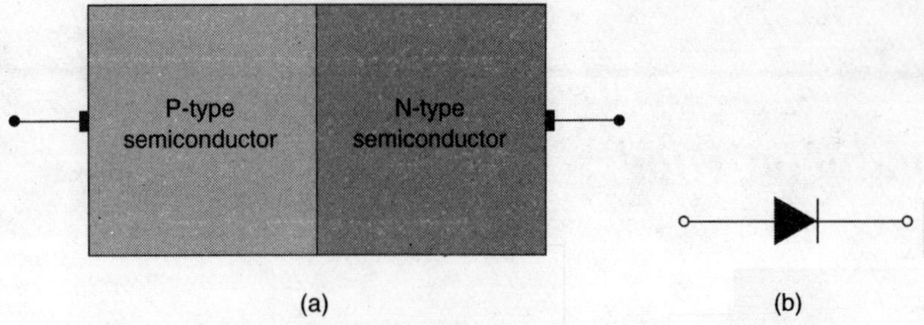

Figure 2.1 (a) P–N junction; (b) symbol of a P–N junction diode.

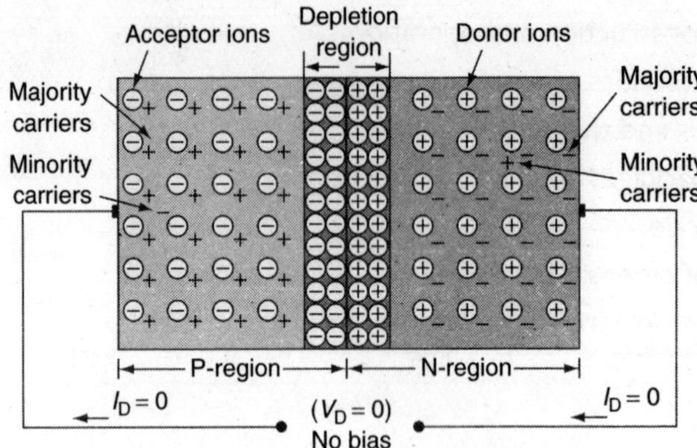

Figure 2.2 P–N junction with no applied bias.

The electrons in the N-region and the holes in the P-region combine near the junction, resulting in a region near the junction that is devoid of free electrons and holes. This region of uncovered positive and negative ions is called the *depletion region* because of the depletion of free carriers in this region. The thickness of this region is of the order of 0.5 μm.

Electrons in the N-region (majority carriers) and negatively charged ions in the P-region repel each other near the junction. Similarly, holes in the P-region (majority carriers) and positively charged ions in the N-region also repel each other near the junction. An effective potential of the order of few tenths of a volt, referred to as the *contact potential* or the *barrier potential,* is developed across the depletion region. However, some of the holes and electrons have sufficient kinetic energy to overcome the contact potential and be able to pass through the depletion region. This results in a flow of electrons from the N-region to the P-region and flow of holes from the P-region to the N-region. This constitutes the majority carrier flow vector.

Also, holes that are present in the depletion region of the N-region (minority carriers) will pass to the P-region. Similarly, electrons that are present in the depletion region of the P-region (minority carriers) will pass to the N-region. This constitutes the minority carrier flow vector. The relative magnitudes of the minority and the majority flow vectors are such that the net flow in either direction is zero. This is referred to as the open-circuit condition of the semiconductor diode where no bias voltage is applied to the diode. In other words, in the absence of an applied bias voltage, the net flow of current in a semiconductor diode is zero. Figure 2.2 shows the P–N junction with no applied bias.

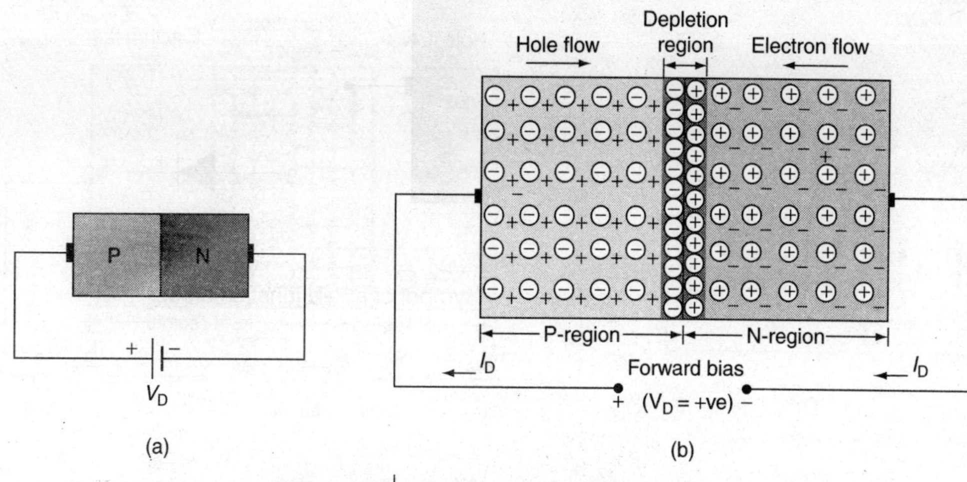

Figure 2.3 Forward-biased P–N junction.

In the subsequent paragraphs, we will discuss the response of the semiconductor diode under forward-bias and reverse-bias conditions.

Forward-Bias Condition

A semiconductor diode is forward-biased by applying a positive potential to the P-region and a negative potential to the N-region as shown in Figure 2.3(a). This applied potential causes the electrons in the N-region and the holes in the P-region to combine with positive and negative ions, respectively, in the depletion region. This results in a reduction of the width of the depletion region [Figure 2.3(b)] and a decrease in the potential barrier at the junction. As the applied bias is increased in magnitude, the width of the depletion region decreases until a point is reached where there is a sharp rise in the number of majority carriers crossing the junction. In other words, a large number of holes cross the junction from the P-region to the N-region and a large number of electrons cross the junction in the reverse direction, that is, from the N-region to the P-region. It may be mentioned here that holes traveling from left to right constitute a current in the same direction as the electrons traveling from right to left. This results in exponential rise in the current due to the majority carriers. The current due to the majority carriers is referred to as the *forward current* and is in the range of few tens of milliamperes (except for power diodes where the current is of the order of few amperes). Typically, the voltage across the forward-biased diode is less than 1 V and depends upon the diode material. As an example, the forward voltage for silicon and germanium diodes is typically 0.7 V and 0.3 V, respectively.

The flow of the minority carriers remains the same as in the case of diode with no applied bias. The current contributed by the minority carriers is referred to as the *reverse saturation current* or *reverse leakage current* and is of the order of a few nanoamperes to a few microamperes. The reverse saturation current is in the opposite direction to the forward current. However, its magnitude is negligible as compared to the forward current. V–I characteristics of the diode are discussed in detail in Section 2.4.

Reverse-Bias Condition

A diode is said to be reverse-biased when an external potential applied across it is such that the positive terminal is connected to the N-region and the negative terminal is connected to the P-region [Figure 2.4(a)].

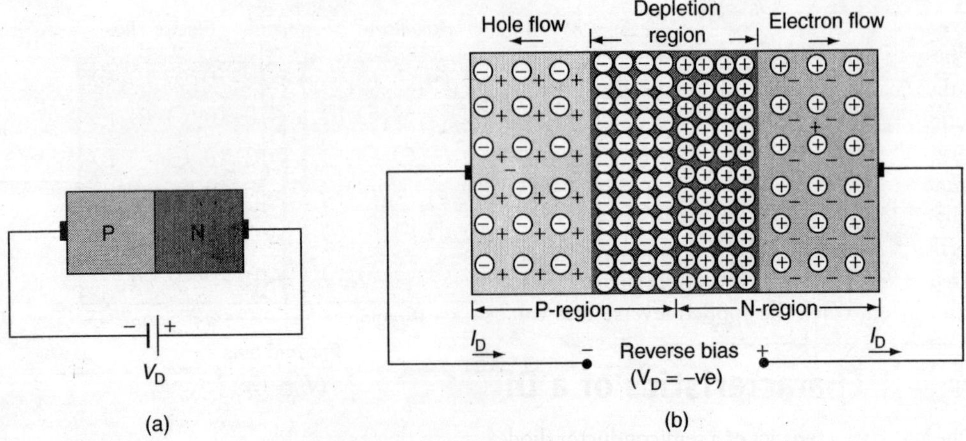

Figure 2.4 | Reverse-biased P–N junction.

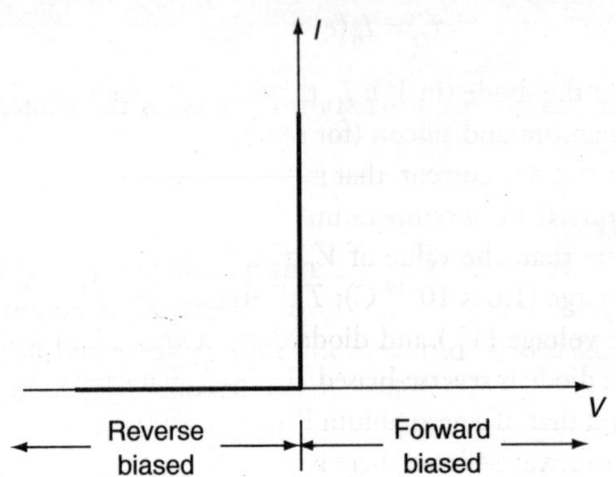

Figure 2.5 | V–I characteristics of an ideal diode.

This results in widening of the depletion region as electrons and holes are drawn away from the junction due to the polarity of the applied voltage [Figure 2.4(b)]. Widening of the depletion region reduces the flow of majority carriers to approximately zero.

The minority carrier flow remains the same as in case of diode with no applied bias. As mentioned before, this current is referred to as the reverse saturation current and is of the order of a few nanoamperes to a few microamperes. The reverse saturation current does not significantly change with change in the reverse-bias potential. However, it is a strong function of the diode temperature and increases with increase in diode temperature. When the applied reverse-bias is increased beyond the breakdown voltage of the diode, there is a sharp increase in the reverse current. This is discussed in detail in Section 2.4.

2.2 Ideal Diode

An ideal diode behaves like a switch that conducts current only in one direction, from anode to cathode. An ideal diode acts as a short circuit when forward-biased and as an open circuit when reverse-biased. Thus, the resistance of the forward-biased diode is zero and the resistance of the reverse-biased diode is infinite. Figure 2.5 shows the V–I characteristics of an ideal diode.

2.3 Practical Diode

The actual diode differs from the ideal diode described in Section 2.2. In the forward-bias condition, the ideal diode acts as a closed switch, with zero ON-resistance that allows the current to flow in one direction, that is, from anode to cathode. However, practical diodes do not conduct until a certain value of forward voltage is applied to them. This voltage, referred to as the *cut-in voltage* or the *knee voltage* or the *threshold voltage*, is of the order of less than 1 V for semiconductor diodes. Also, the ON-resistance of the practical diode is not zero and varies from few ohms to few hundreds of ohms. In the reverse-bias state, the practical diode differs from the ideal open switch as in this condition a small amount of current, referred to as the reverse saturation current, flows through the diode. Also, there is sharp increase in the reverse current when the applied reverse-bias voltage exceeds the reverse breakdown voltage of the diode.

2.4 V–I Characteristics of a Diode

The V–I characteristics of a semiconductor diode both in the forward-bias and reverse-bias conditions are expressed by the universal diode equation also referred to as the *Shockley's diode equation* [Eq. (2.1)]:

$$I_D = I_0(e^{V_D/\eta V_T} - 1) \tag{2.1}$$

where V_D is the voltage across the diode (in V); I_D the diode current (in mA); I_0 the reverse saturation current (in mA); $\eta = 1$ for germanium and silicon (for relatively higher values of diode current) and $\eta = 2$ for silicon at relatively low levels of diode current, that is below the cut-in-voltage or the knee-point of the diode characteristics; V_T the volt equivalent of temperature (in V).

It may be mentioned here that, the value of $V_T = kT/q$, where k is the Boltzmann constant (8.642×10^{-5} eV/K); q the electron charge (1.6×10^{-19} C); T the temperature (in K); V_T the volt equivalent of temperature (in V). Also, diode voltage (V_D) and diode current (I_D) are positive when the diode is forward-biased and negative when the diode is reverse-biased. The V–I characteristics of a silicon P–N junction diode are shown in Figure 2.6(a) and that of a germanium P–N junction diode in Figure 2.6(b). As is evident from the figures, when the diode is forward-biased there is a minimum voltage that must be exceeded before there is sufficient conduction of current through the diode. In other words, current flows through the diode when it is forward-biased, with the applied voltage greater than the cut-in voltage (V_γ) of the diode. The cut-in voltage is 0.7 V in the case of silicon diodes and 0.3 V in the case of germanium diodes.

When the applied forward voltage exceeds the cut-in voltage, there is a sharp rise in the current through the diode. In other words, a very small increment in the forward voltage (V_D) results in a very large increase in the forward current (I_D). For positive values of V_D, we can see from Eq. (2.1) that the first term of the equation will grow exponentially and overpower the effect of the second term. The first term corresponds to the forward current through the diode and the second term corresponds to the reverse saturation current. Thus, the current through the diode varies exponentially with the applied voltage, provided that the applied voltage is greater than the cut-in voltage. The forward current is measured in milliamperes and is generally in the range of few tens of milliamperes.

In the reverse-bias mode, the small current that flows is the reverse saturation current. It is of the order of few nanoamperes for silicon diodes and typically 1 μA for germanium diodes. This current is independent of the applied reverse voltage until the semiconductor junction breaks down at a voltage known as the *reverse breakdown voltage* or the *peak inverse voltage.* The breakdown of the junction results in a sudden rise of current that ends up in damaging the diode. Hence, when the diodes are operated in the reverse-bias mode, their operating voltage should be less than the breakdown voltage. Some diodes known as breakdown diodes are designed to operate in the breakdown region. Breakdown diodes are discussed in detail in Section 2.11.

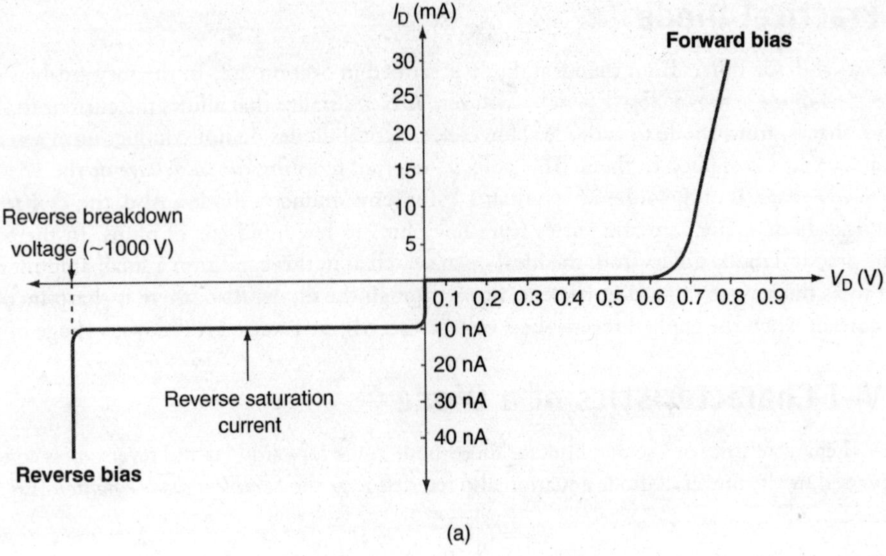

(a)

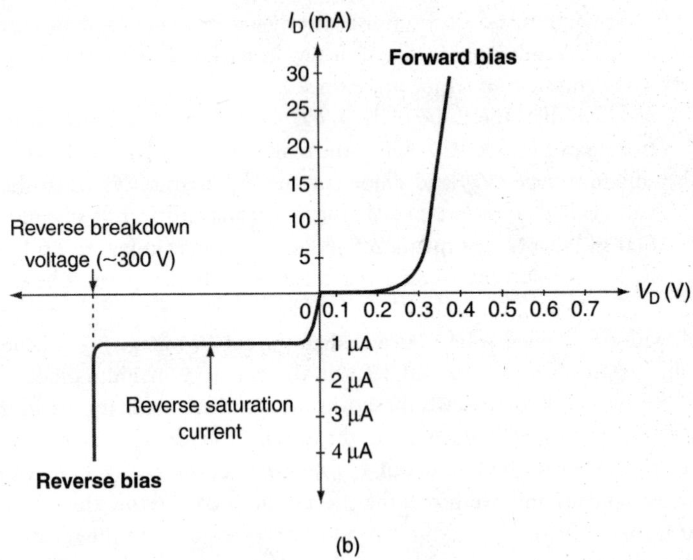

(b)

Figure 2.6 | V–I characteristics of (a) silicon diode and (b) germanium diode.

2.5 Temperature Dependence of the V–I Characteristics

Temperature has a significant effect on the V–I characteristics of the diode. Figure 2.7 shows the variation in the diode characteristic curve with change in temperature. As is evident from the figure, the reverse saturation current, reverse breakdown voltage, cut-in voltage and the diode's forward voltage are strong functions of the diode temperature.

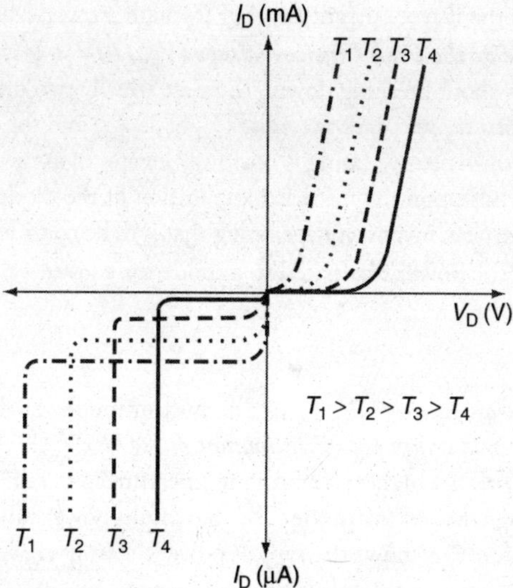

Figure 2.7 Temperature dependence of the diode V–I characteristics.

As an approximation it can be said that reverse saturation current doubles itself for every 10°C rise in diode temperature. As an example, the reverse saturation current of the germanium diode is of the order of 1 μA at 25°C and increases to around 100 μA at 100°C. The variation of the reverse saturation current with temperature is given by

$$I_0(T) = I_0(T_1) \times 2^{(T-T_1)/10} \tag{2.2}$$

where $I_0(T)$ is the reverse saturation current at temperature T and $I_0(T_1)$ the reverse saturation current at temperature T_1.

The reverse breakdown voltage of the diode increases with increase in temperature. Also, the cut-in-voltage (V_γ) and the forward voltage across the diode for a given current decrease with increase in temperature. The variation of cut-in voltage and the forward voltage with temperature is given by

$$\frac{dV}{dT} = -2.5 \text{ m V/°C} \tag{2.3}$$

2.6 Diode Specifications

Diodes have a wide range of performance specifications. These specifications are the basis of the selection criteria when it comes to choosing the right diode for a given application. Some of the major performance specifications for a diode are as follows:

1. ***Forward Voltage*** **(V_F):** It is the voltage applied across a forward-biased diode. It is not a specification in itself. It is given along with the corresponding forward current value at which it has been measured. It indicates the diode's static resistance. For example, general purpose diode 1N3611 is specified as 1.1 V@1000 mA, which also indicates that its static resistance is 1.1 Ω.
2. ***Forward Current*** **(I_F):** It is the direct current flowing through the diode when it is forward-biased.
3. ***Reverse Voltage*** **(V_R):** It is the voltage across a reverse-biased diode. It is specified along with corresponding reverse current value at which it has been measured. It also indicates the diode's reverse-biased resistance.

4. ***Reverse Current*** **(I_R):** It is the direct current flowing through a reverse-biased diode.
5. ***Reverse Breakdown Voltage or the Peak Inverse Voltage*** **(V_{BR}, *PIV*):** It is the maximum reverse voltage that a diode can withstand without breaking down. There are usually two different PIV ratings specified in case of diodes. One is the *repetitive peak inverse voltage* (V_R or V_{RRM}) and the other is the *non-repetitive peak inverse voltage* (V_{RSM}). The non-repetitive rating is obviously greater than the repetitive rating. The one that needs to be considered depends upon the intended application of the diode. As an example, in a rectifier application, it is the repetitive peak inverse voltage rating that is to be considered.
6. ***Power Dissipation*** **(P_D):** The power dissipated in a diode for a given value of diode voltage (V_D) and current (I_D) is given by

$$P_D = V_D \times I_D \tag{2.4}$$

7. ***Maximum Power Dissipation Rating*** **[$P_{D(max)}$]:** The maximum power that can be safely dissipated in a diode is referred to as the *maximum power dissipation rating* [$P_{D(max)}$]. The value of maximum power dissipation is specified at 25°C. At higher operating temperatures, its value should be derated as per the power–temperature derating curve of the diode. The maximum power rating decreases linearly with the increase in temperature. Figure 2.8 shows the typical power derating curve for a diode.
8. ***Maximum Junction Temperature*** **(T_j):** It is the maximum allowable junction temperature of the diode. It is significant in the case of power diodes and helps in finding the size of the heat sink to be used for a given diode current.
9. ***Maximum Average Rectified Current*** **($I_{F(av)}$):** It is the maximum average forward rectified output current that can be allowed to pass through the diode.
10. ***Peak Repetitive Forward Current*:** This is the maximum instantaneous value of the repetitive forward current.
11. ***Peak Forward Surge Current*:** During turn-on, malfunction, switching, etc., high values of current may flow through the diode for brief time intervals. Surge current ratings define the maximum value and time duration of such surges in the current level. For instance, a surge rating of 10 A for 10 ms implies that the diode can handle a maximum of 10 A of forward current for time duration not exceeding 10 ms. The surge current rating is significantly higher than the peak forward current rating.
12. ***Ampere Square Seconds*** **(I^2t):** It indicates the sub-cycle current capability of diode when used as a rectifier. It is usually specified for one complete cycle of a 50 Hz operation.

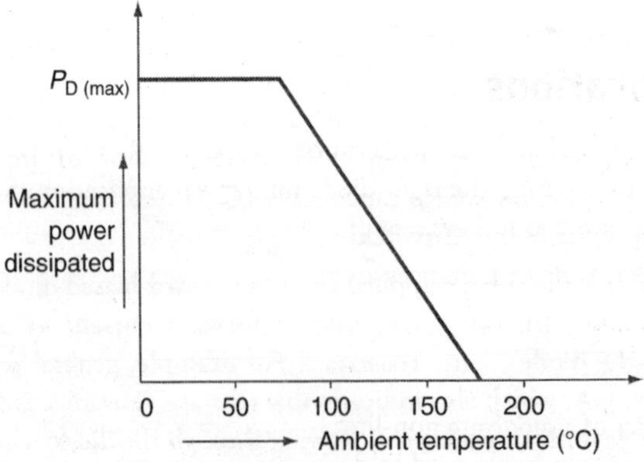

Figure 2.8 Typical power derating curve of a diode.

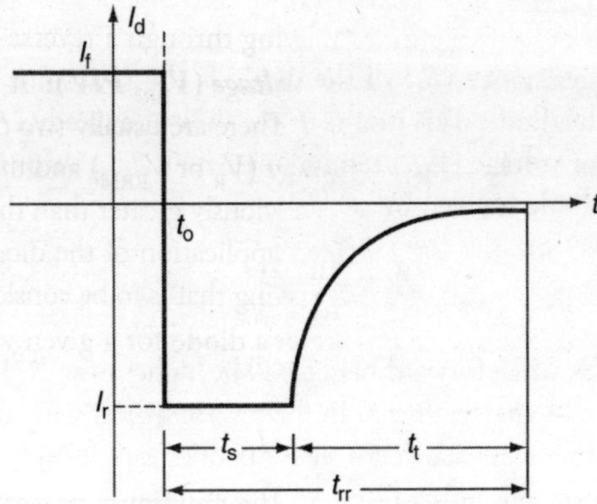

Figure 2.9 | Reverse recovery time.

13. ***Reverse Recovery Time*** **(t_{rr}):** When the diode is switched from the forward-biased condition to the reverse-biased condition abruptly, it is the time required by the reverse current or voltage to reach a specified value. Figure 2.9 shows the current versus time waveform of a diode when the voltage across the diode is abruptly changed to reverse-bias the diode from its forward-bias condition. On application of the reverse voltage, the diode current reverses its direction as shown in the figure and stays at this level for time t_s (storage time). It is the time required for the carriers in the N-region to move to the P-region and the carriers in the P-region to move to the N-region. After this, the current reduces and eventually reaches the reverse saturation value after a certain time called the transition time (t_t). The reverse recovery time is the sum of the storage time and the transition time. The reverse recovery time is a very significant parameter in fast recovery rectifier diodes used in switched mode power supplies and in diodes used for high-frequency switching applications. The reverse recovery time varies from a few nanoseconds (for ultrafast diodes) to about 500 ns (for a typical fast recovery rectifier).
14. ***Forward Recovery Time*** **(t_{ff}):** It is the time required for the forward current or voltage to reach a specified value after the diode has been abruptly switched from the reverse-biased state to the forward-biased state. This parameter too is significant in switching applications.
15. ***Diode Resistance*:** The diode offers resistance both in the forward- and the reverse-biased conditions. The diode resistance in the forward-biased region varies from few ohms to few hundreds of ohms, while in the reverse-biased region it is in the range of few to few hundreds of MΩ. Diode resistance is discussed in detail in Section 2.7.
16. ***Diode Capacitance*:** It is the inherent capacitance of the diode junction. There are two types of capacitances present, namely, the *transition capacitance* and the *diffusion capacitance.* In the reverse-bias condition, the transition or the depletion capacitance (C_T) is of importance whereas in the forward-bias region diffusion or storage capacitance (C_D) dominates. Diode capacitance plays a very significant role in the functioning of switching diodes. Smaller value of diode capacitance results in faster switching times. Diode capacitances are discussed in detail in Section 2.8.

2.7 Diode Resistance

As the V–I characteristics of a diode are non-linear, the diode resistance varies with change in the applied voltage. Two terms very commonly used to define the resistance of a diode are the *static resistance* and the *dynamic resistance.*

Static Resistance

The static resistance or the DC resistance (R_S) of the diode is the resistance offered by the diode when a steady DC voltage is applied to the diode. This results in the flow of a steady DC current through the diode. Let us consider that application of voltage (V_{D1}) results in current (I_{D1}) through the diode [Figure 2.10(a)]. Then the static resistance of the diode is given by

$$R_S = \frac{V_{D1}}{I_{D1}} \tag{2.5}$$

The static resistance of the diode when forward-biased will be higher near the knee region or below it as compared to the vertical region of the V–I characteristics. In the reverse-biased state, the value of the static resistance will be very high. Typical values of static resistance for silicon diodes vary from few tens to hundreds of ohms in the forward-biased region and from few mega-ohms to few hundreds of mega-ohms in the reverse-biased region.

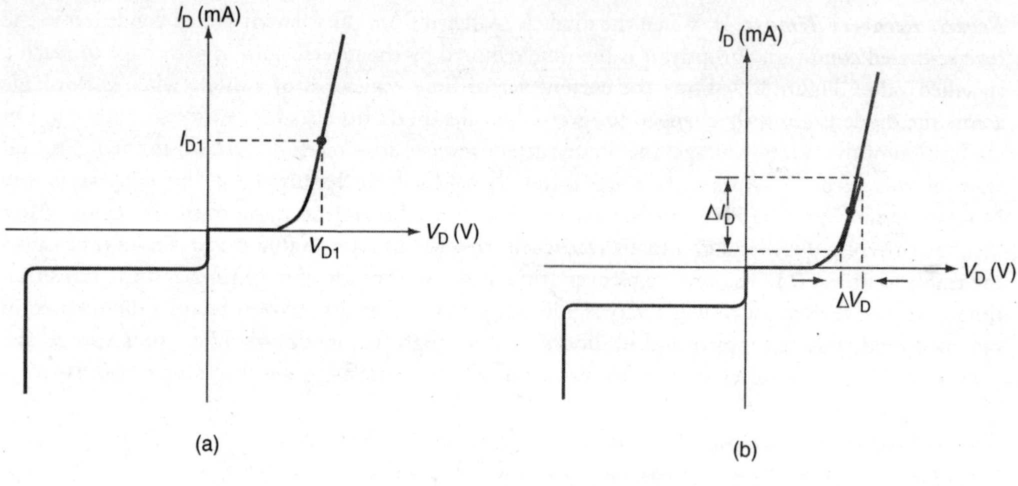

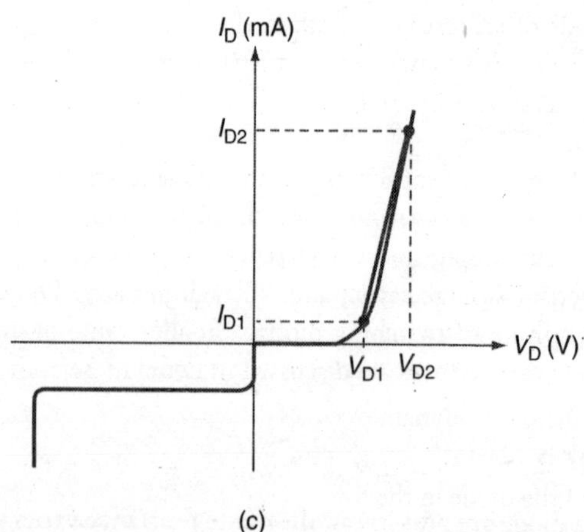

Figure 2.10 (a) Static resistance of a diode; (b) dynamic resistance of a diode; (c) average AC resistance of a diode.

Dynamic Resistance

Dynamic resistance or the AC resistance of a diode is defined as the resistance offered by the diode to a time-varying input signal. The dynamic resistance of the diode having the V–I characteristics shown in Figure 2.10(b) is given by Eq. (2.6). In other words, the dynamic resistance at a particular point in the operating region of the diode is defined by the slope of the tangent drawn at that point.

$$r = \frac{\Delta V_D}{\Delta I_D} \tag{2.6}$$

By taking the derivative of universal diode equation given in Eq. (2.1) with respect to applied forward voltage and reversing the result we get the expression for the dynamic resistance of the diode. The derivation is as follows.

Universal diode equation is $I_D = I_0(e^{V_D/\eta V_T} - 1)$. Substituting $V_T = kT/q$ in the above equation and taking derivative of the equation wrt the forward voltage (V_D) we get

$$\frac{dI_D}{dV_D} = \frac{qI_0 e^{qV_D/\eta kT}}{\eta kT}$$

Substituting $I_0 e^{qV_D/\eta kT} = I_D + I_0$ in the above equation we get

$$\frac{dI_D}{dV_D} = \frac{q(I_D + I_0)}{\eta kT}$$

Now as $I_D \gg I_0$,

$$\frac{dI_D}{dV_D} \cong \frac{qI_D}{\eta kT}$$

Taking the reciprocal of the above equation, we obtain

$$\frac{dV_D}{dI_D} \cong \frac{\eta kT}{qI_D}$$

Substituting the value of $k = 8.642 \times 10^{-5}$ eV/K and $T = 300$ K we get

$$\frac{dV_D}{dI_D} = r \cong \frac{26\eta}{I_D}$$

Dynamic resistance (r) of a diode in the forward-biased region is given by

$$r \cong \frac{26\eta}{I_D} \tag{2.7}$$

where $\eta = 1$ for germanium and silicon (for relatively higher values of diode current); $\eta = 2$ for silicon at relatively low levels of diode current, that is below the cut-in-voltage or the knee-point of the diode characteristics; I_D is the forward diode current (in mA). The dynamic ON resistance for the forward -biased diode is also represented as R_D.

In the reverse-biased region, the value of the dynamic resistance of the diode is given by

$$\text{Dynamic resistance of the diode in the reverse-biased region} \cong \frac{26\eta}{I_0} \tag{2.8}$$

where I_0 is the reverse saturation current. However, the change in the value of reverse saturation current (I_0) is very small with change in the reverse-bias voltage from 0 V to the reverse breakdown voltage resulting in very high value of dynamic resistance. Hence, for all practical purposes the diode can be assumed to be an open circuit in the reverse-bias region. The typical value of dynamic resistance of silicon diodes is of the order of few ohms in the forward-biased region and around few hundreds of mega-ohms in the reverse-biased region.

Average AC Resistance

Another term that is sometimes used to define the resistance of a diode is called the average AC resistance. When a sufficiently large input signal is applied to the diode to produce a broad swing as shown in Figure 2.10(c), the resistance associated with the diode is called the average AC resistance. It is determined by the slope of the straight line formed by joining the two points on the V–I characteristics of the diode corresponding to the maximum and minimum input voltages:

$$\text{Average AC resistance} = \frac{V_{D2} - V_{D1}}{I_{D2} - I_{D1}} \tag{2.9}$$

The static, dynamic and average AC resistances discussed thus far are all contributed by the P–N junction. Other than the junction resistance, the resistance of the semiconductor material (called the body resistance) and the resistance introduced by the connection between the semiconductor material and the external metallic conductor (called the contact resistance) are also present. These resistances together can range from 0.1 Ω to around 2 Ω and in most cases can be ignored.

EXAMPLE 2.1 *Refer to Figure 2.11. Determine the static and the dynamic resistances of the diode at points A and B.*

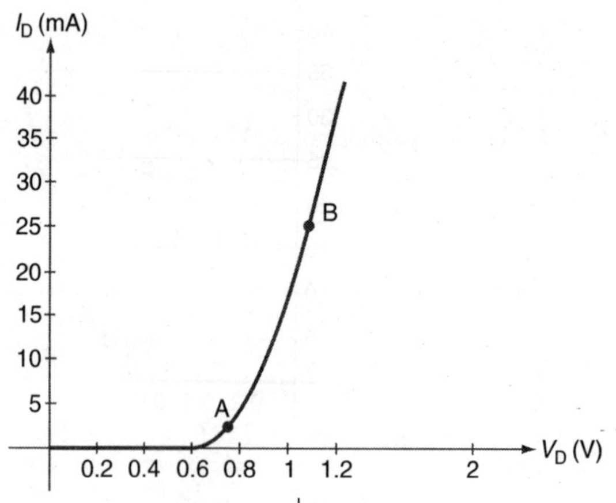

Figure 2.11 Example 2.1.

Solution

1. Let us first consider point A. The diode current and voltage at point A are 2 mA and 0.75 V, respectively.
2. Static resistance at point A = $0.75/2 \times 10^{-3} = 375\ \Omega$.
3. The slope of the tangent line at point A gives the dynamic resistance of the diode at point A. Figure 2.12(a) shows the exploded view of the characteristics near point A.
4. Dynamic resistance = $(0.82 - 0.68)/(4.4 \times 10^{-3} - 0) = 140/4.4 = 31.8\ \Omega$.
5. Let us now consider point B [Figure 2.12(b)].
6. The diode current and voltage are 25 mA and 1.14 V, respectively.

7. Static resistance of the diode at point B = $1.14/25 \times 10^{-3} = 45.6\ \Omega$.
8. The slope of the tangent line at point B gives the dynamic resistance of the diode at point B [Figure 2.12(b)].
9. Dynamic resistance = $(1.195 - 1)/(35 - 15) \times 10^{-3} = 0.195/20 \times 10^{-3} = 9.75\ \Omega$.
10. As is clear from the example, the resistance of a diode in the linear V–I region is much smaller as compared to the resistance near the knee region. Also, the dynamic resistance of a diode is much smaller than the static resistance.

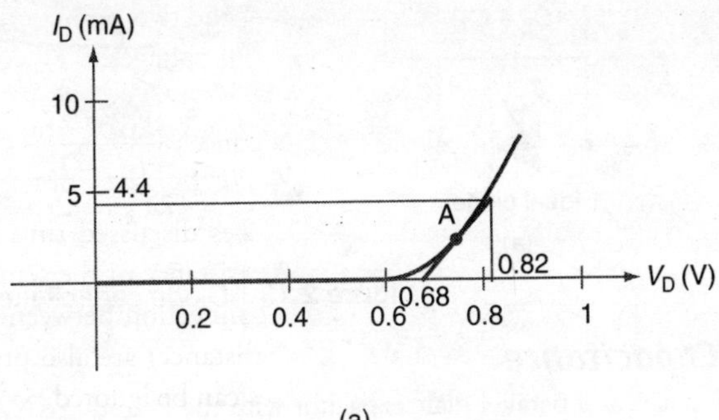

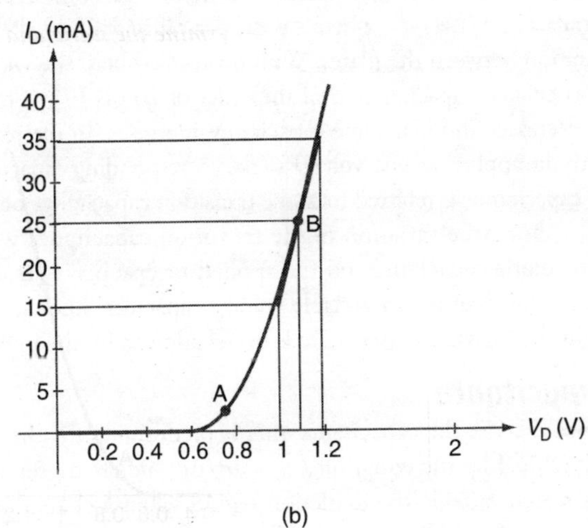

Figure 2.12 Solution to Example 2.1.

2.8 Diode Junction Capacitance

As discussed earlier in Section 2.6 on diode specifications, there are two types of capacitances associated with a junction diode, namely, the *transition capacitance* (C_T) and the *diffusion capacitance* (C_D). These capacitances in effect come in parallel with the ideal diode as shown in Figure 2.13(a). For low- and mid-frequency low-power applications, the effect of these capacitances on the diode performance is negligible and hence can be ignored. However, in high-frequency and high-power applications, the effect of these capacitances have to be taken into consideration. We will discuss these two diode capacitances in detail in the following sub-sections.

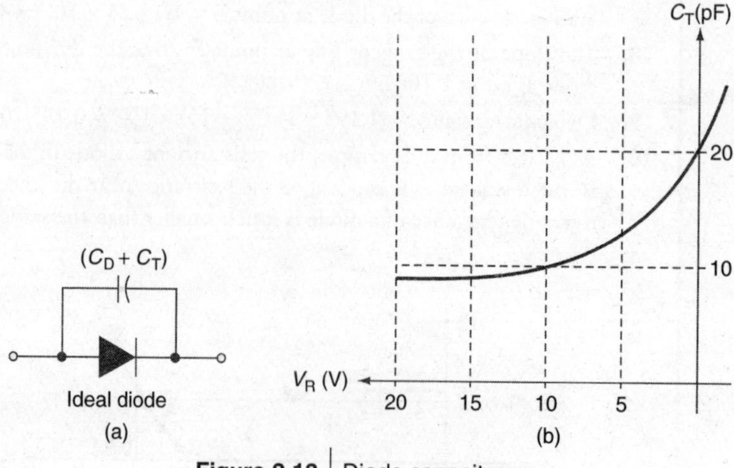

Figure 2.13 Diode capacitance.

Transition Capacitance

The P–N junction acts as a parallel plate capacitor with the P- and the N-regions as the parallel plates and the depletion region as the insulator or the dielectric. As we can recall, the capacitance of a parallel plate capacitor is given by the formula $C_P = (\varepsilon A / d)$, where ε is the permittivity of the dielectric used, A is the area of the plates and d is the separation between the plates. With no applied bias, the width of the depletion region is around 0.5 μm and the associated capacitance is of the order of 20 pF. In the forward-biased state, the width of the depletion region decreases and hence the capacitance increases. In the reverse-biased condition, the depletion region widens with the applied reverse voltage so the corresponding capacitance reduces with increase in applied reverse bias. This capacitance is referred to as the transition capacitance or the space charge capacitance.

Figure 2.13(b) shows the variation of the transition capacitance with the applied reverse voltage. The dependence of the diode capacitance on the applied reverse bias is made use of in a number of electronic devices and systems, for example in variable voltage capacitors known as the varactors. The effect of transition capacitance in the forward-biased state is overshadowed by the presence of diffusion capacitance.

Diffusion Capacitance

In the forward-biased state, the capacitance that is predominant is the diffusion capacitance or the storage capacitance. It is defined by the equation $C_D = \mathrm{d}q/\mathrm{d}v$, where d$q$ represents the change in the number of minority carriers stored outside the depletion region when a change in voltage (dv) is applied across the diode. In other words, it is dependent on the rate at which the charge is inducted into the P- and the N-regions just outside the depletion region. Its value in the forward-biased region is in the range of 10–20 μF. In the reverse-bias region, its value is much smaller than the transition capacitance and hence the transition capacitance predominates in this region.

Diffusion capacitance affects the switching time of the diode. The switching time constant of the diode is equal to $(r_d \times C_D)$, where r_d is the dynamic forward resistance of the diode. The value of switching time constant is very small due to the extremely small value of r_d. Hence, the switching time of the diode is not taken into consideration for normal diode applications and it assumes importance only when the diode is used as a switching device in very high speed applications.

2.9 Diode Equivalent Circuits

An equivalent circuit of a device is a combination of elements suitably connected so as to best represent the actual terminal characteristics of the device. The most accurate equivalent circuit model for a diode is the *piecewise linear equivalent circuit model* in which the diode curves are represented by straight-line segments. The model is shown in Figure 2.14. From the figure it is clear that the assumption has been made that the diode will not conduct until the voltage at the anode exceeds the cathode voltage by the cut-in voltage, which is 0.7 V for silicon diodes and 0.3 V for germanium diodes. Hence, a battery voltage (V_B) has been introduced in the circuit opposite to the conduction direction of the diode. The magnitude of V_B is equal to the cut-in voltage of the diode. When the applied voltage exceeds V_B, the diode starts conducting and the resistance of the diode is expressed as the dynamic-ON resistance (r_d) in the forward-biased condition. A line is drawn on the equivalent model curve with a slope equal to the inverse of the value of the dynamic resistance ($1/r_d$). The ideal diode shown in the circuit is an ideal switch that conducts only in one direction. The piecewise linear equivalent circuit model is the most accurate equivalent model of a diode. However, it does not result in the actual duplication of the diode characteristics, especially in the knee region. Also, the model is equally valid for both DC as well as AC applications.

When the network resistance is much larger than the value of the diode resistance (r_d) then the above model can be simplified as shown in Figure 2.15. Here the diode resistance is assumed to be zero. The model makes an assumption that the diode will not conduct until the cut-in voltage is reached and after that it acts as an ideal closed switch that conducts only in one direction.

Another possible simplification model is shown in Figure 2.16. Here, the curve has been approximated by a straight line through the origin and the slope of the straight line is given by the inverse of the static diode resistance at the point of intersection of the line with the diode V–I characteristics.

Ideal diode is the most simple equivalent diode model. This model is applicable when the applied voltage levels are much larger than the diode's cut-in voltage and the network resistance is of a much larger value

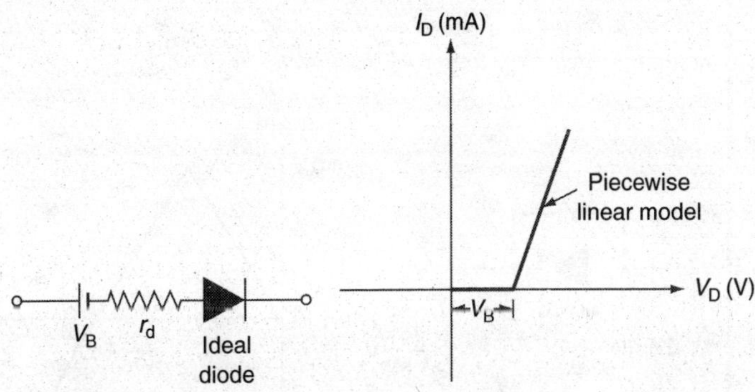

Figure 2.14 Piecewise linear equivalent model of a diode.

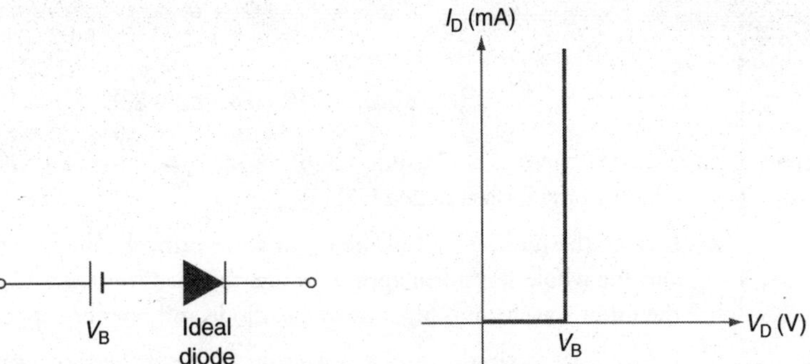

Figure 2.15 Simplified equivalent diode model.

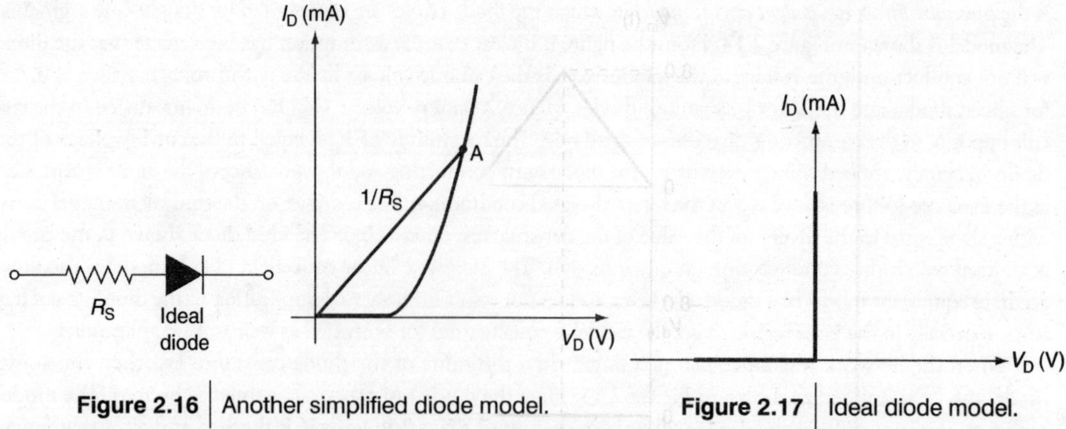

Figure 2.16 Another simplified diode model.

Figure 2.17 Ideal diode model.

than the diode's dynamic-ON resistance. The V–I characteristics of an ideal diode were shown in Figure 2.5. They are reproduced again in Figure 2.17 for reference.

EXAMPLE 2.2 *Figure 2.18(a) shows a simple diode circuit. The input waveform applied to the circuit is shown in Figure 2.18(b). Draw the waveforms for the output voltage (V_o) and voltage across the diode (V_d) assuming the diode to be ideal.*

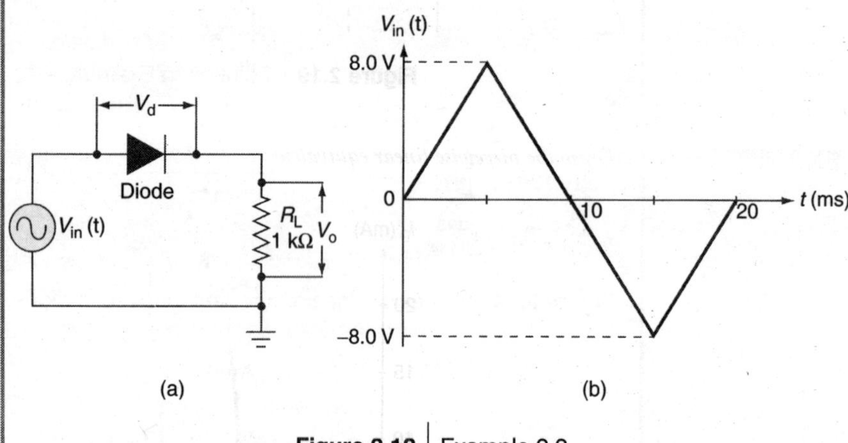

Figure 2.18 Example 2.2.

Solution

1. The ideal diode acts as a short circuit in the forward-biased region and as an open circuit in the reverse-biased region.
2. During the positive half of the input waveform, the diode acts as a short circuit and the whole waveform appears across the load resistance (R_L). Negative half of the input waveform is blocked by the diode and does not appear across R_L.
3. Figure 2.19 shows the output waveform (V_o) and the diode waveform (V_d).

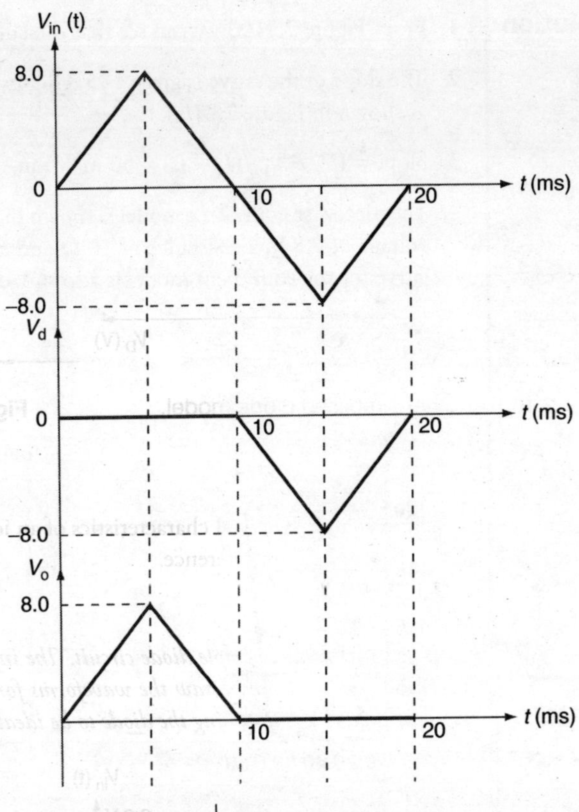

Figure 2.19 | Solution to Example 2.2.

EXAMPLE 2.3 *Draw the piecewise linear equivalent circuit model for the diode shown in Figure 2.20.*

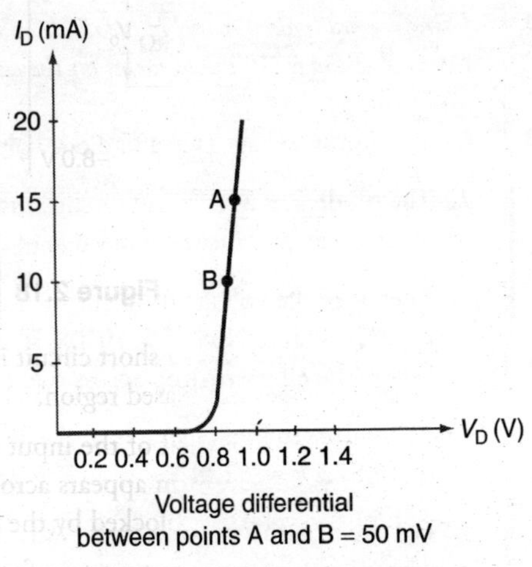

Figure 2.20 | Example 2.3.

Solution

1. From Figure 2.21(a) we can see that the cut-in voltage is 0.8 V (approx.).
2. The slope of the curve is given by taking two points A and B in the linear region as shown in Figure 2.21(a).
3. Slope = $(V_A - V_B)/(I_A - I_B) = 50$ mV/5 mA = 10 Ω.
4. The piecewise equivalent model is shown in Figure 2.21(b). It comprises a battery voltage of 0.8 V, a resistance of 10 Ω and an ideal diode. The V–I characteristic curve for the equivalent model is also shown in the figure.

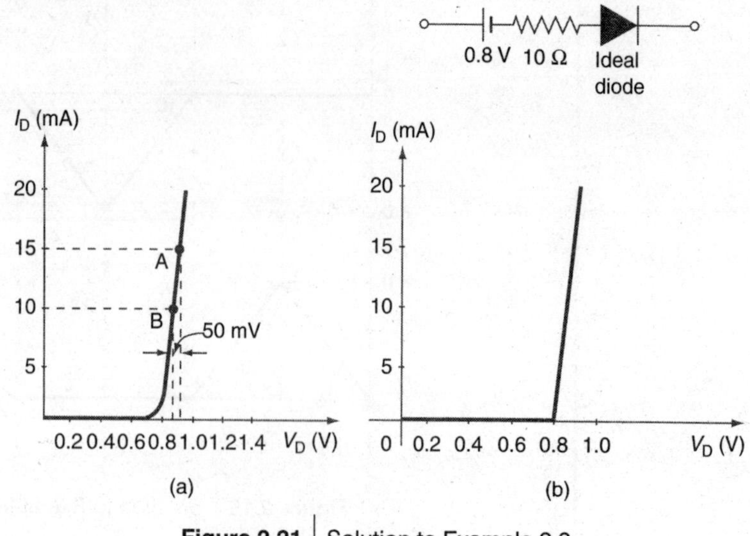

Figure 2.21 Solution to Example 2.3.

EXAMPLE 2.4 *Using the equivalent model of the diode in Example 2.3, draw the output voltage (V_o) and the diode voltage (V_d) waveforms for the circuit and the input waveform of Example 2.2.*

Solution

1. The output voltage (V_o) and diode voltage (V_d) waveforms are shown in Figure 2.22.
2. The diode acts as an open circuit until the input voltage reaches 0.8 V. After that it acts as a resistance with a value of 10 Ω.
3. Therefore the voltage drop across the diode resistance when input voltage is 8 V is given by $[(8 - 0.8)/1 \times 10^3] \times 10 = 72$ mV. Therefore, when the input voltage is 8 V, the effective drop across the diode is 0.872 V.
4. Therefore, the voltage across the load resistance when input voltage is 8 V is $8 - 0.872$ V = 7.128 V.
5. For the negative portion of the waveform, the diode acts as an open circuit. The whole input voltage appears across the diode and the output voltage (V_o) is zero.

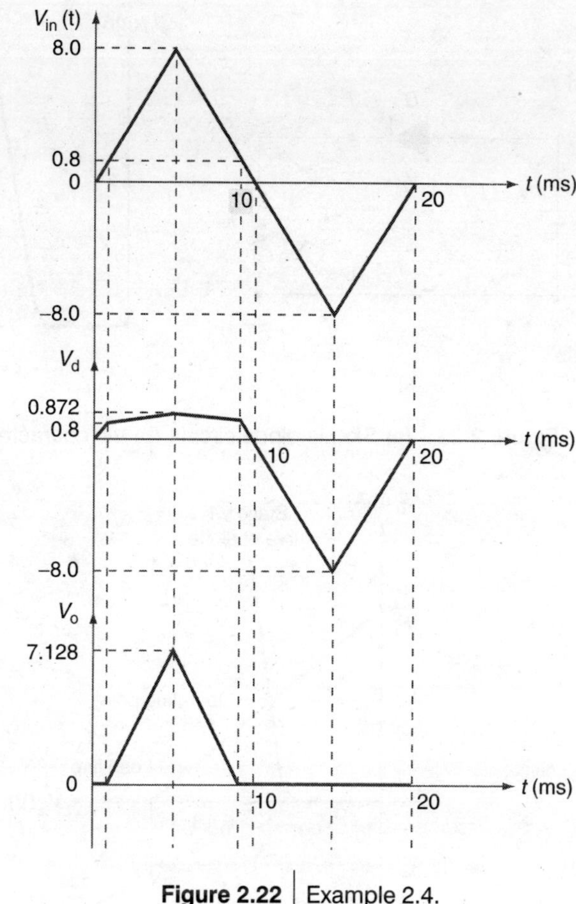

Figure 2.22 Example 2.4.

2.10 Load-Line Analysis of a Diode Circuit

Load-line analysis is a graphical method of analyzing a circuit. In this method, a load line is drawn on the actual characteristic curve or on the equivalent model curve of the active device used in the circuit. It provides a very accurate method of analyzing the circuit when the actual characteristic curve of the active device is used for analysis. The slope of the load line depends on the applied load. It may be mentioned here that the applied load generally has an important impact on the point or region of operation of the device. The active device of concern in this section is the semiconductor diode.

DC Applied Voltage

Figure 2.23(a) shows the basic diode circuit where a DC input voltage source (V_I) is applied to a series connection of a diode (D) and load resistance (R_L). Applying Kirchhoff's voltage law to the circuit of Figure 2.23(a) we get

$$V_I = V_D + I_D R_L \tag{2.10}$$

where V_D is the diode voltage and I_D the diode current.

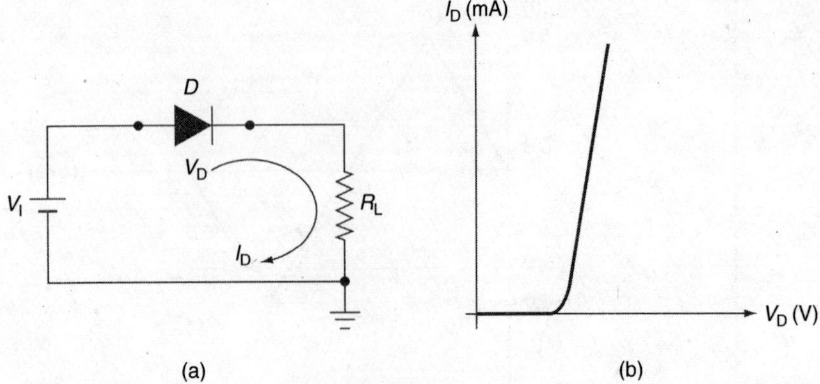

Figure 2.23 (a) Simple diode circuit; (b) V–I characteristics of a diode.

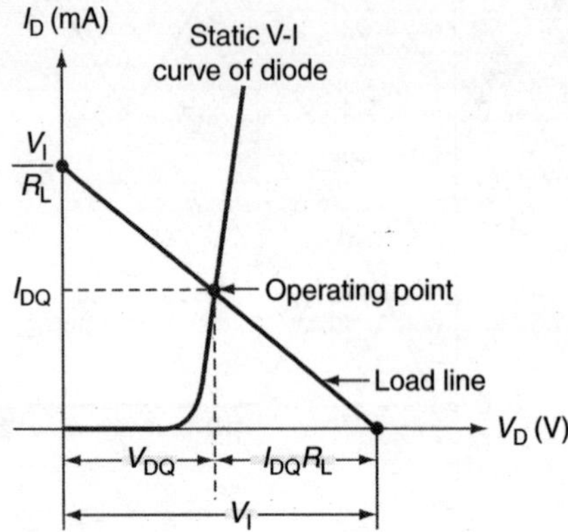

Figure 2.24 Load-line analysis of a diode circuit for DC input voltage.

The straight line represented by Eq. (2.10) is called the *load line*. This single equation is not sufficient to determine the two unknown variables: diode voltage (V_D) and diode current (I_D). However, these two variables are the same as the diode's V–I characteristic axis variables [Figure 2.23(b)]. Therefore, a second relationship between the two variables is given by the V–I characteristic curve of the diode. The intersection of the load line with the V–I characteristic curve of the diode determines the *operating point* of the circuit also called the *quiescent point* or the *Q-point*.

The load line can be drawn by determining its intercepts on the voltage and the current axis. For $V_D = 0$, $I_D = V_I/R$ and for $I_D = 0$, $V_D = V_I$. The straight line joining these two points is the load line. The slope of the line is dependent on the value of load resistance (R_L) and is given by $-1/R_L$. Thus, for a given input voltage (V_I), lower the value of the load resistance steeper is the load line resulting in a higher value of the current at the Q-point. The process of drawing the load line and determining the Q-point is better illustrated in Figure 2.24. The operating point for the circuit is (V_{DQ}, I_{DQ}), where $V_{DQ} = V_I - I_{DQ} \times R_L$.

AC Applied Voltage

Let us consider the case when a time-varying input signal is applied to the circuit shown in Figure 2.25(a). Since the voltage applied is time-variant, separate load lines need to be drawn for the instantaneous values of the input voltage. The various load lines are parallel to each other as the value of load resistance (R_L) is

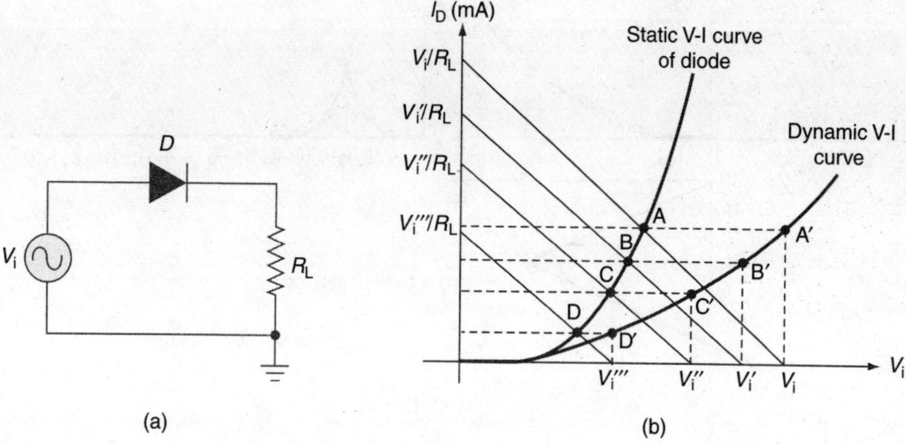

Figure 2.25 Dynamic characteristic curve.

fixed. The intersection of these lines with the static V–I characteristic curve of the diode gives the value of the current in the circuit corresponding to different instantaneous values of the input signal. A better method to determine the current is to draw the dynamic characteristic curve of the circuit which is a plot between the diode current and the input voltage. Figure 2.25(b) shows the procedure for drawing the dynamic characteristic curve. The load line for the maximum value of the input signal is drawn. From the Q-point a horizontal line is drawn. The point where this line intersects with the vertical line drawn from the X-axis corresponding to that input voltage gives a point on the dynamic curve. The process is repeated for a few other values of input voltage to yield sufficient points to construct the dynamic curve.

Let us assume that the waveform shown in Figure 2.26(a) is applied to the circuit shown in Figure 2.25(a). The dynamic curve can be used to draw the output current waveform as shown in Figure 2.26(b). The figure is self-explanatory. It may be mentioned here that the dynamic curve applies only to the circuit containing the same value of load resistance for which it is drawn. Also, in the discussion we have assumed the diode to be an open circuit in the reverse bias region. However, the dynamic curve for the diode in the reverse-bias region can be drawn on similar lines as drawn for the forward-bias region.

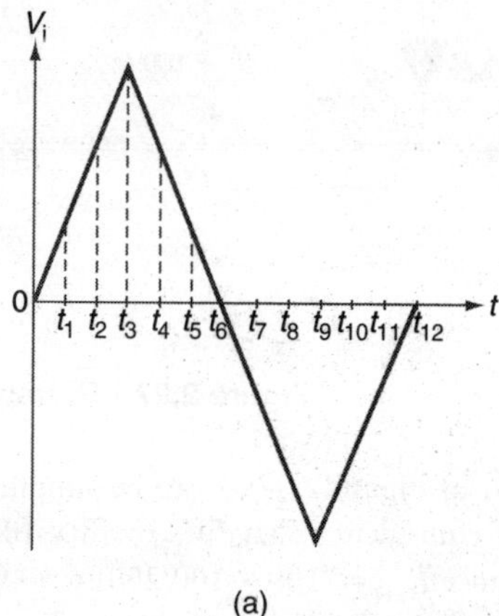

Figure 2.26 (a) Input waveform; (b) output waveform construction of a diode circuit for AC input voltage.

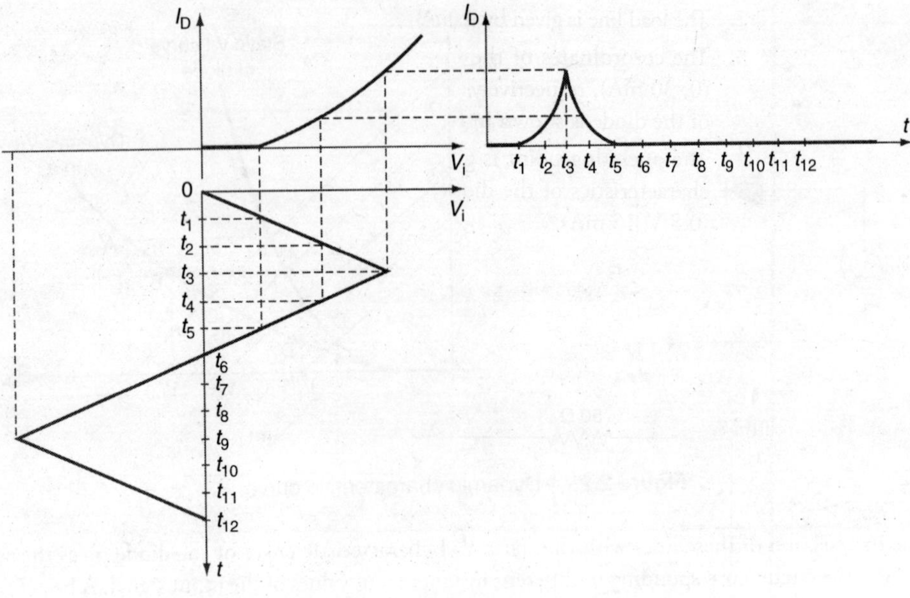

Figure 2.26 *Continued.*

EXAMPLE 2.5 *Draw the load line for the diode circuit of Figure 2.27(a). The forward characteristics of the diode are shown in Figure 2.27(b). Also determine the operating point.*

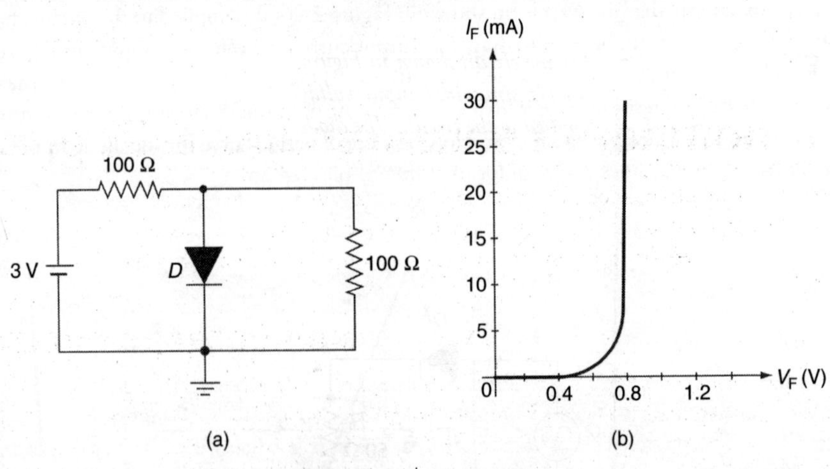

Figure 2.27 Example 2.5.

Solution

1. The circuit of Figure 2.27(a) can be simplified using the Thevenin's theorem. Thevenin's equivalent voltage $V_{TH} = (3 \times 100/200) = 1.5$ V. Thevenin's equivalent resistance $R_{TH} = (100 \times 100/200) = 50\ \Omega$. The simplified equivalent circuit is shown in Figure 2.28(a).

2. The load line is given by the equation $V_{TH} = V_D + I_D \times R_{TH}$ or $1.5 = V_D + I_D \times 50$.
3. The co-ordinates of the load line on the X- and the Y-axis are (1.5 V, 0) and (0, 30 mA), respectively. The load line superimposed on the V–I characteristics of the diode is shown in Figure 2.28(b).
4. The operating point is given by the intersection of the load line with the V–I characteristics of the diode. From Figure 2.28(b), we can see that the point is (0.8 V, 15 mA).

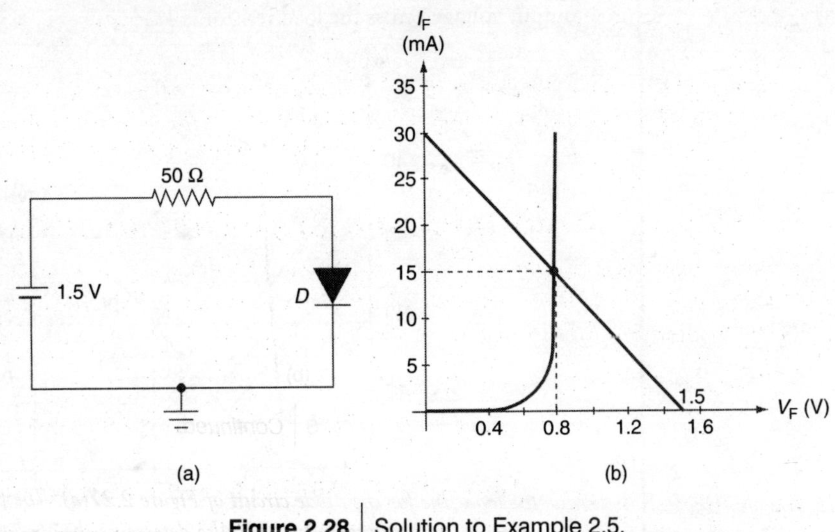

Figure 2.28 | Solution to Example 2.5.

EXAMPLE 2.6 *For the circuit shown in Figure 2.29(a), draw the output waveform of the circuit when a 50 Hz sinusoidal input voltage with a root mean square (RMS) voltage of 1.44 V is applied to the circuit. The diode characteristics are shown in Figure 2.29(b).*

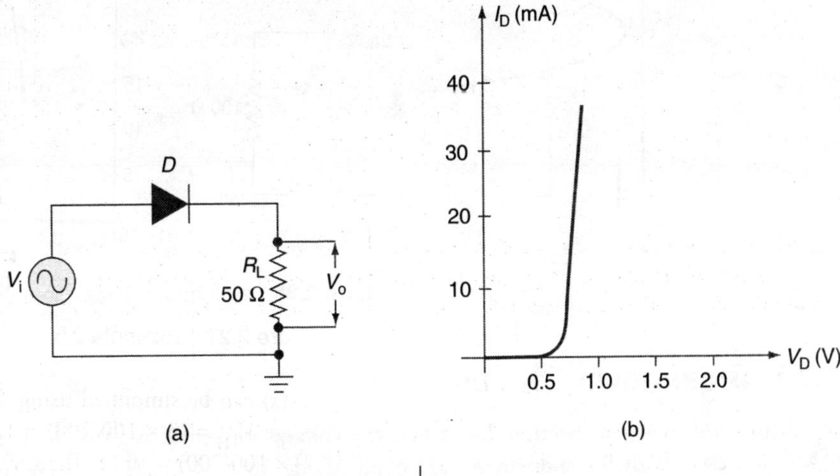

Figure 2.29 | Example 2.6.

Solution

1. The RMS voltage of 1.44 V implies a peak value of 2 V and a frequency of 50 Hz implies a time period of 20 ms.
2. Load line is drawn for the peak value of the input waveform. The load line equation is $2 = V_D + I_D \times 50$. The coordinates of the line on the voltage and the current axes are (2 V, 0) and (0, 40 mA), respectively.
3. The procedure is repeated for other values of the input waveform and the dynamic curve is drawn. The relevant waveforms are shown in Figure 2.30.
4. From the figure, we see that the maximum output current is 24 mA. The peak output voltage across the load resistor is 1.2 V.

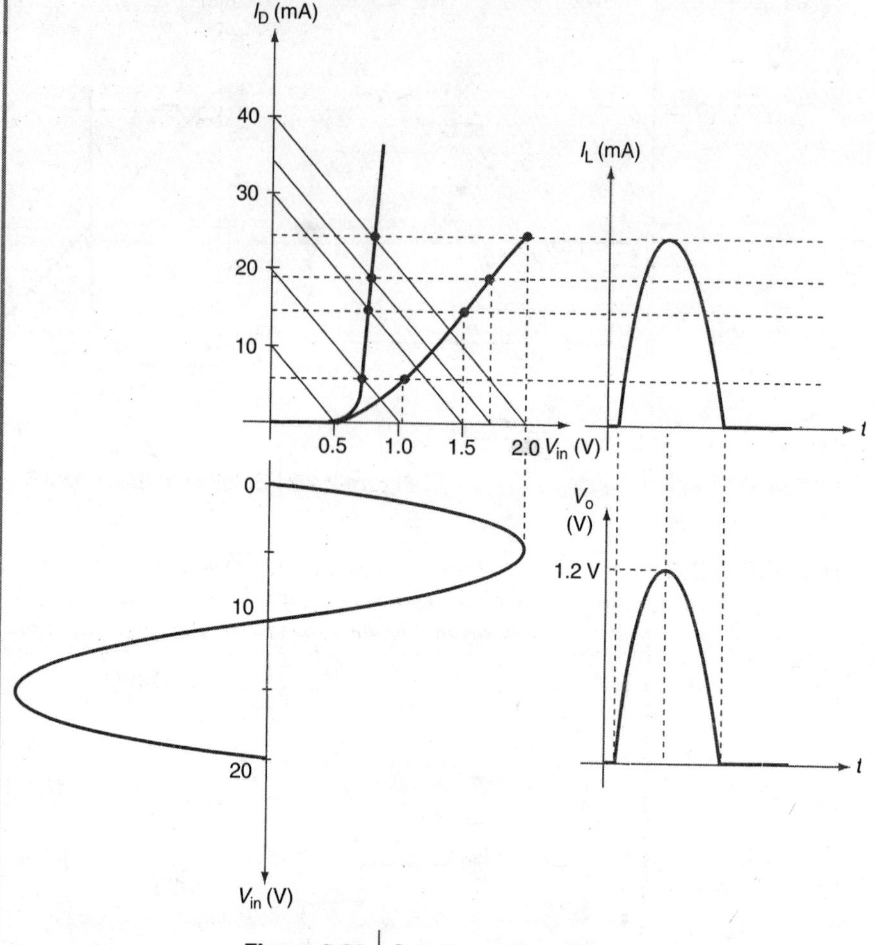

Figure 2.30 Solution to Example 6.

2.11 Breakdown Diodes

As discussed earlier in Section 2.4, when the voltage applied across the diode in the reverse-biased region exceeds the breakdown voltage of the diode, there is a sharp increase in the current flowing through the diode. This region is known as the breakdown region. Breakdown diodes are designed with sufficient power dissipation capabilities to operate in the breakdown region. They are generally employed as

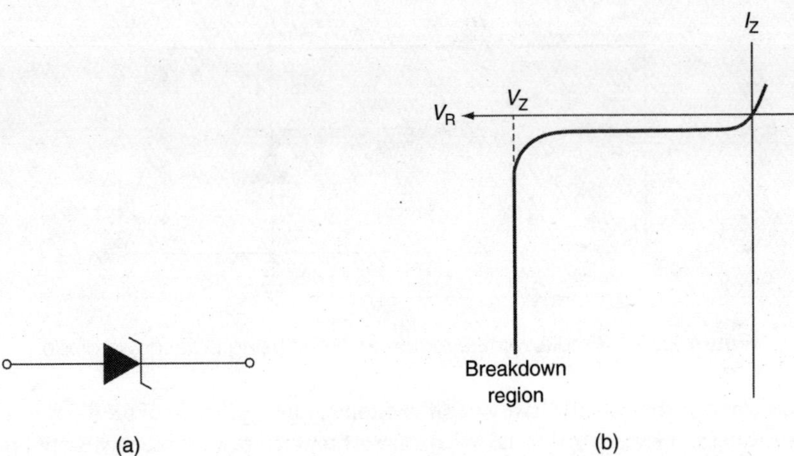

Figure 2.31 (a) Circuit symbol of breakdown diodes; (b) V–I characteristic of breakdown diodes.

constant-voltage devices or as voltage references. Depending upon the mechanism which leads to breakdown they can be further classified as *Zener diodes* and *avalanche diodes.*

The symbol and the V–I characteristics of breakdown diodes are shown in Figures 2.31(a) and (b), respectively. As is clear from Figure 2.31(b), for reverse voltages less than the breakdown voltage (V_Z), the diode acts as an open circuit, and for voltages greater than the breakdown voltage it acts as a constant voltage reference with the voltage across it equal to the breakdown voltage. It may be mentioned here that the shape of the V–I characteristics is the same for both the Zener and avalanche diodes. The parameters of interest for the breakdown diodes are the breakdown voltage, the dynamic impedance and the power dissipation capability.

Avalanche Diodes

In the case of avalanche diodes, on the application of reverse-bias voltage the thermally generated carriers have sufficient energies to disrupt covalent bonds, thereby resulting in free electrons. These free electrons knock out more electrons from the adjacent bonds. The process is regenerative and is referred to as *avalanche multiplication*. Avalanche breakdown mechanism is predominant in lightly doped diodes with broad depletion region and low field intensity. Generally, the avalanche diodes have breakdown voltages greater than 6 V and their breakdown voltage increases with increase in temperature, that is, they have positive temperature coefficient of breakdown voltage. As the temperature increases, the vibrational displacement of atoms in the crystal grows which increases the probability of collision of carriers with the lattice atoms as they cross the depletion region. Hence, they do not have sufficient energy to start the avalanche process resulting in an increase in the breakdown voltage. Silicon diodes with avalanche breakdown phenomenon are available with breakdown voltages ranging from several volts to several hundreds of volts and with power ratings up to 50 W.

Zener Diodes

The breakdown phenomenon in the case of a Zener diode is the result of electrons breaking their covalent bonds due to the existence of a strong electric field at the junction. The new hole–electron pair created increases the reverse current. It does not involve collisions of carriers with the lattice atoms. A Zener breakdown phenomenon occurs for heavily doped diodes having a narrow depletion-region width and high-field intensity. They have breakdown voltages below 6 V. With increase in temperature, the energy of the valence electrons increases, making it easier for these electrons to break the covalent bonds and hence the breakdown

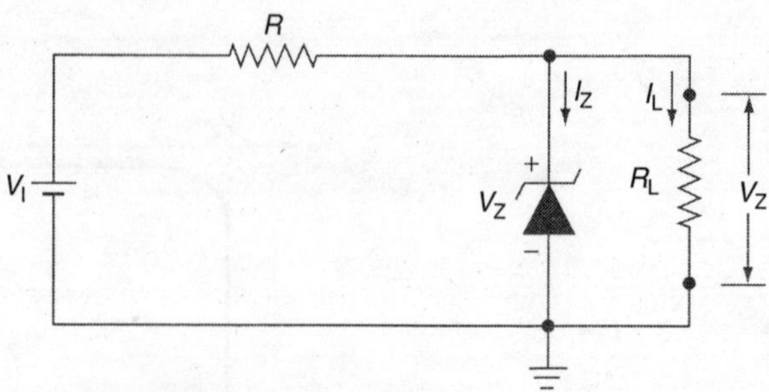

Figure 2.32 | Simple voltage regulator circuit using breakdown diode.

voltage decreases. Hence, these diodes have a negative temperature coefficient of breakdown voltage. Diodes with breakdown voltages between 5 V and 6 V have almost zero temperature coefficient of breakdown voltage. It may be mentioned here that the term Zener diode is generally used for breakdown diodes even with avalanche breakdown phenomenon.

Both Zener and avalanche diodes are used in voltage regulators to regulate the load voltage against variations in load current and input voltage. They are used in these applications because in the breakdown region large change in the diode current produces only a small change in the diode voltage. Figure 2.32 shows a simple voltage regulator circuit employing a Zener diode. The voltage across the load resistor is the same as the Zener breakdown voltage. The topic of voltage regulators is covered in the chapter on linear power supplies (Chapter 14).

2.12 Varactor Diodes

Varactor diodes are used as variable voltage capacitors. They are also referred to as *varicaps* or *variable voltage capacitance diodes* or *tunable diodes*. Their mode of operation depends on the transition capacitance that exists at the P–N junction when the diode is reverse-biased. Junction capacitances were discussed in detail in Section 2.8. Figure 2.33 shows the characteristics of a typical commercially available varactor diode. As shown in the figure, there is a sharp decrease in the transition capacitance initially with increase in reverse-bias voltage. As the reverse-bias voltage increases further, the rate of change of capacitance with voltage decreases. Varactor diodes are normally operated with reverse voltages upto 20–30 V. The relationship between the transition capacitance and the applied reverse bias is expressed by

$$C_T = \frac{K}{(V_\gamma + V_R)^n} \tag{2.11}$$

where K is a constant (depends on the semiconductor material and the diode construction technique); V_γ the knee potential of the diode; V_R the magnitude of the applied reverse bias; $n = 1/2$ for alloy junction and 1/3 for diffused junction.

The circuit symbol and the equivalent circuit of varactor diodes are shown in Figures 2.34(a) and (b), respectively. The variable R_R is the resistance of the diode in the reverse-bias region and is of the order of greater than equal to 1 MΩ; R_S is the geometric resistance of the diode and is of the order of few ohms. The magnitude of C_T varies from few picofarads to around hundred picofarads. In different varactor diode types, the values of minimum and maximum capacitances may vary; however, the ratio of maximum to minimum capacitance is typically 2.5 to 3. Typical application areas of varactor diodes include FM modulators, automatic frequency control devices, adjustable bandpass filters and parametric amplifiers.

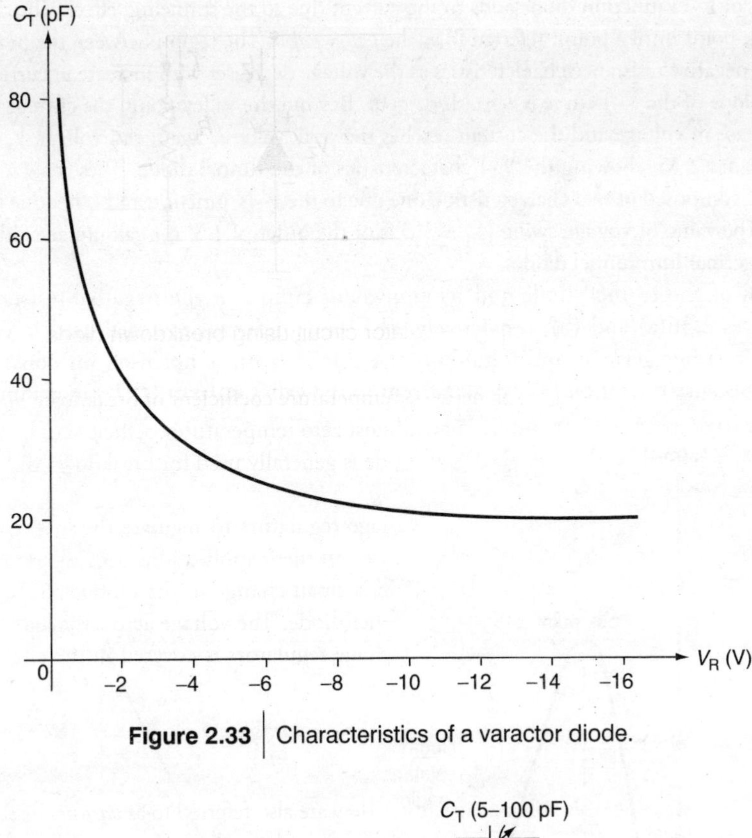

Figure 2.33 Characteristics of a varactor diode.

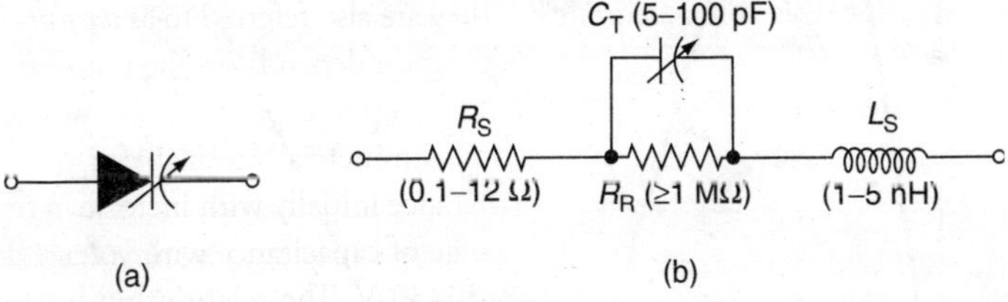

Figure 2.34 (a) Circuit symbol of a varactor diode; (b) equivalent circuit of a varactor diode.

2.13 Tunnel Diodes

Tunnel diodes have heavily doped P- and N-regions, about 100–1000 times dopant concentration than that of a typical semiconductor diode. Heavy doping results in narrowing of the depletion region. The width of the depletion region of a tunnel diode is about 100–1000 times less than that of a typical semiconductor diode. Owing to this narrow depletion region, the charge carriers instead of climbing up the potential barrier may pierce through the potential barrier resulting in "tunneling" of carriers both in the forward-bias and the reverse-bias regions, hence rendering the diode bi-directional conduction property. In the forward direction, the current reaches the maximum value I_P (called the peak current) at a voltage V_P (peak voltage). At this point, referred to as *peak point,* slope of the V–I curve is zero, that is, di/dv = 0. Beyond the peak point, the current starts to decrease with increase in voltage as there are no more carriers available for tunneling. The current approaches zero for a forward voltage of 0.4 V to 0.5 V but then the normal P–N junction effect starts. The forward current of P–N junction diode adds to the current due to the tunneling effect. The current decreases beyond the peak point until a point, referred to as the *valley point.* The region between the peak point and the valley point has negative resistance characteristics as the voltage decreases with increase in current. At the valley point also, the slope of the V–I curve is zero ($di/dv = 0$). Beyond the valley point, the current starts increasing again with increase in voltage and the current reaches the peak value I_P again at a voltage V_F. This is further illustrated in Figure 2.35, showing the V–I characteristics of the tunnel diode. These characteristics may be considered to be composed of two characteristics, one due to the P–N junction and other due to the tunneling phenomenon. The value of voltage swing ($V_F - V_P$) is of the order of 1 V for gallium arsenide tunnel diodes and 0.45 V for germanium tunnel diodes.

The symbol of the tunnel diode and its equivalent circuit in the negative resistance region are shown in Figures 2.36(a) and (b), respectively. The semiconductor material used in construction of tunnel diodes is either germanium or gallium arsenide. Silicon is not used for constructing tunnel diodes. This is because the ratio of the peak current to the valley current (I_P/I_V) in gallium arsenide and

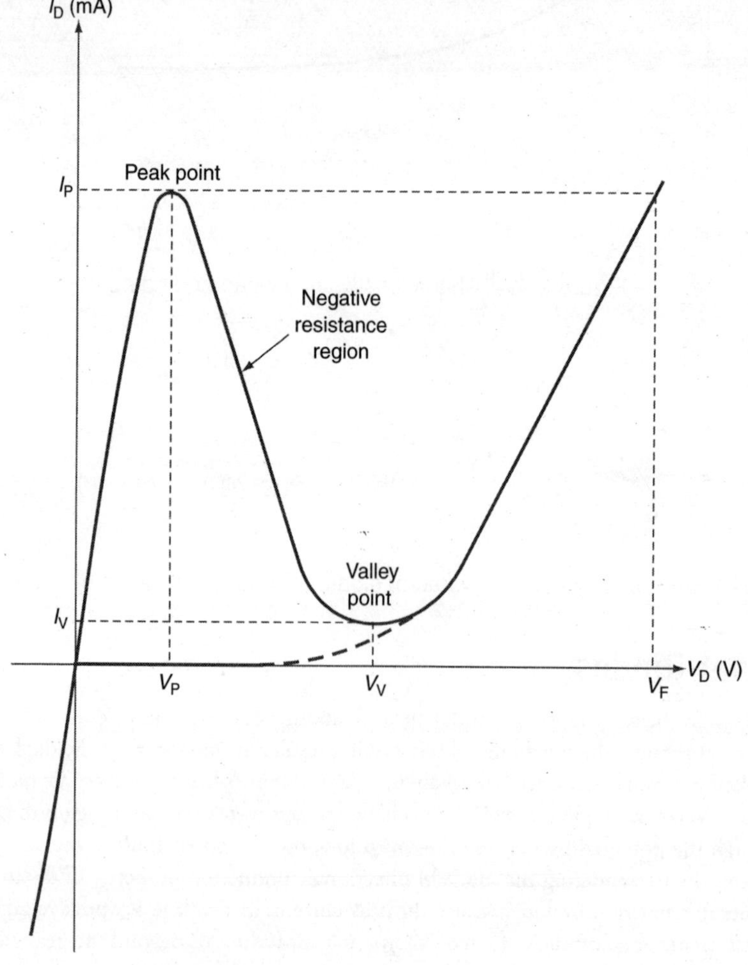

Figure 2.35 | V–I characteristics of a tunnel diode.

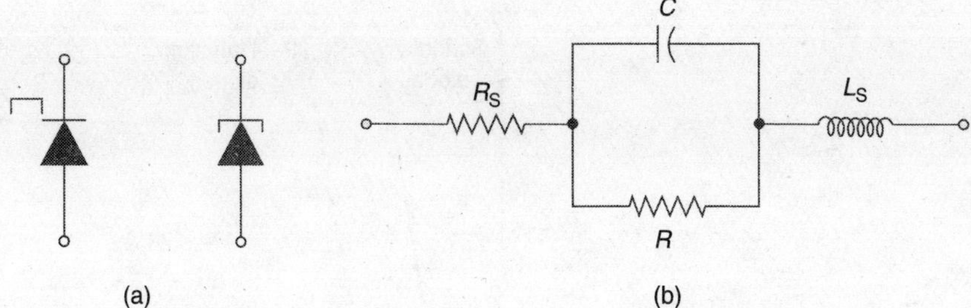

Figure 2.36 (a) Circuit symbol of a tunnel diode; (b) equivalent circuit of the tunnel diode in the negative resistance region.

germanium is quite high, approximately 15 for gallium arsenide and 8 for germanium. The value in the case of silicon is very small (approximately 3).

Tunnel diodes are used in high-speed applications such as in computers with switching times of the order of few nanoseconds to several picoseconds. Owing to their negative resistance characteristics these diodes were earlier used as microwave oscillators. However, now they have been replaced by other devices that have surpassed them in performance.

2.14 Schottky Diodes

Schottky diodes, also known as *hot-carrier diodes*, have a metal–semiconductor junction instead of a semiconductor–semiconductor junction (P–N junction) of a conventional P–N junction diode. Normally N-type silicon is used as the semiconductor while the metal used can be aluminum, platinum, tungsten or molybdenum. This different construction technique renders these diodes some special characteristics as compared to P–N junction diodes such as lower cut-in voltage, increased frequency of operation, etc.

Schottky barrier diodes are majority carrier conduction devices. In both the materials (metal and semiconductor) electrons are the majority carriers. The circuit symbol and the equivalent circuit model for a Schottky diode are shown in Figures 2.37(a) and (b), respectively. The equivalent circuit is an ideal diode in parallel with a capacitor which is equivalent to the junction capacitance. The V–I characteristics of a Schottky diode as compared to a conventional P–N junction diode are shown in Figure 2.38.

The junction barrier for a Schottky diode, in both the forward- and reverse-bias regions, is less than that of P–N junction diode. This results in lower cut-in voltage of the order of 0.3 V for silicon-metal Schottky diode as compared to a cut-in voltage of 0.7 V for silicon P–N junction diodes. Lower junction barrier also results in higher currents at the same applied voltage in both the forward- and the reverse-bias conditions. Thus, they dissipate less power than a normal diode. This, however, results in larger reverse saturation current as compared to a conventional P–N junction diode which is highly undesirable. Also, the peak inverse voltage (PIV) rating for a Schottky barrier diode is less than that of a comparable P–N junction diode.

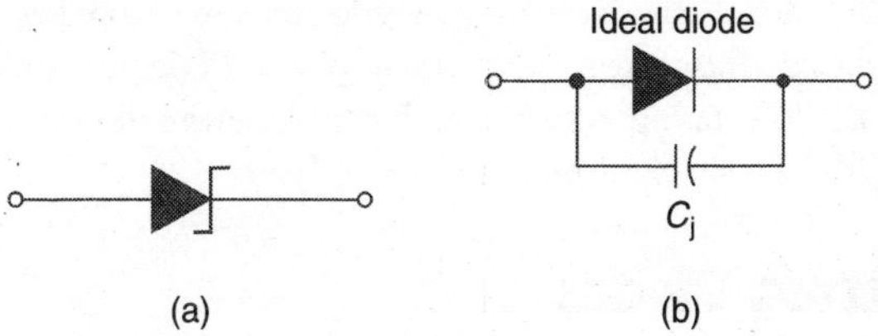

Figure 2.37 (a) Circuit symbol of a Schottky diode; (b) equivalent circuit of a Schottky diode.

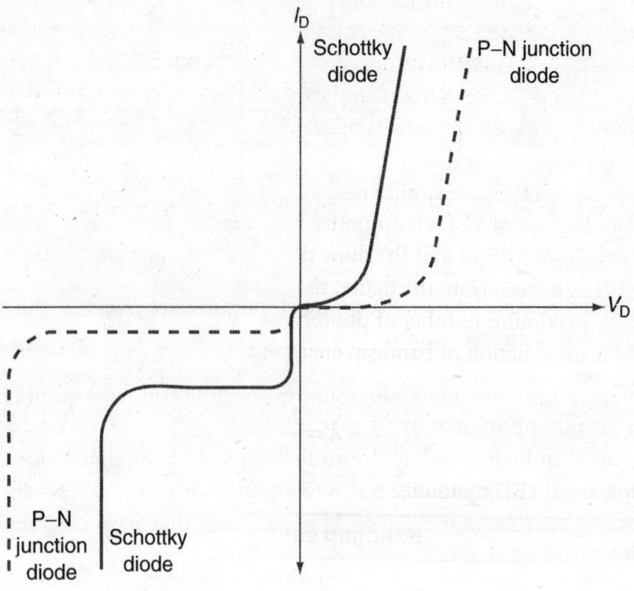

Figure 2.38 V–I characteristics of a Schottky diode.

Schottky diodes are used as high-efficiency rectifiers which are essential in applications such as switched mode power supplies (SMPS), switching regulators, etc. The absence of minority carriers in Schottky diodes results in significantly lower value of reverse recovery time (as low as 20 ns). Thus, they are effective at operating frequencies extending up to several gigahertz. Other application areas include low-voltage/high-current power supplies, AC to DC converters, mixers and detectors in communication systems.

2.15 Point-Contact Diodes and Power Diodes

Point-Contact Diodes

These diodes are intended primarily for radio frequency (RF) applications owing to their extremely small internal capacitance, considerably less than that of a conventional junction diode. They basically have a metal–semiconductor junction and have been replaced by Schottky barrier diodes because Schottky diodes offer lower forward resistance, wide dynamic range and better noise performance as compared to point-contact diodes.

Power Diodes

Power diodes are designed to operate at high-power levels and at high operating temperatures. They are mainly used as rectifiers. They are generally constructed using silicon because silicon offers higher current, temperature and PIV ratings. Such diodes have large junction area to ensure low forward diode resistance so that the I^2R loses can be reduced. The current capability of power diodes is increased by placing two or more diodes in parallel whereas the PIV rating is increased by stacking the diodes in series. Generally, they are mounted in conjunction with heat sinks for thermal management.

2.16 Light-Emitting Diodes

A semiconductor P–N junction diode designed to emit light when forward-biased is called a light-emitting diode (LED). When a P–N junction is forward-biased, the electrons in the N-type material and the holes in the P-type material travel towards the junction. Some of these holes and electrons recombine with each other and in the process radiate energy. The energy will be released either in the form of photons of light or in the form of heat. In silicon and germanium diodes, most of the energy is released as heat and the emitted light is insignificant. However, in some materials such as gallium phosphide (GaP), gallium arsenide (GaAs) and gallium arsenide phosphide (GaAsP) substantial photons of light are emitted. Hence, these materials are used in the construction of LEDs.

The V–I characteristics of LEDs are similar to that of a normal P–N junction diode with the difference that the cut-in voltage in the case of LEDs is around 1.5 V as compared to 0.7 V for silicon diodes and 0.3 V for germanium diodes. Figures 2.39(a) and (b) show the process of light emission in an LED and its circuit symbol, respectively. As can be seen from the figure, the conducting surface connected to the P-type material is smaller in size to allow maximum number of photons to contribute to the output light energy. The wavelength of emitted light is the function of bandgap energy of the semiconductor material and is expressed by the empirical formula

$$\lambda = \frac{1240}{\Delta E} \tag{2.12}$$

Table 2.1 | Commonly used LED materials

Material	Bandgap energy (eV)	Wavelength (nm)
GaAs	1.43	910
GaP	2.24	560
$GaAs_{60}P_{40}$	1.91	650
AlSb	1.60	775
InSb	0.18	6900

where λ is the wavelength (nm); ΔE the bandgap energy (eV). Table 2.1 enlists some of the materials used for making LEDs along with their bandgap energies and wavelengths. LEDs are discussed in detail in the chapter on optoelectronic devices (Chapter 7).

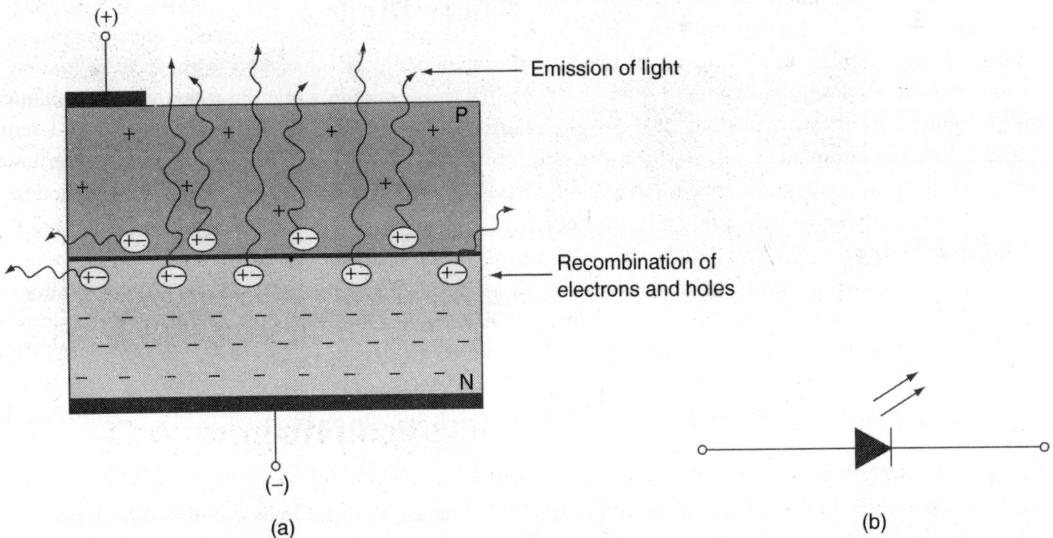

Figure 2.39 | (a) Process of light emission in an LED; (b) circuit symbol of an LED.

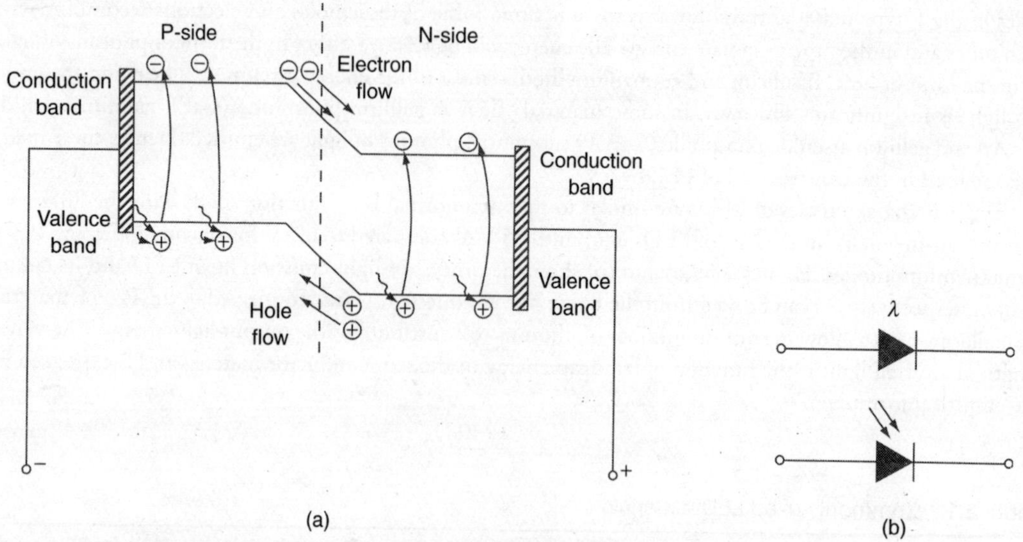

Figure 2.40 (a) Photoeffect in a photodiode; (b) circuit symbol of a photodiode.

2.17 Photodiodes

Photodiode is a junction diode through which significant current flows when light falls on it. Photodiodes are operated either in the reverse-bias mode (referred to as the photoconductive mode) or with no external bias (referred to as the photovoltaic mode). When no light is incident on the photodiode, the current flowing through it is the reverse saturation current. This current is also referred to as the *dark current.* When operated in the photoconductive mode, the impinging photons of incident light create electron–hole pairs on both sides of the junction. The number of electron–hole pairs generated is directly proportional to the number of incident photons. The photo-induced electrons in the conduction band of the P-region will move across the junction down the potential hill along with the thermally generated minority carriers. Similarly, holes produced in the valence band of the N-region are available to add to the current flow by moving across to the P-region. Figures 2.40(a) and (b) show the photoeffect in a photodiode and its circuit symbol. Figure 2.41 shows the variation of the photocurrent with the incident light. In the figure, I_{L1}, I_{L2}, I_{L3} and I_{L4} are the photocurrent levels corresponding to light levels L_1, L_2, L_3 and L_4, respectively. When operated in the photovoltaic mode, a voltage is developed across the anode and the cathode terminals. The dark current in the photovoltaic mode is nearly zero.

The spectral response of photodiodes is a function of the energy bandgap of the material used in its construction. Some of the commonly used materials are silicon (200–1100 nm), germanium (500–1900 nm), indium gallium arsenide (700–1700 nm) and mercury cadmium telluride (1900–10,000 nm). Detailed description of photodiodes is given in the chapter on optoelectronic devices (Chapter 7).

2.18 Connecting Diodes in Series and in Parallel

Diodes in Series

Semiconductor junction diodes are connected in series to enhance the peak inverse voltage rating beyond what is available in a single diode. In order to ensure that there is equal division of reverse voltage across the individual diodes, the diodes should have closely matched reverse-bias characteristics. Equal division of

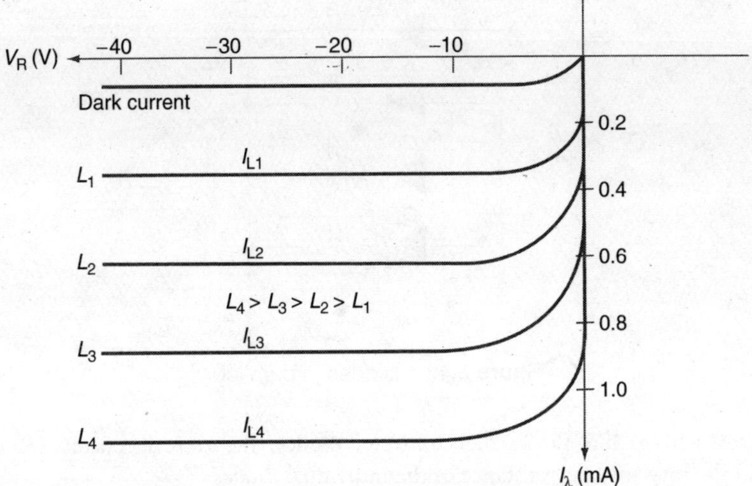

Figure 2.41 Variation of photocurrent with the incident light in a photodiode.

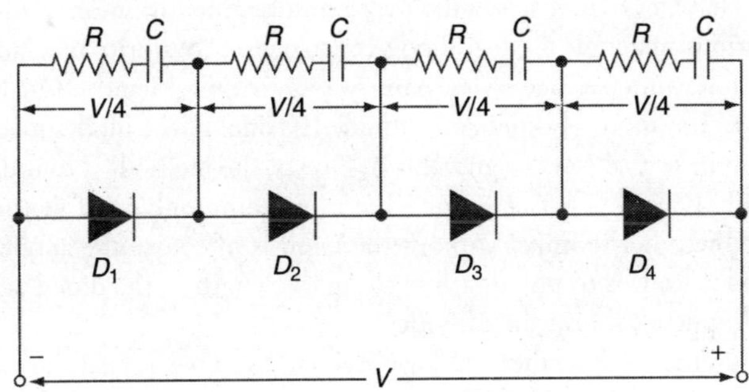

Figure 2.42 Connecting diode in series.

reverse voltage can however be forced by connecting series R-C networks across individual diodes. An arrangement for series connection of four diodes is shown in Figure 2.42. The value of the resistors (R) used should be much smaller than the reverse-bias resistance of the individual diodes.

Diodes in Parallel

Semiconductor diodes are connected in parallel to enhance the forward current capability. Parallel connection of diodes is trickier than the series connection of the same. Parallel connected diodes must have closely matched forward characteristics, lest they will not have equal division of current. The diode with the lowest forward voltage drop draws larger current initially. This heats the diode junction, thus further reducing the forward voltage drop. (The forward voltage drop reduces at a rate of 2.5 mV/°C.) This process is cumulative and ends up with the diode getting damaged. As a result, the other diodes in the parallel connection have to share a larger burden of current. Again the diode with comparatively lower forward voltage becomes the target and is thus prone to damage. The process continues until all the diodes get damaged. An equal division of forward current can be forced by using series resistors (Figure 2.43) or

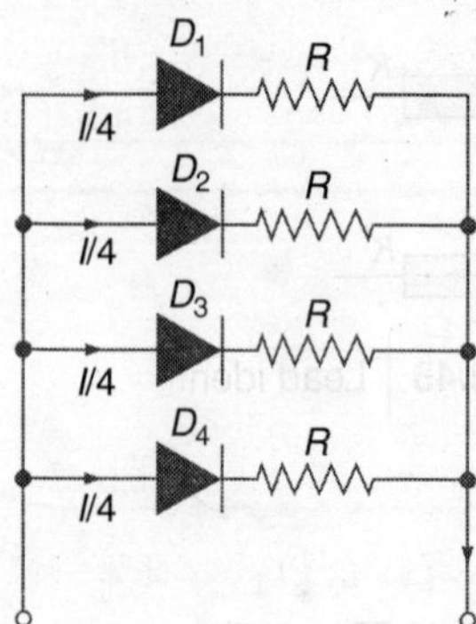

Figure 2.43 Diodes in parallel.

balancing inductors with each of the parallel connected diodes. The value of resistors (*R*) used should be much larger than the forward-bias resistance of the individual diodes.

2.19 Diode Numbers and Lead Identification

Semiconductor diodes have a "1" prefixed in their type number identification. However, no distinction is made among the various materials used in diode construction. Majority of semiconductor diodes are fabricated in one of the following package styles, namely DO-7, DO-35 and DO-41. These package styles are shown in Figure 2.44. The anode (P-side) and cathode (N-side) of the diodes made in these and similar package styles are marked in several ways (Figure 2.45). One of the methods is to indicate the anode with a positive sign and the cathode with a negative sign. The most commonly used method is to put a circular band near the cathode. The other terminal without the band is of course the anode. Yet another popular style of marking the diode's leads is to put an arrow along the length of the diode with the arrow pointing towards the cathode or to put a dot near the cathode.

In the case of Zener diodes made in these package styles, a band is put near the cathode. In some Zener diodes, a positive sign is put near one of the leads with the other lead usually unmarked. In this case, a

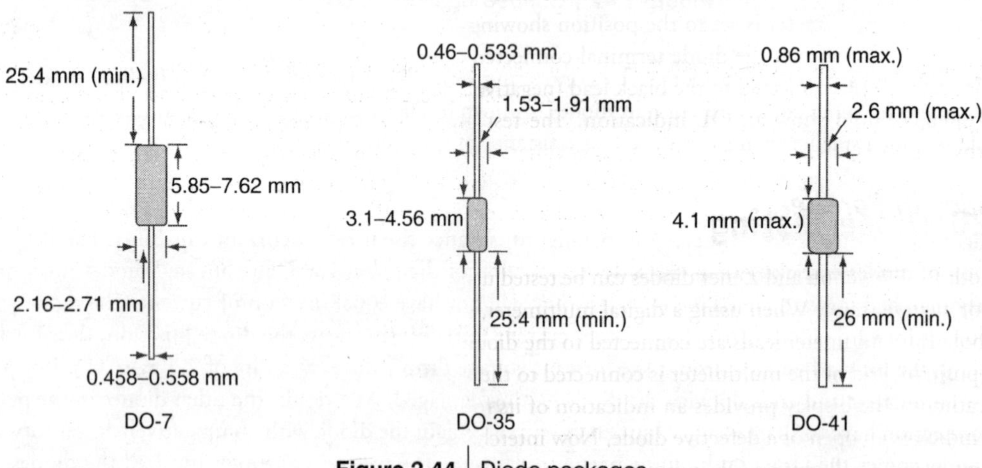

Figure 2.44 Diode packages.

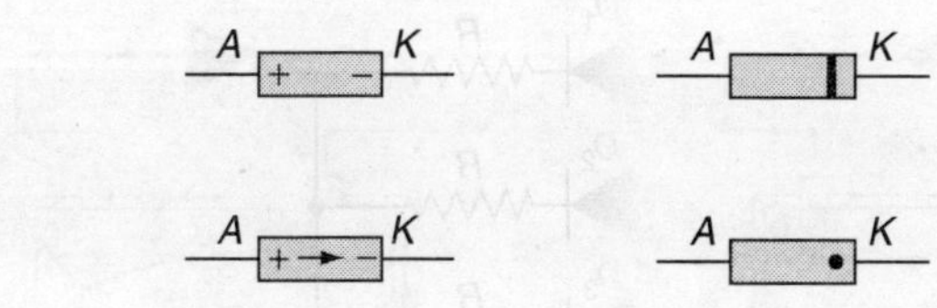

Figure 2.45 | Lead identification of diodes.

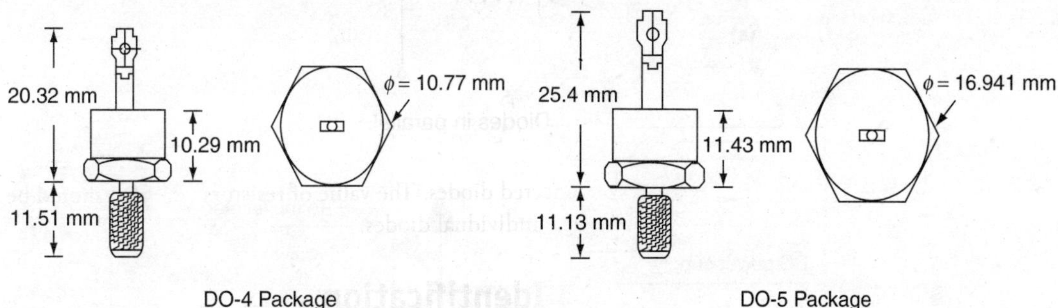

Figure 2.46 | Stud-mounted metal packages for diodes.

plus (+) sign indicates cathode and not the anode as stated in the case of conventional diodes. Remember that in the usual mode of operation of a Zener diode, cathode is more positive with respect to the anode.

High-current versions of semiconductor diodes are usually made in stud-mounted metal packages such as DO-4, DO-5 and so on. The DO-4 and the DO-5 packages are shown in Figure 2.46. The stud-mounted diodes are made both with the stud acting as the anode and the stud as the cathode. The stud-mounted diodes are marked by either putting the plus (+) and minus (–) signs, respectively, on the anode and the cathode or by showing the diode symbol with the anode pointing towards the anode terminal and the cathode pointing towards the cathode terminal.

Lead identification in diodes can also be done using a multimeter. Multimeter leads are connected to the diode and the multimeter is set to the position showing the diode symbol. If the display shows the cut-in voltage of the diode then the diode terminal connected to the red (positive) lead of the multimeter is the anode and the one connected to the black lead (negative) is the cathode. If the connections are reversed, the multimeter should show an OL indication. The test gives correct results only when the diode used is healthy.

2.20 Diode Testing

Both P–N junction and Zener diodes can be tested using a digital or an analog multimeter, an ohmmeter or a curve tracer. When using a digital multimeter, set the multimeter at a position showing the diode symbol. The multimeter leads are connected to the diode such that the diode is forward-biased, that is, the red (positive) lead of the multimeter is connected to the anode and the black (negative) lead is connected to the cathode. The display provides an indication of its forward-bias voltage. An OL indication in this position indicates an open or a defective diode. Now interchange the multimeter leads to reverse-bias the diode. The multimeter will give an OL indication (open circuit) if the diode under test is healthy. A low resistance or a short circuit in this position indicates a shorted or a defective diode.

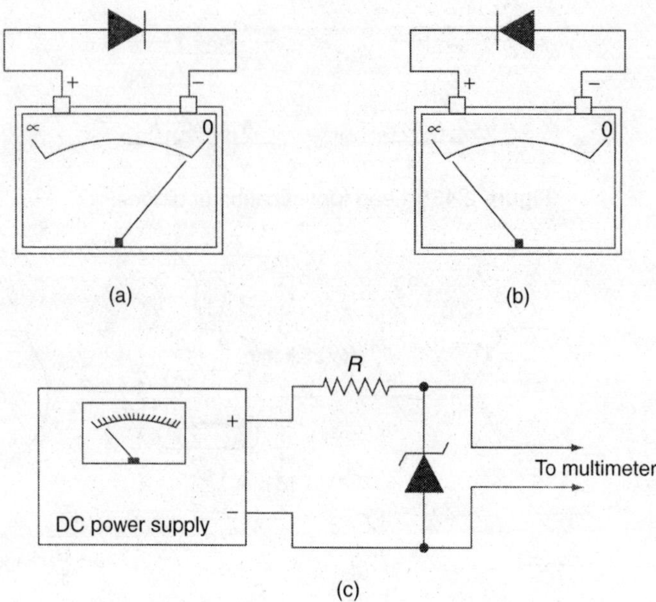

Figure 2.47 | Testing diodes using multimeter.

The diode can be tested using an analog multimeter or an ohmmeter in a similar manner. Select the meter in one of the lower resistance ranges. The leads are connected to the diode in such a way that the diode is forward-biased. For a healthy diode the meter shows a very low resistance confirming that the diode is working properly in the forward-bias mode [Figure 2.47(a)]. The resistance shown by the meter is a function of the current established through the diode by the internal battery of the meter. Now, interchange the leads to reverse-bias the diode. The multimeter would show an open circuit if the diode is healthy [Figure 2.47(b)]. An open circuit in both the tests and a low resistance or short in both the tests indicates an open and a shorted diode, respectively.

Zener diodes can also be tested in the same fashion. Another important parameter one would like to check in the case of Zener diodes is the Zener breakdown voltage. The breakdown voltage of a given diode can be ascertained by rigging up a small test circuit as shown in Figure 2.47(c). Resistance R is typically 100 Ω. The input DC voltage being fed from a regulated DC power supply is gradually increased while continuously monitoring the voltage across the Zener diode with a multimeter. The voltage across the Zener diode is observed to increase with the increase in the input voltage. Infact, the voltage across the Zener diode is almost equal to the input voltage, until it reaches the breakdown voltage. Beyond that, the output voltage stays put despite changes in the input voltage. After having reached the breakdown voltage, the current through the diode is given by the input–output voltage differential divided by the resistance (R). The power dissipated in the Zener diode in this case would be equal to the product of the breakdown voltage and the current flowing through the circuit. So, while carrying out this test, one should remember not to exceed the input voltage to a point that forces the Zener diode under test to dissipate more power than it can safely handle. Typically, the current through the diode should not be allowed to exceed 10 mA while carrying out the test.

KEY TERMS

Ampere square seconds (I^2t)
Avalanche diode
Average AC resistance
Breakdown diode
Cut-in voltage or the knee voltage

Diffusion capacitance or the storage capacitance
Diode capacitance
Dynamic resistance
Equivalent circuit
Forward bias
Forward current (I_F)
Forward recovery time (t_{ff})
Forward voltage (V_F)
Ideal diode
LED
Load-line analysis
Maximum average rectified current ($I_{F(av)}$)
Peak forward surge current
Peak repetitive forward current
Photodiode
Piecewise linear equivalent circuit model
Point-contact diode
Power diode
Power dissipation (P_D)
Reverse bias
Reverse breakdown voltage or the peak inverse voltage
Reverse current (I_R)
Reverse recovery time (t_{rr})
Reverse voltage (V_R)
Schottky diode
Semiconductor diode
Static resistance
Transition capacitance
Tunnel diode
Varactor diode
Zener diode

OBJECTIVE-TYPE EXERCISES

Multiple-Choice Questions

1. P-side of a semiconductor diode is applied a potential of 0.5 V whereas the N-side is applied a potential of −1.0 V. The diode will
   a. conduct.
   b. not conduct.
   c. conduct partially.
   d. breakdown.

2. In a semiconductor diode, V–I relationship is such that
   a. current varies linearly with voltage.
   b. current increases exponentially with voltage.
   c. current varies inversely with voltage.
   d. none of these.

3. The capacitance appearing across a reverse-biased semiconductor junction
   a. increases with increase in bias voltage.
   b. decreases with increase in bias voltage.
   c. is independent of bias voltage.
   d. none of these.

4. There are two semiconductor diodes A and B. One of them is Zener whereas other is avalanche. Their ratings are 5.6 V and 24 V, respectively, then
   a. A is Zener, B is avalanche.
   b. A is avalanche, B is Zener.
   c. both of them are Zener diodes.
   d. both of them are avalanche diodes.

5. The static resistance of a diode is
   a. its opposition to the DC current flow.
   b. its opposition to AC current flow.
   c. resistance of diode when forward-biased.
   d. none of these.

6. The important specifications of a Zener diode are
   a. its breakdown voltage and power dissipation.
   b. breakdown voltage, dynamic impedance and power dissipation.
   c. breakdown voltage and dynamic impedance.
   d. none of these.

7. Typical value of impurity concentration in a tunnel diode is
   a. 1 part in 10^8 parts.
   b. 1 part in 10^6 parts.
   c. 1 part in 10^3 parts.
   d. 1 part in 10 parts.

8. The photodiodes are operated in
   a. reverse-bias condition.
   b. zero-bias condition.
   c. either of the two.
   d. none of the two.

9. The cut-in voltage for a LED is of the order
   a. 1 V.
   b. 0.7 V.
   c. 0.3 V.
   d. 1.5 V.

10. A varactor diode may be advantageous at microwave frequencies (indicate false answer)
    a. for electronic tuning.
    b. as an oscillator.
    c. as a parametric amplifier.
    d. for frequency multiplication.

Fill in the Blanks

1. The ideal diode acts as a _______ switch when forward-biased and acts as a _______ switch when reverse-biased.
2. In an open-circuit P–N junction diode, the current due to majority carrier flow is _______ to/than the current due to the minority carrier flow.
3. The Schottky diodes have a _______ junction.
4. The reverse-bias current of a diode _______ with increase in temperature.
5. _______ is the most accurate diode equivalent model.

REVIEW QUESTIONS

1. Show the basic diode action diagrammatically when it is
   a. Unbiased
   b. Reverse-biased
   c. Forward-biased
2. Sketch V–I characteristics of a semiconductor junction diode for both silicon and germanium diodes. Indicate differences, if any, in the characteristics curve of the two types.
3. Briefly describe the following terms:
   a. Static resistance
   b. Dynamic resistance
   c. Junction capacitance
   d. Tunneling effect
4. Why do we need to connect diodes in series and in parallel and what are the precautions to be observed while doing so?
5. What are breakdown diodes? How are they classified on the basis of breakdown mechanism?
6. Show how a Zener diode may be used to regulate the output voltage.
7. Explain in detail
   a. The effect of temperature on Zener diode.
   b. The depletion region and the N- and the P-regions of a P–N junction diode form a parasitic capacitance. What is the effect of the applied reverse-bias voltage on this capacitance?
   c. How is it possible to determine the polarity of a rectifying diode (which terminal is the anode and which terminal is the cathode) from its physical appearance?
   d. What do you understand by the term "derating"? What is its significance for semiconductor devices?
   e. The effect of temperature on the reverse saturation current of the diode.
8. "*Tunnel diode is a voltage controllable device.*" Comment.
9. What are Schottky diodes? How are they different from conventional P–N junction diodes? What are their major applications?
10. Explain the principle of operation of a LED.

11. What is meant by the term "reverse-recovery time"? Is it due to the majority carriers or the minority carriers?

12. What is the difference between the static and dynamic resistance of a P–N junction diode? Using the diode equation show that the dynamic resistance of an ideal P–N junction diode under forward-bias condition is inversely proportional to the forward current.

13. For a silicon diode, calculate the amount by which the diode voltage would have to be increased to double the diode current.

14. Mention two instruments which can be used to check the health of a diode. Also explain the checking procedure.

15. Explain in detail the operating principle of a photodiode. Also, draw its V–I characteristics.

PROBLEMS

1. Refer to Figure 2.48. Determine the static resistance of the diode at points A and B.

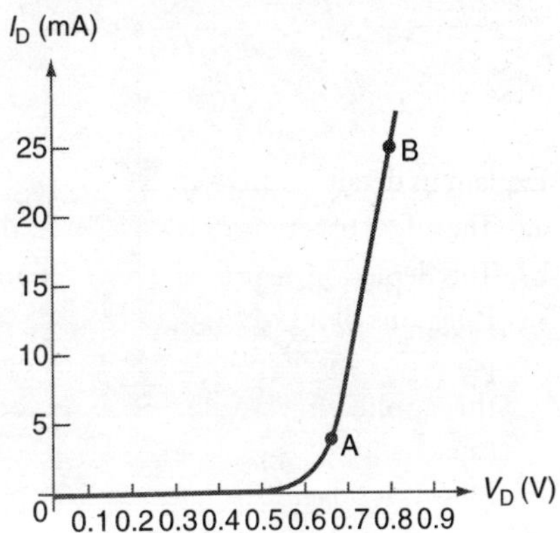

Figure 2.48 | Problem 1.

2. Draw the piecewise linear equivalent circuit model for the diode in Problem 1.

3. A simple diode circuit is shown in Figure 2.49(a). Assuming the diode to be ideal, draw the output waveform (V_o) and waveform across the resistance (V_r) for the input waveform (V_{in}) shown in Figure 2.49(b).

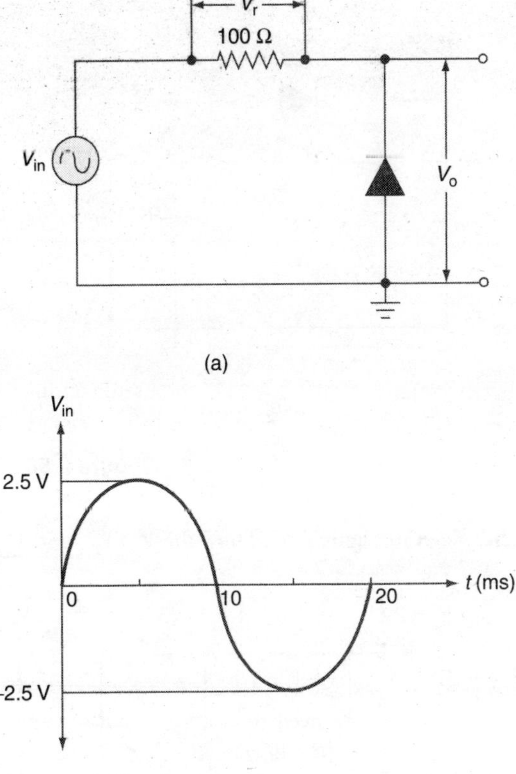

Figure 2.49 | Problem 3.

4. Sketch the output waveform when the input waveform (V_{in}) of Figure 2.50(a) is fed to the circuits of Figures 2.50(b) and (c).

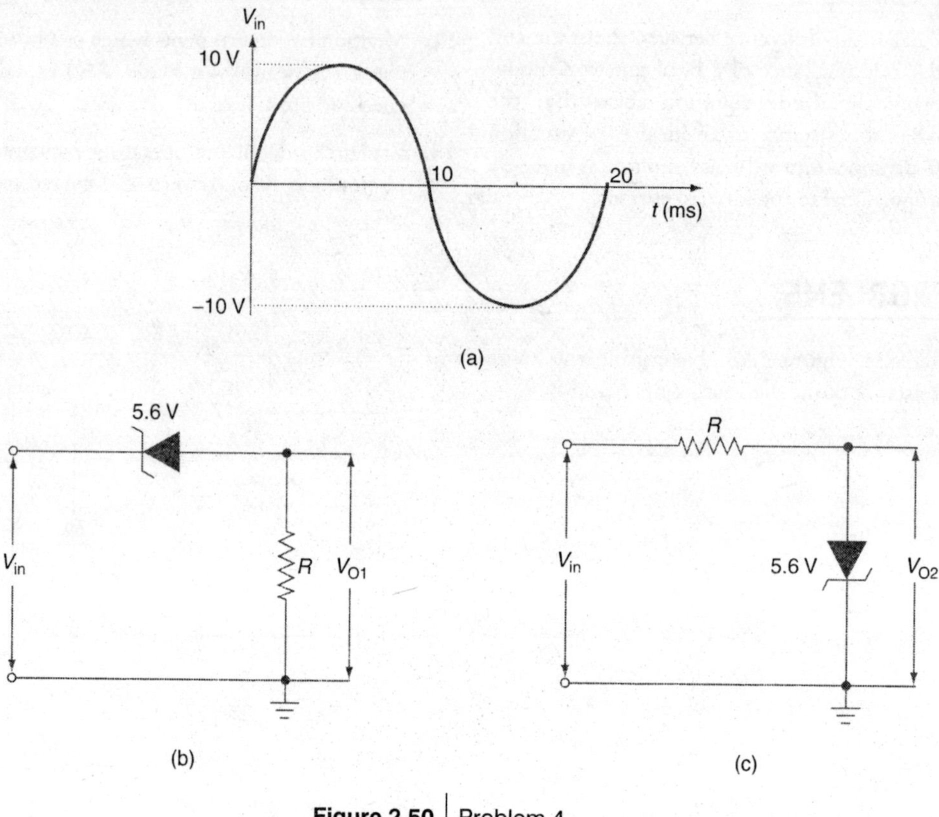

Figure 2.50 Problem 4.

5. Refer to Figure 2.51. Draw the V_O, V_{O1} and V_{O2} waveforms assuming the diode to be ideal.

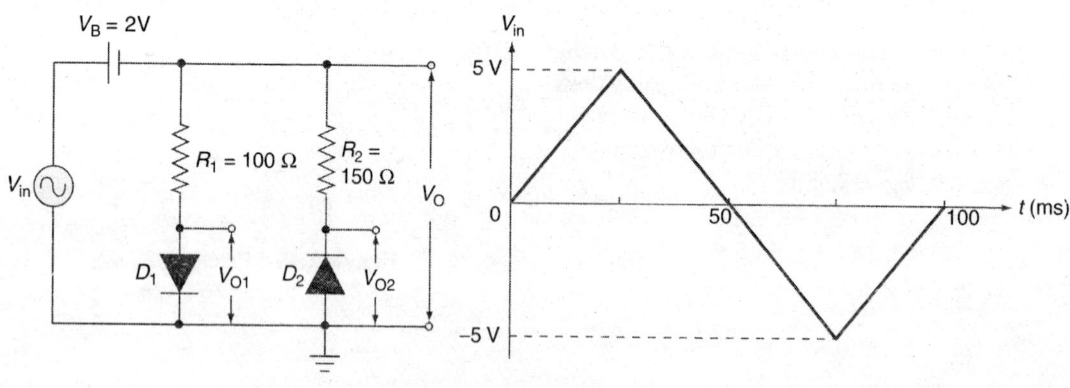

Figure 2.51 Problem 5.

ANSWERS

Multiple-choice Questions

1. (a)
2. (b)
3. (b)
4. (a)
5. (a)
6. (b)
7. (c)
8. (c)
9. (d)
10. (b)

Fill in the Blanks

1. Closed, open
2. Equal
3. Metal-semiconductor
4. Increases
5. Piecewise linear equivalent model

Problems

1. 170 Ω, 32 Ω
2.

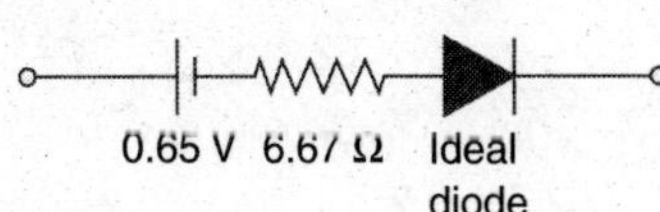

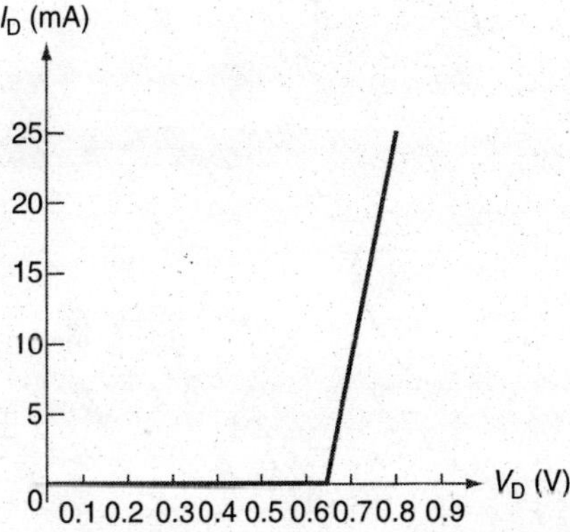

Figure 2.52 Solution to Problem 2.

3.

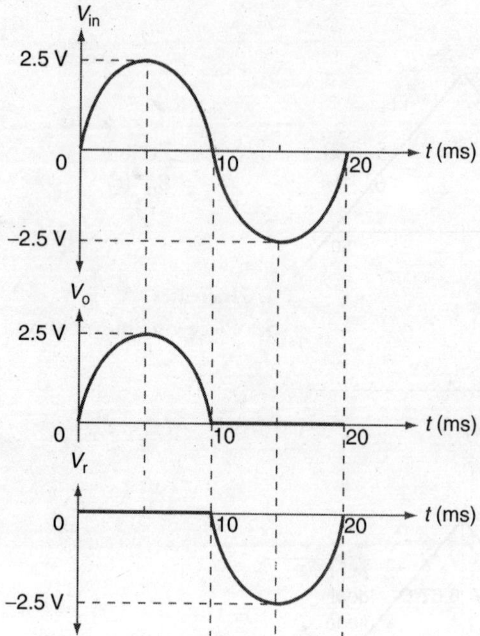

Figure 2.53 Solution to Problem 3.

4.

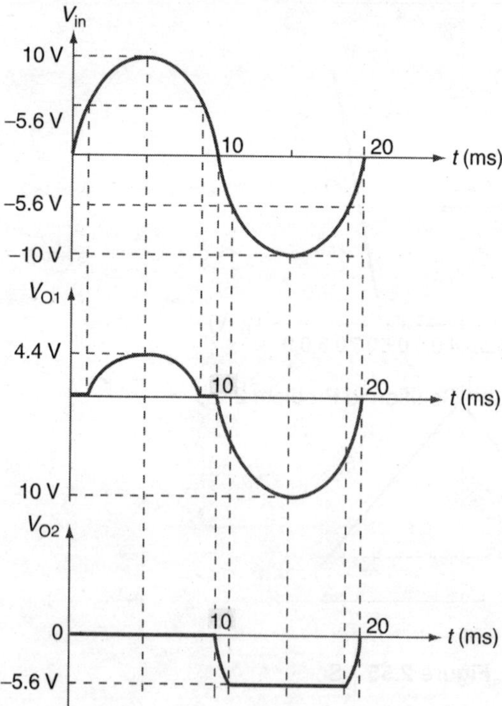

Figure 2.54 Solution to problem 4.

5.

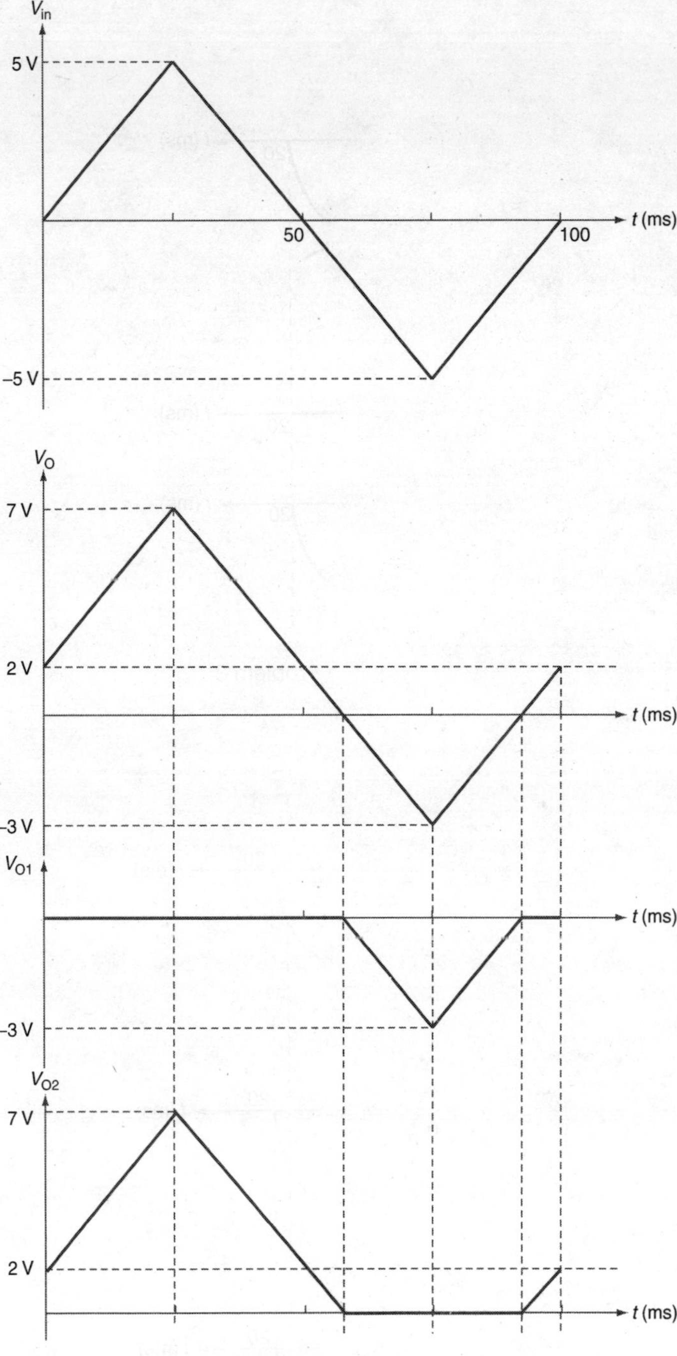

Figure 2.55 | Solution to Problem 5.

CHAPTER 3

Bipolar Junction Transistors

Learning Objectives

After completing this chapter, you will learn the following:

- Comparison between a bipolar junction transistor and a vacuum triode.
- Basics of transistor construction and types (PNP and NPN transistors).
- Different transistor configurations – common base, common emitter and common collector.
- Transistor input and output characteristics.
- Ebers–Moll model of a transistor.
- Transistor specifications and maximum ratings.
- Different transistor packages and lead identification.
- How to test a transistor.
- Phototransistors and power transistors.

Bipolar junction transistors (BJTs) are three-layer, three-terminal semiconductor devices. They comprise either an N-type semiconductor layer sandwiched between two P-type semiconductor layers or a P-type layer sandwiched between two N-type layers. The former is referred to as a PNP transistor while the latter as an NPN transistor. The first transistor was developed a long time back in the year 1947 by Walter H. Brattain and John Bardeen at the Bell Telephone Laboratories, USA. Before the invention of transistors, vacuum tubes were used extensively. Transistors have replaced the vacuum tubes in most of the applications as they offer considerable advantages over the vacuum tubes, such as smaller size, lighter weight, better efficiency, no warm-up period, lower operating voltages and so on. Transistors form the fundamental building block of the circuitry that governs the operation of computers, cellular phones, power electronics and many other modern electronic systems. In these systems, transistors are used as either amplifiers or electrically controlled switches. In fact, the invention of transistors has revolutionized the field of electronics.

This chapter covers all the fundamental topics related to transistors. We will begin the chapter with a brief comparison of transistors with vacuum triodes, followed by fundamental topics such as transistor construction, types, different transistor configurations and transistor input and output characteristics. Topics of practical interest, such as transistor specifications, maximum ratings, lead identification and transistor testing, are covered towards the end of the chapter.

3.1 Bipolar Junction Transistor versus Vacuum Triode

Both bipolar junction transistors and vacuum triodes are three-terminal devices. Transistors can be considered as solid-state analogs of vacuum triodes. The three terminals of a triode are referred to as cathode, plate and control grid. The corresponding terminals of a transistor are emitter, collector and base, respectively. Although both transistors and vacuum triodes are three-terminal devices, their modes of operation are fundamentally different. Transistors are current-controlled devices whereas vacuum triodes are voltage-controlled devices. In a vacuum triode, the output voltage is directly related to the input voltage. The amplification factor (μ) of a vacuum triode is defined as the ratio of the change in the plate voltage to the change in the grid voltage for a constant plate current. In a transistor the output current is a function of the input current, and the transistor gain (β) is defined as the ratio of the change in the collector current to the change in the base current for a constant collector–emitter voltage.

3.2 Transistor Construction and Types

A BJT is a three-layer, three-terminal semiconductor device having two PN junctions. It comprises three differently doped semiconductor regions, namely the emitter region, the base region and the collector region. The base region is physically sandwiched between the emitter and the collector regions. BJT are so named as both holes and electrons contribute to the flow of current.

The width of the base region is much smaller than the width of the emitter and the collector regions. Typical ratio of the total width of the transistor to the width of the base region is of the order of few hundreds. The emitter region is the most heavily doped, the collector region moderately doped and the base region very lightly doped. The doping of the base region is around 10 times less than that of the emitter region. This results in reduced conductivity of the base region. Bipolar transistors can be classified as NPN and PNP transistors depending upon the type of doping of the three regions.

NPN Transistor

Figure 3.1(a) shows the structure of an NPN transistor. As is evident from the figure, the collector and the emitter regions are N-type semiconductors and the base region is a P-type semiconductor. The collector, emitter and base terminals are designated as C, E and B, respectively. Figure 3.1(b) shows the circuit symbol of an NPN transistor. The arrow on the emitter lead specifies the direction of the conventional current flow when the emitter–base junction is forward-biased. In an NPN transistor most of the current flow is due to flow of electrons.

PNP Transistor

Figure 3.2(a) shows the structure of a PNP transistor. The collector and the emitter regions are P-type semiconductors and the base region is an N-type semiconductor. Figure 3.2(b) shows the circuit symbol of a PNP

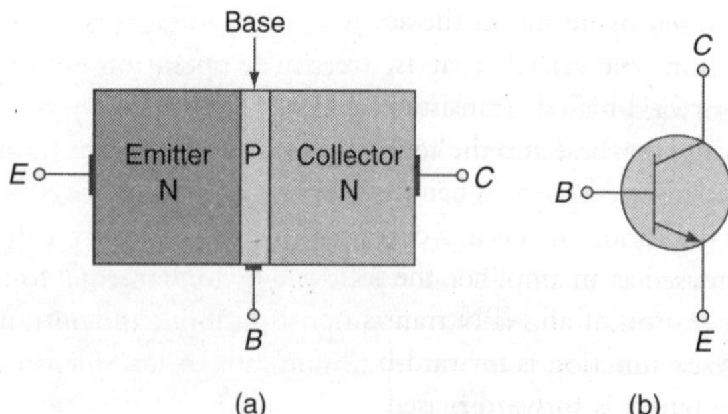

Figure 3.1 (a) Structure; (b) circuit symbol of an NPN transistor.

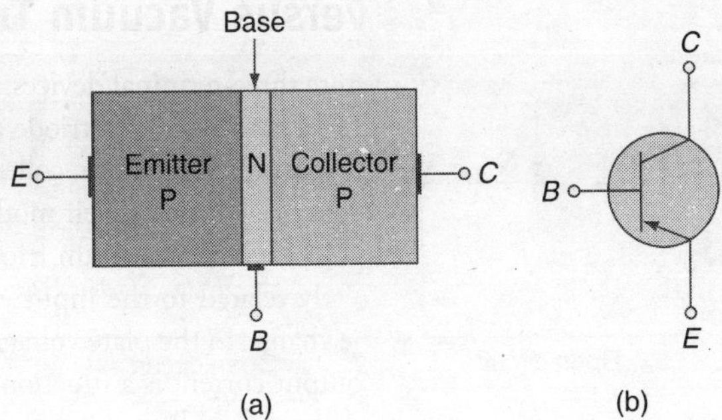

Figure 3.2 | (a) Structure; (b) circuit symbol of a PNP transistor.

transistor. The arrow on the emitter lead specifies the direction of the conventional current flow when the emitter–base junction is forward-biased. In a PNP transistor, holes contribute mostly to the flow of current.

NPN transistors are more commonly used as compared to PNP transistors as they offer higher current density and faster switching times. This is so because the electron mobility is higher than the hole mobility.

3.3 Transistor Operation

The basic operation of an NPN transistor is described in this section. The operation of a PNP transistor is same as that of an NPN transistor except that the roles of electrons and holes are interchanged and the polarities of the voltages and the direction of current reversed. Transistors may be looked upon as two PN junction diodes connected back to back. The two junctions are the emitter–base junction and the collector–base junction. The fundamentals of semiconductor junction diodes covered in Chapter 2 apply to transistors also and will be used to explain the operation of a transistor. As we have studied in Chapter 2, when the PN junction diode is an open circuit no current flows through it and the diode voltage is equal to the diode's contact potential. Similarly, when no external voltage is applied to the transistor, the currents flowing through the transistor are zero and the potential at the two junctions is equal to their respective contact potentials.

Transistors operate in four regions, namely the active region, the reverse-active region, the saturation region and the cut-off region depending upon the polarity of voltages applied to the emitter–base and the collector–base junctions. In the active region, the emitter–base junction is forward-biased and the collector–base junction is reverse-biased. Transistors when operating in the active region function as amplifiers. In the reverse-active region, the biasing condition is reversed, that is, the emitter–base junction is reverse-biased and the collector–base junction is forward-biased. Transistors are seldom operated in the reverse-active region. In the saturation region, both the emitter–base and the collector–base junctions are forward-biased and in the cut-off region both the junctions are reverse-biased. When the transistor is used as a switching device, it operates either in the saturation or the cut-off region. It acts as a closed switch in the saturation region and as an open switch in the cut-off region. When used as an amplifier, the transistor is operated in the active region.

Let us consider the operation of an NPN transistor in the active region. As mentioned before, in the active region the emitter–base junction is forward-biased and the collector–base junction is reverse-biased. When the emitter–base junction is forward-biased with an open collector–base junction [Figure 3.3(a)], normal PN junction diode action takes place. The width of the depletion region decreases due to the applied bias and there is a heavy flow of electrons from the N-type emitter to the P-type base. As the base is lightly doped,

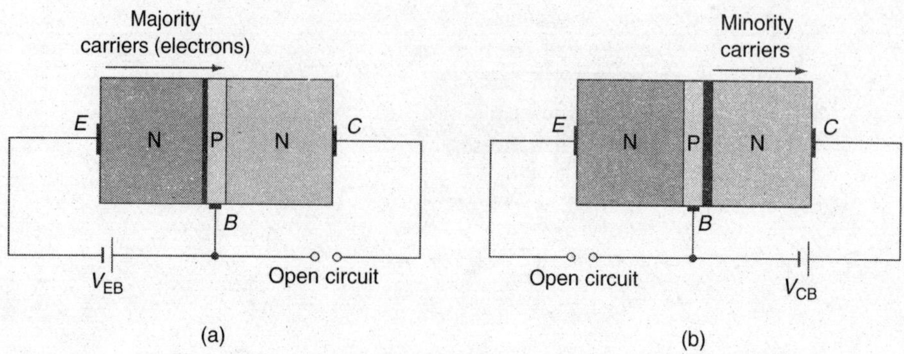

Figure 3.3 (a) Forward-biased emitter–base junction; (b) reverse-biased collector–base junction.

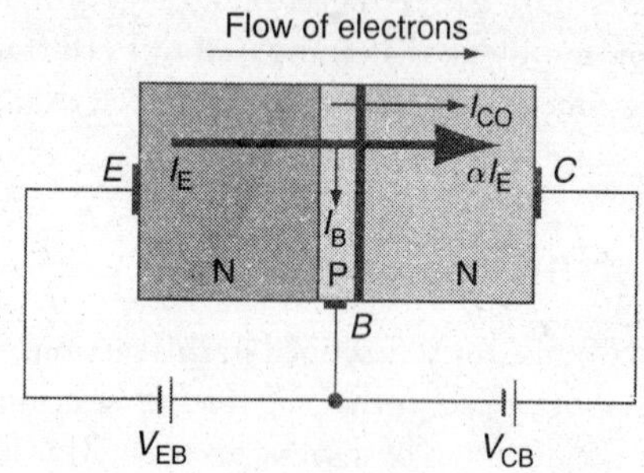

Figure 3.4 Flow of current in an NPN transistor in the active region.

a very small hole current flows from the P-type base to the N-type emitter region. The width of the depletion region is larger in the base region as compared to that in the emitter region as the base is lightly doped compared to the emitter region. If the collector–base junction is reverse-biased with the emitter–base junction open [Figure 3.3(b)], it behaves like a normal reverse-biased junction diode. There is a small current flow due to the minority carriers, that is, the flow of electrons from the base region to the emitter region and flow of holes from the emitter to the base. The depletion width increases with the increase in the reverse-bias voltage and is larger in the base region than that in the collector region.

Figure 3.4 shows the flow of current in an NPN transistor in the active region, that is, both the forward and the reverse voltages are applied simultaneously to the emitter–base and the collector–base junctions, respectively. The emitter current (I_E) comprises electron current (due to flow of electrons from emitter to base) and hole current (due to the flow of holes from base to emitter). As the base is very lightly doped as compared to the emitter, the emitter current consists mainly of electrons. Not all the electrons crossing the emitter–base junction reach the collector–base junction as some of them remain in the base region and constitute the base current (I_B). As the base region is very thin and has low level of conductivity (as it is lightly doped), only a very few electrons remain in the base region. The rest of the electrons diffuse into the reverse-biased collector–base junction. They travel across the collector–base junction easily as they are minority carriers in the P-type base region of the collector–base junction. This is referred to as the injection of the minority carriers into the P-type base region. (It may be recalled that in a reverse-biased PN junction diode, the minority carriers easily cross the junction). These electrons diffuse across the reverse-biased junction to reach the N-type collector and constitute the collector current (I_C). The magnitude of the base current is of the order of few microamperes as compared to several milliamperes for the collector and the emitter current.

Applying Kirchhoff's current law to the transistor, considering it as a node, we get

$$I_E = I_C + I_B \tag{3.1}$$

where I_E is the emitter current, I_C the collector current and I_B the base current.

From Eq. (3.1) we can infer that the emitter current is the sum of the collector current and the base current. The collector current comprises two components: the majority-carrier component and the leakage-current component. The majority-carrier component is due to the electrons that have traveled from the emitter region across the base to the collector region. This component is equal to αI_E, where α is the fraction of emitter electrons that reach the collector region. The leakage current (I_{CO}) is the minority current of the reverse-biased collector–base junction with an open-circuit emitter–base junction. I_{CO} is in the range of few hundreds of nanoamperes to few microamperes. The expression for collector current is given by

$$I_C = \alpha I_E + I_{CO} \tag{3.2}$$

The above equation is only valid in the active region of the transistor. The generalized expression for the collector current in a transistor is given by

$$I_C = \alpha I_E + I_{CO}\left[1 - \exp\left(-\frac{V_{CB}}{V_T}\right)\right] \tag{3.3}$$

where V_{CB} is the voltage across the collector–base junction and V_T the volt equivalent of temperature.

When the collector–base junction is sufficiently reverse-biased, the term $\exp(-V_{CB}/V_T)$ tends to zero and Eq. (3.3) reduces to Eq. (3.2).

3.4 Common-Base Configuration

Transistors are connected in any of the following three configurations:

1. Common-base (CB) configuration.
2. Common-emitter (CE) configuration.
3. Common-collector (CC) configuration.

CB configuration is discussed in this section. CE and the CC configurations are covered in Sections 3.5 and 3.6, respectively.

In the CB configuration, the base terminal is common to both the input and the output sections. Figures 3.5(a) and (b) show the basic circuit of the transistor in the CB configuration for the NPN and the PNP transistors, respectively. The directions of currents shown are used for conventional current flow. Also, the current flowing into the transistor is taken as positive and the current leaving the transistor is taken as negative.

Input Characteristics

The input characteristics of a transistor are a plot of the input current versus the input junction voltage for different values of output junction voltage. The input characteristics of CB configuration relate the emitter current (I_E) to the emitter–base voltage (V_{EB}) for various levels of the collector–base voltage (V_{CB}). Figure 3.6 shows the input characteristics of a common-base NPN Silicon transistor. The current

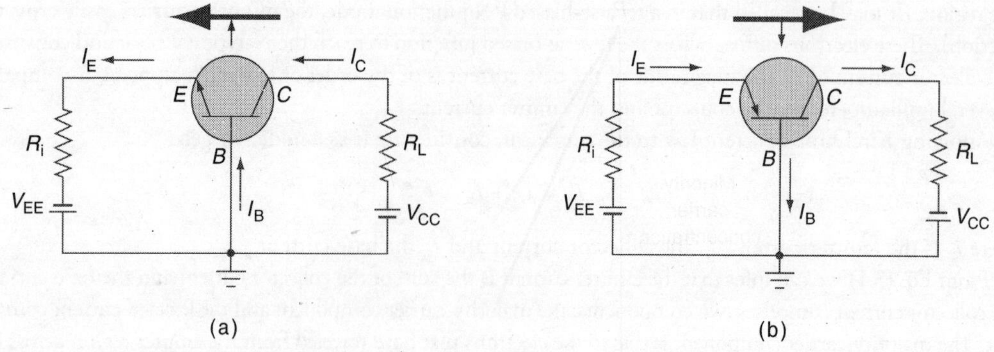

Figure 3.5 Common-base configuration.

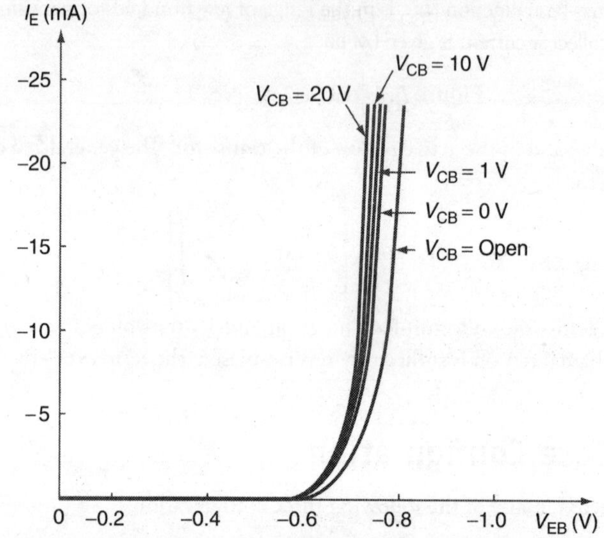

Figure 3.6 Input characteristics of CB transistor.

I_E is considered negative as the current flows out of the emitter terminal. The input characteristics of PNP transistors are same with the reversal of polarity of the voltages and direction of currents.

From the figure we can infer that there is a cut-in or threshold voltage below which the value of emitter current is very small. The typical values of cut-in voltage for silicon and germanium transistors are approximately 0.5 and 0.1 V, respectively. The curve for open condition is the same as that for a forward-biased PN junction diode. Another feature of the input characteristics is that for a fixed value of collector–base voltage (V_{CB}), the emitter–base voltage (V_{EB}) increases with increase in the emitter current (I_E). This behavior is the same as that of a PN junction diode in the forward-biased state. Since a small change in the emitter–base voltage causes a very large change in the emitter current, the input resistance (r_i) of the common-base configuration is very small. The value of r_i in the linear portion of the input characteristics is of the order of hundred ohms. Also it can be interpreted from the figure that for fixed value of emitter–base voltage (V_{EB}), the emitter current (I_E) increases with increase in the collector–base voltage (V_{CB}). This is because of the early effect phenomenon in transistors.

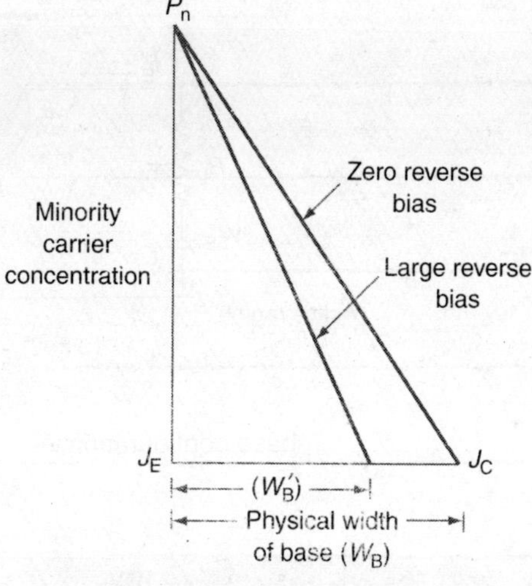

Figure 3.7 | Early effect.

Early effect or the *base width modulation* phenomenon refers to the change in the width of the base region with the change in the collector–base voltage. As the emitter–base junction is forward-biased, the width of the depletion region is negligible. For the reverse-biased collector–base junction, the width of the depletion region is substantial. The width of the depletion region increases with increase in the reverse voltage at the collector–base junction. As the base region is lightly doped, the penetration of the depletion region is much larger in the base region than in the collector region. As a result of this the effective width of the base region decreases. This phenomenon of change in the effective width of the base region with change in the collector–base voltage is referred to as the early effect.

As a result of the early effect, at increased reverse potential the rate of recombination of the electrons and holes decreases. This results in increase in the value of α. Also, the concentration of the minority carriers becomes zero at effective base width (W_B') instead of W_B (Figure 3.7). Hence, the concentration gradient of minority carriers (P_n) is increased within the base region. As the emitter current is proportional to the gradient of minority carriers at the emitter junction (J_E), the value of emitter current also increases.

Output Characteristics

The output characteristics of a transistor are a plot of the output current and the output junction voltage for different values of input current. The output characteristics of common-base configuration (Figure 3.8) relate the collector current (I_C) to the collector–base voltage (V_{CB}) for various levels of the emitter current (I_E). For a fixed value of emitter current, the collector current almost remains constant with changes in the value of the collector–base voltage. However, near the origin the collector current drops rapidly with the decrease in the value of the collector–base voltage. The output characteristics can be divided into three regions, namely the active region, the cut-off region and the saturation region.

Active Region

In the active region the collector–base junction is reverse-biased while the emitter–base junction is forward-biased. The unshaded portion of Figure 3.8 corresponds to the active region. The collector current (I_C) is almost independent of the collector–base voltage (V_{CB}) and depends only on the value of the emitter current (I_E). Therefore, the output characteristics curves are straight parallel lines. Actually the collector

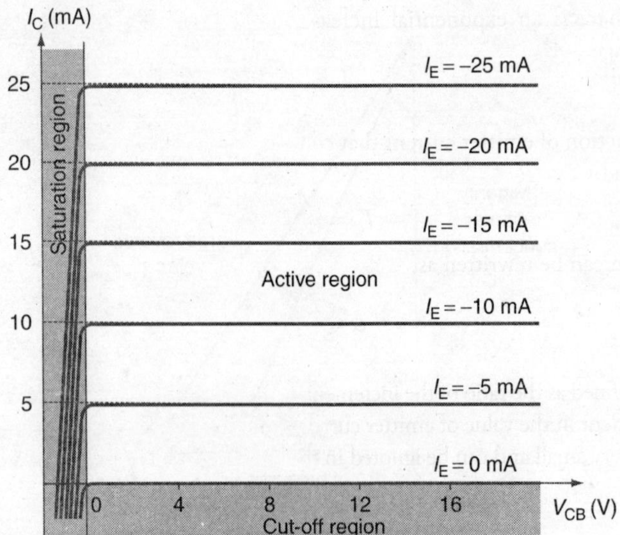

Figure 3.8 | Output characteristics of the common-base transistor.

current increases slowly with the collector–base voltage (around 0.5%). This is because of the early effect phenomenon. But for most applications this increase can be ignored and the collector current can be considered to be constant for a fixed value of emitter current. The output resistance (r_o) offered by the CB configuration is very high as a very large change in the collector–base voltage produces a very small change in the collector current.

When the emitter–base junction is open-circuited, the emitter current is zero. The collector current that flows in this condition is the reverse saturation current (I_{CO}). This condition corresponds to the lowest curve in the output characteristics. The current I_{CO} is of the order of few microamperes for germanium transistors and several nanoamperes for silicon transistors.

Cut-off Region

In the cut-off region, both the collector–base and the emitter–base junctions of a transistor are reverse-biased. The region below the $I_E = 0$ curve corresponds to the cut-off region. In this region, the transistor acts as an open circuit and does not conduct any current. As mentioned before, the value of collector current at $I_E = 0$ is equal to the reverse saturation current (I_{CO}).

I_{CO} increases rapidly with increase in temperature. As an example, for a general purpose silicon transistor 2N2222, the values of I_{CO} at a collector–base voltage of 50 V for ambient temperatures 25°C and 150°C are 10 nA and 10 μA, respectively. This implies that there is a change of the order of 1000 times for 125°C change in temperature. I_{CO} is also referred to as I_{CBO}, the collector current with base open-circuited. I_{CBO} can be ignored in most transistor applications except for power transistors and transistors operating at high temperatures.

Saturation Region

In the saturation region, both the collector–base and the emitter–base junctions are forward-biased. The region to the left of $V_{CB} = 0$ line corresponds to the saturation region. As is clear from the figure, the collector–base voltage (V_{CB}) is slightly negative in the saturation region. This is because the collector–base junction is also forward-biased. There is an exponential increase in the collector current with a small increase in the collector–base voltage.

Alpha (α)

Alpha (α) is the fraction of emitter current that contributes to the collector current. The current equation in a transistor is given by

$$I_C = I_{CO} + \alpha I_E \tag{3.4}$$

The above equation can be rewritten as

$$\alpha = \frac{I_C - I_{CO}}{I_E - 0} \tag{3.5}$$

Alpha (α) can be defined as the ratio of the increment in the value of collector current from its value in the cut-off region to the increment in the value of emitter current from its value in the cut-off region. As mentioned earlier, the value of I_{CO} is very small and can be ignored in the large-signal analysis. Therefore Eq. (3.4) reduces to

$$I_C = \alpha I_E \tag{3.6}$$

Therefore, α is also referred to as the large-signal current gain for a common-base transistor. In the active region, the value of α is nearly equal to 1, the exact value being between 0.90 and 0.998. Therefore, the current gain of the transistor in the CB mode is less than unity. The value of α is not constant but varies with the emitter current (I_E), collector voltage (V_{CB}) and the operating temperature. The voltage gain of the CB configuration is in the range of 50–300. Therefore, a CB transistor acts as a voltage amplifier and not as a current amplifier.

When a time-varying input is applied, the point of operation moves on the output characteristics curve. In that case an ac alpha (α_{ac}) is defined as the ratio of the change in the collector current to the change in the emitter current for a fixed value of collector–base voltage. Mathematically,

$$\alpha_{ac} = \left(\frac{\Delta I_C}{\Delta I_E}\right)_{V_{CB}=\text{constant}} \tag{3.7}$$

where α_{ac} refers to common-base, short circuit amplification factor.

EXAMPLE 3.1 *For the common-base configuration shown in Figure 3.9, determine the values of base current (I_B), emitter current (I_E) and collector current (I_C). It is given that the value of α is 0.95.*

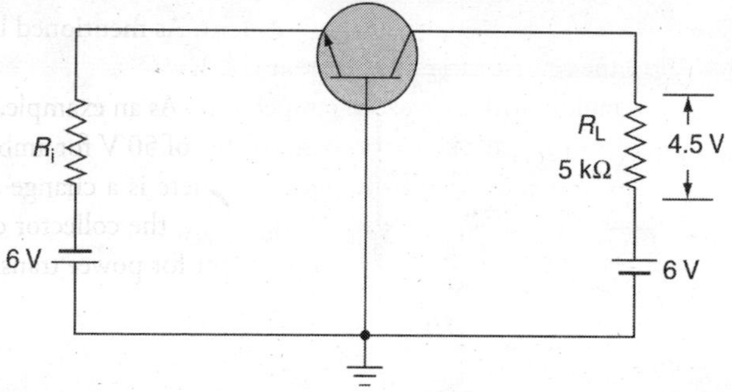

Figure 3.9 Example 3.1.

Solution

1. The value of load resistance $R_L = 5$ kΩ.
2. The voltage drop across the resistor is 4.5 V.
3. Therefore, the current flowing through the resistor = $4.5/(5 \times 10^3)$ A = 0.9 mA.
4. The current flowing through the resistor is the collector current. Therefore, collector current is equal to 0.9 mA.
5. The emitter current is $I_C/\alpha = 0.9 \times 10^{-3}/0.95$ A = 0.947 mA.
6. The base current is $I_E - I_C = (0.947 \times 10^{-3} - 0.9 \times 10^{-3}) = 47$ μA.

Answer: The value of I_C, I_E and I_B are 0.9 mA, 0.947 mA and 47 μA, respectively.

3.5 Common-Emitter Configuration

The common-emitter (CE) configuration has emitter terminal common to both the input and the output sections, as shown in Figures 3.10(a) and (b), for the NPN and the PNP transistors, respectively. The input signal is applied to the emitter–base section and the output is taken from the collector–emitter section. It is the most commonly used transistor configuration. Salient features of CE transistor configuration are high values of voltage and current gains, medium values of input and output impedances.

Input Characteristics

The input characteristics of the transistor in the common-emitter configuration relate the base current (I_B) to the emitter–base voltage (V_{BE}) for different values of the collector-emitter voltage (V_{CE}). The input characteristics for a common-emitter NPN transistor are shown in Figure 3.11. We can see from the figure that the magnitude of base current (I_B) is in range of several tens of microamperes. For fixed value of emitter–base voltage (V_{BE}), an increase in the value of collector–emitter voltage (V_{CE}) results in a decrease in the value of the base current (I_B). This is because of the early effect which results in reduction of the base width with increase in the collector–emitter voltage (V_{CE}).

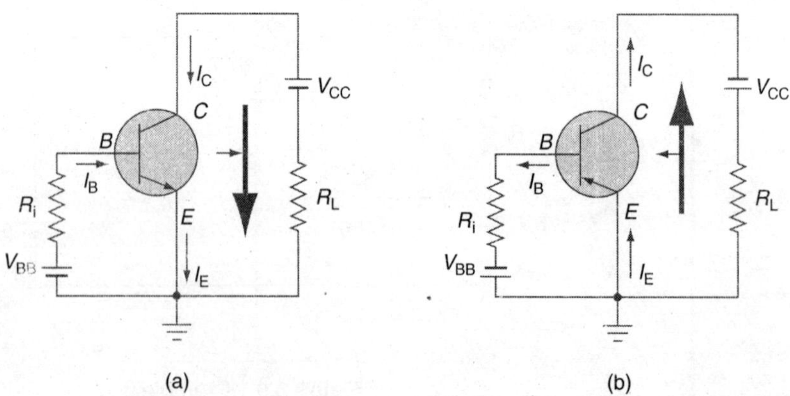

Figure 3.10 Common-emitter configuration for (a) NPN transistor; (b) PNP transistor.

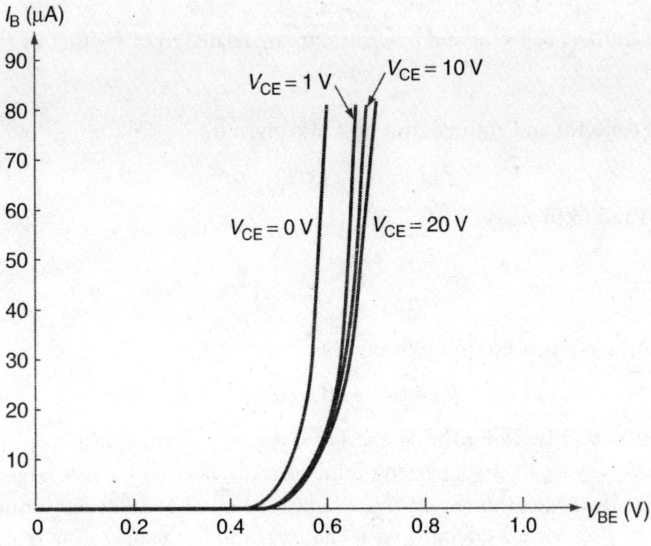

Figure 3.11 | Input characteristics of CE transistor.

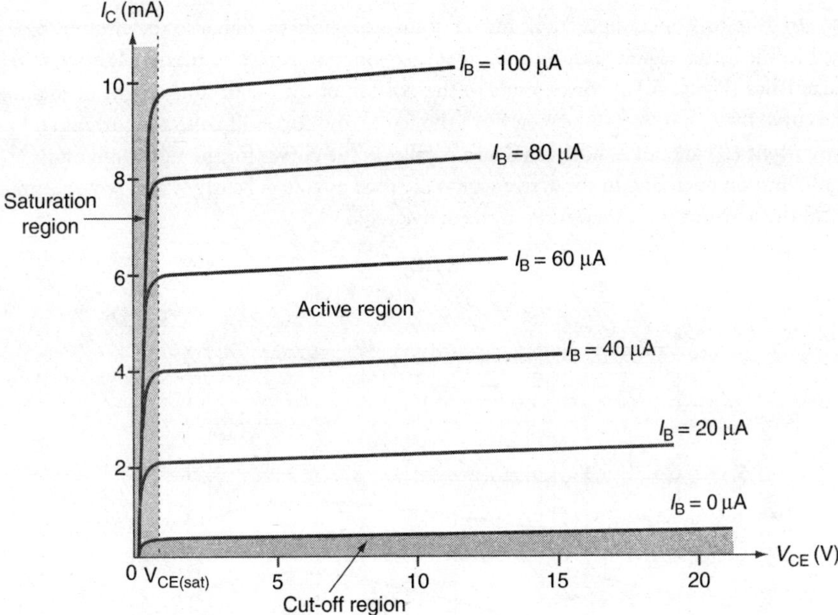

Figure 3.12 | Output characteristics of CE transistor.

Output Characteristics

Output characteristics of the CE configuration relate the collector current (I_C) to the collector–emitter voltage (V_{CE}) for different values of base current (I_B). The output characteristics of a CE transistor are shown in Figure 3.12. The output curves for CE configuration are not as horizontal as that for CB configuration, indicating that the collector–emitter voltage has an influence on the value of collector current.

Beta (β)

For any transistor the emitter, collector and base currents are related to each other by the equation

$$I_E = I_C + I_B \tag{3.8}$$

Relationship between collector and emitter current is also given by

$$I_C = I_{CO} + \alpha I_E \tag{3.9}$$

Combining Eqs. (3.8) and (3.9) we get

$$I_C = \frac{\alpha}{(1-\alpha)} I_B + \frac{1}{(1-\alpha)} I_{CO} \tag{3.10}$$

If we substitute $\beta = \alpha/(1-\alpha)$ then Eq. (3.10) becomes

$$I_C = \beta I_B + (\beta + 1) I_{CO} \tag{3.11}$$

Here, β (also denoted as h_{FE}) is referred to as the DC forward current transfer ratio or the DC current gain of the transistor. A very small change in the value of α is reflected as a very large change in the value of β. The CE characteristics of the transistors of the same type number differ significantly from one device to another. The value of β varies considerably with changes in both the operating temperature and collector current (Figure 3.13).

Active Region

As in the case of CB transistor configuration, for CE transistor configuration also the emitter–base junction is forward-biased in the active region and the collector–base junction is reverse-biased. The active region in the output characteristics (Figure 3.12) corresponds to the portion of the graph to the right of the line at $V_{CE(sat)}$ and above the curve for $I_B = 0$. As can be seen from the figure, the curves of collector current (I_C) for different values of base current (I_B) are not as horizontal and parallel as the curves for the CB configuration. Transistors in the CE configuration operating in the active region are used as voltage, current and power amplifiers.

As $I_B >> I_{CO}$ in the active region, therefore, in the active region

$$I_C = \beta I_B$$

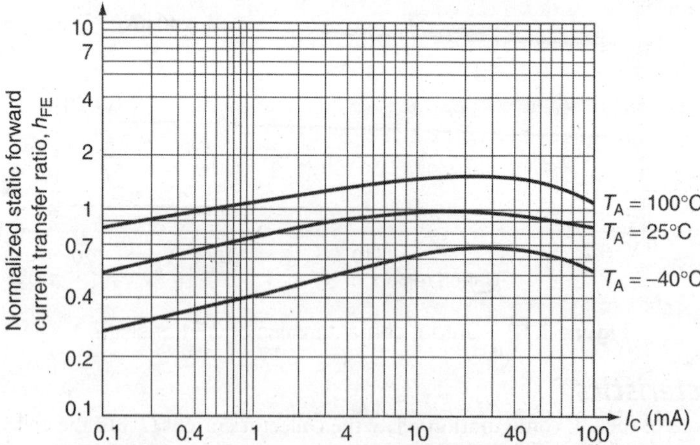

Figure 3.13 Variation of h_{FE} with change in temperature and collector cur-

Typical value of β is in the range of 50–100. Hence, the CE configuration provides a high current gain. It also provides a large value of voltage and power gain.

For AC applications ac beta (β_{ac}) is defined as

$$\beta_{ac} = \left(\frac{\Delta I_C}{\Delta I_B}\right)_{V_{CE}=\text{constant}}$$

β_{ac} is referred to as the CE forward-current amplification factor and is also denoted by h_{fe}.

Saturation Region

The CE transistor is in the saturation region when both the collector–base and the emitter–base junctions are forward-biased. Magnitudes of collector–base voltage (V_{CB}) and emitter–base voltage (V_{EB}) are equal to the cut-in voltages of the collector–base and the emitter–base junctions, respectively. Therefore, the value of V_{CE} ($V_{CB} + V_{BE}$) is few tenths of volts in the saturation region. The region to the left of $V_{CE} = V_{CE(sat)}$ line in the output characteristics is the saturation region. In the saturation region, the value of the collector current is independent of the base current and depends on the value of resistor connected between the collector terminal and the supply terminal. For the CE circuit of Figure 3.10, the value of collector current in the saturation region is given by V_{CC}/R_L. The minimum base current required to saturate the transistor is given by I_C/β.

The parameter which is important in the saturation region is the CE saturation resistance ($R_{CE(sat)}$), which is defined as the ratio of the collector–emitter voltage at saturation to the collector current ($V_{CE(sat)}/I_C$). The curves to the left of the $V_{CE} = V_{CE(sat)}$ line can be approximated as straight lines whose slope can be determined using the value of $R_{CE(sat)}$.

Cut-off Region

In the cut-off region, both the collector–base and the emitter–base junctions are reverse-biased. Also, the base current is equal to zero ($I_B = 0$) in this region. In the CE configuration, for $I_B = 0$, there is a considerable amount of collector current flowing through the transistor. Its value is given by substituting the value $I_B = 0$ in Eq. (3.11):

$$I_C = (\beta+1)I_{CO} = \frac{I_{CO}}{1-\alpha} \tag{3.12}$$

This current is denoted by the symbol I_{CEO}.

For silicon transistors, the value of α near cut-off region is nearly zero. Therefore, the value of collector current is equal to I_{CO}. Hence, the silicon transistor is in the cut-off region when $I_B = 0$ both for short circuit ($V_{BE} = 0$) and reverse-biased emitter–base junction.

For germanium transistors, the value of α near cut-off region may be as large as 0.9. Therefore, the value of the collector current flowing through the transistor can be as large as 10 times the value of leakage current I_{CO}. Hence, the germanium transistor is not in the cut-off region for $I_B = 0$. A reverse bias needs to be applied to the emitter–base junction to bring the transistor to cut-off. The bias voltage applied should bring the value of collector current (I_C) less than or equal to reverse saturation current (I_{CO}). Reverse-bias voltage of 0.1 V is sufficient to reduce the collector current to this value. Therefore, the germanium transistor is in cut-off region when $I_B = 0$ for reverse-biased emitter–base junction with V_{BE} greater than 0.1 V.

EXAMPLE 3.2 *For a transistor, the value of α is specified to be 0.98 at a particular collector–base voltage. The value of α increases by 0.5% when the collector–base voltage is increased. Find the percentage change in the value of β. Comment on the result.*

Solution

1. Original value of $\alpha = 0.98$.
2. Value of $\beta = \alpha/(1 - \alpha) = 0.98/(1 - 0.98) = 49$.
3. New value of $\alpha = 0.98 + 0.5 \times 0.98/100 = 0.985$.
4. Value of β for $\alpha = 0.985$ is $\beta = 0.985/(1 - 0.985) = 66$.
5. Percentage change in $\beta = [(66 - 49)/49] \times 100\% = 34.69\%$.
6. From the above result it is clear that a small change in the value of $\alpha = 0.5\%$ results in a large change in the value of $\beta = 34.69\%$.

Answer: Percentage change in β is 34.69%.

EXAMPLE 3.3 *For the circuit shown in Figure 3.14, find the values of emitter current (I_E), collector current (I_C) and base current (I_B) It is given that $\beta = 50$, $V_{BE} = 0.7$ V and $I_{CO} = 0$ μA.*

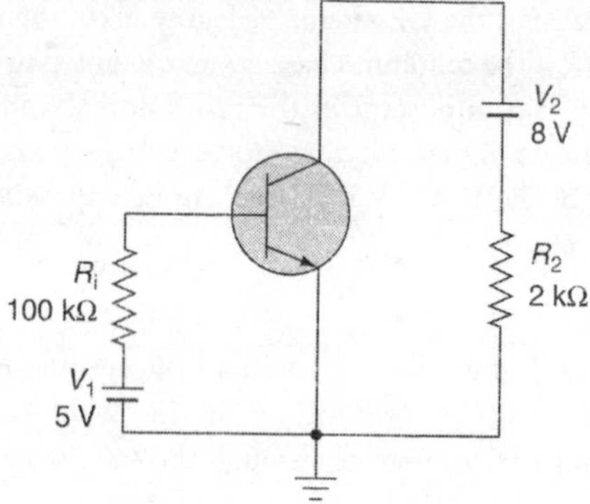

Figure 3.14 Example 3.3.

Solution

1. The polarity of the voltage V_1 applied to the input section forward biases the emitter–base junction. Therefore the transistor is in active region or in the saturation region. Let us assume that the transistor is in the active region.
2. Applying Kirchhoff's voltage law to the input section:
$$5 - 100 \times 10^3 \times I_B - V_{BE} = 0$$
3. Substituting $V_{BE} = 0.7$ V, $I_B = (5 - 0.7)/(100 \times 10^3) = 43$ μA.
4. $I_C = \alpha I_B$ (as $I_{CO} \cong 0$)
Therefore, $I_C = 50 \times 43 \times 10^{-6}$ A $= 2.15$ mA.
5. Applying Kirchhoff's voltage law to the output section, we get
$$8 - 2 \times 10^3 \times 2.15 \times 10^{-3} - V_{CE} = 0$$
$$V_{CE} = 8 - 2 \times 10^3 \times 2.15 \times 10^{-3}$$
$$= 8 - 4.3 = 3.7 \text{ V}$$
6. $V_{CE} = V_{CB} + V_{BE}$
Therefore, $V_{CB} = 3.7 - 0.7 = 3$ V.

7. For the NPN transistor, positive value of V_{CB} represents a reverse-biased collector–base junction and hence the assumption that the transistor is in the active region is correct.

8. $I_E = I_C + I_B$. Therefore

$$I_E = 2.15 \times 10^{-3} + 43 \times 10^{-6} = 2.193 \text{ mA}$$

Answer: $I_C = 2.15$ mA, $I_B = 43$ μA and $I_E = 2.193$ mA.

3.6 Common-Collector Configuration

In the common-collector (CC) configuration, also known as the emitter-follower configuration, the collector terminal is common to both the input and the output sections. Figures 3.15(a) and (b) show the NPN and PNP transistors connected in the CC configuration. The configuration is similar to the common-emitter configuration with the output taken from the emitter terminal rather than the collector terminal.

CC configuration offers high input impedance and low output impedance and hence it is used for impedance matching applications, that is, for driving low-impedance load from a high-impedance source. The voltage gain offered by CC configuration is less than unity and the value of current gain is high.

Input Characteristics

The input characteristics of CC configuration relate the base current (I_B) to the collector–base voltage (V_{BC}) for different values of the emitter–collector voltage (V_{EC}). The input characteristics for a CC NPN transistor are shown in Figure 3.16.

Output Characteristics

Output characteristics of the CC configuration relate the emitter current (I_E) to the emitter–collector voltage (V_{EC}) for different values of base current (I_B). Figure 3.17 shows the output characteristics for an NPN transistor in the CC configuration. The characteristics are similar to that for the CE configuration.

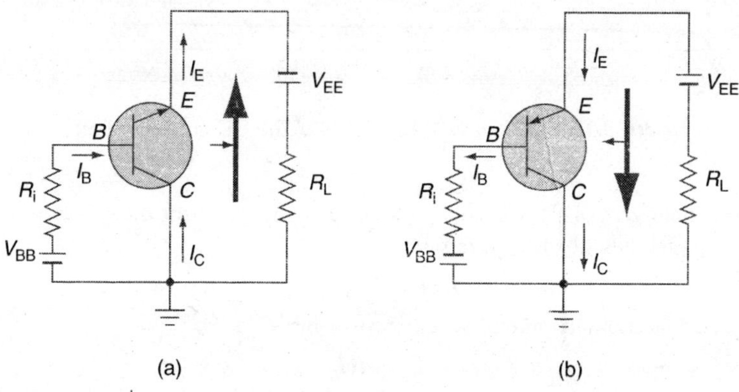

Figure 3.15 | CC configuration for (a) NPN transistor; (b) PNP transistor.

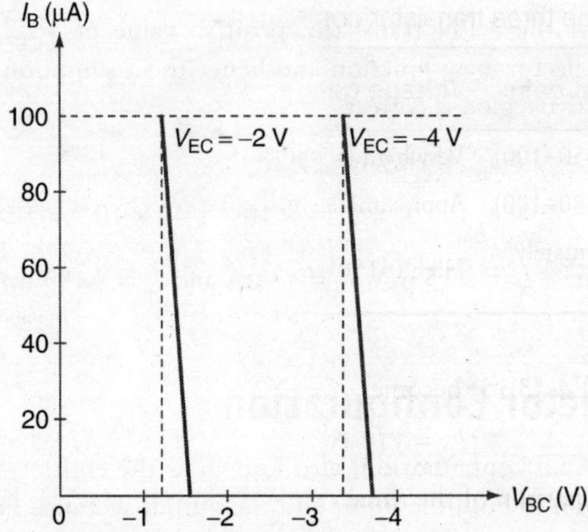

Figure 3.16 | Input characteristics of the CC configuration.

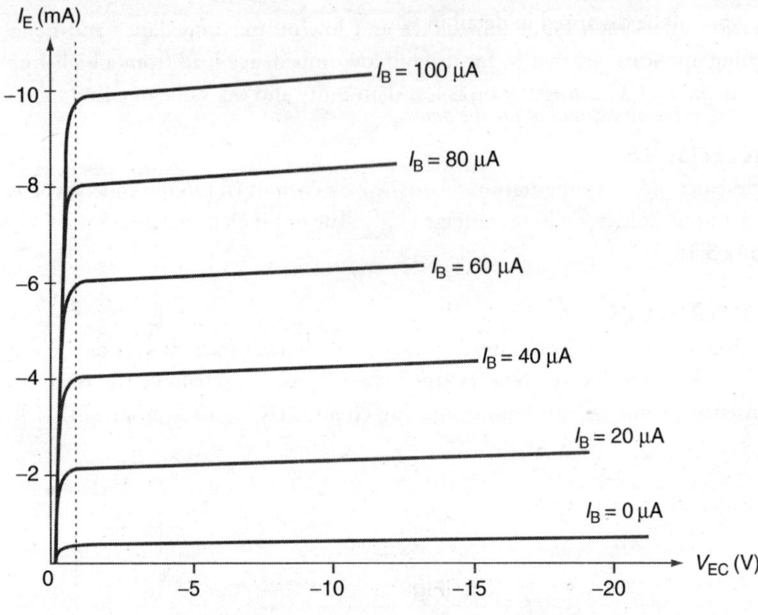

Figure 3.17 | Output characteristics of the CC configuration.

Gamma (γ)

Gamma (γ) is the current gain in the CC configuration. For any transistor the collector–emitter and base currents are related to each other by the expression

$$I_E = I_C + I_B \tag{3.13}$$

Relationship between collector and emitter current is given by

$$I_C = I_{CO} + \alpha I_E \tag{3.14}$$

Combining Eqs. (3.13) and (3.14) we get

$$I_E = \frac{I_B}{1-\alpha} + \frac{I_{CO}}{1-\alpha} \tag{3.15}$$

Table 3.1 | Salient features of the three transistor configurations

Configuration	Current gain	Voltage gain	Input impedance	Output impedance
Common emitter (CE)	High (≈50–100)	Very high (≈500)	Medium (≈800 Ω)	Medium (≈50 kΩ)
Common collector (CC)	High (≈80–100)	Approximately unity	Very high (≈800 kΩ)	Very low (≈50 Ω)
Common base (CB)	Approximately unity	High (≈150)	Low (≈100 Ω)	Very high (≈500 kΩ)

If $\gamma = (\beta + 1) = 1/(1 - \alpha)$ then Eq. (3.15) becomes

$$I_C = \gamma I_B + \gamma I_{CO} \tag{3.16}$$

Table 3.1 gives a qualitative comparison of the three configurations in terms of current and voltage gains, input and output impedances.

The configurations discussed in Sections 3.4–3.6 are the basic ones and only show the mode of operation of the transistor. The associated circuitry to be used in these configurations for providing required biasing to the two junctions will be discussed in detail in Chapter 4.

EXAMPLE 3.4 *Derive an expression for the power gain provided by the transistor in Figure 3.18.*

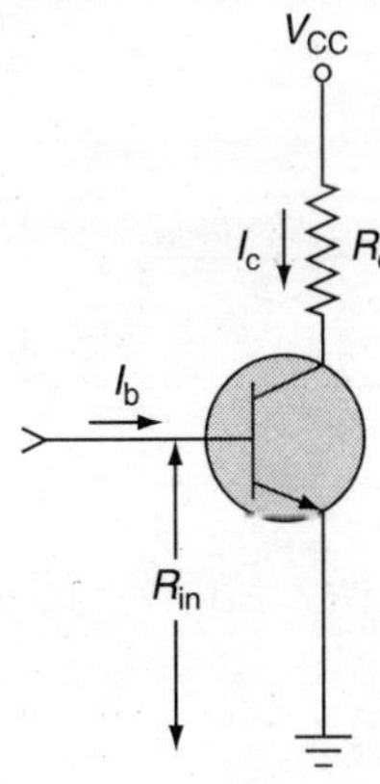

Figure 3.18 | Example 3.4.

Solution

1. Input power = Input voltage × Input current.
2. Input voltage = $I_b \times R_{in}$.
3. Therefore, Input power = $I_b \times R_{in} \times I_b = I_b^2 \times R_{in}$.
4. Output power = Output voltage × Output current
   $= I_c^2 \times R_c$
   $= \beta^2 \times I_b^2 \times R_c$
5. Power gain = Output power/Input power
   $= (\beta^2 \times I_b^2 \times R_c)/(I_b^2 \times R_{in})$
   $= (\beta^2 \times R_c)/R_{in}$

3.7 Ebers–Moll Model of Transistors

Ebers–Moll transistor model was developed by Ebers and Moll in the year 1954. It is also known as the coupled diode model. It is an ideal model for a bipolar transistor and is applicable for all four regions of transistor operation. The model involves two ideal diodes and two ideal current sources. Figures 3.19(a) and (b) show the Ebers–Moll model for the NPN and the PNP transistor, respectively.

To understand the model let us consider the generalized current equation of a transistor given in Eq. (3.3). It is repeated here for convenience of the readers.

$$I_C = I_{CO}\left[1-\exp\left(-\frac{V_{CB}}{V_T}\right)\right] + \alpha I_E \tag{3.17}$$

Equation (3.17) can be rewritten for the active region as

$$I_C = I_{CS}\left[1-\exp\left(-\frac{V_{CB}}{V_T}\right)\right] + \alpha_F I_E \tag{3.18}$$

where α_F is the CB current gain in the normal operating mode (emitter–base junction is forward-biased and collector–base junction is reverse-biased) and I_{CS} the saturation current of the collector–base diode.

For the reverse-active region the Eq. (3.17) can be rewritten as

$$I_E = I_{ES}\left[1-\exp\left(-\frac{V_{EB}}{V_T}\right)\right] + \alpha_R I_C \tag{3.19}$$

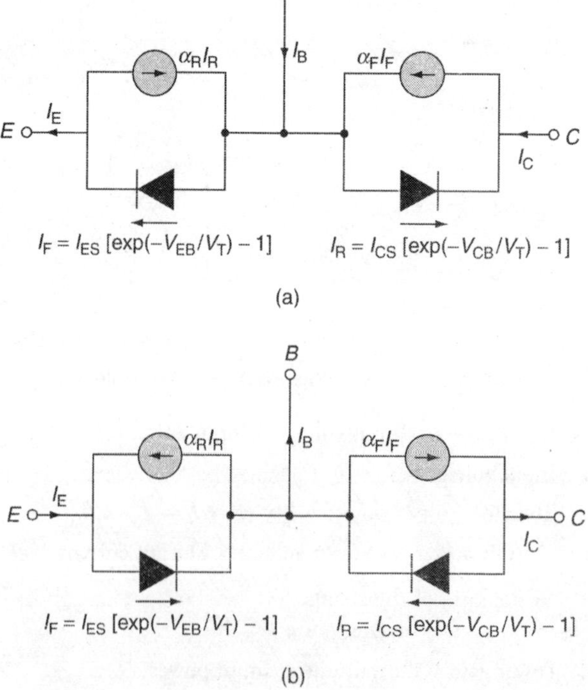

Figure 3.19 Ebers–Moll model for (a) NPN transistor; (b) PNP transistor.

where α_R is the CB current gain in the inverting operating mode (emitter–base junction is reverse-biased and the collector–base junction is forward-biased) and I_{ES} the saturation current of the emitter–base diode.

The two diodes shown in Figure 3.19 represent the base-emitter and the collector–base diodes and are connected back-to-back. The reverse saturation currents through the emitter–base and the collector–base diodes are I_{ES} and I_{CS}, respectively. Two current sources are in shunt with the diodes and their values depend upon the current flowing through the diodes. They quantify the transport of minority carriers through the base region, that is, they account for the minority-carrier transport across the base.

From Figure 3.19, the equations for the collector, emitter and base currents in the Ebers–Moll model are given by

$$I_C = -I_R + \alpha_F I_F \tag{3.20}$$

$$I_E = I_F - \alpha_R I_R \tag{3.21}$$

$$I_B = (1 - \alpha_R)I_R + (1 - \alpha_F)I_F \tag{3.22}$$

The Ebers–Moll parameters are related by the expression

$$I_{ES}\alpha_F = I_{CS}\alpha_R \tag{3.23}$$

This expression is referred to as the reciprocity relation.

In the discussion above, we have not taken into consideration the base-spreading resistance ($r_{bb'}$) of a transistor. It is the resistance offered by the base region to the flow of current through it. Typical value of $r_{bb'}$ is of the order of 100 Ω and it increases with the increase in the reverse-bias collector–base voltage. Its value also depends on the doping level of the base region. The effects of $r_{bb'}$ are important at high frequencies.

It may be mentioned here that it is impossible to construct a transistor by simply connecting two diodes back-to-back in series. A cascade arrangement of two diodes exhibits transistor properties only if the carriers injected by one junction diffuse into the second junction.

3.8 Transistor Specifications and Maximum Ratings

Selecting the right transistor type number suiting one's requirements becomes a simple exercise provided we can appreciate the critical specifications of a transistor and also their significance for different applications. Some of the important transistor specifications are: DC current gain (β or h_{FE}), AC current gain (β_{ac} or h_{fe}), gain-bandwidth product (f_T), transistor breakdown voltages and maximum power dissipation ($P_{D(max)}$).

DC Current Gain (β or h_{FE})

The variable β (also denoted as h_{FE}) is called the DC current gain, that is, the ratio of the collector current to the base current of the transistor in common-emitter configuration. It specifies the base current required to keep the transistor conducting for a given collector current. It is an important parameter for switching transistors as it tells about the minimum base current required to drive the transistor in the saturation region for a certain collector current. A transistor with smaller h_{FE} needs a harder base drive for a given collector current.

AC Current Gain (β_{ac} or h_{fe})

AC current gain is defined as the ratio of the change in the collector current to a small change in the base current for a constant collector–emitter voltage:

$$h_{fe} = \left(\frac{\Delta I_C}{\Delta I_B}\right)_{V_{CE}=\text{constant}} \tag{3.24}$$

Gain-Bandwidth Product (f_T)

The gain-bandwidth product (f_T) tells us about the high frequency response of the transistor. It is the frequency for which gain on the high-frequency side falls to unity or 0 dB. It is an important parameter that needs to be considered when the transistor is to be used for intermediate frequency/radio frequency (IF/RF) applications.

Transistor Breakdown Voltages

There are two types of breakdown phenomena possible in a transistor, namely the avalanche breakdown and reach-through phenomenon. The breakdown voltages associated with the avalanche multiplication are V_{CEO} and V_{CBO}. V_{CEO} is the maximum voltage that can be applied across the collector–emitter junction with the base open in the CE configuration. It is the worst case of collector–emitter breakdown voltage and is a very important specification particularly in switching transistors used in switched-mode power supplies. This parameter is often specified in different ways. Quite often, V_{CER} (collector–emitter breakdown voltage with a specified resistance typically of the value of 100–200 Ω connected between the base and emitter) and V_{CES} (collector–emitter breakdown voltage with base shorted to the emitter) ratings are also given in addition to the V_{CEO} rating of the switching transistors. It may be mentioned that V_{CEO} is the lowest of all and if the design is such that the V_{CEO} rating is not exceeded, the possibility of collector–emitter junction breakdown gets eliminated. V_{CBO} is the reverse output breakdown voltage when the transistor is connected in the CB configuration with the emitter terminal open.

The second mechanism that leads to transistor breakdown is the reach-through or the punch-through effect. It results from the increase in the width of the collector–base junction depletion region with increase in the reverse voltage. As the base region is very thin, even at moderate values of reverse voltages, the depletion region spreads completely across the base and reaches the emitter junction. This results in large flow of emitter current leading to transistor breakdown. The collector–base breakdown voltage due to the punch-through effect is independent of the transistor configuration.

The lower of the breakdown voltages either due to avalanche or reach-through breakdown is considered as the maximum voltage limit.

$I_{C(max)}$

It is the peak collector current rating of the transistor. It is specified for continuous or pulsed mode of operation of a transistor.

Power Dissipation ($P_{D(max)}$)

It is the maximum power dissipation capability of a transistor. The curve for maximum power dissipation can be plotted using the formula

$$P_{D(max)} = V_{CE} \times I_C \tag{3.25}$$

The maximum collector current, collector–emitter voltage and the power ratings limit the active region of operation of a transistor as shown in Figure 3.20. $V_{CE(sat)}$ specifies the minimum collector–emitter voltage required to drive the transistor in the active region. The area enclosed by dotted lines represents the safe operating area of the transistor.

$P_{D(max)}$ is usually specified at a given ambient temperature and it should be derated at higher temperatures as per the derating curve supplied by the manufacturers. The use of heat sink results in increased power dissipation capability of the transistor. The actual dissipation capability can be determined from known values of maximum operating junction temperature, ambient temperature and the thermal resistance involved. There are two types of thermal resistances associated with a transistor: the junction-to-case thermal resistance and the case-to-ambient thermal resistance. The former tells about how effectively heat is conducted away from the junction to the case, and the latter tells about how effectively the heat is conducted away from the case to ambient.

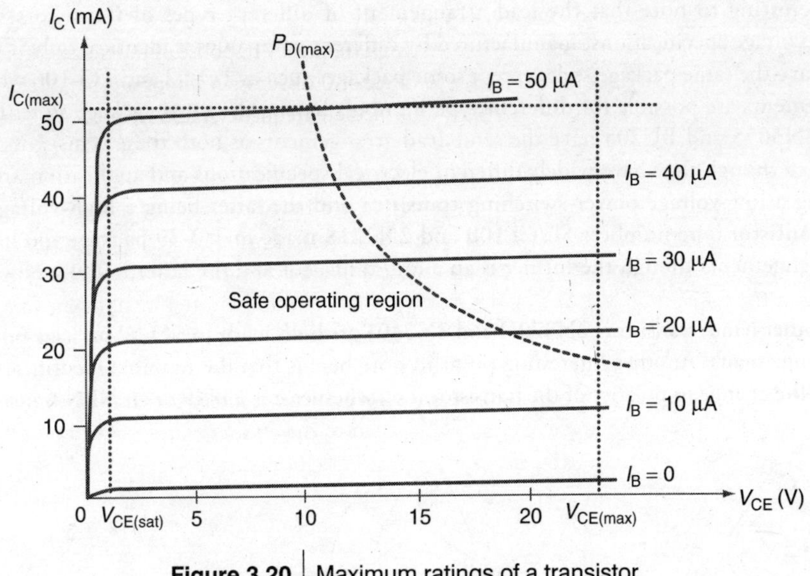

Figure 3.20 Maximum ratings of a transistor.

Table 3.2 Typical transistor applications and important specifications

S. No.	Application requirements	Important specifications
1.	General purpose, low-level amplifier and switching transistors	h_{FE}, $I_{C(max)}$, f_T, V_{CEO}
2.	Power-switching applications	V_{CEO}, V_{CBO}, h_{FE}, $I_{C(max)}$, f_T, $P_{D(max)}$
3.	Low-level IF/RF amplification	$I_{C(max)}$, f_T, V_{CEO}
4.	Audio amplification	h_{FE}, $I_{C(max)}$, $P_{D(max)}$, V_{CEO}
5.	High-voltage transistors	V_{CEO}, V_{CBO}, h_{FE}, $I_{C(max)}$, f_T

The case-to-ambient thermal resistance depends upon the transistor's package size. It is, for instance 300°C/W for TO-18 package, 150°C/W for TO-5 and TO-39 packages, 60°C/W for TO-66 package and only 30°C/W for TO-3 package. The effective case-to-ambient thermal resistance can be reduced by using an appropriate heat sink that basically increases the effective radiating area.

All specifications are not equally important for all application requirements. Table 3.2 lists some typical applications and the corresponding transistor parameters that would significantly affect the choice criteria.

3.9 Lead Identification

Bipolar junction transistors are made in a large variety of package styles. Some of the more popular package styles include the TO-5, TO-18, TO-39, TO-72, TO-237, TO-92, TO-3, TO-66 and TO-220 packages. Transistors in TO-3 and TO-66 packages are high-power devices, while those with small metal can or plastic body (TO-5, TO-18, TO-39, TO-72, TO-237, TO-92, TO-220) are low- to medium-power devices. Transistor leads are made of gold, aluminum or nickel and then encapsulated in a container. The lead arrangement for different transistor package styles is shown in Figure 3.21.

It is interesting to note that the lead arrangement of different types of transistors with varying current and voltage specifications, manufactured by different companies is identical only if these devices happen to have the same package style, except some packages such as TO-92 and TO-106 where different lead arrangements are possible for different type numbers having the same package style. For instance, transistors 2N3055 and BU205 have the same lead arrangements as both these transistors are made in TO-3 package though they have widely different electrical specifications and application areas, with the former being a low-voltage power-switching transistor and the latter being a high-voltage transistor. Similarly, transistor type numbers SL/CL100 and 2N2218 made in TO-39 package too have identical terminal arrangements though the former is an audio transistor and the latter is a low-power switching transistor.

On the other hand, transistors 2N370H and 2N5401 are both made in TO-92 package but have different lead arrangements. Another interesting point to note here is that the terminal identification does not change with the change in polarity of the transistor (i.e., whether it is a PNP or an NPN transistor), as long

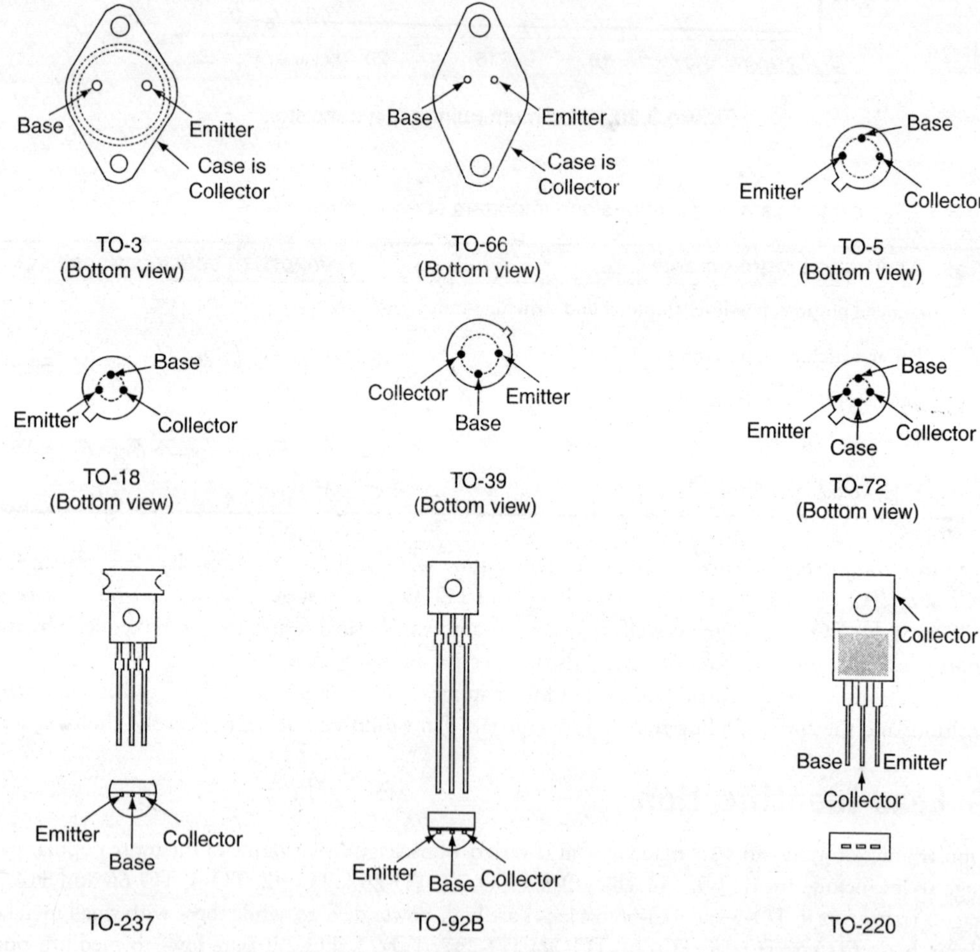

Figure 3.21 | Transistor package styles and lead identification.

as the package is the same. For instance, transistor type numbers 2N2222 and 2N2907 have the same lead arrangements though the former is an NPN transistor and the latter is a PNP transistor.

Remembering the lead arrangement of different transistor package styles becomes simple if we take into account of the following points

1. Metal can transistor packages (TO-5, TO-18, TO-39) invariably have a notch and the lead adjacent to the notch is the emitter. The leads are identified as emitter–base–collector starting from the emitter and moving clockwise.
2. The collector is usually connected internally to the metal can in such packages. One can easily identify the lead that is common to the metal body by careful observation and even a continuity check with the multimeter is not needed.
3. In some of the plastic packages like TO-106 for instance, there is a dot near the emitter lead.
4. The lead arrangements of TO-66 and TO-3 package styles are identical when both types are viewed in the same way. The metal body in both these types is the collector and there is no separate lead for the collector.
5. Transistors with TO-72 package have four leads with the fourth lead connected to the case internally. The package has a notch near the emitter lead and the leads are identified as emitter–base–collector starting from the emitter and moving clockwise just like other similar packages with a notch but having three leads.
6. Another widely used package designation for the transistors is the "SOT" designation, which has much larger number of package styles than the popular "TO" designation. But for most of the popular transistor numbers there is a corresponding "TO" designation for a given "SOT" designation and vice versa. For example, SOT-18 is nothing but TO-72 and SOT-54 is the same as TO-92 package. Also, there are some popular SOT packages that are only a slight variation of the popular TO packages, for example SOT-93 is similar to TO-220 but with a slightly larger width. As far as lead identification is concerned, for a given SOT package, it is the same as that for the corresponding TO package.
7. RF power transistors are packaged in different styles when compared with conventional power transistors. The popular package styles in this category are SOT-119, SOT-120, SOT-121, SOT-122 and SOT-123 (Figure 3.22). Identifying the leads of these transistors is quite straight forward. Packages SOT-120 to SOT-123 are more or less identical except for a slight variation in dimensions. Each one of them has four strips (leads in RF power transistors are in the form of strips) placed 90° with respect to each other over a 360° circle. The strip with a slight angular cut is always the collector and the strip opposite to the collector is always the base. The other two strips are both emitters. In SOT-119, there are six strips out of which the four outer ones are all emitters, the smaller of the two middle ones is always the collector and the remaining one is the base.

Transistor leads can also be identified using a multimeter. The procedure for identifying the leads is the same as that for PN junction diodes. The collector–base and emitter–base junctions can be checked with the multimeter to identify the leads. But such a test gives the correct result only if the device under test is healthy.

In the multimeter identification of transistor leads, if either the collector or the emitter lead is known, the other two leads can be identified without any problem from a single junction test. If the emitter terminal is known (emitter is the terminal adjacent to the notch in TO-5, TO-18, TO-39, TO-72 package styles) then the base and the collector terminals are identified by performing the collector–base diode junction test. If the collector terminal is known (it is usually connected to the body in the case of TO-5, TO-18, TO-39, TO-72 package styles and is in fact the body in case of TO-66 and TO-3 packages) then the base and the emitter terminals can be identified by taking the emitter–base junction diode test. Also, whether the transistor is an NPN or a PNP transistor, the meter shows an open circuit between the collector and the emitter terminals in both the directions.

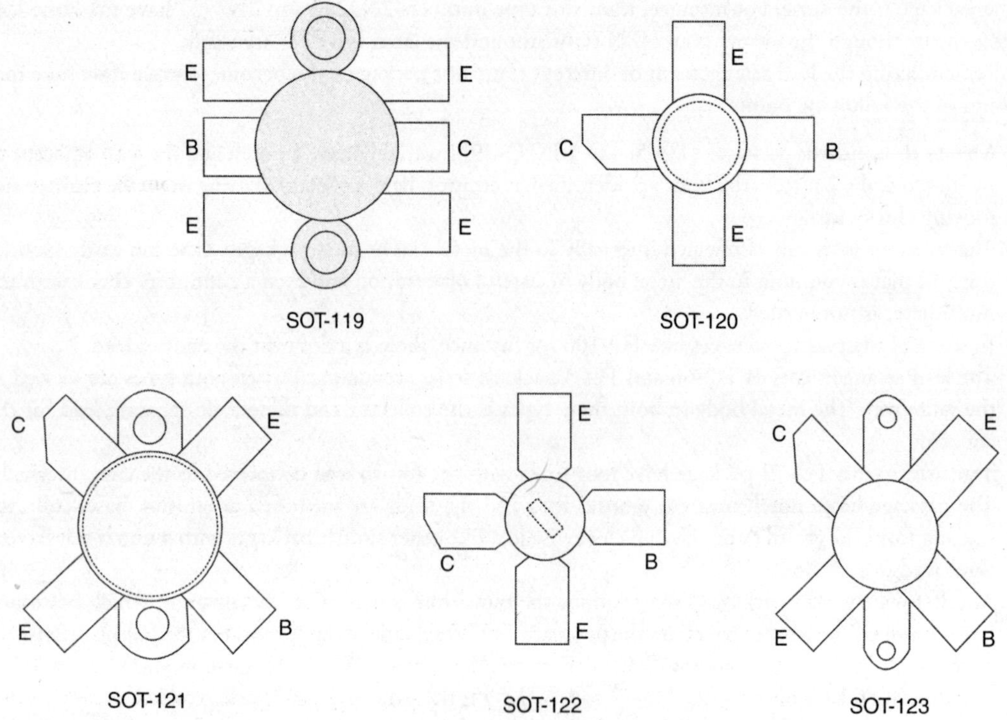

Figure 3.22 | Package styles and lead identification of RF transistors.

The multimeter tests for identifying the leads of a bipolar junction transistor are illustrated in Figures 3.23(a)–(f) for an NPN transistor and in Figures 3.24(a)–(f) for a PNP transistor. The test arrangements depicted in these figures are self-explanatory.

3.10 Transistor Testing

As in case of diodes, transistors also can be checked using a multimeter, an ohmmeter and a curve tracer. Using a multimeter, transistors are tested by checking the emitter–base and collector–base junctions in the same fashion as explained in the case of the PN junction diode. The junction must be tested both in the forward-biased and reverse-biased modes. As an example, in case of an NPN transistor the emitter–base junction is forward-biased by connecting the red lead of the multimeter to the base and the black lead to the emitter. In the case of a healthy transistor, the multimeter will show the voltage corresponding to the forward voltage drop of the emitter–base junction when set to the diode test position. An OPEN reading in this condition indicates a faulty transistor. The emitter–base junction is reverse-biased by interchanging the connections and now the meter should show an OL (open) reading. A short circuit or a low resistance in this case indicates a faulty transistor. Similarly, the collector–base junction can also be checked. In addition, collector–emitter terminals should show an open condition in both the directions.

Advanced digital meters provide the value of h_{fe} by placing the transistor in the socket provided for the purpose. The diode-testing mode provided in these meters can be used to check whether the transistor is working properly or not.

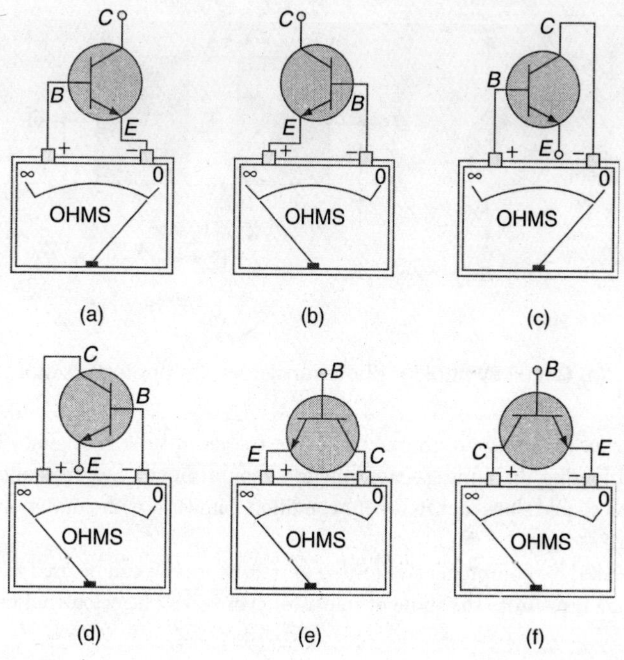

Figure 3.23 | Lead identification of NPN transistors using a multimeter.

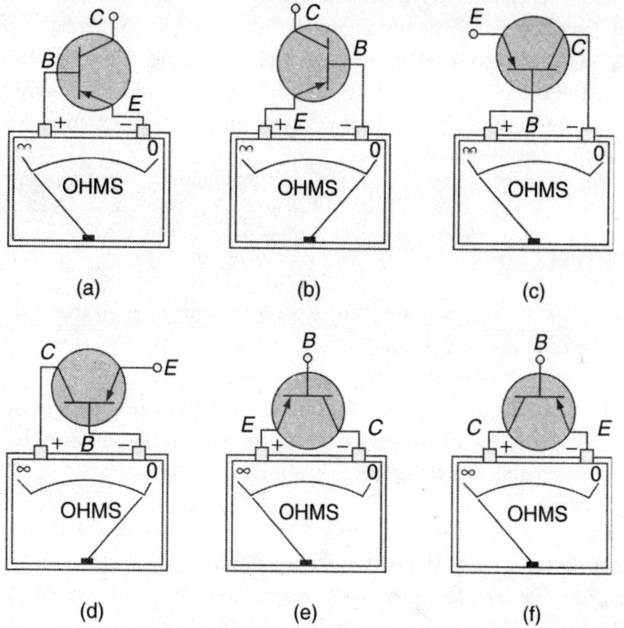

Figure 3.24 | Lead identification of PNP transistors using a multimeter.

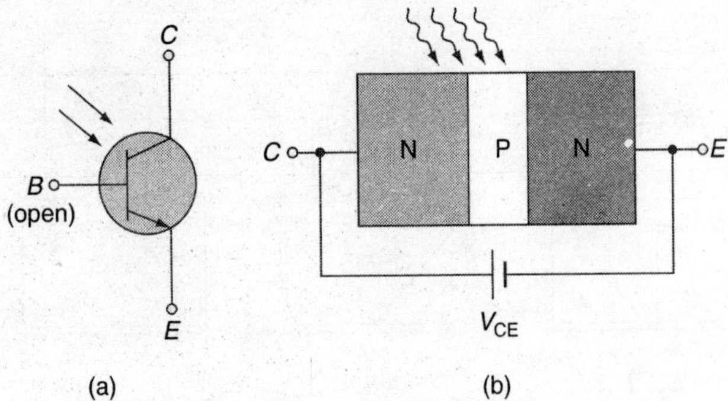

Figure 3.25 (a) Circuit symbol for phototransistors; (b) phototransistor connection.

Transistors can be checked using an ohmmeter or the resistance scale of digital multimeters. With the collector open, forward biasing the emitter–base junction should show a low resistance and reverse biasing the emitter–base junction should show an OL (open) condition. Similarly, with emitter open, the collector–base junction can be checked.

Curve tracer can be used for comprehensive testing of transistors as it can be used to display the input and output characteristics of a transistor. The value of transistor β or h_{fe} can be calculated from these curves.

3.11 Phototransistors

Phototransistors are solid-state light sensors that possess internal gain. Phototransistors can be viewed as photodiodes whose output current is fed to the base of a conventional small signal transistor. Figure 3.25(a) shows the circuit symbol of a phototransistor and Figure 3.25(b) shows its connection diagram. Phototransistor gain is of the order of 100–1500 as compared to unity gain of photodiodes. Although the output of photodiodes can be amplified through the use of an external operational amplifier, phototransistors offer a cost-effective option. However, the response time of phototransistors is of the order of few to hundreds of microseconds, which is much larger than that of photodiodes.

Phototransistors are discussed in detail in the chapter on optoelectronic devices (Chapter 7).

3.12 Power Transistors

Power transistors, as the name suggests, are transistors intended for high-power applications. Improvements in production techniques have resulted in higher transistor power ratings in smaller packages with increased breakdown voltages and faster switching times.

The power handling capability of the transistor and the collector junction temperature are related to each other as the power dissipated by the device causes an increase in the junction temperature of the transistor. The average power dissipated in a transistor is given by the expression

$$P_D = V_{CE} \times I_C \tag{3.26}$$

The maximum power rating ($P_{D(max)}$) is defined as the maximum power that can be safely dissipated in a transistor. The transistor can dissipate this power up to a certain case temperature. Above this temperature the power handling capability of the transistor decreases with increase in the case temperature and becomes zero at the maximum operating temperature (Figure 3.26). Silicon transistors have higher operating temperatures as compared to germanium transistors with typical maximum values for the junction temperatures being 150–200°C for silicon transistors and 100–110°C for germanium transistors.

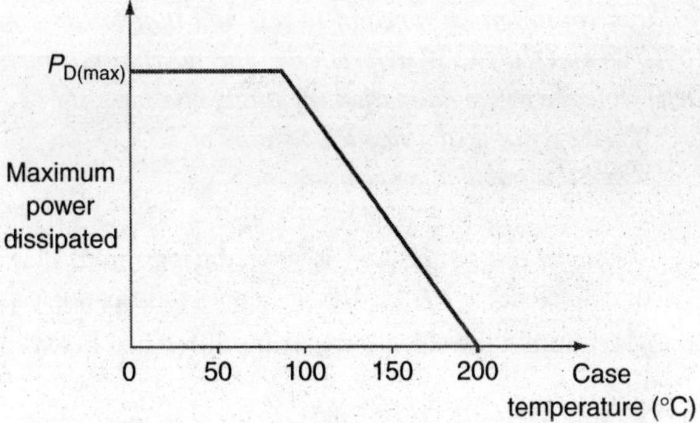

Figure 3.26 | Power derating curve of a transistor.

Power transistors are mounted on large metal cases called heat sinks to provide a large area for better radiation of heat. With the heat sink, the transistor has a larger area from which to radiate the heat into the air, thereby holding the case temperature to a much lower value than would be possible without the heat sink.

Let us now consider how the transistor junction temperature (T_J), the case temperature (T_C) and the ambient temperature (T_A) are related to the power handling capability of the power transistor. One of the most important parameters that defines the power handling capability of any device is its thermal resistance. It provides information about how much temperature change occurs for a given amount of power dissipation. Thermal resistance is measured in °C/W. Lower the value of the thermal resistance of the device more is its power handling capability. The temperature of the transistor junction is given by the formula

$$T_J = P_D\theta_{JA} + T_A \tag{3.27}$$

where T_J is the transistor junction temperature, P_D the power dissipated in the transistor, θ_{JA} the junction-ambient thermal resistance and T_A the ambient temperature.

Also

$$T_J = P_D\theta_{JC} + T_C \tag{3.28}$$

where θ_{JC} is the junction-case thermal resistance and T_C the case temperature.

Without the heat sink the typical value of θ_{JA} ($\theta_{JC} + \theta_{CA}$) is in the range of 40–50°C/W (θ_{CA} is the case–ambient thermal resistance), and with the heat sink the value of θ_{JA} ($\theta_{JC} + \theta_{CS} + \theta_{SA}$) is reduced to around 2–5°C/W (θ_{CS} is the case-heatsink thermal resistance; θ_{SA} is the heatsink-ambient thermal resistance). Thus, the use of heat sink results in reduced value of transistor junction to ambient thermal resistance and increase in power dissipation capability of the transistor.

EXAMPLE 3.5 *What should be the maximum value of junction-to-case thermal resistance of a certain silicon transistor that has a maximum junction operating temperature of 200°C and that can safely dissipate a power of 300 W at a case temperature of 25°C.*

Solution

1. The said transistor can safely dissipate a power of 300 W at a case temperature of 25°C. Therefore, maximum allowable junction-case temperature differential is (200–25) = 175°C.
2. Therefore, the maximum value of junction-to-case thermal resistance = 175/300 = 0.583°C/W.

Answer: Maximum value of junction-to-case thermal resistance is 0.583°C/W.

EXAMPLE 3.6 *A silicon transistor has junction-to-case and junction-to-ambient thermal resistances of 10°C/W and 100°C/W, respectively. The maximum junction temperature is 200°C. Determine the power dissipation capability of a transistor:*

1. *When operating at a case temperature of 50°C.*
2. *When the ambient temperature is 25°C.*

Solution

1. When the case temperature is 50°C, the maximum allowable junction-case temperature difference is 150°C. This gives power dissipation capability as 150/10 = 15 W.
2. Maximum allowable temperature difference between ambient and junction = 175°C.
   Ambient-junction thermal resistance = 100°C/W
   This gives power dissipation capability as 175/100 = 1.75 W

Answer: The power dissipation capability of transistor is (1) 15 W and (2) 1.75 W.

3.13 Transistor Construction Techniques

Transistors can be constructed using various techniques, the important ones being point contact, grown-junction, alloy-junction, diffusion, epitaxial and annular techniques.

Point-Contact Transistors

The earliest transistors fabricated were point-contact transistors. Point-contact transistors are constructed by placing two wires into the semiconductor wafer. The wires are N-type and the wafer is P-type for an NPN transistor (Figure 3.27) and vice versa for a PNP transistor. PN junction is formed between the wire and the wafer by applying electrical pulses to each of the wire. These transistors suffer from poor reliability and are no longer used.

Grown-Junction Type Transistors

Grown-junction type transistors are fabricated from a single crystal. The crystal is drawn from a melt of silicon or germanium whose impurity concentration is changed by adding the N-type and the P-type dopants during the crystal drawing operation. The crystal is then sliced into a large number of devices and the contacts are then made (Figure 3.28).

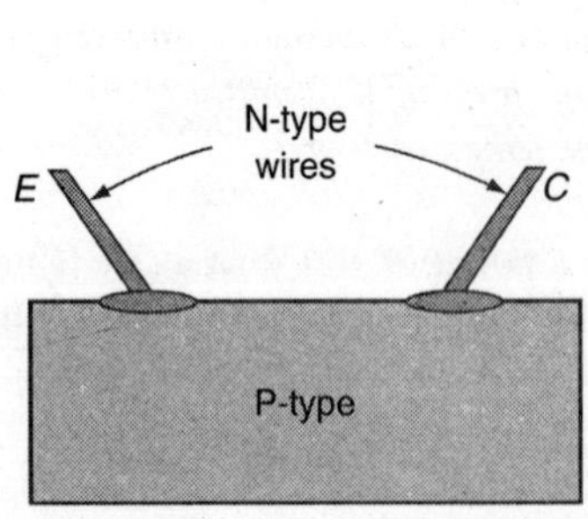

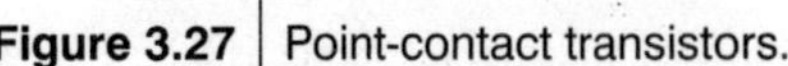
Figure 3.27 | Point-contact transistors.

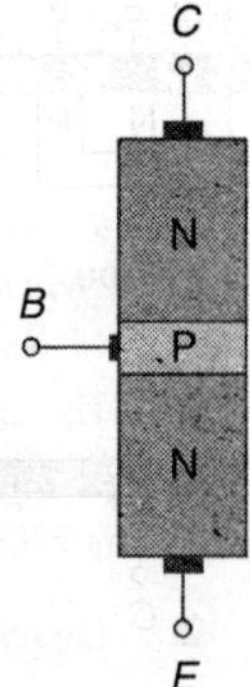

Figure 3.28 | Grown-junction type transistors.

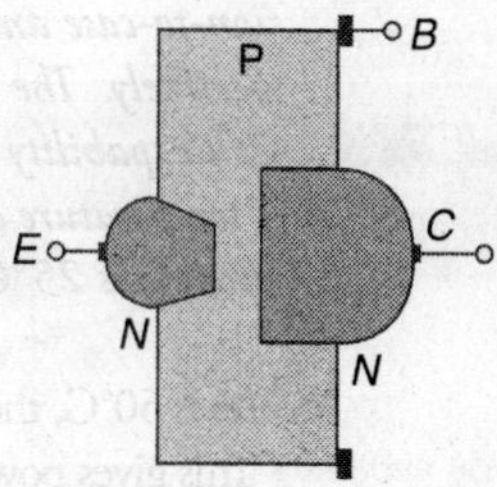

Figure 3.29 | Alloy-junction transistors.

Alloy-Junction Transistors

In the case of alloy-junction transistors, the base is a thin wafer. Two dots of impurity elements are placed on opposite sides of this wafer. In the case of an NPN transistor the wafer is a P-type material and the dots are of N-type material (Figure 3.29), whereas in the case of PNP transistors the wafer is an N-type material and the dots are of P-type material. The whole structure is raised for a short time to a temperature high enough to melt the impurity into the base material. As is clear from Figure 3.29, the collector region is made larger than the emitter region. This is done so that the collector region collects maximum number of majority carriers from the emitter region and prevents them from diffusing into the base region.

Diffusion Transistors

The most frequently used technique for transistor fabrication is the diffusion technique. In this technique the semiconductor wafer is subjected to gaseous diffusions of both N-type and P-type impurities to form the emitter–base and the collector–base junctions. Two types of transistors are fabricated using the diffusion technique, namely, the planar transistors and the mesa transistors. The planar NPN silicon transistor of the diffusion type is shown in Figure 3.30(a). The collector–base region is photo-etched on the block of N-type silicon and a P-type base region is formed by a gaseous diffusion-masking process. The emitter is then diffused onto the base and the whole structure is covered by a layer of silicon oxide.

Mesa transistor is essentially a planar transistor that has been etched at the collector–base junction leaving a mesa or a flat-topped peak [Figure 3.30(b)]. Mesa transistors are rugged devices with high power-dissipation capability and can operate at higher frequencies. However, they have higher value of saturation voltage because of highly resistive collector region. Hence, they are unsuitable for switching applications.

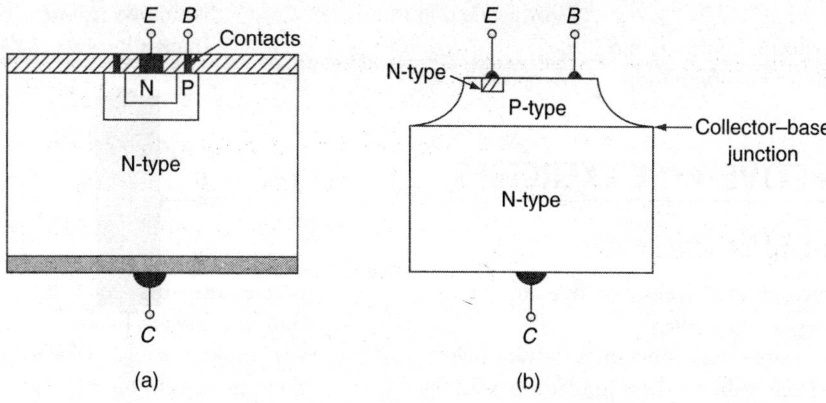

Figure 3.30 | (a) Planar diffusion transistors; (b) mesa diffusion transistors.

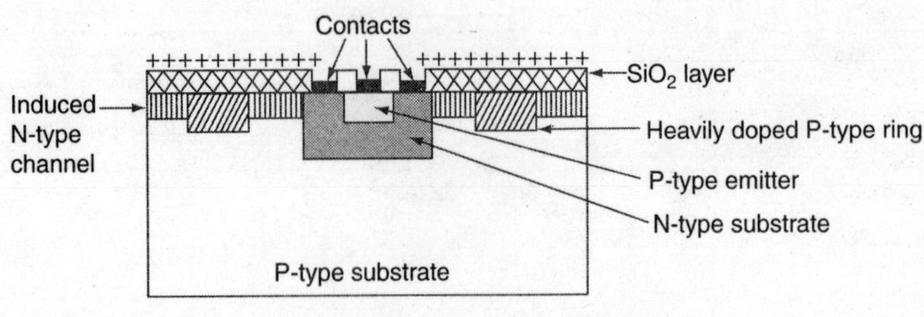

Figure 3.31 | Annular transistors.

Epitaxial Transistors

The epitaxial technique consists of growing a very thin, high purity, single-crystal layer of silicon or germanium on a heavily doped substrate of the same material. This augmented crystal forms the collector on which the base and the emitter regions are diffused. Both planar and mesa transistors can be constructed using this technique.

Annular Transistors

In annular transistors, a heavily doped ring is introduced around the base region. The ring is of the P-type material for PNP transistors (Figure 3.31) and of the N-type for NPN transistors. It interrupts the induced channel and isolates the collector–base junction from the surface of the device. It is therefore a high-voltage device with low collector–base leakage.

KEY TERMS

AC current gain (h_{fe})
Active region
Alloy-junction transistors
Alpha (α)
Annular transistors
Base-spreading resistance ($r_{bb'}$)
Beta (β)
Common-collector configuration
Common-emitter configuration
Common-base configuration
Diffusion technique
Early effect
Ebers–Moll transistor model
Epitaxial technique
Gain-bandwidth product (f_T)
Grown-junction transistor
$I_{C(max)}$
Mesa transistor
NPN transistor
PNP transistor
Point-contact transistors
Reach-through or the punch-through effect
Reverse-active region
Saturation region
Transistor

OBJECTIVE-TYPE EXERCISES

Multiple-Choice Questions

1. A semiconductor transistor operates in the active region only when
   a. the emitter–base junction is forward-biased and the collector–base junction is reverse-biased.
   b. both emitter–base and collector–base junctions are forward-biased.
   c. both emitter–base and collector–base junctions are reverse-biased.

d. the collector–base junction is forward-biased and emitter–base junction is reverse-biased.

2. Which of the following is/are metal can package/s:
   a. TO-5
   b. TO-18
   c. TO-92
   d. Both (a) and (b)

3. When a healthy NPN transistor is connected to an ohmmeter such that the base terminal is connected to the red lead of the meter and the emitter terminal to the black lead then the meter shows
   a. an open circuit.
   b. some medium resistance.
   c. a very small resistance.
   d. none of the above.

4. A conducting bipolar transistor dissipates least power when operating in the
   a. saturation region.
   b. cut-off region.
   c. active region.
   d. reverse-active region.

5. A bipolar transistor in sinusoidal oscillator configuration is operating in the
   a. active region.
   b. saturation region.
   c. cut-off region.
   d. reverse-active region.

6. The maximum reverse collector to emitter breakdown voltage with base open is referred to as
   a. V_{CEO}
   b. V_C
   c. V_{CBO}
   d. V_{EBO}

7. When a transistor is used as a switch, the base current required to switch on the transistor for a given collector current is calculated from
   a. h_{fe}
   b. α
   c. γ
   d. σ

8. For $\alpha = 0.9$ the value of β is
   a. 1
   b. 0.9
   c. 9
   d. 10

9. With increase in the collector–base reverse voltage
   a. the base width increases.
   b. the base width decreases.
   c. the base width is not affected.
   d. the base width can increase or decrease.

10. Which of the transistor configurations is capable of providing both voltage and current gains?
    a. Common base
    b. Common collector
    c. Common emitter
    d. Both common emitter and common base

Match the Following

Match the terms in Column (a) with the figures in Column (b).

S. No.	Column (a)	S. No.	Column (b)
1.	NPN transistor	A.	C, B, E (transistor symbol)

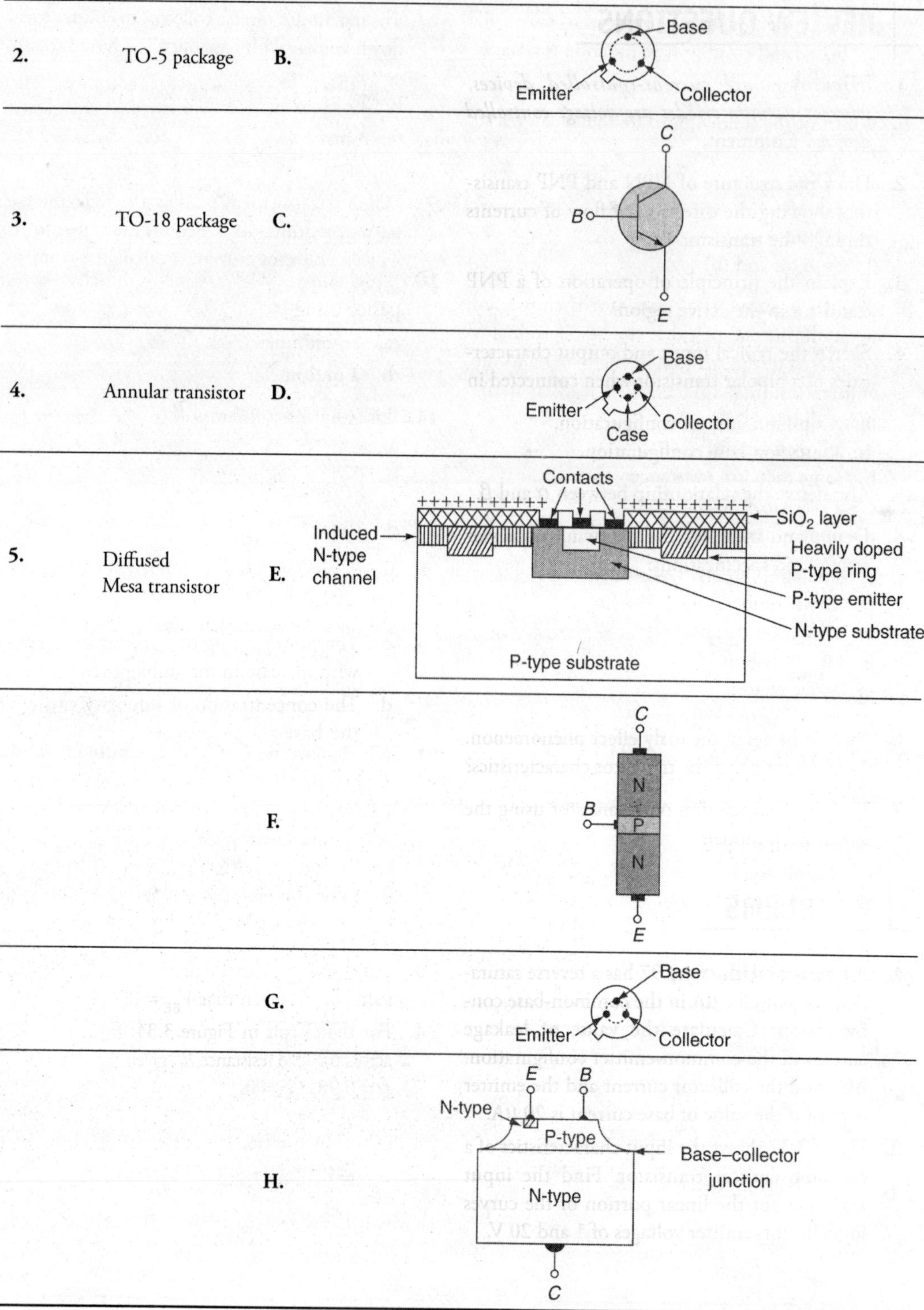
2.
TO-5 package
B.
Base
Emitter
Collector
C
3.
TO-18 package
C.
B
E
4.
Annular transistor
D.
Base
Emitter
Collector
Case
Contacts
5.
Diffused
Mesa transistor
E.
Induced
N-type
channel
SiO2 layer
Heavily doped
P-type ring
P-type emitter
N-type substrate
P-type substrate
C
F.
B
N
P
N
E
G.
Base
Emitter
Collector
E
B
N-type
P-type
Base–collector
junction
H.
N-type
C

REVIEW QUESTIONS

1. "*Transistors are current-controlled devices, whereas vacuum triodes are voltage-controlled devices.*" Comment.

2. Draw the structure of NPN and PNP transistors showing the direction of flow of currents through the transistor.

3. Explain the principle of operation of a PNP transistor in the active region?

4. Sketch the typical input and output characteristics of a bipolar transistor when connected in

   a. Common-emitter configuration.
   b. Common-base configuration.

   Also derive the relationship between α and β.

5. Define and interpret the following transistor ratings and specifications:

   a. V_{CBO}
   b. V_{CEO}
   c. $P_{D(max)}$
   d. α

6. Explain in detail the early effect phenomenon. How does it affect the transistor characteristics?

7. Explain the operation of a transistor using the Ebers–Moll model?

8. Compare the common-base, common-emitter and common-collector configurations of a transistor?

9. Explain the manufacturing process for diffused mesa and annular transistors. Give one merit and one demerit for each configuration.

10. How will you identify the terminals of a transistor using

    a. an ohmmeter?
    b. a multimeter?

11. List any four differences in the characteristic curves of silicon and germanium transistors.

12. Give reasons for the following:

    a. Why is the collector current slightly less than the emitter current?
    b. Why is a transistor referred to as a bipolar junction device?
    c. The power rating of a transistor decreases with increase in the ambient temperature.
    d. The concentration of minority carriers in the base region increases with increase in the reverse-bias voltage of the collector-base junction.

PROBLEMS

1. A transistor with $\alpha = 0.97$ has a reverse saturation current of 1 μA in the common-base configuration. Calculate the value of leakage current in the common-emitter configuration. Also find the collector current and the emitter current if the value of base current is 20 μA.

2. Figure 3.32 shows the input characteristics of a common-emitter transistor. Find the input resistance for the linear portion of the curves for collector–emitter voltages of 1 and 20 V.

3. For the circuit in Figure 3.33, determine the value of R_1, given that $V_{BE} = 0.7$ V, $I_{CO} = 0$.

4. For the circuit in Figure 3.34, find the voltage across the load resistance R_L, given that $V_{BE} = 0.7$ V, $\alpha = 0.98$, $I_{CO} = 0$.

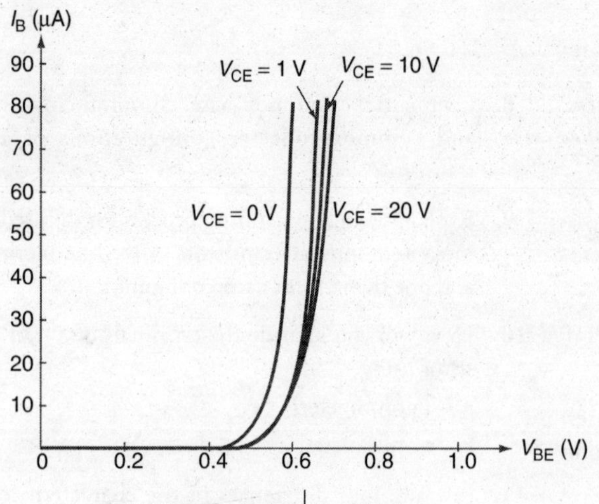

Figure 3.32 | Problem 2.

Figure 3.33 | Problem 3.

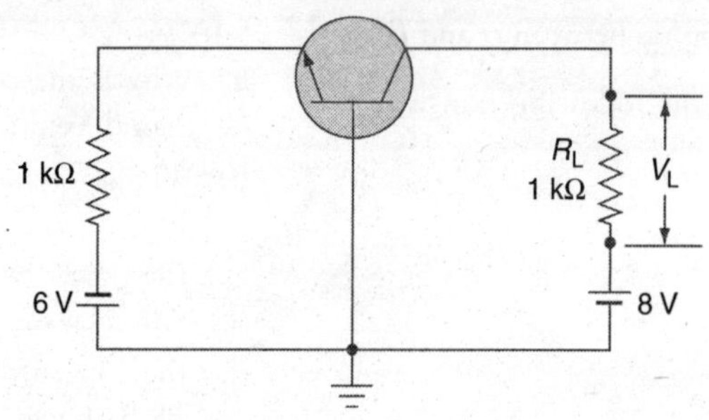

Figure 3.34 | Problem 4.

ANSWERS

Multiple-Choice Questions

1. (a)
2. (d)
3. (c)
4. (a)
5. (a)
6. (a)
7. (a)
8. (c)
9. (b)
10. (c)

Match the Following

1. C
2. B
3. G
4. E
5. H

Problems

1. 33.33 μA; 0.68 mA; 0.7 mA
2. 666.67 Ω; 1500 Ω
3. 17.12 kΩ
4. 5.2 V

CHAPTER 4

Transistor Biasing and Thermal Stabilization

Learning Objectives

After completing this chapter, you will learn the following:

- Importance of transistor biasing.
- Designing a transistor-biasing circuit.
- Detailed analysis of fixed-bias, emitter-bias, collector-to-base-bias and voltage-divider-bias with emitter-bias configurations.
- Design of common base and common-collector configurations.
- Understanding the importance of stability factors $S_{I_{CO}}$, S_{β} and $S_{V_{BE}}$.
- Derivation of expressions for stability factors for different biasing configurations.
- Phenomenon of thermal runaway.
- Bias compensation techniques.
- Operation of transistor as a switch.

In the last chapter the fundamentals of transistor construction and operation were discussed. After understanding the fundamentals of transistor operation, we are in a position to design a transistor-based amplifier circuit. The design of any electronic amplifier involves two important aspects, namely, the DC response and the AC response. The choice of parameters to establish the desired DC levels affect the AC response and vice versa. The DC analysis and the AC analysis are done separately and then superposition theorem is applied for the complete analysis.

To design a transistor-based amplifier circuit it is necessary to operate the transistor in the active region. This is done using a transistor-biasing circuit. This chapter focuses on the importance of transistor biasing and the various transistor-biasing configurations including fixed-bias, emitter-bias, collector-to-base-bias and voltage-divider-bias with emitter-bias configuration. The stability offered by each of the configurations against variations in temperature and other parameters is another topic covered in the chapter. Towards the end of the chapter, the phenomenon of thermal runaway and design of transistor switch is covered.

4.1 Operating Point

We have studied in Chapter 3 that a transistor acts as an amplifier when it is operated in the active region of its output characteristics. Therefore, the first step in designing a transistor amplifier is to design a circuit so as to enable the transistor to operate in its linear active region. This is done by using external components such as resistors and capacitors and applying DC voltages to the transistor so as to establish proper collector current (I_C) and collector–emitter voltage (V_{CE}) across the transistor. This process is referred to as *transistor biasing* and the circuit used for transistor biasing is called a *biasing circuit.* Transistor biasing is done so that the transistor amplifies the input signal linearly and without distortion.

There are four conditions that should be met for a transistor to act as a faithful amplifier. First, the emitter–base junction should be forward-biased and the collector–base junction should be reverse-biased for all levels of input signal. For the emitter–base junction to be forward-biased, the base–emitter voltage (V_{BE}) should not fall below 0.3 V for germanium transistors and below 0.7 V for silicon transistors for all values of input signal. Second, the collector–emitter voltage (V_{CE}) should not fall below the knee voltage ($V_{CE(sat)}$) for any part of the input signal. For V_{CE} less than the $V_{CE(sat)}$ (0.5 V for germanium transistor and 1.0 V for silicon transistor), the collector–base junction is not properly reverse-biased. Third, the value of collector current (I_C) when no signal is applied should be at least equal to the maximum collector current due to signal alone. Finally, the maximum ratings of the transistor ($I_{C(max)}$, $V_{CE(max)}$ and $P_{D(max)}$) should not be exceeded at any value of the input signal.

The DC collector current (I_C) and the collector–emitter voltage (V_{CE}) when no input signal is applied are collectively referred to as the *operating point.* Since the operating point is a fixed point on the output characteristics of the transistor, it is also referred to as the *quiescent point* (Q-point). Judicious selection of the operating point is important for faithful amplification of the input signal. Figure 4.1 shows the output characteristics of a common-emitter amplifier with four different operating points. The functioning of the transistor amplifier for each of these operating points is discussed in the following paragraphs. This will help in understanding the importance of selecting the correct operating point.

Operating point A represents a condition when no bias is applied to the transistor. The transistor is in the cut-off region and there is no collector current through the transistor. Also, the base–emitter voltage is zero. It does not satisfy any of the conditions necessary for faithful amplification and hence A is not a suitable operating point.

Point B would allow some positive and negative variations of the output signal but the peak-to-peak output voltage is limited due to the proximity of the operating point to the knee point ($V_{CE(sat)}$). Also, non-linearities will be introduced in the amplification as the spacing between the I_C curves is not linear near the knee region.

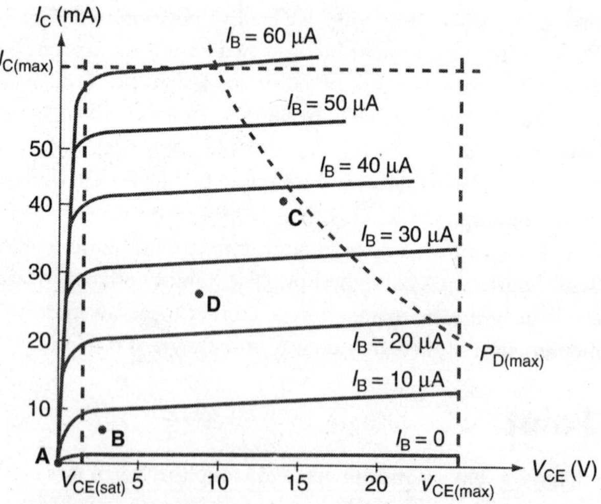

Figure 4.1 Selecting a suitable operating point.

Point C is too close to the $P_{D(max)}$ curve of the transistor. Therefore, the output voltage swing in the positive direction is limited.

Point D is located in the middle of the active region of the transistor characteristics. It will allow both the positive and the negative excursions in the output signal. It also provides linear gain and largest possible output voltage and current swing. Therefore, the operating point for a transistor amplifier is selected to be in the middle of the active region.

It may be mentioned here that after having selected the operating point, the effect of temperature should also be taken into account. A rise in the temperature results in increase in the value of transistor gain (β) and the leakage current (I_{CO}). This results in a shift in the operating point. The biasing network should also provide temperature stability so that there is minimum variation in the operating point with change in temperature. The concept of bias stabilization is discussed in detail in Section 4.5.

4.2 Common-Emitter Configuration

Common-emitter configuration is the most popular of the three transistor amplifier configurations because it offers considerable current gain as well as voltage gain. There are several common-emitter biasing circuits, namely the fixed-bias, emitter-bias, voltage-divider-bias with emitter-bias and collector-to-base-bias circuits. The various biasing circuits are discussed in detail in this section. Also DC analysis, load-line analysis and merits and demerits of each of the configurations are covered.

Fixed-Bias Circuit

Consider the circuit shown in Figure 4.2. It is referred to as the fixed-bias circuit and is one of the simplest possible transistor-biasing circuits. The biasing components include two resistors, base resistor (R_B) and collector resistor (R_C), and a supply voltage (V_{CC}). The base–emitter junction gets forward-biased through V_{CC} and R_B. The supply voltage also reverse biases the collector–base junction through resistor R_C. Resistor R_B is of the order of few hundreds of kilo-ohms whereas typical value of R_C is of few kilo-ohms. Capacitors C_i and C_o are referred to as the input and the output coupling capacitors, respectively.

DC Analysis

DC analysis of a circuit refers to analyzing a circuit so as to establish the operating point in the absence of any input AC signal. For the purpose of DC analysis, the input and output capacitors are considered as open and it is assumed that all AC sources are zero (Figure 4.3).

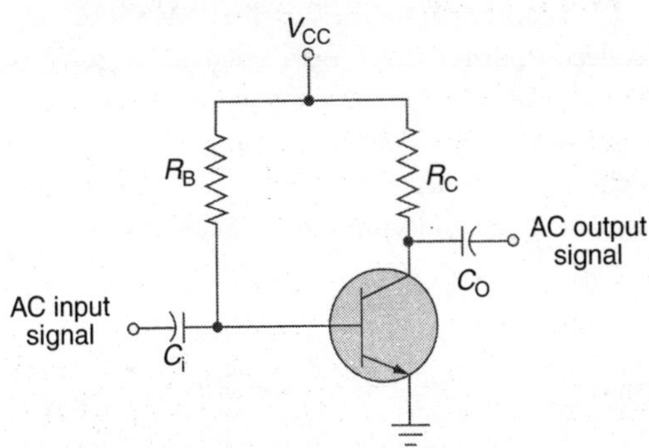

Figure 4.2 | Fixed-bias circuit.

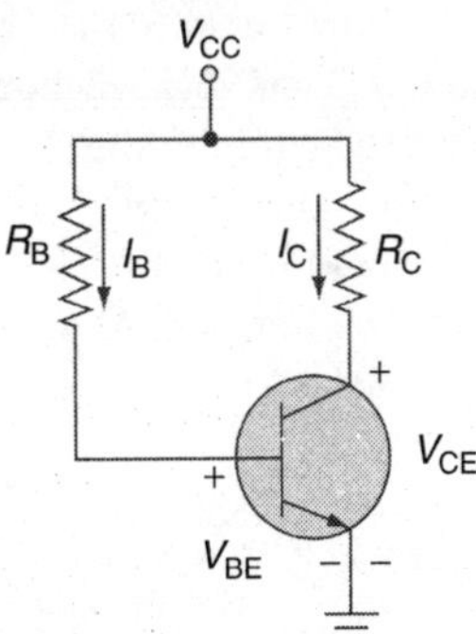

Figure 4.3 | DC equivalent of fixed-bias circuit.

Before going into detailed analysis of the circuit, let us discuss the notations used in the chapter. Base–emitter voltage is the voltage at the base terminal with respect to the emitter terminal or the base–emitter differential voltage. It is denoted by V_{BE} and is given by

$$V_{BE} = V_B - V_E \tag{4.1}$$

where V_B is the base voltage wrt ground; V_E the emitter voltage w.r.t. ground.

Collector–emitter voltage is the voltage at the collector terminal w.r.t. the emitter terminal or the collector–emitter differential voltage. It is denoted by V_{CE} and is given by

$$V_{CE} = V_C - V_E \tag{4.2}$$

where V_C is the collector voltage wrt ground; V_E the emitter voltage w.r.t. ground.

The base–emitter section of the fixed-bias circuit comprises the supply voltage (V_{CC}), the base resistor (R_B) and the transistor base–emitter junction. Base current (I_B) can be determined by applying Kirchhoff's voltage law to the base–emitter section:

$$V_{CC} - I_B R_B - V_{BE} = 0 \tag{4.3}$$

Rearranging the terms in Eq. (4.3) we get the value of base current (I_B) as

$$I_B = \frac{V_{CC} - V_{BE}}{R_B} \tag{4.4}$$

From Eq. (4.4) it is clear that the base current (I_B) is given by ratio of the voltage drop across the base resistor (R_B) to the value of R_B. The value of base–emitter voltage (V_{BE}) is small as compared to the supply voltage (V_{CC}) and hence can be neglected without causing much error. Therefore, Eq. (4.4) can be approximated as

$$I_B \cong \frac{V_{CC}}{R_B} \tag{4.5}$$

The collector current (I_C) of the transistor is directly related to the base current (I_B) and is expressed as

$$I_C = \beta I_B$$

that is

$$I_C = \beta\left(\frac{V_{CC} - V_{BE}}{R_B}\right) \cong \frac{\beta V_{CC}}{R_B} \tag{4.6}$$

where β is the transistor current gain.

We can infer from Eq. (4.6) that the collector current (I_C) is dependent on the supply voltage (V_{CC}) and the base resistor (R_B) and is independent of the value of collector resistor (R_C). Any change in the value of R_C will not have any effect on the base current or the collector current as long as the transistor is operating in the active region. However, the transistor collector–emitter voltage (V_{CE}) depends on the value of R_C.

The collector–emitter section comprises the supply voltage (V_{CC}), collector resistor (R_C) and the transistor collector–emitter junction. Applying Kirchhoff's voltage law to the collector–emitter section we get

$$V_{CC} - I_C R_C - V_{CE} = 0 \tag{4.7}$$

Rearranging the terms we get

$$V_{CE} = V_{CC} - I_C R_C \tag{4.8}$$

Thus, the collector–emitter voltage (V_{CE}) is equal to the difference between the supply voltage (V_{CC}) and the voltage across the collector resistor (R_C).

The values of collector current (I_C) and collector–emitter voltage (V_{CE}) given in Eqs. (4.6) and (4.8) represent the operating point or the quiescent point and are denoted as I_{CQ} and V_{CEQ}, respectively. The quiescent point for a fixed-bias circuit is given by

$$I_{CQ} = \beta\left(\frac{V_{CC} - V_{BE}}{R_B}\right), \quad V_{CEQ} = V_{CC} - I_{CQ} R_C \tag{4.9}$$

Load-Line Analysis

The expression given in Eq. (4.8) relates to two variables, namely, the collector current (I_C) and the collector–emitter voltage (V_{CE}). The transistor output characteristics curve also relates these two variables. If we superimpose the straight line defined by Eq. (4.8) on the transistor output characteristics, we can determine the operating point of the circuit and also how the operating point changes with change in the value of circuit parameters. This is referred to as load-line analysis (Figure 4.4).

To draw the load line, substitute $I_C = 0$ in Eq. (4.8). We get

$$V_{CE} = V_{CC}\Big|_{I_C = 0}$$

This point appears on the horizontal axis (0, V_{CC}) of the output characteristics. I_C can be evaluated by substituting $V_{CE} = 0$ in Eq. (4.8) as

$$I_C = \frac{V_{CC}}{R_C}\Bigg|_{V_{CE} = 0}$$

This point appears on the vertical axis (V_{CC}/R_C, 0) of the output characteristics.

The load line is obtained by joining these two points as shown in Figure 4.4. The operating point is established on the load line by determining the level of base current (I_B) using Eq. (4.4) or Eq. (4.5). The point of intersection of the load line with the curve corresponding to the calculated value of I_B gives the operating point as shown in the figure. The operating point shifts with the change in the value of circuit parameters.

The operating point moves up the load line if the value of I_B increases and moves down the load line when the value of I_B decreases (Figure 4.5). The value of I_B can be changed by changing the value of resistor

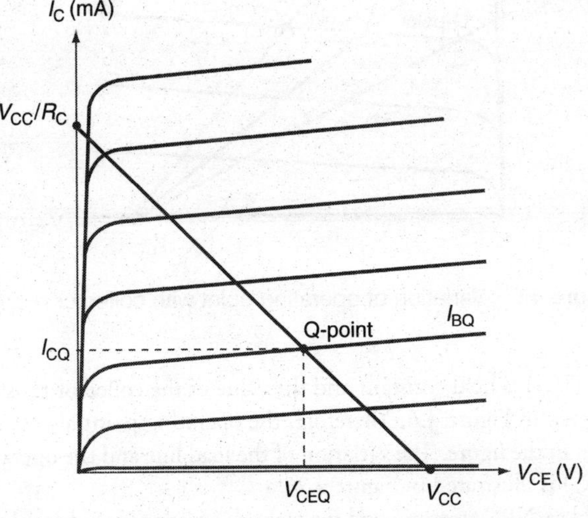

Figure 4.4 | Load-line analysis of the fixed-bias circuit.

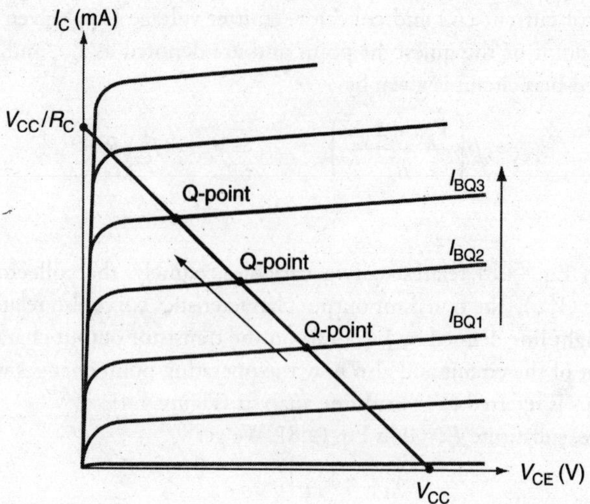

Figure 4.5 Variation of operating point with base current.

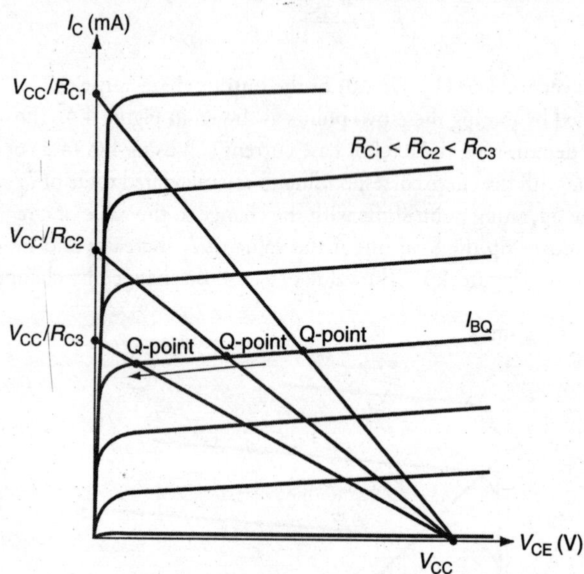

Figure 4.6 Variation of operating point with collector resistor.

R_B. If the supply voltage (V_{CC}) is held constant and the value of the collector resistor (R_C) is changed, then the load line shifts as shown in Figure 4.6. Therefore, the operating point also shifts for the same value of base current (I_B) as shown in the figure. The variation of the load line and the operating point due to change in the supply voltage (V_{CC}) is illustrated in Figure 4.7.

The circuit shown employs NPN transistor and the network equations have been derived for NPN transistors. Same analysis applies to PNP transistors with the direction of currents and the polarities of the voltages reversed.

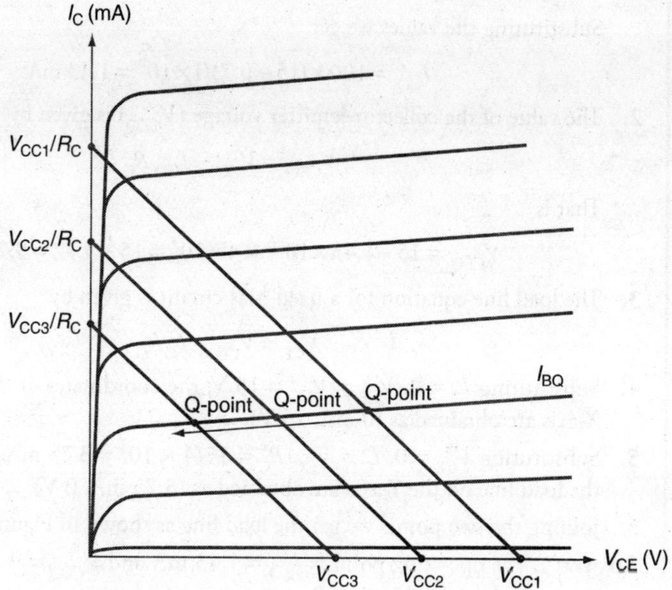

Figure 4.7 Variation of operating point with supply voltage.

Advantages and Disadvantages

Fixed-bias circuit is the simplest possible biasing circuit requiring a very few components. However, the circuit offers worst stability against variations in temperature or transistor gain (β) as compared to the other configurations. It is therefore prone to thermal runaway and is very rarely used.

EXAMPLE 4.1 *For the fixed-bias circuit of Figure 4.8, determine the operating point (given that transistor gain $\beta = 100$, $V_{BE} = 0.7$ V). Also draw the load line for the circuit.*

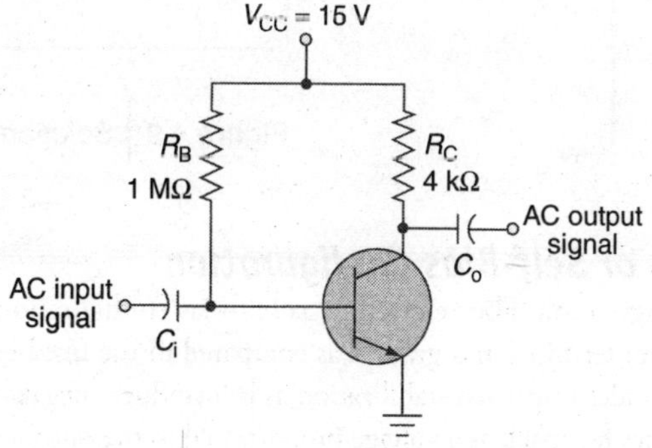

Figure 4.8 Example 4.1.

Solution

1. The value of collector current (I_{CQ}) is given by

$$I_{CQ} = \beta\left(\frac{V_{CC} - V_{BE}}{R_B}\right)$$

Substituting the values we get

$$I_{CQ} = 100 \times (15 - 0.7)/1 \times 10^6 = 1.43 \text{ mA}$$

2. The value of the collector–emitter voltage (V_{CEQ}) is given by

$$V_{CEQ} = V_{CC} - I_{CQ} R_C$$

That is

$$V_{CEQ} = 15 - 1.43 \times 10^{-3} \times 4 \times 10^3 = 15 - 5.72 = 9.28 \text{ V}$$

3. The load line equation for a fixed-bias circuit is given by

$$V_{CE} = V_{CC} - I_C R_C$$

4. Substituting $I_C = 0$, $V_{CE} = V_{CC} = 15$ V, the coordinates of the load line on the X-axis are obtained as (0 mA, 15 V).
5. Substituting $V_{CE} = 0$, $I_C = V_{CC}/R_C = 15/4 \times 10^3 = 3.75$ mA, the coordinates of the load line on the Y-axis are obtained as (3.75 mA, 0 V).
6. Joining the two points we get the load line as shown in Figure 4.9.

Answer: The operating point is $I_{CQ} = 1.43$ mA and $V_{CEQ} = 9.28$ V. The load line is shown in Figure 4.9.

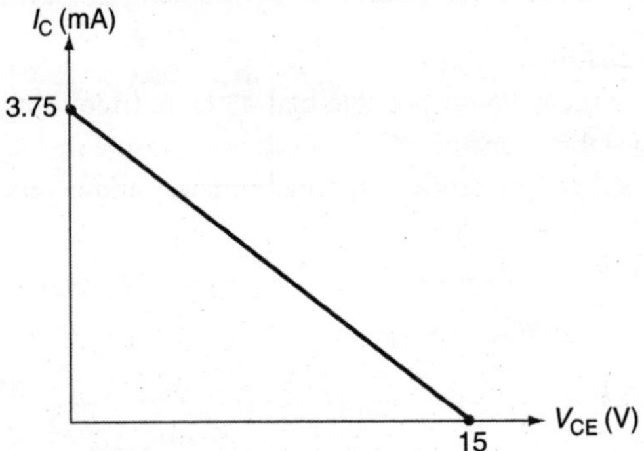

Figure 4.9 Solution to Example 4.1.

Emitter-Bias or Self-Bias Configuration

Emitter-bias configuration, also referred to as self-bias configuration, has an additional emitter resistor (R_E) between the emitter terminal and ground as compared to the fixed-bias circuit (Figure 4.10). The addition of the resistor R_E provides improved stabilization as it introduces negative feedback into the circuit. The feedback type is current-series feedback as a voltage proportional to the output current is fed-back in series to the input.

DC Analysis

The DC equivalent of the emitter-bias circuit of Figure 4.10 is shown in Figure 4.11. The DC analysis is done on similar lines as that done for the fixed-bias circuit. Applying Kirchhoff's voltage law to the base–emitter loop we get

$$V_{CC} - I_B R_B - V_{BE} - I_E R_E = 0$$

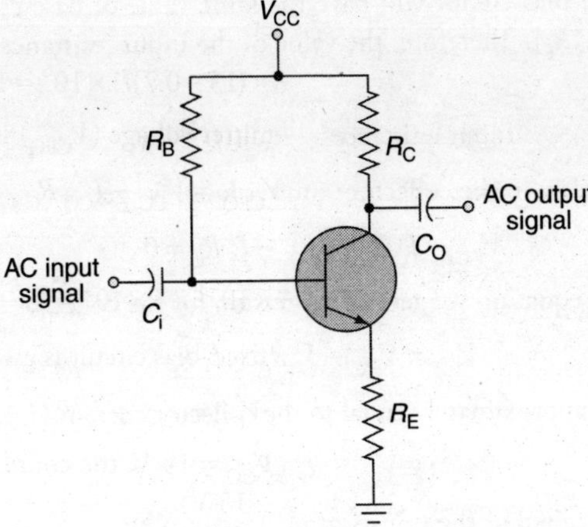

Figure 4.10 Emitter-bias or self-bias circuit.

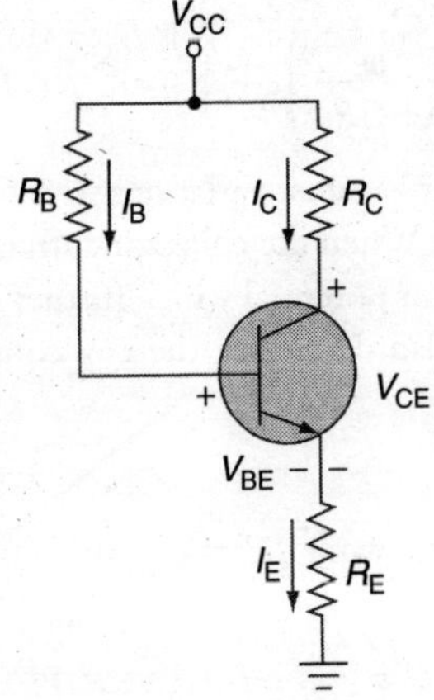

Figure 4.11 DC equivalent of the emitter-bias circuit.

Substituting the value of emitter current (I_E) as $I_E = (\beta + 1)I_B$ in the above equation and rearranging the terms, the expression for I_B can be written as

$$I_B = \frac{V_{CC} - V_{BE}}{R_B + (\beta + 1)R_E} \tag{4.10}$$

Voltage V_{BE} is small as compared to V_{CC} and can therefore be neglected. The expression for base current (I_B) is then given by

$$I_B \cong \frac{V_{CC}}{R_B + (\beta + 1)R_E} \tag{4.11}$$

From Eq. (4.10) we can infer that the emitter resistor (R_E) is reflected into the input circuit as $(\beta + 1)R_E$. In other words, R_E which is a part of the collector–emitter loop appears as $(\beta + 1)R_E$ in the base–emitter loop. The fixed-bias circuit will have the same value of base current (I_B) when it has a base resistor equal to $[R_B + (\beta + 1)R_E]$. Therefore, the value of the input resistance for the emitter-bias circuit is given by

$$\text{Input resistance} = R_B + (\beta + 1)R_E \tag{4.12}$$

Applying Kirchhoff's voltage law to the collector–emitter loop, we get

$$V_{CC} - I_C R_C - V_{CE} - I_E R_E = 0$$

Rearranging the terms of the equation we get the expression for the collector–emitter voltage (V_{CE}) as

$$V_{CE} = V_{CC} - I_C R_C - I_E R_E$$

As the emitter current (I_E) is approximately equal to the collector current (I_C), therefore

$$V_{CE} \cong V_{CC} - I_C(R_C + R_E) \tag{4.13}$$

The voltage of the emitter terminal of the transistor (V_E) is given by

$$V_E = I_E R_E \cong I_C R_E \tag{4.14}$$

The Q-point for the emitter-bias circuit is given by

$$I_{CQ} = \beta\left(\frac{V_{CC} - V_{BE}}{R_B + (\beta+1)R_E}\right), \; V_{CEQ} = V_{CC} - I_{CQ}(R_C + R_E) \tag{4.15}$$

The emitter-bias circuit offers stability against variations in collector current due to change in temperature or change in the transistor gain (β). When the collector current increases, the emitter voltage increases. This results in decrease in the base–emitter potential which further leads to decrease in the value of base current. Therefore, the collector current also decreases, thereby compensating for the initial increase in its value.

Load-Line Analysis

The load-line analysis of the emitter-bias network differs slightly from that of the fixed-bias configuration. The load line in this configuration is given by

$$V_{CE} = V_{CC} - I_C(R_C + R_E) \tag{4.16}$$

To draw the load line, substitute $I_C = 0$ in Eq. (4.16) following which we get

$$V_{CE} = V_{CC}\Big|_{I_C = 0}$$

This point appears on the horizontal axis (0, V_{CC}) of the output characteristics. Substituting $V_{CE} = 0$ in Eq. (4.16), we obtain I_C as

$$I_C = \frac{V_{CC}}{(R_C + R_E)}\Bigg|_{V_{CE} = 0}$$

This point appears on the vertical axis ($V_{CC}/(R_C + R_E)$, 0) of the output characteristics. The load line is obtained by joining these two points as shown in Figure 4.12. The operating point is established on the load line by determining the level of I_B using Eq. (4.10) or Eq. (4.11).

Advantages and Disadvantages

The emitter-bias circuit offers better stability than the fixed-bias circuit. However, maximum stability is offered by the circuit when the ratio of the base resistor (R_B) to the emitter resistor (R_E), that is R_B/R_E, is as

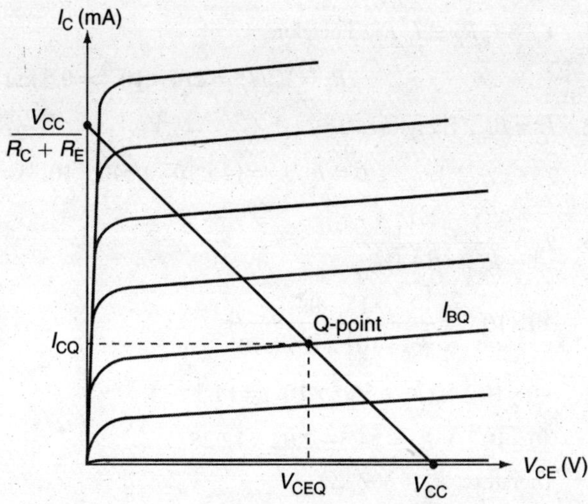

Figure 4.12 Load-line analysis of the emitter-bias circuit.

small as possible. Thus, R_E should have a large value or R_B should be small. For large values of resistor R_E, larger collector supply voltage (V_{CC}) is needed. Also increase in R_E increases the negative feedback and reduces the gain of the circuit. For small values of resistor R_B, a separate base supply voltage is needed which adds to circuit complexity and is often not feasible. The disadvantages of the emitter-bias circuit are removed in the voltage-divider-bias with emitter-bias circuit.

EXAMPLE 4.2 *Refer to Figure 4.13. Find the values of resistors R_B, R_C and R_E and the transistor gain β, given that $I_B = 40\ \mu A$, $I_C = 4\ mA$, $V_E = 2\ V$, $V_{CE} = 12\ V$ and supply voltage $V_{CC} = 15\ V$. Assume that the transistor used in the circuit is a silicon transistor.*

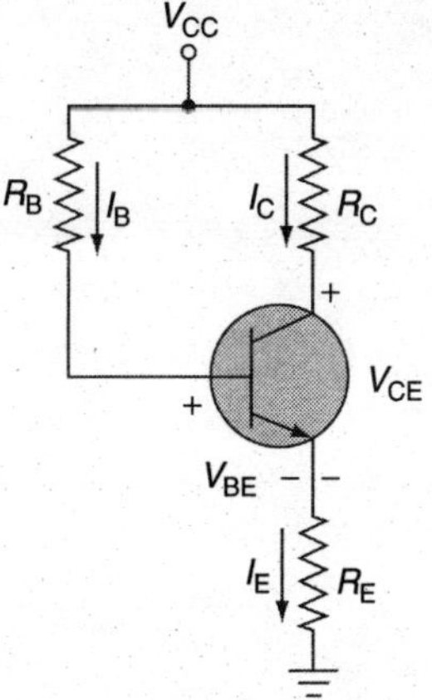

Figure 4.13 Example 4.2.

Solution

1. $V_E = I_E R_E \cong I_C R_E$. Therefore

$$R_E = V_E / I_C = 2/4 \times 10^{-3} = 0.5\ \text{k}\Omega$$

2. $I_C = \beta I_B$. Therefore,

$$\beta = I_C / I_B = (4 \times 10^{-3})/(40 \times 10^{-6}) = 100$$

3. $I_B = \dfrac{V_{CC} - V_{BE}}{R_B + (\beta + 1) R_E}$

$$40 \times 10^{-6} = \frac{15 - 0.7}{R_B + 101 \times 0.5 \times 10^3}$$

$$40 \times 10^{-6} \times (R_B + 50.5 \times 10^3) = 14.3$$

$$40 \times 10^{-6} \times R_B = 14.3 - 2.02 = 12.28$$

Therefore, $R_B = 307\ \text{k}\Omega$.

4. $V_{CE} = V_{CC} - I_C (R_C + R_E)$

$$12 = 15 - 4 \times 10^{-3} \times (R_C + 0.5 \times 10^3)$$

$$4 \times 10^{-3} \times R_C = 15 - 12 - 2 = 1$$

Therefore, $R_C = 0.25\ \text{k}\Omega$.

Answer: $R_E = 0.5\ \text{k}\Omega$, $R_B = 307\ \text{k}\Omega$, $R_C = 0.25\ \text{k}\Omega$, $\beta = 100$.

EXAMPLE 4.3

For the circuit shown in Figure 4.14, $V_{CC} = 15$ V, $V_{EE} = -10$ V, $R_C = 2$ kΩ, $R_E = 5$ kΩ, $R_B = 400$ kΩ and $\beta = 60$. Find the value of collector current (I_C) and the collector-to-emitter voltage (V_{CE}).

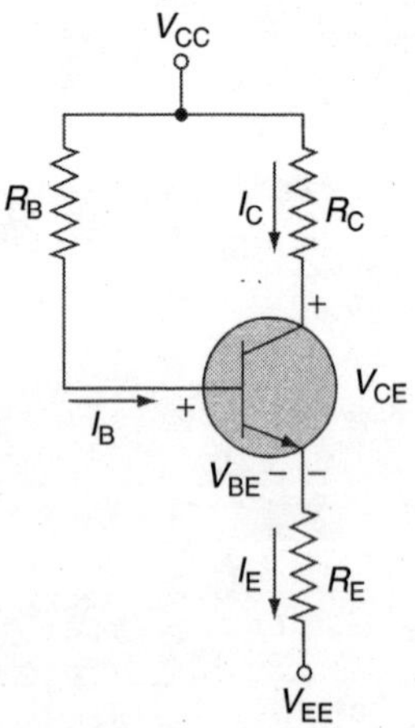

Figure 4.14 Example 4.3.

Solution

1. Applying Kirchhoff's voltage law to the base–emitter loop of the circuit in Figure 4.14, we get

$$V_{CC} - I_B R_B - V_{BE} - I_E R_E - V_{EE} = 0$$

2. Substituting $I_E = (\beta + 1)I_B$ in the above equation, we obtain the expression for I_B as

$$I_B = \frac{V_{CC} - V_{EE} - V_{BE}}{R_B + (\beta + 1)R_E}$$

$$I_B = \frac{15 + 10 - 0.7}{400 \times 10^3 + 61 \times 5 \times 10^3}$$

$$= 24.3/(705 \times 10^3) = 34.46\ \mu\text{A}$$

3. $I_C = \beta I_B$. Therefore, $I_C = 60 \times 34.46 \times 10^{-6}$ A = 2.07 mA.

4. Applying Kirchhoff's law to the collector–emitter loop of the circuit in Figure 4.14, we get

$$V_{CC} - I_C R_C - V_{CE} - I_E R_E - V_{EE} = 0$$

As $I_C \cong I_E$, therefore $V_{CE} = V_{CC} - V_{EE} - I_C(R_C + R_E)$.

5. $V_{CE} = 15 + 10 - 2.07 \times 10^{-3} \times (2 \times 10^3 + 5 \times 10^3) = 25 - 14.49 = 10.51$ V.

Answer: $I_C = 2.07$ mA, $V_{CE} = 10.51$ V.

Voltage-Divider-Bias with Emitter-Bias Configuration

The stability of the emitter-bias configuration is further improved if its input side is modified as shown in Figure 4.15. The circuit configuration is referred to as voltage-divider-bias with emitter-bias or simply the voltage-divider-bias configuration. It is the most commonly used transistor-biasing configuration. The name

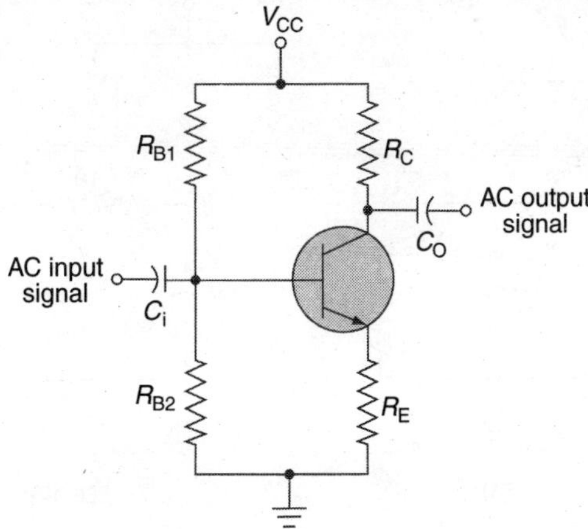

Figure 4.15 | Voltage-divider-bias with emitter-bias circuit.

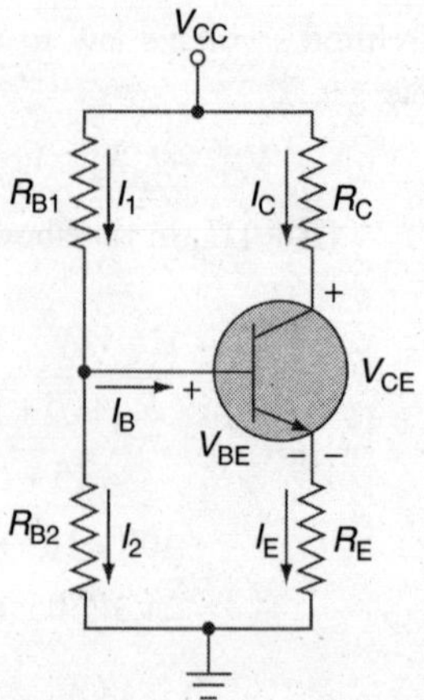

Figure 4.16 DC equivalent of voltage-divider-bias circuit.

voltage-divider comes from the fact that the input section comprises a voltage divider of resistors R_{B1} and R_{B2} across the supply voltage V_{CC}. The circuit offers improved stability against variations in the temperature and the transistor gain.

DC Analysis

The DC equivalent of the voltage-divider-bias circuit of Figure 4.15 is shown in Figure 4.16. The circuit can be analyzed using two methods, namely, the accurate method and the approximate method. The accurate method is applicable to all circuits whereas the approximate method can be applied if certain conditions are met. We will discuss both the methods in subsequent paragraphs.

Accurate Method: Accurate method makes use of Thevenin's equivalent model of the input section. The input section of the circuit can be redrawn as shown in Figure 4.17(a) and can be simplified using Thevenin's equivalent theorem. Figure 4.17(b) shows the Thevenin's equivalent model. R_{TH} is the Thevenin's equivalent resistance and is determined by replacing the voltage source by a short circuit and calculating the resultant resistance of the circuit. R_{TH} is equal to the parallel combination of resistors R_{B1} and R_{B2} and is given by

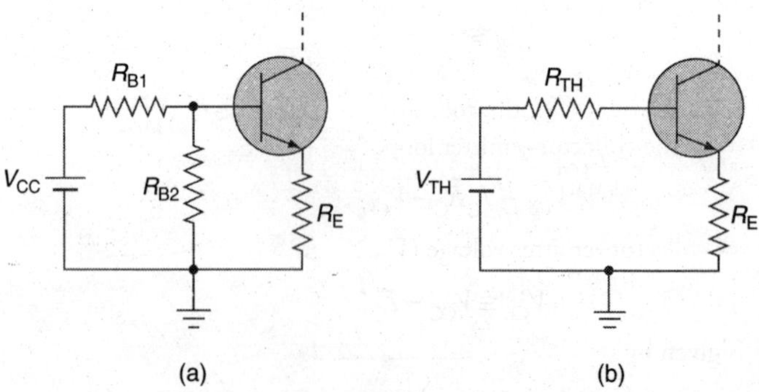

Figure 4.17 (a) Input section of the voltage-divider-bias configuration; (b) Thevenin's equivalent of the input section of voltage-divider-bias configuration.

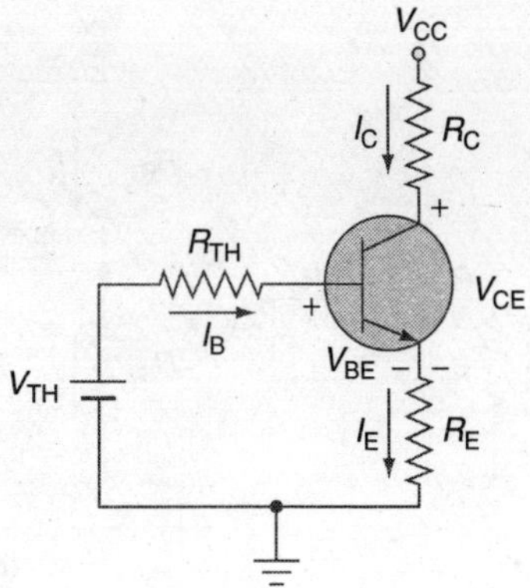

Figure 4.18 Thevenin's equivalent of voltage-divider-bias configuration.

$$R_{TH} = R_{B1} \| R_{B2} = \frac{R_{B1} R_{B2}}{R_{B1} + R_{B2}} \tag{4.17}$$

V_{TH} is the open-circuit Thevenin's voltage and is equal to the voltage drop across the resistor R_{B2}:

$$V_{TH} = \frac{R_{B2} V_{CC}}{R_{B1} + R_{B2}} \tag{4.18}$$

Figure 4.18 shows the complete circuit using Thevenin's equivalent model. Applying Kirchhoff's voltage law to the base–emitter loop of the circuit in Figure 4.18, we get

$$V_{TH} - I_B R_{TH} - V_{BE} - I_E R_E = 0 \tag{4.19}$$

Substituting $I_E = (\beta + 1)I_B$, we get the expression for I_B as

$$I_B = \frac{V_{TH} - V_{BE}}{R_{TH} + (\beta + 1)R_E} \tag{4.20}$$

The expression is similar to the one derived for emitter-bias configuration with the term R_B being replaced by R_{TH}. If the base–emitter voltage (V_{BE}) is small as compared to the Thevenin's voltage (V_{TH}), then Eq. (4.20) can be approximated as

$$I_B \cong \frac{V_{TH}}{R_{TH} + (\beta + 1)R_E} \tag{4.21}$$

After determining the base current (I_B), the collector–emitter voltage (V_{CE}) can be determined by applying Kirchhoff's voltage law to the collector–emitter loop,

$$V_{CC} - I_C R_C - V_{CE} - I_E R_E = 0$$

As $I_C \cong I_E$, the value of collector–emitter voltage (V_{CE}) is given by

$$V_{CE} \cong V_{CC} - I_C (R_C + R_E) \tag{4.22}$$

The operating point is given by

$$I_{CQ} = \beta \left(\frac{V_{TH} - V_{BE}}{R_{TH} + (\beta + 1)R_E} \right), \; V_{CEQ} = V_{CC} - I_{CQ} (R_C + R_E) \tag{4.23}$$

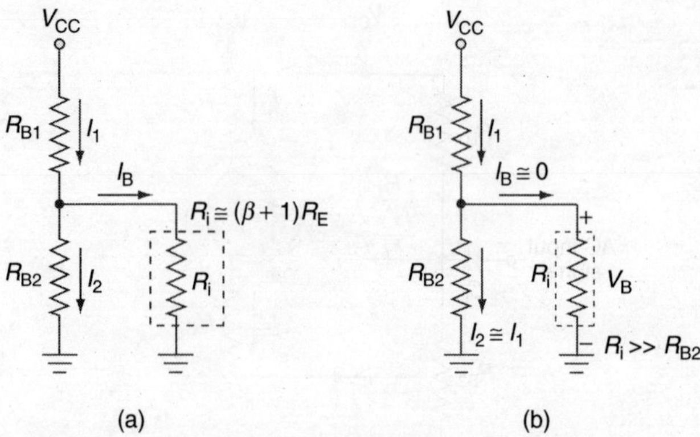

Figure 4.19 | Approximate method for analysis of voltage-divider-bias configuration.

Approximate Method: The input section of the voltage-divider with emitter-bias configuration can be redrawn as shown in Figure 4.19(a). The resistance R_i is the equivalent resistance between the base terminal and the ground and is referred to as the input resistance. Its value is given by

$$R_i \cong (\beta+1)R_E \tag{4.24}$$

If the value of resistance R_i is much larger than the resistance R_{B2}, then the base current (I_B) will be much smaller than the current I_2 and can be neglected. In that case it is assumed that the base current I_B is equal to zero and current I_1 is equal to current I_2 [Figure 4.19(b)]. Therefore, resistors R_{B1} and R_{B2} can be considered as series elements and the voltage at the base terminal (V_B) is given by

$$V_B = \frac{R_{B2}V_{CC}}{R_{B1}+R_{B2}} \tag{4.25}$$

The emitter voltage (V_E) is expressed as

$$V_E = V_B - V_{BE} \tag{4.26}$$

and the emitter current (I_E) is given by

$$I_E = \frac{V_E}{R_E} \tag{4.27}$$

As collector current (I_C) and emitter current (I_E) are approximately equal, the value of I_C is

$$I_C \cong \frac{V_E}{R_E} \tag{4.28}$$

The collector–emitter voltage (V_{CE}) is given by

$$V_{CE} = V_{CC} - I_C(R_C + R_E) \tag{4.29}$$

It may be mentioned here that the approximate method can be applied if the value of the input resistance R_i is equal to greater than 10 times the resistance R_{B2}. That is

$$(\beta+1)R_E \geq 10R_{B2} \tag{4.30}$$

Load-line Analysis: The output circuit of the voltage-divider-bias configuration is the same as that of the emitter-bias configuration. This results in the same load line for the two configurations. The level of base current (I_B) is however determined by a different equation in this case.

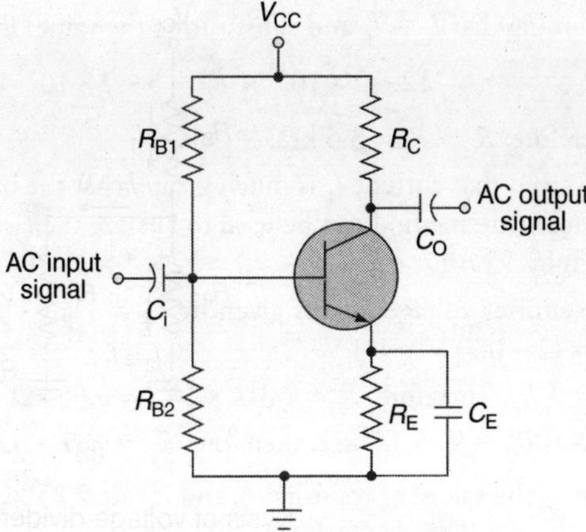

Figure 4.20 | Voltage-divider-bias configuration with emitter capacitor.

Advantages and Disadvantages

Voltage-divider-bias configuration is the most commonly used configuration as it provides excellent stabilization against variations in temperature and transistor gain (β). This is because the emitter resistor introduces negative feedback in the circuit. But negative feedback results in reduction of AC gain of the circuit. This problem can be solved by using a capacitor C_E in parallel with resistor R_E (Figure 4.20). The capacitor does not affect the DC analysis as it acts as an open circuit for DC voltages. For AC inputs, it acts as a short circuit, making the voltage across the emitter resistor (R_E) equal to zero and thus removing the problem of AC negative feedback.

EXAMPLE 4.4 *Determine the values of the resistors R_C and R_E for the circuit in Figure 4.21 given that $R_1 = 5\ k\Omega$, $R_2 = 1\ k\Omega$, $\beta = 200$, $V_{BE} = 0.7\ V$, $I_1 >> I_B$, $V_{CEQ} = 5\ V$ and $I_{CQ} = 2\ mA$.*

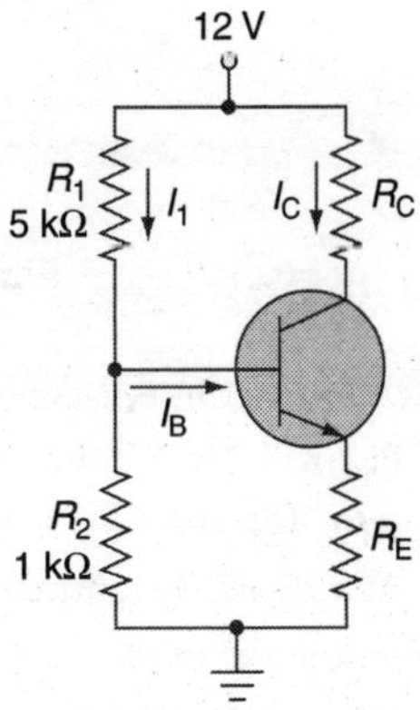

Figure 4.21 | Example 4.4.

Solution

1. Applying Kirchhoff's voltage loop to the collector–emitter loop of the circuit, we get

$$V_{CC} - I_C R_C - V_{CE} - I_E R_E = 0$$

2. Assuming that $I_C \cong I_E$ and substituting the values in the above equation, we get

$$12 - 2\times10^{-3} \times R_C - 5 - 2\times10^{-3} \times R_E = 0$$

Therefore, $R_C + R_E = 3.5$ kΩ.

3. It is given that current I_1 is much greater that the base current I_B. Therefore, the approximate method can be used to analyze the circuit. The base voltage (V_B) is given by $V_B = 12 \times R_2/(R_1 + R_2) = 12 \times 1 \times 10^3/(5 \times 10^3 + 1 \times 10^3) = 2$ V.
4. The emitter voltage (V_E) is given by $V_E = V_B - V_{BE}$. As $V_{BE} = 0.7$ V, therefore $V_E = (2 - 0.7)$ V $= 1.3$ V.
5. $V_E = I_E R_E$. Therefore, $R_E = 1.3/2 \times 10^{-3} = 0.65$ kΩ.
6. Also as $R_C + R_E = 3.5$ kΩ, therefore, $R_C = (3.5 - 0.65)$ kΩ $= 2.85$ kΩ.

Answer: The values of resistors R_C and R_E are 2.85 kΩ and 0.65 kΩ, respectively.

EXAMPLE 4.5 *For the circuit in Figure 4.22, determine the output voltage of the circuit when the adjust terminal of the potentiometer is at*

(a) full-down position (position C);
(b) middle position (position B);
(c) top-most position (position A).

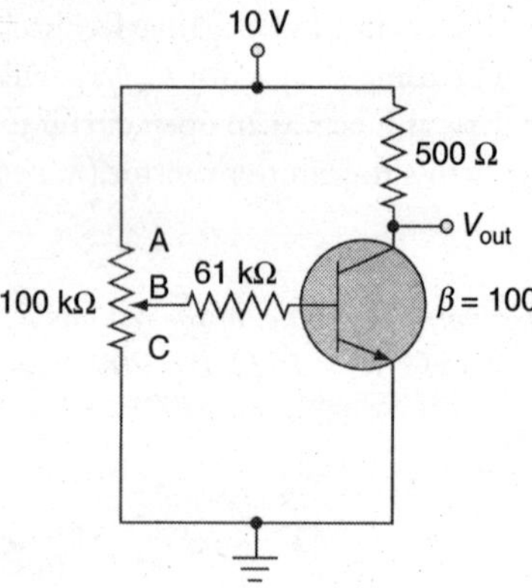

Figure 4.22 Example 4.5.

Solution

(a) Potentiometer in full-down position (position C)

1. Figure 4.23(a) shows the circuit. Both the base and the emitter voltages are zero. Therefore $V_{BE} = 0$. Hence, the transistor is not conducting.
2. As a result, the output voltage is equal to the supply voltage, that is 10 V.

(b) Potentiometer in the middle position (position B)

1. Figure 4.23(b) shows the circuit. Applying Thevenin's theorem to the input section of the circuit in Figure 4.23(b), Thevenin's equivalent resistance (R_{TH}) is: $R_{TH} = (50 \times 10^3 \times 50 \times 10^3)/(50 \times 10^3 + 50 \times 10^3) = 25$ kΩ.
2. The open-circuit Thevenin's equivalent voltage (V_{TH}) is given by

$$V_{TH} = (10 \times 50 \times 10^3)/(50 \times 10^3 + 50 \times 10^3) = 5 \text{ V}$$

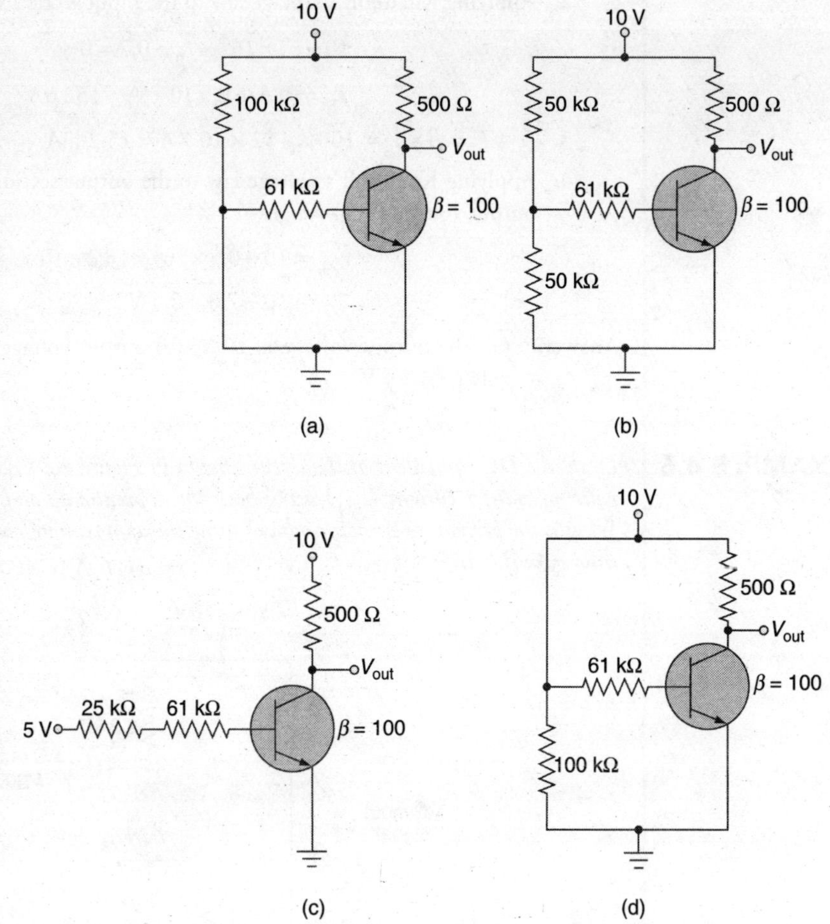

Figure 4.23 (a) Solution to part (a) Example 4.5; (b) and (c) solution to part (b) Example 4.5; (d) solution to part (c) Example 4.5.

3. The simplified circuit is shown in Figure 4.23(c).
4. Applying Kirchhoff's voltage law to the input circuit, we get
$$5 - 25 \times 10^3 \times I_B - 61 \times 10^3 \times I_B - 0.7 = 0$$
5. Therefore, $I_B = (4.3/86) \times 10^{-3}$ A = 50 μA.
6. $I_C = \beta \times I_B$. Therefore, $I_C = 100 \times 50 \times 10^{-6} = 5$ mA.
7. Applying Kirchhoff's voltage law to the output section of the circuit and solving for output voltage (V_{out}) we get
$$V_{out} = 10 - 0.5 \times 10^3 \times 5 \times 10^{-3} = 7.5 \text{ V}$$

(c) Potentiometer in top-most position (position A)

1. Figure 4.23(d) shows the circuit when the adjust terminal of the potentiometer is at position A.

2. Applying Kirchhoff's voltage law to the input section we get

$$10 - 61\times10^3 \times I_B - 0.7 = 0$$

$$I_B = (9.3/61)\times10^{-3}\ \text{A} = 152\ \mu\text{A}$$

3. $I_E \cong I_C = \beta\times I_B = 100\times152\times10^{-6}\ \text{A} = 15.2\ \text{mA}$.

4. Applying Kirchhoff's voltage law to the output section and solving for the output voltage (V_{out}) we get

$$V_{out} = 10 - 0.5\times10^3\times15.2\times10^{-3}$$

$$= 10 - 7.6 = 2.4\ \text{V}$$

Answer: (a) The output voltage is 10 V; (b) output voltage is 7.5 V; (c) output voltage is 2.4 V.

EXAMPLE 4.6 *Draw the DC equivalent of the circuit shown in Figure 4.24. Calculate the quiescent value of emitter current (I_{EQ}) using both the approximate and the accurate method. What is the percentage error introduced using the approximate method, given that transistor gain β is 165?*

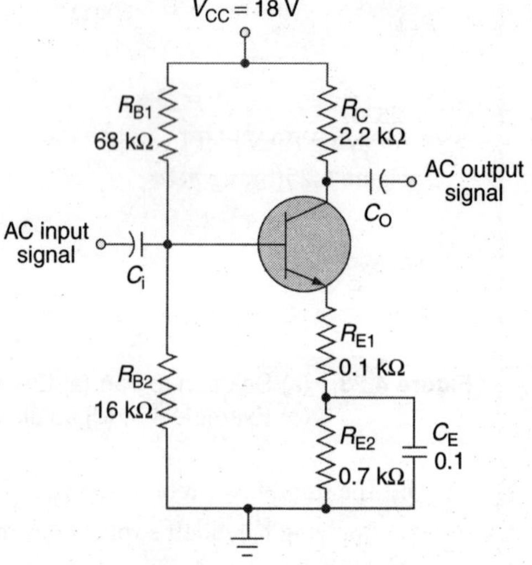

Figure 4.24 | Example 4.6.

Solution

1. The DC equivalent circuit is shown in Figure 4.25(a). The DC equivalent circuit is drawn by making all capacitors open and all the AC sources are considered to be zero. Resistor R_E is equal to the sum of the resistors R_{E1} and R_{E2}.

Using the Accurate Method

2. Applying Thevenin's theorem to the input section, the circuit reduces to the one shown in Figure 4.25(b).

3. The value of the Thevenin's equivalent resistance R_{TH} is 68 kΩ‖16 kΩ = 12.95 kΩ.

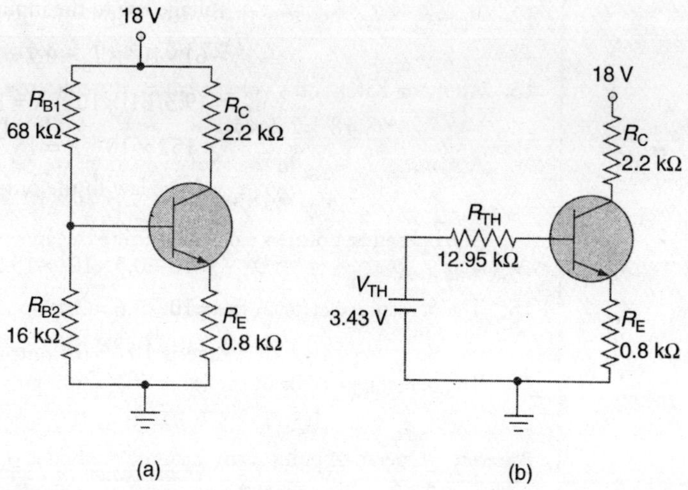

Figure 4.25 | Solution to Example 4.6.

4. The value of the Thevenin's equivalent voltage (V_{TH}) is

$$V_{TH} = (18 \times R_{B2})/(R_{B1} + R_{B2})$$
$$= (18 \times 16 \times 10^3)/(68 \times 10^3 + 16 \times 10^3)$$
$$= 3.43 \text{ V}$$

5. Applying Kirchhoff's voltage law to the emitter–base loop of the circuit in Figure 4.25(b), we get

$$3.43 - 12.95 \times 10^3 \times I_B - 0.7 - 0.8 \times 10^3 \times I_E = 0$$

6. Substituting $I_E = (\beta + 1)I_B = 166 \times I_B$ in the above equation, we obtain

$$2.73 - 12.95 \times 10^3 \times I_B - 132.8 \times 10^3 \times I_B = 0$$
$$I_B = 18.7\,\mu\text{A}$$

7. $I_C = \beta I_B$. Therefore, $I_C = 165 \times 18.7 \times 10^{-6} = 3.08$ mA.
8. Applying Kirchhoff's voltage law to the collector–emitter loop of the circuit in Figure 4.25(b), we get

$$18 - 2.2 \times 10^3 \times I_C - V_{CE} - 0.8 \times 10^3 \times I_E = 0$$

Assuming, $I_C \cong I_E$ in the above equation, we get

$$V_{CE} = 18 - 3 \times 10^3 \times I_C = 18 - 3 \times 10^3 \times 3.08 \times 10^{-3} = 18 - 9.24 = 8.76 \text{ V}$$

Therefore, $V_{CE} = 8.76$ V.

9. The operating point as calculated using accurate method is ($I_C = 3.08$ mA, $V_{CE} = 8.76$ V).

Using the Approximate Method

10. The voltage at the base terminal (V_B) is

$$V_B = 18 \times R_{B2}/(R_{B1} + R_{B2}) = 18 \times 16 \times 10^3/(68 \times 10^3 + 16 \times 10^3) = 3.43 \text{ V}$$

11. Therefore, the voltage at the emitter terminal (V_E) is

$$V_E = V_B - V_{BE} = (3.43 - 07)\text{V} = 2.73 \text{ V}$$

12. $V_E = R_E \times I_E$, therefore the emitter current (I_E) is equal to

$$I_E = 2.73/0.8 \times 10^3 = 3.41 \text{ mA}$$

13. Applying Kirchhoff's voltage law to the collector–emitter loop, we get

$$18 - 2.2 \times 10^3 \times I_C - V_{CE} - 0.8 \times 10^3 \times I_E = 0$$

Assuming, $I_C \cong I_E$, in the above equation, we get

$$V_{CE} = 18 - 3 \times 10^3 \times 3.41 \times 10^{-3} = 7.77 \text{ V}$$

14. The operating point as calculated using the approximate method is (I_C = 3.41 mA, V_{CE} = 7.77 V).
15. The percentage error in the value of I_C using approximate method is

$$[(3.41 - 3.08)/3.08] \times 100\% = 10.71\%$$

16. The percentage error in the value of V_{CE} using the approximate method is

$$[(7.77 - 8.76)/8.76] \times 100\% = -11.3\%$$

Answer: Operating point using accurate method is (I_C = 3.08 mA, V_{CE} = 8.76 V).
Operating point using approximate method is (I_C = 3.41 mA, V_{CE} = 7.77 V).
Percentage error in I_C is 10.71% and in V_{CE} is −11.3%.

Collector-to-Base-Bias Configuration

In collector-to-base-bias configuration, the base-bias voltage is obtained from the collector of the transistor instead of the collector supply voltage (V_{CC}) as shown in Figure 4.26. This configuration is also referred to as feedback-bias configuration. The circuit offers better stability of the operating point against variations in temperature and transistor gain (β) due to negative feedback. The configuration has voltage-shunt feedback as the output voltage is fed-back in shunt to the input through base resistor (R_B).

DC Analysis

Figure 4.27 shows the DC equivalent of the collector-to-base-bias circuit in Figure 4.26. The current in the resistor R_C through supply voltage V_{CC} is split into two parts at the collector junction, one flowing into the collector terminal (I_C) and the other flowing through the base resistor (R_B). The current in resistor R_B is equal to the base current (I_B). Therefore, the current through resistor R_C is the sum of the base current (I_B) and the collector current (I_C).

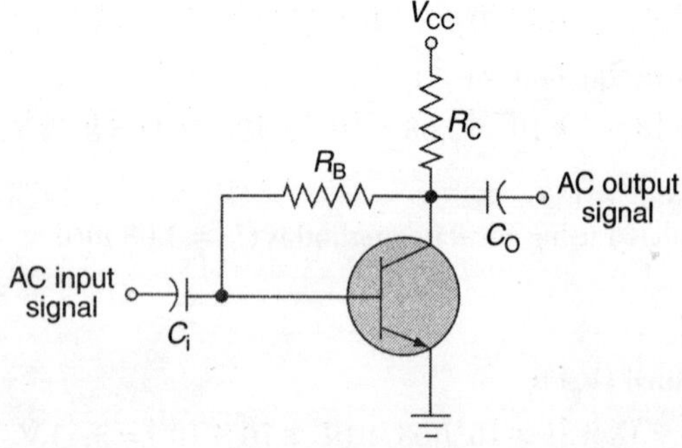

Figure 4.26 | Collector-to-base-bias configuration.

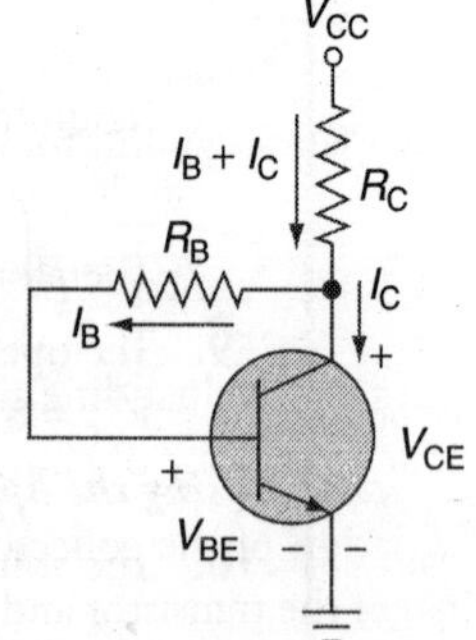

Figure 4.27 | DC equivalent of collector-to-base-bias configuration.

Applying Kirchhoff's voltage law to the base–emitter loop of the circuit in Figure 4.27, we obtain

$$V_{CC} - (I_B + I_C)R_C - I_B R_B - V_{BE} = 0$$

Substituting $I_C = \beta I_B$ in the above equation and solving the equation for I_B we get

$$I_B = \frac{V_{CC} - V_{BE}}{R_B + (\beta + 1)R_C} \tag{4.31}$$

This equation can be compared with that of emitter-bias configuration where the base current (I_B) was given by

$$I_B = \frac{V_{CC} - V_{BE}}{R_B + (\beta + 1)R_E}$$

The term R_E in the expression for base current (I_B) for emitter-bias configuration has been replaced by the term R_C in the collector-to-base-bias configuration.

The value of collector current (I_C) is given by $I_C = \beta I_B$. Therefore,

$$I_C = \beta\left(\frac{V_{CC} - V_{BE}}{R_B + (\beta + 1)R_C}\right) \tag{4.32}$$

As the value of β is very large, (β + 1) can be approximated as β. Therefore, collector current (I_C) is equal to

$$I_C \cong \beta\left(\frac{V_{CC} - V_{BE}}{R_B + \beta R_C}\right)$$

If the value of βR_C is much greater than R_B, then the term $R_B + \beta R_C$ can be approximated as βR_C and in this case the value of collector current I_C is

$$I_C \cong \beta\left(\frac{V_{CC} - V_{BE}}{\beta R_C}\right) = \frac{V_{CC} - V_{BE}}{R_C}$$

Therefore, the collector current becomes independent of the value of transistor gain (β). In other words, the stability offered by the collector-to-base configuration improves as the value of the collector resistor (R_C) increases.

Applying Kirchhoff's voltage law to the collector–emitter loop, we get

$$V_{CC} - (I_B + I_C)R_C - V_{CE} = 0$$

Ignoring base current (I_B) because its value is negligible compared to the collector current (I_C), we get

$$V_{CE} \cong V_{CC} - I_C R_C \tag{4.33}$$

The value of the operating point for collector-to-base-bias configuration is given by

$$I_{CQ} = \beta\left(\frac{V_{CC} - V_{BE}}{R_B + (\beta + 1)R_C}\right), V_{CEQ} = V_{CC} - I_{CQ} R_C \tag{4.34}$$

Load-line Analysis: The load-line analysis for collector-to-base-bias configuration can be carried on similar lines to that done in the case of emitter-bias configuration.

Another variation of the collector-to-base-bias circuit is to place an emitter resistor (R_E) between the emitter terminal of the transistor and the ground as shown in Figure 4.28. In that case, the equations for the base current (I_B), collector current (I_C) and the collector–emitter voltage (V_{CE}) are as follows:

$$I_B = \frac{V_{CC} - V_{BE}}{R_B + (\beta + 1)(R_C + R_E)} \tag{4.35}$$

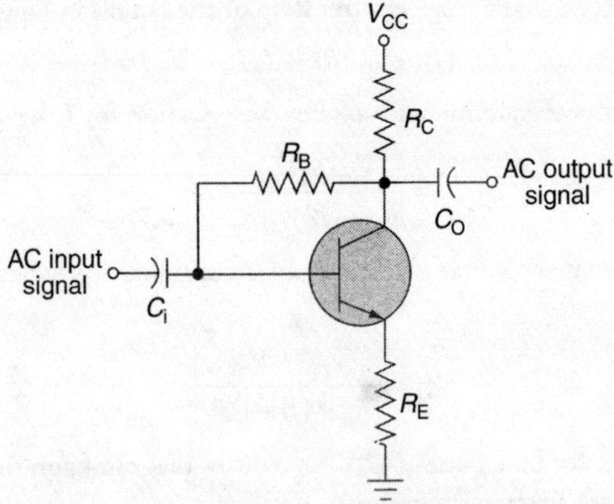

Figure 4.28 Collector-to-base-bias configuration with emitter resistor.

$$I_C = \beta\left(\frac{V_{CC} - V_{BE}}{R_B + (\beta+1)(R_C + R_E)}\right) \tag{4.36}$$

$$V_{CE} = V_{CC} - I_C(R_C + R_E) \tag{4.37}$$

The collector-to-base-bias configuration with emitter resistor offers better stability than emitter-bias configuration and collector-to-base-bias configuration without emitter resistor.

Advantages and Disadvantages

The collector-to-base-bias circuit provides stability to the operating point against variations in temperature and transistor gain (β). However, due to negative feedback, the AC voltage gain of the amplifier is reduced. This problem is partially solved by splitting the resistor R_B into two parts and by connecting a capacitor C_B as shown in Figure 4.29. For the AC signal, capacitor C_B acts as a short circuit and the effective base resistance R_B is reduced to half. This reduces the AC negative feedback and increases the AC voltage gain offered by the circuit.

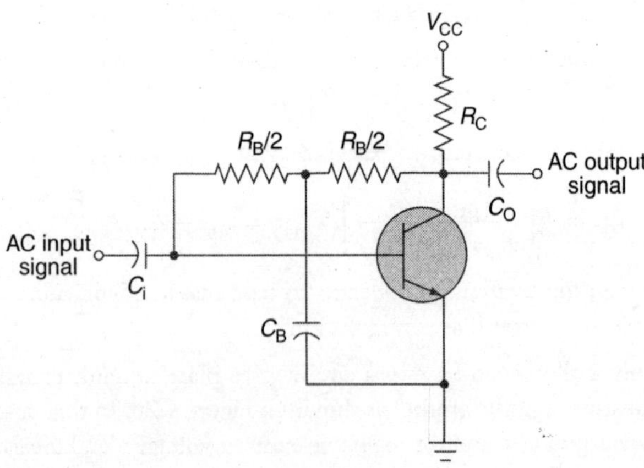

Figure 4.29 Collector-to-base bias with capacitor to reduce AC negative feedback.

Also, the base resistor (R_B) in collector-to-base-bias configuration has a smaller value than that used in fixed-bias or the emitter-bias configurations. Therefore, in this case the base current changes more with temperature. Hence, the advantage of better stability factor offered by collector-to-base-bias configuration is offset by the larger variation in the base current.

EXAMPLE 4.7 *Determine the operating point of the collector-to-base-bias circuit of Figure 4.30. The value of the transistor gain β is 100 and the base–emitter voltage (V_{BE}) of the transistor is 0.7 V. Also find the percentage change in the value of operating point when the value of β increases by 50%.*

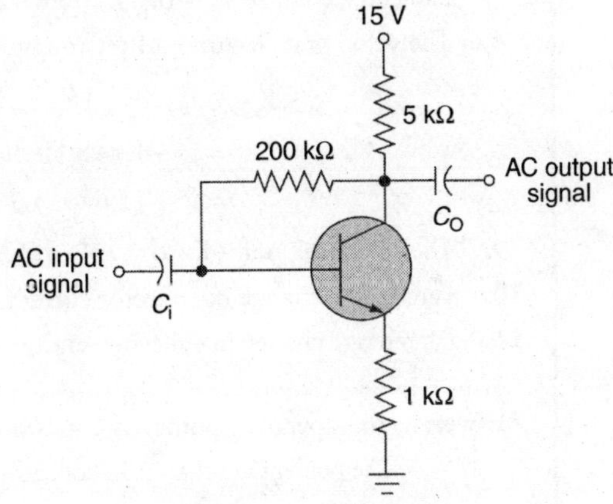

Figure 4.30 Example 4.7.

Solution

1. The value of base current is

$$I_B = \frac{V_{CC} - V_{BE}}{R_B + (\beta + 1)(R_C + R_E)}$$

$$= \frac{15 - 0.7}{200 \times 10^3 + 101 \times (5 \times 10^3 + 1 \times 10^3)}$$

$$= \frac{14.3}{806 \times 10^3}$$

$$= 17.74\ \mu A$$

2. Collector current $I_C = \beta I_B = 100 \times 17.74 \times 10^{-6} = 1.77$ mA.
3. The value of collector–emitter voltage is

$$V_{CE} = V_{CC} - I_C(R_C + R_E)$$

$$= 15 - 1.77 \times 10^{-3} \times (5 \times 10^3 + 1 \times 10^3)$$

$$= 15 - 10.62 = 4.38\ V$$

4. The operating point for $\beta = 100$ is (1.77 mA, 4.38 V).
5. When the value of β increases by 50%, value of new β is equal to 150.

6. The value of base current is

$$I_B = \frac{V_{CC} - V_{BE}}{R_B + (\beta+1)(R_C + R_E)}$$

$$= \frac{15 - 0.7}{200\times10^3 + 151\times(5\times10^3 + 1\times10^3)}$$

$$= \frac{14.3}{1106\times10^3}$$

$$= 12.93\ \mu\text{A}$$

7. Collector current $I_C = \beta I_B = 150 \times 12.93 \times 10^{-6} = 1.94$ mA.
8. The value of collector–emitter voltage is

$$V_{CE} = V_{CC} - I_C(R_C + R_E)$$

$$= 15 - 1.94\times10^{-3} \times (5\times10^3 + 1\times10^3)$$

$$= 15 - 11.64 = 3.36\ \text{V}$$

9. The operating point for $\beta = 150$ is (1.94 mA, 3.36 V).
10. Percentage change in collector current = [(1.94–1.77)/1.77] × 100% = 9.6%.
11. Percentage change in collector–emitter voltage = [(3.36–4.38)/4.38] × 100% = –23.3%.

Answer: The operating point for $\beta = 100$ is (1.77 mA, 4.38 V).
The percentage change in collector current is 9.6% and in collector–emitter voltage is –23.3%.

4.3 Common-Base Circuit

In the common-base circuit, as we have studied in Chapter 3, the input is applied to the emitter terminal and the output is taken from the collector terminal. The base terminal is common to both the input and the output sections. Figure 4.31 shows the circuit for common-base configuration. The DC equivalent of the circuit is shown in Figure 4.32.

The analysis of the input section determines the emitter current (I_E). Applying Kirchhoff's voltage law to the input section (emitter–base loop), we get

$$V_{EE} - I_E R_E - V_{BE} = 0$$

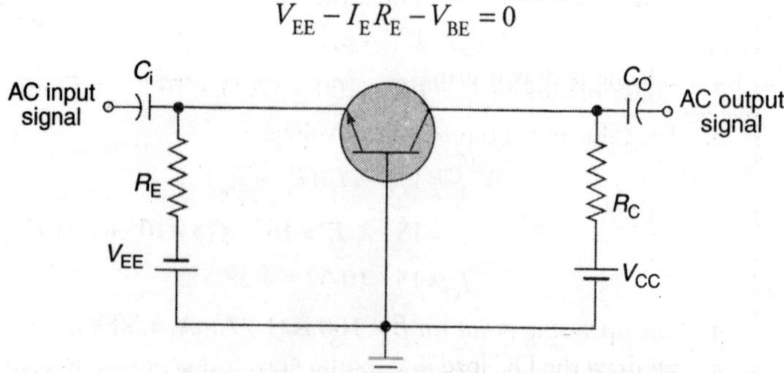

Figure 4.31 | Common-base circuit.

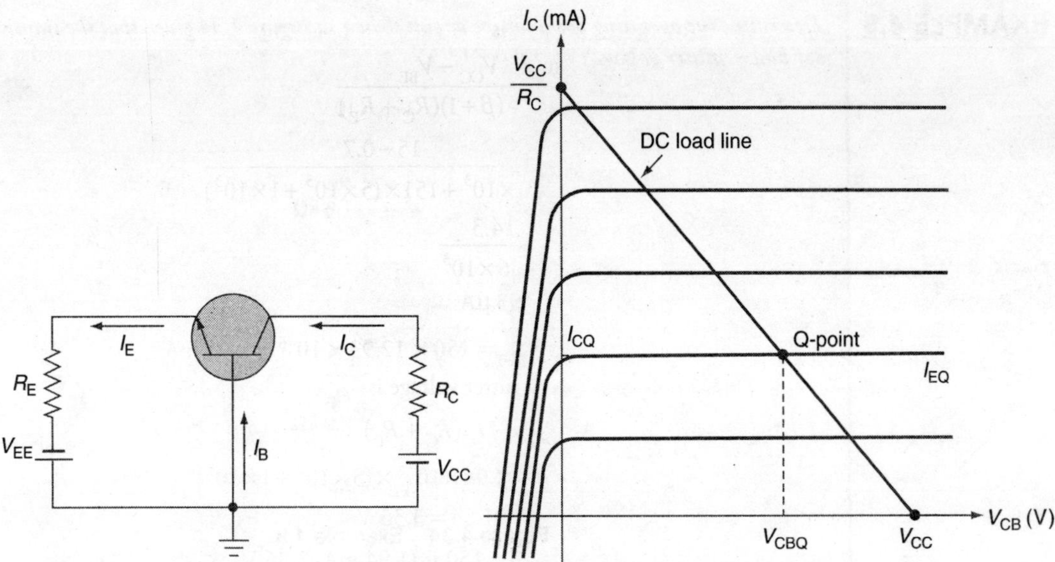

Figure 4.32 DC equivalent of common-base circuit.

Figure 4.33 Load-line analysis of common-base configuration.

Therefore, the emitter current (I_E) is equal to

$$I_E = \frac{V_{EE} - V_{BE}}{R_E} \tag{4.38}$$

As the collector current (I_C) ≅ emitter current (I_E), the value of collector current (I_C) is also given by Eq. (4.38). Applying Kirchhoff's voltage law to the output section (collector–base loop), we get

$$V_{CC} - V_{CB} - I_C R_C = 0$$

Therefore,

$$V_{CB} = V_{CC} - I_C R_C \tag{4.39}$$

The operating point for the common base configuration is given by

$$I_{CQ} = \frac{V_{EE} - V_{BE}}{R_E}, \; V_{CBQ} = V_{CC} - I_{CQ} R_C \tag{4.40}$$

Load-line Analysis The load line is drawn using the output equation given by Eq. (4.39). Substituting $I_C = 0$ in Eq. (4.39), we get

$$V_{CB} = V_{CC}\Big|_{I_C=0}$$

Substituting $V_{CB} = 0$ in Eq. (4.39), we get

$$I_C = \frac{V_{CC}}{R_C}\Bigg|_{V_{CB}=0}$$

Joining the two points we can draw the DC load line on the output characteristics (Figure 4.33). The operating point (I_{CQ}, V_{CBQ}) is determined by the point of intersection of the load line with the characteristic curves at the quiescent value of emitter current given by Eq. (4.38).

EXAMPLE 4.8 *Determine the operating point for the circuit shown in Figure 4.34 given that the transistor base–emitter voltage (V_{BE}) is 0.7 V.*

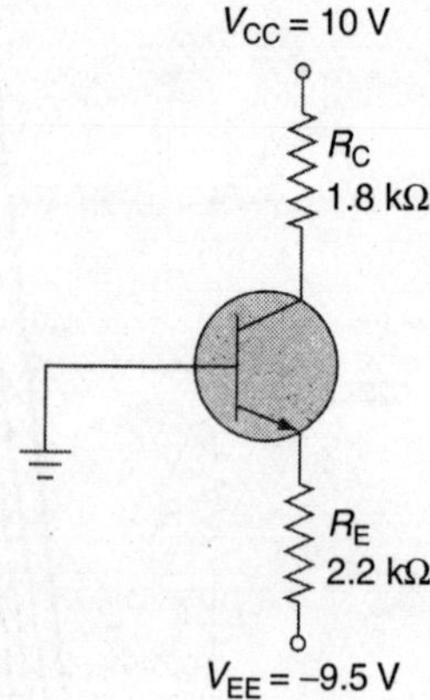

Figure 4.34 | Example 4.8.

Solution

1. The value of the emitter current is

$$I_E = \frac{-V_{EE} - V_{BE}}{R_E}$$

$$I_E = (9.5 - 0.7) / 2.2 \times 10^3 = 4 \text{ mA}$$

2. The value of collector current $I_C \cong I_E$. Therefore, $I_C = 4$ mA.

$$V_{CB} = V_{CC} - I_C R_C$$

3. The output voltage is given by $= 10 - 4 \times 10^{-3} \times 1.8 \times 10^3$.

$$= 10 - 7.2 = 2.8 \text{ V}$$

4. The operating point is $I_C = 4$ mA, $V_{CB} = 2.8$ V.

Answer: The operating point is $I_C = 4$ mA, $V_{CB} = 2.8$ V.

4.4 Common-Collector Circuit

In the common-collector configuration, also referred to as emitter-follower configuration, the input voltage is applied to the base terminal and the output is taken from the emitter terminal. The collector terminal is common to both the input and the output sections. Common-collector configuration exhibits 100% voltage-series feedback as whole of the output voltage is fed-back in series with the input voltage.

Figure 4.35 shows one of the possible circuits of common-collector configuration. The circuit is similar to that of voltage-divider bias with the difference that there is no collector resistor (R_C) and the output is taken from the emitter terminal instead of the collector terminal.

Figure 4.36(a) shows another possible common-collector circuit. Figure 4.36(b) shows the DC equivalent of the circuit. Applying Kirchhoff's voltage law to the base–emitter loop, we get

$$-I_B R_B - V_{BE} - I_E R_E + V_{EE} = 0$$

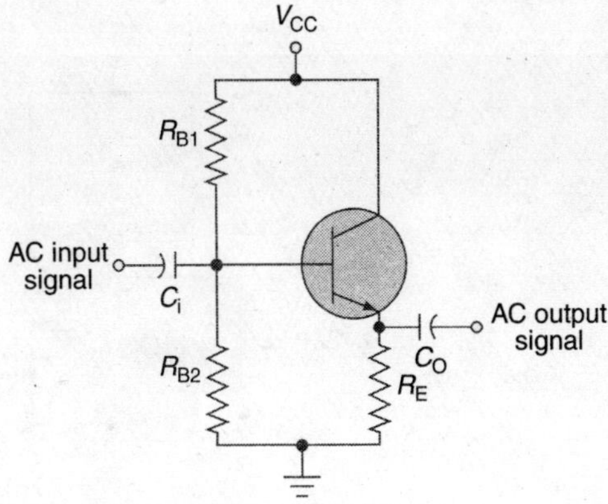

Figure 4.35 One possible common-collector configuration.

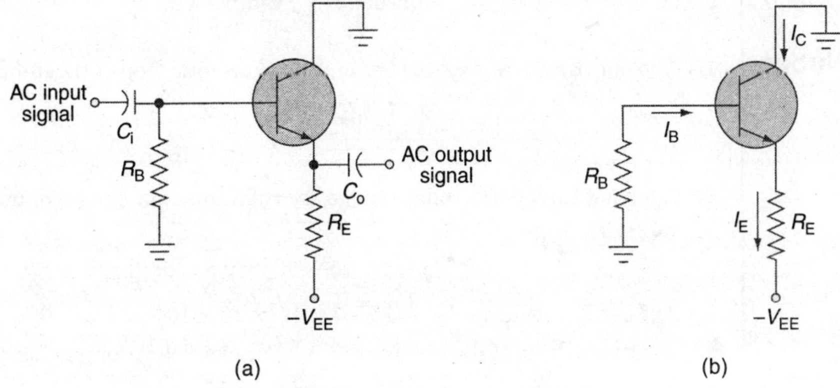

Figure 4.36 (a) Another possible common-collector configuration; (b) DC equivalent of the circuit in part (a).

Substituting $I_E = (\beta + 1)I_B$ in the above equation and solving for base current (I_B), we get

$$I_B = \frac{V_{EE} - V_{BE}}{R_B + (\beta + 1)R_E} \tag{4.41}$$

Applying Kirchhoff's voltage law to the emitter–collector loop, we get

$$-V_{EE} + I_E R_E + V_{CE} = 0$$

$$V_{CE} = V_{EE} - I_E R_E \tag{4.42}$$

Load-line analysis can be done on similar lines as for the common-emitter configuration.

EXAMPLE 4.9 *Determine the output voltage (V_{out}) of the circuit shown in Figure 4.37 given that V_{BE} voltage for transistors Q_1 and Q_2 is 0.7 V.*

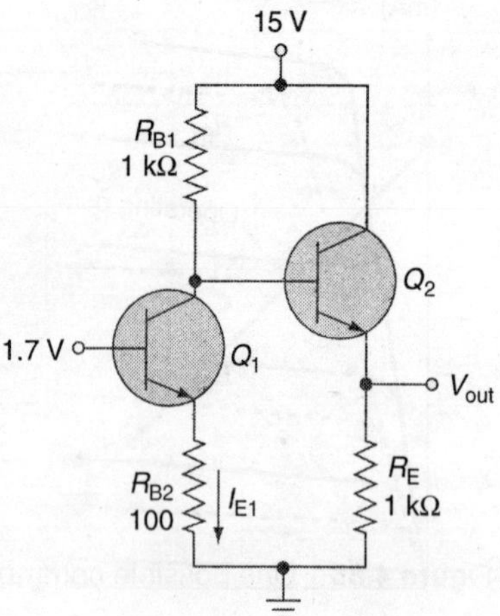

Figure 4.37 Example 4.9.

Solution

1. Applying Kirchhoff's voltage law to the base–emitter loop of transistor Q_1, we get
$$1.7 - 0.7 - 100 \times I_{E1} = 0$$
$$I_{E1} = 10 \text{ mA}$$
2. Applying Kirchhoff's voltage law to the collector–emitter loop of transistor Q_1, we get
$$15 - 1 \times 10^3 \times I_{C1} - V_{C1} = 0$$
3. As $I_{E1} \cong I_{C1}$, therefore $V_{C1} = 15 - 1 \times 10^3 \times 10 \times 10^{-3} = 5$ V.
4. The base voltage of the transistor Q_2 = Collector voltage of transistor Q_1.
5. Therefore, base voltage of the transistor Q_2 = 5 V.
6. Emitter voltage of transistor Q_2 is given by $V_{E2} = V_{B2} - V_{BE2} = 5 - 0.7 = 4.3$ V.
7. Therefore, output voltage $V_{out} = V_{E2} = 4.3$ V.

Answer: The output voltage V_{out} is 4.3 V.

4.5 Bias Stabilization

Bias stabilization refers to the ability of a bias circuit to maintain a fixed operating point against variations in temperature and transistor gain (β). Bias stabilization is important as the transistor parameters are strongly dependent on temperature. The transistor gain (β) increases with increase in temperature, the base–emitter voltage (V_{BE}) of the transistor decreases with increase in temperature at a rate of 2.5 mV/°C for constant collector current and the leakage current (I_{CO}) doubles itself for every 10°C rise in temperature. As the base current (I_B) depends on V_{BE}, therefore it also varies with temperature. Collector current (I_C) is given by the expression $I_C = \beta I_B + (\beta + 1)I_{CO}$. Therefore, it varies with change in temperature as all the three parameters in its expression (β, I_B and I_{CO}) are temperature-dependent.

Figure 4.38 shows the typical output characteristics of a common–emitter transistor at two different temperatures. As it is evident from the figure, the CE output characteristics shift upwards with increase in

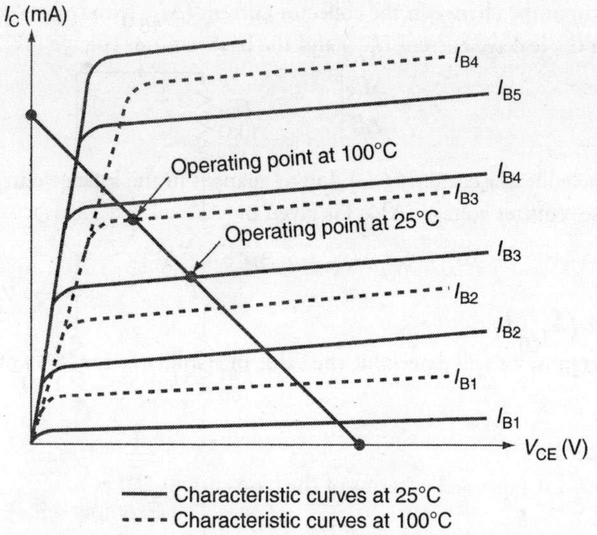

Figure 4.38 | Variation in the output characteristics of a transistor with change in temperature.

temperature as the leakage current (I_{CO}) increases with increase in temperature. The spacing between the adjacent curves also increases as the gain (β) of the transistor increases. Thus for the same base current, the operating point shifts and it may be possible that the transistor biased in the active region at one temperature finds itself in the saturation region at an elevated temperature.

Another important cause of variation in collector current (I_C) is the widespread variation in the value of transistor gain (β) of the order of three times for two transistors of the same type number. Thus for the same base current, the collector current varies with change in the transistor used in the circuit. Each of the biasing circuit described in preceding sections offers different amount of stability to the operating point. The amount of stability offered by the circuit is measured in terms of stability factor.

Stability Factor

Stability factor defines the extent to which the collector current (I_C) of a transistor is stable against variations in the transistor parameters, namely, the leakage current (I_{CO}), the transistor gain (β) and the base–emitter voltage (V_{BE}). The three types of stability factors are defined with respect to transistors, namely, $S_{I_{CO}}$, S_β and $S_{V_{BE}}$. Small value of stability factor indicates good bias stability whereas large value of stability factor indicates poor bias stability. Ideal value of stability factor is zero.

$S_{I_{CO}}$ is defined as the ratio of the change in the collector current (ΔI_C) with respect to change in the leakage current (ΔI_{CO}) with the base–emitter voltage (V_{BE}) and the transistor gain (β) held constant. It can be expressed mathematically as

$$S_{I_{CO}} = \left.\frac{\Delta I_C}{\Delta I_{CO}}\right|_{V_{BE} = \text{const.},\ \beta = \text{const.}} \tag{4.43}$$

$S_{V_{BE}}$ is defined as the ratio of change in the collector current (ΔI_C) with respect to change in the base–emitter voltage (ΔV_{BE}) with both the leakage current (I_{CO}) and the transistor gain (β) held constant:

$$S_{V_{BE}} = \left.\frac{\Delta I_C}{\Delta V_{BE}}\right|_{I_{CO} = \text{const.},\ \beta = \text{const.}} \tag{4.44}$$

S_β is defined as the ratio of the change in the collector current (ΔI_C) with respect to change in the transistor gain (β) keeping both the leakage current (I_{CO}) and the base–emitter voltage (V_{BE}) as constant:

$$S_\beta = \left.\frac{\Delta I_C}{\Delta\beta}\right|_{I_{CO} = \text{const.},\ V_{BE} = \text{const.}} \tag{4.45}$$

The total change in the collector current (ΔI_C) due to changes in the leakage current (ΔI_{CO}), the transistor gain ($\Delta\beta$) and the base–emitter voltage (ΔV_{BE}) is given by

$$\Delta I_C = S_{I_{CO}}\Delta I_{CO} + S_\beta\Delta\beta + S_{V_{BE}}\Delta V_{BE} \tag{4.46}$$

Stability Factor ($S_{I_{CO}}$)

In the following paragraphs, we will determine the value of stability factor ($S_{I_{CO}}$) offered by different biasing circuits.

Fixed-Bias Configuration

The collector current (I_C) is expressed in terms of the base current (I_B) as

$$I_C = \beta I_B + (\beta+1)I_{CO}$$

Differentiating collector current (I_C) with respect to the leakage current (I_{CO}) and keeping the transistor gain (β) and the base–emitter voltage (V_{BE}) as constant, we get

$$\frac{dI_C}{dI_{CO}} = (\beta+1)$$

The stability factor $S_{I_{CO}}$ for a fixed-bias circuit is given by

$$S_{I_{CO}} = \beta+1 \tag{4.47}$$

If $\beta = 100$, then $S_{I_{CO}} = 101$, which implies that the collector current increases by 101 times than the increase in the leakage current. Therefore, for fixed-bias circuit the collector current (I_C) is strongly dependent on the change in the leakage current (I_{CO}) and hence on the temperature. In other words, fixed-bias circuit offers very poor stability against variations in the leakage current.

Emitter-Bias Configuration

As derived in Section 4.1, the voltage-current equation for the base–emitter loop of the emitter-bias configuration is given by

$$V_{CC} - V_{BE} - I_E R_E - I_B R_B = 0 \tag{4.48}$$

Substituting $I_E = I_B + I_C$ in Eq. (4.48) and rearranging the terms, we get

$$(R_B + R_E)I_B = V_{CC} - V_{BE} - I_C R_E$$

$$I_B = \frac{V_{CC} - V_{BE} - I_C R_E}{R_B + R_E} \tag{4.49}$$

As $V_{BE} << V_{CC}$, Eq. (4.49) can be rewritten as

$$I_B = \frac{V_{CC} - I_C R_E}{R_B + R_E} \tag{4.50}$$

The collector current (I_C) is expressed as

$$I_C = \beta I_B + (\beta+1)I_{CO} \tag{4.51}$$

Substituting the value of I_B given by Eq. (4.50) in Eq. (4.51) we get

$$I_C = \beta \frac{(V_{CC} - I_C R_E)}{R_B + R_E} + (\beta + 1) I_{CO} \tag{4.52}$$

Rearranging the terms of Eq. (4.52) we get

$$\frac{(R_B + R_E + \beta R_E) I_C}{R_B + R_E} = \frac{\beta V_{CC}}{R_B + R_E} + (\beta + 1) I_{CO}$$

$$I_C = \frac{\beta V_{CC}}{R_B + (\beta + 1) R_E} + \frac{(\beta + 1)(R_B + R_E) I_{CO}}{R_B + (\beta + 1) R_E} \tag{4.53}$$

Differentiating I_C in Eq. (4.53) with respect to I_{CO} keeping β and V_{BE} constant we get

$$\frac{dI_C}{dI_{CO}} = \frac{(\beta + 1)(R_B + R_E)}{R_B + (\beta + 1) R_E} = \frac{(\beta + 1)(1 + R_B/R_E)}{1 + \beta + R_B/R_E}$$

Therefore, the stability factor $S_{I_{CO}}$ for emitter-bias configuration is given as

$$S_{I_{CO}} = \frac{(\beta + 1)(1 + R_B/R_E)}{1 + \beta + R_B/R_E} \tag{4.54}$$

For $R_B/R_E >> (\beta + 1)$, Eq. (4.54) becomes

$$S_{I_{CO}} \cong \beta + 1 \tag{4.55}$$

For the other extreme, when $R_B/R_E << 1$

$$S_{I_{CO}} \cong 1 \tag{4.56}$$

Thus the stability factor ($S_{I_{CO}}$) for an emitter-bias circuit varies from approximately 1 to ($\beta + 1$) as the ratio of base resistor (R_B) to emitter resistor (R_E) increases from a very small value to a very large value (Figure 4.39). As we know, the stability factor should be as small as possible, therefore the ratio R_B/R_E should be as small as possible. Thus, resistor R_E should be sufficiently large. Increase in the value of R_E increases the negative feedback factor and reduces the gain of the circuit. Therefore, a trade-off needs to be applied that satisfies both the stability and circuit gain criteria.

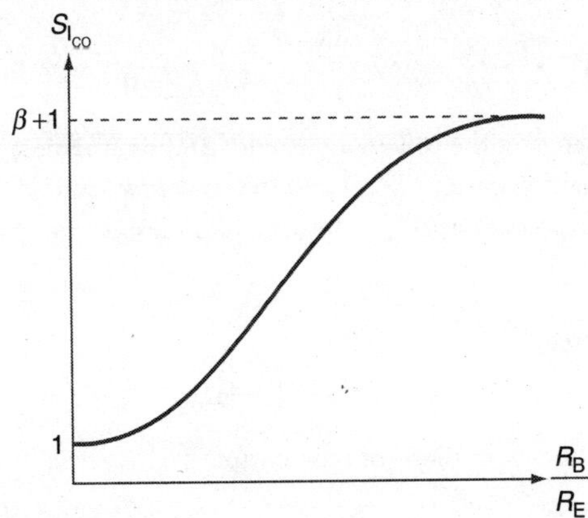

Figure 4.39 | Stability factor for emitter-bias circuit.

To sum up, the emitter-bias configuration offers some stability against variations in the leakage current I_{CO}. However, the stability offered is not very high as the ratio of R_B/R_E cannot be reduced beyond a certain value. This problem is overcome in the voltage-divider bias with emitter-bias configuration.

The fact that the emitter-bias configuration offers stability can also be explained logically, without going deep into mathematical calculations, with the help of the expression for the base current (I_B) for the configuration given as

$$I_B = \frac{V_{CC} - V_{BE} - I_C R_E}{R_B + R_E} \tag{4.57}$$

When the value of collector current (I_C) increases due to increase in the leakage current (I_{CO}), the value of the base current (I_B) decreases, which in turn reduces the value of the collector current (I_C). This compensates for the initial increase in I_C. Thus, the circuit tries to maintain a constant collector current.

Voltage-Divider-Bias with Emitter-Bias Configuration

In the case of voltage-divider-bias configuration, the expression for $S_{I_{CO}}$ is similar to that of emitter-bias configuration, with the base resistor (R_B) being replaced by Thevenin's equivalent resistance (R_{TH}):

$$S_{I_{CO}} = \frac{(\beta+1)(1+R_{TH}/R_E)}{1+\beta+R_{TH}/R_E} \tag{4.58}$$

The circuit offers highest stability when the value of emitter resistor (R_E) is much larger than the Thevenin's equivalent resistance (R_{TH}). It must be remembered that in voltage-divider configuration, Thevenin's equivalent resistance (R_{TH}) is much smaller than the corresponding base resistor (R_B) of the emitter-bias configuration. Thus, the ratio R_E/R_{TH} is higher as compared to R_E/R_B in emitter-bias configuration. Hence, this configuration offers better stability as compared to the emitter-bias configuration.

Collector-to-Base-Bias Configuration

The expression for $S_{I_{CO}}$ for collector-to-base-bias configuration can be obtained in a manner similar to that for the emitter-bias configuration. The expression is given as

$$S_{I_{CO}} = \frac{(\beta+1)(1+R_B/R_C)}{1+\beta+R_B/R_C} \tag{4.59}$$

Hence, the ratio R_B/R_C should be as small as possible for better stability.

Stability Factor ($S_{V_{BE}}$)

$S_{V_{BE}}$ is defined as the ratio of change in the collector current (ΔI_C) with respect to change in the base–emitter voltage (ΔV_{BE}) with both the leakage current (I_{CO}) and the transistor gain (β) held constant. In the following sub-sections we derive the expression for $S_{V_{BE}}$ for different biasing circuits.

Fixed-Bias Circuit

The expression for collector current (I_C) is

$$I_C = \beta I_B + (\beta+1)I_{CO}$$

In the case of fixed-bias circuit, the expression for base current (I_B) is given by

$$I_B = \frac{V_{CC} - V_{BE}}{R_B} \tag{4.60}$$

Substituting the value of base current (I_B) in the expression for collector current (I_C), we get

$$I_C = \frac{\beta(V_{CC} - V_{BE})}{R_B} + (\beta + 1)I_{CO} \tag{4.61}$$

Differentiating Eq. (4.61) with respect to V_{BE} with I_{CO} and β constant, we get

$$\frac{dI_C}{dV_{BE}} = \frac{-\beta}{R_B}$$

Therefore, the stability factor $S_{V_{BE}}$ for a fixed-bias configuration is given by

$$S_{V_{BE}} = \frac{-\beta}{R_B} \tag{4.62}$$

As is clear from this equation, the stability factor ($S_{V_{BE}}$) of the fixed-bias circuit improves as the value of base resistor (R_B) increases.

Emitter-Bias Configuration

In the emitter-bias configuration the base current (I_B) is given by

$$I_B = \frac{V_{CC} - V_{BE} - I_C R_E}{R_B + R_E} \tag{4.63}$$

The equation for collector current (I_C) is

$$I_C = \beta I_B + (\beta + 1)I_{CO} \tag{4.64}$$

Substituting the value of base current (I_B) in Eq. (4.64), we get

$$I_C = \frac{\beta(V_{CC} - V_{BE} - I_C R_E)}{R_B + R_E} + (\beta + 1)I_{CO} \tag{4.65}$$

Rearranging the terms in Eq. (4.65), we get

$$I_C = \frac{\beta(V_{CC} - V_{BE}) + (\beta + 1)(R_B + R_E)I_{CO}}{R_B + (\beta + 1)R_E} \tag{4.66}$$

Differentiating I_C in Eq. (4.66) with respect to V_{BE} keeping β and I_{CO} constant, we get

$$\frac{dI_C}{dV_{BE}} = \frac{-\beta}{R_B + (\beta + 1)R_E} = \frac{-\beta / R_E}{R_B / R_E + (\beta + 1)}$$

Thus the stability factor $S_{V_{BE}}$ for the emitter-bias configuration is given by

$$S_{V_{BE}} = \frac{-\beta / R_E}{R_B / R_E + (\beta + 1)} \tag{4.67}$$

When $(\beta + 1) >> R_B/R_E$, the value of stability factor is given by

$$S_{V_{BE}} = \frac{-\beta / R_E}{\beta + 1} \cong \frac{-1}{R_E} \tag{4.68}$$

We can see from Eq. (4.68) the stability of the emitter–bias circuit against variations in base–emitter voltage (V_{BE}) improves with increase in the value of emitter resistance (R_E).

Voltage-Divider Bias with Emitter-Bias Configuration

In the case of voltage-divider-bias configuration, the expression for $S_{V_{BE}}$ is similar to that of emitter-bias configuration with the base resistor (R_B) replaced by Thevenin's equivalent resistance (R_{TH}):

$$S_{V_{BE}} = \frac{-\beta / R_E}{R_{TH}/R_E + (\beta + 1)} \tag{4.69}$$

Collector-to-Base-Bias Configuration

In the case of collector-to-base-bias configuration, the expression for $S_{V_{BE}}$ is similar to that of emitter-bias configuration except that the emitter resistor (R_E) is replaced by collector resistor (R_C):

$$S_{V_{BE}} = \frac{-\beta / R_C}{R_B/R_C + (\beta + 1)} \tag{4.70}$$

Stability Factor (S_β)

S_β is defined as the ratio of the change in the collector current (ΔI_C) with respect to change in the transistor gain (β) keeping both I_{CO} and V_{BE} constant.

Fixed-Bias Configuration

The expression for collector current is

$$I_C = \beta I_B + (\beta + 1) I_{CO}$$

As $I_{CO} << I_B$, therefore $I_C = \beta I_B$.
For $\beta = \beta_1$,

$$I_{C1} = \beta_1 I_B \tag{4.71}$$

For $\beta = \beta_2$,

$$I_{C2} = \beta_2 I_B \tag{4.72}$$

Subtracting Eq. (4.71) from Eq. (4.72), we get

$$I_{C2} - I_{C1} = (\beta_2 - \beta_1) I_B \tag{4.73}$$

Substituting $(I_{C2} - I_{C1})$ as ΔI_C and $(\beta_2 - \beta_1)$ as $\Delta\beta$ in Eq. (4.73), we get

$$\Delta I_C = \Delta\beta I_B \tag{4.74}$$

Equation (4.74) can be rewritten as

$$\frac{\Delta I_C}{\Delta\beta} = I_B = \frac{I_{C1}}{\beta_1} \tag{4.75}$$

Therefore, the value of stability factor S_β for the fixed-bias circuit is given by

$$S_\beta = \frac{I_{C1}}{\beta_1} \tag{4.76}$$

Emitter-Bias Configuration

In the emitter-bias configuration the base current (I_B) is given by

$$I_B = \frac{V_{CC} - V_{BE} - I_C R_E}{R_B + R_E} \tag{4.77}$$

As we know, the expression for collector current (I_C) is given by

$$I_C = \beta I_B + (\beta+1)I_{CO} \tag{4.78}$$

Substituting this value of I_B given by Eq. (4.77) in Eq. (4.78), we get

$$I_C = \frac{\beta(V_{CC} - V_{BE} - I_C R_E)}{R_B + R_E} + (\beta+1)I_{CO} \tag{4.79}$$

Rearranging the terms in Eq. (4.79), we get

$$I_C(R_B + R_E + \beta R_E) = \beta V_{CC} - \beta V_{BE} + (\beta+1)(R_B + R_E)I_{CO} \tag{4.80}$$

As $V_{BE} << V_{CC}$ and $I_{CO} << I_C$, Eq. (4.80) can be approximated as

$$I_C(R_B + R_E + \beta R_E) = \beta V_{CC} \tag{4.81}$$

For $\beta = \beta_1$, Eq. (4.81) can be written as

$$I_{C1}(R_B + R_E + \beta_1 R_E) = \beta_1 V_{CC} \tag{4.82}$$

For $\beta = \beta_2$, Eq. (4.81) can be written as

$$I_{C2}(R_B + R_E + \beta_2 R_E) = \beta_2 V_{CC} \tag{4.83}$$

Subtracting Eq. (4.82) from Eq. (4.83), we get

$$(I_{C2} - I_{C1})(R_B + R_E) + I_{C2}\beta_2 R_E - I_{C1}\beta_1 R_E = (\beta_2 - \beta_1)V_{CC} \tag{4.84}$$

Substituting $(I_{C2} - I_{C1})$ as ΔI_C and $(\beta_2 - \beta_1)$ as $\Delta\beta$ in Eq. (4.84), we get

$$\Delta I_C(R_B + R_E) + I_{C2}\beta_2 R_E - I_{C1}\beta_1 R_E = \Delta\beta V_{CC} \tag{4.85}$$

Adding and subtracting $I_{C1}\beta_2 R_E$ in Eq. (4.85) and then solving we get

$$\Delta I_C(R_B + R_E) + \Delta I_C \beta_2 R_E + I_{C1}\Delta\beta R_E = \Delta\beta V_{CC} \tag{4.86}$$

Rearranging the terms in Eq. (4.86) we get

$$\Delta I_C(R_B + R_E + \beta_2 R_E) = \Delta\beta(V_{CC} - I_{C1}R_E) \tag{4.87}$$

Rearranging the terms in Eq. (4.82) we get

$$V_{CC} = \frac{I_{C1}(R_B + R_E + \beta_1 R_E)}{\beta_1} \tag{4.88}$$

Substituting this value of V_{CC} in Eq. (4.87), we get

$$\Delta I_C(R_B + R_E + \beta_2 R_E) = \Delta\beta\left[\frac{I_{C1}(R_B + R_E + \beta_1 R_E)}{\beta_1} - I_{C1}R_E\right]$$

Therefore,

$$\frac{\Delta I_C}{\Delta\beta} = \frac{I_{C1}(R_B + R_E)}{\beta_1(R_B + R_E + \beta_2 R_E)}$$

$$\frac{\Delta I_C}{\Delta\beta} = \frac{I_{C1}(1 + R_B/R_E)}{\beta_1(1 + \beta_2 + R_B/R_E)}$$

Table 4.1 | Important parameters of different biasing configurations

	I_{CQ}	V_{CEQ}	$S_{I_{CO}}$	$S_{V_{BE}}$	S_β
Fixed bias	$\beta\left(\frac{V_{CC}-V_{BE}}{R_B}\right)$	$V_{CC}-I_{CQ}R_C$	$\beta+1$	$\frac{-\beta}{R_B}$	$\frac{I_{C1}}{\beta_1}$
Emitter bias	$\beta\left(\frac{V_{CC}-V_{BE}}{R_B+(\beta+1)R_E}\right)$	$V_{CC}-I_{CQ}(R_C+R_E)$	$\frac{(\beta+1)(1+R_B/R_E)}{1+\beta+R_B/R_E}$	$\frac{-\beta/R_E}{R_B/R_E+(\beta+1)}$	$\frac{I_{C1}(1+R_B/R_E)}{\beta_1(1+\beta_2+R_B/R_E)}$
Voltage-divider bias	$\beta\left(\frac{V_{TH}-V_{BE}}{R_{TH}+(\beta+1)R_E}\right)$	$V_{CC}-I_{CQ}(R_C+R_E)$	$\frac{(\beta+1)(1+R_{TH}/R_E)}{1+\beta+R_{TH}/R_E}$	$\frac{-\beta/R_E}{R_{TH}/R_E+(\beta+1)}$	$\frac{I_{C1}(1+R_{TH}/R_E)}{\beta_1(1+\beta_2+R_{TH}/R_E)}$
Collector-to-base bias	$\beta\left(\frac{V_{CC}-V_{BE}}{R_B+(\beta+1)R_C}\right)$	$V_{CC}-I_{CQ}R_C$	$\frac{(\beta+1)(1+R_B/R_C)}{1+\beta+R_B/R_C}$	$\frac{-\beta/R_C}{R_B/R_C+(\beta+1)}$	$\frac{I_{C1}(1+R_B/R_C)}{\beta_1(1+\beta_2+R_B/R_C)}$

The value of stability factor (S_β) for the emitter-bias configuration is given by

$$S_\beta = \frac{I_{C1}(1+R_B/R_E)}{\beta_1(1+\beta_2+R_B/R_E)} \tag{4.89}$$

Voltage-Divider Bias with Emitter-Bias Configuration

In the case of voltage-divider-bias configuration, the expression for S_β is similar to that of emitter-bias configuration with the base resistor (R_B) being replaced by Thevenin's equivalent resistance (R_{TH}):

$$S_\beta = \frac{I_{C1}(1+R_{TH}/R_E)}{\beta_1(1+\beta_2+R_{TH}/R_E)} \tag{4.90}$$

Collector-to-Base-Bias Configuration

In the case of collector-to-base-bias configuration, the expression for S_β is similar to that of emitter-bias configuration with the resistance R_E being replaced by R_C:

$$S_\beta = \frac{I_{C1}(1+R_B/R_C)}{\beta_1(1+\beta_2+R_B/R_C)} \tag{4.91}$$

Table 4.1 summarizes the values of quiescent collector current (I_{CQ}), quiescent collector-to-emitter voltage (V_{CEQ}) and stability factors $S_{I_{CO}}$, $S_{V_{BE}}$ and S_β for the various transistor-biasing configurations.

EXAMPLE 4.10 *Determine the stability factors $S_{I_{CO}}$, $S_{V_{BE}}$ and S_β for each of the following bias arrangements. Also determine the total change in collector current when the temperature changes from +25°C to +175°C. The various transistor parameters at different temperatures are listed in Table 4.2.*

(a) Fixed-bias circuit ($R_B = 300\ k\Omega$, $I_C = 2\ mA$, $\beta = 50$).

(b) Emitter-bias circuit ($R_B = 300\ k\Omega$, $R_E = 2\ k\Omega$, $I_C = 2\ mA$, $\beta = 50$).

(c) Voltage-divider-bias circuit ($R_{B1} = 50\ k\Omega$, $R_{B2} = 10\ k\Omega$, $R_E = 2\ k\Omega$, $I_C = 2\ mA$, $\beta = 50$).

Table 4.2 | Example 4.10.

T(°C)	I_{CO} (nA)	β	V_{BE} (V)
−65	2×10^{-4}	25	0.85
25	0.2	50	0.7
100	25	80	0.5
175	3×10^{3}	125	0.32

Solution

(a) ***Fixed-bias circuit***

1. $S_{I_{CO}} = \beta + 1$. Therefore, $S_{I_{CO}} = 51$.
2. $S_\beta = \dfrac{I_{C1}}{\beta_1}$

   where I_{C1} and β_1 are the values of collector current and transistor gain at 25°C, $I_{C1} = 2$ mA and $\beta_1 = 50$.
3. Therefore, $S_\beta = 2\times10^{-3}/50 = 4\times10^{-5}$.
4. $S_{V_{BE}} = -\beta/R_B$. Therefore, $S_{V_{BE}} = -50/(300\times10^3) = -16.6\times10^{-5}$.
5. Total change in the collector current ΔI_C is
$$\Delta I_C = S_{I_{CO}}\Delta I_{CO} + S_\beta \Delta\beta + S_{V_{BE}}\Delta V_{BE}$$
6. $\Delta I_{CO} = (3\times10^3 - 0.2)$ nA $\cong 3\times10^3$ nA $= 3$ μA.
7. $\Delta\beta = 125 - 50 = 75$.
8. $\Delta V_{BE} = 0.32 - 0.7 = -0.38$.
9. $\Delta I_C = [51\times3\times10^{-6} + 4\times10^{-5}\times75 + (-16.6\times10^{-5})(-0.38)]$ A
   $= (153 + 3000 + 63.08)$ μA $= 3.22$ mA

(b) ***Emitter-bias circuit***

10. $S_{I_{CO}} = \dfrac{(1+\beta)(1+R_B/R_E)}{1+\beta+R_B/R_E}$

    $S_{I_{CO}} = (51)[1+\{(300\times10^3)/(2\times10^3)\}]/[1+50+\{(300\times10^3)/(2\times10^3)\}]$

    $= 51\times151/201 = 38.31$
11. $S_\beta = \dfrac{I_{C1}(1+R_B/R_E)}{\beta_1(1+\beta_2+R_B/R_E)}$

    where I_{C1} and β_1 are the values of collector current and transistor gain at 25°C. $I_{C1} = 2$ mA and $\beta_1 = 50$. β_2 is the transistor gain at 175°C with $\beta_2 = 125$.
12. Therefore, $S_\beta = (2\times10^{-3})[1+\{(300\times10^3)/(2\times10^3)\}]/[50(1+125+\{(300\times10^3)/(2\times10^3)\}] = (302\times10^{-3})/(50\times276) = 2.19\times10^{-5}$.
13. $S_{V_{BE}} = \dfrac{-\beta/R_E}{R_B/R_E+(\beta+1)}$

    $S_{V_{BE}} = \{-50/(2\times10^3)\}/[\{(300\times10^3)/(2\times10^3)\}+51]$

    $= -25\times10^{-3}/201 = -0.1243\times10^{-3} = -12.43\times10^{-5}$

14. Total change in the collector current ΔI_C is

$$\Delta I_C = S_{I_{CO}} \Delta I_{CO} + S_\beta \Delta\beta + S_{V_{BE}} \Delta V_{BE}$$

15. $\Delta I_C = [38.31 \times 3 \times 10^{-6} + 2.19 \times 10^{-5} \times 75 + (-12.43 \times 10^{-5})(-0.38)]\text{A}$
$= 1.8 \text{ mA}$

(c) ***Voltage-divider bias with emitter-bias circuit***

16. $$R_{TH} = \frac{R_{B1} \times R_{B2}}{R_{B1} + R_{B2}}$$

$$R_{TH} = (50 \times 10^3 \times 10 \times 10^3)/(50 \times 10^3 + 10 \times 10^3) = 500/60 = 8.3 \text{ k}\Omega$$

$$S_{I_{CO}} = \frac{(1+\beta)(1+R_{TH}/R_E)}{1+\beta+R_{TH}/R_E}$$

17. $S_{I_{CO}} = [(51)\{1 + (8.3 \times 10^3)/(2 \times 10^3)\}]/\{1 + 50 + (8.3 \times 10^3)/(2 \times 10^3)\}$

$= 51 \times 5.15/55.15 = 4.76$

18. $$S_\beta = \frac{I_{C1}(1+R_{TH}/R_E)}{\beta_1(1+\beta_2+R_{TH}/R_E)}$$

where I_{C1} and β_1 are the values of collector current and transistor gain at 25°C. $I_{C1} = 2$ mA and $\beta_1 = 50$. β_2 is the transistor gain at 175°C, that is $\beta_2 = 125$.

Therefore,

$$S_\beta = [(2 \times 10^{-3})\{1 + (8.3 \times 10^3)/(2 \times 10^3)\}]/(50[1 + 125 + \{(8.3 \times 10^3)/(2 \times 10^3)\}])$$
$$= 10.3 \times 10^{-3}/6507.5 = 1.58 \times 10^{-6}$$

19. $$S_{V_{BE}} = \frac{-\beta/R_E}{R_{TH}/R_E + (\beta+1)}$$

$$S_{V_{BE}} = \{-50/(2 \times 10^3)\}/[\{(8.3 \times 10^3)/(2 \times 10^3)\} + 50 + 1]$$
$$= -25 \times 10^{-3}/55.15 = 0.453 \times 10^{-3} = -45.3 \times 10^{-5}$$

20. Total change in the collector current ΔI_C is

$$\Delta I_C = S_{I_{CO}} \Delta I_{CO} + S_\beta \Delta\beta + S_{V_{BE}} \Delta V_{BE}$$

$$\Delta I_C = [4.76 \times 3 \times 10^{-6} + 1.58 \times 10^{-6} \times 75 + (-45.3 \times 10^{-5})(-0.38)] \text{ A}$$
$$= 0.305 \text{ mA}$$

Answer: Fixed-bias circuit: $S_{I_{CO}} = 51$, $S_{V_{BE}} = -16.6 \times 10^{-5}$, $S_\beta = 4 \times 10^{-5}$, $\Delta I_C =$ 3.22 mA.

Emitter-bias circuit: $S_{I_{CO}} = 38.31$, $S_\beta = 2.19 \times 10^{-5}$, $S_{V_{BE}} = -12.43 \times 10^{-5}$, $\Delta I_C = 1.8$ mA.

Voltage-divider bias with emitter-bias circuit: $S_{I_{CO}} = 4.76$, $S_\beta = 1.58 \times 10^{-6}$, $S_{V_{BE}} = -45.3 \times 10^{-5}$, $\Delta I_C = 0.305$ mA.

EXAMPLE 4.11 *Design an emitter-bias circuit with the following specifications:*

(a) change in collector current due to change in leakage current for a temperature range of 25° C to 100° C to be less than or equal to 1 μA;

(b) change in collector current due to change in transistor gain β for a temperature range of 25° C to 100° C to be less than or equal to 400 μA;

(c) change in collector current due to change in base–emitter voltage (V_{BE}) for a temperature range of 25° C to 100° C to be less than or equal to 50 μA;

(d) the quiescent collector-to-emitter voltage is 4 V.

Given that:

$$\text{At } 25°\text{C } I_{CO} = 0.1 \text{ nA}, \beta = 50, V_{BE} = 0.7;$$
$$\text{at } 100°\text{C } I_{CO} = 25.1 \text{ nA}, \beta = 70, V_{BE} = 0.4.$$

Solution

1. The desired value of the stability factor $S_{I_{CO}} \leq 1 \times 10^{-6}/(25.1 - 0.1) \times 10^{-9} \leq 40$. Therefore, the maximum value of $S_{I_{CO}}$ is 40.
2. For an emitter-bias circuit,
$$S_{I_{CO}} = \frac{(1+\beta)(1+R_B/R_E)}{1+\beta+R_B/R_E}$$
3. Substituting $\beta = 50$ in the above expression we get
$$40 = [51 \times (1 + R_B/R_E)]/(51 + R_B/R_E)$$
Therefore, $40\,(51 + R_B/R_E) = [51 \times (1 + R_B/R_E)]$. Therefore, $R_B/R_E = 180.8$.
4. The desired value of the stability factor
$$S_{V_{BE}} \leq 50 \times 10^{-6}/(-0.3) \leq -16.6 \times 10^{-5}$$
5. The maximum value of $S_{V_{BE}}$ is -16.6×10^{-5}.
6. For an emitter-bias circuit,
$$S_{V_{BE}} = \frac{-\beta/R_E}{R_B/R_E + (\beta+1)}$$
7. Substituting $\beta = 50$ in the above equation, we get
$$-16.6 \times 10^{-5} = (-50/R_E)/(R_B/R_E + 51)$$
8. Therefore, $-16.6 \times 10^{-5}\,(R_B/R_E + 51) = -50/R_E$. That is $R_B/R_E + 51 = 3 \times 10^5/R_E$.
9. Substituting $R_B/R_E = 180.8$ in the above equation, we get
$$R_E = (3 \times 10^5)/231.8 = 1.294\ \text{k}\Omega$$
10. The value of $R_B = 180.8 \times 1.294\ \text{k}\Omega = 234\ \text{k}\Omega$.
11. The desired value of the stability factor $S_\beta \leq (400 \times 10^{-6})/(20) \leq 2 \times 10^{-5}$.
12. For an emitter-bias circuit,
$$S_\beta = \frac{I_{C1}(1+R_B/R_E)}{\beta_1(1+\beta_2+R_B/R_E)}$$
13. Substituting the value of β_1 as 50 and β_2 as 70 in the above expression, we get
$$2 \times 10^{-5} = I_{C1} \times 181.8/50(71 + 180.8)$$

14. $I_{C1} = 2 \times 10^{-5} \times 50 \times 251.8/181.8 = 1.38$ mA.

15. For the emitter-bias circuit the collector current (I_C) is given by

$$I_C = \frac{\beta(V_{CC} - V_{BE})}{R_B + (\beta + 1)R_E}$$

Therefore,

$$1.38 \times 10^{-3} = 50(V_{CC} - 0.7)/(234 \times 10^3 + 51 \times 1.294 \times 10^3)$$

$$V_{CC} = 8.98 \text{ V} \cong 9 \text{ V}$$

16. Applying Kirchhoff's voltage law to the collector–emitter loop, we get

$$9 - I_C R_C - V_{CE} - I_E R_E = 0$$

$$9 - 1.38 \times 10^{-3} \times R_C - 4 - 1.38 \times 10^{-3} \times 1.294 \times 10^3 = 0$$

17. Therefore, $R_C = 2.3$ kΩ.

18. Figure 4.40 shows the design.

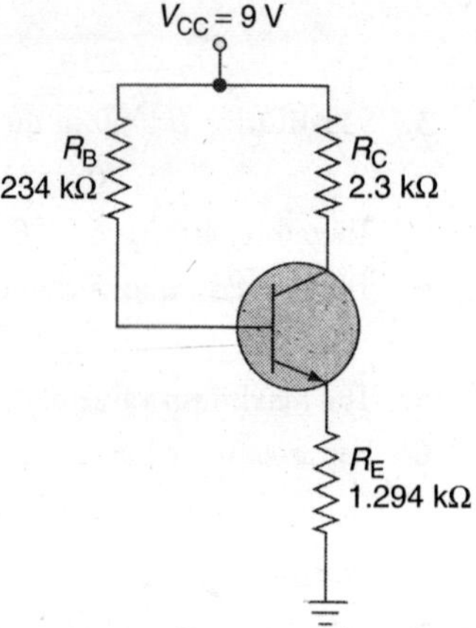

Figure 4.40 | Example 4.11.

4.6 Bias Compensation

The biasing techniques discussed so far offer stability to the operating point (I_{CQ}, V_{CEQ}) by virtue of negative feedback. Although, negative feedback improves stability but it also reduces the gain of the circuit. In applications where the reduction in gain is intolerable, compensation techniques are used to reduce the drift in the operating point.

Compensation techniques make use of temperature-sensitive devices such as diodes, thermistors, transistors, sensitors, etc. to compensate for the changes in the operating point caused due to changes in temperature. In the following sub-sections, we will discuss few of the commonly used compensation circuits.

Diode Compensation for Base–Emitter Voltage (V_{BE})

Figure 4.41 shows a circuit using diode for compensation against variations in base–emitter voltage (V_{BE}) due to change in temperature. The diode is made of the same material as the transistor so that there is same variation

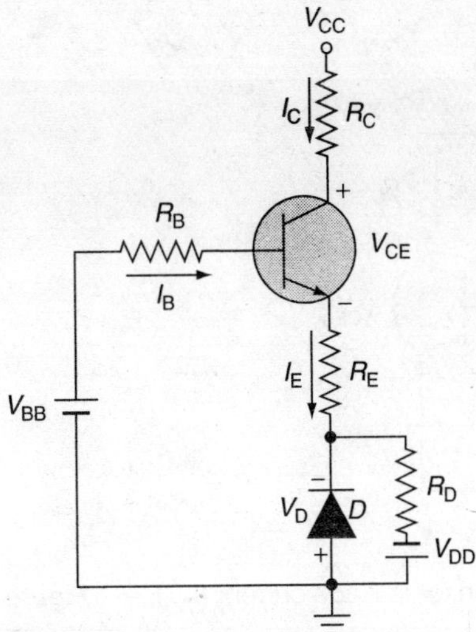

Figure 4.41 Diode compensation for base−emitter voltage (V_{BE}).

in the transistor's base–emitter voltage (V_{BE}) and diode's forward voltage (V_D) due to temperature. If we examine the circuit, we will see that the circuit is basically an emitter-bias circuit with an additional diode circuitry in the emitter leg. The diode is kept in forward-bias mode through voltage (V_{DD}) and resistance (R_D).

Applying Kirchhoff's voltage law to the base–emitter loop, we get

$$V_{BB} - I_B R_B - V_{BE} - I_E R_E + V_D = 0$$

Substituting $I_E = (\beta + 1)I_B$ in the above equation and solving for base current (I_B), we get

$$I_B = \frac{V_{BB} - (V_{BE} - V_D)}{R_B + (\beta + 1)R_E} \tag{4.92}$$

Collector current (I_C) is related to the base current by the expression

$$I_C = \beta I_B + (\beta + 1)I_{CO}$$

Substituting the value of I_B in the expression for collector current, we get

$$I_C = \frac{\beta[V_{BB} - (V_{BE} - V_D)]}{R_B + (\beta + 1)R_E} + (\beta + 1)I_{CO} \tag{4.93}$$

As is clear from Eq. (4.93), the change in the base–emitter voltage (V_{BE}) of the transistor due to the change in temperature will be nullified by a similar change in the forward voltage (V_D) of the diode. In other words, the diode's forward voltage (V_D) tracks the changes in the base–emitter voltage (V_{BE}) of the transistor and compensates for its changes.

Diode Compensation for Leakage Current (I_{CO})

To compensate for the variation in the leakage current (I_{CO}), a diode is placed across the base–emitter terminals of the transistor as shown in Figure 4.42. The diode is reverse-biased and hence the reverse saturation current (I_D) flows through it. The diode is chosen to be of the same material as the transistor, so that the reverse saturation current of the diode increases with temperature at the same rate as the leakage current of the transistor.

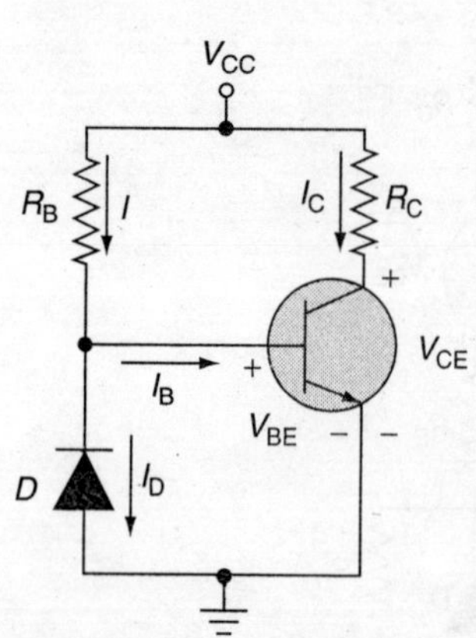

Figure 4.42 | Diode compensation for leakage current (I_{CO}).

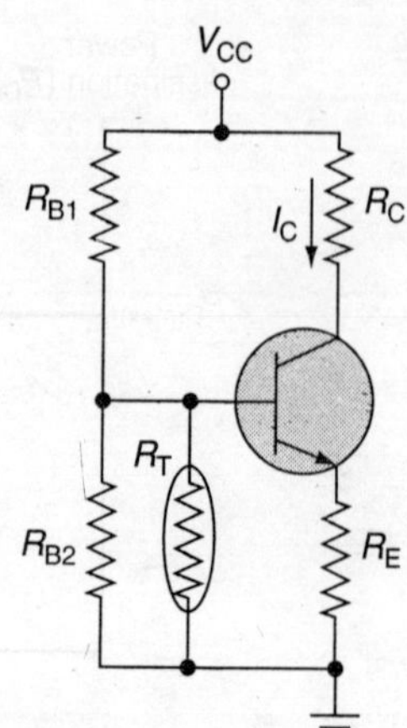

Figure 4.43 | Thermistor compensation.

The base current (I_B) in Figure 4.42 is equal to

$$I_B = I - I_D$$

Substituting this value of base current (I_B) in the expression for collector current (I_C), we get

$$I_C = \beta(I - I_D) + (\beta + 1)I_{CO}$$

As β and $(\beta + 1)$ are nearly equal, the expression for I_C can be written as

$$I_C = \beta I - \beta I_D + \beta I_{CO}$$

Rearranging the terms we get

$$I_C = \beta I - \beta(I_D - I_{CO}) \tag{4.94}$$

The diode reverse current (I_D) tracks the transistor leakage current (I_{CO}) over the desired temperature range.

Thermistor Compensation

Figure 4.43 shows a thermistor-based compensation circuit. The thermistor having negative temperature coefficient of resistance is placed in parallel with resistor R_{B2}. Values of the resistances are so chosen as to establish the desired value of collector current (I_C) at the normal operating temperature. As the temperature increases, the value of the thermistor resistance decreases. This reduces the forward bias and hence the base and collector currents of the transistor. When the temperature decreases, the thermistor resistance increases which results in an increase in the value of base–emitter voltage. This in turn increases the base and the collector currents. Therefore, the thermistor compensates for the change in collector current due to change in temperature.

4.7 Thermal Runaway

The power dissipation capability of a transistor depends upon its physical size, its construction and its mounting arrangement in the system. The maximum power rating is limited by the temperature that the collector-to-base junction can withstand and the ambient temperature. As the ambient temperature increases, the power rating of the transistor decreases. This is referred to as power derating. The power dissipation capability of transistors vary from few to several hundreds of milliwatts in the case of small signal transistors to

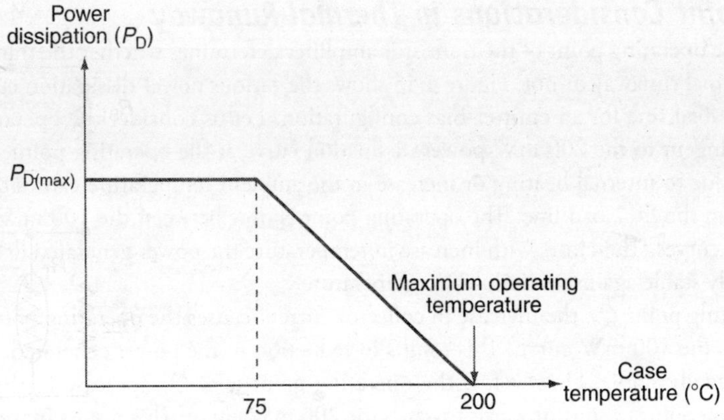

Figure 4.44 Typical power derating curve of a transistor.

around 250 W in the case of power transistors. As mentioned in Chapter 3, the maximum permissible temperature that the collector-to-base junction of a transistor can handle is in the range of 150°C to 225°C for silicon transistors and 60°C to 100°C for germanium transistors. Figure 4.44 shows the typical power derating curve of a silicon transistor with change in transistor case temperature. It may be mentioned here that in the case of small signal transistors, the case temperature is slightly larger than the ambient temperature and the case and the ambient temperatures are generally considered to be equal. However, in the case of power transistors, case temperature may exceed the ambient temperature by a large amount.

If the transistor circuit is not designed properly, it may lead to the phenomenon of *thermal runway*. When the transistor is in operation it dissipates power and its junction temperature rises, which in turn causes the collector current to increase. This may lead to more power dissipation and further increase in temperature and subsequently a further increase in collector current. If this cycle continues, it may result in permanently damaging the transistor. This phenomenon is referred to as thermal runaway. Proper design of the transistor circuit and selection of a suitable operating point is necessary to prevent the phenomenon of thermal runaway.

The steady-state temperature rise at the transistor collector junction is given by

$$T_J - T_A = \Theta P_D \tag{4.95}$$

where T_J is the transistor junction temperature; T_A the ambient temperature; P_D the power dissipated in the transistor; Θ the thermal resistance (°C/W). *Thermal resistance* is defined as the ratio of the rise in transistor junction temperature to the amount of power dissipated. The value of thermal resistance depends upon the transistor size, the size of heat sink used and other cooling methods used such as forced-air cooling, etc.:

$$\Theta = \frac{T_J - T_A}{P_D} = \frac{dT_J}{dP_D} \tag{4.96}$$

The inverse of the thermal resistance gives the temperature rate at which the power is dissipated under steady-state conditions:

$$\frac{dP_D}{dT_J} = \frac{1}{\Theta} \tag{4.97}$$

The condition for thermal stability is that the rate at which heat is generated at the collector junction should not exceed the rate at which it can be dissipated under steady-state conditions.

Operating-Point Considerations in Thermal Runaway

The position of the operating point of the transistor amplifier determines whether the transistor is inherently stable against thermal runaway or not. Figure 4.45 shows the various power dissipation curves of a transistor and a typical DC load line for an emitter-bias configuration. Let us consider the operating point Q_1. The DC load line is tangent to the 200 mW power dissipation curve at the operating point. An increase in the collector current due to internal heating or increase in the ambient temperature causes the operating point to shift upwards on the DC load line. The operating point is now between the 100 mW and the 200 mW power dissipation curves. Therefore, with increase in temperature the power generated decreases. Hence, the circuit is inherently stable against variations in temperature.

For the operating point Q_2, the increase in collector current causes the operating point to shift upwards and move towards the 100 mW curve. This results in reduction in the power generated. Hence, the circuit is inherently thermally stable. However, if the operating point is at Q_3, increase in the collector current causes the operating point to shift upwards towards the 200 mW curve. This results in increase in the power generated. Hence, the circuit is not inherently thermally stable and may lead to thermal runaway. Such a circuit needs to be checked for thermal stability.

The thumb rule to decide whether the operating point is in the safe region of operation is that for operating point with collector-to-emitter voltage (V_{CEQ}) less than $V_{CC}/2$ the circuit is thermally stable as increase in collector current results in reduced power generation. In the case of operating points having V_{CEQ} greater than $V_{CC}/2$, the circuit is not inherently thermally stable. In such cases, it is necessary to check the thermal characteristics of the transistor and the circuit design to ensure thermal stability.

For such circuits to be thermally stable they should satisfy the following condition:

$$[V_{CC} - 2I_C(R_E + R_C)](S_{I_{CO}})(0.07I_{CO}) < 1/\Theta \tag{4.98}$$

where V_{CC} is the supply voltage; I_C the collector current; R_E the emitter resistor; R_C the collector resistor; $S_{I_{CO}}$ the stability factor; I_{CO} the leakage current; Θ the thermal resistance of the transistor. This equation is valid for the emitter-bias circuit of Figure 4.11 redrawn again in Figure 4.46 for the convenience of the readers. In the case of fixed-bias circuit, Eq. (4.98) is valid with $R_E = 0$.

The mathematical treatment to the theoretical concepts described for thermal runaway phenomenon is given in the subsequent paragraphs.

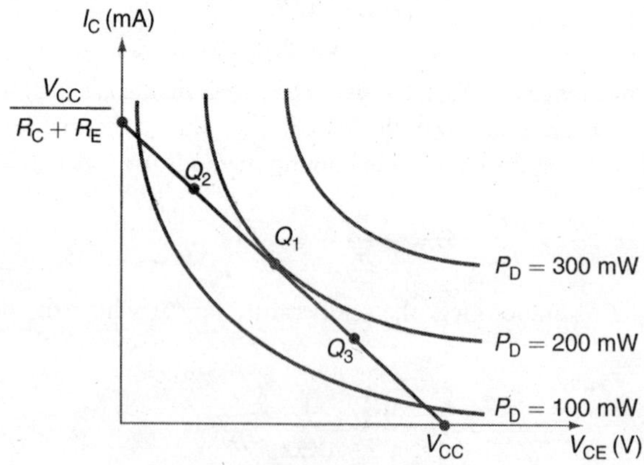

Figure 4.45 Operating-point considerations against thermal runaway.

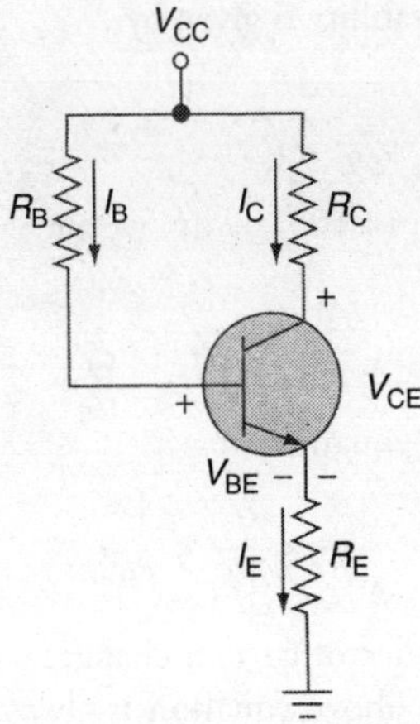

Figure 4.46 | Emitter-bias circuit.

For the emitter-bias circuit in Figure 4.46, the power produced in the transistor is given by

$$P_G = I_C V_{CB} \cong I_C V_{CE} \tag{4.99}$$

where P_G is the power produced in the transistor; I_C the collector current; V_{CB} the collector–base voltage; V_{CE} the collector–emitter voltage. Now $V_{CE} = V_{CB} + V_{BE}$. Assuming V_{BE} to be negligible as compared to V_{CB} and V_{CE}, we have $V_{CE} \cong V_{CB}$.

The collector–emitter voltage (V_{CE}) in emitter-bias circuit is expressed by

$$V_{CE} = V_{CC} - I_E R_E - I_C R_C \tag{4.100}$$

As $I_E \cong I_C$, Eq. (4.100) can be approximated as

$$V_{CE} \cong V_{CC} - I_C(R_E + R_C) \tag{4.101}$$

Substituting the value of V_{CE} given in Eq. (4.101) in Eq. (4.99), we get

$$P_G = I_C V_{CC} - I_C^2(R_E + R_C) \tag{4.102}$$

Differentiating Eq. (4.102) with respect to collector current (I_C), we get

$$\frac{dP_G}{dI_C} = V_{CC} - 2I_C(R_E + R_C) \tag{4.103}$$

The required condition for thermal stability is that the rate at which heat is produced at the collector junction should not exceed the rate at which it can be dissipated by the transistor under steady-state conditions. Rate of heat generated at the collector junction is given by differentiating the power generated (P_G) with respect to the junction temperature. Therefore, for thermal stability the following equation should be satisfied:

$$\frac{dP_G}{dT_J} < \frac{dP_D}{dT_J} \tag{4.104}$$

From Eq. (4.97) we know that

$$\frac{dP_D}{dT_J} = \frac{1}{\Theta}$$

Therefore, the requirement for thermal stability is given by

$$\frac{dP_G}{dT_J} < \frac{1}{\Theta} \tag{4.105}$$

Multiplying and dividing the LHS of Eq. (4.105) by dI_C we get

$$\frac{dP_G}{dT_J} \times \frac{dI_C}{dI_C} < \frac{1}{\Theta}$$

Rearranging the terms in the LHS of the equation we get

$$\frac{dP_G}{dI_C} \times \frac{dI_C}{dT_J} < \frac{1}{\Theta} \tag{4.106}$$

where dI_C/dT_J is the rate at which the collector current changes with junction temperature. Since $1/\Theta$ and dI_C/dT_J are both positive, therefore the above equation is always true when dP_G/dI_C is negative. From Eq. (4.103) we know that

$$\frac{dP_G}{dI_C} = V_{CC} - 2I_C(R_E + R_C)$$

Therefore to ensure thermal stability, the following equation should be satisfied:

$$V_{CC} - 2I_C(R_E + R_C) < 0 \tag{4.107}$$

Rearranging the terms in Eq. (4.107), we get

$$I_C > \frac{V_{CC}}{2(R_E + R_C)} \tag{4.108}$$

We know that in emitter-bias configuration

$$V_{CE} = V_{CC} - I_C(R_E + R_C)$$

Substituting the value of I_C in the equation we infer that when the collector–emitter voltage (V_{CE}) is less that half the supply voltage ($V_{CE} < V_{CC}/2$), then the circuit is thermally stable under all conditions. For $V_{CE} > V_{CC}/2$, the term dP_G/dI_C is positive and therefore the circuit design should be done such that Eq. (4.106) is satisfied.

The collector current (I_C) changes with the change in temperature as the leakage current (I_{CO}), the base–emitter voltage (V_{BE}) and the transistor gain (β) change with temperature. The rate of change of collector current with junction temperature is given by

$$\frac{dI_C}{dT_J} = S_{I_{CO}} \frac{dI_{CO}}{dT_J} + S_{V_{BE}} \frac{dV_{BE}}{dT_J} + S_\beta \frac{d\beta}{dT_J} \tag{4.109}$$

However in most cases the effect of leakage current (I_{CO}) is far more than that of transistor gain (β) and the base–emitter voltage (V_{BE}). Therefore,

$$\frac{dI_C}{dT_J} \cong S_{I_{CO}} \frac{dI_{CO}}{dT_J} \tag{4.110}$$

Substituting the value of dI_C/dT_J in Eq. (4.106), we get

$$\left(\frac{dP_G}{dI_C}\right)(S_{I_{CO}})\left(\frac{dI_{CO}}{dT_J}\right) < \frac{1}{\Theta} \tag{4.111}$$

$dI_{CO}/dT_J = 0.07I_{CO}$ as the reverse saturation current increases at a rate of approximately 7%/°C. Substituting the value of dP_G/dI_C [Eq. (4.103)] and the value of dI_{CO}/dT_J in Eq. (4.111), we get

$$[V_{CC} - 2I_C(R_C + R_E)](S_{I_{CO}})(0.07I_{CO}) < \frac{1}{\Theta} \tag{4.112}$$

From Eq. (4.112) we can infer that for small signal transistors the problem of thermal runaway is not so critical as these transistors have small value of collector current (I_C) and small value of stability factor ($S_{I_{CO}}$). However, power transistors have higher value of collector current (I_C) and stability factor and hence thermal management is a major problem in the case of power transistors. One of the thermal management techniques to increase the power handling capability of transistors is to make use of heat sinks. Design of heat sinks is discussed in detail in the chapter on power transistors.

EXAMPLE 4.12 *Figure 4.47 shows the circuit of a transformer-coupled power amplifier. Determine whether the circuit is thermally stable. If not, determine the junction to ambient thermal resistance ($\Theta_{J\text{-}A}$) required so that the transistor operates safely at an ambient temperature of 25°C. It is given that the transistor gain β at 25°C is 100, the leakage current I_{CO} at 25°C is 1 mA, the maximum junction operating temperature is 100°C, the base–emitter voltage of the transistor is 0.7 V.*

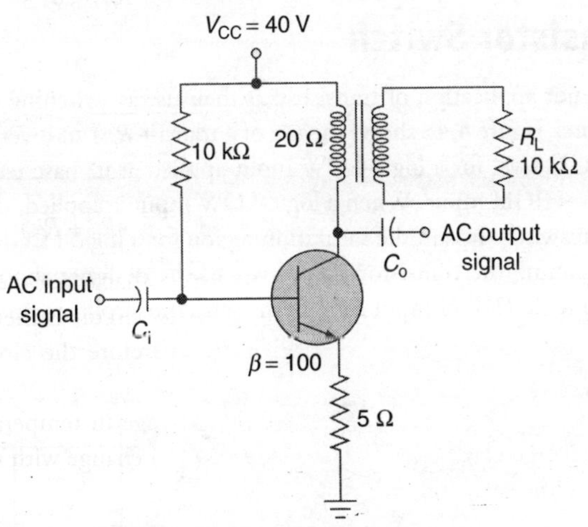

Figure 4.47 Example 4.12.

Solution

1. $I_C = \beta I_B + (\beta+1)I_{CO}$

$$= 100 \times I_B + 101 \times 1 \times 10^{-3}$$

$$= 100I_B + 0.101$$

2. Applying Kirchhoff's voltage law to the emitter–base loop, we get

$$40 - 10 \times 10^3 \times I_B - 0.7 - 5 \times I_E = 0$$

Subtituting $I_E = (\beta + 1)I_B = 101I_B$, we get $I_B = 3.74$ mA, $I_C = 374$ mA and $I_E \cong I_C = 374$ mA.

3. Applying Kirchhoff's voltage law to the collector–emitter loop, we get

$$40 - 20 \times I_C - V_{CE} - 5 \times I_E = 0$$

$$V_{CE} = 40 - 20 \times 374 \times 10^{-3} - 5 \times 374 \times 10^{-3} = 30.65$$

4. As $V_{CE} > V_{CC}/2$, therefore the circuit is not inherently thermally stable.
5. The quiescent power generated is given by

$$V_{CEQ} \times I_{CQ} = 30.65 \times 374 \times 10^{-3} = 11.46 \text{ W}$$

6. The power dissipation capability is given by $(T_J - T_A)/\Theta_{J\text{-}A}$.
7. For thermal stability $(100 - 25)/(\Theta_{J-A}) \geq 11.46$. Therefore, $(\Theta_{J-A}) \leq 6.54$°C/W.

   Infact, transformer-coupled transistor amplifiers are very much susceptible to thermal runaway as they have very small DC resistance in the collector circuit (transformer primary and the emitter resistor).

Answer: The circuit is not thermally stable. The maximum value of thermal resistance is 6.54°C/W.

4.8 Transistor Switch

Another major application of transistors is their use as switching devices in computers and other control applications. Figure 4.48 shows the use of a transistor as an inverting switch, that is the transistor output is at logic-HIGH level for a logic-LOW input applied at its base terminal and the output is at logic-LOW level for a logic-HIGH input. When a logic-LOW input is applied, the transistor is in the cut-off region and acts as an open switch. It is in the saturation region for a logic-HIGH input and acts as a closed switch.

While designing the transistor-based switch, the designer should ensure that the transistor is heavily saturated for a logic-HIGH input signal. The saturation collector current ($I_{C(sat)}$) is given by the equation

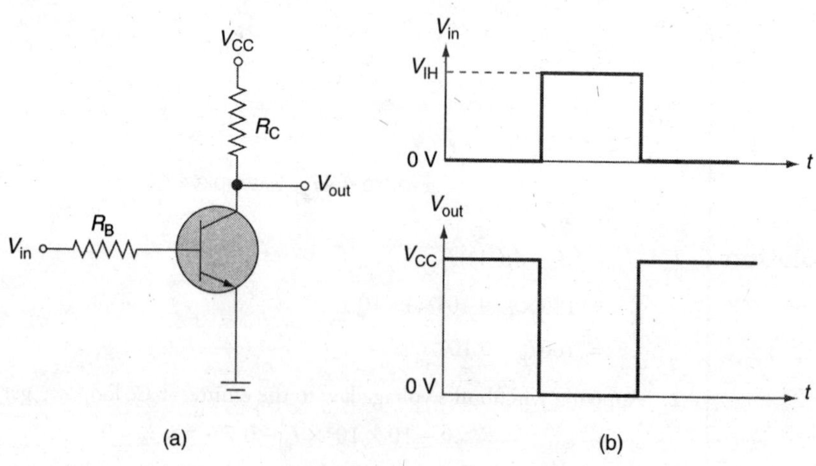

Figure 4.48 Transistor switch.

$$I_{C(sat)} = \frac{V_{CC}}{R_C} \tag{4.113}$$

The level of base current (I_B) in the active region just before the saturation region can be approximated by

$$I_{B(sat)} = \frac{I_{C(sat)}}{\beta}$$

The base current ($I_{B(max)}$) is generally kept to be 20–25% more than the value of $I_{B(sat)}$ so as to ensure that the transistor is in deep saturation. Therefore, the ratio of the collector current to the base current when the logic-HIGH input is applied is less than the transistor current gain (β). The minimum value of input voltage (V_{IH}) required to drive the transistor into deep saturation so that it acts as a closed switch is given by

$$V_{IH} = I_{B(max)} R_B + V_{BE} \tag{4.114}$$

The resistance between the emitter and the collector terminals when the transistor is in saturation is given by

$$R_{sat} = \frac{V_{CE(sat)}}{I_{C(sat)}} \tag{4.115}$$

The resistance offered by the transistor switch when in saturation is equal to R_{sat}. The value of R_{sat} is in the range of few ohms to few tens of ohms.

For input voltage equal to zero, the collector current (I_C) is equal to the leakage current (I_{CO}) which is negligible. Therefore the collector voltage is at the logic-HIGH level and the value of collector–emitter resistance is very high in the range of several hundreds of kilo-ohms to few mega-ohms. The circuit thus acts as an open circuit.

Transistor Switching Delays

Figure 4.49 shows the response of a transistor switch when an input pulse is applied to it. When the input voltage is 0 V, the transistor is in the cut-off region. It is in the saturation region when the input voltage is at

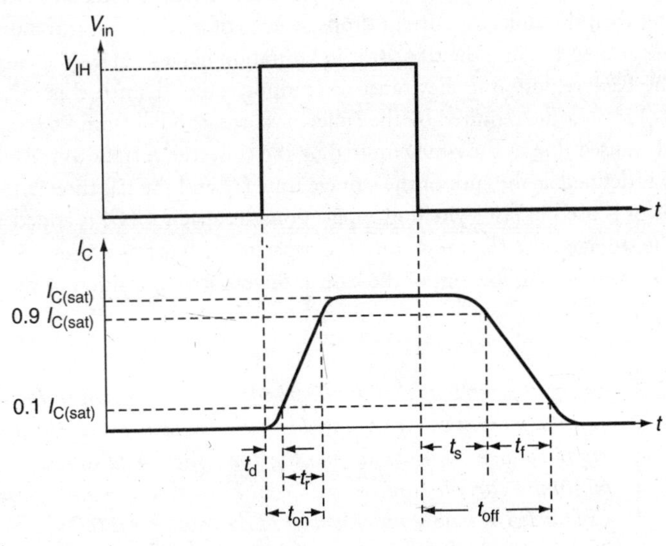

Figure 4.49 Transistor switching times.

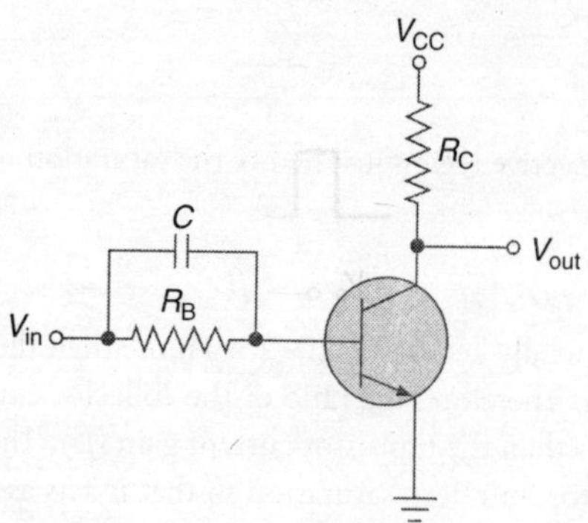

Figure 4.50 | Fast switching transistor circuit.

the voltage level V_{IH}. When the input voltage changes from 0 V to V_{IH}, the transistor does not immediately respond to the input signal and there is a time delay before the collector current reaches the saturation value. The time delay between the time the input pulse is applied to the time the collector current rises to 10% of the final value is called the *delay time* (t_d).

The time required for the collector current to rise from 10% to 90% of the final value is called the *rise time* (t_r). The total time ($t_d + t_r$) is known as the *turn-ON time* (t_{on}) of the transistor. Delay time (t_d) is contributed by three factors: First, the time required to charge the emitter-junction capacitance so that the transistor is brought from the cut-off to the active region; second, the time required to move the carriers from the base junction to the collector junction; third, the time required by the collector current to rise to 10% of its final value. Rise time (t_r) is due to the time taken by the collector current to traverse the active region.

When the input signal returns to 0 V, again there is a delay between the transition of the input waveform and the time when the collector current reduces to zero. The time interval between the input pulse transition to the time when the collector current drops to 90% of its value at saturation is called the *storage time* (t_s). Storage time delay is because the transistor in saturation has a saturation charge of excess minority carriers stored in the base region and the transistor cannot respond until this excess charge has been removed. *Fall time* (t_f) is the time required by the collector current to fall from 90% to 10% of the saturation level. Fall time is caused due to the time required by the collector current to traverse the active region. *Turn-OFF time* (t_{off}) is defined as the sum of the storage time (t_s) and the fall time (t_f).

When the transistor is used in fast switching applications, a capacitor (C) is added across the base resistor (R_B) to reduce the storage time (Figure 4.50). The capacitor will act as a short circuit when switching occurs and an impulse current will flow out of the base at the negative transition of the input pulse.

EXAMPLE 4.13 *An input pulse is applied to the transistor switch shown in Figure 4.51. What is the minimum input voltage required to make the LED glow? Also, find out the minimum input voltage required to put the transistor in saturation. It is given that the minimum current required by the LED to glow is 10 mA, voltage drop across the LED is 1.5 V, base–emitter voltage of the transistor is 0.7 V, collector–emitter voltage of the transistor in saturation is 0.5 V.*

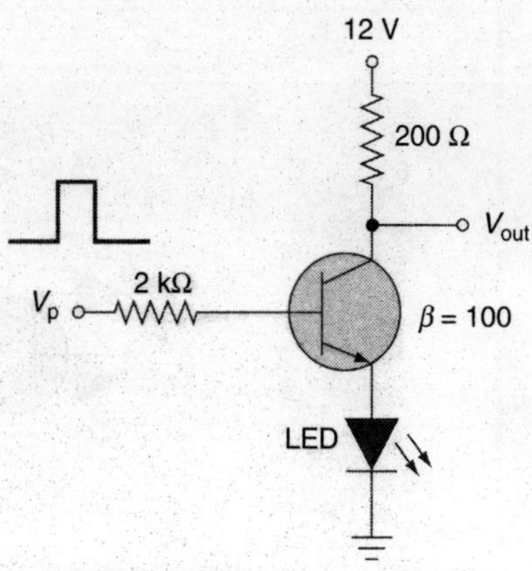

Figure 4.51 | Example 4.13.

Solution

1. The minimum current required to make the LED glow is 10 mA and the voltage drop across the LED is 1.5 V.
2. Therefore, the collector current required to make the LED glow is 10 mA. As β of the transistor is 100, therefore the base current (I_B) required is 100 μA.
3. Applying Kirchhoff's voltage law to the base–emitter loop, we get
$$V_P - 2 \times 10^3 \times 100 \times 10^{-6} - 0.7 - 1.5 = 0$$
$$V_P = 2.4 \text{ V}$$
4. Therefore, the minimum voltage required to make the LED glow is 2.4 V.
5. When the transistor is in saturation, $V_{CE(sat)} = 0.5$ V. Therefore, applying Kirchhoff's voltage law to the collector–emitter loop, we get
$$12 - 200 \times I_{C(sat)} - 0.5 - 1.5 = 0$$
$$I_{C(sat)} = 50 \text{ mA}$$
6. The value of $I_{B(sat)}$ corresponding to this value of $I_{C(sat)}$ is 500 μA.
7. The value of $I_{B(max)}$ is kept 1.25 times this value of $I_{B(sat)}$ to ensure that the transistor is in saturation. Therefore, $I_{B(max)} = 625$ μA.
8. Applying Kirchhoff's voltage law to the base emitter loop and solving for V_P, we get
$$V_P = 0.7 + 1.5 + 2 \times 10^3 \times 625 \times 10^{-6} = 3.45 \text{ V}$$
9. The input voltage required to put the transistor into saturation is 3.45 V.

Answer: The minimum voltage required to make the LED glow is 2.4 V. The input voltage required to put the transistor into saturation is 3.45 V.

EXAMPLE 4.14

A simple logic circuit is configured as shown in Figure 4.52(a). The input voltages V_3 and V_4 applied to the circuit are plotted in Figure 4.52(b). Draw the output waveform across resistor R_5. Assume $V_{CE(sat)} = 0$.

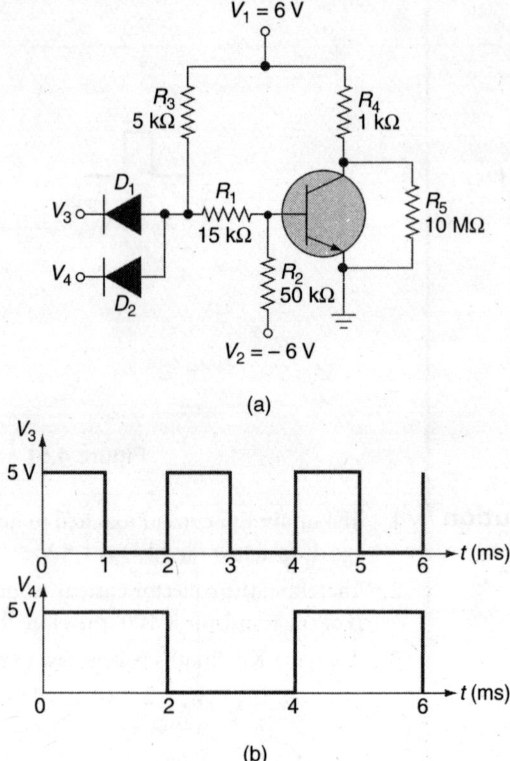

Figure 4.52 | Example 4.14.

Solution

1. When either or both of the inputs are low, then one or both of the diodes D_1 and D_2 are conducting. Therefore, the voltage at the R_1–R_3 node is 0.7 V. The transistor is not-conducting and the collector–emitter voltage is 6 V.
2. When both inputs are high, then both the diodes D_1 and D_2 are not conducting and the base voltage is determined by voltages V_1 and V_2 and resistors R_1, R_2 and R_3.
3. The base voltage can be determined using superposition theorem.
4. Assuming $V_1 = 0$ [Figure 4.53(a)], the voltage due to V_2 at base terminal is
$$V_{B2} = -(5+15)\times\frac{6}{5+15+50} = -20\times\frac{6}{70} = -1.7\text{ V}$$
5. Assuming $V_2 = 0$ [Figure 4.53(b)], the voltage due to V_1 at base terminal
$$V_{B1} = 50\times\frac{6}{5+15+50} = 50\times\frac{6}{70} = 4.3\text{ V}$$
6. Base voltage = 4.3 V – 1.7 V = 2.6 V.
7. This base voltage drives the transistor into saturation. As is given, the value of collector–emitter voltage when the transistor is in saturation is zero. The waveform across R_5 is the same as that of the collector–emitter voltage of the transistor (Figure 4.54).

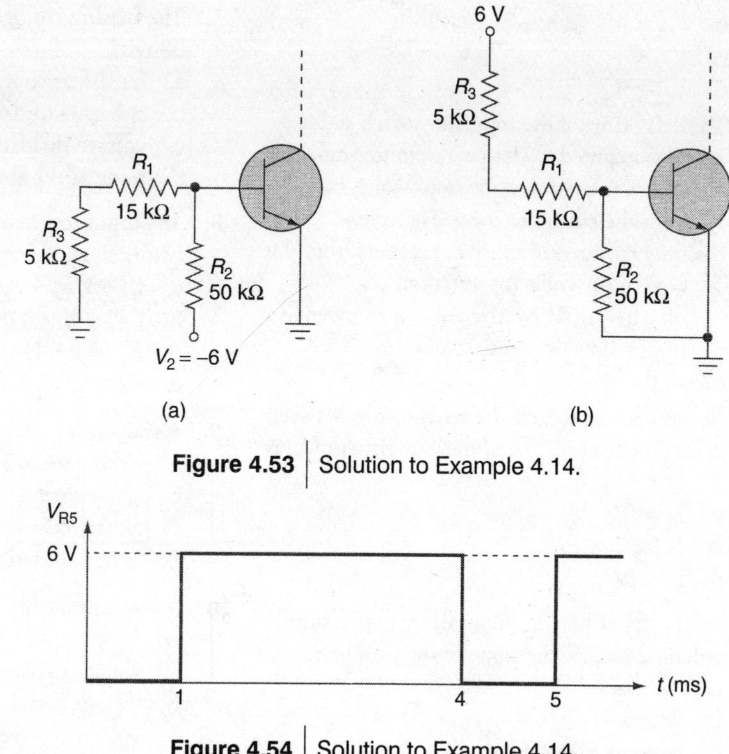

Figure 4.53 Solution to Example 4.14.

Figure 4.54 Solution to Example 4.14.

KEY TERMS

Collector-to-base-bias configuration
Compensation techniques
Emitter-bias configuration
Fixed-bias configuration
Operating point
Stability factor
Voltage-divider bias with emitter-bias configuration

OBJECTIVE-TYPE EXERCISES

Multiple-Choice Questions

1. In the fixed-bias circuit if the base resistor is shorted then
   a. the transistor may get damaged.
   b. the base voltage will be zero.
   c. the collector voltage will be equal to the supply voltage.
   d. the collector current is zero.
2. The common-collector bias and emitter-bias are examples of
   a. voltage-series feedback.
   b. voltage-series feedback and voltage-shunt feedback, respectively.
   c. voltage-series feedback and current-series feedback, respectively.
   d. current-series feedback and current-shunt feedback, respectively.
3. Which of the following conditions ensures that the transistor does not undergo thermal run-away?
   a. $V_{CE} = V_{CC}/2$

b. $V_{CE} < V_{CC}/2$
c. $V_{CE} < V_{CC}$
d. $V_{CE} > V_{CC}/2$

4. The delay time of the transistor switch is due to
   a. time required to charge the emitter-junction capacitance so that the transistor is brought from the cut-off to the active region.
   b. time required to move the carriers from the base to the collector junction.
   c. time required by the collector current to rise to 10% of its final value.
   d. all the above.
5. In a transistor switch the relationship between collector current (I_C) and the base current (I_B) is
   a. $I_C = I_B$
   b. $I_C = \beta I_B$
   c. $I_C > \beta I_B$
   d. $I_C < \beta I_B$
6. In the fixed-bias configuration if the supply voltage changes, the slope of the load line
   a. increases.
   b. decreases.
   c. remains the same.
   d. may increase or decrease.
7. The biasing configuration that offers least stability is
   a. fixed-bias configuration.
   b. collector-to-base-bias configuration.
   c. voltage-divider-bias configuration.
   d. none of the above.
8. The input resistance in case of emitter-bias circuit is equal to
   a. $(\beta + 1)R_B + R_E$
   b. $\beta R_B + (\beta + 1)R_E$
   c. $R_B + (\beta + 1)R_E$
   d. $R_B + R_E$
9. A transistor switch operates in
   a. either saturation or cut-off region.
   b. active region.
   c. either active or cut-off region.
   d. either saturation or active region.
10. In the emitter-bias circuit the voltage across the emitter resistance is equal to
   a. voltage between the emitter and collector.
   b. voltage between the emitter and ground.
   c. voltage between the collector and base.
   d. voltage between the collector and ground.

Match the Following

Choose the correct one from among the alternatives A, B, C, D after matching an item from Group 1 with the most appropriate item in Group 2.

Group 1	Group 2
1: Emitter bias	P: operating point
2: Transistor switch	Q: negative feedback
3: Thermal runaway	R: positive feedback
4: Active region	S: forward-biased base–emitter junction and reverse-biased collector–emitter junction
	T: cut-off and saturation
	U: zero V_{BE} and V_{CE}

(A) 1-Q, 2-T, 3-P, 4-S
(B) 1-R, 2-T, 3-R, 4-Q
(C) 1-U, 2-P, 3-S, 4-R
(D) 1-T, 2-Q, 3-P, 4-S

REVIEW QUESTIONS

1. With the help of common-emitter amplifier configuration, explain the criteria for selection of a suitable operating point and the factors affecting its stability.

2. Derive the mathematical expression to prove that the operating point in voltage-divider-bias configuration is independent of transistor gain β.
3. Draw the circuit for collector-to-base-bias configuration and derive the value of stability factors $S_{I_{CO}}$, S_β and $S_{V_{BE}}$ for the circuit.
4. Explain the operation of a transistor switch. What are the steps to be followed to design a transistor switch?
5. Derive the expressions for the stability factor ($S_{I_{CO}}$) for
   a. fixed-bias configuration;
   b. self-bias configuration;
   c. voltage-divider-bias configuration.
6. What is the drawback of emitter-bias configuration? How is the drawback removed in the voltage-divider bias with emitter-bias configuration?
7. Draw the following circuits using PNP transistors and derive the expressions for the operating point for each of the cases:
   a. fixed-bias configuration;
   b. voltage-divider-bias configuration;
   c. collector-to-base-bias configuration.
8. When is a transistor amplifier circuit inherently stable against thermal runaway? Support the answer with relevant mathematical expressions.
9. Give reasons for the following:
   a. Why is bias compensation required?
   b. Power transistors are more prone to thermal runaway as compared to small signal transistors?
   c. Why is fixed-bias circuit not commonly used?
   d. Why is the operating point chosen near the center of the active region of the transistor characteristics in a transistor amplifier?
10. Define the following terms
    a. power derating;
    b. thermal resistance of a transistor;
    c. turn-ON time of a transistor switch;
    d. bias compensation.

PROBLEMS

1. Figures 4.55(a) and (b) show a fixed-bias circuit and the output characteristics of the transistor used in the circuit (assume base–emitter voltage of transistor = 0.7 V). Determine:
   a. DC load line;
   b. the value of resistor R_B for base current of 40 μA;
   c. the operating point (I_C, V_{CE});
   d. the value of transistor gain β.

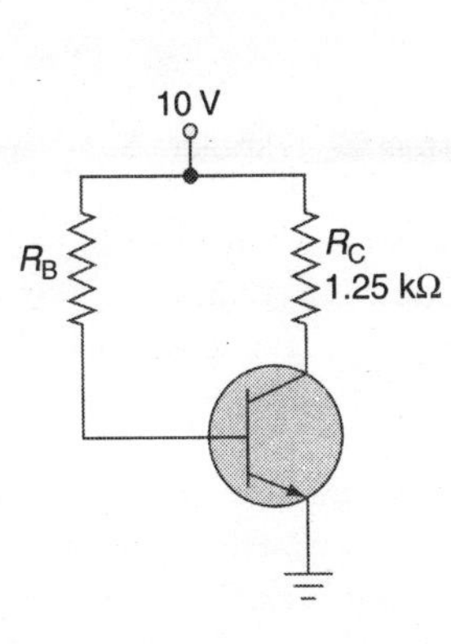

(a)

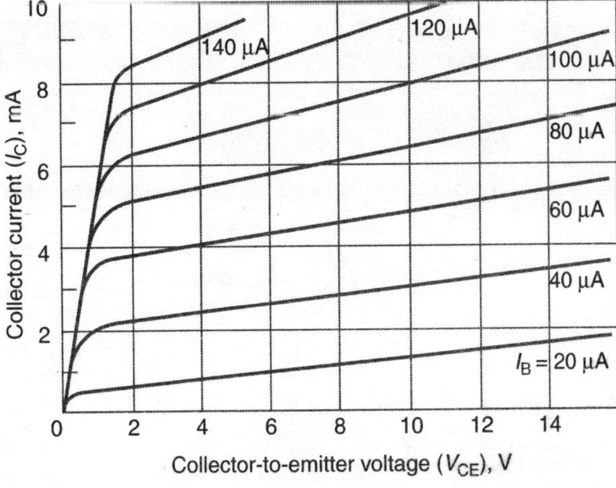

(b)

Figure 4.55 | Problem 1.

2. Find the operating point of the emitter-bias circuit shown in Figure 4.56. Design a voltage-divider bias with emitter-bias circuit having the same operating point (assume base–emitter voltage of transistor = 0.7 V).

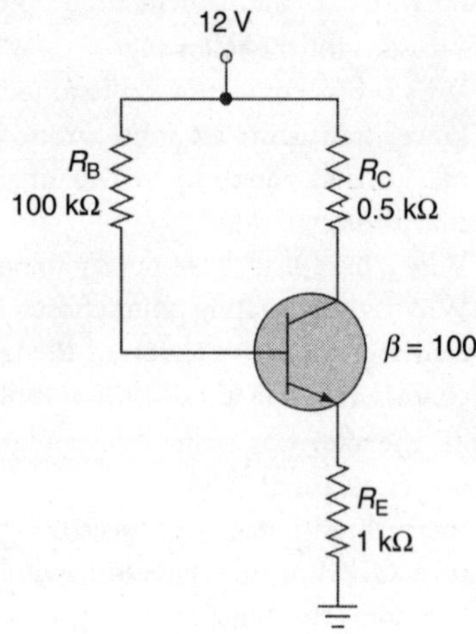

Figure 4.56 Problem 2.

3. Figure 4.57 shows a circuit using a PNP transistor. Find the value of V_{out}. Assume base–emitter voltage of transistor = 0.7 V.

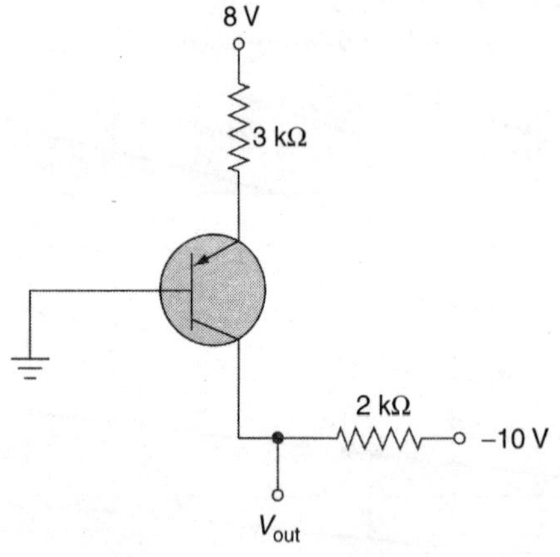

Figure 4.57 Problem 3.

4. Draw the DC equivalent of the circuit shown in Figure 4.58. Also find the collector voltage of transistors Q_1 and Q_2? Assume V_{BEQ1} = V_{BEQ2} = 0.7 V.

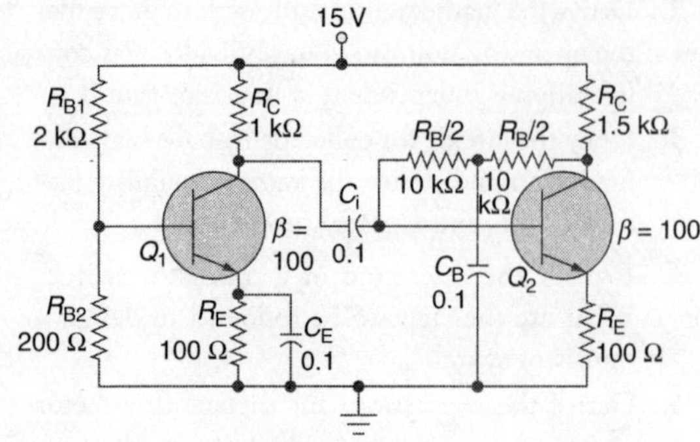

Figure 4.58 Problem 4.

5. For the network in Figure 4.59, find the value of $S_{I_{CO}}$, $S_{V_{BE}}$ and S_β and the total change in collector current for a temperature change of 25°C to +100°C. It is given that at 25°C: I_{CO} = 0.2 nA, β = 50 and V_{BE} = 0.7 V; and at 100°C: I_{CO} = 25 nA, β = 80 and V_{BE} = 0.5 V.

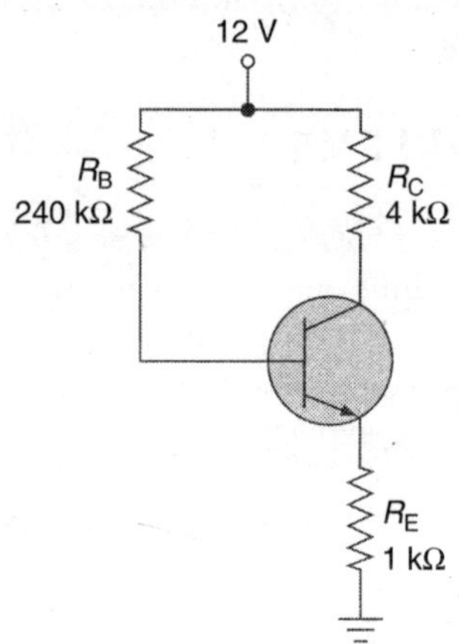

Figure 4.59 Problem 5.

6. Design an emitter-bias circuit with the following specifications: I_C = 10 mA, V_{CE} = 4 V, V_{CC} = 15 V, R_C/R_E = 10. It is given that β is 130 and V_{BE} is 0.7 V.

7. Figure 4.60 shows the transistor-based inverter circuit with the desired output waveform for the given input waveform. Find the value of V_{CC}, R_C and R_B given that β = 80, $I_{C(sat)}$ = 10 mA, the output voltage V_{out} when the transistor is off is 12 V, V_{BE} = 0.7 V.

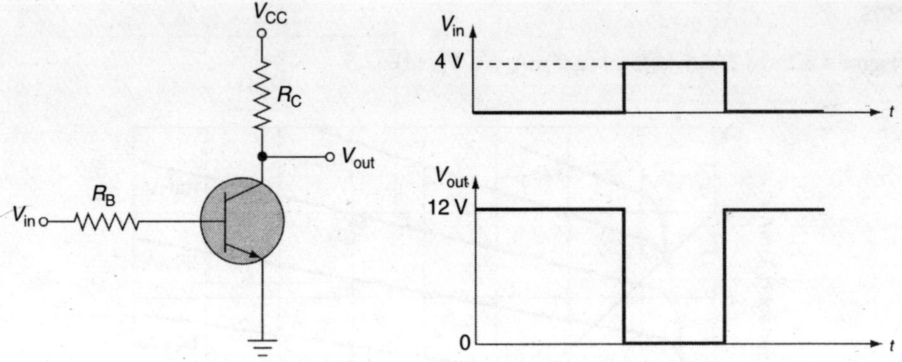

Figure 4.60 | Problem 7.

8. (a) Refer to Figure 4.61. Calculate the value of R_B if $V_{CE} = 5$ V.

   (b) For $R_B = 50$ kΩ, determine the value of V_{CEQ}. Also, determine whether the circuit is inherently thermally stable. It is given that the base–emitter voltage of the transistor is 0.7 V.

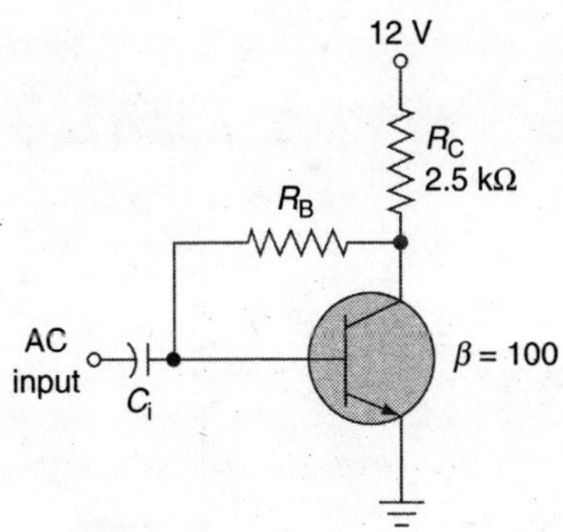

Figure 4.61 | Problem 8.

ANSWERS

Multiple-Choice Questions

1. (a)
2. (c)
3. (b)
4. (d)
5. (d)
6. (c)
7. (a)
8. (c)
9. (a)
10. (b)

Match the Following

Answer (A).

Problems

1. (a) Figure 4.62; (b) 232.5 kΩ; (c) (2.7 mA, 6.6 V); (d) 67.5

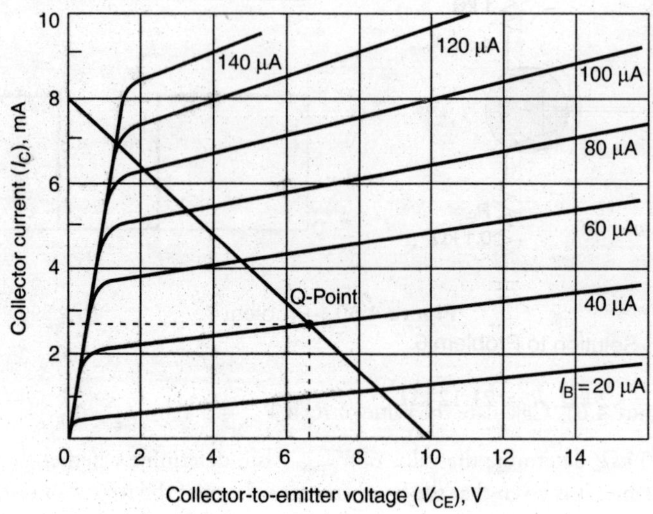

Figure 4.62 Solution to part (a) of Problem 1.

2. (5.62 mA, 3.57 V); Figure 4.63

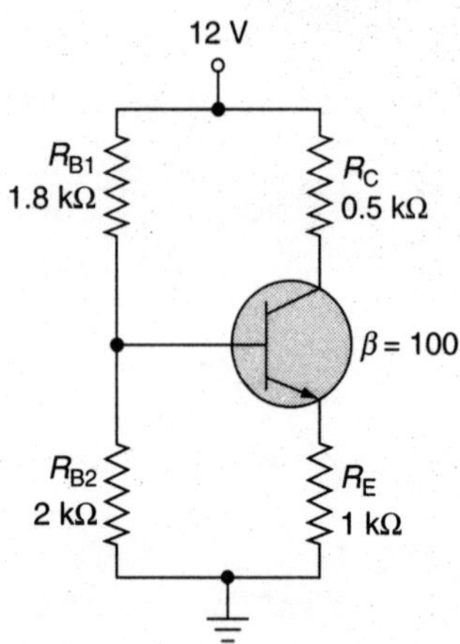

Figure 4.63 Solution to Problem 2.

3. −5.14 V

4. Figure 4.64; V_{CQ1} = 8.58 V; V_{CQ2} = 3.07 V

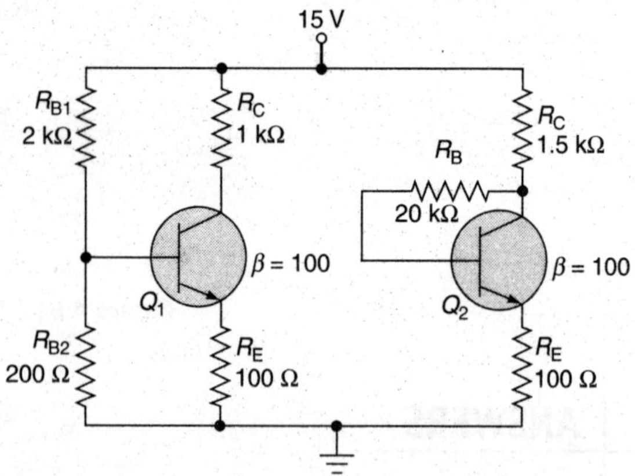

Figure 4.64 Solution to Problem 4.

5. $S_{I_{CO}} = 42.24$, $S_{V_{BE}} = -0.17 \times 10^{-3}$, $S_\beta = 2.92 \times 10^{-5}$, $\Delta I_C = 0.911$ mA

6.

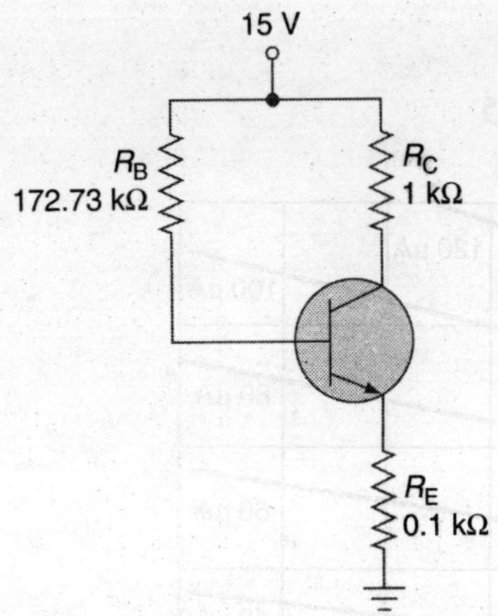

Figure 4.65 Solution to Problem 6.

7. $V_{CC} = 12$ V, $R_C = 1.2$ kΩ, $R_B = 21.12$ kΩ

8. (a) 153.57 kΩ, (b) 2.6 V; the circuit is thermally stable

CHAPTER 5

Field Effect Transistors

Learning Objectives

After completing this chapter, you will learn the following:

- Comparison between FETs and BJTs.
- Types of FETs: JFETs and MOSFETs.
- Construction and operation of JFETs.
- Construction and operation of MOSFETs.
- Comparison between JFETs and MOSFETs.
- FET biasing configurations: common-gate, common-source (fixed-bias, self-bias, voltage-divider-bias and feedback-bias configurations) and common-drain configurations.
- Handling and testing of FET devices.
- Introduction to VMOS, CMOS and IGBT devices.

Field effect transistors (FETs) are three-terminal semiconductor devices where the conduction path is controlled by an electric field established by the carriers present in the device. The concept of FETs predates that of bipolar junction transistors (BJTs) but they were physically implemented after BJTs due to limitations of semiconductor technology. FETs can be classified into two types, namely, the junction FETs (JFET) and metal-oxide-semiconductor FETs (MOSFET) depending upon their construction and mode of operation. MOSFETs are further classified as enhancement MOSFETs and depletion MOSFETs. The focus in this chapter is FETs. The topics covered include comparison between FETs and BJTs, construction and operation of JFETs and MOSFETs, followed by commonly used biasing circuits for both types of devices. Testing and handling FET devices is also covered in the chapter. The chapter concludes with a brief description of vertical MOS (VMOS), complementary MOS (CMOS) and insulated gate bipolar transistors (IGBT).

5.1 Bipolar Junction Transistors versus Field Effect Transistors

Both BJTs and FETs are semiconductor devices. The major difference between the two devices is that BJTs are current-controlled devices whereas FETs are voltage-controlled devices. In a BJT, the collector current (I_C) is a direct function of the base current (I_B) whereas in an FET, the drain current (I_D) depends upon the gate-source voltage (V_{GS}). In other words, in a BJT the output current is controlled by the input current whereas in an FET it is controlled by the input voltage.

Another important difference between the two devices is that BJTs are bipolar devices whereas FETs are unipolar devices. In other words, in a BJT both electrons and holes contribute to the flow of current whereas in an FET either holes or electrons contribute to the current. In an N-channel FET electrons are the current carriers whereas in a p-channel FET holes are the current carriers.

The input impedance of FET devices is very high (of the order of several hundred mega-ohms) as compared to that of BJT transistor configurations (varying from hundred ohms to less than 1 MΩ). Input impedance is a very important characteristic parameter in the design of linear AC amplifiers. In addition, FET devices, in general, are more temperature stable and smaller in construction as compared to BJTs. Owing to their smaller size, FETs are extensively used in the fabrication of integrated circuits. However, the gain of an FET-based amplifier is smaller as compared to a BJT amplifier, that is, FET amplifiers have poorer sensitivity to changes in the input signal. Also FETs are more sensitive to handling than BJTs.

5.2 Junction Field Effect Transistors

Junction FET (JFET) is the simplest of the FETs. It is a three-terminal device where the voltage applied at one terminal controls the current through the other two terminals. JFETs comprise a semiconductor channel embedded into semiconductor layers of opposite polarity. Depending upon whether the semiconductor channel is an N-type semiconductor or a P-type semiconductor, JFETs are classified as N-channel or P-channel JFETs, respectively.

Construction and Principle of Operation

Figures 5.1(a) and (b) show the cross-sectional view of N-channel and P-channel JFETs, respectively. As we can see from the figures, in an N-channel JFET, an N-type semiconductor material forms a channel between embedded layers of P-type material whereas in a P-channel JFET, a P-type semiconductor forms a channel between the embedded layers of N-type material. Therefore, two P–N junctions are formed between the semiconductor channel and the embedded semiconductor layers. Ohmic contacts are made at the top and bottom of the channel and are referred to as the drain (D) and the source (S) terminals, respectively. The channel behaves as a resistive element between its drain and source terminals. In an N-channel JFET, both the embedded P-type layers are connected together and form the gate (G) terminal. Similarly in a P-channel JFET, the gate terminal is formed by connecting the two N-type embedded layers. Figures 5.2(a) and (b) show the circuit symbols for the N-channel and P-channel JFETs, respectively.

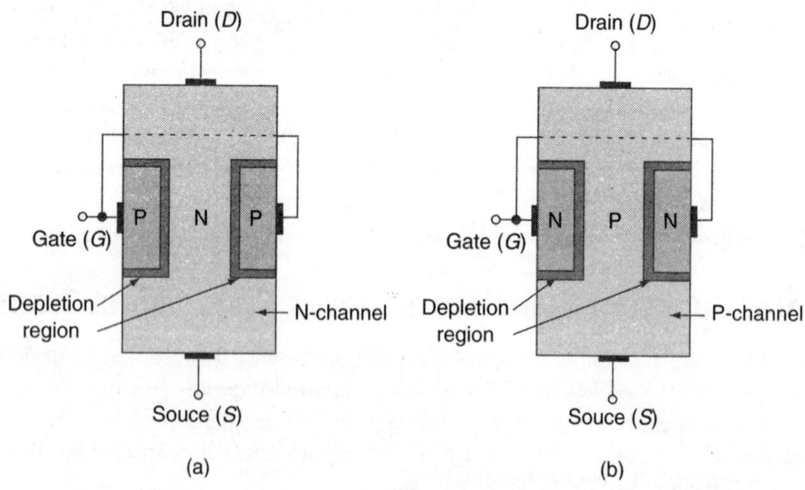

Figure 5.1 Cross-section of (a) an N-channel JFET; (b) a P-channel JFET.

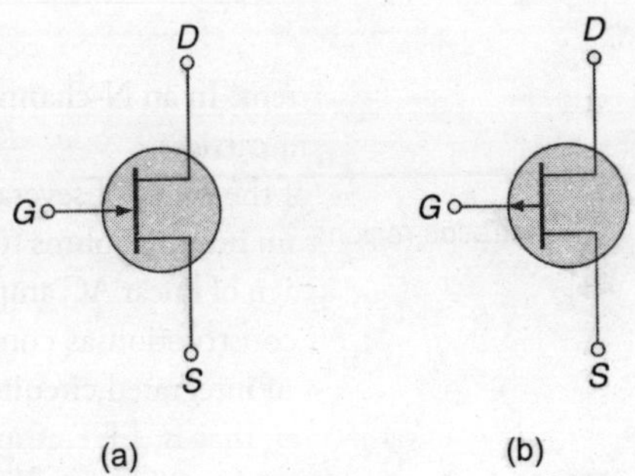

Figure 5.2 | Circuit symbol of (a) an N-channel JFET; (b) a P-channel JFET.

In the absence of any externally applied potential, both the P–N junctions are open circuit and a small depletion region is formed at each of the junctions as shown in Figure 5.1. The externally applied potential between gate and source terminals controls the flow of drain current for a given potential between the drain and source terminals. The operation of JFET devices is explained in the subsequent sections.

Characteristic Curves

In this section, the principle of operation of an N-channel JFET is explained. The operation of a P-channel JFET is similar to that of an N-channel JFET with the polarities of voltages and direction of currents reversed. Let us consider the situation when a positive drain-source voltage (V_{DS}) is applied to the JFET with gate terminal shorted to the source terminal ($V_{GS} = 0$).

Figure 5.3(a) shows the circuit connection. When the drain-source voltage is applied, the electrons in the N-channel are attracted to the drain-terminal establishing the flow of drain current (I_D) as shown in Figure 5.3(b). The value of I_D is determined by the value of the applied V_{DS} and the resistance of the N-channel between the drain and the source terminals. Owing to the flow of I_D, there is a uniform voltage drop across the

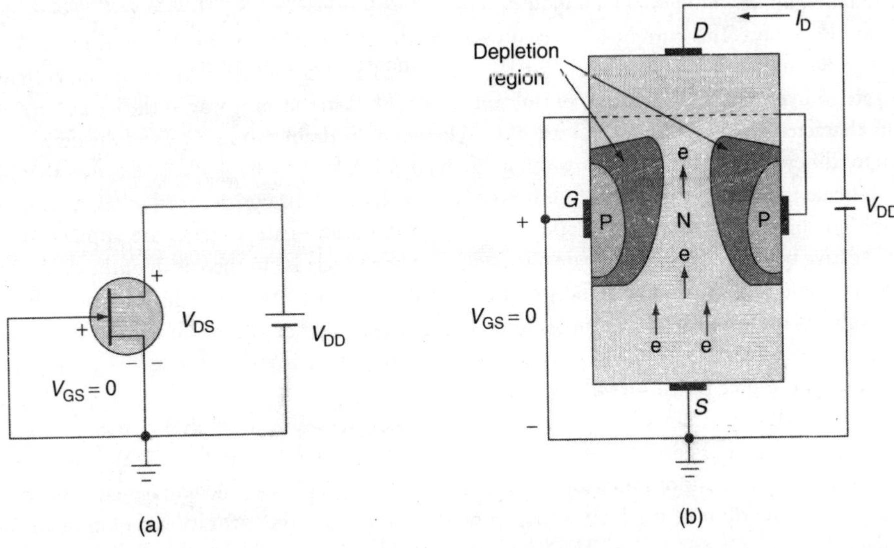

Figure 5.3 | N-channel JFET with $V_{GS} = 0$ and positive value of V_{DS}.

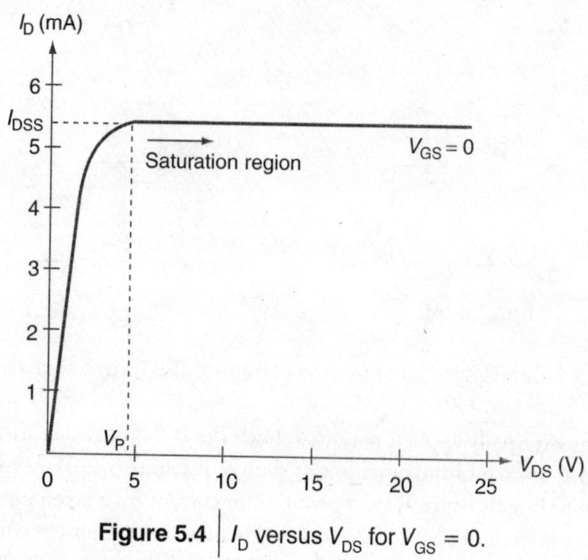

Figure 5.4 I_D versus V_{DS} for $V_{GS} = 0$.

channel resistance, which reverse biases the two P–N junctions. This results in increase in the width of the depletion region. It may be mentioned here that the depletion region is wider near the drain-region than the source-region. This is because I_D and the channel resistance establish more reverse-bias voltage at the P–N junction near the drain-region than near the source-region.

I_D increases linearly with increase in V_{DS} till the V_{DS} reaches a value where the saturation effect sets in. This is evident from Figure 5.4 which shows the relationship between I_D and V_{DS} for zero V_{GS} ($V_{GS} = 0$). The value of V_{DS} where the saturation effect sets in is referred to as the pinch-off voltage (V_P). When V_{DS} reaches V_P, the value of I_D does not change with further increase in the value of V_{DS}. This condition is referred to as the pinch-off condition. This happens because the width of the depletion regions of the P–N junctions has increased significantly near the drain-region resulting in reduction of the channel width (Figure 5.5). Therefore, I_D essentially remains constant for $V_{DS} > V_P$. This current is referred to as the drain-to-source current for short circuit connection between gate and source (I_{DSS}). In nutshell, for $V_{DS} > V_P$, JFET has characteristics of a constant current source.

The gate-source voltage (V_{GS}) is the control voltage for JFETs in the same way as the base current (I_B) is for BJTs. The characteristic curves for a JFET are plotted between the drain current (I_D) and the drain-source voltage (V_{DS}) for different values of V_{GS}. In case of an N-channel JFET, the voltage V_{GS} is negative, that is, the gate terminal is made more negative than the source terminal. Voltage V_{GS} is positive for P-channel JFETs.

Figure 5.6 shows the circuit connection when both drain and gate voltages are applied to the JFET. When a negative bias is applied to the gate terminal, there is an increase in the width of the depletion region. Therefore, the pinch-off phenomenon occurs at lower values of V_{DS}. Also, the value of saturation drain current decreases. As the value of V_{GS} becomes more negative the value of saturation current decreases further. The drain current becomes zero for V_{GS} equal to $-V_P$. This voltage is referred to as the gate-source cut-off voltage or the gate-source pinch-off voltage ($V_{GS(off)}$).

In fact, the value of drain-source pinch-off voltages decreases in a parabolic manner with the V_{GS} becoming more negative. Figure 5.7 shows the output characteristic curves for the N-channel JFET. The region to the left of the locus of pinch-off voltages is the Ohmic region or the voltage-controlled resistance region. Region to the right of the locus of the pinch-off voltages is the saturation region or the constant-current region. In the Ohmic region, JFET acts as a variable resistor whose resistance is controlled by the applied gate-source voltage.

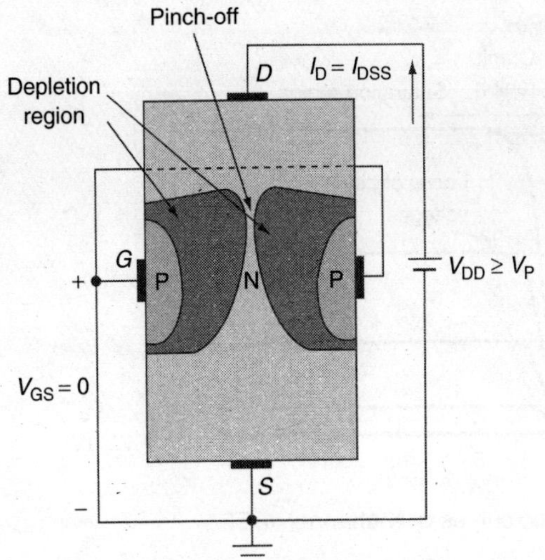

Figure 5.5 N-channel JFET with $V_{GS} = 0$ and $V_{DS} \geq V_P$.

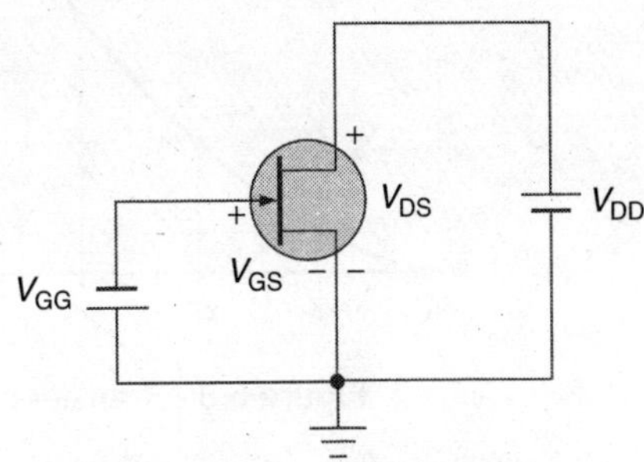

Figure 5.6 N-channel JFET biasing circuit.

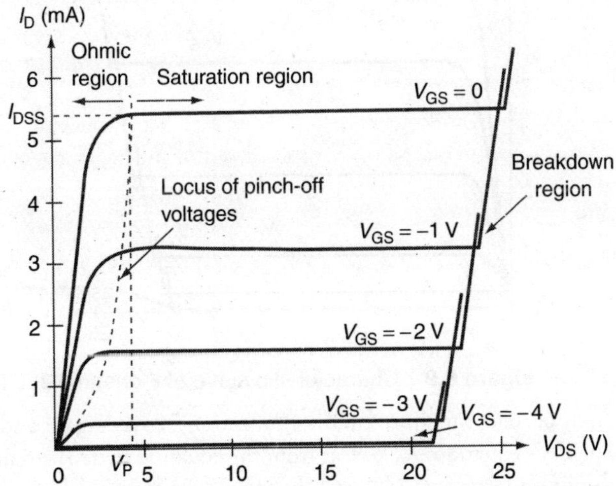

Figure 5.7 Output characteristic curves of an N-channel JFET.

The drain resistance (r_d) in the saturation region is given by Eq. (5.1)

$$r_d = \frac{r_o}{(1 - V_{GS} / V_p)^2} \tag{5.1}$$

where r_o is the resistance at $V_{GS} = 0$; r_d is the resistance at a particular value of V_{GS}; V_P is the pinch-off voltage.

The relationship between the output current I_D in the saturation region for a given value of input V_{GS} is given by

$$I_D = I_{DSS}\left(1 - \frac{V_{GS}}{V_P}\right)^2 \tag{5.2}$$

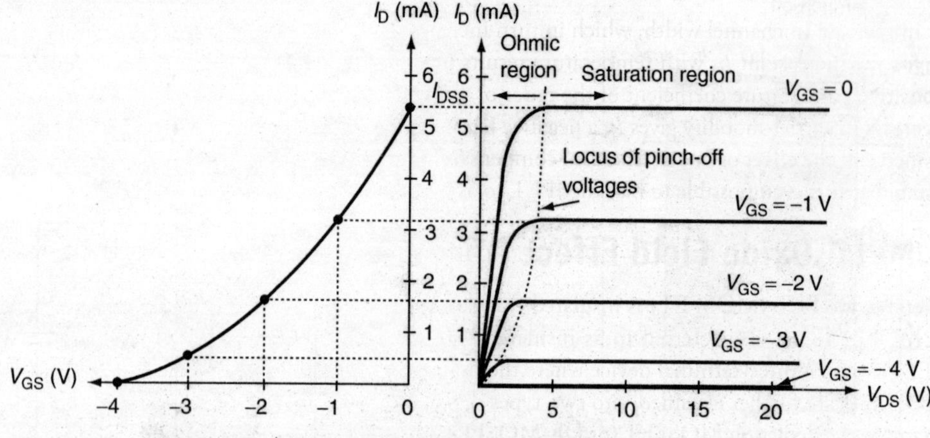

Figure 5.8 Transfer characteristic curves of N-channel JFET.

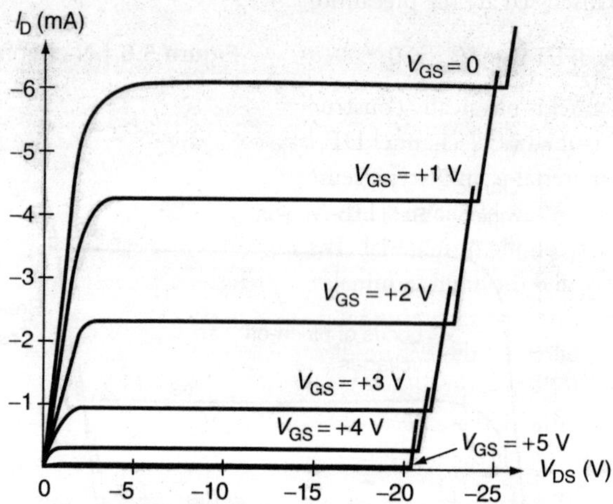

Figure 5.9 Characteristic curve of P-channel JFET.

where I_{DSS} is the drain current for short circuit connection between gate and source. This expression is referred to as the Shockley's equation. As is clear from the equation there is a non-linear square law relationship between the output drain current (I_D) and the input gate-source voltage (V_{GS}) as opposed to a linear relation between the output collector current (I_C) and the input base current (I_B) in case of BJTs. Because of the square law characteristics, JFETs are very useful devices in radio tuners and TV receivers.

The transfer characteristics of an FET device is a plot between I_D and V_{GS} and can be plotted using Shockley's equation or using the output characteristic curves. Figure 5.8 shows how we can obtain the transfer characteristics curves using the output characteristics curves.

As mentioned before, P-channel JFETs behave in the same manner as the N-channel JFETs with the direction of currents and polarities of voltages reversed. Figure 5.9 shows the output characteristic curves for P-channel JFETs.

Effect of Temperature on JFET Parameters

JFETs offer better thermal stability as compared to BJTs. Increase in JFET temperature results in decrease in the depletion region width and decrease in the carrier mobility. Decrease in the width of depletion region results in increase in channel width, which in turn increases in I_D. This results in positive temperature coefficient for I_D. Increase in I_D with temperature results in increase in $V_{GS(off)}$ with temperature. $V_{GS(off)}$ also has a positive temperature coefficient of the order of 2.2 mV/°C.

Decrease in carrier mobility gives I_D a negative temperature coefficient. Since both the mechanisms occur simultaneously, the effect of one mechanism compensates for the other. Therefore, JFETs offer better temperature stability. It is even possible to bias the JFET so as to establish zero temperature coefficient.

5.3 Metal Oxide Field Effect Transistors

Metal oxide FET (MOSFET) is insulated from the semiconductor channel by a very thin oxide layer. MOSFETs are also referred to as insulated gate field effect transistors (IGFETs). Like a JFET, a MOSFET is also a three-terminal device where the drain current is controlled by the applied gate voltage.

MOSFETs are further classified into two types depending upon their construction and mode of operation, namely, the depletion MOSFET (or DE-MOSFET) and the enhancement MOSFET (or E-MOSFET). In this section, we discuss the construction, principle of operation and characteristic parameters of both the types of MOSFETs. Also discussed are the precautions to be taken while handling MOSFETs.

Depletion MOSFETs

In a DE-MOSFET, a channel is physically constructed between the drain and the source terminals. DE-MOSFETs are further classified as N-channel DE-MOSFETs and P-channel DE-MOSFETs depending on whether the channel material is an N-type semiconductor or a P-type semiconductor.

The cross-sectional view of an N-channel DE-MOSFET is shown in Figure 5.10. It comprises a substrate made of a P-type semiconductor material. Two N+ type regions linked by an N-channel are formed on the substrate. The source and the drain terminals are formed by connecting metal contacts to the two N+ regions as shown in Figure 5.10. The gate terminal is connected to the insulating silicon dioxide (SiO_2) layer on top of the N-channel. Therefore, there is no direct electrical connection between the gate terminal and the channel of a DE-MOSFET. (In case of E-MOSFETs also, there is no direct electrical connection between the gate terminal and the channel.) There is a capacitance that exists between the gate and the channel as the metal gate contact and the channel act as walls of a parallel plate capacitor and the SiO_2 layer forms the dielectric. Hence the input impedance of a DE-MOSFET is very high of the order of 10^{10}–10^{15} Ω.

The construction of a P-channel DE-MOSFET (Figure 5.11) is similar to that of an N-channel DE-MOSFET with the difference being that the substrate is an N-type semiconductor while the channel is a P-type material. Figures 5.12(a) and (b) show the circuit symbols for N-channel and P-channel DE-MOSFETs, respectively.

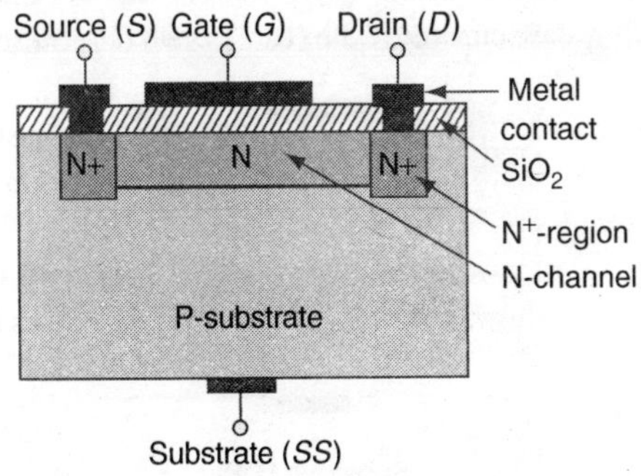

Figure 5.10 Cross-section of an N-channel DE-MOSFET.

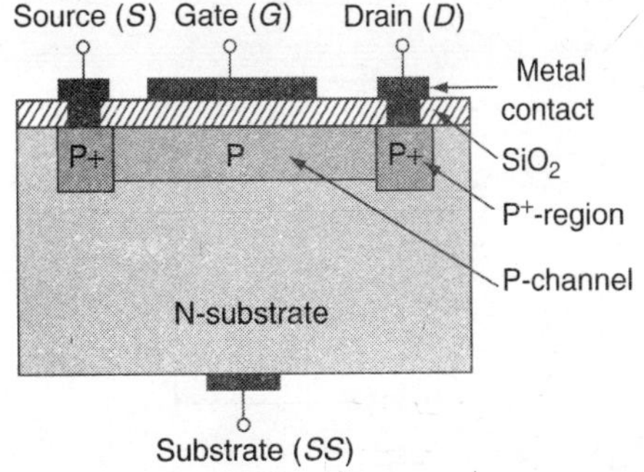

Figure 5.11 Cross-section of a P-channel DE-MOSFET.

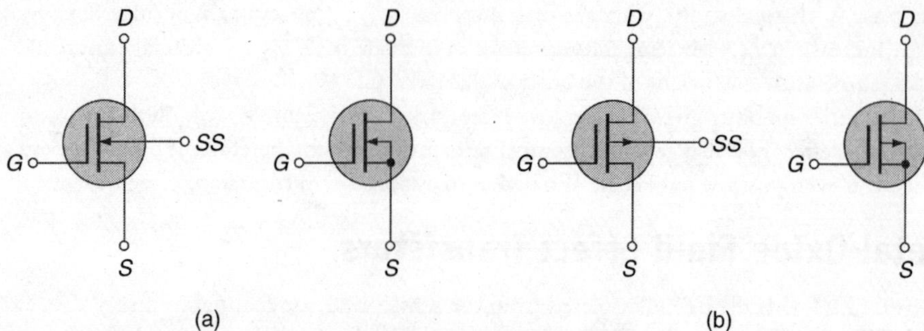

Figure 5.12 Circuit symbol of (a) an N-channel DE-MOSFET; (b) a P-channel DE-MOSFET.

Let us now see how the N-channel DE-MOSFET operates. When the gate and the source terminals are shorted, that is, the voltage $V_{GS} = 0$ and a positive voltage is applied between the drain and the source terminals, that is, voltage V_{DS} is positive (Figure 5.13), there is a flow of current in the N-channel as the electrons are attracted by positive potential at the drain terminal. The current increases with increase in V_{DS} and after a certain value of V_{DS} it becomes constant. This current is represented as I_{DSS} and is similar to that established in a JFET with $V_{GS} = 0$. When the gate terminal is at a negative potential as compared to the source terminal, electrons in the N-channel are repelled by this negative potential towards the P-type substrate. Also, the holes in the P-type substrate are attracted towards the gate. This results in recombination of holes and electrons and there is reduction in the number of free electrons in the N-channel (Figure 5.14). The higher the negative potential, more is the rate of recombination and less the number of free electrons in the channel. Therefore the drain current decreases with increase in the value of the negative gate-source potential.

For positive values of gate-source voltage, electrons (minority carriers) in the P-type substrate are attracted into the channel and establish new carriers through the collisions between accelerating particles. Thus the drain current increases rapidly with increase in the positive value of gate-source voltage. As the application of positive gate-source voltage increases the value of drain current, the region of positive gate-source voltages is referred to as the enhancement region. The region for zero and negative values of gate-source voltage is referred to as the depletion region. It may be mentioned here that Shockley's equation as defined for JFETs is applicable for DE-MOSFETs also in both the depletion and the enhancement regions. Figure 5.15 shows the output characteristic curves for an N-channel DE-MOSFET.

The transfer characteristics for DE-MOSFET can be plotted in a similar fashion for that of a JFET. Figure 5.16 shows the transfer characteristics for an N-channel DE-MOSFET.

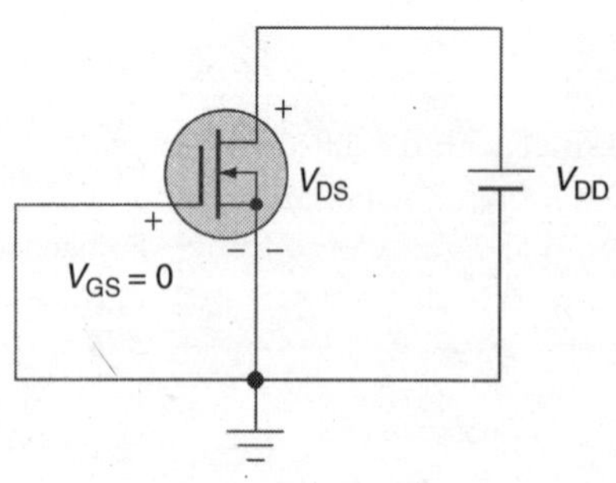

Figure 5.13 Circuit connection of N-channel DE-MOSFET.

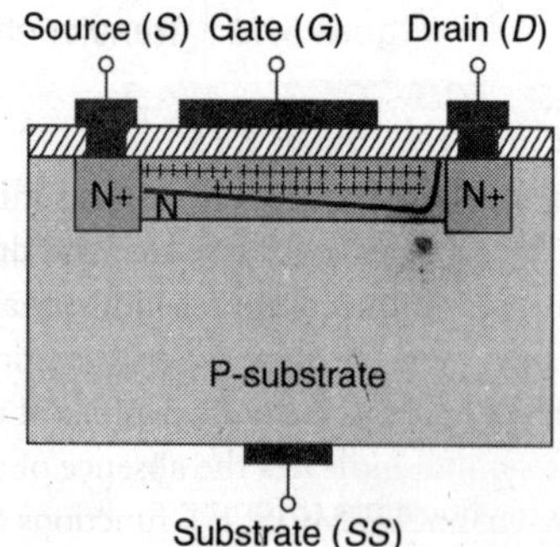

Figure 5.14 N-channel DE-MOSFET.

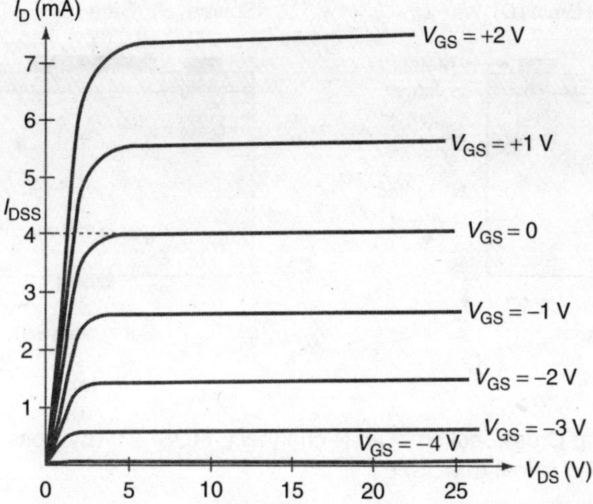

Figure 5.15 Output characteristic curves of N-channel DE-MOSFET.

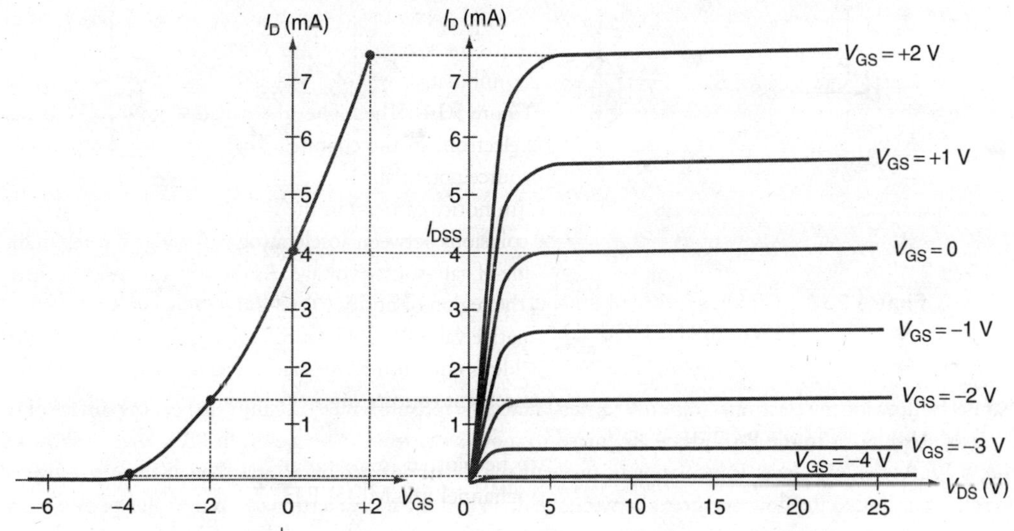

Figure 5.16 Transfer characteristic curves of N-channel DE-MOSFET.

Enhancement MOSFETs

The construction of an E-MOSFET is similar to that of a DE-MOSFET with the difference that there is no physical channel between the source and drain terminals in the E-MOSFET. The invention of E-MOSFETs has revolutionized the computer industry and they are extensively used in digital electronics and computers. Figures 5.17(a) and (b) show the cross-section of N-channel and P-channel E-MOSFETs, respectively. Figures 5.18(a) and (b) show the circuit symbols of the N-channel and P-channel MOSFETs, respectively. The broken line in the symbol indicates the absence of a channel.

The N-channel E-MOSFET functions as follows. When the gate-source voltage is zero and some positive drain-source voltage is applied there is no drain current as there is no channel available for flow of drain current. E-MOSFETs are also normally called OFF MOSFETs as they do not conduct when $V_{GS} = 0$. The drain current flows only when a positive voltage is applied to the gate terminal with respect to the source terminal as this induces

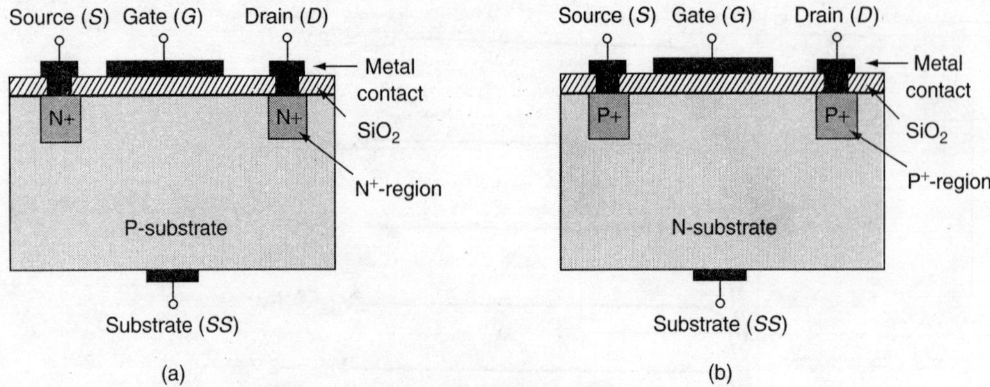

Figure 5.17 (a) Cross-section of an N-channel E-MOSFET; (b) cross-section of a P-channel E-MOSFET.

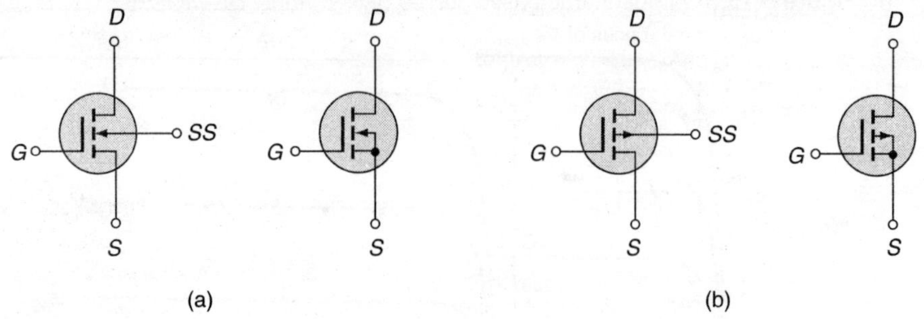

Figure 5.18 Circuit symbol of an N-channel E-MOSFET; (b) circuit symbol of a P-channel E-MOSFET.

a channel by drawing the electrons (minority carriers) in the P-type substrate to accumulate near the surface of the SiO_2 layer. Also, holes in the P-substrate are forced to move away from the edge of the SiO_2 layer as shown in Figure 5.19. As the SiO_2 layer is insulating, it prevents the electrons from being absorbed at the gate terminal. These electrons lead to the flow of current between the drain and the source terminals. As the value of gate-source voltage is increased, more and more electrons accumulate leading to an enhanced flow of drain current. The level of gate-source voltage that leads to significant flow of drain current is referred to as threshold voltage and is denoted by V_T. For a fixed gate-source voltage and increasing the level of drain-source voltage leads to an initial increase in the drain current which eventually saturates due to the reduction in the gate-drain voltage (V_{GD}) with increase in the drain-source voltage (V_{DS}). Reduction in the gate-drain voltage reduces the attractive forces for the free carriers in the induced channel near the drain region, resulting in the reduction of effective channel width near the drain region. This effect is referred to as the pinching effect. Pinching effect refers to the reduction in the width of the channel near the drain region with increase in the drain-source voltage (Figure 5.20). The value of the drain-source voltage at which the drain current saturates is given by $V_{DS(sat)}$.

Figure 5.21 shows the output characteristic curves for an n-channel E-MOSFET. It can be observed from the curve that the $V_{DS(sat)}$ voltage increases with the increase in the applied gate-source voltage. The relationship between $V_{DS(sat)}$ and V_{GS} is given by

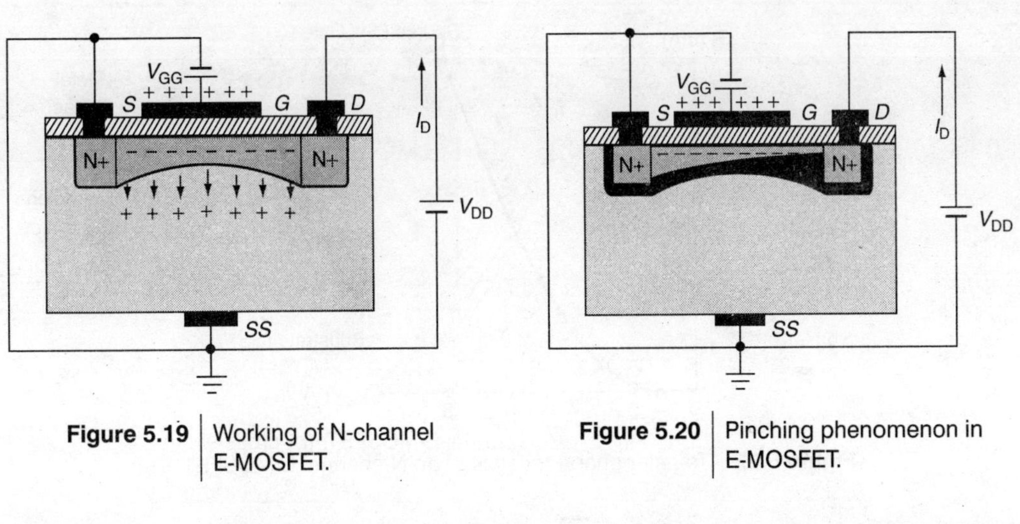

Figure 5.19 Working of N-channel E-MOSFET.

Figure 5.20 Pinching phenomenon in E-MOSFET.

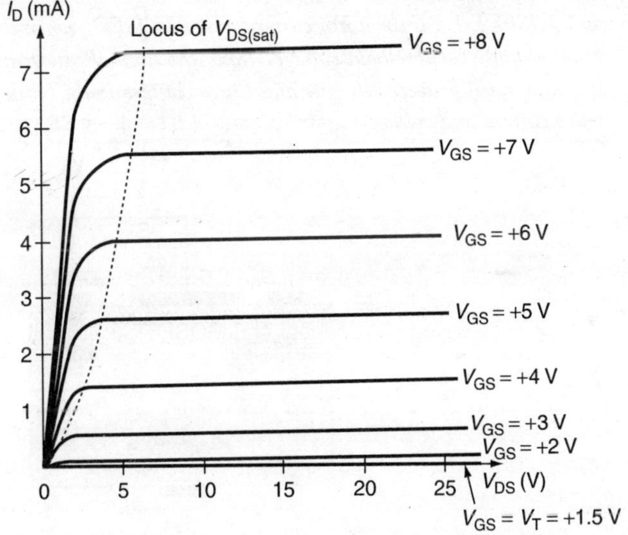

Figure 5.21 Output characteristic curves for an N-channel E-MOSFET.

$$V_{DS(sat)} = V_{GS} - V_T \tag{5.3}$$

where V_T is the threshold gate-source voltage.

Also, the drain current is zero for gate-source voltage less than the threshold voltage V_T. For voltages greater than the threshold voltage the drain current is given by

$$I_D = K(V_{GS} - V_T)^2 \tag{5.4}$$

where K is a constant. As is clear from Eq. (5.4), the relationship between the drain current and the gate-source voltage is non-linear and the current is proportional to the square of the voltage. The relationship is shown in Figure 5.22. The characteristics of Figure 5.22 are referred to as the transfer characteristics.

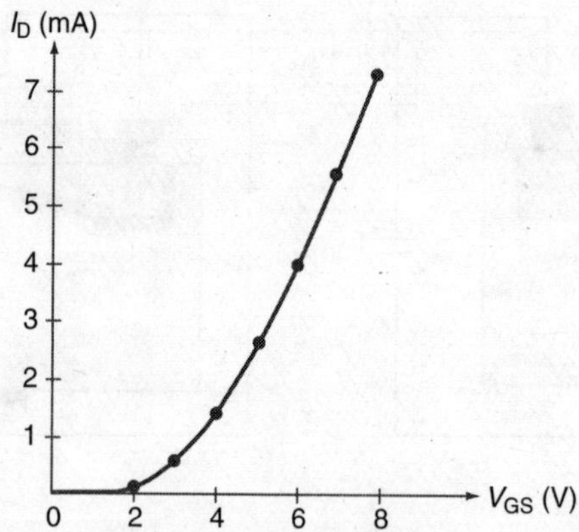

Figure 5.22 Transfer characteristics of an N-channel E-MOSFET.

EXAMPLE 5.1

Identify the MOSFET shown in Figure 5.23. Given that V_T is the threshold voltage of the MOSFET, I_{DS} is the drain current of the MOSFET when the gate-source voltage is equal to twice the threshold voltage, draw its output characteristics. An external supply V_{GG} is applied between the gate and the drain terminals. Draw the curve between the drain current and voltage V_D for $V_{GG} = V_T/2$.

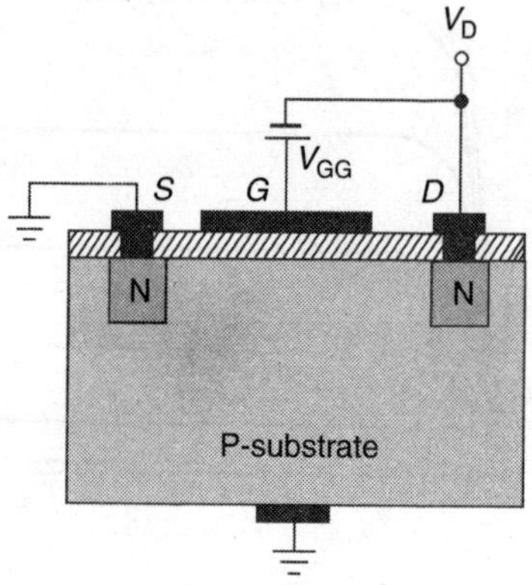

Figure 5.23 Example 5.1.

Solution

1. The MOSFET shown in the figure is an N-channel E-MOSFET. As we have studied, E-MOSFET conducts for V_{GS} greater than the threshold voltage (V_T). The current in an E-MOSFET is given by $I_D = K(V_{GS} - V_T)^2$. As I_{DS} is the current for $V_{GS} = 2V_T$, therefore $K = I_{DS}/V_T^2$.
2. The output characteristics can be plotted using the equations

$$I_D = \frac{I_{DS}}{V_T^2}(V_{GS} - V_T)^2$$

$$V_{DS(sat)} = V_{GS} - V_T$$

As an example consider $V_{GS} = 3.5V_T$, $I_D = 6.25I_{DS}$ and $V_{DS(sat)} = 2.5V_T$. By calculating the values of I_D for different values of V_{GS} we can plot the output characteristic curves for the given MOSFET. Figure 5.24 shows the output characteristics of the given E-MOSFET.

3. The voltage V_{GG} is applied between the gate and the drain terminals. The gate-source voltage (V_{GS}) is given by $V_{GS} = V_{GG} + V_{DS} = V_{GG} + V_D$. (The voltage V_D is equal to the drain-source voltage V_{DS}.)
4. As $V_{GG} = V_T/2$, the voltage V_{GS} will be less than the threshold voltage V_T until voltage V_{DS} is less than $V_T/2$. When $V_D = V_T/2$, $V_{GS} = V_T$ and the MOSFET starts conducting after that.
5. Table 5.1 lists the values of V_{GS}, I_D for various values of V_D.
6. Figure 5.25 shows the plot of points corresponding to Table 5.1. The curve obtained by joining the points is the I_D versus V_D plot for $V_{GG} = V_T/2$.

Table 5.1 | Solution to Example 5.1

V_D	V_{DS}	V_{GS}	I_D
0	0	$0.5V_T$	0
$0.5V_T$	$0.5V_T$	V_T	0
V_T	V_T	$1.5V_T$	$0.25I_{DS}$
$1.5V_T$	$1.5V_T$	$2V_T$	I_{DS}
$2V_T$	$2V_T$	$2.5V_T$	$2.25I_{DS}$
$2.5V_T$	$2.5V_T$	$3V_T$	$4I_{DS}$
$3V_T$	$3V_T$	$3.5V_T$	$6.25I_{DS}$

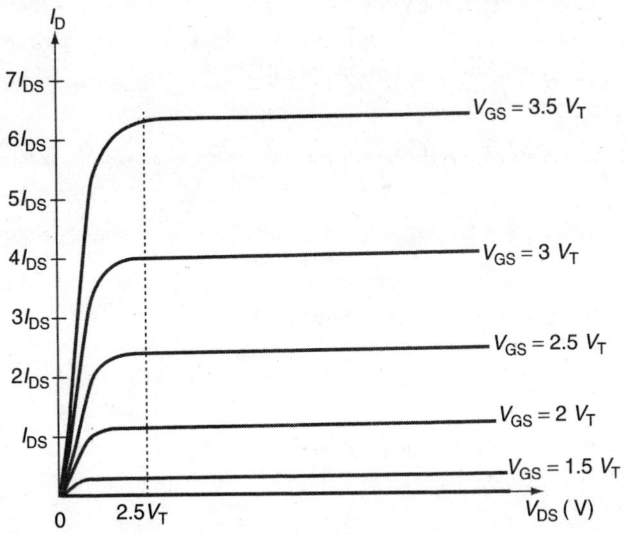

Figure 5.24 | Solution to Example 5.1.

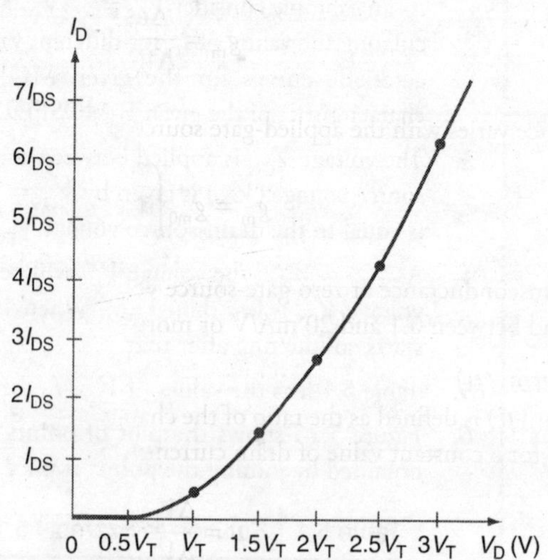

Figure 5.25 Solution to Example 5.1.

Answer: Figure 5.24 shows the output characteristics and Figure 5.25 shows the I_D versus V_D plot.

5.4 FET Parameters and Specifications

In this section we describe the characteristic parameters and specifications of FETs.

Characteristic Parameters

Parameters used to define the performance of an FET device are static and dynamic drain resistance, transconductance (g_m) and amplification factor (μ).

Drain Resistance

Static drain resistance (R_D) is defined as the ratio of the drain-source voltage (V_{DS}) to the drain current (I_D):

$$R_D = \frac{V_{DS}}{I_D} \tag{5.5}$$

Dynamic drain resistance (r_d) is defined as the ratio of change in the drain-source voltage to the change in the drain current at a constant gate-source voltage.

$$r_d = \left.\frac{\Delta V_{DS}}{\Delta I_D}\right|_{V_{GS} = \text{const.}} \tag{5.6}$$

The typical values of r_d lie in the range of 0.1 to 1 MΩ for JFETs and and in the range of 1 to 50 kΩ for MOSFETs.

Transconductance (g_m)

Transconductance (g_m) is defined as the ratio of the change in the drain current to the change in the gate-source voltage for a constant drain-source voltage:

$$g_m = \left.\frac{\Delta I_D}{\Delta V_{GS}}\right|_{V_{DS} = \text{const.}} \tag{5.7}$$

The transconductance varies with the applied-gate source voltage (V_{GS}) as given in Eq. (5.8):

$$g_m = g_{m0}\left(1 - \frac{V_{GS}}{V_P}\right) \tag{5.8}$$

where g_{m0} is the transconductance at zero gate-source voltage. The value of g_m is in the range of 0.1 to 10 mA/V for JFETs and between 0.1 and 20 mA/V or more for MOSFETs.

Amplification Factor (μ)

Amplification factor (μ) is defined as the ratio of the change in the drain-source voltage to the change in the gate-source voltage for a constant value of drain current:

$$\mu = \left.\frac{\Delta V_{DS}}{\Delta V_{GS}}\right|_{I_D = \text{const.}} \tag{5.9}$$

Substituting the value of r_d given in Eq. (5.6) and the value of g_m given in Eq. (5.7) in Eq. (5.9) we get

$$\mu = \frac{\Delta V_{DS}}{\Delta V_{GS}} = \frac{\Delta V_{DS}}{\Delta I_D} \times \frac{\Delta I_D}{\Delta V_{GS}} = r_d \times g_m \tag{5.10}$$

Therefore, the amplification factor is the product of the dynamic drain resistance and the transconductance of the FET. Amplification factor in a JFET can be as high as 100.

EXAMPLE 5.2 *A given JFET device has a drain current of 8 mA when a drain voltage of 5 V is applied to it with gate-source terminals shorted. When the drain voltage is increased to 10 V there is a small increase in the drain current and the new value of drain current is 8.2 mA. When the gate-source voltage is made −0.4 V, the drain current decreases to 7 mA. Determine the type of the JFET, its drain resistance, transconductance and amplification factor.*

Solution

1. Since application of negative gate-source voltage results in decrease of the drain current, the JFET is an N-channel JFET.
2. Drain resistance

$$r_d = \left.\frac{\Delta V_{DS}}{\Delta I_D}\right|_{V_{GS} = \text{const.}}$$

$$r_d = (10 - 5)/(8.2 \times 10^{-3} - 8.0 \times 10^{-3}) = 5/(0.2 \times 10^{-3}) = 25\ \text{k}\Omega.$$

3. Transconductance

$$g_m = \left.\frac{\Delta I_D}{\Delta V_{GS}}\right|_{V_{DS} = \text{const.}}$$

$$g_m = (7\times10^{-3} - 8.2\times10^{-3})/(-0.4 - 0) = -1.2\times10^{-3}/(-0.4) = 3\ \text{mA/V}$$

4. Amplification factor

$$\mu = r_d \times g_m$$
$$= (25\times 10^3)\times(3\times 10^{-3}) = 75$$

Answer: JFET is an N-channel JFET, drain resistance = 25 kΩ, transconductance = 3 mA/V and amplification factor = 75.

EXAMPLE 5.3 *Derive the expression for the transconductance (g_m) of a JFET.*

Solution

1. The equation for the drain current (I_D) in a JFET is given by

$$I_D = I_{DSS}\left(1-\frac{V_{GS}}{V_P}\right)^2$$

2. Differentiating both the sides of the equation w.r.t. the gate-source voltage (V_{GS}) we get

$$\frac{dI_D}{dV_{GS}} = 2I_{DSS}\times\left(1-\frac{V_{GS}}{V_P}\right)\times\left(\frac{-1}{V_P}\right)$$

3. As $g_m = dI_D/dV_{GS}$. Therefore,

$$g_m = 2I_{DSS}\times\left(1-\frac{V_{GS}}{V_P}\right)\times\left(\frac{-1}{V_P}\right)$$

4. Let g_{m0} be the transconductance for $V_{GS} = 0$. Therefore,

$$g_{m0} = 2I_{DSS}\times\left(\frac{-1}{V_P}\right)$$

5. Substituting the value of g_{m0} in the expression for g_m we get

$$g_m = g_{m0}\times\left(1-\frac{V_{GS}}{V_P}\right)$$

Answer: The expression for transconductance of a JFET is given by

$$g_m = g_{m0}\times\left(1-\frac{V_{GS}}{V_P}\right)$$

FET Datasheet Specifications

An FET datasheet provides similar information as a BJT datasheet such as the device's maximum ratings, mechanical data and electrical characteristics. The common electrical specifications mentioned in datasheets of JFET and MOSFET devices are as follows:

1. **Reverse Gate-Source Breakdown Voltage (BV_{GS}):** It is defined as the reverse gate-source voltage with either the drain open (BV_{GSO}) or drain shorted to the source (BV_{GSS}). It is typically few tens of volts.
2. **Power Dissipation (P_D):** Power dissipation rating of the JFET is the product of the drain-source voltage (V_{DS}) and the drain current (I_D). The power dissipation rating must be derated with increase

in temperature. It is usually specified at an ambient of 25°C. JFETs are available in power ratings of hundreds of milliwatts while MOSFETs are available in a wide range of power ratings starting from a few milliwatts to more than hundred watts.

3. **Saturation Drain Current (I_{DSS}):** It is the maximum drain current when the gate terminal is shorted to the source terminal. It is usually specified at a given drain-source voltage somewhere in the channel pinch-off region.
4. **Pinch-Off Voltage (V_P or $V_{GS(off)}$):** It is the gate-source voltage for which the drain current reduces to zero. It is also specified for a given value of drain-source voltage. It is specified in case of JFETs and DE-MOSFETs only.
5. **Gate Leakage current (I_{GSS}):** It is the gate-to-source leakage current with the drain terminal shorted to the source terminal. It is given for a specific value of gate reverse-bias voltage. Typical value of gate leakage current is few nanoamperes for JFETs and few pico-amperes for MOSFETs.
6. **Forward Transconductance (g_{fs}):** It is usually given for specified values of gate-source voltage (V_{GS}) and drain-source voltage (V_{DS}). It is typically few hundred micro-mhos to few milli-mhos for both JFETs and MOSFETs.
7. **Output Conductance (g_{os}):** It is the reciprocal of the dynamic drain resistance (r_d). It is usually specified as an admittance parameter (y_{os}). y_{os} equals g_{os} at low frequencies. Admittance is in the range of few milli-mhos for both JFETs and MOSFETs.
8. **Input Capacitance (C_{iss}):** It is the input capacitance of the FET when connected in common-source configuration. It is typically of the order of few picofarads for both JFET and MOSFET devices. The overall input capacitance (C_i) in a common-source amplifier configuration using an FET is larger than C_{iss} due to the presence of Miller component of the gate-drain inter-electrode capacitance (C_{gd} or C_{rss}). C_{gd} is also referred to as the reverse transfer capacitance. The overall input capacitance is given by:

$$C_i = C_{iss} + (1 - A_V)C_{rss} \tag{5.11}$$

   where A_V is the voltage gain.
9. **Reverse Transfer Capacitance (C_{rss}):** It is the reverse transfer capacitance for the common-source configuration. It is of the order of few picofarads in JFETs but only a small fraction of a picofarad in some MOSFETs.
10. **Output Capacitance (C_{oss}):** It is the drain-source capacitance for the common-source configuration. This too is typically few picofarads for both JFET and MOSFET devices.
11. **Threshold Voltage ($V_{GS(th)}$):** It is the gate-source threshold voltage where the MOSFET begins to conduct. It is specified for E-MOSFETs only.
12. **Drain-Source ON Voltage ($V_{DS(on)}$):** It is the drain-source voltage for a particular level of gate-source voltage and drain current when the MOSFET is in the ON-state. It is specified for E-MOSFETs only.
13. **ON-State Drain Current ($I_{D(on)}$):** It is a typical value of drain current for a particular value of gate-source voltage when the MOSFET is in the ON-state. It is specified for E-MOSFETs only. As mentioned earlier, the drain current in an E-MOSFET is given by

$$I_D = K(V_{GS} - V_T)^2$$

   Therefore, the values of V_T, $V_{GS(on)}$ and $I_{D(on)}$ help in determining the value of K. The value of K is given by

$$K = \frac{I_{D(on)}}{(V_{GS(on)} - V_T)^2} \tag{5.12}$$

5.5 Differences between JFETs and MOSFETs

JFETs and MOSFETs are somewhat similar devices but there are quite a few differences between the two devices in terms of their principle of operation and the values of their characteristic parameters. These differences are as follows:

1. JFETs are operated in depletion mode only. DE-MOSFETs can be operated in both depletion and enhancement modes and E-MOSFETs are operated in enhancement mode only.
2. The input resistance offered by MOSFETs is much higher than that by JFETs. Input resistance for JFETs is greater than $10^9\ \Omega$ whereas that of MOSFETs is around $10^{13}\ \Omega$.
3. JFETs have higher drain resistance than MOSFETs and hence their characteristic curve is more flat than that of MOSFETs. Drain resistance for JFETs is in the range of 100 kΩ to 1 MΩ while that for MOSFETs is in the range of 1 to 50 kΩ.
4. The leakage gate current in MOSFETs is much smaller than that in JFETs. The gate current for the MOSFETs is in the range of 100 nA to 10 pA whereas that for the JFETs is in the range of 100 μA to 10 nA.
5. MOSFETs are easier to construct and are used more widely than JFETs.

5.6 Handling MOSFETs

Owing to the presence of thin SiO_2 layer in MOSFETs, they are prone to damage if not handled properly. A person accumulates static charge from the surroundings. When that person handles a MOSFET device, that charge can lead to potential difference across the SiO_2 layer which can result in its breakdown and establish conduction through it. Therefore, some precautions need to be taken while handling MOSFETs.

A shorting conducting foil or a shorting ring is connected across all the three leads of the device until the device is inserted into the system. The shorting ring prevents the development of potential difference between any two device terminals. The person using the MOSFET should always touch ground before using the device so as to discharge the accumulated charge before handling the device. The person who is soldering should use a shorting strap to discharge static electricity and also should make sure that the tip of the soldering iron is grounded. Also the MOSFET should always be held from the casing. In addition, the MOSFET should be inserted or removed with the supply off.

An effective method to prevent MOSFET damage is to connect Zener diodes back-to-back between the gate and the source terminals so that the gate-to-source voltage never exceeds the specified maximum rating. Figure 5.26 shows the use of Zener diodes for protection of E-MOSFETs. Similar configuration can be used

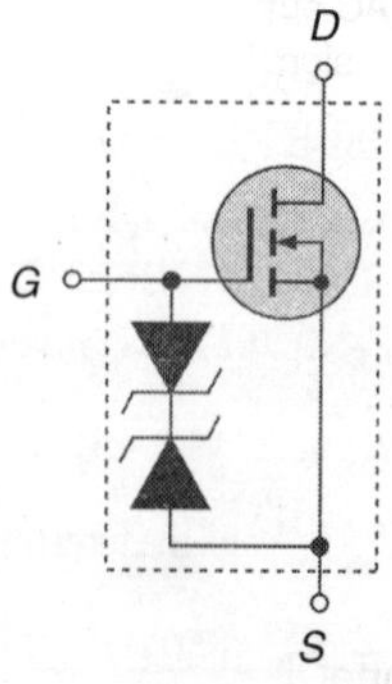

Figure 5.26 Use of Zener diodes to protect E-MOSFET.

for DE-MOSFETs. But the use of Zener diodes results in reduction of input impedance as the impedance of the Zener diode in the reverse-bias mode is less than the input impedance of the MOSFET.

5.7 Biasing JFETs

DC biasing of an FET is done to produce the required gate-to-source voltage (V_{GS}) to get the desired value of drain current (I_D). There are large variations in the maximum and the minimum values of FET parameters even for a given type. The biasing circuits should maintain the drain current and the drain-source voltage within reasonable limits even for the maximum and minimum values of its parameters. It may be mentioned here that the phenomenon of thermal runaway does not occur in FETs. In this section, we discuss the common configurations used for biasing JFETs. The biasing configurations for DE-MOSFETs and E-MOSFETs are discussed in the next section. There are three biasing configurations used with JFETs, namely, the common-source, common-drain and common-gate configurations. Each of these configurations is discussed in the subsequent paragraphs.

Common-Source Configuration

Common-source configuration offers high input impedance, low output impedance, high voltage gain and the output voltage is 180° out-of-phase with the input voltage. The commonly used common-source biasing configurations include fixed-bias configuration, self-bias configuration and voltage-divider configuration.

Fixed-Bias Configuration

Fixed-bias configuration is the most simplest of the biasing configurations. Figure 5.27 shows the fixed-bias circuit for N-channel JFET. The biasing components include drain resistor (R_D), gate resistor (R_G), input and output coupling capacitors (C_i and C_o), drain supply voltage (V_{DD}) and gate supply voltage (V_{GG}). The gate supply voltage ensures that the gate terminal is negative w.r.t. to the source. Resistor R_G is used so that the input AC signal develops across it. The DC equivalent of the circuit is shown in Figure 5.28.

In a JFET, the gate current (I_G) is approximately equal to zero ($I_G \cong 0$). Therefore, the voltage drop across the resistor R_G, given by the product of the gate current and resistor R_G, is approximately zero.

$$V_{R_G} = I_G \times R_G \cong 0 \tag{5.13}$$

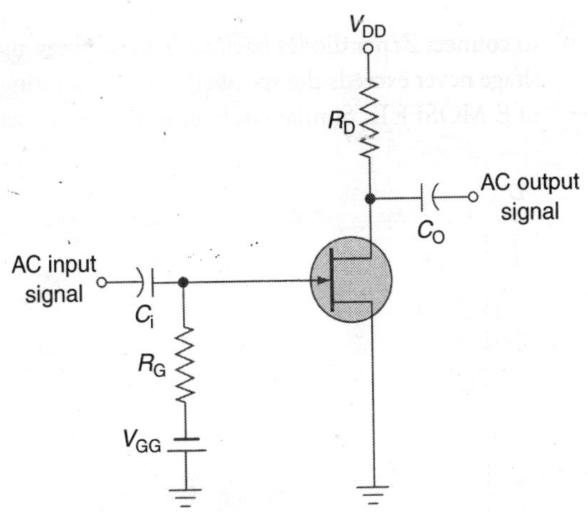

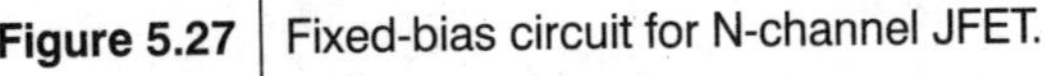
Figure 5.27 Fixed-bias circuit for N-channel JFET.

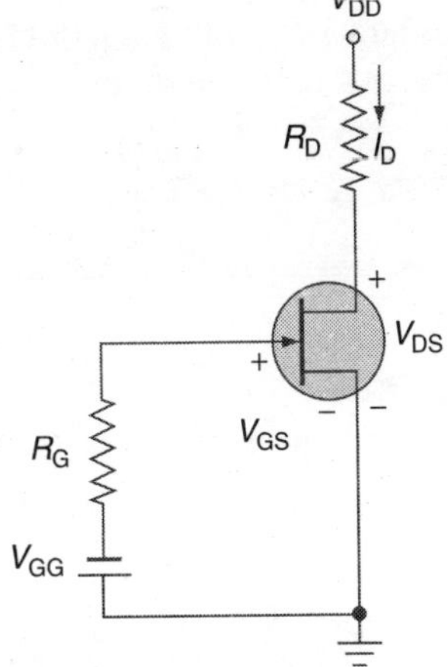

Figure 5.28 DC equivalent of fixed-bias circuit of Figure 5.27.

Applying Kirchhoff's voltage law to the input section we get

$$-V_{GG} - V_{GS} = 0 \tag{5.14}$$

Therefore, the value of gate-source voltage is given by

$$V_{GS} = -V_{GG} \tag{5.15}$$

The gate-source voltage (V_{GS}) is negative and equal in magnitude to the applied gate voltage (V_{GG}). As the voltage V_{GG} is fixed, V_{GS} is also fixed. Therefore, the configuration is named as fixed-bias configuration. This value of gate-source voltage is denoted as V_{GSQ}.

Since the drain current (I_D) in a JFET is given by Shockley's equation

$$I_D = I_{DSS}\left(1 - \frac{V_{GS}}{V_P}\right)^2$$

Therefore, the value of quiescent drain current (I_{DQ}) is given by

$$I_{DQ} = I_{DSS}\left(1 - \frac{V_{GSQ}}{V_P}\right)^2 \tag{5.16}$$

Since the value of gate-source voltage (V_{GS}) in a fixed-bias configuration is fixed, therefore the level of drain current (I_D) is also fixed.

Applying Kirchhoff's voltage law to the output section we get

$$V_{DD} - I_D R_D - V_{DS} = 0 \tag{5.17}$$

Therefore, the value of quiescent drain-source voltage (V_{DSQ}) is given by

$$V_{DSQ} = V_{DD} - I_{DQ} R_D \tag{5.18}$$

The operating point is defined as (I_{DQ}, V_{DSQ}). The operating point can also be obtained graphically, by superimposing the vertical line $V_{GS} = -V_{GG}$ on the transfer characteristics of the JFET (Figure 5.29).

The operating point can also be obtained by superimposing the load line on the output characteristic curves of the JFET. The load line is defined by Eq. (5.17).

Substituting $V_{DS} = 0$ in Eq. (5.17), we get $I_D = V_{DD}/R_D$
Substituting $I_D = 0$ in Eq. (5.17), we get $V_{DS} = V_{DD}$

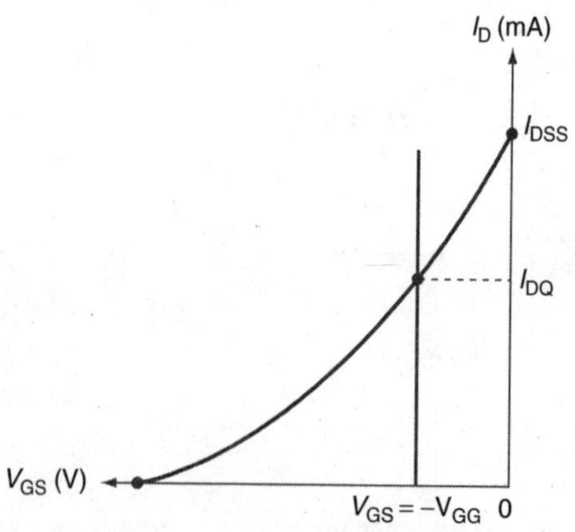

Figure 5.29 Graphical analysis of the fixed-bias circuit of Figure 5.27.

The line formed by joining the two points $(0, V_{DD})$ and $(V_{DD}/R_D, 0)$ is the DC load line. As we have studied in the chapter on BJT biasing, the operating point defines the DC conditions that exist when no input AC signal is applied. The bias point is selected so as to have the maximum possible drain-source voltage swing for the AC input signal. Figure 5.30 shows the load-line analysis.

The fixed-bias configuration is not used much as the wide differences in the minimum and maximum values of the JFET parameters make drain current levels unpredictable with simple fixed-bias circuits. Another disadvantage of the fixed-bias circuit is that it needs an additional supply voltage for biasing the gate terminal. Self-bias and potential-divider biasing configurations require a single supply voltage and maintain the quiescent drain current and drain-source voltage within desirable limits.

Self-Bias Configuration

Self-bias configuration is the most commonly used biasing scheme for FETs. Self-bias configuration offers stabilization of the operating point against variations in FET parameters. Figure 5.31 shows the self-bias circuit for an N-channel JFET. The difference between the fixed-bias and the self-bias configurations is the

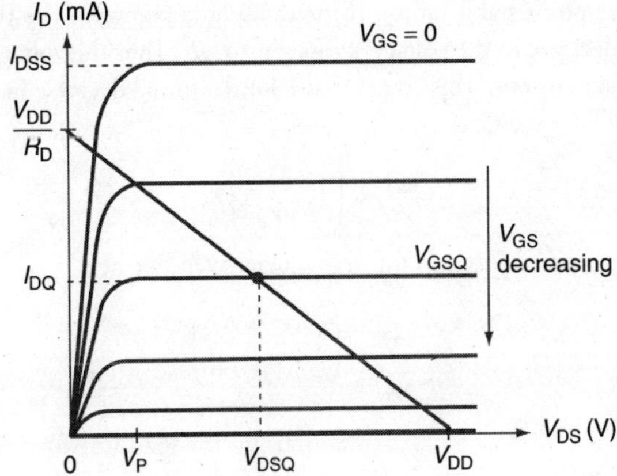

Figure 5.30 | Load-line analysis for the fixed-bias circuit of Figure 5.27.

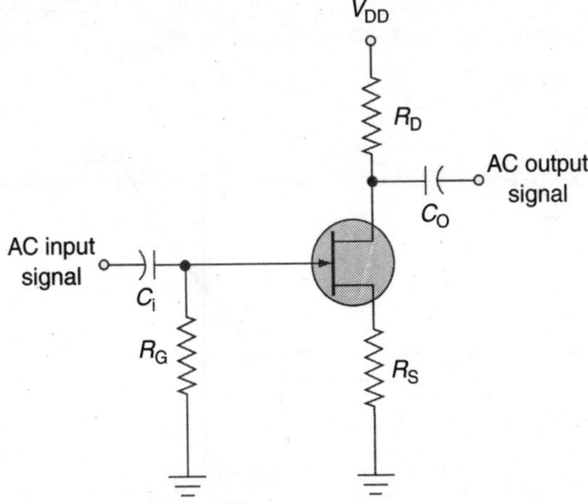

Figure 5.31 | Self-bias configuration for N-channel JFET.

addition of source resistor (R_S) between the source and the ground terminals and the removal of the gate supply voltage. The voltage drop across the resistor (R_S) provides the controlling gate voltage.

The analysis of the self-bias circuit can be done by drawing its DC equivalent circuit as shown in Figure 5.32. As the gate current (I_G) is zero, there is no voltage drop across the resistor R_G. Therefore the gate voltage V_G is equal to zero. Applying Kirchhoff's voltage law to the input section we get

$$-V_{GS} - I_D R_S = 0 \tag{5.19}$$

Therefore, the gate-source voltage is given by

$$V_{GS} = -I_D R_S \tag{5.20}$$

As the gate voltage is zero, the source voltage (V_S) is given by

$$V_S = V_G - V_{GS} = I_D R_S \tag{5.21}$$

The voltage drop (V_S) across source resistor R_S provides the biasing gate-source voltage and hence no external power supply is required for the purpose. Hence this configuration is named self-bias configuration. The voltage (V_S) also results in bias-point stabilization. If the transconductance of the JFET decreases, the drain current decreases resulting in decrease in the voltage across resistor R_S. Thus the voltage V_{GS} becomes less negative resulting in increase in drain current. This compensates for the initial decrease in the drain current.

Drain current (I_D) in a JFT is given by

$$I_D = I_{DSS}\left(1 - \frac{V_{GS}}{V_P}\right)^2$$

Substituting the value of V_{GS} in the expression for drain current (I_D) we get

$$I_D = I_{DSS}\left(1 - \frac{-I_D R_S}{V_P}\right)^2 \tag{5.22}$$

Therefore, the drain current is given by

$$I_D = I_{DSS}\left(1 + \frac{I_D R_S}{V_P}\right)^2 \tag{5.23}$$

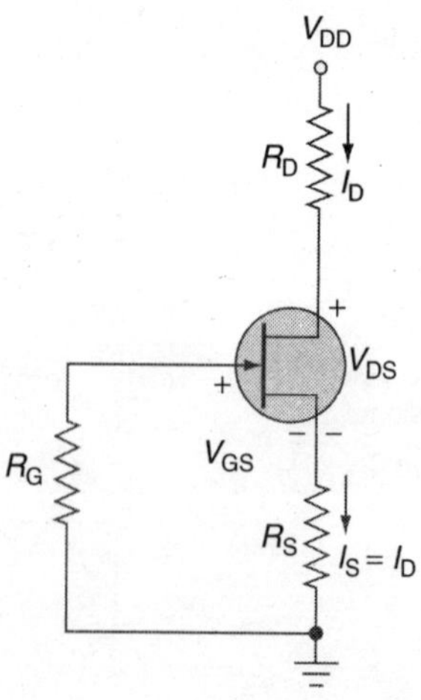

Figure 5.32 DC equivalent of self-bias configuration shown in Figure 5.31.

Applying Kirchhoff's voltage law to the output section we get

$$V_{DD} - I_D R_D - V_{DS} - I_D R_S = 0 \tag{5.24}$$

Therefore, the drain-source voltage (V_{DS}) is given by

$$V_{DS} = V_{DD} - I_D (R_D + R_S) \tag{5.25}$$

The graphical analysis can be done in a similar manner to that for fixed-bias configuration as shown in Figure 5.33. The operating point is determined by superimposing the straight line corresponding to the equation $V_{GS} = -I_D R_S$ on the transfer characteristic curve of the JFET. The load-line analysis can also be done in the same manner as done for the fixed-bias circuit. The only difference is that the load line is now defined by Eq. (5.25).

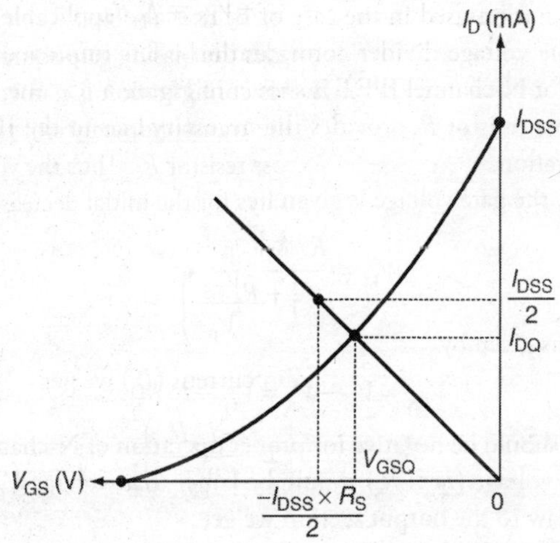

Figure 5.33 | Graphical analysis of self-bias configuration for N-channel JFETs.

EXAMPLE 5.4 *For the self-bias circuit in Figure 5.34, determine the value of drain current (I_D) and gate-source voltage (V_{GS}).*

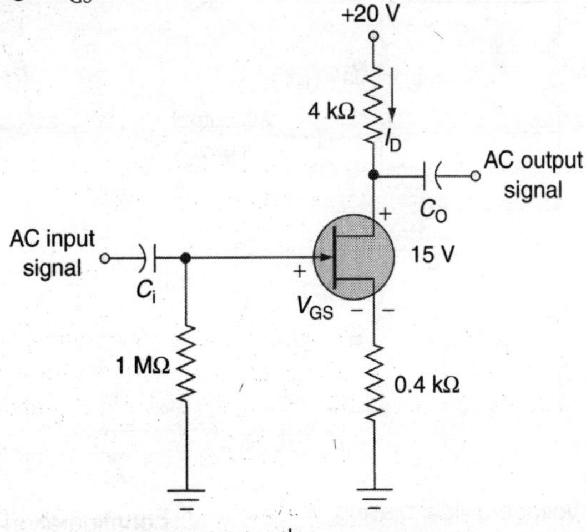

Figure 5.34 | Example 5.4.

Solution

1. The value of drain current is given by

$$I_D = \frac{V_{DD} - V_{DS}}{R_D + R_S}$$

2. Therefore, $I_D = (20 - 15)/(4 \times 10^3 + 0.4 \times 10^3) = 5/4.4 \times 10^3 = 1.14$ mA.
3. The gate-source voltage is given by $V_{GS} = -I_D \times R_S = -1.14 \times 10^{-3} \times 0.4 \times 10^3 = 0.456$ V.

Answer: Drain current $I_D = 1.14$ mA and gate-source voltage $V_{GS} = 0.456$ V.

Voltage-Divider Biasing

Voltage-divider biasing configuration used in the case of BJTs is also applicable to JFETs. As mentioned in Chapter 4 on BJT biasing, the voltage-divider configuration offers improved bias stability. The voltage-divider biasing configuration for N-channel JFET is shown in Figure 5.35. The resistors R_1 and R_2 form the potential divider. Voltage across resistor R_2 provides the necessary bias to the JFET. Figure 5.36 shows the DC equivalent of the configuration.

As the gate current $I_G \cong 0$, the gate voltage is given by

$$V_G = \frac{R_2 \times V_{DD}}{R_1 + R_2} \tag{5.26}$$

The gate-source voltage (V_{GS}) is given by

$$V_{GS} = V_G - V_S = V_G - I_D R_S \tag{5.27}$$

As the gate-source voltage should be negative for proper operation of N-channel JFETs, therefore for the circuit to operate properly the voltage ($I_D \times R_S$) should be larger than voltage V_G.
Applying Kirchhoff's voltage law to the output section we get

$$V_{DS} = V_{DD} - I_D(R_D + R_S) \tag{5.28}$$

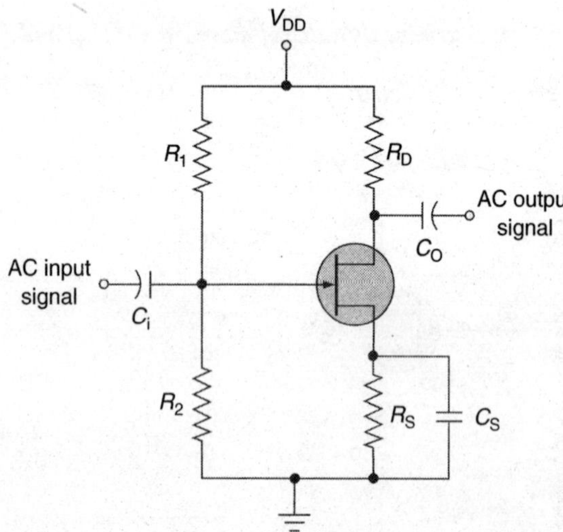

Figure 5.35 | Voltage-divider biasing configuration for N-channel JFET.

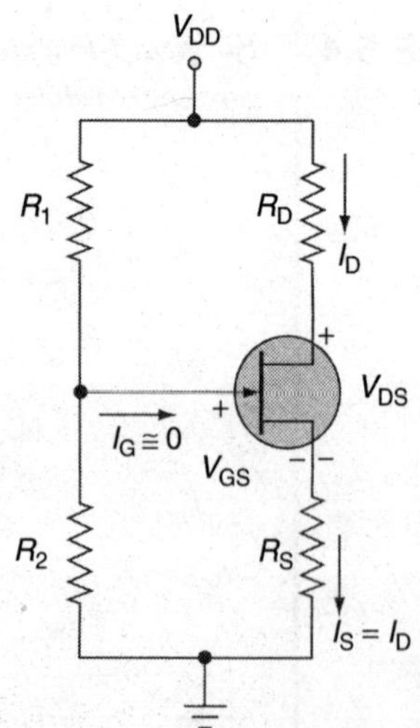

Figure 5.36 | DC equivalent of voltage-divider biasing configuration of Figure 5.35.

The operating point is given by

$$\left(I_{DQ} = \frac{V_G - V_{GS}}{R_S},\ V_{DSQ} = V_{DD} - I_{DQ}(R_D + R_S) \right)$$

Figure 5.37 shows the graphical method to determine the operating point. The figure is self-explanatory. Load-line analysis can also be done to establish the operating point as explained in the case of fixed-bias circuit.

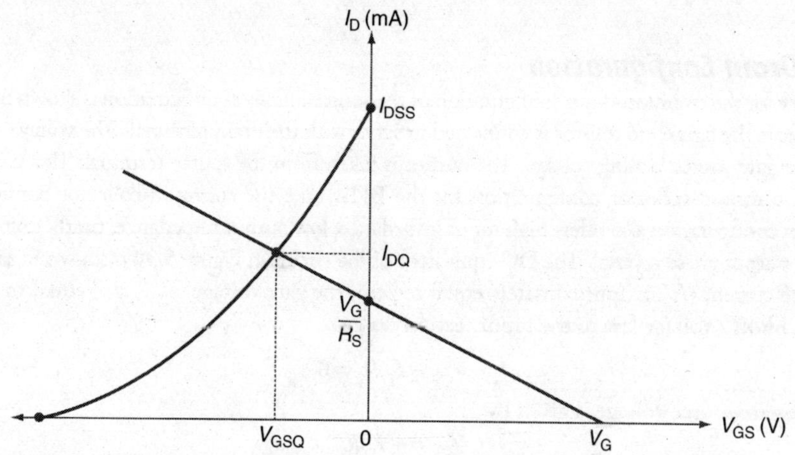

Figure 5.37 Graphical analysis of voltage-divider bias configuration.

EXAMPLE 5.5 *For the circuit in Figure 5.38, determine the value of drain-source voltage (V_{DS}). (Given that the gate-source voltage is −0.8 V.)*

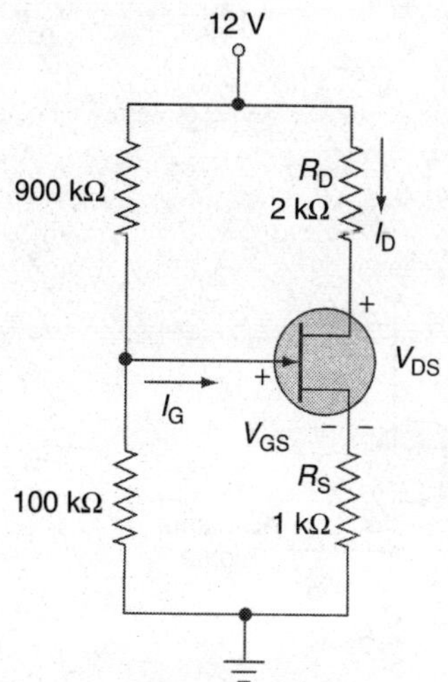

Figure 5.38 Example 5.5.

Solution 1. The gate voltage is given by $V_G = 12 \times 100 \times 10^3/(100 \times 10^3 + 900 \times 10^3) =$ 1.2 V.

2. The gate-source voltage is equal to $V_{GS} = V_G - V_S$.
Therefore, $-0.8 = 1.2 - V_S$ or $V_S = 2.0$ V.
3. The drain current is equal to $I_D = V_S/R_S = 2/(1 \times 10^3) = 2$ mA.
4. The drain-source voltage is $V_{DS} = 12 - 2 \times 10^3 \times 2 \times 10^{-3} - 1 \times 10^3 \times 2 \times 10^{-3}$
$= 12 - 4 - 2 = 6$ V.

Answer: The drain-source voltage is equal to 6 V.

Common-Drain Configuration

The basic circuit for the common-drain configuration or the source follower configuration is shown in Figure 5.39. As is evident from the figure, no resistor is connected in series with the drain terminal. The voltage across resistor R_S provides the gate-source biasing voltage. The output is taken from the source terminal. This configuration is similar to the common-collector configuration for the BJTs. Like the common-collector configuration, the common-drain configuration also offers high input impedance, low output impedance, nearly unity voltage gain and no input–output phase reversal. The DC equivalent of the circuit in Figure 5.39 is shown in Figure 5.40.

As the gate current (I_G) is approximately equal to zero, the gate voltage V_G is also equal to zero. Applying Kirchhoff's voltage law to the input section we get

$$-V_{GS} - I_D R_S = 0$$

Therefore, the gate-source voltage is given by

$$V_{GS} = -I_D R_S \tag{5.29}$$

As the gate voltage is zero, the source voltage (V_S) is given by

$$V_S = I_D R_S \tag{5.30}$$

Applying Kirchhoff's voltage law to the output circuit we get

$$V_{DD} - V_{DS} - I_D R_S = 0$$

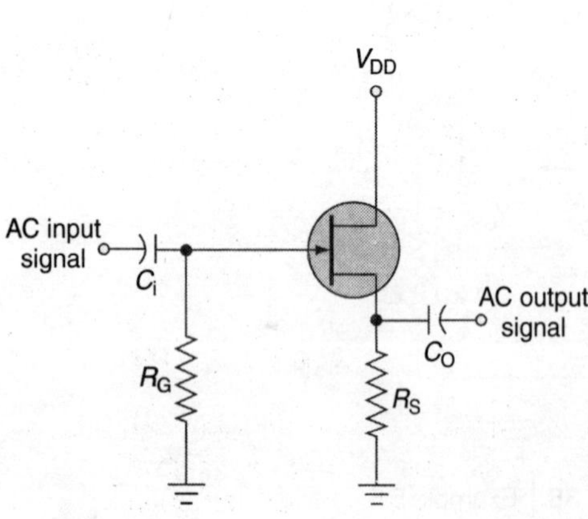

Figure 5.39 Common-drain configuration for N-channel JFET.

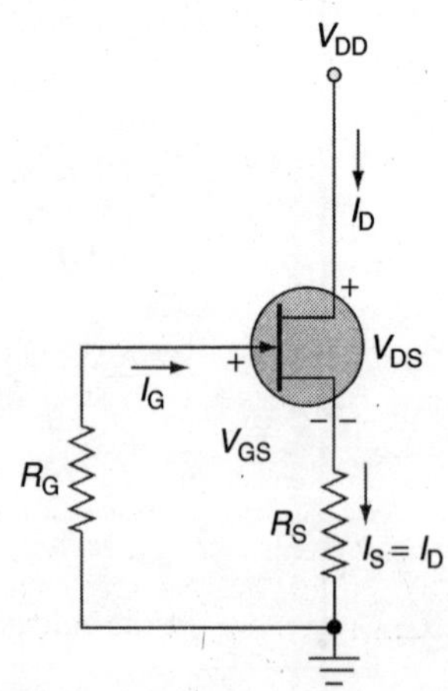

Figure 5.40 DC equivalent of the common-drain configuration of Figure 5.39.

Therefore, the drain-source voltage is given by

$$V_{\mathrm{DS}} = V_{\mathrm{DD}} - I_{\mathrm{D}}R_{\mathrm{S}} \tag{5.31}$$

Another possible common-drain configuration is shown in Figure 5.41(a). This configuration is based on the boot-strapped bias configuration and provides increased input resistance. The concept of boot-strapping is discussed in detail in Chapter 8. Figure 5.41(b) shows the voltage-divider common-drain amplifier. The gate-bias voltage V_{G} is derived from V_{DD} by means of potential divider formed by resistors R_1 and R_2. In this case also, no resistor is connected in series with the drain terminal. The analysis for both the circuits can be done on similar lines as outlined earlier.

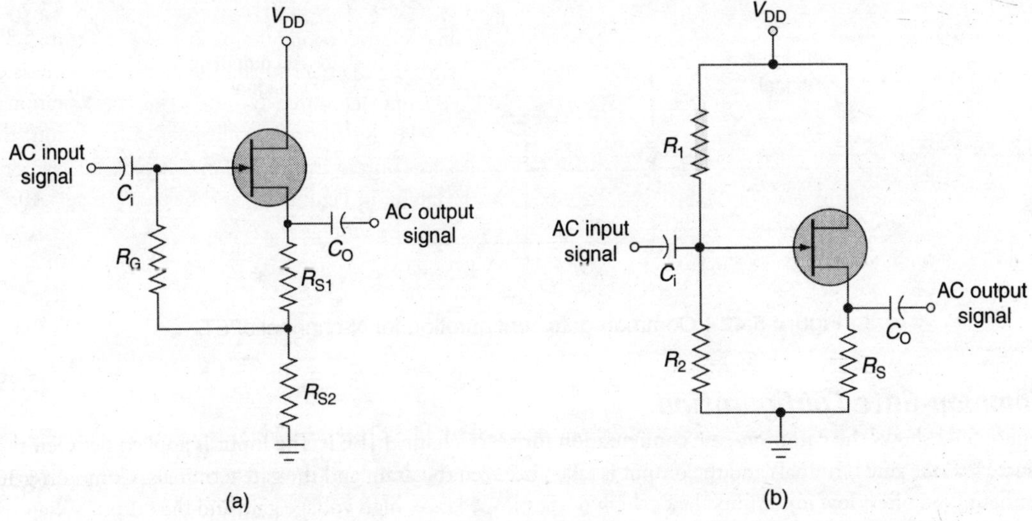

Figure 5.41 (a) Common-drain configuration with boot-strapping for N-channel JFET; (b) voltage-divider common-drain configuration for N-channel JFET.

EXAMPLE 5.6 *In an N-channel JFET-based voltage-divider common-drain configuration, determine the value of resistor (R_{S}) so as to have the operating point as $I_{\mathrm{DQ}} = 5$ mA, $V_{\mathrm{DSQ}} = 10$ V. Given that $V_{\mathrm{DD}} = 28$ V, $R_1 = 1$ MΩ, $R_2 = 0.5$ MΩ, saturation drain current of the JFET = 10 mA and gate-source pinch-off voltage = −5 V.*

Solution

1. In a JFET,

$$I_{\mathrm{D}} = I_{\mathrm{DSS}}\left(1 - \frac{V_{\mathrm{GS}}}{V_{\mathrm{P}}}\right)^2$$

$$5 \times 10^{-3} = 10 \times 10^{-3}\ [1 - V_{\mathrm{GS}}/(-5)]^2$$

$$V_{\mathrm{GS}} = -1.5\ \mathrm{V}$$

2. In the voltage-divider configuration,

$$V_{\mathrm{G}} = \frac{R_2 \times V_{\mathrm{DD}}}{R_1 + R_2}$$

$$V_G = 0.5 \times 10^6 \times 28/(0.5 \times 10^6 + 1 \times 10^6) = 28/3 = 9.33 \text{ V}$$

3. The value of the resistance R_S is given by

$$R_S = \frac{(V_G - V_{GS})}{I_D}$$

$$R_S = [9.33 - (-1.5)]/5 \times 10^{-3} = 2.166 \text{ k}\Omega$$

Answer: The value of the resistor R_S is 2.166 kΩ.

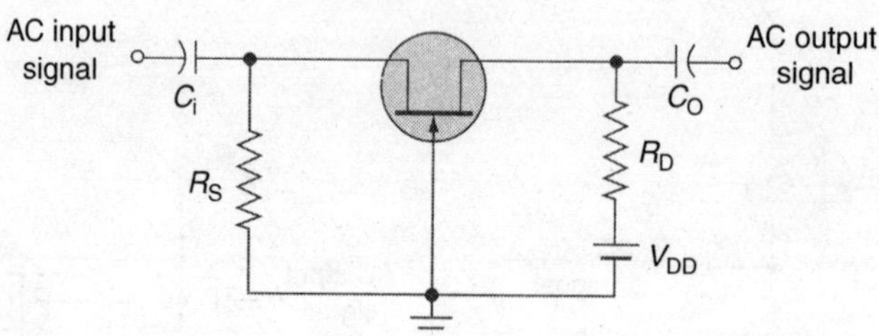

Figure 5.42 Common-gate configuration for N-channel JFET.

Common-Gate Configuration

Figure 5.42 shows the common-gate configuration for an N-channel JFET. The input is applied between the source and the gate terminals and the output is taken between the drain and the gate terminals. Common-gate configuration offers low input impedance, high output impedance, high voltage gain and the output voltage is in phase with the input voltage. The analysis for the circuit can be done on similar lines as that outlined earlier. The values of the gate-source and drain-source voltages are given by Eqs. (5.32) and (5.33), respectively.

$$V_{GS} = -I_D R_S \tag{5.32}$$

$$V_{DS} = V_{DD} - I_D(R_S + R_D) \tag{5.33}$$

5.8 Biasing MOSFETs

In this section we will discuss the commonly used biasing configurations for the DE-MOSFETs and the E-MOSFETs.

Depletion MOSFETs

The biasing schemes for DE-MOSFETs are the same as that for JFETs because of the similarities in their characteristics. The only difference being that DE-MOSFETs also operate in enhancement mode, that is, with positive values of gate-source voltage (V_{GS}) in addition to the depletion mode. The operation of the DE-MOSFET in the enhancement mode is explained with the help of Example 5.7.

EXAMPLE 5.7 *Figure 5.43 shows a biasing configuration using DE-MOSFET. Given that the saturation drain current is 8 mA and the pinch-off voltage is −2 V, determine the value of gate-source voltage, drain current and the drain-source voltage.*

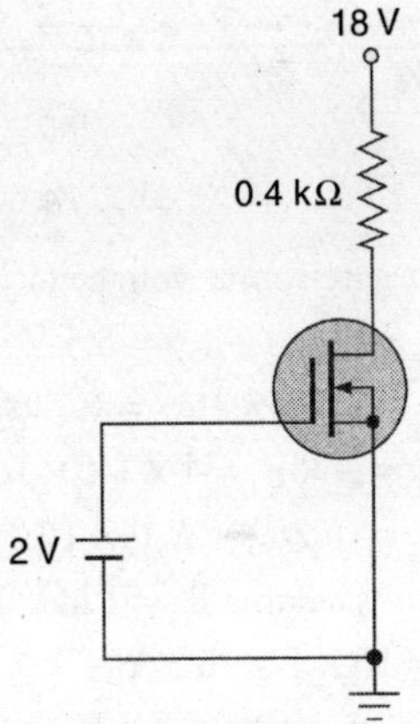

Figure 5.43 | Example 5.7.

Solution

1. The gate-source voltage (V_{GS}) is equal to 2 V.
2. The polarity of the voltage applied between the gate and the source terminals is such that the MOSFET operates in the enhancement region of its output characteristics.
3. In a DE-MOSFET

$$I_D = I_{DSS}\left(1-\frac{V_{GS}}{V_P}\right)^2$$

Now $I_{DSS} = 8$ mA, $V_{GS} = 2$ V, $V_P = -2$ V. Substituting in the above equation we get

$$I_D = 8 \times 10^{-3} \times [1-2/(-2)]^2 = 32 \times 10^{-3}\text{ A} = 32\text{ mA}$$

4. Applying Kirchhoff's voltage law to the output section we get

$$18 - 0.4 \times 10^3 \times 32 \times 10^{-3} - V_{DS} = 0$$

$$V_{DS} = 18 - 12.8 = 5.2\text{ V}$$

Answer: Gate-source voltage = 2 V, drain current = 32 mA, drain-source voltage = 5.2 V.

EXAMPLE 5.8 *Design a voltage-divider-bias network using a DE-MOSFET with supply voltage V_{DD} = 16 V, I_{DSS} = 10 mA and $V_P = -5$ V to have a quiescent drain current of 5 mA and gate voltage of 4 V. (Assume the drain resistor R_D to be four times the source resistor R_S.)*

Solution

1. As the quiescent drain current is less than saturation drain current, the MOSFET is operated in the depletion mode.
2. The drain current (I_D) is given by

$$I_D = I_{DSS}\left(1-\frac{V_{GS}}{V_P}\right)^2$$

$$5\times10^{-3}=10\times10^{-3}\times[1-\{V_{GS}/(-5)\}]^2$$

$$0.5=(1+V_{GS}/5)^2$$

$$V_{GS}/5=0.7-1=-1.5\text{ V}$$

3. The gate-source voltage (V_{GS}) is given by $V_{GS}=V_G-V_S=V_G-I_D R_S$.
4. $I_D\times R_S=4+1.5=5.5$ V.
5. $R_S=5.5/5\times10^{-3}=1.1$ kΩ.
6. $R_D=4\times R_S=4\times1.1\times10^3=4.4$ kΩ.
7. $V_G=[R_2/(R_1+R_2)]\times16$.
8. Let us assume R_2 = 1 kΩ. Therefore,
   $4=16\times1\times10^3/(R_1+1\times10^3)$
   $(R_1+1\times10^3)=4\times10^3$ or $R_1=3\times10^3=3$ kΩ
9. Figure 5.44 shows the circuit configuration.

Answer: Figure 5.44 shows the voltage-divider configuration.

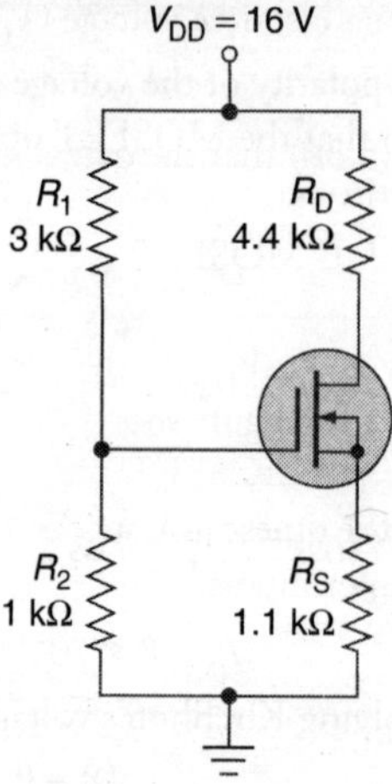

Figure 5.44 Solution to Example 5.8.

Enhancement MOSFETs

Two most popular biasing configurations for E-MOSFETs are the feedback biasing configuration and the voltage-divider configuration. These two biasing configurations are described in this section.

Feedback-Biasing Configuration

Figure 5.45 shows the circuit for the feedback-biasing configuration. The feedback connection to the gate terminal is taken from the drain terminal through resistor R_G. The resistor R_G brings bias voltage to the gate terminal to turn the MOSFET ON. Figure 5.46 shows the DC equivalent circuit. Since the gate current (I_G) is approximately equal to zero, therefore the voltage drop across resistor R_G is also approximately equal to zero. Applying Kirchhoff's voltage law to the input section we get

$$V_{DD}-I_D R_D-V_{GS}=0 \tag{5.34}$$

Therefore, gate-source voltage (V_{GS}) is given by

$$V_{GS}=V_{DD}-I_D R_D \tag{5.35}$$

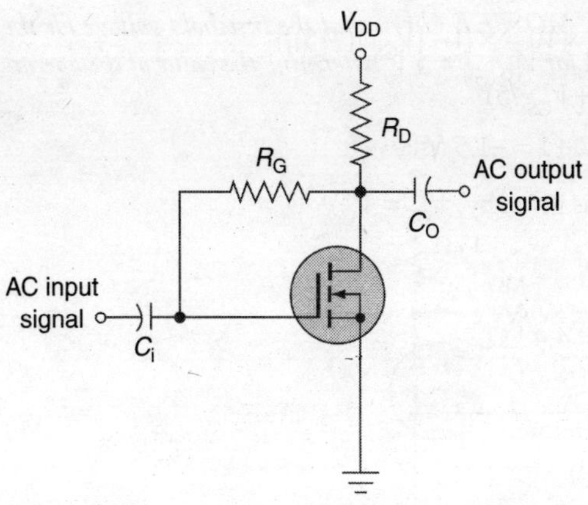

Figure 5.45 | Feedback-biasing configuration for N-channel E-MOSFET.

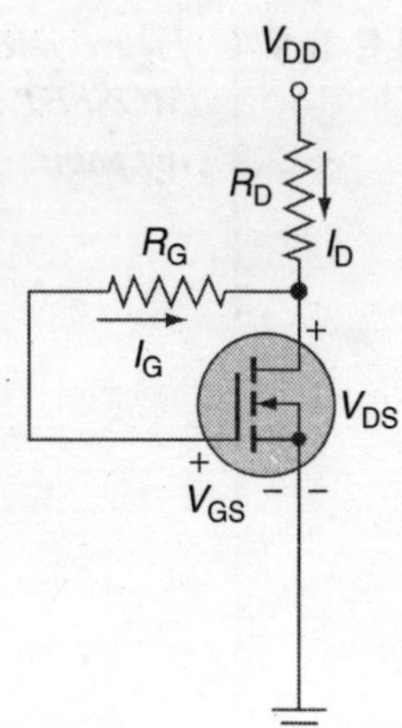

Figure 5.46 | DC equivalent of the circuit.

Applying Kirchhoff's voltage law to the output section and solving for the drain-source voltage (V_{DS}) we get

$$V_{DS} = V_{DD} - I_D R_D \tag{5.36}$$

It is clear from Eqs. (5.35) and (5.36) that the gate-source voltage (V_{GS}) and the drain-source voltage (V_{DS}) are equal, that is,

$$V_{GS} = V_{DS} \tag{5.37}$$

The operating point is given by (I_{DQ}, V_{DSQ}). The operating point can also be established using graphical method as shown in Figure 5.47. The figure shows that the straight line given by Eq. (5.35) is superimposed on the transfer characteristics of the MOSFET. The point of intersection between the straight line and the transfer curve gives the value of the quiescent gate-source voltage and quiescent drain current. The operating point can also be obtained by superimposing the DC load line defined by Eq. (5.36) on the output characteristic curves for the MOSFET.

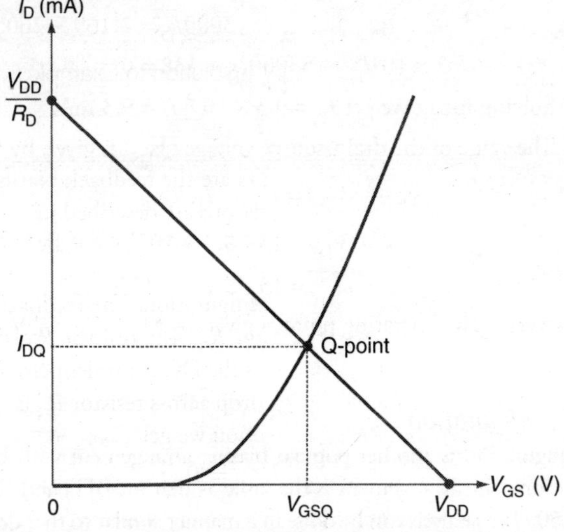

Figure 5.47 | Graphical method for determining the operating point for the circuit in Figure 5.45.

EXAMPLE 5.9 *Figure 5.48 shows a circuit using E-MOSFET. Given that the threshold voltage for the MOSFET is 2 V and $I_{D(on)} = 6$ mA for $V_{GS(on)} = 5$ V, determine the value of the operating point.*

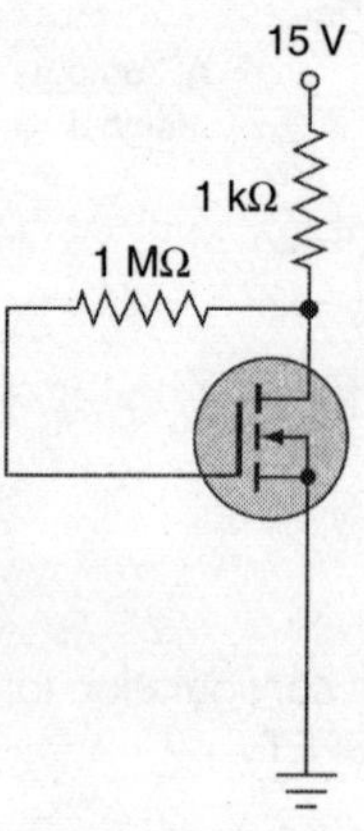

Figure 5.48 | Example 5.9.

Solution

1. Drain current in an E-MOSFET is given by
$$I_D = K(V_{GS} - V_T)^2$$
2. Therefore, $K = 6 \times 10^{-3}/(5-2)^2 = 0.67 \times 10^{-3}$ A/V $= 0.67$ mA/V.
3. Gate-source voltage in the feedback configuration is given by
$$V_{GS} = V_{DD} - I_D R_D$$
$$V_{GS} = 15 - I_D \times 1 \times 10^3 = 15 - 1000 I_D$$
4. Substituting this value of I_D in the expression $I_D = K(V_{GS} - V_T)^2$ we get
$$I_D = 0.67 \times 10^{-3}(15 - 1000I_D - 2)^2$$
$$I_D = 0.67 \times 10^{-3}(13 - 1000I_D)^2$$
$$3000I_D = 2(169 - 26000I_D + 10^6 I_D^2)$$
$$2 \times 10^6 I_D^2 - 55000I_D + 338 = 0$$
5. Solving for I_D we get $I_D = 9.3 \times 10^{-3}$ A $= 9.3$ mA.
6. The value of the drain-source voltage (V_{DS}) is given by
$$V_{DS} = V_{DD} - I_D R_D$$
$$V_{DS} = 15 - 9.3 \times 10^{-3} \times 1 \times 10^3$$
$$= 15 - 9.3 = 5.7 \text{ V}$$

Answer: The operating point is given by (9.3 mA, 5.7 V).

Voltage-Divider-Biasing Configuration

Voltage-divider-biasing configuration is another popular biasing arrangement with E-MOSFETs. Figure 5.49 shows the biasing configuration. The arrangement is the same as that for BJTs and JFETs. The DC equivalent circuit is shown in Figure 5.50. The analysis can be done in a manner similar to that done in the case of JFETs.

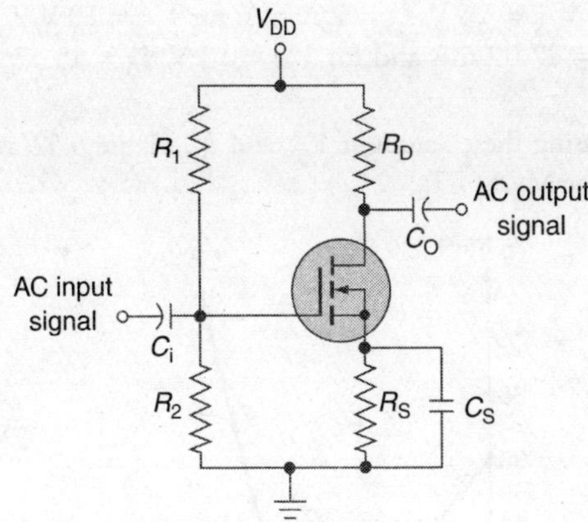

Figure 5.49 Voltage-divider-biasing configuration for N-channel E-MOSFET.

Figure 5.50 DC equivalent of the voltage-divider-biasing configuration in Figure 5.49.

EXAMPLE 5.10 *Figure 5.51 shows a voltage-divider configuration for the E-MOSFET. Given that the threshold voltage for the MOSFET is 4 V and the value of* $I_{D(on)} = 6$ *mA for* $V_{GS(on)} = 8$ *V, use graphical method to determine the value of the quiescent drain current, gate-source voltage and drain-source voltage.*

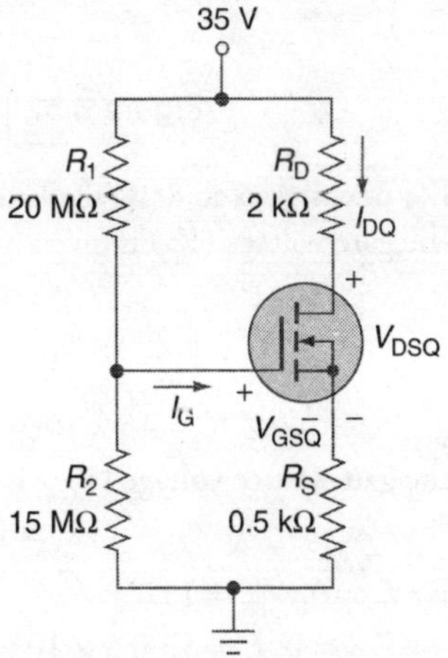

Figure 5.51 Example 5.10.

Solution

1. The transfer characteristics of the MOSFET can be plotted by finding the value of K using

$$K = \frac{I_{D(on)}}{(V_{GS(on)} - V_{GS(th)})^2}$$

2. Given that $I_{D(on)} = 6$ mA, $V_{GS(on)} = 8$ V and $V_{GS(th)} = 4$ V, therefore

$$K = 6 \times 10^{-3}/(8 - 4)^2 = 0.375 \times 10^{-3} \text{ A/V}^2$$

3. Therefore, the value of drain current is given by

$$I_D = 0.375 \times 10^{-3} (V_{GS} - V_{GS(th)})^2$$

4. For $V_{GS} = 5$ V, $I_D = 0.375$ mA; for $V_{GS} = 7.5$ V, $I_D = 4.59$ mA; for $V_{GS} = 10$ V, $I_D = 13.5$ mA; for $V_{GS} = 12.5$ V, $I_D = 27.09$ mA and for $V_{GS} = 15$ V, $I_D = 45.375$ mA.
5. The transfer curve can be plotted using these values of V_{GS} and I_D. Figure 5.52(a) shows the transfer characteristics of the MOSFET.

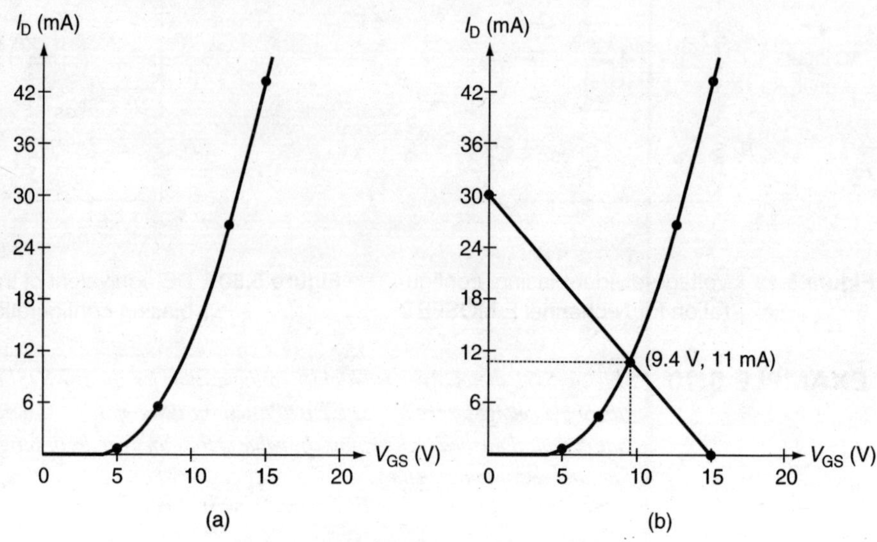

Figure 5.52 Solution to Example 5.10.

6. The next step is to draw the load line.
7. The gate voltage (V_G) is given by

$$V_G = \frac{R_2 \times V_{DD}}{R_1 + R_2}$$

$$V_G = 15 \times 10^6 \times 35/(20 \times 10^6 + 15 \times 10^6) = 15 \text{ V}$$

8. The gate-source voltage (V_{GS}) is given by

$$V_{GS} = V_G - V_S = V_G - I_D R_S$$

9. For $I_D = 0$, $V_{GS} = 15$ V
10. For $V_{GS} = 0$, $I_D = 15/0.5 \times 10^3 = 30$ mA
11. The next step is to draw the load line with coordinates (0, 15 V) and (30 mA, 0) on the transfer characteristics [Figure 5.52(b)].
12. From Figure 5.52(b), the quiescent values of gate-source voltage and drain current are 9.4 V and 11 mA respectively.
13. The value of the drain-source voltage is given by

$$V_{DS} = V_{DD} - I_D (R_D + R_S)$$

$$V_{DS} = 35 - 11 \times 10^{-3} (2 \times 10^3 + 0.5 \times 10^3) = 35 - 11 \times 2.5 = 7.5 \text{ V}$$

Answer: The quiescent values of drain-source voltage, gate-source voltage and drain current are 7.5 V, 9.4 V and 11 mA, respectively.

EXAMPLE 5.11 *Determine the values of voltages V_D and V_C for the circuit shown in Figure 5.53, given that the transistor β is 100, $V_{BE} = 0.7V$, saturation drain current of JFET is 10 mA and the pinch-off voltage is -5 V.*

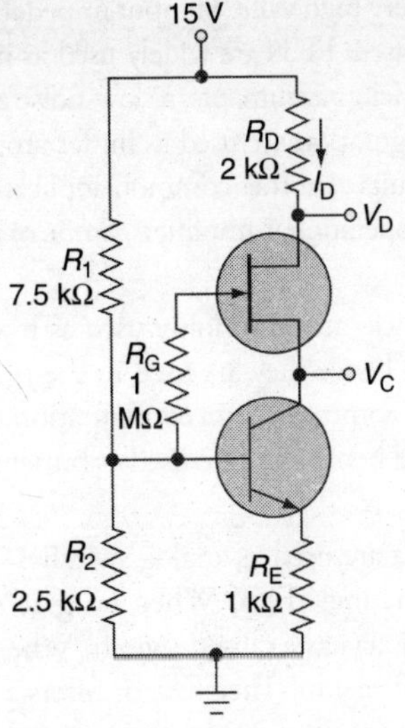

Figure 5.53 Example 5.11.

Solution

1. The figure shows the voltage-divider transistor configuration with an additional JFET connected between the base and the collector terminals.
2. Value of $\beta \times R_E = 100 \times 1 \times 10^3 = 10^5$.
   Value of $10 \times R_2 = 10 \times 2.5 \times 10^3 = 2.5 \times 10^4$.
3. As the value of $(\beta \times R_E)$ is much larger than $(10 \times R_2)$, approximate analysis can be done to analyze the voltage-divider transistor configuration.
4. $V_B = 15 \times 2.5 \times 10^3/(2.5 \times 10^3 + 7.5 \times 10^3) = 3.75$ V.
5. $V_E = V_B - V_{BE} = 3.75 - 0.7 = 3.05$ V.
6. $I_E = V_E/R_E = 3.05/(1 \times 10^3) = 3.05$ mA.
7. $I_C \cong I_E = 3.05$ mA.
8. In the figure shown, $I_D = I_S = I_C = 3.05$ mA.
9. The drain voltage (V_D) is equal to $V_D = 15 - I_D \times 2 \times 10^3$
   $$V_D = 15 - 3.05 \times 10^{-3} \times 2 \times 10^3 = 15 - 6.1 = 8.9 \text{ V}$$
10. As the current through the gate resistor is zero, therefore there is no voltage drop across the resistor R_G. The value of collector voltage (V_C) is equal to $V_C = V_B - V_{GS}$.
11. In a JFET the drain current is given by
   $$I_D = I_{DSS}\left(1 - \frac{V_{GS}}{V_P}\right)^2$$
   $$3.05 \times 10^{-3} = 10 \times 10^{-3}\ [1 - V_{GS}/(-5)]^2$$
   $$V_{GS} = -2.24 \text{ V}$$
12. Therefore, $V_C = 3.75 - (-2.24) = 5.99$ V.

Answer: $V_C = 5.99$ V, $V_D = 8.9$ V.

5.9 FET Applications

The major shortcoming of BJTs is their low value of input impedance which leads to loading of the input source. As FETs offer very high value of input impedance as compared to BJTs, they are ideal for many applications where BJTs can be used. FETs are widely used as input amplifiers in oscilloscopes, electronic voltmeters and other test and measurement instruments, as low-noise amplifiers in front end of TV and radio receivers. FETs in the common-drain configuration are used as buffer amplifiers. E-MOSFETs are very commonly used in the fabrication of integrated circuits. Another common application of FETs is in switching applications and as voltage-variable resistors (VVRs) in operational amplifiers. Some of the common applications of FETs are discussed in this section.

1. **Amplifiers:** FET devices are commonly used as low-noise amplifiers and as buffer amplifiers. FETs are low-noise devices and hence they are used in the front-end of receivers and other electronic equipments and systems. JFETs in common-drain configuration (source follower) offer high input impedance and low output impedance and hence they are used as buffer amplifiers to isolate the preceding stage from the following stage.
2. **Analog Switch:** FETs are used as analog switches. Figure 5.54 shows one possible switching configuration using an N-channel JFET. When no gate voltage (V_{GG}) is applied, the FET operates in the saturation region and acts as a closed switch. When a negative gate voltage (V_{GG}) is applied, the FET operates in the cut-off region. Therefore, it offers a very high resistance and acts as an open switch.
3. **Multiplexers:** FETs are used in multiplexer circuits where each FET device acts as a single-pole single-throw switch. Figure 5.55 shows an N-channel JFET-based multiplexer. The input signals are applied to the drain terminals of the JFETs while the corresponding control inputs are applied to the gate terminals of the JFETs. When the control input corresponding to one of the input channels is made zero, that input is transmitted to the output. The control inputs for the other channels are made more negative than the $V_{GS(off)}$ voltage. Hence all the other input signals are blocked.
4. **Current Limiters:** FETs can also be used in current-limiting applications as shown in Figure 5.56. During the normal operation of the circuit, the JFET acts in the ohmic region. When the load current increases substantially due to short circuit or any other reason, the JFET operates in the saturation region. Hence it acts as a constant current source and prevents excessive current through the load.
5. **Voltage-Variable Resistors (VVRs):** FETs when operated in the ohmic region (for small positive values of drain-to-source voltage V_{DS}) of their characteristics, act as voltage-variable resistors. In this region the drain

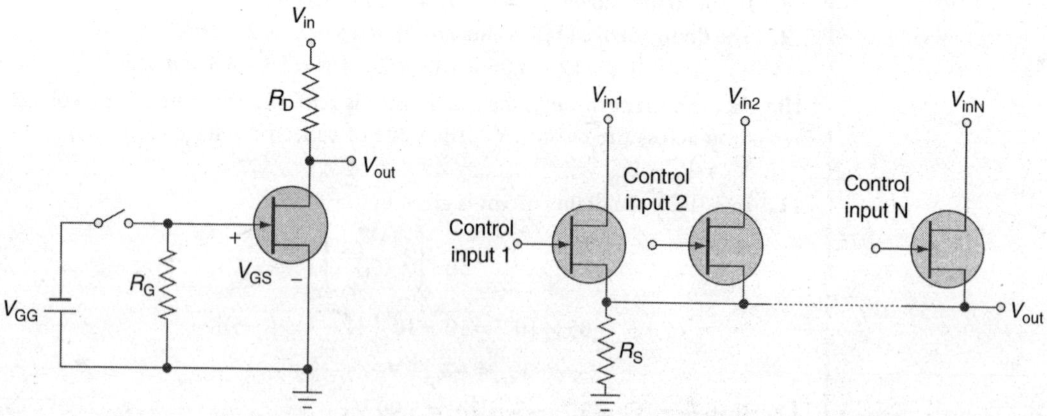

Figure 5.54 | FET as an analog switch.

Figure 5.55 | FET as a multiplexer.

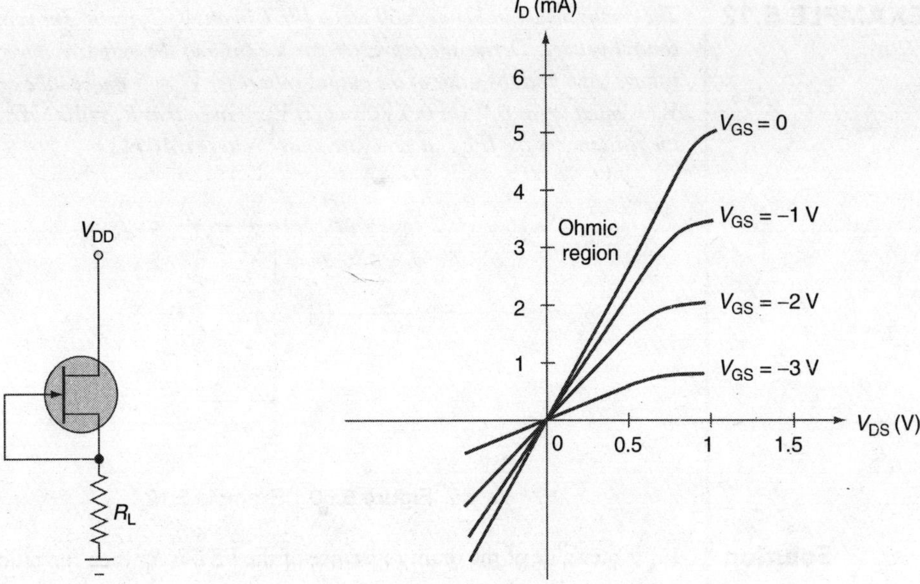

Figure 5.56 FET for current limiting.

Figure 5.57 Characteristics of an N-channel JFET in the ohmic region.

resistance R_D can be controlled by the gate-to-source voltage (V_{GS}). For an N-channel JFET, the value of R_D increases with increase in the negative value of V_{GS} as shown in Figure 5.57. As we can see from the figure, the curve is symmetrical near the origin, that is, for small negative values of drain-source voltage the curves are symmetrical to that of positive values of drain-source voltage. Thus, if an AC voltage (with small peak-to-peak voltage) is applied between the drain and the source terminals, then the FET acts as a linear resistor for a given gate-source voltage. FET-based VVRs are used in automatic gain control circuits.

6. **Oscillators:** FETs are also used in phase-shift oscillators (Figure 5.58) and pierce type of crystal-controlled oscillators (Figure 5.59). Oscillators are described in detail in Chapter 12 on sinusoidal oscillators.

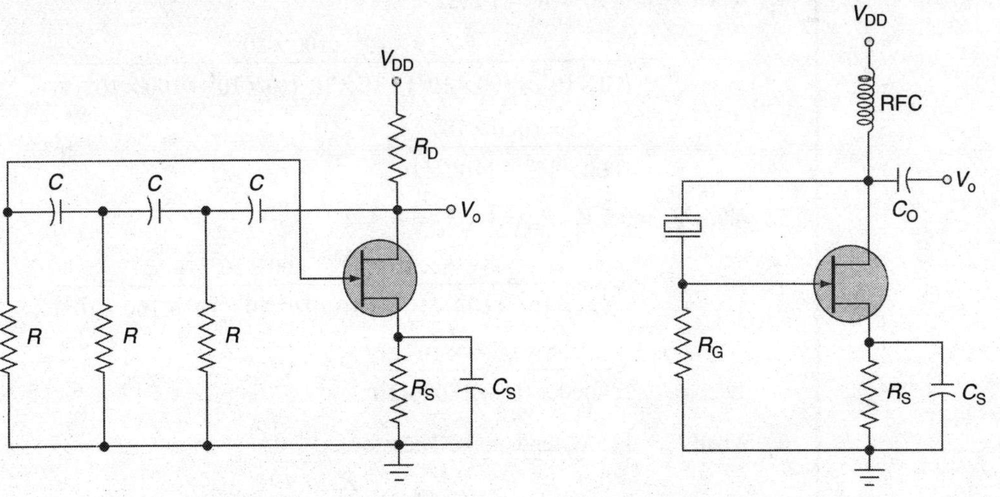

Figure 5.58 FET-based phase-shift oscillator.

Figure 5.59 FET-based Pierce oscillator.

EXAMPLE 5.12 *The circuit shown in Figure 5.60 uses a JFET in an AGC circuit. The voltage V_C is the control voltage. Derive the expression for the ratio of the output voltage to the input voltage. Also find the value of the output voltage for $V_{in} = 5$ V when the control voltage V_C is equal to (a) 0 V, (b) 0.5 V_P and (c) V_P. (Given that $R_L = 100$ kΩ, $R = 10$ kΩ, the resistance of the JFET at zero gate-source voltage is 10 kΩ.)*

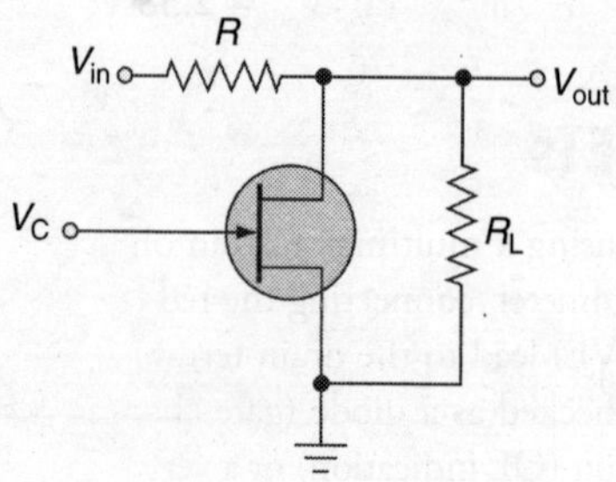

Figure 5.60 Example 5.12.

Solution

1. If the value of the drain resistance of the FET is R_D then the ratio V_{out} to V_{in} is given by

$$\frac{V_{out}}{V_{in}} = \frac{R_D \| R_L}{(R_D \| R_L) + R} = \frac{R_D \times R_L}{(R_D \times R_L) + R(R_D + R_L)}$$

2. The value of the resistance (R_D) is given by the expression

$$R_D = \frac{R_o}{(1 - V_{GS}/V_P)^2}$$

where R_o is the resistance at $V_{GS} = 0$.

3. The control voltage is applied between the gate and the source terminals, therefore $V_C = V_{GS}$.

4. When $V_C = 0$, $R_D = R_o = 10$ kΩ

$$V_{out} = \frac{5 \times 10 \times 10^3 \times 100 \times 10^3}{(10 \times 10^3 \times 100 \times 10^3) + 10 \times 10^3 (10 \times 10^3 + 100 \times 10^3)}$$

$$= \frac{5 \times 1000 \times 10^6}{1000 \times 10^6 + 1100 \times 10^6} = 2.38 \text{ V}$$

5. When $V_C = 0.5\ V_P$, $R_D = 4 \times R_o = 40$ kΩ

$$V_{out} = \frac{5 \times 40 \times 10^3 \times 100 \times 10^3}{(40 \times 10^3 \times 100 \times 10^3) + 10 \times 10^3 (40 \times 10^3 + 100 \times 10^3)}$$

$$= \frac{5 \times 4000 \times 10^6}{4000 \times 10^6 + 1400 \times 10^6} = 3.7 \text{ V}$$

6. When $V_C = V_P$, R_D tends to ∞. Therefore

$$\frac{V_{out}}{V_{in}} = \frac{R_L}{R_L + R}$$

$$= 100 \times 10^3/(100 \times 10^3 + 10 \times 10^3) = 0.91$$

$$V_o = 5 \times 0.91 = 4.55 \text{ V}$$

Answer: $\dfrac{V_{out}}{V_{in}} = \dfrac{R_D \times R_L}{(R_D \times R_L) + R(R_D + R_L)}$

(a) $V_{out} = 2.38$ V; (b) $V_{out} = 3.7$ V; (c) $V_{out} = 4.55$ V

5.10 Testing FETs

FETs can be checked using a multimeter or an ohmmeter. When an N-channel JFET is checked using a multimeter or an ohmmeter, connecting the red (POSITIVE) lead of the multimeter to the gate terminal and the black (NEGATIVE) lead to the drain terminal should show a low resistance [Figure 5.61(a)]. In this condition, the JFET is checked as a diode (gate-channel junction). By reversing the connections, the meter should show an open circuit (OL indication) or a very high resistance [Figure 5.61(b)]. Also, connecting the red (POSITIVE) lead of the multimeter to the gate terminal and the black (NEGATIVE) lead to the source terminal should show a low resistance [Figure 5.61(c)] and by reversing the connections, the meter should show an open circuit (OL indication) or a very high resistance [Figure 5.61(d)]. If the meter shows a high resistance in both cases, it indicates that the gate junction is open. A low resistance in both cases indicates a shorted gate.

When the meter is connected between the drain and the source terminals, it indicates a small resistance of the order of few hundreds of ohms. The resistance check from the source to the drain [Figure 5.61(e)]

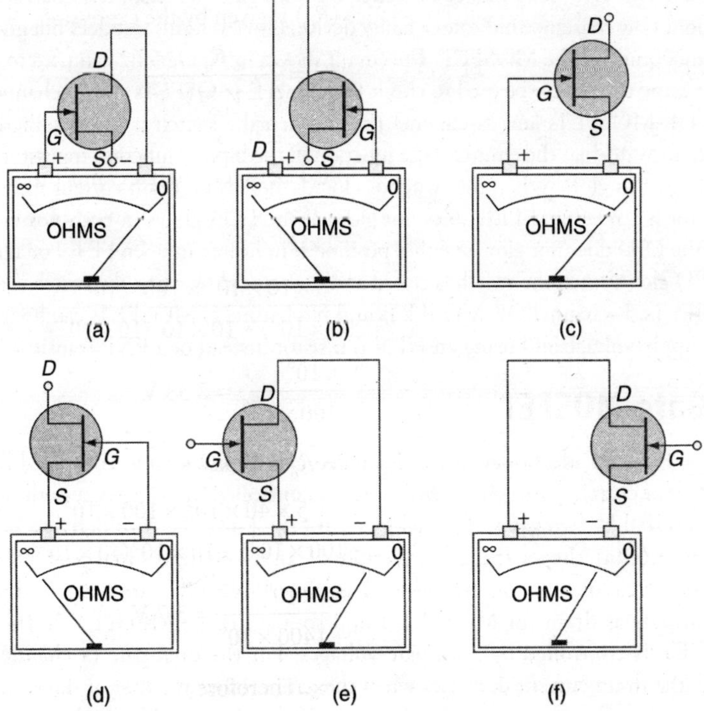

Figure 5.61 | Testing N-channel JFETs with a multimeter.

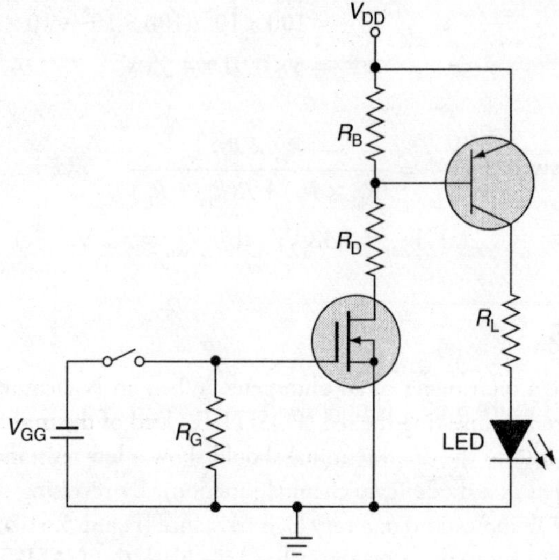

Figure 5.62 | MOSFET test circuit.

should yield similar value as from the drain to the source [Figure 5.61(f)]. While doing the source-drain resistance check, the pins of the JFET should be inserted into an anti-static material prior to testing. This ensures that the residual voltage across the gate-channel PN junction will be neutralized and the test will give accurate results. A P-channel JFET can also be checked in a similar manner.

While checking a MOSFET, the resistance measured between gate and drain terminals should be infinitely high in either direction. Low resistance indicates a faulty device. However, this test does not give complete information about the functioning of the MOSFET. The circuit shown in Figure 5.62 can used to check N-channel DE-MOSFETs. The same circuit can be used to check P-channel E-MOSFETs and N-channel JFETs.

For N-channel DE-MOSFETs and N-channel JFETs when the switch is open, sufficient current flows through resistor R_B to forward-bias the emitter–base junction of the bipolar junction transistor and it starts conducting. The LED begins to glow. When the switch is closed, there is no drain current through the FET and therefore the transistor is cut-off and LED does not glow. If the LED glows in both positions, it indicates a shorted FET and if the LED does not glow in either position it indicates an open FET. For a healthy P-channel E-MOSFET, the LED glows when the switch is closed and does not glow when the switch is open.

The P-channel JFETs, P-channel DE-MOSFETs and N-channel E-MOSFETs can be tested by reversing the polarity of the supply voltage and using an NPN transistor instead of a PNP transistor.

5.11 Dual-Gate MOSFET

In a dual-gate MOSFET, an additional second insulated gate is provided as compared to a conventional MOSFET. The flow of current through the MOSFET is controlled by voltages at both the gate terminals. Since the control is exerted by two gates, the dual-gate MOSFET may be considered to be the counterpart of a tetrode. Figure 5.63(a) shows the cross-section of an N-channel dual-gate DE-MOSFET and Figure 5.63(b) shows the circuit symbol. The device acts if two MOSFETs are connected in series. The N+ region in the middle acts as drain for MOSFET-1 and source for the MOSFET-2. The flow of current through the MOSFET is controlled by both gate voltages. For the dual-gate N-channel DE-MOSFET shown in the figure, the drain current decreases when the gate voltage at either of the two gate terminals is made negative. It may be mentioned here that the gate terminal-1 provides higher transconductance as

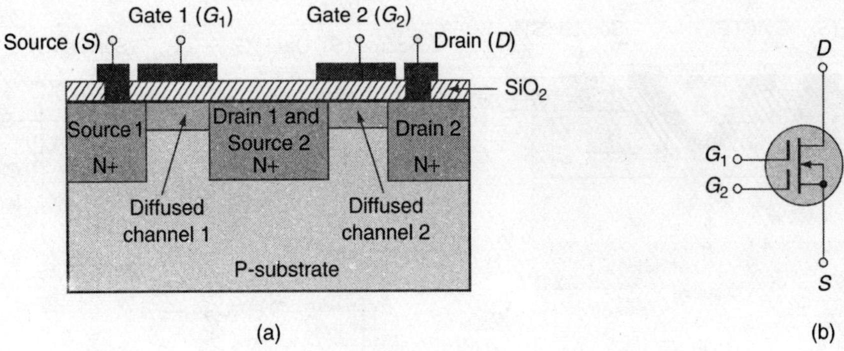

Figure 5.63 | N-channel dual-gate DE-MOSFET.

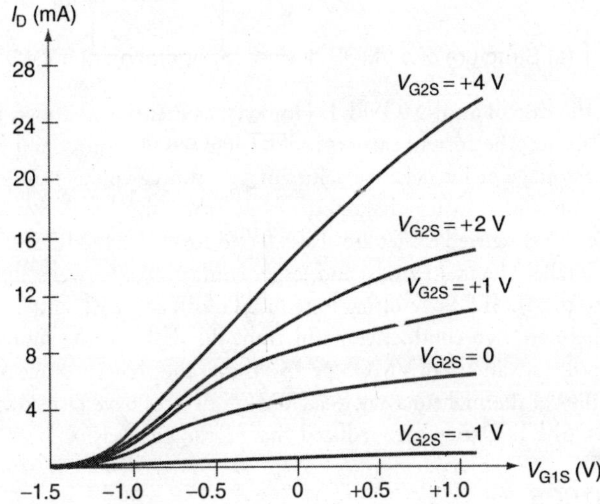

Figure 5.64 | Transfer characteristics of an N-channel dual-gate DE-MOSFET.

compared to the gate terminal-2. Owing to simultaneous control of two gate voltages, the device is used in applications such as AGC amplifiers, mixers and demodulators. When it is used in an AGC amplifier, the signal to be amplified is connected to Gate-1 and the voltage to control the gain is applied to Gate-2.

Figure 5.64 shows the transfer characteristics of a popular N-channel dual-gate DE-MOSFET. The drain characteristics are similar to that of a conventional N-channel DE-MOSFET.

5.12 VMOS Devices

MOSFETs have smaller power-handling capability as compared to BJTs. The power-handling capability of a MOSFET can be improved if the construction of the MOSFET is modified as shown in Figure 5.65(a). The MOSFET shown in the figure is referred to as vertical metal oxide semiconductor (VMOS) FET or as power MOSFET. VMOS has a vertical structure with the channel formed in the vertical direction rather than the horizontal direction. The operation of a VMOS device is similar to that of an E-MOSFET. No channel exists between drain and source terminals until the gate-source voltage is made positive. For positive values of gate-source voltage, an N-channel is formed close to the gate [Figure 5.65(b)]

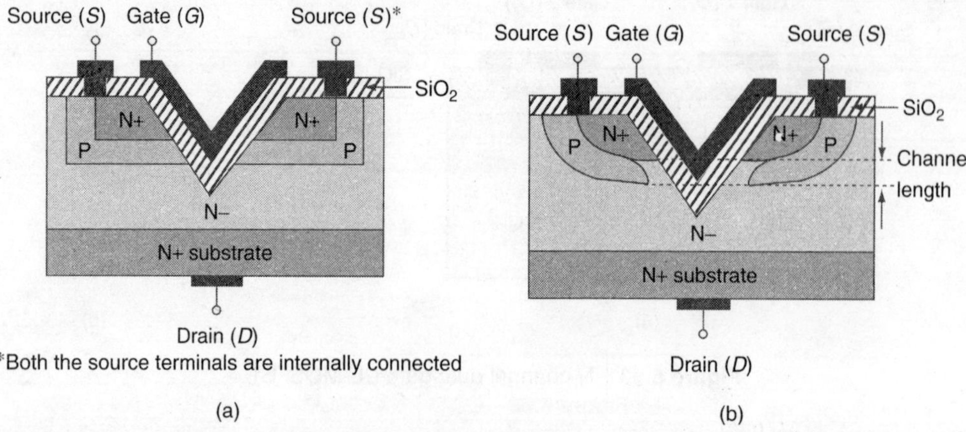

Figure 5.65 (a) Structure of a VMOS device; (b) operation of a VMOS device.

similar to that formed in the case of an E-MOSFET. However, as mentioned above, the channel is formed in the vertical direction. This lets the current carriers to flow between the source and the drain terminals. In the absence of gate-source voltage or for negative values of gate-source voltages, no channel exists and the drain current is zero. Drain and transfer characteristics are the same as shown in the case of planar E-MOSFETs. The MOSFETs discussed earlier are also referred to as planar MOSFETs.

VMOS devices have smaller channel lengths and larger contact area between the channel and the N+ doped regions as compared to MOSFETs, resulting in reduced resistance levels and hence in reduced power-dissipation levels. Also there are two conductive paths from the drain to the source which also leads to higher current rating. Another advantage of VMOS devices is that they have positive temperature coefficient which reduces the possibility of thermal runaway. Also VMOS devices have faster switching times as compared to that of planar MOSFETs as they have reduced charge storage levels.

5.13 CMOS Devices

Complementary metal oxide semiconductor (CMOS) are those semiconductor devices in which both P-type and N-type E-MOSFETs are diffused onto the same chip. The CMOS configuration has extensive applications in computer logic design. CMOS devices offer high input impedance, low power consumption and require far less space as compared to BJT-based logic circuit. However, they offer slower switching speed as compared to BJTs.

Figure 5.66 shows the basic inverter circuit using CMOS configuration. Inverter is a logic circuit that inverts the applied input signal, that is, logic LOW and logic HIGH levels applied at the input terminals result in logic HIGH and logic LOW levels at the output terminals, respectively. The complementary N-type and P-type E-MOSFETs are connected in series, with their gate terminals tied together to form the input terminal. Also, the drain terminals are connected together to form the output terminal. Source terminal of the P-channel MOSFET (S_2) is connected to voltage V_{SS} (between 5 and 15 V) and the source terminal of the N-channel MOSFET (S_1) is connected to the ground.

Figure 5.67 shows the simplified diagram of the CMOS architecture shown in Figure 5.66. The circuit operates as follows: When the input voltage V_{in} is at logic LOW, the gate-source voltage (V_{G2S2}) of the P-channel E-MOSFET is equal to $-V_{SS}$ and the MOSFET is in the ON-state, providing a low resistance path between V_{SS} and the output terminal. The gate-source voltage (V_{G1S1}) of N-channel E-MOSFET is 0 V and therefore it is OFF, resulting in very high impedance between the output terminal and the ground. Therefore, the output voltage V_{out} is equal to the supply voltage V_{SS} or in other words the output voltage (V_{out}) is at logic HIGH.

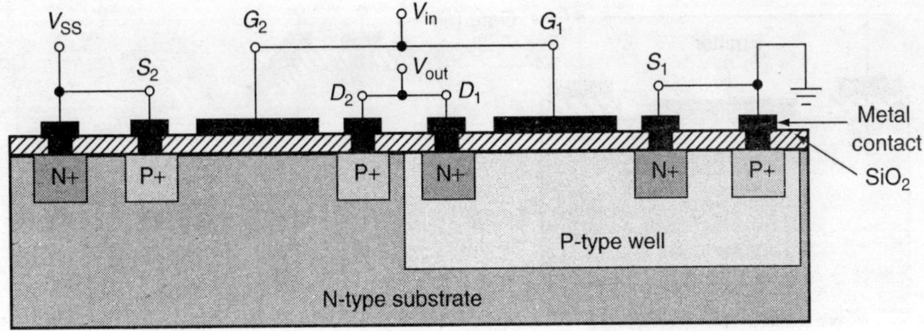

Figure 5.66 | CMOS inverter.

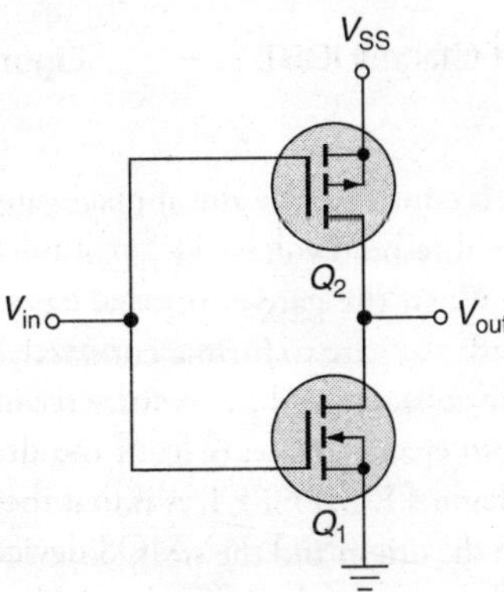

Figure 5.67 | Simplified diagram of CMOS inverter.

When the input voltage V_{in} is at logic HIGH, that is, equal to the supply voltage V_{SS}, the gate-source voltage (V_{G2S2}) of the P-channel E-MOSFET is 0 V and therefore, the MOSFET is in the OFF-state. The gate-source voltage (V_{G1S1}) of the N-channel E-MOSFET is equal to the supply voltage (V_{SS}) and hence it is switched ON, offering a low resistance path. The two MOSFETs form a voltage divider and the output voltage V_{out} is approximately equal to 0 V. Therefore, logic HIGH at the input results in logic LOW at the output. In either state, one of the MOSFETs is OFF. This results in very low power dissipation in the device. Special handling precautions mentioned for MOSFETs are also applicable to CMOS devices.

5.14 Insulated Gate Bipolar Transistors (IGBTs)

IGBTs are three-terminal power semiconductor devices having positive attributes of both BJTs and MOSFETs. IGBTs offer fast switching times similar to that of MOSFETs and lower ON-state voltages and larger blocking voltages similar to that of BJTs. They are used in high efficiency and fast switching applications like switch mode power supplies, traction motor control and induction heating.

Figure 5.68 shows the cross-sectional view of an N-channel IGBT device. We can see from the figure that the construction of IGBT is very similar to that of a VMOS device except that the N+ drain is replaced by P+ collector layer, thus forming a vertical PNP transistor. Figure 5.69 shows the simplified equivalent circuit for the N-channel IGBT. The equivalent circuit shows an N-channel power MOSFET driving a wide base PNP transistor in a Darlington configuration.

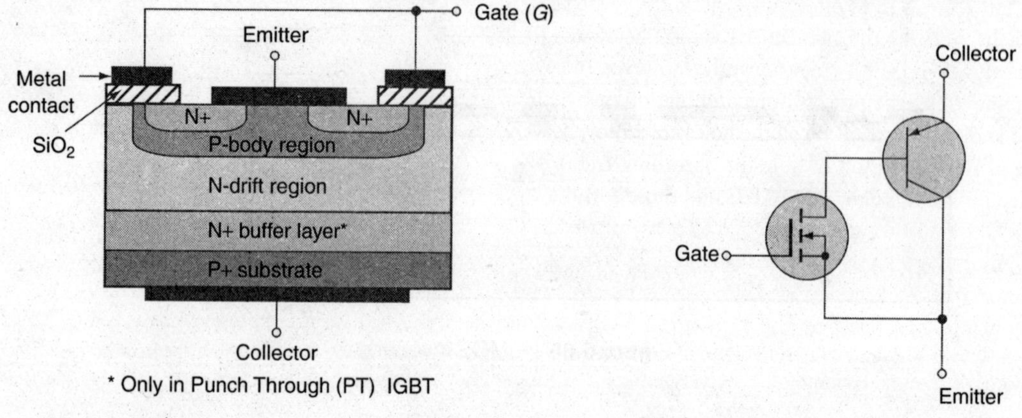

Figure 5.68 | Cross-section of N-channel IGBT.

Figure 5.69 | Simplified equivalent circuit of an N-channel IGBT.

The ON/OFF-state of the device is controlled by the applied gate voltage w.r.t. to the emitter voltage. If the gate-emitter voltage is less that the threshold voltage (V_{TH}) of the MOSFET, no inversion layer is created and the device is in the OFF-state. When the gate-emitter voltage is above the threshold voltage (V_{TH}), enough electrons will be drawn towards the gate to form a conductive channel across the body region, leading to the flow of current between the collector and the emitter terminals.

Figure 5.70 shows the typical output characteristics of an N-channel IGBT device. The output characteristics are quite similar to that of an N-channel E-MOSFET. A noteworthy feature on the IGBT characteristics is the offset of approximately 0.7 V from the origin and the steep slope of the rising portion of the characteristics. The offset is because the ON-state voltage across the IGBT is one diode-drop higher than that of N-channel E-MOSFET. The steep slope of the transfer characteristics is attributed to the fact that current flow in an IGBT is due to flow of both electrons and holes as compared to an N-channel MOSFET where the current flow is due to the flow of electrons only. This reduces the effective resistance to current flow in the drift region. The resulting reduction in the ON-state voltage is the main advantage of IGBTs over power MOSFETs.

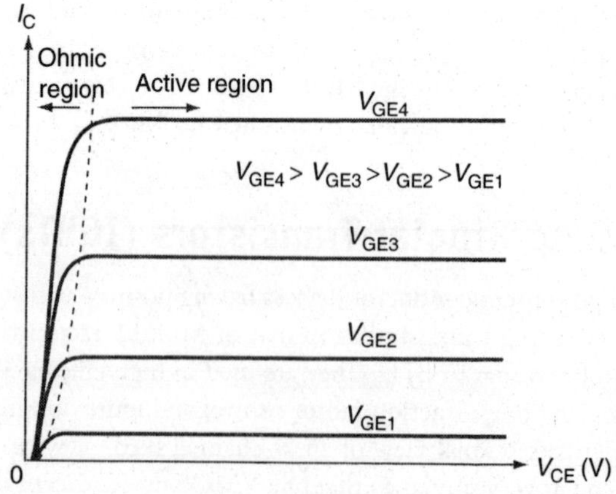

Figure 5.70 | Output characteristics of an N-channel IGBT.

However, IGBTs offer slow switching speeds especially during turn-off. Turn-off in the case of IGBTs is done by reducing the gate-emitter voltage below the threshold voltage. The electron flow in the IGBT as in an N-channel MOSFET stops abruptly. However, in an IGBT holes are left in the drift region and they can only be removed by the process of recombination or by applying a voltage gradient. This results in a tail current in IGBTs during turn-off till all the holes are removed. An N+ buffer layer is added in some IGBTs to control the rate of recombination of holes by absorbing trapped holes during turn-off. IGBTs with N+ buffer layer are called punch-through (PT) IGBTs and those without the N+ buffer layer are called non-punch-through (NPT) IGBTs. PT IGBTs are also referred to as asymmetrical IGBTs and NPT IGBTs as symmetrical IGBTs.

Another problem associated with IGBTs is the occurrence of latch-up phenomenon. Latch-up refers to the failure mode where the IGBT can no longer be turned off by the gate voltage. Latch-up can be explained with the help of a more detailed equivalent circuit of the IGBT as shown in Figure 5.71. The basic structure of an IGBT resembles a thyristor (series of PNPN junctions) and latch-up can occur if the IGBT were not properly used.

Like MOSFETs, IGBTs also are susceptible to gate insulation damage by the electrostatic discharge of energy through the devices. Therefore similar precautions must be taken while handling IGBTs as taken in the case of MOSFETs.

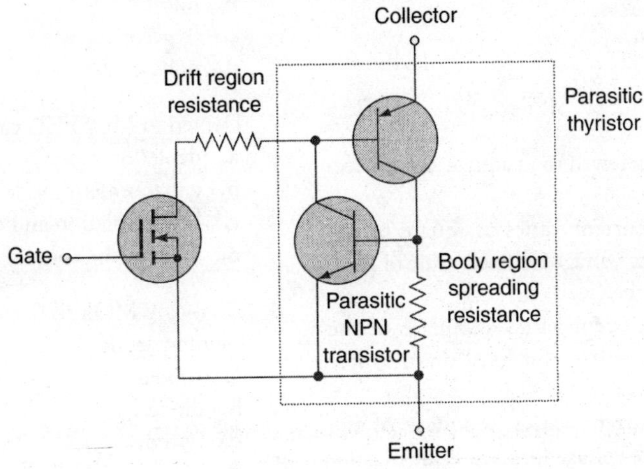

Figure 5.71 Detailed equivalent circuit of an N-channel IGBT.

KEY TERMS

Amplification factor (μ)
Common-drain configuration
Common-gate configuration
Complementary metal oxide semiconductor (CMOS)
Depletion MOSFET
Dual-gate MOSFET
Dynamic drain resistance (r_d)
Enhancement MOSFET
Field effect transistor (FET)
Fixed-bias configuration
Insulated gate bipolar transistor (IGBT)
Junction field effect transistor (JFET)
Metal oxide field effect transistor (MOSFET)
Shockley's equation
Self-bias configuration
Static drain resistance
Transconductance (g_m)
Vertical metal oxide semiconductor (VMOS)
Voltage-divider configuration

OBJECTIVE-TYPE EXERCISES

Multiple-Choice Questions

1. FETs are
   - **a.** voltage controlled devices with high input impedance.
   - **b.** current controlled devices with low input impedance.
   - **c.** voltage controlled devices with low input impedance.
   - **d.** current controlled devices with high input impedance.

2. For low values of drain-source voltages, the JFET acts as a
   - **a.** current source.
   - **b.** voltage source.
   - **c.** BJT.
   - **d.** resistor.

3. JFETs are also referred to as square-law devices because
   - **a.** the drain current varies as square of the drain-source voltage for fixed value of gate-source voltage.
   - **b.** the drain current varies as square of the gate-source voltage for fixed drain-source voltage.
   - **c.** the gate current varies as square of the drain-source voltage for fixed value of gate-source voltage.
   - **d.** the gate current varies as square of the gate-source voltage for fixed drain-source voltage.

4. Which of the following devices has revolutionized the field of computers?
   - **a.** BJTs
   - **b.** enhancement MOSFETs
   - **c.** depletion MOSFETs
   - **d.** JFETs

5. Which of the following statements is/are false?
   - **a.** Noise level of an FET device is more than that of a BJT.
   - **b.** Noise level of an FET device is less than that of a BJT.
   - **c.** Input impedance of a MOSFET is greater than that of a JFET.
   - **d.** Input impedance of a MOSFET is less than that of a JFET.
   - **e.** Both (a) and (c).
   - **f.** Both (b) and (c).

6. The transconductance curve of a JFET is
   - **a.** parabolic.
   - **b.** linear.
   - **c.** hyperbolic.
   - **d.** none of the above.

7. Depletion MOSFETs can operate in
   - **a.** depletion mode only.
   - **b.** enhancement mode only.
   - **c.** both depletion and enhancement modes.
   - **d.** none of the above.

8. Dual-gate MOSFETs can be considered to be counterpart of
   - **a.** triodes.
   - **b.** diodes.
   - **c.** tetrodes.
   - **d.** pentodes.

9. The principle of operation of a VMOS device is similar to that of
   - **a.** enhancement MOSFET.
   - **b.** depletion MOSFET.
   - **c.** insulated gate bipolar transistor.
   - **d.** junction FET.

10. Which of the following statements is/are true?
    - **a.** IGBTs offer fast switching times similar to that of MOSFETs and lower ON-state voltages and larger blocking voltages similar to that of BJTs.

b. IGBTs offer fast switching times similar to that of BJTs and lower-ON-state voltages and larger blocking voltages similar to that of BJTs.

c. The equivalent circuit of an IGBT is an N-channel power MOSFET driving a wide base PNP transistor in a Darlington configuration.

d. The equivalent circuit of an IGBT is an N-channel power MOSFET driving a wide base NPN transistor in a Darlington configuration.

e. Both (a) and (c).

f. Both (a) and (d).

g. Both (b) and (c).

h. Both (b) and (d)

Match the Following

Match the terms in column (a) to those in column (b).

S. No.	Column (a)	S. No.	Column (b)
1.	N-channel enhancement MOSFET	1.	Drain (*D*), Gate (*G*), P, N, P, Source (*S*)
2.	N-channel JFET	2.	Source (*S*) Gate (*G*) Drain (*D*), N+, N, N+, P-substrate, Substrate (*SS*)
3.	P-channel JFET	3.	Source (*S*) Gate (*G*) Drain (*D*), P, P, N-substrate, Substrate (*SS*)

4.	N-channel depletion MOSFET	4.	Source (S) Gate (G) Drain (D) N N P-substrate Substrate (SS)
5.	P-channel enhancement MOSFET	5.	Drain (D) Gate (G) N P N Source (S)
6.	P-channel depletion MOSFET	6.	Source (S) Gate (G) Drain (D) P+ P P+ N-substrate Substrate (SS)

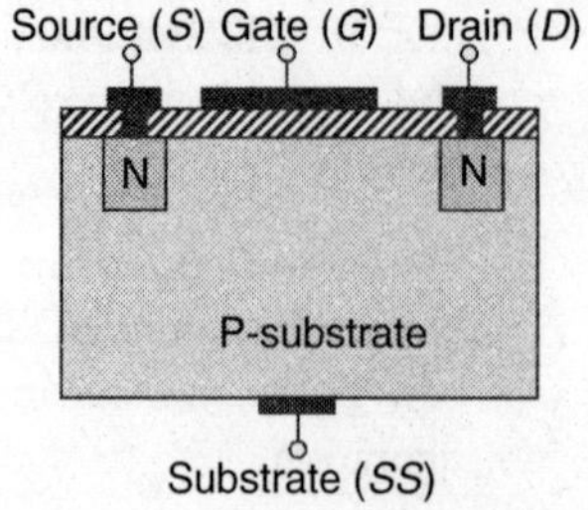

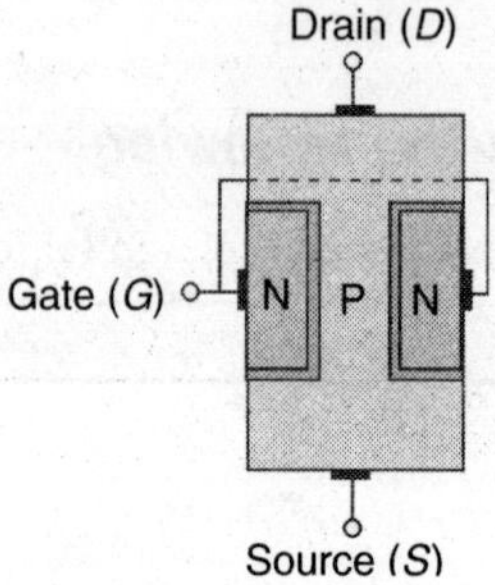

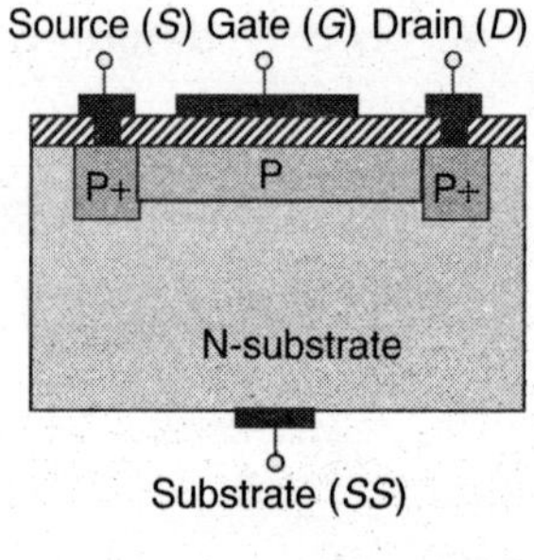

REVIEW QUESTIONS

1. Draw the cross-sectional view of an N-channel JFET and explain its principle of operation. Draw the I_D versus V_{DS} graph for different values of V_{GS} and highlight the different regions of operation.
2. Write short notes on the following:
   a. FET as a voltage variable resistance
   b. Handling MOSFETs
   c. Differences between VMOS and MOSFET
   d. Comparison between BJTs, JFETs and MOSFETs
3. What is an insulated gate bipolar transistor (IGBT)? Is there any difference between IGBT and MOSFET? If yes, then mention any two differences between the two devices.
4. With the help of transfer characteristics for depletion-type and enhancement-type MOSFETs, briefly describe as to how the depletion-type MOSFETs are usually ON devices that can be switched OFF with an appropriate gate signal and the enhancement-type MOSFETs are usually OFF devices that can be switched ON with an appropriate gate signal.

5. With the help of neat diagrams, describe the operation of N-channel depletion and enhancement MOSFETs.
6. Why are FETs known as unipolar devices?
7. Draw the circuit for the voltage-divider configuration using enhancement MOSFETs. Also derive the expression for the operating point.
8. How can one identify the terminals and the type of a MOSFET using laboratory equipments?
9. Explain the principle of operation of a dual-gate MOSFET? Also mention any two of its typical application areas.
10. What are CMOS devices? Explain with the help of relevant diagrams the operation of a CMOS NAND gate.

PROBLEMS

1. An experimental setup using a JFET gave the following readings:
   i. With $V_{GS} = 0$ V and $V_{DS} = 15$ V, $I_D = 15$ mA
   ii. With $V_{GS} = 0$ V and $V_{DS} = 10$ V, $I_D = 14$ mA
   iii. With $V_{GS} = -1$ V and $V_{DS} = 15$ V, $I_D = 13$ mA

   Determine the values of
   a. Drain resistance
   b. Transconductance
   c. Amplification factor
   d. Type of JFET
2. For the circuit shown in Figure 5.72 if the saturation drain current is 5 mA and the pinch-off voltage of the JFET is −4 V, determine the value of quiescent drain current and drain-source voltage. Also determine the value of quiescent gate-source voltage.

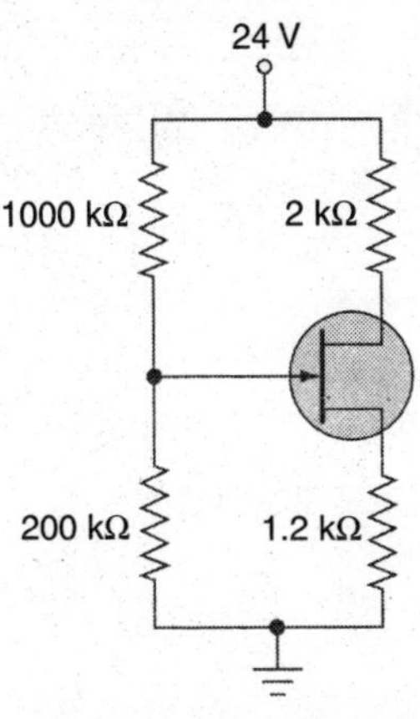

Figure 5.72 | Problem 2.

3. For the AGC circuit shown in Figure 5.73 given that r_o is the drain resistance at $V_{GS} = 0$ V, derive the expression for the voltage gain. Assume that $V_C^2 >> V_P^2$.

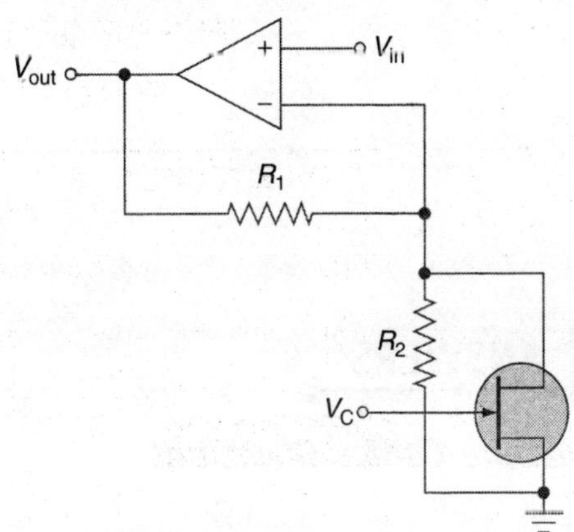

Figure 5.73 | Problem 3.

4. Identify the circuit shown in Figure 5.74. What is the value of current I_{out}?

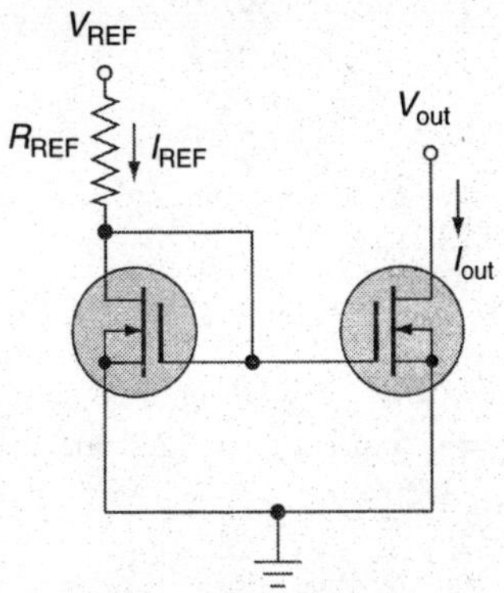

Figure 5.74 | Problem 4.

5. Refer to the circuit shown in Figure 5.75. Given that the transistor β is 100, $V_{BE} = 0.7$ V, saturation drain current of JFET is 10 mA and the pinch-off voltage is −5 V, determine the values of voltages V_D and V_E.

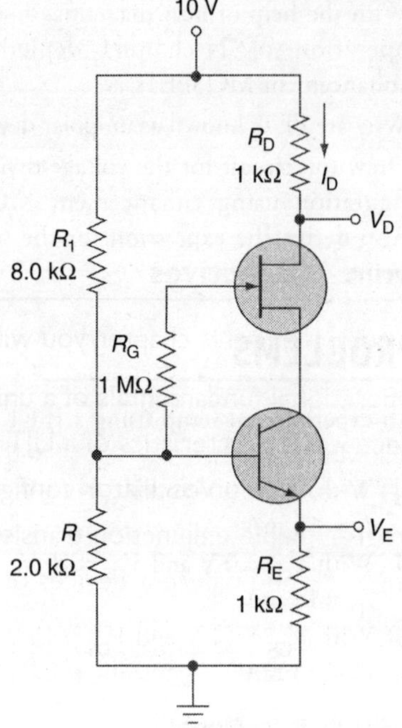

Figure 5.75 | Problem 5.

ANSWERS

Multiple-Choice Questions

1. (a)
2. (d)
3. (b)
4. (b)
5. (f)
6. (a)
7. (c)
8. (c)
9. (a)
10. (e)

Match the Following

1. 2
2. 1
3. 5
4. 4
5. 3
6. 6

Problems

1. (a) 5 kΩ, (b) 2 mA/V, (c) 10, (d) N-channel JFET
2. $I_{DQ} = 3.75$ mA, $V_{DSQ} = 12$ V and $V_{GSQ} = -0.5$ V
3. $1+\frac{R_1}{R_2}+\frac{R_2}{r_o}\times\left(1-\frac{2V_C}{V_P}\right)$
4. The circuit is a current mirror, $I_{out} = I_{REF}$
5. $V_D = 8.7$ V, $V_E = 1.3$ V

CHAPTER 6

UJTs and Thyristors

Learning Objectives

After completing this chapter, you will learn the following:

- Operational fundamentals of a unijunction transistor (UJT).
- Electrical characteristics of a UJT and existence of negative resistance region.
- UJT in relaxation oscillator configuration.
- Programmable unijunction transistor (PUT).
- Thyristor and different devices of thyristor family.
- PNPN diode.
- Silicon-controlled rectifier (SCR).
- DIAC and TRIAC.
- Gate turn-OFF thyristor (GTO).
- Rate effect in thyristors.
- Electrical parameters of thyristors.
- Thyristor applications.

The focus in this chapter is on two very popular current-controllable negative resistance semiconductor devices, that is, thyristors and unijunction transistors (UJTs). Thyristor is a generalized name for solid-state semiconductor devices having four or more semiconductor layers and three or more semiconductor junctions. These devices can be with or without the gate-control terminal and act like a latching type of switch. PNPN diode is the most basic device in the family of thyristors. Other popular devices in the family include silicon-controlled rectifier (SCR) and its variants like silicon unilateral switch (SUS), silicon bilateral switch (SBS), DIAC and TRIAC. SCR is the most widely used device in the family of thyristors and the term thyristor is used interchangeably with SCR. Other devices discussed in the chapter include gate turn-OFF thyristors and programmable unijunction transistors (PUT). The topics covered in the chapter include operational principle, electrical characteristics, major performance specifications and typical circuit applications of these devices.

6.1 Unijunction Transistor

Unijunction transistor commonly known as UJT is a semiconductor device with one PN junction as is evident from the word unijunction in its name. Since it has got three terminals like a transistor, it is called unijunction transistor. 2N 2646 is the most commonly used UJT type number.

Construction

Figures 6.1(a) and (b), respectively, show the constructional features and circuit symbol of a UJT. As shown in Figure 6.1(a), it comprises a lightly doped N-type silicon bar with two ohmic contacts called base terminals, B_1 and B_2, made to its two extreme ends and P-type emitter placed closer to the base B_2 to form a PN junction. Figure 6.2 shows the electrical equivalent circuit of a UJT. The equivalent circuit comprises a potential divider arrangement of two resistors and a PN junction diode. Resistor R_{BB1} represents the resistance of base bar between B_1 terminal and the PN junction and resistor R_{BB2} represents resistance of the base bar between B_2 terminal and the PN junction. R_{BB1} has been shown as a variable resistance as its value depends upon the emitter current flowing through the PN junction when it is forward-biased. For $I_E = 0$, total resistance of the base bar (= $R_{BB1} + R_{BB2}$) is termed as R_{BB}. R_{BB} lies in the range of 4–10 kΩ. Another parameter defined for a UJT is the intrinsic stand-off ratio η equal to $[R_{BB1}/(R_{BB1} + R_{BB2})]$ with value of R_{BB1} taken at $I_E = 0$. η is in the range of 0.5–0.8 and is typically 0.7, which also signifies that the emitter terminal is closer to B_2 terminal.

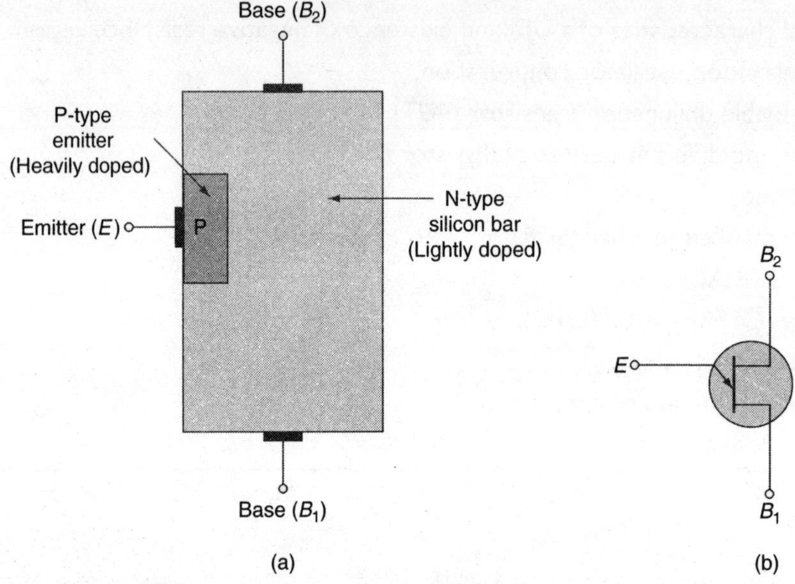

Figure 6.1 Unijunction transistor: (a) Construction; (b) circuit symbol.

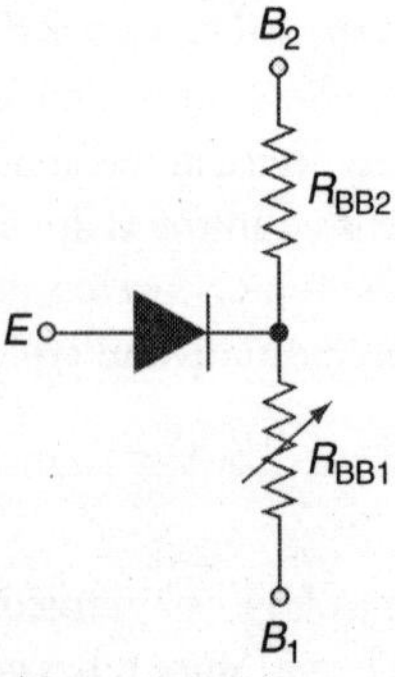

Figure 6.2 Electrical equivalent circuit of UJT.

Operational Principle

The operational principle of a UJT can be best explained with the help of its electrical characteristics or to be more precise its input V–I characteristics. Figure 6.3 shows the electrical circuit for determining the input characteristics. During operation, B_2 terminal is made more positive with respect to B_1 terminal. Also, it is essential to forward bias the PN junction diode by a voltage equal to its cut-in voltage V_γ, which is in the range of 0.35–0.7 V for any significant emitter current I_E to flow through the PN junction. In the absence of the required forward bias, voltage across R_{BB1} is given by ηV_{BB}. Therefore, if the PN junction were to be forward-biased, the externally applied voltage to the emitter terminal must at least be equal to the sum of ηV_{BB} and the cut-in voltage of the diode junction. It is expressed by Eq. (6.1). The emitter voltage V_E at which diode starts conducting is termed as V_P.

$$V_P = \eta V_{BB} + V_\gamma \tag{6.1}$$

As the emitter voltage V_E is increased, initially the current remains negligibly small in magnitude until a voltage ($= V_P$) is reached at which the diode is forward-biased. After that current increases rapidly. It is seen that as the current increases, the voltage decreases giving a negative resistance region. Such behavior can be explained by considering the fact that due to increase in forward current, the resistance of $E-B_1$ region falls rapidly resulting in reduction in the voltage. Finally when I_E becomes very large, it may be considered to be much greater than I_{B2}. Under these conditions, the curve approaches asymptotically the curve for $I_{B2} = 0$ giving rise to a valley point. The curve for $I_{B2} = 0$ is the same as it would be for ordinary PN junction diode. Figure 6.4 shows V_E–I_E characteristics.

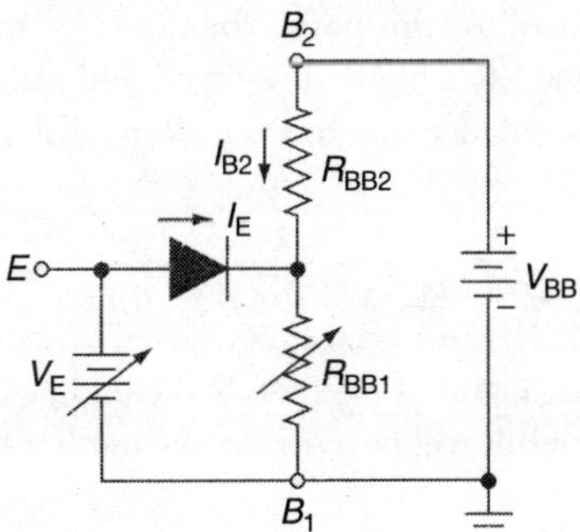

Figure 6.3 Electrical circuit for determining input characteristics of UJT.

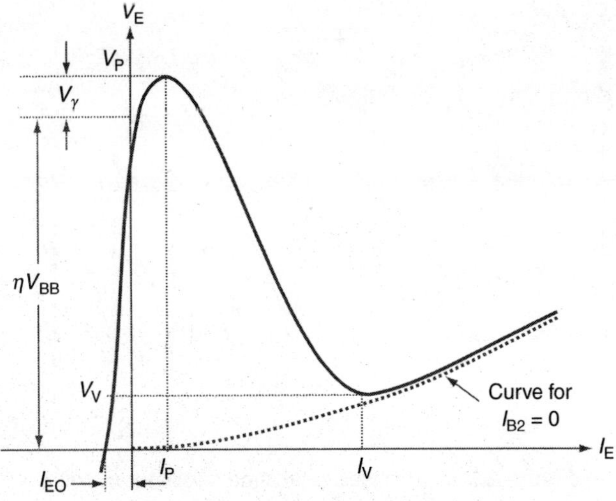

Figure 6.4 V_E–I_E characteristics of UJT.

The region before the peak point (V_P, I_P) is called cut-off region as the input diode remains reverse-biased in this region. The region after the valley point (V_V, I_V) is termed as saturation region as there is not much increase in the emitter voltage for large changes in emitter current.

Current-Controllable Device

As is seen from the V–I characteristics, the curve is a single-valued function of current and a multi-valued function of voltage. A single-valued function of current implies that for each current value, there is a unique voltage. Such a behavior is contrary to the one observed in the case of tunnel diode, which could be expressed by a single-valued function of voltage. That is what made tunnel diode a voltage-controllable device. Owing to single-valued function of current nature of its V--I characteristics, a UJT is called a current-controllable device.

UJT Relaxation Oscillator Circuit

Figure 6.5(a) shows the basic UJT-based relaxation oscillator circuit. The waveform that appears across the capacitor is shown in Figure 6.5(b). Initially UJT is in the cut-off region. That is, the input diode is reverse-biased. The capacitor starts charging from $+V$ through R. When the voltage V_{out} across the capacitor becomes large enough to forward bias the input diode, the capacitor starts discharging through the low resistance between the emitter–base B_1 region and resistor R_1. This discharge process continues until it reaches a point where input diode is again reverse-biased. At this point, the capacitor starts charging again. The process of charging through R, which is comparatively a higher resistance, and discharging through low forward resistance of input diode and R_1 continues and gives rise to a waveform as shown in Figure 6.5(b). The frequency of oscillation is given by

$$f = \frac{1}{RC \times \ln\{1/(1-\eta)\}} \tag{6.2}$$

If the capacitor in the relaxation oscillator of Figure 6.5(a) could be charged through a constant current source as shown in Figure 6.6(a), the result will be a perfect sawtooth waveform [Figure 6.6(b)].

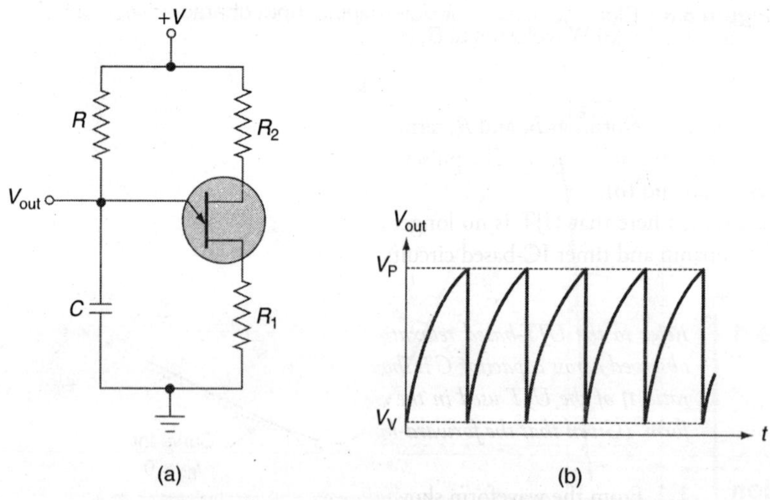

Figure 6.5 | UJT-based relaxation oscillator circuit.

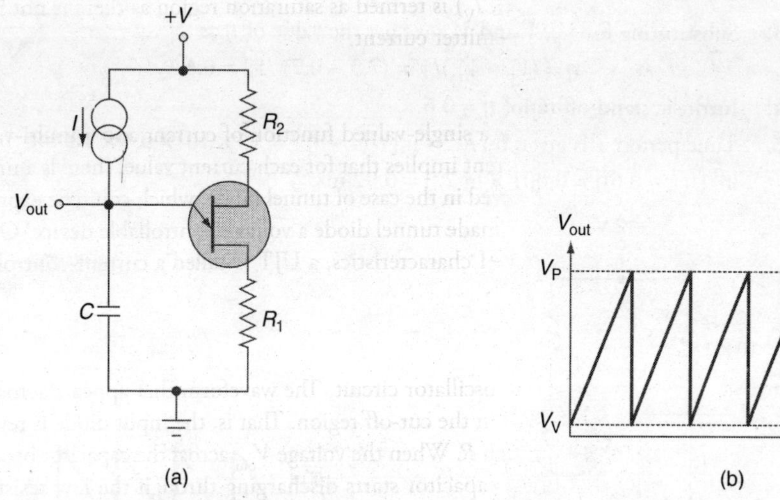

Figure 6.6 Constant current charging in UJT relaxation circuit.

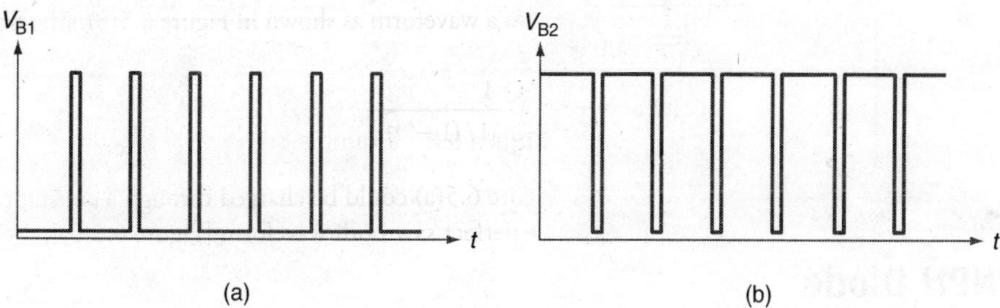

Figure 6.7 (a) Waveforms at B_1 terminal; (b) waveforms at B_2 terminal.

If we see the voltage waveforms at B_1 and B_2 terminals, it is observed that we get a train of positive pulses at B_1 and a train of negative pulses at B_2. The pulses occur during the time UJT is ON. The waveforms are shown in Figures 6.7(a) and (b).

It may be mentioned here that UJT is no longer a popular device for building oscillators. It has been largely replaced by opamp and timer IC-based circuits.

EXAMPLE 6.1 *Refer to the UJT-based relaxation oscillator circuit of Figure 6.8(a). The waveform observed across capacitor C is shown in Figure 6.8(b). Determine the intrinsic stand-off ratio η of the UJT used in the circuit. Also determine the time period T of the waveform. (Given that the forward-biased diode voltage drop = 0.7 V.)*

Solution

1. From the waveform shown in Figure 6.8(b), peak voltage $V_P = 7.9$ V.
2. Also, $V_P = \eta \times V + V_D$, where $V = 12$ V and V_D is the forward-biased diode voltage drop = 0.7 V.

3. Substituting for V_P, V and V_D, we get the value of η as
$$\eta = (V_P - V_D)/V = (7.9 - 0.7)/12 = 0.6$$
4. Intrinsic stand-off ratio, $\eta = 0.6$.
6. Time period T is given by $RC \times \ln[1/(1-\eta)] = 10 \times 10^3 \times 0.1 \times 10^{-6} \times \ln[1/(1-0.6)] = 0.001 \times \ln 2.5 = 0.92$ ms.

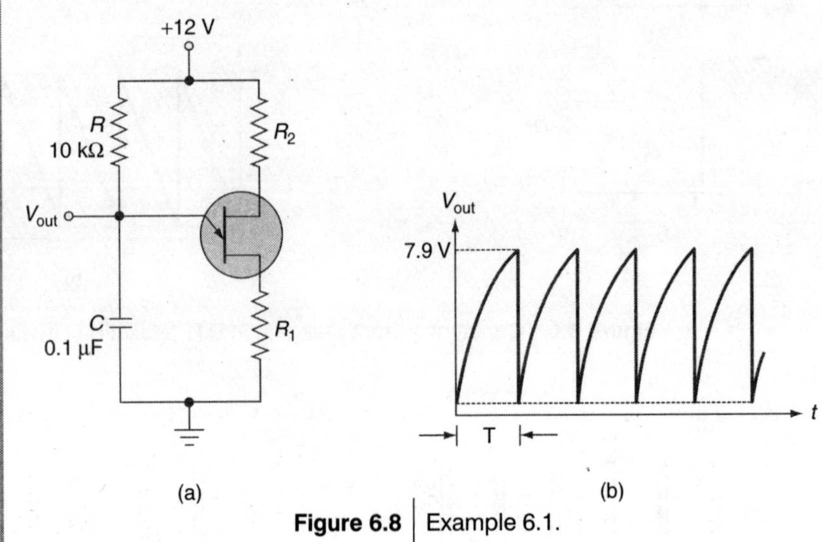

Figure 6.8 | Example 6.1.

6.2 PNPN Diode

It is a four-layer diode consisting of four alternate layers of P-type and N-type materials as shown in Figure 6.9(a). The P-type and N-type semiconductor regions on the extreme are called anode and cathode, respectively. Figure 6.9(b) shows the circuit symbol of the PNPN diode. The PNPN diode is also referred to as a Shockley diode. A device very similar to a PNPN diode is the silicon unilateral switch (SUS), except that its forward voltage drop after firing is higher than the PNPN diode.

If anode (P-type) is made positive with respect to the cathode (N-type), junctions J_1 and J_3 are forward-biased. This applied voltage then effectively appears across junction J_2, thus reverse biasing junction J_2. Now if the applied voltage is increased, a stage comes when the semiconductor junction J_2 breaks down. We have

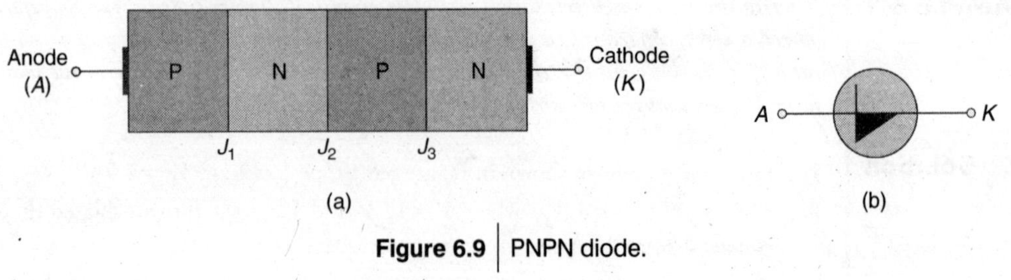

Figure 6.9 | PNPN diode.

studied earlier in Chapter 2 that the breakdown of PN junction occurs when the reverse voltage applied to it exceeds the peak inverse voltage of the diode.

At this breakdown voltage, the current increases all of a sudden from a very small value to a very large value. This increase in current is accompanied by reduction in the voltage giving rise to a negative resistance region. At this point, referred to as break-over point, the PNPN diode switches from its OFF-state (blocking state) to its ON-state.

Operation of a PNPN diode can also be explained by considering it as back-to-back connected NPN and PNP bipolar transistors as shown in Figure 6.10. However, it may be mentioned here that two transistors connected back-to-back do not make a PNPN diode.

The collector current of a bipolar transistor in the active region is given by

$$I_C = -\alpha I_E + I_{CO} \tag{6.3}$$

where I_C is the collector current leaving the transistor; I_E is the emitter current entering the transistor; α the short-circuit gain of CB configuration; I_{CO} the reverse saturation current.

Note that both the transistors will be in active region because the collector junctions of both of them (i.e., J_2) are reverse-biased and their emitter junctions (J_1 of PNP transistor and J_3 of NPN transistor) are forward-biased.

$$I_{E1} = \text{Emitter current of } Q_1 = +I \text{ and } I_{E2} = \text{Emitter current of } Q_2 = -I$$

Also the leakage current for Q_1 (I_{CO1}) is negative and for Q_2 (I_{CO2}) is positive. Let I_{CO} be the total leakage current of the device. Therefore

$$I_{CO2} = -I_{CO1} = I_{CO}/2$$

Equation (6.3) can, therefore, be employed to write expressions for collector currents I_{C1} and I_{C2} as Eqs. (6.4) and (6.5), respectively.

$$I_{C1} = -\alpha_1 I + I_{CO1} \tag{6.4}$$

$$I_{C2} = +\alpha_2 I + I_{CO2} \tag{6.5}$$

Now in the case of transistor Q_1, substituting the sum of all currents entering the transistor equal to zero, we get

$$I + I_{C1} - I_{C2} = 0 \tag{6.6}$$

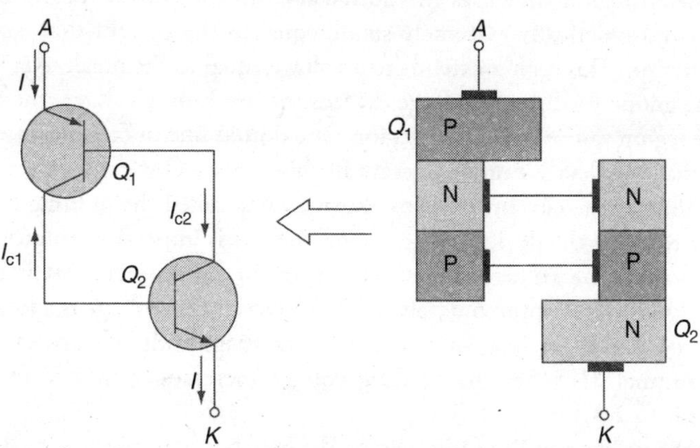

Figure 6.10 | PNPN diode represented as back-to-back connected NPN and PNP transistors.

Combining Eqs. (6.4)–(6.6) and putting $I_{CO2} = -I_{CO1} = I_{CO}/2$, expression for current I can be written as

$$I = \frac{I_{CO2} - I_{CO1}}{1-(\alpha_1+\alpha_2)} = \frac{I_{CO}}{1-(\alpha_1+\alpha_2)} \tag{6.7}$$

Here α_1 and α_2 are the forward current gains of the two transistors in common-base configuration and will have values lying between 0 and 0.95 depending upon the currents flowing through them. When we are increasing the voltage, effectively we are doing nothing but increasing the value of α_1 and α_2 and when $\alpha_1 + \alpha_2$ reaches unity, there is a sudden increase in anode current as is obvious from Eq. (6.7).

$$I = \frac{I_{CO}}{1-(1)} \quad \text{for } (\alpha_1+\alpha_2) \rightarrow 1$$

Please note that if $(\alpha_1 + \alpha_2)$ were to exceed unity, direction of current would not have reversed as is indicated by Eq. (6.7). The reason for this is as follows. The moment $(\alpha_1 + \alpha_2)$ becomes unity or approaches unity, current becomes exceedingly large. This brings all three junction diodes into saturation region. In other words, Q_1 and Q_2 go to saturation due to their collector junctions being forward-biased. As a consequence of transistors going to saturation, magnitudes of α_1 and α_2 decrease so that $(\alpha_1 + \alpha_2)$ never exceeds unity. Put in another way, transistors Q_1 and Q_2 enter saturation only upto the extent that $(\alpha_1 + \alpha_2)$ remains unity.

PNPN Diode Material

The semiconductor material used for making PNPN diodes is always silicon. Germanium is never used as it does not have a stable OFF-state. To elaborate it further, with germanium as the semiconductor material, the magnitudes of α may become large enough to give $(\alpha_1 + \alpha_2)$ equal to unity for a very small value of applied voltage thus leading to an unstable OFF-state.

PNPN Diode Characteristics

The V–I characteristics of a PNPN diode are shown in Figure 6.11. The characteristic curve can be divided into three regions, namely, cut-off region also known as forward-blocking state, saturation region and the transition region shown as the dotted line. In the cut-off region, current through the device is ideally zero and practically extremely small, equal to the current that would flow through a reverse-biased PN junction. This region extends to a voltage equal to the break-over voltage marked V_{BO} in Figure 6.11. As the anode-to-cathode voltage exceeds the break-over voltage, the device switches rapidly from the cut-off region to the saturation region. The dotted line in fact indicates this rapid switching action and also that the device cannot operate in this region. Once the device has broken-over, it stays in that state as long as the current remains above a value called the holding current marked I_H in Figure 6.11. In order to bring the device to the cut-off state, it is imperative to bring the current below the holding current value. The voltage corresponding to the holding current is the holding voltage marked as V_H. The value of V_H is approximately 0.7 V. However, this voltage is a function of the current flowing through the device. It, in fact, increases with the magnitude of current. As an example, for PNPN diode type number 1N5158, the holding voltage increases from 1 V to 2 V as the current increases from 200 mA to 2 A.

A PNPN diode behaves like an ON–OFF switch. The switch is open in the forward-blocking state and is closed in the saturation region. The characteristics of a PNPN diode for a negative anode-to-cathode voltage are similar to that of a reverse-biased diode.

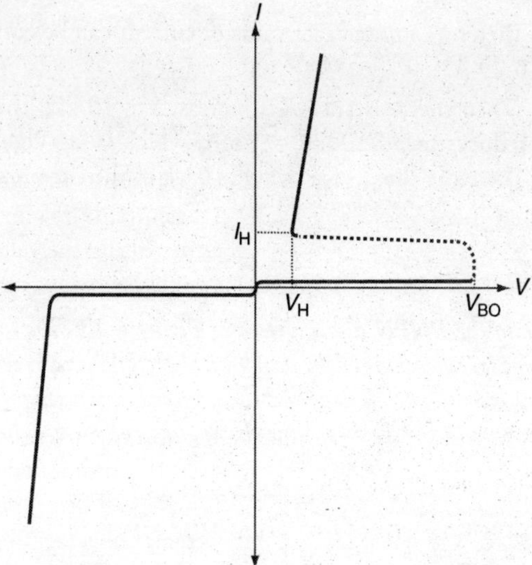

Figure 6.11 | V–I characteristics of PNPN diode.

EXAMPLE 6.2

The PNPN diode used in the circuit of Figure 6.12(a) has a break-over voltage of 20 V and a holding current of 5 mA. The V–I characteristics of the device are shown in Figure 6.12(b). Determine (a) current flowing through the device and (b) the region of operation of the device if the resistance R were increased to 10 kΩ.

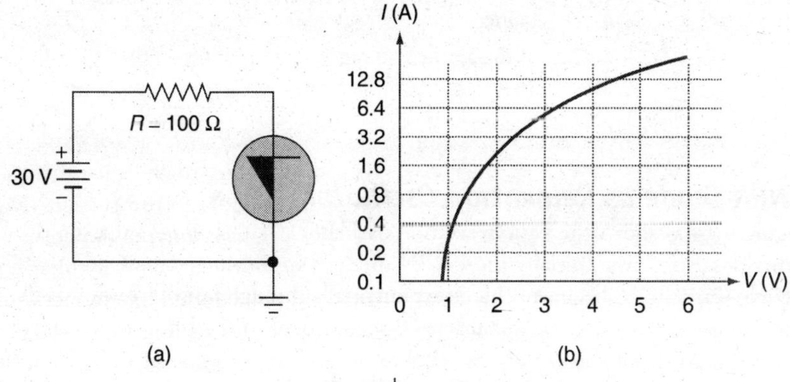

Figure 6.12 | Example 6.2.

Solution

1. The applied voltage is greater than the break-over voltage. The device is therefore in the saturation region. The current flowing through the device to first approximation is given by 30/100 = 0.3 A.
2. For current equal to 0.3 A, the voltage drop across the device as seen from the characteristic curve of Figure 6.12(b) is 1.0 V.

3. Therefore, more exact value of current can be computed from (30 – 1)/100 = 0.29 A.
4. When the resistance R is increased to 10 kΩ, the current through the device reduces to 30/10000 = 3 mA, which is less than the holding current value. Therefore the device switches back to the cut-off state.

EXAMPLE 6.3 *Refer to the PNPN diode circuit of Figure 6.13. The break-over voltage and holding current specifications of the device are 12 V and 4 mA, respectively. The variable voltage source is set in such a way that the device is conducting. If the knee voltage of the device is taken to be 0.7 V, determine the applied voltage at which the device will turn OFF.*

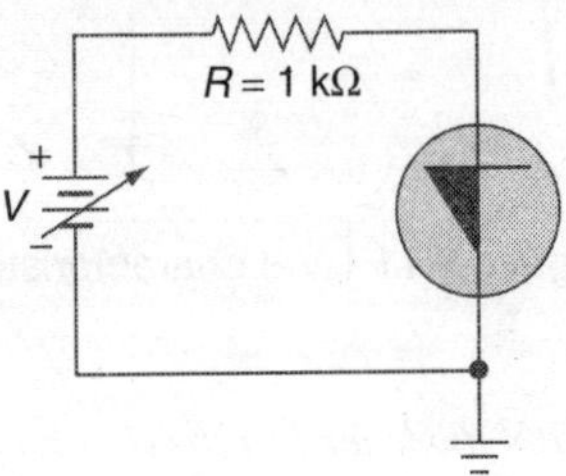

Figure 6.13 Example 6.3.

Solution

1. The device will turn off when the current falls below the holding current value.
2. If the applied voltage at that point is V, then $(V - 0.7)/1 \times 10^3 = 4 \times 10^{-3}$. That is, $V = 4.7$ V.

PNPN Diode as Relaxation Oscillator

Figure 6.14(a) shows the basic relaxation oscillator circuit configured around a PNPN diode. The circuit functions as follows. Initially the PNPN diode is in the cut-off state and therefore behaves like an open switch. Capacitor C begins to charge exponentially through resistor R towards the applied DC voltage V. As the voltage across the capacitor reaches a value equal to the break-over voltage of the PNPN diode, the device breaks down and rapidly switches to the saturation region of its V–I characteristics. PNPN diode is now in the ON-state and behaves like a closed switch or a near short circuit. The capacitor rapidly (almost instantaneously) discharges through the PNPN diode. The discharge process continues as long as the current through the PNPN diode remains above the holding current value. The moment it falls below that value, the PNPN diode rapidly switches to the OFF-state. The capacitor begins to charge again through R and the process is repeated. Thus, the capacitor repetitively charges and discharges through R and PNPN diode, respectively. The charging time is determined by the product of R and C and charging voltage V. Equation (6.8) represents the charging process (assuming $V_H = 0$).

$$V_c = V \times (1 - e^{-t/RC}) \tag{6.8}$$

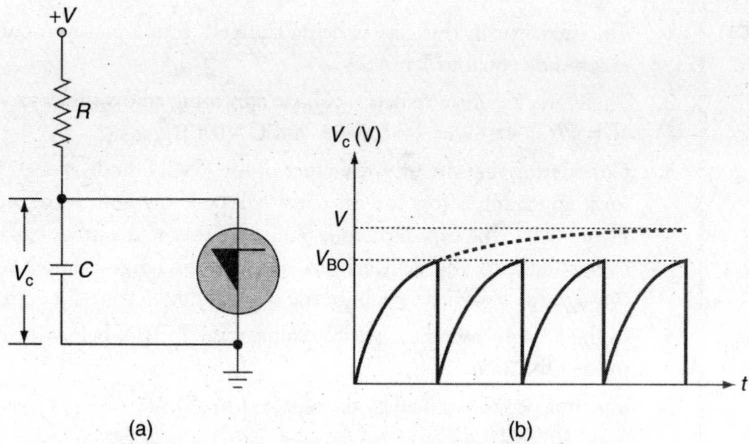

Figure 6.14 PNPN diode relaxation oscillator.

The discharge time is determined by the product of C and ON-resistance of the PNPN diode. The waveform across the capacitor resembles a sawtooth, more so when the charging voltage V is large as compared to the break-over voltage of the PNPN diode. Figure 6.14(b) shows the waveform. The waveform becomes a perfect sawtooth if resistor R were replaced by a constant current source. The charging process in that case would be represented by

$$V_c = I \times t/C \tag{6.9}$$

where I is the magnitude of the constant charging current.

EXAMPLE 6.4 *Refer to the relaxation oscillator circuit of Figure 6.15. The PNPN diode used in the circuit is 1N 5158 having a break-over voltage and holding current specifications of 10 V and 4 mA, respectively. Draw the waveform across the capacitor indicating its timing parameters (assume V_H = 0).*

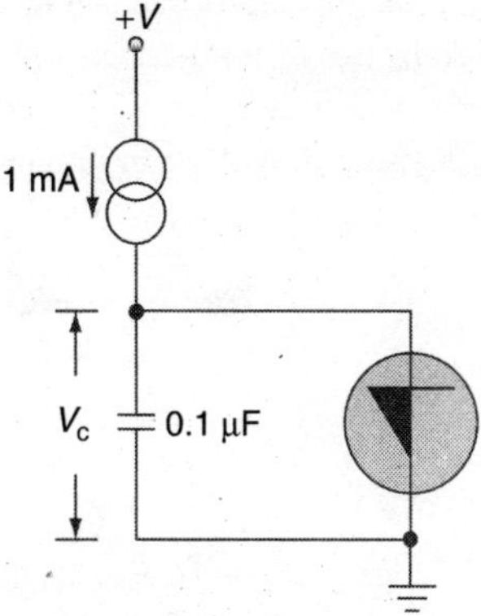

Figure 6.15 Example 6.4.

Solution

1. The capacitor in this case is being charged from a constant current source of magnitude equal to 1 mA.
2. Therefore, the instantaneous voltage appearing across the capacitor is given by $V_c = (I/C) \times t$. Now $I = 1.0$ mA and $C = 0.1$ μF.
3. Considering that the ON-resistance of the PNPN diode is negligible, the waveform appearing across the capacitor will be a sawtooth waveform as shown in Figure 6.16. The capacitor voltage linearly rises to a voltage equal to the break-over voltage of the device from where it discharges almost instantaneously through the device. The voltage rise is linear due to constant current charging.
4. In the present case, the capacitor voltage rises to 10 V before the device switches to the ON-state.
5. The time period required by the capacitor to charge to 10 V is given by $0.1 \times 10^{-6} \times 10/10^{-3} = 1$ ms.
6. The sawtooth waveform therefore has a time period of 1 ms.

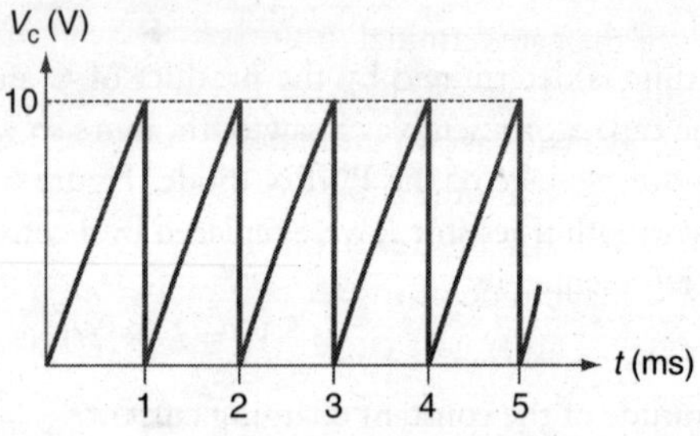

Figure 6.16 | Solution to Example 6.4.

Rate Effect

The effect of rate of change of applied voltage on the break-over voltage is termed as rate effect. When the PNPN diode is in the forward-blocking or OFF-state, the center diode junction J_2 is reverse-biased while the two outermost diode junctions J_1 and J_3 are forward-biased. All reverse-biased diodes have some capacitance across them. A four-layer diode represented by two forward-biased and one reverse-biased diode is shown in Figure 6.17.

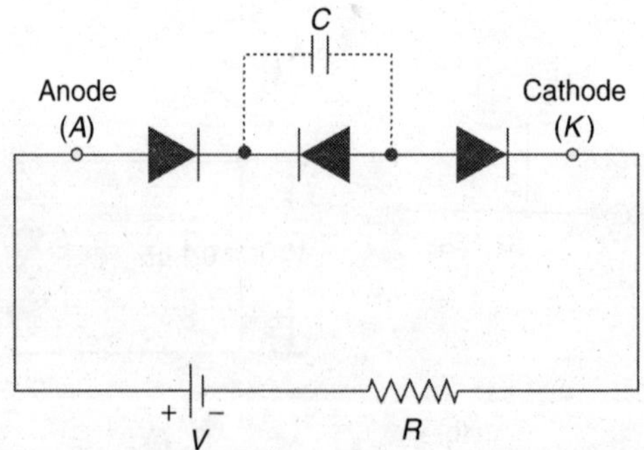

Figure 6.17 | Rate effect in PNPN diodes.

When rate of change of applied voltage is low, capacitance C offers very high reactance with the result that the current through the capacitance can be ignored. When the rate of change of applied voltage is sufficiently large then the current through C, when added to the total current, enables the sum $(\alpha_1 + \alpha_2)$ to reach unity at an applied voltage less than the break-over voltage. In other words, high rate of change of applied voltage effectively reduces the break-over voltage leading to premature firing of the device. This phenomenon is called rate effect.

6.3 Silicon-Controlled Rectifier

The construction of a silicon-controlled rectifier (SCR) is exactly the same as that of a four-layer diode with the only difference that the connection to one of the inner layers adjacent to the cathode layer is brought out to exercise control over the switching characteristics of the device. This control terminal is called the gate-terminal, cathode gate to be more precise. Figure 6.18(a) shows the circuit symbol of an SCR. Considering the PNPN device to be equivalent to back-to-back connection of a PNP and an NPN transistor, we can notice that the gate terminal is nothing but the base terminal of the NPN transistor as shown in Figure 6.18(b).

The control action of the gate terminal in the case of an SCR functions as follows. A momentary pulse applied to the gate terminal increases the base current of the NPN transistor initiating a regenerative feedback action. This regenerative feedback action ultimately drives both the transistors to saturation causing switching-ON action of the device even if the anode-to-cathode voltage were less than the break-over voltage. The anode-to-cathode voltage at which the device can be triggered to the ON-state is a function of the gate trigger current. In other words, magnitude of trigger current required to turn the device ON depends upon the anode-to-cathode voltage. Larger gate current can trigger the device ON for a lower anode-to-cathode voltage.

In the case of SCR, only the cathode gate is available. If the anode gate is also made available, then the device is referred to as the silicon-controlled switch (SCS). In other words, SCS is a four-layer PNPN device where connection to all the four layers are available. The characteristics of the device are essentially the same as those of an SCR. Figure 6.18(c) shows the circuit symbol of SCS.

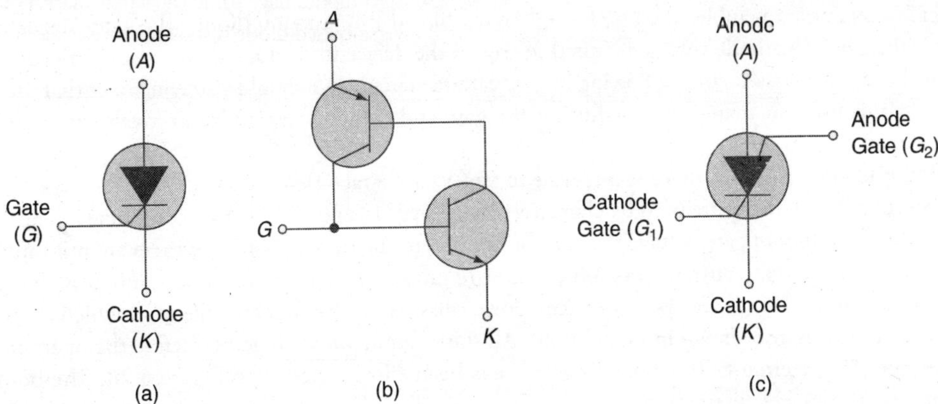

Figure 6.18 (a) Circuit symbol of SCR; (b) equivalent circuit of SCR; (c) circuit symbol of SCS.

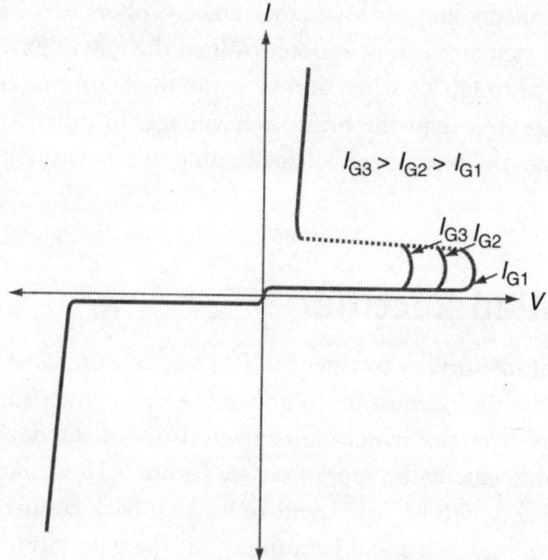

Figure 6.19 | V–I characteristics of an SCR.

V–I Characteristics

V–I characteristics of an SCR are similar to those discussed in the case of a PNPN diode in Section 6.2 (PNPN diode characteristics). However, in the case of SCR, we can plot a family of characteristics in the first quadrant for different values of gate current as shown in Figure 6.19. As is clear from the family of characteristic curves, the break-over voltage reduces with increase in gate trigger current. In other words, as the anode-to-cathode voltage reduces, the magnitude of gate current required to trigger the device to the ON-state increases. The V–I characteristics in the third quadrant are same as that in the case of a PNPN diode. The gate-triggering requirements of an SCR are discussed in the following section.

Gate-Triggering Characteristics

The gate-triggering characteristics of an SCR are a plot of gate voltage (V_G) versus gate current (I_G). As the gate-cathode circuit of an SCR (or a thyristor in general) is nothing but a forward-biased PN junction, the characteristics curve resembles the one for a forward-biased PN junction diode. The gate-trigger voltage (V_{GT}) is the gate-to-cathode voltage required to trigger the device to the ON-state and gate-trigger current (I_{GT}) is the forward-biased current flowing in gate-cathode circuit. We should also remember that the P-and N-type semiconductor materials constituting the gate and cathode regions, respectively, in an SCR are lightly doped.

Owing to light doping, there is a spread in the V–I characteristics even for a given type of SCR. This spread is shown in Figure 6.20 by characteristic curves "1" and "2". In addition, there are minimum and maximum values of gate voltage that can be applied to the device. Similarly there are minimum and maximum values of gate current too. Yet another requirement that needs to be fulfilled is that of the power dissipation. There is always a rated gate power dissipation specified for the SCR which should not be exceeded. This is also shown in Figure 6.20. All these requirements together define the operating area for the gate-trigger circuit. This operating area has been shown shaded in Figure 6.20. The boundary specified by the power dissipation is for the average value of the gate power dissipation. A relatively higher dissipation may be permitted for shorter pulse durations. For example, SCR type number

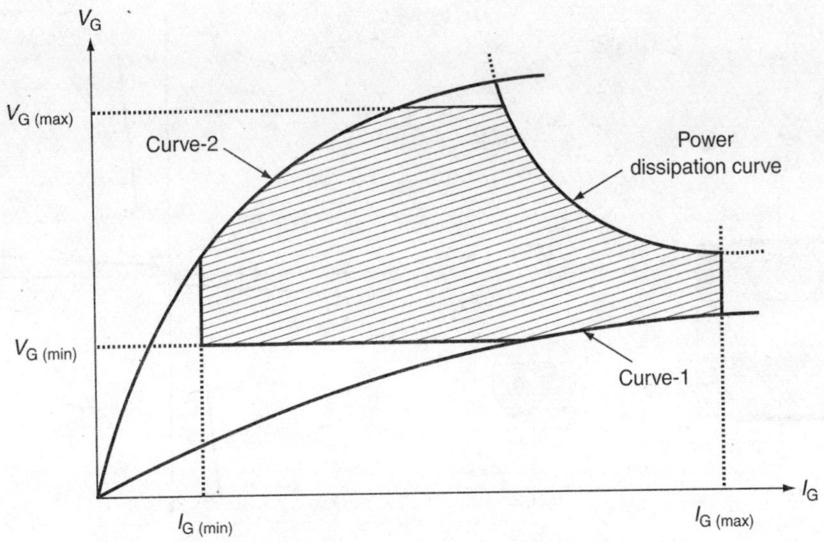

Figure 6.20 | Gate-triggering characteristics.

2N 3668 has P_G(av) rating of 0.5 W and a transient gate power dissipation P_{GM} specification of 40 W for a trigger pulse duration of 10 μs. Now such a device could be triggered by a continuous current of 200 mA at a trigger voltage of 2.5 V. It could also be triggered by a 2 A trigger pulse at 20 V provided that trigger pulse was no wider than 10 μs.

Higher gate-trigger currents yield faster turn-on. But the fast turn-on of the SCR is also not without problems. If the rate of rise of the ON-state current (di/dt) exceeds the critical value of di/dt, the device could get damaged due to creation of localized hot spots. The gate-triggering characteristics vary with temperature. At lower temperatures, one requires higher gate-trigger voltage and current. For example, for SCR type number 2N 3668, the maximum values of V_{GT} and I_{GT} are 2 V and 40 mA, respectively, at a junction temperature of 25°C. At −40°C, these are specified as 3 V and 80 mA, respectively. At 100°C, the values are about 1.5 V and 30 mA. It may be mentioned here that the above discussion is valid for all devices of the thyristor family with gate control.

6.4 DIAC and TRIAC

A DIAC is a bi-directional thyristor. It can be considered to be equivalent to two PNPN devices connected back-to-back [Figure 6.21(a)]. Figure 6.21(b) shows the circuit symbol. As we can see from the figure, it is a two-terminal device with the terminals designated as Main Terminal-1 (MT-1) and Main Terminal-2 (MT-2). The V–I characteristics of a DIAC are similar to those of a four-layer PNPN diode with the difference that a DIAC exhibits identical characteristics both in the forward (first quadrant) and reverse (third quadrant) directions [Figure 6.21(c)].

A TRIAC is equivalent to a DIAC with the gate contact. It is a three-terminal device and the terminals are designated as Main Terminal-1 (MT-1), Main Terminal-2 (MT-2) and Gate (G). Figure 6.22 shows the construction, the circuit symbol and the V–I characteristics of a TRIAC.

A device similar to TRIAC in construction, but without the gate terminal is the silicon bilateral switch (SBS). Its characteristics are symmetrical and it switches ON and breaks down for applied voltage of both polarities.

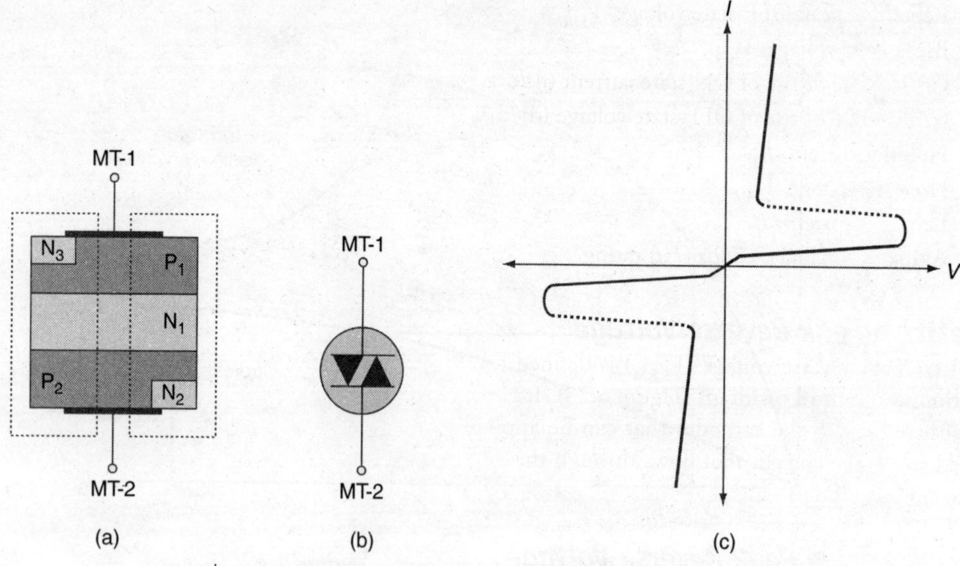

Figure 6.21 DIAC: (a) Construction; (b) circuit symbol; (c) V–I characteristics.

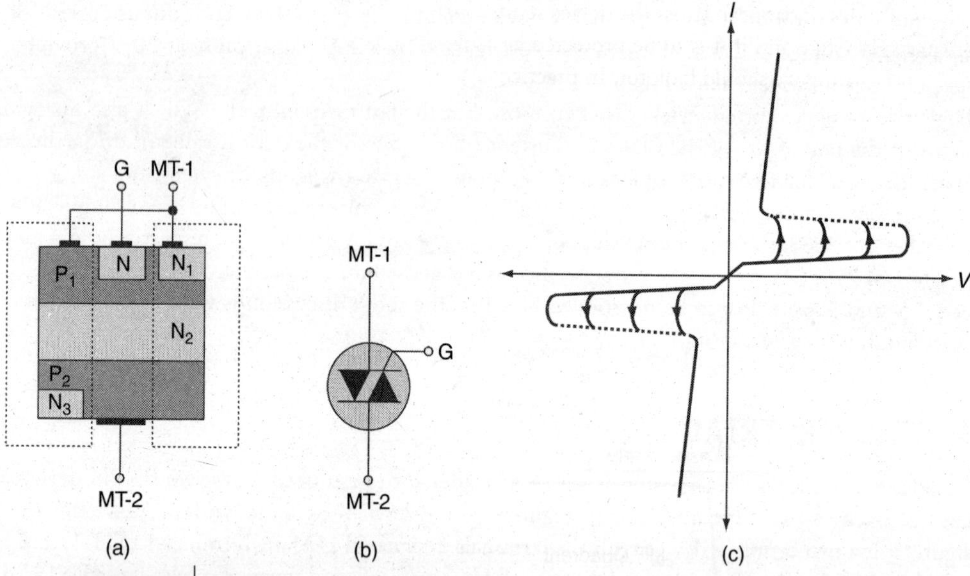

Figure 6.22 TRIAC: (a) Construction; (b) circuit symbol and (c) V–I characteristics.

6.5 Thyristor Parameters

Major performance specifications of a thyristor include the following:

1. Repetitive peak reverse voltage, V_{RRM}.
2. Non-repetitive peak reverse voltage, V_{RSM}.

3. Repetitive peak OFF-state voltage, V_{DRM}.
4. Break-over voltage, V_{BO}.
5. Critical rate of rise of ON-state current (di/dt).
6. Critical rate of rise of OFF-state voltage (dv/dt).
7. Holding current, I_H.
8. Holding voltage, V_H.
9. Latching current, I_L.
10. Amperes squared seconds (I^2t) rating.

Repetitive Peak Reverse Voltage

Repetitive peak reverse voltage (V_{RRM}) is defined for reverse-blocking mode of thyristors like SCRs for operation in the third quadrant (Figure 6.23). It is the maximum repetitive reverse voltage (anode negative with respect to the cathode) that can be applied to the device safely while still keeping it in the blocked state. The current that flows through the device in this state is referred to as the repetitive peak reverse current (I_{RRM}).

Non-Repetitive Peak Reverse Voltage

Non-repetitive peak reverse voltage (V_{RSM}) as shown in Figure 6.23 is also defined in a similar way. For obvious reasons, this rating is little higher than the one discussed above. If the application is such that the reverse voltage does not appear across the device repetitively, may be because the device is being operated in the forward OFF-state and if it is to be protected against any occasional reverse transients, then V_{RSM} and not V_{RRM} is the rating we should look for. In practice, if we do not allow reverse voltage to exceed V_{RRM}, we are very safe.

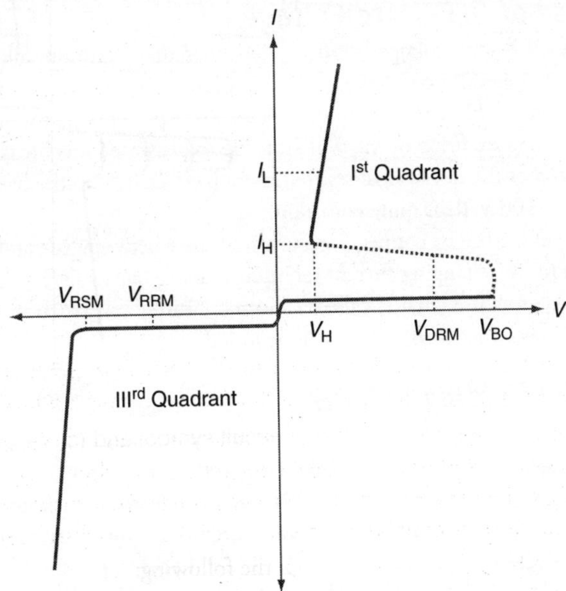

Figure 6.23 | Thyristor parameters.

Repetitive Peak OFF-State Voltage

Repetitive peak OFF-state voltage (V_{DRM}) as shown in Figure 6.23 is the maximum forward OFF-state voltage (anode positive with respect to cathode) that can be allowed to appear across the device when it is being operated in the first quadrant (in the forward-blocking mode). This voltage is usually much less than the actual break-over voltage (V_{BO}) of the device, which is basically a characteristic of the construction of the thyristor. The maximum value of current that can flow in the forward-blocking state is designated as I_{DRM}.

Break-Over Voltage

Break-over voltage (V_{BO}) or peak OFF-state voltage (V_{DM}) is the maximum OFF-state voltage (Figure 6.23). If the applied forward voltage were greater than the break-over voltage, the device is switched to the ON-state even in the absence of any gate signal. The value of V_{BO} does not depend upon the voltage grades of different thyristors in the same family. For instance, SCRs TY 505 F, TY 1005 F, TY 2005F, TY3005 F, TY 4005 F and TY 5005 F, respectively, have V_{DRM} rating of 50, 100, 200, 300, 400 and 500 volts whereas V_{BO} for all these devices belonging to the same class may be larger than the highest available V_{DRM} rating in this class. However, it may be emphasized here that V_{DRM} should not be allowed to exceed in order that the device retains its listed characteristics. The current corresponding to the break-over voltage (V_{BO}) is called break-over current (I_{BO}).

Critical Rate of Rise of ON-State Current

When a thyristor is switched ON, initially, the thyristor can handle a very small current as it is concentrated in a small area of the device pellet. Gradually, the load-current-carrying capability increases to its specified rating. Critical rate-of-rise of ON-state current ($\mathrm{d}i/\mathrm{d}t$) tells us about the maximum rate of change of ON-state current the device can handle safely. If this rating is exceeded during device switch ON, may be due to a faster switch ON, there could be a development of localized hot spots in the pellet at the time of switch ON and this could result in the device getting damaged. $\mathrm{d}i/\mathrm{d}t$ rating of 100 A/μs is typical.

Critical Rate of Rise of OFF-State Voltage

The critical rate of rise of OFF-state voltage ($\mathrm{d}v/\mathrm{d}t$) determines the maximum allowable rate of change of applied forward OFF-state voltage. When applied forward voltage is a time-varying one, a current equal to $C \times \mathrm{d}v/\mathrm{d}t$ flows through the reverse-biased junction capacitance (C) of the thyristor. This current if more than a certain value can cause premature firing of the thyristor due to decrease in its break-over voltage. Maintaining $\mathrm{d}v/\mathrm{d}t$ within $\mathrm{d}v/\mathrm{d}t$ rating of the device ensures that there is no change in the break-over voltage (V_{BO}) of the device. A $\mathrm{d}v/\mathrm{d}t$ rating of 100 V/μs is quite common.

The $\mathrm{d}v/\mathrm{d}t$ rating can be enhanced by connecting a low resistance between gate and cathode, thus providing a low resistance shunt path for the changing current mentioned above bypassing gate-cathode junction. Majority of high $\mathrm{d}v/\mathrm{d}t$-rating thyristors use what is called a shorted emitter construction which is nothing but an internally created low-value resistance across gate-cathode junction.

Holding Current and Holding Voltage

Holding current (I_H) and *holding voltage* (V_H) are defined when the device is in the ON-state and has to be kept there only. Now if the voltage across the device is decreased so that the current decreases, then at a particular stage, the current is not able to keep the device in the ON-state. So, the device goes to OFF-state. Holding current (Figure 6.23) is minimum ON-state current required to keep the thyristor in the low impedance state once it has been triggered to the ON-state. In order to switch off the thyristor, the anode current must be brought below the holding current value. Voltage corresponding to holding current is termed as holding voltage.

The values of these parameters vary from type to type. Typical value of holding current may lie between several milliamperes to several hundreds of milliamperes. Holding voltage may be as small as 0.5 V for smaller units and as large as 20 V for larger devices. Furthermore, these values are subject to change with temperature.

Latching Current

Latching current (I_L) is little larger than the holding current and ON-state current equal to or more than the latching current ensures that once the device is switched ON, it remains in the ON-state even after the gate signal is removed. Once the ON-state current has exceeded the latching current value after switch ON, the current then has to be brought below the holding current to switch it OFF. To further illustrate the difference, let us assume that an SCR is triggered with a narrow gate-trigger pulse and that the gate pulse has been withdrawn before the anode current of the triggered device could reach the latching current amplitude. In such a case, the ON-state will not sustain and the device will come back to the forward-blocking state immediately after the gate-trigger pulse is withdrawn.

Amperes Squared Seconds (I^2t) Rating

The *amperes squared seconds* (I^2t) rating of a thyristor tells us about the surge current-handling capability of the device for sub-cycle time periods when the device is being used as a rectifier. I^2t rating is usually specified in the data sheet. It can also be calculated from the maximum peak surge current that the device can sustain for a given time period which is usually one full cycle of an applied 50 Hz/60 Hz waveform. I^2t rating of the thyristors can be used to calculate the surge current capability when the thyristor conducts for only a part of the full cycle time period.

6.6 Thyristors as Current-Controllable Devices

Thyristors are negative resistance devices as a part of their V–I characteristics exhibits negative resistance where a reduction in the voltage is accompanied by an increase in current. As an example, Figure 6.24 shows the V–I characteristics of a PNPN diode and existence of negative resistance region.

Thyristors are current-controllable devices because their V–I characteristics can be expressed by a single-valued function of current. That is, for every current value, there is one and only one corresponding voltage value (Figure 6.24). For instance, for current equal to 30 mA and 40 mA, the corresponding voltages are 0.5 V and 0.7 V, respectively. On the other hand, these characteristics are representative of a multivalued function

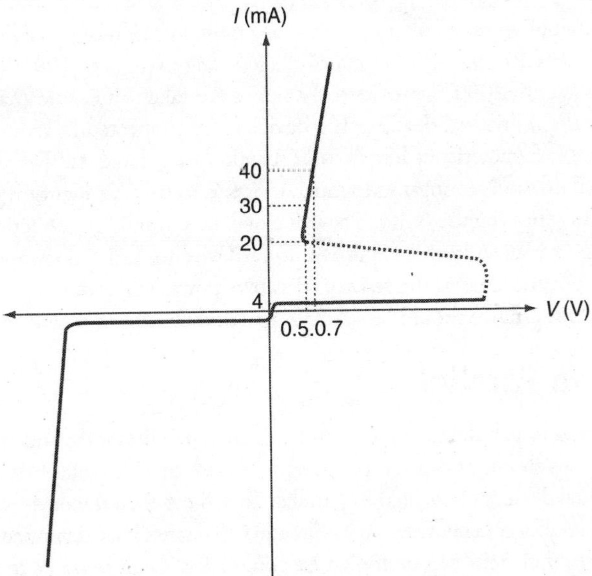

Figure 6.24 V–I characteristics of PNPN diode – negative resistance region.

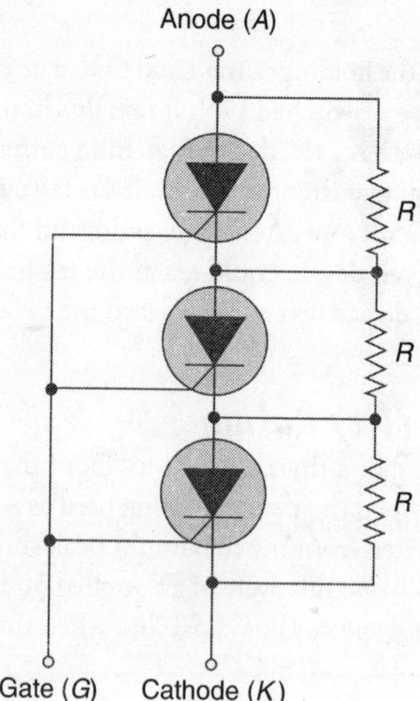

Figure 6.25 | Thyristors in series.

of voltage. That is, for every voltage value, there could be one or more than one corresponding current values. For instance, for a voltage of 0.7 V, the current could be 4 mA or 20 mA or 40 mA. Of course, 20 mA point is in the unstable region and cannot thus sustain. It is because of "single-valued function of current" and "multi-valued function of voltage" nature of the V–I characteristics that thyristors are considered as current-controllable devices. UJTs also belong to the same class.

6.7 Thyristors in Series

Thyristors are connected in series to enhance the voltage rating of the individual devices. For instance, two SCRs each having a repetitive peak OFF-state voltage rating (V_{DRM}) of 1000 V could be connected in series to get an overall V_{DRM} of 2000 V provided that steps are taken to ensure that the applied voltage is equally divided between the individual devices. The device to be connected in series should preferably have closely matched OFF-state characteristics like forward break-over voltage, OFF-state resistance and so on. One way to force an equal division amongst individual devices is to connect identical resistors across each one of the device connected in series (Figure 6.25). The value of *R* here should be a fraction of the forward OFF-state resistance so that any variation in this parameter from device to device does not affect the voltage division. Capacitive dividers are also used as the resistors dissipate power and reduce the efficiency. In the case of capacitive dividers, a series resistance should be used alongwith each capacitor to damp the current pulses.

6.8 Thyristors in Parallel

Thyristors are connected in parallel to enhance the current capability of the individual devices to be connected in parallel. Care should, however, be taken to ensure that the total ON-state current is equally divided amongst individual devices connected in parallel. To achieve this, the devices should preferably have closely matched forward conduction characteristics like the ON-state dynamic impedance, ON-state voltage and so on. Equal division of current can be forced by connecting small resistors in series with each of the parallel connected thyristors (Figure 6.26). *R* in this case is much larger than the ON-state dynamic impedance of the individual thyristors.

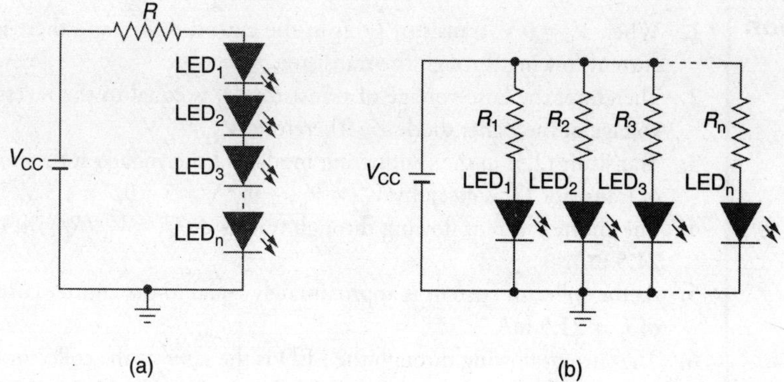

Figure 7.39 (a) Connecting LEDs in series; (b) connecting LEDs in parallel.

large to drive the desired number of LEDs. Also, it should be checked that the series current flowing in the circuit through each LED is in their operating range. The value of the resistor (R) to be connected is given by

$$R = [V_{CC} - (V_{F1} + V_{F2} + V_{F3} + \cdots + V_{Fn})]/I \tag{7.23}$$

where V_{F1}, V_{F2}, …, V_{Fn} are the forward voltages across LED$_1$, LED$_2$, …, LED$_n$ respectively and I is the current flowing through the LEDs.

LEDs can also be connected in parallel to enhance the output light level. However, in the case of parallel connection, one needs to be more careful. Figure 7.39(b) shows the parallel connection of LEDs. The resistors R_1, R_2, …, R_n are used to protect the LEDs. If these resistors were not used, then the LED with the lowest forward voltage will draw excess current and is likely to get damaged. Then the LED with the next smallest forward voltage will get damaged and this process continues till all the LEDs get damaged. The values of these resistors determine the current flowing through individual LEDs.

EXAMPLE 7.8 *For the circuit shown in Figure 7.40, determine the current through the LED when (a) $V_B = 0$ V and (b) $V_B = 10$ V. (V_{BE} of both the transistors is 0.7 V and $V_{CE(sat)}$ of both the transistors is 0.2 V.)*

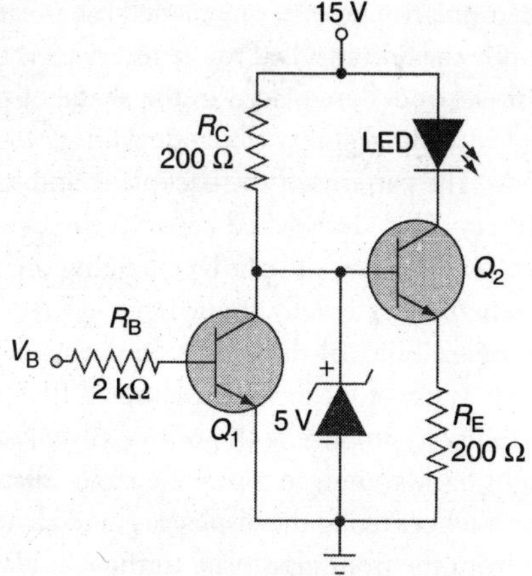

Figure 7.40 Example 7.8.

Solution

1. When $V_B = 0$ V, transistor Q_1 is in the cut-off region and there is no collector current flowing through the transistor.
2. Therefore, the base voltage of transistor Q_2 is equal to the reverse breakdown voltage of the Zener diode Z_1. Therefore, $V_{B2} = 5$ V.
3. Transistor Q_2 is in the conducting mode and the voltage at the emitter terminal of transistor Q_2 is given by $V_{E2} = V_{B2} - 0.7\ \text{V} = 5 - 0.7 = 4.3$ V.
4. The emitter current flowing through transistor $Q_2 = V_{E2}/R_E = 4.3/200 =$ 21.5 mA.
5. As the collector current is approximately equal to the emitter current, the value of $I_C = 21.5$ mA.
6. The current flowing through the LED is the same as the collector current of the transistor. Therefore, the current flowing through the LED is 21.5 mA.
7. When $V_B = 10$ V, transistor Q_1 is in saturation. Therefore, the voltage $V_{CE1} =$ 0.2 V.
8. The base voltage of transistor Q_2, $V_{B2} = 0.2$ V.
9. Hence, transistor Q_2 is in cut-off and the value of collector current is nearly zero. Therefore, the current flowing through the LED is also nearly zero.

7.11 Liquid-Crystal Displays

Liquid crystals are materials that exhibit properties of both solids and liquids, that is, they are an intermediate phase of matter. They can be classified into three different groups: nematic, smectic and cholestric. Nematic liquid crystals are generally used in the fabrication of liquid-crystal displays (LCDs) with the twisted nematic material being the most common.

Construction of an LCD

Figure 7.41(a) shows the construction of a twisted nematic LCD display. As we can see from the figure, it comprises a cell of liquid-crystal fluid, conductive electrodes, a set of polarizers and a glass casing.

The outermost layers are the polarizers which are housed on the outer surface of the glass casing. Polarizers are components that polarize light in one plane. The polarizer attached to the front glass is referred to as the front polarizer, while the one attached to the rear glass is the rear polarizer. On the inner surface of the glass casing, transparent electrodes are placed in the shape of the desired image. The electrode attached to the front glass is referred to as the segment electrode while the one attached to the rear glass is the backplane or the common electrode. The patterns of the backplane and segment electrodes form the numbers, letters, symbols, etc. The liquid crystal is sandwiched between the two electrodes. The basic principle of operation of LCD is to control the transmission of light by changing the polarization of the light passing through the liquid crystal with the help of an externally applied voltage. As LCDs do not emit their own light, backlighting is used to enhance the legibility of the display in dark conditions. A variety of methods exist for backlighting LCD panels such as use of incandescent lamps, LEDs and electro luminescent lamps.

LCDs have the capability to produce both positive as well as negative images. A positive image is defined as a dark image on a light background. In a positive image display, the front and the rear polarizers are perpendicular to each other. Light entering the display is guided by the orientation of the liquid-crystal molecules that are twisted by 90° from the front glass plate to the rear glass plate. This twist allows the incoming light to pass through the second polarizer [Figure 7.41(b)]. When a voltage is applied to the display, the liquid-crystal molecules straighten out and stop redirecting the light. As a result light travels straight through and is filtered out by the second polarizer. Therefore, no light can pass through, making this region darker compared

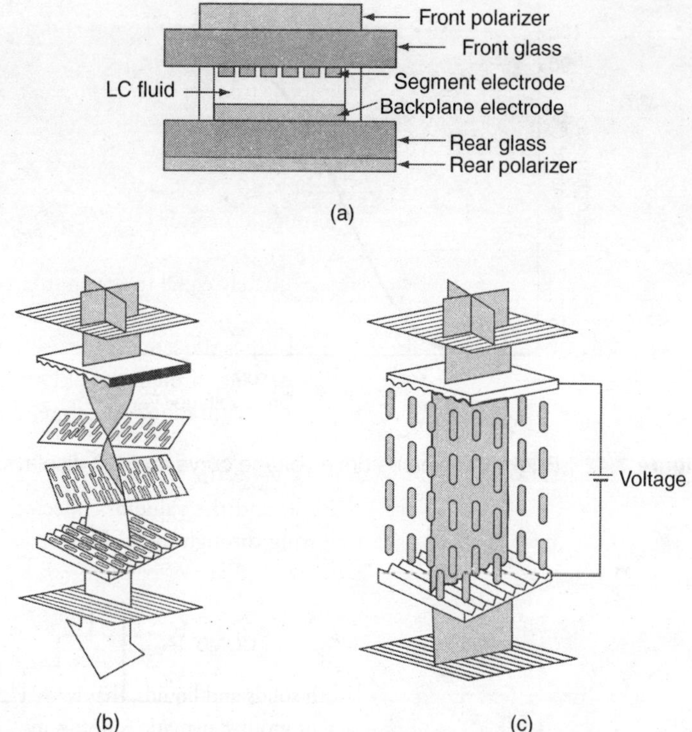

Figure 7.41 (a) Cross-section of a twisted nematic LCD display; (b) and (c) twisted nematic LCD operation.

to the rest of the screen [Figure 7.41(c)]. Hence, in order to display characters or graphics, voltage is applied to the desired regions, making them dark and visible to the eye.

A negative image is a light image on a dark background. In negative image displays, the front and the rear polarizers are aligned parallel to each other.

Driving an LCD

The LCD driver waveforms are designed to create a zero DC potential across all the pixels, as the DC voltage deteriorates the LC fluid such that it cannot be energized. LCDs are driven with symmetrical waveforms with less than 50 mV DC component. Figure 7.42 shows the brightness versus the RMS drive voltage curve for LCDs. V_{ON} is the RMS voltage applied across the liquid crystal that creates an ON pixel that is typically at the 90% contrast level. V_{OFF} or V_{TH} is the RMS voltage across the liquid crystal when the contrast voltage reaches 10% level. Another important specification is the discrimination ratio, which is defined as the ratio of V_{ON} to V_{OFF}. The discrimination ratio defines the contrast levels the LCD panel will achieve.

LCDs can be classified as direct-drive and multiplex-drive displays depending upon the technique used to drive them. Direct-drive displays, also known as static-drive displays, have an independent driver for each pixel. The drive voltage in this case is a square waveform having two voltage levels, namely, ground and V_{CC} [Figure 7.43(a)]. In the figure, segment 0 is the ON segment whereas segment 1 is the OFF segment. Direct-drive displays offer the best contrast ratios over a wide operating temperature range. However, as the display size increases the drive circuitry becomes very complex. Hence, multiplex-drive circuits are used for larger size displays. These displays reduce the total number of interconnections between the LCD and the driver. They have more than one backplane and the driver produces an amplitude-varying, time-synchronized

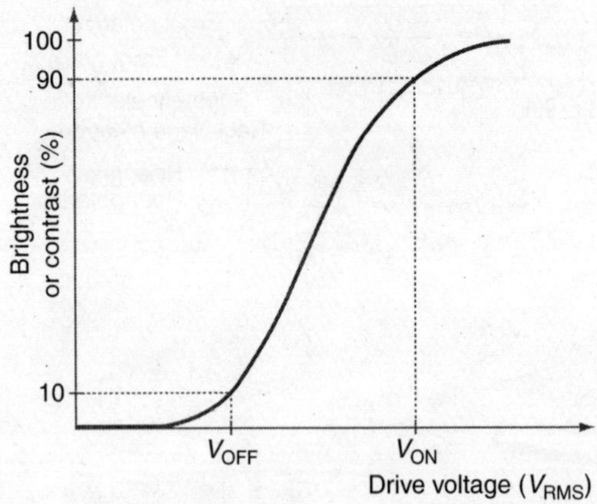

Figure 7.42 Brightness versus drive voltage curve for LCD displays.

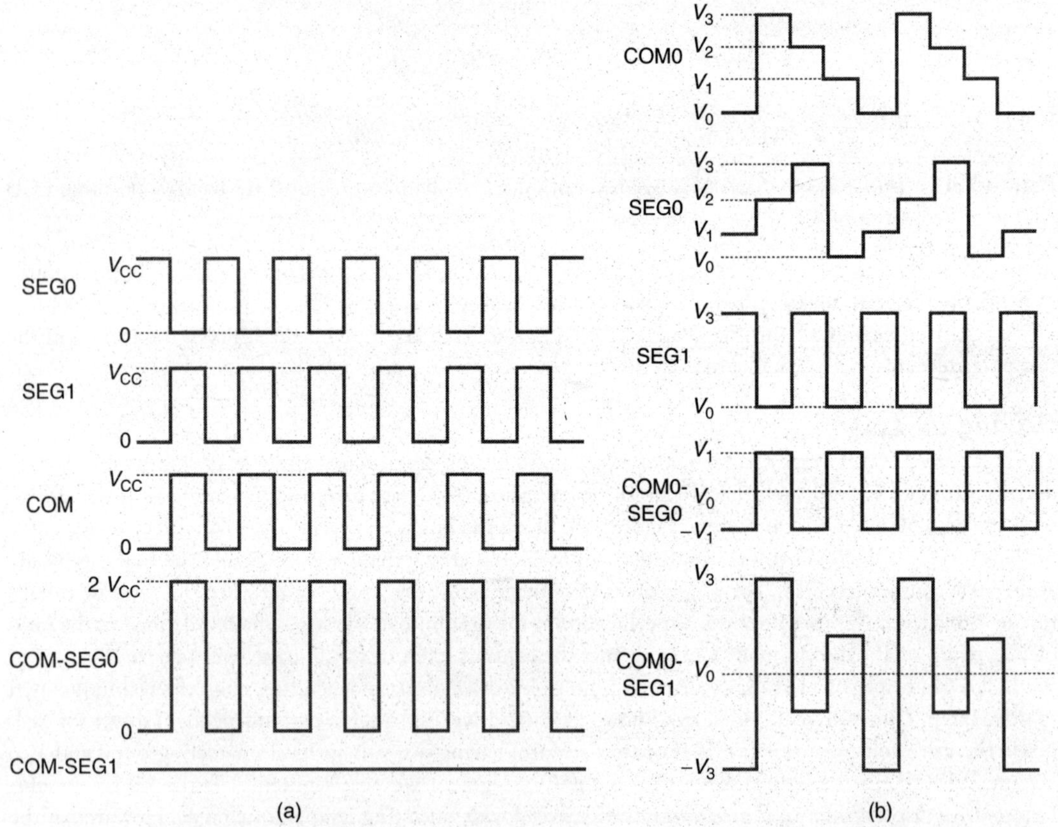

(a) (b)

Figure 7.43 (a) Direct-drive waveforms; (b) multiplex-drive waveforms.

waveform for both segment and backplanes. Figure 7.43(b) shows a typical multiplex-drive waveform showing the segment and the backplane waveforms. Segment 0 is inactive whereas segment 1 is active. Segment 0 is inactive as the voltage across the LCD never crosses its activation threshold voltage.

LCD Response Time

The LCD response time is defined by the ON and OFF response times. ON time refers to the time required by an OFF pixel to become visible after the application of proper drive voltage. The OFF time is defined as the time required by the ON pixel to turn OFF after the application of proper drive voltage. The response time of LCDs varies widely with temperature and increases rapidly at low operating temperatures. Hence, LCDs can only operate at low temperatures when used along with temperature controllers. At high temperatures, the liquid-crystal molecules begin to assume random orientations, resulting in the pixels on the positive image display becoming completely dark, while the pixels on the negative image display becoming completely transparent. Figure 7.44 shows the typical variation of the ON and the OFF times of an LCD display with temperature.

Liquid-Crystal Display Types

LCDs are non-emissive devices, that is, they do not generate light on their own. Depending upon the mode of transmission of light in an LCD, they are classified as reflective, transmissive and transreflective LCD displays.

Reflective LCD displays have a reflector attached to the rear polarizer which reflects incoming light evenly back into the display. Figure 7.45 shows the principle of operation of reflective LCD displays. These displays rely on the ambient light to operate and do not work in dark conditions. They produce only positive images. The front and the rear polarizers are perpendicular to each other. These types of displays are commonly used in calculators and digital wrist watches.

In **transmissive LCD displays**, back light is used as the light source. Most of these displays operate in the negative mode, that is, the text will be displayed in light color and the background is a dark color. Figure 7.46 shows the basic construction of a transmissive display. Negative transmissive displays have the front and the rear polarizers in parallel with each other whereas positive transmissive displays have the front and the rear polarizers perpendicular to each other. Transmissive displays are good for very low light level conditions. They offer very poor contrast when used in direct sunlight because sunlight swamps out the backlighting. Hence, these displays cannot be used in natural sunlight and provide good picture quality indoors. They are generally used in medical devices, electronics test and measuring equipments and in laptops.

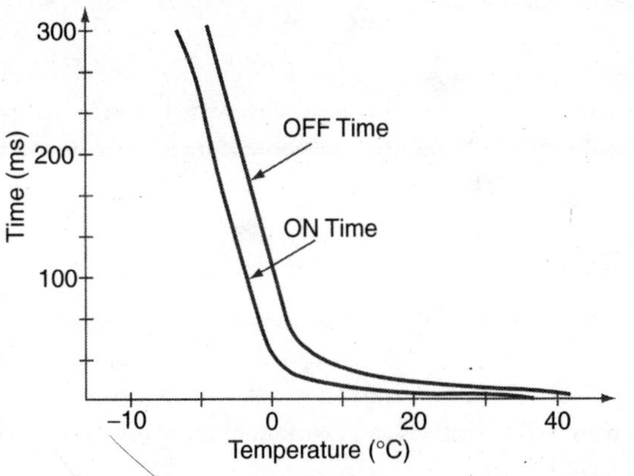

Figure 7.44 Variation of response time of LCD display with temperature.

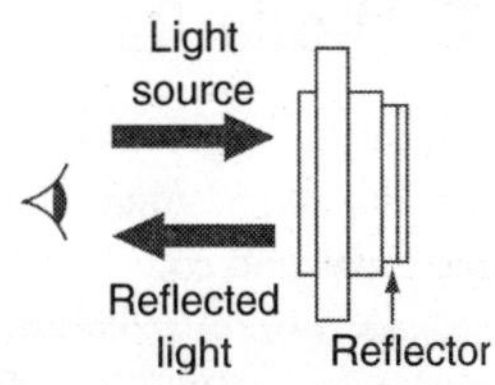

Figure 7.45 Reflective LCD display.

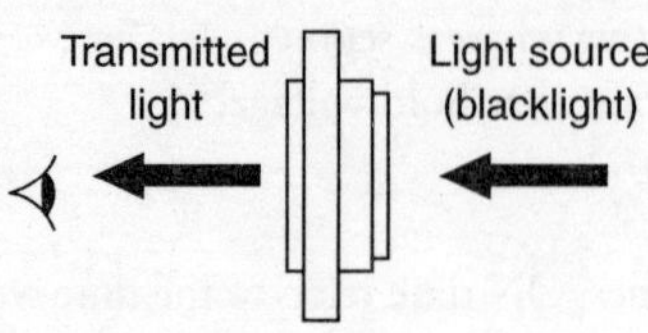

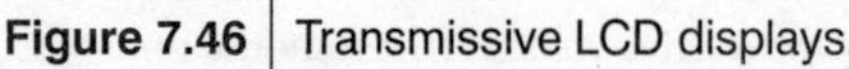
Figure 7.46 | Transmissive LCD displays.

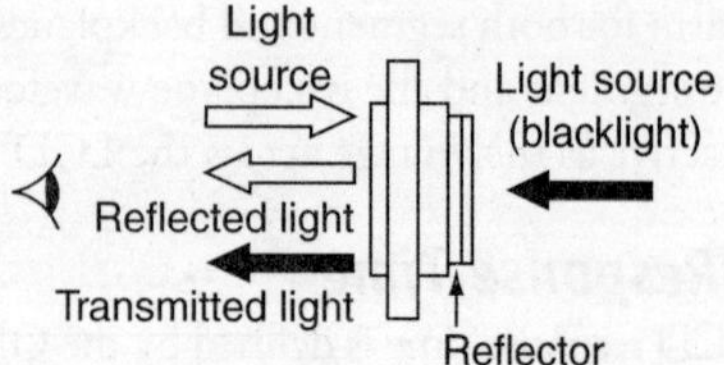

Figure 7.47 | Transreflective LCD displays.

Transreflective displays are a combination of reflective and transmissive displays (Figure 7.47). A white or silver translucent material is applied to the rear of the display, which reflects some of the ambient light back to the observer. It also allows the backlight to pass through. They are good for displays operating in varying light conditions. However, they offer poorer contrast ratios than reflective displays.

LCD displays can also be classified as passive LCD displays and active LCD displays depending upon the nature of the activation circuit. Passive displays use components that do not supply their own energy to turn ON or turn OFF the desired pixels. They are made up of a set of multiplexed transparent electrodes arranged in a two-dimensional pattern of rows and columns. To address a pixel, the column containing the pixel is sent a charge and the corresponding row is connected to the ground. Passive displays can have either direct-drive or multiplex-drive circuitry. For larger displays multiplex-drive circuits are used as it is not possible and economical to have separate connections for each segment. However, as the number of multiplexed lines increase, the contrast ratio decreases due to the cross-talk phenomenon wherein a voltage applied to the desired pixel causes the liquid-crystal molecules in the adjacent pixels to partially untwist.

These inherent problems of passive displays are removed in active displays. Active displays use an active device such as a transistor or a diode in each pixel which acts like a switch that precisely controls the voltage that each pixel receives. Active displays are further classified as thin film transistor (TFT) displays and thin film diode (TFD) displays depending upon whether the active device used is a transistor or a diode. In both these devices a common electrode is placed above the liquid-crystal matrix. Below the liquid crystal is a conductive grid connected to each pixel through a TFT or a TFD. The gate of each TFT is connected to the row electrode, the drain to the column electrode and the source to the liquid crystal. The display is activated by applying the display voltage to each row electrode line by line. One of the major advantages of active displays is that nearly all effects of cross-talk are eliminated.

Advantages and Disadvantages

As LCD displays are not active sources of light, they offer considerable advantages such as very low power consumption, low operating voltages and good flexibility. However, their response time is too slow for many applications, they offer limited viewing angles and are temperature sensitive.

7.12 Cathode Ray Tube Displays

Cathode ray tube (CRT) displays are used in a wide range of systems ranging from consumer electronic systems like television and computer monitors to measuring instruments like oscilloscopes to military systems like radar and so on. CRT display is a specialized vacuum tube in which the images are produced when the electron beam strikes the fluorescent screen. CRT displays can be monochrome displays as well as colored displays.

Monochrome CRT displays comprise a single electron gun, a fluorescent screen and an internal or external mechanism to accelerate and deflect the electron beam. Figure 7.48 shows the cross-sectional view of a CRT

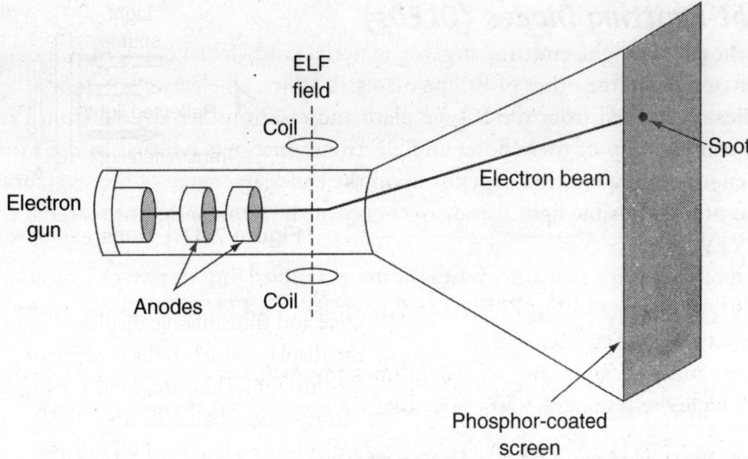

Figure 7.48 | Cross-section of a monochrome CRT display.

display. The electron gun produces a narrow beam of electrons that are accelerated by the anodes. There are two sets of deflecting coils, namely, the horizontal coil and the vertical coil. These coils produce an extremely low frequency electromagnetic field in the horizontal and vertical directions to adjust the direction of the electron beam. CRT tubes also have a mechanism to vary the intensity of the electron beam. In order to produce moving pictures in natural colors on the screen, complex signals are applied to the deflecting coils and to the circuitry responsible for controlling the intensity of the electron beam. This results in movement of the spot from right to left and from top to bottom in a sequence of horizontal lines referred to as a raster. The speed of the spot movement is so fast that the person viewing the screen sees a constant image on the entire screen.

Colored CRT displays comprise three electron guns, one each for the three primary colors, namely, red, blue and green. The CRT produces three overlapping images, one in red (R), one in green (G) and one in blue (B). This is referred to as the RGB color model.

Advantages and Disadvantages

CRT displays offer very high resolution and as these displays emit their own light; therefore, they have very high values of peak luminances. Moreover, these displays offer wide viewing angles of the order of 180°. Also, CRT display technology is more mature as compared to alternate display technologies and they are cheaper as compared to other displays.

Inspite of the significant advantages offered by CRT displays as mentioned above, alternate display technologies are slowly replacing the CRT displays due to the drawbacks of these displays. CRT displays are bulky and consume significant power. Moreover they require high voltages to operate and they cause fatigue and strain to the human eye.

7.13 Emerging Display Technologies

This section gives an introduction to the emerging display technologies including organic light-emitting diodes (OLEDs), digital light-processing technology (DLP), plasma displays, field emission displays (FEDs) and electronic ink displays. All these display technologies are explained in brief in this section. Detailed description of these technologies is beyond the scope of the book.

Organic Light-Emitting Diodes (OLEDs)

OLEDs are composed of a light-emitting organic material sandwiched between two conducting plates, one of N-type material and the other of P-type material. When an electric potential is applied between these plates, holes are ejected from the P-type plate and electrons are ejected from the N-type plate. Owing to the recombination of these holes and electrons, energy is released in the form of light photons. The wavelength of light emitted depends upon the bandgap energy of the semiconductor material used. In order to produce visible light, bandgap energy of the semiconductor material should be of the order of 1.5–3.5 eV.

Depending upon their basic structure, OLEDs can be classified into three types, namely, small molecule OLEDs (SMOLEDs), polymer LEDs (PLEDs) and dendrimer OLEDs. OLEDs can be driven using passive as well as active matrix driver circuits.

As OLEDs are emissive devices, they offer significant advantages as compared to LCD displays like faster switching speeds, higher refresh rates, lower operating voltages and larger viewing angles.

Digital Light Processing (DLP) Technology

DLP technology makes use of an optical semiconductor device referred to as digital micromirror device (DMD) which is basically a precise light switch that can digitally modulate light through a large number of microscopic mirrors arranged in a rectangular array. These mirrors are mounted on tiny hinges and can be tilted away or towards the light source with the help of the DMD chip and thus projecting a light or a dark pixel on the screen. Use of DLP technology is currently limited to large projection systems.

Plasma Display Panels (PDP)

Plasma displays are composed of millions of cells sandwiched between two panels of glass. Two electrodes, namely, the address electrodes and display electrodes, are also placed between the two glass plates covering the entire screen. The address electrodes are printed on the rear glass plate and the transparent display electrodes are located above the cells along the front glass plate. These electrodes are perpendicular to each other forming a grid network.

Each cell is filled with xenon and neon gas mixture. The electrodes intersecting at a specific cell are charged to excite the gas mixture in that cell. When the gas mixture is excited, a plasma is created releasing ultraviolet light which then excites the phosphor electrons located on the sides of the cells. These electrons in turn release visible light and return to their lower energy state. Each pixel is composed of three cells containing red, green and blue phosphors.

Plasma displays offer several advantages like each pixel generates its own light offering large viewing angles, generates superior image quality and the image quality is not affected by the area of the display. However, these displays are fragile in nature and are susceptible to burn-out from static images.

Field Emission Displays (FEDs)

FEDs function much like the CRT displays with the main difference being that these displays use millions of small electron guns to emit electrons at the screen instead of just one as in case of CRT displays. The extraction of electrons in FEDs is based on the "tunneling effect." FED displays produce the same quality of image as produced by the CRT displays without being bulky as the CRT displays. Infact these displays can be as thin as LCD displays and as large as plasma displays.

Electronic Ink Displays

Electronic ink displays, also referred to as electronic paper, are active matrix displays making use of pigments that resemble the ink used in print.

7.14 Optocouplers

An optocoupler, also referred to as an optoisolator, is a device that uses a short optical transmission path to transfer signals between the elements of a circuit. Optocouplers are sealed units that house an optical transmitting device and a photosensitive device that are coupled together optically. The optical path may be air or a dielectric waveguide. Figure 7.49 shows the basic structure of an optocoupler.

The transmitter unit contains either a lamp, an LED or in some cases a laser diode. The receiver unit may be a photodiode, a phototransistor, a photoFET, a photoSCR, a photoDIAC, a photoTRIAC, a photoconductor or any other photosensitive material. As the coupling between the source and the photosensor is optical, high isolation exists between the input and the output circuitry. Hence, low power level, sensitive circuits can be used to actuate high power devices using optocouplers. In other words, optocouplers are used in applications that require isolation between input and output signals. Optocouplers have also replaced low power relays and pulse transformers in many applications. They can also be used for applications like detection of objects, liquid-level detection, smoke and fog detection, end-of-tape detection and so on.

Optocouplers with photodiodes [Figure 7.50(a)], phototransistors [Figure 7.50(b)], photo-Darlington transistors [Figure 7.50(c)], photoconductor [Figure 7.50(d)] and photoFET [Figure 7.50(e)] detectors at the receiving end are referred to as non-latching optocouplers. Optocouplers with photoSCR [Figure 7.51(a)], photoDIAC [Figure 7.51(b)] and photoTRIAC [Figure 7.51(c)] at the receiving side are referred to as latching optocouplers.

Optocoupler Parameters

The important parameters that define the performance of an optocoupler include forward optocoupling efficiency, input-to-output isolation voltage, input current, bandwidth and temperature response.

1. **Forward Optocoupling Efficiency:** The forward optocoupling efficiency is specified in terms of the current transfer ratio (CTR). CTR is the ratio of the output current to the input current. For logic output optocouplers, the coupling efficiency is defined as the input current to the LED that would cause a change in the logic state of the optocoupler's output. To ensure high coupling efficiency, the wavelength response of the receiver is matched to the emission spectrum of the phototransmitter. Typical values of CTR range from 10% to 50% for optocouplers having phototransistors as the photosensor and can be even as high as 200% for optocouplers having photo-Darlington transistors at the output.
2. **Isolation Voltage:** It is the maximum permissible DC potential that can be allowed to exist between the input and the output circuits. Typical values of isolation voltages offered by optocouplers are in the range of 500–4000 V.

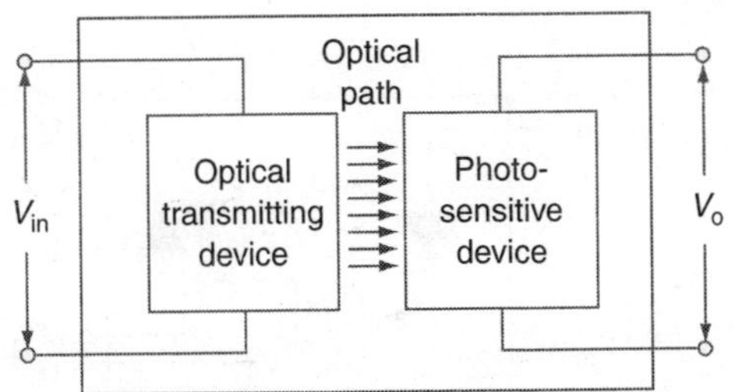

Figure 7.49 | Basic structure of an optocoupler.

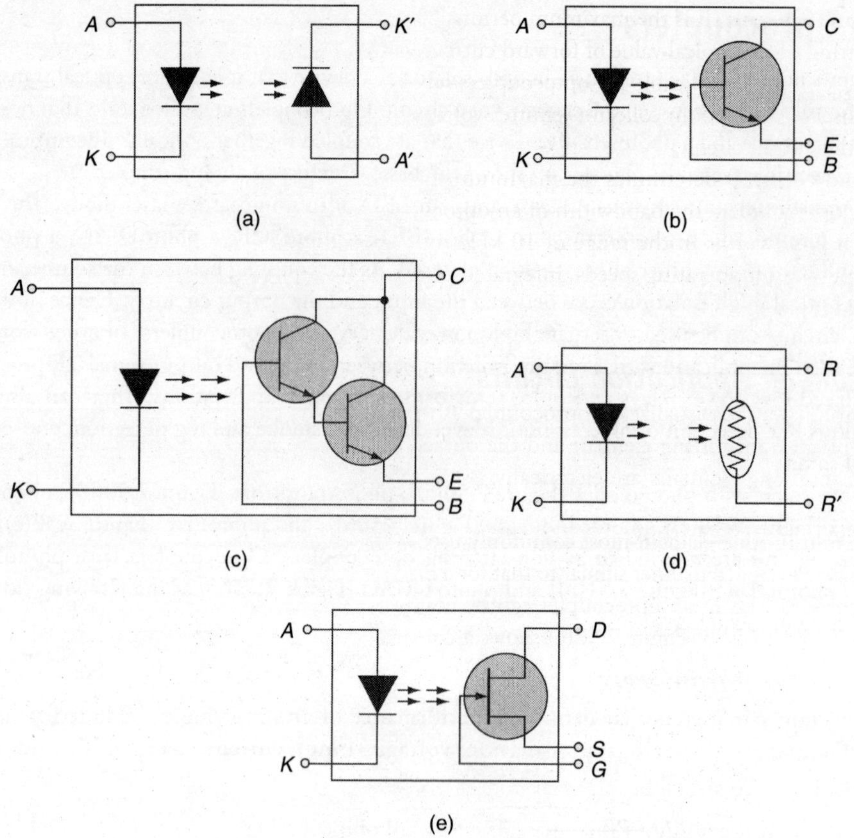

Figure 7.50 Non-latching optocoupler configurations.

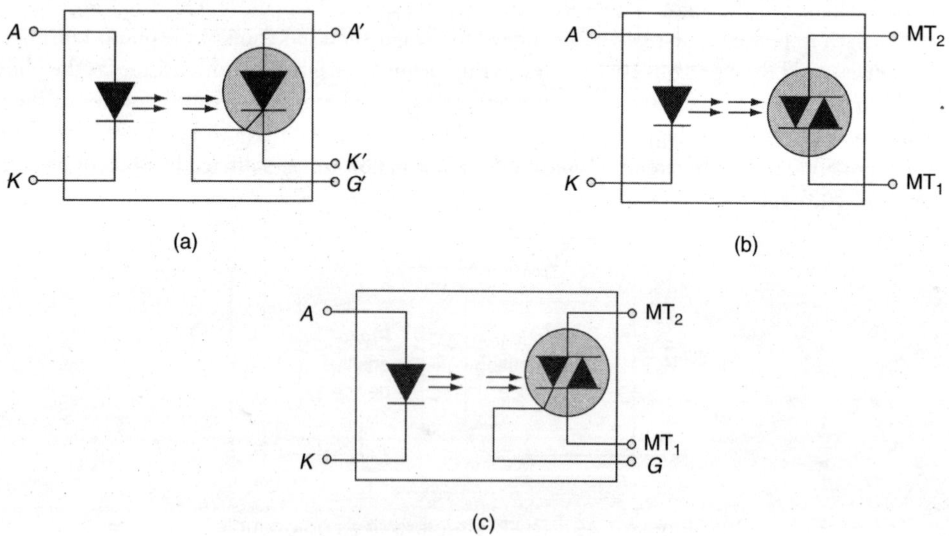

Figure 7.51 Latching optocoupler configurations.

3. **Input Current:** It is the maximum permissible forward current that is allowed to flow into the transmitting LED. Typical value of forward current varies in the range of 10–100 mA.
4. $V_{CE(max)}$**:** It is applicable for optocouplers having phototransistors at the output. It is defined as the transistor's maximum collector–emitter voltage rating. It limits the supply voltage that can be applied to the output circuit.
5. **Bandwidth:** It determines the maximum signal frequency that can be successfully passed through the optocoupler. The bandwidth of an optocoupler depends upon its switching speed. Optocouplers offer bandwidths in the range of 10 kHz to 1 MHz, depending upon the device construction. To achieve faster operating speeds, integrated photodiode-transistor detectors or Schottky transistors are used.

Optocoupler Application Circuits

The simplest way to visualize an optocoupler is in terms of its two important components, namely, the input optical transmitting element and the output photosensor. As in an optocoupler, the transmitting and the receiving elements are electrically isolated; hence there exists a lot of flexibility in connecting them.

The transmitting element most commonly used in an optocoupler is an LED. The LED in an optocoupler can be driven in a manner similar to that for a discrete LED. Figure 7.52 shows the various configurations in which the LEDs in an optocoupler can be connected. These circuits are similar to those discussed in Section 7.10 on LEDs. Figure 7.52(a) shows a conventional circuit for driving the LED. The diode across

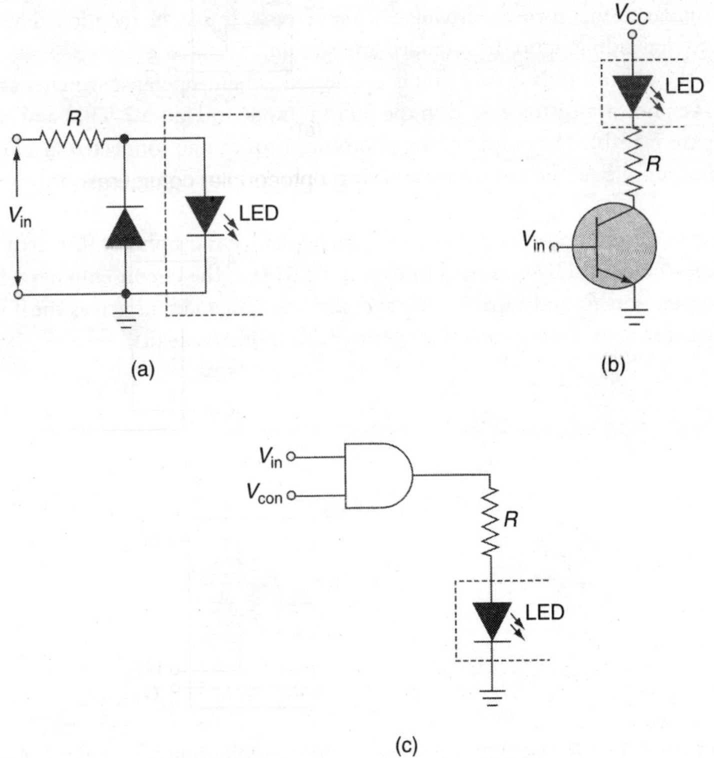

Figure 7.52 Driving LEDs of an optocoupler.

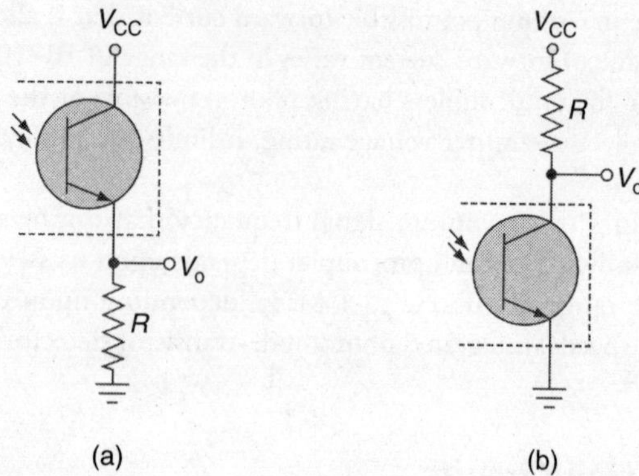

Figure 7.53 Driving the phototransistors of an optocoupler.

the LED is used for protecting the LED against reverse polarity voltages. Figures 7.52(b) and (c) show how to drive an LED using a transistor and a logic buffer, respectively. For both the circuits, the LED is ON for logic HIGH input and is OFF for logic LOW input.

At the receiving side of the optocoupler, the photosensor used may be a photodiode, a phototransistor, a photo-Darlington transistor, a photoFET, a photoDIAC or a photoTRIAC. Circuits for driving these photosensors are similar to that used for driving discrete sensors. It may be mentioned here that the output circuit is configured depending upon the intended application.

In many cases, the phototransistors are simply connected as light-operated switches as shown in Figures 7.53(a) and (b). The phototransistor is used in the pull-up mode in Figure 7.53(a) and is used in the pull-down mode in Figure 7.53(b). The output of the phototransistor can be connected to a logic gate, a transistor or an operational amplifier. The optocoupler having a photo-Darlington transistor can also be driven in a similar manner.

Figure 7.54 shows the application circuit of an optocoupler having a photoDIAC as a photosensing element. In the circuit, the photoDIAC is used to trigger a TRIAC. The circuit employs a filter/delay circuit comprising resistors R_1 and R_2 and capacitor C_1 and also a snubber circuit across the TRIAC comprising resistor R_S and capacitor C_S to ensure correct triggering with inductive loads.

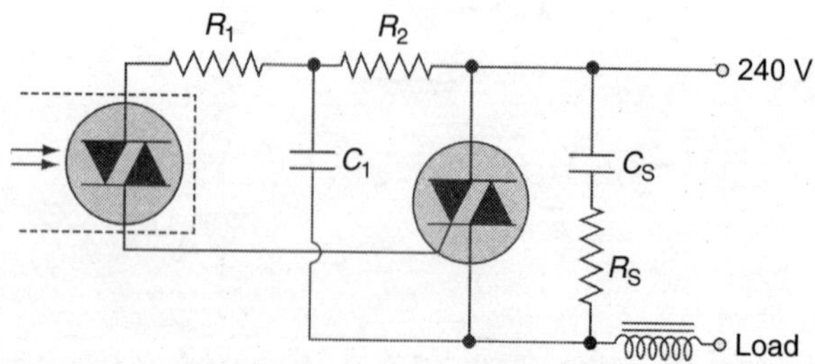

Figure 7.54 Application circuit of an optocoupler having a photoDIAC.

EXAMPLE 7.9 *For the optocoupler circuit of Figure 7.55(a), the voltage across the resistor R is 4 V. Determine the value of the voltage V_B applied to the base of the transistor Q_1. The relationship between the input current flowing through the LED and the output phototransistor collector current is shown in Figure 7.55(b). The base–emitter voltage of transistor Q_1 is equal to 0.7 V.*

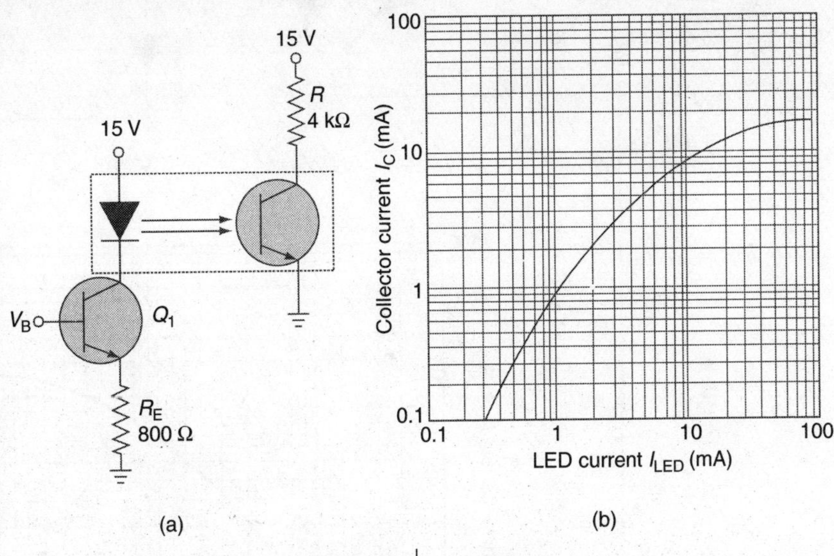

Figure 7.55 Example 7.9.

Solution

1. The current flowing across the resistor $R = 4/(4 \times 10^3) = 1 \times 10^{-3}$ A = 1 mA.
2. The collector current of the phototransistor (I_C) is equal to the current across resistor R. Therefore, $I_C = 1$ mA.
3. From the curve of Figure 7.55(b), the input current flowing through the LED is approximately equal to 1.1 mA.
4. The current flowing through the LED is equal to the collector current of transistor Q_1.
5. As the collector current of the transistor is approximately the same as its emitter current, therefore the emitter current is equal to 1.1 mA.
6. The voltage drop across resistor $R_E = 800 \times 1.1 \times 10^{-3} = 0.88$ V.
7. The voltage $V_B = V_E + V_{BE} = 0.88 + 0.7 = 1.58$ V.

EXAMPLE 7.10 *The optocoupler-based circuit of Figure 7.56(a) is used to provide isolation from the power line and detect zero crossings of the line voltage. The relationship between the input LED current and the output current of the phototransistor for the optocoupler is shown in Figure 7.56(b). Draw the output waveform $V_o(t)$. Assume the diodes to be ideal.*

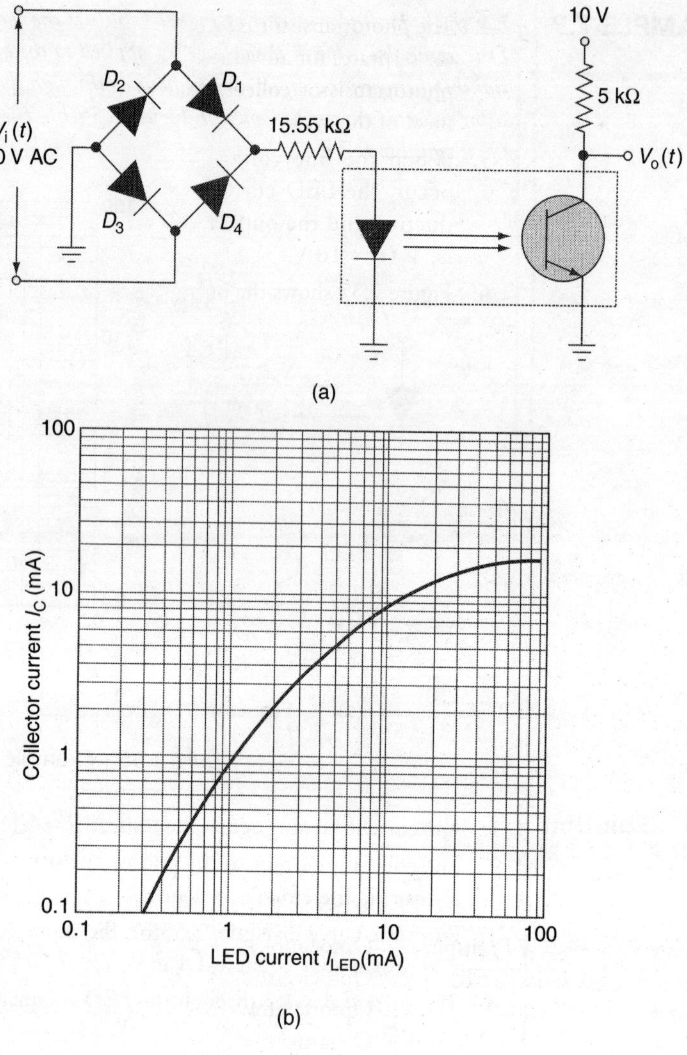

Figure 7.56 Example 7.10.

Solution

1. The bridge rectifier produces a full-wave rectified output. Therefore, the current through the LED is also a full-wave rectified waveform. The peak current through the LED is $I_{\text{LEDpeak}} = (1.414 \times 220)/(15.55 \times 10^3) = 20 \times 10^{-3}$ A = 20 mA.

2. The value of collector current when the phototransistor is in saturation $I_{\text{Csat}} = 10/(5 \times 10^3) = 2 \times 10^{-3} = 2$ mA.

3. From Figure 7.53(b), the collector current corresponding to the LED current of 20 mA is 14 mA. The collector current of the phototransistor never reaches 14 mA as it saturates at 2 mA.

4. The phototransistor is saturated during most of the cycle as the phototransistor saturates for all values of LED currents that produce more than 2 mA of phototransistor collector current. Therefore, the output voltage is zero for most of the cycle.
5. When the line voltage changes polarity, that is, when zero crossings occur, the LED current drops to zero. The phototransistor stops conducting and the output voltage is equal to the supply voltage 10 V, that is, $V_o(t) = 10$ V.
6. Figure 7.57 shows the output waveform.

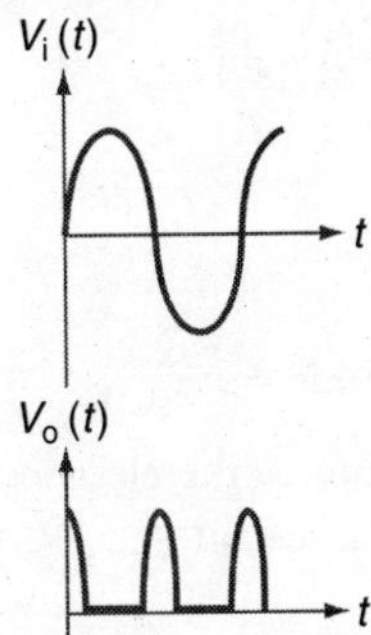

Figure 7.57 | Solution to Example 7.10.

KEY TERMS

Avalanche photodiode
Cathode ray tube (CRT) display
Current transfer ratio (CTR)
Dee-star
Detectivity
Digital light processing (DLP)
Field emission display (FED)
Flicker noise
Flux
Illuminance
Image intensifier
Intensity
Johnson noise
Light dependent resistor (LDR)
Light-emitting diode (LED)
Liquid-crystal display (LCD)
Luminous intensity
Noise equivalent power (NEP)
Optocoupler
Optoelectronic device
Optoisolator
Organic light-emitting diode (OLED)
Photoconductive mode
Photoconductor
Photodiode
Photoelectric sensor
Photoemitter
PhotoFET
Photometry
Photomultiplier tube
Photoresistor
Photosensor
Phototransistor
Photovoltaic mode
PIN photodiode
Plasma display
PN photodiode
Quantum efficiency
Radiant incidence
Radiometeric intensity
Radiometry
Response time
Responsivity
Rise time
Schottky photodiode
Shot noise
Spectral response
Thermal sensor
Time constant
Vacuum photodiode

OBJECTIVE-TYPE EXERCISES

Multiple-Choice Questions

1. What factors determine the type of photodetector you select?
   - a. Speed of response
   - b. Minimum and maximum light levels
   - c. Spectral response
   - d. (a) and (b)
   - e. All the above
2. A photocell's resistance versus light can vary as much as
   - a. 10:1.
   - b. 20:1.
   - c. 50:1.
   - d. several orders of magnitude.
3. LED's efficiency is a measure of the electrical energy required to produce a certain
   - a. current.
   - b. resistance.
   - c. photometric efficiency.
   - d. light output.
4. The resistance of a photoconductor
   - a. decreases with increase in light intensity.
   - b. increases with increase in light intensity.
   - c. does not change with light intensity.
   - d. can increase or decrease with increase in light intensity.
5. Increase in reverse-bias voltage across the photodiode
   - a. increases the rise time and decreases the width of the depletion region of the photodiode.
   - b. decreases the rise time and decreases the width of the depletion region of the photodiode.
   - c. decreases the rise time and increases the width of the depletion region of the photodiode.
   - d. increases the rise time and increases the width of the depletion region of the photodiode.
6. The noise current and responsivity of a sensor are 10 nA and 1 A/W, respectively. Its NEP is
   - a. 10 nW.
   - b. 1 nW.
   - c. 100 nW.
   - d. 0.1 nW.
7. The output wavelength of an LED is
   - a. directly proportional to the bandgap energy of the semiconductor material.
   - b. inversely proportional to the bandgap energy of the semiconductor material.
   - c. proportional to the square of the bandgap energy of the semiconductor material.
   - d. inversely proportional to the square of the bandgap energy of the semiconductor material.
8. The best parameter to compare the noise performance of any two sensors is
   - a. NEP.
   - b. dee-star.
   - c. detectivity.
   - d. none of these.
9. Which of the following statements is true?
   - a. Drive waveform for a LCD display is a DC voltage.
   - b. Drive waveform for a LCD display is an AC waveform with zero RMS value.
   - c. Drive waveform for a LCD display is an AC waveform with zero DC value.
   - d. Drive waveform for a LCD display can be a DC or an AC waveform.
10. Typical range of CTR value for an optocoupler having a phototransistor at the output is
    - a. 10% to 50%.
    - b. 1% to 10%.
    - c. 60% to 90%.
    - d. 10% to 70%.

Fill in the Blanks

1. Dark current in a photodiode is a measure of its __________ current.
2. __________ photosensor can be used to count even a single photon.

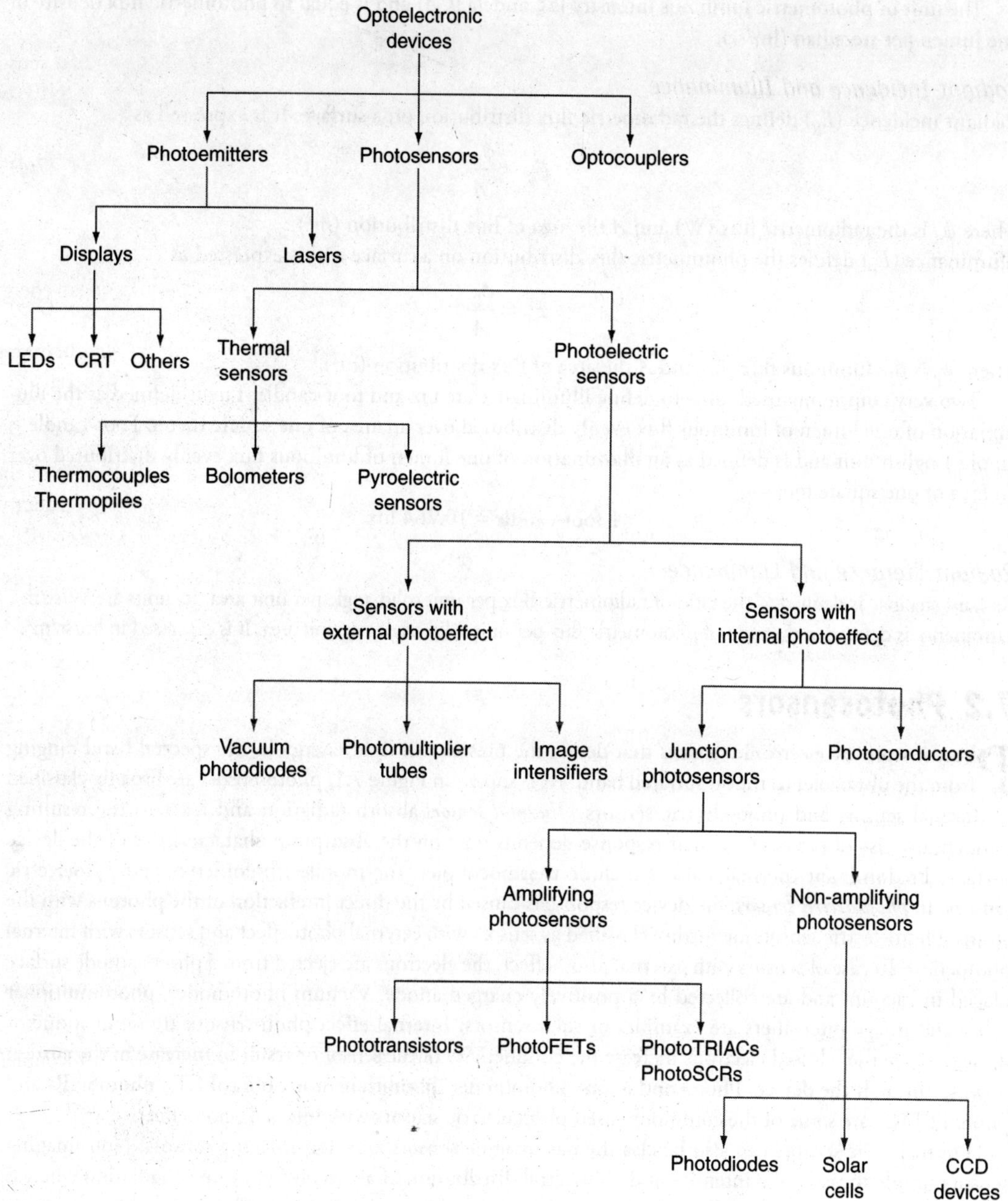

Figure 7.1 | Classification of optoelectronic devices.

Photometric or luminous intensity (I_P) is defined as the ratio of photometric flux density per steradian. It is given by

$$I_P = \frac{\phi_P}{\Omega} \tag{7.3}$$

where ϕ_P is the photometric flux (lm) and Ω the solid angle (sr).

The unit of photometric luminous intensity is Candela (Cd) and is equal to photometric flux density of one lumen per steradian (lm/sr).

Radiant Incidence and Illuminance

Radiant incidence (E_R) defines the radiometric flux distribution on a surface. It is expressed as

$$E_R = \frac{\phi_R}{A} \tag{7.4}$$

where ϕ_R is the radiometric flux (W) and A the area of flux distribution (m^2).
Illuminance (E_P) defines the photometric flux distribution on a surface and is expressed as

$$E_P = \frac{\phi_P}{A} \tag{7.5}$$

where ϕ_P is the luminous flux (lu) and A the area of flux distribution (m^2).

Two very commonly used units to define illuminance are lux and foot-candle. Lux is defined as the illumination of one lumen of luminous flux evenly distributed over an area of one square meter. Foot-candle is an old English unit and is defined as an illumination of one lumen of luminous flux evenly distributed over an area of one square foot.

$$1 \text{ foot-candle} = 10.764 \text{ lux}$$

Radiant Sterance and Luminance

Radiant sterance is defined as the ratio of radiometric flux per unit solid angle per unit area. Its units are W/sr/m^2. Luminance is defined as the ratio of photometric flux per unit solid angle per unit area. It is expressed in lm/sr/m^2.

7.2 Photosensors

Photosensors are electronic devices that detect the presence of light energy in the spectral band ranging from the ultraviolet to the far infrared band. As is shown in Figure 7.1, photosensors are broadly classified as thermal sensors and photoelectric sensors. *Thermal sensors* absorb radiation and react to the resulting temperature rise of the device. Their response depends only on the absorption characteristics of the device surface. Predominant thermal sensors include thermocouples, thermopiles, bolometers and pyroelectric sensors. In *photoelectric sensors,* the device response is caused by the direct interaction of the photons with the atoms. Photoelectric sensors are further classified as sensors with external photoeffect and sensors with internal photoeffect. In case of sensors with external photoeffect, the electrons are ejected from a photocathode surface placed in vacuum and are collected by a positively charged anode. Vacuum photodiodes, photomultiplier tubes and image intensifiers are examples of such sensors. Internal effect photosensors are semiconductor devices where the released electrons increase the conductivity of the sensor or result in increase in the current flowing through the device. Photoconductors, photodiodes, phototransistors, photoFETs, photoSCRs and photoTRIACs are some of the commonly used photoelectric sensors with internal photoeffect.

Photoelectric sensors can also be classified as imaging sensors and non-imaging sensors. Non-imaging sensors simply measure the intensity and/or spectral distribution of an incoming beam of radiation whereas imaging sensors also preserve the intensity versus position information in a two-dimensional field of view. Photodiodes, photomuliplier tubes (PMTs), photoconductors are all examples of non-imaging sensors. Imaging sensors include image intensifier tubes, CCDs and so on.

Characteristic Parameters

Major characteristic parameters used to characterize the performance of photosensors include responsivity, noise equivalent power (NEP), sensitivity (detectivity and dee-star), quantum efficiency, response time, noise and spectral response.

1. **Responsivity (R):** It is defined as the ratio of electrical output to radiant light input and is measured in A/W or V/W. Reponsivity is a function of wavelength of incident radiation and bandgap energy of the photosensor material. For most sensors it is specified at a particular wavelength. However in the case of some sensors like for measuring black-body radiation, it is integrated over a given wavelength range. It is also referred to as the figure of merit for the sensor system as the design of the signal processing stages depends on the amount of signal voltage or current generated by the photosensor.

   Responsivity figures for silicon PIN photodiodes are in the range of 0.4 to 0.6 A/W whereas for avalanche photodiodes, they are in the range of 40 to 80 A/W. Thermal sensors have poorer responsivity as compared to photoelectric sensors. As an example, the responsivity figure for pyroelectric sensors is in the range of 0.5 to 5 μA/W.
2. **Noise Equivalent Power (NEP):** NEP is the radiant power applied to the sensor that produces an output signal equal to the root mean square (RMS) noise output from the sensor, that is, the signal-to-noise ratio equals one. In other words, it is the minimum detectable radiation level of the sensor. The value of NEP is computed using the ratio of noise current to responsivity. For detection of weak signals, responsivity and NEP parameters are of utmost importance.
3. **Detectivity and Dee-Star:** Detectivity of a sensor is the reciprocal of its NEP. A sensor with higher detectivity value is more sensitive than a sensor with lower detectivity value. Detectivity, like NEP depends upon noise bandwidth and sensor area. To eliminate these factors, a normalized figure of detectivity referred to as "Dee-star" is used. It is defined as the detectivity normalized to an area of 1 cm^2 and a noise bandwidth of 1 Hz. The value of Dee-star (D^*) can be calculated using

$$D^* = D\sqrt{A\Delta f} \tag{7.6}$$

   where D^* is the Dee-star (W^{-1} cm Hz$^{1/2}$); D the detectivity (W^{-1}); A the detector area (cm^2); Δf the bandwidth (Hz).
4. **Quantum Efficiency or Quantum Yield:** An ideal photosensor should produce 1 photoelectron per incident photon of light. This is not true for practical sensors. The ratio of the number of photoelectrons released to the number of photons of incident light absorbed is referred to as the quantum efficiency of the sensor. It is the intrinsic efficiency of the sensor. The value of quantum efficiency (η) is computed using the formula

$$\eta = \frac{1240 \times R}{\lambda} \tag{7.7}$$

   where R is the responsivity in A/W and λ is the wavelength in nm.
5. **Response Time:** It is expressed as *rise time* parameter in photoelectric sensors and as *time constant* parameter in thermal sensors. Rise time is the time required by the output to reach from 10% to 90% of the final response and it determines the highest signal frequency to which a sensor can respond. Time constant is defined as the time required by the output to reach to 63% of the final response from zero initial value.

   Bandwidth of photoelectric sensors is related to its rise time by the following formula:

$$BW = \frac{0.35}{t_r} \tag{7.8}$$

   where BW is the bandwidth in MHz and t_r is the rise time is in μs.
6. **Sensor Noise:** Noise is the most critical factor in designing sensitive radiation detection systems. Noise in these systems is generated in photosensors, radiation sources and post-detection circuitry. Sensor noise includes Johnson noise, shot noise, generation-recombination noise and flicker noise.
   - **Johnson noise also known as Nyquist or thermal noise** is caused by the thermal motion of charged particles in a resistive element. The RMS value of the noise voltage depends on the resistance value, temperature and the system bandwidth and is given by

$$V_{RMS} = \sqrt{4kRT\Delta f} \tag{7.9}$$

where V_{RMS} is the RMS noise voltage (V); R the resistance value in Ω; k the Boltzmann constant (1.38×10^{-23} J/K); T the absolute temperature (K); Δf the system bandwidth (Hz).

- **Shot noise** in a photosensor is caused by the discrete nature of the photoelectrons generated. It depends on the average current through the photosensor and system bandwidth and is expressed by

$$I_{SRMS} = \sqrt{2eI_{av}\Delta f} \tag{7.10}$$

where I_{SRMS} is the RMS shot noise current (A); I_{av} the average current through the photosensor (A); e the charge of an electron (1.60×10^{-19} C); Δf the system bandwidth (Hz). In the case of a photodiode, the shot noise is generated both due to the dark current and the photocurrent.

- **Generation-recombination noise** is caused by the fluctuation in current generation and the recombination rates in a photosensor. This type of noise is predominant in photoconductive sensors operating at infrared wavelengths. The generation-recombination noise can be calculated using

$$I_{GRMS} = 2eG\sqrt{\eta EA\Delta f} \tag{7.11}$$

where I_{GRMS} is the RMS generation-recombination noise current (A); e the charge of an electron (1.60×10^{-19} C); Δf the system bandwidth (Hz); E the radiant incidence (W/cm^2); A the sensor-receiving area (cm^2); G the photoconductive gain; η the quantum efficiency.

- **Flicker noise or 1/f noise** occurs in all conductors where the conducting medium is not a metal and exists in all semiconductor devices that require bias current for their operation. Its amplitude is inversely proportional to the frequency and usually the flicker noise is predominant at frequencies below 100 Hz. The total equivalent noise (I_{NEQ}) is calculated by adding the noise voltages or currents in the RMS manner as given in the following equation:

$$I_{NEQ} = \sqrt{I_{JRMS}^{\ 2} + I_{SRMS}^{\ 2} + I_{GRMS}^{\ 2} + I_{FRMS}^{\ 2}} \tag{7.12}$$

where I_{JRMS} is the RMS Johnson noise current (A); I_{SRMS} is the RMS shot noise current (A); I_{GRMS} is the RMS generation–recombination noise current (A) and I_{FRMS} is the RMS flicker noise current (A).

7. **Spectral Response:** It describes the wavelength range over which a sensor responds. Most photoelectric materials have narrow spectral response whereas most thermal sensors have wide spectral response. As an example, the spectral response of silicon, germanium, indium gallium arsenide (InGaAs) photodiodes are in the range of 200–1100 nm, 500–1900 nm and 700–1700 nm, respectively, whereas that of thermistors is from 0.5 to 10 μm.

EXAMPLE 7.1 *A photodiode has a noise current of 1 fA, responsivity figure of 0.5 A/W, active area of 1 mm² and rise time of 3.5 ns. Determine its (a) NEP, (b) detectivity, (c) D*, (d) quantum efficiency at 850 nm.*

Solution

1. NEP = Noise current/Responsivity = $1 \times 10^{-15}/0.5 = 2 \times 10^{-15}$ W = 2 fW.
2. Detectivity = 1/NEP = $1/\ 2 \times 10^{-15} = 0.5 \times 10^{15}$ W^{-1}.
3. $D^* = D \times \sqrt{A \times \Delta f}$

   $A = 1\text{ mm}^2 = 1 \times 10^{-2}\text{ cm}^2$

   Δf(in MHz) $= 0.35/t_r$ (in μs) $= 0.35/3.5 \times 10^{-3} = 100$ MHz $= 1 \times 10^8$ Hz

   Therefore, $D^* = 0.5 \times 10^{15} \times \sqrt{(1 \times 10^{-2} \times 1 \times 10^8)} = 5 \times 10^{17}$ W^{-1} cm Hz$^{1/2}$.
4. Quantum efficiency, $\eta = \left[\dfrac{1240 \times R}{\lambda}\right]$

   $\eta = [(1240 \times 0.5)/850] = 0.729$

EXAMPLE 7.2 *An oscilloscope is used to measure the output of a photodiode. Determine the rise time of the pulse as seen on the oscilloscope, given that the rise time of the photodiode is 1 ns, rise time of the light pulse is 5 ns and the bandwidth of the oscilloscope is 350 MHz.*

Solution

1. Given that the rise time of the light pulse is 5 ns and the rise time of the photodiode is 1 ns.
2. Bandwidth of the oscilloscope = 350 MHz. Therefore, rise time of the oscilloscope is t_r (in μs) = 0.35/BW (in MHz) = 0.35/350 = 1×10^{-3} μs = 1 ns.
3. Therefore, overall rise time = $\sqrt{(5\times10^{-9})^2 + (1\times10^{-9})^2 + (1\times10^{-9})^2}$
$= 5.20 \times 10^{-9}$ s = 5.20 ns

7.3 Photoconductors

Photoconductors, also referred to as photoresistors, light-dependent resistors (LDRs) and photocells, are semiconductor photosensors whose resistance decreases with increasing incident light intensity. They are bulk semiconductor devices with no PN junction and having a structure as shown in Figure 7.2(a). When light is incident on the photoconductor, electrons jump from the valence band to the conduction band. Hence, the resistance of the semiconductor material decreases. The resistance change in a photoconductor is of the order of 6 decades, ranging from few tens of megaohms under dark conditions to few tens or hundreds of ohms under bright light conditions. Other features include wide dynamic response, spectral coverage from ultraviolet to far infrared and low cost. However, they are sluggish devices having response time of the order of hundreds of milliseconds.

The resistance–illuminance relation in photoconductors is described by

$$R_a = R_b \times \left(\frac{E_a}{E_b}\right)^{-\alpha} \tag{7.13}$$

where R_a and R_b are the resistances at illuminance levels of E_a and E_b, respectively. E_a and E_b are the illuminance levels in lux or foot-candles. α is the characteristic slope of the resistance–illuminance curve.

The value of α is in the range of 0.55 to 0.9. Figure 7.2(b) shows the circuit symbol of a photoconductor and Figure 7.2(c) shows the typical resistance–illuminance curve of a photoconductor.

Commonly used materials in photoconductors are cadmium sulphide (CdS), lead sulphide (PbS), lead selenide (PbSe), mercury cadmium telluride (HgCdTe) and germanium copper (Ge:Cu). Spectral response of some of these photoconductor materials is shown in Figure 7.3. Inexpensive CdS photoconductors are used in many consumer items like camera light meters, clock radios, security alarms, street lights and so on. On the other hand, Ge:Cu cells are used for infrared astronomy and infrared spectroscopy applications.

Photoconductors are further classified as intrinsic or extrinsic photoconductors depending upon whether an external dopant has been added or not to the semiconductor material. Intrinsic photoconductors operate at shorter wavelengths as the electrons have to jump from the valence to the conduction band. Extrinsic photoconductors have spectral response covering longer wavelengths.

Application Circuits

Photoconductors are usually used for detection of infrared radiation. When a bias is applied to the photoconductor in the absence of radiation, a current is generated that can be referred to as the dark current. When light is incident on the photoconductor, its resistance decreases and the current flowing through it increases. Photosignal is the increase in the current caused by radiation. Generally this photosignal is much smaller (of the order of few parts in thousand) than the dark current. Extracting this small signal from the dark current is the primary task of the front-end circuit.

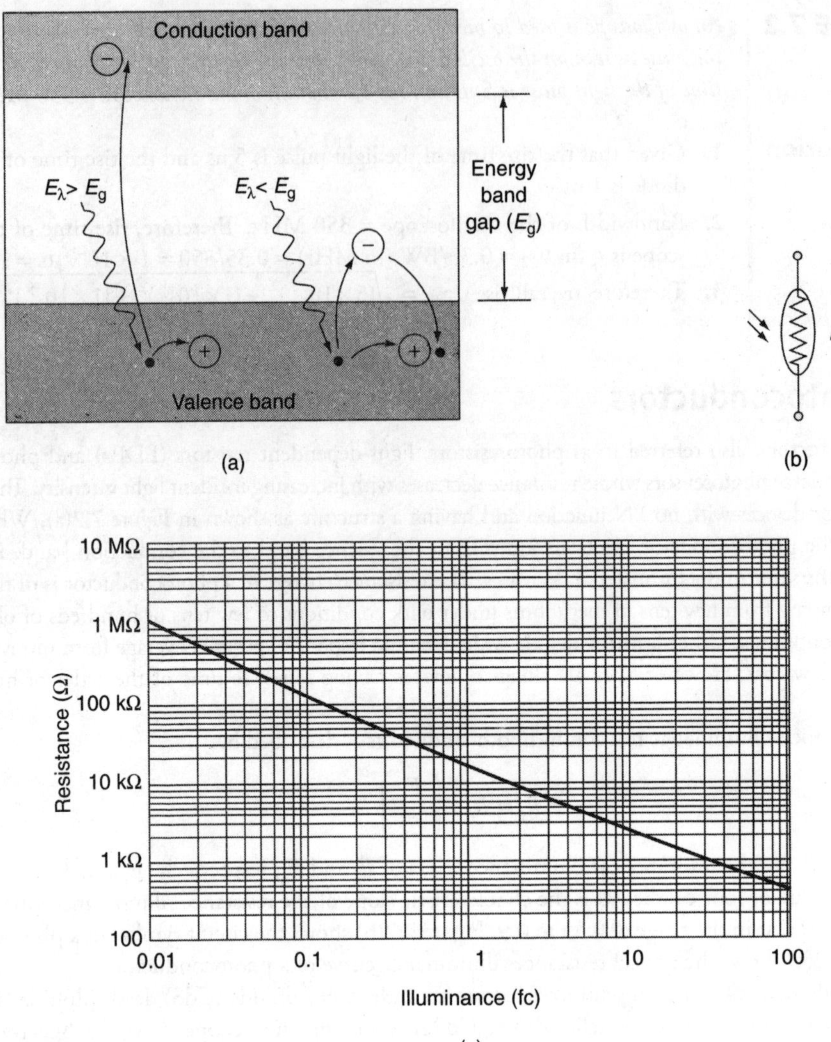

Figure 7.2 (a) Cross-section of a photoconductor; (b) circuit symbol of a photoconductor; (c) typical resistance–illuminance curve of a photoconductor.

Figures 7.4(a) and (b) show the simplest possible circuits using photoconductors. However, using photoconductors in these configurations reduces the responsivity of the conductor as the relative change in the circuit resistance is smaller because of the load resistance R. The choice of R and R_{sen} also affects the output voltage from the circuit. For Figure 7.4(a), higher the value of R, higher is the output voltage but the relative responsivity is poorer. Similarly, in case of circuit in Figure 7.4(b), higher the value of R, lower is the output voltage but the relative responsivity is better.

To overcome these problems, photoconductors are used in conjunction with operational amplifiers (also referred to as opamps) to obtain both better responsivity and high output voltage. There are two possible circuit configurations, namely, voltage mode amplifiers and current mode or transimpedance amplifiers. The basic transimpedance amplifier is shown in Figure 7.4(c). The non-inverting input of the opamp is connected to ground through resistance R_{com} to minimize the DC offset voltage.

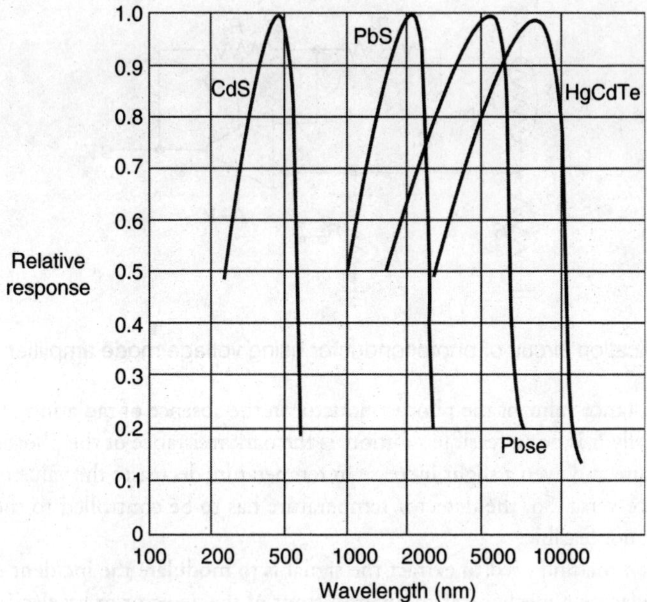

Figure 7.3 Spectral response of commonly used photoconductor materials.

The output voltage V_o is given by

$$V_o = -(R_f / R_{sen}) \times V_{bias} \tag{7.14}$$

The gain of the transimpedance amplifier should be so set that the amplifier does not saturate at the maximum expected radiation intensity. Also, if the bias voltage of the photoconductor is more than the maximum rated input voltage of the opamp then a Zener diode should be connected between the inverting input of the opamp and the ground terminal.

Theoretically, the signal voltage can be obtained by subtracting the output voltage in dark condition from the voltage signal in Eq. (7.14) and is given by

$$V_o = -[R_f / R_{sen} - R_f / R_{dark}] \times V_{bias} \tag{7.15}$$

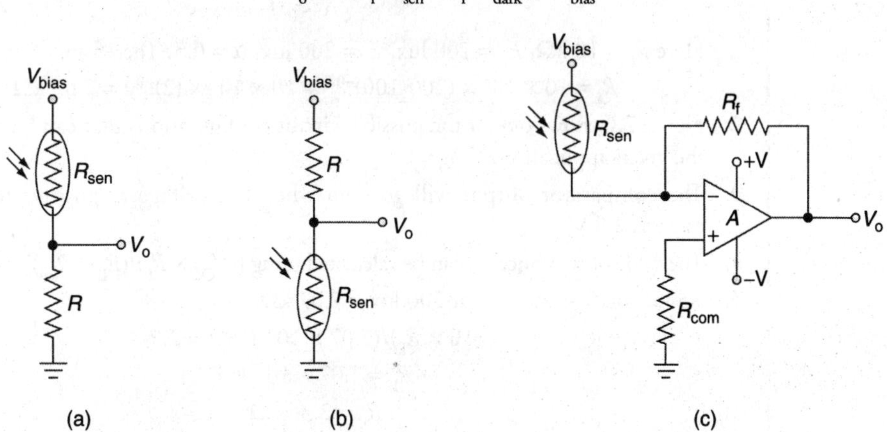

Figure 7.4 (a) and (b) Simplest application circuits using photoconductors; (c) application circuit of photoconductor using opamp in the transimpedance mode.

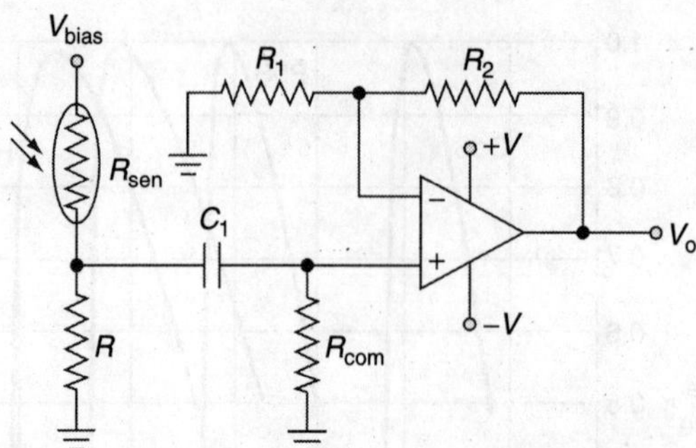

Figure 7.5 Application circuit of photoconductor using voltage mode amplifier with AC coupling.

where R_{dark} is the resistance value of the photoconductor in the absence of radiation.

However, practically it is not a feasible solution as the dark resistance of the photoconductor is a strong function of temperature and even a slight increase in temperature decreases the value of dark resistance by a large amount and vice-versa. So, the detector temperature has to be controlled to the order of 0.01°C or better, which is often not feasible.

The most common method used to extract the signal is to modulate the incident radiation at a specific frequency, either by placing a mechanical chopper in front of the detector or by electrically modulating the radiation source. The signal generated due to radiation is now an AC signal while the dark current is a DC signal. The AC signal can be separated from the DC background signal using an AC coupled amplifier. A voltage mode amplifier using AC coupling is shown in Figure 7.5.

EXAMPLE 7.3 *Design a circuit using a photoconductor that generates a logic HIGH voltage when the light incident on it is above 200 lux, given that the photoconductor has a resistance of 10 kΩ at light level of 100 lux, $\alpha = 0.5$, power supply voltage (V_{CC}) = 10 V and the reference voltage of the Zener diode is 2.5 V.*

Solution

1. The resistance of the photoconductor at 200 lux can be calculated using the expression

$$R_a = R_b \times \left(\frac{E_a}{E_b}\right)^{-\alpha}$$

Here $R_b = 10$ kΩ, $E_b = 100$ lux, $E_a = 200$ lux, $\alpha = 0.5$. Therefore,

$$R_a = 10 \times 10^3 \times (200/100)^{-0.5} = 10 \times 10^3 \times (2)^{-0.5} = 7.07 \text{ k}\Omega$$

2. Figure 7.6 shows one of the possible circuit configurations that can be used for the given application.
3. The comparator output will go high when the voltage at positive terminal exceeds 2.5 V.
4. The value of resistance R_L can be calculated using $[(V_{CC} \times R_L)/(R_L + R_{sen})] = 2.5$ V.
5. As $V_{CC} = 10$ V and R_{sen} at 200 lux is 7.07 kΩ.

$$(10 \times R_L)/(7.07 \times 10^3 + R_L) = 2.5$$
$$4R_L = 7.07 \times 10^3 + R_L$$
$$R_L = 2.36 \text{ k}\Omega$$

6. For a 10 mA current through the Zener diode, value of resistor R can be calculated using the expression $R = [(V_{CC} - V_Z)/I_Z] = (10 - 2.5)/(10 \times 10^{-3}) = 750\ \Omega$.

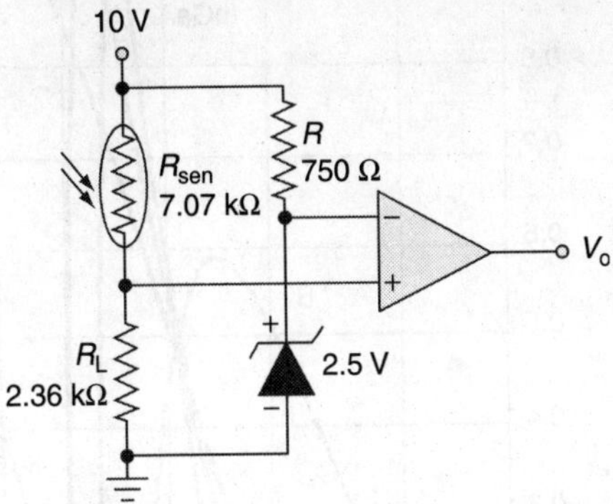

Figure 7.6 | Solution to Example 7. 3.

7.4 Photodiodes

Photodiodes are junction semiconductor light sensors that generate current or voltage when the PN junction in the semiconductor is illuminated by light of sufficient energy. The spectral response of the photodiode is a function of the bandgap energy of the material used in its construction. The upper cut-off wavelength of a photodiode is given by

$$\lambda_c = \frac{1240}{E_g} \tag{7.16}$$

where λ_c is the cut-off wavelength (nm) and E_g the bandgap energy (eV).

Photodiodes are mostly constructed using silicon, germanium, indium gallium arsenide (InGaAs), lead sulphide (PbS) and mercury cadmium telluride (HgCdTe). Figure 7.7 shows the spectral characteristics of these photodiodes.

Photodiode Types

Depending upon their construction there are several types of photodiodes. These include PN photodiodes, PIN photodiodes, Schottky-type photodiodes and avalanche photodiodes (APDs).

PN Photodiodes

PN photodiodes comprise a PN junction as shown in Figure 7.8(a). When light with sufficient energy strikes the diode, photoinduced carriers are generated which include electrons in the conduction band of the P-type material and holes in the valence band of the N-type material. When the photodiode is reverse-biased, the photoinduced electrons will move down the potential hill from the P-side to the N-side. Similarly, the photoinduced holes will add to the current flow by moving across the junction to the P-side from the N-side. Shorter wavelengths are absorbed at the surface while the longer wavelengths penetrate deep into the diode. Figure 7.8(b) shows the mechanism of conversion of incident light photons into electric current in a PN photodiode. PN photodiodes are used for precision photometry applications like medical instrumentation, analytical instruments, semiconductor tools and industrial measurement systems.

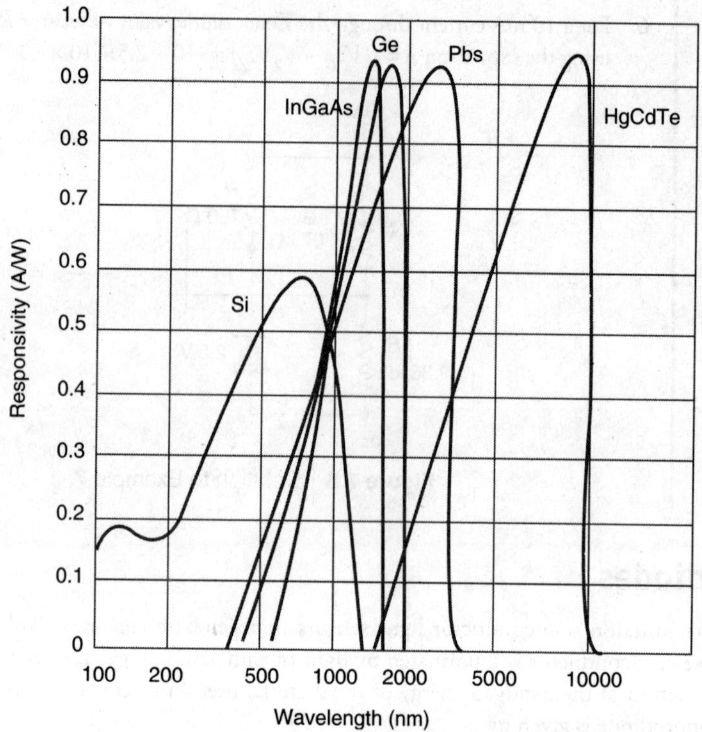

Figure 7.7 Spectral characteristics of photodiodes.

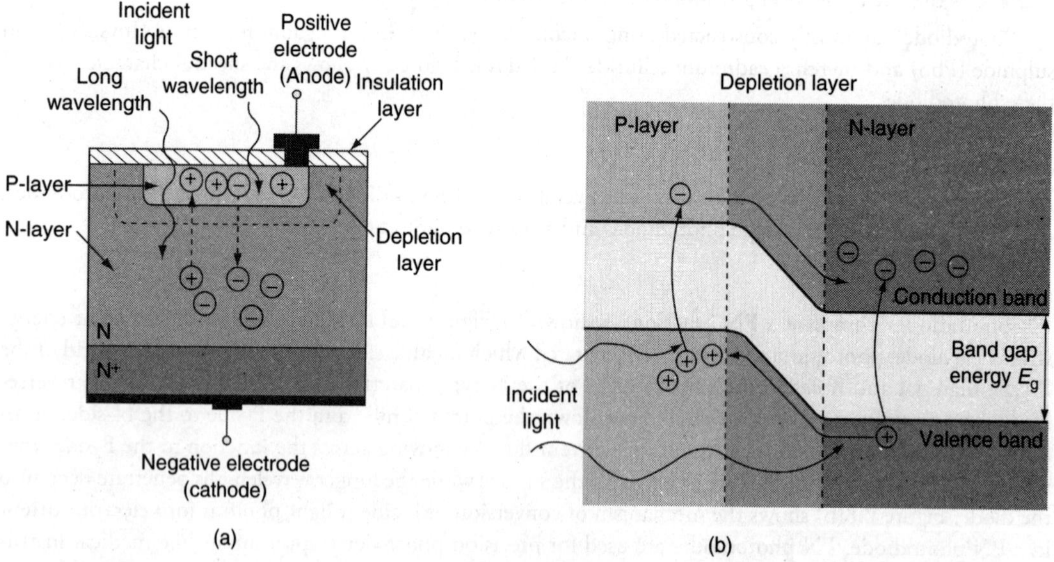

Figure 7.8 (a) Cross-section of a PN photodiode; (b) generation of current in a PN photodiode.

PIN Photodiodes

In PIN photodiodes, an extra high resistance intrinsic layer is added between the P and the N layers (Figure 7.9). This has the effect of reducing the transit or diffusion time of the photoinduced electron-hole pairs which in turn results in improved response time. PIN photodiodes feature low capacitance, thereby offering high bandwidth making them suitable for high-speed photometry as well as optical communication applications.

Schottky Photodiodes

In Schottky-type photodiodes, a thin gold coating is sputtered onto the N material to form a Schottky effect PN junction. Schottky photodiodes have enhanced ultraviolet (UV) response.

Avalanche Photodiodes (APD)

APDs are high-speed, high-sensitivity photodiodes utilizing an internal gain mechanism that functions by applying a relatively higher reverse-bias voltage than that is applied in the case of PIN photodiodes.

Figure 7.10 shows the cross-section of an APD. APDs are so constructed as to provide a very uniform junction that exhibits the avalanche effect at reverse-bias voltages between 30 V and 200 V. The electron-hole pairs that are generated by incident photons are accelerated by the high electric field to force the new electrons to move from the valence band to the conduction band. In this way, the multiplication of the order of 50–100 is achieved. APDs have fast response times similar to that of PIN photodiodes. Responsivity figures for silicon PIN photodiodes are in the range of 0.4–0.6 A/W whereas for APDs they are between 40 and 80 A/W, around

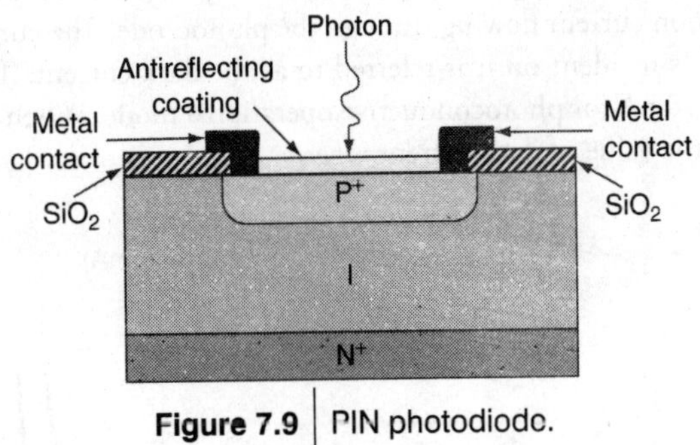

Figure 7.9 | PIN photodiode.

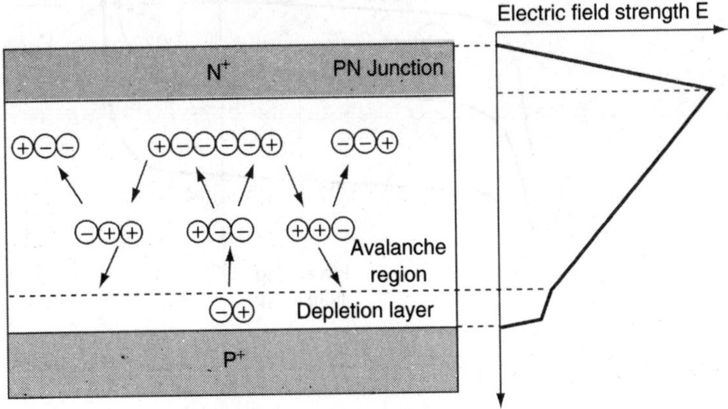

Figure 7.10 | Avalanche photodiode.

100 times more than that of PIN photodiodes. Moreover, they offer excellent signal-to-noise ratio similar to that offered by photomultiplier tubes. Hence, they are used in a variety of applications requiring high sensitivity such as long distance optical communication and optical distance measurement.

V–I Characteristics of a Photodiode

Figures 7. 11(a) and (b) show the circuit symbol and V–I characteristics of a photodiode. As we can see from Figure 7.11(b), the V–I characteristic curve of the photodiode in the dark state curve ① is similar to that of a conventional rectifier diode. However, when light strikes, curve shifts downwards with increasing intensity of light. If the photodiode terminals are shorted, a photocurrent proportional to the light intensity will flow in a direction from anode to cathode. If the circuit is open, then an open circuit voltage will be generated with the positive polarity at the anode. It may be mentioned here that the short circuit current is linearly proportional to light intensity while the open circuit voltage has a logarithmic relationship with the light intensity.

Photodiodes can be operated in two modes namely the *photovoltaic* mode and *photoconductive* mode. In the photovoltaic mode of operation, no bias voltage is applied and due to the incident light, a forward voltage is produced across the photodiode. In photoconductive operational mode, a reverse-bias voltage is applied across the photodiode. This widens the depletion region, resulting in higher speed of response. As a thumb rule, all applications requiring bandwidth less than 10 kHz can use photodiodes in photovoltaic mode. For all other applications, photodiodes are operated in photoconductive mode. Moreover, the linearity of a photodiode is also improved when it is operated in the photoconductive mode. However, there is an increase in the noise current of the photodiode when it is operated in the photoconductive mode. This is due to the reverse saturation current flowing through the photodiode. The current that flows through the photodiode when no light is incident on it is referred to as the dark current. The value of dark current is typically in the range of 1–10 nA for photoconductive operational mode. When the photodiode is operated in the photovoltaic mode, the value of dark current is zero.

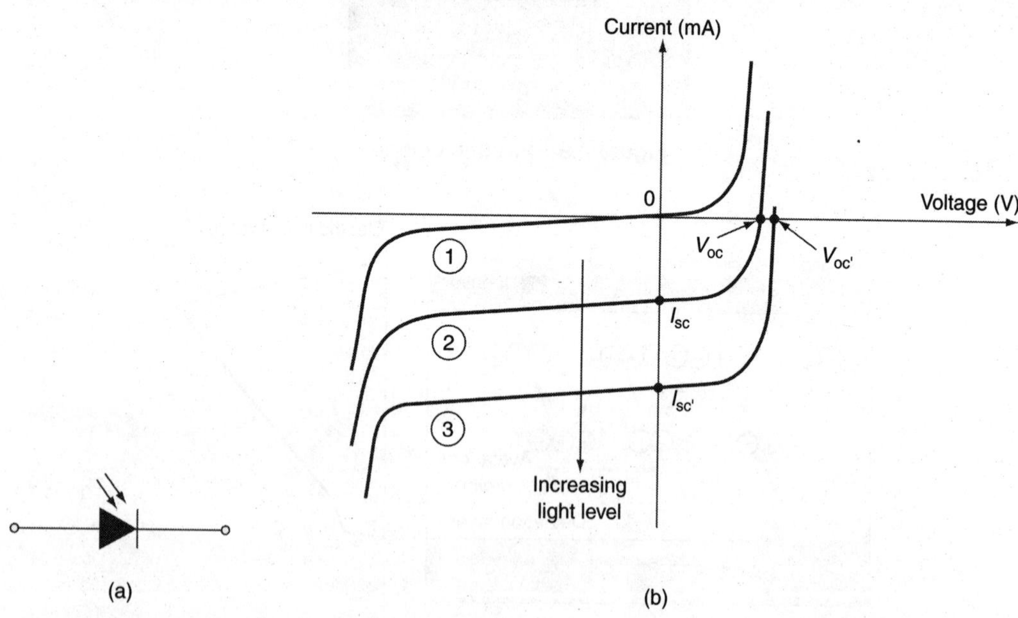

Figure 7.11 (a) Circuit symbol of a photodiode; (b) V–I characteristics of a photodiode.

Photodiode Application Circuits

As discussed above, photodiodes can be operated in two modes, namely, the photovoltaic mode and the photoconductive mode. In the photovoltaic mode, the photodiode is operated with zero external bias voltage and is generally used for low-speed applications or for detecting low light levels. Figures 7.12(a) and (b) show two commonly used application circuits employing photodiodes in the photovoltaic mode. The output voltages for these circuits are given by ($I_{det} \times R$) and ($I_{det} \times R_f$), respectively, where I_{det} is the current through the photodiode. The circuit in Figure 7.12(b) offers better linearity than the circuit in Figure 7.12(a) as the equivalent input resistance across the photodiode in this case is R_f/A, where A is the open-loop gain of the operational amplifier. It is obvious that value of R_f/A is much smaller as compared to that of R in the case of Figure 7.12(a). Figure 7.13 shows the load-line analysis of a photodiode operating in the photovoltaic mode. The load line corresponding to the smaller load is closer to the current axis and the one corresponding to a larger load is close to the voltage axis. As is evident from the figure, for a better linear response the equivalent resistance across the photodiode should be as small as possible.

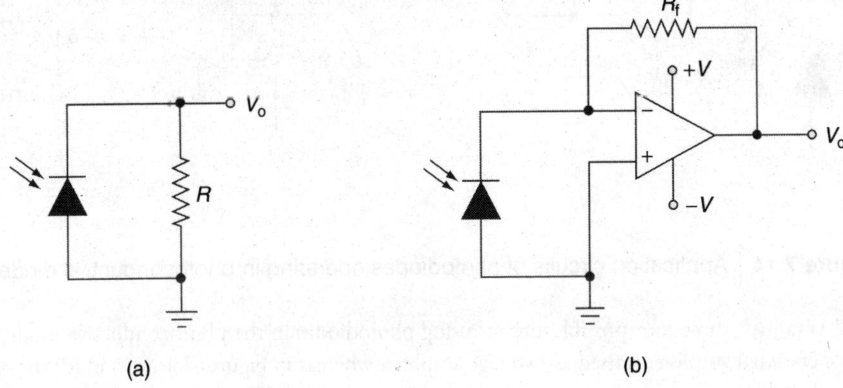

Figure 7.12 Application circuits of photodiodes in photovoltaic mode.

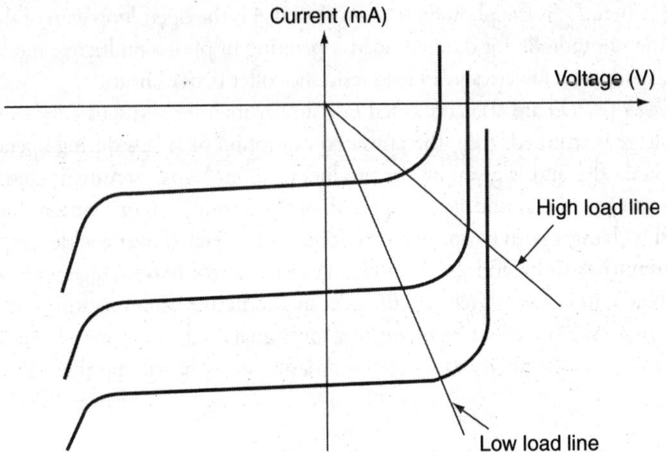

Figure 7.13 Load-line analysis of photodiode in photovoltaic mode.

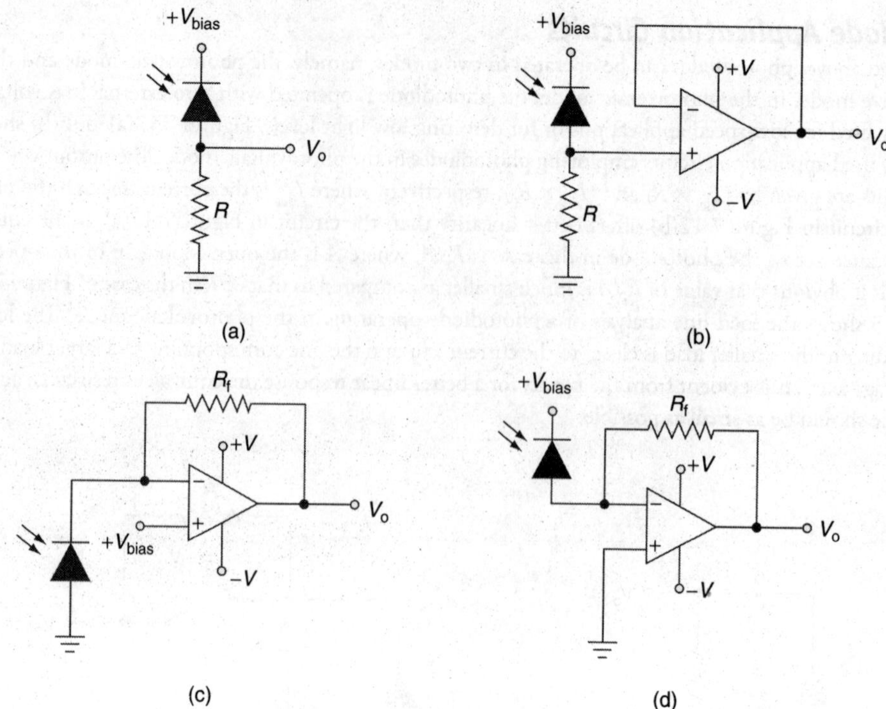

Figure 7.14 Application circuits of photodiodes operating in photoconductive mode.

Figures 7.14(a)–(d) show four possible circuits using photodiodes in the photoconductive mode. In Figure 7.14(b), the operational amplifier is used as a voltage amplifier whereas in Figures 7.14(c) and (d) the operational amplifier is used in the transimpedance mode. For the circuit in Figure 7.14(b), the output voltage and the effective resistance across the photodiode are ($I_{det} \times R$) and R, respectively. I_{det} is the current flowing through the photodiode. The output voltage and the effective resistance across the photodiode in Figures 7.14(c) and (d) are ($I_{det} \times R_f$) and R_f/A, respectively, where I_{det} is the photodiode current and A is the open-loop gain of the operational amplifier. The response of the photodiode for different loads operating in photoconductive mode is shown in Figure 7.15. As we can see, circuits with lower value of load resistance offer better linearity.

Avalanche photodiodes (*APDs*) are also connected in a similar manner as discussed above except that a much higher reverse-bias voltage is required. Also, the power consumption of APDs during operation is much higher than that of PIN photodiodes and is given by the product of input signal, sensitivity and reverse-bias voltage. Hence a protective resistor is added to the bias circuit as shown in Figure 7.16 or a current-limiting circuit is used.

As the gain of APDs changes with temperature, so if they are operated over a wide temperature range, some temperature offset circuit has to be added which changes the reverse-bias voltage with temperature so as to compensate for the change in gain with temperature. As an alternative, a temperature controller can be added to keep the temperature of APD constant. For detecting low signal levels, shot noise from the background light should be limited by using optical filters, by source modulation or by restricting the field-of-view.

Solar Cells

Solar cell is a device whose operation is very similar to that of a photodiode operating in the photovoltaic mode. The operational principle of the basic solar cell is based on the photovoltaic effect. As mentioned above, due to the photovoltaic effect, there is a generation of an open circuit voltage across a PN junction

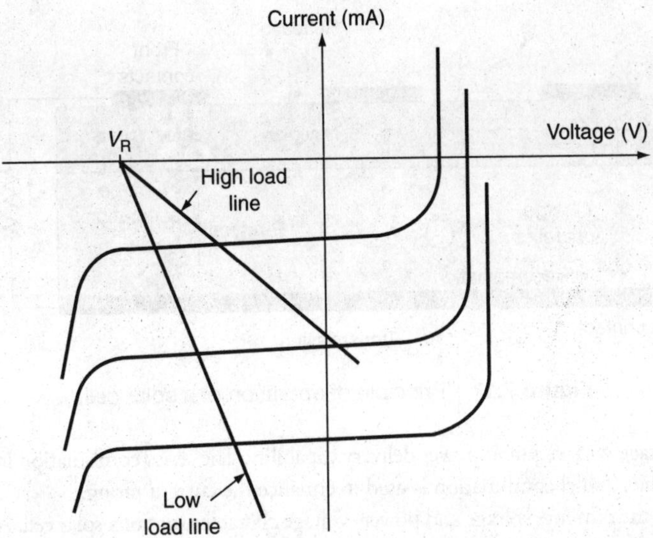

Figure 7.15 | Load-line analysis of photodiodes operating in photoconductive mode.

when it is exposed to light, which is the solar radiation in case of a solar cell. This open circuit voltage leads to the flow of electric current through a load resistance connected across it as shown in Figure 7.17.

As is evident from the figure, the impinging photon energy leads to generation of electron-hole pairs. The electron-hole pairs either recombine and vanish or start drifting in the opposite directions with electrons moving towards the N-region and holes moving towards the P-region. This accumulation of positive and negative charge carriers constitutes the open circuit voltage. This voltage can cause a current to flow through an external load or when the junction is shorted, the result is a short circuit current whose magnitude is proportional to input light intensity. The output voltage and the current-delivering capability of an individual solar cell are very small for it to be of any use as an electrical power input to any system. As an example, a typical solar cell would produce 500 mV output with a load current capability of about 150 mA. The series-parallel arrangement of solar cells is done to get

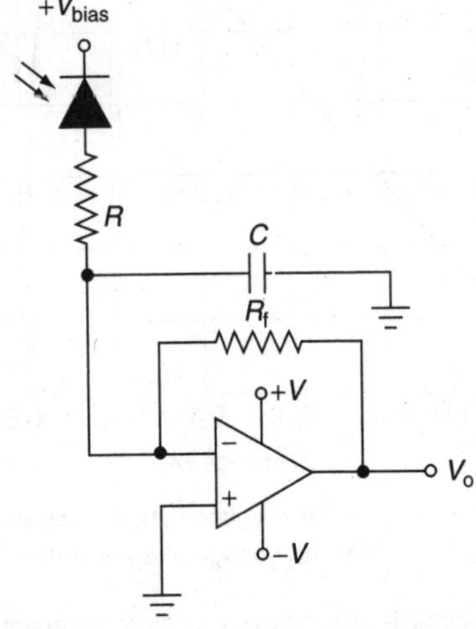

Figure 7.16 | Application circuit using avalanche photodiode.

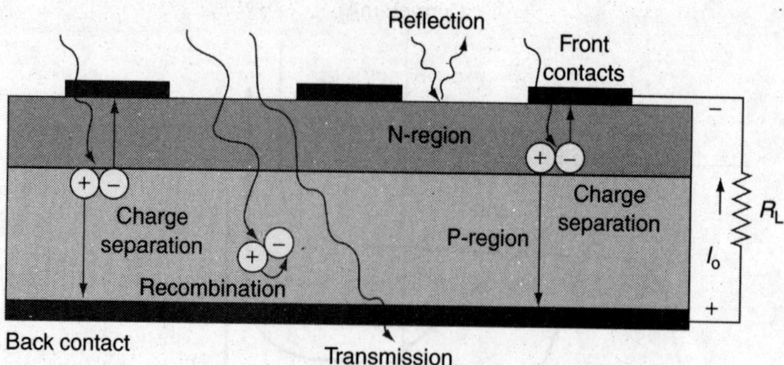

Figure 7.17 Principle of operation of a solar cell.

the desired output voltage with required power delivery capability. The series combination is used to enhance the output voltage while the parallel combination is used to enhance the current rating.

Figure 7.18 shows the current–voltage and power–voltage characteristics of a solar cell. As is evident from the figure, solar cell generates its maximum power at a certain voltage. The point of maximum power is called maximum power point (MPP). The cell voltage and the corresponding current are less than the open circuit voltage (V_{OC}) and the short circuit current (I_{SC}), respectively, at the maximum power point.

Solar cell efficiency is the ratio of maximum electrical power produced by the solar cell to the radiant power incident on the solar cell area. The efficiency figure for some crystalline solar cells is in excess of 20%. The most commonly used semiconductor material for making solar cells is silicon. Both crystalline and amorphous forms of silicon are used for the purpose. Another promising material for making solar cells is gallium arsenide (GaAs). Gallium arsenide solar cells when perfected will be light weight and more efficient.

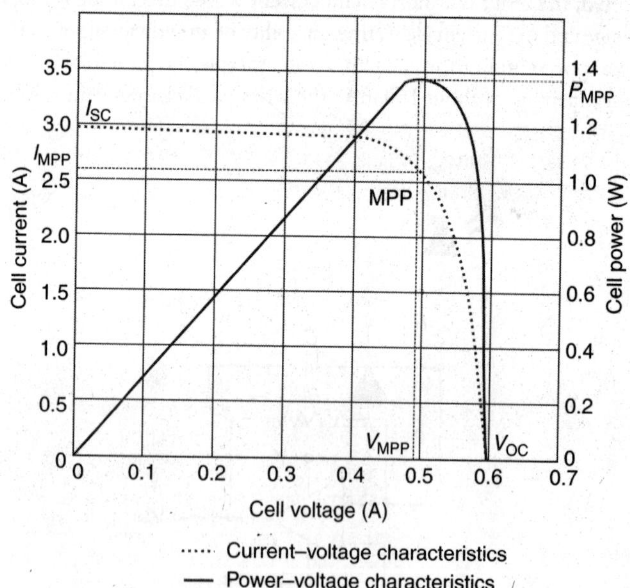

Figure 7.18 Current–voltage and power–voltage characteristics of a solar cell.

EXAMPLE 7.4 *Determine the cut-off wavelengths for silicon and germanium photodiodes, given that their bandgap energies are 1.1 eV and 0.72 eV, respectively, at 25°C. How will the cut-off wavelength change when the operating temperature changes from 25°C to 200°C?*

Solution

1. The cut-off wavelength is given by the formula
$$\lambda_c = \frac{1240}{E_g}$$
2. At 25°C, for silicon photodiode, $E_g = 1.1$ eV, therefore $\lambda_c = 1240/1.1 = 1127.27$ nm.
3. The temperature variation of the bandgap energy of silicon semiconductor, as discussed in Chapter 1, is given by $E_g(T) = 1.21 - 3.60 \times 10^{-4}T$, where T is the temperature in Kelvin.
4. Therefore, bandgap energy of silicon photodiodes at 200°C is given by
$$E_g = 1.21 - 3.60 \times 10^{-4} \times 473 = 1.21 - 0.17 = 1.04 \text{ eV}$$
5. The cut-off wavelength of silicon photodiodes at 200°C is given by
$$\lambda_c = 1240/1.04 = 1192.31 \text{ nm}$$
6. At 25°C, for germanium photodiode, $E_g = 0.72$ eV, therefore $\lambda_c = 1240/0.72 = 1722.22$ nm.
7. The temperature variation of the bandgap energy of germanium semiconductor, as discussed in Chapter 1, is given by $E_g(T) = 0.785 - 2.23 \times 10^{-4}T$, where T is the temperature in Kelvin.
8. Therefore, bandgap energy of germanium photodiodes at 200°C is given by
$$E_g = 0.785 - 2.23 \times 10^{-4} \times 473 = 0.785 - 0.105 = 0.68 \text{ eV}$$
9. The cut-off wavelength of germanium photodiodes at 200°C is given by $\lambda_c = 1240/0.68 = 1823.53$ nm.

EXAMPLE 7.5 *For the circuit shown in Figure 7.19, determine the amplitude of the output voltage pulse when the light pulse having wavelength of 1000 nm, pulse width of 1 s and energy*

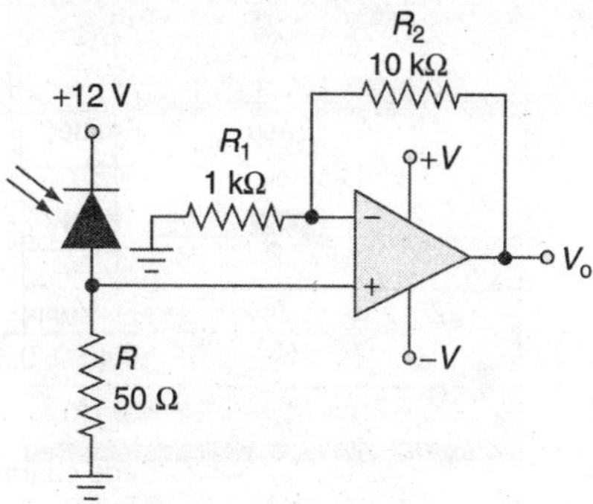

Figure 7.19 | Example 7.5.

of 10 mJ is incident on the active area of the photodiode. The responsivity of the photodiode is 0.5 A/W at 1000 nm.

Solution

1. The incident light pulse has an energy of 10 mJ and a pulse width of 1 s.
2. Therefore, the input peak power = $10 \times 10^{-3}/1 = 10$ mW.
3. Output current from the photodiode = $0.5 \times 10 \times 10^{-3} = 5$ mA.
4. Voltage across the resistance $R = 50 \times 5 \times 10^{-3} = 250$ mV.
5. Gain of the amplifier = $(1 + R_2/R_1) = [1 + (10 \times 10^3/1 \times 10^3)] = 11$.
6. Voltage amplitude of the output pulse = $250 \times 10^{-3} \times 11 = 2.75$ V.

7.5 Phototransistors

Figure 7.20 shows the construction of a phototransistor. Phototransistors are usually connected in the common-emitter configuration with base open and the radiation is concentrated on the region near the collector–base junction. Figure 7.21(a) shows the circuit symbol of the phototransistor and Figure 7.21(b) shows the typical V–I characteristics of a phototransistor. When there is no radiation incident on the phototransistor, the collector current is due to the thermally generated carriers and is given by

$$I_C = (\beta + 1)I_{CO} \tag{7.17}$$

where I_{CO} is the reverse saturation current.

In phototransistors, this current is referred to as the dark current. When light is incident on the phototransistor, photocurrent is generated and the magnitude of the collector current increases. The expression for the collector current is given by

$$I_C = (\beta + 1)(I_{CO} + I_\lambda) \tag{7.18}$$

where I_λ is the current generated due to incident light photons.

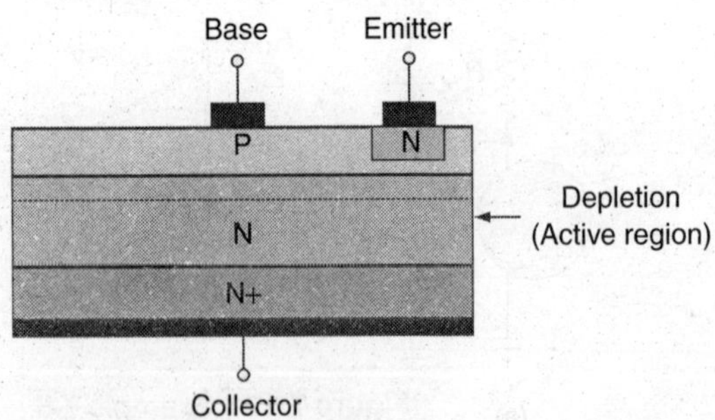

Figure 7.20 Cross-section of a phototransistor.

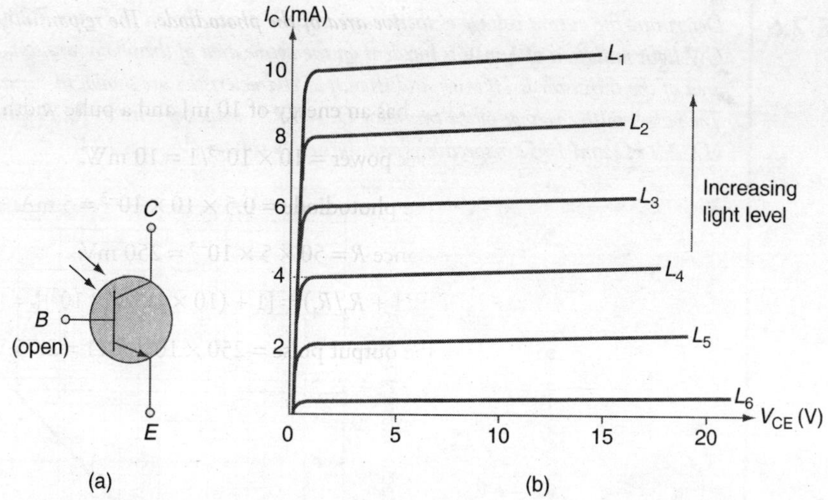

Figure 7.21 | (a) Circuit symbol of a phototransistor; (b) V–I characteristics of a phototransistor.

Phototransistor Application Circuits

Phototransistors can be used in two configurations, namely, the common-emitter configuration [Figure 7.22(a)] and the common-collector configuration [Figure 7.22(b)]. In the common-emitter configuration, the output is high and goes low when light is incident on the phototransistor, whereas in common-collector configuration, the output goes from low to high when light is incident on the phototransistor. The transistor in both the configurations can act in two modes, namely, the active mode and the switched mode. In the active mode, the transistor operates in the active region of its characteristics and the output voltage is proportional to input light intensity. In the switched mode, phototransistor is switched between cut-off and saturation and the output is either in the HIGH state or the LOW state. The modes are controlled by the value of the resistor R. The output of the phototransistor can be amplified using an opamp or a transistor-based amplifier circuit.

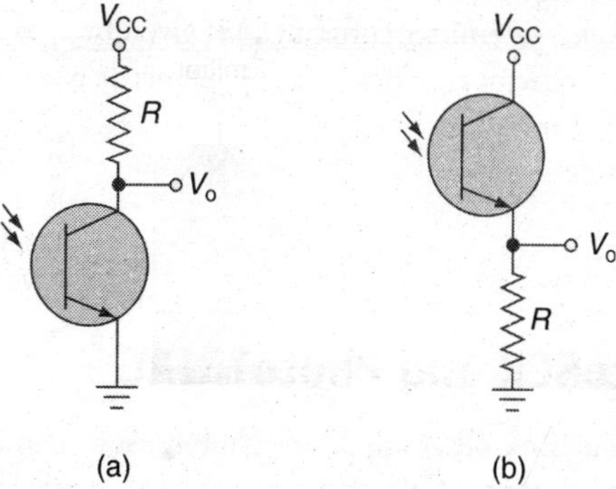

Figure 7.22 | Application circuits of phototransistors.

EXAMPLE 7.6 *Determine the output voltage of the phototransistor circuit shown in Figure 7.23(a) when a CW light radiation of 1 mW is incident on the active area of the phototransistor. The active area of the transistor is 10 mm² and its output characteristics are shown in Figure 7.23(b). The base–emitter voltage of the transistor $Q_2 = 0.7$ V, values of resistors R_1, R_C and R_E are 1 kΩ, 2.2 kΩ and 1 kΩ, respectively, and the supply voltage (V_{CC}) is 12 V.*

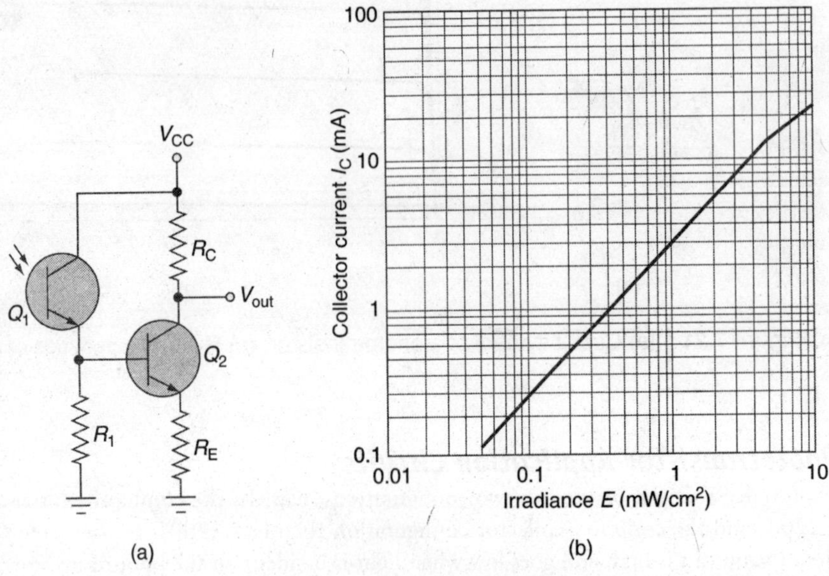

Figure 7.23 Example 7.6.

Solution

1. The incident irradiance on the phototransistor $= 1 \times 10^{-3}/\ (10 \times 10^{-1})^2$ W/cm² = 1 mW/cm².
2. From output characteristics of the transistor, collector current generated is 3 mA.
3. The voltage generated across the resistor R_1 is $3 \times 10^{-3} \times 1 \times 10^3 = 3$ V.
4. Therefore, the voltage applied to the base of the transistor Q_2 is 3 V. So the transistor Q_2 goes into the conducting mode.
5. The voltage across resistor $R_E = 3 - 0.7\text{ V} = 2.3$ V.
6. The value of emitter current (I_E) is given by $I_E = 2.3/(1 \times 10^3) = 2.3$ mA.
7. As the collector current (I_C) is approximately equal to the emitter current, therefore $I_C = 2.3$ mA.
8. The output voltage $V_{out} = V_{CC} - I_C \times R_C = 12 - 2.3 \times 10^{-3} \times 2.2 \times 10^3 = 12 - 5.06 =$ 6.94 V.

7.6 PhotoFET, PhotoSCR and PhotoTRIAC

In this section we will discuss the three other important photosensors, namely, the photoFETs, photoSCRs and the photoTRIACs. While photoSCRs and photoTRIACs are latching type of photosensors, photoFETs are non-latching photosensors like photodiodes and phototransistors.

PhotoFET

PhotoFETs are light-sensitive FET devices wherein the diode formed by the reverse-biased gate-channel junction acts as a photodiode. Incident light generates additional photocarriers resulting in increased conductivity level. Gate current flows if the gate is connected to an external resistor. Figure 7.24(a) shows the circuit symbol of a photoFET. When no light is incident on the photoFET, the value of gate impedance is very high. When light is incident on the photoFET, the value of gate impedance decreases. Figure 7.24(b) shows the typical application circuit using a photoFET. When no light is incident, the gate voltage is approximately equal to the voltage $-V_{GG}$. When light is incident, the negative gate voltage decreases resulting in increase in the value of drain current (I_D) and the value of the output voltage (V_o) decreases.

PhotoSCR

PhotoSCRs, generally referred to as light-activated SCRs (LASCRs), are essentially the same as conventional SCRs except that they are triggered by light incident on the gate junction area. They comprise a window and lens to focus more light on the gate junction area, more specifically on the middle junction J_2 of the SCR. They conduct current in one direction when activated by light of sufficient amount and continue to conduct until the current falls below a specified value referred to as holding current. In other words, photoSCRs act as a latch that can be triggered ON by the light incident on the gate junction but it does not turn OFF when the light source is removed. They can be turned

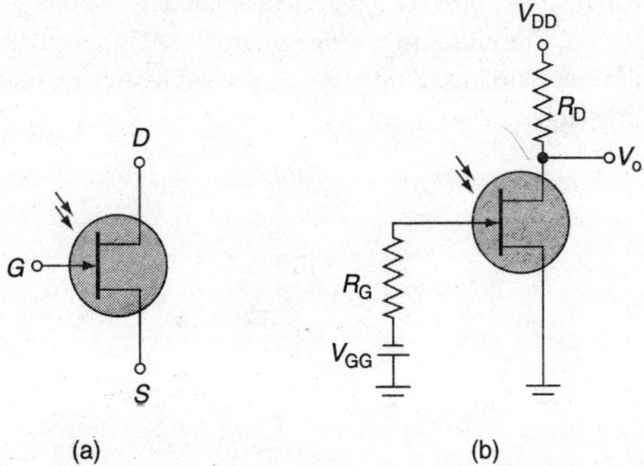

Figure 7.24 (a) Circuit symbol of photoFET; (b) a simple application circuit using photoFET.

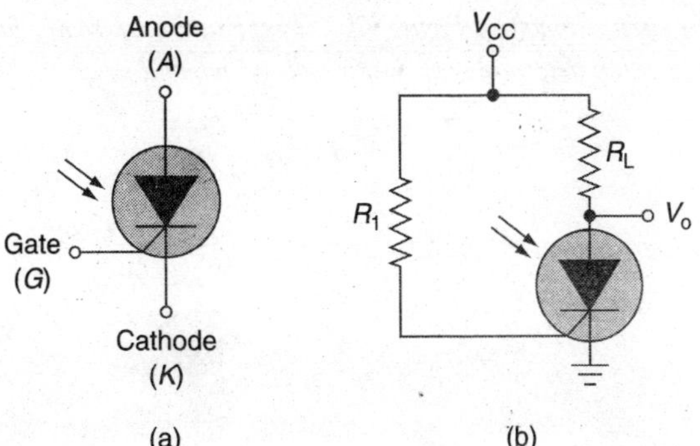

Figure 7.25 (a) Circuit symbol of photoSCR; (b) simple application circuit using photoSCR.

OFF by reducing the current below the holding current value of the SCR. PhotoSCRs can handle large amount of current as compared to a photodiode or a phototransistor. They have high value of rate of change of voltage with time, that is, high dv/dt rating which is important for triggering the SCR on application of light input. PhotoSCRs are most sensitive to light when their gate terminal is open. They are generally used in the receiving channel of optocouplers.

Figure 7.25(a) shows the circuit symbol of a photoSCR and Figure 7.25(b) shows a simple application circuit built around it. When no light is incident on the photoSCR, it is OFF and no current flows through the load resistor R_L. When the photoSCR is illuminated, it turns ON and hence allowing current to flow through the load resistor R_L.

PhotoTRIAC

PhotoTRIACs, also referred to as light-activated TRIACs, are bidirectional thyristors that are designed to conduct current in both directions when the incident light radiation exceeds a specified threshold value. PhotoTRIACs are generally used as solid-state AC switches and as photosensors in optocouplers to provide isolation from the driving source to the load. Figure 7.26 shows the circuit symbol of a photoTRIAC. The operation of photoTRIAC is similar to that of a standard TRIAC, except that the trigger current is generated indirectly in the case of a photoTRIAC by the light incident on it whereas in the case of a standard TRIAC it is supplied directly. One of the most important parameters to describe the performance of a photoTRIAC is its output dv/dt rating. Other important parameters are the break-down voltage and the power rating of the device.

There are two different types of photoTRIACs available, namely, the non-zero-crossing photoTRIACs and zero-crossing photoTRIACs. The non-zero-crossing photoTRIACs are used for applications that require fine control involving small time constants. Zero-crossing photoTRIACs are used in applications where the control time constant is fairly large.

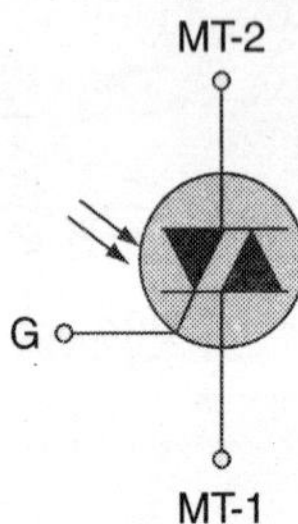

Figure 7.26 | Circuit symbol of a photoTRIAC.

EXAMPLE 7.7 *The circuit shown in Figure 7.27 is kept in a dark room. Determine the output voltage (V_o). Also, determine the output voltage when a bright light is flashed on the circuit.*

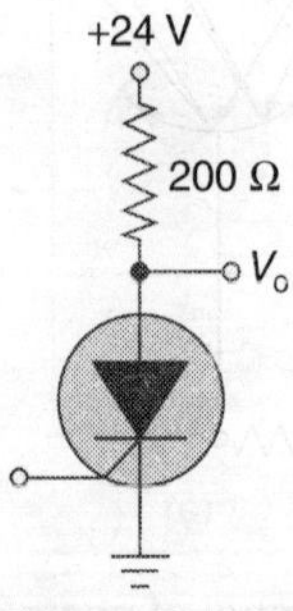

Figure 7.27 | Example 7.7.

Solution

1. When the circuit is kept in the dark room with no incident light, the photoSCR is in the non-conducting state. Therefore, the output voltage V_o is equal to the supply voltage, that is, $V_o = +24$ V.
2. When a bright light is incident on the photoSCR, it goes into the conducting state and ideally the output voltage is zero, that is, $V_o = 0$ V.

7.7 Photoemissive Sensors

The photosensors discussed so far have internal photoeffect where the photoelectrons generated by the incident radiation remain within the semiconductor material. Other category of photosensors include those photosensors which have external photoeffect wherein the photogenerated electrons travel beyond the physical boundaries of the material. These sensors are also referred to as photoemissive sensors. In this section we discuss some of the commonly used photoemissive sensors including vacuum photodiodes, photomultiplier tubes and image intensifiers.

Vacuum Photodiodes

Vacuum photodiode is the oldest photosensor. It comprises an anode and a cathode placed in a vacuum envelope. Cathode, when irradiated, releases electrons that are attracted by the positively charged anode, thus producing a photocurrent proportional to the light intensity.

Photomultiplier Tubes

Photomultiplier tubes (PMT) are extremely sensitive photosensors operating in the ultraviolet, visible and near infrared spectrum. PMTs have internal gain of the order of 10^8 and can even detect single photon of light. They are constructed from a glass vacuum tube which houses a photocathode, several dynodes and an anode. When the incident photons strike the photocathode, electrons are produced as a result of the

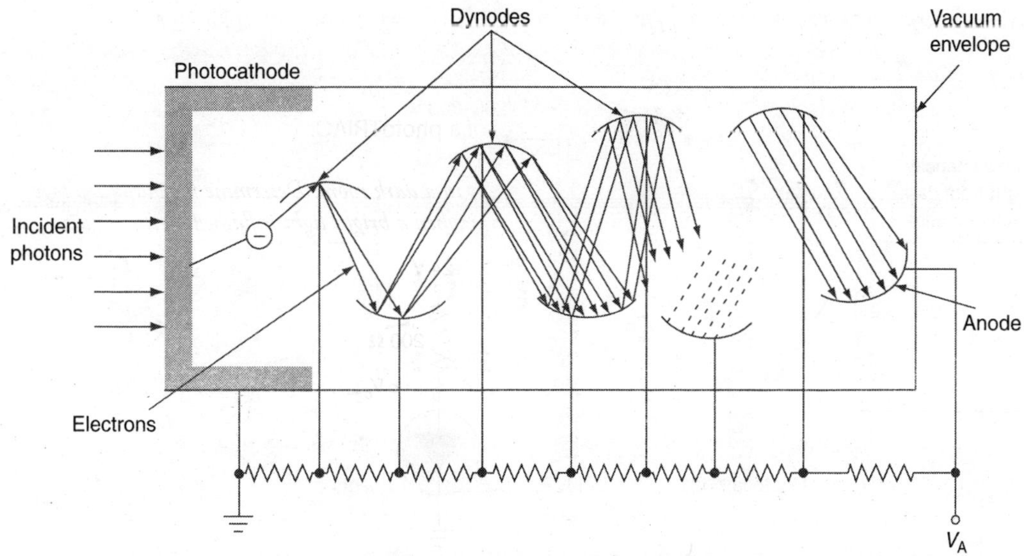

Figure 7.28 Cross-section of a photomultiplier tube.

photoelectric effect. These electrons accelerate towards the anode and in the process electron multiplication takes place due to secondary emission process from the dynodes. PMTs require few kilo-volts of biasing voltages for proper operation. Figure 7.28 shows the cross-section of a PMT. As we can see from the figure, the dynodes are given progressively increasing positive voltages with the dynode nearest to the cathode having the lowest voltage and the dynode nearest to the anode having the maximum voltage.

Salient features of PMTs include low-noise, high-frequency response and large active area. By virtue of these features, PMTs are used in nuclear and particle physics, astronomy, medical imaging and motion picture film scanning. APDs have replaced PMTs in some applications, but PMTs are still used in many application areas.

Image Intensifiers

Image intensifiers are devices that amplify visible and near infrared light from an image so that a dimly lit scene can be viewed by a camera or by human eye. Contemporary image intensifiers comprise an objective lens, vacuum tube with photocathode at one end, tilted microchannel plate (MCP) and a phosphor screen (Figure 7.29). Objective lens focuses the image onto the photocathode. When the photons strike the photocathode, electrons are released due to the photoelectric effect. These photoelectrons are accelerated through around 4–5 kV into a tilted microchannel plate where secondary electron multiplication takes place. The electrons all move together due to the potential difference across the tube and for each photoelectron hundreds or even thousands of electrons are created. All these electrons hit the phosphor screen at the other end, releasing one photon for every electron. Thus the screen converts the high-energy electrons into photons, which correspond to the input image radiation but with the incident flux being amplified many times.

Image intensifiers are classified into the following categories: generation 0, generation 1, generation 2 and generation 3. Generation 0 and generation 1 devices did not have the MCP and the stream of electrons generated by the photocathode was accelerated towards the phosphor screen by the applied potential. Generation 1 devices were a tremendous improvement upon generation 0 devices and had three times the photosensitivity than that of generation 0 devices. Generation 2 devices introduced the concept of microchannel plates. Generation 3 devices are the same as generation 2 devices except that the photocathode material in these devices is gallium arsenide (GaAs) whereas it was S-25 in the case of generation 2 devices. Also, generation 3 devices had a better MCP. Generation 3 ultra and generation 4 tubes are also available which offer slight improvement over generation 3 devices. Image intensifiers are used in night vision devices (NVD) used for military applications.

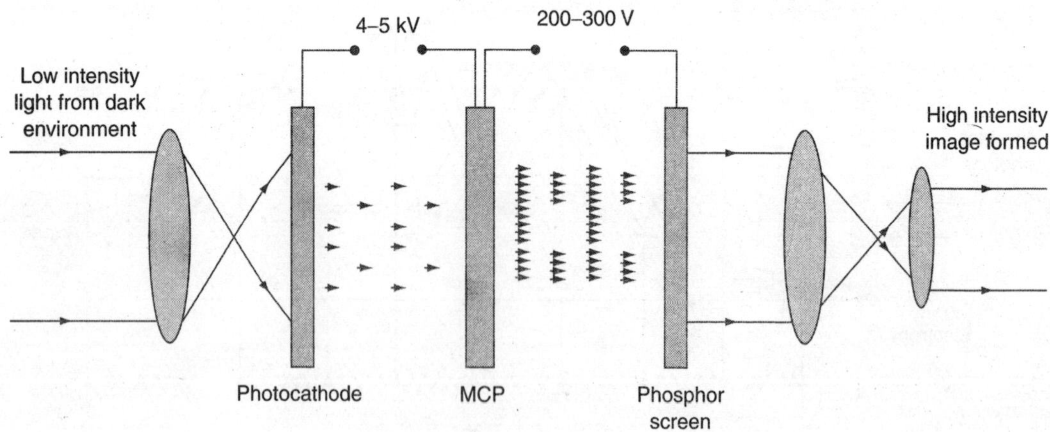

Figure 7.29 Image intensifier tube.

7.8 Thermal Sensors

Thermal sensors absorb radiation, which produces a temperature change that in turn causes a change in the physical or the electrical property of the sensor. In other words, thermal sensors respond to change in their bulk temperature caused by the incident radiation. Thermocouples, thermopiles, bolometers and pyroelectric sensors come in the category of thermal sensors. Thermal sensors lack the sensitivity of photoelectric sensors and are generally slow in response, but have a wide spectral response. Most of these sensors are passive devices, requiring no bias. In this section, we will discuss about the different types of thermal sensors and their application circuits.

Thermocouple and Thermopile

Thermocouple sensors are based on the Seeback effect, that is, the temperature change at the junction of two dissimilar metals generates an electromagnetic force (EMF) proportional to the temperature change. The commonly used thermocouple materials are bismuth–antimony, iron–constantan and copper–constantan. Their temperature coefficients are 100 μV/°C, 54 μV/°C and 39 μV/°C, respectively. To compensate for the changes in the ambient temperature, thermocouples generally have two junctions, namely, the measuring junction and the reference junction.

The responsivity of a single thermocouple is very low and therefore to increase the responsivity, several junctions are connected in series to form a thermopile. Thermopiles are series combination of around 20–200 thermocouples. Spectral response of thermocouples and thermopiles extends into the far infrared band up to 40 μm. They are suitable for making measurements over a large temperature range up to 1800 kΩ. However, thermocouples are less suitable for applications where smaller temperature differences need to be measured with great accuracy such as 0–100°C measurement with 0.1°C accuracy. For such applications, thermistors and resistance temperature detectors (RTDs) are more suitable.

The responsivity of thermopiles is of the order of 10–100 V/W and the typical signal output varies from few tens of micro-volts to few milli-volts. Hence, they need low noise and very low offset operational amplifiers for providing the gain. The gain required varies from as small as 10 to as large as 10,000 or more. Generally, for gain less than 1000, a single-stage amplifier is used. For gain values more than 1000, two amplifier stages are used. Figure 7.30 shows the application circuit where two amplifier stages are used. As we can see from the figure, thermopiles require no bias voltage.

The thermopile signal would be positive or negative depending upon whether the temperature of the object filling the thermopile's field-of-view is greater than or less than that of the thermopile. Also, the

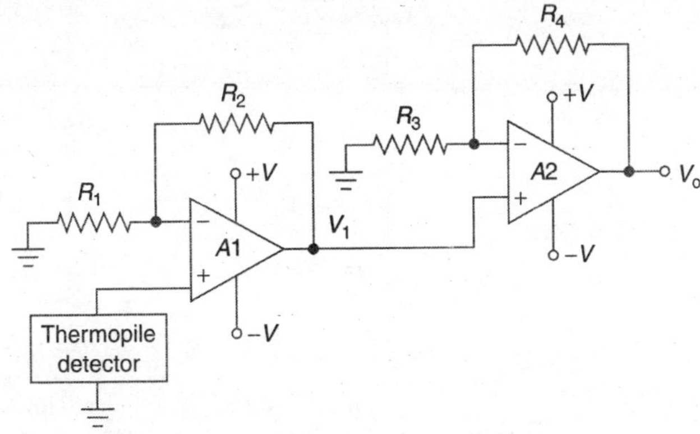

Figure 7.30 Application circuit using thermopiles.

output of the circuit varies with change in the ambient temperature. It is therefore necessary to compensate for the ambient temperature variations. Many thermopile modules have an inbuilt thermistor to compensate for the ambient temperature variations.

Bolometers

Bolometer is the most popular type of thermal sensor. The sensing element in a bolometer is a resistor with a high temperature coefficient. Bolometers are different from photoconductors, as in a photoconductor a direct photon–electron interaction causes a change in the conductivity of the material whereas in a bolometer the increased temperature and the temperature coefficient of the element causes the resistance change. Bolometers can be further categorized as metal bolometers, thermistor bolometers and low-temperature germanium bolometers.

Metal bolometers use metals such as bismuth, nickel or platinum having temperature coefficients in the range of 0.3–0.5%/°C. Thermistor bolometers are the most popular and they find applications in burglar alarms, smoke sensors and other similar devices. The sensor in this case is a thermistor, an element made of manganese, cobalt and nickel oxide. They have high temperature coefficients up to 5%/°C that varies with temperature as $1/T^2$. They are classified as negative temperature coefficient (NTC) and positive temperature coefficient (PTC) thermistors depending upon whether their temperature coefficient of resistance is negative or positive. Figure 7.31(a) shows the circuit symbol of a thermistor. Spectral response of thermistors extends from 0.5 to 10 μm. More sensitive thermistors typically have NEP and response time of the order of 10^{-10} W and 100 ms. Less sensitive thermistors have NEP and response time figures of 10^{-8} W and 5 ms, respectively. Figures 7.31(b) and (c) show the simplest possible configurations in which a thermistor can be used for measurement of light intensity. The figures are self-explanatory. The output of the circuits in Figures 7.31(b) and (c) can be fed to an operational amplifier or to a comparator for linear light control or light ON–OFF control, respectively.

Low temperature germanium bolometers are sensitive laboratory-type bolometers that use germanium as the sensor. They have the highest responsivity when operated at few degrees above the absolute zero temperature.

Pyroelectric Sensors

Pyroelectric sensors are characterized by spontaneous electric polarization, which is altered by temperature changes as light illuminates these sensors. Pyroelectric sensors are low-cost, high-sensitivity devices that are stable against temperature variations and electromagnetic interference. Pyroelectric sensors only respond to modulating light radiation and there will be no output for a CW incident radiation. Figure 7.32(a) shows the circuit symbol of pyroelectric sensors.

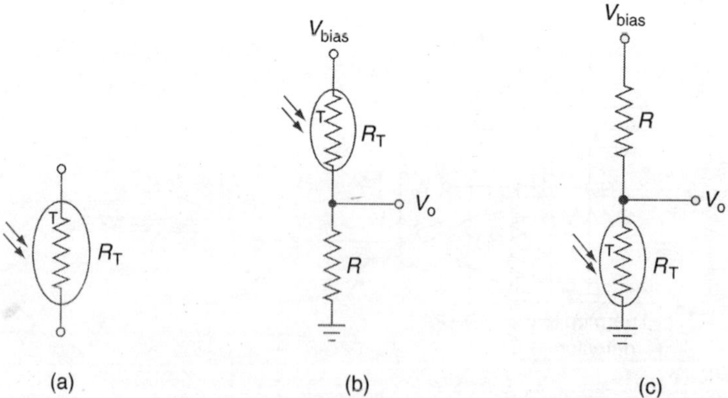

Figure 7.31 (a) Circuit symbol of a thermistor; (b) and (c) application circuits of a thermistor.

Pyroelectric sensors operate in two modes, namely, the voltage mode and the current mode. In the voltage mode, the voltage generated across the entire pyroelectric crystal is detected. In the current mode of operation, current flowing on and off the electrode on the exposed face of the crystal is detected. Voltage mode is more commonly used than the current mode.

The circuit for voltage mode is shown in Figure 7.32(b). The operational amplifier chosen should have very high input impedance of the order of 10^{12} to 10^{14} Ω. But the circuit is sensitive to ambient temperature variations. Ambient temperature variations can be compensated by employing AC coupling between the amplifier stages or by adding a compensation crystal in opposition, either in series or in parallel. One crystal is exposed to radiation and the other is shielded from radiation. As the ambient temperature changes, the surface charge generated on one crystal is cancelled by the equal and opposite charge generated on the other crystal. The incident radiation, however, generates charge only on one crystal and is not cancelled.

Voltage mode pyroelectric sensors are generally integrated with an FET. A shunt resistor (R_S) in the range of 10^{10}–10^{11} Ω is added to provide thermal stabilization. External connections include a power supply (V_{DD}) and load resistor (R_L) [Figure 7.32(c)]. The output voltage appears across R_L.

The circuit for current mode operation is shown in Figure 7.32(d). The modulation frequency can be much higher in the case of current mode operation than it is for voltage mode operation. Hence, it is much easier to separate the signal generated from the ambient temperature drift.

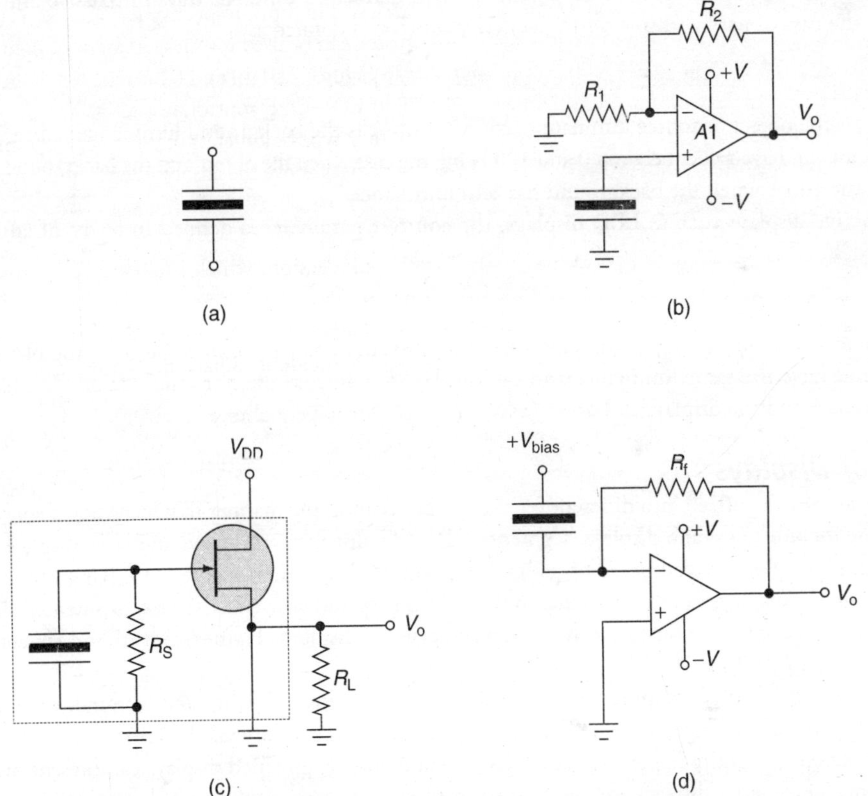

Figure 7.32 (a) Circuit symbol of pyroelectric sensors; (b) and (c) voltage mode pyroelectric sensor application circuits; (d) current mode pyroelectric sensor application circuit.

7.9 Displays

Displays are output devices that are used for visual presentation of information. Displays form an interface between the machine and the human. In this section, we will discuss different types of displays and the characteristic parameters used to define the quality of displays.

Display Characteristics

Three factors are critical for a good visual display, namely, legibility, brightness and contrast.

Legibility

Legibility is the property of a display by virtue of which the characters are easy to read with speed and accuracy. The factors which contribute to the legibility of the display are its style, size, character sharpness and shape.

Brightness

Brightness refers to the perception of luminance by the visual world.

Contrast

Contrast of a display depends on the background luminance and the source luminance. The readability of the display depends upon the contrast parameter. It is defined in different ways for passive and active displays. In the case of passive displays such as LCD, contrast is defined as

$$C = (L_O - L_B) / L_O \tag{7.19}$$

where L_O is the object or source luminance (cd/m^2) and L_B is the background luminance (cd/m^2).

Contrast can have values between 0 and 1, 0 being the case when the object and the background luminance are the same and 1 when the background has zero luminance.

For active displays such as LED displays, the contrast parameter is defined in terms of contrast ratio which is defined as

$$CR = L_O / L_B \tag{7.20}$$

The contrast ratio can have values between 1 and ∞. For contrast ratio equal to 1, the object and the background have the same luminance and the displayed characters are not visible at all. The background luminance is 0 and the display has best visibility at contrast value equal to ∞.

Types of Displays

Displays can be categorized into different types depending upon the manner in which they display information. These include bar graph displays, segmented displays, dot-matrix displays and large displays.

Bar graph displays are composed of several bar elements as shown in Figure 7.33. Bar graph displays are replacing analog displays as indicators due to their simplicity and cost-effectiveness. Segmented displays are available in two configurations, namely, the seven-segment displays [Figure 7.34(a)] and sixteen-segment displays [Figure 7.34(b)].

Seven-segment display comprises seven bars and one or two decimal points and is an industry standard for numeric displays. These displays are used for displaying numerals and limited alphabets. Sixteen-segment displays can present the entire upper-case alphabets and numerals. Segmented displays can present only limited information. Dot-matrix displays are the simplest displays that represent the set of lower-case and upper-case alphabets and numerals at reasonable cost and complexity. The most commonly used dot-matrix display is the 5×7 display which comprises 35 display elements set in a pattern of 5 rows and 7 columns (Figure 7.35). Each element is addressed by selecting the proper row and column. Bar, segmented and 5×7 dot-matrix displays

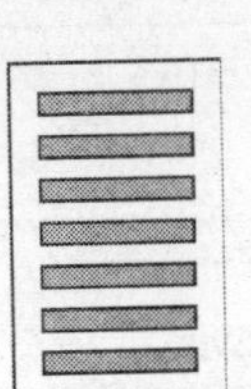

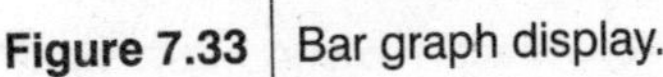

Figure 7.33 | Bar graph display.

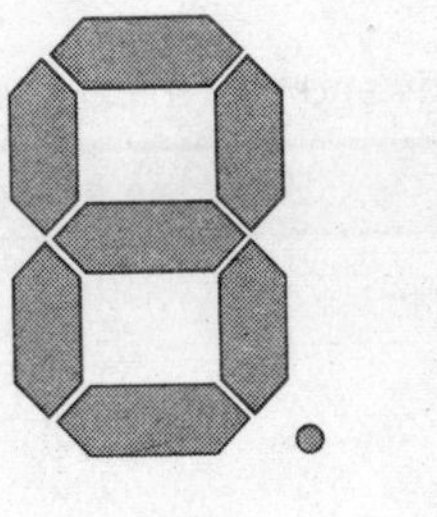

(a) (b)

Figure 7.34 | (a) Seven-segment displays; (b) sixteen-segment displays.

can be constructed using LEDs or liquid-crystal displays (LCDs). Large-scale displays include cathode ray tube (CRT) displays, plasma displays, LCD thin film transistor (TFT) displays and so on.

LEDs and LCDs are discussed in Sections 7.10 and 7.11, respectively, followed by CRT displays and emerging trends in display technology in Sections 7.12 and 7.13, respectively.

7.10 Light-Emitting Diodes

LED is a semiconductor PN junction diode designed to emit light when forward-biased. It is one of the most popular optoelectronic source. LEDs consume very little power and are inexpensive.

We have studied in Chapter 2 that when a PN junction is forward-biased, the electrons in the N-type material and the holes in the P-type material travel towards the junction. Some of these holes and electrons recombine with each other and in the process radiate energy. The energy will be released either in the form of photons of light or in the form of heat. In silicon and germanium diodes, most of the energy is released as heat and the emitted light is insignificant. However, in some materials like gallium phosphide (GaP), gallium arsenide (GaAs) and gallium arsenide phosphide (GaAsP) substantial photons of light are emitted. Hence, these materials are used in the construction of LEDs.

In the absence of an externally applied voltage, the N-type material contains electrons while the P-type material contains holes that can act as current carriers. When the diode is forward-biased, the energy levels shift and hence there is a significant increase in the concentration of electrons in the conduction band on the N-side and that of holes in valence band on the P-side. These electrons and holes combine near the junction to release energy in the form of photons (Figure 7.36). It may be mentioned here that the process of light emission in an LED is that of spontaneous emission, that is, the photons emitted are not in phase and travel in different directions.

Figure 7.35 | 5 × 7 Dot-matrix display.

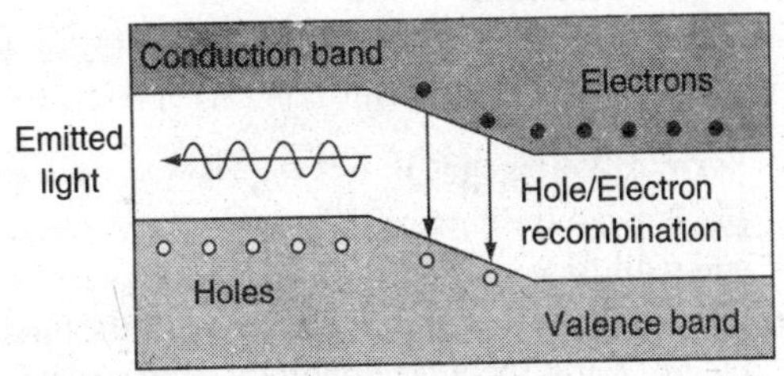

Figure 7.36 | PN junction of an LED.

Table 7.1 | Bandgap energy and the typical wavelengths of commonly used LED materials

Material	Bandgap energy (eV)	Wavelength (nm)
GaAs	1.43	910
GaP	2.24	560
$GaAs_{60}P_{40}$	1.91	650
AlSb	1.60	775
InSb	0.18	6900

The energy of the photon resulting from this recombination is equal to the bandgap energy of the semiconductor material and is expressed by the following empirical formula:

$$\lambda = \frac{1240}{\Delta E} \tag{7.21}$$

where λ is the wavelength (nm) and ΔE the bandgap energy (eV).

Some of the commonly used semiconductor materials used for fabricating LEDs are gallium arsenide (GaAs), gallium phosphide (GaP), gallium arsenic phosphide (GaAsP), aluminum antimonide (AlSb) and indium antimonide (InSb). Table 7.1 enlists the bandgap and the typical wavelengths emitted by these materials.

LED Characteristic Curves

The characteristics of interest in an LED are the V–I characteristics, spectral distribution curve, light output versus input current and the directional characteristics.

1. **V–I Characteristics:** Figure 7.37(a) shows the V–I characteristics of LEDs of different colors. As the LED is operated in the forward-biased mode, the V–I characteristics in the forward-biased region are shown. V–I characteristics of LEDs are similar to that of conventional PN junction diodes except that the cut-in voltage in the case of LEDs is in the range of 1.3–3 V as compared to 0.7 V for silicon diodes and 0.3 V for germanium diodes.
2. **Spectral Distribution Curve:** Spectral distribution curve shows the variation of light intensity with wavelength. Figure 7.37(b) shows the typical spectral curves for yellow, green and red LEDs.
3. **Light Output versus Input Current:** Figure 7.37(c) shows a typical light output versus input current curve depicting the dependence of emitted light on forward current flowing through the LED.
4. **Directional Characteristics:** Directional characteristics refer to the variation in the light output with change in the viewing angle [Figure 7.37(d)].

LED Parameters

The parameters of interest in the case of LEDs are forward voltage (V_F), candle power (CP), radiant power output (P_o), peak spectral emission (λ_P) and spectral bandwidth.

1. **Forward Voltage (V_F):** It is the DC voltage across the LED when it is ON. The typical values of V_F for LEDs are in the range of 1.3–3.0 V. As we can see from Figure 7.37(a), V_F is near 1.5 V for yellow, green and red LEDs.
2. **Candle Power (CP):** It is a measure of the luminous intensity or the brightness of the light emitted by the LED. It is the most important parameter of an LED. It is a non-linear function of LED current and the value of CP increases with increase in the current flowing through the LED.

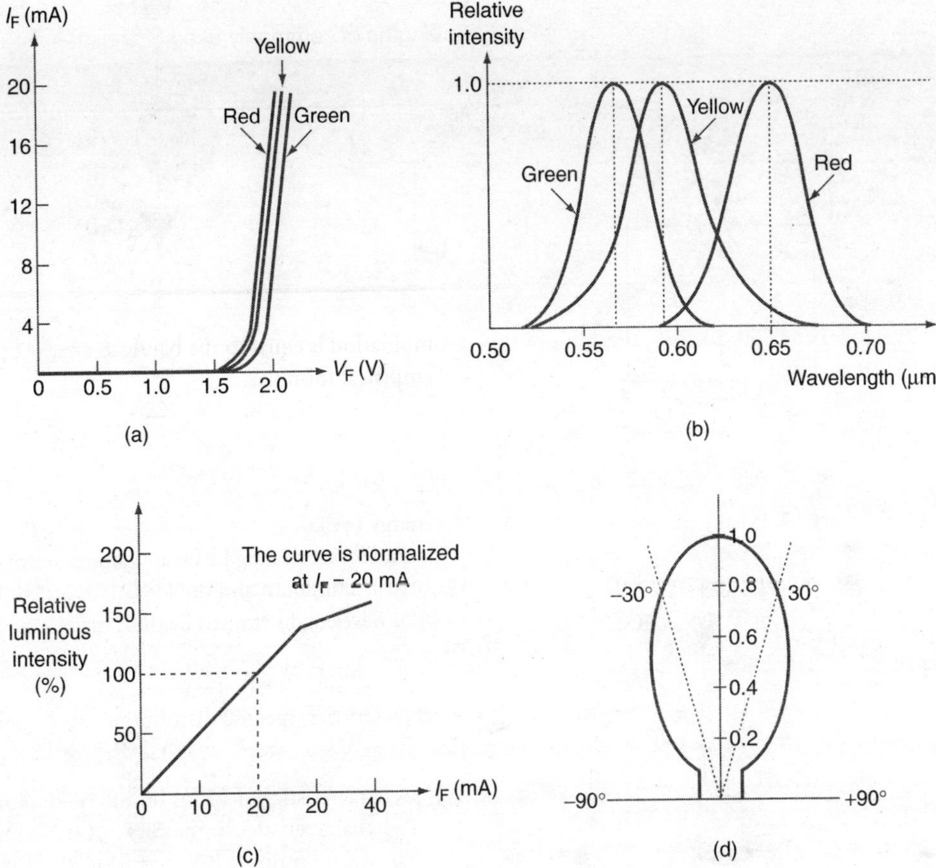

Figure 7.37 (a) V–I characteristics of an LED; (b) spectral characteristics of an LED; (c) light output versus input current characteristics of an LED; (d) directional characteristics of an LED.

3. **Radiant Power Output (P_o):** It is the light power output of the LED.
4. **Peak Spectral Emission (λ_P):** It is the wavelength where the intensity of light emitted by the LED is maximum.
5. **Spectral Bandwidth:** It gives an indication as to how concentrated the brightest color is around its nominal wavelength.

LED Drive Circuits

LEDs are operated in the forward-biased mode. As the current through the LED changes very rapidly with change in the forward voltage above the threshold voltage, LEDs are current-driven devices. Figure 7.38(a) shows a simple circuit for driving an LED. The resistor (R) is the current-limiting resistor used to limit the current flowing through the LED. In this case the V–I characteristics of the LED is used to determine the voltage that needs to be applied to the LED to generate the desired forward current. A silicon diode can be placed inversely parallel to the LED for reverse polarity voltage protection. The current that will flow through the LED is given by

$$I = (V_{CC} - V_F)/R \tag{7.22}$$

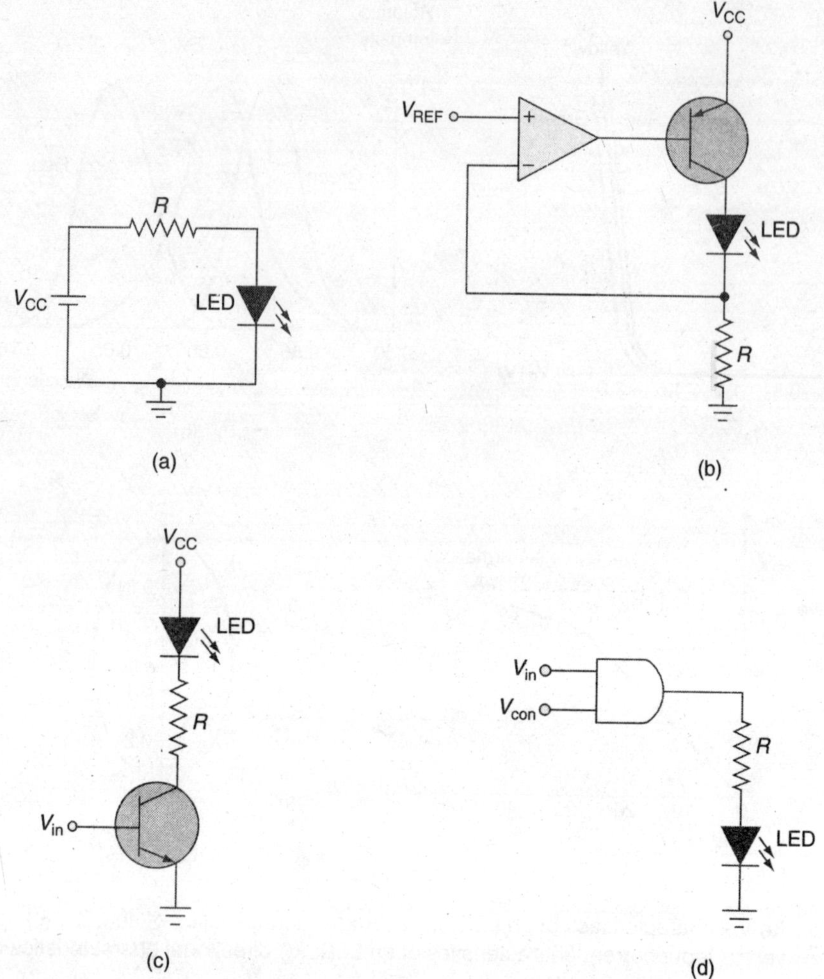

Figure 7.38 (a) Simple LED driver circuit; (b) constant current source based LED driver circuit; (c) and (d) logic circuits for driving LEDs.

where V_{CC} is the supply voltage; V_F is the forward diode voltage; R is the current-limiting resistor. However, any change in the forward voltage of the LED due to temperature changes or variation from device to device causes a change in the LED current. Moreover, there is power dissipation across the series resistor R, resulting in reduced efficiency. A better drive circuit configuration is the one that employs a constant current source as shown in Figure 7.38(b). The current flowing through the LED is determined by the reference voltage (V_{REF}) and the resistor R.

LEDs can also be used to display the logic output states. Figures 7.38(c) and (d) show two typical logic circuits that can be used to drive LEDs. Figure 7.38(c) uses a transistor-based switch while Figure 7.38(b) employs a logic gate/buffer. In both the circuits, the LED glows when the voltage V_{in} is in the logic HIGH state.

When the light emitted by one LED is not sufficient, several LEDs can be connected in series to enhance the light level to the desired value. LEDs can be connected in series as shown in Figure 7.39(a). In a series connection, the current flowing through each LED is the same. The value of the supply voltage (V_{CC}) should be sufficiently

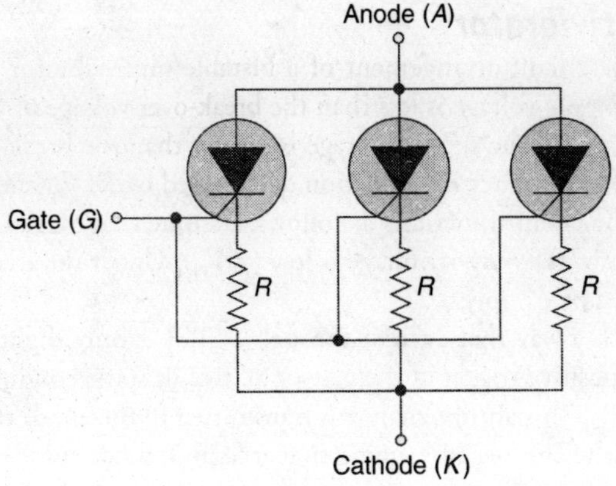

Figure 6.26 | Thyristors in parallel.

6.9 Applications of Thyristors

Some common applications of devices of thyristor family are briefly discussed in the following sub-sections.

SCR as Pulse Generator

Figure 6.27 shows the use of an SCR as a pulse generator. In the normal state, the output voltage would be at ground level as the capacitor C_1 would have been sitting charged to V volts. It may be at mentioned that the break-over voltage of the SCR must be greater than the voltage V. When a triggering pulse is applied at the gate of the SCR, it fires and the capacitor C_1 discharges through ON resistance (r) of the SCR and resistance R_1. It does so with a time constant R_1C_1 if $r < R_1$. The capacitor can discharge only upto a voltage V_H (called holding voltage) as beyond that holding current of the SCR can no longer be supplied and the SCR turns off. When the SCR fires, the voltage across SCR tends to change abruptly to V_H from V changing by $(V–V_H)$. Since, voltage across a capacitor cannot change abruptly, the output voltage (V_o) changes abruptly from 0 to $-(V–V_H)$ and then rises exponentially as C_1 discharges. The output abruptly goes to zero when voltage across C_1 has decayed to V_H which can no longer supply the holding current (I_H) and at that instant $V_o = I_HR_1$. The output pulse-width in this case is about $3R_1C_1$.

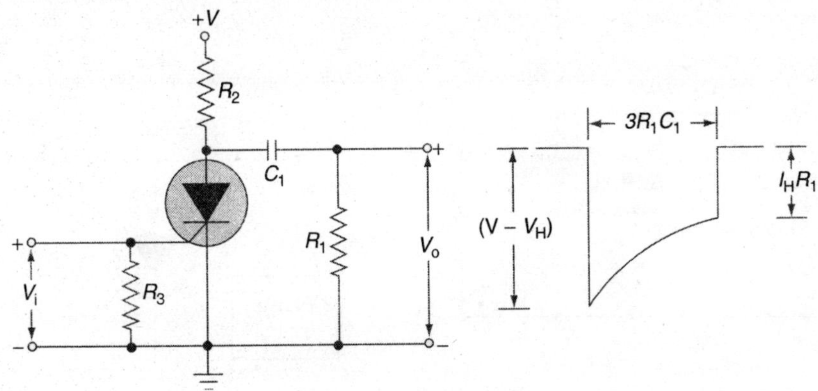

Figure 6.27 | SCR-based pulse generator.

SCR as Bistable Multivibrator

Figure 6.28 shows the basic circuit arrangement of a bistable multivibrator using SCRs. In the circuit arrangement shown, if the supply voltage is less than the break-over voltage of the SCRs, the circuit can be used as a bistable multivibrator. If the supply voltage is greater than the break-over voltage, it becomes an astable multivibrator with the frequency of oscillation determined by R_1, R_2 and C.

In the bistable mode, the circuit functions as follows. Assume that SCR-1 is initially conducting and SCR-2 is in cut-off. Obviously, the output voltage is low (= V_H). Under these conditions, the current flowing through SCR-1 is limited by R_1 only.

R_1 can be chosen in such a way that current through SCR-1 is only slightly greater than the holding current. Now if we apply a positive trigger at the gate of SCR-2, it starts conducting and the anode voltage of SCR-2 drops from V to V_H. This abrupt change is transmitted to the anode of SCR-1 as voltage across C cannot change instantaneously. This negative-going step at SCR-1 anode turns it OFF. Also the current that flows through C as a result of SCR-2 anode going to an almost zero potential has to be supplied through R_1. As mentioned above, R_1 cannot supply both the holding current for SCR-1 as well as current through C. As a result, current through SCR-1 falls below its holding current value and its turn-OFF is ensured. As SCR-1 goes to OFF-state, output goes high (= V). A positive trigger at SCR-1 gate again changes state.

Half-Wave Controlled Rectifier

The basic circuit diagram is shown in Figure 6.29. The point at which the gate-trigger pulse is applied to the SCR gate during the positive half cycle of the AC source is controlled by a suitable circuitry in the box labeled "phase control". During the negative half cycle, SCR remains reverse-biased and there is no current through the load. Thus, input AC power appears across the load only during the conduction period of the SCR. The AC power in the load thus can be controlled by controlling the firing angle of SCR.

Figure 6.30 shows the relevant waveforms. Figure 6.30(a) shows the waveforms appearing across the load and Figure 6.30(b) shows SCR anode waveform. In the half-wave rectifier control of AC power using SCR, the firing angle can be anywhere between 0° and 180°.

Full-Wave Controlled Rectifier

The basic circuit arrangement is shown in Figure 6.31. Typical input and output waveforms are shown in Figure 6.32. Conduction angle is 90°. Diodes D_1 and D_3 conduct during positive half cycles of

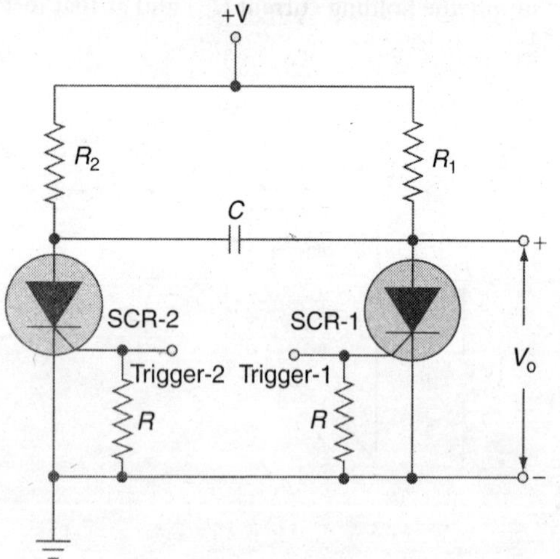

Figure 6.28 SCR-based bistable multivibrator.

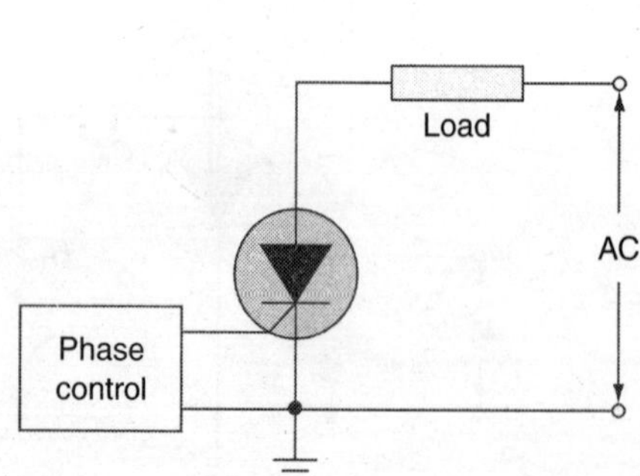

Figure 6.29 Half-wave controlled rectifier.

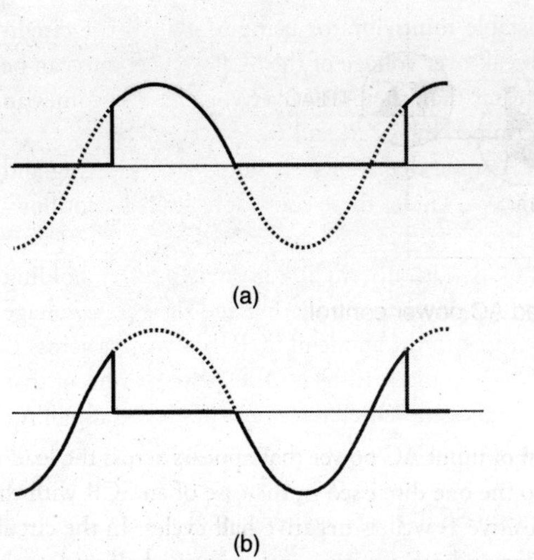

Figure 6.30 | Relevant waveforms in half-wave controlled rectifier.

Figure 6.31 | Full-wave controlled rectifier.

input whereas diodes D_2 and D_4 conduct during negative half cycles of input. The power control is provided by SCR.

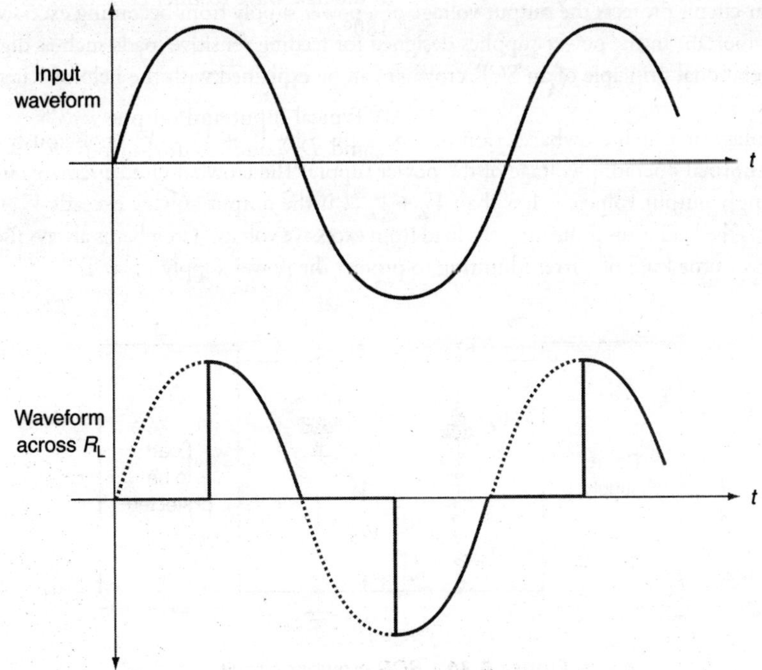

Figure 6.32 | Relevant waveforms in full-wave controlled rectifier.

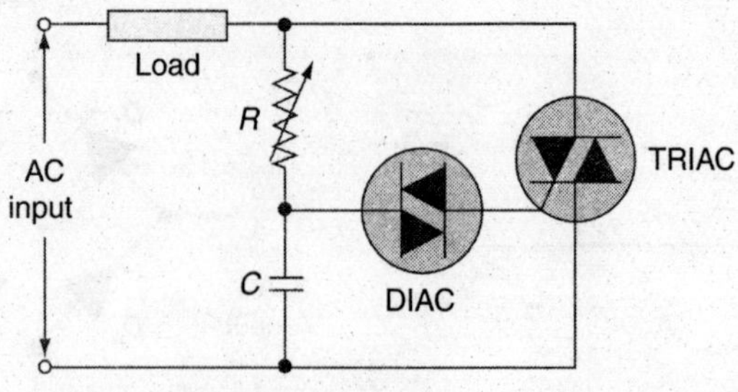

Figure 6.33 | TRIAC-based AC power control.

TRIAC-Based AC Power Control

Figure 6.33 shows basic circuit arrangement. The portion of input AC power that appears across the load is during the time the TRIAC is ON. The idea is similar to the one discussed in the case of an SCR with the TRIAC having an advantage that it can control both positive as well as negative half cycles. In the circuit shown, phase angle is being controlled by a DIAC. During both positive and negative half cycles, the TRIAC conducts as and when the break-over voltage of the DIAC is exceeded.

The TRIAC turns off when the current falls below its holding value. Another trigger during the negative half cycle turns the TRIAC ON again. The period for which the TRIAC conducts during positive and negative half cycles of AC input can be controlled by varying *R*. By controlling time constant (*RC*), we can control the time instant at which DIAC would fire which in turn triggers the TRIAC.

SCR-Based Crowbar Protection

An SCR crowbar circuit protects the output voltage of a power supply from becoming excessively high. This is particularly important in the power supplies designed for feeding sensitive loads such as digital integrated circuits. The operational principle of an SCR crowbar can be explained with the help of schematic arrangement of Figure 6.34.

The over-voltage at which crowbar action occurs is given by $V_Z + V_{GT}$. V_Z is obviously selected to be higher than the normal operating voltage of the power supply. The crowbar circuit remains inactive as long as the power supply output voltage is less than $V_Z + V_{GT}$. If the output voltage exceeds $V_Z + V_{GT}$, SCR is triggered. It shorts the load, thus protecting the load from excessive voltage. Crowbar is always used in conjunction with a fuse or some kind of current limiting to protect the power supply.

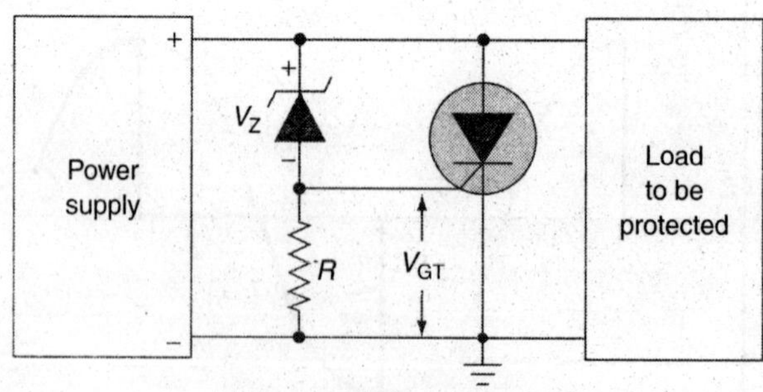

Figure 6.34 | SCR crowbar circuit.

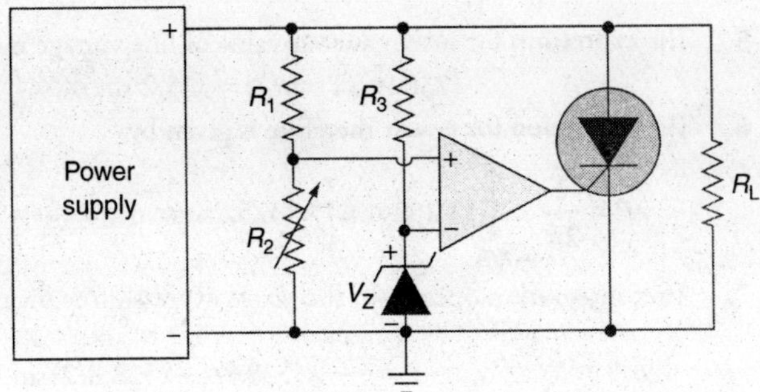

Figure 6.35 Modified SCR crowbar circuit.

An important aspect of crowbar circuit is its turn-ON time. Since SCRs with turn-ON time as fast as a microsecond are commercially available, it suits the application. In the basic circuit of Figure 6.34, the turn-ON of SCR is dependent on the breakdown of Zener diode. Owing to a slightly curved knee of the Zener diode characteristics at the breakdown point, the device becomes a bit sluggish. The problem can be overcome by adding gain to the trigger circuit of SCR. One such circuit is shown in Figure 6.35. The circuit is self-explanatory.

Crowbar action occurs at an output voltage given by

$$V_O \times \frac{R_2}{R_1 + R_2} = V_Z \tag{6.10}$$

$$V_O = V_Z \times \left(1 + \frac{R_1}{R_2}\right) \tag{6.11}$$

Crowbar circuits are now available in IC form for a range of standard operating voltages. These ICs just need to be connected across the load. The IC crowbar has a built-in Zener diode, some kind of gain circuit and SCR. SK 9345 series of IC crowbars offer protection to +5 V (SK 9345), +12 V (SK 9346) and +15 V (SK 9347) power supplies.

EXAMPLE 6.5 *Refer to the SCR-based half-wave power control circuit of Figure 6.36. The 230 V AC source of supply feeds a 100 Ω load through a controlled rectifier. If the trigger circuit of the SCR was so adjusted as to start conduction at 30° after the start of each cycle, determine the total power delivered to the load by the AC supply. Assume holding voltage of the SCR to be zero.*

Solution

1. The instantaneous value of the power drawn from the AC supply is the product of the instantaneous values of line current and line voltage. The average value of this product will be the power delivered by the AC supply.
2. The SCR conducts only for a period from 30° ($\pi/6$ rad) to 180° (π rad) during each cycle. For rest of the period, the SCR remains in the cut-off state.
3. Therefore, the current flows through the load only for a period from 30° ($\pi/6$ rad) to 180° (π rad).
4. The expression for instantaneous value of line current is given by

$$(230 \times \sqrt{2}/100) \sin \alpha = 3.252 \sin \alpha$$

5. The expression for instantaneous value of line voltage is given by

$$(230 \times \sqrt{2}) \sin \alpha = 325.2 \sin \alpha$$

6. The expression for power therefore is given by

$$P = \frac{1}{2\pi} \times \int_{\pi/6}^{\pi} (3.252\sin\alpha) \times (325.2\sin\alpha)d\alpha = \frac{1}{2\pi} \times \int_{\pi/6}^{\pi} 1057.6\sin^2\alpha d\alpha$$

7. After integration operation, the above expression reduces to

$$P = \frac{1}{2\pi} \times \left|528.8\alpha - (528.8/2)\sin 2\alpha\right|_{\pi/6}^{\pi}$$

8. This simplifies to $P = 256.78$ W.

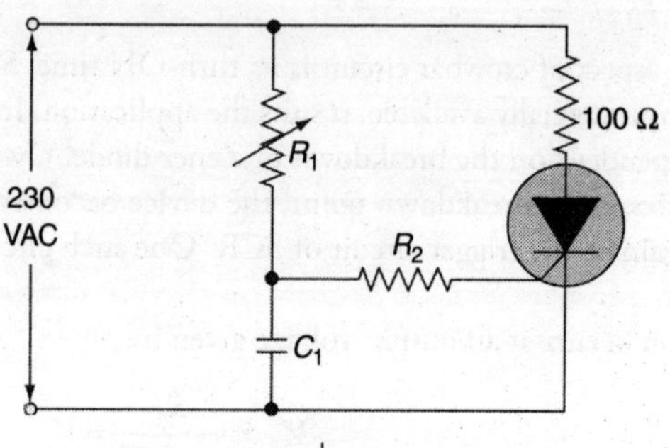

Figure 6.36 | Example 6.5.

EXAMPLE 6.6 *Refer to the SCR crowbar circuit of Figure 6.37. Determine the required breakdown voltage of the Zener diode if the load voltage could at the most be allowed to increase to 10 V. Take V_{GT} of SCR to be equal to 0.8 V.*

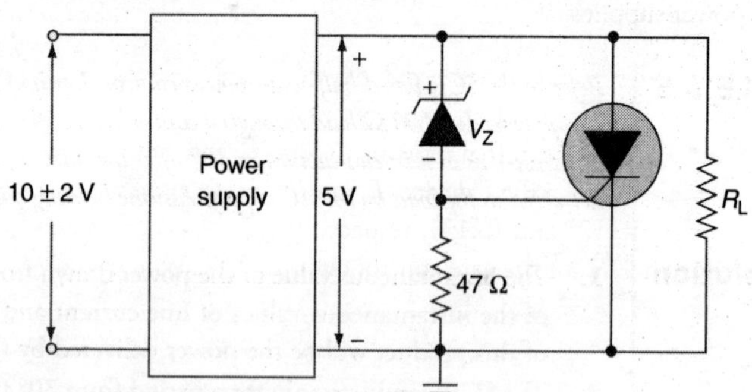

Figure 6.37 | Example 6.6.

Solution

1. In the present case, $V_Z + V_{GT} = 10$ V.
2. This gives $V_Z = 10 - V_{GT} = 10 - 0.8 = 9.2$ V.

6.10 Gate Turn-OFF Thyristors

A conventional thyristor as described in the preceding sections is a solid-state semiconductor device with at least four layers of alternating P and N types of semiconductor material. These devices can be with or without the gate control terminal and act like a latching-type switch. These devices continue to stay in the conducting state once they are appropriately triggered as long as the voltage across the device is not reduced to zero or reversed or the forward current brought below a certain threshold value called the holding current.

A gate turn-OFF thyristor (GTO), on the other hand, is a special type of thyristor, which can be switched to the ON and OFF states by applying appropriate trigger pulses to the gate terminal. The GTO can be turned ON by a positive current pulse applied between gate and cathode terminals. The turn-ON phenomenon in a GTO is not as reliable as it is in the case of a conventional thyristor. A small magnitude of positive gate current therefore must be maintained even after turn-ON to improve reliability.

The turn-OFF of the GTO is accomplished by applying a suitable negative voltage pulse. Application of negative voltage initiates a reduction in the forward current by about 20–30%. This reduction in forward current induces a cathode-to-gate voltage which further reduces the forward current. The process ultimately culminates in the device transitioning to the blocking state.

As compared to conventional thyristors, GTO thyristors have relatively higher ON-state voltage drop, longer turn-ON and turn-OFF times and also require higher turn-ON gate current.

GTO thyristors are available without or with reverse-blocking capability. The former are known as asymmetrical GTO thyristors, abbreviated as A-GTO. The GTO thyristors with reverse-blocking capability are known as symmetrical GTO thyristors, abbreviated as S-GTO. The major application areas of GTO thyristors include their use in variable speed motor drives, high power inverters and traction.

6.11 Programmable Unijunction Transistor

The conventional unijunction transistor is essentially a lightly doped bar of N-type semiconductor material with heavily doped P-type diffusion region somewhere along the length of the bar. The diffusion point is usually closer to one of the ends of the N-type bar.

Programmable unijunction transistor (PUT) behaves more or less like a UJT and has similar applications. A PUT is designed to enable the engineer to program UJT parameters, which include inter-base resistance (R_{BB}), intrinsic stand-off ratio (η), peak current (I_P) and valley current (I_V). Programming is possible with the help of two external resistors. Figure 6.38(a) shows the circuit symbol and Figure 6.38(b) the constructional features of a PUT device. R_1 and R_2 are programming resistors. R_{BB} and η in the case of PUT are given by Eqs. (6.12) and (6.13), respectively. The peak current and valley current depend upon the equivalent resistance R_G of the gate control circuit. R_G is given by Eq. (6.14).

$$R_{BB} = R_1 + R_2 \tag{6.12}$$

$$\eta = R_1/(R_1 + R_2) \tag{6.13}$$

$$R_G = R_1 \times R_2/(R_1 + R_2) \tag{6.14}$$

As is obvious from Figure 6.38(b), the name PUT is a misnomer. PUT is a four-layer device like a thyristor with contacts, namely, anode (A) and cathode (K) made to the two extreme layers and a control contact called gate (G) made to one of the inner layers. In this case, the inner layer chosen is the one closer to the

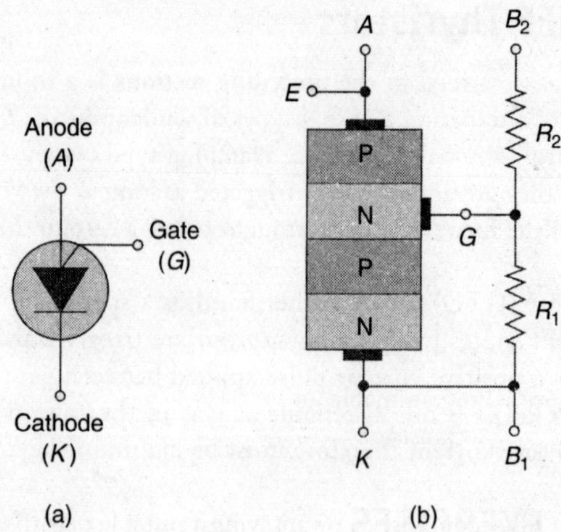

Figure 6.38 Programmable unijunction transistor: (a) Circuit symbol; (b) construction.

anode contact. The device is so called because it can perform functions similar to that of a UJT. Note that a PUT device is directly interchangeable with a UJT device.

Figure 6.39 shows the V–I characteristics of a PUT device. The voltage V_S appearing at the control terminal is given by

$$V_S = V_B \times [R_1/(R_1 + R_2)] \tag{6.15}$$

where V_B is the DC voltage applied between B_2 and B_1 terminals.

As anode to cathode voltage exceeds V_S by one diode voltage drop, the device goes to conduction. We can notice the similarity in the V–I characteristics of a PUT and a UJT device. 2N 6027 and 2N 6028 are commonly used PUTs. Like UJT devices, the most common application of PUT devices also is in triggering of thyristors. Figure 6.40 shows one such circuit, which is self-explanatory.

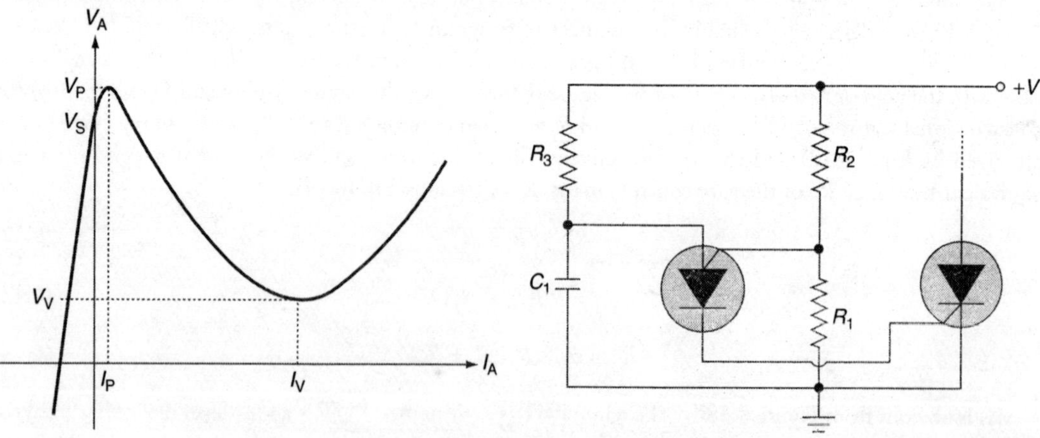

Figure 6.39 V–I characteristics of PUT.

Figure 6.40 Thyristor triggering with a PUT device.

KEY TERMS

Amperes squared seconds rating
Asymmetrical gate turn-OFF thyristor
Break-over voltage
Critical rate of rise of OFF-state voltage
Critical rate-of-rise of ON-state current
DIAC
Gate turn-OFF thyristor
Holding current
Holding voltage
Intrinsic stand-off ratio
Latching current
Non-repetitive peak reverse voltage
Peak OFF-state voltage
PNPN diode
Programmable unijunction transistor
Rate effect
Repetitive peak OFF-state voltage
Repetitive peak reverse voltage
Silicon-controlled rectifier
Symmetrical gate turn-OFF thyristor
Unijunction transistor
TRIAC

OBJECTIVE-TYPE EXERCISES

Multiple-Choice Questions

1. SCRs are connected in series to enhance
a. their overall d*v*/d*t* rating.
b. the overall voltage rating.
c. their current-handing capability.
d. none of these.

2. While connecting SCRs in series, the individual SCRs chosen for the purpose should have closely matched
a. d*i*/d*t* rating.
b. reverse-biased characteristics.
c. forward- and reverse-blocking characteristics.
d. forward ON-state characteristics.

3. SCRs are connected in parallel to enhance
a. voltage-handing capability.
b. current-handing capability.
c. d*i*/d*t* rating.
d. none of these.

4. While connecting SCRs in parallel, the SCRs to be connected in parallel should have closely matched
a. forward ON-state characteristics.
b. forward and reverse OFF-state characteristics.
c. forward OFF-state and ON-state characteristics.
d. SCRs cannot be connected in parallel.

5. A UJT relaxation oscillator circuit produces a sawtooth like waveform
a. at B_1 terminal.
b. at B_2 terminal.
c. across the capacitor.
d. none of these.

6. V–I characteristics of a UJT can be expressed by
a. a single-valued function of voltage.
b. a multi-valued function of current.
c. a single-valued function of current.
d. none of these.

7. Which of the following device type numbers is not a thyristor?
a. 2N2646
b. OE 104
c. TY 1005 F
d. OE 106

8. Pick the odd one out.
a. Tunnel diode
b. UJT
c. SCR
d. TRIAC

9. When we want to know the sub-cycle surge current capability of a thyristor, we should look for
a. d*i*/d*t* rating.
b. surge current rating, I_{FSM}.
c. I^2t rating.
d. none of these.

10. In half-wave SCR power control circuit, if the firing angle is 30°, then for one complete cycle of operation, the load gets power for
    a. 60°
    b. 150°
    c. 330°
    d. 30°

11. The construction of a programmable unijunction transistor (PUT) is
    a. similar to that of a conventional unijunction transistor except for the fact that both resistors forming the inter-base resistance R_{BB} are variable.
    b. similar to that of a four-layer PNPN diode.
    c. different from the conventional unijunction transistor in the sense that in the case of a PUT, the silicon bar is heavily doped and the P-type emitter is lightly doped.
    d. different from the conventional unijunction transistor in the sense that a PUT is made from germanium and not silicon.

12. Which of the following thyristors does not have a control terminal?
    a. DIAC
    b. TRIAC
    c. SCR
    d. GTO thyristor

13. While switching an SCR from the forward-blocking state to the ON-state by applying a gate-trigger pulse, it is important for a successful switch on that the gate-trigger pulse is present till one of the following parameters is exceeded.
    a. Holding current
    b. Latching current
    c. Holding voltage
    d. di/dt rating

14. Which of the following parameters is programmable in a programmable unijunction transistor?
    a. Intrinsic stand-off ratio
    b. Inter-base resistance R_{BB}
    c. Peak and valley currents
    d. All the above

15. Once an SCR has been switched to the ON-state, the minimum value of the anode current required to keep the device in the ON-state is called
    a. latching current.
    b. trigger current.
    c. holding current.
    d. break-over current.

Match the Following

Column 2 of Table 6.1 lists some of the devices belonging to family of UJTs and thyristors from S. No. 1 to 6. Their circuit symbols and the V–I characteristics are given in a haphazard manner in columns 3 and 4 respectively. For each of the listed devices in column 2, identify the corresponding circuit symbol and the V–I characteristics. For example, if you feel that the device listed at S. No. 1 has its circuit symbol and its V–I characteristics, respectively, listed at S. No. 3 and 6, then your answer for this part will be (1–3–6).

Table 6.1

S. No.	Device type	Circuit symbol	V–I characteristics
1.	Silicon-controlled rectifier (SCR)	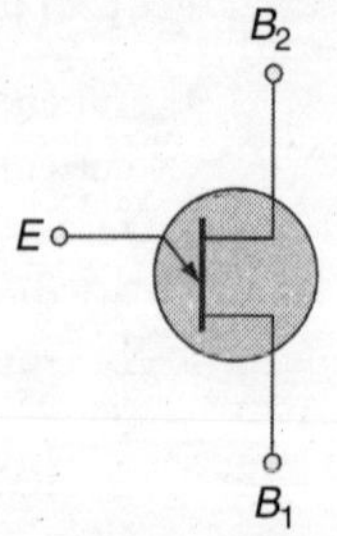 B_2, E, B_1	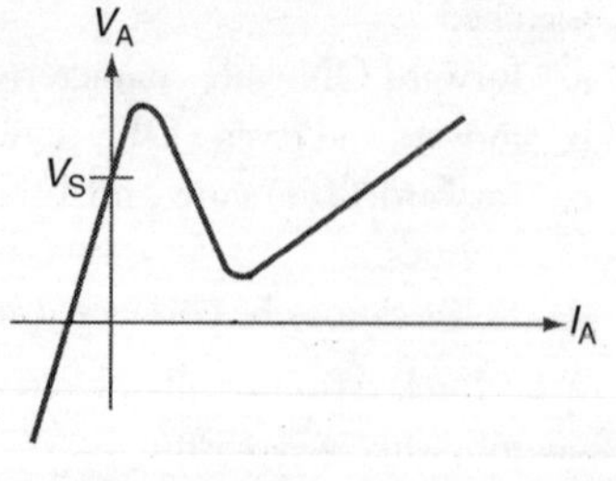 V_A, V_S, I_A

2. Unijunction transistor (UJT)

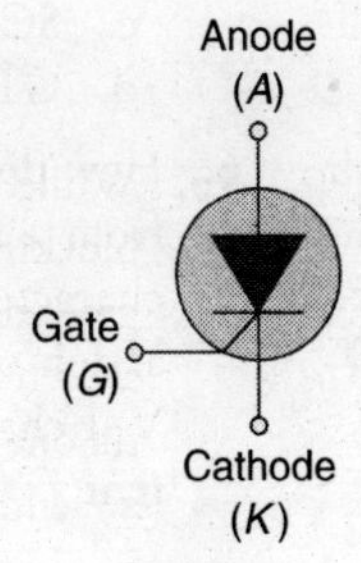

3. Programmable unijunction transistor (PUT)

4. DIAC

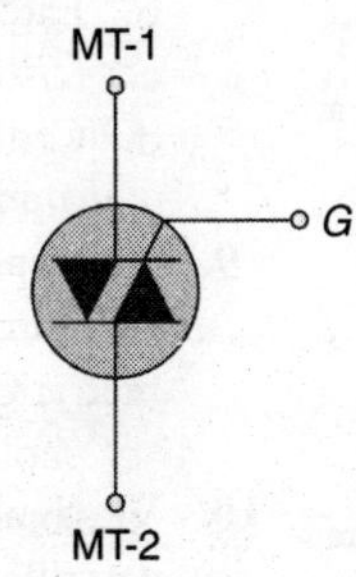

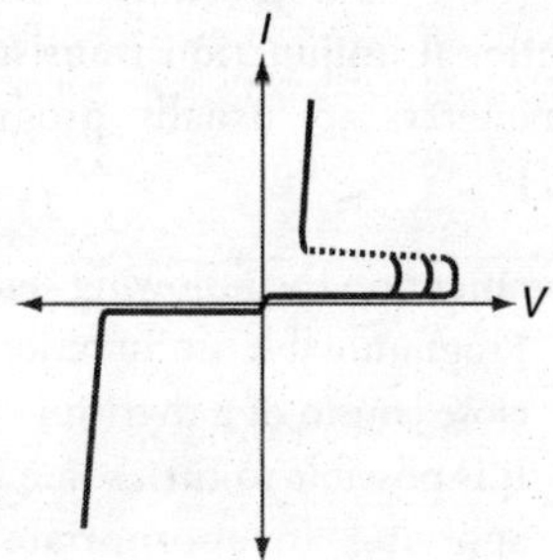

5. TRIAC

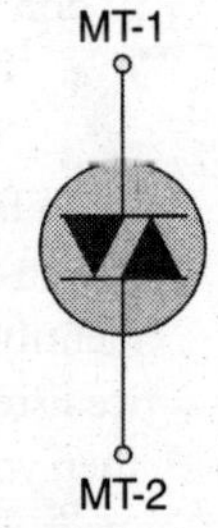

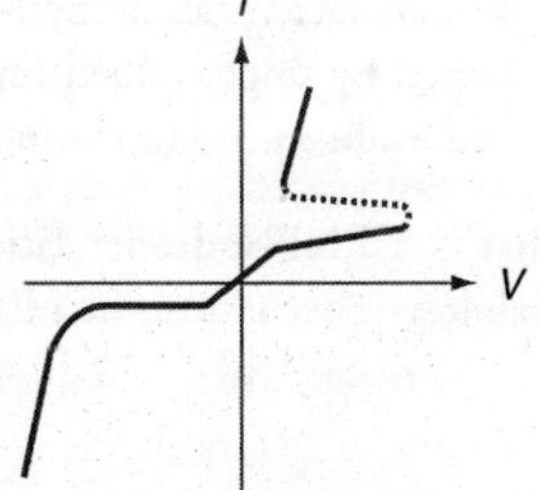

6. Silicon-controlled switch (SCS)

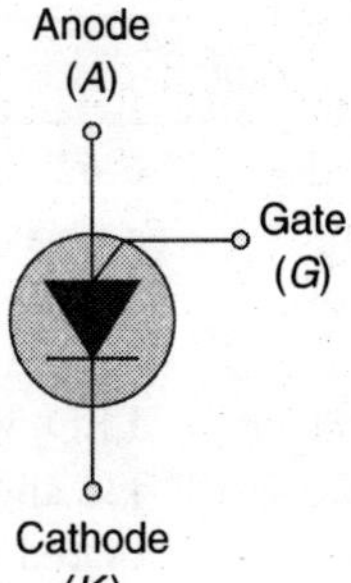

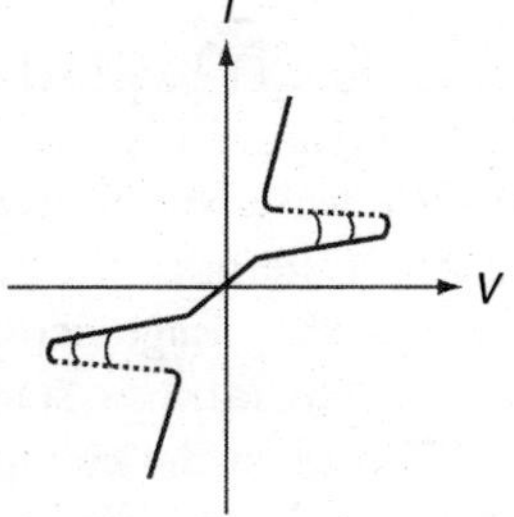

REVIEW QUESTIONS

1. What is a unijunction transistor (UJT)? With the help of relevant schematic diagram, briefly describe the operational principle of a UJT with particular reference to its V–I characteristics.

2. Why is UJT referred to as a current-controllable device and not a voltage-controllable device? Draw the basic circuit diagram of a UJT-based relaxation oscillator circuit and derive an expression for its frequency of operation.

3. What is a programmable unijunction transistor (PUT) and how does it differ from a conventional unijunction transistor? What UJT parameters are usually programmable in a PUT?

4. Comment on the following statements.
   a. Programmable unijunction transistor is a close cousin of a thyristor.
   b. It is possible to turn some thyristors off by applying an appropriate signal to the gate.
   c. V–I characteristics of thyristors can be represented by single-valued function of current and multi-valued function of voltage.

5. What is a PNPN diode? Briefly describe the breakdown mechanism in a PNPN diode.

6. How does a silicon-controlled rectifier differ from a PNPN diode? With the help of V–I characteristics, briefly describe the control action of the gate in terms of change in the V–I characteristics as a function of gate current.

7. What do you understand by rate effect in thyristors? How does this lead to premature firing of the device?

8. Define and briefly describe the significance of following electrical parameters of thyristors.
   a. Holding current
   b. Latching current
   c. Critical rate of rise of OFF-state voltage
   d. Critical rate of rise of ON-state current

9. What are gate turn-OFF (GTO) thyristors? Differentiate between asymmetric and symmetric GTO thyristors.

10. With the help of basic circuit diagrams, briefly describe the operation of the following application circuits.
    a. Half-wave AC power control using an SCR
    b. SCR-based crowbar circuit
    c. SCR triggering using a programmable unijunction transistor

PROBLEMS

1. Refer to the UJT-based relaxation oscillator circuit of Figure 6.41 and the associated sawtooth waveform observed across the capacitor. Determine the peak value (V_P) of the sawtooth voltage across the capacitor given that the intrinsic stand-off ratio η of the UJT used in the circuit is 0.4. Assume the forward-biased diode voltage drop of 0.65 V.

2. Refer to the PNPN diode circuit of Figure 6.42. The PNPN diode used in the circuit has a break-over voltage of 12 V and holding and latching current specifications of 5 mA and 10 mA, respectively. Determine the status of LED, whether it is ON or OFF, for (a) $R = 1$ kΩ and (b) $R = 10$ kΩ. Assume the forward-biased drop across PNPN diode and LED to be 1.5 V each.

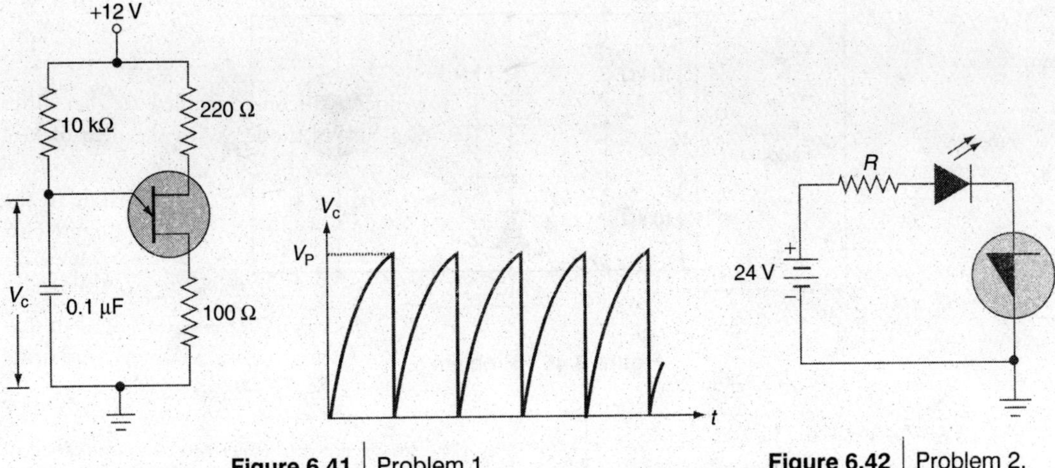

Figure 6.41 Problem 1.

Figure 6.42 Problem 2.

3. The PNPN diode circuit of Figure 6.43 has break-over voltage and holding current specifications of 18 V and 5 mA, respectively. The variable voltage source is set in such a way that the LED is glowing. If the knee voltage of the PNPN diode is taken to be 1.0 V and the forward-biased LED voltage drop to be 1.5 V, determine the applied voltage at which the LED will turn OFF.

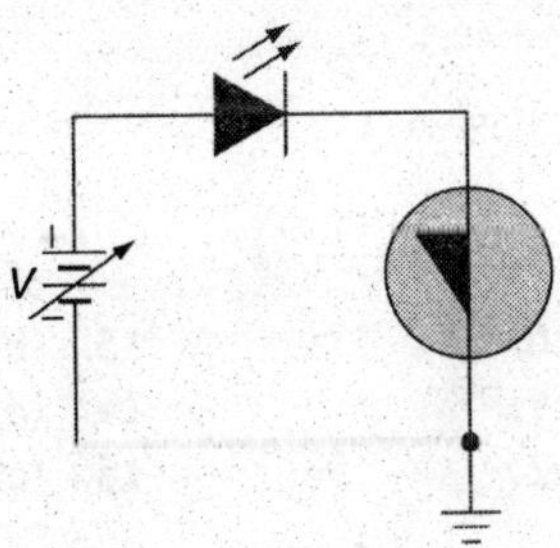

Figure 6.43 Problem 3.

4. Refer to the relaxation oscillator circuit of Figure 6.44. The PNPN diode used in the circuit has break-over voltage and holding current specifications of 12.5 V and 5 mA, respectively. Determine the peak value and frequency of the sawtooth voltage waveform appearing across the capacitor. Assume the ON-resistance of the PNPN device to be negligible.

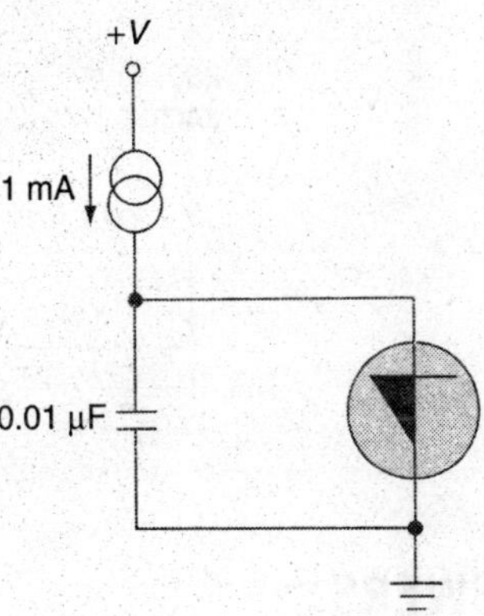

Figure 6.44 Problem 4.

5. Refer to the SCR crowbar circuit of Figure 6.45. Determine the required breakdown voltage of the Zener diode if the load voltage could at the most be allowed to increase to 30 V. Take V_{GT} of SCR to be equal to 0.8 V.

6. Refer to the SCR-based half-wave power control circuit of Figure 6.46. The 230 V AC source of supply feeds a 200 Ω load through a controlled rectifier. If the trigger circuit of the SCR was so adjusted as to start conduction at 60° after the start of each cycle, determine (a) the RMS value of the load current and (b) the total power delivered to the load by the AC supply. Assume holding voltage of the SCR to be zero.

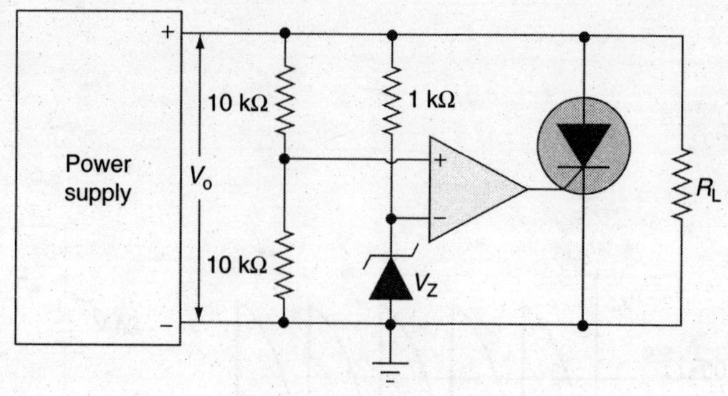

Figure 6.45 | Problem 5.

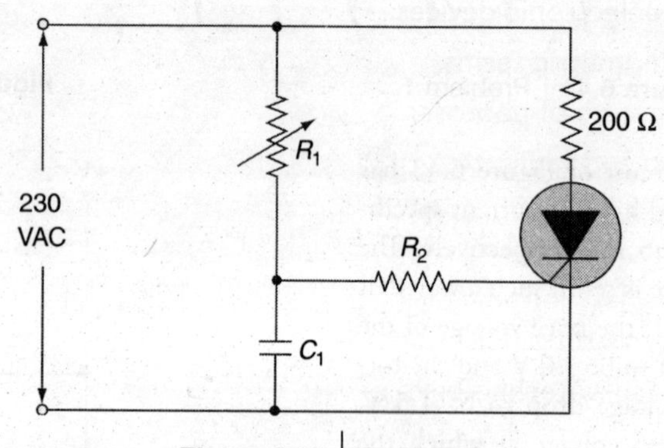

Figure 6.46 | Problem 6.

ANSWERS

Multiple-Choice Questions

1. (b) **2.** (c) **3.** (b) **4.** (a) **5.** (c) **6.** (c) **7.** (a) **8.** (a) **9.** (c) **10.** (b) **11.** (b) **12.** (a) **13.** (b) **14.** (d) **15.** (c)

Match the Following

(1–2–4)
(2–1–3)
(3–6–1)
(4–5–2)
(5–4–6)
(6–3–5)

Problems

1. 5.45 V
2. (a) ON; (b) OFF
3. 7.5 V
4. Peak value = 12.5 V; frequency = 8 kHz
5. 15 V
6. (a) 0.73 A, (b) 107 W

CHAPTER 7

Optoelectronic Devices

Learning Objectives

After completing this chapter, you will learn the following:

- Classification of optoelectronic devices.
- Photometric and radiometric terms.
- Characteristic parameters of photosensors.
- Principle of operation and application circuits of different types of photosensors, namely, photoconductors, photodiodes, solar cells, phototransistors, photoFETs, photoSCRs, photoTRIACs, vacuum photodiodes, photomultiplier tubes and image intensifier tubes.
- Different types of displays including light-emitting diodes (LEDs), liquid-crystal displays (LCDs) and cathode-ray tube (CRT) displays.
- Emerging trends in display technology.
- Optocoupler basics.

Optoelectronics is the field related to the study of electronic devices that emit, detect and control light. These devices are collectively referred to as the optoelectronic devices. Photoemitters, photosensors, displays and optocouplers are the popular optoelectronic devices. Photoemitters are electrical-to-optical transducers that are used to convert the electrical energy into output light. Some of the common photoemitters include light-emitting diodes (LEDs) and different types of displays. Photosensors are optical-to-electrical transducers that are used for converting the incident light energy into electrical output. Photoconductors, photodiodes, phototransistors, photomultiplier tubes and image intensifiers are some of the commonly used photosensors. Optocouplers are devices that use short optical transmission path to transfer signals between elements of a circuit. Optoelectronic devices constitute the heart of a variety of systems ranging from the simple gadgets like light meters to the most complex of military systems like precision guided munitions, laser range finders, target trackers, etc.; from instrumentation, measurement and diagnostic systems to space-based weather forecasting and remote sensing systems; from fiber-optic and laser-based communication applications to spectrophotometry and photometry applications and so on.

This chapter discusses in detail the fundamentals and application circuits of different types of optoelectronic devices. The chapter begins with classification of optoelectronic devices, followed by the definition of various radiometric and photometric terms commonly used in the field of optoelectronics. Discussion on photosensors, their characteristic parameters and principle of operation of different types of photosensors including photoconductors, photodiodes, phototransistors, photoSCRs and photoemissive devices follows next. After that different types of photoemitting devices and displays are discussed. The chapter concludes with a brief description on optocouplers. The text is adequately illustrated with practical circuits and a large number of solved examples.

7.1 Optoelectronic Devices

Optoelectronics is the field that deals with the study of devices that emit, detect and control light in the wavelength spectrum ranging from ultraviolet to far infrared. Optoelectronic devices include electrical-to-optical and optical-to-electrical transducers that covert electrical energy into light energy and light energy into electrical energy, respectively. Optocouplers also come in the broad category of optoelectronic devices.

Classification

As mentioned in the introductory section of the chapter, optoelectronic devices can be classified into photo-emitters, photosensors and optocouplers. Figure 7.1 lists the different types of optoelectronic devices. Photosensors, their characteristic parameters, types and their application circuits are discussed in Sections 7.2–7.8. Different types of photoemitters are covered in Sections 7.9–7.13. Optocouplers are discussed in Section 7.14.

Radiometric and Photometric Units

Optoelectronics is the study of devices and systems emitting, sensing or controlling radiation in the infrared, visible and ultraviolet bands in the wavelength spectrum of 1 nm to 1 mm. There are two approaches used to define the units and quantities related to the filed of optoelectronics, namely, *radiometry* and *photometry*.

Radiometry is the study of properties and characteristics of electromagnetic radiation and the sources and receivers of electromagnetic radiation. Radiometry covers a wide frequency spectrum; however for the present chapter we will limit our discussion to frequencies from ultraviolet to infrared.

Photometry is the science that deals with visible light and its perception by human vision. The most important difference between radiometry and photometry is that in radiometry, the measurements are made with objective electronic instruments whereas in case of photometry, measurements are done with reference to the response of human eye.

In this section, we define the commonly used radiometric and photometric quantities.

Radiometric and Photometric Flux

Flux is defined as a flow phenomenon or a field condition occurring in space. It is a measure of the total power emitted from a source or incident on a particular surface. The symbol for radiometric flux is ϕ_R and for photometric flux it is ϕ_P. Radiometric flux is measured in watts (W) while photometric flux is measured in lumens (lm). Lumen is defined as the amount of photometric flux generated by 1/683 W of radiometric flux at 555 nm where the photopic vision sensitivity of eye is maximum.

Efficacy of a radiation source is defined as the ratio of photometric or luminous flux to the total radio-metric flux from the source. It is given by

$$K = \frac{\phi_P}{\phi_R} \tag{7.1}$$

where K is the efficacy (lm/W), ϕ_P the photometric flux (lm), ϕ_R the radiometric flux (W).

Radiometric and Photometric Intensity

Intensity function describes the flux distribution in space. Radiometric intensity (I_R) is defined as the radiometric flux density per steradian. It is given by the following equation and is expressed in watts per steradian (W/sr):

$$I_R = \frac{\phi_R}{\Omega} \tag{7.2}$$

where ϕ_R is the radiometric flux (W) and Ω is the solid angle (sr).

3. The width of the depletion region of a photodiode is __________ proportional to the applied reverse-bias voltage.
4. __________ is the most important photosensor parameter to be considered for low noise applications.
5. When you are looking for an ultra low noise performance and the frequency of operation is less than 1 kHz, you operate the photodiode in __________ mode.
6. LCD displays offer __________ viewing angle as compared to the LED displays.
7. Main component of a CRT display is an __________.
8. LEDs are __________ biased for their normal operation.
9. Optocouplers are mostly used in applications to provide __________ between the input and output circuits.
10. Phototransistors offer __________ response time as compared to photodiodes.

REVIEW QUESTIONS

1. Name the two operating modes of a photodiode? Describe the difference between these two modes using schematic diagrams to highlight the operation of the photodiode in both the modes.
2. What is a phototransistor? Draw the schematic symbol of a phototransistor. State any two application areas of phototransistors.
3. Explain in detail the principle of operation of an LED. Also explain the factors that determine the output wavelength of LEDs.
4. Name the most sensitive photosensor. Also explain in brief its principle of operation.
5. What are optocouplers? Also explain the important characteristic parameters of optocouplers.
6. Explain the following terms:
   a. NEP
   b. Illuminance
   c. Thermal noise
   d. Current transfer ratio
7. Compare and contrast the following:
   a. Radiometry and photometry
   b. Detectivity and Dee-star
   c. Thermal detectors and photoelectric detectors
   d. Radiant intensity and illuminance
8. How does the response time of an LCD display vary with temperature?
9. Explain the different modes of operation of an LCD display. Also mention the advantages and disadvantages of each of these operating modes.
10. Mention any two important applications of optocouplers. Draw the basic circuits that can be used for these applications.
11. Explain in detail the difference between bolometers and photoconductors.
12. Which photosensor is used in night vision devices? Explain in brief its principle of operation.
13. Which parameters of a photosensor are of utmost importance while designing a receiver for detecting weak optical signals?
14. How does the wavelength of an LED vary with change in the bandgap energy of the semiconductor material?
15. What are the design considerations to be kept in mind while connecting LEDs in series and in parallel?

PROBLEMS

1. For the circuit shown in Figure 7.58, determine the current flowing through the LED? The base–emitter voltage of the PNP transistor is –0.6 V and the forward voltage drop of the LED is 1.4 V.

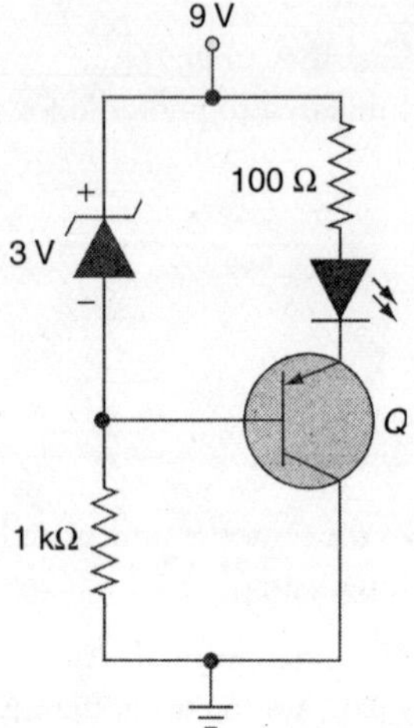

Figure 7.58 | Problem 1.

2. Design a panel of solar cells capable of delivering an output voltage of 5 V with a load-delivering capability of 1 A. Each of the solar cell is capable of generating an output voltage of 0.48 V with an output current of 150 mA.

3. A laser pulse with a rise time of 10 ns is incident on a PIN photodiode. The electrical pulse is seen on an oscilloscope having a bandwidth of 35 MHz and the rise time is measured to be 20 ns. Determine the rise time of the photodiode.

4. **a.** A photosensor has total noise current of 100 pA, responsivity of 1 A/W, active area of 2 mm^2 and rise time of 3.5 ns. Determine its (i) NEP; (ii) detectivity and (iii) Dee-star.

   b. Compare the NEP, detectivity and Dee-star parameters of the sensor in Problem 4(a) with another photosensor having same parameters as that of the sensor in Problem 4(a) except that the active area of the photosensor is 8 mm^2 and the noise current is 10 nA.

5. For the optocoupler circuit of Figure 7.59(a), determine the voltage across the resistor R, given that the value of the voltage V_B applied to the base of the transistor Q_1 is 1 V. The relationship between the input current flowing through the LED and the output phototransistor collector current is shown in Figure 7.59(b). The base–emitter voltage of transistor Q_1 is equal to 0.7 V.

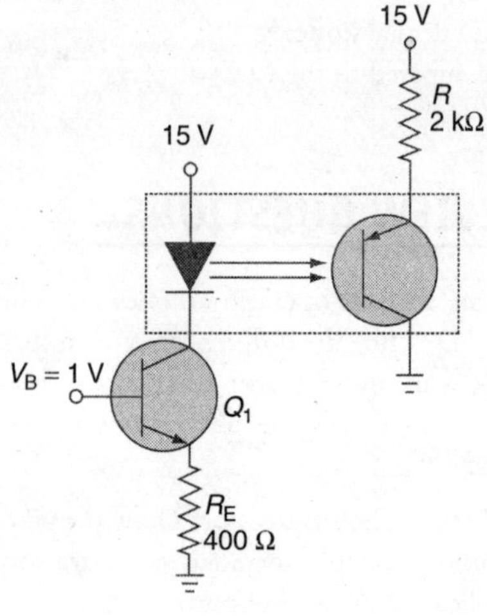

(a)

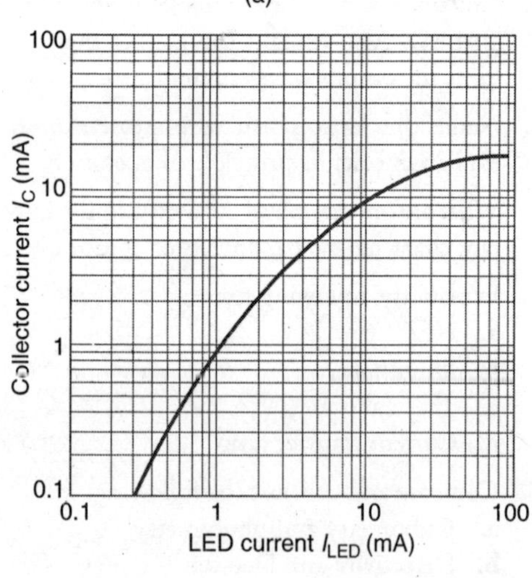

(b)

Figure 7.59 | Problem 5.

ANSWERS

Multiple-Choice Questions

1. (e)
2. (d)
3. (d)
4. (a)
5. (c)
6. (a)
7. (b)
8. (b)
9. (c)
10. (a)

Fill in the Blanks

1. Reverse saturation
2. Photomultiplier tube
3. Directly
4. NEP
5. Photovoltaic
6. Smaller
7. Electron gun
8. Forward
9. Isolation
10. Larger

Problems

1. 10 mA
2. Figure 7.60
3. 14.14 ns
4. **a.** 0.1 nW, 10^{10} W^{-1} and 1.414×10^{13} $W^{-1}cmHz^{1/2}$
   b. 10 nW, 10^{8} W^{-1} and 2.828×10^{11} $W^{-1}cmHz^{1/2}$
5. 1.24 V

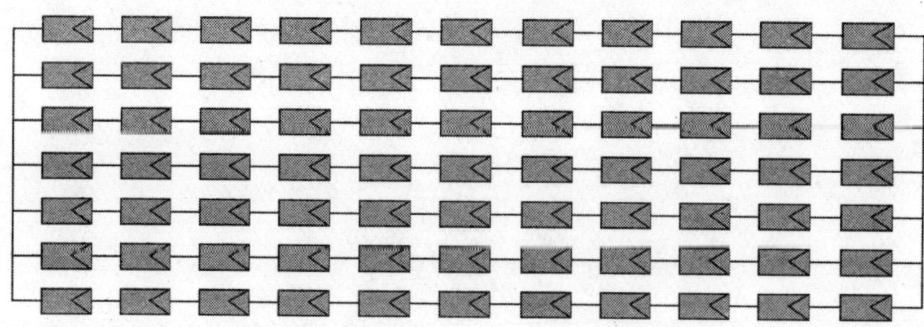

Figure 7.60 Solution to Problem 2.

CHAPTER 8

Small Signal Analysis of Amplifiers

Learning Objectives

After completing this chapter you, will learn the following:

- Frequency response of amplifiers.
- h-parameter model of amplifiers.
- h-parameter model of BJT amplifiers.
- Analysis of different BJT amplifier configurations using h-parameters.
- Small signal response of FET amplifiers.
- Cascading amplifiers.
- Darlington amplifiers.
- Cascode amplifiers.
- Low-frequency response of BJT amplifiers.
- Low-frequency response of FET amplifiers.
- Effect of cascading amplifier stages on the overall frequency response.

The chapter focuses on the small signal response of BJT and FET amplifiers. The small signal response of BJT amplifiers is mostly analyzed using the h-parameter model. In the chapter, the h-parameter model for the three BJT configurations is covered and detailed analysis of BJT amplifiers using the h-parameter model has been carried out. The small signal response of FET amplifiers is also discussed. In addition to the mid-band analysis, the low-frequency response of both BJT and FET amplifiers is also discussed in the chapter.

Cascading of amplifiers is done to increase the value of gain, to match the input and output impedances of the amplifier with the source and the load impedance, respectively. Cascading of BJT and FET amplifiers with particular reference to its effect on the overall frequency response of the amplifier is also described. Other topics covered in the chapter include Darlington amplifiers and Cascode amplifiers.

8.1 Amplifier Bandwidth: General Frequency Considerations

The response of an amplifier to an input signal depends upon the frequency of the signal. Figure 8.1 shows the typical frequency response curves for the RC-coupled, transformer-coupled and the direct-coupled amplifiers. The horizontal scale is a logarithmic scale to permit the plot to highlight both the low-frequency and the high-frequency regions of the response curve. For each curve three regions have been defined, namely, the low-frequency region, the mid-frequency region and the high-frequency region.

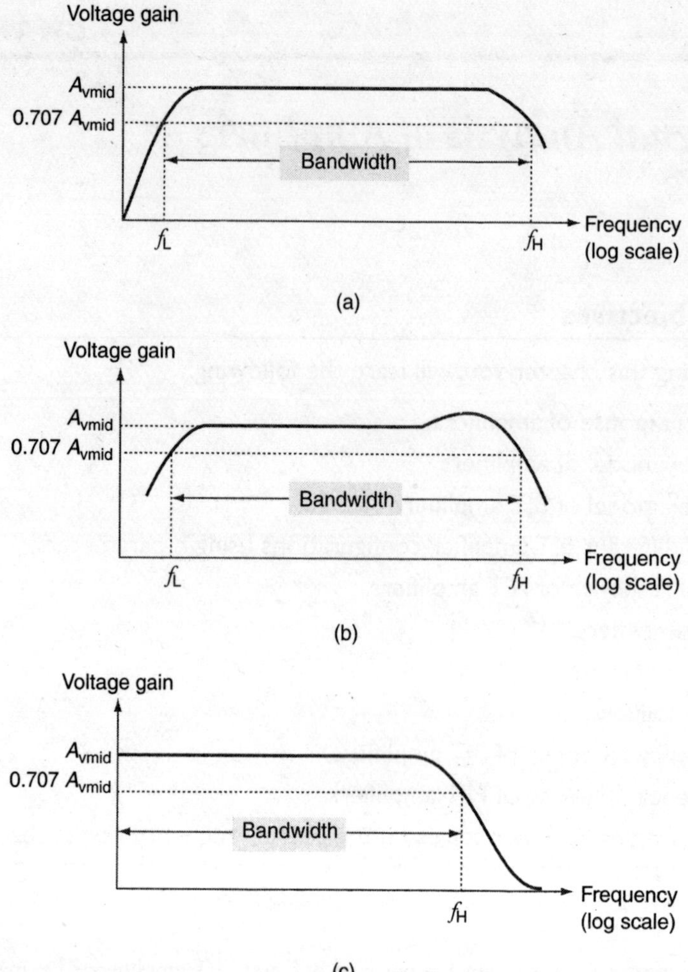

Figure 8.1 (a) Typical frequency response curve of RC-coupled amplifier; (b) typical frequency response curve of transformer-coupled amplifier; (c) typical frequency response curve of direct-coupled amplifier.

Low-frequency response of an amplifier is affected by the input and the output coupling capacitors and the bypass capacitors. At low frequencies, these capacitors cannot be replaced by short-circuit approximations as their reactances increase at low frequencies. The stray capacitances and the capacitive elements related to the active device and the network limit the high-frequency response of the system.

For each amplifier there is a region of frequencies where the magnitude of gain is relatively close to the mid-band value. The cut-off levels are defined by the frequencies where the gain value in decibels falls below the mid-band value by 3 decibels. In other words, the cut-off frequencies are defined as those frequencies where the magnitude of the gain in 0.707 times its value at the mid-band frequencies or the magnitude of the power gain is half of the magnitude of the power gain at the mid-band frequencies. The cut-off frequencies are referred to as the lower cut-off frequency (f_L) and the upper cut-off frequency (f_H). The difference between the upper cut-off and the lower cut-off frequencies is referred to as the bandwidth of the system.

8.2 Hybrid h-Parameter Model for an Amplifier

A two-port, four-terminal device or an amplifier (Figure 8.2) with two input and two output terminals can be represented in terms of an equivalent circuit model making use of two currents and two voltages provided that it meets the following two conditions. First, there is a common connection between the input and the output. Second, it should contain only linear elements. Two of the four variables (input and output currents, input and output voltages) can be chosen as the independent variables and the remaining two variables can be expressed in terms of these independent variables. The choice of the independent variables depends upon the nature of the device.

Transistors are generally modeled using the hybrid parameter model or the h-parameter model and the transistor datasheets provide the values of the h-parameters. Hence, the hybrid parameter model is described here in detail. In the case of h-parameter model, input current (I_i) and output voltage (V_o) are taken as independent variables. The other two variables, namely, the input voltage (V_i) and the output current (I_o) are related to these variables by the following equations:

$$V_i = h_{11}I_i + h_{12}V_o \tag{8.1}$$

$$I_o = h_{21}I_i + h_{22}V_o \tag{8.2}$$

The quantities h_{11}, h_{12}, h_{21} and h_{22} are referred to as the hybrid parameters or the h-parameters. The term "hybrid" is chosen as these terms have different dimensions, that is, they are not alike dimensionally. Figure 8.3 shows the representation of the network in terms of the h-parameters. As we can see from the figure, the h-parameter model makes use of the Thevenin's voltage equivalent model at the input and the Norton's current equivalent model at the output. It may be mentioned here that V_i and I_i are the RMS voltage and current values, respectively, of the applied input signal. V_o and I_o are the RMS voltage and current values of the resulting output signal.

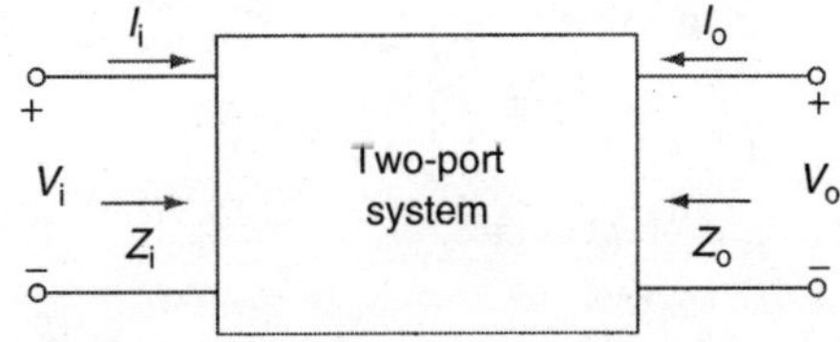

Figure 8.2 Block diagram of a two-port, four-terminal device.

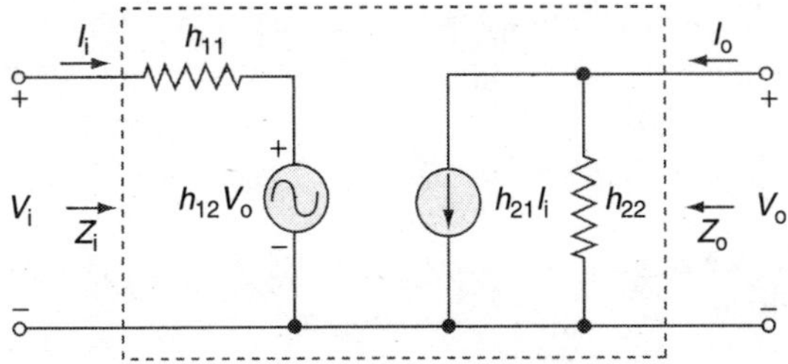

Figure 8.3 h-parameter model of a two-port network.

Determination of h-Parameters

1. **Parameter h_{11}:** In Eq. (8.1), substituting $V_o = 0$, that is, the output terminals are short circuited, we get

$$h_{11} = \left.\frac{V_i}{I_i}\right|_{V_o=0} \tag{8.3}$$

where V_i and I_i are the RMS values of input voltage and current, respectively. Using partial calculus, the value of h_{11} can be calculated as

$$h_{11} = \left.\frac{\partial v_i}{\partial i_i}\right|_{V_o=\text{const.}} = \left.\frac{\Delta v_i}{\Delta i_i}\right|_{V_o=\text{const.}} \tag{8.4}$$

Therefore, the parameter h_{11} is the ratio of the instantaneous change in the input voltage to the instantaneous change in the input current for constant value of output voltage. Hence, the parameter h_{11} has the units of impendance, that is, ohms. It is referred to as the short-circuit input impedance parameter. The subscript 11 indicates that it is dependent on the values of the input quantities. h_{11} is also represented as h_i.

2. **Parameter h_{12}:** In Eq. (8.1), if we substitute $I_i = 0$, that is, the input terminals are open circuited, then

$$h_{12} = \left.\frac{V_i}{V_o}\right|_{I_i=0} \tag{8.5}$$

Using partial calculus, the value of h_{12} can be determined as

$$h_{12} = \left.\frac{\partial v_i}{\partial v_o}\right|_{I_i=\text{const.}} = \left.\frac{\Delta v_i}{\Delta v_o}\right|_{I_i=\text{const.}} \tag{8.6}$$

Here h_{12} is the ratio of the instantaneous change in the input voltage to the instantaneous change in the output voltage for constant value of input current and is referred to as the open-circuit reverse transfer voltage ratio parameter. It is a dimensionless quantity. h_{12} is also represented as h_r.

3. **Parameter h_{21}:** If in Eq. (8.2), we substitute $V_o = 0$, that is, the output terminals are shorted, then

$$h_{21} = \left.\frac{I_o}{I_i}\right|_{V_o=0} \tag{8.7}$$

Applying partial calculus, the value of h_{21} is given by

$$h_{21} = \left.\frac{\partial i_o}{\partial i_i}\right|_{V_o=\text{const.}} = \left.\frac{\Delta i_o}{\Delta i_i}\right|_{V_o=\text{const.}} \tag{8.8}$$

Parameter h_{21} is the ratio of the change in the instantaneous value of output current to the change in the instantaneous value of the input current for constant value of output voltage. It is dimensionless parameter and is referred to as the short-circuit forward transfer current ratio parameter. h_{21} is also represented as h_f.

4. **Parameter h_{22}:** If the input terminals are open circuit, that is, $I_i = 0$, then Eq. (8.2) simplifies to

$$h_{22} = \left.\frac{I_o}{V_o}\right|_{I_i=0} \tag{8.9}$$

Applying partial calculus we get

$$h_{22} = \left.\frac{\partial i_o}{\partial v_o}\right|_{I_i=\text{const.}} = \left.\frac{\Delta i_o}{\Delta v_o}\right|_{I_i=\text{const.}} \tag{8.10}$$

Parameter h_{22} is the ratio of the change in the instantaneous value of output current to the change in the instantaneous value of the output voltage for constant value of input current. It is referred to as the open-circuit output admittance parameter and is measured in siemens. h_{22} is also represented as h_o.

8.3 Transistor Hybrid Model

The h-parameter model is widely used for bipolar junction transistors. The basic assumption here is that the variations in the Q-point are small, so that the transistor parameters can be considered constant over the complete signal excursion. It may be mentioned here that the h-parameter model is applicable to all the three transistor configurations. The values of h-parameters are more or less constant for a given transistor, although they vary slightly with change in collector current. However, they have different values for each of the three transistor configurations. In this section we discuss the h-parameter model for the three transistor configurations.

h-Parameter Model for the Common-Emitter Configuration

Figures 8.4(a) and (b) show the circuit symbol and the h-parameter equivalent model for the common-emitter configuration, respectively. As we can see from the figure, a second subscript has been added to the nomenclature of the h-parameters. This is done so as to distinguish between the h-parameters of the three transistor configurations. The parameter h_{11} is denoted as h_{ie} and is referred to as the input impedance of the transistor in the common-emitter configuration. Parameter h_{21} is denoted as h_{fe} and stands for forward current transfer ratio for the common-emitter transistor configuration; parameter h_{12} is denoted as h_{re} and is referred to as the reverse voltage transfer ratio for the common-emitter transistor configuration. Parameter h_{22} is denoted as h_{oe} and it means the output admittance for the common-emitter configuration. Note that in this case, current I_i is the base current I_b, current I_o is the collector current I_c, voltage V_i is the voltage V_{be} and voltage V_o is the voltage V_{ce}. The h-parameter equations for the common-emitter configuration are given by the following two equations:

$$V_{be} = h_{ie}I_b + h_{re}V_{ce} \tag{8.11}$$

$$I_c = h_{fe}I_b + h_{oe}V_{ce} \tag{8.12}$$

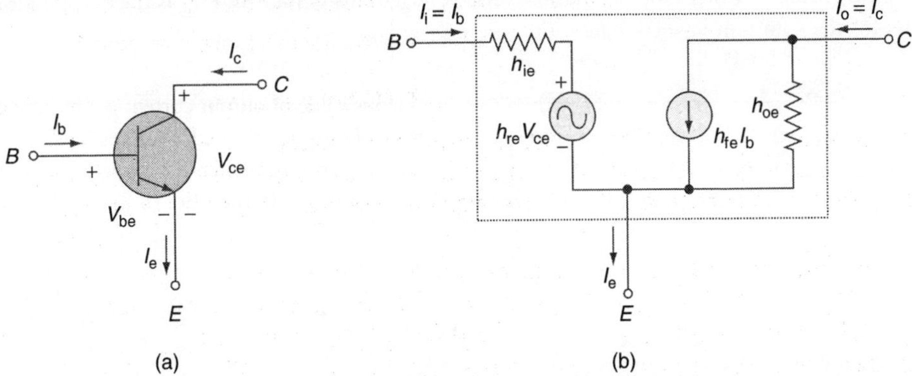

Figure 8.4 (a) Circuit symbol of common-emitter transistor configuration; (b) h-parameter model for the common-emitter transistor configuration.

The values of the parameters h_{ie}, h_{fe}, h_{re} and h_{oe} are given by the following set of equations, respectively.

$$h_{ie} = \left.\frac{\partial v_{be}}{\partial i_b}\right|_{V_{ce}=\text{const.}} = \left.\frac{\Delta v_{be}}{\Delta i_b}\right|_{V_{ce}=\text{const.}} \tag{8.13}$$

$$h_{re} = \left.\frac{\partial v_{be}}{\partial v_{ce}}\right|_{I_b=\text{const.}} = \left.\frac{\Delta v_{be}}{\Delta v_{ce}}\right|_{I_b=\text{const.}} \tag{8.14}$$

$$h_{fe} = \left.\frac{\partial i_c}{\partial i_b}\right|_{V_{ce}=\text{const.}} = \left.\frac{\Delta i_c}{\Delta i_b}\right|_{V_{ce}=\text{const.}} \tag{8.15}$$

$$h_{oe} = \left.\frac{\partial i_c}{\partial v_{ce}}\right|_{I_b=\text{const.}} = \left.\frac{\Delta i_c}{\Delta v_{ce}}\right|_{I_b=\text{const.}} \tag{8.16}$$

The symbol Δ refers to a small variation around the quiescent point of operation, that is, the h-parameters are determined in the region of operation for the applied signal. The effect of the parameter h_{re} is so small on the transistor amplifier that it can be neglected. Figure 8.5 shows the simplified h-parameter model for the common-emitter transistor configuration. Here, h_{re} is assumed to be zero, therefore the magnitude of the voltage source $h_{re}V_{ce}$ is also equal to zero. In other words, it results in short-circuit equivalent for the feedback element. In cases where the value of $1/h_{oe}$ is very large as compared to the value of load resistance, it is assumed to be open in comparison with the parallel load to be connected across the output terminals.

Figures 8.6(a), (b) and (c) respectively show the circuit symbol, complete h-parameter model and simplified h-parameter model of the common-collector configuration. The parameter h_{ic} is referred to as the input impedance of the transistor in the common-collector configuration. Parameter h_{fc} stands for forward current transfer ratio for the common-collector configuration and parameter h_{rc} is referred to as the reverse voltage transfer ratio for the common-collector configuration. Parameter h_{oc} is the output admittance in the common-collector configuration. The h-parameters for the common-collector configuration can be determined in a similar fashion as that for the common-emitter configuration.

Figures 8.7(a), (b) and (c) respectively show the circuit symbol, complete h-parameter model and the simplified h-parameter model for the common-base configuration. h_{ib} is the input impedance parameter, h_{fb} is the forward current transfer ratio, h_{rb} is the reverse voltage transfer ratio and h_{ob} is the output admittance parameter for the common-base configuration.

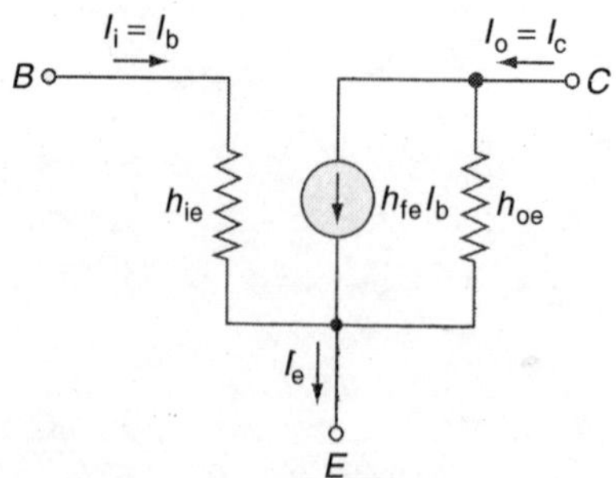

Figure 8.5 | Simplified h-parameter model for the common-emitter transistor configuration.

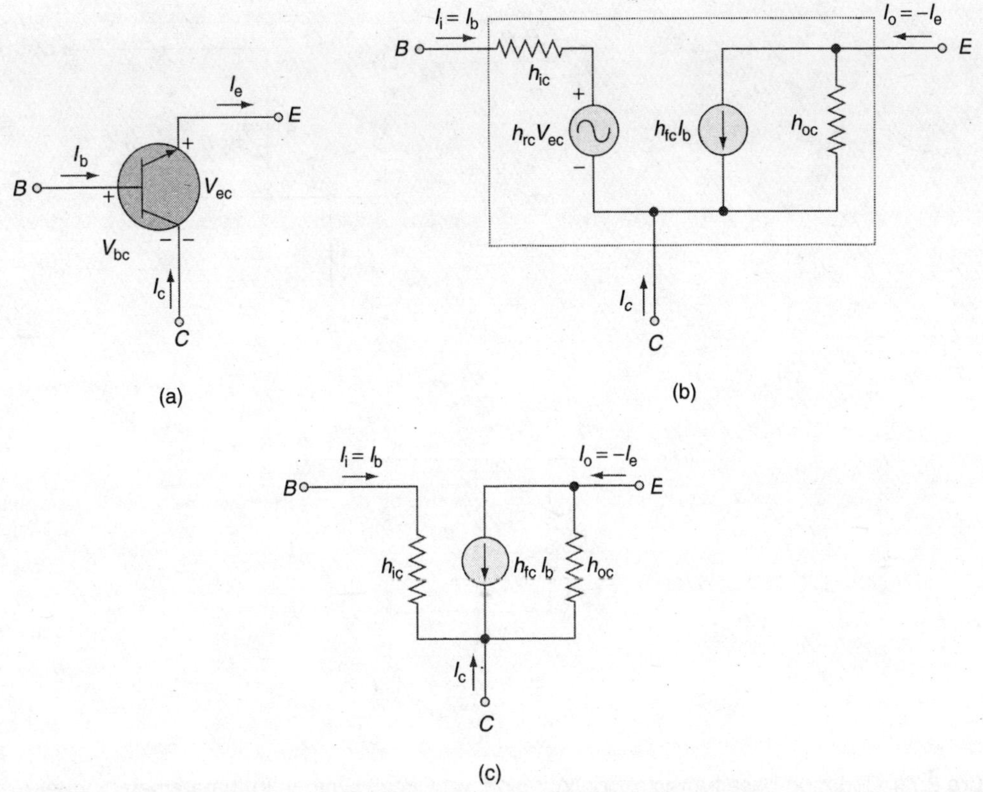

Figure 8.6 Common-collector transistor configuration: (a) Circuit symbol; (b) h-parameter model; (c) simplified h-parameter model.

Relationships between h-Parameters of Different Transistor Configurations

While designing a transistor-based amplifier, it may be necessary to convert from one set of transistor's h-parameters of a given configuration to another for the other configurations. Table 8.1 gives the approximate conversion formulae for the h-parameters. Derivation of the formulae is beyond the scope of the book.

Table 8.1 Approximate conversion formulae for the h-parameters

$h_{ic} = h_{ie}$	$h_{rc} = 1$	$h_{fc} = -(1 + h_{fe})$	$h_{oc} = h_{oe}$
$h_{ib} = \dfrac{h_{ie}}{1 + h_{fe}}$	$h_{rb} = \dfrac{h_{ie}h_{oe}}{1 + h_{fe}} - h_{re}$	$h_{fb} = -\dfrac{h_{fe}}{1 + h_{fe}}$	$h_{ob} = \dfrac{h_{oe}}{1 + h_{fe}}$
$h_{ie} = \dfrac{h_{ib}}{1 + h_{fb}}$	$h_{re} = \dfrac{h_{ib}h_{ob}}{1 + h_{fb}} - h_{rb}$	$h_{fe} = -\dfrac{h_{fb}}{1 + h_{fb}}$	$h_{oe} = \dfrac{h_{ob}}{1 + h_{fb}}$
$h_{ic} = \dfrac{h_{ib}}{1 + h_{fb}}$	$h_{rc} = 1$	$h_{fc} = -\dfrac{1}{1 + h_{fb}}$	$h_{oc} = \dfrac{h_{ob}}{1 + h_{fb}}$

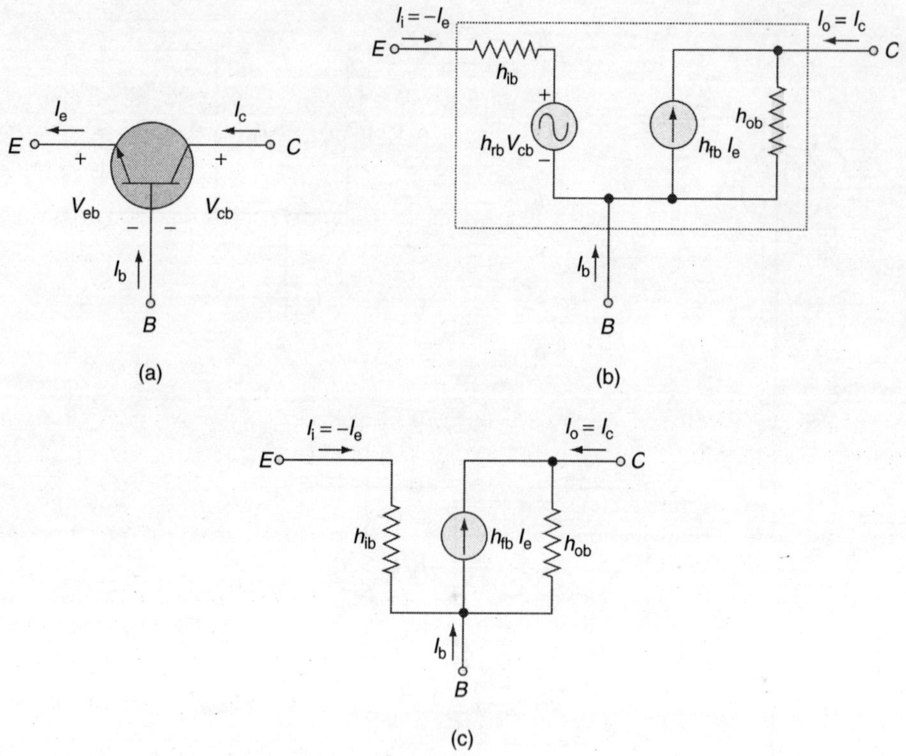

Figure 8.7 Common-base transistor configuration: (a) Circuit symbol; (b) h-parameter model; (c) simplified h-parameter model.

EXAMPLE 8.1 *Given that the hybrid parameters for the transistor are h_{ie} = 1.5 kΩ, h_{fe} = 150, $h_{re} = 1 \times 10^{-4}$ and h_{oe} = 20 μmhos. Draw the hybrid equivalent circuit of the transistor in all the three configurations.*

Solution

1. Figure 8.8(a) shows the hybrid equivalent circuit for the transistor in the common-emitter configuration.
2. The values of hybrid parameters in the common-collector configuration are
$$h_{ic} = h_{ie},\ h_{rc} = 1,\ h_{fc} = -(1 + h_{fe}) \text{ and } h_{oc} = h_{oe}$$
3. Therefore, h_{ic} = 1.5 kΩ, h_{rc} = 1, h_{fc} = −151 and h_{oc} = 20 μmhos.
4. Figure 8.8(b) shows the hybrid equivalent circuit of the transistor in the common-collector configuration.
5. The values of hybrid parameters in the common-base configuration are
$$h_{ib} = \frac{h_{ie}}{1 + h_{fe}}$$
$$= (1.5 \times 10^3)/151 = 9.93\ \Omega$$

$$h_{rb} = \frac{h_{ie}h_{oe}}{1+h_{fe}} - h_{re}$$
$$= [(1.5\times10^{3}\times20\times10^{-6})/151] - 1\times10^{-4} = 0.99\times10^{-4}$$

$$h_{fb} = -\frac{h_{fe}}{1+h_{fe}}$$
$$= -150/151 = -0.99$$

$$h_{ob} = \frac{h_{oe}}{1+h_{fe}}$$
$$= (20\times10^{-6})/151 = 0.13\ \times10^{-6}$$

6. Figure 8.8(c) shows the hybrid equivalent of the transistor in the common-base configuration.

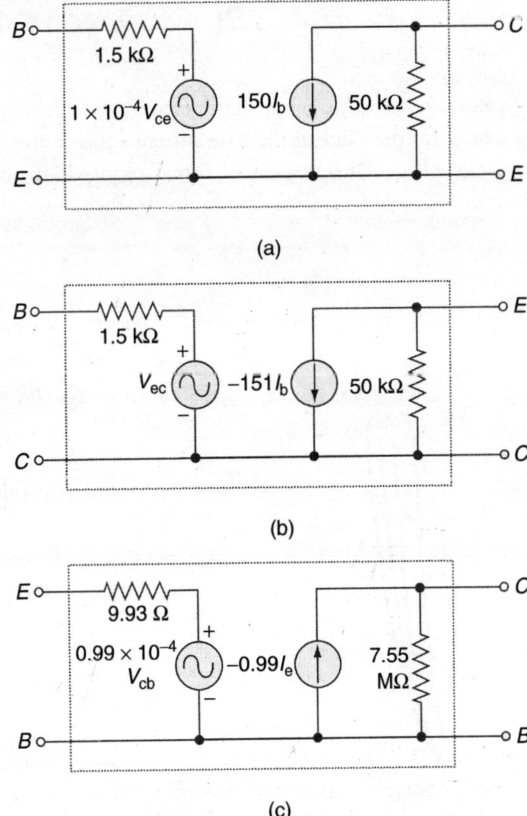

Figure 8.8 | Solution to Example 8.1.

Graphical Determination of h-Parameters

The values of the h-parameters can be determined graphically by making use of the transistor's input and output characteristics. The parameters h_i and h_r are determined from the input characteristic curves of the transistor whereas the parameters h_f and h_o are determined from the output characteristic curves. In this section we describe the procedure for determining the h-parameters graphically for common-emitter transistor configuration. The procedure for determining the h-parameters of the common-base and common-collector configurations is similar to that for the common-emitter configuration.

The first step in determining the h-parameters is to determine the Q-point or the operating point. Figure 8.9 shows the typical input characteristic curve for a transistor in the common-emitter configuration. As we can see from the characteristic curve, the values of the emitter–base voltage, collector–emitter voltage and the base current at the Q-point are given by V_{BEQ}, V_{CEQ} and I_{BQ}, respectively. The parameter h_{ie} is determined by drawing a line tangent to the input characteristic curve corresponding to V_{CEQ} at the Q-point. The value of the parameter h_{ie} is given by the slope of this line. In other words, h_{ie} is the ratio of small change in the value of emitter–base voltage to the small change in the value of base current around the operating point as shown in the figure. Therefore, the value of h_{ie} is given by

$$h_{ie} = \left.\frac{V_{BE2} - V_{BE1}}{I_{B2} - I_{B1}}\right|_{V_{CE} = V_{CEQ}} = \left.\frac{\Delta v_{be}}{\Delta i_b}\right|_{V_{CE} = V_{CEQ}} \tag{8.17}$$

The parameter h_{re} is also determined using the input characteristic curve (Figure 8.10). A horizontal line is drawn at I_B equal to I_{BQ}, that is, for the value of the base current equal to the quiescent value of the base current. The change in emitter–base voltage is determined for a small change in the value of collector–emitter voltage around the operating point. The value of h_{re} is then determined by the ratio of the change in the value of emitter–base

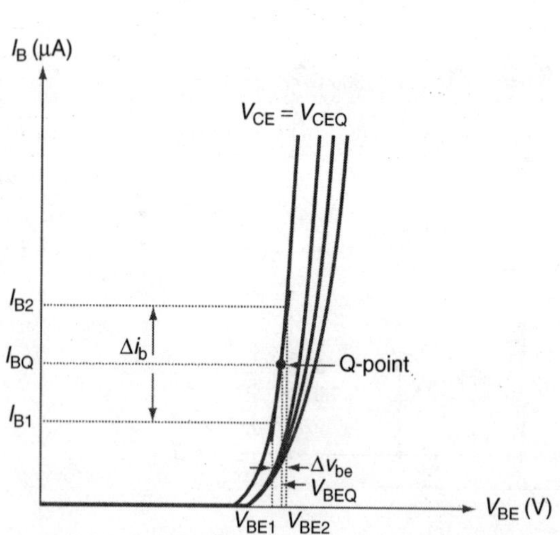

Figure 8.9 Determination of h-parameter h_{ie}.

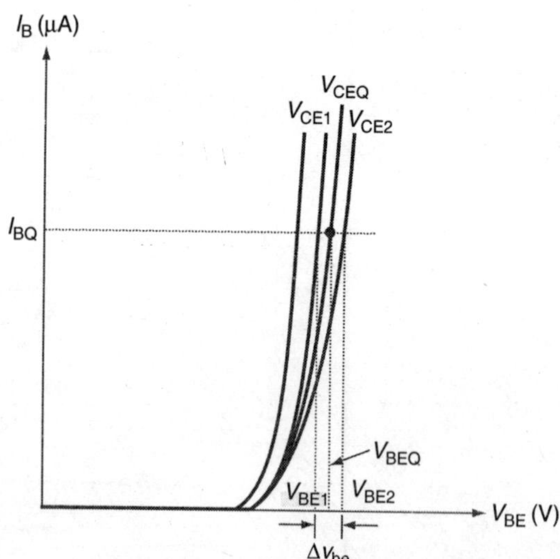

Figure 8.10 Determination of h-parameter h_{re}.

voltage to the change in the value of collector–emitter voltage for a constant value of base current. The value of h_{re} is given by

$$h_{re} = \left.\frac{V_{BE2} - V_{BE1}}{V_{CE2} - V_{CE1}}\right|_{I_B = I_{BQ}} = \left.\frac{\Delta v_{be}}{\Delta v_{ce}}\right|_{I_B = I_{BQ}} \tag{8.18}$$

The other two parameters, that is, h_{fe} and h_{oe} are determined from the output characteristics. The value of parameter h_{fe} is determined by drawing a vertical line corresponding to the quiescent value of collector–emitter voltage (V_{CEQ}). The value of h_{fe} is then determined by taking a small change in the base current and then determining the corresponding change in the collector current. h_{fe} is the ratio of the change in the collector current to the change in the base current (Figure 8.11). It may be mentioned here that the accuracy of the results improves for small values of the changes. The value of h_{fe} is given by

$$h_{fe} = \left.\frac{I_{C2} - I_{C1}}{I_{B2} - I_{B1}}\right|_{V_{CE} = V_{CEQ}} = \left.\frac{\Delta i_c}{\Delta i_b}\right|_{V_{CE} = V_{CEQ}} \tag{8.19}$$

The value of the parameter h_{oe} is determined by drawing a tangent to the output curve corresponding to base current equal to the quiescent base current. The value of the h_{oe} parameter is then determined by taking the ratio of the change in the collector current corresponding to a small change in the collector–emitter voltage (Figure 8.12). The value of h_{oe} is given by

$$h_{oe} = \left.\frac{I_{C2} - I_{C1}}{V_{CE2} - V_{CE1}}\right|_{I_B = I_{BQ}} = \left.\frac{\Delta i_c}{\Delta v_{ce}}\right|_{I_B = I_{BQ}} \tag{8.20}$$

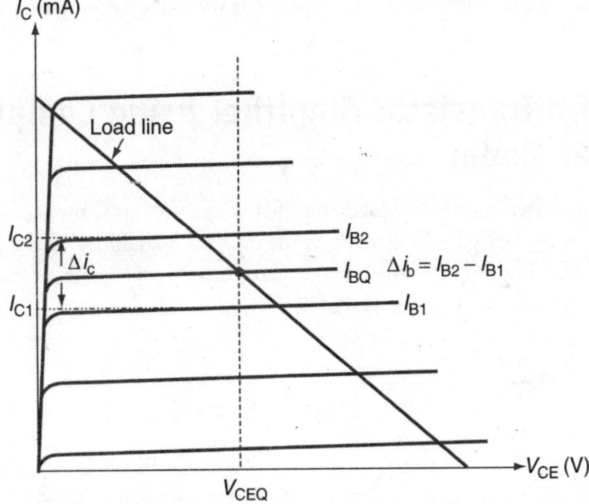

Figure 8.11 Determination of h-parameter h_{fe}.

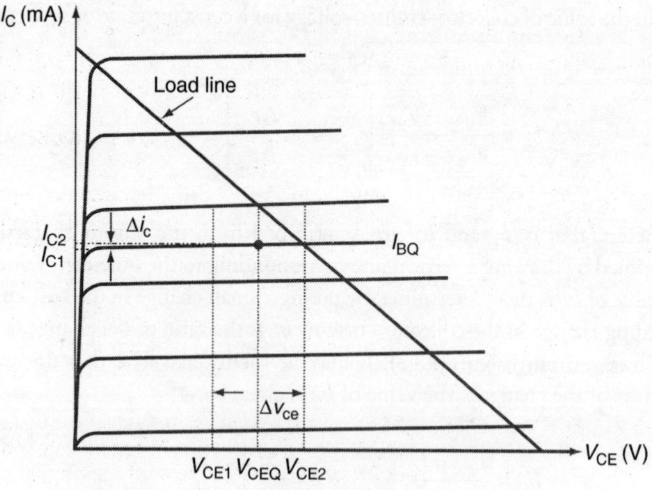

Figure 8.12 Determination of h-parameter h_{oe}.

Table 8.2 Typical h-parameter values for silicon transistor

Parameter	Common-emitter	Common-collector	Common-base
h_i	1–6.5 kΩ	1–6.5 kΩ	20–30 Ω
h_r	$(1.5 \times 10^{-4}) - (2.5 \times 10^{-4})$	1	$(0.1 \times 10^{-4}) - (3 \times 10^{-4})$
h_f	50–250	(−50) – (−250)	−1
h_o	5–25 µmhos	5–25 µmhos	0.02–0.5 µmhos

Typical h-parameter values of the NPN silicon transistor for the three amplifier configurations are given in Table 8.2.

8.4 Analysis of a Transistor Amplifier using Complete h-Parameter Model

Figure 8.13 shows a generalized transistor-based amplifier where the transistor is replaced by its h-parameter model. As we can see from the figure, resistor R_L is the external load and V_s is the input signal source. The important parameters of any amplifier are the current gain, input impedance, voltage gain and the output impedance. The expressions for these parameters will be derived in this section.

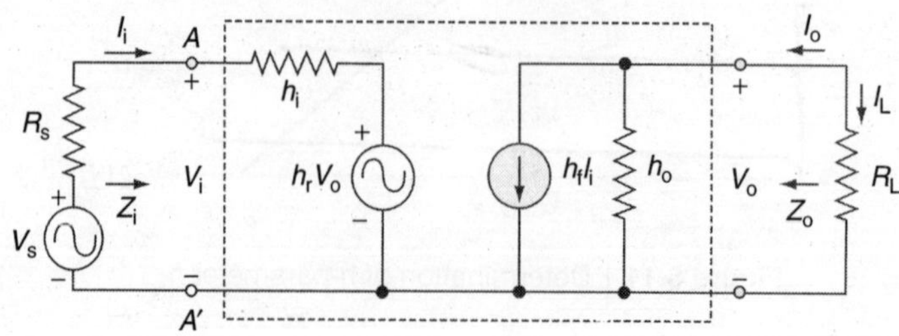

Figure 8.13 Generalized h-parameter model of a transistor-based amplifier.

1. **Current gain or the current amplification (A_i):** Current gain is defined as the ratio of the current through the load resistance (I_L) to the input current (I_i). The following equation gives the expression for the current gain:

$$A_i = \frac{I_L}{I_i} \tag{8.21}$$

As the current $I_L = -I_o$, therefore

$$A_i = -\frac{I_o}{I_i} \tag{8.22}$$

Applying Kirchhoff's current law to the output section of the circuit shown in Figure 8.13, the value of I_o is given by

$$I_o = h_f I_i + h_o V_o \tag{8.23}$$

The value of the output voltage V_o is given by

$$V_o = I_L R_L = -I_o R_L \tag{8.24}$$

Therefore, the current gain (A_i) is given by

$$A_i = -\frac{h_f}{1 + h_o R_L} \tag{8.25}$$

This is the current gain without taking the source resistor (R_s) into account. The overall current gain taking source resistor into account can be determined by replacing the voltage source with its Norton's equivalent as shown in Figure 8.14.

The overall current gain is determined using the following expression:

$$A_{is} = -\frac{I_o}{I_s} \tag{8.26}$$

The above equation can be rewritten as

$$A_{is} = -\frac{I_o}{I_i} \times \frac{I_i}{I_s} = A_i \times \frac{I_i}{I_s}$$

The value of current I_i is given by

$$I_i = I_s \times \left(\frac{R_s}{Z_i + R_s} \right) \tag{8.27}$$

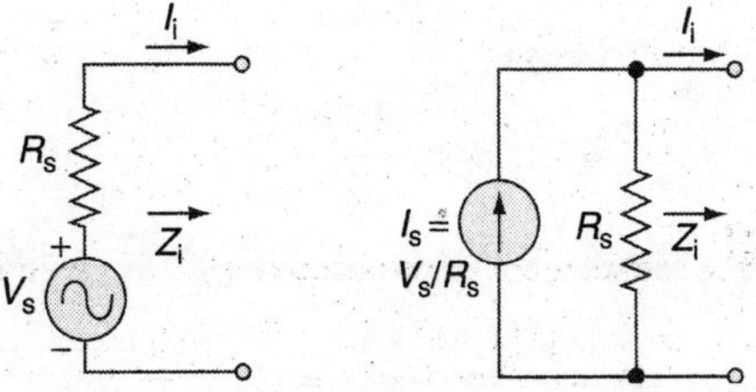

Figure 8.14 | Norton's equivalent of a voltage source.

Therefore, the overall current gain (A_{is}) is given by

$$A_{is} = A_i \times \left(\frac{R_s}{Z_i + R_s} \right) \quad (8.28)$$

From Eq. (8.28), it is clear that when $R_s \to \infty$, $A_{is} \to A_i$. Therefore, A_i is the current gain for an ideal current source.

2. **Input impedance (Z_i):** The input impedance Z_i is defined as the impedance seen looking into the input terminals A–A' of the amplifier. It is given by

$$Z_i = \frac{V_i}{I_i} \quad (8.29)$$

Applying Kirchhoff's voltage law to the input section of the amplifier we get

$$V_i = h_i I_i + h_r V_o \quad (8.30)$$

Substituting the value of V_i given by Eq. (8.30) in Eq. (8.29), we get

$$Z_i = \frac{h_i I_i + h_r V_o}{I_i} \quad (8.31)$$

The output voltage V_o is given by

$$V_o = -I_o R_L = A_i I_i R_L \quad (8.32)$$

Substituting the value of V_o in Eq. (8.31), we get

$$Z_i = \frac{h_i I_i + h_r A_i I_i R_L}{I_i} = h_i + h_r A_i R_L$$

Substituting the value of A_i given in Eq. (8.25) in the above equation we get

$$Z_i = h_i - \frac{h_r h_f R_L}{1 + h_o R_L} \quad (8.33)$$

3. **Voltage gain (A_v):** The voltage gain A_v is given by the ratio of the output voltage (V_o) to the input voltage (V_i).

$$A_v = \frac{V_o}{V_i}$$

Substituting the value of V_o given in Eq. (8.32) in the above equation, we get

$$A_v = \frac{A_i I_i R_L}{V_i} \quad (8.34)$$

Substituting the value of $V_i/I_i = Z_i$, we get

$$A_v = \frac{A_i R_L}{Z_i}$$

The voltage gain taking source resistance R_s into account (A_{vs}) is given by

$$A_{vs} = \frac{V_o}{V_s} = \frac{V_o}{V_i} \times \frac{V_i}{V_s} = A_v \times \frac{V_i}{V_s} \quad (8.35)$$

From the equivalent input circuit of the amplifier, the voltage (V_i) is expressed in terms of the signal voltage (V_s) by

$$V_i = \frac{V_s Z_i}{Z_i + R_s} \tag{8.36}$$

Therefore, the expression for A_{vs} is given by

$$A_{vs} = \frac{A_v Z_i}{Z_i + R_s} \tag{8.37}$$

When $R_s \to 0$ then $A_{vs} \to A_v$. In other words, A_v is the voltage gain for an ideal voltage source, that is, the one with zero internal resistance.

4. **Output admittance (Y_o):** The output admittance (Y_o) is defined as the reciprocal of the output impedance (Z_o). The output impedance (Z_o) is determined by setting the voltage source (V_s) to zero and the load impedance R_L to infinity and by driving the output terminals from a voltage source (V_o). Z_o is then given by the ratio of the applied voltage (V_o) to output current (I_o).

$$Y_o = \left.\frac{I_o}{V_o}\right|_{V_s = 0, R_L = \infty} \tag{8.38}$$

Substituting the value of I_o from Eq. (8.23) in Eq. (8.38), we get

$$Y_o = h_f \frac{I_i}{V_o} + h_o \tag{8.39}$$

Applying Kirchhoff's voltage law to the input section of the circuit in Figure 8.13, we get

$$V_s - R_s I_i - h_i I_i - h_r V_o = 0 \tag{8.40}$$

As $V_s = 0$, therefore

$$R_s I_i + h_i I_i + h_r V_o = 0 \tag{8.41}$$

Rearranging the terms in Eq. (8.41), we get

$$\frac{I_i}{V_o} = -\frac{h_r}{h_i + R_s} \tag{8.42}$$

Substituting the value of I_i/V_o given by Eq. (8.42) in Eq. (8.39), we get

$$Y_o = h_o - \frac{h_f h_r}{h_i + R_s} \tag{8.43}$$

In this expression, it is assumed that the load R_L is external to the amplifier. If the effect of load resistor R_L is included, then the total impedance is given by the parallel combination of Z_o and R_L.

EXAMPLE 8.2 *For the circuit shown in Figure 8.15, determine the input impedance, voltage gain, current gain and output impedance. The values of the h-parameters of the transistor are $h_{ie} = 1.5\ k\Omega$, $h_{fe} = 100$, $h_{re} = 1 \times 10^{-4}$ and $h_{oe} = 25\ \mu A/V$.*

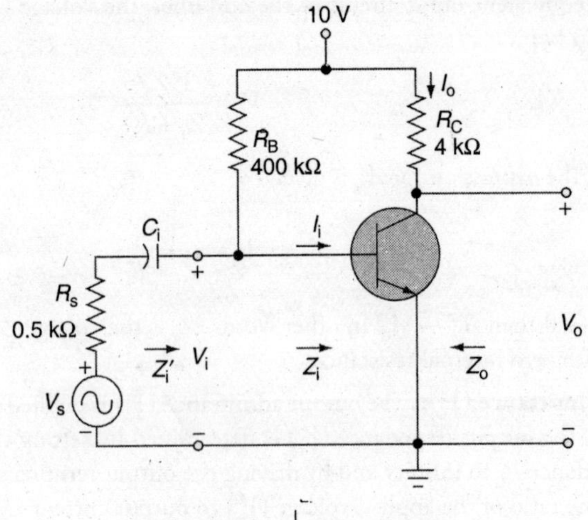

Figure 8.15 Example 8.2.

Solution 1. The complete hybrid equivalent model for the network in Figure 8.15 is shown in Figure 8.16(a). Figure 8.16(b) shows the simplified circuit of the network shown in Figure 8.16(a) with the input section being replaced by its Thevenin's equivalent circuit.

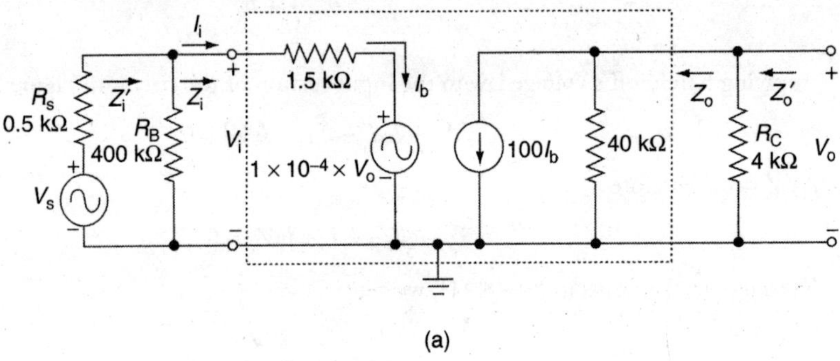

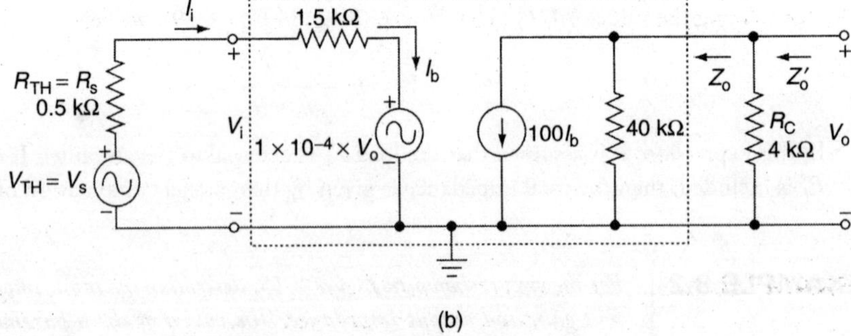

Figure 8.16 Solution to Example 8.2.

As the resistor $R_B >> R_s$, therefore the Thevenin's equivalent voltage V_{TH} is approximately equal to the source voltage V_s and the Thevenin's equivalent resistance R_{TH} is approximately equal to the resistor R_s.

2. The input impedance Z_i is equal to

$$Z_i = h_{ie} - \frac{h_{fe}h_{re}R_C}{1+h_{oe}R_C}$$

$$= 1.5\times10^3 - \frac{100\times1\times10^{-4}\times4\times10^3}{1+25\times10^{-6}\times4\times10^3}$$

$$= 1.5\times10^3 - \frac{40}{1.1}$$

$$= 1500 - 36.36 = 1.464\ \text{k}\Omega$$

3. The voltage gain A_v is equal to

$$A_v = \frac{V_o}{V_i} = \frac{-h_{fe}R_C}{h_{ie} + (h_{ie}h_{oe} - h_{fe}h_{re})R_C}$$

$$= \frac{-100\times4\times10^3}{1.5\times10^3 + (1.5\times10^3\times25\times10^{-6} - 100\times1\times10^{-4})\times4\times10^3}$$

$$= \frac{-4\times10^5}{1.5\times10^3 + 0.0275\times4\times10^3}$$

$$= \frac{-4\times10^5}{1.61\times10^3} = -248.45$$

4. The current gain A_i is equal to

$$A_i = -\frac{h_{fe}}{1+h_{oe}R_C}$$

$$= \frac{-100}{1+25\times10^{-6}\times4\times10^3}$$

$$= -90.91$$

5. The output impedance Z_o' is parallel combination of Z_o and R_C.
6. Z_o is given by

$$Z_o = \frac{1}{h_{oe} - [h_{fe}h_{re}/(h_{ie}+R_s)]}$$

$$= \frac{1}{25\times10^{-6} - [(100\times1\times10^{-4})/(1.5\times10^3+500)]}$$

$$= \frac{1}{25\times10^{-6} - 5\times10^{-6}} = 50\ \text{k}\Omega$$

7. The overall output impedance $Z_o' = 50\times10^3 \,\|\, 4\times10^3 = 3.7\times10^3 = 3.7\ \text{k}\Omega$.

8.5 Analysis of Transistor Amplifier Configurations using Simplified h-Parameter Model

The simplified h-parameter model of a transistor was discussed in the Section 8.3. In this section, we will discuss the analysis of the various transistor amplifier configurations using the simplified h-parameter model.

Common-Emitter Configuration

The analysis for the fixed-bias configuration, voltage-divider configuration, emitter-bias configuration with unbypassed emitter resistor is discussed in the following subsections.

Fixed-Bias Configuration

Figure 8.17(a) shows the circuit diagram of the fixed-bias configuration and Figure 8.17(b) shows the simplified h-parameter equivalent model.

The input impedance Z_i is given by a parallel combination of resistor R_B and transistor's h_{ie} parameter:

$$Z_i = R_B \| h_{ie} \tag{8.44}$$

The output impedance (Z_o) is given by the parallel combination of resistor R_C and the inverse of the output admittance h-parameter h_{oe}:

$$Z_o = R_C \| (1/h_{oe}) \tag{8.45}$$

The voltage gain A_v is given by

$$A_v = \frac{V_o}{V_i} \tag{8.46}$$

The magnitude of the output voltage V_o is given by

$$V_o = -I_o Z_o = -I_c Z_o \tag{8.47}$$

The collector current (I_c) is given by

$$I_c = h_{fe} I_b \tag{8.48}$$

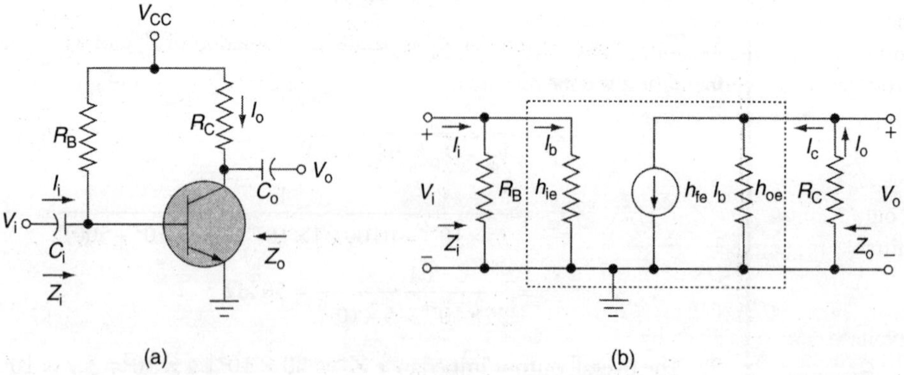

Figure 8.17 (a) Circuit diagram of fixed-bias configuration; (b) simplified h-parameter equivalent model.

The base current (I_b) in turn is expressed in terms of the input voltage V_i as

$$I_b = \frac{V_i}{h_{ie}} \tag{8.49}$$

Substituting the value of I_c given by Eq. (8.48) and value of I_b given by Eq. (8.49) in Eq. (8.47), we get

$$V_o = -h_{fe} \times \frac{V_i}{h_{ie}} \times Z_o \tag{8.50}$$

Substituting this value of V_o in the Eq. (8.46), the voltage gain is given by

$$A_v = \frac{-h_{fe} \times (V_i/h_{ie}) \times Z_o}{V_i} = \frac{-h_{fe} \times Z_o}{h_{ie}} = \frac{-h_{fe} \times [R_C \| (1/h_{oe})]}{h_{ie}} \tag{8.51}$$

The current gain A_i is given by

$$A_i = \frac{I_o}{I_i} \tag{8.52}$$

The magnitude of I_o is given by

$$I_o = I_c = h_{fe} I_b \tag{8.53}$$

Base current I_b is expressed in terms of the input current I_i as

$$I_b = \frac{R_B}{R_B + h_{ie}} \times I_i \tag{8.54}$$

Therefore, the current gain A_i is given by

$$A_i = \frac{h_{fe} I_b}{I_i} = \frac{h_{fe}}{I_i} \times \frac{R_B}{R_B + h_{ie}} \times I_i = \frac{h_{fe} \times R_B}{R_B + h_{ie}} \tag{8.55}$$

Assuming $R_B >> h_{ie}$, $A_i \cong h_{fe}$.

Voltage-Divider Configuration

Figure 8.18(a) shows the voltage-divider configuration and Figure 8.18(b) shows its h-parameter equivalent model. As we can see from the figure, the equivalent circuit is the same as in the case of fixed-bias circuit with the difference that the resistor R_B is replaced by parallel combination of resistors R_{B1} and R_{B2}. The analysis for the voltage-divider configuration is done on similar lines as that for the fixed-bias configuration.

Input impedance Z_i is given by

$$Z_i = (R_{B1} \| R_{B2}) \| h_{ie} \tag{8.56}$$

The output impedance Z_o is given by the parallel combination of resistor R_C and the inverse of the output admittance h-parameter h_{oe}:

$$Z_o = R_C \| (1/h_{oe}) \tag{8.57}$$

The voltage gain A_v is given by

$$A_v = \frac{-h_{fe} \times [R_C \| (1/h_{oe})]}{h_{ie}} \tag{8.58}$$

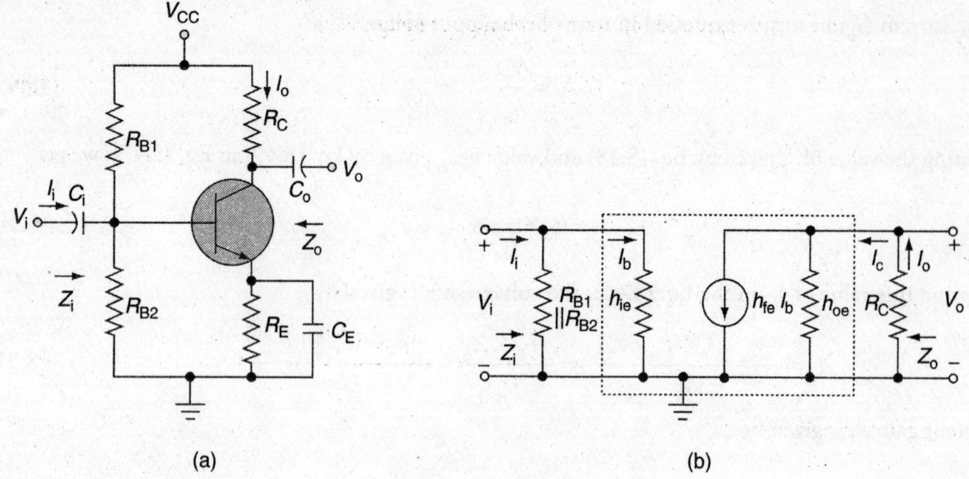

Figure 8.18 (a) Circuit diagram of voltage-divider configuration; (b) simplified h-parameter model.

The current gain A_i is given by

$$A_i = \frac{h_{fe} \times (R_{B1} \| R_{B2})}{(R_{B1} \| R_{B2}) + h_{ie}} \tag{8.59}$$

Emitter-Bias Configuration with Unbypassed Emitter Resistor

Figure 8.19(a) shows the circuit diagram of the emitter-bias configuration with unbypassed emitter resistor and Figure 8.19(b) shows its h-parameter model representation.

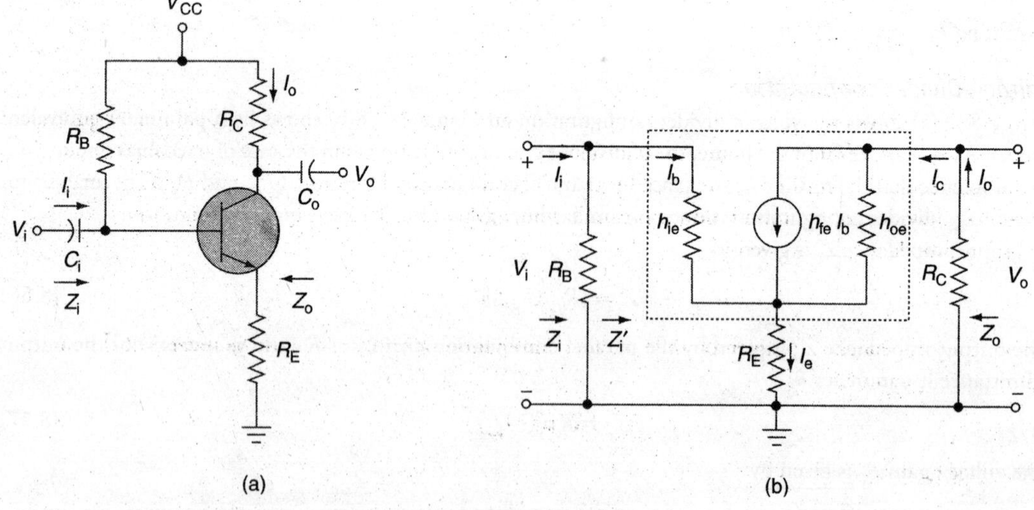

Figure 8.19 (a) Circuit diagram of emitter-bias configuration with unbypassed emitter capacitor; (b) simplified h-parameter model.

Applying Kirchhoff's voltage law to the input section we get

$$V_i = I_b h_{ie} + I_e R_E = I_b h_{ie} + (h_{fe}+1) I_b R_E = [h_{ie} + (h_{fe}+1) R_E] I_b$$

The input impedance looking into the network to the right of resistor R_B is given by

$$Z_i' = \frac{V_i}{I_b} = h_{ie} + (h_{fe}+1) R_E \tag{8.60}$$

The overall input impedance Z_i is given by parallel combination of resistor R_B and impedance Z_i':

$$Z_i = R_B \| Z_i' \tag{8.61}$$

The voltage gain A_v is given by

$$A_v = \frac{V_o}{V_i} \tag{8.62}$$

The output voltage V_o is given by

$$V_o = -I_o R_C = -I_c R_C = -h_{fe} I_b R_C \tag{8.63}$$

The base current I_b is given by

$$I_b = \frac{V_i}{Z_i'} \tag{8.64}$$

Therefore, the magnitude of voltage gain A_v is given by

$$A_v = -\frac{h_{fe} I_b R_C}{V_i} = -\frac{h_{fe} R_C}{Z_i'} = -\frac{h_{fe} R_C}{h_{ie} + (h_{fe}+1) R_E} \tag{8.65}$$

The magnitude of current gain A_i is given by

$$A_i = \frac{I_o}{I_i} \tag{8.66}$$

The output current I_o is given by

$$I_o = I_c = h_{fe} I_b \tag{8.67}$$

The base current I_b is expressed in terms of the input current I_i as

$$I_b = \frac{R_B}{R_B + Z_i'} \times I_i \tag{8.68}$$

The value of the current gain A_i is then given by

$$A_i = \frac{h_{fe} I_b}{I_i} = \frac{h_{fe} R_B}{R_B + Z_i'} = \frac{h_{fe} R_B}{R_B + h_{ie} + (h_{fe}+1) R_E} \tag{8.69}$$

Emitter–Follower Configuration

Figure 8.20(a) shows the emitter–follower configuration and Figure 8.20(b) shows its h-parameter equivalent model.

The input impedance is determined in a similar manner as that for the emitter-bias configuration with unbypassed emitter resistor. The input impedance looking into the network to the right of resistor R_B is given by

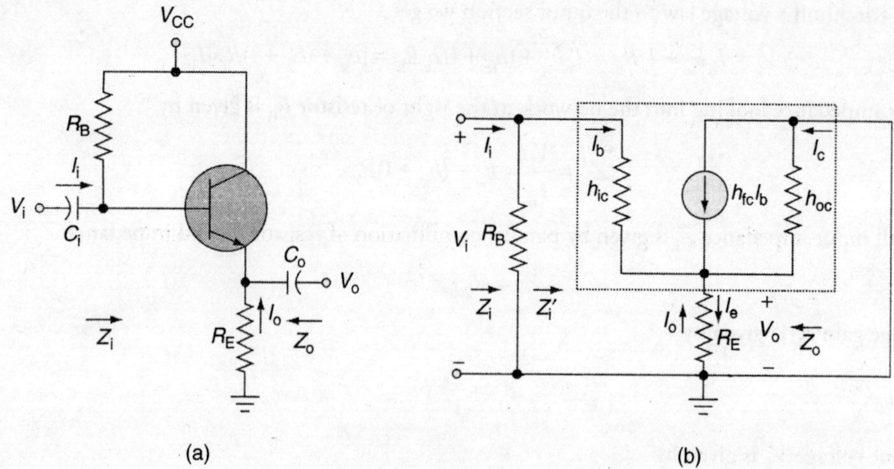

Figure 8.20 (a) Circuit diagram of emitter–follower configuration; (b) simplified h-parameter equivalent model.

$$Z_i' = \frac{V_i}{I_b} = h_{ic} - h_{fc}R_E = h_{ie} + (h_{fe} + 1)R_E \tag{8.70}$$

The overall input impedance Z_i is given by parallel combination of resistor R_B and impedance Z_i':

$$Z_i = R_B \| Z_i' \tag{8.71}$$

The output impedance Z_o can be determined as follows.

The base current I_b is given by

$$I_b = \frac{V_i}{Z_i'} \tag{8.72}$$

The emitter current I_e is then given as

$$I_e = -h_{fc}I_b = (h_{fe} + 1)I_b = (h_{fe} + 1) \times \frac{V_i}{Z_i'} \tag{8.73}$$

Substituting the value of Z_i' in the above equation we get

$$I_e = (h_{fe} + 1) \times \frac{V_i}{h_{ie} + (h_{fe} + 1)R_E} = \frac{V_i}{h_{ie}/(h_{fe} + 1) + R_E} \tag{8.74}$$

Figure 8.21 shows the network defined by Eq. (8.74).

The output impedance Z_o is defined by setting the input voltage V_i equal to zero. The output impedance Z_o is a parallel combination of resistor R_E and impedance defined by $h_{ie}/(h_{fe} + 1)$.

$$Z_o = R_E \| [h_{ie}/(h_{fe} + 1)] \tag{8.75}$$

From Figure 8.21, the output voltage V_o is expressed in terms of the input voltage V_i as

$$V_o = \frac{R_E}{R_E + h_{ie}/(h_{fe} + 1)} \times V_i \tag{8.76}$$

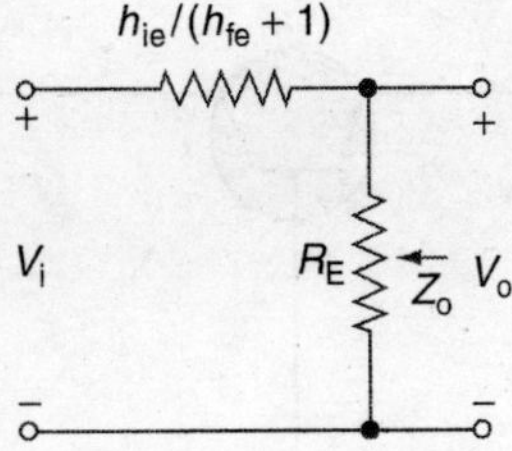

Figure 8.21 | Equivalent network.

The voltage gain A_v is then given by

$$A_v = \frac{V_o}{V_i} = \frac{R_E}{R_E + h_{ie}/(h_{fe}+1)} \tag{8.77}$$

The current gain A_i is given by

$$A_i = \frac{I_o}{I_i}$$

The output current I_o is given by

$$I_o = -I_e = h_{fc}I_b = -(h_{fe}+1)I_b$$

From Figure 8.20(b), the base current I_b is given by

$$I_b = \frac{R_B}{R_B + Z_i'} \times I_i \tag{8.78}$$

Therefore, A_i is given by

$$A_i = \frac{-(h_{fe}+1)I_b}{I_i} = \frac{-(h_{fe}+1)R_B}{R_B + Z_i'} \tag{8.79}$$

Common-Base Configuration

Figure 8.22(a) shows the circuit diagram of common-base configuration and Figure 8.22(b) shows its simplified h-parameter equivalent model.

Input impedance Z_i is given by parallel combination of resistor R_E and parameter h_{ib}:

$$Z_i = R_E \| h_{ib} = R_E \| [h_{ie}/(h_{fe}+1)] \tag{8.80}$$

The output impedance Z_o is equal to the parallel combination of collector resistor R_C and $1/h_{ob}$:

$$Z_o = R_C \| (1/h_{ob}) \cong R_C \tag{8.81}$$

The output voltage V_o is given by

$$V_o = -I_o R_C = h_{fb} I_e R_C \tag{8.82}$$

The emitter current I_e is expressed in terms of the input voltage V_i as

$$I_e = -\frac{V_i}{h_{ib}} \tag{8.83}$$

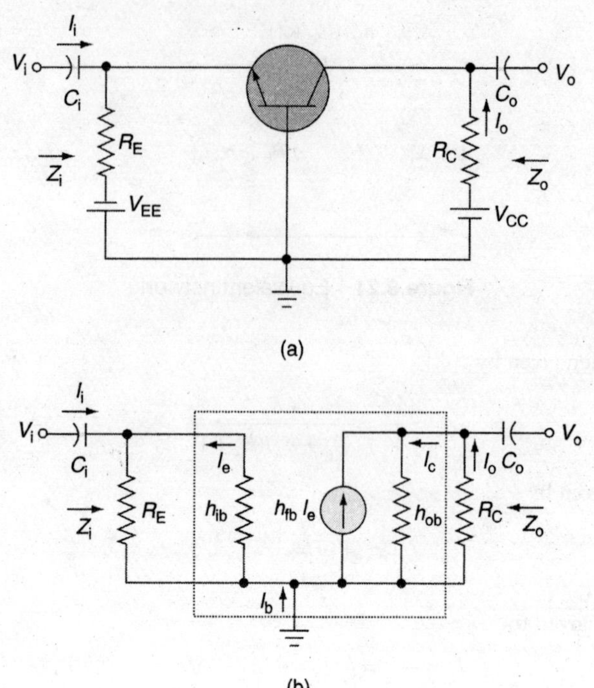

Figure 8.22 (a) Circuit diagram of common-base configuration; (b) simplified h-parameter equivalent model.

Therefore, voltage gain A_v is given by

$$A_v = \frac{V_o}{V_i} = \frac{+h_{fb} I_e R_C}{-h_{ib} I_e} = -\frac{h_{fb} R_C}{h_{ib}} = \frac{h_{fe} R_C}{h_{ie}} \tag{8.84}$$

The current gain A_i is given by

$$A_i = \frac{I_o}{I_i} = \frac{-h_{fb} I_e}{I_i} \tag{8.85}$$

The emitter current I_e is expressed in terms of the input current I_i by

$$I_e = \frac{-R_E}{R_E + h_{ib}} \times I_i \tag{8.86}$$

Therefore, current gain is given by

$$A_i = \frac{h_{fb} R_E}{R_E + h_{ib}} = \frac{h_{fb} R_E}{R_E + h_{ie}/(1+h_{fe})} \cong h_{fb} \tag{8.87}$$

EXAMPLE 8.3 *Determine the following parameters for the amplifier shown in Figure 8.23. Given that the h-parameters of the transistor are h_{ie} = 1 kΩ, h_{fe} = 100, $h_{oe} = 40 \times 10^{-6}$ mhos.*
(a) Z_i; (b) Z_o; (c) A_v; (d) A_i

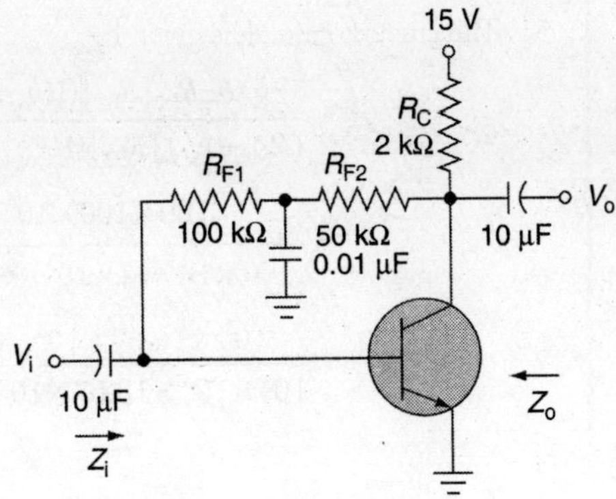

Figure 8.23 | Example 8.3.

Solution 1. The AC equivalent circuit for the amplifier in Figure 8.23 is shown in Figure 8.24.

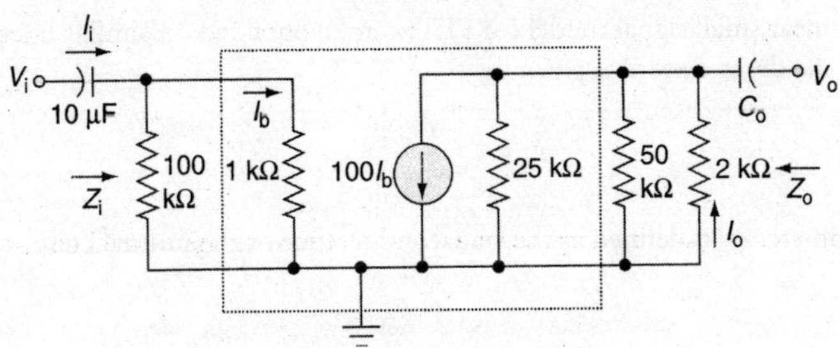

Figure 8.24 | Solution to Example 8.3.

2. Input impedance

$$Z_i = R_{F1} \| h_{ie}$$

$$= 100 \times 10^3 \| 1 \times 10^3$$

$$= 0.99 \text{ k}\Omega$$

3. Output impedance (Z_o) is given by

$$Z_o = R_{F2} \| R_C \| (1/h_{oe})$$

$$= 50 \times 10^3 \| 2 \times 10^3 \| 25 \times 10^3$$

$$= 1.79 \times 10^3 \ \Omega$$

$$= 1.79 \text{ k}\Omega$$

4. Voltage gain A_v is given by

$$A_v = \frac{-h_{fe} \times [R_{F2} \| R_C \| (1/h_{oe})]}{h_{ie}}$$

$$= \frac{-100 \times 1.79 \times 10^3}{1 \times 10^3}$$

$$= -179$$

5. The current gain A_i is given by

$$A_i = \frac{h_{fe} R_{F1} [R_{F2} \| (1/h_{oe})]}{(R_{F1} + h_{ie}) [R_{F2} \| (1/h_{oe}) + R_C]}$$

$$= \frac{100 \times 100 \times 10^3 \times (50 \times 10^3 \| 25 \times 10^3)}{(100 \times 10^3 + 1 \times 10^3) \times (50 \times 10^3 \| 25 \times 10^3 + 2 \times 10^3)}$$

$$= \frac{10^7 \times 16.67 \times 10^3}{101 \times 10^3 \times 18.67 \times 10^3} = 88.4$$

8.6 Small Signal Analysis of FET Amplifiers

The linear small signal model for FETs can be obtained on similar lines as that for BJTs. The expression for the drain current is given by

$$I_d = V_{gs} \left. \frac{\partial i_d}{\partial v_{gs}} \right|_{V_{DS} = \text{const.}} + V_{ds} \left. \frac{\partial i_d}{\partial v_{ds}} \right|_{V_{GS} = \text{const.}} \tag{8.88}$$

The parameter g_m is defined as the transconductance or the mutual conductance and is given by

$$g_m = \left. \frac{\partial i_d}{\partial v_{gs}} \right|_{V_{DS} = \text{const.}} \tag{8.89}$$

It is also designated as y_{fs} or g_{fs} and is also referred to as forward transadmittance. The second important parameter used to define the operation of FETs is the drain resistance designated as r_d. It is defined by Eq. (8.90). The reciprocal of drain resistance r_d is referred to as the drain conductance (designated as g_d). It is also known as output conductance and is also denoted as y_{os}.

$$r_d = \left. \frac{\partial v_{ds}}{\partial i_d} \right|_{V_{GS} = \text{const.}} \tag{8.90}$$

Substituting the values of g_m given by Eq. (8.89) and r_d given by Eq. (8.90) in Eq. (8.88) we get

$$I_d = g_m V_{gs} + \frac{1}{r_d} V_{ds} \tag{8.91}$$

The amplification factor m of an FET is defined as

$$\mu = \left. \frac{\partial v_{ds}}{\partial v_{gs}} \right|_{I_D = \text{const.}} \tag{8.92}$$

The parameters g_m, r_d and m are related by the following equation:

$$\mu = r_d g_m \tag{8.93}$$

The low-frequency model of an FET is defined by Eq. (8.91) and is shown in Figure 8.25. As we can see from the figure, it has a Norton's equivalent output circuit with a voltage-dependent current source whose current output is proportional to the gate-source voltage (V_{gs}). Also, the input impedance between the gate and the source

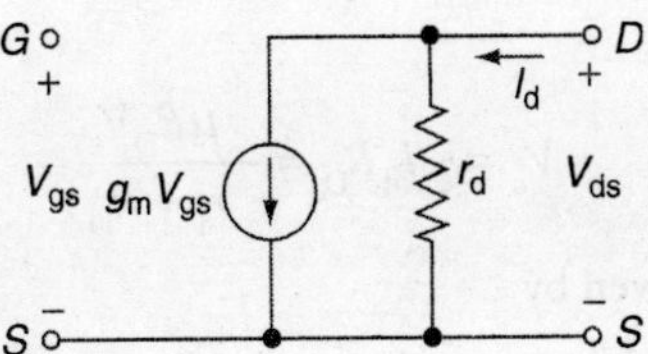

Figure 8.25 Low-frequency model of an FET.

terminals is infinite because it is assumed that there is no current flowing through the reverse-biased gate terminal. The above equations and the model in Figure 8.25 are applicable for both JFETs as well as MOSFETs.

When we compare this model of the FET with that of the BJT, we find that there a few major differences. First, the value of the current generated by the output current source in the case of an FET depends on the input voltage whereas in the case of a BJT it depends upon the input current. Second, in the case of an FET, there is no feedback from the output to the input whereas in the case of a BJT there is feedback between the output and the input sections through parameter h_{re}. Lastly, the input impedance of an FET is much larger than that of a BJT. In nutshell, FET is more closer to being an ideal amplifier than a BJT at low frequencies.

Common-Source FET Amplifier

The common-source FET amplifier is shown in Figure 8.26(a). Replacing the FET by its low-frequency small signal model, the equivalent circuit of Figure 8.26(b) is obtained.

Applying Kirchhoff's voltage law to the output section we get

$$I_d R_D + (I_d - g_m V_{gs}) r_d = 0 \tag{8.94}$$

The voltage between the gate and the source terminals (V_{gs}) is equal to the input voltage V_i. Rearranging the terms in Eq. (8.94) and substituting $V_{gs} = V_i$, we get

$$I_d = \frac{g_m r_d V_i}{r_d + R_D} = \frac{\mu V_i}{r_d + R_D} \tag{8.95}$$

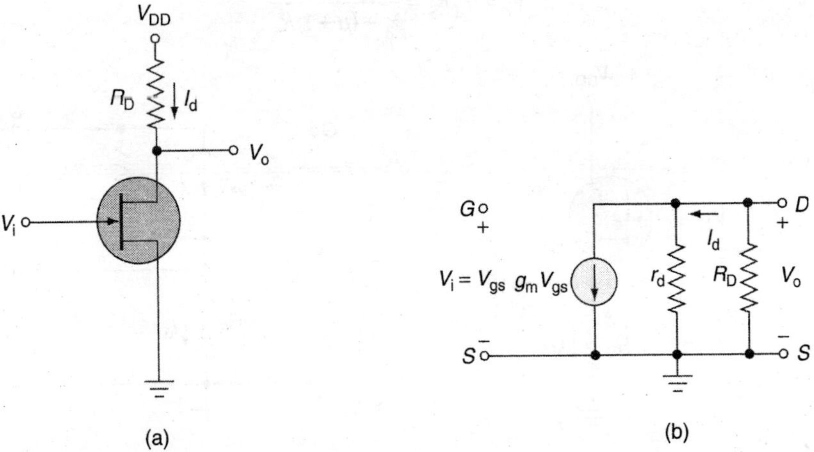

Figure 8.26 (a) Common-source FET amplifier; (b) low-frequency small signal equivalent model of the amplifier in (a).

The output voltage V_o is given by

$$V_o = -I_d R_D = -\frac{\mu R_D V_i}{r_d + R_D} \tag{8.96}$$

Therefore, the voltage gain A_v is given by

$$A_v = \frac{V_o}{V_i} = -\frac{\mu R_D}{r_d + R_D} \tag{8.97}$$

For the common-source amplifier with an unbypassed source resistor (R_S), the analysis can be carried out on similar lines and the voltage gain is given by

$$A_v = -\frac{\mu R_D}{r_d + R_D + (\mu + 1) R_S} \tag{8.98}$$

Common-Drain FET Amplifier

The common-drain FET amplifier is shown in Figure 8.27(a). Replacing the FET by its low-frequency small signal model, the equivalent circuit of Figure 8.27(b) is obtained. The analysis is carried on similar lines to that of the common-source FET amplifier.

Applying Kirchhoff's voltage law to the output section we get

$$I_d R_S + (I_d - g_m V_{gs}) r_d = 0 \tag{8.99}$$

The gate-source voltage is expressed as

$$V_{gs} = V_i - I_d R_S \tag{8.100}$$

Combining Eqs. (8.99) and (8.100) we get

$$I_d = \frac{g_m r_d V_i}{r_d + R_S + g_m r_d R_S} = \frac{\mu V_i}{r_d + (\mu + 1) R_S} \tag{8.101}$$

The output voltage V_o is given by

$$V_o = I_d R_S = \frac{\mu R_S V_i}{r_d + (\mu + 1) R_S} \tag{8.102}$$

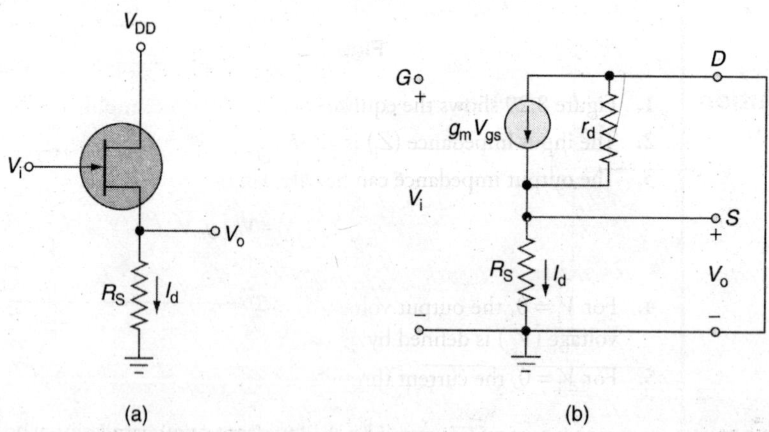

Figure 8.27 (a) Common-drain amplifier; (b) low-frequency small signal equivalent model of the amplifier in part (a).

Therefore, the voltage gain A_v is given by

$$A_v = \frac{V_o}{V_i} = \frac{\mu R_S}{r_d + (\mu+1)R_S} \tag{8.103}$$

For the common-drain amplifier with an unbypassed drain resistor (R_D), the analysis can be carried out on similar lines and the voltage gain is given by

$$A_v = \frac{\mu R_S}{r_d + R_D + (\mu+1)R_S} \tag{8.104}$$

As the value of μ is very large, therefore the term $(\mu + 1)R_S >> (r_d + R_D)$. Therefore, Eq. (8.104) can by approximated as

$$A_v \cong \frac{\mu R_S}{(\mu+1)R_S} \cong \frac{\mu}{\mu+1} \cong 1 \tag{8.105}$$

EXAMPLE 8.4 *For the self-bias JFET amplifier shown in Figure 8.28, determine the value of (a) Z_i, (b) Z_o and (c) A_v. Given that I_{DSS} = 10 mA, V_p = −5 V and r_d = 50 kΩ. The quiescent operating point is V_{GSQ} = −2.5 V and I_{DQ} = 2.5 mA.*

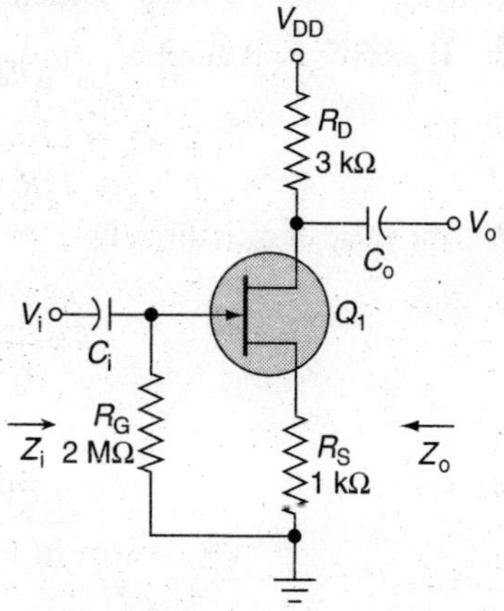

Figure 8.28 | Example 8.4.

Solution

1. Figure 8.29 shows the equivalent circuit for the amplifier in Figure 8.28.
2. The input impedance (Z_i) is given by $Z_i = R_G$. Therefore, Z_i = 2 MΩ.
3. The output impedance can be calculated as

$$Z_o = \left.\frac{V_o}{I_o}\right|_{V_i=0}$$

4. For $V_i = 0$, the output voltage V_o is defined by $V_o = -I_d R_D$ and the gate-source voltage (V_{gs}) is defined by $V_{gs} = -I_d R_S$.
5. For $V_i = 0$, the current through resistor r_d is equal to

$$I' = \frac{V_{rd}}{r_d} = \frac{V_o + V_{gs}}{r_d} = \frac{-I_d(R_D + R_S)}{r_d}$$

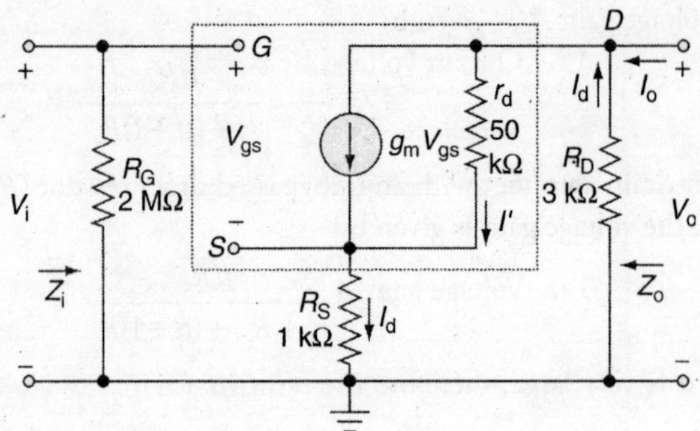

Figure 8.29 Solution to Example 8.4.

6. Applying KCL at the drain node (*D*), $I_d + I_o = I' + g_m V_{gs}$.
7. Therefore,

$$I_o = -I_d\left(1 + g_m R_S + \frac{R_D + R_S}{r_d}\right)$$

8. Therefore, Z_o is given by

$$Z_o = \frac{R_D}{1 + g_m R_S + [(R_D + R_S)/r_d]}$$

9. The value of g_m is given by

$$g_m = g_{mo}\left(1 - \frac{V_{GSQ}}{V_P}\right)$$

10.
$$g_{mo} = \frac{2I_{DSS}}{|V_P|} = \frac{2\times 10\times 10^{-3}}{5} = 4 \text{ mS}$$

11. Therefore, $g_m = 4 \times 10^{-3}\,[1 - (-2.5)/(-5)] = 2$ mS
12. Output impedance Z_o is given by

$$Z_o = 3\times 10^3/[1 + 2\times 10^{-3}\times 1\times 10^3 + (3\times 10^3 + 1\times 10^3)/(50\times 10^3)]$$
$$= (3\times 10^3)/(3 + 0.08) = 0.97 \text{ k}\Omega$$

13. The value of voltage gain A_v can be calculated as follows:

Applying KVL to the input section we get $V_{gs} = V_i - I_d R_S$

14. Applying KCL to the drain node (*D*) we get

$$I_d = g_m V_{gs} + \frac{V_o - V_{RS}}{r_d}$$

15. Output voltage V_o is equal to $V_o = -I_d R_D$.

16. Therefore, I_d is given by

$$I_d = \frac{g_m V_i}{1 + g_m R_S + [(R_D + R_S)/r_d]}$$

17. Voltage gain A_v is equal to

$$A_v = \frac{V_o}{V_i} = -\frac{g_m R_D}{1 + g_m R_S + [(R_D + R_S)/r_d]}$$

$$= \frac{-2 \times 10^{-3} \times 3 \times 10^3}{1 + 2 \times 10^{-3} \times 1 \times 10^3 + [(3 \times 10^3 + 1 \times 10^3)/(50 \times 10^3)]}$$

$$= -1.95$$

8.7 Cascading Amplifiers

Many times, the gain of a single-amplifier stage is not sufficient for the intended application or the input or the output impedance of the amplifier is not of the correct magnitude for the given application. In such cases, two or more amplifier stages are cascaded, that is, the output of a given stage is connected to the input of the next amplifier stage. A cascade connection of amplifiers is a series connection where the output of one stage is applied to the input of the next stage. As an example, the common-emitter amplifier is used for cascading to provide power gain, common-collector amplifier may be used as the last stage to drive a low-resistance load as it has low output resistance or it may be used as first stage of the amplifier by virtue of its high input impedance.

Figure 8.30 shows a generalized cascaded amplifier connection. The total gain is the product of the gains of the individual amplifier stages under loaded conditions. The overall gain (A_v) is therefore given by

$$A_v = A_{v1} \times A_{v2} \times A_{v3} \times \cdots \times A_{vn} \tag{8.106}$$

where A_v is the overall voltage gain; A_{v1} is the voltage gain of stage 1 with the input impedance of stage 2 acting on it; A_{v2} is the voltage gain of stage 2 with the input impedance of stage 3 acting on it and its source impedance is the output impedance of stage 1; A_{v3} is the voltage gain of stage 3 with the input impedance of stage 4 acting on it and its source impedance is the output impedance of stage 2; A_{vn} is the voltage gain of stage n with the load impedance acting on it and its source impedance is the output impedance of stage $(n-1)$.

The overall current gain is given by

$$A_i = -A_v \times \left(\frac{Z_{i1}}{R_L}\right) \tag{8.107}$$

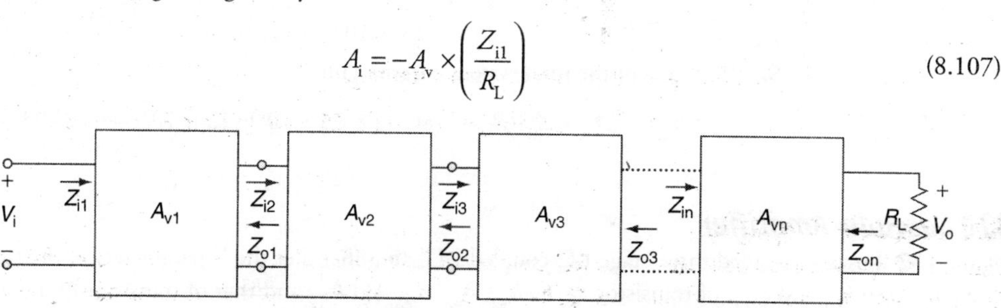

Figure 8.30 Generalized cascaded amplifier connection.

where A_i is the overall current gain; A_v is the overall voltage gain; Z_{i1} is the input impedance of the stage 1; R_L is the load resistance.

It may be mentioned here that the DC bias conditions for the cascaded amplifier stages can be determined on similar lines as that discussed in Chapter 4 for BJT amplifiers and in Chapter 5 for FET amplifiers.

EXAMPLE 8.5 *Figure 8.31 shows a two-stage CC-CB amplifier. The values of input and output impedances and the voltage gains for each stage are shown in the figure. All the values are for no-load conditions. However, the input impedance and the output impedance of the first stage are under loaded conditions. Determine*

(a) The loaded voltage gain for each stage.

(b) The overall voltage gain of the amplifier.

(c) The total system voltage and current gain.

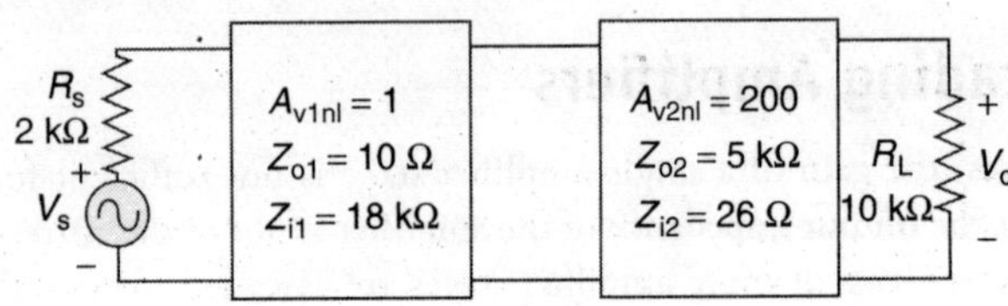

Figure 8.31 Example 8.5.

Solution

1. The loaded voltage gain of the second-stage, that is, the CB amplifier is given by

$$A_{v2} = A_{v2nl} \times [R_L/(R_L + Z_{o2})]$$
$$= 200 \times [(10 \times 10^3)/(10 \times 10^3 + 5 \times 10^3)]$$
$$= 133.33$$

2. The loaded voltage gain of the first stage, that is, the CC amplifier is given by

$$A_{v1} = A_{v1nl} \times [Z_{i2}/(Z_{i2} + Z_{o1})] = 1 \times [26/(26+10)] = 26/36 = 0.722$$

3. The overall voltage gain of the amplifier $= A_{v1} \times A_{v2} = 0.722 \times 133.33 = 96.26$.

4. The value of total system voltage gain

$$A_{vs} = A_v \times [Z_{i1}/(Z_{i1} + R_s)] = 96.26 \times [(18 \times 10^3)/(18 \times 10^3 + 2 \times 10^3)]$$
$$= -86.63$$

5. The value of the total system current gain

$$A_{is} = -(A_{vs} \times Z_{i1})/R_L = -(86.63 \times 18 \times 10^3)/(10 \times 10^3) = -155.93$$

BJT Cascade Amplifier

Figure 8.32 shows a cascaded three-stage RC-coupled BJT amplifier. Let the h-parameters of the transistor Q_1 be h_{ie1}, h_{fe1}, h_{re1} and h_{oe1}; of transistor Q_2 be h_{ie2}, h_{fe2}, h_{re2} and h_{oe2} and that of transistor Q_3 be h_{ie3}, h_{fe3}, h_{re3} and h_{oe3}.

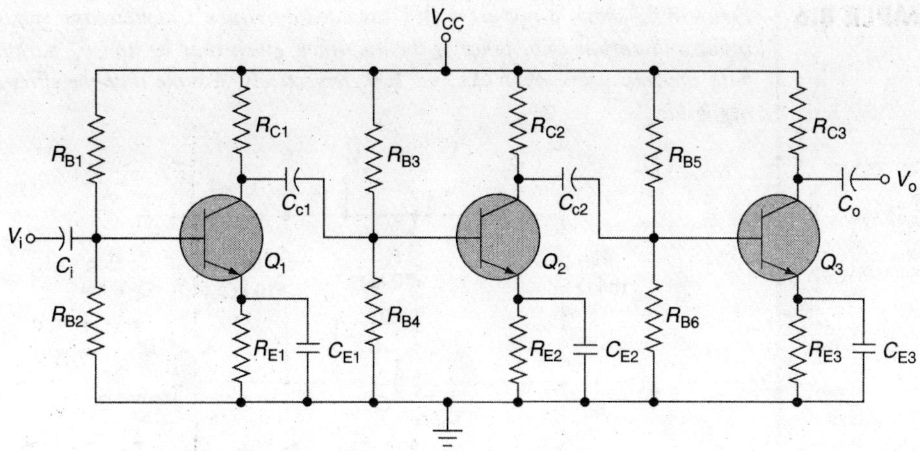

Figure 8.32 Cascaded three-stage RC-coupled BJT amplifier.

The voltage gain of the third stage is given by

$$A_{v3} = \frac{-h_{fe3} \times [R_{C3} \| (1/h_{oe3})]}{h_{ie3}} \tag{8.108}$$

Assuming $1/h_{oe} >> R_{C3}$, the equation can be simplified as

$$A_{v3} = \frac{-h_{fe3} \times R_{C3}}{h_{ie3}} \tag{8.109}$$

Similarly, the gain for the second stage A_{v2}, assuming $1/h_{oe2} >> R_{B5} \| R_{B6} \| R_{C2} \| h_{ie3}$ is given by

$$A_{v2} = \frac{-h_{fe2} \times (R_{B5} \| R_{B6} \| R_{C2} \| h_{ie3})}{h_{ie2}} \tag{8.110}$$

The gain for the first stage A_{v1}, assuming $1/h_{oe1} >> R_{B3} \| R_{B4} \| R_{C1} \| h_{ie2}$ is given by

$$A_{v1} = \frac{-h_{fe1} \times (R_{B3} \| R_{B4} \| R_{C1} \| h_{ie2})}{h_{ie1}} \tag{8.111}$$

The overall voltage gain A_v is given by the product of the voltage gains of the three stages:

$$A_v = A_{v1} \times A_{v2} \times A_{v3} \tag{8.112}$$

The overall input impedance of the amplifier is the same as the input impedance of stage 1 and is given by

$$Z_i = R_{B1} \| R_{B2} \| h_{ie1} \tag{8.113}$$

The output impedance of the amplifier is equal to the output impedance of the last stage and is given by

$$Z_o = R_{C3} \| (1/h_{oe3}) \tag{8.114}$$

EXAMPLE 8.6 *Figure 8.33 shows a two-stage BJT cascaded amplifier. Calculate the voltage gain, input and output impedance of the amplifier, given that h_{ie} and h_{fe} parameters of both the transistors are 1 kΩ and 100, respectively. Assume that the effect of h_{oe} is negligible.*

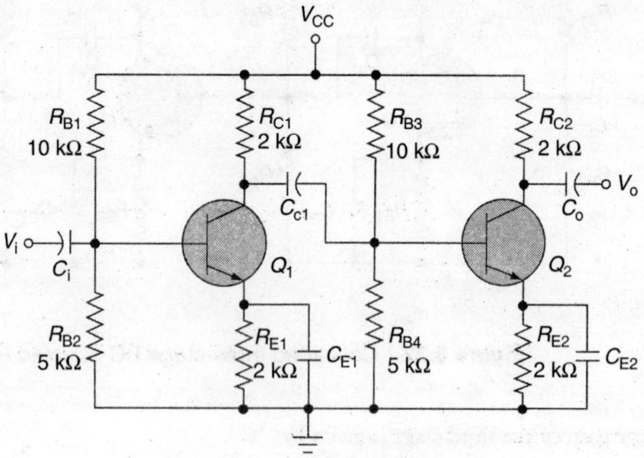

Figure 8.33 Example 8.6.

Solution

1. Voltage gain of the second stage is given by

$$A_{v2} = \frac{-h_{fe2} \times R_{C2}}{h_{ie2}}$$

$$= \frac{-100 \times 2 \times 10^3}{1 \times 10^3} = -200$$

2. Voltage gain of the first stage is given by

$$A_{v1} = \frac{-h_{fe1} \times (R_{B3} \| R_{B4} \| R_{C1} \| h_{ie2})}{h_{ie1}}$$

$$= \frac{-100 \times (10 \times 10^3 \| 5 \times 10^3 \| 2 \times 10^3 \| 1 \times 10^3)}{1 \times 10^3}$$

$$= \frac{-100 \times 555.56}{1 \times 10^3} = -55.556$$

3. Overall voltage gain is given by $A_v = A_{v1} \times A_{v2} = -200 \times -55.556 = 11111.2$.

4. The input impedance of the amplifier Z_i is given by

$$Z_i = R_{B1} \| R_{B2} \| h_{ie1}$$

$$= 10 \times 10^3 \| 5 \times 10^3 \| 1 \times 10^3 = 769.05\ \Omega$$

5. The output impedance of the amplifier is given by $Z_o = R_{C2} \| (1/h_{oe2})$. As the effect of h_{oe} is negligible, therefore $Z_o = R_{c2} = 2$ kΩ.

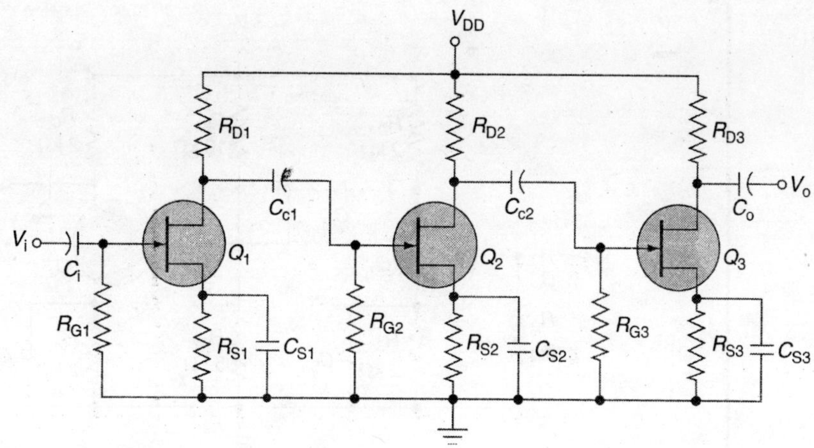

Figure 8.34 Cascaded three-stage RC-coupled JFET amplifier.

FET Cascade Amplifier

Figure 8.34 shows a cascaded three-stage RC-coupled JFET amplifier. The gains of the first, second and third stages are given respectively by the following three equations:

$$A_{v1} = -g_{m1}R_{D1} \tag{8.115}$$

$$A_{v2} = -g_{m2}R_{D2} \tag{8.116}$$

$$A_{v3} = -g_{m3}R_{D3} \tag{8.117}$$

where R_{D1}, R_{D2} and R_{D3} are the drain resistors for stage-1, stage-2 and stage-3 amplifiers respectively; g_{m1}, g_{m2} and g_{m3} are the transconductance values for the stage-1, stage-2 and stage-3 amplifiers, respectively. The overall gain A_v is given by

$$A_v = A_{v1} \times A_{v2} \times A_{v3} \tag{8.118}$$

The input impedance Z_i of the cascaded amplifier is the same as the input impedance of the stage 1:

$$Z_i = R_{G1} \tag{8.119}$$

The output impedance Z_o is given by the output impedance of the last stage:

$$Z_o = R_{D3} \tag{8.120}$$

A combination of FET and BJT stages can also be used to provide both high value of voltage gain as well as high value of input impedance.

EXAMPLE 8.7 *Figure 8.35 shows a two-stage cascaded amplifier with the first stage as a common-source JFET amplifier and the second stage as a common-emitter BJT amplifier. Calculate the voltage gain, input and output impedances of the amplifier. Given that h_{ie} and h_{fe} parameters of the transistor are 1 kΩ and 100, respectively. Assume that the effect of h_{oe} is negligible. The transconductance g_m of the JFET is 2.6 mS.*

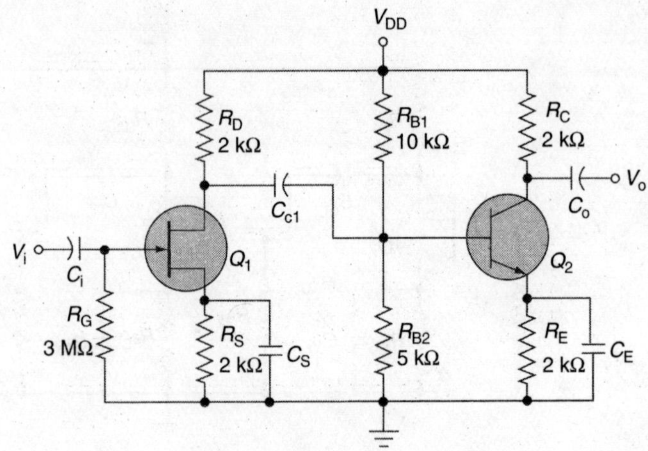

Figure 8.35 Example 8.7.

Solution

1. Voltage gain of the second stage is given by

$$A_{v2} = \frac{-h_{fe} \times R_C}{h_{ie}}$$

$$= \frac{-100 \times 2 \times 10^3}{1 \times 10^3} = -200$$

2. Voltage gain of the first stage is given by

$$A_{v1} = -g_m (R_D \| R_{B1} \| R_{B2} \| h_{ie})$$

$$= -2.6 \times 10^{-3} \times (2 \times 10^3 \| 10 \times 10^3 \| 5 \times 10^3 \| 1 \times 10^3)$$

$$= -2.6 \times 10^{-3} \times 555.56 = -1.45$$

3. Overall voltage gain is given by $A_v = A_{v1} \times A_{v2} = -200 \times -1.45 = 290$.
4. The input impedance of the amplifier Z_i is given by $Z_i = R_G$. Therefore, $Z_i = 3$ MΩ.
5. The output impedance of the amplifier is given by $Z_o = R_C \| (1/h_{oe})$. As the effect of h_{oe} is negligible, therefore $Z_o = R_C = 2$ kΩ.

8.8 Darlington Amplifiers

Darlington transistors refer to the connection of two BJTs wherein their collector terminals are tied together and the emitter terminal of one of the transistors is connected to the base terminal of the other transistor. In other words, the Darlington connection can be considered as two cascaded emitter–followers, with the first stage having an infinite emitter resistance. The composite transistor acts as a single unit (Figure 8.36) with a current gain approximately equal to the product of the current gains of the individual transistors. If the individual transistors have current gains of β_1 and β_2, then the Darlington connection provides an approximate current gain of β_D given by

$$\beta_D = \beta_1 \times \beta_2 \tag{8.121}$$

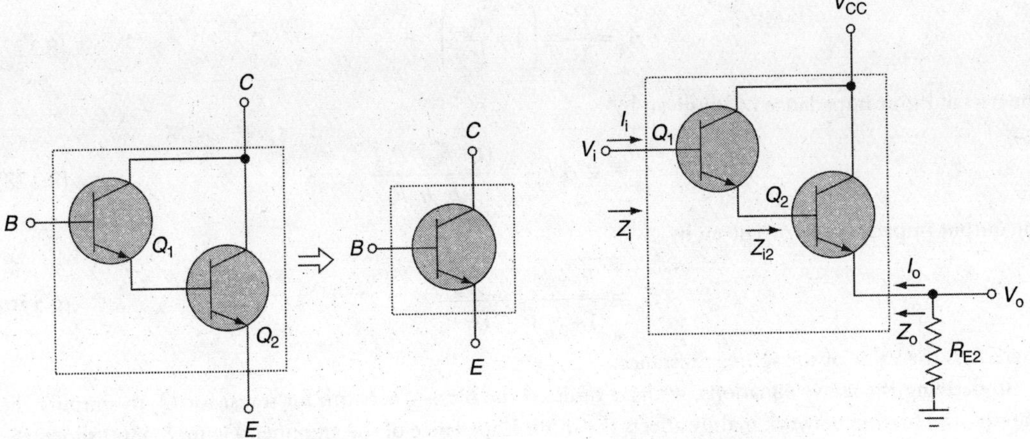

Figure 8.36 Darlington transistor.

Figure 8.37 Circuit using a Darlington transistor.

It offers other advantages like increased value of input impedance and reduced value of output impedance. The values of these parameters are derived in the subsequent paragraphs. Figure 8.37 shows a circuit configuration employing a Darlington pair. The biasing network for Q_1 has not been included for simplicity of analysis. The current gain for the second transistor Q_2 is given by

$$A_{i2} = \frac{I_o}{I_{b2}} = \frac{1+h_{fe2}}{1+h_{oe2}R_{E2}} \cong 1+h_{fe2} \tag{8.122}$$

The input resistance of the second stage is given by

$$Z_{i2} = h_{ie2} + (1+h_{fe2})R_{E2} \cong (1+h_{fe2})R_{E2} \tag{8.123}$$

Z_{i2} is the effective load resistance for the first-stage Q_1 and the current gain for the first stage (A_{i1}) is given by

$$\begin{aligned} A_{i1} &= \frac{I_{e1}}{I_1} = \frac{I_{b2}}{I_1} = \frac{1+h_{fe1}}{1+h_{oe1}Z_{i2}} \\ &\cong \frac{1+h_{fe1}}{1+h_{oe1}(1+h_{fe2})R_{E2}} \\ &\cong \frac{1+h_{fe1}}{1+h_{oe1}h_{fe2}R_{E2}} \end{aligned} \tag{8.124}$$

The overall current gain (A_i) is given by

$$A_i = \frac{I_o}{I_i} = \frac{I_o}{I_{b2}} \times \frac{I_{b2}}{I_i} = A_{i2} \times A_{i1} \cong (1+h_{fe2})\left(\frac{1+h_{fe1}}{1+h_{oe1}h_{fe2}R_{E2}}\right) \tag{8.125}$$

Assuming that the h-parameters for both the transistors are equal, that is, $h_{fe1} = h_{fe2} = h_{fe}$ and $h_{oe1} = h_{oe2} = h_{oe}$, the above equation can be rewritten as

$$A_i \cong \left(\frac{(1+h_{fe})^2}{1+h_{oe}h_{fe}R_{E2}}\right) \tag{8.126}$$

The overall voltage gain (A_v) is less than unity, because it consists of two emitter–followers in cascade, each offering value of voltage gain slightly less than unity.

$$A_v = \frac{V_o}{V_i} \cong \left(1 - \frac{h_{ie}}{Z_{i2}}\right) \tag{8.127}$$

The overall input impedance (Z_i) is given by

$$Z_i = \frac{A_i R_{E2}}{A_v} \cong A_i R_{E2} \cong \frac{(1+h_{fe})^2 R_{E2}}{1+h_{oe}h_{fe}R_{E2}} \tag{8.128}$$

The output impedance (Z_o) is given by

$$Z_o \cong \frac{R_s + h_{ie}}{(1+h_{fe})^2} + \frac{h_{ie}}{1+h_{fe}} \tag{8.129}$$

where R_s is the value of the source resistance.

In deriving the above equations, we have omitted the biasing network for transistor Q_1 to simplify the analysis. The biasing network mainly affects the input impedance of the amplifier. Figure 8.38(a) shows the biasing arrangement. Let us now consider the effect of the biasing network of transistor Q_1 on the input impedance of the network.

The overall input impedance (Z_i') is given by

$$Z_i' = Z_i \| R \tag{8.130}$$

where $R = R_{B1} \| R_{B2}$. The value of R (i.e., parallel combination of R_{B1} and R_{B2}) is much less than the value of Z_i. Therefore, the overall input impedance (Z_i') is appreciably smaller than Z_i. This nullifies one of the major advantages offered by a Darlington amplifier of high input impedance.

This can be partially overcome by adding a resistor R_{B3} as shown in Figure 8.38(b). The new value of R is now

$$R = R_{B1} \| R_{B2} + R_{B3} \tag{8.131}$$

The value of R is still less than Z_i. The value of R can be substantially improved if we add a capacitor C_B in addition to resistor R_{B3} [Figure 8.38(c)]. The reactance of the capacitor is negligible at low frequencies at which the amplifier is to be used. Hence, the capacitor (C_B) directly couples the output voltage V_o to the lower side of resistor R_{B3}. The other end of the resistor R_{B3} is connected to the input voltage V_i. As the

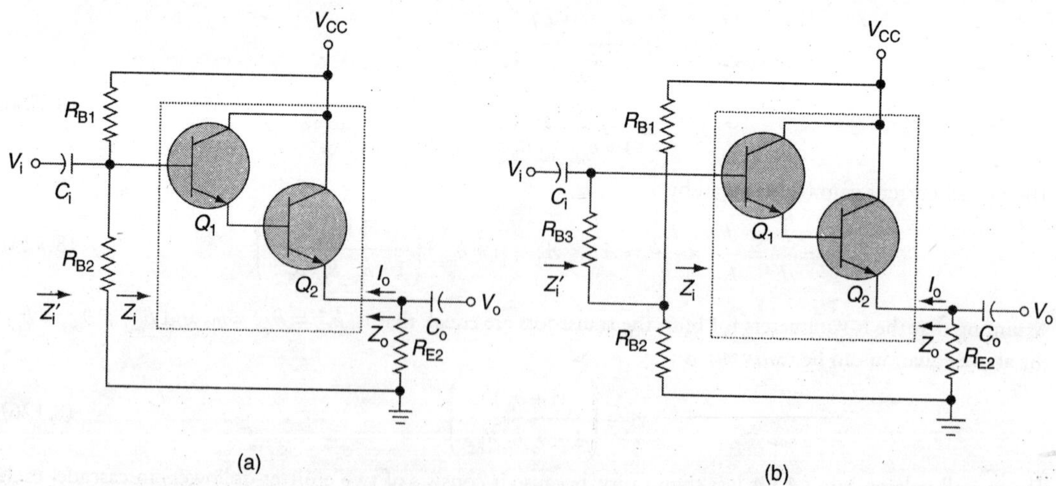

Figure 8.38 (a) Darlington amplifier with input bias circuit; (b) Darlington amplifier with modified input bias circuit; (c) bootstrapping in Darlington amplifier.

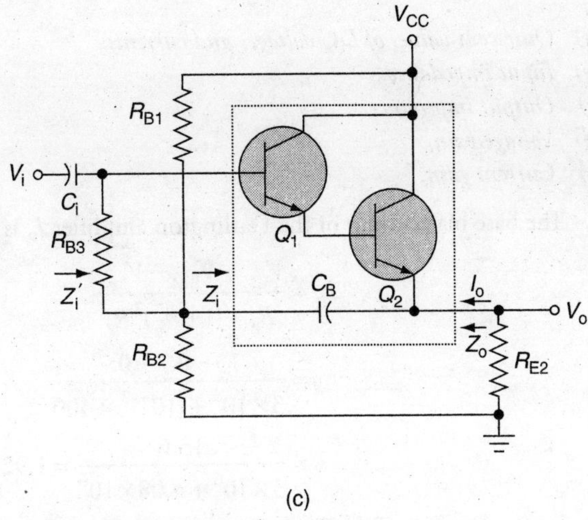

(c)

Figure 8.38 *Continued.*

voltage gain of the amplifier is nearly unity, the input voltage V_i is approximately equal to the output voltage V_o. Therefore, there is very small AC voltage drop across the resistor R_{B3}. Hence, it draws a very small AC current from the input voltage V_i. Therefore, the effective value of R_{B3} has increased manifold. The effective value of R_{B3} can be calculated by making use of Miller's effect:

$$R_{B3(eff)} = \frac{R_{B3}}{1 - A_v} \tag{8.132}$$

As the value of voltage gain (A_v) is close to unity, value of $R_{B3(eff)}$ is very large. The effect of the voltage gain (A_v) approaching unity on the resistor $R_{B3(eff)}$ is referred to as bootstrapping. For unity value of A_v both ends of R_{B3} increase by the same potential as if R_{B3} were pulling it by its bootstraps.

EXAMPLE 8.8 *Figure 8.39 shows a Darlington amplifier. The two transistors Q_1 and Q_2 are identical and the h-parameters for both the transistors are h_{ie} = 1 kΩ, h_{fe} = 100 and $h_{oe} = 40 \times 10^{-6}$ mhos. The values of the voltages V_{CC} = 15 V, V_{BE1} = 0.7 V and V_{BE2} = 0.7 V. Determine the following:*

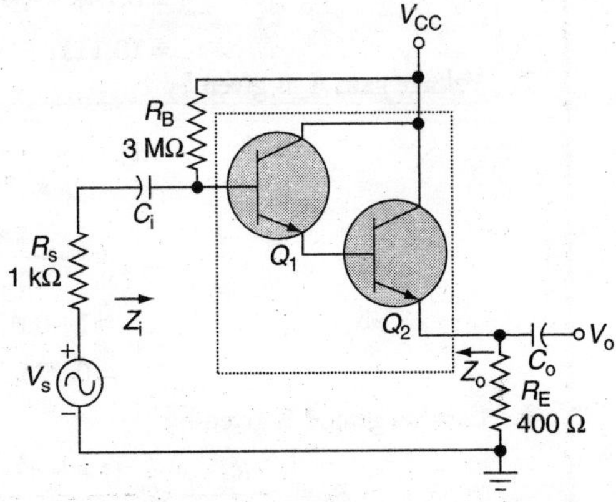

Figure 8.39 Example 8.8.

(a) Quiescent values of DC voltages and currents.
(b) Input impedance.
(c) Output impedance.
(d) Voltage gain.
(e) Current gain.

Solution

1. The base bias current of the Darlington amplifier I_B is given by

$$I_B = \frac{V_{CC} - V_{BE1} - V_{BE2}}{R_B + (1+h_{fe})^2 R_E}$$
$$= \frac{15 - 0.7 - 0.7}{3\times10^6 + (101)^2 \times 400}$$
$$= \frac{13.6}{3\times10^6 + 4.08\times10^6} = 1.92\ \mu A$$

2. Emitter current of the Darlington amplifier is

$$I_{E2} = (1 + h_{fe})^2 I_{B1} = (101)^2 \times 1.92 \times 10^{-6}\ \mu A = 19.6\ mA$$

3. The collector current of the Darlington amplifier $I_C \cong I_E = 19.6$ mA.
4. The collector–emitter voltage $V_{CE} = V_C - V_E = 15 - 19.6 \times 10^{-3} \times 400 = 7.16$ V.
5. $$Z_i = R_B \left\| \frac{(1+h_{fe})^2 R_E}{1 + h_{oe} h_{fe} R_E} \right.$$
$$= 3\times10^6 \left\| \frac{(101)^2 \times 400}{1 + 40\times10^{-6} \times 100 \times 400} \right.$$
$$= 3\times10^6 \| 1.57\times10^6 = 1.03\ M\Omega$$

6. $$Z_o \cong \frac{R_s + h_{ie}}{(1+h_{fe})^2} + \frac{h_{ie}}{1+h_{fe}}$$
$$= \frac{1\times10^3 + 1\times10^3}{(101)^2} + \frac{1\times10^3}{101}$$
$$= 0.196 + 9.9$$
$$= 10.1\ \Omega$$

7. Voltage gain A_v is given by

$$A_v = 1 - \frac{h_{ie}}{(1+h_{fe})R_E}$$
$$= 1 - \frac{1\times10^3}{101\times400}$$
$$= 1 - 0.025$$
$$= 0.975$$

8. Current gain A_i is given by

$$A_i = \frac{R_B}{Z_i' + R_B} \times \left(\frac{(1+h_{fe})^2}{1 + h_{oe} h_{fe} R_E} \right)$$

$$Z_i' = \frac{(1+h_{fe})^2 R_E}{1+h_{oe} h_{fe} R_E} = 1.57\times10^6$$

Therefore, A_i is given by

$$A_i = \frac{3\times10^6}{3\times10^6 + 1.57\times10^6} \times \frac{(101)^2}{1+40\times10^{-6}\times100\times400}$$
$$= 0.66\times3923.46 = 2589.49$$

8.9 Cascode Amplifiers

Cascode amplifiers are two-stage amplifiers comprising a transconductance amplifier followed by a current buffer. They offer advantages like high input–output isolation, high input impedance and high output impedance. In a BJT cascode amplifier configuration, the common-emitter transistor amplifier is followed by a common-base transistor amplifier. Figure 8.40(a) shows the circuit diagram of a cascode amplifier wherein the transistor Q_1 is configured as common-emitter amplifier and Q_2 is configured as common-base amplifier. The common-base amplifier Q_2 offers large bandwidth but its input impedance is low. Because of the low input impedance of Q_2, the voltage gain of Q_1 is low. Therefore, the Miller's component of capacitance of transistor Q_1 is small and the bandwidth of the cascode amplifier is wider than that for the common-emitter stage. Hence, cascode amplifiers are used for high-frequency applications.

In the case of an FET-based cascode amplifier, common-source amplifier is followed by common-gate amplifier as shown in Figure 8.40(b).

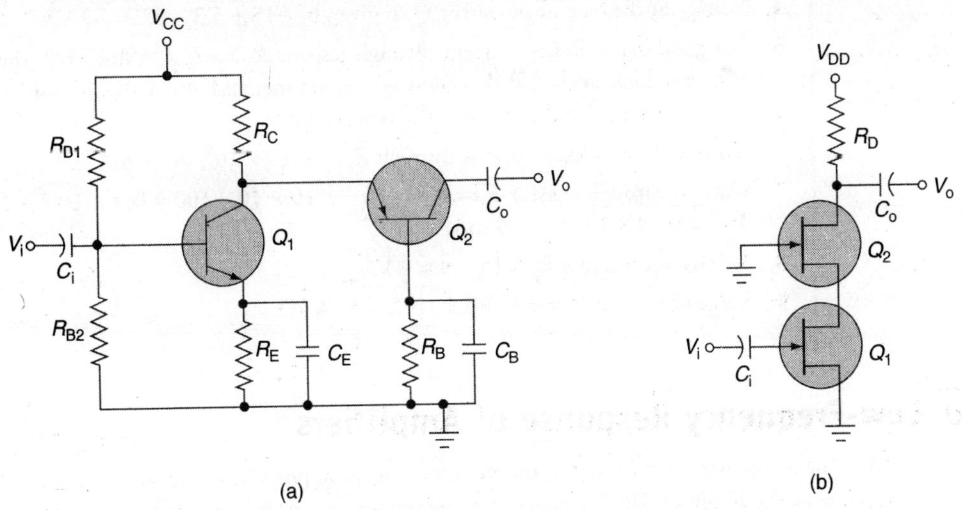

Figure 8.40 (a) BJT cascode amplifier; (b) FET cascode amplifier.

EXAMPLE 8.9 *For the cascode amplifier circuit shown in Figure 8.41, determine the values of resistors R_E, R_1 and R_2 such that the operating point is $I_{CQ} = 10$ mA and $V_{CEQ} = 10$ V. Given that the value of $\beta = 100$ and V_{BE} of each transistor is 0.7 V.*

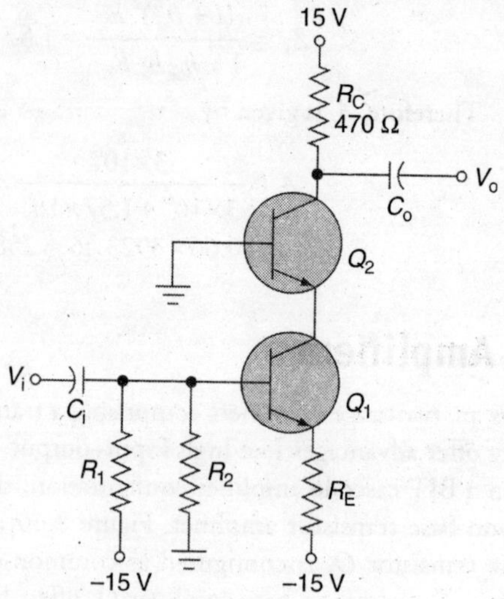

Figure 8.41 Example 8.9.

Solution

1. DC voltage drop across the resistor R_C is given by $470 \times 10 \times 10^{-3} = 4.7$ V.
2. Therefore, the voltage drop across the resistor R_E is $15 - 4.7 - 10 - 10 - (-15) = 30 - 24.7 = 5.3$ V.
3. Value of resistor R_E is approximately equal to $5.3/10 \times 10^{-3} = 530\ \Omega$.
4. Voltage at the base of transistor Q_1 is given by $-15 + 5.3 + 0.7 = -9$ V.
5. For good bias stability, current through resistor $R_2 >> I_{BQ1}$. Value of R_2 should not be so large such that this condition is not met and also it should not be too small to have an undue load on the power supply.
6. Assume $R_2 = 10$ kΩ. Current through R_2 is $9/(10 \times 10^3) = 0.9$ mA.
7. Current through resistor $R_1 = 0.9 \times 10^{-3} - 10 \times 10^{-3}/100 = 0.9 \times 10^{-3} - 10 \times 10^{-5} = 0.89 \times 10^{-3} = 0.89$ mA.
8. Voltage drop across R_1 is $15 - 9 = 6$ V.
9. Value of resistor $R_1 = 6/(0.89 \times 10^{-3}) = 6.74$ kΩ.

8.10 Low-Frequency Response of Amplifiers

As discussed in the earlier part of the chapter, the frequency of the applied input signal has a great effect on the response of the amplifier. The low-frequency response is limited by the coupling and the bypass capacitors as they can no longer be considered as short circuits. The high-frequency response is affected by the stray capacitive elements associated with the active device. Moreover, as the number of amplifier stages increases, the low- and the high-frequency response gets further limited. In this section, we will discuss the low-frequency response of the BJT and FET amplifiers. This is followed by a discussion on the effect of cascading amplifier stages on the overall frequency response of the amplifier in the next section. The high-frequency response of amplifiers is discussed in Chapter 9.

Low-Frequency *Response of BJT Amplifiers*

In the low-frequency region of operation, a BJT or an FET amplifier's response is affected by the R–C combinations formed by the network capacitors including the coupling and bypass capacitors and the network resistive elements. In this section we discuss the effect of these capacitors on the low-frequency response of the voltage-divider BJT amplifier configuration. The results can be generalized to any transistor configuration. Figure 8.42 shows the voltage-divider BJT amplifier configuration. C_i is the input-coupling capacitor and is connected between the applied input source and the active device. C_o is the output-coupling capacitor and is connected between the output of the active device and the load.

Effect of Input Coupling Capacitor

The capacitor C_i forms an *RC* network as shown in Figure 8.43. R_i is the input resistance of the amplifier as seen by the source and is given by parallel combination of R_1, R_2 and h_{ie}:

$$R_i = R_1 \| R_2 \| h_{ie} \tag{8.133}$$

The voltage V_i applied to the input of the active device is calculated by using the voltage-divider rule. Therefore, voltage V_i is given by

$$V_i = \frac{R_i}{R_s + R_i - jX_{C_i}} \times V_s \tag{8.134}$$

At mid- and high frequencies the reactance of capacitors C_i and C_o will be sufficiently small to permit a short-circuit approximation. Therefore, the input voltage at mid-band frequencies ($V_{i\text{-mid}}$) is given by

$$V_{i\text{-mid}} = \frac{R_i}{R_s + R_i} \times V_s \tag{8.135}$$

The cut-off frequency established by the capacitor C_i is given by

$$f_{LC_i} = \frac{1}{2\pi(R_i + R_s)C_i} \tag{8.136}$$

At f_{LC_i} the voltage V_i will be 0.707 times the voltage $V_{i\text{-mid}}$ assuming that C_i is the only capacitive element effecting the low-frequency response.

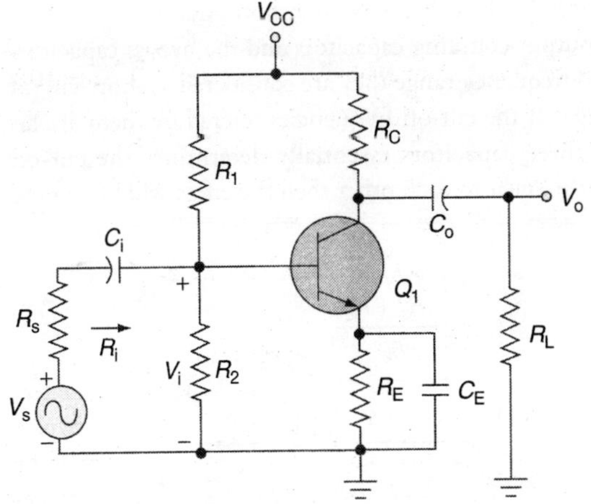

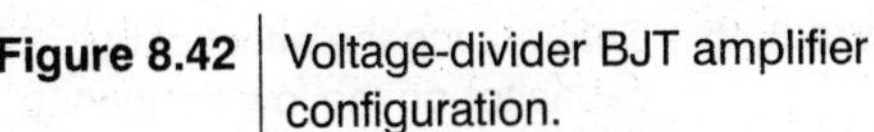
Figure 8.42 Voltage-divider BJT amplifier configuration.

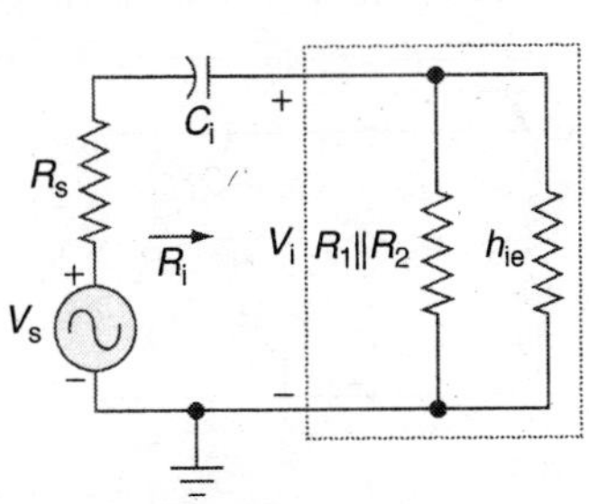

Figure 8.43 Determining the effect of input-coupling capacitor on the low-frequency response.

Effect of the Output Coupling Capacitor

The output coupling capacitor (C_o) is connected between the output of the active device and the load. Figure 8.44 shows the simplified configuration highlighting the effect of C_o on the low-frequency response of the amplifier. R_o is the total output resistance and is given by

$$R_o = R_C \| r_o \cong R_C \tag{8.137}$$

The cut-off frequency as established by C_o is given by

$$f_{LC_o} = \frac{1}{2\pi(R_o + R_L)C_o} \cong \frac{1}{2\pi(R_C + R_L)C_o} \tag{8.138}$$

The output voltage V_o will be 70.7% of its mid-band value at the frequency f_{LC_o} assuming that C_o is the only capacitive element controlling the low-frequency response.

Effect of Bypass Capacitor

Figure 8.45 shows the network as seen by the bypass capacitor C_E. The value of the equivalent resistance R_E is given by

$$R_e = R_E \| [(R_s' + h_{ie})/h_{fe}] \tag{8.139}$$

where

$$R_s' = R_s \| R_1 \| R_2$$

The cut-off frequency as established by resistance R_E and capacitor C_E is given by

$$f_{LC_E} = \frac{1}{2\pi R_e C_E} \tag{8.140}$$

The effect of bypass capacitor C_E can be explained qualitatively by considering that at low frequencies the capacitor C_E acts like an open circuit and whole of the resistor R_E appears in the gain equation, resulting in minimum value of gain. As the frequency increases, the reactance of the capacitor C_E decreases resulting in decrease in the value of parallel impedance of resistor R_E and capacitor C_E. The gain is maximum when the impedance of the capacitor C_E reduces so much that it can be considered as a short circuit.

It may be mentioned here that the input and the output coupling capacitors and the bypass capacitors effect only the low-frequency response. At the mid-band frequency range they are considered as short-circuit equivalent and do not affect the gain at these frequencies. If the cut-off frequencies offered by them are far apart then the highest cut-off frequency due to the three capacitors essentially determines the cut-off frequency of the entire system. If the cut-off frequencies are near to each other then the effect will be to raise

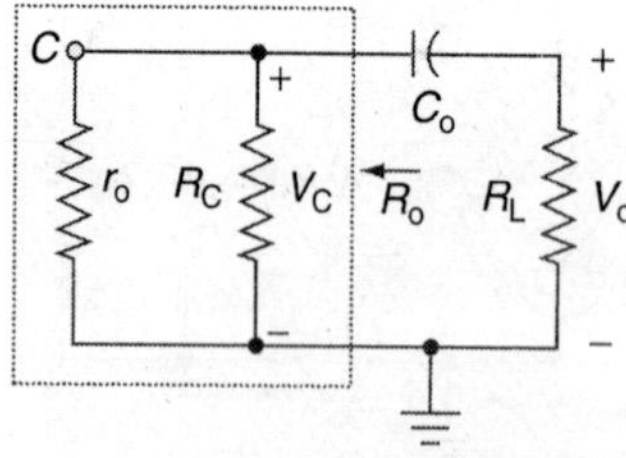

Figure 8.44 Determining the effect of output coupling capacitor on the low-frequency response.

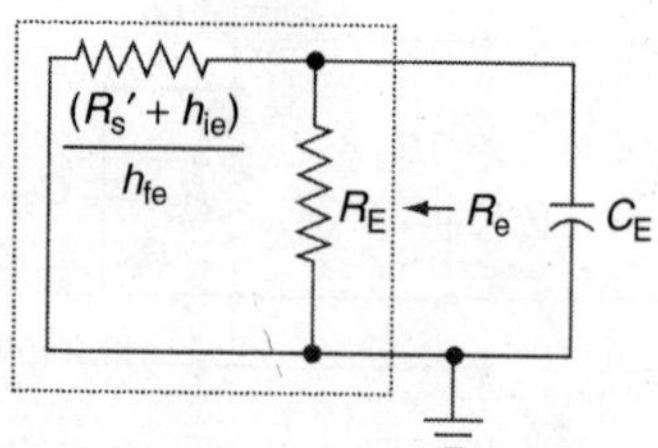

Figure 8.45 Determining the effect of bypass capacitor on the low-frequency response.

the lower cut-off frequency of the entire system, that is, there is an interaction between the capacitive elements resulting in increased lower cut-off frequency for the entire system.

Low-Frequency Response of FET Amplifiers

The low-frequency response of FET amplifiers is quite similar to that of BJT amplifiers discussed in the preceding subsection. In the case of FET amplifiers also, there are three capacitors that affect the low-frequency response, namely, the coupling capacitor C_i between the source and the FET, the coupling capacitor C_o between the FET and the load and the source capacitor C_S. Figure 8.46 shows the circuit of a JFET-based amplifier. In this section, we will discuss the effect of all the three capacitors on the low frequency response for the amplifier. The fundamental equations and the procedure apply to other amplifier configurations as well.

Effect of Input Coupling Capacitor

Figure 8.47 shows the equivalent network seen by the input coupling capacitor C_i. The cut-off frequency as determined by the capacitor C_i is given by

$$f_{LC_i} = \frac{1}{2\pi(R_i + R_s)C_i} \cong \frac{1}{2\pi(R_G + R_s)C_i} \tag{8.141}$$

In most of the applications, the value of resistor R_G is much larger than the value of the resistor R_s. Therefore, the low cut-off frequency (f_{LC_i}) is primarily determined by the values of resistor R_G and capacitor C_i.

Effect of Output Coupling Capacitor

Figure 8.48 shows the network as seen by the output coupling capacitor. The output resistance (R_o) is determined by

$$R_o = R_D \parallel r_d \tag{8.142}$$

The resulting cut-off frequency f_{LC_o} is given by

$$f_{LC_o} = \frac{1}{2\pi(R_o + R_L)C_o} = \frac{1}{2\pi(R_D \parallel r_d + R_L)C_o} \tag{8.143}$$

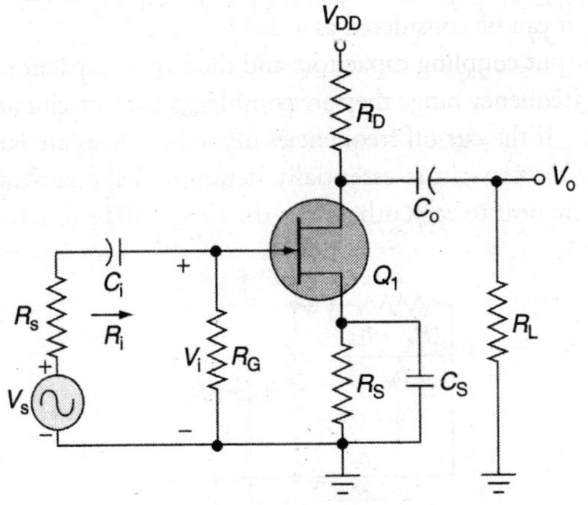

Figure 8.46 JFET-based amplifier.

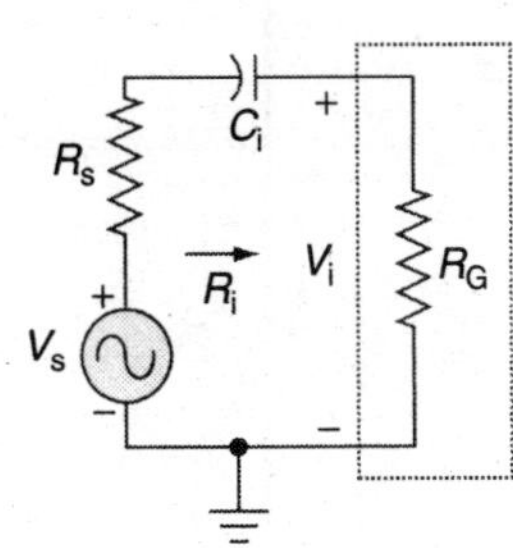

Figure 8.47 Determining the effect of input coupling capacitor on the low-frequency response.

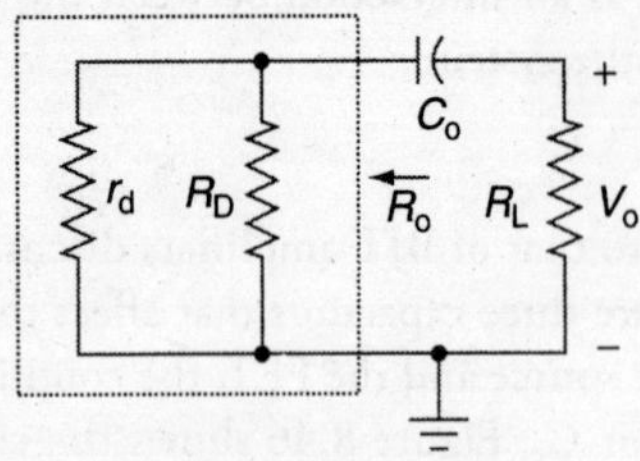

Figure 8.48 Determining the effect of output coupling capacitor on the low-frequency response.

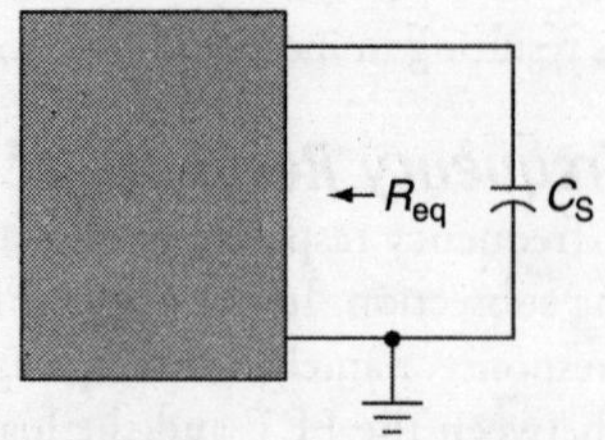

Figure 8.49 Determining the effect of source capacitor on the low-frequency response.

Effect of Source Capacitor

The equivalent network seen by the source capacitor C_S is shown in Figure 8.49. The equivalent resistance as seen by the capacitor C_S is given by

$$R_{eq} = \frac{R_S(r_d + R_D \| R_L)}{R_S(1+g_m r_d) + r_d + R_D \| R_L} \tag{8.144}$$

As the value of resistance r_d is very large, assuming $r_d = \infty$ we get

$$R_{eq} = R_S \| (1/g_m) \tag{8.145}$$

The cut-off frequency due to the capacitor C_S is defined as

$$f_{LC_S} = \frac{1}{2\pi R_{eq} C_S} \tag{8.146}$$

EXAMPLE 8.10 *Determine the lower cut-off frequency of the BJT amplifier shown in Figure 8.50. Sketch the frequency response using Bode plot. Given that the h-parameters of the transistor are h_{ie} = 1.5 kΩ and h_{fe} = 100.*

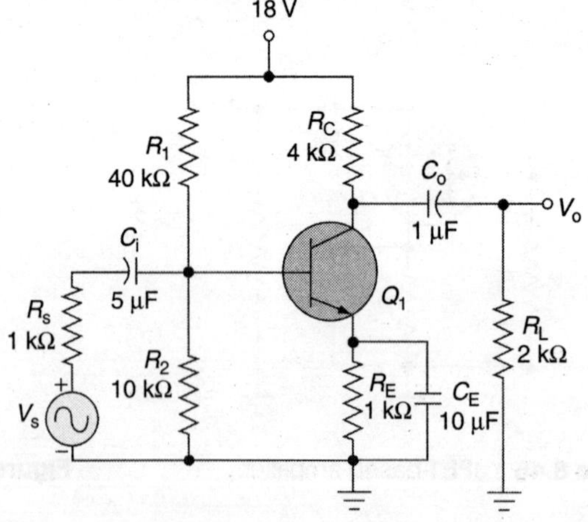

Figure 8.50 Example 8.10.

Solution

1. The cut-off frequency due to the capacitor C_i is given by

$$f_{LC_i} = \frac{1}{2\pi(R_i + R_s)C_i}$$

$$R_i = R_1 \| R_2 \| h_{ie}$$

$$= 40\times10^3 \| 10\times10^3 \| 1.5\times10^3$$

$$= 1.26\times10^3 = 1.26\ \text{k}\Omega$$

Therefore $f_{LC_i} = 1/2 \times \pi \times (1.26 \times 10^3 + 1 \times 10^3) \times 5 \times 10^{-6} = 14.08$ Hz.

2. The cut-off frequency due to capacitor C_E is given by

$$f_{LC_E} = \frac{1}{2\pi R_e C_E}$$

3. $$R_e = R_E \| [(R_s \| R_1 \| R_2 + h_{ie})/h_{fe}]$$

$$= 1\times10^3 \| [(1\times10^3 \| 40\times10^3 \| 10\times10^3 + 1.5\times10^3)/100]$$

$$= 23.33\ \Omega$$

4. Therefore $f_{LC_E} = 1/2 \times \pi \times (23.33) \times 10 \times 10^{-6} = 682$ Hz.

5. The cut-off frequency due to capacitor C_o is given by

$$f_{LC_o} = \frac{1}{2\pi(R_C + R_L)C_o}$$

$$= \frac{1}{2\pi(4\times10^3 + 2\times10^3)\times1\times10^{-6}}$$

$$= 26.53\ \text{Hz}$$

6. As we can see f_{LC_E} is significantly higher than f_{LC_o} and f_{LC_i}, hence f_{LC_E} is the predominant factor in determining the low-frequency response for the complete system.

7. Hence the cut-off frequency for the overall system is approximately equal to 682 Hz.

8. Figure 8.51 shows the asymptotic curves using the Bode plot.

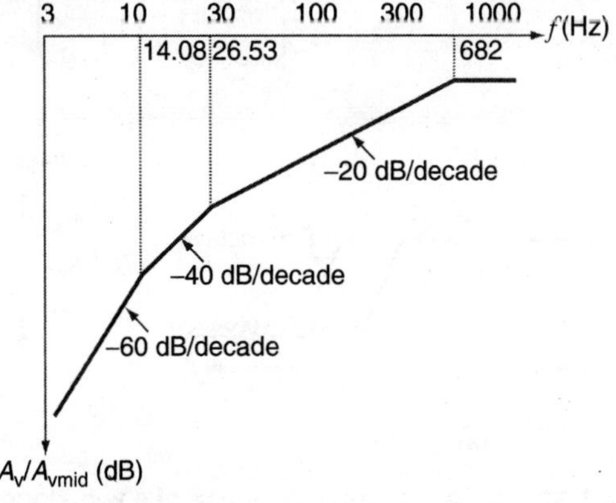

Figure 8.51 Solution to Example 8.10.

8.11 Low-Frequency Response of Cascaded Amplifier Stages

The overall frequency response of an amplifier changes if an additional stage is added to it. In a multi-stage amplifier, the lower cut-off frequency is determined by the stage having the highest value of the lower cut-off frequency and the upper cut-off frequency is determined by the stage having the lowest value of the upper cut-off frequency. This also results in reduction of the overall bandwidth of the amplifier. The effect of adding additional stages can be best understood by considering that all stages are identical with the same lower and upper cut-off frequencies. Let the lower cut-off frequency and upper cut-off frequency of each stage be f_L and f_H, respectively. The drop-off rate in the low- and the high-frequency regions for each stage is −6 dB/octave or −20 dB/decade.

For a two-stage amplifier, the drop-off rates increase to −12 dB/octave or −40 dB/decade. The lower cut-off frequency (f_L') where the amplitude falls by 3 dB is given by

$$f_L' = \frac{f_L}{\sqrt{2^{1/2}-1}} = \frac{f_L}{0.64} = 1.56 f_L \tag{8.147}$$

The upper cut-off frequency f_H' is given by

$$f_H' = f_H\sqrt{2^{1/2}-1} = 0.64 f_H \tag{8.148}$$

Figure 8.52 shows the response of the two-stage amplifier with each stage having a unity gain. The asymptotic response is shown in Figure 8.52(a) whereas the actual response is shown in Figure 8.52(b). Also the response of single-stage amplifiers is shown to highlight the effect of cascading the two stages.

The above discussion can be generalized for n stages. Let the gain of each individual stage in the mid frequency region be A_{vmid} and the gain in the low-frequency region be A_{vlow}. Let the overall mid-frequency gain be $A_{\text{vmid-overall}}$ and the overall low-frequency gain be $A_{\text{vlow-overall}}$. Also, the lower and the upper cut-off frequencies for the individual stages are f_L and f_H, respectively, and the lower and the upper cut-off frequencies for the overall amplifier are f_{Ln} and f_{Hn}, respectively. Therefore,

$$A_{\text{vmid-overall}} = (A_{\text{vmid}})^n \tag{8.149}$$

$$A_{\text{vlow-overall}} = (A_{\text{vlow}})^n \tag{8.150}$$

Taking the ratio of Eq. (8.149) and (8.150) we get

$$\frac{A_{\text{vlow-overall}}}{A_{\text{vmid-overall}}} = \left(\frac{A_{\text{vlow}}}{A_{\text{vmid}}}\right)^n \tag{8.151}$$

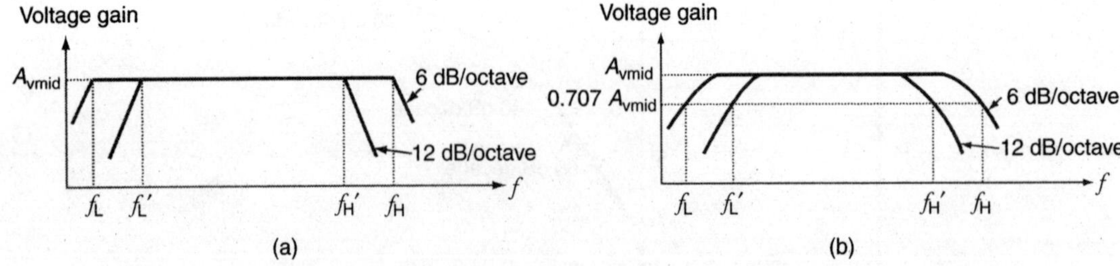

Figure 8.52 (a) Asymptotic response of a two-stage amplifier; (b) actual response of a two-stage amplifier.

$$\frac{A_{\text{vlow-overall}}}{A_{\text{vmid-overall}}} = \left(\frac{1}{(1 - jf_L/f)}\right)^n \tag{8.152}$$

Let the frequency at which the magnitude of the expression given by Eq. (8.152) become $1/\sqrt{2}$ (-3 dB) be f_{Ln}. Therefore,

$$\frac{1}{\sqrt{[1+(f_L/f_{Ln})^2]^n}} = \frac{1}{\sqrt{2}} \tag{8.153}$$

On solving Eq. (8.153), we get

$$f_{Ln} = \frac{f_L}{\sqrt{2^{1/n} - 1}} \tag{8.154}$$

Similarly, the overall upper cut-off frequency (f_{Hn}) is given by

$$f_{Hn} = f_H\sqrt{2^{1/n} - 1} \tag{8.155}$$

It may be mentioned here that increase in the number of stages is not always associated with decrease in the bandwidth. If the value of mid-band gain is kept fixed and independent of the number of amplifier stages then the bandwidth may increase with increase in the number of stages.

KEY TERMS

Cascade amplifier
Cascode amplifier
Darlington amplifier
h-parameter model
Open-circuit output admittance parameter (h_{22})
Open-circuit reverse transfer voltage ratio (h_{12})
Short-circuit forward transfer current ratio (h_{21})
Short-circuit input impedance parameter (h_{11})

OBJECTIVE-TYPE EXERCISES

Multiple-Choice Questions

1. The parameter h_{oe} can be determined by
   a. taking the slope of the output characteristic curve at the operating point.
   b. taking the slope of the input characteristic curve at the operating point.
   c. cannot be determined using the input and output characteristic curves.
   d. by taking the collector current increment for a fixed value of collector–emitter voltage.

2. What is the unit of the output conductance parameter?
   a. Ohms
   b. It is dimensionless
   c. Mhos
   d. Ampere

3. Increase in the value of transistor's h_{fe} parameter results in
   a. decrease in the value of input impedance and increase in the value of current gain.
   b. decrease in the values of both the input impedance and the current gain.
   c. increase in the values of both the input impedance and the current gain.
   d. increase in the value of input impedance and decrease in the value of current gain.

4. Increase in the junction temperature of a transistor results in
   a. increase in the values of all the four h-parameters.
   b. decrease in the values of all the four h-parameters.
   c. increase in the values of h_{ie} and h_{fe} parameters and decrease in the values of h_{re} and h_{oe} parameters.
   d. decrease in the values of h_{ie} and h_{fe} parameters and increase in the values of h_{re} and h_{oe} parameters.

5. Which of the following statement(s) is/are true?
   a. The low-frequency response of an amplifier is due to the bypass and the coupling capacitors.
   b. The high-frequency response of an amplifier is due to the bypass and the coupling capacitors.
   c. The low-frequency response of an amplifier is due to the junction capacitances and the stray-wiring capacitances.
   d. The high-frequency response of an amplifier is due to the junction capacitances and the stray-wiring capacitances.
   e. Both (a) and (d).
   f. Both (b) and (c).

6. The voltage gain of an amplifier decreases at 20 dB/decade above 100 kHz. If the mid-band frequency gain is 80 dB, what is the value of the voltage gain at 2 MHz?
   a. 60 dB
   b. 52 dB
   c. 54 dB
   d. 64 dB

7. In the h-parameter model, the input and the output sections are modeled as
   a. voltage sources.
   b. current sources.
   c. input section as voltage source and output section as current source.
   d. input section as current source and output section as voltage source.

8. Larger the spacing between the curves of the output characteristics of a transistor
   a. smaller is the value of h_{fe}.
   b. larger is the value of h_{fe}.
   c. h_{fe} is independent of the spacing.
   d. h_{fe} can increase or decrease depending upon the circuit configuration.

9. Which of the following statement(s) is/are true?
   a. In the case of an FET amplifier, there is no feedback from the output to the input whereas in the case of a BJT amplifier there is feedback between the output and the input circuits through the parameter h_{re}.
   b. In the case of a BJT amplifier, there is no feedback from the output to the input whereas in the case of an FET amplifier there is feedback between the output and input sections through the parameter g_m.
   c. BJT is a more ideal amplifier as compared to an FET.
   d. FET is a more ideal amplifier as compared to a BJT.
   e. Both (a) and (d).
   f. Both (b) and (c).

10. Which of the following statement(s) is/are false?
   a. The parameters h_i and h_r are determined from the input characteristic curves of the transistors whereas the parameters h_f and h_o are determined from the output or the collector characteristics.
   b. Cascode amplifiers are two-stage amplifiers comprising a transconductance amplifier followed by a current buffer.
   c. Darlington connection refers to the connection of two bipolar junction transistors wherein their collector terminals are tied together and the emitter terminal of one transistor is connected to the base terminal of the other transistor.
   d. Darlington connection refers to the connection of two bipolar junction transistors wherein their emitter terminals are tied together and the collector terminal of one transistor is connected to the base terminal of the other transistor.

Fill in the Blanks

1. For a multistage amplifier, the lower cut-off frequency will be determined by the stage having the ________ lower cut-off frequency and the upper cut-off frequency is determined by the stage having the ________ upper cut-off frequency.

2. The low-frequency response is limited by the ________ and the ________ capacitors while the high frequency response is affected by the ________ capacitive elements associated with the active device.

3. Darlington connection can be considered as two cascaded ________, with the first stage having an ________ emitter resistance.

4. The parameter h_{11} is the ratio of the instantaneous change in the ________ voltage due to instantaneous change in the ________ current and has the units ________.

5. The low-frequency model of an FET has a ________ output circuit with a dependent current source whose current output is proportional to the ________.

REVIEW QUESTIONS

1. Draw the frequency response of an RC-coupled amplifier and a DC-coupled amplifier. Also explain the main difference between the response of the two amplifiers.

2. Draw the comprehensive h-parameter model of a transistor. Also draw the approximate h-parameter model, highlighting the assumptions made in drawing it.

3. Derive the expressions for the voltage and current gains, input and output impedances of a collector-to-base feedback common-emitter amplifier configuration using simplified h-parameter equivalent model.

4. Why are Darlington transistors also referred to as superbeta transistors? Explain the concept using the internal schematic of Darlington transistors.

5. Explain the effect of coupling and bypass capacitors on the low-frequency response of the transistor-based amplifier.

6. Explain the effect of cascading amplifier stages on the overall frequency response of the amplifier.

7. Derive the expression for the cut-off frequencies due to the bypass and the coupling capacitors for the common-collector configuration.

8. What are cascode amplifiers? What are the advantages offered by the cascode amplifiers?

9. How can we determine the h-parameters of a transistor using its input and output characteristics curves?

10. Derive the relationship between the h_{fe} parameter of the three amplifier configurations using bipolar transistors.

PROBLEMS

1. Figure 8.53 shows a two-stage cascaded amplifier with the first stage as a common-emitter BJT amplifier and the second stage as a common-source JFET amplifier. Calculate the values of voltage gain, input and output impedances of the amplifier. Given that h_{ie} and h_{fe} parameters of the transistor are 1.2 kΩ and 120, respectively. Assume that the effect of h_{oe} is negligible. The transconductance g_m of the JFET is 3 mS.

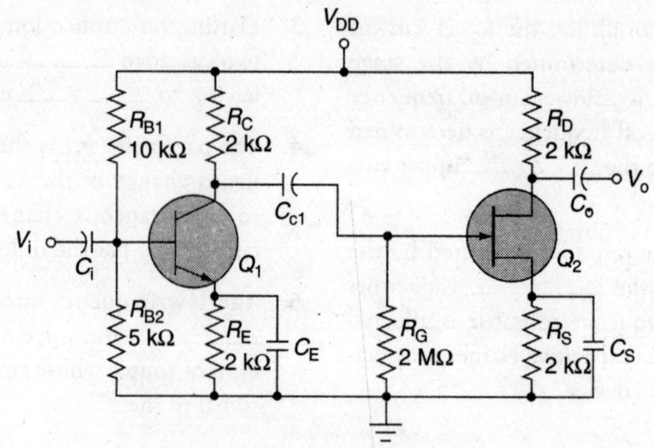

Figure 8.53 | Problem 1.

2. For the voltage-divider JFET amplifier shown in Figure 8.54, determine the value of the following parameters:

a. Z_i
b. Z_o
c. A_v

Given that the values of the FET parameters $I_{DSS} = 10$ mA, $V_p = -5$ V and $r_d = 50$ kΩ. The quiescent operating point is $V_{GSQ} = -2.5$ V and $I_{DQ} = 2.5$ mA.

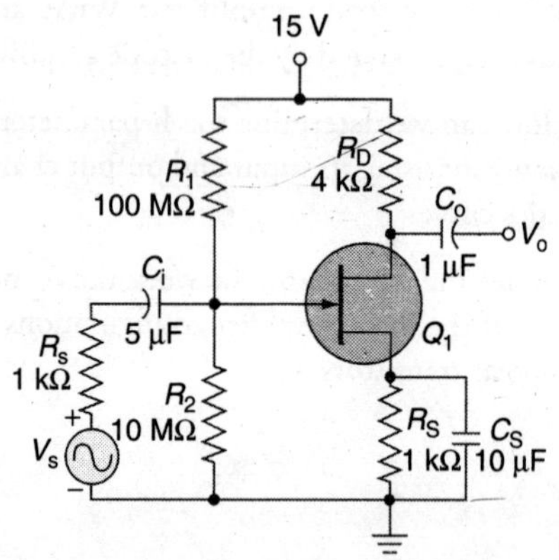

Figure 8.54 | Problem 2.

3. For the single-stage amplifier shown in Figure 8.55, determine the values of

a. $A_{vs} = V_o/V_s$
b. $A_v = V_o/V_i$
c. $A_i = I_o/I_i$

(Given that $h_{fe} = 100$, $h_{ie} = 1$ kΩ and that the effect of h_{oe} can be neglected.)

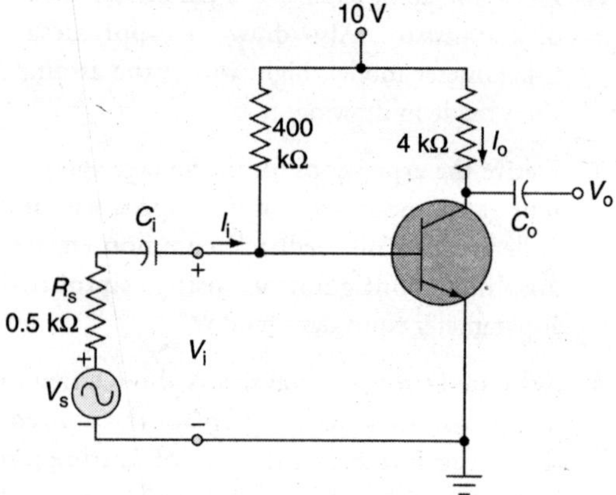

Figure 8.55 | Problem 3.

4. For the BJT configuration shown in Figure 8.56, determine the following:

a. V_i
b. Z_i
c. A_{vnl}
d. A_{vs}

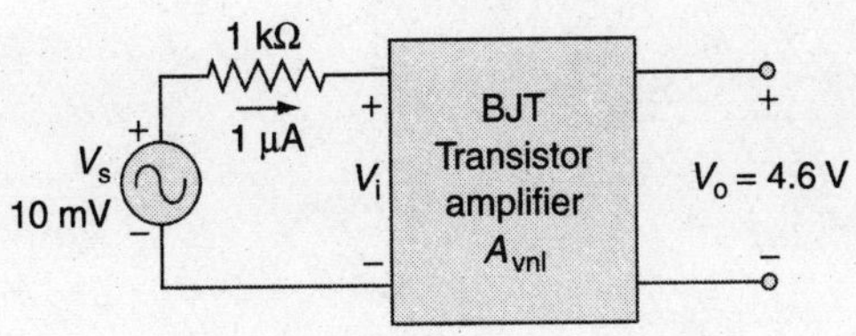

Figure 8.56 Problem 4.

5. For the amplifier shown in Figure 8.57, determine the following:
   a. DC bias currents and voltages to produce a quiescent output voltage of 7.5 V
   b. Z_i
   c. Z_o

   (Given that the h_{fe}, h_{ie} and h_{oe} parameters of both the transistors are 149, 1 kΩ and 25 × 10^{-4} Ω^{-1}, respectively, $V_{BE1} = V_{BE2} = 0.7$ V and $R_s = 500$ Ω.)

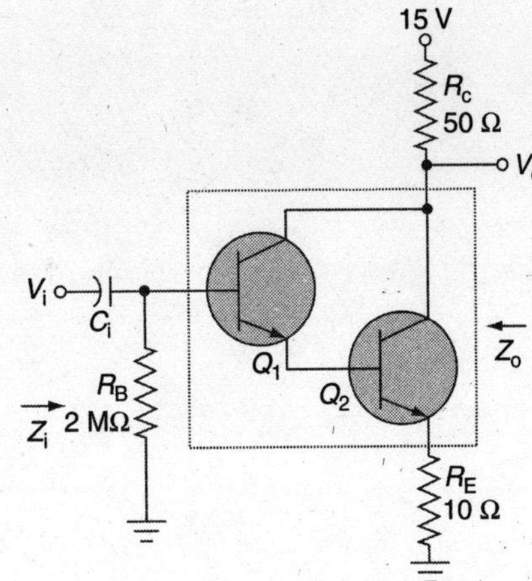

Figure 8.57 Problem 5.

ANSWERS

Multiple-Choice Questions

1. (a)
2. (c)
3. (a)
4. (a)
5. (e)
6. (d)
7. (c)
8. (b)
9. (e)
10. (d)

Fill in the Blanks

1. Highest, lowest
2. Coupling, bypass, stray
3. Emitter–follower, infinite
4. Input, input, impedance
5. Norton's equivalent, gate-source voltage (V_{gs})

Problems

1. 1200, 882.12 Ω, 2 kΩ
2. 9.09 MΩ, 3.7 kΩ, –7.41
3. –266.31, –400, 99.75
4. 9 mV, 9 kΩ, 511.11, 460
5. I_{CQ2} = 150 mA, I_{EQ2} = 150 mA, I_{BQ2} = 1 mA, I_{EQ1} = 1 mA, I_{BQ1} = 6.67 μA, I_{CQ1} = 1 mA, V_{CQ2} = 7.5 V, V_{CQ1} = 7.5 V, V_{EQ2} = 1.5 V, V_{EQ1} = 2.2 V, V_{BQ2} = 2.2 V, V_{BQ1} = 2.9 V, Z_i = 46.51 kΩ, Z_o = 6.73 Ω

CHAPTER 9

High-Frequency Response of Small Signal Amplifiers

Learning Objectives

After completing this chapter, you will learn the following:

- High-frequency model for the common-emitter transistor amplifier configuration.
- Common-emitter short-circuit current gain.
- β cut-off frequency and α cut-off frequency.
- High-frequency response of common-collector transistor amplifier configuration.
- High-frequency response of cascaded amplifier stages.
- High-frequency response of an FET amplifier.
- Amplifier rise time and sag.

The focus in this chapter is on the high-frequency response of small signal amplifiers. The high-frequency response of BJT amplifiers is studied using the hybrid-Π model. High-frequency response of common-emitter, common-collector and common-base BJT amplifiers and FET amplifiers is discussed in the chapter. This is followed by discussion on high-frequency response of cascaded amplifier stages. Other topics discussed in the chapter are Miller's Theorem and amplifier's response to a square input waveform. The chapter is amply illustrated with solved examples.

9.1 High-Frequency Model for the Common-Emitter Transistor Amplifier

The h-parameter model of a transistor is not applicable at high frequencies as at these frequencies the transistor behaves in quite a different manner to what it does at low frequencies. At low frequencies, it is assumed that the transistor responds to the input voltage and current instantly as the diffusion time of the carriers is very small as compared to the rise time of the input signal. However, at high frequencies this is not the case and hence the h-parameter model is not valid at high frequencies. A commonly used model at high frequencies is the hybrid-Π model or the Giacoletto model. This model gives a fairly good approximation of the transistor's behavior at high frequencies.

Figures 9.1(a) and (b) show the circuit of a common-emitter NPN transistor and its hybrid-Π model, respectively. The node B′ is an internal node and is not physically accessible. All the components, both capacitive as well as resistive, are assumed to be independent of frequency. They are dependent on the quiescent operating conditions, but under a given bias condition they do not vary much for small input signal variations.

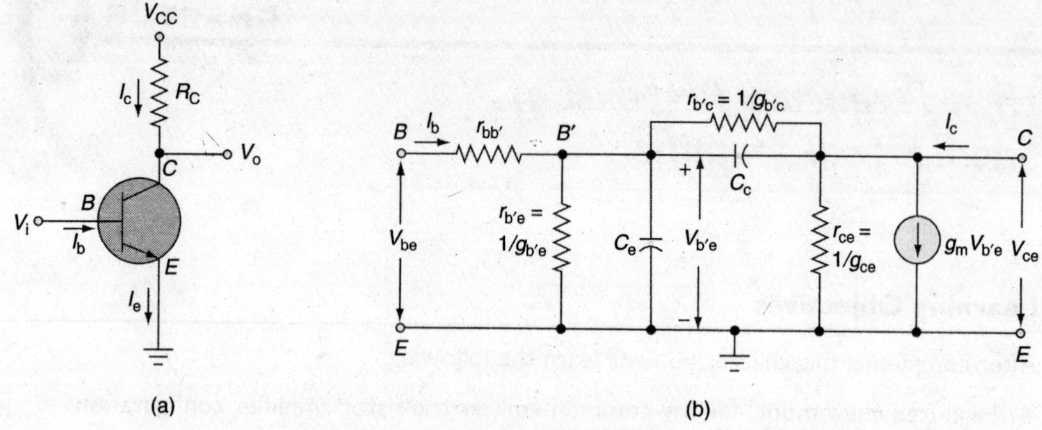

Figure 9.1 (a) Common-emitter NPN transistor; (b) hybrid-Π model of the common-emitter transistor of part (a).

Various circuit components are the base-spreading resistance ($r_{bb'}$), conductance between terminals B′ and E ($g_{b'e}$), conductance between terminals C and E (g_{ce}), conductance between terminals B′ and C ($g_{b'c}$), current source between terminals C and E ($g_m V_{b'e}$), collector-junction barrier capacitance (C_c) and diffusion capacitance between terminals B′ and E (C_e). The ohmic base-spreading resistance ($r_{bb'}$) is represented as a lump parameter between the external base terminal (B) and the node B′. The conductance ($g_{b'e}$) takes into account the increase in the recombination base current due to the increase in the minority carriers in the base region. g_{ce} is the conductance between the collector and the emitter terminals. The conductance ($g_{b'c}$) takes into account the feedback effect between the output and the input due to Early effect. Early effect results in modulation of the width of the base region due to varying collector–emitter voltage which in turn causes a change in the emitter and the collector currents as the slope of the minority-carrier distribution in the base region changes.

Small changes in the value of voltage $V_{b'e}$ cause excess minority carriers, proportional to the voltage $V_{b'e}$, to be injected in to the base region. This results in small signal collector current. Hence, the magnitude of the collector current for shorted collector and emitter terminals is proportional to the voltage $V_{b'e}$. The current generator $g_m V_{b'e}$ takes into account this effect. Note that g_m is the transconductance of the transistor. C_c is the collector-junction barrier capacitance. Sometimes, this capacitance is split into two parts, namely, the capacitance between C and B′ terminals and the capacitance between C and B terminals. The capacitance between C and B terminals is also referred to as the overlap-diode capacitance.

In this section, we will derive the expressions for the components of hybrid-Π model in terms of h-parameters.

Hybrid-Π Conductances

Figure 9.2(a) shows the hybrid-Π model for the common-emitter transistor amplifier applicable at low frequencies and Figure 9.2(b) shows the h-parameter model for the same. As the hybrid-Π model is drawn for low frequencies, the capacitive elements are considered as open circuit.

Base-Spreading Resistance ($r_{bb'}$)

In the circuit shown in Figure 9.2(b), the value of input resistance when the output terminals are shorted, that is $V_{ce} = 0$, is equal to h_{ie}. Under these conditions for the circuit in Figure 9.2(a), the input resistance is given by

$$Z_i\Big|_{V_{ce}=0} = r_{bb'} + r_{b'e} \| r_{b'c} \qquad (9.1)$$

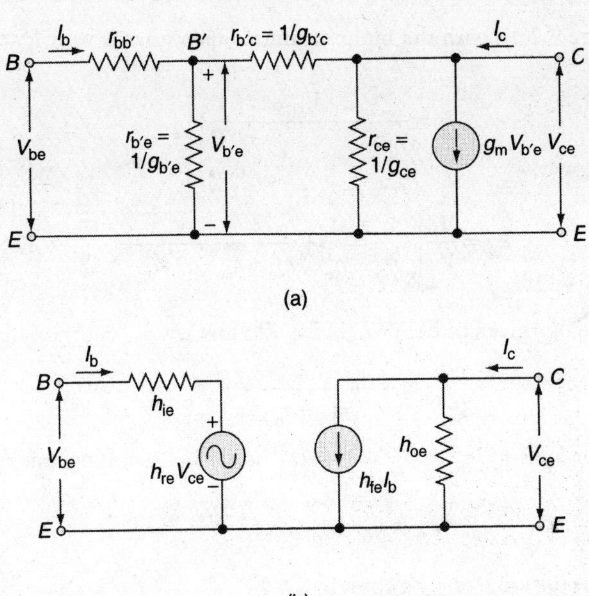

Figure 9.2 (a) Hybrid-Π model for a common-emitter transistor at low frequencies; (b) h-parameter model for a common-emitter transistor at low frequencies.

Therefore

$$h_{ie} = r_{bb'} + r_{b'e} \| r_{b'c} \tag{9.2}$$

As $r_{b'c} >> r_{b'e}$, therefore Eq. (9.2) can be approximated as

$$h_{ie} = r_{bb'} + r_{b'e} \tag{9.3}$$

Conductance between Terminals B′ and C or the Feedback Conductance ($g_{b'c}$)

For the circuit in Figure 9.2(b), if the input terminals are open-circuited, then h_{re} is the reverse voltage gain. In terms of the circuit in Figure 9.2(a), the value of h_{re} is given by

$$h_{re} = \frac{V_{b'e}}{V_{ce}} = \frac{r_{b'e}}{r_{b'e} + r_{b'c}} \tag{9.4}$$

Arranging the terms in Eq. (9.4), we get

$$r_{b'e}(1 - h_{re}) = h_{re} r_{b'c} \tag{9.5}$$

As the value of h_{re} is in the range of 10^{-4}, that is, $h_{re} << 1$, therefore Eq. (9.5) can be approximated by

$$r_{b'e} = h_{re} r_{b'c} \text{ or } g_{b'c} = h_{re}\, g_{b'e} \tag{9.6}$$

The equation also verifies that the value of resistance $r_{b'c}$ is much larger than resistance ($r_{b'e}$), that is, $r_{b'c} >> r_{b'e}$.

Conductance between Terminals C and E (g_{ce})

For the circuit in Figure 9.2(b), if the input terminals are open circuit then

$$V_{b'e} = h_{re} V_{ce} \tag{9.7}$$

For the circuit in Figure 9.2(a), with the input terminals open, that is with $I_b = 0$, the collector current I_c is given by

$$I_c = \frac{V_{ce}}{r_{ce}} + \frac{V_{ce}}{r_{b'e} + r_{b'c}} + g_m V_{b'e} \tag{9.8}$$

Value of h_{oe} is given by

$$h_{oe} = \left.\frac{I_c}{V_{ce}}\right|_{I_b=0} = \frac{1}{r_{ce}} + \frac{1}{r_{b'e} + r_{b'c}} + \frac{g_m V_{b'e}}{V_{ce}} \tag{9.9}$$

Substituting the value of $V_{b'e}$ given in Eq. (9.7) in Eq. (9.9) we get

$$h_{oe} = \frac{1}{r_{ce}} + \frac{1}{r_{b'e} + r_{b'c}} + g_m h_{re} \tag{9.10}$$

Substituting the value of h_{re} as $g_{b'c}/g_{b'e}$, $1/r_{ce}$ as g_{ce}, $1/r_{b'c}$ as $g_{b'c}$ and assuming that $r_{b'c} >> r_{b'e}$, Eq. (9.10) can be rewritten as

$$h_{oe} = g_{ce} + g_{b'c} + g_m \frac{g_{b'c}}{g_{b'e}} \tag{9.11}$$

We will derive latter that the value of g_m is given by

$$g_m = h_{fe}\, g_{b'e} \tag{9.12}$$

Substituting the value of g_m given by Eq. (9.12) in Eq. (9.11), we get

$$h_{oe} = g_{ce} + g_{b'c} + g_{b'c} h_{fe} \tag{9.13}$$

Rearranging the terms in the above equation we get

$$g_{ce} = h_{oe} - (1 + h_{fe}) g_{b'c} \tag{9.14}$$

As the value of $h_{fe} >> 1$, Eq. (9.14) can be approximated as

$$g_{ce} \cong h_{oe} - h_{fe} g_{b'c} \cong h_{oe} - g_m h_{re} \tag{9.15}$$

Conductance between Terminals B′ and E or the Input Conductance ($g_{b'e}$)

In the circuit shown in Figure 9.2(a) as the value of resistance ($r_{b'c}$) is much greater than resistance ($r_{b'e}$), most of the current I_b flows into $r_{b'e}$ and the value of the voltage ($V_{b'e}$) is given by

$$V_{b'e} \cong I_b r_{b'e} \tag{9.16}$$

The short-circuit collector current (I_c) is given by

$$I_c = g_m V_{b'e} \cong g_m I_b r_{b'e} \tag{9.17}$$

As we have studied in Chapter 8, the short-circuit current gain (h_{fe}) is defined as

$$h_{fe} = \left.\frac{I_c}{I_b}\right|_{V_{ce} = \text{const.}} = g_m r_{b'e} \tag{9.18}$$

Rearranging the terms in Eq. (9.18), we get

$$r_{b'e} = \frac{h_{fe}}{g_m} \text{ or } g_{b'e} = \frac{g_m}{h_{fe}} \tag{9.19}$$

Transistor's Transconductance (g_m)

The transconductance of a transistor (g_m) is defined as the ratio of the change in the value of collector current to change in the value of voltage $V_{b'e}$ for constant value of collector–emitter voltage.

For a common-emitter transistor configuration, the expression for collector current is given by

$$I_c = I_{CO} + \alpha I_e \tag{9.20}$$

The value of g_m is given by

$$g_m = \left.\frac{\partial I_c}{\partial V_{b'e}}\right|_{V_{CE} = \text{const.}} = \alpha \frac{\partial I_e}{\partial V_{b'e}} = \alpha \frac{\partial I_e}{\partial V_e} \tag{9.21}$$

The partial derivative of the emitter voltage w.r.t. to the emitter current (i.e., $\partial V_e/\partial I_e$) can be represented as the emitter diode resistance (r_e). As we have studied in Chapter 2 on semiconductor diodes, the dynamic resistance of a forward-biased diode (r_d) is given as

$$r_d = \frac{V_T}{I_D} \tag{9.22}$$

where V_T is the volt equivalent of temperature and I_D is the diode current. Therefore, the value of g_m can be generalized as

$$g_m = \frac{\alpha I_e}{V_T} = \frac{I_c - I_{CO}}{V_T} \tag{9.23}$$

As the value of $I_c >> I_{CO}$, therefore the value of g_m for an NPN transistor is positive. For a PNP transistor, the analysis can be carried out on similar lines and the value of g_m in the case of a PNP transistor is also positive. Therefore, the expression for g_m can be written as

$$g_m = \frac{|I_c|}{V_T} \tag{9.24}$$

Hybrid-Π Capacitances

In the hybrid-Π model shown in Figure 9.1(b), there are two capacitances namely the collector-junction barrier capacitance (C_c) and the emitter-junction diffusion capacitance (C_e).

Collector-Junction Capacitance (C_c)

The capacitance C_c is the output capacitance of the common-base transistor configuration with the input open ($I_e = 0$). It is also specified as C_{ob}. As the collector–base junction is reverse-biased, C_c is the transition capacitance and it varies as $(V_{CB})^{-n}$, where n is 1/2 for abrupt junction and 1/3 for a graded junction.

Emitter-Junction Capacitance (C_e)

The capacitance C_e is the diffusion capacitance of the forward-biased emitter junction and is proportional to the emitter current (I_e) and is almost independent of temperature.

Variation of Hybrid-Π Parameters

The variations in the values of hybrid-Π parameters with change in collector current (I_C), collector–emitter voltage (V_{CE}) and temperature (T) are highlighted in Table 9.1.

Table 9.1 | Variations in the values of hybrid-Π parameters

Parameter	$I_C\uparrow$	$V_{CE}\uparrow$	$T\uparrow$
g_m	Linear	Independent	Inverse
$r_{bb'}$	Decreases	Complex relation	Increases
$r_{b'e}$	Inverse	Increases	Increases
C_e	Linear	Decreases	Complex relation
C_c	Independent	Decreases	Increases

9.2 Common-Emitter Short-Circuit Current Gain

Let us consider a single-stage common-emitter amplifier with the value of the collector resistor (R_C) equal to zero. In this case as the collector resistor acts as the load resistor, this means that the load is short circuit. Figure 9.3(a) shows the circuit connection and Figure 9.3(b) shows the hybrid-Π equivalent model for the circuit. The input source is a sinusoidal source and furnishes a sinusoidal input current I_i. The load current produced is I_L. The equivalent model shown in the figure can be simplified to that shown in Figure 9.3(c). The assumptions made in the simplified model are that the conductance $g_{b'c}$ can be neglected as the value of $g_{b'c} << g_{b'e}$. The conductance g_{ce} has also been removed as it is placed across short-circuited terminals. Another approximation is that the current delivered directly to the output through the conductance $g_{b'c}$ and capacitance C_c has been neglected.

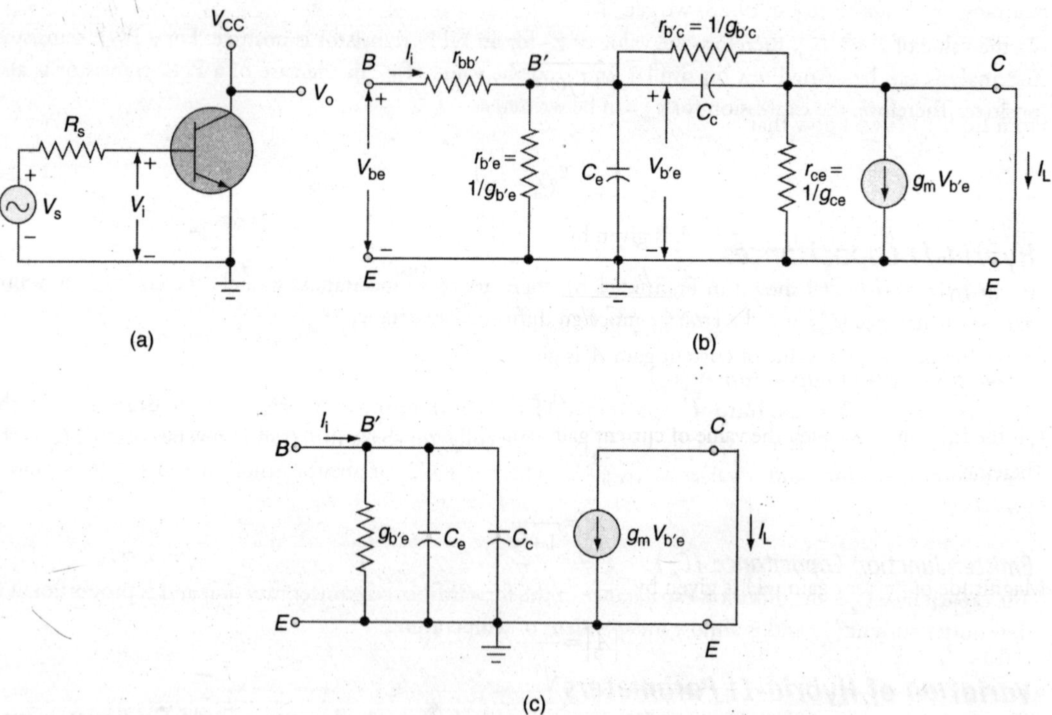

Figure 9.3 | (a) Common-emitter amplifier with short-circuit load; (b) hybrid-Π equivalent model for the amplifier in part (a); (c) simplified hybrid-Π equivalent model.

The parameters of interest are the β cut-off frequency (f_β) and the short-circuit gain bandwidth product (f_T). f_β is the frequency at which the value of short-circuit common-emitter gain reduces to 0.707 times its mid-band value. In other words, at the β cut-off frequency, the short-circuit common-emitter current gain is 3 dB below its mid-band value. Thus, f_β represents the maximum attainable current gain bandwidth for the common-emitter amplifier. The actual maximum bandwidth depends upon the circuit connections. f_T is the frequency at which the short-circuit common-emitter current gain value is unity or 0 dB.

β Cut-Off Frequency

For the circuit shown in Figure 9.3(c), the value of load current (I_L) is given by

$$I_L = -g_m V_{b'e} \tag{9.25}$$

The value of $V_{b'e}$ is given by

$$V_{b'e} = \frac{I_i}{g_{b'e} + j\omega(C_e + C_c)} \tag{9.26}$$

The value of current gain (A_i) under short-circuit condition is

$$A_i = \frac{I_L}{I_i} \tag{9.27}$$

Substituting the values of I_L and I_i given by Eqs. (9.25) and (9.26), respectively, in Eq. (9.27) we get

$$A_i = \frac{-g_m}{g_{b'e} + j\omega(C_e + C_c)} \tag{9.28}$$

Rearranging the terms in Eq. (9.28) we get

$$A_i = \frac{-g_m / g_{b'e}}{1 + [j\omega(C_e + C_c) / g_{b'e}]} \tag{9.29}$$

From Eq. (9.19) we know that

$$g_{b'e} = \frac{g_m}{h_{fe}}$$

Therefore, the value of current gain A_i is given by

$$A_i = \frac{-h_{fe}}{1 + [j\omega(C_e + C_c)/g_{b'e}]} = \frac{-h_{fe}}{1 + [j2\pi f(C_e + C_c)/g_{b'e}]} \tag{9.30}$$

At low frequencies, the value of current gain A_i is given by

$$A_i = -h_{fe} \tag{9.31}$$

f_β is the frequency at which the value of current gain reduces to 0.707 times the gain value given in Eq. (9.31). Therefore,

$$A_i = \frac{-h_{fe}}{1 + j(f/f_\beta)} \tag{9.32}$$

Magnitude of current gain (A_i) is given by

$$|A_i| = \frac{h_{fe}}{\sqrt{1 + (f/f_\beta)^2}}$$

The value of f_β is given by

$$f_\beta = \frac{g_{b'e}}{2\pi(C_e + C_c)} \tag{9.33}$$

As we can see from Eq. (9.31), the value of A_i is equal to $-h_{fe}$ at zero and low frequencies. Remember that h_{fe} is the low-frequency short-circuit current gain of the common-emitter amplifier configuration.

Gain-Bandwidth Product

The frequency f_T is the frequency at which the magnitude of the short-circuit current gain of the common-emitter amplifier configuration becomes unity. As the value of $h_{fe} >> 1$, the magnitude of the current gain A_i becomes unity at the frequency given by the product of h_{fe} and f_β. Therefore, f_T is given by

$$f_T \cong h_{fe} f_\beta \cong \frac{h_{fe} g_{b'e}}{2\pi(C_e + C_c)} \cong \frac{g_m}{2\pi(C_e + C_c)} \tag{9.34}$$

The parameter f_T is a strong function of the collector current of the transistor. The variation of f_T with collector current (I_c) is highlighted in Figure 9.4.

The expression for current gain A_i can be written as

$$A_i \cong \frac{-h_{fe}}{1 + jh_{fe}(f/f_T)} \tag{9.35}$$

Figure 9.5 shows the variation of the current gain of the short-circuit common-emitter amplifier configuration with frequency. The dotted bold lines indicate the asymptotic curves while the regular bold line shows the actual curve. The two asymptotes intersect each other at $f = f_\beta$ and the gain thereafter decreases at a rate of 20 dB/decade. The actual gain at $f = f_\beta$ is 3 dB down (or 0.707 times) the value of mid-band gain.

α Cut-Off Frequency

The α cut-off frequency is the frequency at which the short-circuit current gain value of the common-base configuration drops by 3 dB to its value at low frequencies. It is represented as f_α. It may be mentioned here that the transistor used in common-base configuration has a much higher value of 3 dB frequency as compared to the transistor used in common-emitter configuration. In other words, the value of f_α is much larger than the value of f_β.

The expression for the current gain of the common-base amplifier configuration is given by

$$A_i = \frac{-h_{fb}}{1 + j(f/f_\alpha)} \tag{9.36}$$

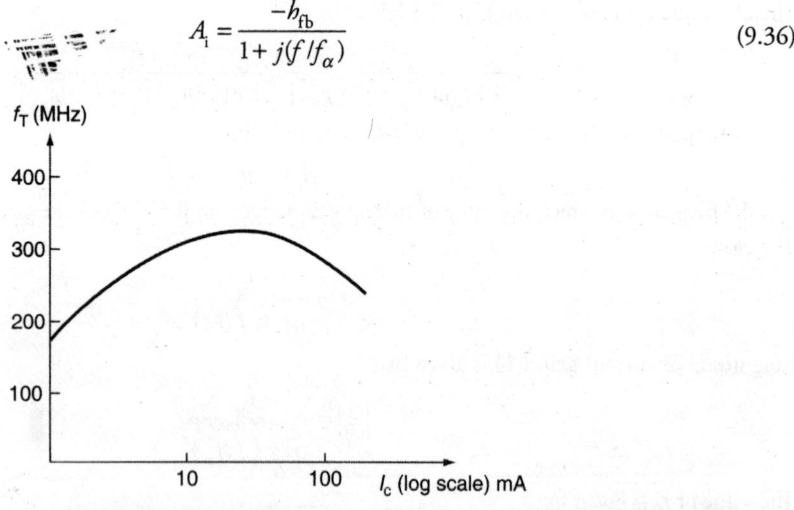

Figure 9.4 Variation of the frequency f_T with collector current.

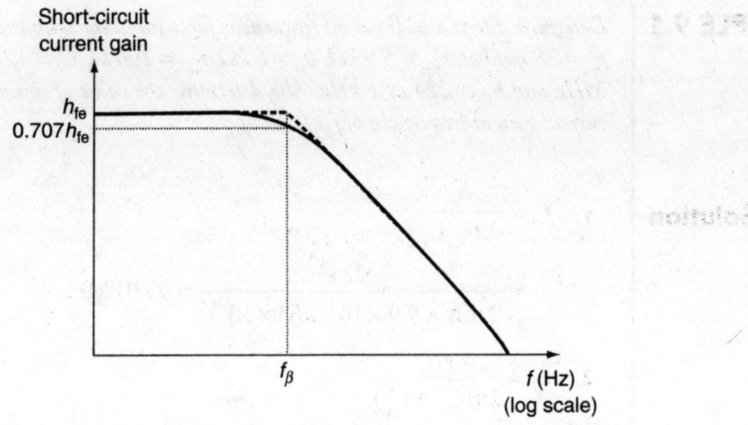

Figure 9.5 Variation of short-circuit common-emitter current gain with frequency.

where f_α is the α cut-off frequency. The expression for the α cut-off frequency is given by

$$f_\alpha = \frac{1}{2\pi r_{b'e}(1+h_{fb})C_e} \tag{9.37}$$

As the value of $h_{fe} \cong 1/(1 + h_{fb})$, Eq. (9.37) can be rewritten as

$$f_\alpha \cong \frac{h_{fe}}{2\pi r_{b'e}C_e} \tag{9.38}$$

Multiplying and dividing Eq. (9.38) by $(C_e + C_c)$ and substituting the value of f_β in the equation, we get

$$f_\alpha \cong \frac{h_{fe}f_\beta(C_e + C_c)}{C_e} \tag{9.39}$$

From the above equation, it is clear that the bandwidth offered by the common-base amplifier is much higher than that offered by the common-emitter amplifier, although the latter has much higher value of gain. Figure 9.6 shows the comparison of the manner in which short-circuit current gains for the common-emitter and common-base amplifier configurations vary with frequency.

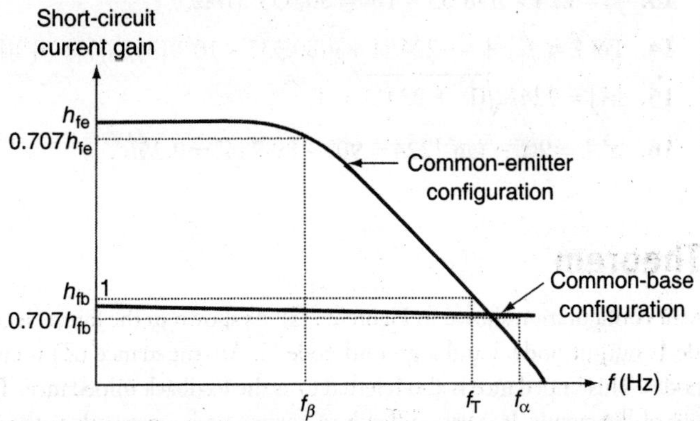

Figure 9.6 Comparison of variations of short-circuit current gains of common-emitter and common-base amplifier configurations with frequency.

EXAMPLE 9.1 *Determine the α and β cut-off frequencies for a transistor with the following specifications: $g_m = 38$ mmhos, $r_{b'e} = 5.9\ k\Omega$, $h_{ie} = 6\ k\Omega$, $r_{bb'} = 100\ \Omega$, $C_c = 12\ pF$, $C_e = 63\ pF$, $f_T = 80$ MHz and $h_{fe} = 224$ at 1 kHz. Also determine the value of common-emitter short-circuit current gain at frequencies of f_β, f_T and f_α.*

Solution

1. $$f_\alpha = \frac{h_{fe}}{2\pi r_{b'e} C_e}$$
$$= \frac{224}{2\times\pi\times 5.9\times 10^3 \times 63\times 10^{-12}} = 95.91\ \text{MHz}$$
2. $$f_\beta = \frac{g_{b'e}}{2\pi(C_e + C_c)}$$
3. $g_{b'e} = 1/r_{b'e} = 1/(5.9 \times 10^3) = 1.69 \times 10^{-4}$.
4. $f_\beta = 1.69 \times 10^{-4}/[2 \times \pi \times (63 \times 10^{-12} + 12 \times 10^{-12})] = 358.63$ kHz.
5. Common-emitter short-circuit current gain is given by
$$A_i = \frac{-h_{fe}}{1 + j(f/f_\beta)}$$
6. For $f = f_\alpha$, $A_i = -224/[1 + j\{(95.91 \times 10^6)/(358.63 \times 10^3)\}] = -224/(1 + 267.43j)$.
7. $|A_i| = 224/\sqrt{(1^2 + 267.43^2)} = 0.838$.
8. $\angle A_i = 90° - \tan^{-1}(267.43) = 90° - 89.786° = 0.21°$.
9. For $f = f_\beta$, $A_i = -224/[1 + j\{(358.63 \times 10^3)/(358.63 \times 10^3)\}] = -224/(1 + j)$.
10. $|A_i| = 224/\sqrt{2} = 158.39$.
11. $\angle A_i = 90° - \tan^{-1}1 = 90° - 45° = 45°$.
12. $f_T = h_{fe} f_\beta$.
13. $f_T = 224 \times 358.63 \times 10^3 = 80.333$ MHz.
14. For $f = f_T$, $A_i = -224/[1 + j\{(80.333 \times 10^6)/(358.63 \times 10^3)\}] = -224/(1 + 224j)$.
15. $|A_i| = 224/\sqrt{(1^2 + 224^2)} = 1$.
16. $\angle A_i = 90° - \tan^{-1}224 = 90° - 89.744° = 0.256°$.

9.3 Miller's Theorem

Let us consider a circuit configuration shown in Figure 9.7(a). As shown in the figure, it comprises three nodes, namely, input node 1, output node 2 and a ground node G. An impedance (Z) is connected between the input and the output nodes. This impedance is also referred to as the feedback impedance. This impedance has an effect on the functioning of the circuit. It is very difficult to analyze such a network as the impedance affects the input and the output simultaneously. Miller's theorem helps to analyze such circuit configurations. According to Miller's theorem, the circuit with feedback impedance can be replaced by an equivalent circuit such that the

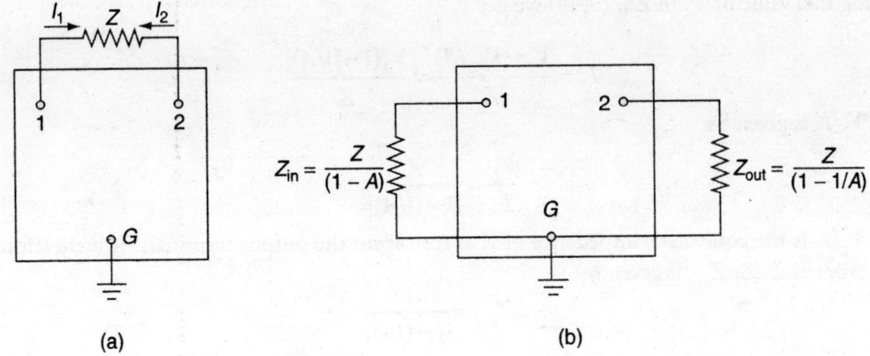

Figure 9.7 (a) Circuit configuration with feedback impedance; (b) Miller's equivalent circuit of the network in part (a).

feedback impedance is split into two impedances: one between the input terminal and ground (Z_{in}) and the other between the output terminal and ground (Z_{out}). Figure 9.7(b) shows the Miller's equivalent circuit of the network shown in Figure 9.7(a). In the subsequent paragraphs, we derive the expressions for Z_{in} and Z_{out}.

Let the voltages at nodes 1 and 2 be V_1 and V_2, respectively. Let the ratio of V_2/V_1 be represented as A. Using Miller's theorem, the impedance connected between nodes 1 and 2 can be replaced by two impedances: one between node 1 and ground node G (Z_{in}) and the other between node 2 and ground node G (Z_{out}). The value of current I_1 is given by

$$I_1 = \frac{V_1 - V_2}{Z} \tag{9.40}$$

The value of V_2 is given by

$$V_2 = AV_1$$

Therefore, current I_1 is given as

$$I_1 = \frac{V_1 - AV_1}{Z} = \frac{V_1(1-A)}{Z} \tag{9.41}$$

From Eq. (9.41), the ratio of V_1/I_1 is given by

$$\frac{V_1}{I_1} = \frac{Z}{1-A} \tag{9.42}$$

V_1/I_1 is the equivalent impedance of Z as seen from the input side of the circuit. Therefore, Z_{in} is equal to the ratio V_1/I_1 and is given by

$$Z_{in} = \frac{Z}{1-A} \tag{9.43}$$

The impedance Z_{in} appears in parallel with the input terminals of the network. The expression for output impedance Z_{out} can be derived as follows. The value of current I_2 is given by

$$I_2 = \frac{V_2 - V_1}{Z} \tag{9.44}$$

Voltage V_1 is expressed in terms of voltage V_2 as

$$V_1 = \frac{V_2}{A}$$

Substituting this value of V_1 in Eq. (9.44) we get

$$I_2 = \frac{V_2 - (V_2/A)}{Z} = \frac{V_2[1-(1/A)]}{Z} \tag{9.45}$$

The ratio V_2/I_2 is given by

$$\frac{V_2}{I_2} = \frac{Z}{[1-(1/A)]} \tag{9.46}$$

The ratio V_2/I_2 is the equivalent impedance of Z as seen from the output terminals. It is therefore equal to Z_{out}. The expression for Z_{out} is given by

$$Z_{out} = \frac{Z}{1-(1/A)} \tag{9.47}$$

EXAMPLE 9.2 *For the circuit shown in Figure 9.8, determine the values of following parameters: (a) R_i; (b) R_i'; (c) amplifier voltage gain (A_v); (d) system voltage gain (A_{vs}); (e) amplifier current gain (A_i) and (f) system current gain (A_i'). The value of transistor's h-parameters are $h_{ie} = 1\ k\Omega$, $h_{re} = 1 \times 10^{-4}$, $h_{fe} = 100$ and $h_{oe} = 25 \times 10^{-6}\ \Omega^{-1}$.*

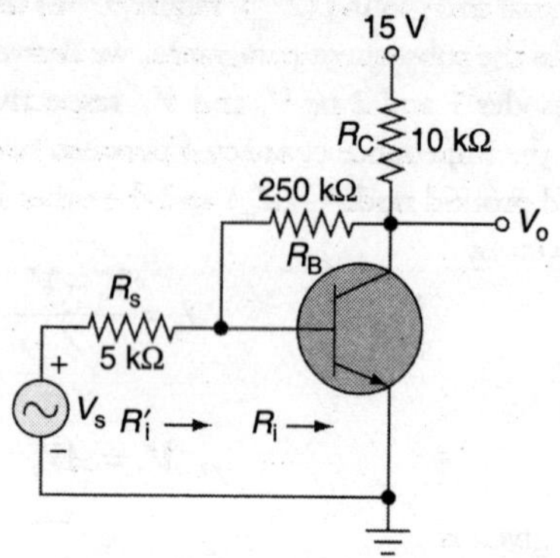

Figure 9.8 Example 9.1.

Solution

1. The resistor R_B is the feedback resistor between the input and the output terminals. It can be replaced by the Miller's equivalent components as shown in Figure 9.9. The equivalent impedance of R_B as seen from the output terminals (R_{BO}) is given by $R_B/[1 - (1/A_v)]$. A_v is the voltage gain from base to collector. As the value of voltage gain is much larger than 1, therefore, value of $R_{BO} \cong R_B \cong 250\ k\Omega$.
2. The effective load resistance $(R_L') = R_C \parallel R_{BO} = 10 \times 10^3 \parallel 250 \times 10^3 = 9.61 \times 10^3\ \Omega = 9.61\ k\Omega$.
3. The value of input resistance R_i is given by

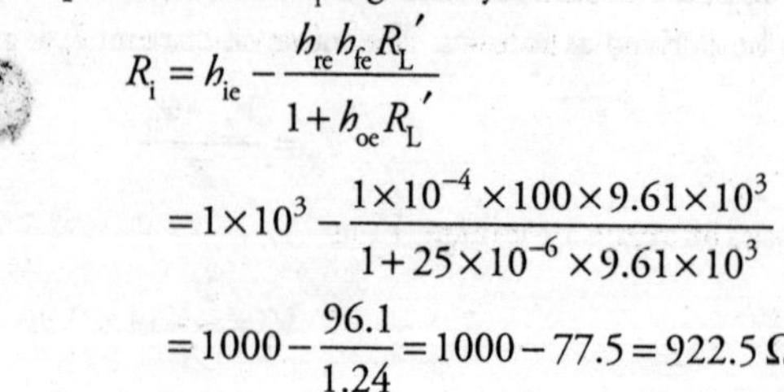

$$R_i = h_{ie} - \frac{h_{re} h_{fe} R_L'}{1 + h_{oe} R_L'}$$

$$= 1\times10^3 - \frac{1\times10^{-4}\times100\times9.61\times10^3}{1+25\times10^{-6}\times9.61\times10^3}$$

$$= 1000 - \frac{96.1}{1.24} = 1000 - 77.5 = 922.5\ \Omega$$

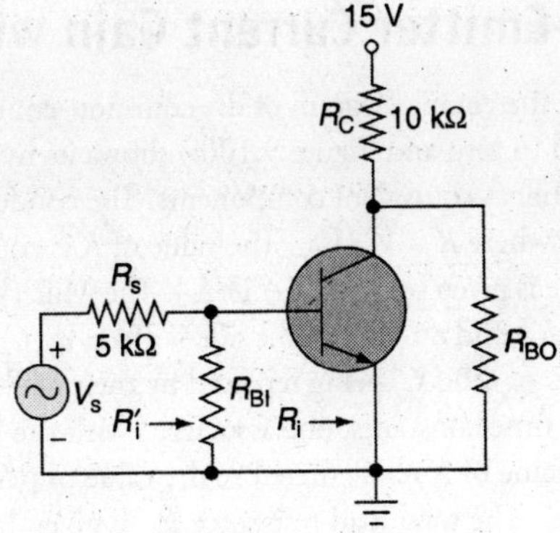

Figure 9.9 Solution to Example 9.2.

4. Current gain is given by

$$A_i = -\frac{h_{fe}}{1 + h_{oe} R_L'}$$

$$= \frac{-100}{1 + 25 \times 10^{-6} \times 9.61 \times 10^3} = -80.63$$

5. The value of voltage gain is given by

$$A_v = \frac{A_i R_L'}{R_i}$$

$$= \frac{-80.63 \times 9.61 \times 10^3}{922.5} = -839.95$$

6. The value of the effective resistance of R_B from the input side $(R_{BI}) = R_B/[1 - A_v]$ $= 250 \times 10^3 / [1 - (-839.95)] = (250 \times 10^3)/840.95 = 297.28\ \Omega$.

7. The value of $R_i' = R_i \,||\, R_{BI} = 922.5 \,||\, 297.28 = 224.83\ \Omega$.

8. System voltage gain A_{vs} is given by

$$A_{vs} = A_v \times [R_i'/(R_i' + R_s)]$$
$$= -839.95 \times [224.83/(224.83 + 5 \times 10^3)]$$
$$= -839.95 \times 0.043 = -36.12$$

9. The value of system current gain A_i' is given by

$$A_i' = A_i \times \left(\frac{R_{RI}}{R_i + R_{BI}}\right) \times \left(\frac{R_{BO}}{R_{BO} + R_C}\right)$$

$$= -80.63 \times \frac{297.28}{922.5 + 297.28} \times \frac{250 \times 10^3}{250 \times 10^3 + 10 \times 10^3}$$

$$= -80.63 \times \frac{297.28}{1219.78} \times \frac{250}{260}$$

$$= -80.63 \times 0.244 \times 0.96 = -18.89$$

9.4 Common-Emitter Current Gain with Resistive Load

Figure 9.10(a) shows the circuit diagram of the common-emitter amplifier configuration when the load resistor (R_L) is not equal to zero and Figure 9.10(b) shows its hybrid-Π equivalent model. The conductance $g_{b'c}$ can be replaced by its Miller's equivalent components. The conductance component due to $g_{b'c}$ on the input side is given by $g_{b'c}$ $(1 - K)$, where $K = V_{ce}/V_{b'e}$. The value of K is equal to $-g_m R_L$. The conductance component due to $g_{b'c}$ on the output side is given by $g_{b'c}$ $[(K - 1)/K]$. The Miller's component of the capacitance C_c on the input side is given by C_c $(1 - K)$ and on the output side is given by C_c $[(K - 1)/K]$. Figure 9.11 shows the equivalent circuit with components $g_{b'c}$ and C_c being replaced by their Miller's equivalent components.

The circuit has two time constants, one associated with the input section and the other associated with the output section. As the value of $K >> 1$, therefore the value of $[(K - 1)/K] \cong 1$. Therefore, $g_{b'c}$ $[(K - 1)/K] \cong g_{b'c}$ and C_c $[(K - 1)/K] \cong C_c$. The total load resistance R_L' is given by

$$R_L' = R_L \| (1/g_{b'c}) \| (1/g_{ce}) \tag{9.48}$$

In most cases, the value of $g_{b'c} << g_{ce}$ ($r_{b'c} \approx$ 4–5 MΩ and $r_{ce} \approx$ 80–100 kΩ), therefore $g_{b'c}$ can be ignored from the output section. The value of load resistor R_L is in the range of 2–5 kΩ. Therefore, the conductance g_{ce} can be neglected as compared to $1/R_L$. Therefore, resistor $R_L' \cong R_L$.

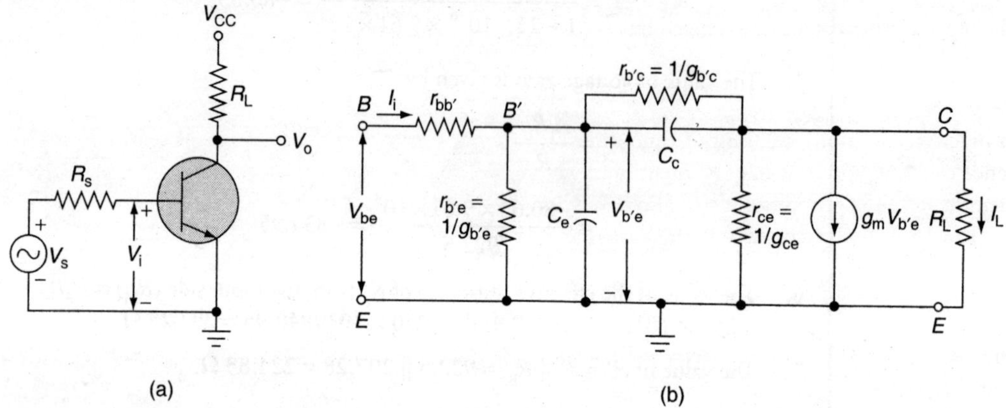

Figure 9.10 (a) Circuit diagram of common-emitter amplifier configuration with load resistance (R_L); (b) hybrid-Π equivalent model of the circuit in part (a).

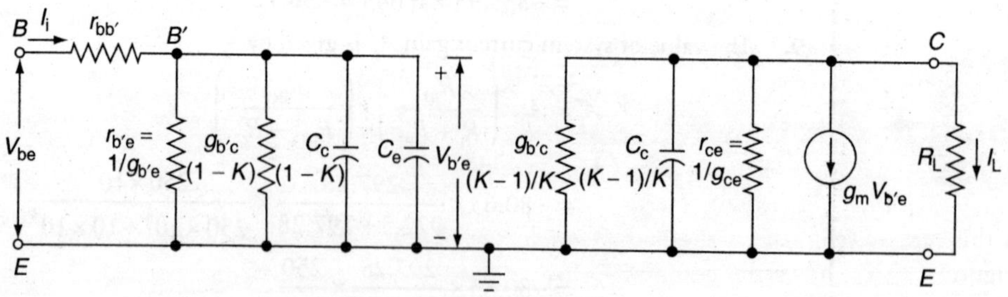

Figure 9.11 Simplified hybrid-Π model making use of Miller's theorem for the model shown in Figure 9.10(b).

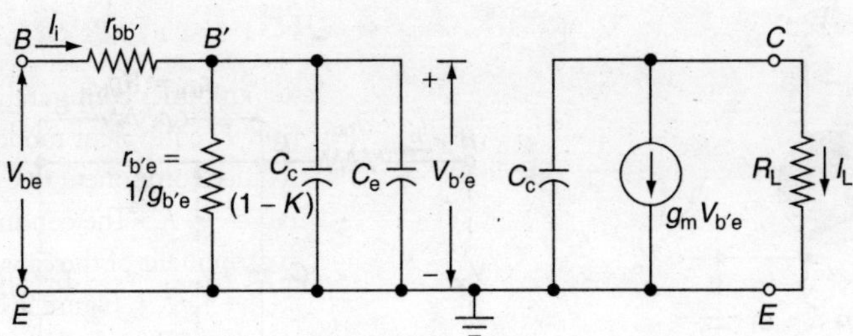

Figure 9.12 Further simplified hybrid-Π model for the model shown in Figure 9.10(b).

The input conductance (g_i) is given by

$$g_i = g_{b'e} + g_{b'c}(1-K) \tag{9.49}$$

In most of the cases, the magnitude of the conductance $g_{b'c}(1-K)$ is very small as compared to the value of $g_{b'e}$. Therefore, $g_i \cong g_{b'e}$. Figure 9.12 shows the further simplified hybrid-Π equivalent model.
The output time constant (t_{oc}) is given by

$$t_{oc} = R_L{'}C_c \approx R_L C_c \tag{9.50}$$

The input time constant (t_{ic}) is given by

$$t_{ic} = (1/g_i) \times [C_e + C_c(1 + g_m R_L) \approx (1/g_{b'e})] \times [C_e + C_c(1 + g_m R_L)] \tag{9.51}$$

In practical situations, the output time constant is negligible as compared to the input time constant and hence can be ignored. It may be mentioned here that if the transistor works into a highly capacitive load, then the output time constant will also be predominant and cannot be ignored.

The upper 3 dB frequency in this case is given by

$$f_H = \frac{1}{2\pi r_{b'e}[C_e + C_c(1 + g_m R_L)]} \tag{9.52}$$

The above equation has been derived by neglecting the effect of the base-spreading resistance ($r_{bb'}$) and source resistor (R_s). The value of source resistor has a very strong influence on the upper cut-off frequency. The cut-off frequency taking into account the effect of R_s and $r_{bb'}$ is given by

$$f_H = \frac{1}{2\pi[(R_s + r_{bb'}) \| r_{b'e}][C_e + C_c(1 + g_m R_L)]} \tag{9.53}$$

When the effect of biasing resistors is taken into account, the term R_s in Eq. (9.53) is replaced by $R_{s'}$, where $R_{s'}$ is a parallel combination of R_s and biasing resistors.

9.5 High-Frequency Response of Common-Collector Transistor Amplifier

In this section, we discuss the high-frequency response of a common-collector transistor amplifier. Figure 9.13(a) shows the common-collector transistor amplifier configuration. Capacitance C_L is included in parallel with the load resistor R_L as the common-collector transistor due to its low output resistance is often used to drive capacitive loads. Figure 9.13(b) shows the hybrid-Π equivalent model for the common-collector amplifier configuration shown in Figure 9.13(a).

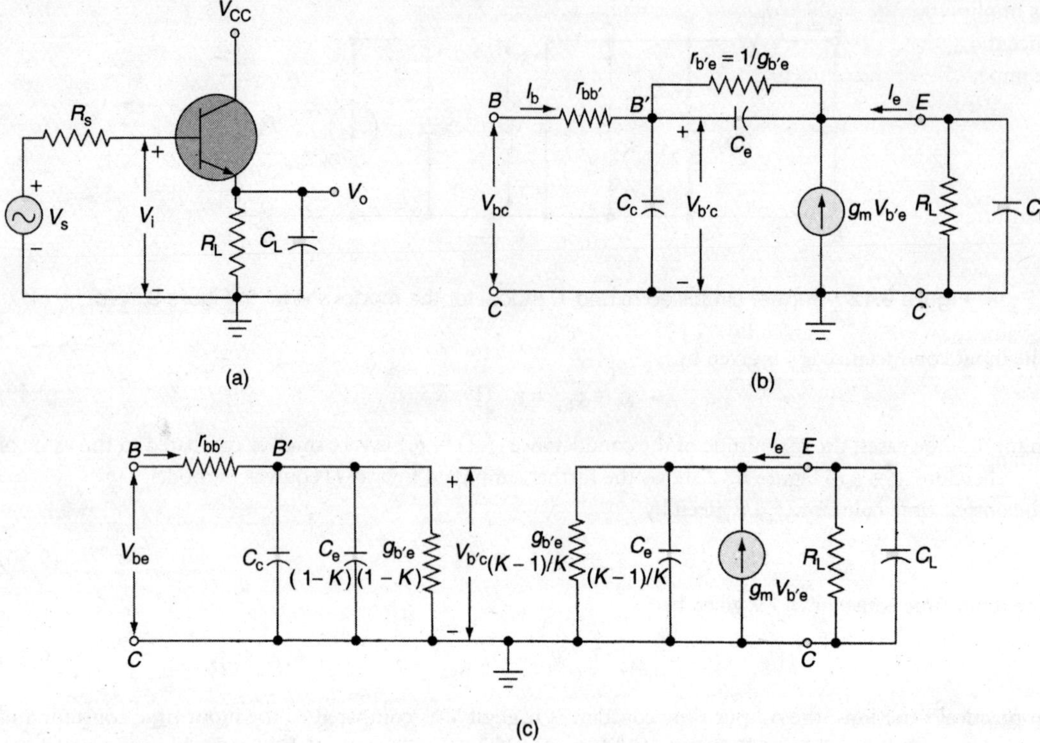

Figure 9.13 (a) Common-collector amplifier; (b) hybrid-Π equivalent model of the common-collector amplifier; (c) simplified hybrid-Π equivalent model of the common-collector amplifier.

Applying Miller's theorem to the hybrid-Π equivalent circuit of Figure 9.13(b), we get the equivalent circuit as shown in Figure 9.13(c). The parameter K is given by the ratio of voltages V_{ec} and $V_{b'c}$ (i.e., $K = V_{ec}/V_{b'c}$). The input time constant t_{ic} is given by

$$t_{ic} = \left[(R_s + r_{bb'}) \middle\| \left\{ \frac{1}{g_{b'e}(1-K)} \right\} \right] [C_c + C_e(1-K)] \tag{9.54}$$

As the low-frequency gain of the emitter–follower configuration is approximately equal to unity, therefore $(1 - K) \cong 0$. Therefore, the expression for t_{ic} can be approximated by

$$t_{ic} \cong (R_s + r_{bb'})C_c \tag{9.55}$$

The output time constant (t_{oc}) is given by

$$t_{oc} = \left[R_L \middle\| \left\{ \frac{1}{g_{b'e}(K-1)/K} \right\} \right] [C_L + C_e(K-1)/K] \tag{9.56}$$

As the value of $(K - 1) \cong 0$, the above equation can be simplified as

$$t_{oc} \cong R_L C_L \tag{9.57}$$

As we have assumed that the output load is highly capacitive, therefore the value of $C_L >> C_c$. Hence,

$$R_L C_L >> (R_s + r_{bb'})C_c \tag{9.58}$$

This implies that the value of output time constant (t_{oc}) is much larger than the input time constant (t_{ic}). Hence the upper 3 dB frequency is determined mostly by the output circuit.
The impedance of the output circuit (Z_o) is given by

$$Z_o = R_L \left\| \frac{1}{g_{b'e}(K-1)/K} \right\| \frac{1}{j\omega\{C_L + C_e(K-1)/K\}} \tag{9.59}$$

Substituting $(K-1) \cong 0$, we get

$$Z_o \cong R_L \left\| \frac{1}{j\omega C_L} \right. \tag{9.60}$$

The value of voltage V_{ec} is given by

$$V_{ec} = g_m V_{b'e} Z_o \cong g_m V_{b'e} \left(R_L \left\| \frac{1}{j\omega C_L} \right. \right) \tag{9.61}$$

Rearranging the terms we get

$$V_{ec} = \frac{g_m V_{b'e}}{(1/R_L) + j\omega C_L} = \frac{g_m V_{b'e} R_L}{1 + j\omega R_L C_L} \tag{9.62}$$

The value of $V_{b'e}$ is given by $V_{b'e} = V_{b'c} - V_{ec}$. Therefore, Eq. (9.62) can be rewritten as

$$V_{ec} = \frac{g_m (V_{b'c} - V_{ec}) R_L}{1 + j\omega R_L C_L}$$

The value of V_{ec} is given by

$$V_{ec} = \frac{g_m R_L V_{b'c}}{1 + g_m R_L + j\omega R_L C_L} \tag{9.63}$$

As $K = V_{ec}/V_{b'c}$, therefore the expression for K is given by

$$K = \frac{V_{ec}}{V_{b'c}} = \frac{g_m R_L}{1 + g_m R_L + j\omega R_L C_L} \tag{9.64}$$

Multiplying and dividing Eq. (9.64) by $(1 + g_m R_L)$ we get

$$A = \left(\frac{g_m R_L}{1 + g_m R_L} \right) \frac{1}{1 + [j\omega R_L C_L/(1 + g_m R_L)]} \tag{9.65}$$

Equation (9.65) can be rewritten as Eq. (9.66)

$$A = \left(\frac{g_m R_L}{1 + g_m R_L} \right) \left(\frac{1}{1 + (jf/f_H)} \right) \tag{9.66}$$

where $f_H = (1 + g_m R_L)/2\pi C_L R_L$. The value of f_H can be expressed as

$$f_H = \frac{1 + g_m R_L}{2\pi R_L C_L} \cong \frac{g_m}{2\pi C_L} \tag{9.67}$$

From Eq. (9.34), the value of unity gain bandwidth (f_T) is given by

$$f_T = \frac{g_m}{2\pi (C_e + C_c)} \tag{9.68}$$

As the value of C_e for a transistor is much larger than C_c, therefore f_T can be approximated by

$$f_T \cong \frac{g_m}{2\pi C_e} \tag{9.69}$$

Substituting this value of f_T in Eq. (9.67) we get

$$f_H \cong \frac{f_T C_e}{C_L} \tag{9.70}$$

Since the input impedance between terminals B′ and C is much larger as compared to $(R_s + r_{bb'})$, therefore K is approximately the overall voltage gain (A_{vs}), that is,

$$K \cong A_{vs} = \frac{V_{ec}}{V_s} \tag{9.71}$$

9.6 High-Frequency Response of an FET Amplifier

The high-frequency response of an FET amplifier is similar to that of a BJT amplifier. Figure 9.14 shows the high-frequency model for an FET (JFET as well as MOSFET). The high-frequency model is similar to the low-frequency model with the addition of junction capacitances.

The capacitance C_{gs} represents the barrier capacitance between the gate and the source terminals. C_{gd} is the barrier capacitance between the gate and the drain terminals. C_{ds} is the drain-to-source capacitance of the channel. These capacitors offer high impedance at lower frequencies and can be considered as open circuit. However, at high frequencies, due to these capacitances feedback exists between the input and output circuits and voltage amplification drops rapidly as the frequency increases.

In this section, we discuss the high-frequency response of the common-source and common-drain FET amplifiers. The derivations are done for JFET-based amplifiers. The expressions derived here apply equally well to MOSFET-based amplifiers as well.

Common-Source Amplifier at High Frequencies

Figure 9.15(a) shows the circuit diagram for the common-source JFET amplifier and Figure 9.15(b) shows its small signal high-frequency equivalent model. The output voltage V_o is given by the product of short-circuit current (I) and the impedance seen between the output terminals (Z). Therefore,

$$V_o = ZI \tag{9.72}$$

Z is determined by shorting the input terminals, that is, $V_s = 0$. Hence, there is no current flowing through the current generator $g_m V_s$. Therefore, the value of Z is given by the parallel combination of R_L, $j\omega C_{ds}$, r_d and $j\omega C_{gd}$ and is given by

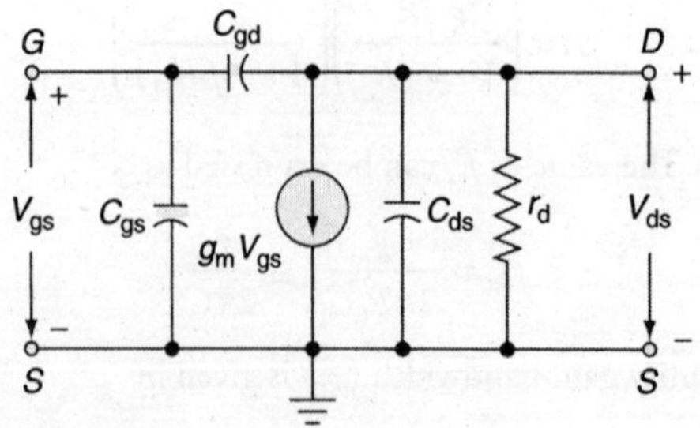

Figure 9.14 High-frequency model of an FET.

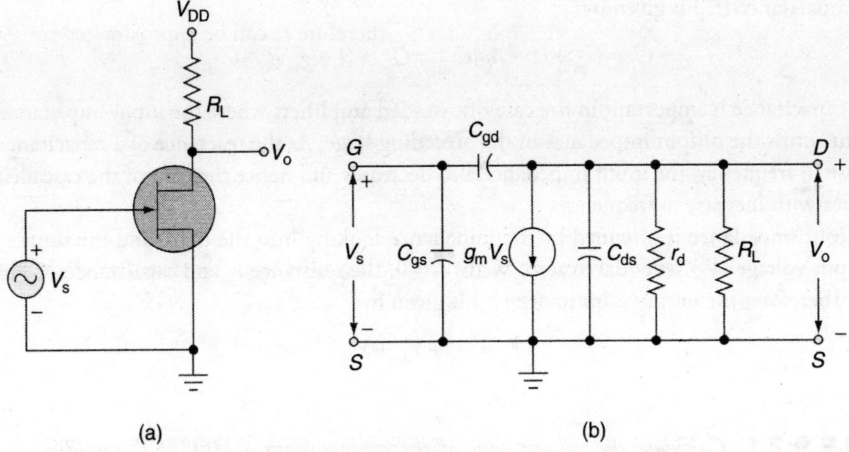

Figure 9.15 (a) Circuit diagram of a common-source JFET amplifier; (b) small signal high-frequency model of the common-source JFET amplifier of part (a).

$$Y = \frac{1}{Z} = G_L + Y_{ds} + g_d + Y_{gd} \tag{9.73}$$

where $G_L = 1/R_L$ is the conductance corresponding to load R_L. If the load is represented by an impedance Z_L, then G_L will be replaced by Y_L (Y_L is the admittance corresponding to impedance Z_L). Also $Y_{ds} = j\omega C_{ds}$ is the admittance corresponding to C_{ds}; $g_d = 1/r_d$ is the conductance corresponding to r_d; $Y_{gd} = j\omega C_{gd}$ is the admittance corresponding to C_{gd}.

The current I flowing from the drain to the source terminal with output terminals shorted is given by

$$I = -g_m V_s + V_s Y_{gd} \tag{9.74}$$

Therefore, the output voltage V_o is given by

$$V_o = \frac{(-g_m + Y_{gd})V_s}{G_L + Y_{ds} + g_d + Y_{gd}} \tag{9.75}$$

The value of voltage gain (A_v) is therefore equal to

$$A_v = \frac{V_o}{V_s} = \frac{-g_m + Y_{gd}}{G_L + Y_{ds} + g_d + Y_{gd}} \tag{9.76}$$

At low frequencies, the FET capacitances can be neglected and hence $Y_{ds} = Y_{gd} = 0$. Therefore, the value of gain at low frequencies is given by

$$A_v = \frac{-g_m}{G_L + g_d} = \frac{-g_m R_L r_d}{R_L + r_d} = -g_m R_L' \tag{9.77}$$

where $R_L' = R_L \| r_d$.

The input admittance and the input capacitance can be calculated as follows. We can see from Figure 9.15(b) that there is a coupling between the gate and the drain terminals through capacitance C_{gd}. The admittance offered by the capacitance (Y_{gd}) can be replaced by $Y_{gd}(1 - A_v)$ between the gate and the source terminals and by $Y_{gd}[1 - (1/A_v)]$ between the drain and the source terminals. The input admittance (Y_i) is therefore given by

$$Y_i = Y_{gs} + (1 - A_v)Y_{gd} = Y_{gs} + (1 + g_m R_L')Y_{gd} \tag{9.78}$$

The input capacitance (C_i) is given by

$$C_i = C_{gs} + (1 - A_v)C_{gd} = C_{gs} + (1 + g_m R_L')C_{gd} \tag{9.79}$$

This input capacitance is important in the case of cascaded amplifiers where the input impedance of a stage acts in shunt across the output impedance of the preceding stage. As the reactance of a capacitance decreases with increase in frequency, the input impedance also decreases and hence the gain of the cascaded amplifier also decreases with increase in frequency.

The output impedance is obtained by the impedance looking into the drain and the source terminals, with the input voltage (V_i) set equal to zero. With $V_i = 0$, the resistance r_d and capacitances C_{ds} and C_{gd} are in parallel. Therefore, the output admittance (Y_o) is given by

$$Y_o = g_d + Y_{ds} + Y_{gd} \tag{9.80}$$

EXAMPLE 9.3 *Calculate the voltage gain of the common-source MOSFET amplifier at operating frequencies of 20 kHz and 20 MHz with drain resistance (R_D) of 100 kΩ. The MOSFET parameters are g_m = 1.5 mA/V, R_D = 50 kΩ, C_{gs} = 2.5 pF, C_{ds} = 1.0 pF and C_{gd} = 2.8 pF.*

Solution For operating frequency of 20 kHz

1. $Y_{gs} = j\omega C_{gs} = j \times 2 \times \pi \times 20 \times 10^3 \times 2.5 \times 10^{-12} = j3.14 \times 10^{-7}\ \Omega^{-1}$.
2. $Y_{ds} = j\omega C_{ds} = j \times 2 \times \pi \times 20 \times 10^3 \times 1.0 \times 10^{-12} = j1.26 \times 10^{-7}\ \Omega^{-1}$.
3. $Y_{gd} = j\omega C_{gd} = j \times 2 \times \pi \times 20 \times 10^3 \times 2.8 \times 10^{-12} = j3.52 \times 10^{-7}\ \Omega^{-1}$.
4. $g_d = 1/r_d = 1/(50 \times 10^3) = 2 \times 10^{-5}\ \Omega^{-1}$.
5. $G_D = 1/R_D = 1/(100 \times 10^3) = 1 \times 10^{-5}\ \Omega^{-1}$.
6. The value of voltage gain (A_v) is given by

$$A_v = \frac{-g_m + Y_{gd}}{G_D + Y_{ds} + g_d + Y_{gd}}$$

$$= \frac{-1.5\times10^{-3} + j3.52\times10^{-7}}{1\times10^{-5} + j1.26\times10^{-7} + 2\times10^{-5} + j3.52\times10^{-7}}$$

$$= \frac{-1.5\times10^{-3} + j3.52\times10^{-7}}{3\times10^{-5} + j4.78\times10^{-7}}$$

7. The imaginary terms are negligible in comparison with the real terms. Therefore, the value of voltage gain $A_v = (-1.5 \times 10^{-3})/(3 \times 10^{-5}) = -50$.

For operating frequency of 20 MHz

1. $Y_{gs} = j\omega C_{gs} = j \times 2 \times \pi \times 20 \times 10^6 \times 2.5 \times 10^{-12} = j3.14 \times 10^{-4}\ \Omega^{-1}$.
2. $Y_{ds} = j\omega C_{ds} = j \times 2 \times \pi \times 20 \times 10^6 \times 1.0 \times 10^{-12} = j1.26 \times 10^{-4}\ \Omega^{-1}$.
3. $Y_{gd} = j\omega C_{gd} = j \times 2 \times \pi \times 20 \times 10^6 \times 2.8 \times 10^{-12} = j3.52 \times 10^{-4}\ \Omega^{-1}$.

4. $g_d = 1/r_d = 1/(50 \times 10^3) = 2 \times 10^{-5}\ \Omega^{-1}$.
5. $G_D = 1/R_D = 1/(100 \times 10^3) = 1 \times 10^{-5}\ \Omega^{-1}$.
6. The value of voltage gain (A_v) is given by

$$A_v = \frac{-g_m + Y_{gd}}{G_D + Y_{ds} + g_d + Y_{gd}}$$

$$= \frac{-1.5\times10^{-3} + j3.52\times10^{-4}}{1\times10^{-5} + j1.26\times10^{-4} + 2\times10^{-5} + j3.52\times10^{-4}}$$

$$= \frac{-1.5\times10^{-3} + j3.52\times10^{-4}}{3\times10^{-5} + j4.78\times10^{-4}}$$

7. Multiplying and dividing by $(3 \times 10^{-5} - j4.78 \times 10^{-4})$, we get

$$A_v = \frac{(-1.5\times10^{-3} + j3.52\times10^{-4})\times(3\times10^{-5} - j4.78\times10^{-4})}{(3\times10^{-5} + j4.78\times10^{-4})\times(3\times10^{-5} - j4.78\times10^{-4})}$$

$$= \frac{-4.5\times10^{-8} + j7.17\times10^{-7} + j10.56\times10^{-9} + 16.83\times10^{-8}}{9\times10^{-10} + 22.85\times10^{-8}}$$

$$= \frac{-12.33\times10^{-8} + j7.28\times10^{-7}}{22.94\times10^{-8}}$$

8. $|A_v| = \sqrt{[(12.33 \times 10^{-8})^2 + (7.28 \times 10^{-7})^2]}/(22.94 \times 10^{-8}) = 3.22$.
9. $\angle A_v = \tan^{-1}[(7.28 \times 10^{-7})/(-12.33 \times 10^{-8})] = \tan^{-1}(-5.9) = -80.38°$.

Common-Drain Amplifier at High Frequencies

Figure 9.16(a) shows the circuit of a common-drain or a source-follower amplifier. Figure 9.16(b) shows its small signal high-frequency equivalent model.

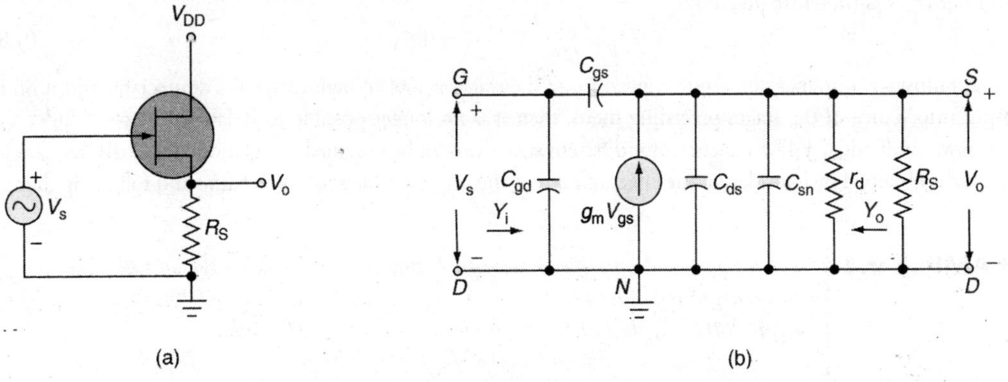

Figure 9.16 (a) Common-drain JFET amplifier; (b) small signal high-frequency equivalent model of the common-drain JFET amplifier shown in part (a).

The output voltage V_o is given by the product of the short-circuit current and the impedance between the source and the ground terminals. By carrying out analysis in a manner similar to that for the common-source amplifier, the expression for the voltage gain (A_v) for a common-drain amplifier is given by

$$A_v = \frac{(g_m + j\omega C_{gs})R_s}{1 + [g_m + g_d + j\omega(C_{gs} + C_{ds} + C_{sn})]R_s} \tag{9.81}$$

At low frequencies, the value of reactance offered by the capacitances C_{gs}, C_{ds} and C_{sn} is infinity. Therefore, at low frequencies, the value of voltage gain (A_v) is given by

$$A_v = \frac{g_m R_s}{1 + (g_m + g_d)R_s} \tag{9.82}$$

As we can see from the above equation, the value of A_v is slightly less than unity as generally $g_m R_s >> 1$.

Input admittance (Y_i) is obtained by using the Miller's theorem in a manner similar to that done for the common-source FET amplifier. The expression for (Y_i) is given by

$$Y_i = Y_{gd} + Y_{gs}(1 - A_v) = j\omega C_{gd} + j\omega C_{gs}(1 - A_v) \cong j\omega C_{gd} \tag{9.83}$$

One of the major advantages of the common-drain amplifier over the common-source amplifier is that it offers smaller value of input capacitance as compared to the common-source amplifier.

The output admittance (Y_o) can also be determined in a manner similar to that for the common-drain JFET amplifier. It is given by

$$Y_o = g_m + g_d + j\omega C_T \tag{9.84}$$

9.7 High-Frequency Response of Cascaded Amplifier Stages

We have studied in Chapter 8 that the overall frequency response of an amplifier changes if an additional stage is added to it. In a multistage amplifier, the upper cut-off frequency is determined by the stage having the smallest value of the upper cut-off frequency.

The upper cut-off frequency (f_{Hn}) for "n" identical non-interactive stage amplifier is given by

$$f_{Hn} = f_H\sqrt{2^{1/n} - 1} \tag{9.85}$$

where f_H is the upper cut-off frequency of each individual stage. The upper cut-off frequency of a two-stage amplifier (f_{H2}) is therefore given by

$$f_{H2} = f_H\sqrt{2^{1/2} - 1} = 0.64 f_H \tag{9.86}$$

If in a multistage amplifier, the input impedance of the stages is low enough to act as a appreciable shunt on the output impedance of the stages preceding them, then it is no longer possible to isolate the stages. Under such conditions, individual 3 dB frequencies for different stages cannot be obtained in isolation. The 3 dB frequency in this case is obtained by considering the effect of each of the stages on the stages preceding and following them.

EXAMPLE 9.4 *For the cascaded amplifier shown in Figure 9.17, determine the overall upper cut-off frequency of the amplifier. Given that h_{ie} for each transistor is 1000 Ω, $r_{b'e}$ is 800 Ω, $r_{bb'}$ is 200 Ω, C_c is 5 pF, C_e is 40 pF and $g_m = 60 \times 10^{-3}$ mhos.*

Solution

1. The overall upper cut-off frequency can be determined by determining the upper cut-off frequency for each stage.

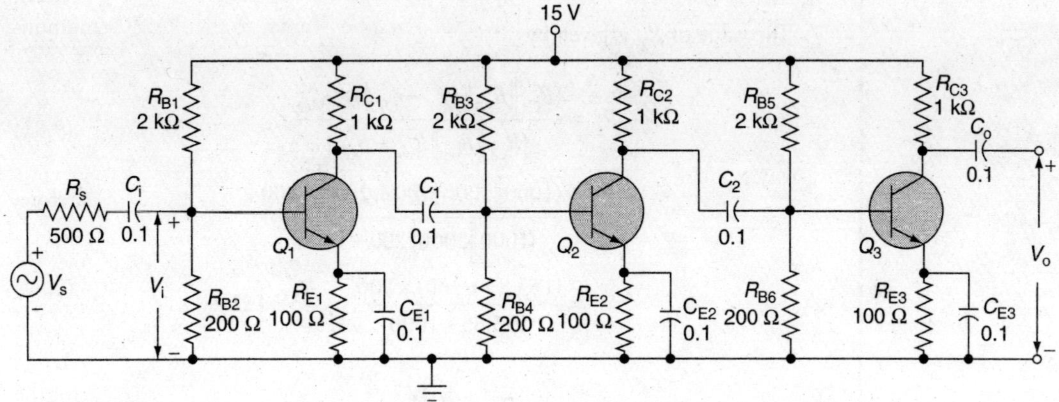

Figure 9.17 | Example 9.4.

2. The upper cut-off frequency for the third stage amplifier (f_{H3}) is given by

$$f_{H3} = \frac{1}{2\pi R_{3'}[C_e + C_c(1 + g_m R_{C3})]}$$

3.
$$R_{3'} = \frac{(R_{C2} \| R_{B5} \| R_{B6} + r_{bb'3}) \times r_{b'e3}}{(R_{C2} \| R_{B5} \| R_{B6} + h_{ie3})}$$

$$= \frac{(1000 \| 2000 \| 200 + 200) \times 800}{(1000 \| 2000 \| 200 + 1000)}$$

$$= \frac{(153.85 + 200) \times 800}{153.85 + 1000} = 245.34\ \Omega$$

4.
$$f_{H3} = \frac{1}{2 \times 3.1414 \times 245.34[40 \times 10^{-12} + 5 \times 10^{-12}(1 + 60 \times 10^{-3} \times 1 \times 10^{3})]}$$

$$= \frac{1}{2 \times 3.1414 \times 245.34 \times 345 \times 10^{-12}} = 1.88\ \text{MHz}$$

5. The upper cut-off frequency for the second stage (f_{H2}) is given by

$$f_{H2} = \frac{1}{2\pi R_{2'}[C_e + C_c(1 + g_m R_{L2'})]}$$

6. The effective value of load resistance for the second stage ($R_{L2'}$) is given by

$$R_{L2'} = R_{C2} \| R_{B5} \| R_{B6} \| h_{ie3}$$

$$= 1000 \| 2000 \| 200 \| 1000 = 133.33\ \Omega$$

7. The value of $R_{2'}$ is given by

$$R_{2'} = \frac{(R_{C1} \| R_{B3} \| R_{B4} + r_{bb'2}) \times r_{b'e2}}{(R_{C1} \| R_{B3} \| R_{B4} + h_{ie2})}$$

$$= \frac{(1000 \| 2000 \| 200 + 200) \times 800}{(1000 \| 2000 \| 200 + 1000)}$$

$$= \frac{(153.85 + 200) \times 800}{153.85 + 1000} = 245.34\ \Omega$$

8. $$f_{H2} = \frac{1}{2 \times 3.1414 \times 245.34[40 \times 10^{-12} + 5 \times 10^{-12}(1 + 60 \times 10^{-3} \times 133.33)]}$$

$$= 7.63\ \text{MHz}$$

9. The upper cut-off frequency for the first stage (f_{H1}) is given by

$$f_{H1} = \frac{1}{2\pi R_{1'}[C_e + C_c(1 + g_m R_{L1'})]}$$

10. The effective load resistance for the first stage ($R_{L1'}$) is given by

$$R_{L1'} = R_{C1} \| R_{B3} \| R_{B4} \| h_{ie2}$$

$$= 1000 \| 2000 \| 200 \| 1000$$

$$= 133.33\ \Omega$$

11. The value of $R_{1'}$ is given by

$$R_{1'} = \frac{(R_s \| R_{B1} \| R_{B2} + r_{bb'1}) \times r_{b'e1}}{(R_s \| R_{B1} \| R_{B2} + h_{ie1})}$$

$$= \frac{(500 \| 2000 \| 200 + 200) \times 800}{(500 \| 2000 \| 200 + 1000)}$$

$$= \frac{(133.33 + 200) \times 800}{133.33 + 1000} = 235.292\ \Omega$$

12. $$f_{H1} = \frac{1}{2 \times 3.1414 \times 235.292[40 \times 10^{-12} + 5 \times 10^{-12}(1 + 60 \times 10^{-3} \times 133.33)]}$$

$$= 7.96\ \text{MHz}$$

13. The overall upper cut-off frequency is limited by the cut-off frequency of the third stage as it is around four times less than the cut-off frequencies of the other two stages.

14. The overall upper cut-off frequency is therefore approximately equal to 1.88 MHz.

9.8 Amplifier Rise Time and Sag

The response of an amplifier to a step input is an effective measure to test its performance. There is a close relationship between the transfer function of the amplifier for the leading edge of the step input and its high-frequency response. In other words, the high-frequency response of the amplifier essentially determines the ability of the amplifier to faithfully respond to rapid variations in the input signal. Similarly, the response of the amplifier to the flat portion of the step input and its low-frequency response are interrelated. That is, the low-frequency response of the amplifier is a measure of the fidelity of the amplifier to respond to slowly varying changes in the input signal.

Rise Time

Let us consider that the step input applied has a pulse width of t_p. Figure 9.18 shows the response of the amplifier to the leading and the falling edge of the step input. The amplifier acts as a low pass filter to the leading and the falling edges of the input signal. The transfer function of the amplifier to the leading edge of the input signal is given by

$$V_o = V(1 - e^{-t/R_1C_1}) \tag{9.87}$$

where R_1 and C_1 are the resistive and the capacitive elements limiting the high-frequency response of the amplifier. The rise-time (t_r) of the amplifier is given by the time required by the output signal to rise from 10% of its final value to 90% of its final value. It is an indication of how fast the amplifier responds to the fast rising edges of the input signal. The value of the rise time is given by

$$t_r = 2.2R_1C_1 = \frac{2.2}{2\pi f_H} = \frac{0.35}{f_H} \tag{9.88}$$

where f_H is the upper cut-off frequency of the amplifier. t_r is specified in *s*, ms and μs respectively, for f_H in Hz, kHz and MHz. Therefore, the rise time of an amplifier is inversely proportional to its upper 3 dB cut-off frequency. The upper 3 dB frequency of the amplifier (f_H) required to amplify the step input signal with pulse width t_p, without much distortion is given by

$$f_H = \frac{1}{t_p} \tag{9.89}$$

Substituting the value of f_H in Eq. (9.88), we get

$$t_r = 0.35t_p \tag{9.90}$$

Tilt or Sag

The response of the amplifier to the flat portion of the step input (Figure 9.19) is affected by the high-pass circuit of the amplifier. The transfer function is expressed as

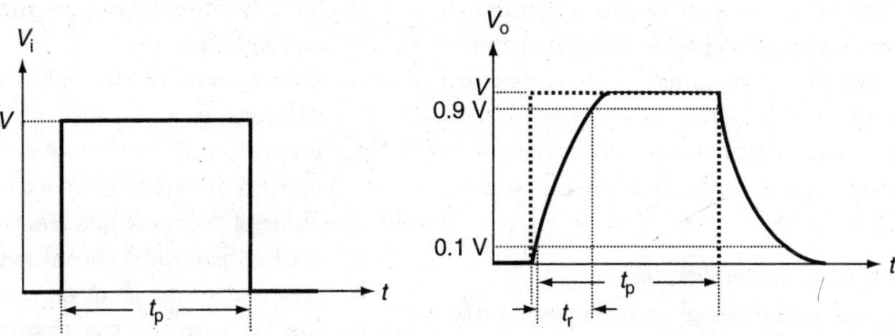

Figure 9.18 | Response of the amplifier to the leading and the falling edges of the step input.

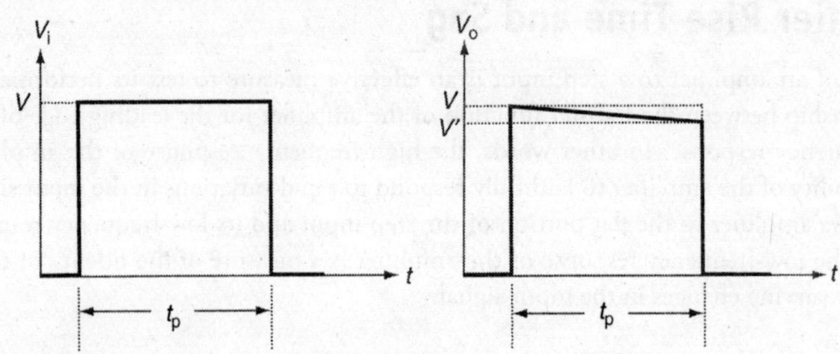

Figure 9.19 Response of the amplifier to the flat portion of the step input.

$$V_o = Ve^{-t/R_2C_2} \tag{9.91}$$

where R_2 and C_2 are the resistive and the capacitive elements limiting the low-frequency response of the amplifier. For time t, much larger than the time constant R_2C_2, Eq. (9.91) can be approximated as

$$V_o = V\left(1 - \frac{t}{R_2C_2}\right) \tag{9.92}$$

From Figure 9.19, the percentage tilt or sag in the output voltage is given by

$$P = \left(\frac{V - V'}{V}\right) \times 100\% = \left(\frac{t_p}{R_2C_2}\right) \times 100\% \tag{9.93}$$

where t_p is the pulse width of the step input.

KEY TERMS

Hybrid-Π model
Giacoletto model
β cut-off frequency (f_β)
Short-circuit gain-bandwidth product (f_T)
α cut-off frequency (f_α)
Miller's theorem
Rise-time
Sag

OBJECTIVE-TYPE EXERCISES

Multiple-Choice Questions

1. The emitter diffusion capacitance for a transistor
   a. is directly proportional to the collector current.
   b. is inversely proportional to the collector current.
   c. is independent of the collector current.
   d. is proportional to the square of collector current.
2. The rise time of an amplifier is
   a. inversely proportional to the upper 3 dB cut-off frequency.
   b. directly proportional to the upper 3 dB cut-off frequency.
   c. independent of the upper 3 dB cut-off frequency.
   d. proportional to the square root of the upper 3 dB cut-off frequency.
3. The value of α cut-off frequency is
   a. smaller than the β cut-off frequency.
   b. greater than the β cut-off frequency.
   c. can be more or less than the β cut-off frequency.

d. equal to the β cut-off frequency.

4. The conductance ($g_{b'c}$) takes into account
   a. the resistance between the emitter and the collector terminals.
   b. the conductance between the base and collector due to flow of majority carriers.
   c. the reduction in the flow of emitter current.
   d. the feedback effect between the output and the input due to the Early effect.

5. The Ohmic base-spreading resistance is represented as
   a. the increase in the recombination base currrent due to the increase in the minority carriers in the base region.
   b. the conductance between the collector and the emitter terminals.
   c. a lump parameter between the external base terminal and the node B′.
   d. the feedback effect between the output and the input due to the Early effect.

State whether True or False

1. The response of the amplifier to the flat portion of the step input is affected by the high-pass circuit of the amplifier.
2. The value of the gain-bandwidth product of the common-emitter amplifier increases with increase in the value of the collector current.
3. The value of the transistor's transconductance decreases with increase in temperature
4. α cut-off frequency is the frequency at which the short-circuit small signal forward current transfer ratio of a common-base amplifier drops by 3 dB to its value at low frequencies.
5. The common-base transistor amplifier has a higher value of upper cut-off frequency than the common-emitter transistor amplifier.

REVIEW QUESTIONS

1. Draw the hybrid-Π model of a transistor, explaining each of the components used in the model.
2. What do you understand by the term "rise-time"? Which parameters affect the rise time in case of a bipolar transistor-based amplifier?
3. When different identical amplifier stages are connected in cascade, which stage has the most influence on the overall high-frequency response of the amplifier and why?
4. What is Miller's effect? What influence does it have on the high-frequency response of the transistor or FET amplifier?
5. Derive the expressions for the upper cut-off frequencies of the common-emitter and the common-base transistor amplifier configurations?
6. Explain why the 3 dB frequency for the current gain is not the same as the 3 dB frequency for the voltage gain.
7. Derive the expression for the short-circuit current gain of a common-emitter transistor amplifier as a function of frequency.
8. Using Miller's theorem, derive the expression for the mid-band input capacitance of a common-emitter transistor amplifier with load resistance.
9. Draw the small signal equivalent circuit for a common-source MOSFET amplifier.
10. Differentiate between:
    a. The α cut-off frequency and the β cut-off frequency.
    b. The high-frequency response of a common-collector amplifier and a common-emitter amplifier.
    c. Hybrid parameters for low-frequency analysis and hybrid-Π parameters for high-frequency analysis.

PROBLEMS

1. Calculate the voltage gain at operating frequencies of 20 kHz and 20 MHz of the common-drain MOSFET amplifier with source resistance (R_S) of 1 kΩ. The MOSFET parameters are $g_m = 1.5$ mA/V, $r_d = 50$ kΩ, $C_{gs} = 2.5$ pF, $C_{ds} = 1.0$ pF, $C_{gd} = 2.8$ pF and $C_{sn} = 2.7$ pF.

2. For the cascaded amplifier shown in Figure 9.20, determine the overall upper cut-off frequency of the amplifier. Given that h_{fe} of each transistor is 100, h_{ie} is 850 Ω, $r_{b'e}$ is 600 Ω, $r_{bb'}$ is 250 Ω, C_c is 10 pF, C_e is 50 pF and $g_m = 1.50 \times 10^{-3}$ mhos.

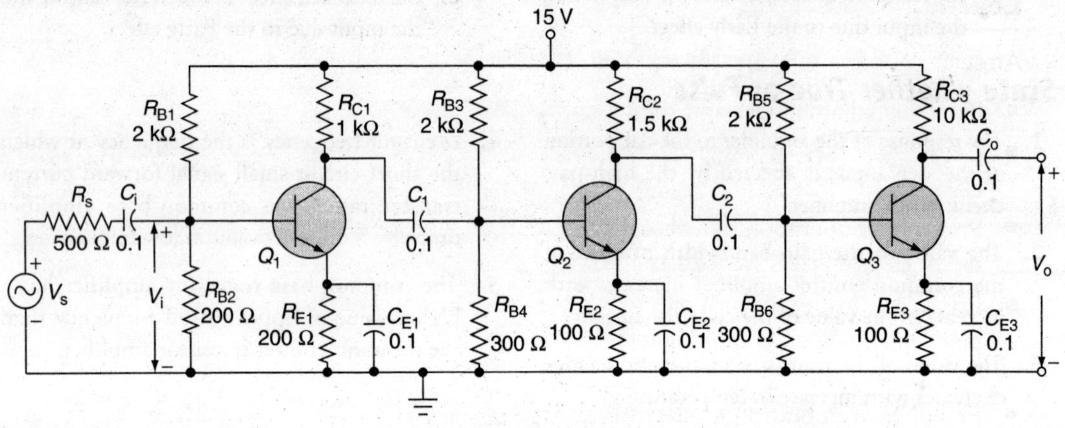

Figure 9.20 | Problem 2.

3. The bandwidth of a single-stage amplifier extends from 10 Hz to 100 kHz. Find the frequencies at which the voltage gain is down by 1 dB from its mid-band value.

4. A three-stage amplifier with identical stages has an overall lower and upper 3 dB cut-off frequencies of 10 Hz and 10 kHz, respectively. Determine the upper and the lower cut-off frequencies of the individual stages assuming that the stages are non-interactive stages.

ANSWERS

Multiple-Choice Questions

1. (a) 2. (a) 3. (b) 4. (d) 5. (c)

State whether True or False

1. True
2. False
3. True
4. True
5. True

Problems

1. 0.595, 0°, 0.581, −5.37°
2. 2.868 MHz
3. 19.65 Hz, 51 kHz
4. 19.61 kHz, 5.1 Hz

CHAPTER 10

Large Signal Amplifiers

Learning Objectives

After completing this chapter, you will learn the following:

- Large signal amplifiers and their characteristic parameters.
- Classification of large signal amplifiers: class A, class B, class AB, class C, class D and other classes.
- Principle of operation of different types of class A amplifiers including class A amplifiers with direct coupled resistive load, transformer coupled load and class A push–pull amplifiers.
- Principle of operation of different types of class B amplifiers including transformer coupled push–pull class B amplifiers, complementary-symmetry push–pull class B amplifiers and quasi-complementary push–pull class B amplifiers.
- Principle of operation of class AB amplifiers.
- Class C amplifiers.
- Class D amplifiers.
- Thermal management of power transistors.

The amplifier circuits we have studied until now are small signal amplifiers where the signal voltage and current levels are small. The focus in this chapter is on large signal or power amplifiers. Large signal or power amplifiers provide power amplification and are used in applications to provide sufficient power to the load or the power device. The output power delivered by these amplifiers is of the order of few watts to few tens of watts. They handle moderate-to-high levels of current and voltage signals as against small levels of current and voltage signals in the case of small signal amplifiers. As we have studied in earlier chapters, the main characteristic specifications in case of small signal amplifiers are amplification linearity and gain magnitude. In the case of large signal amplifiers, the main design specifications are power efficiency, maximum power-handling capability of the amplifier and distortion.

The topics covered in this chapter include classification of large signal amplifiers into different classes, namely, class A, class B, class AB, class C, class D and other classes and the main characteristic specifications of power amplifiers. The principle of operation of different types of class A amplifiers including direct coupled, transformer coupled and push–pull amplifiers is covered next. This is followed up by a discussion on transformer-coupled push–pull, complementary-symmetry push–pull and quasi-complementary push–pull class B amplifiers. Other classes of large signal amplifiers, which include class AB, class C and class D amplifiers, are covered next. The chapter ends with a discussion on thermal management of power transistors. The chapter is amply illustrated with a large number of solved examples.

10.1 Large Signal Amplifiers

Large signal or power amplifiers provide power amplification and are used in applications to provide sufficient power to the load or the power device. The output power delivered by these amplifiers is of the order of few Watts to few tens of Watts. In this section we will discuss different classes of power amplifiers and their characteristic specifications.

Classification

On the basis of their circuit configurations and principle of operation, amplifiers are classified into different classes. Different classes of large signal amplifiers include class A, class B, class AB, class C, class D, class E and class F amplifiers. Each of these amplifiers offers different advantages and disadvantages as compared to each other. In this section, a brief introduction to these classes and general large signal amplifier characteristic specifications is given. Class E and F amplifiers are very rarely used. Hence, only class A, class B, class AB, class C and class D amplifiers are described in detail later in the chapter.

Class A Amplifiers

The active device in a class A amplifier operates during the whole of the input cycle and the output signal is an amplified replica of the input signal with no clipping. In other words, in class A amplifiers, the amplifying element is so biased that it operates over the linear region of its output characteristics during the full period of the input cycle and is always conducting to some extent. Class A amplifiers offer very poor efficiency and a theoretical maximum of 50% efficiency is possible in these amplifiers. They are generally used for implementing small signal amplifiers. Figure 10.1 shows the input and output waveforms of class A amplifiers.

Class B Amplifiers

Class B amplifiers operate only during the half of the input cycle as shown in Figure 10.2. Class B amplifiers offer much improved efficiency over class A amplifiers with a possible theoretical maximum of 78.5%.

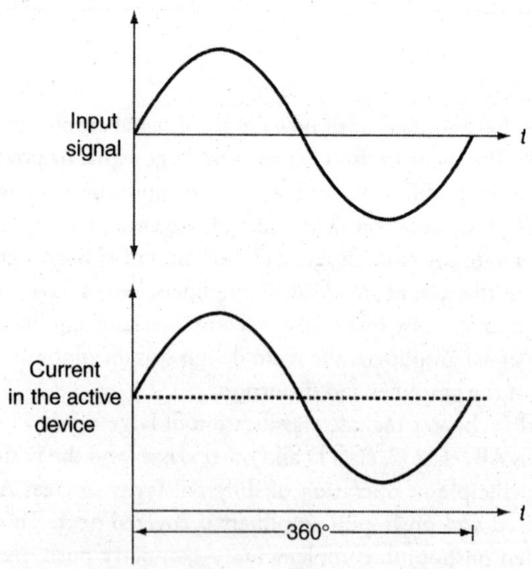

Figure 10.1 | Waveforms of class A amplifiers.

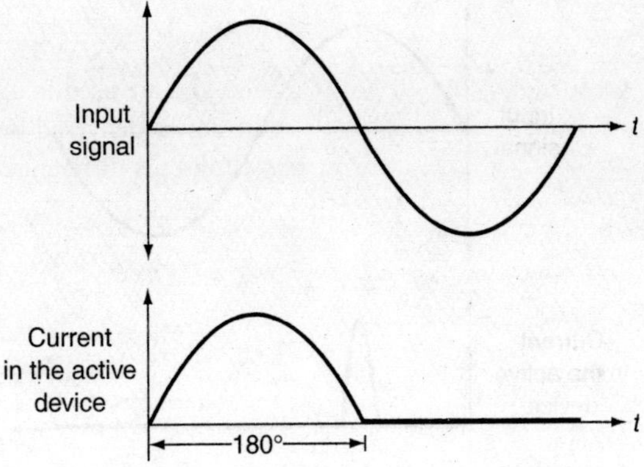

Figure 10.2 | Waveforms of class B amplifiers.

However they also create a large amount of distortion. A single class B amplifier is rarely used in practical systems. Two class B amplifiers are used either as a complementary pair or in a push–pull arrangement. Thesc configurations are discussed in detail in Section 10.3.

Class AB Amplifiers

In a class AB amplifier, the amplifying device conducts for a little more than half of the input waveform. They sacrifice some efficiency over class B amplifiers but they offer better linearity than class B amplifiers. However, they offer much more efficiency than class A amplifiers. Figure 10.3 shows the waveforms of class AB amplifiers. Operation of class AB amplifiers is explained in Section 10.4.

Class C Amplifiers

Class C amplifiers conduct for less than half cycle of the input signal (Figure 10.4) resulting in a very high efficiencies upto 90%. However, they are associated with a very high level of distortion at the output. Class C amplifiers operate in two modes, namely, the tuned mode and the untuned mode. Class C amplifiers are discussed in detail in Section 10.5.

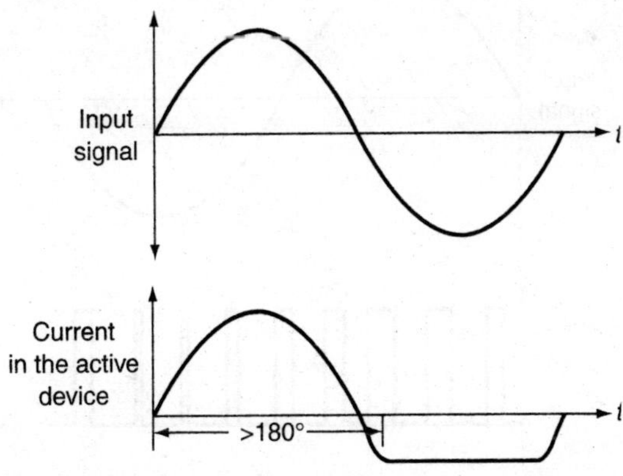

Figure 10.3 | Input and output waveforms of class AB amplifiers.

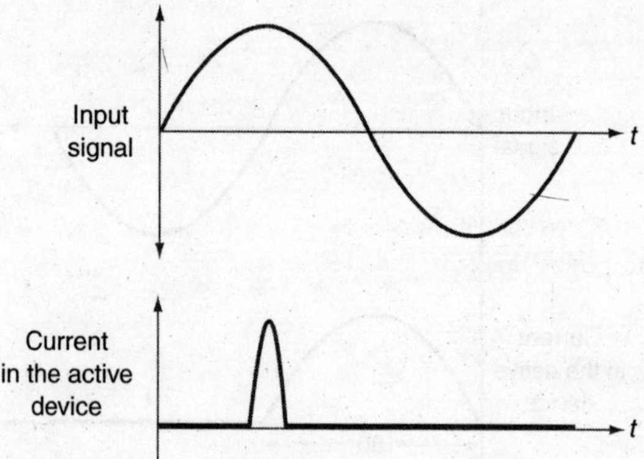

Figure 10.4 | Input and output waveforms of class C amplifiers.

Class D Amplifiers

Class D amplifiers use the active device in switching mode to regulate the output power. Hence, these amplifiers offer high efficiencies and do not require heat sinks and transformers. These amplifiers use pulse width modulation (PWM), pulse density modulation or sigma delta modulation to convert the input signal into a string of pulses. Figure 10.5 shows how a sinusoidal input waveform is converted into a string of digital pulses using PWM technique. As we can see from the figure, the pulse width of the PWM output waveform at any time instant is directly proportional to the amplitude of the input signal.

Other Classes

Class E and class F amplifiers are switching power amplifiers offering very high efficiency levels. They are used at very high frequencies where the switching time is comparable to the duty time. Class G amplifiers are efficient versions of class AB amplifiers. They employ rail switching to decrease power consumption and increase efficiency. The amplifier has several power rails at different voltages and it switches between the rails as the output signal approaches each rail value. Class H amplifiers create infinite number of supply rails by modulating the supply rails. Detailed description of these classes is beyond the scope of the book.

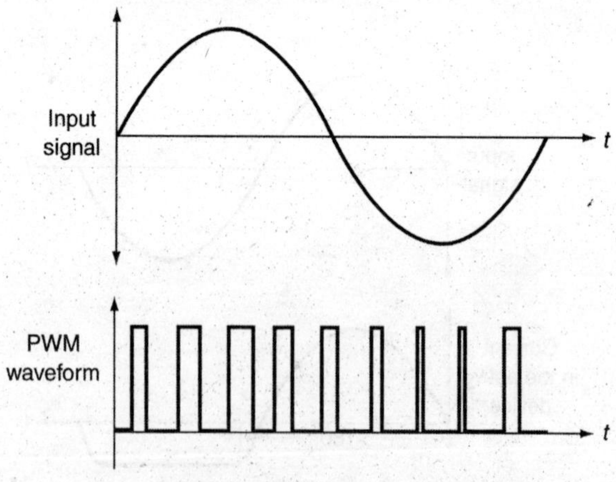

Figure 10.5 | Class D amplifier waveforms.

Large Signal Amplifier Characteristics

The main characteristics that define the performance of a power amplifier are efficiency, distortion level and output power. These characteristics are discussed in detail in this section.

Efficiency

Efficiency of an amplifier is defined as the ability of the amplifier to convert the DC input power of the supply into an AC output power that can be delivered to the load. The expression for efficiency is given by

$$\eta = \frac{P_o}{P_i} \times 100\% \tag{10.1}$$

where P_o is the AC output power delivered to the load and P_i the DC input power.

Harmonic Distortion

Distortion in large signal amplifiers is mainly caused due to harmonic distortion. Harmonic distortion refers to the distortion in the amplitude of the output signal of an amplifier caused due to the non-linearity in the characteristics of the active device used for amplification. In other words, the active device does not equally amplify all portions of the input signal over its positive and negative excursions. The distortion is more in the case of a large input signal level. Figure 10.6 shows how the non-linear dynamic transfer curve of the active device results in harmonic distortion.

The dynamic transfer curve of an active device can be generalized using the following equation

$$I_o = k_1 I_i + k_2 I_i^2 + k_3 I_i^3 + \ldots \tag{10.2}$$

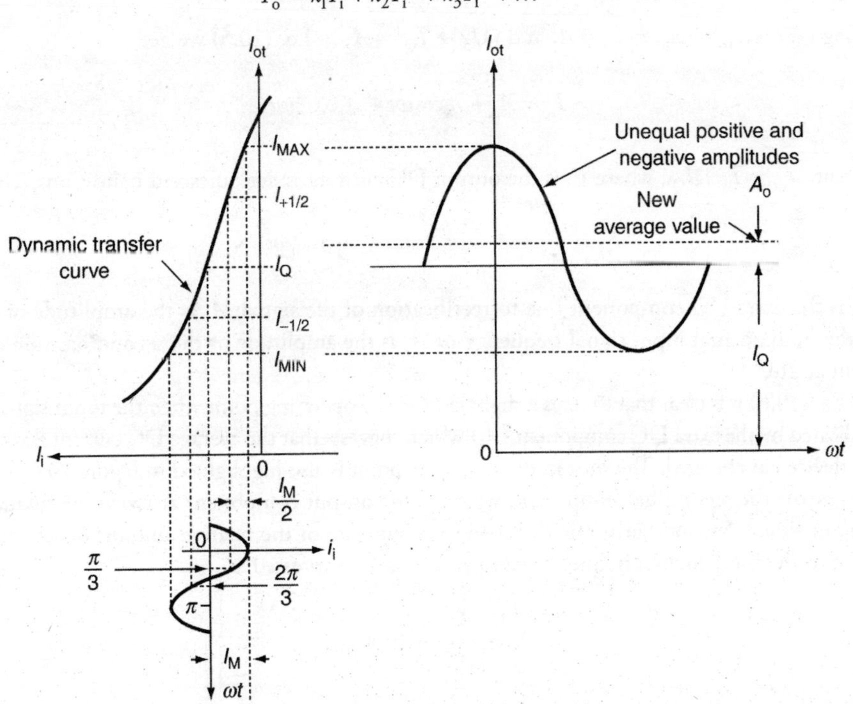

Figure 10.6 Harmonic distortion due to the non-linearity in the transfer characteristics of the active device.

where I_o is the alternating portion of the output current; I_i the input current; k_1, k_2, k_3 are constants.

In case the input signal is not sufficiently large to drive the amplifier to the extremes of its dynamic transfer curve, then the slight curvature of the dynamic curve over the region of operation may be described by the following parabolic relation:

$$I_o = k_1 I_i + k_2 I_i^2 \tag{10.3}$$

Let us assume that the input signal is a sinusoidal signal and is expressed as

$$I_i = I_M \cos\omega t \tag{10.4}$$

Substituting Eq. (10.4) in Eq. (10.3) we get

$$I_o = k_1 I_M \cos\omega t + k_2 I_M^2 \cos^2\omega t$$

As

$$\cos^2\omega t = \frac{1}{2} + \frac{\cos 2\omega t}{2}$$

we get

$$I_o = k_1 I_M \cos\omega t + \frac{1}{2} k_2 I_M^2 + \frac{1}{2} k_2 I_M^2 \cos 2\omega t \tag{10.5}$$

Substituting $(1/2)k_2 I_M^2 = A_0$, $k_1 I_M = A_1$ and $(1/2)k_2 I_M^2 = A_2$ in Eq. (10.5) we get

$$I_o = A_0 + A_1 \cos\omega t + A_2 \cos 2\omega t$$

Total current, $I_{ot} = I_o + I_Q$, where I_Q is the output DC current under quiescent conditions. Therefore,

$$I_{ot} = I_Q + A_0 + A_1 \cos\omega t + A_2 \cos 2\omega t \tag{10.6}$$

where A_0 is the extra DC component due to rectification of the signal; A_1 is the amplitude of the desired signal at the fundamental input signal frequency ω; A_2 is the amplitude of the second harmonic frequency component at 2ω.

From Eq. (10.6) it is clear that there is a slight shift in the operating point when the input signal is applied. This is indicated by the extra DC component (A_0) which suggests that the average DC current flowing through the active device has changed. The shift in the operating point is also highlighted in Figure 10.6.

A_2 represents the second harmonic term which is the output component at twice the frequency of the applied input signal. Second harmonic distortion is a measure of the relative amount of second harmonic component to the fundamental frequency component and is expressed as

$$D_2 = \left|\frac{A_2}{A_1}\right| \times 100\% \tag{10.7}$$

The values of A_0, A_1 and A_2 can be determined in terms of the values of the output signal from the Figure 10.6.

1. When $\omega t = 0$, $I_{ot} = I_{MAX}$.
2. When $\omega t = \pi/2$, $I_{ot} = I_Q$.
3. When $\omega t = \pi$, $I_{ot} = I_{MIN}$.

Substituting these values in Eq. (10.6) and solving we get

$$A_0 = A_2 = \frac{I_{MAX} + I_{MIN} - 2I_Q}{4} = \frac{(I_{MAX} + I_{MIN})}{4} - \frac{I_Q}{2} \quad (10.8)$$

$$A_1 = \frac{I_{MAX} - I_{MIN}}{2} \quad (10.9)$$

When the magnitude of the input signal is large enough to drive the amplifier to the extremes of its dynamic transfer curve, which is mostly true for power amplifiers, the higher harmonic terms cannot be neglected. As given in Eq. (10.2), the output current I_o is expressed in terms of the input signal as

$$I_o = k_1 I_i + k_2 I_i^2 + k_3 I_i^3 + \ldots$$

Let us assume that the input signal is a sinusoidal signal and is expressed as

$$I_i = I_M \cos\omega t$$

The output signal is then expressed as

$$I_o = k_1 I_M \cos\omega t + k_2 I_M{}^2 \cos^2\omega t + k_3 I_M{}^3 \cos^3\omega t + \ldots \quad (10.10)$$

Solving Eq. (10.10) in terms of multiples of the signal frequency ω and expressing the constant terms as A_0, A_1 and A_2 for the DC component, input signal frequency component and the second harmonic component, respectively, we get

$$I_o = A_0 + A_1 \cos\omega t + A_2 \cos 2\omega t + A_3 \cos 3\omega t + \ldots \quad (10.11)$$

The total current I_{ot} is then given by

$$I_{ot} = I_Q + A_0 + A_1 \cos\omega t + A_2 \cos 2\omega t + A_3 \cos 3\omega t + \ldots \quad (10.12)$$

The values of the harmonic components can be determined in a manner similar to that described earlier in previous paragraphs. In order to obtain the expression for upto fourth harmonic, five values of output current are necessary to solve the equations. The output current values are chosen for maximum value of the input signal, minimum value of the input signal, zero value of the input signal, one-half the maximum positive value of input signal and one-half the maximum negative value of input signal. Let I_{MAX}, I_{MIN}, I_Q, $I_{+1/2}$ and $I_{-1/2}$ be the corresponding output currents for the above-mentioned values of the input signals, respectively. Solving in a manner similar as explained before, we get

$$A_0 = \frac{1}{6} \times (I_{MAX} + 2I_{+1/2} + 2I_{-1/2} + I_{MIN}) - I_Q \quad (10.13)$$

$$A_1 = \frac{1}{3} \times (I_{MAX} + I_{+1/2} - I_{-1/2} - I_{MIN}) \quad (10.14)$$

$$A_2 = \frac{1}{4} \times (I_{MAX} - 2I_Q + I_{MIN}) \tag{10.15}$$

$$A_3 = \frac{1}{6} \times (I_{MAX} - 2I_{+1/2} + 2I_{-1/2} - I_{MIN}) \tag{10.16}$$

$$A_4 = \frac{1}{12} \times (I_{MAX} - 4I_{+1/2} + 6I_Q - 4I_{-1/2} + I_{MIN}) \tag{10.17}$$

The second harmonic distortion component (D_2) is given by

$$D_2 = \left|\frac{A_2}{A_1}\right| \times 100\% \tag{10.18}$$

The third harmonic distortion component (D_3) is given by

$$D_3 = \left|\frac{A_3}{A_1}\right| \times 100\% \tag{10.19}$$

The fourth harmonic distortion component (D_4) is given by

$$D_4 = \left|\frac{A_4}{A_1}\right| \times 100\% \tag{10.20}$$

The total harmonic distortion (D) is given by the square root of the mean square values of the individual harmonic components:

$$D = \sqrt{D_2^2 + D_3^2 + D_4^2 + \ldots} \tag{10.21}$$

The power delivered at the fundamental frequency is

$$P_1 = \frac{A_1^2 R_L}{2} \tag{10.22}$$

The total power output is given by

$$P = (A_1^2 + A_2^2 + A_3^2 + \ldots) \times \frac{R_L}{2} \tag{10.23}$$

Therefore,

$$P = (1 + D_2^2 + D_3^2 + \ldots) \times P_1 = (1 + D^2) \times P_1 \tag{10.24}$$

EXAMPLE 10.1 *Calculate the values of harmonic distortion components for an output signal having amplitude of 5 V at the fundamental frequency, second harmonic component of 0.5 V, third harmonic component of 0.2 V and fourth harmonic component of 0.05 V. Also calculate the total harmonic distortion.*

Solution

1. The second harmonic distortion component is given by

$$D_2 = \left|\frac{A_2}{A_1}\right| \times 100\%$$

$$D_2 = \frac{0.5\text{ V}}{5\text{ V}} \times 100\% = 10\%$$

2. The third harmonic distortion component is given by

$$D_3 = \left|\frac{A_3}{A_1}\right| \times 100\%$$

$$D_3 = \frac{0.2\text{ V}}{5\text{ V}} \times 100\% = 4\%$$

3. The fourth harmonic distortion component is given by

$$D_4 = \left|\frac{A_4}{A_1}\right| \times 100\%$$

$$D_4 = \frac{0.05\text{ V}}{5\text{ V}} \times 100\% = 1\%$$

4. The total harmonic distortion (D) is equal to

$$D = \sqrt{D_2^{\,2} + D_3^{\,2} + D_4^{\,2}}$$

$$D = \sqrt{(10)^2 + (4)^2 + (1)^2} = \sqrt{117} = 10.8\%$$

5. Total harmonic distortion in percentage = 10.8%.

10.2 Class A Amplifiers

As mentioned before, the active device in a class A amplifier operates during the whole of the input cycle. Class A amplifiers can have direct-coupled resistive load or a transformer-coupled resistive load. Class A amplifiers are also configured using push–pull arrangement. In this section, all three types of class A amplifiers are discussed in detail with emphasis on their design procedure.

Class A Amplifier with Direct-Coupled Resistive Load

A simple transistor amplifier shown in Figure 10.7 is a class A amplifier with direct-coupled resistive load or a series-fed class A amplifier. The resistor R_C is the load resistor. The difference between this circuit and the amplifier circuits studied earlier in Chapter 4 is that the signal levels in this case are of the order of few tens of Volts and the transistor used here is a power transistor which is capable of operating in the range of several watts to few tens of Watts.

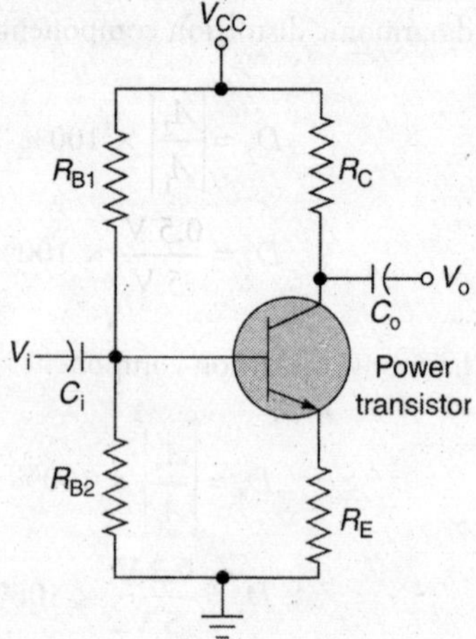

Figure 10.7 Class A amplifier with direct-coupled resistive load.

The value of the quiescent base current is given by

$$I_B = \frac{V_{TH} - V_{BE}}{R_{TH} + (\beta + 1)R_E} \tag{10.25}$$

where

$$R_{TH} = R_{B1} \| R_{B2} = \frac{R_{B1}R_{B2}}{R_{B1} + R_{B2}}$$

$$V_{TH} = \frac{R_{B2}V_{CC}}{R_{B1} + R_{B2}}$$

The value of collector current (I_C) is equal to βI_B and the collector–emitter voltage (V_{CE}) is given by

$$V_{CE} = V_{CC} - I_C(R_C + R_E)$$

The DC bias determines the quiescent point, which in turn determines the maximum possible collector current swing and the collector–emitter voltage swing when the AC signal is applied at the input. Figure 10.8 shows the output characteristics and the current and voltage waveforms for the amplifier. Figure 10.8(a) shows the waveforms for a small input signal and Figure 10.8(b) shows the waveforms for a large input signal. The input signal applied to the base is a sinusoidal waveform and assuming the output characteristics to be equidistant, the output current and voltage waveforms are also sinusoidal. When an AC signal is applied to the base of the amplifier, the base current will vary above and below the DC bias point, which in turn will cause the collector current and the collector–emitter voltage to vary around its DC bias point. The output current and voltage varying around the bias point provide AC power to the load.

Output Power

The AC output power delivered to the load (resistor R_C in this case) is given by

$$P_o = V_{ce(RMS)} I_{c(RMS)} = I^2_{c(RMS)} R_C \tag{10.26}$$

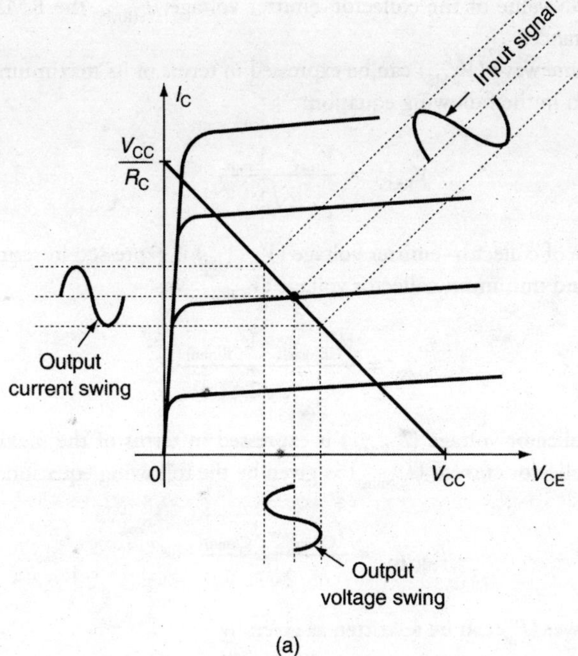

(a)

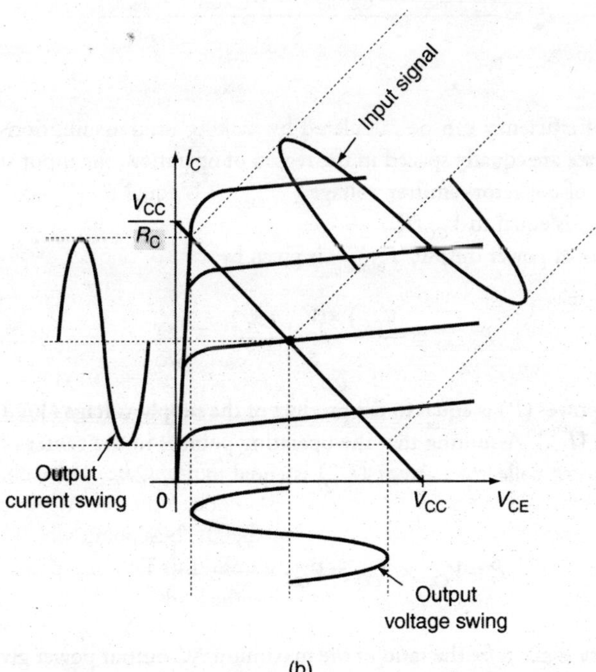

(b)

Figure 10.8 (a) Input and output waveforms for the series-fed class A amplifier – small input signal; (b) input and output waveforms for the series-fed class A amplifier – large input signal.

where $V_{ce(RMS)}$ is the RMS value of the collector–emitter voltage; $I_{c(RMS)}$ the RMS value of the collector current; R_C the load resistance.

The RMS value of a sine wave (V_{RMS}) can be expressed in terms of its maximum value (V_{max}) and minimum value (V_{min}) as given in the following equation:

$$V_{RMS} = \frac{V_{max} - V_{min}}{2\sqrt{2}} \tag{10.27}$$

Therefore, the RMS value of collector–emitter voltage ($V_{ce(RMS)}$) is expressed in terms of the maximum collector voltage ($V_{CE(max)}$) and minimum collector voltage ($V_{CE(min)}$) as

$$V_{ce(RMS)} = \frac{V_{CE(max)} - V_{CE(min)}}{2\sqrt{2}} \tag{10.28}$$

The RMS value of collector voltage ($I_{c(RMS)}$) is expressed in terms of the maximum collector current ($I_{C(max)}$) and minimum collector current ($I_{C(min)}$) as given by the following equation:

$$I_{c(RMS)} = \frac{I_{C(max)} - I_{C(min)}}{2\sqrt{2}} \tag{10.29}$$

Therefore, output AC power (P_o) can be rewritten as given by

$$P_o = \frac{(V_{CE(max)} - V_{CE(min)}) \times (I_{C(max)} - I_{C(min)})}{8} \tag{10.30}$$

Maximum Efficiency

The maximum value of efficiency can be calculated by making ideal assumptions like the characteristics curves of the active device are equally spaced in the region of operation, the input signal has zero minimum value, maximum value of collector–emitter voltage ($V_{CE(max)}$) is equal to V_{CC} and the maximum value of collector current ($I_{C(max)}$) is equal to V_{CC}/R_C.

The maximum value of power output ($P_{o(max)}$) is given by

$$P_{o(max)} = \frac{(V_{CC}) \times (V_{CC}/R_C)}{8} = \frac{V_{CC}^2}{8R_C} \tag{10.31}$$

The value of the input power (P_i) is equal to the product of the supply voltage (V_{CC}) and the quiescent value of the collector current (I_{CQ}). Assuming that the operating point is in the center of the output characteristics, the value of quiescent collector current (I_{CQ}) is equal to $V_{CC}/2R_C$. The value of input power (P_i) is therefore given by

$$P_i = V_{CC} \times I_{CQ} = V_{CC} \times \frac{V_{CC}}{2R_C} = \frac{V_{CC}^2}{2R_C} \tag{10.32}$$

The maximum efficiency is given by the ratio of the maximum AC output power given in Eq. (10.31) to the input power given in Eq. (10.32). The maximum value of efficiency is equal to 25%. In other words, the upper limit of the conversion efficiency in case of a series-fed class A amplifier is 25%. It may be mentioned here that in most of the practical series-fed class A amplifiers, the efficiency is much less than 25%.

EXAMPLE 10.2 *Calculate the efficiency of the amplifier circuit shown in Figure 10.9. The input voltage applied is such that it produces a base current of 10 mA peak. The emitter–base voltage of the transistor is equal to 0.7 V.*

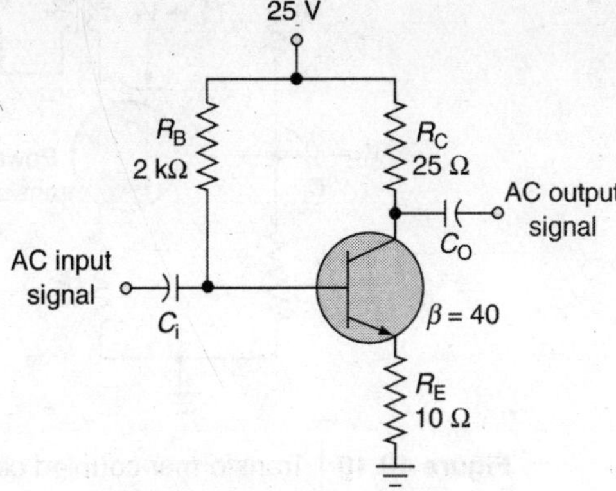

Figure 10.9 Example 10.2.

Solution

1. The value of the base current at the Q-point is given by $I_{BQ} = (V_{CC} - 0.7)/[R_B + (\beta + 1)R_E] = (25 - 0.7)/(2 \times 10^3 + 41 \times 10) = 24.3/2410 = 10.08 \times 10^{-3}\text{A} = 10.08\text{ mA}$.

2. The value of the collector current I_{CQ} is given by $\beta \times I_{BQ} = 40 \times 10.08 \times 10^{-3} = 403.3 \times 10^{-3}\text{ A} = 403.3\text{ mA}$.

3. The input power $P_i = V_{CC} \times I_{CQ} = 25 \times 403.3 \times 10^{-3} = 10.08\text{ W}$.

4. The output power $P_o = [I_{C(p)}{}^2 \times R_C]/2$.

5. $I_{C(p)} = \beta \times I_{B(p)} = 40 \times 10 \times 10^{-3} = 400 \times 10^{-3} = 400\text{ mA}$.

6. $P_o = [(400 \times 10^{-3})^2 \times 25]/2 = 2\text{ W}$.

7. Efficiency $\eta = (P_o/P_i) \times 100\% = (2/10.08) \times 100\% = 19.84\%$.

Transformer-Coupled Class A Amplifiers

Class A amplifier with transformer-coupled load employs a transformer-coupled output stage as shown in Figure 10.10. This configuration offers better efficiency as compared to a class A amplifier with a resistive load. This is so because in the case of direct coupling, the transistor quiescent current passes through the load resistance which results in wastage of power as it does not contribute to the AC component of the output power. In the case of a transformer-coupled load, the primary of the transformer has negligible DC resistance; therefore there is negligible power loss. In fact, the efficiency can be increased by a factor of two by using transformer coupling. However, in this case it is important to use an output-matching transformer in order to transfer a significant power to the load.

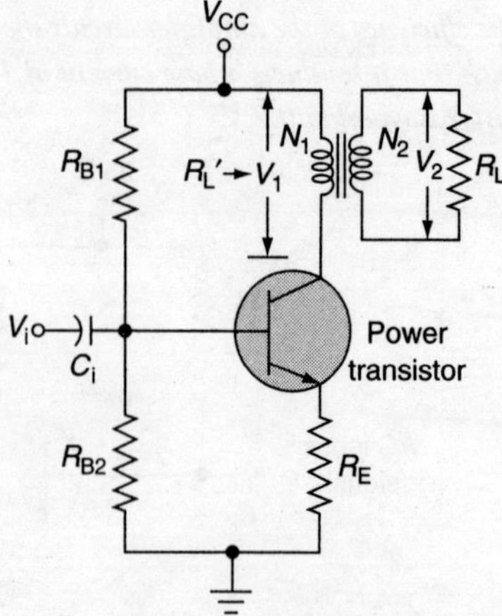

Figure 10.10 | Transformer-coupled class A amplifier.

The relationship between the transformer's primary and secondary voltages and currents and its turn ratio are given by Eqs. (10.33) and (10.34), respectively:

$$\frac{V_1}{V_2} = \frac{N_1}{N_2} \tag{10.33}$$

where V_1 is the primary voltage; V_2 the secondary voltage; N_1 the number of primary turns; N_2 the number of secondary turns:

$$\frac{I_1}{I_2} = \frac{N_2}{N_1} \tag{10.34}$$

where I_1 is the primary current; I_2 the secondary current; N_1 the number of primary turns; N_2 the number of secondary turns.

From Eqs. (10.33) and (10.34) we get

$$\frac{V_1}{I_1} = n^2 \times \frac{V_2}{I_2} \tag{10.35}$$

where V_1/I_1 represents reflected load resistance R_L', V_2/I_2 is equal to the output resistance load resistance R_L, n is equal to the ratio of the primary turns to the secondary turns (N_1/N_2).

Equation (10.35) can be rewritten as

$$R_L' = n^2 \times R_L \tag{10.36}$$

Figure 10.11 shows the transistor collector characteristics along with the DC and the AC load lines for the transformer-coupled class A amplifier. The output current and voltage waveforms are also shown.

For transformer-coupled amplifiers, the DC load line is drawn vertically from $V_{CE} = V_{CC}$. This is so as the resistance of the transformer's primary is negligible. The AC load line is drawn with a slope proportional to $-1/R_L'$.

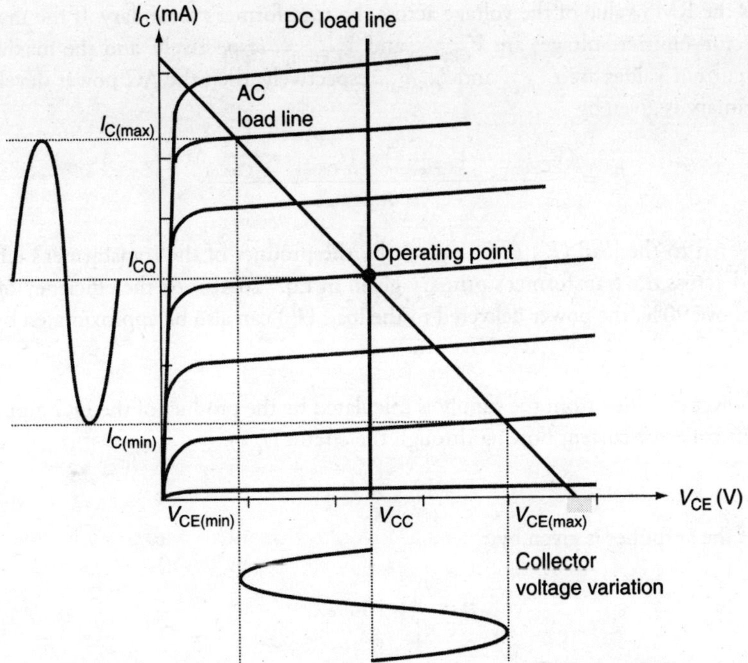

Figure 10.11 Transistor collector characteristics along with the DC and the AC load lines for the transformer-coupled class A amplifier.

The main design objective is to design a circuit that will deliver maximum output power to the load for a small allowable distortion. To deliver maximum output power, the AC load line is drawn tangent to the hyperbola curve of maximum power dissipation. The point of tangency is where the DC load line intersects the hyperbola. As already discussed in Chapter 4, the load line must be drawn so as not to violate the maximum collector emitter voltage rating of transistor. This is usually done by making $V_{CC} \le V_{CE(max)}/2$.

In the case of transformer-coupled class A amplifier, the maximum power dissipated ($P_{D(max)}$) is twice the AC output power (P_o'). Here P_o' is the power developed across the transformer's primary. The Q-point is located at

$$I_{CQ} = \frac{2P_o'}{V_{CC}}, \quad V_{CEQ} = V_{CC} \tag{10.37}$$

If the Q-point is located at the mid-point of the load line then

$$R_L' = \frac{V_{CC}^2}{2P_o'} \tag{10.38}$$

R_L' is the reflected load resistance seen by the transformer's primary. The transformer chosen should be such that the actual load R_L on the secondary looks like R_L' in the primary.

Output Power

The output AC power delivered to the load can be determined using

$$P_o = \frac{V_{2(RMS)}^2}{R_L} \tag{10.39}$$

where $V_{2(\text{RMS})}$ is the RMS value of the voltage across the transformer's secondary. If the maximum and the minimum collector–emitter voltages are $V_{\text{CE(max)}}$ and $V_{\text{CE(min)}}$, respectively, and the maximum and minimum collector current values are $I_{\text{C(max)}}$ and $I_{\text{C(min)}}$, respectively, then the AC power developed across the transformer's primary is given by

$$P_o' = \frac{(V_{\text{CE(max)}} - V_{\text{CE(min)}}) \times (I_{\text{C(max)}} - I_{\text{C(min)}})}{8} \tag{10.40}$$

The power delivered to the load (P_o) is then given by the product of the transformer's efficiency and the power developed across the transformer's primary given in Eq. (10.40). As the efficiency of efficient transformers is well above 90%, the power delivered to the load (P_o) can also be approximated by Eq. (10.40).

Efficiency

The DC input power obtained from the supply is calculated by the product of the DC supply voltage (V_{CC}) and the quiescent collector current flowing through the circuit (I_{CQ}).

$$P_i = V_{\text{CC}} \times I_{\text{CQ}} \tag{10.41}$$

The efficiency of the amplifier is given by

$$\eta = \frac{P_o}{P_i} \times 100\% \tag{10.42}$$

The main source of power loss is that dissipated by the transistor in the form of heat and is approximately equal to the difference between the power that is drawn from the DC supply and the AC power delivered to the load. When the input signal is small, little AC power is delivered to the load and maximum power is dissipated by the transistor. When the input signal is large, large amount of power is delivered to the load and less power is dissipated by the transistor. In other words, in a transformer-coupled class A amplifier the power loss is minimum when the load is drawing maximum power from the amplifier and is maximum when the load is disconnected from the amplifier.

The maximum value of efficiency can be calculated by making certain assumptions like the characteristic curves of the active device are equally spaced in the region of operation, the input signal has zero minimum value and the operating point is in the center of the output characteristics.
Under the already mentioned ideal conditions,

$$I_{\text{CQ}} = \frac{I_{\text{C(max)}} - I_{\text{C(min)}}}{2} \text{ and } V_{\text{CC}} = \frac{V_{\text{CE(max)}} + V_{\text{CE(min)}}}{2}$$

Therefore,

$$P_i = \frac{(V_{\text{CE(max)}} + V_{\text{CE(min)}})}{2} \times \frac{(I_{\text{C(max)}} - I_{\text{C(min)}})}{2} \tag{10.43}$$

Substituting the values of P_o and P_i in Eq. (10.42) we get

$$\eta = 50\left(\frac{V_{\text{CE(max)}} - V_{\text{CE(min)}}}{V_{\text{CE(max)}} + V_{\text{CE(min)}}}\right)\% \tag{10.44}$$

Therefore, the upper limit for theoretical efficiency of a transformer-coupled class A amplifier is 50%, which is twice that of a series-fed class A amplifier.

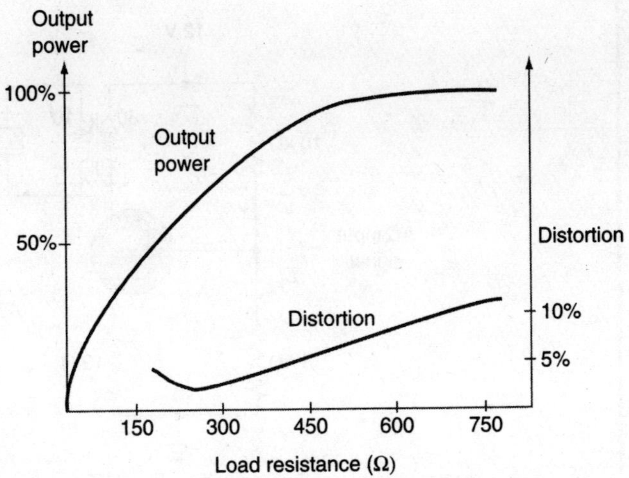

Figure 10.12 Variation of output power and total distortion with load resistance.

Variation of Output Power with Load

Figure 10.12 shows the variation of output power and total distortion with the load resistance. As we can see from the curve, the load that provides minimum value of total distortion is different from the load that yields maximum value of output power. However, the output power curve is largely flat in the region of maximum power, so a well-designed amplifier would work properly for a load that gives slightly less than maximum output power as it will give significantly lower value of total distortion.

Disadvantages of Transformer-Coupled Class A Amplifier

The value of total distortion is quite large in the case of these amplifiers. Moreover, the maximum output power is generated at a load resistance value that is different from the value that offers minimum harmonic distortion. Also, the output transformer is subject to saturation problems as a relatively large DC collector current flows under zero signal conditions.

EXAMPLE 10.3 *Determine the AC power delivered to the speaker in the circuit shown in Figure 10.13(a). The value of the quiescent base current is 8 mA and the input signal results in a peak-to-peak base current swing of 8 mA. The output characteristics of the transistor are shown in Figure 10.13(b).*

Solution

1. The DC load line is obtained by drawing a vertical line from the point (0, V_{CC}), that is, from (0, 12 V).
2. The intersection of this DC load line with the curve corresponding to quiescent base current of 8 mA gives the operating point. From Figure 10.14, we can determine that the operating point is I_{CQ} = 160 mA and V_{CEQ} = 12 V.
3. The effective AC resistance seen by the transformer's primary $R_L' = (N_1/N_2)^2 \times R_L = (30/10)^2 \times R_L = 9 \times 8\ \Omega = 72\ \Omega$.

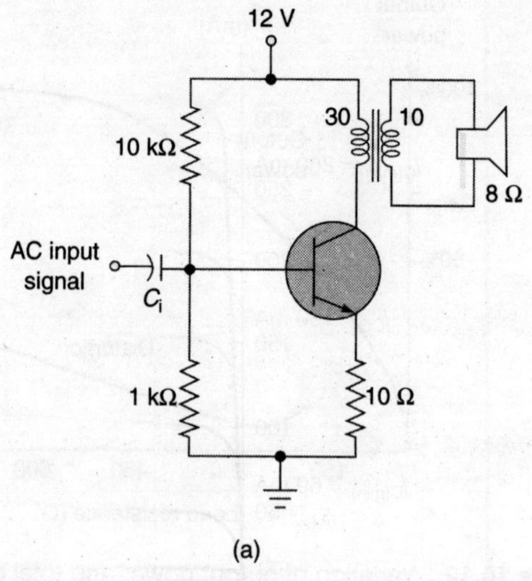

(a)

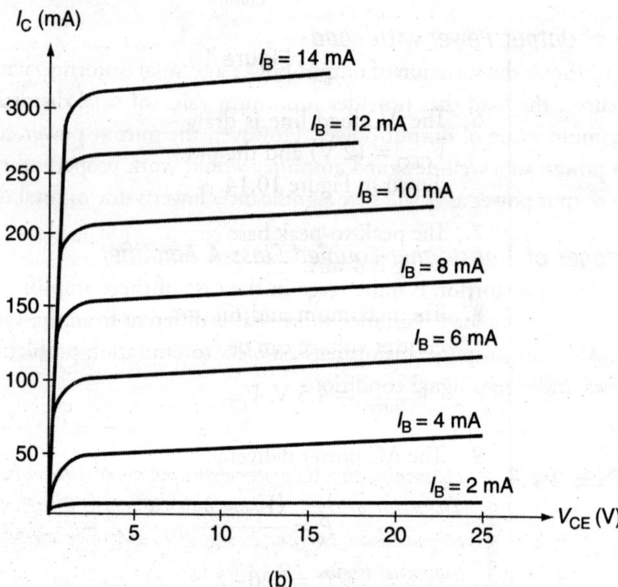

(b)

Figure 10.13 | Example 10.3.

4. The AC load line is drawn with a slope of (−1/72) going through the operating point.

5. The intercept of the load line on the Y-axis = $I_{CQ} + V_{CC}/R'_L$ = [160 + (12 × 10^3)/72] mA = 160 mA + 166.67 mA = 326.67 mA.

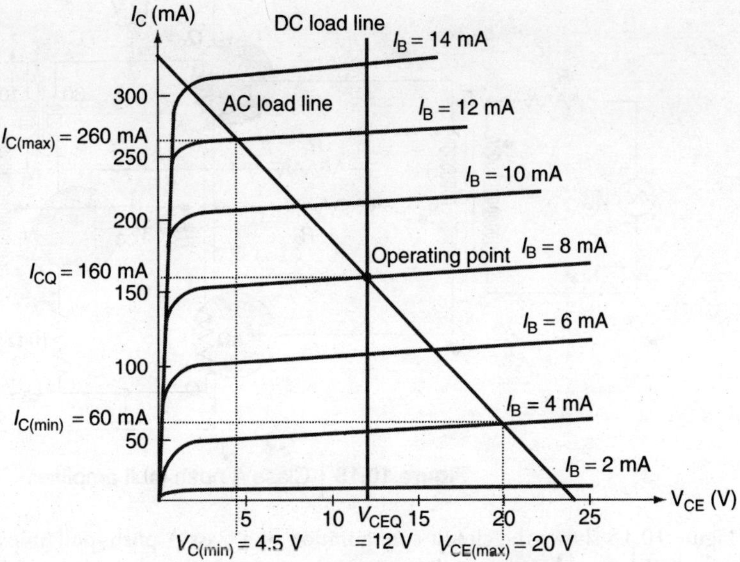

Figure 10.14 | Solution to Example 10.3.

6. The AC load line is drawn by joining the operating point (I_{CQ} = 160 mA, V_{CEQ} = 12 V) and the point (I_C = 326.67 mA, V_{CE} = 0). The AC load line is shown in Figure 10.14.

7. The peak-to-peak base current swing is 8 mA. Therefore, the peak base current swing is 4 mA.

8. The maximum and minimum values of the collector current and collector–emitter voltage can be obtained from Figure 10.14:

$$V_{CE(min)} = 4.5\text{ V},\ V_{CE(max)} = 20\text{ V},\ I_{C(min)} = 60\text{ mA and } I_{C(max)} = 260\text{ mA}$$

9. The AC power delivered to the load is equal to

$$P_o = \frac{(V_{CE(max)} - V_{CE(min)}) \times (I_{C(max)} - I_{C(min)})}{8}$$

$$P_o = [(20 - 4.5) \times (260 - 60)]/8 \text{ mW}$$
$$= (15.5 \times 200)/8 \text{ mW} = 387.5 \text{ mW} = 0.3875 \text{ W}$$

Class A Push–Pull Amplifiers

Push–pull amplifiers employ two active devices which are fed with input signals that are 180° out-of-phase with each other. These amplifiers usually have a center-tapped output transformer. Push–pull configuration offers advantages such as cancellation of second harmonic distortion term and reduction in the power supply ripple voltage.

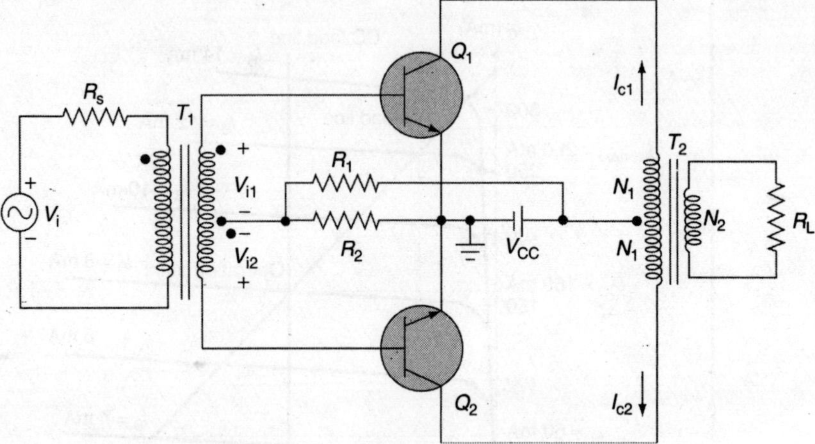

Figure 10.15 | Class A push–pull amplifier.

Figure 10.15 shows the circuit configuration of a class A push–pull amplifier. The transformer at the input end (T_1) provides phase-splitting and the two voltages to the base of the transistors Q_1 and Q_2 are 180° out-of-phase w.r.t. each other. Resistors R_1 and R_2 are so chosen that both the transistors conduct for the whole input signal cycle. The collector currents of both the transistors pass through the windings of the output transformer (T_2) in opposite directions. Therefore, their magnetizing effects cancel with the result that there is no magnetic saturation problem in the output transformer.

When the input signal V_i becomes positive, the base of transistor Q_1 becomes more positive and the base of the transistor Q_2 becomes less positive. Therefore, the collector current of transistor Q_1 will increase in magnitude whereas the collector current of transistor Q_2 will decrease in magnitude. Hence, the voltage across resistor R_L which is proportional to the difference between the collector currents flowing through the two transistors will be positive.

When the input signal V_i becomes negative, the reverse action takes place and the output voltage across resistor R_L becomes negative. This pushing and pulling of the output currents results in decrease in the magnitude of harmonic distortion as the even harmonic terms get cancelled without increase in the values of the odd harmonic terms.

Let us assume that the input signal applied to the amplifier is a sinusoidal signal. This results in base currents that are also sinusoidal in shape. Let the base current of transistor Q_1 be $I_{b1} = I_B\cos\omega t$. Therefore, the base current of the transistor Q_2 is equal to $I_{b2} = I_B\cos(\omega t + 180) = -I_B\cos\omega t$, as the base current flowing through transistor Q_2 is 180° out-of-phase to the base current flowing through transistor Q_1.
The collector current of transistor Q_1 is given by

$$I_{c1} = I_{CQ} + A_0 + A_1\cos\omega t + A_2\cos 2\omega t + A_3\cos 3\omega t + A_4\cos 4\omega t + \ldots \tag{10.45}$$

The collector current through transistor Q_2 is given by

$$I_{c2} = I_{CQ} + A_0 + A_1\cos(\omega t + \pi) + A_2\cos 2(\omega t + \pi) + A_3\cos 3(\omega t + \pi) + A_4\cos 4(\omega t + \pi) + \ldots \tag{10.46}$$

On simplifying Eq. (10.46) we get

$$I_{c2} = I_{CQ} + A_0 - A_1\cos\omega t + A_2\cos 2\omega t - A_3\cos 3\omega t + A_4\cos 4\omega t + \ldots \tag{10.47}$$

The output voltage is directly proportional to the difference of the collector currents flowing through transistors Q_1 and Q_2. The difference between the collector currents flowing through transistors Q_1 and Q_2 is given by

$$I_{c1} - I_{c2} = 2A_1\cos\omega t + 2A_3\cos 3\omega t + \dots \tag{10.48}$$

We can see from Eq. (10.48) that the DC component and the even harmonic terms have been cancelled. The main source of distortion is the third harmonic component instead of the second harmonic component. The third harmonic distortion term (D_3) is given by

$$D_3 = \left|\frac{2A_3}{2A_1}\right| \times 100\% = \left|\frac{A_3}{A_1}\right| \times 100\% \tag{10.49}$$

The total harmonic distortion D is given by

$$D = \sqrt{D_3^2 + D_5^2 + \dots} \tag{10.50}$$

The discussion above has assumed that the two transistors are identically matched, which is not practically feasible. Hence, a small amount of even harmonic component will be present at the output. The push–pull configuration also results in reduction of the ripple present in the power supply voltage (V_{CC}).

10.3 Class B Amplifiers

In a class B amplifier, the active device is biased at zero DC level. Therefore, it provides an output signal varying over one-half of the input signal cycle as the active device conducts for only one-half of the input signal cycle. To obtain output for full input cycle, push–pull configuration is used, that is, two active devices are used wherein each conducts for opposite half-cycles and the combined operation provides full cycle of the output signal. Figure 10.16 shows the block schematic of a push–pull configuration. It may be mentioned here that class B amplifiers offer higher efficiency than class A amplifiers using a single active device.

A number of circuit arrangements are possible for obtaining class B operation. These include transformer-coupled push–pull configuration, complementary-symmetry push–pull configuration and quasi-complementary push–pull configuration. Each of these circuit configurations is explained in the following sections.

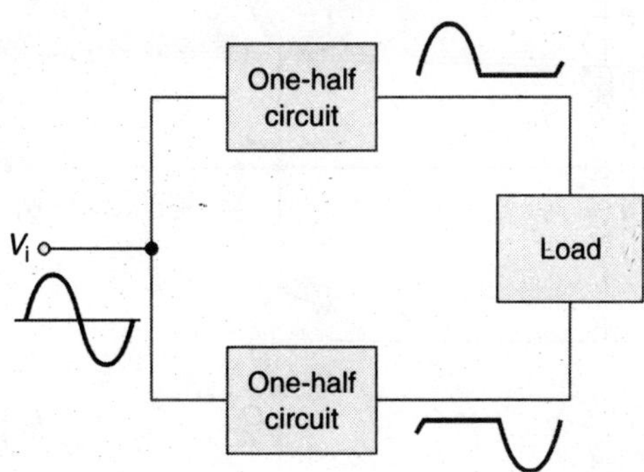

Figure 10.16 Block schematic of push–pull configuration.

Transformer-Coupled Push–Pull Class B Amplifier

Figure 10.17 shows the circuit for a transformer-coupled push–pull class B amplifier. It is essentially the same as a push–pull class A amplifier except that the active devices in this case are biased in the cut-off region. If we compare the circuit of Figure 10.17 with the circuit of class A push–pull amplifier in Figure 10.15, we can see that the resistor $R_2 = 0$ in Figure 10.17, as silicon transistor, is essentially in the cut-off region if its base terminal is shorted to the emitter terminal. Class B amplifier offers higher power output, higher efficiency and there is negligible power loss under quiescent conditions, that is, when no input signal is applied. However, they have higher harmonic distortion, self-bias configuration cannot be used and power supply voltages must have good regulation.

Conversion Efficiency

To determine the conversion efficiency, let us assume that the output characteristics of the active device are equally spaced and also that the minimum collector current is zero. Figure 10.18(a) shows the graphical schematic for determining the output waveform of a single class B transistor stage. As we can see that for a sinusoidal input excitation, the output is sinusoidal during the first half of the input cycle and is zero during the second half cycle.

The effective value of load resistance (R_L') is given by

$$R_L' = \left(\frac{N_1}{N_2}\right)^2 \times R_L \tag{10.51}$$

where N_1 is the number of primary turns to the center tap and N_2 the number of secondary tutns.

Figure 10.18(b) shows that the collector current waveforms of transistors Q_1 and Q_2. As is clear from the figure, the output waveform of transistor Q_2 is 180° out-of-phase to that of transistor Q_1. The load current is proportional to the difference between the collector currents flowing through the transistors Q_1 and Q_2. It is therefore a perfect sine wave for ideal conditions. The output power (P_o) is given by

$$P_o = \frac{I_M V_M}{2} = \frac{I_M}{2} \times (V_{CC} - V_{MIN}) \tag{10.52}$$

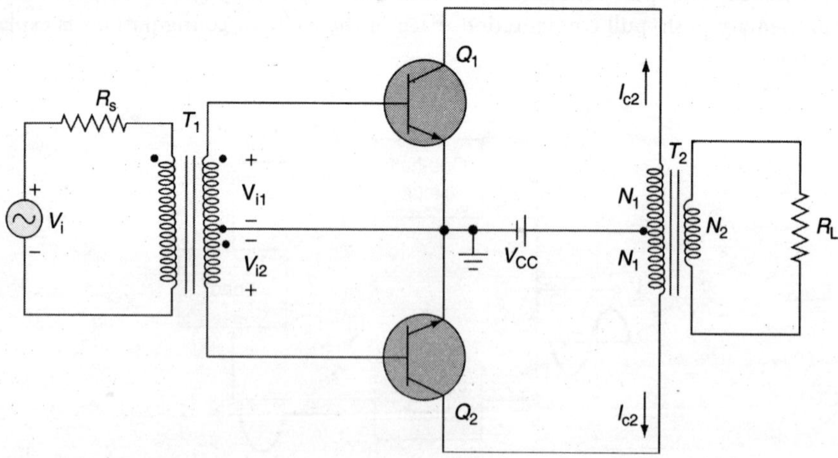

Figure 10.17 Transformer-coupled push–pull class B amplifier.

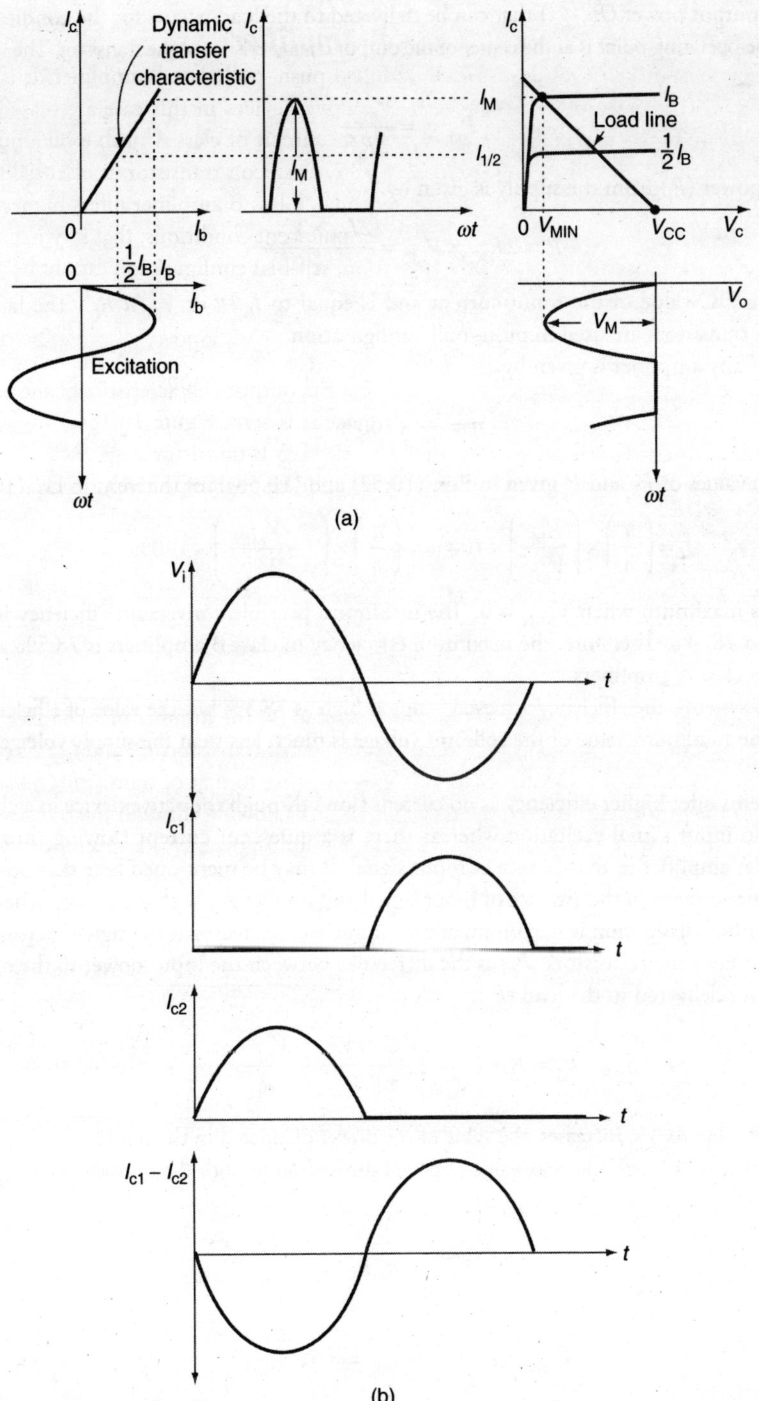

Figure 10.18 (a) Waveform of a single class B transistor stage; (b) output waveforms for class B push–pull amplifiers.

The maximum output power ($P_{o(max)}$) that can be delivered to the load occurs for the conditions $V_M = V_{CC}$, $V_{MIN} = 0$ and the operating point is at the center of the output characteristics of the transistor. The value of $P_{o(max)}$ is given by

$$P_{o(max)} = \frac{V_{CC}^2}{2R_L'} \tag{10.53}$$

The DC input power (P_i) from the supply is given by

$$P_i = 2I_{DC} \times V_{CC} = \frac{2I_M \times V_{CC}}{\pi} \tag{10.54}$$

where I_{DC} is the DC value of the input current and is equal to I_M/π or $V_M/\pi R_L'$. The factor of 2 arises because the two transistors are used in push–pull configuration.

Efficiency of any amplifier is given by

$$\eta = \frac{P_o}{P_i} \times 100\% \tag{10.55}$$

Substituting the values of P_o and P_i given in Eqs. (10.52) and (10.54), respectively, in Eq. (10.55), we get

$$\eta = \left(\frac{\pi}{4}\right) \times \left(\frac{V_M}{V_{CC}}\right) \times 100\% = \left(\frac{\pi}{4}\right) \times \left(1 - \frac{V_{MIN}}{V_{CC}}\right) \times 100\% \tag{10.56}$$

The efficiency is maximum when $V_{MIN} = 0$. The maximum possible conversion efficiency is equal to 25π which is equal to 78.5%. Therefore, the maximum efficiency in class B amplifiers is 78.5% as compared to that of 50% in a class A amplifiers.

For practical systems, the efficiency achieved is not as high as 78.5% but the value of efficiency is higher in systems where the minimum value of the collector voltage is much less than the supply voltage (i.e., $V_{MIN} \ll V_{CC}$).

Class B systems offer higher efficiency as no current flows through the active device in a class B amplifier when there is no input signal excitation whereas there is a quiescent current flowing through the active device in a class A amplifier in the absence of input signal. It may be mentioned here that power dissipation in class B amplifiers is zero in the absence of input signal and it increases with excitation, whereas in the case of a class A amplifier, dissipation is maximum at zero input and decreases as the signal increases. The collector dissipation in both the transistors (P_C) is the difference between the input power to the collector circuit (P_i) and the power delivered to the load (P_o):

$$P_C = P_i - P_o = \frac{2V_{CC} \times V_M}{\pi R_L'} - \frac{V_M^2}{2R_L'} \tag{10.57}$$

When $V_M = 0$, $P_C = 0$. As V_M increases, the value of the power dissipated in the transistors (P_C) increases and it is maximum for $V_M = 2V_{CC}/\pi$. The peak value of power dissipation in both the transistors ($P_{C(max)}$) is given by

$$P_{C(max)} = \frac{2V_{CC}^2}{\pi^2 R_L'} \tag{10.58}$$

Therefore,

$$P_{C(max)} = \frac{4}{\pi^2} \times P_{o(max)} \cong 0.4P_{o(max)} \tag{10.59}$$

Hence, we can obtain a power output of five times the specified power dissipation of a single transistor. As an example, to deliver 10 W from a class B push–pull amplifier, the transistors should have a collector dissipation of 2 W each.

Harmonic Distortion

The output of a push–pull system has a mirror symmetry. Therefore, $I_Q = 0$, $I_{MAX} = -I_{MIN}$ and $I_{+1/2} = -I_{-1/2}$. The values of different harmonic distortion components are given by

$$A_0 = A_2 = A_4 = 0 \tag{10.60}$$

$$A_1 = \frac{2}{3} \times (I_{MAX} + I_{+1/2}) \tag{10.61}$$

$$A_3 = \frac{1}{3} \times (I_{MAX} - 2I_{+1/2}) \tag{10.62}$$

Therefore, there is no even-harmonic distortion. The principal contributor to the harmonic distortion is the third harmonic distortion component (D_3) given by

$$D_3 = \left|\frac{A_3}{A_1}\right| \times 100\% \tag{10.63}$$

The total output power (P_o), taking harmonic distortion into account, is given by

$$P_o = (1 + D_3^{\,2}) \times \frac{A_1^2 R'_L}{2} \tag{10.64}$$

Crossover Distortion

Crossover distortion refers to the non-linearity in the output signal when the output signal crosses from positive to negative or from negative to positive. In other words, crossover distortion refers to the distortion resulting at low values of the input signal in the vicinity of the zero region. The output of the transistor collector current is not a perfect half-sine-wave and it results in crossover distortion. This arises as the value of the transistor's β is quite low near the cut-off region for small values of collector current compared to the rest of the input signal. Figure 10.19 shows the output waveform with crossover distortion.

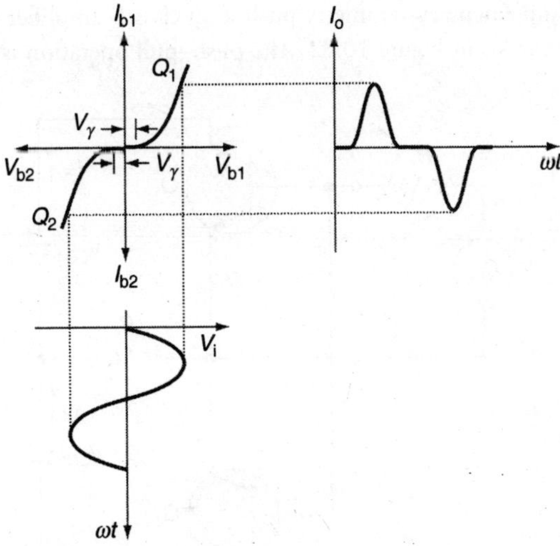

Figure 10.19 | Crossover distortion.

EXAMPLE 10.4 *A class B amplifier provides a 20 V peak output signal to 15 Ω load. The system operates on a power supply of 25 V. Determine the efficiency of the amplifier.*

Solution

1. The peak load current $I_L(p) = 20/15 = 1.33$ A.
2. The DC value of current drawn from the supply $I_{DC} = (2/\pi) \times I_L(p) = 0.847$ A.
3. Input power delivered by the supply voltage $P_i = V_{CC} \times I_{DC} = 25 \times 0.847 = 21.175$ W.
4. Output power delivered to the load $P_o = V_L(p)^2/2R_L = 20^2/(2 \times 15) = 400/30 = 13.33$ W.
5. Efficiency $\eta = (P_o/P_i) \times 100\% = (13.33/21.175) \times 100\% = 62.95\%$.

Complementary-Symmetry Push–Pull Class B Amplifier

Complementary-symmetry push–pull class B amplifiers dispense with the input and the output transformers as shown in Figure 10.20. They make use of complementary transistors (NPN and PNP) to obtain a full-cycle output across the load with each transistor operating for half cycle. The same input is applied to the base terminals of both the transistors. The NPN transistor is so biased that it conducts during the positive half of the input signal whereas the PNP transistor conducts during the negative half of the input signal. The output appears across the load for the full cycle of the input signal.

However, there are two main drawbacks of this configuration. First, it requires two different voltage supplies. Second, the output signal suffers from crossover distortion. This is so because the transistors conduct partially near the zero-voltage condition.

A more practical version of a complementary-symmetry push–pull class B amplifier is the one employing darlington-connected transistors as shown in Figure 10.21. The circuit offers higher output current capability and lower output resistance.

Quasi-Complementary Push–Pull Class B Amplifier

Another variation of the complementary-symmetry push–pull class B amplifier is the quasi-complementary push–pull class B amplifier shown in Figure 10.22. The push–pull operation is achieved by using a pair of

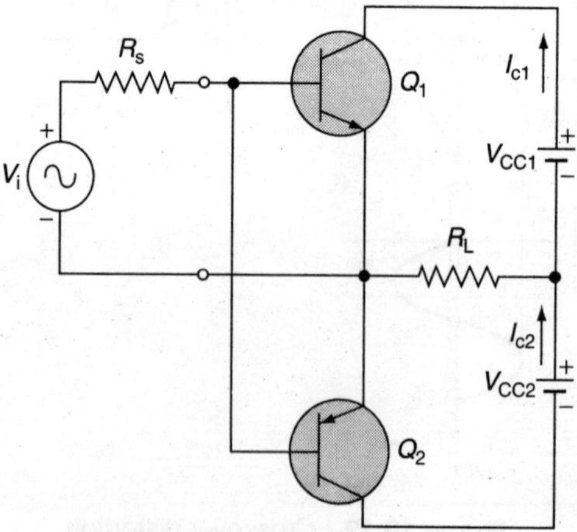

Figure 10.20 Complementary-symmetry push–pull class B amplifier.

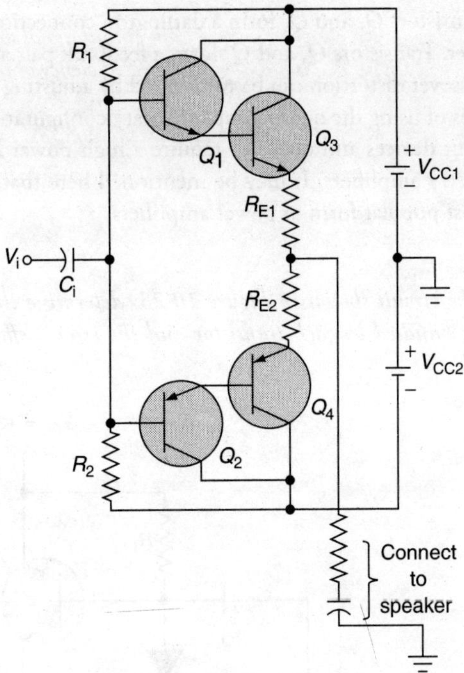

Figure 10.21 | Complementary-symmetry push–pull class B amplifier with Darlington transistors.

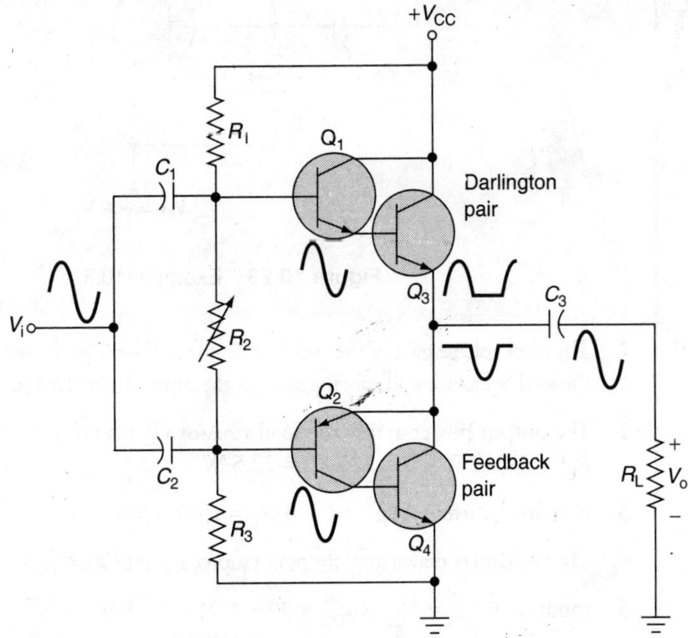

Figure 10.22 | Quasi-complementary push–pull class B amplifier.

complementary transistors. Transistors Q_1 and Q_3 form a darlington connection that provides output from a low-impedance emitter–follower. Transistors Q_2 and Q_4 form a feedback pair and they provide a low-impedance drive to the load. The crossover distortion can be minimized by adjusting the value of the resistor R_2.

One of the main advantages of using the quasi-complementary configuration is that it employs matched NPN transistors as high current devices and does not require a high-power PNP transistor as required in case of complementary-symmetry amplifiers. It may be mentioned here that quasi-complementary push–pull class B amplifier is the most popular form of power amplifiers.

EXAMPLE 10.5 *For the circuit shown in Figure 10.23, determine the input power, output power, power handled by each transistor and the circuit efficiency for a 15 V peak input signal.*

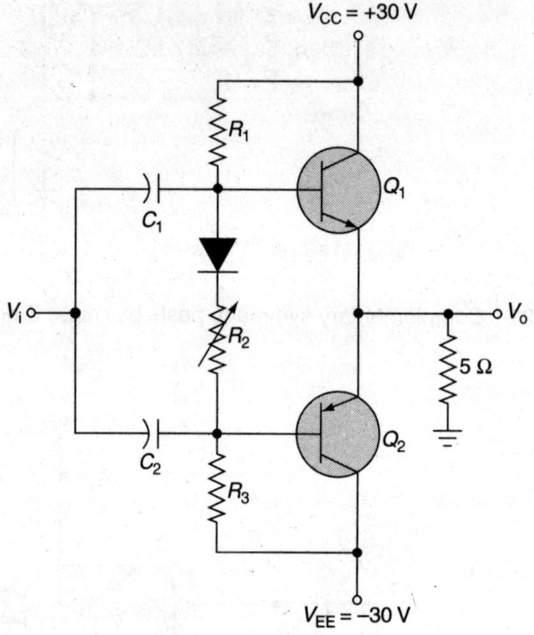

Figure 10.23 | Example 10.5.

Solution

1. The ideal voltage gain of the amplifier is unity. Therefore, the resulting voltage across the load resistance is ideally the same as the input signal. That is, $V_L(p) = 15$ V.
2. The output power across the load resistor (R_L) is given by $P_o = [V_L(p)]^2/(2 \times R_L) = (15)^2/(2 \times 5) = 225/10 = 22.5$ W.
3. Peak load current $I_L(p) = V_L(p)/R_L = 15/5 = 3$ A.
4. The DC current drawn from the power supply $I_{DC} = (2/\pi) \times I_L(p) = (2/\pi) \times 3 = 1.91$ A.
5. Input power $P_i = V_{CC} \times I_{DC} = 30 \times 1.91 = 57.3$ W.

6. Total power dissipated $P_D = P_i - P_o = 57.3 - 22.5 = 34.8$ W.
7. Power dissipated in each transistor $= P_D/2 = 34.8/2 = 17.4$ W.
8. The efficiency at the given input signal is $\eta = (P_o/P_i) \times 100\% = (22.5/57.3) \times 100\% = 39.27\%$.

10.4 Class AB Amplifiers

Class AB amplifiers do not suffer from the problem of crossover distortion as in these amplifiers a small current flows even at zero input signal level. Figure 10.24 shows the configuration of a class AB push–pull amplifier. The circuit is essentially the same as that for class A amplifier. The voltage drop across resistor R_2 is approximately equal to the cut-in voltage of the transistor. When an AC signal is applied to the base, the collector current starts flowing immediately. This biases the transistor away from class B slightly towards class A. Resistors R_E are referred to as the emitter-stabilizing resistors and reduce the amount of distortion produced. However they cause a decrease in the output power due to the negative feedback effect.

10.5 Class C Amplifiers

The amplifiers discussed so far, that is, class A, class B and class AB amplifiers, are linear amplifiers where the amplitude and phase of the output signal is directly related to the amplitude and phase of the input signal. In applications where linearity is not the main issue and efficiency is of primary concern, class C, class D, class E and class F amplifiers are used.

The active device in case of class C amplifiers is so biased that it conducts for less than one half of the input cycle, that is, it operates for less than 180° of the input cycle. Only a small portion of the input cycle is passed through the amplifier. This distorts the input signal and hence class C amplifiers are not used for

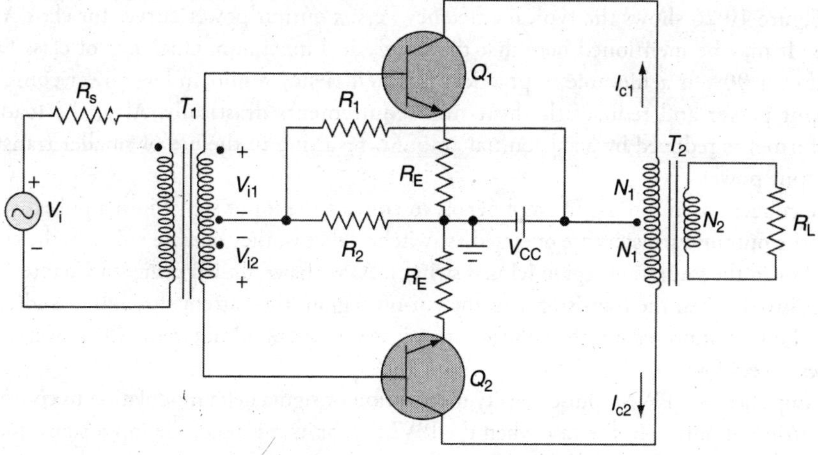

Figure 10.24 Class AB amplifier.

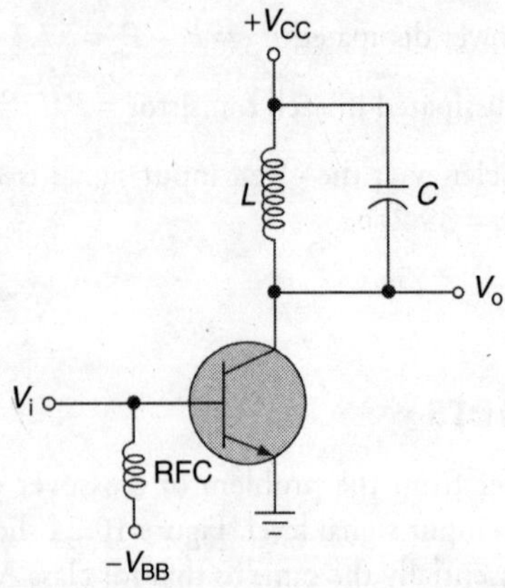

Figure 10.25 | Tuned class C amplifier.

audio applications. They are widely used as radio frequency (RF) and intermediate frequency (IF) amplifiers. They offer very high efficiencies of the order of 90%.

Class C amplifiers operate in two modes, namely, the untuned mode and the tuned mode. However, mostly they are operated in the tuned mode. Figure 10.25 shows a tuned class C amplifier configuration. The tuned circuit provides a full cycle of the output signal at the fundamental or the resonant frequency of the tuned circuit. Hence, the unwanted frequencies are drastically suppressed. Other residual harmonics can be removed by using a filter. Class C amplifiers are generally used in RF transmitters and are primarily not intended for use as large signal or power amplifiers.

10.6 Class D Amplifiers

Class D amplifiers operate with digital or pulsed signals. Class D amplifiers offer very high efficiency levels of the order of 90%; hence they are quite desirable in power amplifiers and audio amplifiers. Figure 10.26 shows the typical efficiency versus output power curves for class AB and class D amplifiers. It may be mentioned here that the theoretical maximum efficiency of class D amplifiers is 100% and over 90% is achievable in practice. High efficiency results in less power consumption for a given output power and reduces the heat-sink requirements drastically. Also, the loading on the power transformer is reduced by a substantial amount, resulting in the use of smaller transformers for the same output power.

The basic concept used in class D amplifiers is to convert the input signal into a pulsed waveform. In other words, the output transistors are operated as switches, that is, they operate either in the cut-off region (open switch) or in the saturation region (closed switch). As we have studied earlier in Chapter 3 on bipolar junction transistors, when the transistor is in the cut-off region, the current through it is ideally zero and when it is in the saturation region, the voltage across it is very small, ideally zero. The power dissipation in both the cases is very low.

Class D amplifiers use PWM, pulse density modulation or sigma delta modulation to convert the input signal into a string of pulses. In the case when the PWM technique is used, the input signal modulates the duty cycle of the drive waveform applied to the input of the switching transistors. In other words, when the amplitude of the input signal increases, the time of the HIGH state increases and that of the LOW state

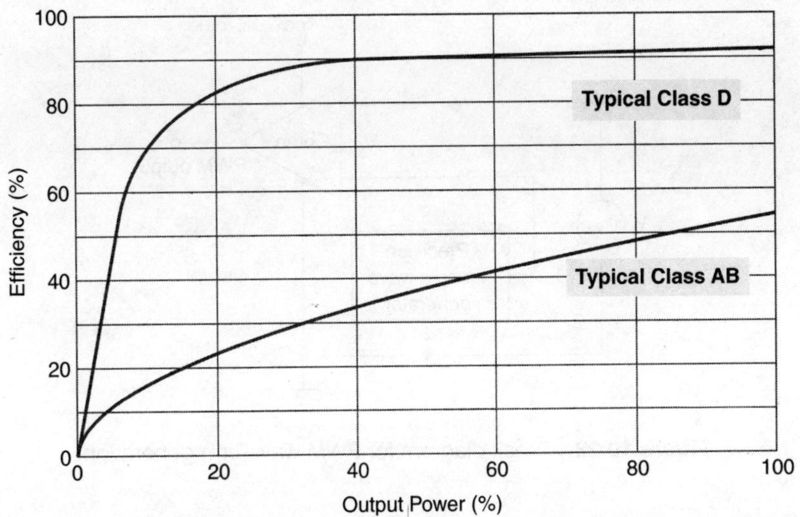

Figure 10.26 Efficiency versus output power curves for class AB and class D amplifiers.

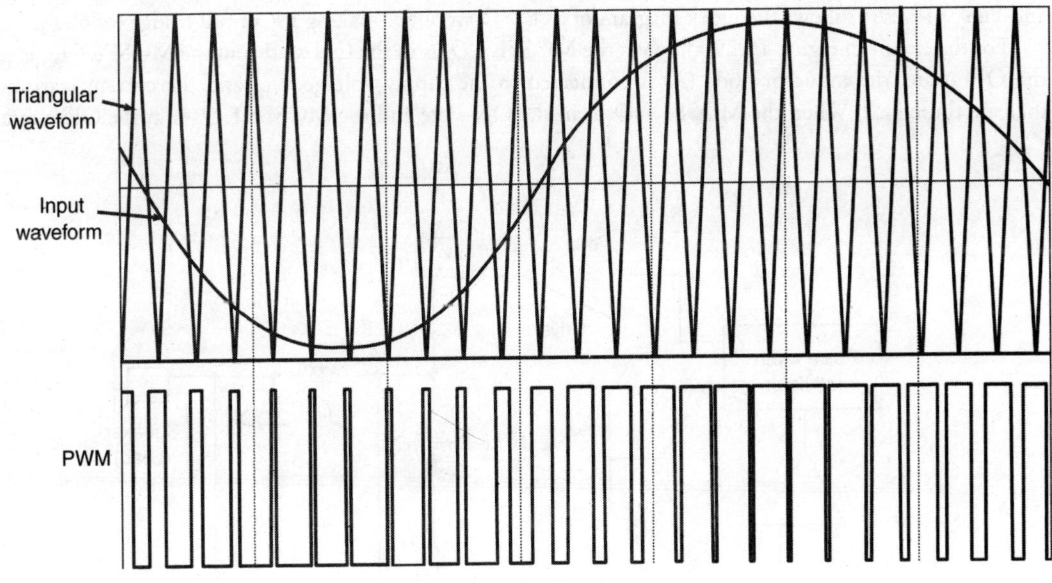

Figure 10.27 Generation of PWM waveform.

decreases. When the amplitude of input signal decreases, the time of HIGH state decreases and that of LOW state increases. PWM is usually generated by comparing the input signal with a triangular waveform (Figure 10.27) or a sawtooth waveform. Figure 10.28 shows the block diagram of the circuit used to generate the PWM waveform used to drive the switching transistors.

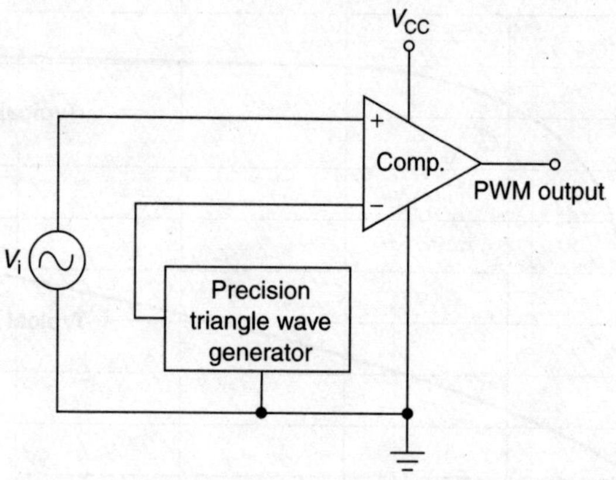

Figure 10.28 Block diagram for PWM waveform generation.

Class D amplifiers can be built using two basic topologies, namely, the half-bridge topology and the full-bridge topology. The half-bridge topology makes use of two active devices whereas the full-bridge topology makes use of four active devices. The half-bridge topology is simpler as compared to the full-bridge topology. Figure 10.29(a) shows the block diagram of a class D amplifier making use of half-bridge topology and Figure 10.29(b) shows the block diagram of a class D amplifier making use of full-bridge topology.

For the circuit in Figure 10.29(a), when the MOSFET Q_1 is in the ON-state and the MOSFET Q_2 is in the OFF-state, the inductor node (A) is connected to the supply voltage V_{DD} and the current starts to increase through it. When the MOSFET Q_2 is in the ON-state and the MOSFET Q_1 is in the OFF-state,

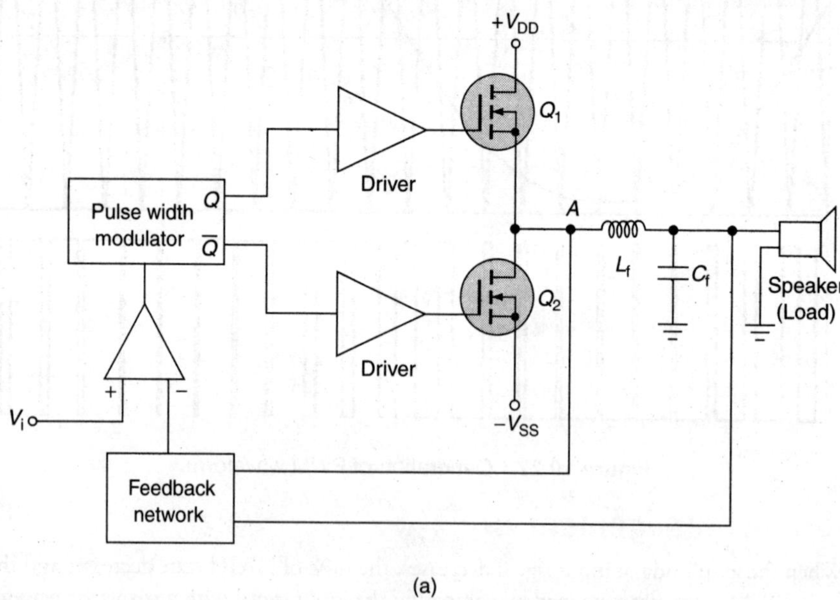

Figure 10.29 (a) Half-bridge topology for class D amplifiers; (b) full-bridge topology for class D amplifiers.

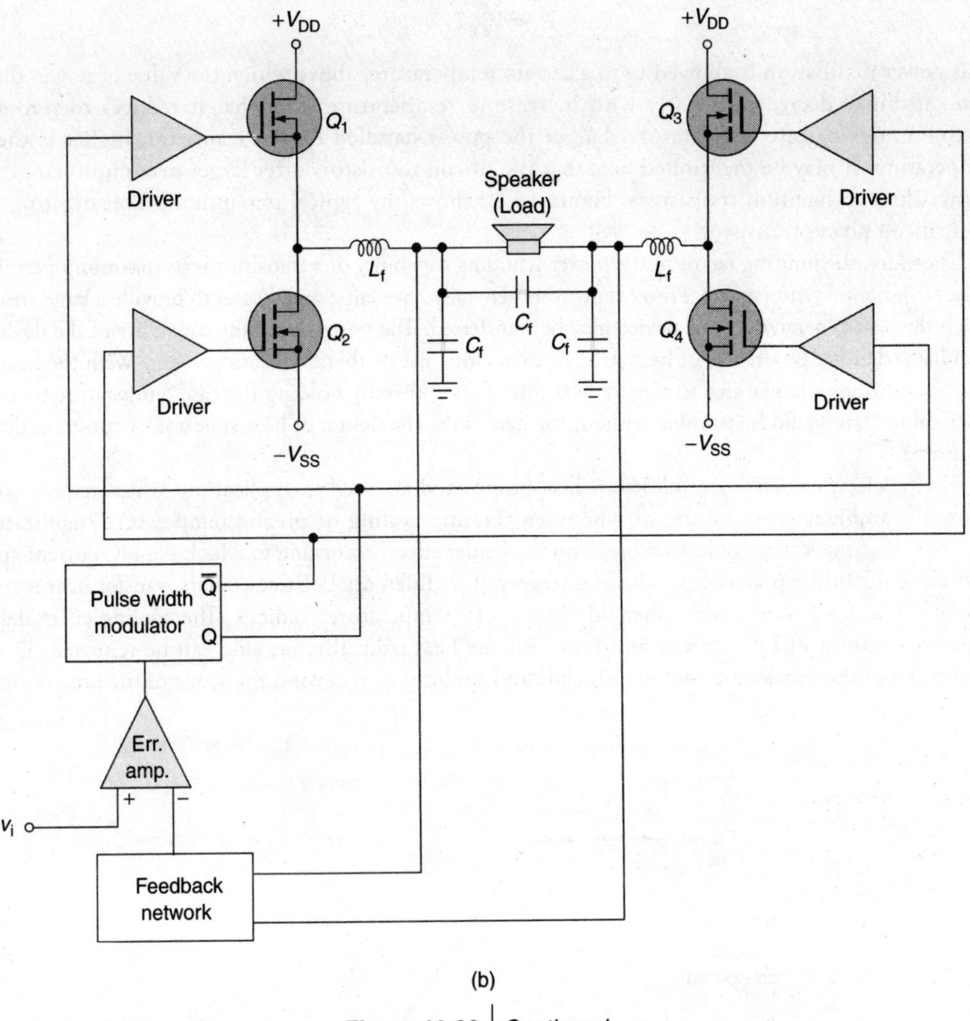

Figure 10.29 | *Continued.*

the current through the inductor L_f starts to decrease. Therefore, the current waveform in the inductor L_f is a triangular waveform. It may be mentioned here that only one of the MOSFETs is in the ON-state at any given time instant. The inductor L_f in conjunction with the capacitor C_f and the output load forms a low-pass filter that reconstructs the input signal by averaging the switching node voltage. Feedback is provided in order to reduce the timing errors.

10.7 Thermal Management of Power Transistors

Power transistors are used as active devices in power amplifiers. The maximum power that can be handled by an active device is related to its junction temperature, as the power dissipated by the device causes an increase in its junction temperature. The average power dissipated by the transistor can be approximated by the following equation:

$$P_D = V_{CE} I_C \tag{10.65}$$

This power dissipation is allowed upto a certain temperature, above which the value of power dissipation capability decreases linearly with increase in temperature such that it reduces to zero at the maximum device case temperature. Larger the power handled by the transistor, higher is the case temperature. It may be mentioned here that the silicon transistors offer larger maximum temperature ratings than germanium transistors. Figure 10.30 shows the typical maximum power derating curve for a silicon power transistor.

Therefore, the limiting factor in the power-handling capability of a transistor is its maximum permissible collector-junction temperature. Power transistors generally have large metal cases to provide a large area from which the heat generated by the device may be transferred. The power-handling capability of the device can be enhanced either by the use of heat sinks or by making use of thermoelectric coolers. With the heat sink, the transistor has a larger area to radiate heat into the air, thereby holding the case temperature to a much lower value than would be possible without the heat sink. The design of heat sink was discussed in detail in Chapter 3.

Thermoelectric coolers are solid-state heat pumps and are used in applications which require cooling below the ambient temperature, or where temperature cycling or precise temperature stabilization is required. Thermoelectric coolers are based on the Peltier effect, according to which the DC current applied across two dissimilar materials results in a temperature differential. These coolers transfer heat from one side of the active device to the other side against the temperature gradient. The cooling effect depends upon the amount of DC current and how well the heat from the hot side can be removed. Detailed description of thermoelectric cooling principle and application is beyond the scope of the present text.

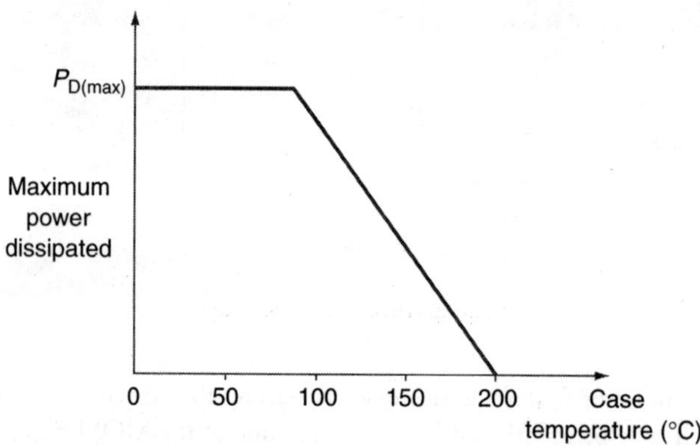

Figure 10.30 | Typical power derating curve for a silicon power transistor.

KEY TERMS

Class A amplifier
Class AB amplifier
Class C amplifier
Class D amplifier
Crossover distortion
Efficiency
Harmonic distortion
Thermal resistance
Large signal amplifier
Power amplifier

OBJECTIVE-TYPE EXERCISES

Multiple-Choice Questions

1. Which of the following amplifier class suffers mainly from the problem of crossover distortion?
   a. Class A
   b. Class B
   c. Class AB
   d. Class C

2. Which of the following best describes a class A amplifier?
   a. High efficiency and high distortion
   b. Low efficiency and high distortion
   c. Low efficiency and low distortion
   d. High efficiency and low distortion

3. Heat sinks are used in power transistors to
   a. reduce the transistor power.
   b. reduce the junction temperature.
   c. increase the ambient temperature.
   d. increase the collector current.

4. In which class of amplifiers it is theoretically possible to achieve 100% efficiency?
   a. Class D
   b. Class A
   c. Class AB
   d. Class C

5. In which of the following amplifier classes, the active device operates for the whole of the input signal cycle?
   a. Class A
   b. Class AB
   c. Class B
   d. Class C

6. The maximum possible efficiency in series-fed class A and transformer coupled class A amplifiers are
   a. 50% and 25% respectively.
   b. 25% and 50% respectively.
   c. Both have 25%.
   d. Both have 50%.

7. How much percentage of maximum power can be dissipated by a transistor for an operating temperature equal to its maximum junction temperature?
   a. 100%
   b. 10%
   c. 50%
   d. 0%

8. A 10 W class B push–pull amplifier should have transistors with minimum individual collector dissipation of
   a. 2 W.
   b. 1 W.
   c. 5 W.
   d. 10 W.

9. Which of the following harmonic component has the main contribution in the total distortion in an amplifier?
   a. Third harmonic component
   b. Second harmonic component
   c. Fourth harmonic component
   d. Fifth harmonic component

10. Class C amplifiers are generally used as
    a. power amplifiers.
    b. RF amplifiers.
    c. audio amplifiers.
    d. none of these.

Match the Following

Figure 10.31 shows six power amplifier configurations. Identify the amplifier configurations from the list given below:

a. Series-fed class A amplifier
b. Tuned class C amplifier
c. Half-bridge class D amplifier
d. Complementary-symmetry push–pull class B amplifier
e. Push–pull class A amplifier
f. Push–pull class B amplifier

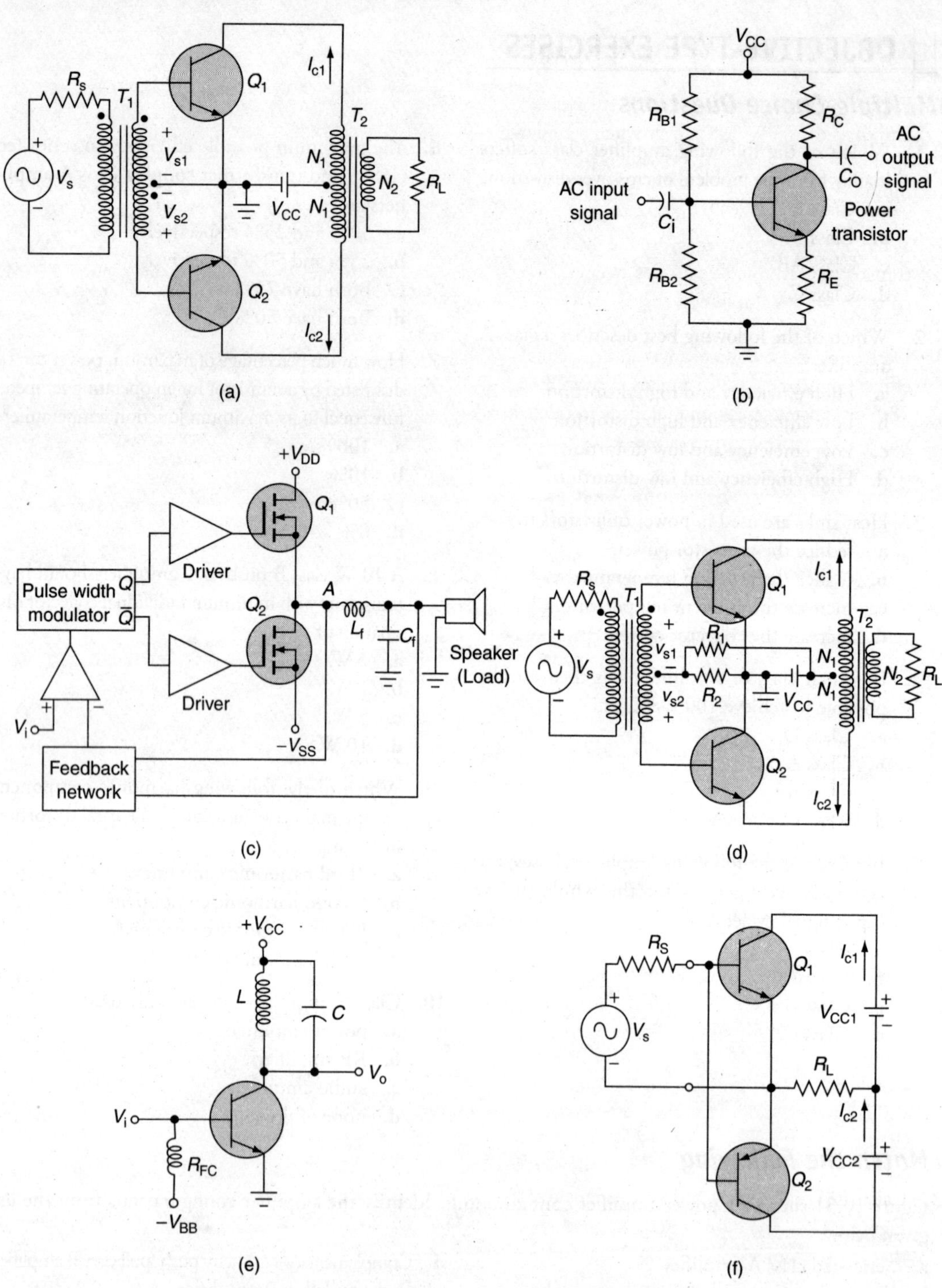

Figure 10.31 | Match the following.

REVIEW QUESTIONS

1. Explain how the active device in a class A amplifier dissipates less power when a signal is applied to it as compared to when there is no input signal.

2. What are the advantages offered by class A transformer-coupled amplifier over a direct-coupled class A amplifier?

3. Derive an expression to prove that the maximum efficiency in the case of a class B amplifier is 78.5%. What assumptions are made in calculating the maximum theoretical efficiency?

4. What is crossover distortion? What are the main factors that lead to crossover distortion and how can they be removed?

5. What are power amplifiers? How are they classified into different classes depending upon their mode of operation?

6. Sketch the circuit diagram of a quasi-complementary push–pull class B amplifier. Also draw the relevant current and voltage input and output waveforms.

7. Draw the circuit diagram of class A push–pull amplifier and explain its principle of operation.

8. What are class C amplifiers? How do they differ from class A and class B amplifiers?

9. Explain in detail how the use of heat sinks results in enhancement in the power dissipation capability of the transistor.

10. Write short notes on the following:
    a. Crossover distortion
    b. Harmonic distortion
    c. Complementary-symmetry push–pull class B amplifier
    d. Maximum efficiency of a class A amplifier

PROBLEMS

1. A class B amplifier provides a 15 V peak output signal to 10 Ω load. The system operates on a power supply of 20 V. Determine the efficiency of the amplifier.

2. Calculate the harmonic distortion components for an output signal having fundamental amplitude of 6 V, second harmonic component of 0.5 V, third harmonic component of 0.1 V and fourth harmonic component of 0.04 V. Also calculate the total harmonic distortion.

3. Calculate the efficiency of the amplifier circuit in Figure 10.32. The input voltage applied is such that it produces a peak-to-peak base current of 16 mA. The emitter–base voltage of the transistor is equal to 0.7 V.

4. For the circuit of Figure 10.33, determine the input power, output power, power handled by each transistor and the circuit efficiency for an input of 15 V peak.

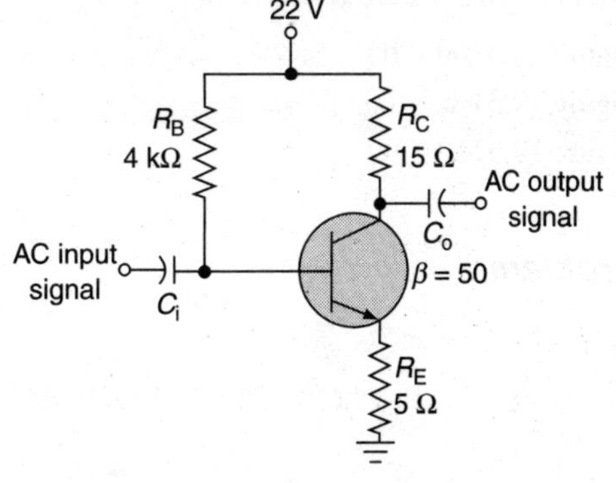

Figure 10.32 | Problem 3.

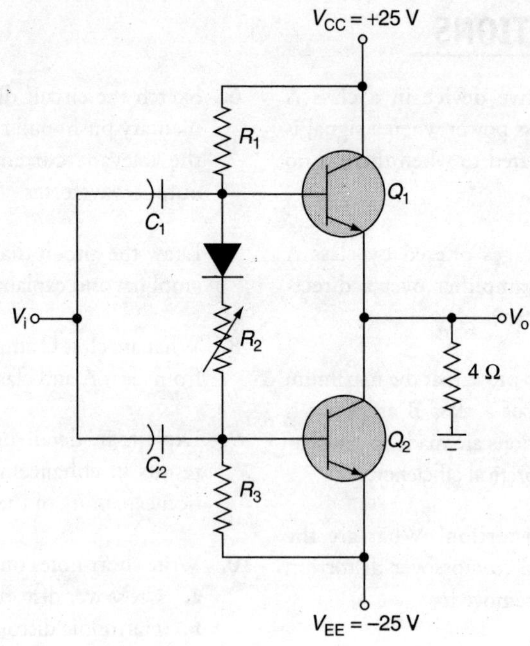

Figure 10.33 | Problem 4.

ANSWERS

Multiple-Choice Questions

1. (b) **3.** (b) **5.** (a) **7.** (d) **9.** (b)
2. (c) **4.** (a) **6.** (b) **8.** (a) **10.** (b)

Match the Following

Figure 10.31(a) – (f)
Figure 10.31(b) – (a)
Figure 10.31(c) – (c)
Figure 10.31(d) – (e)
Figure 10.31(e) – (b)
Figure 10.31(f) – (d)

Problems

1. 58.87%

2. D_2=8.33%, D_3=1.67%, D_4=0.67%, D=8.52%

3. 21.82%

4. Input power = 59.71 W; output power = 28.125 W; power handled by each transistor = 15.794 W; efficiency = 47.1%

CHAPTER 11

Feedback Amplifiers

Learning Objectives

After completing this chapter, you will learn the following:

- Classification of amplifiers based on input and output parameters of interest.
- Types of negative feedback.
- Examples of voltage-series, current-series, voltage-shunt and current-shunt feedback in amplifier circuits.
- Effect of negative feedback on input and output impedances.
- Effect of negative feedback on gain (or conversion) and bandwidth parameters.
- Effect of negative feedback on noise performance.

Practical amplifier circuits always have some kind of negative feedback inherent to their operation. As we will see during the course of our discussion, presence of negative feedback in amplifiers brings along with it many advantages. In this chapter are introduced the basic concepts of negative feedback in amplifiers. The chapter begins with a brief outline on the classification of amplifiers based on input (current or voltage) and output (current or voltage) parameters of interest. This is followed by different types of feedback encountered in amplifiers. The classification of types of feedback is based on the type of output signal (current or voltage) fed back to the input and also the mode in which it is fed back (series or shunt). Also, each of the different types of feedback enhances the performance of a particular type of amplifier circuit. Effect of different types of negative feedback on the performance parameters of the amplifier is also discussed in detail. The text is adequately illustrated with practical circuits and a large number of solved examples.

11.1 Classification of Amplifiers

On the basis of the input and output parameters of interest, amplifiers are classified as voltage amplifiers, current amplifiers, transresistance amplifiers and transconductance amplifiers. In the case of a voltage amplifier, a small change in the input voltage produces a large change in the output voltage. Voltage gain, which is the ratio of the change in the output voltage to change in the input voltage, is the gain parameter. The input and output circuits of a voltage amplifier are represented by Thevenin's equivalent circuits as shown in Figure 11.1. In order that the circuit of Figure 11.1 acts like a true voltage amplifier, the input resistance of the amplifier represented by R_i in Figure 11.1 should ideally be infinite so that the whole applied input voltage appears across the amplifier input irrespective of the value of source resistance R_s. In a practical voltage amplifier circuit, R_i is much larger than R_s. Also, the output resistance R_o should ideally be

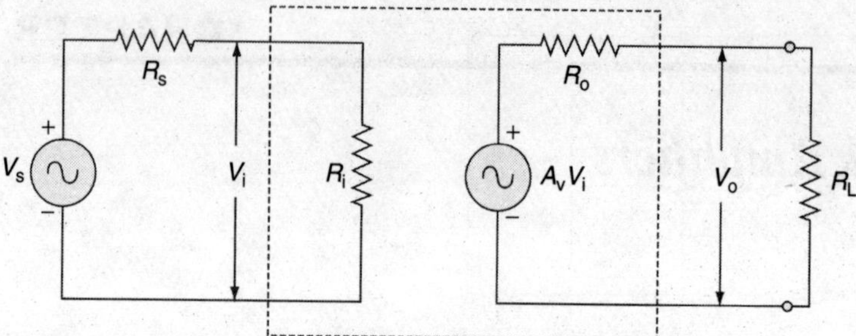

Figure 11.1 Equivalent circuit of voltage amplifier.

zero so that whole of amplified input voltage appears across the load resistance R_L irrespective of the value of R_L. In a practical voltage amplifier circuit, R_o is much smaller than R_L.

In the case of a current amplifier, a small change in the input current produces a large change in the output current. Current gain, which is the ratio of change in the output current to the change in the input current, is the gain parameter. The input and output circuits of a current amplifier are represented by Norton's equivalent circuits as shown in Figure 11.2. In order that the circuit of Figure 11.2 acts like a true current amplifier, the input resistance of the amplifier represented by R_i in Figure 11.2 should ideally be zero so that the whole applied input current flows through the amplifier input irrespective of the value of source resistance R_s. In a practical current amplifier circuit, R_i is much smaller than R_s. Also, the output resistance R_o should ideally be infinite so that whole of amplified input current flows through the load resistance R_L irrespective of the value of R_L. In a practical current amplifier circuit, R_o is much larger than R_L.

In the case of a transresistance amplifier, a small change in the input current produces a large change in the output voltage. Ratio of the change in the output voltage to change in the input current is the gain parameter. The gain parameter has the units of resistance. The input and output circuits of a transresistance amplifier are, respectively, represented by Norton's and Thevenin's equivalent circuits as shown in Figure 11.3. For the circuit of Figure 11.3 to behave like a true transresistance amplifier, the input resistance of the amplifier represented by R_i in Figure 11.3 should ideally be zero so that the whole of applied input current flows through the amplifier input irrespective of the value of source resistance R_s. In a practical transresistance amplifier circuit, R_i is much smaller than R_s. Also, the output resistance R_o should ideally be zero so that the output voltage appears across the load resistance R_L irrespective of the value of R_L. In a practical circuit, R_o is much smaller than R_L.

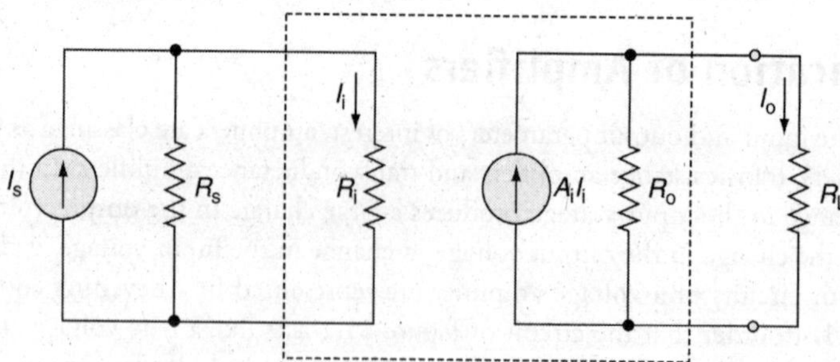

Figure 11.2 Equivalent circuit of current amplifier.

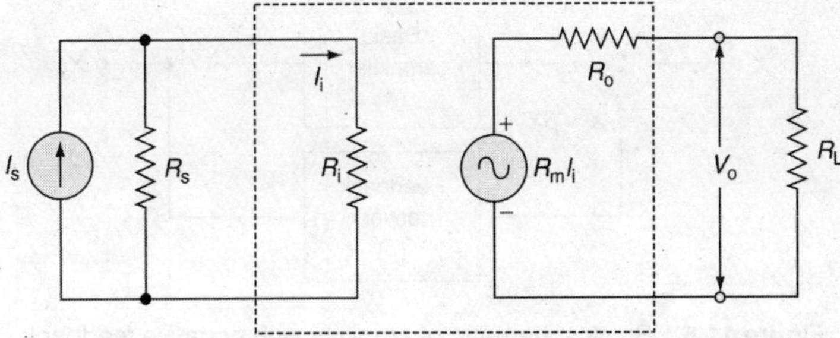

Figure 11.3 | Equivalent circuit of transresistance amplifier.

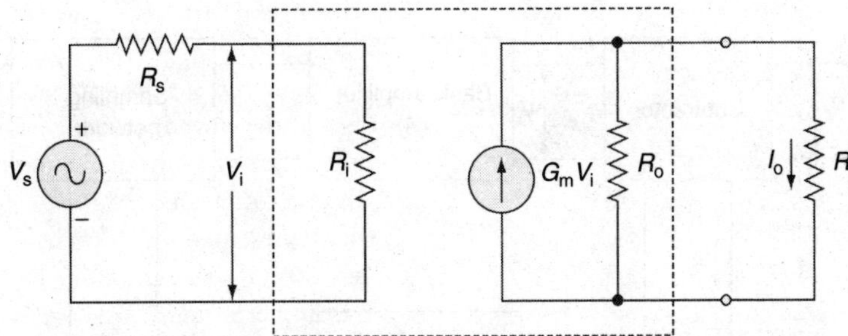

Figure 11.4 | Equivalent circuit of transconductance amplifier.

In the case of a transconductance amplifier, a small change in the input voltage produces a large change in the output current. Ratio of the change in the output current to the change in the input voltage is the gain parameter. The gain parameter has the units of conductance. The input and output circuits of a transconductance amplifier are, respectively, represented by Thevenin's and Norton's equivalent circuits as shown in Figure 11.4. For the circuit of Figure 11.4 to behave like a true transconductance amplifier, the input resistance of the amplifier represented by R_i in Figure 11.4 should ideally be infinite so that the whole of applied input voltage appears across the amplifier input irrespective of the value of source resistance R_s. In a practical transconductance amplifier circuit, R_i is much larger than R_s. Also, the output resistance R_o should ideally be infinite so that the output current flows through the load resistance R_L irrespective of the value of R_L. In a practical circuit, R_o is much larger than R_L.

11.2 Amplifier with Negative Feedback

In a negative-feedback amplifier, a sample of the output signal is fed back to the input and the feedback signal is combined with the externally applied input signal in a subtractor circuit as shown in Figure 11.5. As a result, the actual signal X_i applied to the basic amplifier is the difference of the externally applied input signal X_s and the feedback signal X_f. The generalized representation of input and output signals is intended to indicate that the signal could either be a current or a voltage signal.

Figure 11.6 shows a more elaborate schematic arrangement of an amplifier with negative feedback depicting different circuit blocks. The source of external input signal could either be a voltage source or a current source. The basic amplifier produces either an output current or voltage proportional to the input

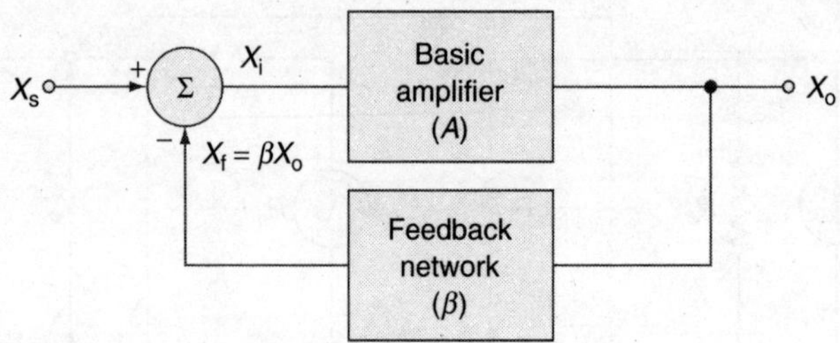

Figure 11.5 Block schematic of amplifier with negative feedback.

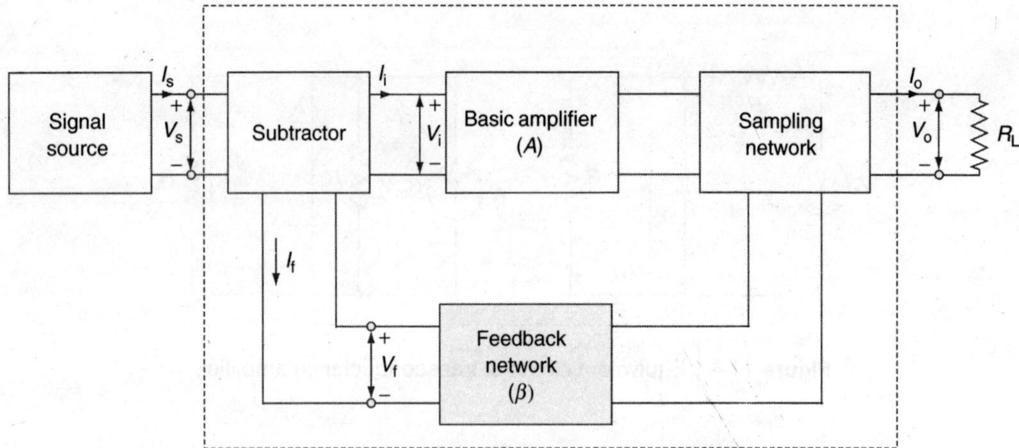

Figure 11.6 Schematic arrangement of various building blocks of a negative-feedback amplifier.

current or voltage. The nature of input and output parameters decides the nature of gain parameter of the amplifier as outlined earlier in Section 11.1.

The sampling network samples either the output voltage by connecting the input side of the feedback network in shunt across the output [Figure 11.7(a)] or the output current where the input side of the feedback network is connected in series with the output [Figure 11.7(b)]. The two sampling techniques are, respectively, known as voltage and current sampling.

The combining operation of externally applied input signal and the feedback signal is carried out in a differential amplifier (or subtractor) circuit. It is done in either of the two ways, namely, series connection [Figure 11.8(a)] and shunt connection [Figure 11.8(b)].

The gain parameter – which could be a voltage gain, current gain, transresistance or transconductance – has two values, namely, the gain of the basic amplifier without feedback and the gain of the amplifier with feedback. With reference to Figure 11.5, gain values without and with feedback are, respectively, given by X_o/X_i and X_o/X_s.

Effect of Negative Feedback on Gain

We will now derive an expression for gain with feedback in terms of gain without feedback (open-loop gain) and the feedback factor for the negative-feedback amplifier of Figure 11.5. The actual signal applied to the amplifier input X_i is the difference of externally applied input signal X_s and the feedback signal X_f. It is given by

$$X_i = X_s - X_f \tag{11.1}$$

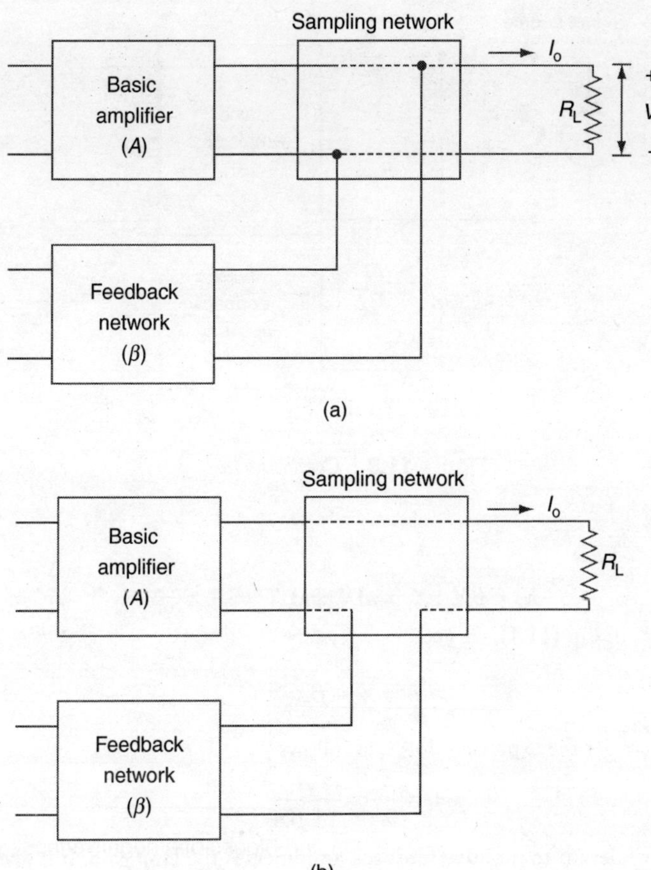

Figure 11.7 Sampling in negative-feedback amplifiers: (a) Voltage sampling; (b) current sampling.

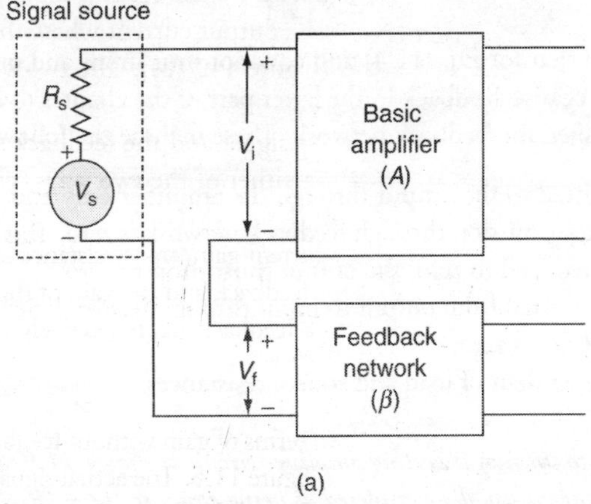

Figure 11.8 Mixing operation in negative-feedback amplifiers: (a) Series input connection; (b) shunt input connection.

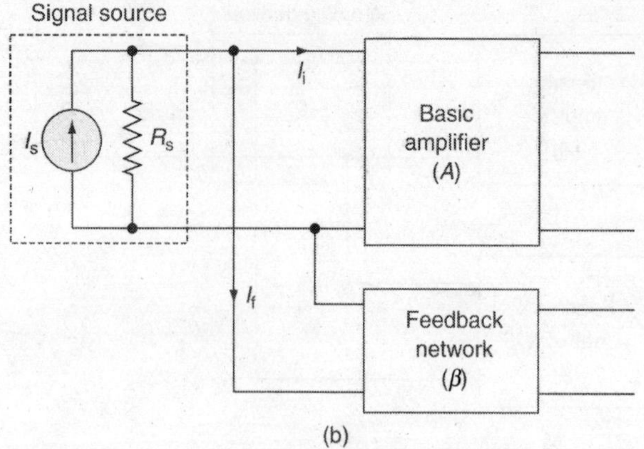

Figure 11.8 | *Continued.*

Also,

$$X_f = \beta X_o,\ X_o = AX_i \text{ and } X_o = A_f X_s \tag{11.2}$$

Substituting for X_i and X_f in Eq. (11.1), we get

$$\frac{X_o}{A} = X_s - \beta X_o \tag{11.3}$$

Simplifying Eq. (11.3), we get the expression for A_f as follows:

$$A_f = \frac{X_o}{X_s} = \frac{A}{1+\beta A} \tag{11.4}$$

An important parameter relevant to negative-feedback amplifiers is the loop gain. It is given by ($-\beta A$) with minus sign indicating negative feedback. Another relevant term is the quantum of feedback expressed in decibels. It is given by

$$\text{dB of feedback} = 20\log\left|\frac{A_f}{A}\right| = 20\log\left|\frac{1}{1+\beta A}\right| \tag{11.5}$$

It may be mentioned here that for Eq. (11.4) and equations for input and output impedances derived in the case of amplifiers with negative feedback in the latter part of the chapter to be valid, three fundamental assumptions should be satisfied for feedback network. These include the following:

1. The input signal is transmitted to the output through the amplifier only and not through the feedback network. That is, forward transmission through feedback network is zero. This further implies that if the gain of the amplifier were reduced to zero, the output must drop to zero.
2. The feedback signal is transmitted from output to input through feedback network only. That is, reverse transmission through amplifier is zero.
3. The feedback factor is independent of load and source resistances.

EXAMPLE 11.1 *Refer to the non-inverting amplifier circuit of Figure 11.9. The closed-loop gain of this amplifier is usually considered as being equal to $[(1 + (R_2/R_1)]$. Given that the open-loop gain of the opamp is 10,000, values of R_1 and R_2 are 10 kΩ and 100 kΩ, respectively, and the value of the applied input voltage V_i is 1 V, determine the percentage error incurred in computing the output voltage by using this expression.*

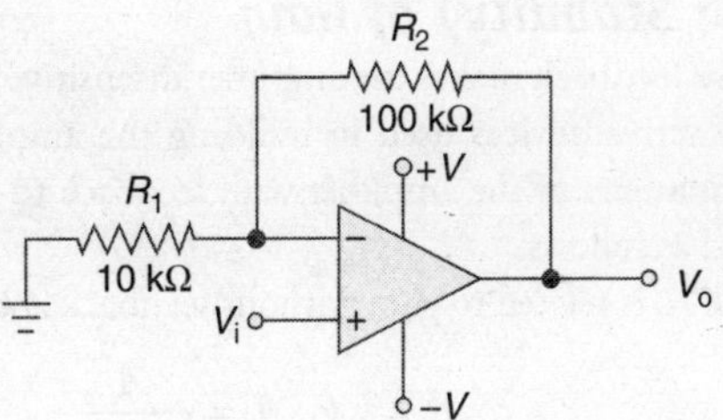

Figure 11.9 | Example 11.1.

Solution

1. Closed-loop gain ignoring the effect of finite value of open loop gain = $1 + (R_2/R_1)$.
2. Substituting for R_1 and R_2, it comes out to be 11.
3. The output voltage is, therefore, 11 V.
4. The true value of closed-loop gain is given by $[A/(1 + \beta A)]$. A is the open-loop gain and is equal to 10,000. β is the feedback factor and is given by $[R_1/(R_1 + R_2)]$. This equals 1/11.
5. The true value of the closed-loop gain is, therefore, given by [10,000/{(1 + 10,000)/11}] = 10.988.
6. The true value of output voltage is, therefore, 10.988 V.
7. Percentage error = [(11 − 10.988)/10.988] × 100 = 0.11%.

11.3 Advantages of Negative Feedback

Introduction of negative feedback in amplifiers gives them many desirable features, which include the following:

1. It desensitizes the gain parameter to variation in values of components used in building the basic amplifier.
2. It increases the bandwidth.
3. It reduces distortion and increases linearity. It may be mentioned here that fundamentally all electronic devices (bipolar transistors, MOSFETs, etc.) that provide power gain are non-linear. Negative feedback allows the gain to be traded for higher linearity.
4. It reduces noise.
5. It can decrease or increase the input resistance depending upon the feedback topology. To be more specific, it depends upon how the feedback signal is mixed with the externally applied input signal. Series and shunt mixing, respectively, increase and decrease the input resistance.
6. It can decrease or increase the output resistance depending upon the feedback topology. More precisely, it depends upon how the output signal is sampled. Voltage sampling decreases the output resistance while current sampling increases it.

Most of the above-mentioned advantages (increased linearity, increased bandwidth, etc.) come at the cost of reduced gain. Closed-loop gain is smaller than the open-loop gain and the quantum of reduction depends upon the open-loop gain and the feedback factor. It, in fact, depends upon the product of the two called the loop gain.

Second disadvantage is the sensitivity of the input and output impedances to variation in open-loop gain. Third, negative feedback may sometimes lead to instability. But this can be taken care of in a carefully designed amplifier. Each one of these features is discussed in detail in the following sections.

Desensitivity (or Stability) of Gain

Introduction of negative feedback makes the amplifier insensitive to variations in the values of the components and parameters of the active devices used in building the amplifier. The expression that relates percentage variation in the gain parameter of the amplifier with feedback to the percentage variation in the same without feedback can be derived as follows.

Gain with feedback A_f is related to gain without feedback A by Eq. (11.4) and the equation is reproduced as follows:

$$A_f = \frac{A}{1+\beta A}$$

Differentiating the above equation with respect to A, we get

$$\frac{dA_f}{dA} = \frac{d}{dA}\left[\frac{A}{1+\beta A}\right] = \frac{(1+\beta A)-\beta A}{(1+\beta A)^2} = \frac{1}{(1+\beta A)^2}$$

$$dA_f = \frac{dA}{(1+\beta A)^2} = \left(\frac{dA}{A}\right)\times\left[\frac{A}{(1+\beta A)^2}\right] = \left(\frac{dA}{A}\right)\times\left[\frac{A_f}{1+\beta A}\right]$$

$$\frac{dA_f}{A_f} = \left[\frac{1}{1+\beta A}\right]\times\left(\frac{dA}{A}\right)$$

$$\left|\frac{dA_f}{A_f}\right| = \left|\frac{1}{1+\beta A}\right|\times\left|\frac{dA}{A}\right| \tag{11.6}$$

$|(1+\beta A)|$ is called the desensitivity parameter D. Thus, percentage variation in gain with feedback is equal to the percentage variation in gain without feedback divided by the desensitivity parameter D. As a special case, when $\beta A >> 1$, A_f equals $1/\beta$ and therefore becomes independent of the open-loop gain of the amplifier. In that case, the stability of the gain parameter depends only on the stability of the components used in the feedback network. By using stable passive components in the feedback network, it is indeed possible to have a stable amplifier that is immune to variations in parametric values of the amplifier. Remember that all this comes at the cost of reduced gain. This implies that the gain without feedback needs to be much larger than the desired value of the gain with feedback. If increase in instability of the amplifier on account of having a larger gain without feedback is not significantly higher than the instability of the amplifier without feedback at a lower gain value, then introduction of negative feedback certainly improves the stability by a significant margin.

Effect on Bandwidth

Bandwidth increases with introduction of negative feedback. Increase in bandwidth results from the fact that amplifiers exhibit a constant gain-bandwidth product. Reduction in gain is, therefore, accompanied by increase in bandwidth. Bandwidth increases by the same desensitivity factor $D = 1 + \beta A$ by which the gain reduces. Bandwidth of amplifier with feedback is given by

$$(BW)_f = BW\times(1+\beta A) \tag{11.7}$$

Figure 11.10 shows the gain-bandwidth curve of a typical operational amplifier. The gain-bandwidth product is given by the unity gain crossover frequency. We can see how bandwidth can be traded for closed-loop gain. Increase in bandwidth with introduction of negative feedback can also be explained as follows. As the gain rolls off with increase in frequency, reduced output signal amplitude means reduced feedback. Reduced negative feedback means increase in the magnitude of effective input signal which increases the output. In other words, output remains at its mid-band value up to a higher frequency.

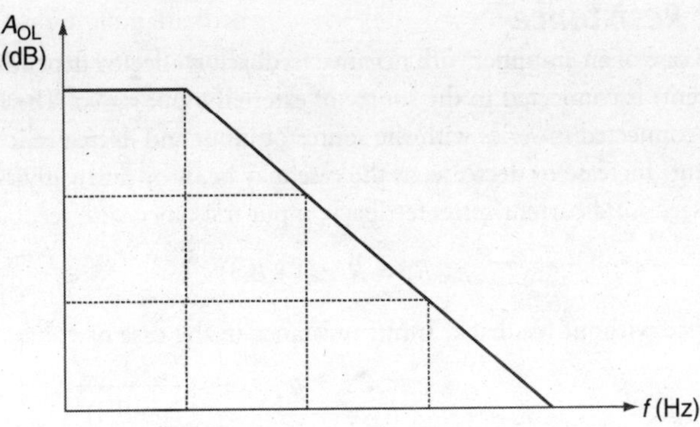

Figure 11.10 | Effect of negative feedback on bandwidth.

Effect on Non-Linear Distortion

As discussed in Chapter 10 on large signal amplifiers, non-linear distortion arises from the existence of non-linear transfer characteristics of the active device and large input and output signal swings that are large enough to drive the active device to operate in the non-linear region of its characteristics. Non-linear distortion can be assumed to be predominantly second harmonic distortion. Introduction of negative feedback reduces distortion provided that reduction in gain caused by negative feedback is compensated by increased gain in the preamplifier stages rather than introducing an additional gain stage. Remember that the non-linear distortion mainly occurs in the last stage of amplification and increasing the gain of previous stages does not add significantly to the overall distortion level.

It can be proved that non-linear distortion decreases by the desensitivity factor $D = 1 + \beta A$. Let us assume that the distortion levels without and with negative feedback are D_2 and D_{2f}, respectively. Suffix "2" implies second harmonic distortion. D_2 is the distortion contributed by the active device. In the presence of feedback, D_{2f} appears as $-\beta AD_{2f}$ at the input of the amplifier. The following gives the expression for D_{2f}:

$$D_2 - \beta AD_{2f} = D_{2f} \tag{11.8}$$

$$D_{2f} = \frac{D_2}{1+\beta A} \tag{11.9}$$

Derivation of above expression makes use of superposition principle. Equation (11.9) is, therefore, valid only when the active device operates close to the linear region. This further means that the above expression is valid for small distortion levels. Also, small amount of additional distortion arising out of small fraction of distortion present at the output being fed back to the input is assumed to be negligible in deriving the above expression.

Effect on Noise

Introduction of negative feedback acts on the noise generated in the amplifier in the same manner as it does on the non-linear distortion. Reduction in noise is governed by

$$N_f = \frac{N}{1+\beta A} \tag{11.10}$$

N_f and N are, respectively, the noise levels with and without negative feedback. However, if reduction in gain resulting from introduction of negative feedback is compensated by adding an amplifier stage, the overall system may turn out to be noisier than before. In order to benefit from the positive effect of negative feedback on noise, it is important that the reduced gain is compensated by readjustment of amplifier parameters for a higher gain without feedback so that the amplifier with feedback gives the desired gain.

Effect on Input Resistance

Input resistance in the case of an amplifier with negative feedback is affected depending upon how the feedback signal (voltage or current) is connected to the source of external input signal. The input resistance increases if the feedback signal is connected in series with the source of input and decreases if the feedback signal is connected across it in shunt. Increase or decrease, as the case may be, is by desensitivity factor $D = 1 + \beta A$. Thus, in the case of voltage-series and current-series feedback, input resistance with feedback R_{if} is given by

$$R_{if} = R_i \times (1 + \beta A) \tag{11.11}$$

R_i is the input resistance without feedback. Input resistance in the case of voltage-shunt and current-shunt feedback is given by

$$R_{if} = \frac{R_i}{1 + \beta A} \tag{11.12}$$

Equations (11.11) and (11.12) will be derived subsequently in the relevant sections for different feedback topologies.

Effect on Output Resistance

Negative feedback affects the output resistance of the amplifier depending upon the nature of the output signal fed back to the input. In case output voltage is sampled, output resistance decreases. In case output current or a voltage proportional to the output current is sampled, output resistance increases. Output resistance with feedback R_{of} in the case of current-series and current-shunt feedback is given by Eq. (11.13). R_o is the output resistance without feedback. Output resistance in the case of voltage-series and voltage-shunt feedback is given by Eq. (11.14):

$$R_{of} = R_o \times (1 + \beta A) \tag{11.13}$$

$$R_{of} = \frac{R_o}{1 + \beta A} \tag{11.14}$$

Equations (11.13) and (11.14) will be derived subsequently in the relevant sections for different feedback topologies.

EXAMPLE 11.2 *An amplifier without feedback has a voltage gain of 100. The designer decides to use 10% negative feedback to bring the non-linear distortion to an acceptable level. Determine the gain of the amplifier in the presence of feedback. If the desired value of gain with feedback is 50, what should in that case be the feedback factor?*

Solution

1. Gain with feedback = $A/(1 + \beta A)$, where A is the gain without feedback and β is the feedback factor.
2. Gain with feedback = $100/(1 + 0.1 \times 100) = 100/11 = 9.09$.
3. If the gain with feedback needs to be equal to 50, then $50 = 100/(1 + \beta \times 100)$.
4. Solving for β, we get $100\beta + 1 = 2$. That is, $\beta = 0.01$ or 1%.

EXAMPLE 11.3 *The total harmonic distortion of an amplifier reduces from 10% to 1% on introduction of 10% negative feedback. Determine the open-loop and closed-loop gain values.*

Solution

1. Distortion (with feedback) = Distortion (without feedback)/(1 + βA), where A is the open-loop gain.
2. $0.01 = 0.1/(1 + 0.1A)$, which gives $1 + 0.1A = 10$ or $A = 90$.
3. Therefore, open-loop gain = 90.
4. Closed-loop gain = $90/(1 + 0.1 \times 90) = 9$.

EXAMPLE 11.4 *A negative-feedback amplifier has −20 dB of feedback. Determine the loop gain.*

Solution

1. Negative feedback in dB = 20 log (Gain with feedback/Gain without feedback) = −20.
2. Log (Gain with feedback/Gain without feedback) = −1.
3. Gain with feedback/Gain without feedback = 0.1 = $1/(1 + \beta A)$.
4. This gives $(1 + \beta A) = 10$, or $\beta A = 9$.
5. Loop gain = $\beta A = 9$.

EXAMPLE 11.5 *A voltage amplifier is characterized by voltage gain of 100, input resistance of 100 kΩ and output resistance of 1 kΩ in the absence of any feedback. Find the modified values of these parameters if 5% of output voltage were feedback in series and phase opposition with the input.*

Solution

1. Open-loop gain $A = 100$ and feedback factor $\beta = 0.05$.
2. Closed-loop gain = $100/(1 + 0.05 \times 100) = 100/6 = 16.67$.
3. Since the feedback signal is in series with input, modified input resistance is given by $100 \times 10^3 \times (1 + 0.05 \times 100) = 600$ kΩ.
4. Since it is fraction of the output voltage that is fed back to the input, modified output resistance is given by $1 \times 10^3 / (1 + 0.05 \times 100) = 1000/6\ \Omega = 166.67\ \Omega$.

EXAMPLE 11.6 *A voltage amplifier is a cascade arrangement of three identical amplifier stages each having an open loop gain of A_1. The output from the final stage is fed back in series and phase opposition with the input of the first stage to get an overall closed loop gain of A_f. Derive an expression for overall open-loop gain A in terms of open loop gain stability $|dA_1/A_1|$ of individual stages and overall closed loop gain stability $|dA_f/A_f|$.*

Solution

1. Open-loop gain, $A = A_1^3$. Therefore, $dA = 3A_1^2 dA_1$.
2. This gives $dA/A = 3A_1^2 \times (dA_1/A_1^3) = 3dA_1/A_1$.
3. Now, $dA_f/A_f = [1/|1+\beta A|] \times (dA/A)$.
4. $|dA_f/A_f| = [1/|1+\beta A|] \times 3 \times dA_1/A_1$.
5. Also, $1/|1+\beta A| = A_f/A$.
6. Therefore, $A = 3A_f \times [|dA_1/A| / |dA_f/A_f|]$.

11.4 Feedback Topologies

On the basis of the nature of sampled signal and the mode in which it is fed back to the input, there are four feedback topologies. These include the following:

1. Voltage-series feedback topology (also known as series–shunt topology).
2. Voltage-shunt feedback topology (also known as shunt–shunt topology).
3. Current-series feedback topology (also known as series–series topology).
4. Current-shunt feedback topology (also known as shunt–series topology).

Each one of these feedback topologies is described in the following sections.

11.5 Voltage-Series (Series–Shunt) Feedback

In the case of voltage-series (series–shunt) feedback, output voltage is sampled and mixed in series with the externally applied input signal. Figure 11.11 shows the block schematic arrangement of a generalized feedback amplifier with voltage-series feedback. Figure 11.12 shows the equivalent circuit for the schematic arrangement of Figure 11.11.

Gain

The gain parameter in this case is the voltage gain. Equation (11.15) gives the expression for voltage gain with feedback in terms of gain without feedback and the feedback factor:

$$A_{\mathrm{Vf}} = \frac{A_{\mathrm{V}}}{1+\beta A_{\mathrm{V}}} \tag{11.15}$$

where A_{V} and A_{Vf} are the voltage gains without and with feedback taking into account the load resistance R_{L}.

Input Resistance

Expression for input resistance is derived as follows:

$$R_{\mathrm{if}} = \frac{V_{\mathrm{s}}}{I_{\mathrm{s}}} = \frac{V_{\mathrm{s}}}{I_{\mathrm{i}}} \tag{11.16}$$

Now $I_{\mathrm{i}} = V_{\mathrm{i}}/R_{\mathrm{i}}$ and $V_{\mathrm{i}} = V_{\mathrm{s}} - \beta V_{\mathrm{o}}$. Substituting for V_{i}, we get

$$I_{\mathrm{i}} = \frac{V_{\mathrm{s}} - \beta V_{\mathrm{o}}}{R_{\mathrm{i}}} \tag{11.17}$$

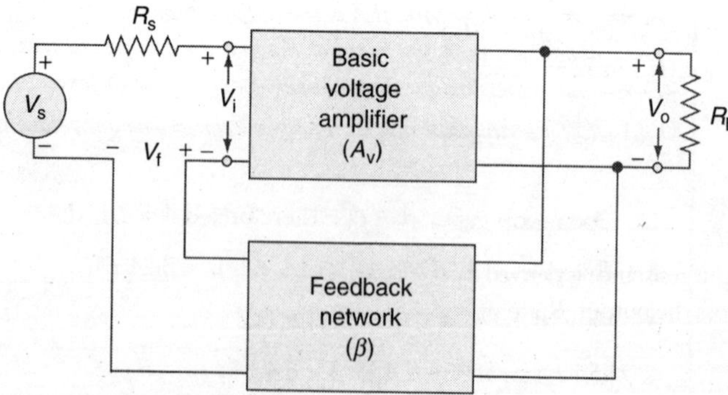

Figure 11.11 | Schematic arrangement of voltage-series (series–shunt) feedback.

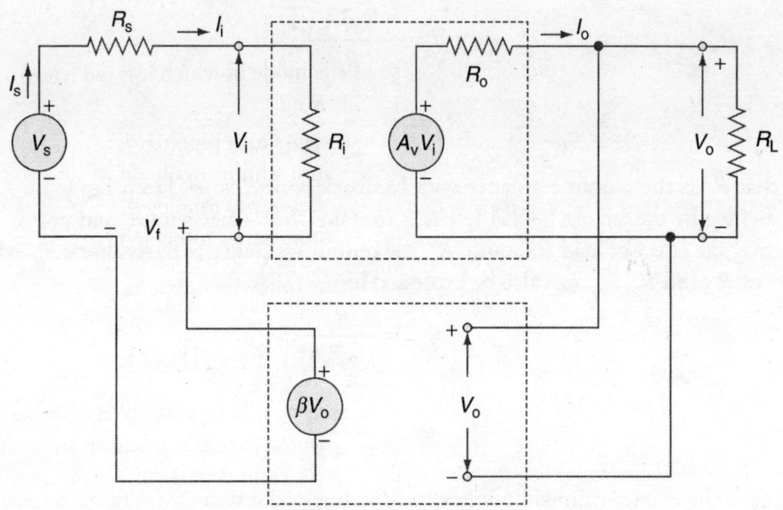

Figure 11.12 | Equivalent circuit for schematic arrangement of Figure 11.11.

Substituting for I_i from Eq. (11.17) in Eq. (11.16), we get

$$R_{if} = V_s \times \frac{R_i}{V_s - \beta V_o} = \frac{R_i}{1-\beta(V_o/V_s)}$$

Since $V_o/V_s = A_{Vf}$, where A_{Vf} is the voltage gain with feedback taking load resistance (R_L) into account, therefore

$$R_{if} = \frac{R_i}{1-\beta A_{Vf}} \tag{11.18}$$

Now

$$A_{Vf} - \frac{A_V}{1+\beta A_V}$$

where A_V is the voltage gain without feedback taking load resistance (R_L) into account. It is given by

$$A_V = A_v \times \left(\frac{R_L}{R_o + R_L}\right)$$

A_v is the open-circuited voltage gain without feedback, that is, the voltage gain without feedback without taking load resistance (R_L) into account. Therefore

$$R_{if} = \frac{R_i}{1-(\beta A_V/1+\beta A_V)} = R_i \times (1+\beta A_V) \tag{11.19}$$

Output Resistance

Expression for output resistance is derived by considering $V_s = 0$ or $I_s = 0$, letting load resistance $R_L = \infty$ and applying a voltage V across the output. Ratio of applied voltage V to the resulting current I gives the output resistance.

$$I = \frac{V - A_v V_i}{R_o}$$

For $V_s = 0$, $V_i = -V_f = -\beta V$. Therefore

$$I = \frac{V + \beta A_v V}{R_o}$$

$$R_{of} = \frac{V}{I} = \frac{R_o}{1 + \beta A_v} \tag{11.20}$$

Remember that R_{of} is the output resistance with feedback with $R_L = \infty$. From Eq. (11.20) we see that it is equal to R_o divided by the factor $(1 + \beta A_v)$, which contains the voltage gain A_v and not A_V.

Considering the effect of load resistance R_L, the output resistance with feedback $R_{of'}$ is given by parallel combination of R_{of} and R_L. $R_{of'}$ can also be expressed by

$$R_{of'} = \frac{R_{o'}}{1 + \beta A_V}$$

where

$$R_{o'} = \frac{R_o \times R_L}{R_o + R_L} \tag{11.21}$$

Remember, A_V is the voltage gain without feedback taking load resistance (R_L) into account.

Practical Circuits

Common-drain amplifier (source follower) circuit as shown in Figure 11.13 is an example of voltage-series feedback as the output voltage appearing across the source resistor (R_S) is fed back in series with the externally applied input signal. The bipolar transistor counterpart of source follower is the emitter–follower, which is another example of voltage-series feedback. Source–follower and emitter–follower are examples of 100% feedback with the result that the closed-loop gain is approximately unity.

A non-inverting amplifier circuit configured around an opamp (Figure 11.14) is yet another example of voltage-series feedback. In this case, the feedback voltage (V_f) appears across R_1. It equals $V_o \times R_1/(R_1 + R_2)$. The feedback voltage V_f is in series with externally applied input voltage V_s. Also, it is in phase opposition with the external input as V_s and V_f are, respectively, applied to non-inverting and inverting inputs of the opamp.

Another non-inverting amplifier configuration with voltage-series feedback is shown in Figure 11.15. The circuit shown is a cascade arrangement of two common-emitter amplifier stages. The emitter resistor of the first stage is split into two series-connected resistors. Relatively much smaller of the two resistance values is un-bypassed and forms a part of the potential divider arrangement with another resistor connected from the output. The feedback factor is given by $R_1/(R_1 + R_2)$.

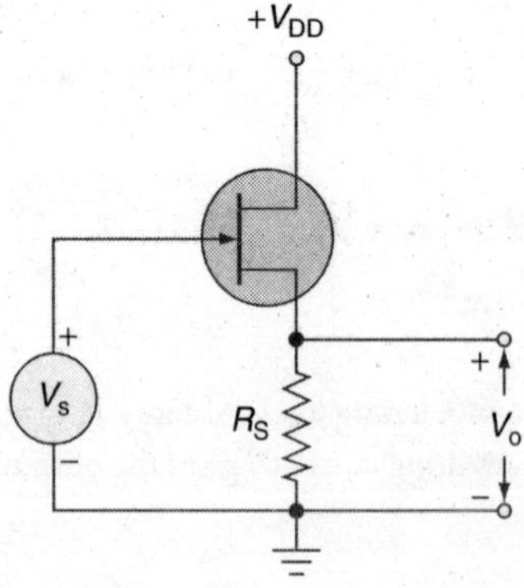

Figure 11.13 Source–follower amplifier circuit.

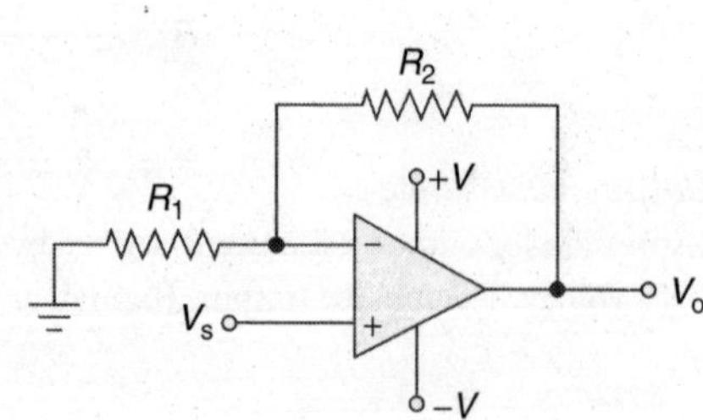

Figure 11.14 Voltage-series feedback in non-inverting amplifier.

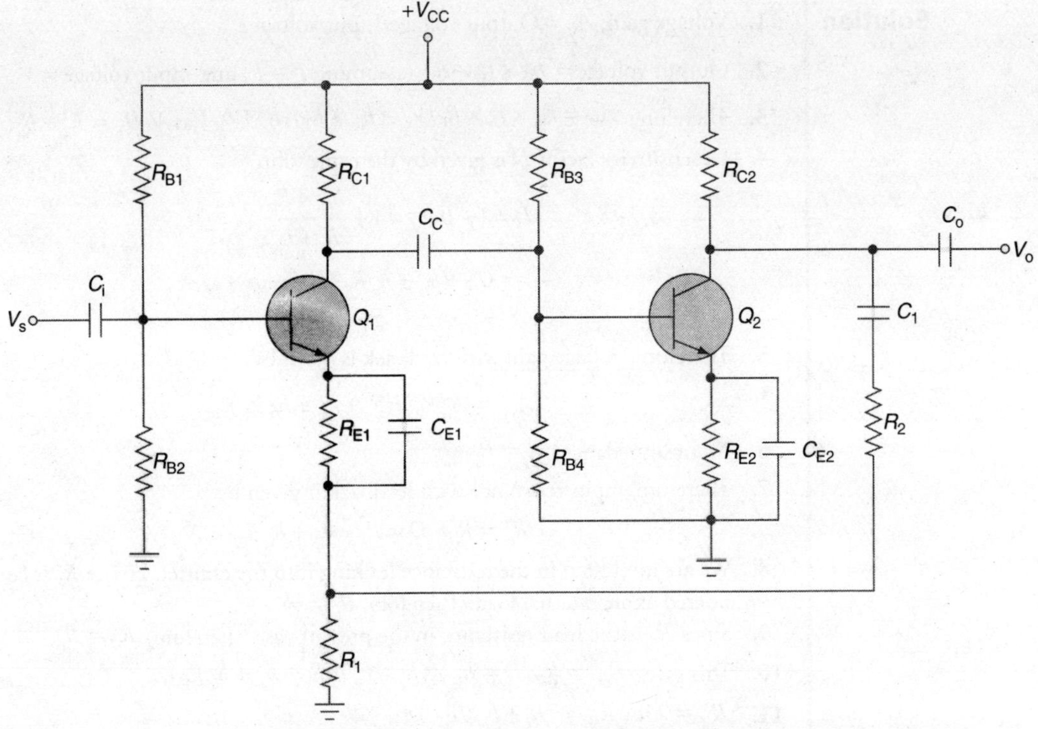

Figure 11.15 | Two-stage common-emitter amplifier with voltage-series feedback.

EXAMPLE 11.7 *For the common-collector circuit of Figure 11.16, determine expressions for voltage gain, input resistance and output resistance in the presence of negative feedback.*

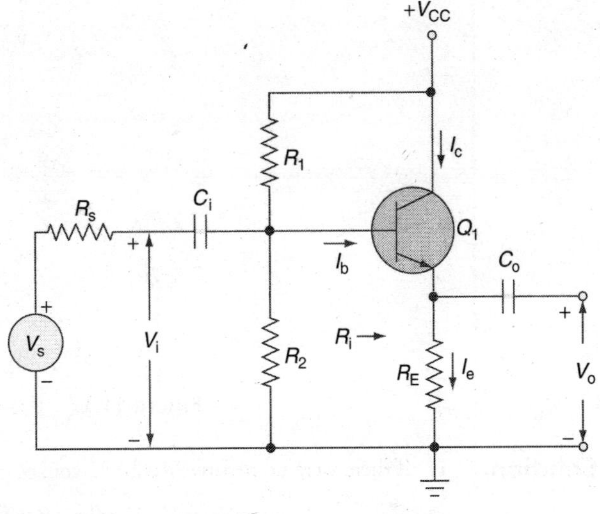

Figure 11.16 | Example 11.7.

Solution

1. Voltage gain, A_V = Output voltage/Input voltage.
2. Output voltage = $h_{fe} \times I_b \times R_E$ (assuming $I_c \cong I_e$) and input voltage = V_s.
3. Therefore, $A_V = h_{fe} \times I_b \times R_E / V_s \cong h_{fe} \times R_E / (R_s + h_{ie})$ as $V_s / I_b = R_s + h_{ie}$.
4. Desensitivity factor D is given by the expression

$$D = 1 + \beta A_V = 1 + \frac{h_{fe} \times R_E}{R_s + h_{ie}}$$
$$= (R_s + h_{ie} + h_{fe} R_E) / (R_s + h_{ie})$$

as $\beta = 1$.

5. Therefore, voltage gain with feedback is given by

$$A_{Vf} = (h_{fe} R_E) / (R_s + h_{ie} + h_{fe} R_E)$$

6. Input impedance, $R_i = R_s + h_{ie}$.
7. Therefore, input resistance with feedback is given by

$$R_{if} = R_i \times D = R_s + h_{ie} + h_{fe} R_E$$

8. We are interested in the resistance looking into the emitter. Hence R_E is considered as an external load. Therefore, $R_{of} = \infty$.
9. Since R_E is the load resistance in the present case, therefore, $R_{o'} = R_E$.
10. This gives $R_{of'} = R_{o'} / D = R_E \times (R_s + h_{ie}) / (R_s + h_{ie} + h_{fe} R_E)$.
11. $R_{of} = \lim_{R_E \to \infty} R_{of'} = (R_s + h_{ie}) / h_{fe}$.

EXAMPLE 11.8 *For the source follower circuit of Figure 11.17, determine the voltage gain, input resistance and output resistance in the presence of voltage-series feedback.*

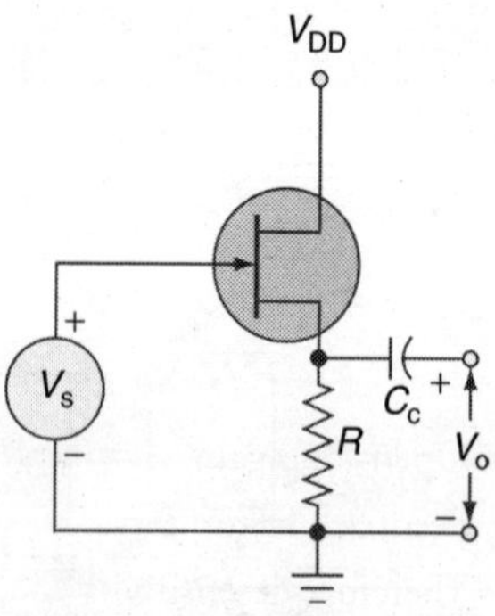

Figure 11.17 | Example 11.8.

Solution

1. If there were no negative feedback, voltage gain A_V would have been expressed by

$$A_V = V_o / V_s = \{g_m \times (r_d \| R) \times V_s\} / V_s$$
$$= (g_m \times r_d \times R \times V_s) / \{(r_d + R) \times V_s\}$$

Therefore, $A_V = (g_m \times r_d \times R)/(r_d + R)$.

2. Also $g_m \times r_d = \mu$. This gives $A_V = (\mu \times R)/(r_d + R)$.
3. Desensitivity factor,
$$D = 1 + \beta A_V = 1 + [(\mu \times R)/(r_d + R)]$$
$$= [\{r_d + (1+\mu) \times R\}/(r_d + R)]$$
as $\beta = 1$
4. Therefore, $A_{Vf} = A_V/D = [(\mu \times R)/\{r_d + (1+\mu)R\}]$.
5. The input impedance of an FET for all practical purposes is infinite. Therefore, input resistance with feedback $R_{if} = R_i \times D$ is also infinite.
6. Output resistance with feedback $R_{of} = R_o/(1+\beta A_v)$. Here $R_o = r_d$ considering the load resistance R to be an open circuit. Also, $A_v = \mu$. Therefore, $R_{of} = r_d/(1+\mu)$.
7. Now $R_{of'} = R_{o'}/D$, $R_{o'} = (r_d \times R)/(r_d + R)$ and $D = \{r_d + (1+\mu) \times R\}/(r_d + R)$. $R_{of'}$ is the output resistance with feedback taking load resistance into account.
8. This gives
$$R_{of'} = [(r_d \times R)/\{r_d + (1+\mu) \times R\}]$$
9. The value of R_{of} can also be determined by using the expression
$$R_{of} = \lim_{R\to\infty} R_{of'} = \lim_{R\to\infty}[(r_d \times R)/\{r_d + (1+\mu) \times R\}] = r_d/(1+\mu)$$

EXAMPLE 11.9 *For the opamp based non-inverting amplifier circuit of Figure 11.18, determine the voltage gain and the input impedance in the presence of feedback given that open-loop gain and the input impedance of the opamp are 80 dB and 1 MΩ, respectively.*

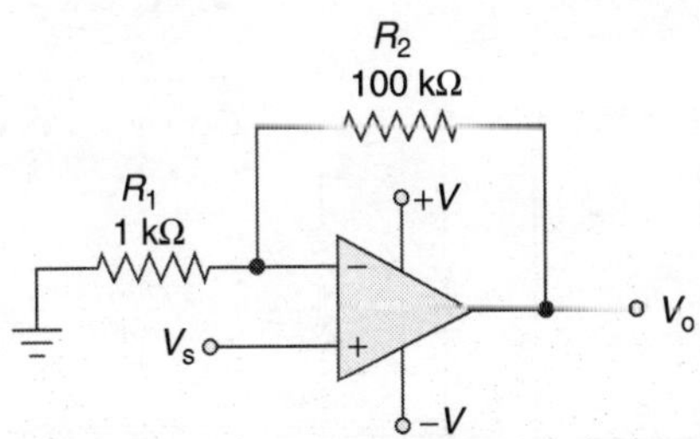

Figure 11.18 | Example 11.8

Solution

1. Open-loop gain, $A = 80$ dB = 10000.
2. Feedback factor, $\beta = R_1/(R_1 + R_2) = 1 \times 10^3/(1 \times 10^3 + 100 \times 10^3) = 1/101$.
3. Therefore desensitivity factor, $D = 1 + \beta A = 1 + 10000/101 = 100.0099$.
4. Gain with feedback = 10000/100.0099 = 99.99.
5. Input impedance of the opamp = 1 MΩ.
6. Since it is a case of series feedback, input impedance would increase by the desensitivity factor.
7. That is, input impedance with feedback = $1 \times 10^6 \times 100.0099$ = 100 MΩ.

11.6 Voltage-Shunt (Shunt–Shunt) Feedback

In the case of voltage-shunt (shunt–shunt) feedback, output voltage is sampled and mixed in shunt with the externally applied input signal. Figure 11.19 shows the block schematic arrangement of a generalized feedback amplifier with voltage-shunt feedback. Figure 11.20 shows the equivalent circuit for the schematic arrangement of Figure 11.19.

Gain

The gain parameter in this case is the transresistance. Equation (11.22) gives the expression for transresistance with feedback R_{Mf} in terms of transresistance without feedback R_M and the feedback factor β.

$$R_{Mf} = \frac{R_M}{1+\beta R_M} \tag{11.22}$$

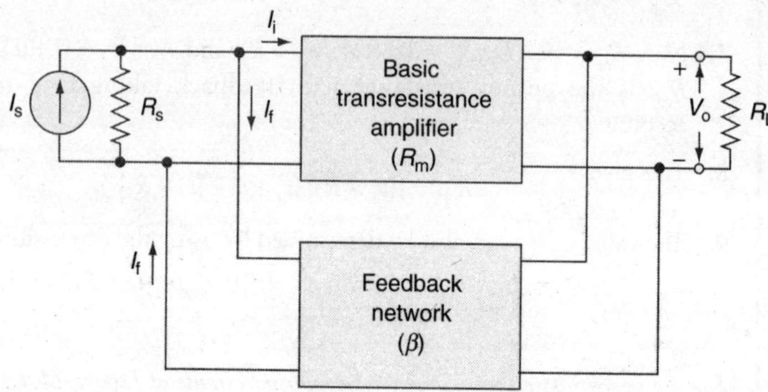

Figure 11.19 | Schematic arrangement of voltage-shunt (shunt–shunt) feedback.

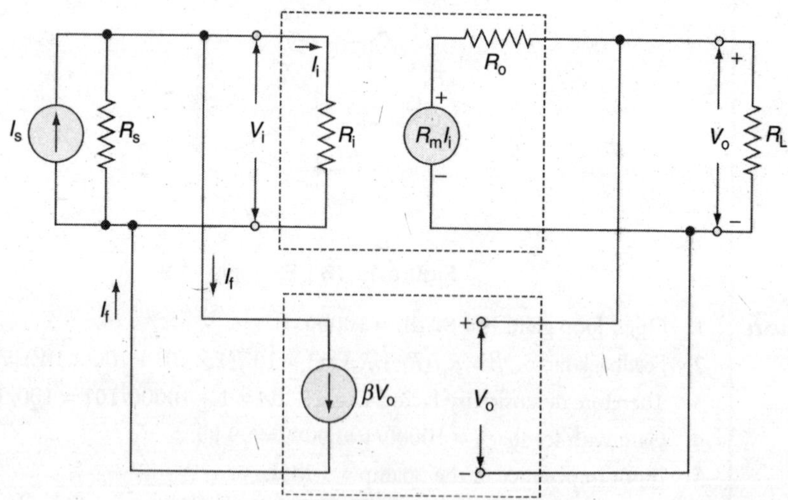

Figure 11.20 | Equivalent circuit for schematic arrangement of figure 11.19.

Input Resistance

Expression for input resistance is derived as follows.

$$R_{\text{if}} = \frac{V_{\text{i}}}{I_{\text{s}}} = \frac{R_{\text{i}} \times I_{\text{i}}}{I_{\text{s}}} \tag{11.23}$$

Substituting $I_{\text{s}} = I_{\text{i}} + I_{\text{f}}$ in Eq. (11.23), we get

$$R_{\text{if}} = \frac{R_{\text{i}} \times I_{\text{i}}}{I_{\text{i}} + I_{\text{f}}} = \frac{R_{\text{i}}}{(I_{\text{i}} + I_{\text{f}})/I_{\text{i}}} = \frac{R_{\text{i}}}{1 + (I_{\text{f}}/I_{\text{i}})}$$

Now, $I_{\text{f}} = \beta V_{\text{o}}$. Therefore, $R_{\text{if}} = R_{\text{i}}/[1 + (\beta V_{\text{o}}/I_{\text{i}})]$.

Also, $V_{\text{o}}/I_{\text{i}} = R_{\text{M}}$. This gives

$$R_{\text{if}} = R_{\text{i}}/(1 + \beta R_{\text{M}}) \tag{11.24}$$

R_{M} is the transresistance taking load resistance R_{L} into account and is given by

$$R_{\text{M}} = R_{\text{m}} \times \left(\frac{R_{\text{L}}}{R_{\text{o}} + R_{\text{L}}} \right)$$

where R_{m} is the open-circuit transresistance, that is, without taking the load resistance R_{L} into account and can be expressed as

$$R_{\text{m}} = \lim_{R_{\text{L}} \to \infty} R_{\text{M}}$$

Output Resistance

Expression for output resistance is derived by considering $I_{\text{s}} = 0$, letting load resistance $R_{\text{L}} = \infty$ and applying a voltage V across the output. Ratio of applied voltage V to the resulting current I gives the output resistance.

$$I = (V - R_{\text{m}} I_{\text{i}})/R_{\text{o}}$$

For $I_{\text{s}} = 0$, $I_{\text{i}} = -I_{\text{f}} = -\beta V_{\text{o}} = -\beta V$. Therefore,

$$I = (V + \beta R_{\text{m}} V)/R_{\text{o}} = V(1 + \beta R_{\text{m}})/R_{\text{o}}$$

$$R_{\text{of}} = V/I = R_{\text{o}}/(1 + \beta R_{\text{m}}) \tag{11.25}$$

Remember that R_{of} is the output resistance with feedback with $R_{\text{L}} = \infty$. Considering the effect of load resistance R_{L}, the output resistance with feedback $R_{\text{of}'}$ is given by parallel combination of R_{of} and R_{L}. $R_{\text{of}'}$ can also be expressed by

$$R_{\text{of}'} = R_{\text{o}'}/(1 + \beta R_{\text{M}}) \tag{11.26}$$

where

$$R_{\text{o}'} = (R_{\text{o}} \times R_{\text{L}})/(R_{\text{o}} + R_{\text{L}})$$

Practical Circuits

Common-emitter amplifier with collector-to-base feedback as shown in Figure 11.21 is an example of voltage-shunt feedback. As is evident from the circuit diagram, a current proportional to the output voltage is fed back in the shunt with the source of input signal. Since $V_{\text{o}} >> V_{\text{i}}$, the feedback current is equal to $V_{\text{o}}/R_{\text{B}}$ and the feedback factor β equals $1/R_{\text{B}}$. The amplifier nearly achieves the characteristics of a transresistance amplifier.

Figure 11.22 shows the opamp version of voltage-shunt feedback topology. The circuit shown is that of an inverting amplifier. The input current given by $V_{\text{s}}/R_{\text{s}}$ flows through the feedback resistance R_{f} to produce an output voltage equal to $-I_{\text{s}} \times R_{\text{f}}$. The gain parameter is the transresistance R_{f}.

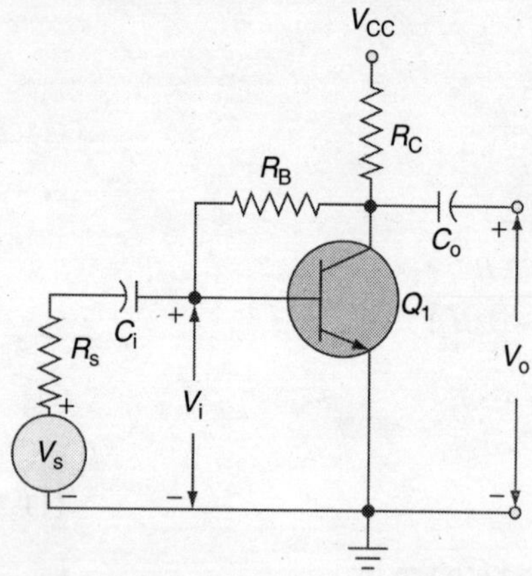

Figure 11.21 | Common-emitter amplifier circuit with voltage-shunt feedback.

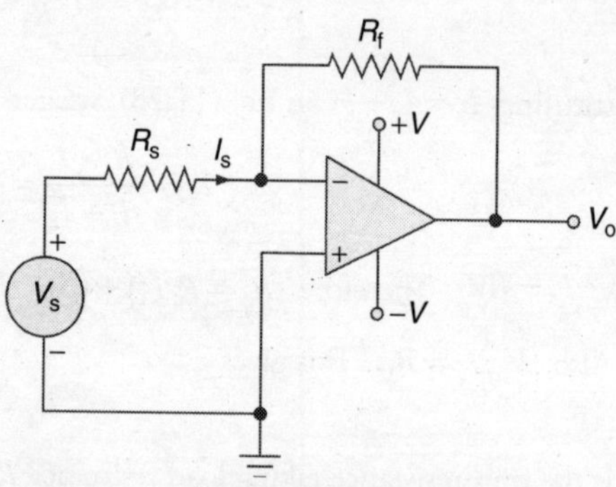

Figure 11.22 | Inverting amplifier with voltage-shunt feedback.

EXAMPLE 11.10 *Refer to the opamp-based inverting amplifier circuit of Figure 11.23. Identify the type of negative feedback. Determine the transimpedance gain, the input impedance and output impedance of the amplifier, given that transimpedance, input impedance and output impedance parameters of the opamp are 100 MΩ, 10 MΩ and 100 Ω, respectively.*

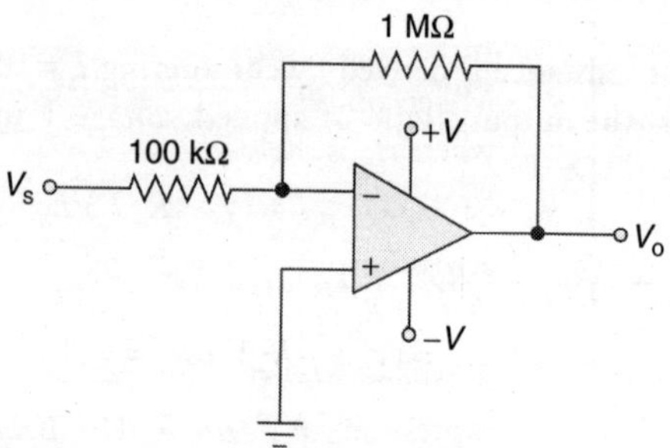

Figure 11.23 | Example 11.10.

Solution

1. The feedback is of voltage-shunt type.
2. Transimpedance, $R_M = 100\ \text{M}\Omega = 100 \times 10^6\ \Omega = 10^8\ \Omega$
3. Feedback factor, $\beta = 1/10^6\ (\Omega)^{-1} = 10^{-6}\ (\Omega)^{-1}$
4. Therefore, transimpedance with feedback,

$$R_{Mf} = R_M/(1+\beta R_M)$$

$$= 10^8/(1+10^{-6}\times 10^8) = 10^8/101 = 0.99\times 10^6\ \Omega = 990\ \text{k}\Omega$$

5. Input impedance, $R_{if} = R_i/(1+\beta R_M) = 10^7/(1 + 10^{-6} \times 10^8) = 10^7/101 = 99\ \text{k}\Omega$
6. As the output is seen across an open-circuit, $R_m = R_M$
7. Output impedance, $R_{of} = R_o/(1+\beta R_m) = 100/(1 + 10^{-6} \times 10^8) = 100/101 = 0.99\ \Omega$

EXAMPLE 11.11 *Refer to the voltage-shunt feedback circuit of Figure 11.24. Derive expressions for feedback factor, transresistance, input resistance and output resistance with feedback.*

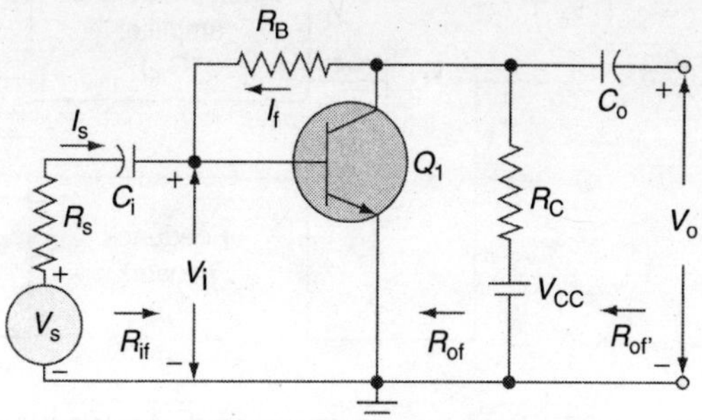

Figure 11.24 Example 11.11.

Solution

1. Feedback factor β is given by I_f/V_o.
2. Now, $I_f = (V_o - V_i)/R_B$.
3. Since $V_o \gg V_i$, therefore $I_f = V_o/R_B$. That is, $\beta = I_f/V_o = 1/R_B$.
4. Transresistance with feedback, $R_{Mf} = V_o/I_s \cong 1/\beta = R_B$.
5. Input resistance with feedback is given by parallel combination of h_{ie} and Miller component of R_B appearing across input. That is, $R_{if} = h_{ie} \parallel R_B/(1 - A_V)$ where A_V is the voltage gain.
6. $A_V = -h_{fe}R_C'/h_{ie}$, where $R_C' = R_C \parallel$ (Miller component of R_B appearing across output). That is, $R_C' = R_C \parallel R_B$. Remember that the Miller component of R_B appearing across output will be equal to $R_B \times [A_V/(A_V - 1)] \cong R_B$.
7. R_{if} therefore can be determined by substituting the value of A_V in the expression for R_{if} and simplifying the resultant expression.
8. Output resistance with feedback R_{of} is given by parallel combination of Miller component of R_B appearing across output and R_C. This is approximately equal to $R_C \parallel R_B$, which is further equal to $(R_C \times R_B)/(R_C + R_B)$.

11.7 Current-Series (Series–Series) Feedback

In the case of current-series (series–series) feedback, output current (usually a voltage proportional to the output current) is sampled and mixed in series with the externally applied input signal. Figure 11.25 shows the block schematic arrangement of a generalized feedback amplifier with current-series feedback. Figure 11.26 shows the equivalent circuit for the schematic arrangement of Figure 11.25.

Gain

The gain parameter in this case is the transconductance. Equation (11.27) gives the expression for transconductance with feedback G_{Mf} in terms of transconductance without feedback G_M and the feedback factor β.

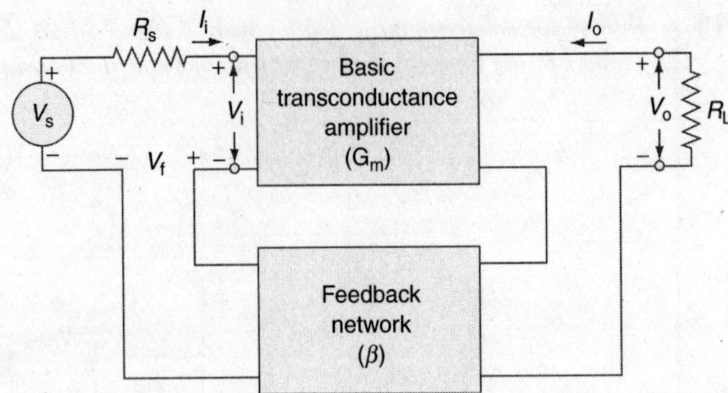

Figure 11.25 Schematic arrangement of current-series (series–series) feedback.

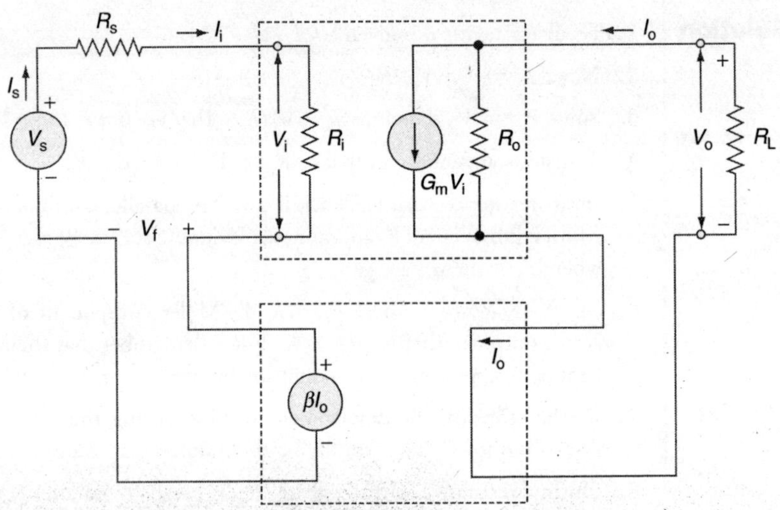

Figure 11.26 Equivalent circuit for schematic arrangement of Figure 11.25.

$$G_{Mf} = \frac{G_M}{1+\beta G_M} \tag{11.27}$$

Input Resistance

Expression for input resistance is derived as follows:

$$R_{if} = V_s/I_s = V_s/I_i = (V_i + V_f)/I_i \tag{11.28}$$

Now, $I_i = V_i/R_i$. Substituting the value of I_i in Eq. (11.28), we get

$$R_{if} = (V_i + V_f)\times(R_i/V_i) = R_i \times [1+(V_f/V_i)]$$

Also, $V_f = \beta I_o$. Therefore,

$$R_{if} = R_i \times [1+(\beta I_o/V_i)] = R_i \times (1+\beta G_M) \tag{11.29}$$

G_M is the transconductance taking load resistance R_L into account. It is expressed as

$$G_M = G_m \times \left(\frac{R_o}{R_o + R_L}\right)$$

where G_m is the short-circuit transconductance, that is, without taking the load resistance R_L into account. It is also expressed as

$$G_m = \lim_{R_L \to 0} G_M$$

Output Resistance

Expression for output resistance is derived by considering $V_s = 0$, letting load resistance $R_L = \infty$ and applying a voltage V across the output. Ratio of applied voltage V to the resulting current I gives the output resistance:

$$I = (V/R_o) - G_m V_i$$

For $V_s = 0$, $V_i = -V_f = -\beta I_o = +\beta I$. Therefore,

$$I = (V/R_o) - \beta I G_m$$

$$R_{of} = V/I = R_o \times (1 + \beta G_m) \quad (11.30)$$

Remember that R_{of} is the output resistance with feedback with $R_L = \infty$. Considering the effect of load resistance R_L, the output resistance with feedback $R_{of'}$ is given by parallel combination of R_{of} and R_L. $R_{of'}$ can also be expressed by

$$R_{of'} = R_{o'} \times [(1 + \beta G_m)/(1 + \beta G_M)]$$

where

$$R_{o'} = R_o \| R_L \quad (11.31)$$

Practical Circuits

Common-emitter amplifier with unbypassed emitter resistor as shown in Figure 11.27 is an example of current-series feedback. As is evident from the circuit diagram, a voltage proportional to the output current is fed back in series with the source of input signal. This is true if the base current were considered as negligible. The

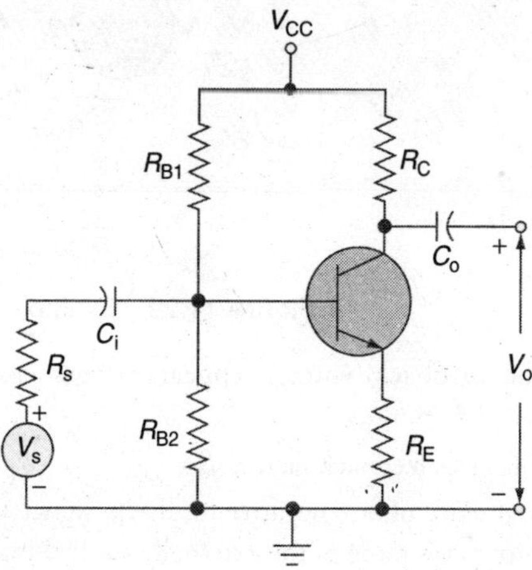

Figure 11.27 Common-emitter amplifier with current-series feedback.

feedback factor β in this case equals $-R_E$. The amplifier nearly achieves the characteristics of a transconductance amplifier. Although the output current is proportional to the output voltage, this configuration should not be misunderstood as a case of voltage-series feedback. If it were considered one, then the feedback factor would equal $-R_E/R_C$. This violates one of the fundamental assumptions of negative-feedback amplifiers according to which the feedback factor should be independent of load and source resistances.

Similarly, common-source amplifier with un-bypassed source resistor is also a case of current-series feedback. Also, an opamp wired as a non-inverting amplifier where the output taken is the current I_o across the feedback resistor R_2 is an example of current-series feedback. As shown in Figure 11.28, it is the voltage developed across R_1 $(= -I_o \times R_1)$ that is fed back in series with the input.

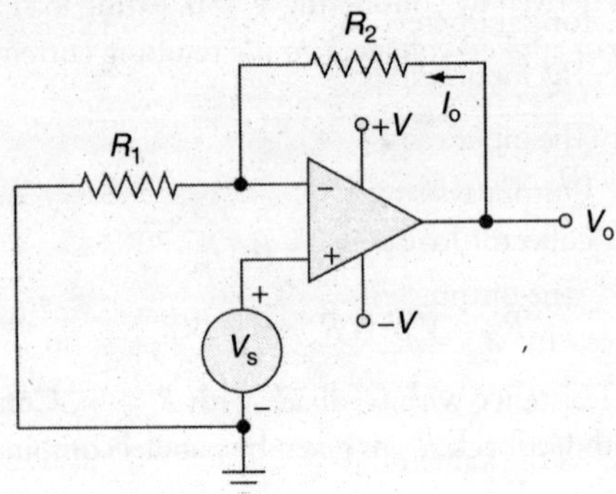

Figure 11.28 Opamp-based amplifier circuit with current-series feedback.

EXAMPLE 11.12 *Figure 11.29 shows the basic common-emitter amplifier circuit with unbypassed emitter resistor. Derive expressions for transconductance, input resistance and output resistance with and without feedback. Also prove that the transconductance parameter in this circuit is stabilized due to presence of current-series feedback.*

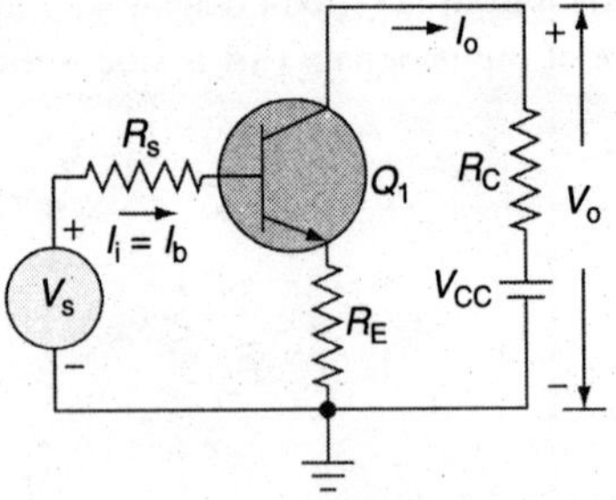

Figure 11.29 Example 11.12.

Solution

1. The feedback voltage appears across emitter resistor R_E. Therefore, $V_f = -I_o \times R_E$.
2. This gives feedback factor, $\beta = V_f / I_o = -R_E$.
3. In absence of any negative feedback, signal V_i appearing across the input of amplifier is same as the externally applied input signal V_s.
4. Therefore, transconductance without feedback G_M is given by

$$I_o/V_i = I_o/V_s = -(h_{fe} \times I_b)/V_s$$

5. Now, $V_s/I_b = R_s + h_{ie} + R_E$. Therefore, $G_M = -h_{fe}/(R_s + h_{ie} + R_E)$.
6. Desensitivity factor, $D = (1+\beta G_M) = 1 + [(h_{fe} \times R_E)/(R_s + h_{ie} + R_E)]$.
   Therefore, $D = [\{R_s + h_{ie} + (1+h_{fe}) \times R_E\}/(R_s + h_{ie} + R_E)]$.
7. This gives expression for transconductance with feedback G_{Mf} as
   $$G_{Mf} = G_M/D = -h_{fe}/[R_s + h_{ie} + (1+h_{fe}) \times R_E]$$
8. Since $(1+h_{fe}) \times R_E >> (R_s + h_{ie})$ and also $h_{fe} >> 1$, expression for G_{Mf} simplifies to $G_{Mf} \cong -1/R_E$. This proves that G_{Mf} is independent of transistor parameters and is only dependent on R_E.
9. The input resistance in the absence of feedback is given by $R_i = R_s + h_{ie} + R_E$.
10. The input resistance with feedback is $R_{if} = R_i \times D = R_s + h_{ie} + (1+h_{fe}) \times R_E$.
11. Output resistance in the absence of feedback (R_o) without considering the collector load resistance R_C is infinity.
12. The output resistance with feedback R_{of} without considering R_C is given by $R_{of} = R_o \times (1+\beta G_m)$. G_m is short-circuited value of G_M. That is,
    $$G_m = \lim_{R_C \to 0} G_M$$
    As the value of R_o is infinity, R_{of} is also infinity.
13. Since G_M is independent of R_C, therefore, $G_m = G_M$.
14. Output resistance with feedback $R_{of'}$ considering the effect of R_C is given by the parallel combination of R_{of} and R_C. As the value of R_{of} is infinity, $R_{of'}$ equals R_C.
15. An alternative expression for $R_{of'}$ is given by $R_{of'} = R_{o'} \times [(1+\beta G_m)/(1+\beta G_M)]$.

EXAMPLE 11.13

Refer to the common-source FET amplifier circuit with un-bypassed source resistor as shown in Figure 11.30. Derive expressions for transconductance, input resistance and output resistance with and without feedback

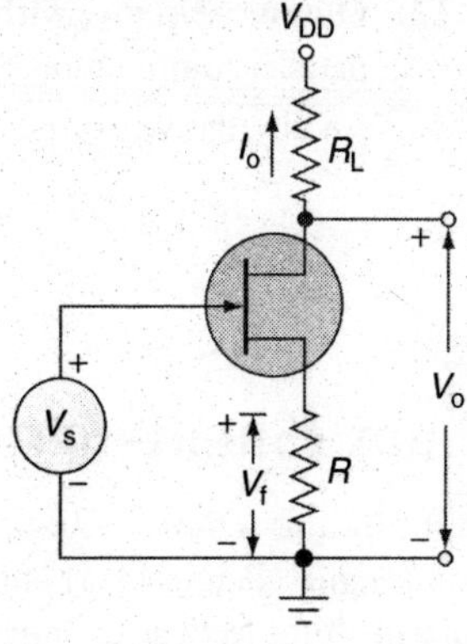

Figure 11.30 Example 11.13.

Solution

1. The feedback voltage appears across source resistor R. Therefore, $V_f = -I_o \times R$.
2. This gives feedback factor, $\beta = V_f / I_o = -R$.
3. In the absence of any negative feedback, the signal V_{gs} appearing across the input of the amplifier is the same as the externally applied input signal V_s. Therefore, transconductance without feedback G_M is given by $I_o / V_{gs} = I_o / V_s$.
4. I_o is given by $I_o = -(g_m \times V_{gs} \times r_d)/(r_d + R_L + R)$. This gives $G_M = -(g_m \times r_d)/(r_d + R_L + R)$.
5. Now, $g_m \times r_d = \mu$. Therefore, $G_M = -\mu/(r_d + R_L + R)$.
6. Desensitivity factor,
$$D = 1 + \beta G_M = 1 + [(\mu \times R)/(r_d + R_L + R)]$$
$$= [\{r_d + R_L + (1+\mu) \times R\}/(r_d + R_L + R)]$$
7. This gives expression for transconductance with feedback G_{Mf} as
$$G_{Mf} = G_M / D = -\mu / [r_d + R_L + (1+\mu) \times R]$$
8. The input resistance R_i in the absence of feedback is infinity.
9. The input resistance with feedback $R_{if} = R_i \times D = \infty$.
10. If R_L is considered to be an external load, the output resistance R_o in the absence of feedback without considering the load resistance R_L is given by $r_d + R$. Therefore, output resistance with feedback R_{of} without considering R_L is given by $R_{of} = R_o \times (1 + \beta G_m)$. G_m is the short-circuited value of G_M. That is,
$$G_m = \lim_{R_L \to 0} G_M$$
11. Now, $G_m = -\mu/(r_d + R)$. This gives
$$R_{of} = R_o \times (1 + \beta G_m)$$
$$= (r_d + R) \times [\{r_d + (1+\mu) \times R\} / (r_d + R)]$$
$$= r_d + (1+\mu) \times R$$
12. Output resistance with feedback $R_{of'}$ considering the effect of R_L is given by parallel combination of R_{of} and R_L.
13. An alternative expression for $R_{of'}$ is given by
$$R_{of'} = R_{o'} \times [(1 + \beta G_m)/(1 + \beta G_M)]$$

11.8 Current-Shunt (Shunt–Series) Feedback

In the case of current-shunt (shunt–series) feedback, output current is sampled and mixed in shunt with the externally applied input signal. Figure 11.31 shows the block schematic arrangement of a generalized feedback amplifier with current-shunt feedback. Figure 11.32 shows the equivalent circuit for the schematic arrangement of Figure 11.31.

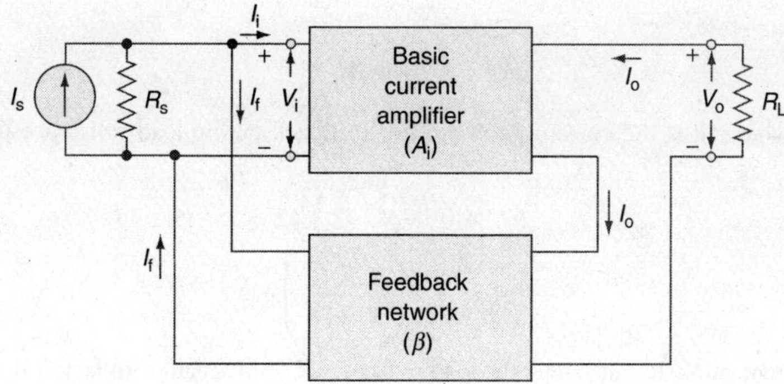

Figure 11.31 Schematic arrangement of current-shunt (shunt–series) feedback.

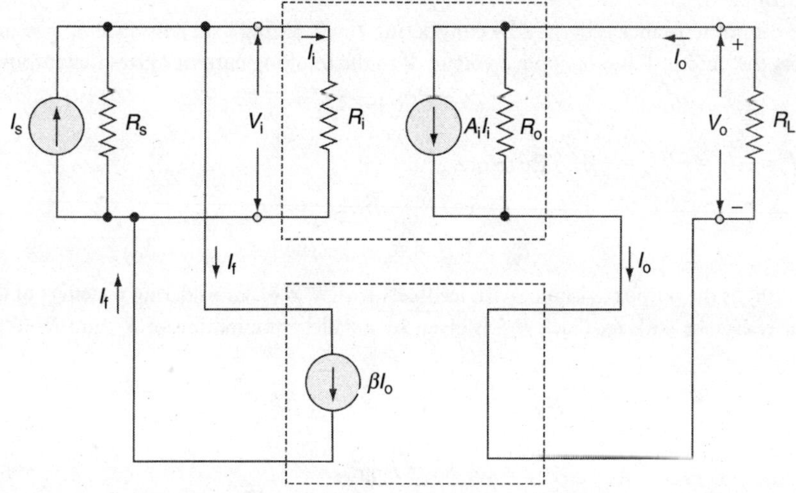

Figure 11.32 Equivalent circuit for schematic arrangement of Figure 11.31.

Gain

The gain parameter in this case is the current gain. Equation (11.32) gives the expression for current gain with feedback A_{If} in terms of current gain without feedback A_{I} and the feedback factor β.

$$A_{\mathrm{If}} = \frac{A_{\mathrm{I}}}{1+\beta A_{\mathrm{I}}} \tag{11.32}$$

Input Resistance

The expression for input resistance is derived as follows:

$$R_{\mathrm{if}} = V_{\mathrm{i}}/I_{\mathrm{s}} = (R_{\mathrm{i}} \times I_{\mathrm{i}})/I_{\mathrm{s}} \tag{11.33}$$

Substituting $I_{\mathrm{s}} = I_{\mathrm{i}} + I_{\mathrm{f}}$ in Eq. (11.33), we get

$$R_{\mathrm{if}} = R_{\mathrm{i}} \times [I_{\mathrm{i}}/(I_{\mathrm{i}}+I_{\mathrm{f}})] = R_{\mathrm{i}}/[(I_{\mathrm{i}}+I_{\mathrm{f}})/I_{\mathrm{i}}] = R_{\mathrm{i}}/[1+(I_{\mathrm{f}}/I_{\mathrm{i}})]$$

Now, $I_f = \beta I_o$. Therefore,

$$R_{if} = R_i/[1+(\beta I_o/I_i)]$$

Also, $I_o/I_i = A_I$, where A_I is the current gain without feedback taking load resistance into account. This gives

$$R_{if} = R_i/(1+\beta A_I) \tag{11.34}$$

A_I is given by

$$A_I = A_i \times \left(\frac{R_o}{R_o + R_L}\right)$$

where A_i is the current gain without taking the load resistance R_L into account. In fact, it is the short-circuited current gain. It can also be expressed as

$$A_i = \lim_{R_L \to 0} A_I$$

Output Resistance

Expression for output resistance is derived by considering $I_s = 0$, letting load resistance $R_L = \infty$ and applying a voltage V across the output. Ratio of applied voltage V to the resulting current I gives the output resistance.

$$I = (V/R_o) - A_i I_i$$

For $I_s = 0$, $I_i = -I_f = -\beta I_o = +\beta I$. Therefore,

$$I = (V/R_o) - \beta I A_i$$

$$R_{of} = V/I = R_o \times (1+\beta A_i) \tag{11.35}$$

Remember that R_{of} is the output resistance with feedback with $R_L = \infty$. Considering the effect of load resistance R_L, the output resistance with feedback $R_{of'}$ is given by parallel combination of R_{of} and R_L. $R_{of'}$ can also be expressed by

$$R_{of'} = R_{o'} \times [(1+\beta A_i)/(1+\beta A_I)] \tag{11.36}$$

where

$$R_{o'} = R_o \| R_L$$

Also, for $R_L = \infty$, $R_{o'} = R_o$ and $A_I = 0$, Eq. (11.36) then reduces to

$$R_{of'} = R_o \times (1+\beta A_i) \tag{11.37}$$

Practical Circuits

A cascade arrangement of two common-emitter amplifier stages with feedback from emitter of the second stage to the base of the first stage as shown in Figure 11.33 is an example of current-shunt feedback. The voltage across emitter resistor of the second stage is out of phase with the base voltage of the first stage, which confirms this to be a case of negative feedback. Also, it can be proved that the feedback current, that is the current flowing through resistor R, is proportional to the output current and the proportionality factor β is equal to $[R_E/(R_E + R)]$. Current-shunt feedback leads to very high output impedance and very low input impedance. These are the desirable traits of a good current amplifier.

Figure 11.34 shows opamp-based inverting current amplifier. This circuit too has current-shunt feedback. One can see the similarities between this circuit and the transistorized circuit shown in Figure 11.33. The feedback factor in this case is given by $[R_1/(R_1 + R_2)]$.

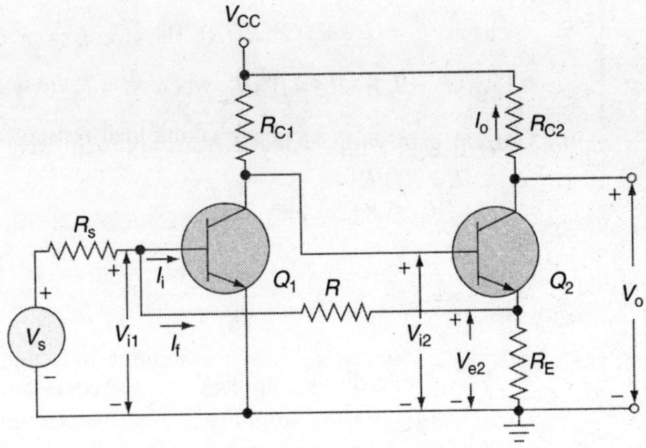

Figure 11.33 Cascade arrangement of common-emitter amplifier stages with current-shunt feedback.

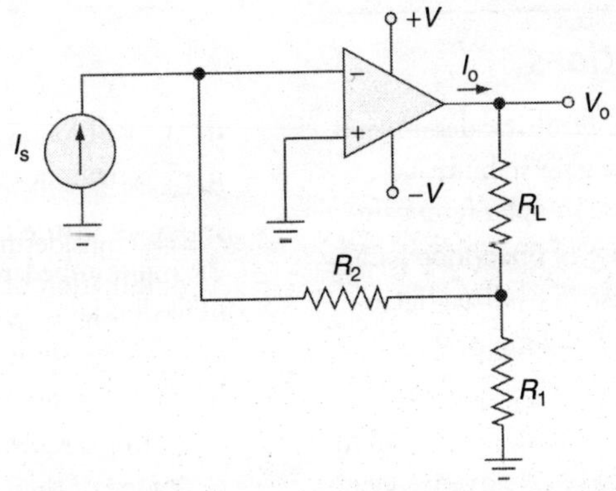

Figure 11.34 Opamp-based current amplifier with current-shunt feedback.

EXAMPLE 11.14 *Refer to the cascade arrangement of two CE amplifier stages as shown in Figure 11.33. Prove that the circuit has current-shunt feedback. Derive an expression for the feedback factor β. What is the current gain with feedback?*

Solution

1. Refer to the circuit of Figure 11.33. As the output current is sampled and fed back in shunt with the input current I_i, it is a current-shunt feedback.
2. The feedback current I_f is given by $I_f = (V_{i1} - V_{e2})/R$.
3. Assuming $V_{e2} \gg V_{i1}$, we get $I_f = -V_{e2}/R$.
4. $V_{e2} = (I_f - I_o) \times R_E$ considering base current of Q_2 to be negligible as compared to its collector current.

5. Therefore, $I_f = (I_o - I_f) \times (R_E/R)$. This gives $I_f = (R_E/R) \times [R/(R+R_E)] \times I_o = [R_E/(R+R_E)] \times I_o = \beta \times I_o$, where $\beta = R_E/(R+R_E)$.
6. Current gain with feedback A_{If} is approximately given by $1/\beta$. That is $A_{If} \cong (R+R_E)/R_E$.

KEY TERMS

Current amplifier
Current-series feedback
Current-shunt feedback
Desensitivity parameter
Negative-feedback amplifier
Transconductance amplifier
Transresistance amplifier
Shunt–series feedback
Series–series feedback
Voltage amplifier
Voltage-series feedback
Voltage-shunt feedback

OBJECTIVE-TYPE EXERCISES

Multiple-Choice Questions

1. Introduction of negative feedback desensitizes or stabilizes the gain. The gain stability
   a. increases with increase in open-loop gain.
   b. decreases with increase in open-loop gain.
   c. decreases with increase in feedback factor.
   d. increases with increase in loop gain.
2. A voltage amplifier has an open-loop gain of 100. If 10% negative feedback were introduced in the amplifier, then an 11% change in open-loop gain would cause
   a. 1% change in closed-loop gain.
   b. 11% change in closed-loop gain.
   c. 1.1% change in closed-loop gain.
   d. 0.1% change in closed-loop gain.
3. In the case of a negative-feedback amplifier, which of the following is true?
   a. Closed-loop gain can be less than or more than the open-loop gain depending upon the type and amount of feedback.
   b. Closed-loop gain is always less than the open-loop gain.
   c. Closed-loop gain is always more than the open-loop gain.
   d. Closed-loop gain and bandwidth are always less than the corresponding open-loop values.
4. In which of the following feedback topologies, the input impedance increases with introduction of feedback.
   a. Voltage-shunt feedback
   b. Current-shunt feedback
   c. Voltage-series feedback
   d. None of these
5. In which of the following feedback topologies, the input impedance decreases with introduction of feedback.
   a. Voltage-shunt feedback
   b. Current-series feedback
   c. Voltage-series feedback
   d. None of these
6. In which of the following feedback topologies, the output impedance increases with introduction of feedback.
   a. Voltage-shunt feedback
   b. Current-shunt feedback
   c. Voltage-series feedback
   d. None of these

7. In which of the following feedback topologies, both input as well as output impedances decrease with introduction of feedback.
   a. Voltage-shunt feedback
   b. Current-shunt feedback
   c. Voltage-series feedback
   d. None of these

8. Which of the following amplifier configurations has an inherent current-series feedback?
   a. Emitter–follower
   b. Common-base amplifier
   c. Common-emitter amplifier by bypassed emitter resistor
   d. Common-emitter amplifier with unbypassed emitter resistor

9. It is desired to design a voltage controlled current source. What type of negative feedback should preferably be introduced to make it a stable source?
   a. Voltage-series feedback
   b. Current-series feedback
   c. Current-shunt feedback
   d. Voltage-shunt feedback

10. A voltage amplifier consists of cascade arrangement of two identical stages. Negative feedback is introduced from output of second stage to input of first stage to get a stable overall closed-loop gain of 45. In order that 10% variation in open-loop gain of each stage does not produce more than 1% variation in overall closed-loop gain, the minimum value of open-loop gain of each stage should be
    a. 30.
    b. 900.
    c. 45.
    d. none of these.

11. A voltage amplifier has 5% negative feedback. Its voltage gain is
    a. indeterminate from given data.
    b. approximately 20.
    c. approximately 5.
    d. 100.

12. For the expression of gain with feedback $A_f = A/(1 + \beta A)$ in the case of negative-feedback amplifier to be valid,
    a. feedback factor β should be independent of load and source resistances.
    b. forward transmission through the feedback network should be zero.
    c. reverse transmission through amplifier should be zero.
    d. all the above should be true.

13. Voltage-shunt feedback stabilizes
    a. voltage gain.
    b. current gain.
    c. transresistance.
    d. transconductance.

14. An amplifier with open-loop input resistance of 100 kΩ has −20 dB of voltage-series feedback. Closed-loop input resistance would be
    a. 10 kΩ.
    b. 1000 kΩ.
    c. 2000 kΩ.
    d. 5 kΩ.

15. In a negative-feedback amplifier with a high open-loop gain, doubling the feedback factor
    a. doubles the closed-loop gain too.
    b. has no effect on closed-loop gain.
    c. reduces the closed-loop gain to one-fourth.
    d. reduces the closed-loop gain to one-half.

Identify the Feedback Topology

Figure 11.35 shows some circuit configurations. Identify the feedback topology used in each of these circuit configurations.

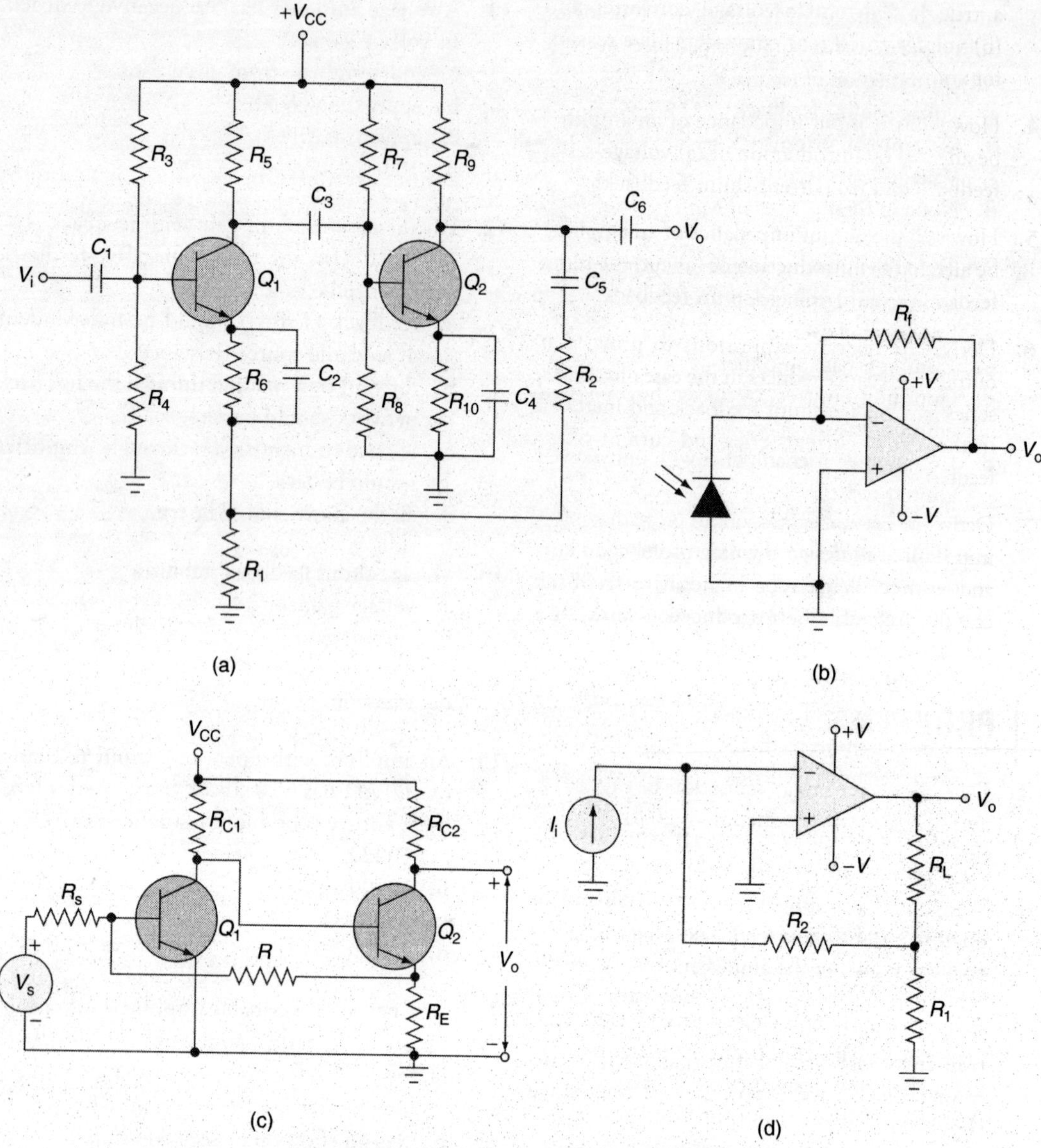

Figure 11.35 Identify the feedback topology.

REVIEW QUESTIONS

1. How do you classify amplifiers based on the nature of input and output signals of interest? What is the gain parameter of interest in each of these types?

2. What are the merits/demerits of introduction of negative feedback in amplifiers?

3. What type of negative feedback should be introduced in an amplifier to make it work like

a true (a) current-to-voltage converter and (b) voltage-to-current converter? Give reasons for your answer.

4. How will the input impedance of an amplifier be affected by introduction of (a) voltage-series feedback and (b) current-shunt feedback?

5. How will the output impedance of an amplifier be affected by introduction of (a) current-series feedback and (b) voltage-shunt feedback?

6. Derive the relevant expressions to prove that output impedance reduces in the case of voltage-series and voltage-shunt feedback and increases in the case of current-series and current-shunt feedback.

7. Derive the relevant expressions to prove that input impedance reduces in the case of voltage-shunt and current-shunt feedback and increases in the case of voltage-series and current-series feedback.

8. Give two examples of practical amplifier circuits representative of the following types of negative feedback.
   a. Series–series feedback
   b. Series–shunt feedback

9. Outline the three fundamental assumptions that must be true in order that introduction of negative feedback has the desired effect on gain parameter stability, input and output impedances.

10. Justify the following.
   a. A common-emitter amplifier with unbypassed emitter resistor is representative of current-series feedback and not voltage-series feedback.
   b. The gain parameter in a negative-feedback amplifier depends exclusively on the components of feedback network when the open-loop gain becomes very large.

PROBLEMS

1. Determine percentage reduction in gain of an amplifier due to introduction of 20 dB of negative feedback.

2. The gain of an amplifier reduces to 10 by introduction of –40 dB of feedback. Determine the open-loop gain of the amplifier.

3. A voltage amplifier is characterized by an open-loop voltage gain of 100, input resistance of 50 kΩ and output resistance of 2 kΩ. Negative feedback of 10% of output voltage is introduced in series with the input to bring the distortion below acceptable level. Find the modified values of these parameters.

4. For the opamp-based non-inverting amplifier circuit of Figure 11.36, determine the voltage gain and the input impedance in the presence of feedback. Given that open-loop gain and the input impedance of the opamp are 70 dB and 10 MΩ, respectively.

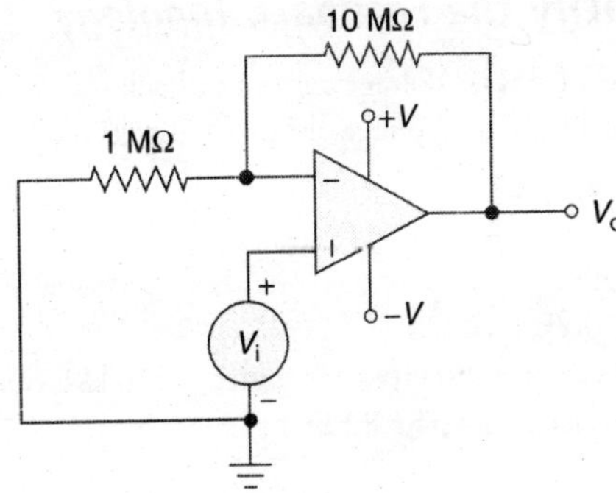

Figure 11.36 Problem 4.

5. Two identical amplifier stages each having an open-loop gain of A_1 are connected in cascade to build a voltage amplifier with an overall open-loop voltage gain of A. The output from the second stage is fed back in series and phase opposition with the input of the first stage to get an overall closed-loop gain of A_f. Derive an expression for overall open-loop gain A in

terms of open-loop gain stability $|dA_1/A_1|$ of individual stages and overall closed-loop gain stability $|dA_f/A_f|$.

6. A voltage amplifier is specified to have a voltage gain of 1000 ± 50. It is desired that the voltage gain does not vary by more than ±0.1%. Find the value of feedback factor β and the value of closed-loop gain.
7. Figure 11.37 shows an FET-based common-source amplifier circuit with voltage-series feedback provided by series combination of R_1 and R_2. FET is characterized by g_m = 4000 μS and r_d = 10 kΩ. Calculate the voltage gain with feedback.

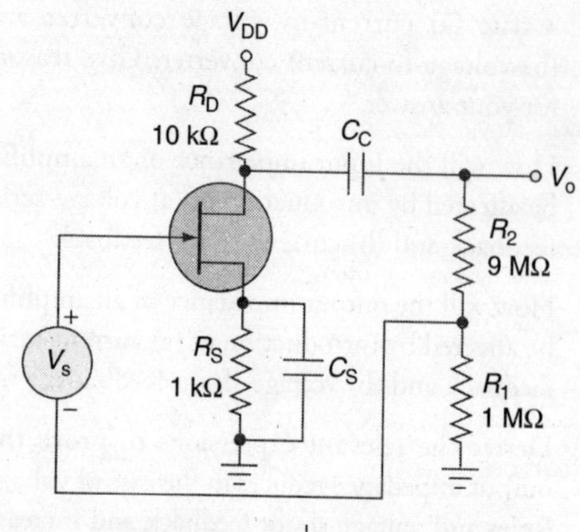

Figure 11.37 | Problem 7.

ANSWERS

Multiple-Choice Questions

1. (d)
2. (a)
3. (b)
4. (c)
5. (a)
6. (b)
7. (a)
8. (d)
9. (b)
10. (a)
11. (b)
12. (d)
13. (c)
14. (b)
15. (d)

Identify the Feedback Topology

Figure 11.35(a): Voltage-series feedback
Figure 11.35(b): Voltage-shunt feedback
Figure 11.35(c): Current-shunt feedback
Figure 11.35(d): Current-shunt feedback

Problems

1. 90%
2. 1000
3. Gain = 9.09; input resistance = 550 kΩ; output resistance = 181.82 Ω
4. Voltage gain = 10.96; input impedance = 2884.80 MΩ
5. $A = 2A_f \times |dA_1/A_1| / |dA_f/A_f|$
6. $\beta = 0.049$; closed-loop gain = 20
7. −6.56

CHAPTER 12

Sinusoidal Oscillators

Learning Objectives

After completing this chapter, you will learn the following:

- Broad classification of oscillators based on the type of output waveform.
- Different constituents of an oscillator circuit.
- Barkhausen criterion of oscillations including gain and phase shift conditions.
- Different types of oscillator circuits.
- RC oscillators including RC phase shift, Wien bridge, Quadrature, Twin-T and Bubba oscillators.
- LC oscillators including Hartley, Colpitt and Clapp oscillators.
- Crystal oscillators including Pierce oscillator.
- Voltage-controlled oscillators.
- Frequency stability considerations.

Discussion on amplifiers is almost invariably followed by the one on oscillators. There are two broad categories of oscillators, namely, the sinusoidal and the non-sinusoidal oscillators. Sinusoidal oscillators discussed in this chapter generate sine wave output. Important types in the non-sinusoidal category are the ones that generate square wave or pulsed outputs. A multivibrator is type of non-sinusoidal oscillator. Multivibrator circuits are discussed in Chapter 13 on wave-shaping circuits. An amplifier is in fact the central building block of an oscillator. While the former has a negative feedback to have increased stability and reduced distortion, the latter is an amplifier with a positive feedback. Major topics discussed in this chapter include oscillator fundamentals like the Barkhausen criterion for oscillations, popular oscillator circuit configurations, which include different types of RC, LC and crystal oscillators and oscillator frequency stability considerations.

12.1 Classification of Oscillators

On the basis of the type of output waveform generated, oscillators are classified as *sinusoidal* and *non-sinusoidal* oscillators. Sinusoidal oscillators produce a sine wave output where as non-sinusoidal oscillators produce square or pulsed output. A multivibrator circuit is a type of non-sinusoidal oscillator. Different types of multivibrator circuits are discussed in detail in Chapter 13 on wave-shaping circuits for reasons that would be obvious as we go through the operational basics of the two types of oscillator circuits in respective chapters. The only thing common between the two types of oscillator circuits is that both types have an inherent regenerative feedback.

Depending upon the nature of the feedback network used, sinusoidal oscillators are further classified as RC, LC and crystal oscillators.

12.2 Conditions for Oscillations: Barkhausen Criterion

An oscillator circuit is essentially an amplifier circuit with a frequency-selective feedback network. The feedback network feeds a fraction of the amplifier output back to its input in such a way as to satisfy the two fundamental requirements for occurrence of sustained oscillations. These requirements are commonly known by the name of *Barkhausen criterion.*

Barkhausen criterion can be best explained by considering the canonical form of negative and positive feedback systems as shown in Figures 12.1(a) and (b), respectively. Canonical form is the simplest form of representation of any class of systems without any loss of generality. The transfer function in the case of negative feedback system of Figure 12.1(a) can be derived as follows. Remember that in the case of a negative feedback system, the summing point is a subtractor. That is, the error signal is the sum of input signal and the phase-inverted feedback signal:

$$E = V_{in} - \beta \times V_{out} \tag{12.1}$$

Substituting $E = V_{out}/A$, we get

$$\frac{V_{out}}{A} = V_{in} - \beta \times V_{out} \tag{12.2}$$

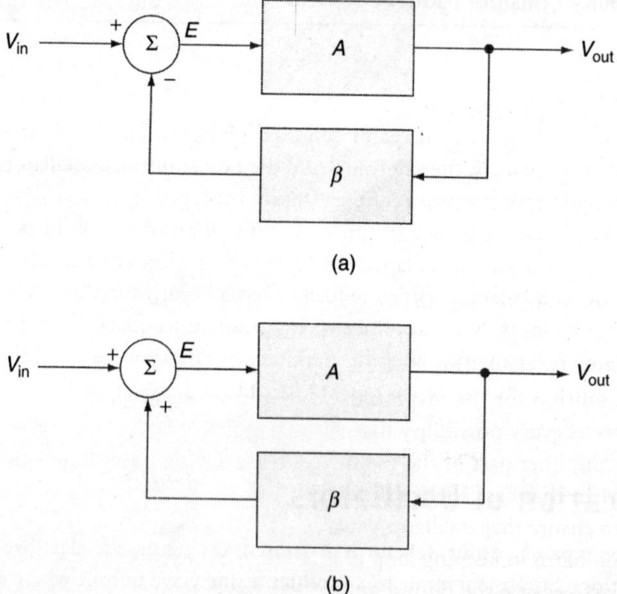

Figure 12.1 Canonical form of feedback systems: (a) Negative feedback system; (b) positive feedback system.

This simplifies to

$$\frac{V_{out}}{V_{in}} = \frac{A}{1+\beta A} \tag{12.3}$$

In the case of a positive feedback system in which the summing point is an adder, the transfer function is given by

$$\frac{V_{out}}{V_{in}} = \frac{A}{1-\beta A} \tag{12.4}$$

If $\beta A = -1 = 1\angle -180°$ in the case of negative feedback system and $\beta A = 1 = 1\angle 0°$ in the case of positive feedback system, the system works like an oscillator. In the case of the former, the conditions specify magnitude of loop gain as unity and loop phase shift as 180°. In the case of latter, the conditions specify magnitude of loop gain as unity and loop phase shift as 0° or 360°. The condition for the magnitude of the loop gain is the same in the two cases. If we carefully examine the two cases, we will find that the loop phase shift condition in both the cases is also the same as phase inversion implied by the negative sign at the summing point of the negative feedback system restores the overall phase shift at the amplifier input. Essentially the two conditions mean the following:

1. The magnitude of loop gain is unity, which ensures that the feedback signal has the same magnitude as that of the input signal.
2. The magnitude of loop phase shift is such that the feedback signal is in-phase with the input signal when it reaches the input of the amplifier.

These two conditions define what is known as Barkhausen criterion of oscillations. Satisfying Barkhausen criterion ensures that oscillator circuits do not need an external applied input signal. Instead they use fraction of the output signal as the input signal.

In practical oscillator circuits, the summing point is an adder and therefore the Barkhausen criterion of oscillations is written as follows:

1. $|\beta A| = 1$. That is, loop gain should be unity.
2. $\angle \beta A = 0°$ or integral multiple of 360°. That is, loop phase shift should be zero or integral multiple of 360°.

Initiation of Oscillations

The process of generation of oscillations is initiated due to some inevitable noise present at the amplifier input. The amplified output due to noise has all frequency components. Since the feedback network is a frequency selective one and the loop phase shift condition is satisfied only at one frequency, the signal fed back to the input has a single frequency component at which the loop phase shift condition of the Barkhausen criterion is satisfied. This leads to the oscillator circuit producing a sinusoidal output.

The essential condition for the magnitude of loop gain for oscillations to occur is that loop gain is precisely unity. There is every possibility that with change in parameters of the transistor or other active devices used in the amplifier part of the oscillator due to ageing or replacement, one lands up with loop gain less than unity. In that case there will be no oscillations. So, in practice, loop gain is kept slightly greater than unity to ensure that oscillator works even if there is a slight change in the circuit parameters. Moreover, there is no harm in keeping loop gain slightly greater than unity as the output cannot increase infinitely as it appears because the output amplitude will be limited due to onset of non-linearity of the active device used. However, if magnitude of loop gain is much larger than unity, the oscillator output will have lot of distortion.

12.3 Types of Oscillators

Sinusoidal oscillators are classified on the basis of the type of frequency-selective network used in the feedback loop. Different types include the following.

1. RC oscillators;
2. LC oscillators;
3. Crystal oscillators.

RC Oscillators

In the case of RC oscillators, multiple RC sections are used to provide the required phase shift. Remember that a single section RC or RL network provides up to a maximum of 90° of phase shift due to existence of a single pole in its transfer function. A minimum of two sections would therefore be required to provide the required 180° of phase shift. In practice, cascade arrangement of three RC sections is used in practical RC phase shift oscillators with each section providing 60° of phase shift. This provides a larger value of rate of change of phase with frequency around the operational frequency ($d\phi/d\omega$), which gives improved performance in terms of frequency stability. Frequency stability issues are discussed in detail in the latter part of the chapter. Figure 12.2 shows the plot of phase as a function of frequency in the case of multiple RC sections.

Prominent candidates in the category of RC oscillators include the RC phase shift oscillator, Twin-T oscillator, Wien bridge oscillator, Bubba oscillator and Quadrature oscillator.

LC Oscillators

A single-section LC circuit has two poles and therefore can provide the required 180° of phase shift. Prominent members include Hartley oscillator, Colpitt oscillator and Clapp oscillator. LC oscillators are suitable for relatively higher operational frequencies due to low-frequency inductors being expensive, bulky and highly non-ideal. RC oscillators are preferred at lower frequencies.

Crystal Oscillators

In crystal oscillators, crystal resonator provides the electrical equivalent of frequency-selective network. Crystal oscillators are the most stable of the three types due to their extremely high rate of change of phase with frequency at the operating frequency ($d\phi/d\omega$). Crystal oscillators are not practical at lower operating frequencies due to their size, weight and cost restrictions.

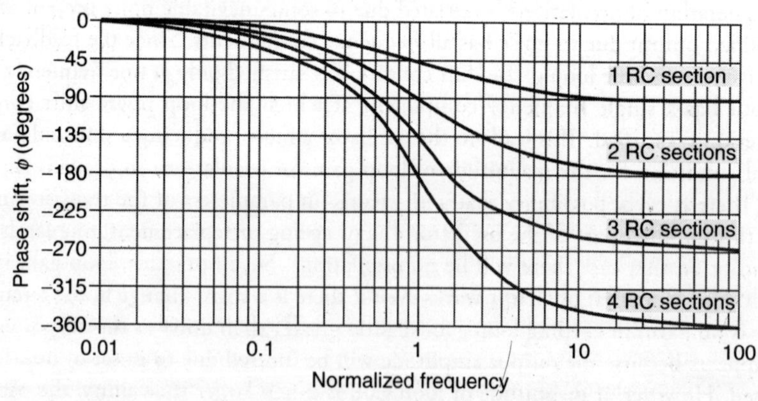

Figure 12.2 Phase versus frequency plot of RC sections.

Oscillators belonging to each one of the three above-mentioned categories are described in the following sections.

EXAMPLE 12.1 *Determine the gain or phase shift as the case may be for the following oscillator circuits.*

Case 1: *If the feedback network of a certain oscillator provides 1% positive feedback, what should be the minimum gain for the amplifier section of the oscillator for sustained oscillations?*

Case 2: *If in an oscillator, the amplifier portion is a two-stage CE configuration, what should be the phase shift to be introduced by the feedback network at the oscillation frequency for sustained oscillations?*

Case 3: *The amplifier gain in an oscillator is 50. What should be the percentage feedback for sustained oscillations?*

Solution

Case 1

1. A feedback of 1% means $\beta = 0.01$.
2. Therefore, amplifier's minimum gain is $1/\beta = 100$.

Case 2

1. A two-stage CE amplifier provides a phase shift of 2π radians.
2. Therefore, the feedback network must not introduce any more phase shift or introduce phase shift equal to multiples of 2π radians in order to satisfy Barkhausen criterion for sustained oscillations.

Case 3

1. Amplifier gain = 50.
2. Therefore, feedback factor $\beta = 1/50 = 0.02$.
3. Percentage feedback = 2%.

12.4 RC Phase Shift Oscillator

The basic RC phase shift oscillator comprises a single-stage amplifier whose output is fed back to its input through a feedback network. The amplifier portion is usually implemented by either a bipolar junction transistor-based common-emitter amplifier stage or an operational amplifier wired as an inverting amplifier. The feedback network comprises a cascade arrangement of three identical sections of either lag- or lead-type RC network. Figure 12.3 shows the circuit schematic of an RC phase shift oscillator using a common-emitter amplifier stage and a lag-type RC feedback network. This circuit could have been as well implemented using a junction FET-based common-source amplifier stage in place of bipolar junction transistor-based common-emitter stage.

Figure 12.4 shows another version of RC phase shift oscillator in which the amplifier portion is implemented using an operational amplifier configured as an inverting amplifier. In both cases, the amplifier provides a phase shift of 180° at the frequency of operation, which means that the feedback network must also provide an additional phase shift of 180° at the operating frequency to satisfy the loop phase shift condition of the Barkhausen criterion. Also the gain to be provided by the amplifier stage must be at least equal to the inverse of the attenuation factor of the feedback network. In fact, in the phase shift oscillator, while the amplifier gain is dictated by the feedback network attenuation factor; the phase shift provided by the amplifier stage decides the phase shift to be provided by the feedback network.

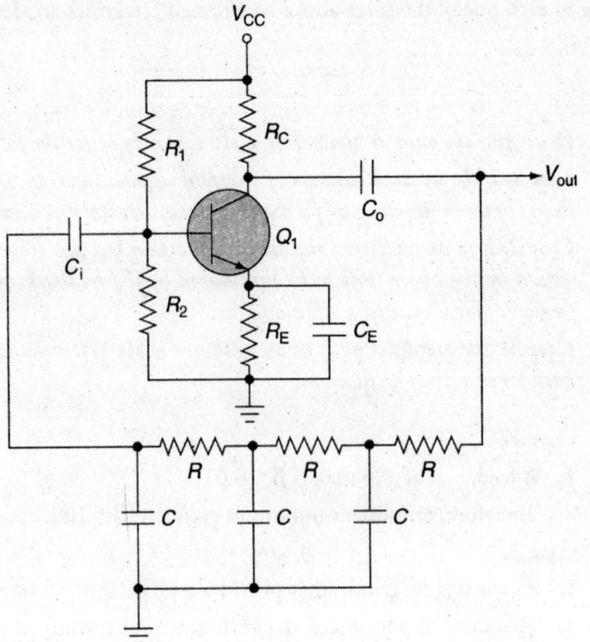

Figure 12.3 | RC phase shift oscillator with lag-type feedback network using common-emitter amplifier.

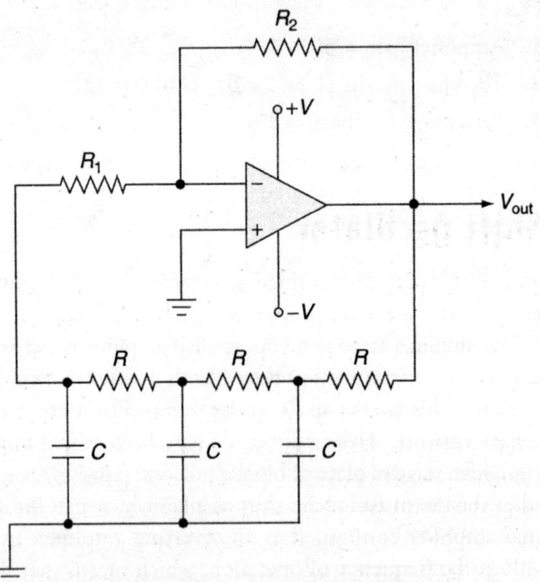

Figure 12.4 | RC phase shift oscillator with lag-type feedback network using operational amplifier.

In order to analyze the oscillator circuits of Figures 12.3 and 12.4, we need to analyze the transfer function of the feedback network. The transfer function will tell us about both the attenuation and the phase shift provided by this network as a function of frequency.

The transfer function of a single-stage lag-type RC network is give by

$$T(s) = \frac{1}{1 + RCs} \tag{12.5}$$

where $s = j\omega$.

Assuming that the RC sections in the cascade arrangement are independent of each other, that is, individual RC sections do not load each other, then the transfer function of the cascade arrangement of three RC sections is given by

$$T(s) = \left[\frac{1}{1 + RCs}\right]^3 \tag{12.6}$$

Now, the single-section RC network provides a phase shift (θ) given by

$$\theta = \tan^{-1}(-\omega RC) \tag{12.7}$$

$$\tan\theta = -\omega RC$$

$$\omega = -\frac{\tan\theta}{RC} \tag{12.8}$$

If this single RC section were to provide the desired lagging phase shift of 60° so as to produce a total lagging phase shift of 180° from the feedback network, then the operational frequency of the oscillator would be given by

$$\omega = \frac{-\tan(-60°)}{RC} = \frac{\sqrt{3}}{RC}\text{, which gives } f = \frac{\sqrt{3}}{2\pi RC} \tag{12.9}$$

Attenuation factor provided by single-section RC network is given by

$$\text{Attenuation factor (single-section RC network)} = \frac{1}{\sqrt{1 + \omega^2 R^2 C^2}} \tag{12.10}$$

Substituting the value of (ω) from Eq. (12.9), we get

$$\text{Attenuation factor} = 1/\sqrt{(1+3)} = 1/2$$

The overall attenuation factor (β) of the feedback network is then given by

$$\beta - (1/2)^3 = 1/8 \tag{12.11}$$

Equation (12.11) implies that the amplifier gain must at least be equal to 8. In practice, it is observed that the required gain is much higher than 8 and also that the oscillation frequency is also higher than that computed by using Eq. (12.9). This is due to the loading effect of different RC sections when they are in cascade arrangement. This is explained in the following paragraphs.

Without going into the mathematics of network analysis, considering the loading effect, it can be proved that the transfer function of the three-section RC network of the lag type is given by

$$T(s) = \frac{(1/RC)^3}{s^3 + (5/RC)s^2 + (6/R^2C^2)s + (1/R^3C^3)} \tag{12.12}$$

Substituting $s = j\omega$, we get

$$T(j\omega) = \frac{(1/RC)^3}{[(1/R^3C^3) - (5\omega^2/RC)] + j[(6\omega/R^2C^2) - \omega^3]}$$

Multiplying both numerator and denominator by R^3C^3, we get

$$T(j\omega) = \frac{1}{(1-5\omega^2R^2C^2)+j(6\omega RC-\omega^3R^3C^3)} \tag{12.13}$$

If the feedback network were to provide an overall phase shift of 180°, then the imaginary part should be equal to zero. That is, $6\omega RC-\omega^3R^3C^3=0$, which gives

$$\omega = \sqrt{6}/RC \tag{12.14}$$

Substituting the value of ω in Eq. (12.13), we get the expression for the feedback factor as

$$\text{Feedback factor, } \beta = 1/(1-30) \tag{12.15}$$

This gives

$$|\beta| = 1/29 \tag{12.16}$$

Equations (12.14) and (12.16) specify the required conditions for loop phase shift and loop gain. The oscillation frequency is given by Eq. (12.14) and Eq. (12.16) tells that the amplifier gain must at least be equal to 29.

A similar analysis can be done in the case of lead-type RC phase shift network too. The expressions for the transfer function and the phase shift provided by single-section lead network are given by Eqs. (12.17) and (12.18), respectively.

$$T(s) = \frac{RCs}{1+RCs} \tag{12.17}$$

$$\theta = \tan^{-1}(1/\omega RC)$$

which gives $\omega = 1/\sqrt{3}RC$ for $\theta = 60°$. (12.18)

Considering the loading effect, the transfer function for the cascade arrangement of three-section lead-type RC network is given by Eq. (12.19). This equation is similar to Eq. (12.13) written for the cascade arrangement of lag network.

$$T(j\omega) = \frac{1}{\{1-5/(\omega^2R^2C^2)\}-j\{6/(\omega RC)-1/(R^3C^3\omega^3)\}} \tag{12.19}$$

Again, if the feedback network were to provide an overall phase shift of 180°, then the imaginary part should be equal to zero. That is,

$$6/\omega RC - 1/R^3C^3\omega^3 = 0$$

which gives

$$\omega = 1/(\sqrt{6}RC) \tag{12.20}$$

Substituting the value of ω in Eq. (12.19), we get expression for the feedback factor:

$$\text{Feedback factor, } \beta = 1/(1-30) \tag{12.21}$$

$$\text{This gives, } |\beta| = 1/29 \tag{12.22}$$

Equations (12.20) and (12.22) specify the required conditions for loop phase shift and loop gain for RC phase shift oscillators employing lead-type RC phase shift network. The oscillation frequency is given by Eq. (12.20) and Eq. (12.22) tells that the amplifier gain must at least be equal to 29. Figure 12.5 shows circuit schematic of RC phase shift oscillator using lead-type phase shift network. The circuit uses opamp-based amplifier stage. The oscillator circuit using transistorized amplifier stage would be similar to the one shown in Figure 12.3 except for the feedback network.

To summarize, in the case of an RC phase shift oscillator, the frequency of oscillation is given by $f = \sqrt{6}/(2\pi RC)$ if the feedback network employed lag-type RC sections and $f = 1/(2\pi\sqrt{6}RC)$ if the feedback circuit used lead-type RC sections. Minimum amplifier gain in both cases is 29.

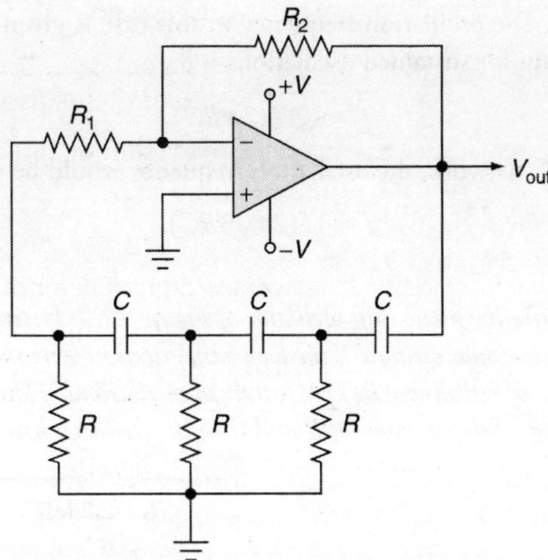

Figure 12.5 | RC phase shift oscillator with lead-type feedback network using operational amplifier.

RC phase shift oscillator has limitations when it comes to designing a variable frequency oscillator as it is impractical to simultaneously vary three capacitance values equally. Also, adjustment of resistance values is not recommended because variation of resistance values will alter the loop gain of the oscillator circuit and there is likelihood of it not satisfying Barkhausen criterion for sustained oscillations. However, higher $d\phi/d\omega$ resulting from steep phase versus frequency slope provided by the three-section RC network gives a reasonably high frequency stability.

12.5 Buffered RC Phase Shift Oscillator

The buffered RC phase shift oscillator (Figure 12.6) overcomes the loading effect of different RC sections in the conventional phase shift oscillator. The oscillator performs very nearly at the computed values of

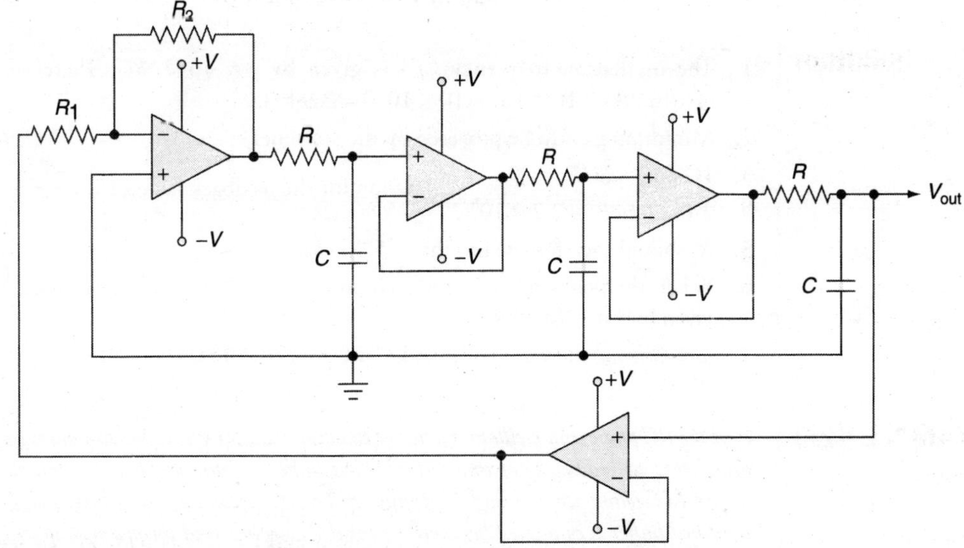

Figure 12.6 | Buffered RC phase shift oscillator.

frequency and amplifier gain. The oscillation frequency in this case is given by Eq. (12.23) and the minimum value of the amplifier gain for sustained oscillations is 8.

$$f = \sqrt{3}/(2\pi RC) \tag{12.23}$$

In the case of lead-type RC network, the oscillation frequency would be given by

$$f = 1/(2\pi\sqrt{3}RC) \tag{12.24}$$

EXAMPLE 12.2 *Refer to the phase shift oscillator of Figure 12.7. Determine the frequency at which this circuit would oscillate if the loop gain criterion were met. Also determine the maximum value of resistance (R_1) for sustained oscillations. How would the oscillation frequency change if the positions of R and C in the feedback network were interchanged?*

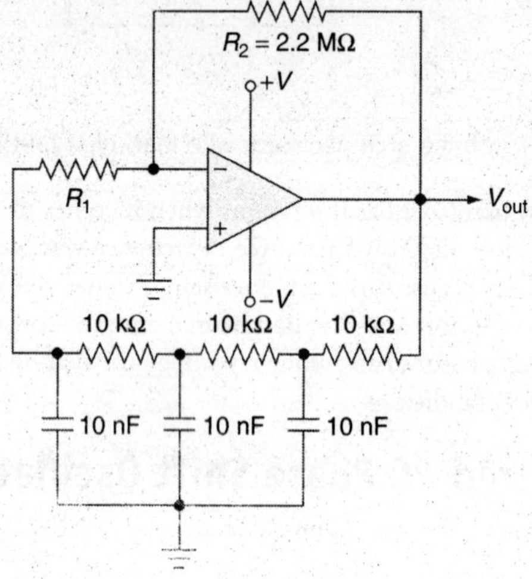

Figure 12.7 Example 12.2.

Solution

1. The oscillation frequency (f) is given by $f = \sqrt{6}/2\pi RC$. Therefore, $f = \sqrt{6}/(6.283 \times 10 \times 10^3 \times 10 \times 10^{-9}) = 3.9$ kHz.
2. Minimum gain to be provided by the amplifier = 29.
3. $|\text{Gain}| = R_2/R_1 = 29$.
4. This gives $R_1 = 2.2 \times 10^6/29 = 75.86$ kΩ.
5. R_1 should therefore be less than 75.86 kΩ.
6. When the positions of R and C are interchanged, the oscillation frequency is given by $f = 1/2\pi\sqrt{6}RC$.
7. Substituting the values of R and C, we get $f = 650$ Hz.

EXAMPLE 12.3 *If in the RC phase shift oscillator circuit of Example 12.2, the three RC sections were separated from each other by opamp buffers. First buffer is connected between the first and second RC sections; second buffer is connected between second and third RC sections and the third buffer is connected between the third RC section and the opamp input. Determine the new values of oscillation frequency and resistor (R_1) for sustained oscillations.*

Solution

1. The oscillation frequency (f) in this case is given by $f = \sqrt{3}/2\pi RC$. Therefore, $f = \sqrt{3}/(6.283 \times 10 \times 10^3 \times 10 \times 10^{-9}) = 2.758$ kHz.
2. Minimum gain to be provided by the amplifier in this case is 8.
3. Therefore, R_1 should be less than $2.2 \times 10^6/8 = 275$ kΩ.

EXAMPLE 12.4

Figure 12.8 shows an RC phase shift oscillator using an opamp as the active device. The oscillator is oscillating at the correct frequency but the output is distorted severely near the signal peaks. What could be the possible causes?

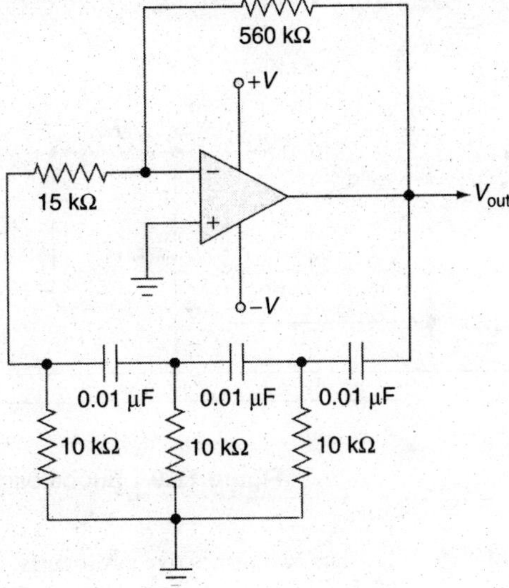

Figure 12.8 Example 12.4.

Solution

1. The minimum amplifier gain requirement is 29.
2. In order to ensure that we get sustained oscillations and the device replacement and ageing have no effects, the amplifier gain is chosen to be slightly more than what is demanded by the Barkhausen criterion.
3. It may exceed the minimum required gain value by 10–15%. Too large a gain can cause signal clipping near the peaks.
4. The gain magnitude in the present case is given by $560 \times 10^3/15 \times 10^3 \cong 37.3$, which exceeds the required minimum by approximately 30%. This explains the distortion observed in the output.

12.6 Bubba Oscillator

Bubba oscillator is a slight variation of the buffered RC phase shift oscillator discussed in Section 12.5. Figure 12.9 shows the circuit schematic of the Bubba oscillator. The difference between the two is that the Bubba oscillator uses four RC sections in the feedback network with each RC section contributing a

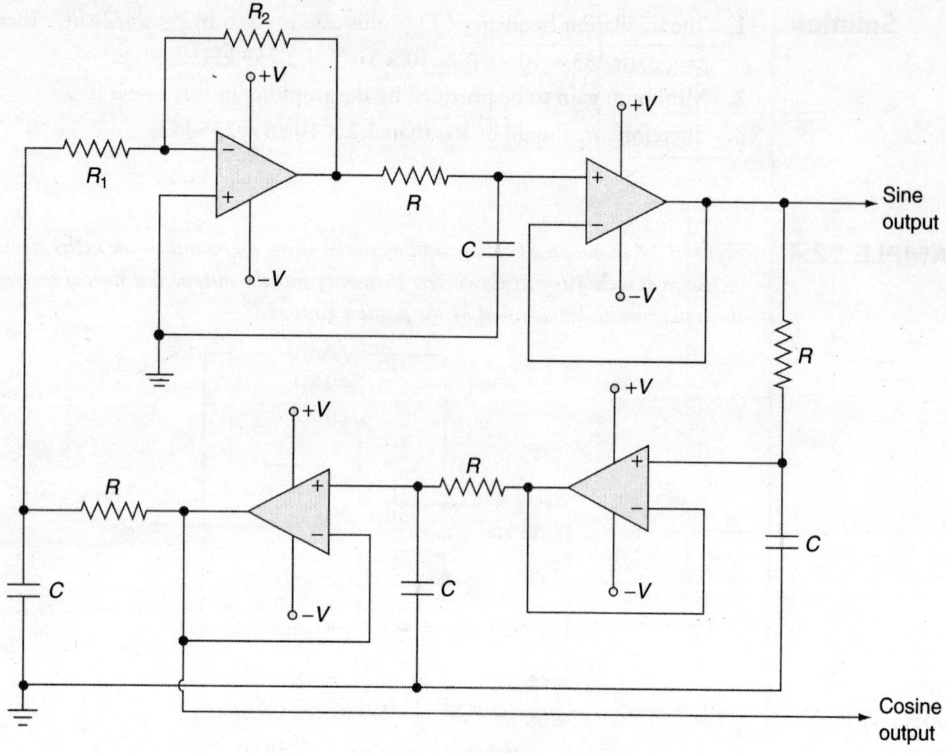

Figure 12.9 Bubba oscillator.

phase difference of 45°. This offers two distinctive advantages. One, taking outputs from alternate sections yields low impedance quadrature outputs. Two, use of four RC sections provides higher $d\phi/d\omega$, which in turn leads to relatively higher frequency stability. The expression for the transfer function of the feedback network is given by Eq. (12.25). Remember that different sections in the feedback network are buffered and therefore there is no loading effect.

$$T(s) = \left[\frac{1}{1+RCs}\right]^4 \tag{12.25}$$

Single RC section provides a phase shift of 45° for $\omega = 1/RC$. Substituting for ω in Eq. (12.25) we get

$$|\beta| = \left|\frac{1}{(1+j)^4}\right| = \frac{1}{4} \tag{12.26}$$

Equation (12.26) tells that the gain of the amplifier must at least be 4 for oscillations to occur. As explained earlier, the gain is chosen to be 10–15% higher than this value.

12.7 Quadrature Oscillator

Quadrature oscillator is yet another type of RC phase shift oscillator (Figure 12.10). As is evident from the circuit schematic of Figure 12.10, the circuit employs three RC sections. The circuit takes advantage

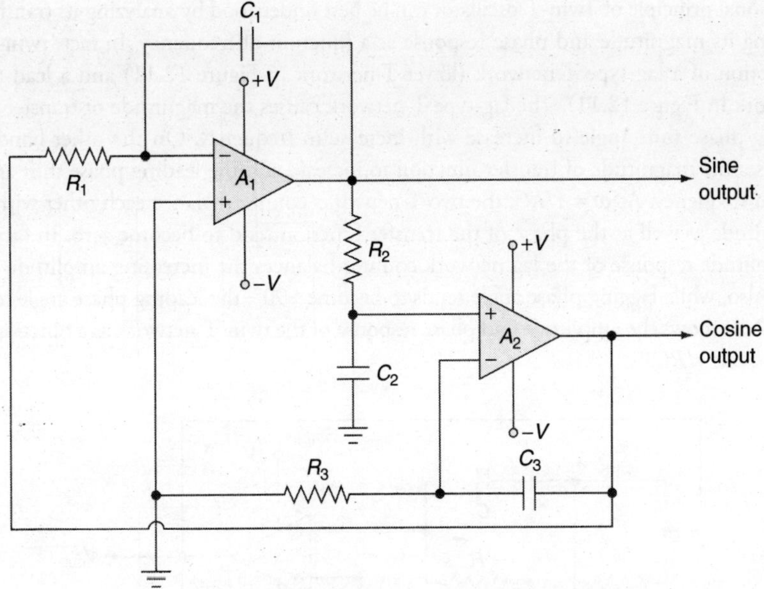

Figure 12.10 Quadrature oscillator.

of the fact that double integral of a sine wave is a negative sine wave of the same frequency and phase. This implies that the original waveform is 180° phase-shifted after double integration. The phase of the output from second integrator is then inverted to provide positive feedback to induce oscillations.

The transfer function of the feedback network is nothing but a cascade arrangement of a three networks. The first one comprises R_1–C_1 configured around opamp A_1. The second one comprises R_2–C_2 and the third one comprises R_3–C_3 configured around opamp A_2. The expression for loop gain is given by

$$\text{Loop gain} = \left[\frac{1}{R_1C_1s}\right] \times \left[\frac{1}{1+R_2C_2s}\right] \times \left[\frac{1+R_3C_3s}{R_3C_3s}\right] \tag{12.27}$$

If $R_1C_1 = R_2C_2 = R_3C_3 = RC$ and if we substitute $\omega = 1/RC$, the first network provides a phase shift of 90°, the second and third networks provide phase shift of 45° so as to provide a total phase shift of 180°. Opamp A_1 too provides a phase shift of 180°, which leads to loop phase shift of 0°. Also, Eq. (12.27) reduces to the following equation:

$$\text{Loop gain} = \frac{1}{(RCs)^2} = 1\angle -180° \tag{12.28}$$

The circuit provides sine and cosine outputs (quadrature outputs) because of 90° phase difference between the two signals present at the outputs of the two opamps.

12.8 Twin-T Oscillator

The Twin-T oscillator employs a twin-T-type of notch filter network as the frequency selective component in the feedback network. Figure 12.11 shows the basic circuit schematic of a Twin-T oscillator. The circuit employs both positive as well as negative feedback. The positive feedback necessary to produce oscillations is provided by a voltage divider network of R_1 and R_2. The negative feedback is through the frequency selective twin-T network.

The operational principle of Twin-T oscillator can be best understood by analyzing its transfer function and thereby studying its magnitude and phase response as a function of frequency. In fact, twin-T network is a parallel connection of a lag-type T-network (lower T-network in Figure 12.11) and a lead-type T-network (upper T-network in Figure 12.11). The lag-type T-network causes the magnitude of transfer function to fall and the lagging phase shift angle to increase with increase in frequency. On the other hand, the lead-type T-network causes the magnitude of transfer function to increase and the leading phase shift angle to decrease with increase in frequency. At $\omega = 1/RC$, the two T-networks counter-balance each other with the result that both the magnitude as well as the phase of the transfer function tend to become zero. In fact, at $\omega = 1/RC$, decreasing amplitude response of the lag network counter-balances the increasing amplitude response of the lead network. Also, while lagging phase angle tends to become –90°, the leading phase angle tends to become +90°. Figure 12.12 shows the amplitude and phase response of the twin-T network as a function of normalized frequency. ω_c equals $1/RC$.

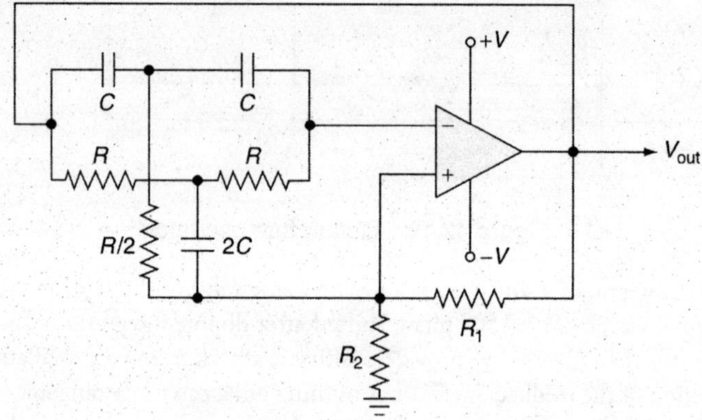

Figure 12.11 Twin-T oscillator.

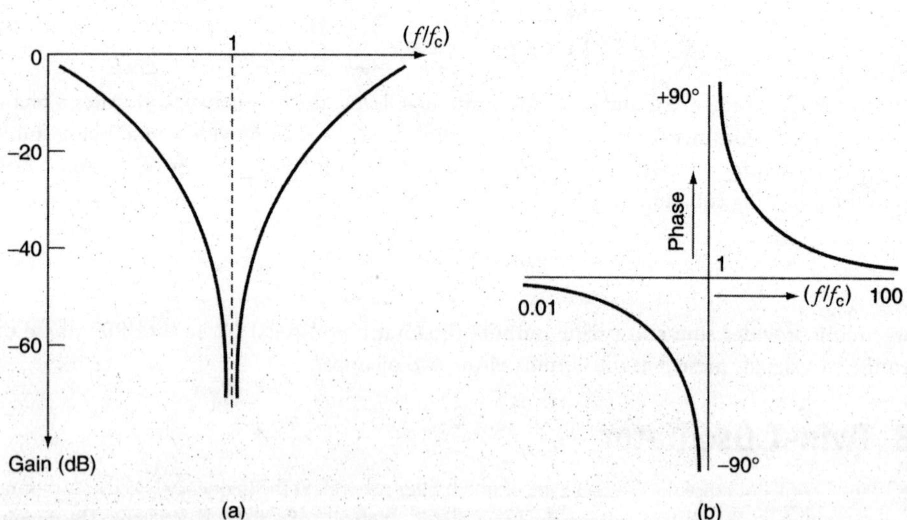

Figure 12.12 (a) Magnitude; (b) phase response of twin-T network.

The same can be explained with the help of expression for transfer function of the twin-T network. Without going into mathematical details, the transfer function of the twin-T network can be expressed as

$$T(j\omega)=\frac{1-\omega^2R^2C^2}{1-\omega^2R^2C^2+j4\omega CR} \tag{12.29}$$

The magnitude of $T(j\omega)$ is

$$\left|T(j\omega)\right|=\frac{1-\omega^2R^2C^2}{\sqrt{(1-\omega^2R^2C^2)^2+(4\omega CR)^2}} \tag{12.30}$$

The phase angle of $T(j\omega)$ is

$$\theta=\tan^{-1}[4\omega CR/(1-\omega^2C^2R^2)] \tag{12.31}$$

Substituting $\omega = 1/RC$ in Eqs. (12.30) and (12.31), we get the magnitude of transfer function as zero and the phase angle as either −90° or +90°. This small computation thus vindicates what was said in the preceding paragraph.

A zero amplitude for the transfer function implies zero negative feedback at $\omega = 1/RC$. The frequency corresponding to $\omega = 1/RC$ is referred to as notch frequency. At all other frequencies, there will be very high negative feedback thus allowing the circuit to oscillate only very close to the notch frequency. Resistance R_2 is a thermistor with a positive temperature coefficient. An incandescent lamp may also be used in place of thermistor. The positive temperature coefficient of resistance of tungsten filament used in incandescent lamp is used for the purpose. A low value of R_2 initially produces a large amount of positive feedback to initiate oscillations. Once the oscillations build up, the current flowing through R_2 heats it and thus raises its temperature. Increase in temperature increases the value of R_2 thus reducing the positive feedback to stabilize the magnitude of oscillations.

Twin-T oscillator produces a low distortion sinusoidal output. This is primarily because of two reasons. First, harmonics are subjected to a very high level of negative feedback, thus severely attenuating them. Second, the operating point of the oscillator is very delicately balanced between positive and negative feedback. This necessitates a very small amount of non-linearity to stabilize the amplitude.

12.9 Wien Bridge Oscillator

The *Wien bridge oscillator* is the most widely used RC oscillator configuration for low-frequency applications due to simplicity of the circuit, very good frequency stability and its amenability to variable frequency operation. The only major disadvantage is its relatively higher amplitude distortion unless special measures are taken to minimize it. Modified Wien bridge oscillator designs that minimize distortion are also discussed in the subsequent paragraphs in this section. The basic Wien bridge oscillator circuit comprises a single-stage amplifier whose output is fed back to its input through a feedback network. The amplifier portion is usually implemented by an operational amplifier wired as a non-inverting amplifier. The feedback network comprises a cascade arrangement of a series RC and a parallel RC network. Figure 12.13 shows the circuit schematic of the basic Wien bridge oscillator configured around an operational amplifier.

In order to analyze the oscillator circuit of Figure 12.13, we need to analyze the transfer function of the feedback network. The transfer function will tell us about both the attenuation and the phase shift provided by this network as a function of frequency.

The transfer function of the feedback network can be computed as follows:

1. The impedance of series RC network = $[R_1+(1/C_1s)]$.
2. Impedance of parallel RC network = $[R_2/(1+R_2C_2s)]$.

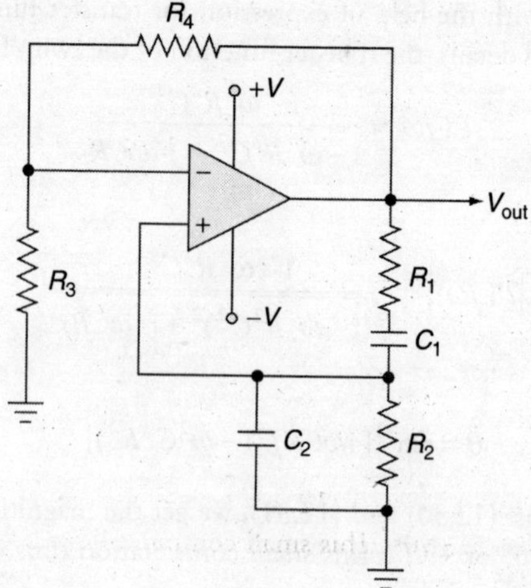

Figure 12.13 | Basic Wien bridge oscillator.

The transfer function of the feedback network can therefore be written as

$$T(s) = \beta = \frac{R_2/(1+R_2C_2s)}{(R_1 + 1/C_1s) + R_2/(1+R_2C_2s)} \tag{12.32}$$

Equation (12.32) can be simplified to

$$\beta = \frac{R_2C_1s}{R_1C_1R_2C_2s^2 + (R_1C_1 + R_2C_2 + R_2C_1)s + 1} \tag{12.33}$$

Substituting $s = j\omega$ in Eq. (12.33), we get

$$\beta = \frac{j\omega R_2C_1}{(1-\omega^2 R_1C_1R_2C_2) + j\omega(R_1C_1 + R_2C_2 + R_2C_1)} \tag{12.34}$$

The magnitude and phase responses of β are

$$\text{Magnitude of } \beta,\ |\beta| = \frac{\omega R_2C_1}{\sqrt{(1-\omega^2 R_1C_1R_2C_2)^2 + \omega^2(R_1C_1 + R_2C_2 + R_2C_1)^2}} \tag{12.35}$$

$$\text{Phase angle, } \theta = 90° - \tan^{-1}[\{\omega(R_1C_1 + R_2C_2 + R_2C_1)\}/(1-\omega^2 R_1C_1R_2C_2)] \tag{12.36}$$

In order that the loop phase shift is zero, the feedback network must provide a phase shift of zero only. From Eq. (12.36), this implies the following:

$$1 - \omega^2 R_1C_1R_2C_2 = 0$$

which gives the frequency of oscillation as

$$\omega = \frac{1}{\sqrt{R_1C_1R_2C_2}} \tag{12.37}$$

Substituting for ω in Eq. (12.35) and simplifying, we get

$$|\beta| = \frac{R_2C_1}{R_1C_1 + R_2C_2 + R_2C_1} \tag{12.38}$$

If in the Wien bridge oscillator, $R_1 = R_2 = R$ and $C_1 = C_2 = C$, then

$$|\beta| = 1/3 \tag{12.39}$$

This implies that the amplifier gain should at least be equal to 3. Also

$$\omega = \frac{1}{RC} \tag{12.40}$$

If we carefully examine the feedback network, we will notice that it is a combination of a lag network formed by R_1 and C_2 and a lead network formed by R_2 and C_1. The operating frequency is the geometric mean of the two cut-off frequencies given by $(1/2\pi R_1C_2)$ and $(1/2\pi R_2C_1)$.

Distortion in Wien Bridge Oscillator

As outlined earlier, Wien bridge oscillator is associated with relatively higher output distortion unless design measures are taken to minimize it. High output distortion results from the fact that the output amplitude is at power supply rails. This saturates the output transistors inside the opamp and causes clipping of the output signal at both the supply rails, thus producing several odd and even harmonics.

Distortion can be minimized by applying non-linear feedback. Figure 12.14 shows one such circuit. Initially, diodes D_1 and D_2 are non-conducting. The feedback resistance in that case is sum of R_2 and R_3. For larger signals, voltage across R_3 is large enough to make D_1 and D_2 conduct, respectively, during positive and negative half cycles. Conducting diodes (D_1 or D_2) decrease effective R_3, thus reducing the gain.

In another configuration, a non-linear component such as an incandescent lamp or a thermistor with positive temperature coefficient of resistance replaces the gain determining resistance connected from inverting input of the opamp to ground. Figure 12.15 shows the modified circuit schematic. The nominal value of resistance of the non-linear component is chosen to be equal to half of the feedback resistance at the current established by the two resistors. In the absence of any oscillations, the non-linear resistance value will be lower, causing the gain to be

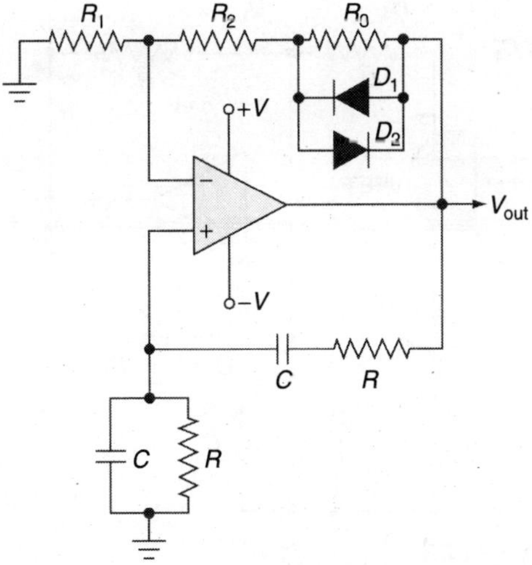

Figure 12.14 Wien bridge oscillator with non-linear feedback.

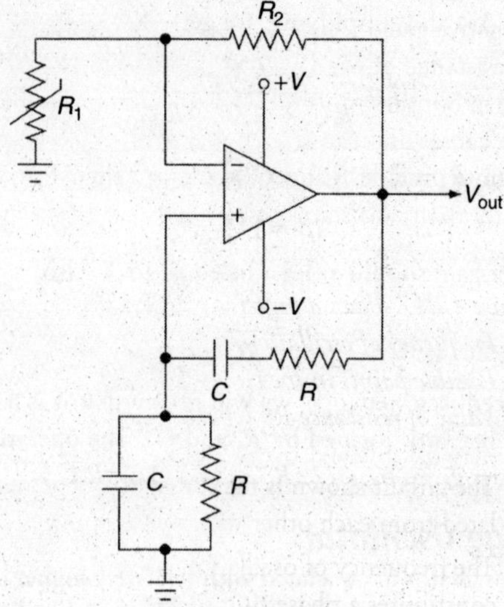

Figure 12.15 | Wien bridge oscillator with a non-linear resistor.

greater than 3. This initiates oscillations. As the oscillations build up, the current through the non-linear resistance heats it up and causes its resistance to increase thus lowering the gain and stabilizing the output. The non-linear relationship between the current and the resistance ensures that a small change in output voltage causes a large change in the resistance value. This keeps the opamp output away from saturation and hence distortion is minimized. It is observed that the distortion in the circuit of the type shown in Figure 12.15 is more than an order of magnitude better than that observed in the case of oscillator circuit of Figure 12.13.

Another possible circuit configuration that achieves low level of output distortion is shown in Figure 12.16. The circuit employs an N-channel JFET whose drain-to-source ON-resistance $R_{DS(ON)}$ is controlled by a

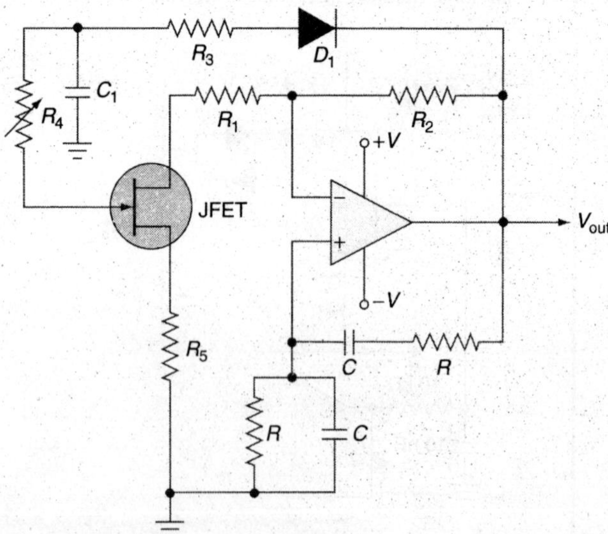

Figure 12.16 | Wien bridge oscillator with automatic gain control.

negative gate voltage. This negative gate voltage is in turn proportional to the peak amplitude of the output signal. The drain-to-source resistance of the JFET is a part of the gain-determining network as is evident from the circuit. Any increase in output amplitude causes increased negative voltage at the JFET gate terminal. Increased negative voltage causes drain-to-source resistance to increase and therefore the gain to decrease. The circuit arrangement therefore provides automatic gain control. Various resistance values are so chosen as to have an initial gain of greater than 3 to start oscillations. Thereafter, the gain is automatically controlled.

EXAMPLE 12.5

Figure 12.17 shows a buffered RC oscillator circuit. Determine the following:
(a) Frequency of oscillation.
(b) Possible points in the circuit for quadrature outputs.
(c) Value of resistance R_G (choose from 220 kΩ, 290 kΩ, 300 kΩ and 330 kΩ).

Solution

1. The circuit shown is that of Bubba oscillator. It employs four RC sections isolated from each other with opamp buffers.
2. The frequency of oscillation is given by $f = 1/2\pi RC$ as each of the four sections contributes a phase shift of 45°.
3. Therefore $f = 1/(6.283 \times 10 \times 10^3 \times 10 \times 10^{-9}) = 1.592$ kHz.
4. Quadrature outputs may be taken from the outputs of opamps A_2 and A_4. Remember outputs of A_2 and A_4 will be 90° apart.
5. Each RC section provides attenuation of $(1/\sqrt{2})$ at the operating frequency.
6. Since RC sections are buffered, attenuation provided by feedback network will be $(1/\sqrt{2})^4 = 1/4$.
7. Therefore the gain of the amplifier should be slightly more than 4.
8. This implies that the input resistance R_G should be slightly less than 300 kΩ. That is, 290 kΩ is the correct choice.

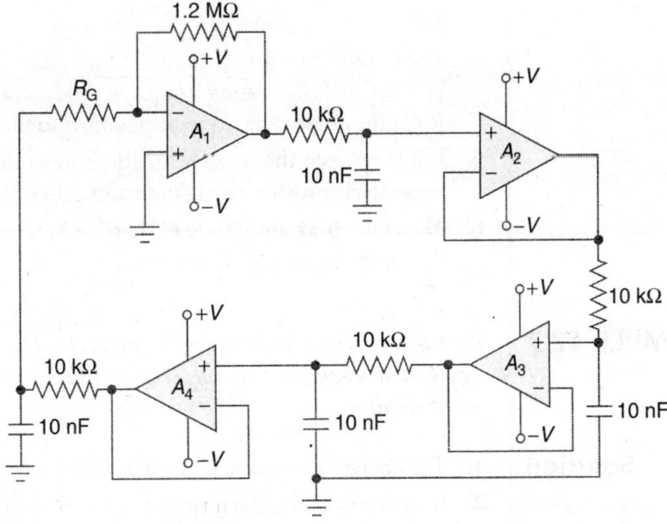

Figure 12.17 | Example 12.5.

EXAMPLE 12.6 *Figure 12.18 shows the circuit diagram of a Quadrature oscillator. Determine the operating frequency. Also determine the phase difference between the signals appearing at the outputs of opamps A_1 and A_2. If the peak amplitude of the signal appearing at the output of A_1 is 2 V, determine the peak amplitude of the signal at the junction of R_2 and C_2 and also at the output of A_2.*

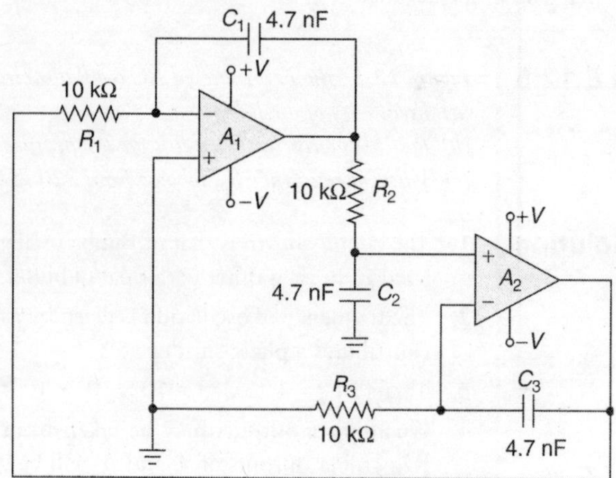

Figure 12.18 Example 12.6.

Solution

1. The frequency of oscillation is given by $f = 1/2\pi RC$.
2. Substituting the values of R and C, we get
$$f = 1/(6.283 \times 10 \times 10^3 \times 4.7 \times 10^{-9}) = 3.386 \text{ kHz}$$
3. The transfer function from output of A_1 to junction of R_2–C_2 is given by $1/(1 + R_2C_2s)$. At $\omega = 1/R_2C_2$, it produces a phase shift of $-45°$.
4. The transfer function from junction of R_2–C_2 to the output of A_2 is given by $(1 + R_3C_3s)/R_3C_3s$. At $\omega = 1/R_3C_3$, it produces a phase shift of $-45°$. Since $R_2C_2 = R_3C_3$, the phase shift from output of A_1 to the output of A_2 will be $-90°$.
5. It is clear from the transfer functions mentioned above that the two networks respectively provide attenuation and gain of $1/\sqrt{2}$ and $\sqrt{2}$.
6. Therefore, peak amplitude of signal at junction of R_2–C_2 is $2/\sqrt{2} = \sqrt{2}$ V and that at the output of A_2 is $\sqrt{2} \times \sqrt{2} = 2$ V.

EXAMPLE 12.7 *Refer to the Twin-T oscillator of Figure 12.19. Determine the frequency of the output signal. How would the frequency change if all component values in the twin-T network are doubled?*

Solution

1. The operating frequency (f) is given by $f = 1/2\pi RC$.
2. If we compare the given twin-T network with the standard form of twin-T, we will find that $R = 2 \times 10 \times 10^3\ \Omega = 20$ kΩ and $C = 0.01 \times 10^{-6}/2 = 0.005$ μF.
3. Therefore, $f = 1/(6.283 \times 20 \times 10^3 \times 0.005 \times 10^{-6}) = 1.592$ kHz.

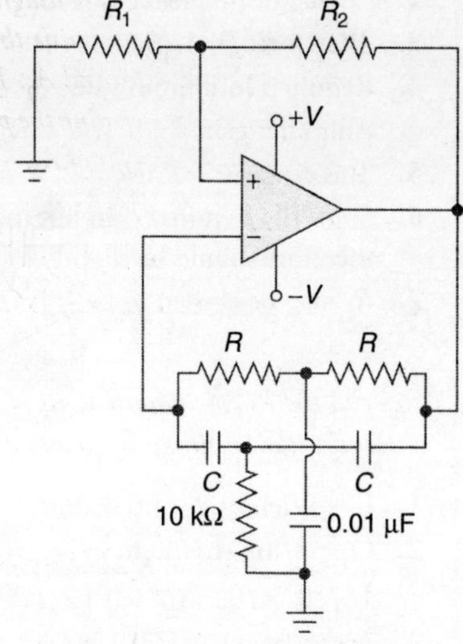

Figure 12.19 | Example 12.7.

4. When all component values are doubled, the operating frequency will be reduced to one-fourth. That is, changed value of frequency = 1.592/4 = 398 Hz.

EXAMPLE 12.8 *Refer to the Wien bridge oscillator circuit of Figure 12.20. Determine the oscillator frequency and the preferred value of* R_1.

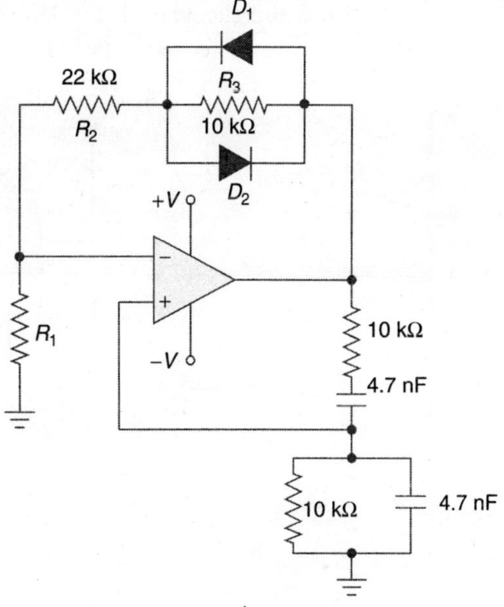

Figure 12.20 | Example 12.8.

Solution

1. Oscillator frequency is given by $f = 1/2\pi RC$ where $R = 10$ kΩ and $C = 4.7$ nF.
2. Therefore, $f = 1/(6.283 \times 10 \times 10^3 \times 4.7 \times 10^{-9}) = 3.386$ kHz.
3. Required minimum value of amplifier gain = 3.
4. Amplifier gain = $1 + [(R_2 + R_3)/R_1]$.
5. This gives $(R_2 + R_3)/R_1 = 2$, $R_1 = (22 \times 10^3 + 10 \times 10^3)/2 = 16 \times 10^3\ \Omega = 16$ kΩ.
6. Since the required gain has to be slightly greater than 3, preferred value of R_1 therefore should be slightly less than 16 kΩ.
7. R_1 may be chosen to be 15 kΩ.

EXAMPLE 12.9

Refer to the RC oscillator circuit of Figure 12.21. Identify the type of oscillator. Also, determine the operating frequency and preferred value of R_3.

Solution

1. It is Wien bridge oscillator.
2. Operating frequency is given by $\omega = 1/\sqrt{R_1R_2C_1C_2}$. Therefore, $\omega = 1/\sqrt{10^3 \times 100 \times 10^3 \times 0.1 \times 10^{-6} \times 10^{-9}} = 10^4$ rad/s.
3. $f = \omega/2\pi = 10^4/6.283$ Hz = 1.592 kHz.
4. Attenuation provided by feedback network is given by
$$|\beta| = R_2C_1/(R_1C_1 + R_2C_2 + R_2C_1)$$
$$|\beta| = (100 \times 10^3 \times 0.1 \times 10^{-6})/(10^3 \times 0.1 \times 10^{-6} + 100 \times 10^3 \times 10^{-9} + 100 \times 10^3 \times 0.1 \times 10^{-6})$$
$$= 10^{-2}/(10^{-4} + 10^{-4} + 10^{-2}) = 1/1.02$$
5. Therefore, minimum value of required gain = 1.02. That is, $1 + (R_4/R_3) = 1.02$, $R_4/R_3 = 0.02$.
6. $R_3 = 2.2 \times 10^3/0.02 = 110$ kΩ.
7. Since the required gain has to be slightly greater than 1.02, preferred value of R_3 therefore should be slightly less than 110 kΩ.
8. R_3 may be chosen to be 100 kΩ.

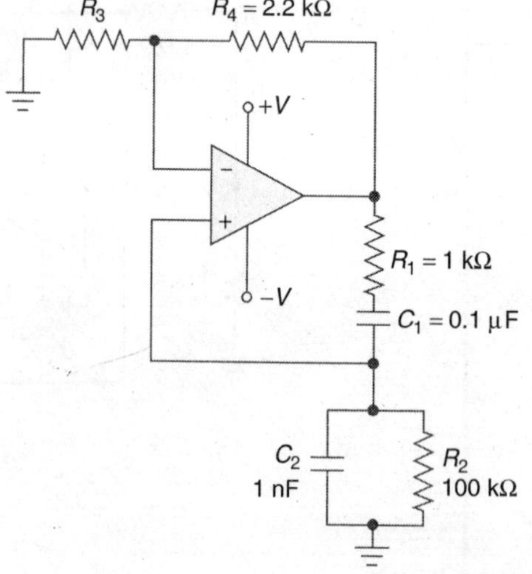

Figure 12.21 Example 12.9.

12.10 LC Oscillators

As outlined earlier, in essence, every oscillator has three main sections. These are the amplifier, the frequency-determining network and the feedback arrangement. The frequency-determining network decides the operating frequency and the feedback arrangement ensures that part of the output signal fed back to the input has the correct amplitude and phase at the operating frequency. In fact, the feedback network together with the amplifier ensures that Barkhausen criterion for sustained oscillations is satisfied at the operating frequency.

In the case of LC oscillators, the operating frequency is determined by an LC tank circuit and is given by $(1/2\pi\sqrt{LC})$. The exact frequency of oscillation is determined by $(1/2\pi\sqrt{LC}) \times \sqrt{Q^2/(Q^2+1)}$. Here Q is the quality factor of the tank circuit. The amplifier may be configured around a bipolar transistor, a junction FET, a MOSFET or an operational amplifier.

LC oscillators are usually classified by the name of its inventor. The common ones are Armstrong oscillator, Hartley oscillator, Colpitt oscillator and Clapp oscillator. They are also classified as series-fed or shunt-fed oscillators depending upon the manner in which DC power is applied to the active device. In the case of series-fed LC oscillators, DC power is applied to the active device through the tank circuit or a part of the tank circuit. In shunt-fed LC oscillators, DC power is applied through a separate path that is parallel to the tank circuit. Each of the LC oscillators mentioned in the preceding paragraph can be constructed either way.

Also, LC oscillators (Armstrong, Hartley, Colpitt and Clapp) are identifiable by the manner in which feedback signal is coupled to the input. In the case of Armstrong oscillator, the feedback signal is magnetically coupled [Figure 12.22(a)]. In the case of Hartley oscillator, a tapped or a split coil is used for the purpose [Figure 12.22(b)]. Split capacitor arrangement is used in the case of Colpitt and Clapp oscillators [Figure 12.22(c)]. Each of these oscillators is described in the following sections.

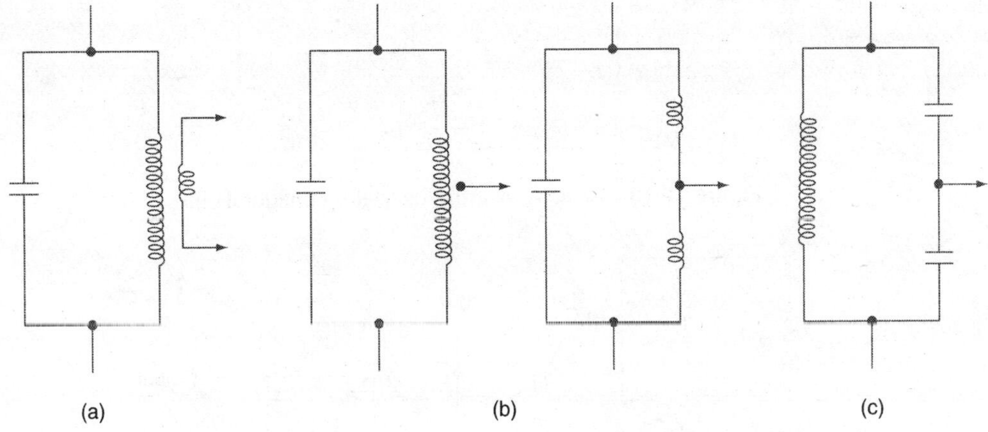

Figure 12.22 | Feedback coupling arrangement in LC oscillators.

12.11 Armstrong Oscillator

Armstrong oscillator, also known as Meissner oscillator, uses magnetic coupling as means of feeding part of output signal back to input to provide oscillations. It is also called a Tickler oscillator due to use of magnetic coupling between the tickler coil and the coupling coil. Tickler coil is the name given to a small coil connected in series with the plate circuit of a vacuum tube and coupled inductively to the grid circuit to provide feedback. In the case of a BJT or an FET, the tickler coil is placed in series with the collector or drain circuit and is inductively coupled to the base or gate circuit. A capacitor is placed across either the coupling coil or the tickler coil to form a tank circuit that decides the operating frequency.

Figures 12.23(a) and (b) show the basic circuit arrangements in the two cases with n-channel junction FET used as the active device. Biasing components are omitted for the sake of simplicity.

The frequency of oscillation is primarily determined by the tank circuit and is given by

$$f = \frac{1}{2\pi\sqrt{LC}} \tag{12.41}$$

Here L is the inductance of the coupling coil in the case of circuit shown in Figure 12.23(a) and that of tickler coil in the case of circuit shown in Figure 12.23(b). In practice, the frequency of oscillations is slightly different from the one computed by using Eq. (12.41) because of stray capacitances, loading of tank circuit, etc. The feedback factor in this case is given by ratio of mutual inductance between the two coils to the inductance in the tank circuit. Minimum gain required to start oscillations is reciprocal of the feedback factor.

Figure 12.24 shows the circuit schematic of an Armstrong oscillator configured around a bipolar junction transistor. The transistor is wired in common-emitter configuration and thus provides a phase shift of

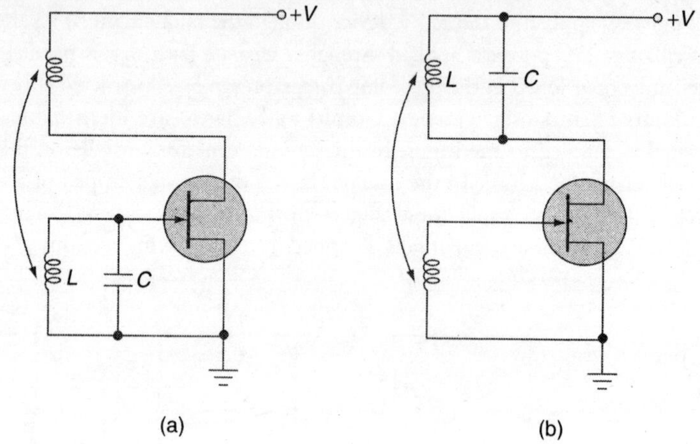

Figure 12.23 Basic Armstrong oscillator configurations.

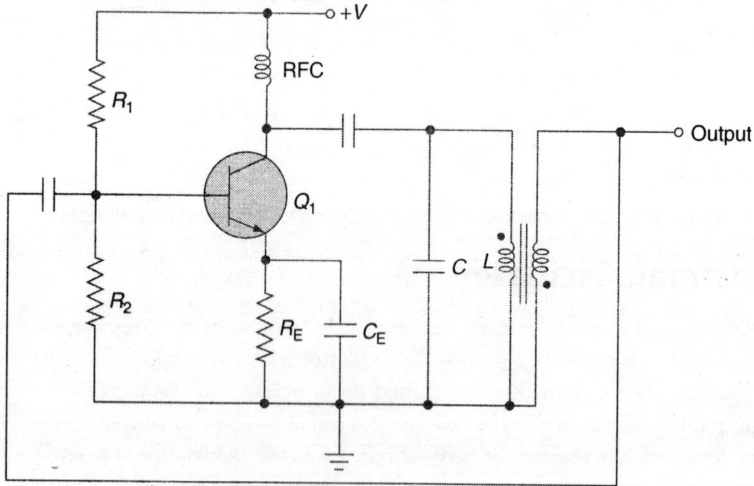

Figure 12.24 Shunt-fed Armstrong oscillator.

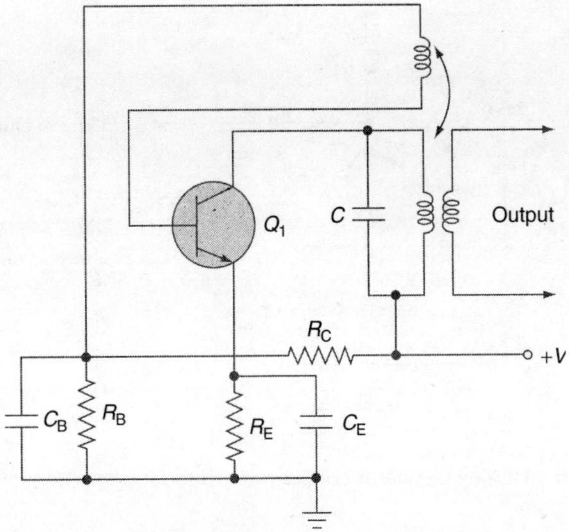

Figure 12.25 | Series-fed Armstrong oscillator.

180°. Another 180° phase shift is provided by magnetic coupling as indicated by placement of dots. Operating frequency is decided by tank circuit comprising capacitor C and inductance L of transformer primary. Note that Armstrong oscillator of Figure 12.24 is a shunt-fed oscillator. The circuit schematic of a series-fed Armstrong oscillator would look like the one shown in Figure 12.25.

12.12 Hartley Oscillator

Hartley oscillator uses a tapped or split coil for the purpose of generating feedback signal. This is where a Hartley oscillator differs from an Armstrong oscillator, which uses a separate coil called tickler coil. In the case of Hartley oscillator, current flowing through one section of the tapped coil induces a voltage in the other section to provide feedback. The feedback signal is 180° out-of-phase with the one that produces it.

Figure 12.26 shows the circuit schematic of Hartley oscillator configured around a bipolar junction transistor. Incidentally, the circuit shown is that of a series-fed oscillator. Figure 12.27 shows the Hartley oscillator configured around an opamp.

The attenuation factor and the phase shift provided by the feedback network can be determined from the transfer function of the feedback network. The feedback network in the present case is a π-network with capacitive series element and inductive shunt elements. The transfer function is given by

$$T(j\omega) = \beta = \frac{-\omega^2 L_2 C}{1-\omega^2 L_2 C} = \frac{-(1-\omega^2 L_1 C)}{\omega^2 L_1 C} \tag{12.42}$$

Negative sign implies phase shift of 180°. Also,

$$|\beta|^2 = \left[\frac{\omega^2 L_2 C}{1-\omega^2 L_2 C}\right] \times \left[\frac{1-\omega^2 L_1 C}{\omega^2 L_1 C}\right]$$

$$= \left(\frac{L_2}{L_1}\right) \times \left[\frac{1-\omega^2 L_1 C}{1-\omega^2 L_2 C}\right]$$

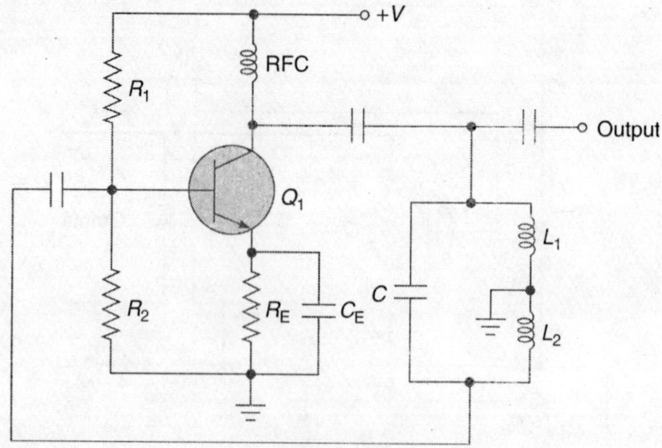

Figure 12.26 Hartley oscillator configured around bipolar junction transistor.

Substituting $\omega = 1/\sqrt{(L_1 + L_2)C}$, we get

$$|\beta|^2 = \left(\frac{L_2}{L_1}\right)^2 \tag{12.43}$$

$$|\beta| = \left(\frac{L_2}{L_1}\right)$$

Equations (12.42) and (12.43) imply that the feedback network introduces a phase shift of 180° and signal attenuation by a factor of (L_2/L_1) at the operating frequency (ω) provided that $\omega = 1/\sqrt{(L_1 + L_2)C}$. This further implies that the amplifier must provide a gain of greater than L_1/L_2 to satisfy the loop gain criterion and a phase shift of 180° to satisfy the loop phase shift criterion.

The advantage of using Hartley oscillator lies in its capability to generate a wide range of frequencies and its easy tunability.

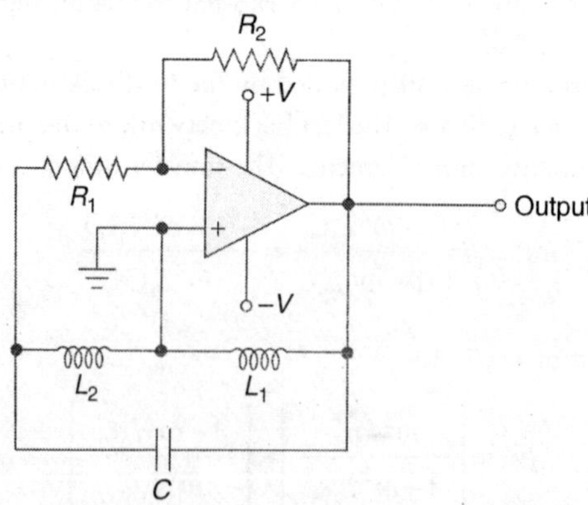

Figure 12.27 Hartley oscillator configured around opamp.

12.13 Colpitt Oscillator

Colpitt oscillator uses a pair of capacitors and an inductor in the tank circuit to produce the regenerative-feedback signal. In fact, the feedback network in this case is an electrical dual of the feedback network of Hartley oscillator. Figures 12.28 and 12.29 show the Colpitt oscillator circuits configured around bipolar junction transistor and opamp, respectively. An FET could also be used as the active device instead. As is obvious from the two circuit schematics, the output signal is developed across C_1 and the feedback signal is generated across C_2.

The attenuation factor and the phase shift provided by the feedback network can be determined from the transfer function of the feedback network. The feedback network in the present case is a π-network with inductive series element and capacitive shunt elements. The transfer function is given by

$$T(j\omega) = \beta = -(\omega^2 LC_1 - 1) = \frac{-1}{\omega^2 LC_2 - 1} \tag{12.44}$$

Negative sign implies phase shift of 180°. We will subsequently see that for $\omega = 1/\sqrt{LC_1C_2/(C_1 + C_2)}$, both $(\omega^2 LC_1 - 1)$ and $(\omega^2 LC_2 - 1)$ are positive.

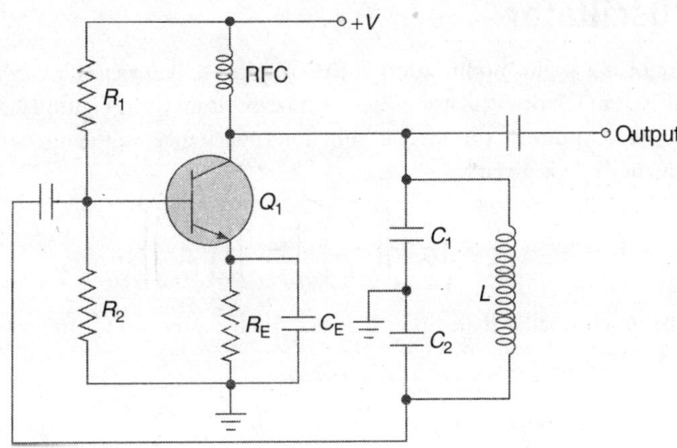

Figure 12.28 Colpitt oscillator configured around bipolar transistor.

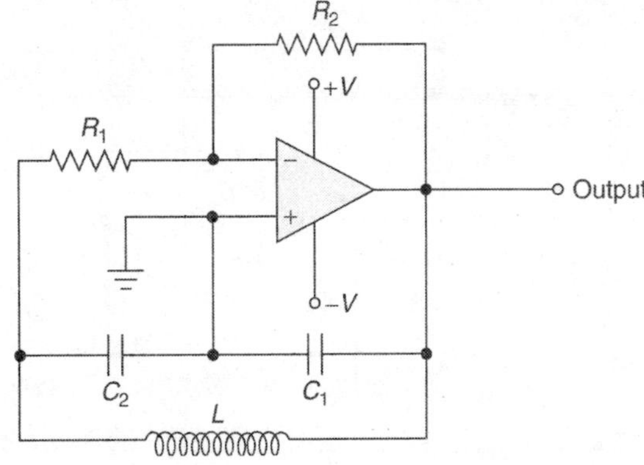

Figure 12.29 Colpitt oscillator configured around opamp.

Also,

$$|\beta|^2 = \frac{\omega^2 LC_1 - 1}{\omega^2 LC_2 - 1}$$

For $\omega = 1/\sqrt{LC_1C_2/(C_1+C_2)}$, this simplifies to

$$|\beta| = \frac{C_1}{C_2} \qquad \text{12.45)}$$

Equations (12.44) and (12.45) imply that the feedback network introduces a phase shift of 180° and signal attenuation by a factor of C_1/C_2 at the operating frequency (ω) provided that $\omega = 1/\sqrt{LC_1C_2/(C_1+C_2)}$. This further implies that the amplifier must provide a gain of greater than (C_2/C_1) to satisfy the loop gain criterion and a phase shift of 180° to satisfy the loop phase shift criterion.

In practice, the operating frequency is affected by the junction capacitance whose Miller components appear across C_1 and C_2. This is overcome in Clapp oscillator configuration.

12.14 Clapp Oscillator

Clapp oscillator circuit is a slight modification of the Colpitt oscillator circuit configuration. The feedback circuit in the case of Clapp oscillator uses an extra capacitor (C_3 in Figure 12.30) in series with the coil. The function of C_3 is to minimize the effect of junction capacitance on the operating frequency.

The operating frequency (f) is given by

$$f = \frac{1}{2\pi} \times \sqrt{\frac{1}{L} \times \left\{ \left(\frac{1}{C_1}\right) + \left(\frac{1}{C_2}\right) + \left(\frac{1}{C_3}\right) \right\}} \qquad (12.46)$$

If C_3 is chosen to be much smaller than either C_1 or C_2, then expression for frequency (f) simplifies to

$$f = \frac{1}{2\pi\sqrt{LC_3}} \qquad (12.47)$$

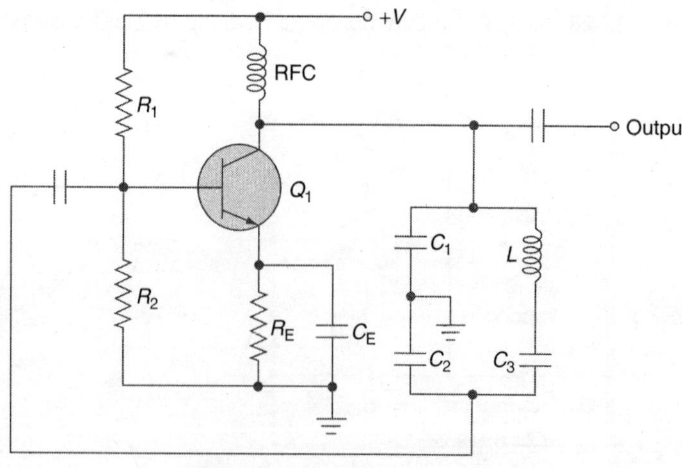

Figure 12.30 | Clapp oscillator.

Remember that we still need C_1 and C_2 to provide the required phase shift for regenerative feedback. Clapp oscillator is preferred over Colpitt oscillator for designing variable frequency oscillators. The adjustment of tuning element (C_3 in Clapp oscillator) does not alter the attenuation factor in Clapp oscillator. The attenuation factor is decided by C_1 and C_2. In the case of Colpitt oscillator, any attempt to vary the frequency by varying either C_1 or C_2 might cause cessation of oscillations over a portion of desired frequency range.

EXAMPLE 12.10 *Refer to the Armstrong oscillator circuit of Figure 12.31. Determine (a) frequency of oscillations and (b) minimum amplifier gain required to start oscillations. How would the oscillation frequency change if the loaded Q-factor of the tank circuit were given to be 5?*

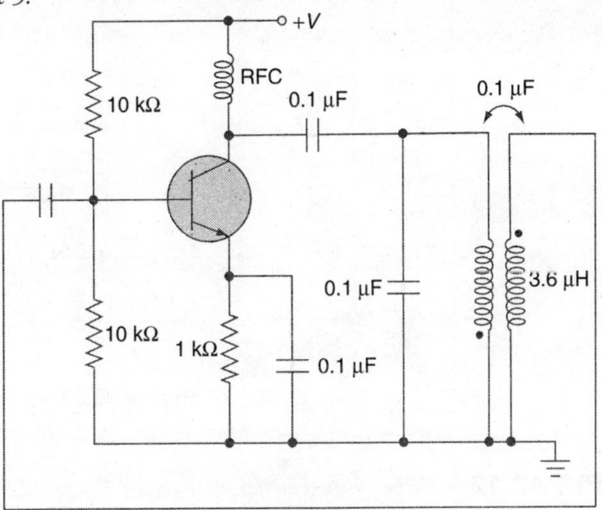

Figure 12.31 Example 12.10.

Solution

1. Frequency of oscillations, $f = 1/2\pi\sqrt{LC} = 1/(6.283\sqrt{3.6\times10^{-6}\times0.1\times10^{-6}})$ $= 265.3$ kHz.
2. Feedback factor $= 0.1 \times 10^{-6}/3.6 \times 10^{-6} = 1/36$.
3. Therefore, minimum value of amplifier gain required to start oscillations = 36.
4. Q-factor of the tank circuit = 5.
5. Frequency of oscillation will reduce by a factor equal to $\sqrt{Q^2/(Q^2+1)}$.
6. Therefore, new frequency of oscillations will be $265.3 \times 10^3 \times \sqrt{5^2/(5^2+1)} =$ 260.1 kHz.

EXAMPLE 12.11 *Refer to the Colpitt oscillator of Figure 12.32. Determine (a) frequency of oscillations and (b) minimum gain required to start oscillations.*

Solution

1. Equivalent value of capacitance, C, in the tank circuit
   $C = 0.1 \times 10^{-6} \times 0.01 \times 10^{-6}/(0.1 \times 10^{-6} + 0.01 \times 10^{-6}) = 0.009$ μF
2. Inductance, $L = 10$ μH.

3. Therefore, frequency of oscillations, $f = 1/(2\pi\sqrt{10\times10^{-6}\times0.009\times10^{-6}})$ = 530.5 kHz.
4. Feedback factor = $0.01 \times 10^{-6}/0.1 \times 10^{-6} = 1/10$.
5. Therefore, minimum value of amplifier gain = 10.

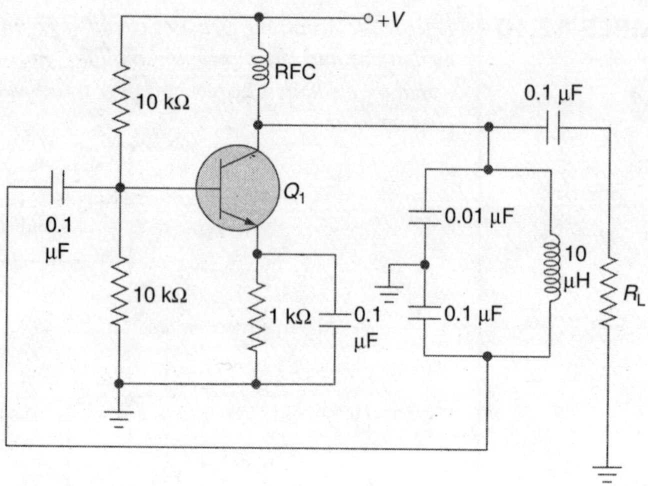

Figure 12.32 | Example 12.11.

EXAMPLE 12.12 *Refer to the Hartley oscillator of Figure 12.33. Determine (a) operating frequency and (b) maximum acceptable value of resistance (R) for oscillations to start.*

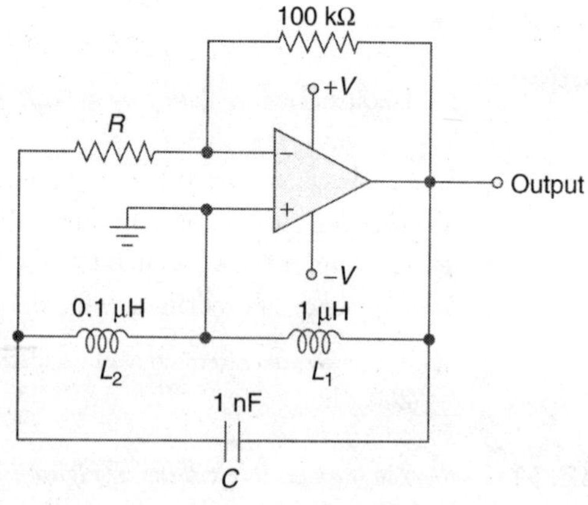

Figure 12.33 | Example 12.12.

Solution

1. Frequency of oscillations is given by $f = 1/2\pi\sqrt{LC}$.
2. $L = L_1 + L_2 = 1.0 \times 10^{-6} + 0.1 \times 10^{-6} = 1.1$ μH and $C = 1$ nF.

3. Therefore, $f = 1/(6.283 \times \sqrt{1.1\times10^{-6} \times 1\times10^{-9}}) = 4.799$ MHz.
4. Feedback factor = $(0.1\times10^{-6})/(1.0 \times 10^{-6}) = 0.1$.
5. Therefore, minimum required gain = 10.
6. Now, $|\text{gain}| = 100 \times 10^3/R$.
7. Therefore maximum value of $R = 10^5/10 = 10^4\ \Omega = 10\ \text{k}\Omega$.

EXAMPLE 12.13

Refer to the Colpitt oscillator of Figure 12.32. The circuit is slightly modified by connecting an additional capacitor of 1.0 nF in series with the inductance (L) as shown in Figure 12.34. Does the modified oscillator configuration resemble any standard oscillator configuration? Determine frequency of oscillations in this case.

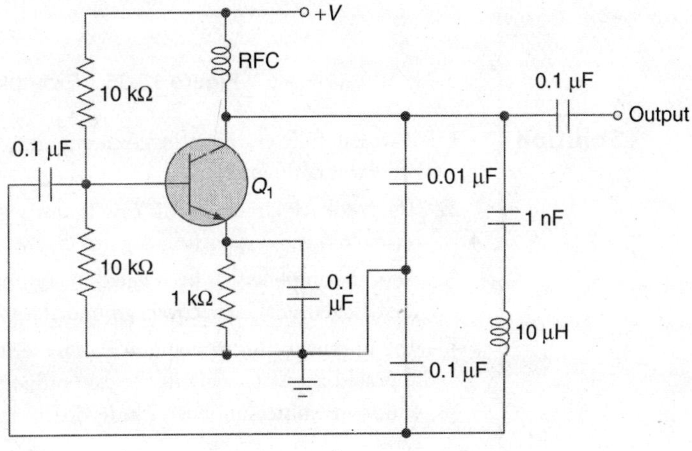

Figure 12.34 | Example 12.13.

Solution

1. The modified circuit is the Clapp oscillator configuration.
2. The frequency of oscillations is given by $f = 1/2\pi\sqrt{LC}$.
3. In the present case, C, is given by $1/C = (1/C_1) + (1/C_2) + (1/C_3)$.
4. Substituting for C_1, C_2 and C_3, we get $1/C = 1/(0.01 \times 10^{-6}) + 1/(0.1 \times 10^{-6}) + 1/(1 \times 10^{-9})$.
5. This gives $C = 0.0009$ µF.
6. Therefore, $f = 1/(6.283 \times \sqrt{10\times10^{-6} \times 0.0009\times10^{-6}}) = 1.677$ MHz.

EXAMPLE 12.14

Refer to the oscillator of Figure 12.35. Does the given oscillator circuit resemble any standard oscillator configuration? If yes, identify the oscillator configuration. Also, determine its frequency of oscillations and the required minimum value of amplifier gain.

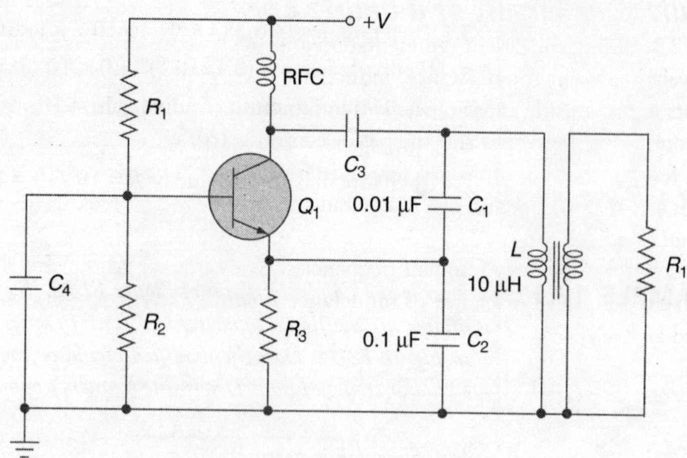

Figure 12.35 Example 12.14.

Solution

1. If we carefully examine the given circuit, we find that it follows the Colpitt oscillator configuration.
2. The feedback circuit in this case is also a tank circuit comprising a pair of series connected capacitors C_1 and C_2 and an inductor L.
3. Also, the amplifier has been wired in common-base configuration. Note that the base terminal is effectively grounded for AC signal through capacitor C_4.
4. The output in this case appears across series combination of C_1 and C_2. It appeared across C_1 only in the case of Colpitt oscillator configured around common-emitter amplifier. The feedback signal appears across C_2 in both the cases.
5. The feedback factor in this case is therefore given by $[C_1 \times C_2/(C_1 + C_2)]/C_2$, which simplifies to $C_1/(C_1 + C_2)$.
6. The required minimum value of amplifier gain is therefore $(C_1 + C_2)/C_1$.
7. Frequency of oscillations can be computed from $f = 1/2\pi\sqrt{LC}$, where $C = C_1 \times C_2/(C_1 + C_2)$.
8. Now $C = 0.01 \times 10^{-6} \times 0.1 \times 10^{-6}/(0.01 \times 10^{-6} + 0.1 \times 10^{-6}) = 0.009$ μF.
9. Therefore, $f = 1/2\pi\sqrt{10\times10^{-6}\times0.009\times10^{-6}} = 530.5$ kHz.
10. Feedback factor $= 0.01 \times 10^{-6}/(0.01 \times 10^{-6} + 0.1 \times 10^{-6}) = 1/11$.
11. Also, required minimum value of amplifier gain = 11.

12.15 Crystal Oscillator

In the case of a crystal oscillator, a quartz crystal with the desired value of resonant frequency forms part of the frequency-selective feedback network. Crystal oscillator is the natural choice when the accuracy and stability of oscillation frequency is of paramount importance. In order to understand the operation of crystal oscillators, it is important that we first study and analyze the AC equivalent circuit of the crystal as a component.

AC Equivalent Circuit of a Quartz Crystal

Figure 12.36 shows the circuit representation and AC equivalent circuit of the quartz crystal. R, L and C_S, respectively, represent the resistance, inductance and capacitance of the piezoelectric crystal element. C_M represents the mounting capacitance. It is in fact the capacitance due to the parallel-plate capacitor formed by the connecting electrodes and the piezoelectric element constituting the dielectric. Typically, R is in the range of few hundreds of ohms to a few kilo-ohms; L is of the order of few tens of milli-henries to few henries, C_S is a very small fraction of a pico-farad and C_M is few pico-farads. The Q-factor of the crystal is given by $Q = \omega L/R = 1/\omega C_S R$.

The crystal exhibits two resonant frequencies. One is the series resonant frequency f_S. It is the frequency at which the inductive reactance of inductance L equals the capacitive reactance of capacitance C_S. It is expressed as

$$f_S = \frac{1}{2\pi\sqrt{LC_S}} \tag{12.48}$$

Figure 12.37 shows the plot of reactance versus frequency for the equivalent circuit of Figure 12.36. Quite understandably, the impedance is a capacitive reactance below the series resonant frequency and an

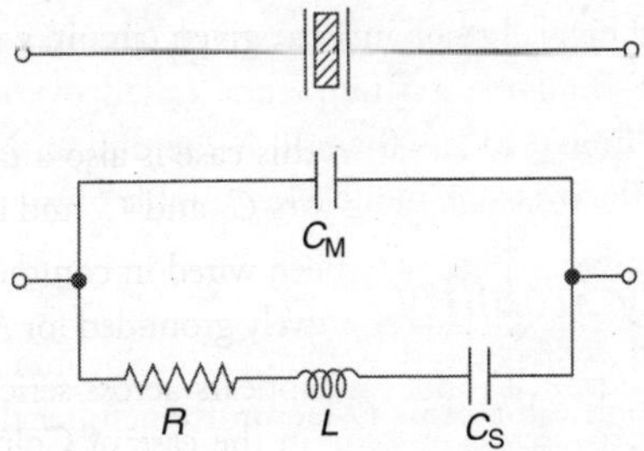

Figure 12.36 Circuit representation and AC equivalent circuit of a quartz crystal.

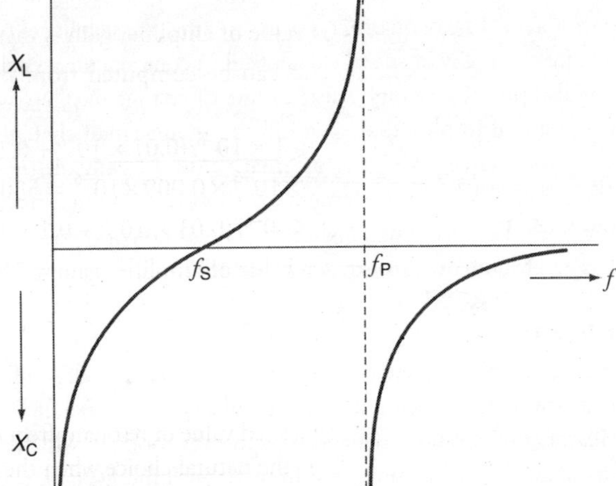

Figure 12.37 Reactance versus frequency plot of a quartz crystal.

inductive reactance above it. The second resonant frequency called the parallel resonant frequency (f_P) occurs at a value where the inductive reactance equals the capacitive reactance due to equivalent capacitance of the tank circuit. Parallel resonance occurs at a frequency where the circulating loop current is at its maximum. Since circulating loop current flows through series combination of C_S and C_M, therefore the equivalent capacitance of the parallel tuned circuit is given by

$$C_P = \frac{C_M \times C_S}{C_M + C_S} \tag{12.49}$$

Parallel resonant frequency is given by

$$f_P = \frac{1}{2\pi\sqrt{LC_P}} \tag{12.50}$$

Since C_S is much smaller than C_M, C_P is only marginally less than C_S with the result that f_S and f_P are very close to each other. The apparent difference between f_S and f_P as shown in Figure 12.37 is an exaggerated one to explain the operation of the crystal.

The two resonant frequencies described in the previous paragraph are the fundamental resonant frequencies. Remember that the specified crystal frequency is between f_S and f_P. This area of frequencies between f_S and f_P is known as the area of usual parallel resonance or simply the area of parallel resonance. A crystal can also resonate at harmonics of the fundamental frequency called overtones. The fundamental resonant frequency of the crystal is usually limited to less than 30 MHz due to the smallest physical dimension the crystal can be cut to. Operation in the overtone mode allows stable output at much higher frequencies.

Extremely High Frequency Stability

The extremely high frequency stability of a crystal oscillator comes from its extremely stable values of inductance and capacitance and a very high value of its *Q*-factor. Remember that the oscillation frequency of an *LC* oscillator in addition to the values of *L* and *C* also depends upon the *Q*-factor of the *LC* circuit. The generalized expression is given by

$$f = [1/(2\pi\sqrt{LC})] \times \sqrt{Q^2/(Q^2+1)} \tag{12.51}$$

A very high value of *Q*-factor in the case of quartz crystal ensures that the stability of oscillation frequency exclusively depends upon the operational stability of crystal elements. As a component, crystal is extremely stable.

A high value of *Q*-factor also produces a high value of rate of change of phase with respect to frequency ($d\theta/d\omega$), where θ represents phase. It implies that even infinitesimally small change in ω will produce a sufficient change in θ to restore the frequency to the original value. In general, the frequency-determining network of an oscillator should be made up of elements with extremely high operational stability and its Q-factor should be high. On both these accounts, quartz crystal has no competitor. It has *Q*-factor approaching tens of thousands and as a component, it is extremely stable.

Crystal Oscillator Circuits

As is evident from the impedance versus frequency characteristics of a crystal, depending upon the circuit characteristics, it can act like a capacitor, an inductor, a series-tuned circuit or a parallel-tuned circuit. There are a large number of crystal oscillator configurations depending upon the mode in which the crystal is used. In one of the categories of crystal oscillator, crystal is connected in series with the *LC* tank circuit in the feedback path. Each of the *LC* oscillator circuits discussed in Section 12.14 (Armstrong, Hartley, Colpitt and Clapp) can be configured as a crystal-controlled oscillator by connecting a crystal in series with the tank circuit.

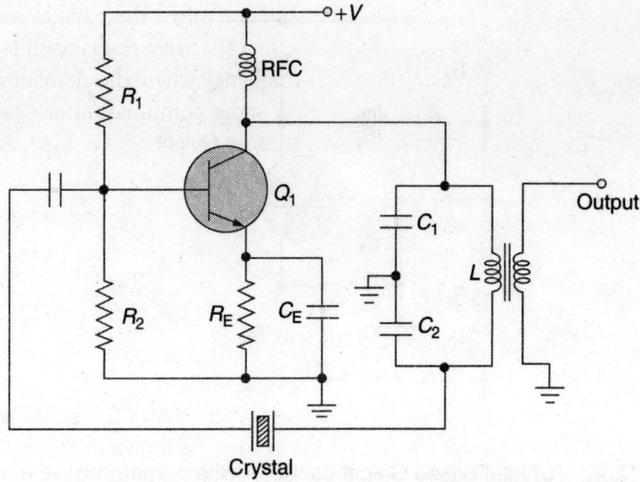

Figure 12.38 | Crystal-controlled Colpitt oscillator.

Figure 12.38 shows one such oscillator circuit. It is the modified Colpitt oscillator circuit. The circuit operates as follows. The *LC* tank circuit is tuned to the series resonant frequency of the crystal. The crystal offers minimum impedance at the series resonant frequency and thus allows the feedback signal to reach the input with practically no additional attenuation. A slight variation in frequency introduces very high impedance. The feedback signal is further attenuated to an extent that loop gain criterion is not met and the oscillations stop. Thus the oscillator can oscillate only at the resonant frequency of the crystal, thus significantly improving the frequency stability of the oscillator. Armstrong, Hartley and Clapp oscillator circuits can similarly be modified by introducing a quartz crystal in series with the respective tank circuits.

Figure 12.39 shows another variation of crystal-controlled Colpitt oscillator circuit. Here crystal forms a part of the tank circuit. The crystal acts like an inductor that resonates with capacitors C_1 and C_2. The resonant frequency is somewhere between the series and parallel resonant frequencies of the quartz crystal.

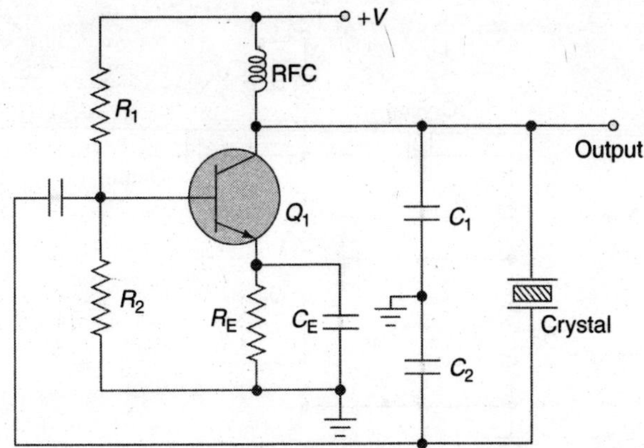

Figure 12.39 | Crystal-based Colpitt oscillator with common-emitter amplifier.

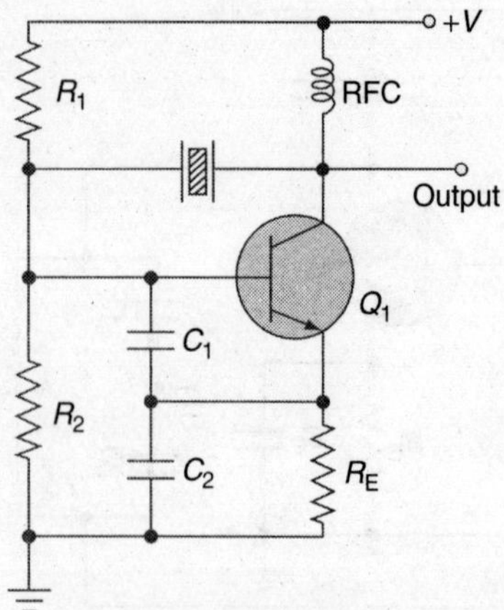

Figure 12.40 | Crystal-based Colpitt oscillator with common-base amplifier.

Figure 12.40 shows a slightly modified Colpitt oscillator circuit that uses common-base amplifier configuration instead of common-emitter configuration used in the oscillator circuit of Figure 12.39. Common-base amplifier configuration allows operation at relatively higher oscillation frequencies.

Yet another application of Colpitt oscillator configuration is found in what is popularly known as *Pierce oscillator*. Figure 12.41 shows the basic circuit implementation of a Pierce oscillator. An FET (JFET or MOSFET) is used as the active device and the crystal along with the inter-electrode capacitances C_{gs} and C_{ds} constitute the feedback network. Pierce oscillator of Figure 12.41 is redrawn in Figure 12.42 to demonstrate its resemblance to Colpitt oscillator configuration. The oscillation frequency is the parallel resonant frequency of the crystal and the inter-electrode capacitances do not play any role in determining oscillation frequency. The feedback factor and therefore the required amplifier gain are determined by C_{gs} and C_{ds}. In fact, it is observed that the oscillator stops oscillating as the oscillation frequency is reduced to below about 2 MHz due to insufficient feedback. In a situation like this, it becomes imperative to have external capacitors between gate-source and drain-source terminals. Pierce oscillator works very well in very high frequency (VHF) and ultra high frequency (UHF) frequency ranges. Purpose of putting radio-frequency choke (RFC) is to prevent the high-frequency output from getting grounded through drain power supply.

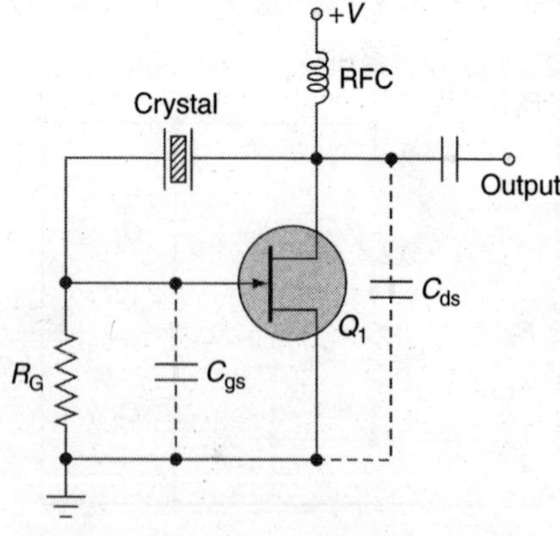

Figure 12.41 | Basic Pierce oscillator.

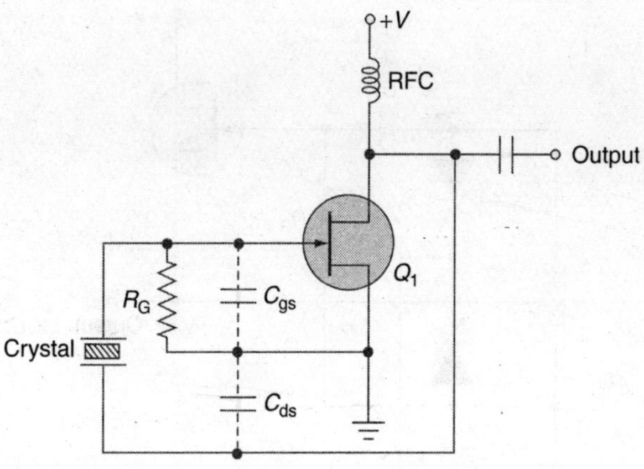

Figure 12.42 Basic Pierce oscillator

EXAMPLE 12.15 *A quartz crystal is characterized by L = 2.5 H, R = 1 kΩ, C_S = 0.01 pF and C_M = 10 pF. Determine the series and parallel resonant frequencies of the crystal.*

Solution

1. Series resonant frequency, $f_S = 1/2\pi\sqrt{LC_S} = 1/(6.283\sqrt{2.5\times 0.01\times 10^{-12}}$ = 1.006614 MHz.
2. Equivalent capacitance C_P for the parallel resonant circuit $C_P = 0.01\times 10^{-12}\times 10\times 10^{-12}/(0.01\times 10^{-12}+10\times 10^{-12})$ pF = 0.00999 pF
3. Parallel resonant frequency, $f_P = 1/2\pi\sqrt{LC_P}$.
4. Substituting the values, we get $f_P = 1/(6.283\sqrt{2.5\times 0.00999\times 10^{-12}})$ = 1.007117 MHz.

12.16 Voltage-Controlled Oscillators

A voltage-controlled oscillator (VCO) is an oscillator circuit in which the frequency of oscillations can be varied by an applied DC control voltage. This is achieved by having a voltage-dependent capacitor commonly known as varicap or a varactor diode as a part of the frequency-determining tank circuit.

Hartley and Clapp oscillator configurations are particularly suited to building VCOs as in both cases, the frequency-determining *LC* circuit has a single capacitor and tuning can be easily done by replacing this capacitor by a varactor diode. Figure 12.43 shows the basic voltage-controlled Hartley oscillator configured around a junction FET. A similar circuit could be configured around a bipolar transistor also. In the circuit shown in Figure 12.43, the amplifier is configured as common-drain amplifier with voltage gain slightly less than unity. In this case, the feedback factor is greater than one as the output signal appears across portion of the coil between source terminal and ground and the feedback signal appears across the whole of the coil winding.

Use of a single varactor diode is usually discouraged. This is because of the reason that for small values of DC control voltages, the varactor diode may start conducting at either of the peaks of the RF signal depending upon how it is connected in the circuit. Conducting diode reduces the Q-factor of the tank circuit and deteriorates the phase noise performance. Back-to-back connection of two varactor diodes overcomes this problem.

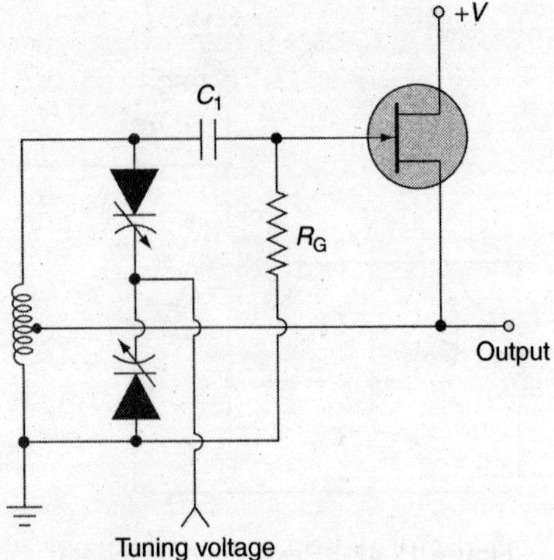

Figure 12.43 Voltage-controlled Hartley oscillator.

Another application of VCO is in fine tuning of crystal oscillators. The oscillator frequency may be varied by few tens of parts per million as the high value of *Q*-factor in the case of crystals allows pulling only over a small range. Fine tuning of crystal oscillator frequency may be needed to adjust output frequency to either match or be an exact multiple of some external reference. Voltage-controlled fine tuning of crystal oscillators may also be employed in temperature-compensated VCOs (TCVCXO) to correct the temperature dependence of oscillator frequency.

12.17 Frequency Stability

Frequency stability of an oscillator is a measure of its ability to maintain a constant oscillation frequency for as long a time period as possible. The oscillation frequency depends upon a large number of circuit features, which include circuit components, stray elements, supply voltages, characteristic parameters of active devices and so on. While one could pay due attention to choice of circuit components, use of clean and regulated supply voltages, etc., it may not be practical to identify location and estimation of magnitude of stray capacitances and inductances. This implies that it would be extremely hard to take remedial measures to counter the frequency drift caused by these elements. Equally impractical would be neutralizing the ill effects of instability of characteristic parameters of active devices.

Fortunately though, not all circuit features influence the oscillation frequency to the same extent. Oscillation frequency is usually far more sensitive to variation in a small number of circuit features than it is to the large number of remaining circuit features. For example, in the case of RC phase shift and Wien bridge oscillator circuits, frequency stability is largely dependent upon stability of *R* and *C*. Similarly, in an *LC* oscillator, it would mainly depend upon stability of *L* and *C*.

Frequency Stability Criterion

According to the frequency stability criterion, if there exists a small set of elements which introduces a large phase change ($d\theta$) for a given change in frequency ($d\omega$), then higher the value of $d\theta/d\omega$, more will be the dependence of ω on this set of elements as compared to its dependence on other circuit features. In the limit when $d\theta/d\omega$ approaches infinity; ω becomes independent of all other features and depends only on this small set of elements.

It can also be argued that $d\theta/d\omega$ is a measure of frequency stability of the oscillator and a higher value of $d\theta/d\omega$ means higher frequency stability. The argument goes as follows. Let us assume that one of the circuit features other than one of the elements of the small set mentioned above undergoes a variation. As a consequence of this variation, if the loop phase shift criterion were earlier satisfied at the operational frequency, it would no longer be satisfied after the variation takes place. The operational frequency must therefore shift in order to restore the loop phase shift back to zero. But if there were a small set of elements which at the nominal oscillation frequency produced a large change in phase for a given change in frequency, then the required frequency change to restore the loop phase shift condition would also be very small. This, in other words, means that the oscillator exhibits a high level of frequency stability.

This concept can be used to explain relatively higher frequency stability of *LC* oscillators in general, which improves with increase in the value of the *Q*-factor of the *LC* resonant circuit. It can similarly be used to explain the exceptionally high-frequency stability of crystal oscillators. In the case of *LC* oscillators, the reactance changes from capacitive to inductive around the frequency of resonance. Higher the *Q*-factor of the *LC* circuit, more abrupt is this change of phase. This further implies that higher *Q*-factor leads to a higher $d\theta/d\omega$ and consequently higher frequency stability. The frequency stability can be quantified by computing the magnitude of $d\theta/d\omega$ at the nominal oscillation frequency by differentiating the expression for the phase angle for the transfer function of the feedback network with respect to ω.

EXAMPLE 12.16 *Derive the relevant expression to prove that the Wien bridge oscillator exhibits better frequency stability at relatively lower oscillation frequencies and that the frequency stability deteriorates with increase in oscillation frequency.*

Solution

1. The expression for phase angle (θ) as a function of frequency (ω) in the case of Wien bridge oscillator can be written as $\theta = 90° - \tan^{-1}[3\,\omega RC/(1 - \omega^2R^2C^2)]$. This equation is obtained by substituting $R_1 = R_2 = R$ and $C_1 = C_2 = C$ in Eq. (12.36).
2. The above equation can also be written as $\theta = \tan^{-1}[(1 - \omega^2R^2C^2)/3\omega RC]$.
3. In general $(d/dx)(\tan^{-1}u) = [1/(1 + u^2)] \times du/dx$.
4. Using this formula, $d\theta/d\omega = KRC$, where K is a constant.
5. The above expression implies that product RC needs to have a higher value in order to have higher $d\theta/d\omega$ and therefore higher stability.
6. Higher RC means lower operating frequency.
7. This proves that the Wien bridge oscillator exhibits better frequency stability at lower oscillation frequencies and that the frequency stability deteriorates as the frequency of oscillation increases.

KEY TERMS

Armstrong oscillator
Barkhausen criterion
Bubba oscillator
Buffered RC phase shift oscillator
Clapp oscillator
Colpitt oscillator
Crystal oscillator
Frequency stability

Hartley oscillator	RC oscillators	Tickler oscillator
LC oscillators	RC phase shift oscillator	Twin-T oscillator
Meissner oscillator	Series-fed LC oscillator	Wien bridge oscillator
Pierce oscillator	Shunt-fed LC oscillator	Voltage-controlled oscillator
Quadrature oscillator	Tickler coil	

OBJECTIVE-TYPE EXERCISES

Multiple-Choice Questions

1. According to Barkhausen criterion for sustained oscillations,
   a. $\beta A < 1$.
   b. $\beta A > 1$.
   c. $\beta A = 1$.
   d. $\beta A = 0$.
2. The condition that decides the oscillator's output frequency is
   a. loop gain should at least be unity.
   b. loop phase shift should be zero or integral multiple of 2π radians.
   c. loop gain should be precisely unity.
   d. loop phase shift should be precisely zero radian.
3. In a conventional transistor RC phase shift oscillator using lead-type feedback network, frequency of oscillations is given by
   a. $f = \dfrac{1}{2\pi RC}$
   b. $f = \dfrac{1}{2\pi\sqrt{RC}}$
   c. $f = \dfrac{1}{2\pi\sqrt{6}RC}$
   d. $f = \dfrac{1}{2\pi\sqrt{3}RC}$
4. In a Wien bridge oscillator, frequency of oscillations is given by
   a. $f = \dfrac{1}{2\pi RC}$
   b. $f = \dfrac{1}{RC}$
   c. $f = \dfrac{1}{2\pi\sqrt{6}RC}$
   d. $f = \dfrac{1}{2\pi\sqrt{3}RC}$
5. Most popular oscillator configuration for audio applications is
   a. Hartley oscillator.
   b. Colpitt oscillator.
   c. Wien bridge oscillator.
   d. RC phase shift oscillator.
6. Which of the following oscillator types provides extremely stable output frequency?
   a. Hartley oscillator.
   b. Wien bridge oscillator.
   c. Crystal oscillator.
   d. Clapp oscillator.
7. Pick the odd-one out.
   a. Hartley oscillator.
   b. Colpitt oscillator.
   c. Clapp oscillator.
   d. Wien bridge oscillator.
8. Of the following, the oscillator with the most stable oscillation frequency is
   a. Clapp oscillator.
   b. Colpitt oscillator.
   c. Hartley oscillator.
   d. Armstrong oscillator.
9. The series and parallel resonant frequencies of a quartz crystal are
   a. the same.
   b. spaced far apart.
   c. very close to each other.
   d. in the range of tens of MHz.
10. The feedback network of a conventional RC phase shift oscillator uses

a. three lag-type RC sections.
b. three lead-type RC sections.
c. three RC sections of either lead or lag type.
d. twin-T notch filter.

11. In the case of a buffered RC phase shift RC oscillator, the required minimum value of amplifier gain is
a. 29.
b. 8.
c. 3.
d. 16.

12. According to the frequency stability criterion,
a. higher $|d\theta/d\omega|$ means higher frequency stability.
b. higher $|d\theta/d\omega|$ means lower frequency stability.
c. frequency stability is independent of $|d\theta/d\omega|$.
d. higher value of *Q*-factor means lower frequency stability.

Identify the Oscillator Configuration

Identify the oscillator circuits of Figure 12.44. Choose from Hartley oscillator, Colpitt oscillator, Clapp oscillator, Tickler oscillator, Pierce oscillator, Wien bridge oscillator, RC phase shift oscillator, Crystal oscillator, Bubba oscillator and Twin-T oscillator.

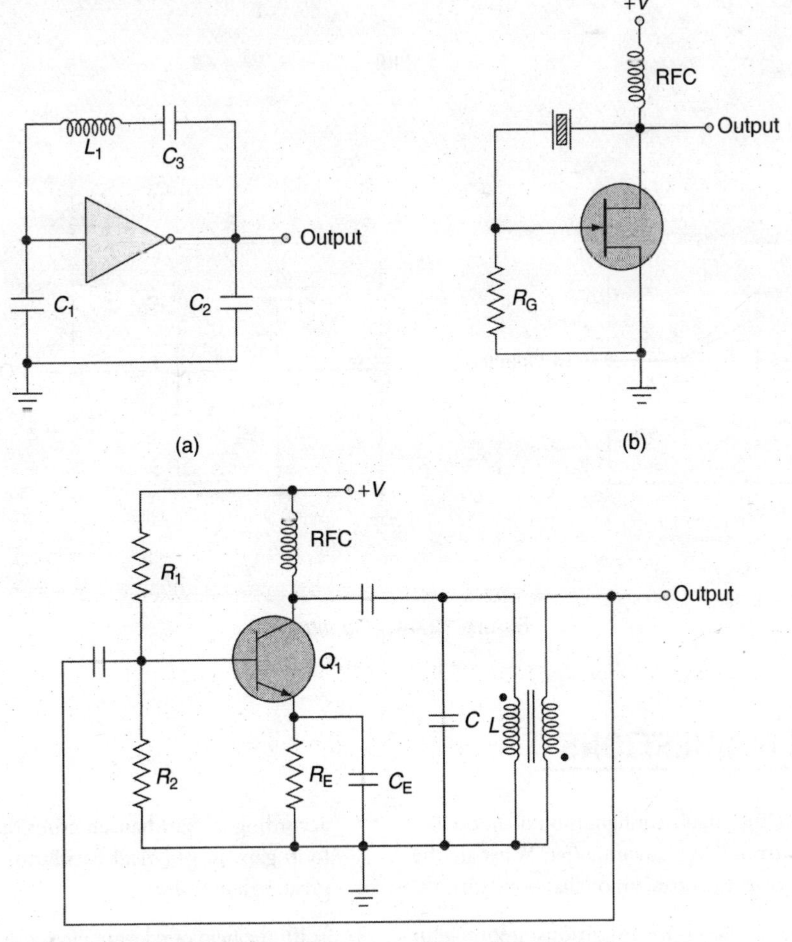

Figure 12.44 Identify the oscillator configuration.

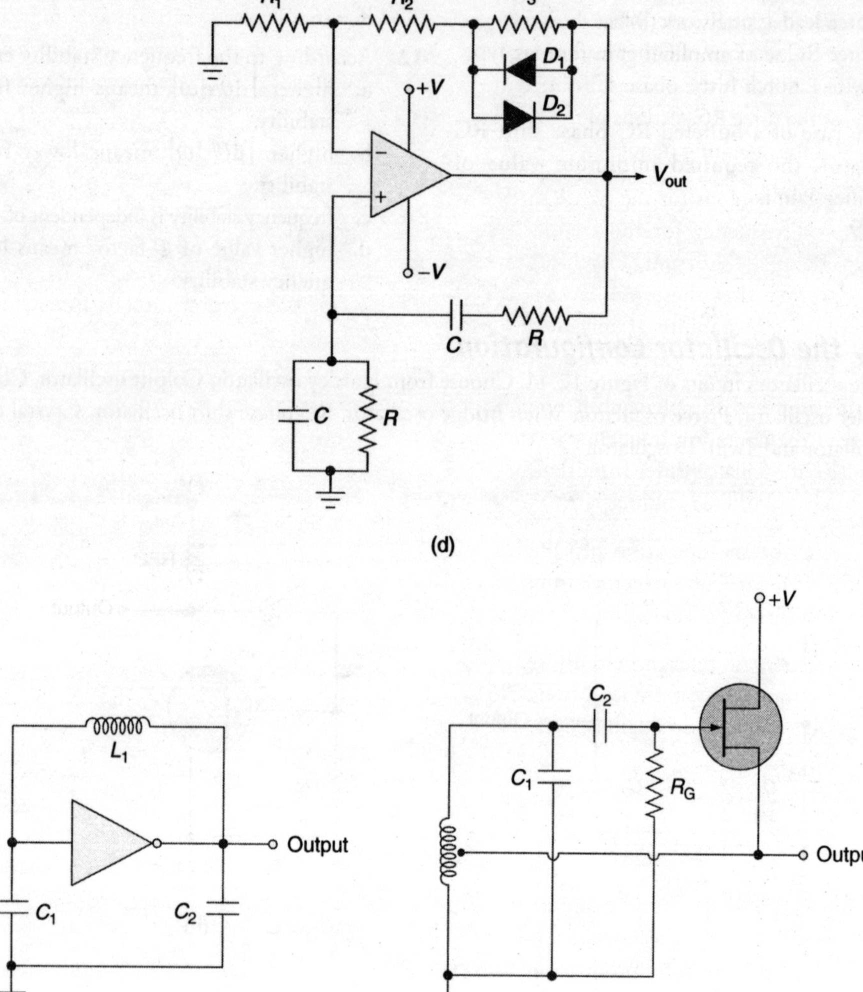

Figure 12.44 *Continued.*

REVIEW QUESTIONS

1. How does the circuit configuration of an oscillator differ from that of an amplifier? What are the different constituents of an oscillator circuit?

2. What are the necessary conditions of loop gain and loop phase shift for sustained oscillations according to Barkhausen criterion? Why is the loop gain in practical oscillators kept slightly greater than unity?

3. With the help of relevant circuit diagram, briefly describe the operation of an RC phase shift

oscillator configured around an opamp and a lead-type feedback network. What should be the minimum value of amplifier gain for sustained oscillations? What is the phase shift introduced by each of the three RC sections in the feedback network at the operating frequency?

4. Derive the expressions for the phase shift as a function of frequency for the feedback networks of RC phase shift and Wien bridge oscillators to prove that these oscillators exhibit better frequency stability at relatively lower operating frequencies.

5. What are buffered RC phase shift oscillators? How does the operating frequency in the case of a buffered oscillator differ from that of conventional non-buffered counterpart?

6. Briefly describe the operation of Quadrature oscillator with particular reference to its ability to produce sine and cosine outputs.

7. With the help of relevant circuit diagram, describe the operation of a Wien bridge oscillator configured around an opamp. What are the phase shifts introduced by the feedback and amplifier parts? Derive the relevant expression to prove that the amplifier should have a gain of at least 3 for sustained oscillations.

8. Why are LC oscillators not suitable for relatively lower frequencies? How does the frequency stability of an LC oscillator depend upon the *Q*-factor of the LC circuit?

9. What are crystal oscillators? What makes crystal oscillator exhibit exceptionally high frequency stability?

10. With the help of basic circuit diagram, briefly describe the operation of a Pierce oscillator. How does it differ from a Colpitt oscillator?

11. What is a voltage-controlled oscillator? Why is it important to use back-to-back connected varactor diodes instead of a single diode?

12. Briefly outline the frequency stability criterion in the case of oscillators. Which parameter can be used to quantify the frequency stability and why?

PROBLEMS

1. Figure 12.45 shows a possible RC phase shift oscillator configured around a junction FET and designed to produce a sinusoidal output at 6.5 kHz. Will this oscillator produce the output at the expected frequency? If not, why? Assume $g_m = 5000$ µmhos and $r_d = 10$ kΩ for the junction FET.

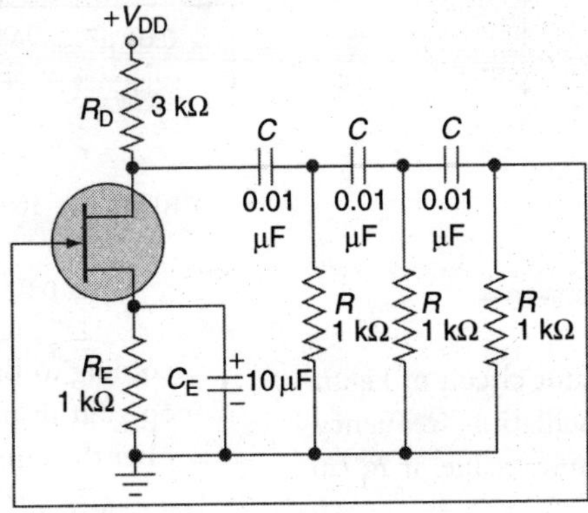

Figure 12.45 Problem 1.

2. Refer to the Wien bridge oscillator circuit of Figure 12.46. Determine different component values for this oscillator to produce a sine wave output at 10 kHz.

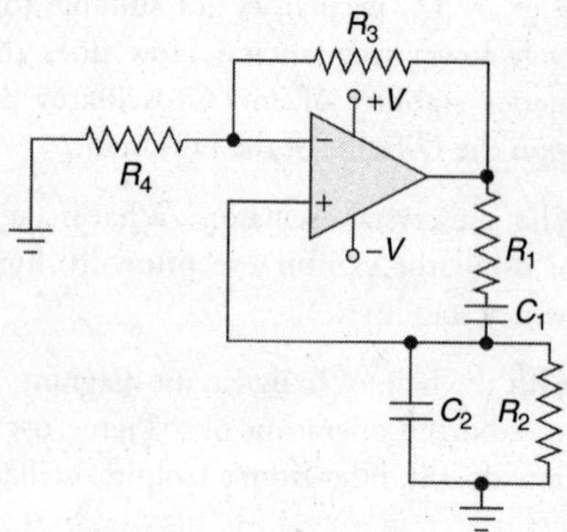

Figure 12.46 Problem 2.

3. Derive an expression to prove that in the case of a buffered RC phase shift oscillator using a lag-type feedback network, $|d\theta/d\omega|$ equals $RC/4$.

4. Refer to the Hartley oscillator circuit of Figure 12.47. Determine the oscillation frequency. Also determine the minimum value of R_1 for sustained oscillations.

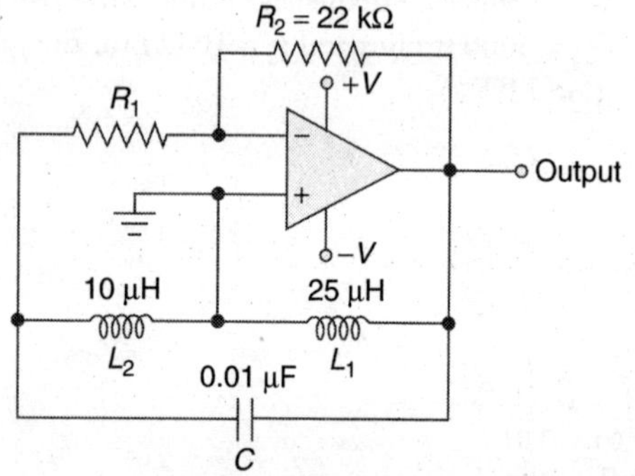

Figure 12.47 Problem 4.

5. Refer to the Colpitt oscillator circuit of Figure 12.48. Determine the oscillation frequency. Also determine the minimum value of R_1 for sustained oscillations.

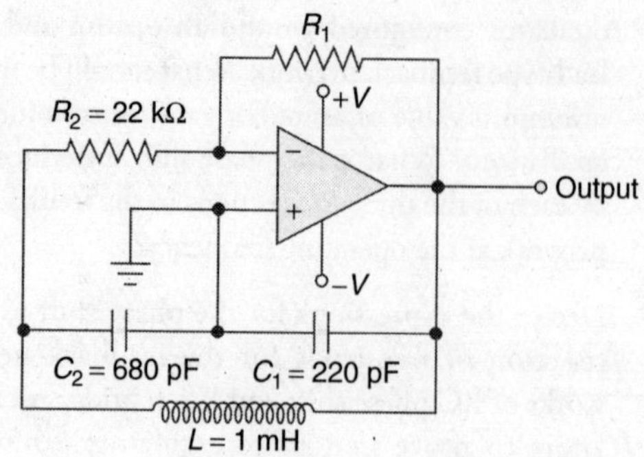

Figure 12.48 Problem 5.

6. An LC oscillator is observed to produce sine wave output at 10 MHz when the Q-factor of the LC circuit was 100. How would the operating frequency change if at all it would with the Q-factor dropping to 10?

7. Determine the minimum amplifier gain and the phase shift required to be introduced by the amplifier for the following cases.
   a. Feedback factor = 2%, oscillator type = Hartley oscillator
   b. Feedback factor = 5%, oscillator type = Wien bridge oscillator

8. A conventional RC phase shift oscillator operates at a frequency of 10 kHz. How would its operating frequency change if different RC sections were buffered and the feedback network used lead-type RC sections?

9. Refer to the RC oscillator of Figure 12.49. Determine oscillation frequency.

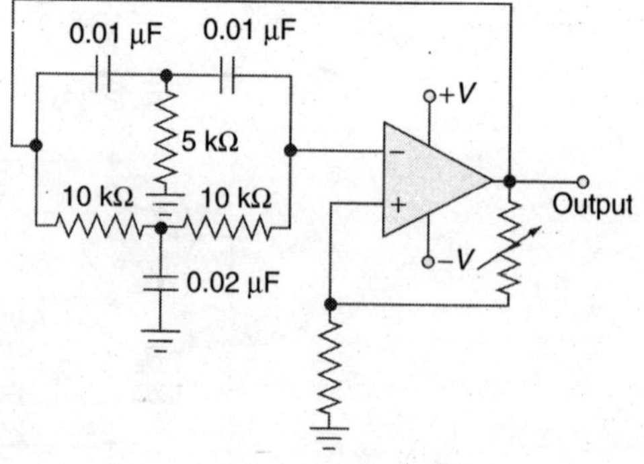

Figure 12.49 Problem 9.

10. A quartz crystal is characterized by series resistance, inductance and capacitance of 1000 Ω, 3 H and 0.05 pF, respectively. The mounting capacitance of the crystal is 10 pF. Determine (a) series resonant frequency of the crystal; (b) parallel resonant frequency of the crystal and (c) operating frequency of the oscillator using this crystal in Pierce oscillator configuration.

ANSWERS

Multiple-Choice Questions

1. (c)
2. (b)
3. (c)
4. (a)
5. (c)
6. (c)
7. (d)
8. (a)
9. (c)
10. (c)
11. (b)
12. (a)

Identify the Oscillator Configuration

Figure 12.44(a): Clapp oscillator

Figure 12.44(b): Pierce oscillator

Figure 12.44(c): Tickler oscillator

Figure 12.44(d): Wien bridge oscillator

Figure 12.44(e): Colpitt oscillator

Figure 12.44(f): Hartley oscillator

Problems

1. No, the gain criterion is not satisfied
2. $R_1 = R_2 = 1.59$ kΩ, $C_1 = C_2 = 0.01$ μF, $R_3 = 20$ kΩ, $R_4 = 10$ kΩ
4. $f = 269$ kHz, $R_1 = 8.8$ kΩ
5. $f = 390.4$ kHz, $R_1 = 68$ kΩ
6. 9.95 MHz
7. (a) Amplifier gain = 50, phase shift = 180°
   (b) Amplifier gain = 20, phase shift = 0°
8. 14.14 kHz
9. 1.592 kHz
10. (a) 411 kHz; (b) 412 kHz; (c) 412 kHz

CHAPTER 13

Wave-Shaping Circuits

Learning Objectives

After completing this chapter, you will learn the following:

- RC and RL low-pass and high-pass circuits.
- RC and RL integrator and differentiator circuits.
- Different types of diode-based clipping circuits.
- Basic clamping circuit, its limitations and practical clamping circuit.
- Bistable, monostable and astable multivibrator circuits configured around discrete semiconductor devices.
- Schmitt trigger circuit and its applications.
- Multivibrator circuits configured around digital integrated circuits.
- Multivibrator circuits configured around timer IC 555.

The topics discussed in this chapter include basic linear and non-linear wave shaping circuits like the RC and RL integrator, RC and RL differentiator, clipping circuits, clamping circuits and multivibrator circuits. Though a clamping circuit is not a wave-shaping circuit in the true sense, it has been chosen to be discussed here because the concepts relevant to the operation of clamping circuits are similar to those that explain the operation of RC wave-shaping and clipping circuits. A clamper circuit acts on an AC waveform, sinusoidal or non-sinusoidal, and gives it a DC level though it does not alter the wave shape. It is an important building block of voltage-multiplying circuits. Keeping in view the scope of the present text, a separate chapter on clamping circuits would not be justified.

13.1 Basic RC Low-Pass Circuit

Figure 13.1 shows the basic RC low-pass circuit comprising a single-section RC circuit with output taken across the capacitor. The output voltage is given by

$$V_o = \left(\frac{X_C}{\sqrt{R^2 + X_C{}^2}}\right) \times V_i \tag{13.1}$$

Qualitatively, since the output is taken across the capacitor and the reactance of a capacitor is inversely proportional to the frequency, the output voltage will fall with increase in frequency (Figure 13.2). That is how

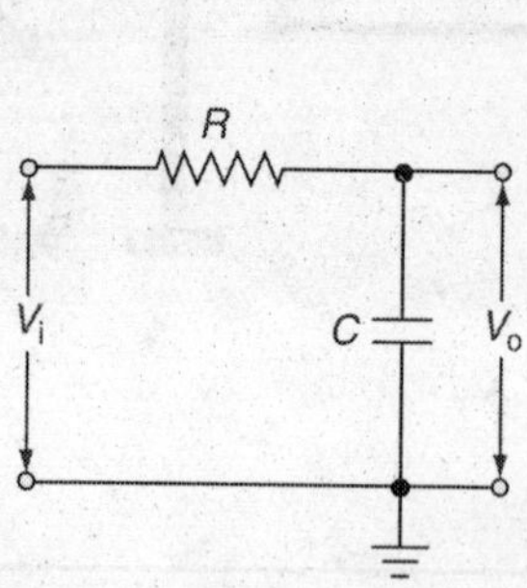

Figure 13.1 | RC low-pass circuit.

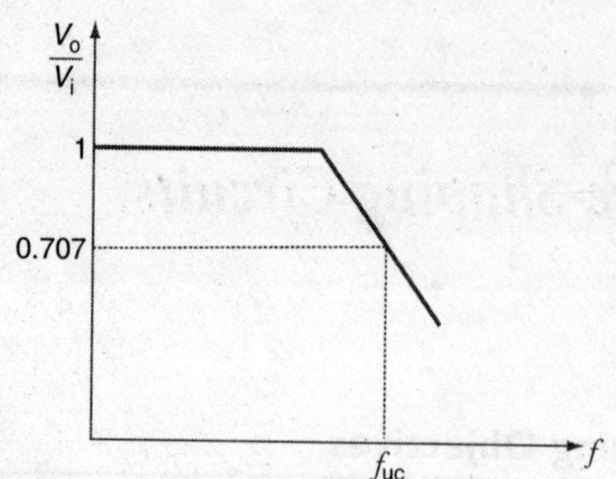

Figure 13.2 | Frequency response of a RC low-pass circuit.

an RC network of the type shown in Figure 13.1 behaves as a low-pass circuit. The upper 3 dB cut-off frequency is the frequency at which output amplitude is 0.707 times (or 3 dB below) the nominal maximum amplitude. The nominal maximum output amplitude is same as the input amplitude; therefore, the ratio (V_o/V_i) equals 0.707 at 3 dB cut-off frequency.

The ratio (V_o/V_i) becomes 0.707 when the resistance (R) equals capacitive reactance (X_C). Therefore, the cut-off frequency (f_{uc}) is given by

$$f_{uc} = \frac{1}{2\pi RC} \tag{13.2}$$

We will now study the behavior of this circuit toward step and pulse inputs.

Step Input

For a step input (V_i) of Figure 13.3(a), the output voltage (V_o), which is also voltage across C, rises exponentially towards the final value of V with a time constant (RC). The output voltage (V_o) is given by

$$V_o = V(1 - e^{-t/RC}) \tag{13.3}$$

This expression is valid only when the capacitor is initially fully discharged. If the capacitor were initially charged to a voltage V_o, less than V, then the exponential charging equation would be

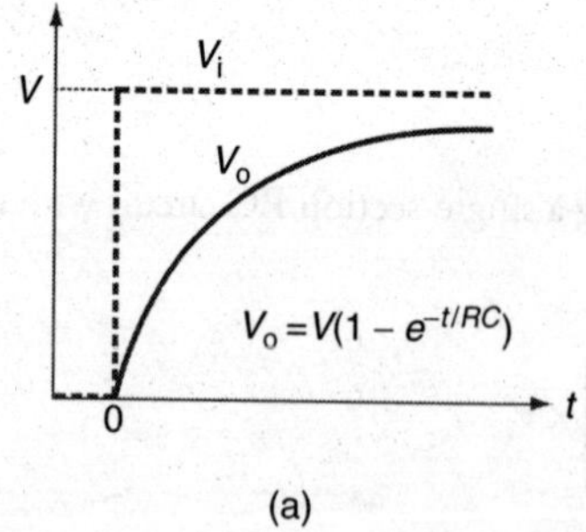

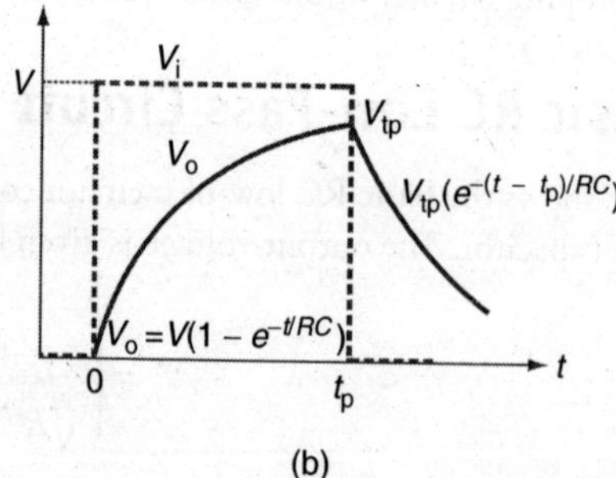

Figure 13.3 | (a) Step response of low-pass circuit; (b) pulse response of low-pass circuit.

$$V_o = V - (V - V_o)e^{-t/RC} \tag{13.4}$$

If this input step occurs at time $t = t_1$, then the following equation represents the charging process:

$$V_o = V[1 - e^{-(t-t_1)/RC}] \tag{13.5}$$

Pulse Input

For the pulse input of Figure 13.3(b), output (V_o) during the high time of the pulse is given by

$$V_o = V(1 - e^{-t/RC}) \tag{13.6}$$

At $t = t_p$, the amplitude of the output voltage is given by

$$V_o(t = t_p) = V(1 - e^{-t_p/RC}) = V_{tp} \tag{13.7}$$

The output (V_o) during the low time of the pulse is given by

$$V_o = V_{tp}(e^{-(t-t_p)/RC}) \tag{13.8}$$

We are often interested in knowing the quality with which the leading and the trailing edges will be passed through the RC low-pass circuit. Such a situation arises particularly in the analysis of high-frequency amplifiers where the amplifier input has a finite capacitance and this capacitance along with source resistance constitutes a low-pass RC network. We will see that the capability of the network to pass fast transitions depends upon the upper 3 dB cut-off frequency of the network.

The quality with which this network reproduces fast transitions is expressed by the magnitude of the rise time (t_r) which is the time taken by the output to change from 10% to 90% of the impressed transition or step. From the exponential charging relationship, it can be verified that

$$t_r = 2.2\,RC \tag{13.9}$$

The relationship between the upper 3 dB cut-off frequency (f_{uc}) and the rise time (t_r) is given by

$$f_{uc} = \frac{0.35}{t_r} \tag{13.10}$$

where f_{uc} is specified in MHz and t_r is specified in μs. This expression indicates that higher the upper 3 dB cut-off frequency, smaller is the rise time. Therefore, for faithful reproduction of fast transitions, f_{uc} should be as high as possible.

13.2 RC Low-Pass Circuit as Integrator

If the circuit shown in Figure 13.1 is an integrator circuit, the output voltage V_o should be integral of the input voltage (V_i), that is,

$$V_o = K\int V_i \mathrm{d}t$$

where K is a constant. In the given RC circuit, if the product RC is much larger than the time period (T) of the applied input, the capacitor voltage (or the output voltage in the present case) would change by only a very small amount as the input goes through a complete cycle. In such a case, it is not wrong to assume that whole of input voltage (V_i) appears across the resistor (R) only. As a result current (I_i) can be expressed as

$$I_i = \frac{V_i}{R}$$

The output voltage (V_o) across the capacitor is given by

$$V_o = \frac{1}{C}\int I_i dt = \frac{1}{C}\int \frac{V_i}{R} dt = \frac{1}{RC}\int V_i dt \qquad (13.11)$$

Therefore, output voltage (V_o) is integral of input voltage (V_i) provided that the time constant is much larger than the time period of the input signal, that is, $RC >> T$. In fact, if $RC \geq 15T$ integration is near ideal.

EXAMPLE 13.1 *Refer to Figure 13.4. Determine the amplitude of V_o at the time of input pulse going low and also 1 ms after it has gone low.*

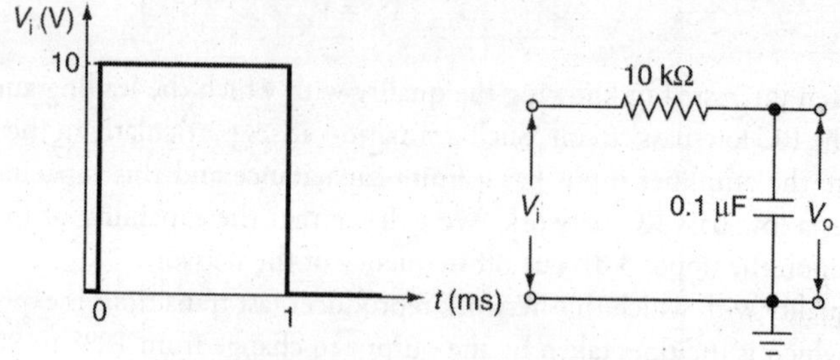

Figure 13.4 | Example 13.1.

Solution

1. The time constant = $R \times C = 10 \times 10^3 \times 0.1 \times 10^{-6} = 10^{-3}$ s = 1 ms.
2. Coincidentally, the time constant equals the pulse width. The output V_o will be 63.1% of the final value of 10 V, that is, $V_o = 6.31$ V at the time of pulse going high to low.
3. In general, the charging process is governed by the expression

$$V_o = V(1 - e^{-t/RC})$$

For t = RC, output voltage V_o is 63.1% of the final voltage (V).

4. When the input pulse goes low, the capacitor starts discharging as per

$$V_o = V'(e^{-(t-t_p)/RC})$$

Here, $V' = 6.31$ V and $t_p = 1$ ms. Again V_o will be 36.9% of (V') 1 ms after the capacitor starts discharging as 1 ms happens to be equal to circuit time constant. Therefore, the output voltage after 1 ms = 0.369 × 6.31 V = 2.33 V.

5. The output waveform is shown in Figure 13.5.

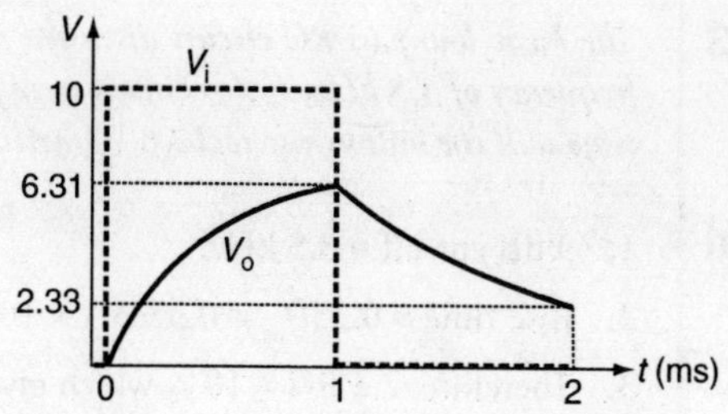

Figure 13.5 | Solution to Example 13.1.

EXAMPLE 13.2 *How will the circuit of Figure 13.6(a) respond to a 10 V step input of Figure 13.6(b)? In what time will the output rise from 1 V to 9 V?*

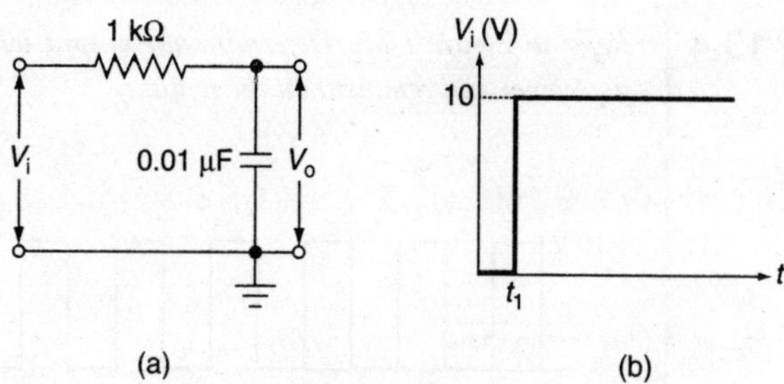

Figure 13.6 | Example 13.2.

Solution

1. Circuit time constant = $RC = 10^3 \times 0.01 \times 10^{-6} = 10\ \mu s$.
2. The response is governed by the equation

$$V_o = 10(1 - e^{-t/10^{-5}})$$

$$= 10(1 - e^{-10^5 t})$$

3. For $t = 10\ \mu s$, $V_o = 10(1 - e^{-1}) = 0.631 \times 10 = 6.31$ V.
4. The output voltage (V_o) is shown in Figure 13.7.
5. The time taken for the output voltage (V_o) to rise from 1 V to 9 V is equal to the rise time (t_r):

$$t_r = 2.2RC = 2.2 \times 10^3 \times 0.01 \times 10^{-6} = 22\ \mu s$$

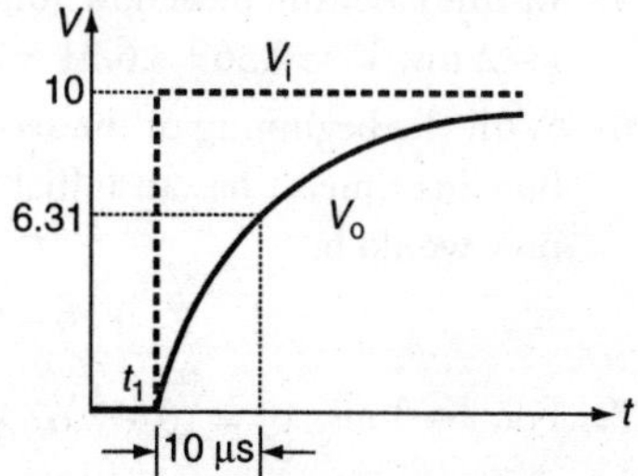

Figure 13.7 | Solution to Example 13.2.

EXAMPLE 13.3 *The basic low-pass RC circuit discussed in the previous examples has 3 dB cut-off frequency of 3.5 kHz. If this circuit were fed at the input with a 20 V step, in what time will the output rise to 12.6 V starting from the time of receiving the step?*

Solution

1. 3 dB cut-off = 3.5 kHz.
2. Rise time = $0.35/f_{uc} = 0.35/3.5 \times 10^3 = 10^{-4}$ s.
3. Therefore, 2.2 RC = 10^{-4}, which gives RC = $10^{-4}/2.2 = 45.5$ μs.
4. The output will rise to 12.6 V (which is 63% of the final value of 20 V) in 45.5 μs (=time constant).

EXAMPLE 13.4 *Refer to Figure 13.8. Determine the output waveform (V_o) for 10 cycles of input waveform and comment on the results.*

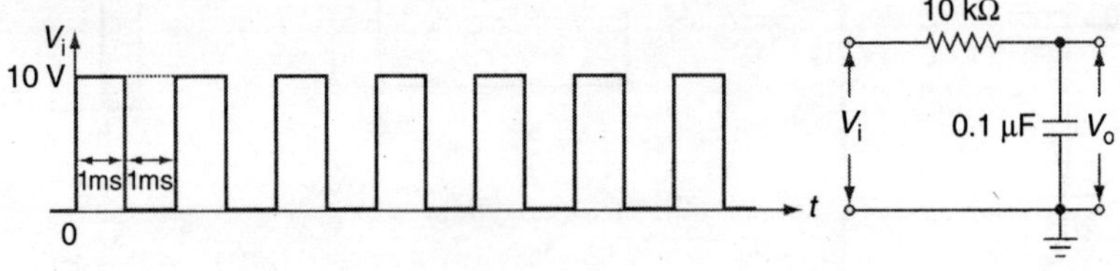

Figure 13.8 Example 13.4.

Solution

1. With the leading edge of the first cycle, the capacitor starts charging and charging is governed by the following equation, $V_o = 10(1 - e^{-t/RC})$.
2. The time constant = RC = $10 \times 10^3 \times 0.1 \times 10^{-6} = 10^{-3}$ s = 1 ms.
3. Since the pulse high time equals the time constant (= 1 ms), the output will rise to 6.31 V at the end of the first pulse.
4. The capacitor starts discharging from the time instant of the trailing edge of the first pulse and the discharge equation is given by
$$V_o = 6.31(e^{-(t-10^{-3})/RC})$$
5. In this case, the pulse low time also equals the time constant. Therefore, at $t = 2$ ms, $V_o = 0.369 \times 6.31 = 2.33$ V.
6. With the beginning of the second pulse, the capacitor starts charging again but this time, it has an initial voltage of 2.33 V and the charging equation now would be
$$V_o = 10 - (10 - 2.33)e^{-(t-2\times10^{-3})/10^{-3}}$$
7. For, $t = 3$ ms, $V_o = 10 - 7.67 \times e^{-1} = 7.18$ V.
8. For $t = 4$ ms, $V_o = 7.18 \times 0.369 = 2.65$ V.

9. Similarly, at $t = 5$ ms,

$$V_o = 10 - (10 - 2.65) \times e^{-1} = 10 - 7.35 \times e^{-1} = 7.3 \text{ V}$$

10. At $t = 6$ ms, $V_o = 7.3 \times 0.369 = 2.69$ V.
11. At $t = 7$ ms, $V_o = 10 - (10 - 2.69) \times e^{-1} = 10 - 7.31 \times e^{-1} = 7.31$ V.
12. At $t = 8$ ms, $V_o = 7.31 \times 0.369 = 2.70$ V.
13. At $t = 9$ ms, $V_o = 10 - (10 - 2.70) \times e^{-1} = 10 - 7.30 \times e^{-1} = 7.31$ V.
14. At $t = 10$ ms, $V_o = 7.31 \times 0.369 = 2.70$ V.
15. In the subsequent cycles, the output will swing between 2.70 V and 7.31 V. It is clear from the above calculations that the steady state is achieved after four cycles. It can be verified that if the circuit time constant is much smaller than the input waveform time period, the steady state would be arrived at very quickly, most likely in the first cycle itself. If the time constant is much larger than the input waveform period, it would require comparatively larger number of cycles to reach steady state. Figure 13.9 shows the output waveform.

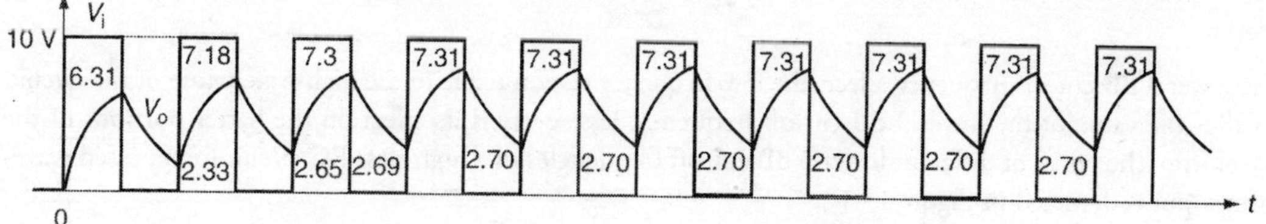

Figure 13.9 | Solution to Example 13.4.

13.3 Basic RC High-Pass Circuit

Figure 13.10 shows the basic RC high-pass circuit. The operation of this circuit can be explained on lines similar to the description of RC low-pass circuit. The output voltage (V_o) is given by

$$V_o = \left(\frac{R}{\sqrt{R^2 + X_C^2}} \right) \times V_i \tag{13.12}$$

Since the reactance of a capacitor is inversely proportional to the frequency, it would increase with decrease in frequency. Consequently, the output voltage falls with decrease in frequency of the input waveform thus lending the circuit of Figure 13.10 its high-pass characteristics as shown in Figure 13.11. The frequency where the ratio V_o/V_i falls to 0.707 of its maximum value is known as the lower 3 dB cut-off frequency. Expression for lower 3 dB cut-off frequency can be computed as follows:
At the lower 3 dB cut-off frequency (f_{lc}),

$$\frac{V_o}{V_i} = \frac{R}{\sqrt{R^2 + X_C^2}} = 0.707$$

Therefore at f_{lc},

$$R = X_C$$

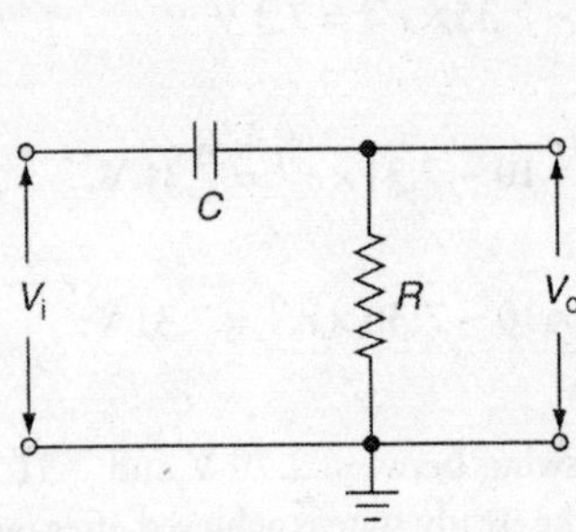

Figure 13.10 | RC high-pass circuit.

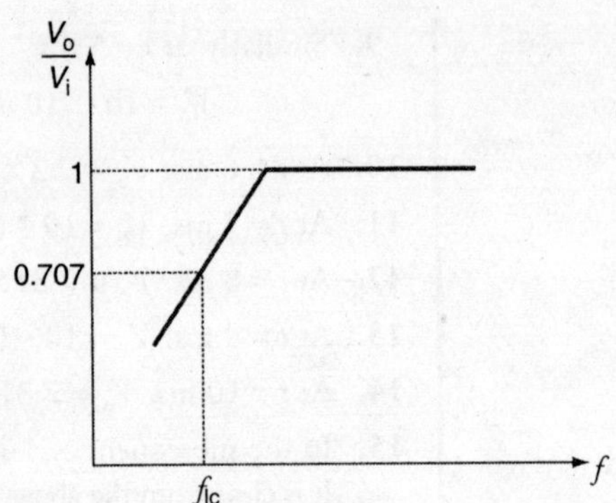

Figure 13.11 | Frequency response of high-pass circuit.

The lower 3 dB cut-off frequency is given by

$$f_{lc} = \frac{1}{2\pi RC} \tag{13.13}$$

The lower 3 dB cut-off frequency affects the low-frequency response due to the high-pass nature of the circuit. Smaller the value of the lower 3 dB cut-off frequency, less severe is its effect on the flatter portions of the waveform. The effect of different lower 3 dB cut-off frequencies in a high-pass RC circuit for a pulsed waveform input is depicted in Figure 13.12.

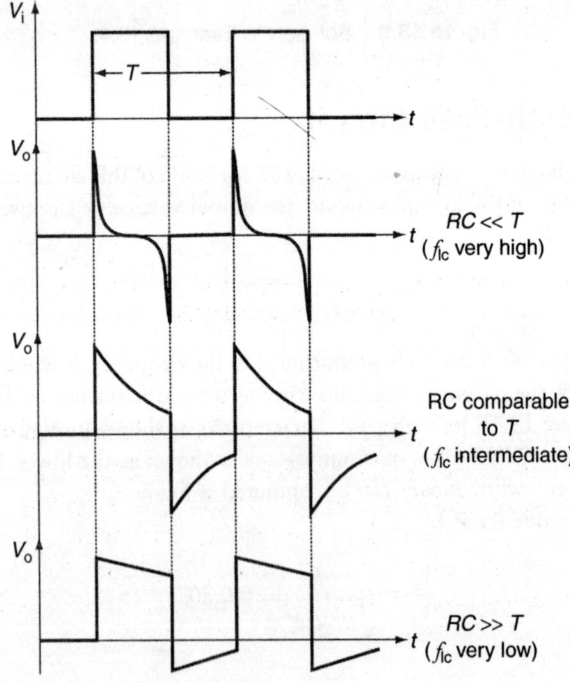

Figure 13.12 | Effect of lower 3 dB cut-off frequency on pulsed waveform input.

13.4 RC High-Pass Circuit as Differentiator

A differentiator circuit is the one in which the output response is proportional to the differential of the input excitation. In other words, the output is proportional to the slope of the input. In the case of the RC circuit of Figure 13.10 where the output is taken across R, if the time constant (RC) is much smaller than the input waveform time period, it is safe to assume that whole of input (V_i) appears across (C) only as the input goes through one complete cycle. The current (I_i) flowing in the circuit is given by

$$I_i = C\frac{dV_i}{dt}$$

The output voltage (V_o) is given by

$$V_o = I_i \times R$$

$$V_o = RC\frac{dV_i}{dt} \propto \frac{dV_i}{dt} \quad (13.14)$$

This explains why RC high-pass circuit behaves as a differentiator under specified conditions.

EXAMPLE 13.5 *Refer to Figure 13.13. Sketch the output waveform preferably without doing any mathematical calculations.*

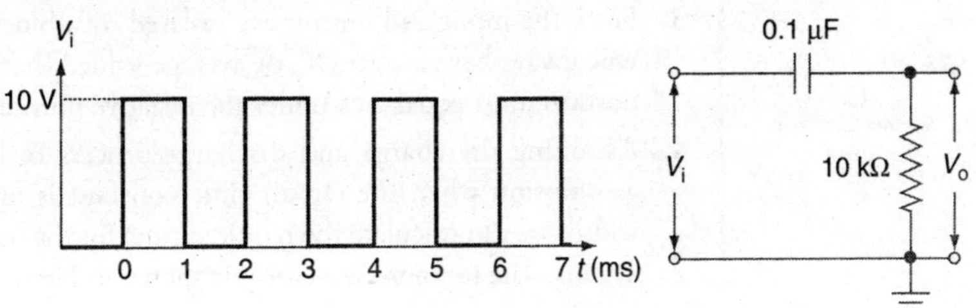

Figure 13.13 Example 13.5.

Solution

1. The output waveform is shown Figure 13.14. The waveform is self-explanatory. The fact that the circuit time constant is 1 ms and so are the high and low times of the input waveform, all voltage levels can be determined without doing any calculations.

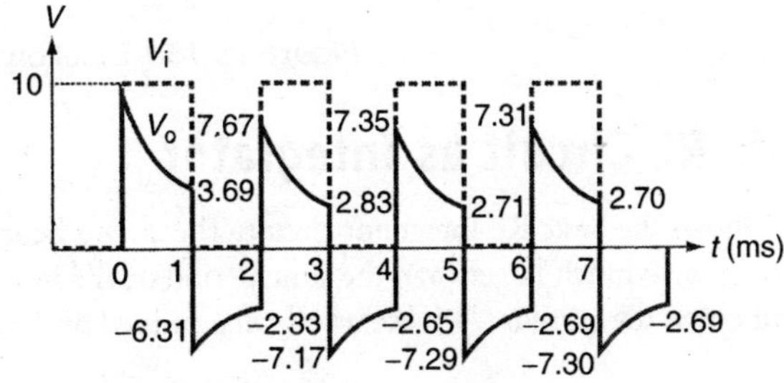

Figure 13.14 Solution to Example 13.5.

EXAMPLE 13.6 *A 100 μs pulse is applied to the RC high-pass circuit of Figure 13.15. Sketch the response waveform. Also calculate the time taken by output pulse to go to near zero after the input pulse goes low.*

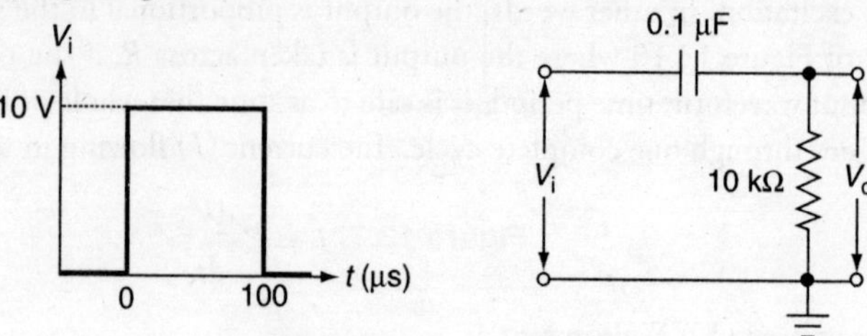

Figure 13.15 Example 13.6.

Solution

1. The output voltage at the time of termination of input pulse, that is, at $t = 100$ μs can be calculated from

$$10 - 10(1 - e^{-10^{-4}/RC}) = 10e^{-10^{-4}/10^{-3}} = 10/e^{0.1} = 9 \text{ V}$$

2. As the input pulse goes to zero, the output goes to –1 V as the voltage across capacitor cannot change instantaneously. The output then gradually rises towards zero as the capacitor discharges.
3. Since the input and output are isolated by a blocking capacitor, the output will always have a zero DC or average value. That is, area under the positive portion must equal area under the negative portion.
4. Assuming the charge and discharge process to be linear which is a valid assumption when the circuit time constant is much larger than the pulse width, we can calculate the required time for the output to decay to zero to be 1.9 ms. The response waveform is shown in Figure 13.16.

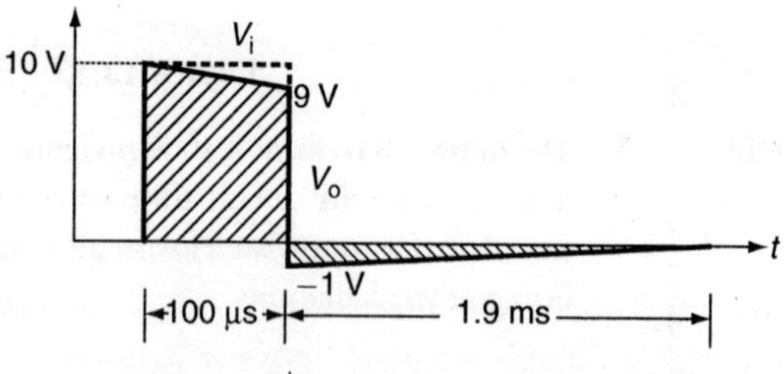

Figure 13.16 Solution to Example 13.6.

13.5 Basic RL Circuit as Integrator

Figure 13.17 shows the basic RL integrator circuit. The circuit behaves as an integrator circuit, if the time constant (L/R) were much larger than the time period of the input waveform. If it were so, it would be justified to assume that the current (I_i) is exclusively determined by L as the input goes through one complete cycle. That is,

$$I_i = \frac{1}{L}\int V_i \mathrm{d}t$$

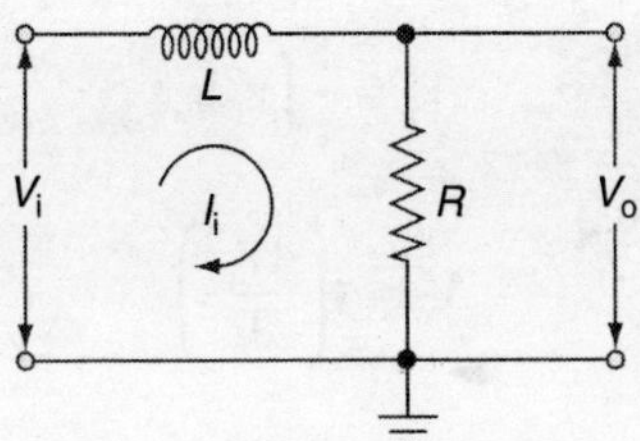

Figure 13.17 | Basic RL integrator.

As the output voltage (V_o) is equal to $V_o = I_i \times R$, therefore

$$V_o = \frac{R}{L}\int V_i \mathrm{d}t$$

$$V_o \propto \int V_i \mathrm{d}t \qquad (13.15)$$

13.6 Basic RL Circuit as Differentiator

Figure 13.18 shows the basic RL differentiator circuit. If the time constant (L/R) were much smaller than the input waveform time period, the current (i) very quickly reaches the steady state and the transient portion takes negligible time. It can thus be assumed that the current (I_i) is exclusively determined by R. That is,

$$I_i = \frac{V_i}{R}$$

As the output voltage (V_o) is equal to

$$V_o = L\frac{\mathrm{d}I_i}{\mathrm{d}t}$$

Therefore V_o is given by

$$V_o = \frac{L}{R}\frac{\mathrm{d}V_i}{\mathrm{d}t}$$

$$V_o \propto \frac{\mathrm{d}V_i}{\mathrm{d}t} \qquad (13.16)$$

We can see that the results obtained in the case of RL circuits are analogous to those obtained in the case of RC circuits. In general, for a simple integrator circuit (RL or RC),

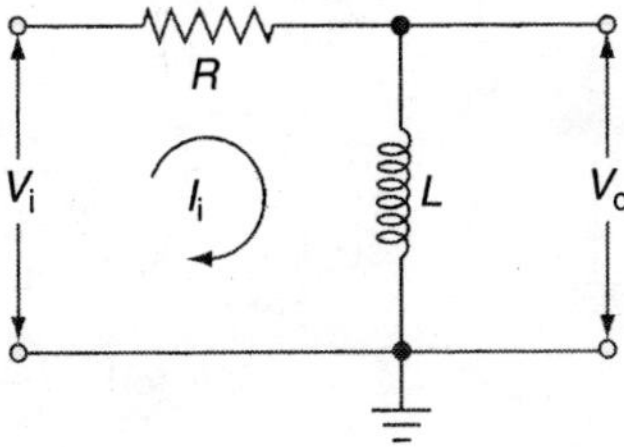

Figure 13.18 | RL differentiator circuit.

$$V_o = \frac{1}{\tau}\int V_i dt \tag{13.17}$$

and for differentiator circuit (RL or RC)

$$V_o = \tau\left(\frac{dV_i}{dt}\right) \tag{13.18}$$

where τ is the time constant which is equal to RC (for RC circuit) or L/R (for RL circuit).

13.7 Diode Clipper Circuits

Diode-based clipper circuits can be used for clipping or removing whole or part of positive or negative portions of bidirectional waveforms. This class of wave-shaping circuits is also called non-linear wave-shaping circuits as one or more than one element has non-linear current–voltage characteristics. Four basic diode-based clipper circuits are shown in Figures 13.19(a)–(d). The non-linear element in the circuits of Figure 13.19 is the diode. In the following paragraphs, we will study the response of each of these circuits to a sinusoidal input. Diodes are assumed to be ideal. That is, the cut-in voltage of the diodes is zero.

1. The input and output waveforms for the clipping circuit of Figure 13.19(a) are shown in Figure 13.20(a). The figure is self-explanatory. The circuit configuration is similar to that of a half-wave rectifier circuit. During the positive and negative half cycles of the input waveform, the diode is respectively forward- and reverse-biased. The positive half cycles therefore appear across the output.

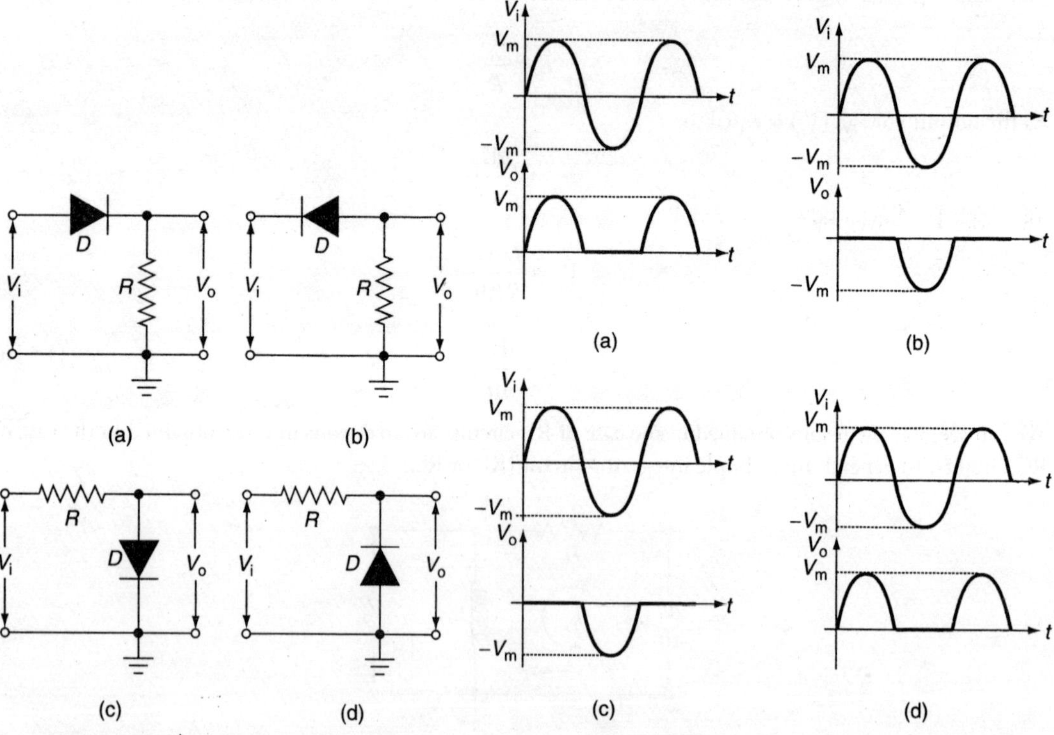

Figure 13.19 | Basic clipper circuits.

Figure 13.20 | Input and output waveforms for the clipper circuits of Figure 13.19.

2. Similarly the output waveform for the circuit of Figure 13.19(b) is shown in Figure 13.20(b). The circuit is again a half-wave rectifier circuit that allows negative half cycles to appear across the output. The diode in this case is forward-biased during negative half cycles of the input waveform.
3. For the clipping circuit of Figure 13.19(c), the diode is forward-biased during positive half cycles and reverse-biased during negative half cycles. The output is therefore clipped to zero during positive half cycles and the negative half cycles are allowed to appear across the output as the diode is then reverse-biased.
4. For the circuit of Figure 13.19(d), the negative half cycles would be clipped to zero.

In case the diodes used in the circuits of Figure 13.19 were non-ideal, the output waveforms would be similar to those shown in Figure 13.20 except that the diode would have a cut-in voltage of 0.7 V for silicon diodes and 0.3 V for germanium diodes instead of zero as assumed in the case of ideal diodes. The waveforms for clipping circuits of Figure 13.19 with silicon diodes are shown in Figure 13.21. The other important issue is that of choice of resistance (R). In the case of non-ideal diodes, the forward-biased resistance of the diode (R_f) is not zero and also the reverse-biased resistance of the diode (R_r) is not infinite. In such a situation, it is desirable that resistance (R) is so chosen that it satisfies the condition $R_f << R << R_r$. The optimum value of R is given by geometric mean of R_f and R_r. That is

$$R = \sqrt{R_f \times R_r} \tag{13.19}$$

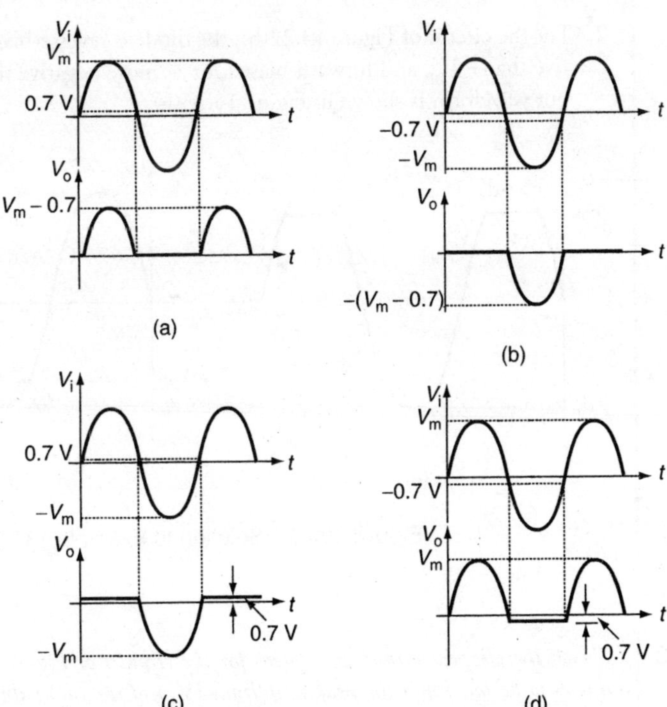

Figure 13.21 Output waveforms for clipper circuits of Figure 13.19 when the diodes are non-ideal.

EXAMPLE 13.7 *Sketch the output waveform for the clipping circuits of Figure 13.22. Assume the diodes to be ideal and the peak amplitude (V_m) of the input sinusoidal signal to be greater than the battery voltage (V_{BB}).*

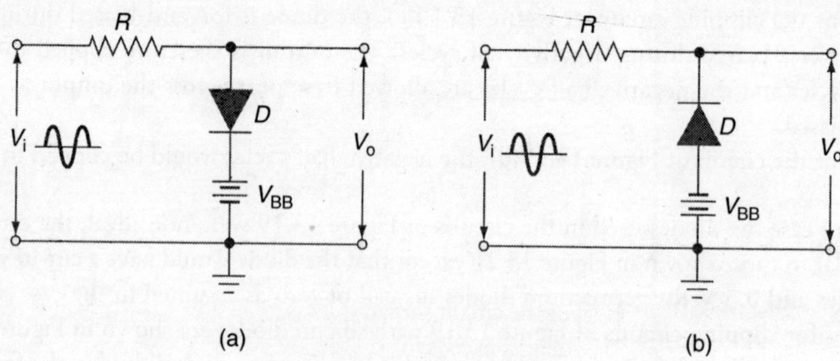

Figure 13.22 Example 13.7.

Solution

1. In the case of the circuit shown in Figure 13.22(a), the diode gets forward-biased when the input exceeds V_{BB} and thus the output remains clamped at V_{BB} as long as input remains greater than V_{BB}. For $V_i < V_{BB}$, the diode is reverse-biased and the output is same as the input. The output waveform is shown in Figure 13.23(a).
2. For the circuit of Figure 13.22(b), the diode is reverse-biased for V_i less negative than $-V_{BB}$ and forward-biased for V_i more negative than $-V_{BB}$. The output waveform is shown in Figure 13.23(b).

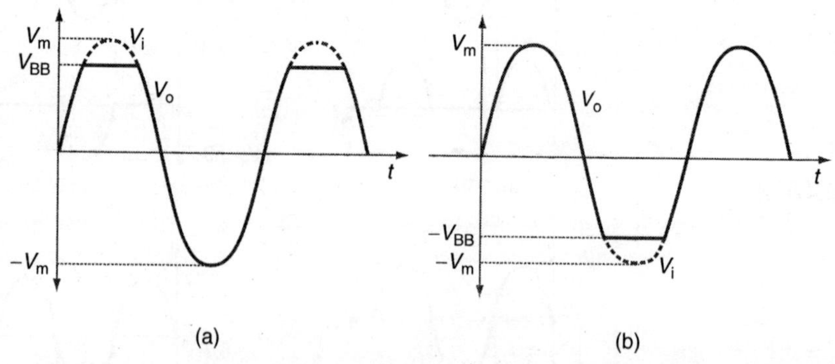

Figure 13.23 Solution to Example 13.7.

EXAMPLE 13.8 *Sketch the clipped output waveforms for the circuits of Figure 13.24. Assume the diodes to be ideal and the peak amplitude (V_m) of the input sinusoidal signal to be greater than battery voltage (V_{BB}).*

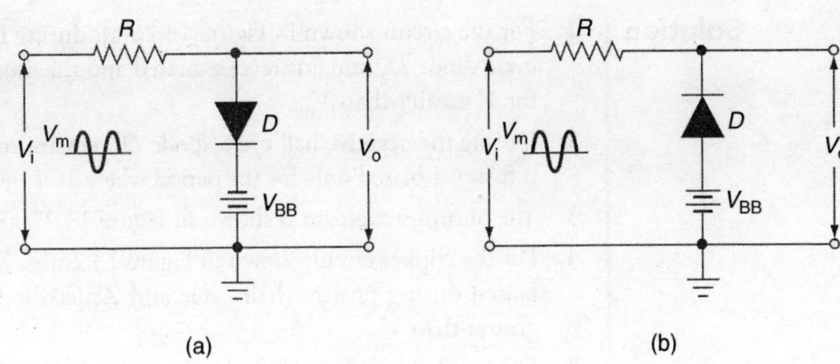

Figure 13.24 | Example 13.8.

Solution

1. For the circuit shown in Figure 13.24(a), the diode is forward-biased for all input voltages except for the period when V_i is more negative than the battery voltage ($-V_{BB}$) where it is reverse-biased. Figure 13.25(a) shows the output waveform.
2. For the circuit shown in Figure 13.24(b), the diode is forward-biased for V_i less than equal to battery voltage (V_{BB}) and reverse-biased for V_i greater than V_{BB}. Figure 13.25(b) shows the output waveform.

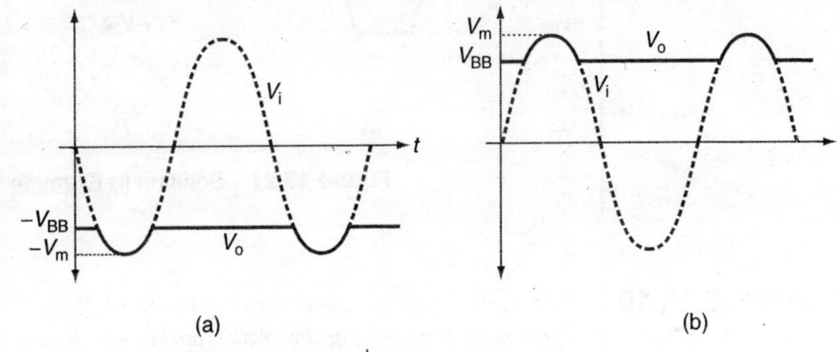

Figure 13.25 | Solution to Example 13.8.

EXAMPLE 13.9 *Sketch the clipped output waveforms for the double-diode circuits of Figures 13.26(a) and (b). Assume diodes D_1 and D_2 to be ideal and the forward-biased voltage drops of the Zener diodes to be zero.*

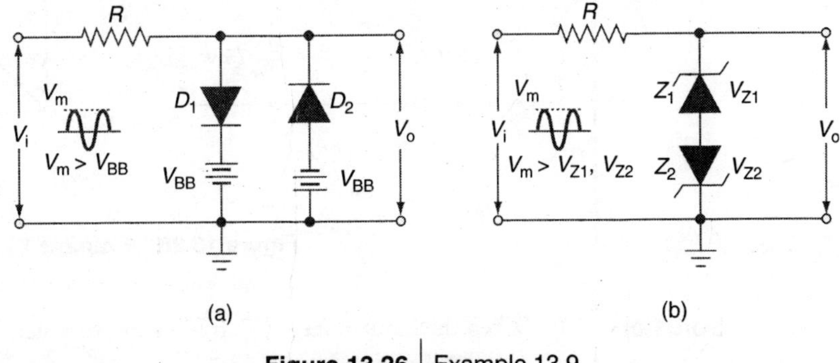

Figure 13.26 | Example 13.9.

Solution

1. For the circuit shown in Figure 13.26(a), during the whole of positive half-cycle diode D_2 remains reverse-biased and the diode D_1 gets forward-biased for V_i greater than V_{BB}.
2. During the negative half cycle, diode D_1 remains reverse-biased and diode D_2 is forward-biased only for the period where V_i is more negative than $-V_{BB}$.
3. The output waveform is shown in Figure 13.27(a).
4. For the clipper circuit shown in Figure 13.26(b), Zener diode Z_2 is forward-biased during positive half cycle and Zener diode Z_1 breaks down for V_i greater than V_{Z1}.
5. During the negative half cycle, Zener diode Z_1 is forward-biased and Zener diode Z_2 breaks down for V_i more negative than $-V_{Z2}$.
6. The output waveform is shown in Figure 13.27(b).

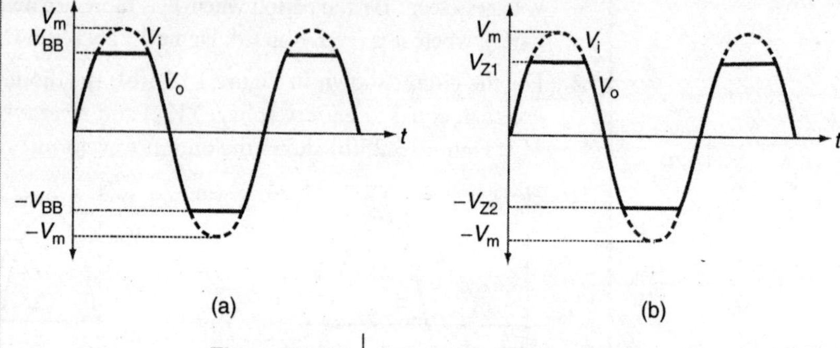

Figure 13.27 | Solution to Example 13.9.

EXAMPLE 13.10

Refer to the two diode clipper circuit of Figure 13.28(a). The input to this circuit is a linear ramp varying from 0 to 100 V as shown in Figure 13.28(b). Plot the output waveform. The diodes can be assumed to be ideal.

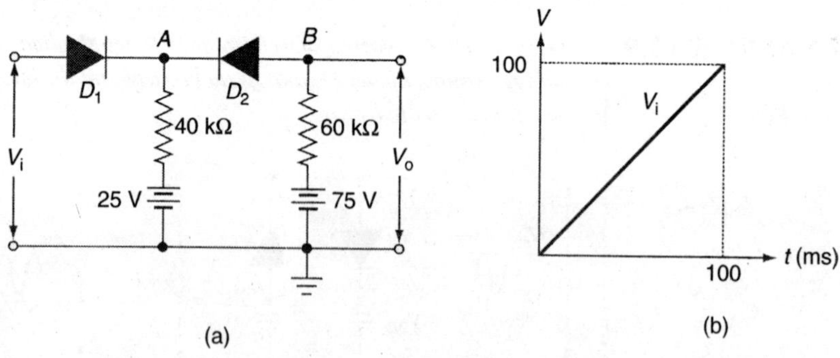

Figure 13.28 | Example 13.10.

Solution

1. When the input voltage (V_i) is less than the potential at node A, the diode D_1 is reverse-biased.

2. When diode D_1 is reverse-biased and the diode D_2 is forward-biased, potential at node A is equal to potential at node B. The potential at nodes A and B is equal to

$$[75 - \{(75 - 25)/(60 \times 10^3 + 40 \times 10^3)\} \times 60 \times 10^3] = 45 \text{ V}$$

3. Therefore, for V_i less than 45 V, diode D_1 is reverse-biased and diode D_2 is forward-biased with nodes A and B at a potential of 45 V.
4. As V_i exceeds 45 V, D_1 gets forward-biased and from then onwards, potential at A is same as V_i. Diode D_2 remains forward-biased as long as V_i does not exceed 75 V. Thus, for V_i greater than 45 V and less than 75 V, V_o is same as V_i.
5. As V_i exceeds 75 V, D_2 is also reverse-biased. From then onwards, the output is constant at 75 V.
6. The input and output waveforms are shown in Figure 13.29.

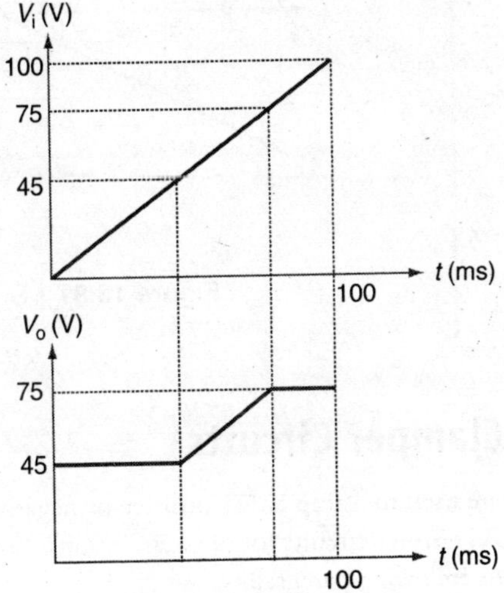

Figure 13.29 Solution to Example 13.10.

EXAMPLE 13.11 *Draw the transfer characteristics (i.e., V_o versus V_i) for the two diode clipper circuit of Figure 13.30. Assume the diodes to be ideal.*

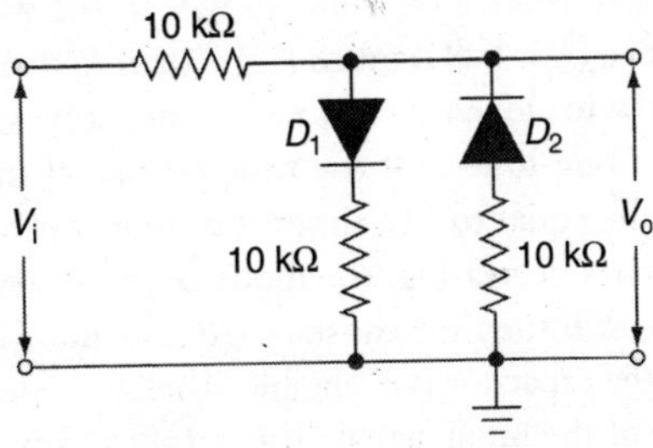

Figure 13.30 Example 13.11.

Solution

1. As V_i increases in the positive direction, D_1 is forward-biased and D_2 is reverse-biased. V_o in this case is always equal to $V_i/2$.
2. For negative values of V_i, diode D_2 is forward-biased and diode D_1 is reverse-biased. Again the output is $V_i/2$.
3. The transfer characteristics are shown in Figure 13.31.

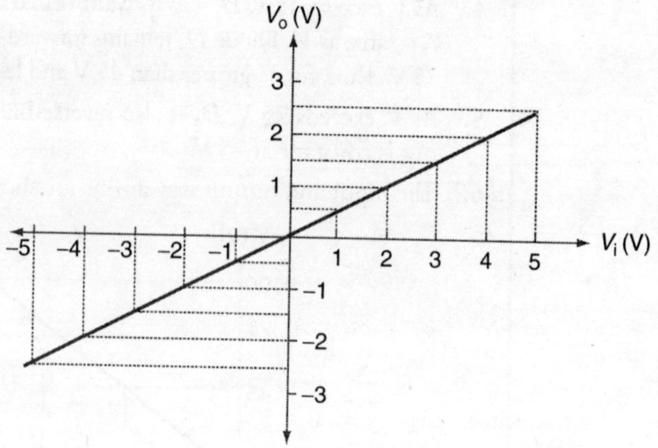

Figure 13.31 Solution to Example 13.11.

13.8 Diode Clamper Circuits

Clamper circuits are used to clamp either positive or negative extremities of an AC signal to zero. These are also called DC restorer circuits for obvious reasons. Both positive and negative clamper circuits are briefly described in the following paragraphs.

Negative Clamper

Figure 13.32(a) shows the negative clamper circuit, which clamps the positive peaks of the AC signal to zero. Figure 13.32(b) shows the clamped output waveform for a given sinusoidal input. The circuit functions as follows. As the input V_i rises towards the positive peak V_m from zero in the first quarter of the cycle, capacitor (C) charges to V_m through the forward-biased diode. The overall charging resistance is sum of source resistance (R_s), not shown in the figure, and the parallel combination of R and diode's forward resistance (R_f). If R is much larger than R_f then the capacitor C charges with a time constant of $[(R_s + R_f) \times C]$. Now for given R_s and R_f, C should be such that it charges to V_m in a time which in no case is greater than one-fourth of the time period of the input waveform. The total charging time may be considered to be equal to five times the time constant.

When the input starts decreasing, the diode becomes reverse-biased. The capacitor now tends to discharge through resistor R. If the time constant (RC) is much larger than the time period of the input waveform, the discharge of the capacitor is negligible. Therefore, the voltage across the capacitor remains constant at the maximum value of the input signal. The output at any instant of time is then equal to algebraic sum of input voltage and voltage across the capacitor. Thus, all positive peaks (V_m) are clamped to zero and all

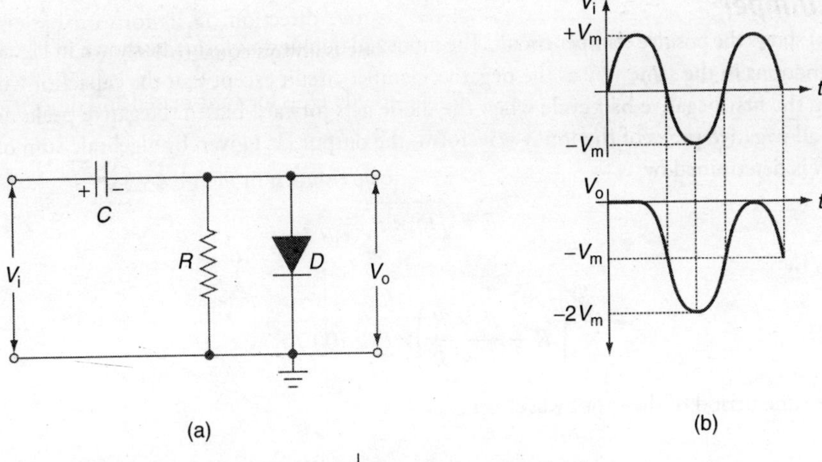

Figure 13.32 | Negative clamper circuit.

negative peaks ($-V_m$) go to $-2V_m$. The clamping circuit as can be seen from the clamped output waveform, does not alter the wave shape, it only changes the DC level.

If the peak amplitude of the input changes, the capacitor must charge or discharge to the new value depending upon whether input amplitude has increased or decreased. When the peak value of the input signal increases, the capacitor charges through the forward-biased diode again to the new larger value and when the peak value of the input signal decreases, it discharges through R to the new lower value.

In the absence of R, the capacitor will be forced to discharge through the reverse-biased diode resistance (R_r) which may be as large as 100 MΩ. Therefore, it may even be seconds before the capacitor discharges to new lower value, in case the peak amplitude of the input waveform decreases and the output again gets clamped to the desired voltage. As R is chosen to be much smaller than R_r, this problem is not encountered and the claming is usually restored within a few cycles of the input waveform at the most even after the input undergoes a step change in peak amplitude. The optimum value of R is given by geometric mean of R_f and R_r. That is,

$$R = \sqrt{R_f \times R_r} \tag{13.20}$$

It may be mentioned here that the clamping circuit will function even in the absence of R provided that the peak input amplitude remains constant. In the event of peak input amplitude decreasing, one has to wait for a sufficiently long time depending upon $R_r \times C$ time constant before normal clamping operation is restored.

After having calculated the value of R for a given diode, C should be so chosen that it does not discharge appreciably during the time the diode remains reverse-biased. The time constant when the diode is reverse-biased is given by

$$\left[R_s + \frac{R_r \times R}{R_r + R}\right] \times C \tag{13.21}$$

The time constant of the discharge circuit should at least be 100 times the reverse-biased time period. It is more appropriate to choose C to meet extremely slow discharge requirement rather than fast charging requirement through R_f. R_f is usually so small that C chosen by the discharge criterion almost always satisfies the charge criterion.

Positive Clamper

Figure 13.33(a) shows the positive clamper circuit. The input and output waveforms are shown in Figure 13.33(b). The circuit functions in the same way as the negative clamper circuit except that the capacitor would charge to $-V_m$ during the first negative half cycle when the diode gets forward-biased. Negative peaks are clamped to zero as for all negative peaks of the input waveform, the output (V_o) given by algebraic sum of V_i and V_c will be zero. R is determined by

$$R = \sqrt{R_f \times R_r} \tag{13.22}$$

and C is given by

$$\left(R_s + \frac{R_r \times R}{R_r + R}\right) \times C \geq 100\,T \tag{13.23}$$

where T is the time period of the input waveform.

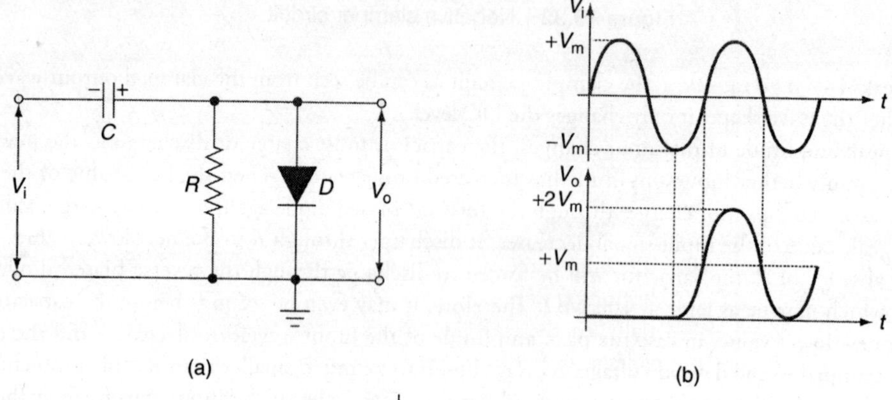

Figure 13.33 Positive clamper circuit.

EXAMPLE 13.12 *For the clamping circuit of Figure 13.34(a) and the input waveform of Figure 13.34(b), plot the output waveform for the first five cycles. Comment on the results obtained. (Assume the diodes to be ideal.)*

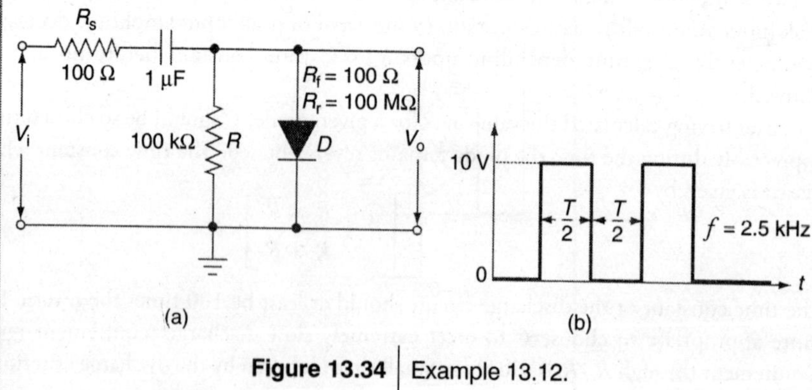

Figure 13.34 Example 13.12.

Solution

1. As the input goes from 0 to +10 V, the diode gets forward-biased. As the voltage across the capacitor cannot change instantaneously, the output voltage (V_o) abruptly rises to only +5 V due to the potential divider arrangement of R_s (= 100 Ω) and R_f (= 100 Ω).
2. The capacitor then starts charging towards +10 V with a time constant $(R_f + R_s) \times C$.
3. The time constant = (100 + 100) × 10^{-6} = 200 μs.
4. The time period of input waveform = 400 μs (for f = 2.5 kHz).
5. Therefore, during the first cycle, when the diode is forward-biased the capacitor would exponentially charge as per the following equation:

$$V_c = 10(1 - e^{-t/(200\times10^{-6})})$$

6. For, t = 200 μs, $V_c = 10(1 - e^{-1}) = 6.3$ V.
7. This gives, V_o = (10 – 6.3)/2 = 1.85 V.
8. When the input drops to zero, the diode gets reverse-biased and the output drops to –6.3 V (= capacitor voltage) as the value of R_r is much larger than R_s.
9. For the second half of the first cycle, when the input is zero, the output remains equal to the capacitor voltage of –6.3 V. Here, it is assumed that the capacitor does not discharge through R during this time which is quite valid as the time constant (RC) equal to 100 ms is 500 times the half cycle time of 200 μs.
10. The output returns to +1.85 V as the input goes to +10 V again with the beginning of the second cycle. The capacitor will start charging exponentially. At the end of the HIGH time of the second cycle, the capacitor voltage $V_c = 10 - (10 - 6.3)e^{-1} = 8.64$ V.
11. This gives, V_o = (10 – 8.64)/2 = 0.68 V.
12. When the input drops to zero, the output drops to –8.64 V. The output waveform progresses in the same fashion for the subsequent cycles.
13. As shown in Figure 13.35, the output is nearly clamped in the fifth cycle. From then onwards, the output has the positive extremities of the input waveform clamped to zero.

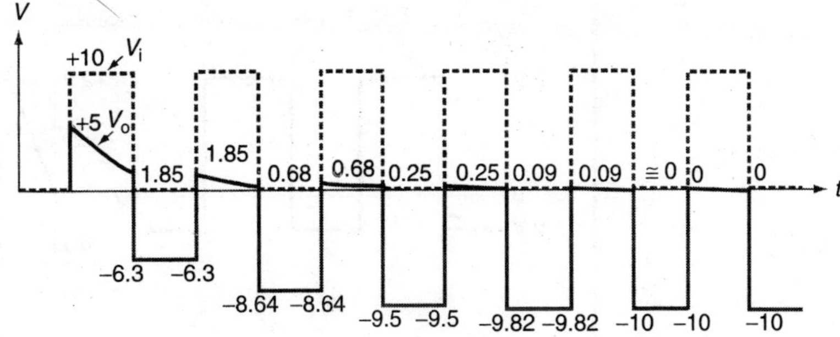

Figure 13.35 | Solution to Example 13.12.

EXAMPLE 13.13 *Sketch the steady-state clamped output waveforms for the circuits shown in Figures 13.36(a)–(c). Assume a zero forward-biased voltage drop for diodes.*

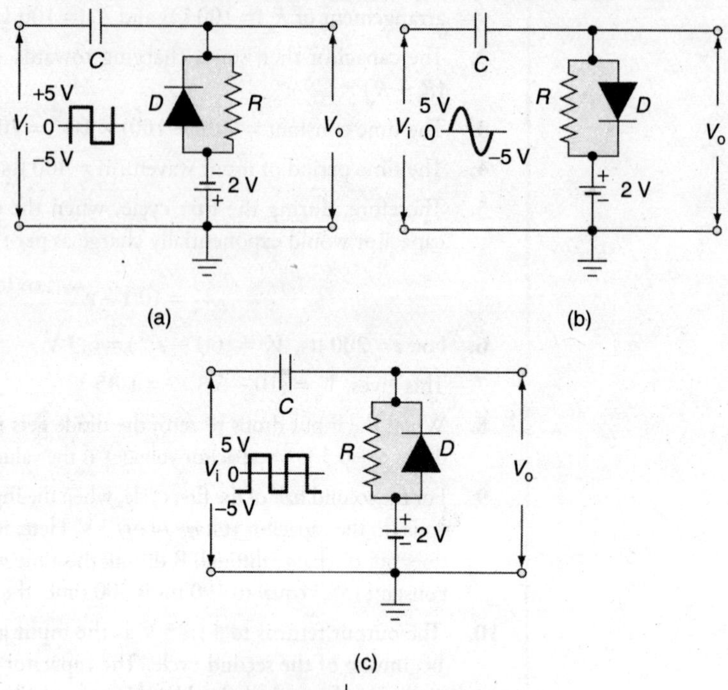

Figure 13.36 Example 13.13.

Solution

1. **Refer to Figure 13.36(a):** In the absence of the 2 V battery, the negative extremities of the input waveform would be clamped to zero. In the presence of the battery the waveform will be clamped to –2 V. Figure 13.37(a) shows the clamped waveform.
2. **Refer to Figure 13.36(b):** In this case, the positive peaks instead of being clamped to zero are clamped to +2 V. Figure 13.37(b) shows the clamped waveform.

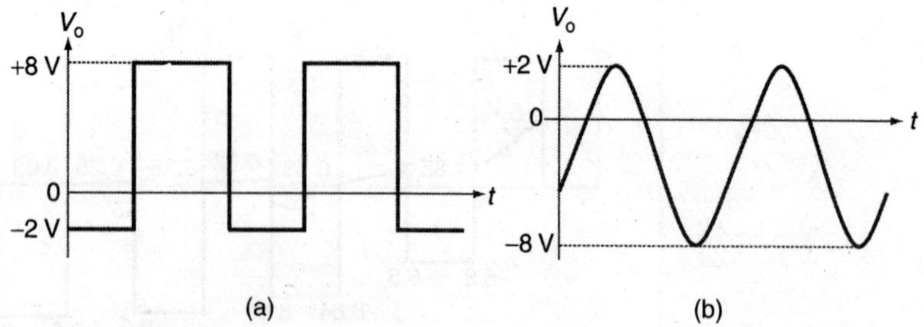

Figure 13.37 Solution to Example 13.13.

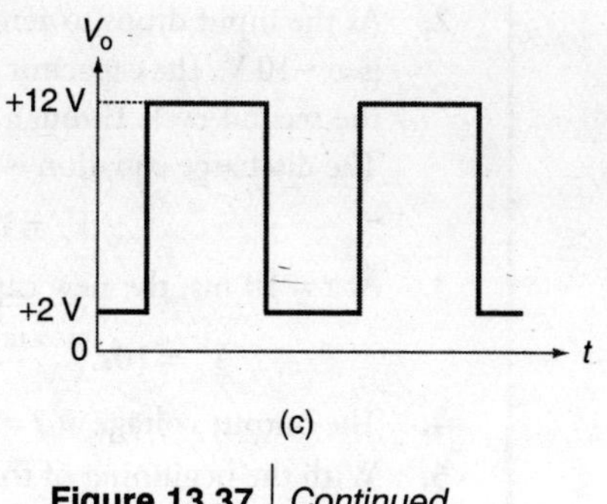

Figure 13.37 | *Continued.*

3. **Refer to Figure 13.36(c):** The circuit is similar to the one shown in Figure 13.36(a) except that the polarity of battery has been reversed. As a result, the negative peak is clamped to +2 V. Figure 13.37(c) shows the waveform.

EXAMPLE 13.14 *Refer to the clamping circuit of Figure 13.38(a). The input waveform to this circuit is shown in Figure 13.38(b) for the first six cycles. Sketch the clamped output waveform for the first six cycles.*

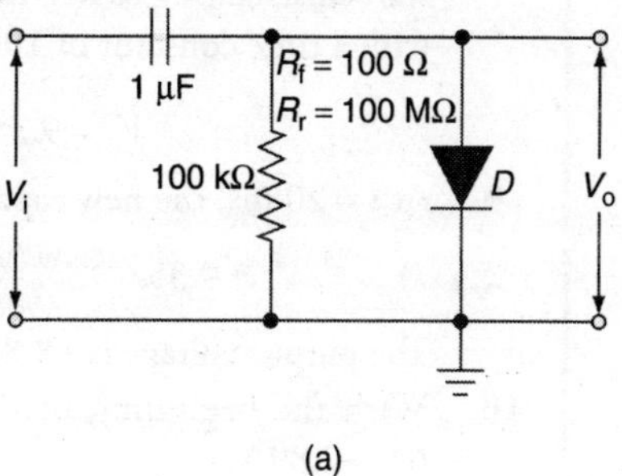

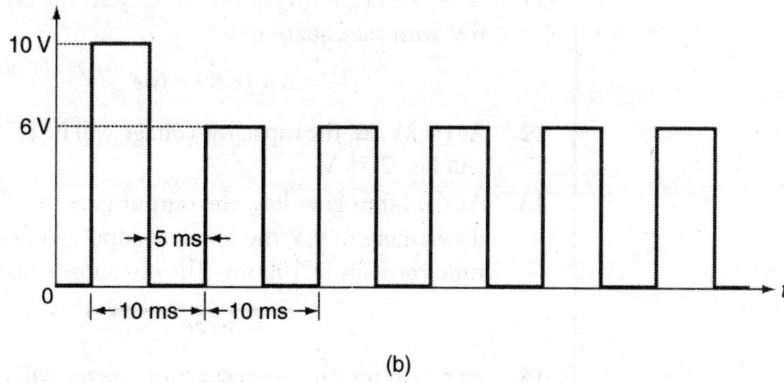

Figure 13.38 | Example 13.14.

Solution

1. With $C = 1$ μF and $R_f = 100$ Ω, the capacitor (C) would charge to 10 V in about half a millisecond (100 μs being the charging time constant) during the 5 ms high time of the first cycle.

2. As the input drops to zero, the output too drops by 10 V and the output is at −10 V. The capacitor starts discharging the moment input goes low in the second cycle through the resistor R with a time constant of 100 ms. The discharge equation is given by
$$V_c = 10e^{-(t-5\times10^{-3})/(100\times10^{-3})}$$
3. At t = 10 ms, the new capacitor voltage will be
$$V_c = 10e^{-(5\times10^{-3})/(100\times10^{-3})} = 10e^{-1/20} = 9.52 \text{ V}$$
4. The output voltage at t = 10 ms is −9.52 V.
5. With the beginning of the second cycle, the peak amplitude of the input decreases by 4 V as compared to the first cycle and as a result, the output can go up to −3.52 V and is not zero.
6. The capacitor starts discharging to 6 V with the equation
$$V_c = 6 + (9.52 - 6)e^{-(t-10\times10^{-3})/(100\times10^{-3})}$$
7. At t = 15 ms, the capacitor voltage will be 9.35 V and the output voltage will be −3.35 V.
8. As the input goes low, the output voltage goes to −9.35 V. The capacitor starts discharging to 0 V the moment input goes low in the second cycle with a time constant of 100 ms. The discharge equation is given by
$$V_c = 9.35e^{-(t-15\times10^{-3})/(100\times10^{-3})}$$
9. At t = 20 ms, the new capacitor voltage will be
$$V_c = 9.35e^{-(5\times10^{-3})/(100\times10^{-3})} = 9.35e^{-1/20} = 8.89 \text{ V}$$
The output voltage is −8.89 V.
10. With the beginning of the third cycle, the output will be −8.89 + 6 = −2.89 V.
11. With the beginning of the third cycle, the capacitor starts discharging to 6 V with the equation
$$V_c = 6 + (8.89 - 6)e^{-(t-20\times10^{-3})/(100\times10^{-3})}$$
12. At t = 25 ms, the capacitor voltage will be 8.75 V and the output voltage will be −2.75 V.
13. As the input goes low, the output goes to −8.75 V. The capacitor starts discharging to 0 V the moment input goes low in the third cycle with a time constant of 100 ms. The discharge equation is given by
$$V_c = 8.75e^{-(t-25\times10^{-3})/(100\times10^{-3})}$$
14. At t = 30 ms, the new capacitor voltage will be
$$V_c = 8.75e^{-(5\times10^{-3})/(100\times10^{-3})} = 8.75e^{-1/20} = 8.32 \text{ V}$$
15. The output voltage is −8.32 V.
16. Similar calculations can be done for the fourth, fifth and sixth cycles.
17. The output waveform is plotted in Figure 13.39.

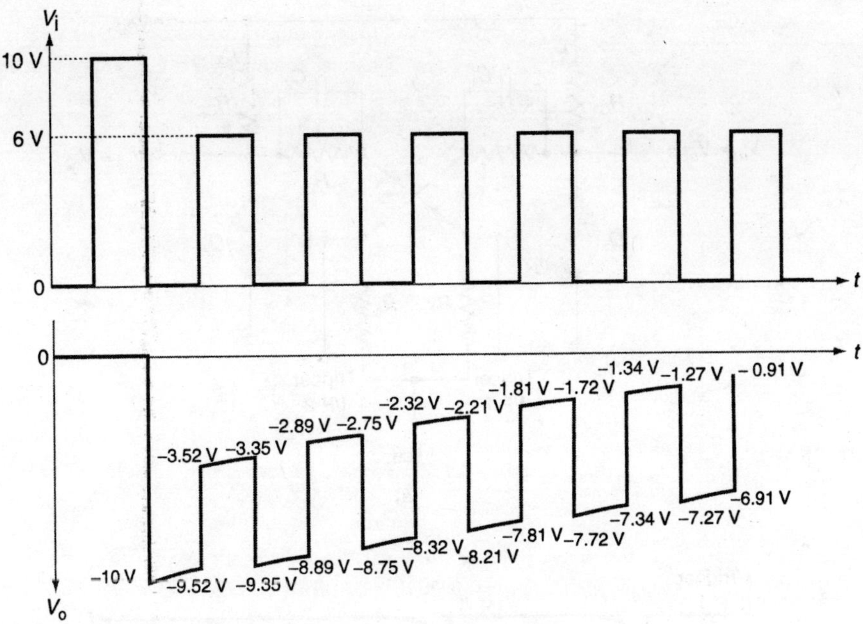

Figure 13.39 Solution to Example 13.14.

13.9 Multivibrators

A multivibrator like the familiar sinusoidal oscillator is a circuit with regenerative feedback with the difference that it produces a pulsed output. There are three basic types of multivibrator circuits. These include bistable multivibrator, monostable multivibrator and astable multivibrator.

Bistable Multivibrator

A *bistable multivibrator* circuit is the one in which both LOW and HIGH output states are stable. Irrespective of the logic status of the output, LOW or HIGH, it stays in that state unless a change is induced by applying an appropriate trigger pulse. As we will see subsequently, the operation of a bistable multivibrator is identical to that of a flip-flop. Figure 13.40(a) shows the basic bistable multivibrator circuit. This is the fixed-bias type of bistable multivibrator. Other configurations are self-bias type and the emitter-coupled type. However, operational principle of all types is the same. The multivibrator circuit of Figure 13.40(a) functions as follows.

In the circuit arrangement of Figure 13.40(a), it can be proved that both the transistors (Q_1 and Q_2) cannot be simultaneously ON or OFF. If Q_1 is ON, the regenerative feedback ensures that Q_2 is OFF and when Q_1 is OFF, the feedback drives transistor Q_2 to the ON-state. In order to vindicate this statement, let us assume that both the transistors Q_1 and Q_2 are conducting simultaneously. Owing to slight circuit imbalance, which is always there, collector current in one transistor will always be greater than that in the other. Let us assume that $I_{c2} > I_{c1}$. Lesser I_{c1} means a higher V_{c1}. Since V_{c1} is coupled to Q_2-base, rise in V_{c1} leads to increase in Q_2-base voltage. Increase in Q_2-base voltage results in increase in I_{c2} and associated reduction in V_{c2}. Reduction in V_{c2} leads to reduction of Q_1-base voltage and an associated fall in I_{c1} with the result that V_{c1} increases further. Thus a slight circuit imbalance has initiated a regenerative action which culminates in transistor Q_1 going to cut-off

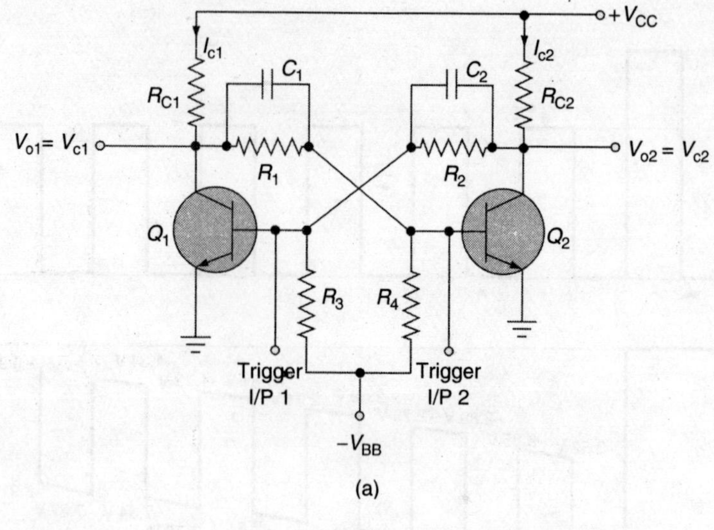

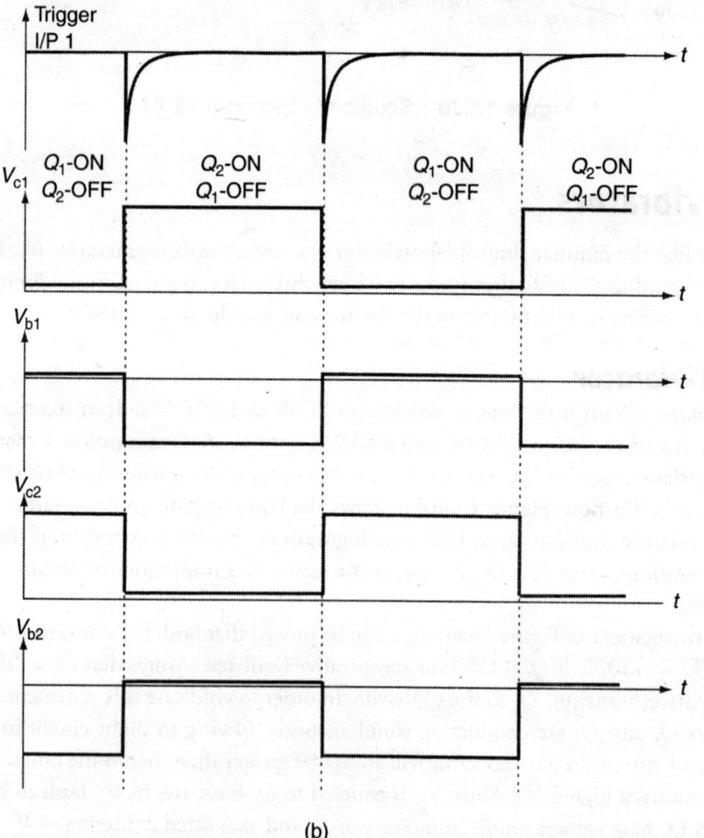

Figure 13.40 (a) Bistable multivibrator; (b) timing waveforms for the bistable multivibrator of (a).

and transistor Q_2 getting driven to saturation. To sum up, whenever there is a tendency of one of the transistors to conduct more than the other, it will end up with that transistor going to saturation and driving the other transistor to cut-off. Now, if we take output from Q_1 collector, it will be LOW ($=V_{CE1(sat)}$) if Q_1 was initially in saturation. If we apply a negative going trigger to Q_1-base to cause a decrease in its collector current, a regenerative action would set in which would drive Q_2 to saturation and Q_1 to cut-off. As a result, output goes to HIGH ($=+V_{CC}$) state. The output will stay HIGH till we apply another appropriate trigger to initiate a transition. Figure 13.40(b) shows the relevant timing diagrams. Thus both of the output states, when output is LOW and also when output is HIGH, are stable and undergo a change only when a transition is induced by means of an appropriate trigger pulse. That is why it is called a bistable multivibrator.

Schmitt Trigger

Schmitt trigger circuit is a slight variation of the bistable multivibrator circuit of Figure 13.40(a). Figure 13.41 shows the basic Schmitt trigger circuit. If we compare the bistable multivibrator circuit of Figure 13.40(a) with the Schmitt trigger circuit of Figure 13.41, we find that coupling from Q_2-collector to Q_1-base in the case of bistable circuit is absent in the case of Schmitt trigger circuit. Instead, resistor R_E provides the coupling. The circuit functions as follows.

When V_{in} is zero, transistor Q_1 is in cut-off. Coupling from Q_1-collector to Q_2-base drives transistor Q_2 to saturation with the result that V_o is LOW. If we assume that $V_{CE2\,(sat)}$ is zero, then voltage across R_E is given by

$$\text{Voltage across } R_E = \frac{V_{CC} \times R_E}{R_E + R_{C2}} \tag{13.24}$$

This is also the emitter voltage of transistor Q_1. In order to make transistor Q_1 conduct, V_{in} must at least be equal to 0.7 V more than the voltage across R_E. That is,

$$V_{in} = \frac{V_{CC} \times R_E}{R_E + R_{C2}} + 0.7 \tag{13.25}$$

When V_{in} exceeds this voltage, Q_1 starts conducting. The regenerative action again drives Q_2 to cut-off. The output goes to the HIGH state. Voltage across R_E changes to a new value given by

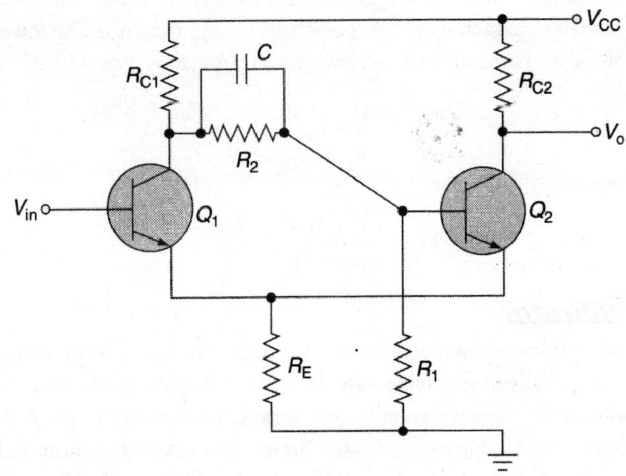

Figure 13.41 | Schmitt trigger.

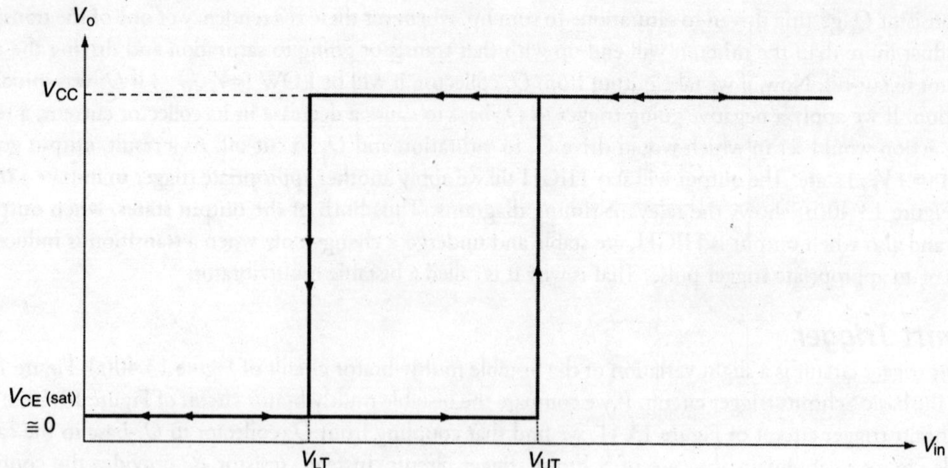

Figure 13.42 Transfer characteristics of the Schmitt trigger circuit.

$$\text{Voltage across } R_E = \frac{V_{CC} \times R_E}{R_E + R_{C1}} \tag{13.26}$$

Q_1 will continue to conduct as long as V_{in} is equal to or greater than the value given by

$$V_{in} = \frac{V_{CC} \times R_E}{R_E + R_{C1}} + 0.7 \tag{13.27}$$

If V_{in} falls below this value, Q_1 tends to come out of saturation and conduct less heavily. The regenerative action does the rest with the process culminating in Q_1 going to cut-off and Q_2 to saturation. Thus the state of output (HIGH or LOW) depends upon input voltage level. The HIGH and LOW states of the output correspond to two distinct input levels given by Eqs. (13.25) and (13.27) and therefore they depend on the values of R_{C1}, R_{C2}, R_E and V_{CC}. Schmitt trigger circuit of Figure 13.41 therefore exhibits hysteresis. Figure 13.42 shows the transfer characteristics of the Schmitt trigger circuit. The lower trip point (V_{LT}) and upper trip point (V_{UT}) of these characteristics are, respectively, given by Eqs. (13.28) and (13.29):

$$V_{LT} = \frac{V_{CC} \times R_E}{R_E + R_{C1}} + 0.7 \tag{13.28}$$

$$V_{UT} = \frac{V_{CC} \times R_E}{R_E + R_{C2}} + 0.7 \tag{13.29}$$

Monostable Multivibrator

A *monostable multivibrator*, also known as *monoshot*, is the one in which one of the states is stable and the other is quasi-stable. The circuit is initially in the stable state. It goes to the quasi-stable state when appropriately triggered. It stays in the quasi-stable state for a certain time period, after which it comes back to the stable state. Figure 13.43 shows the basic monostable multivibrator circuit. The circuit functions as follows. Initially, transistor Q_2 is in saturation as it gets its base bias from $+V_{CC}$ through R. Coupling from Q_2-collector to Q_1-base ensures that Q_1 is in cut-off. When a positive trigger pulse of short duration and sufficient magnitude is applied

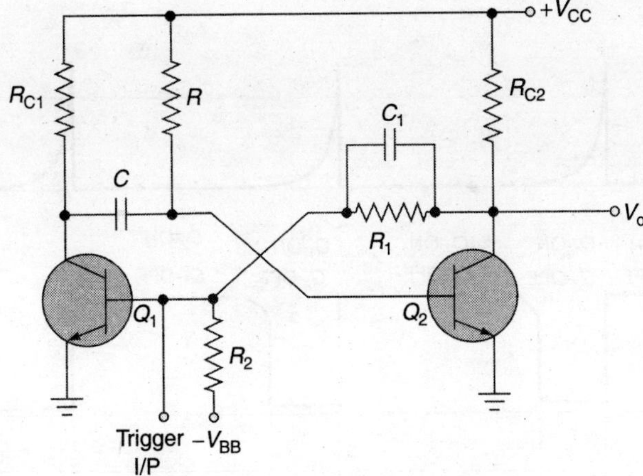

Figure 13.43 | Monostable multivibrator.

to the base of transistor Q_1, Q_1 starts conducting. As the voltage across the capacitor C cannot change instantly, negative voltage is applied to the base of transistor Q_2 and it turns OFF. Therefore, the output goes to the HIGH state. In other words, since there is no direct coupling from Q_1-collector to Q_2-base, which is necessary for a regenerative process to set in, Q_1 is not necessarily in saturation. However, it conducts some current. The Q_1-collector voltage falls by $I_{c1}R_{C1}$ and Q_2-base voltage falls by the same amount as voltage across a capacitor (C in this case) can not change instantaneously. To sum up, the moment we applied the trigger, Q_2 went to cut-off and Q_1 started conducting. But now there is a path for capacitor C to charge from V_{CC} through R and the conducting transistor. The polarity of voltage across C is such that Q_2-base potential rises. The moment Q_2-base voltage exceeds the cut-in voltage, it turns Q_2 ON, which due to coupling through R_1 turns Q_1 OFF. And we are back to the original state, the stable state. Figure 13.44 shows the relevant timing diagrams. Whenever, we trigger the circuit into the other state, it does not stay there permanently and returns back after a time period that depends upon R and C. Larger the time constant (RC), larger is the time for which it stays in the other state called quasi-stable state. The width of the quasi-stable state is given by

$$T = 0.693 \times R \times C \tag{13.30}$$

Retriggerable Monostable Multivibrator

In a conventional monostable multivibrator, once the output is triggered to the quasi-stable state by applying a suitable trigger pulse, the circuit does not respond to subsequent trigger pulses as long as the output is in quasi-stable stable. After the output returns to its original state, it is ready to respond to the next trigger pulse. There is another class of monostable multivibrators called *retriggerable monostable multivibrators*, which responds to trigger pulses even when the output is in quasi-stable state. In this class of monostable multivibrators, if n trigger pulses with a time period of T_t are applied to the circuit, the output pulse width, that is, the time period of the quasi-stable state equals $(n-1)T_t + T$, where T is the output pulse width for the single trigger pulse and $T_t < T$. Figure 13.45 shows output pulse width in the case of a retriggerable monostable multivibrator for repetitive trigger pulses.

Astable Multivibrator

In the case of an astable multivibrator, neither of the two states is stable. Both output states are quasi-stable. The output switches from one state to the other and the circuit functions like a free-running square wave

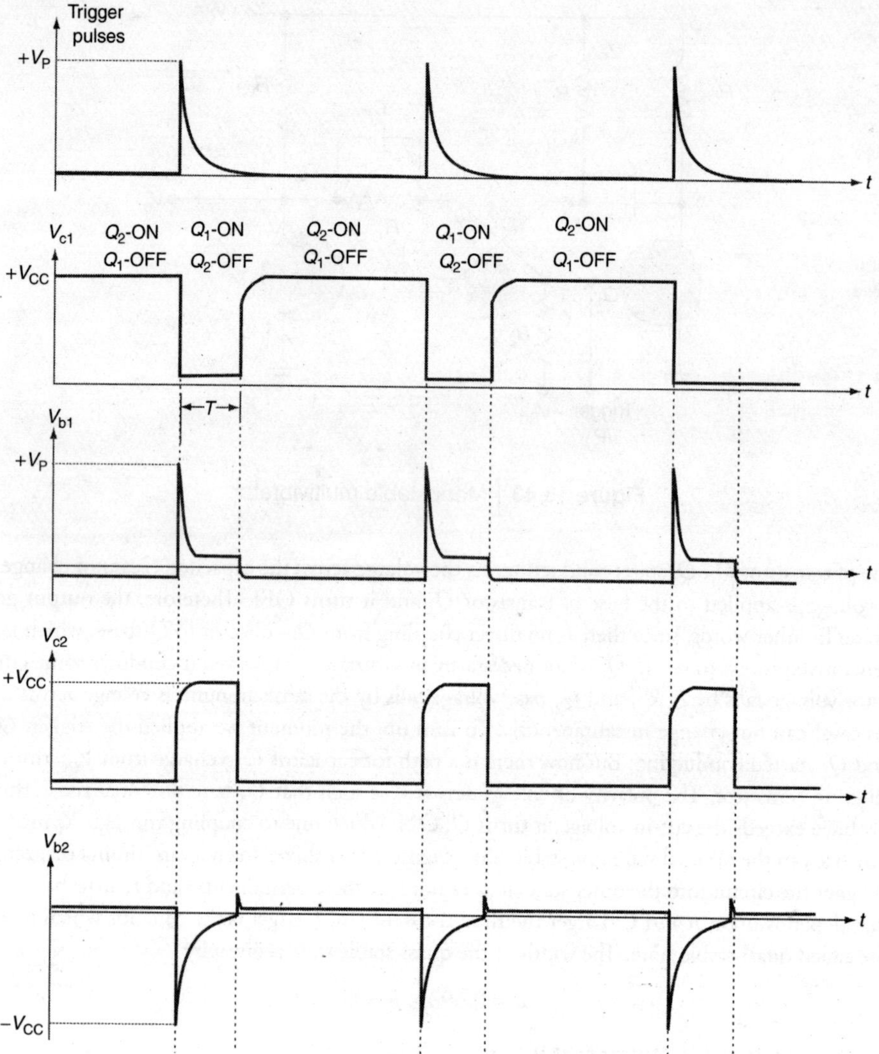

Figure 13.44 Timing waveforms of monostable multivibrator.

oscillator. Figure 13.46 shows the basic astable multivibrator circuit. Value of resistors R_1 and R_2 are typically 10 times the values of R_{C1} and R_{C2}, respectively. It can be proved that in this type of circuit, neither of the output states is stable. Both states, LOW as well as HIGH, are quasi-stable. The time periods for which the output remains LOW and HIGH depends upon R_2C_2 and R_1C_1 time constants, respectively. For $R_1C_1 = R_2C_2$, the output is a symmetrical square waveform. The circuit functions as follows. When power is applied, one transistor will conduct more than the other because of some circuit imbalances. Let us assume that transistor Q_1 conducts more than transistor Q_2. The regenerative action will force transistor Q_1 to saturation and transistor Q_2 to cut-off. Capacitor C_2 will charge rapidly to V_{CC} through resistor R_{C2} and the emitter–base junction of transistor Q_1. This results in momentary increase in the base voltage of transistor Q_1. Capacitor C_1

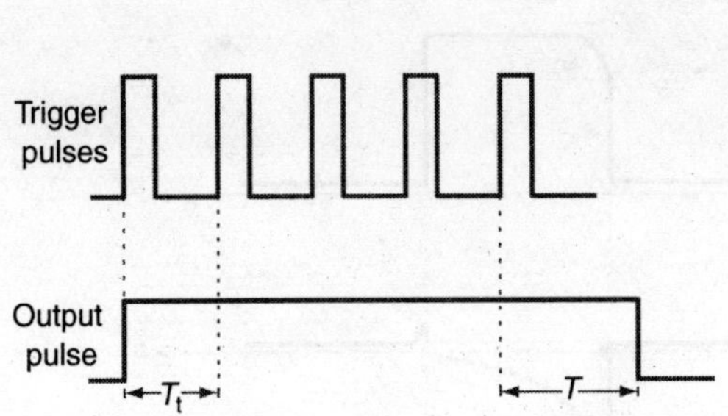

Figure 13.45 Output pulse width for retriggerable monostable multivibrator for repetitive trigger pulses.

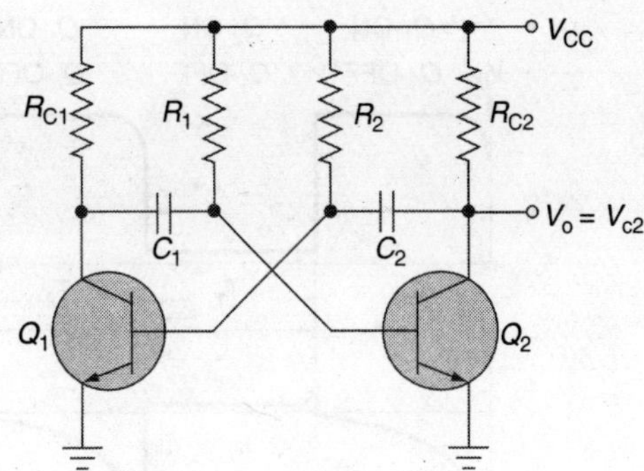

Figure 13.46 Astable multivibrator.

had previously charged through resistor R_{C1} upto V_{CC} when transistor Q_2 was conducting. Now when Q_1 is conducting, C_1 discharges through R_1 and Q_1. The initial pulse of discharge current from C_1 through R_1 results in a negative pulse at the base of transistor Q_2 as shown in Figure 13.47. This turns transistor Q_2 OFF and the output goes to HIGH state. Transistor Q_1 keeps conducting from V_{CC} through resistor R_2. The OFF-time of transistor Q_2 depends upon the time constant R_1C_1. When the base voltage of the transistor reaches the base-switching voltage, transistor Q_2 is no longer in cut-off and starts to conduct allowing capacitor C_1 to be recharged rapidly through resistor R_{C1}. This results in momentary increase in positive voltage at the base of the transistor Q_2 leading to its fast turning ON. Therefore, the output goes to the LOW state. Now capacitor C_2 discharges through transistor Q_2 and resistor R_2. The initial pulse of discharge current from C_2 through R_2 makes the base of transistor Q_1 very negative. This turns OFF Q_1. Q_1 is held in the OFF-state depending upon the time constant R_2C_2 after which Q_1 begins to conduct. This process continues and due to both the couplings (Q_1-collector to Q_2-base and Q_2-collector to Q_1-base) being capacitive, neither of the states is stable. The rounding off in the rising edge of V_{c1} is because of the voltage drop across resistor R_{C1} while capacitor C_1 is recharging. Similarly the rounding off in the rising edge of V_{c2} is because of the voltage drop across resistor R_{C2} while capacitor C_2 is recharging. Figure 13.47 shows the relevant timing diagrams.

Let us now determine the frequency of the output wave for the astable multivibrator of Figure 13.46. The base voltage of transistor Q_2 during discharge of capacitor C_1 is given by

$$V_{b2} = V_{CC} - I_{c1}R_1 \tag{13.31}$$

Since, the capacitor charges to approximately V_{CC}, the initial value of current (I_{c1}) is

$$I_{c1} = \frac{V_{CC} + V_{CC}}{R_1} = \frac{2V_{CC}}{R_1}$$

The current decays exponentially with a time constant of R_1C_1. Therefore, the voltage V_{b2} is given by

$$V_{b2} = V_{CC} - 2V_{CC}e^{-t/R_1C_1} \tag{13.32}$$

The base-switching voltage for silicon transistors is 0.7 V and that for germanium transistors is 0.3 V, which is very small as compared to the V_{CC} voltage. Therefore, it can be assumed that the transistor will switch when $V_{b2} = 0$ V. The time required to switch ON transistor Q_2, that is, the OFF time of the transistor Q_2 (T_2), is given by

$$0 = V_{CC} - 2V_{CC}e^{-T_2/R_1C_1}$$

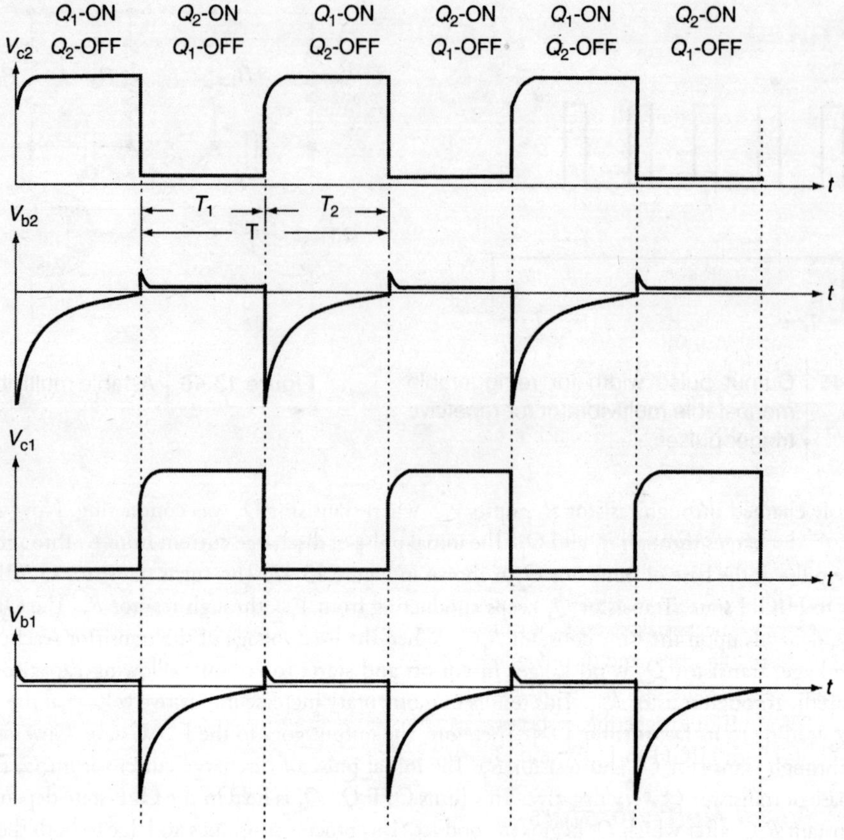

Figure 13.47 Timing waveforms of astable multivibrator.

Therefore,

$$T_2 = R_1C_1 \ln 2 = 0.694R_1C_1 \tag{13.33}$$

T_2 is also the ON time of transistor Q_1. Similarly, the ON time of transistor Q_2 (T_1) which is equal to the OFF time of transistor Q_1 is given by

$$T_1 = R_2C_2 \ln 2 = 0.694R_2C_2 \tag{13.34}$$

The total time period of the wave is T which is given by

$$T = T_1 + T_2 = 0.694(R_1C_1 + R_2C_2) \tag{13.35}$$

For $R_1 = R_2 = R$ and $C_1 = C_2 = C$, the time period is given by $T = 1.388RC$ and the frequency (f) is given by

$$f = \frac{1}{1.388RC}$$

13.10 Integrated Circuit (IC) Multivibrators

In this section, we will discuss monostable and astable multivibrator circuits that can be configured around some of the popular digital and linear integrated circuits.

Digital IC-Based Monostable Multivibrators

Some of the commonly used digital ICs that can be used as monostable multivibrators include 74121 (single monostable multivibrator), 74221 (dual monostable multivibrator), 74122 (single retriggerable monostable multivibrator), 74123 (dual retriggerable monostable multivibrator) – all belonging to TTL family and 4098B (dual retriggerable monostable multivibrator) belonging to CMOS family. Figure 13.48 shows the use of IC 74121 as a monostable multivibrator along with trigger input. The IC provides features for triggering on either LOW-to-HIGH or HIGH-to-LOW edges of the trigger pulses. Figure 13.48(a) shows one of possible application circuits for HIGH-to-LOW edge triggering and Figure 13.48(b) shows one of possible application circuits for LOW-to-HIGH edge triggering. Output pulse width depends on external R and C. The output pulse width can be computed from $T = 0.7RC$. Recommended ranges of values for R and C, respectively, are 4 kΩ to 40 kΩ and 10 pF to 1000 μF. 74121 IC provides complementary outputs. That is, we have stable LOW or HIGH state and corresponding quasi-stable HIGH or LOW state available on Q and $\overline{Q}$ outputs.

Figure 13.49 shows the use of 74123, a dual retriggerable monostable multivibrator. Like 74121, this IC too provides features for triggering on either LOW-to-HIGH or HIGH-to-LOW edges of the trigger pulses. Output pulse width depends on external R and C. It can be computed from $T = 0.28RC \times [1 + (0.7/RC)]$, where R and C are, respectively, in kilo-ohms and pico-farads and T is in nano-seconds. This formula is valid for $C > 1000$ pF. Recommended range of values for R is 5–50 kΩ. Figures 13.49(a) and (b) give application circuits for HIGH-to-LOW and LOW-to-HIGH triggering, respectively. It may be mentioned here that, there can be other triggering circuit options for both HIGH-to-LOW and LOW-to-HIGH edge triggering of the monostable mulitvibrator.

Timer IC-Based Multivibrators

Timer IC 555 is one of the most commonly used general-purpose linear integrated circuits. The simplicity with which monostable and astable multivibrator circuits can be configured around this IC is one of the main reasons for its wide use. Figure 13.50 shows the internal schematic of timer IC 555. It comprises two

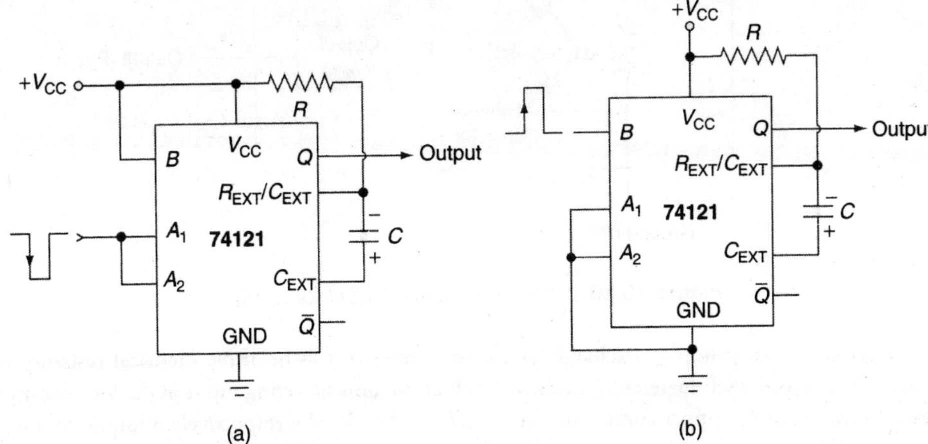

Figure 13.48 (a) HIGH-to-LOW edge triggering of 74121; (b) LOW-to-HIGH edge triggering of 74121.

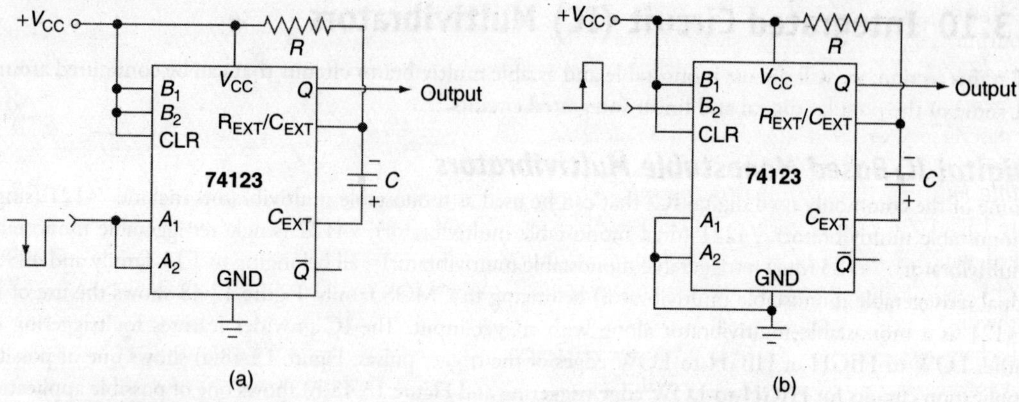

Figure 13.49 (a) HIGH-to-LOW edge triggering of 74123; (b) LOW-to-HIGH edge triggering of 74123.

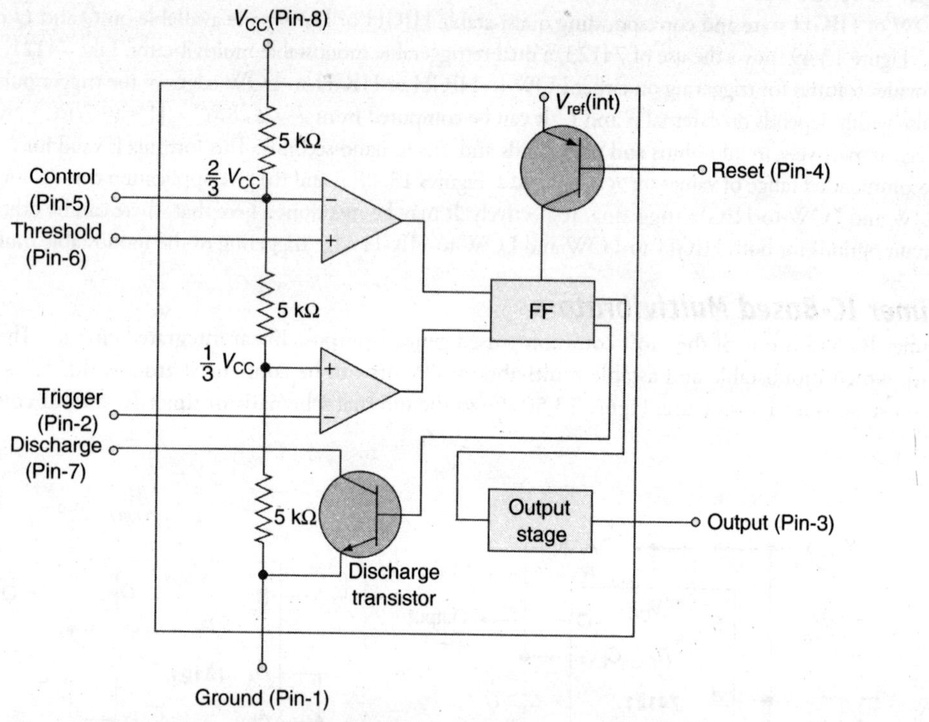

Figure 13.50 Internal schematic of timer IC 555.

opamp comparators, a flip-flop, a discharge transistor, a reset transistor, three identical resistors and an output stage. The resistors set the reference voltage levels at the non-inverting input of the lower comparator and inverting inputs of the upper comparator at $+V_{CC}/3$ and $+2V_{CC}/3$, respectively. Outputs of two comparators feed SET and RESET inputs of the flip-flop and thus decide the logic status of its output and subsequently the final output. The flip-flop's complementary outputs feed the output stage and the base of the discharge transistor. This ensures that when the output is HIGH, the discharge transistor is OFF and when the output is LOW, the discharge transistor is ON. Different terminals of the timer 555 are designated as *Ground* (Terminal-1), *Trigger* (Terminal-2), *Output* (Terminal-3), *Reset* (Terminal-4), *Control* (Terminal-5), *Threshold* (Terminal-6), *Discharge* (Terminal-7) and $+V_{CC}$ (Terminal-8). With this background, we will now describe the astable and monostable multivibator circuits configured around timer IC 555.

Astable Multivibrator Using Timer IC 555

Figure 13.51(a) shows the basic 555 timer-based astable multivibrator circuit. Initially, capacitor C is fully discharged, which forces output to go to the HIGH-state. An open discharge transistor allows capacitor C to charge from $+V_{CC}$ through R_1 and R_2. When the voltage across C exceeds $+2V_{CC}/3$, the output goes to the LOW-state and the discharge transistor is switched ON at the same time. Capacitor C begins to discharge through R_2 and the discharge transistor inside the IC. When the voltage across C falls below $+V_{CC}/3$, the output goes back to the HIGH-state. The charge and discharge cycles repeat and the circuit behaves like a free-running multivibrator. Terminal-4 of the IC is the RESET terminal. Usually, it is connected to $+V_{CC}$. If the voltage at this terminal is driven below 0.4 V, the output is forced to the LOW-state overriding command pulses at Terminal-2 of the IC. HIGH-state and LOW-state time periods are governed by the charge ($+V_{CC}/3$ to $+2V_{CC}/3$) and discharge ($+2V_{CC}/3$ to $+V_{CC}/3$) timings. These are given by Eqs. (13.36) and (13.37), respectively.

$$\text{HIGH-state time period, } T_{\text{HIGH}} = 0.69 \times (R_1 + R_2) \times C \tag{13.36}$$

$$\text{LOW-state time period, } T_{\text{LOW}} = 0.69 \times R_2 \times C \tag{13.37}$$

The relevant waveforms are shown in Figure 13.51(b). The time period (T) and frequency (f) of the output waveform are, respectively, given by Eqs. (13.38) and (13.39), respectively.

$$\text{Time period, } T = 0.69 \times (R_1 + 2R_2) \times C \tag{13.38}$$

$$\text{Frequency, } f = \frac{1}{0.69 \times (R_1 + 2R_2) \times C} \tag{13.39}$$

Remember that when the astable multivibrator is powered, first cycle HIGH-state time period is about 30% longer as the capacitor is initially discharged and it charges from 0 (rather than $+V_{CC}/3$) to $+2V_{CC}/3$.

In the case of the astable multivibrator circuit of Figure 13.51(a), the HIGH-state time period is always greater than the LOW-state time period. Figures 13.51(c) and (d) show two modified circuits where HIGH-state and LOW-state time periods can be chosen independently. For the astable multivibrator circuits of Figures 13.51(c) and (d), the two time periods are given by Eqs. (13.40) and (13.41), respectively.

$$\text{HIGH-state time period} = 0.69 \times R_1 \times C \tag{13.40}$$

$$\text{LOW-state time period} = 0.69 \times R_2 \times C \tag{13.41}$$

For $R_1 = R_2 = R$

$$T = 1.38 \times R \times C$$

$$f = \frac{1}{1.38 \times R \times C} \tag{13.42}$$

Monostable Multivibrator Using Timer IC 555

Figure 13.52(a) shows the basic monostable multivibrator circuit configured around timer 555. It may be mentioned here that monostable multivibrators are also referred to as monoshots. Trigger pulse is applied to Terminal-2

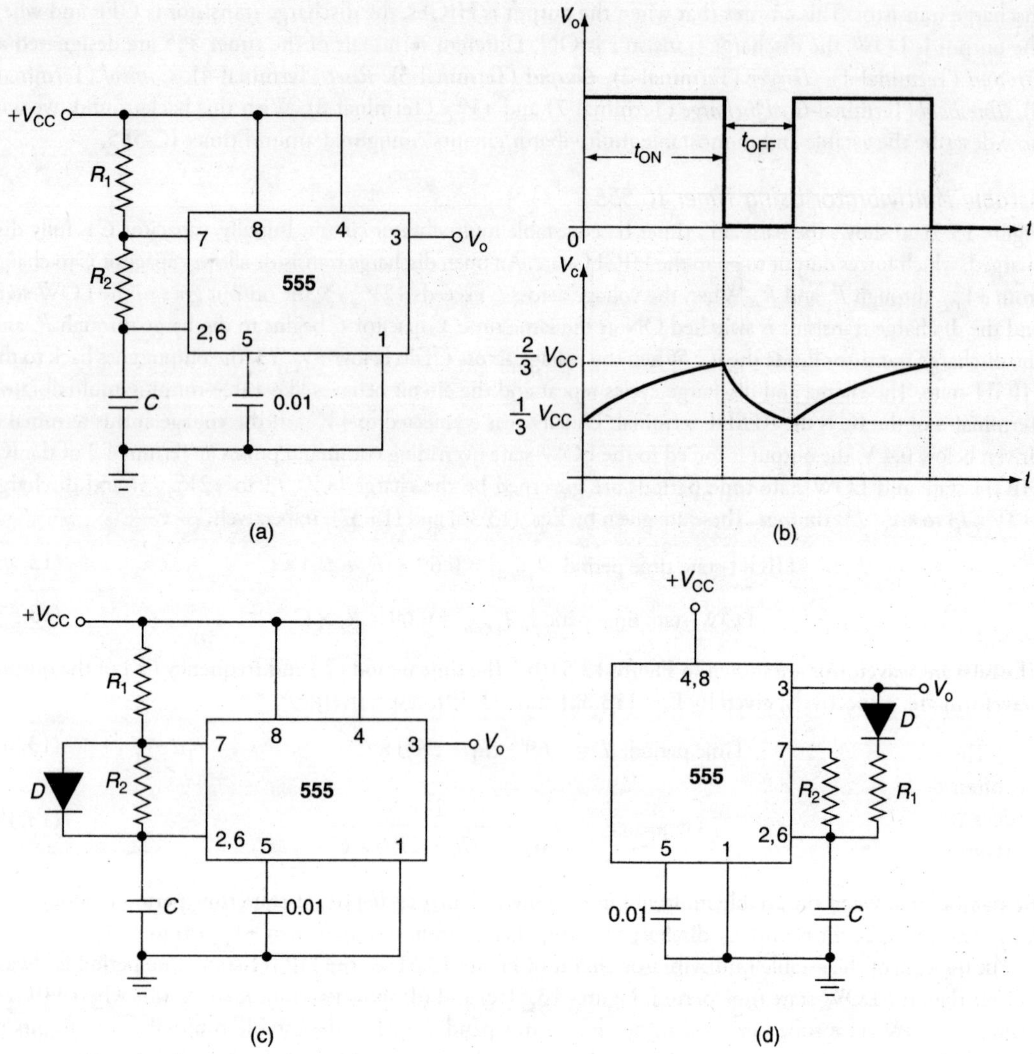

Figure 13.51 (a) Astable multivibrator; (b) relevant waveforms for (a); (c) and (d) modified astable multivibrator circuits.

of the IC, which should initially be kept at $+V_{CC}$. A HIGH at Terminal-2 forces the output to LOW-state. A HIGH-to-LOW trigger pulse at Terminal-2 holds the output in the HIGH-state and simultaneously allows the capacitor to charge from $+V_{CC}$ through R. Remember that LOW-level of the trigger pulse needs to go at least below $+V_{CC}/3$. When the capacitor voltage exceeds $+2V_{CC}/3$, the output goes back to the LOW-state. We will need to apply another trigger pulse to Terminal-2 to make the output go to the HIGH-state again. Every time the timer is appropriately triggered, the output goes to the HIGH-state and stays there for a time period taken by capacitor to charge from 0 to $+2V_{CC}/3$. This time period, which equals the monoshot output pulse width, is given by

$$T = 1.1 \times R \times C \tag{13.43}$$

Figure 13.52(b) shows relevant wacefroms for the circuit of figure 13.52(a).

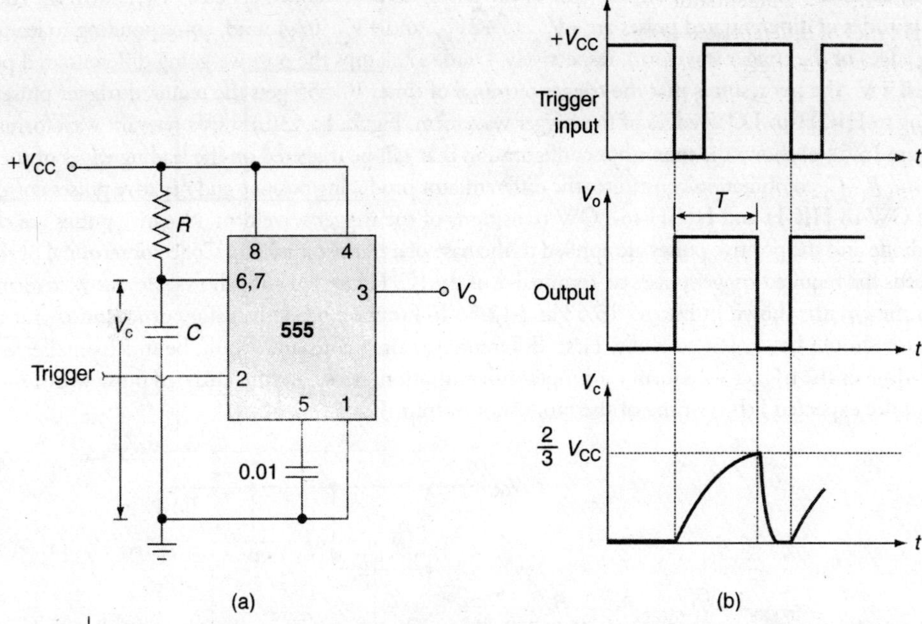

Figure 13.52 (a) Monostable multivibrator circuit configured around timer IC 555; (b) relevant waveforms for the circuit of (a).

The pulse width of the trigger input should be less than the HIGH-time of the monoshot output. Also, it is often desirable to trigger a monostable multivibrator either on the trailing (HIGH-to-LOW) or leading edges (LOW-to-HIGH) of the trigger waveform. In order to achieve that, we will need an external circuit between the trigger waveform input and Terminal-2 of timer IC 555. The external circuit ensures that Terminal-2 of the IC gets the required trigger pulse corresponding to the desired edge of the trigger waveform. Figure 13.53(a) shows the monoshot configuration that can be triggered on the trailing edges of the trigger waveform.

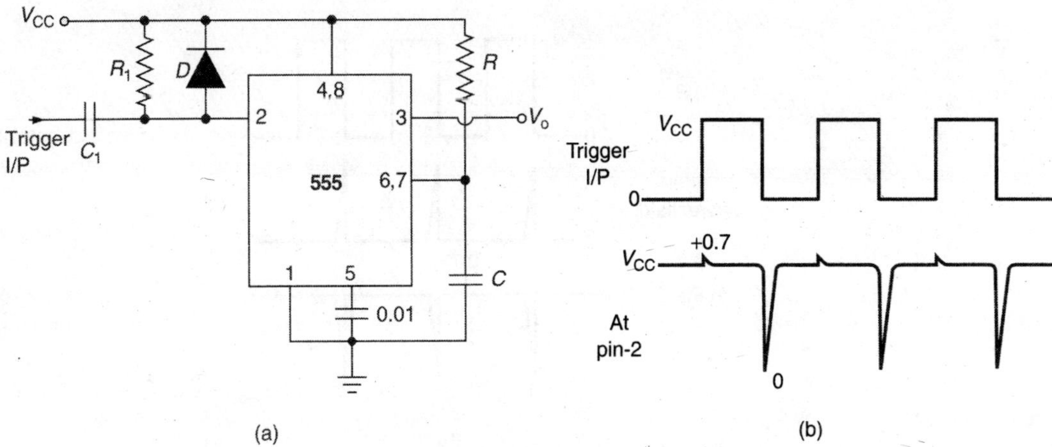

Figure 13.53 (a) Timer IC 555 monoshot configuration triggered on the trailing edges; (b) relevant waveforms.

R_1–C_1 constitutes a differentiator circuit. One of the terminals of resistor R_1 is tied to $+V_{CC}$ with the result that the amplitudes of differentiated pulses are $+V_{CC}$ to $+2V_{CC}$ and $+V_{CC}$ to ground, corresponding to leading and trailing edges of the trigger waveform, respectively. Diode D clamps the positive-going differentiated pulses to about +0.7 V. The net result is that the trigger terminal of timer IC 555 gets the required trigger pulses corresponding to HIGH-to-LOW edges of the trigger waveform. Figure 13.53(b) shows relevant waveforms.

Figure 13.54(a) shows the monoshot configuration that can be triggered on the leading edges of the trigger waveform. R_1–C_1 combination constitutes the differentiator producing positive and negative pulses corresponding to LOW-to-HIGH and HIGH-to-LOW transitions of the trigger waveform. Negative pulses are clamped by the diode and the positive pulses are applied to the base of a transistor switch. Collector terminal of the transistor feeds the required trigger pulses to Terminal-2 of the IC. Figure 13.54(b) shows relevant waveforms.

For the circuits shown in Figures 13.53 and 13.54 to function properly, values of R_1 and C_1 for the differentiator should be chosen carefully. First, differentiator time constant should be much smaller than the HIGH-time of the trigger waveform for proper differentiation. Second, differentiated pulse width should be less than the expected HIGH-time of the monoshot output.

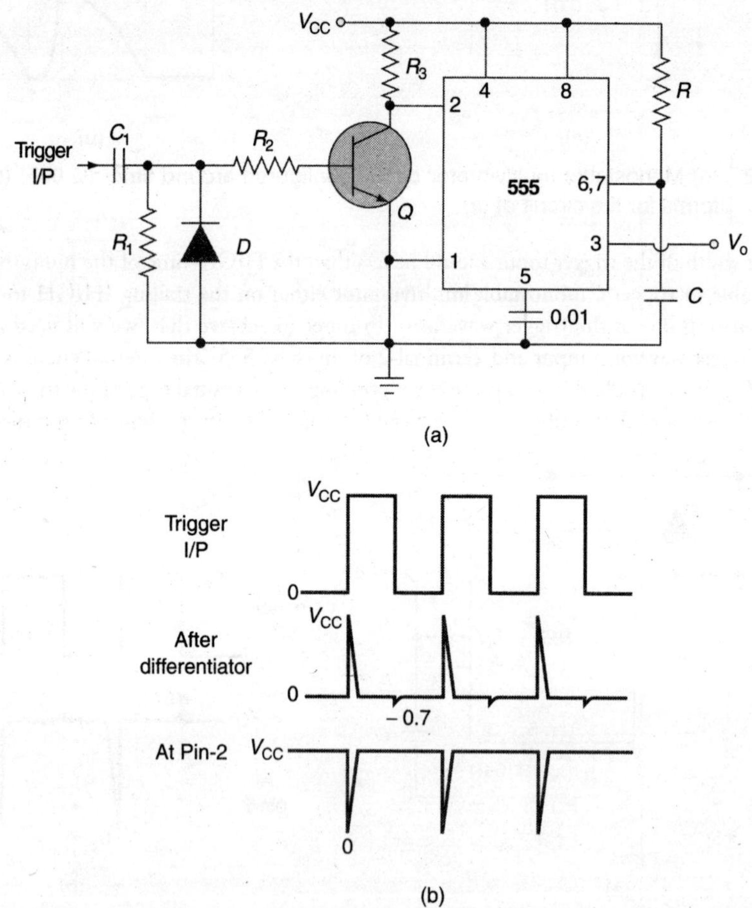

Figure 13.54 (a) Timer IC 555 monoshot configuration triggered on the leading edges; (b) relevant waveforms.

EXAMPLE 13.15 *Pulsed waveform of Figure 13.55(b) is applied to the RESET terminal of astable multivibrator circuit of Figure 13.55(a). Draw the output waveform.*

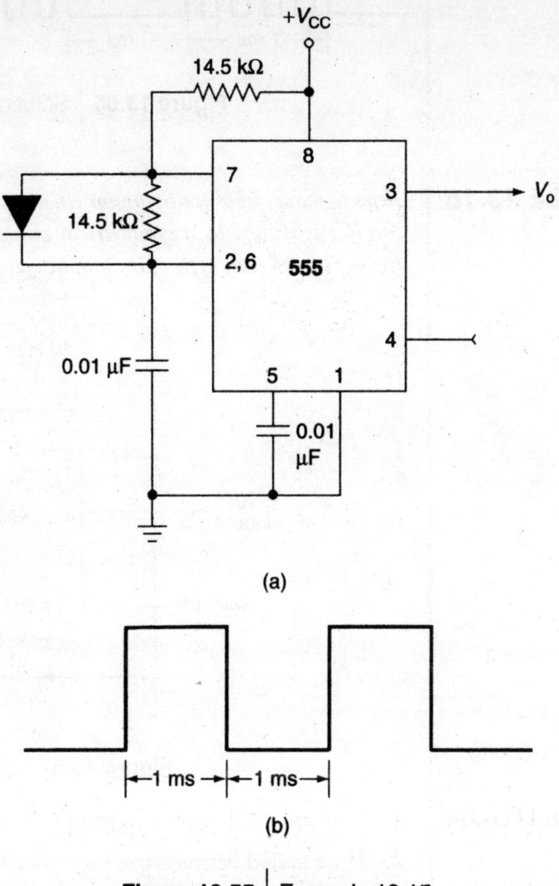

Figure 13.55 | Example 13.15

Solution

1. The circuit shown in Figure 13.55(a) is an astable multivibrator with a 500 Hz symmetrical waveform applied to its RESET terminal. The RESET terminal is alternately HIGH and LOW for 1.0 ms.
2. When the RESET input is LOW, the output is forced to the LOW-state. When the RESET input is HIGH, astable waveform appears at the output.
3. HIGH and LOW time periods of the astable multivibrator are determined as follows:

   HIGH-time $= 0.69 \times 14.5 \times 10^3 \times 0.01 \times 10^{-6} = 100\ \mu s$

   LOW-time $= 0.69 \times 14.5 \times 10^3 \times 0.01 \times 10^{-6} = 100\ \mu s$
4. Astable output is thus a 5 kHz symmetrical waveform. Every time RESET terminal goes HIGH for 1.0 ms, five cycles of 5 kHz waveform appear at the output. Figure 13.56 shows the output waveform appearing at Terminal-3 of timer IC.

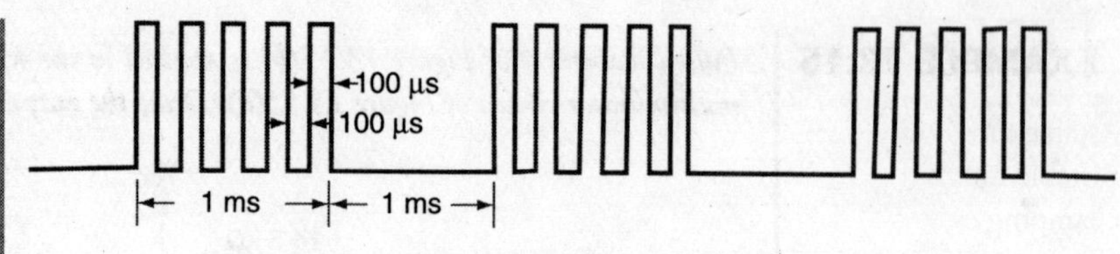

Figure 13.56 | Solution of Example 13.15.

EXAMPLE 13.16 *Refer to monostable multivibrator circuit of Figure 13.57. Trigger terminal (pin-2 of the IC) is driven by a symmetrical pulsed waveform of 10 kHz. Determine the frequency and duty cycle of the output waveform.*

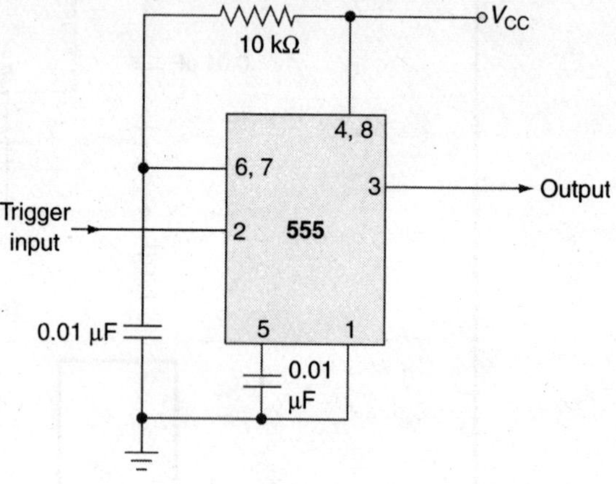

Figure 13.57 | Example 13.16.

SOLUTION

1. Frequency of trigger waveform = 10 kHz.
2. Time period between two successive leading or trailing edges = 100 μs.
3. Expected pulse width of monoshot output = $1.1RC = 1.1 \times 10^4 \times 10^{-8} =$ 110 μs.
4. Trigger waveform is a symmetrical one; it has HIGH and LOW time periods of 50 μs each.
5. Since the LOW-state time period of the trigger waveform is less than the expected output pulse width, it can successfully trigger the monoshot on its trailing edges.
6. Since the time period between two successive trailing edges is 100 μs and the expected output pulse width is 110 μs; therefore, only alternate trailing edges of trigger waveform will trigger the monoshot.
7. Frequency of output waveform = $10 \times 10^3/2 = 5$ kHz.
8. Time period of output waveform = $1/(5 \times 10^3) = 200$ μs.
9. Therefore, duty cycle of output waveform = 110/200 = 0.55.

KEY TERMS

Astable multivibrator
Bistable multivibrator
Clamping circuit
Clipping circuit
Monostable multivibrator
Multivibrator
RC high-pass circuit
RC low-pass circuit
Retriggerable monostable multivibrator
Schmitt trigger
Timer IC 555

OBJECTIVE-TYPE EXERCISES

Multiple-Choice Questions

1. A low-pass circuit can also possibly be
   - **a.** an integrator circuit.
   - **b.** a differentiator circuit.
   - **c.** either a differentiator or an integrator circuit.
   - **d.** none of these.
2. A high-pass circuit can also possibly be
   - **a.** an integrator circuit.
   - **b.** a differentiator circuit.
   - **c.** either a differentiator or an integrator circuit.
   - **d.** none of these.
3. A low-pass circuit with a relatively higher upper 3 dB cut-off frequency will
   - **a.** have relatively more sluggish step response.
   - **b.** have relatively steeper step response.
   - **c.** behave more like an integrator.
   - **d.** none of these.
4. A low-pass circuit is fed with a periodic waveform of time period T. For this circuit to function like an integrator, the necessary condition to be satisfied is
   - **a.** $RC = T$.
   - **b.** $RC << T$.
   - **c.** $RC >> T$.
   - **d.** none of these.
5. In the basic clamper circuit, positive or negative, a resistance R is always connected across the diode. If the forward-biased and reverse-biased resistances of the diode were 10 Ω and 10 MΩ, respectively, the most optimum value of R would then be
   - **a.** 10 Ω
   - **b.** 10 MΩ
   - **c.** 100 kΩ
   - **d.** 10 kΩ
6. An RC integrator circuit with an upper 3 dB cut-off frequency of 3.5 kHz will respond to a step input with a rise time of
   - **a.** 100 μs
   - **b.** 10 μs
   - **c.** 100 ms
   - **d.** indeterminate from given data.
7. An RC differentiator circuit with a lower 3 dB cut-off frequency of 3.5 kHz will respond to a step input with a rise time of
   - **a.** 100 μs
   - **b.** 10 μs
   - **c.** 100 ms
   - **d.** practically nil value.
8. In the case of an timer IC-based monostable multivibrator circuit, the requirement for the trigger pulse appearing at trigger terminal of IC timer is the following:
   - **a.** Trigger pulse width should be equal to the intended output pulse width.
   - **b.** Trigger pulse width should be less than the intended output pulse width.
   - **c.** Trigger pulse width should be greater than the intended output pulse width.
   - **d.** None of these.
9. A retriggerable monostable multivibrator is designed for an output pulse width of 400 μs. If it were fed with 11 trigger pulses with successive trigger pulses separated by 10 μs, the output pulse width would be
   - **a.** 100 μs
   - **b.** 400 μs
   - **c.** 500 μs
   - **d.** 200 μs

10. A Schmitt trigger circuit is a type of
    a. bistable multivibrator circuit.
    b. monostable multivibrator circuit.
    c. astable multivibrator circuit.
    d. none of these.

REVIEW QUESTIONS

1. Draw the basic single-section RC low-pass circuit and briefly explain how does this circuit respond to a step input and a pulse input of given time duration? Under what conditions does this circuit behave as an integrator?
2. Prove that:
   a. Low-pass RC circuit responds to a step input with a rise time of $0.35/f_U$, where f_U is the upper 3 dB cut-off frequency.
   b. Upper 3 dB cut-off frequency in the case of a single-section low-pass RC circuit is given by $1/2\pi RC$.
3. Draw the basic single-section RC high-pass circuit and briefly explain how does this circuit respond to a step input and a pulse input of given time duration? Under what conditions does this circuit behave as a differentiator?
4. With the help of relevant circuit diagrams, briefly describe the operation of clipping circuits that can be used to:
   a. Clip portion of positive half cycles of a sinusoidal input with amplitude greater than a certain specified DC voltage V_{BB}, assuming that the peak amplitude of sinusoidal input is greater than V_{BB}.
   b. Clip portion of negative half cycles of a sinusoidal input with amplitude more negative than a certain specified DC voltage $-V_{BB}$, assuming that the peak amplitude of sinusoidal input is greater than V_{BB}.
5. With the help of circuit diagram, briefly describe the operation of a positive clamper circuit. What is role of resistor (R) in the clamping circuit? How does one choose an optimum value of the resistance?
6. Distinguish between bistable, monostable and astable multivibrators. How does a bistable multivibrator differ from a Schmitt trigger circuit from the viewpoint of both the circuit schematic and function?
7. How does a retriggerable monostable multivibrator differ from a conventional monostable multivibrator? What determines the output pulse width in the case of a retriggerable monostable multivibrator?
8. With the help of circuit diagram, briefly describe the operation of timer IC-based astable multivibrator in which output HIGH- and LOW-state time periods can be set independently.
9. With the help of circuit diagram, briefly describe the operation of timer IC-based monostable multivibrator that can be triggered on
   a. HIGH-to-LOW transitions of input pulse train.
   b. LOW-to-HIGH transitions of input pulse train.
10. Briefly describe reasons for the following:
    a. Why are diode-based clipping circuits also called non-linear wave shaping circuits?
    b. Why should the trigger pulse appearing at trigger terminal of the IC timer 555 in a monostable multivibrator configuration be less than the expected output pulse width for intended operation?
    c. Why does a low-pass RC circuit behave as an integrator when the RC time constant is much larger than the time period of the input waveform?

PROBLEMS

1. A simple low-pass RC network is fed with a 10 V step. If R = 10 kΩ and C = 0.1 μF, what will be the time period in which the output will change from 1.0 V to 9.0 V?

2. The RC network of the type of Problem 1 with different values of R and C gives a rise time of 100 μs to a certain step input. Determine the 3 dB cut-off frequency of the network.

3. Determine the most optimum value of R in the clamper circuit of Figure 13.58 given that forward-biased and reverse-biased resistances of the diode are 10 Ω and 10 MΩ, respectively.

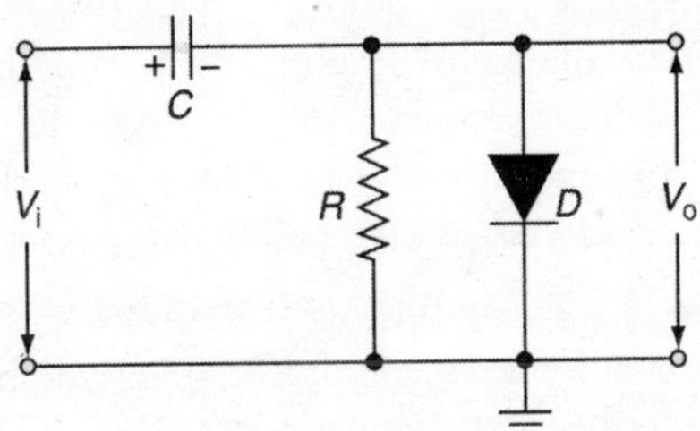

Figure 13.58 Problem 3.

4. Refer to the astable multivibrator circuit of Figure 13.59. It is given that V_{CC} = + 5 V, $R_1 = 2R_2$. If the LOW-state time period of the output waveform were 1 ms, draw the output waveform.

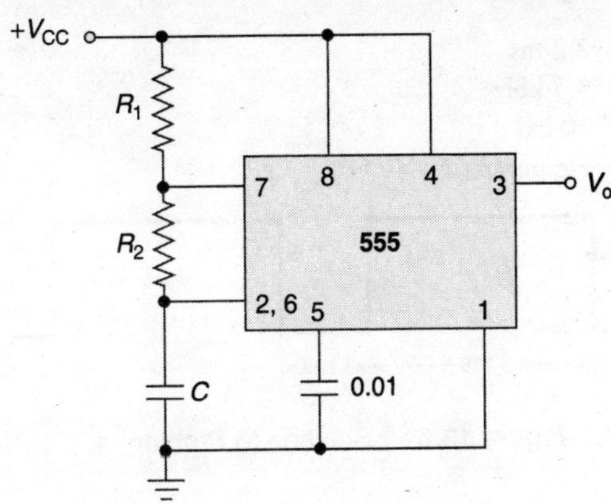

Figure 13.59 Problem 4.

5. The monostable configuration of Figure 13.60 was designed by some one to generate a pulse (pulse width of course depending upon the values of R and C) whenever it was triggered by the available trigger pulse as shown. The circuit did not seem to work. What would be wrong with the circuit?

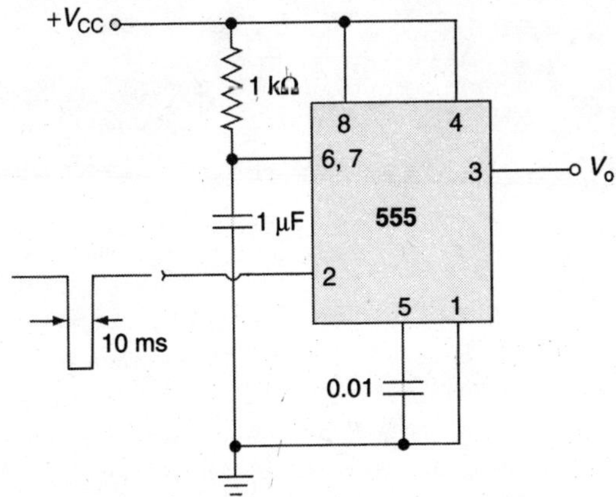

Figure 13.60 Problem 5.

ANSWERS

Multiple-Choice Questions

1. (a)
2. (b)
3. (b)
4. (c)
5. (d)
6. (a)
7. (d)
8. (b)
9. (c)
10. (a)

Problems

1. 2.2 ms
2. 3.5 kHz
3. 10 kΩ
4. Figure 13.61

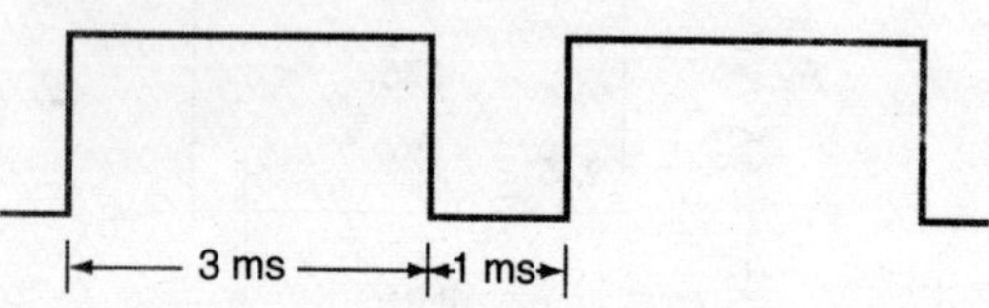

Figure 13.61 | Solution to Problem 4.

5. Trigger pulse width appearing at pin-2 of the IC is greater than the expected output pulse width. It should be less than the expected output pulse width.

CHAPTER 14

Linear Power Supplies

Learning Objectives

After completing this chapter, you will learn the following:

- Constituents of a linear power supply and the role of different building blocks.
- Designing mains transformer.
- Different types of rectifier circuits and their characteristic features.
- Different types of filter circuits and their characteristic features.
- Different types of linear regulator circuits.
- Emitter–follower regulator.
- Series-pass element regulators.
- Shunt regulators.
- Protection circuits.
- IC voltage regulators including general-purpose, fixed output and adjustable output regulators.

Every electronics system, be it an entertainment gadget or a test and measurement equipment, requires one or more DC voltages for its operation. Most of the time it is essential and almost always desirable that these DC voltages are nicely filtered and well regulated. Power supply does the job of providing required DC voltages from available AC mains in the case of mains operated systems and DC input in the case of battery operated systems. Power supplies are often classified as linear power supplies or switched mode power supplies depending upon the nature of regulation circuit. While in the present chapter, the focus is on linear power supplies; switched mode power supplies are discussed in the next chapter.

14.1 Constituents of a Linear Power Supply

A linear power supply essentially comprises a *mains transformer*, a *rectifier circuit*, a *filter circuit* and a *regulation circuit* (Figure 14.1). The transformer provides voltage transformation and produces across its secondary winding(s) AC voltage(s) required for producing desired DC voltages. It also provides electrical isolation between the input power supply, that is, AC mains and the DC output. Step-down transformers required for generating common DC voltages and load current ratings are commercially available. Step-up transformers for generating higher output voltages could be custom designed. Different steps involved in the design of a mains transformer for given primary and secondary voltages and secondary current specifications are outlined in Section 14.2.

The rectifier circuit changes the AC voltage appearing across transformer secondary to DC or more precisely a unidirectional output. Commonly used rectifier circuits include the half-wave rectifier, conventional full-wave rectifier requiring a tapped secondary winding and the bridge rectifier.

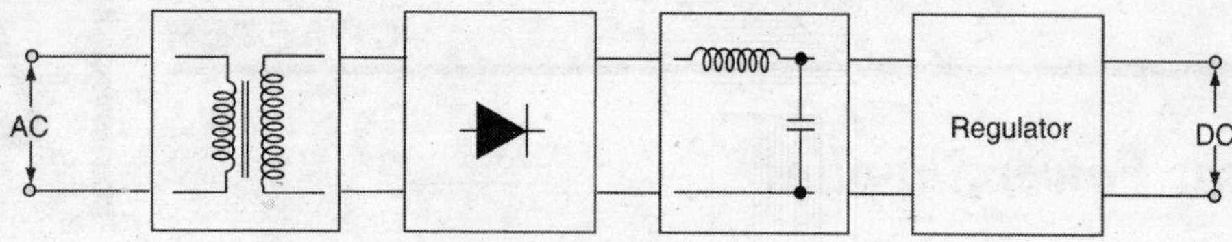

Figure 14.1 Constituents of a linear power supply.

The rectifier voltage always has some AC content known as ripple. The filter circuit smoothens the ripple of the rectifier voltage. The regulator circuit is a type of feedback circuit that ensures that the output DC voltage does not change from its nominal value due to change in line voltage or load current.

In a linearly regulated power supply, the active device used in the regulator, usually a bipolar transistor, is operated anywhere between cut-off and saturation. Commonly used regulator circuit configurations include emitter–follower regulator, series-pass regulator and shunt regulator. Emitter–follower and series-pass regulators are, in fact, now available in IC packages in both fixed output voltage as well as variable output voltage varieties. These are popularly known as *three terminal regulators* and are discussed in Section 14.6.

All power supplies have in-built protection circuits. Common protection features include current limit, short-circuit protection, thermal shutdown and crowbaring. These are also discussed in the chapter.

14.2 Designing Mains Transformer

As outlined earlier, mains transformers for various primary voltages, secondary voltages and a range of secondary current ratings are commercially available to meet most of power supply designers' requirements. In the case of any special requirements, mains transformers can be custom designed by following the under-mentioned steps.

1. The first step is to ensure that the transformer does not saturate at the desired load current or output power requirement. Choosing the transformer core with appropriate cross-section does this. The optimum core cross-section (A_C) is determined with sufficient accuracy using the following equation:
$$A_C = \frac{\sqrt{P}}{5.6} \tag{14.1}$$
where P is the power required to be delivered by the transformer in Watts; A_C the core cross-section in square inches.
2. The ratio of stack thickness (t) to the width of the center limb (W) should be in the range of 1.1 to 1.5 (Figure 14.2).
3. The turns per volt for different windings can be computed as
$$\text{Turns per volt} = \frac{10^8}{4.44 \times f \times A_C \times B} \tag{14.2}$$
where f is the frequency in Hz; B the flux density in lines per square inch (for STALLOY and other similar core materials used for winding power transformers, B may be taken as 50,000 lines per square inch); A_C the core cross-section in square inch. In Eq. (14.2), if core cross-section (A_C) were substituted in cm^2, then the flux density (B) should be substituted in Gauss.
4. Having computed turns per volt, primary and secondary number of turns can be computed from known values of primary and secondary voltages.

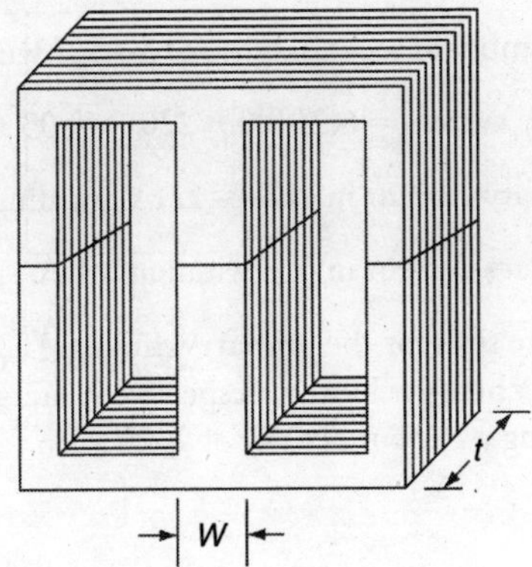

Figure 14.2 Designing mains transformer.

5. Primary current is computed as

$$\text{Primary current} = \frac{P}{\text{Efficiency} \times \text{Primary voltage}} \tag{14.3}$$

Efficiency may be taken as 85–90%.

6. Secondary current is computed as

$$\text{Secondary current} = \frac{\text{Primary current}}{n} \tag{14.4}$$

where n is the ratio of secondary turns (N_S) to primary turns (N_P).

Primary and secondary wire sizes can be determined from known values of primary and secondary currents. Standard wire gauge table can be referred to know the wire gauge number. For power transformers, it is reasonably safe to assume current density figure of 2000 A/in.^{2}. The current handling capability of wires of different sizes in standard wire gauge table is usually given with the assumption of current density figure of 1000 A/in.^{2}.

EXAMPLE 14.1 *Design a power transformer with a multi-output secondary and the following input/output specifications.*

(a) Primary voltage: 220 V, 50 Hz.

(b) Secondary voltage: (a) 12–0–12 V at 100 mA and (b) 5 V at 1 A.

Assume B = 60,000 lines per square inch for the chosen core material and an efficiency of 90%.

Solution

1. Power to be delivered by transformer secondary $= 12 \times 0.1 + 5 \times 1 = 6.2$ W.
2. Core cross-section, $A_C = \sqrt{P}/5.6$, where P is the power to be delivered by transformer secondary. Therefore, $A_C = \sqrt{6.2}/5.6 = 0.444$ in.^{2}.
3. Turns per volt $= 10^8/[4.44 \times f \times A_C \times B] = 10^8/[4.44 \times 50 \times 0.444 \times 60{,}000] = 16.9$.
4. Therefore, number of primary turns $= 16.9 \times 220 = 3718$.
5. The number of secondary turns for one half of (12–0–12) V center-tapped winding $= 16.9 \times 12 = 203$.

6. The number of secondary turns for 5 V winding = 16.9 × 5 = 85.
7. Primary current = 6.2/(0.9 × 220) = 0.03 A.
8. Secondary current in (12–0–12) V winding = 0.1 A.
9. Secondary current in 5 V winding = 1 A.
10. The wire sizes for the primary winding, (12–0–12) V secondary winding and 5 V secondary winding, respectively, are 40 SWG, 35 SWG and 23 SWG assuming a current density of 2000 A/in.^{2}.

14.3 Rectifier Circuits

As outlined earlier, the job of rectifier circuit is to convert the AC voltage appearing across the transformer secondary into a unidirectional voltage. There are three basic rectifier circuit configurations. These include (a) half-wave rectifier, (b) conventional two-diode full-wave rectifier that requires a center-tapped secondary winding and (c) bridge rectifier. Rectifier circuits are characterized by several parameters, which include *ripple frequency, ripple factor, ratio of rectification, transformer utilization factor* and the required *peak inverse voltage* of the rectifier diodes in the circuit. These parameters are briefly discussed in the following subsections. This is then followed up by discussion on different types of rectifier circuits with particular reference to their comparison on the basis of these parameters.

Characteristic Parameters

Performance of a rectifier circuit is often judged on the basis of the parameters outlined in the previous paragraph. These parameters are briefly covered in the following paragraphs.

Ripple Frequency

Ripple frequency is the frequency of the unidirectional periodic voltage waveform present at the output of the rectifier circuit. In the case of half-wave rectifier, as we will see when we discuss different rectifier circuits, it is f, where f is the frequency of AC signal present at the input of rectifier circuit. In the case of full-wave rectifiers, conventional and bridge, it is $2f$. The significance of ripple frequency lies in its direct relationship with ripple factor. Higher ripple frequency means lower ripple factor and less stringent filtering requirement.

Ripple Factor

Ripple factor is ratio of root mean square (RMS) amplitude of AC component (ripple) to the DC component in the rectified waveform. Ripple factor tells how close the rectified waveform is to the true DC. It can be computed as ratio of RMS value of AC component of the rectified voltage signal to the DC component of the rectified voltage signal. It can also be computed from the ratio of RMS value of AC component of rectified current signal to the DC component of the rectified current signal. That is, ripple factor (r) is given by

$$r = \frac{V_\mathrm{r}(\mathrm{RMS})}{V_\mathrm{DC}} = \frac{I_\mathrm{r}(\mathrm{RMS})}{I_\mathrm{DC}}$$

where V_r (RMS) is the RMS value of ripple voltage; V_DC the DC value of rectified voltage; I_r (RMS) the RMS value of ripple current; I_DC the DC value of rectified current. Also,

$$V_\mathrm{r}(\mathrm{RMS}) = \sqrt{{V_\mathrm{RMS}}^2 - {V_\mathrm{DC}}^2}$$

where V_{RMS} is the RMS value of the rectified voltage. I_r (RMS) is given by

$$I_r(\text{RMS}) = \sqrt{I_{RMS}^2 - I_{DC}^2}$$

where I_{RMS} is the RMS value of the rectified current. This gives ripple factor as

$$r = \sqrt{\frac{V_{RMS}^2 - V_{DC}^2}{V_{DC}^2}} = \sqrt{\frac{I_{RMS}^2 - I_{DC}^2}{I_{DC}^2}}$$

$$r = \sqrt{\left(\frac{V_{RMS}}{V_{DC}}\right)^2 - 1} = \sqrt{\left(\frac{I_{RMS}}{I_{DC}}\right)^2 - 1} \tag{14.5}$$

Ratio of Rectification

Ratio of rectification is the ratio of DC power delivered to the load to the AC power input from transformer secondary. Like ripple factor, it also determines the effectiveness of a rectifier circuit in converting AC into DC. DC power delivered to the load resistance (R_L) = $I_{DC}^2 \times R_L$. AC power input from transformer secondary = $I_{RMS}^2 \times (R_f + R_L)$. Here R_f is the resistance offered by forward-biased rectifier diode. Since R_f is much smaller than R_L, AC power available from transformer secondary $\cong I_{RMS}^2 \times R_L$. This gives,

$$\text{Ratio of rectification} = \frac{I_{DC}^2}{I_{RMS}^2} = \left(\frac{I_{DC}}{I_{RMS}}\right)^2 \tag{14.6}$$

From Eqs. (14.5) and (14.6) we can see that ratio of rectification and ripple factor are interrelated. One can be expressed in the form of the other and vice versa. The interrelationship is determined in Example 14.2.

Transformer Utilization Factor

Transformer utilization factor (*TUF*) is defined as the ratio of DC power delivered to the load to the AC power rating of the transformer secondary:

$$\text{TUF} = \frac{\text{DC power delivered to the load}}{\text{AC power rating of transformer secondary}}$$

It may be mentioned here that rating of the transformer in a power supply is governed by the intended DC power to be delivered to the load and the type of rectifier circuit. TUF parameter should not be confused with the ratio of rectification. Rating of transformer secondary is different from the actual AC power delivered by it. AC power rating of transformer secondary is the product of RMS value of voltage across secondary and RMS value of current flowing through secondary. The transformer utilization factor tells us about the maximum DC power that can be delivered to the load for a given transformer rating. A lower TUF implies lower DC power delivered to load for a given power rating of the transformer. We will see in the following paragraphs that TUF values for half-wave and full-wave rectifiers, respectively, are 0.287 and 0.574. This implies that a 1 kVA transformer can at the most deliver a DC power of 287 W to a resistive load when used with a half-wave rectifier. The same for a full-wave rectifier is 574 W.

Peak Inverse Voltage

Peak inverse voltage is the maximum reverse voltage appearing across the diodes used in the rectifier circuit. It is important as it decides the PIV rating of the diode to be used in the rectifier circuit. It is yet another parameter that can be used to compare merits/demerits of different rectifier circuits. It is V_m, $2V_m$ and V_m in the case of half-wave, conventional two-diode full-wave and bridge rectifier circuits, respectively.

Half-Wave Rectifier

Figure 14.3 shows the half-wave rectifier circuit for positive output voltage along with input and output waveforms. Figure 14.4 shows the same for negative output voltage. In the case of positive output rectifier circuit of Figure 14.3, diode D_1 is forward-biased during positive half cycles and reverse-biased during negative half cycles of the input. In the case of negative output rectifier circuit of Figure 14.4, diode D_1 is forward-biased during negative half cycles and reverse-biased during positive half cycles of the input. This explains the output waveforms in the two cases.

Ripple factor in the case of half-wave rectifier circuit can be computed from Eq. (14.5) as

$$r = \sqrt{\left(\frac{I_{\text{RMS}}}{I_{\text{DC}}}\right)^2 - 1}$$

In the case of a half-wave rectified waveform,

$$I_{\text{RMS}} = \frac{I_{\text{m}}}{2} \text{ and } I_{\text{DC}} = \frac{I_{\text{m}}}{\pi}$$

where I_{m} is the peak value of the current waveform across the secondary. This gives

$$r = \sqrt{\left(\frac{I_{\text{m}}/2}{I_{\text{m}}/\pi}\right)^2} - 1 = \sqrt{(\pi^2/4) - 1} = 1.21$$

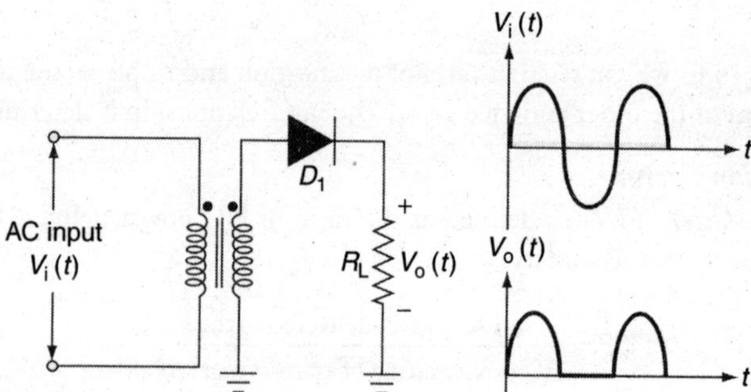

Figure 14.3 | Half-wave rectifier circuit for positive output voltage.

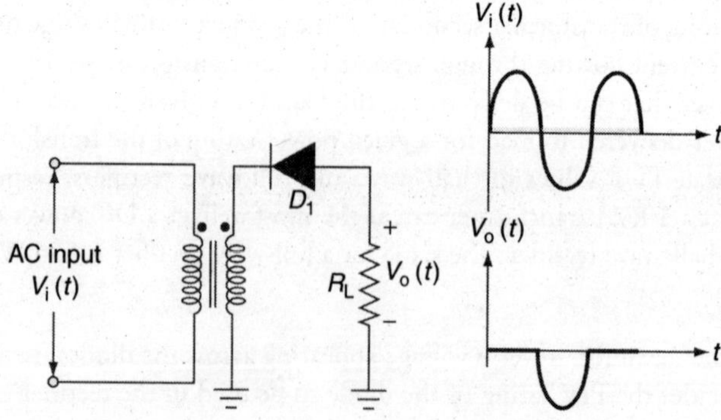

Figure 14.4 | Half-wave rectifier for negative output voltage.

Ratio of rectification can be computed from Eq. (14.6) as

$$\text{Ratio of rectification} = \left(\frac{I_{DC}}{I_{RMS}}\right)^2 = \left(\frac{I_m / \pi}{I_m / 2}\right)^2 = \frac{4}{\pi^2} = 0.406$$

Transformer utilization factor can be computed as follows:

$$\text{DC power delivered to load} = \left(\frac{I_m}{\pi}\right)^2 \times R_L$$

$$\text{AC power rating of transformer secondary} = \frac{V_m}{\sqrt{2}} \times \frac{I_m}{2} = \frac{V_m \times I_m}{2\sqrt{2}}$$

Also, ignoring the forward-biased diode's resistance, $V_m = I_m \times R_L$. This gives

$$\text{AC power rating of transformer secondary} = \frac{V_m \times I_m}{2\sqrt{2}} = \frac{I_m^{\,2} \times R_L}{2\sqrt{2}}$$

Therefore,

$$\text{Transformer utilization factor} = \frac{(I_m / \pi)^2 \times R_L}{(I_m^{\,2} \times R_L) / 2\sqrt{2}} = \frac{2\sqrt{2}}{\pi^2} = 0.287$$

Full-Wave Rectifier

Figure 14.5 shows the full-wave rectifier circuit for positive output voltage along with input and output waveforms. Figure 14.6 shows the same for negative output voltage. In the case of positive output rectifier circuit of Figure 14.5, diode D_1 is forward-biased and diode D_2 is reverse-biased during positive half cycles of the input. During negative half cycles, diode D_2 is forward-biased and diode D_1 is reverse-biased. In both half cycles, current through load resistance R_L flows in the same direction as shown. In the case of negative output rectifier circuit of Figure 14.6, diode D_2 is forward-biased and diode D_1 is reverse-biased during positive half cycles of the input. During negative half cycles, diode D_1 is forward-biased and diode D_2 is reverse-biased. In both half cycles, current through load resistance R_L flows in the same direction, which is opposite to the direction of flow of current in the case of positive output circuit. This explains the output waveforms in the two cases.

Ripple factor in the case of full-wave rectifier circuit can be computed from Eq. (14.5) as

$$r = \sqrt{\left(\frac{I_{RMS}}{I_{DC}}\right)^2 - 1}$$

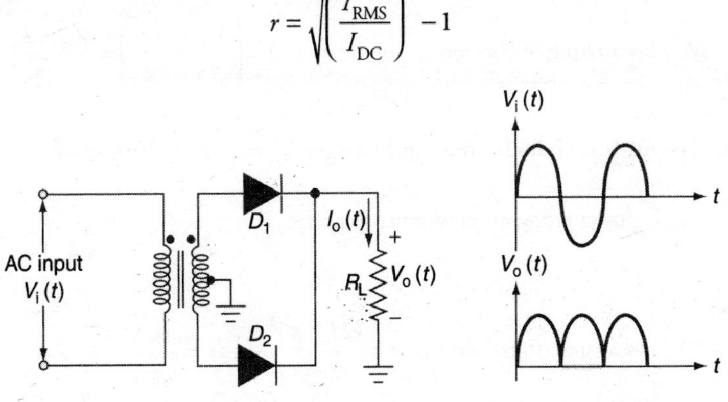

Figure 14.5 Full-wave rectifier circuit for positive output voltage.

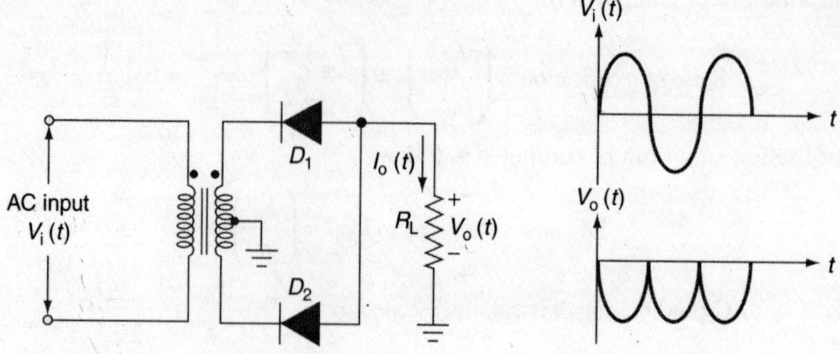

Figure 14.6 | Full-wave rectifier for negative output voltage.

In the case of a full-wave rectified waveform,

$$I_{RMS} = \frac{I_m}{\sqrt{2}} \text{ and } I_{DC} = \frac{2I_m}{\pi}$$

where I_m is the peak value of the current waveform, we have

$$r = \sqrt{\left(\frac{I_m/\sqrt{2}}{2I_m/\pi}\right)^2 - 1} = \sqrt{(\pi^2/8) - 1} = 0.482$$

Ratio of rectification can be computed from Eq. (14.6) as

$$\text{Ratio of rectification} = \left(\frac{I_{DC}}{I_{RMS}}\right)^2 = \left(\frac{2I_m/\pi}{I_m/\sqrt{2}}\right)^2 = \frac{8}{\pi^2} = 0.812$$

Transformer utilization factor can be computed as follows:

$$\text{DC power delivered to load} = \left(\frac{2I_m}{\pi}\right)^2 \times R_L$$

$$\text{AC power rating of transformer secondary} = 2 \times \left(\frac{V_m}{\sqrt{2}} \times \frac{I_m}{2}\right) = \frac{V_m \times I_m}{\sqrt{2}}$$

Also, ignoring the forward-biased diode's resistance, we get $V_m = I_m \times R_L$. This gives

$$\text{AC power rating of transformer secondary} = \frac{V_m \times I_m}{\sqrt{2}} = \frac{I_m^2 \times R_L}{\sqrt{2}}$$

Therefore,

$$\text{Transformer utilization factor} = \frac{(2I_m/\pi)^2 \times R_L}{(I_m^2 \times R_L)/\sqrt{2}} = \frac{4\sqrt{2}}{\pi^2} = 0.574$$

Bridge Rectifier

Figure 14.7 shows the bridge rectifier circuit for positive output voltage along with input and output waveforms. Figure 14.8 shows the same for negative output voltage. In the case of positive output rectifier circuit of Figure 14.7, diodes D_1 and D_3 are forward-biased and diodes D_2 and D_4 are reverse-biased during positive half cycles of the input. During negative half cycles, diode D_2 and D_4 are forward-biased and diodes D_1 and D_3 are reverse-biased. In both half cycles, current through load resistance R_L flows in the same direction as shown. In the case of negative output rectifier circuit of Figure 14.8, diodes D_2 and D_4 are forward-biased and diodes D_1 and D_3 are reverse-biased during positive half cycles of the input. During negative half cycles, diodes D_1 and D_3 are forward-biased and diodes D_2 and D_4 are reverse-biased. In both half cycles, current through load resistance R_L flows in the same direction, which is opposite to the direction of flow of current in the case of positive output circuit. This explains the output waveforms in the two cases.

Ripple factor and ratio of rectification parameters in the case of bridge rectifier are the same as those computed in the case of two-diode full-wave rectifier. That is, ripple factor = 0.482 and ratio of rectification = 0.812. Transformer utilization factor can be computed as follows:

$$\text{DC power delivered to load} = \left(\frac{2I_m}{\pi}\right)^2 \times R_L$$

$$\text{AC power rating of transformer secondary} = \frac{V_m}{\sqrt{2}} \times \frac{I_m}{\sqrt{2}} = \frac{V_m \times I_m}{2}$$

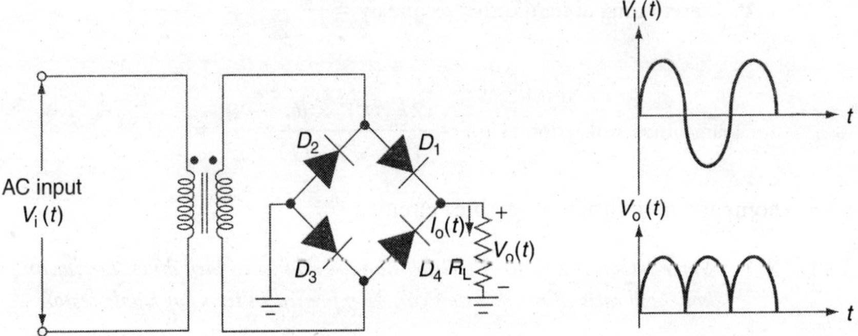

Figure 14.7 | Bridge rectifier for positive output voltage.

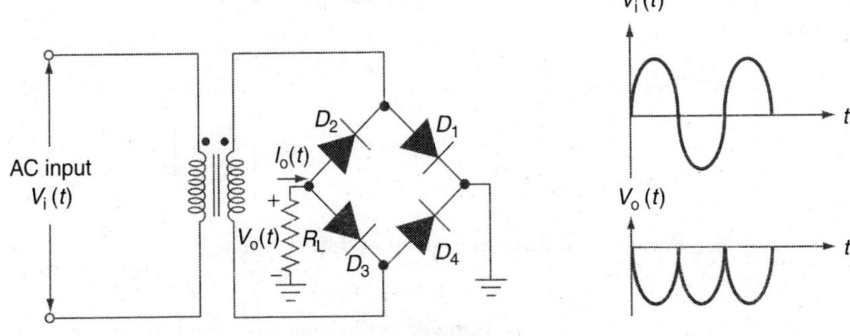

Figure 14.8 | Bridge rectifier for negative output voltage.

Table 14.1 | Comparison of rectifier circuits

Parameter	Half wave	Full wave	Bridge
Secondary voltage Line-to-line (RMS)	$\frac{V_m}{\sqrt{2}}$	$\sqrt{2}\times V_m$	$\sqrt{2}\times V_m$
Number of diodes	1	2	4
Peak inverse voltage	V_m	$\sqrt{2}\times V_m$	V_m
No load DC output	$\frac{V_m}{\pi}$	$\frac{2V_m}{\pi}$	$\frac{2V_m}{\pi}$
Ripple frequency	f	$2f$	$2f$
Ripple factor	1.21	0.482	0.482
Ratio of rectification	0.406	0.812	0.812
TUF	0.287	0.574	0.812

Also, ignoring the forward-biased diode's resistance, we get $V_m = I_m \times R_L$. This gives

$$\text{AC power rating of transformer secondary} = \frac{V_m \times I_m}{2} = \frac{I_m^{\ 2} \times R_L}{2}$$

Therefore,

$$\text{Transformer utilization factor} = \frac{(2I_m/\pi)^2 \times R_L}{(I_m^{\ 2} \times R_L)/2} = \frac{8}{\pi^2} = 0.812$$

Table 14.1 gives a comparison of different rectifier circuits.

EXAMPLE 14.2 *Ripple factor and ratio of rectification are related to each other. Derive an expression to show how ratio of rectification can be expressed in terms of ripple factor.*

Solution

1. Ripple factor, r, is given by Eq. (14.5) as

$$r = \sqrt{\left(\frac{I_{RMS}}{I_{DC}}\right)^2 - 1}$$

2. This gives

$$\left(\frac{I_{RMS}}{I_{DC}}\right)^2 = 1 + r^2 \quad \text{or} \quad \left(\frac{I_{DC}}{I_{RMS}}\right)^2 = \frac{1}{1+r^2}$$

3. Ratio of rectification is given by Eq. (14.6) as

$$\text{Ratio of rectification} = \left(\frac{I_{DC}}{I_{RMS}}\right)^2 = \frac{1}{1+r^2}$$

EXAMPLE 14.3 *Determine the transformer rating if it were to deliver a DC power of 500 W to a resistive load using (a) half-wave rectifier, (b) conventional two-diode full-wave rectifier and (c) bridge rectifier.*

Solution

(a) In the case of half-wave rectifier,

Transformer utilization factor = 0.287 = DC power delivered to load/transformer rating

Therefore, transformer rating = DC power delivered to load/0.287 = 500/0.287 = 1742 W.

(b) In the case of conventional two-diode full-wave rectifier,

Transformer utilization factor = 0.574 = DC power delivered to load/transformer rating

Therefore, transformer rating = DC power delivered to load/0.574= 500/0.574 = 871 W.

(c) In the case of bridge rectifier,

Transformer utilization factor = 0.812 = DC power delivered to load/transformer rating

Therefore, transformer rating = DC power delivered to load/0.812 = 500/0.812 = 616 W.

EXAMPLE 14.4 *A 220 V, 50 Hz AC is applied to the primary of 5:1 step-up transformer with a tapped secondary winding. The transformer along with a two-diode full-wave rectifier feeds a resistive load of 1000 Ω. Determine (a) DC power delivered to the load, (b) power rating of the transformer secondary, (c) PIV across each diode and (d) ripple frequency and ripple factor.*

Solution

(a) Peak value of primary voltage = $220 \times \sqrt{2} = 311$ V.

Peak value of secondary voltage = $311 \times 5 = 1555$ V.

Peak value of secondary current = 1555/1000 = 1.555 A.

DC power delivered to the load = $(2 \times 1.555/\pi)^2 \times 1000 = 981$ W.

(b) In the case of two-diode full-wave rectifier, transformer utilization factor = 0.574. Therefore, power rating of transformer secondary = 981/0.574 = 1709 W.

(c) PIV across each diode = $2 \times 1555 = 3.11$ kV.

(d) Ripple frequency = $2 \times f = 2 \times 50 = 100$ Hz.

$$\text{Ripple factor} = \sqrt{(I_{RMS} / I_{DC})^2 - 1}$$

$$I_{RMS} = 1.555/\sqrt{2} = 1.1 \text{ A}$$

$$I_{DC} = 2 \times 1.555/\pi = 0.99 \text{ A}$$

Therefore, ripple factor = $\sqrt{(1.1/0.99)^2 - 1} = 0.484$.

14.4 Filters

The filter in a power supply helps in reducing the ripple content (the amplitude of AC component), which in the rectified waveform is so large that the waveform can hardly be called a DC. Inductors, capacitors and inductor–capacitor combinations are used for the purpose of filtering. Each one of these types of filters is described in the following sub-sections.

Inductor Filter

The fact that an inductor offers high reactance to AC components is the basis of filtering provided by inductors. Figure 14.9(a) shows the full-wave rectifier circuit with inductor filter. The load current waveforms with and without filter are shown in Figure 14.9(b). The ripple factor (r) can be determined to be equal to $R_L/[3\sqrt{2}(\omega L)]$, which equals $R_L/1333L$ for power line frequency of 50 Hz and $R_L/1600L$ for power line frequency of 60 Hz. Here L is in henries and R_L is in ohms. Equation for ripple factor is derived as follows.

The Fourier series expansion of a full-wave rectified voltage waveform is given by

$$V(t) = \frac{2V_m}{\pi} - \frac{4V_m}{\pi}\left[\left(\frac{\cos 2\omega t}{3}\right) + \left(\frac{\cos 4\omega t}{15}\right) + \left(\frac{\cos 6\omega t}{35}\right) + \cdots\right] \quad (14.7)$$

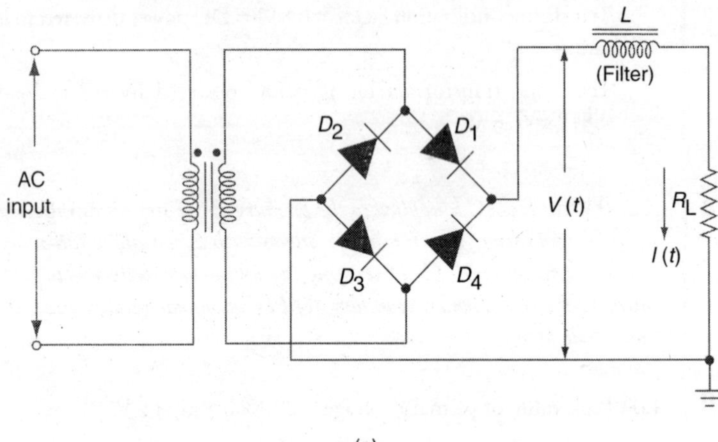

(a)

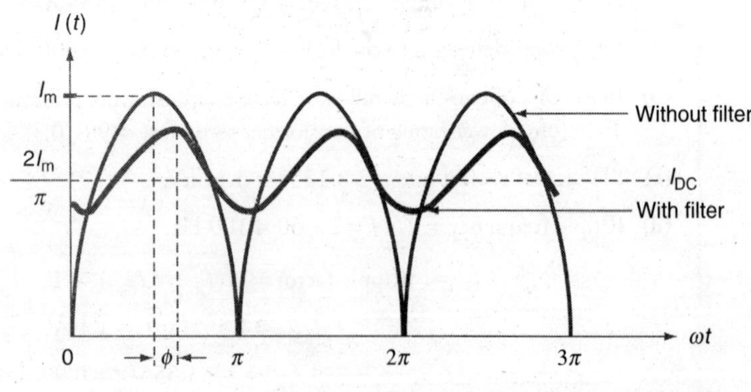

(b)

Figure 14.9 Inductor (or choke) filter.

Neglecting higher order terms beyond second harmonic, Eq. (14.7) reduces to

$$V(t)=\frac{2V_{\mathrm{m}}}{\pi}-\left(\frac{4V_{\mathrm{m}}}{3\pi}\right)\cos 2\omega t \tag{14.8}$$

In Eq. (14.8), the first term represents the DC component and the second term represents the AC component.

Since the AC component of current will lag behind the voltage by an angle (ϕ) given by $\tan^{-1}(2\omega L/R_{\mathrm{L}})$, the expression for resulting current can be written as follows:

$$I(t)=\left(\frac{2V_{\mathrm{m}}}{\pi R_{\mathrm{L}}}\right)-\left(\frac{4V_{\mathrm{m}}}{3\pi}\right)\times\left(\frac{1}{\sqrt{R_{\mathrm{L}}{}^{2}+4\omega^{2}L^{2}}}\right)\times\cos(2\omega t-\phi) \tag{14.9}$$

Ripple factor is nothing but the ratio of RMS value of the AC component to that of the DC component. It can be computed from Eq. (14.9) as it contains both the DC component and the peak value of the AC component. It is given by

$$r=\left(\frac{4V_{\mathrm{m}}}{3\pi\sqrt{2}}\right)\times\left(\frac{1}{\sqrt{R_{\mathrm{L}}{}^{2}+4\omega^{2}L^{2}}}\right)\times\frac{\pi R_{\mathrm{L}}}{2V_{\mathrm{m}}}=\frac{\sqrt{2}}{3\sqrt{1+(4\omega^{2}L^{2}/R_{\mathrm{L}}{}^{2})}} \tag{14.10}$$

For $4\omega^2L^2/R_{\mathrm{L}}{}^2$ much greater than 1, the expression for ripple factor (r) reduces to

$$r=\frac{R_{\mathrm{L}}}{3\sqrt{2}(\omega L)} \tag{14.11}$$

As is clear from the above expression, the ripple factor is directly proportional to load resistance (R_{L}). That is, the ripple content increases with increase in load resistance. In other words, choke filter is not effective for light loads (or high values of load resistance) and is preferably used for relatively higher load currents. In the limit when load resistance tends to infinity (for no load condition), from the exact expression of ripple factor as given in Eq. (14.10), we get $r=\sqrt{2}/3=0.471$. This value is very close to the value derived earlier in the case of full-wave rectifier without filter. The slight difference can be attributed to omission of higher order terms in Eq. (14.7). It therefore implies that presence of inductor filter is as good as not there in the case of load resistance tending to become infinity. In other words, an inductor filter becomes less and less effective with increase in value of load resistance.

It may also be noted that with inductive filtering, the load current never drops to zero. If the value of inductance is suitably chosen, the flow of current through the diodes and the secondary of the transformer are much more even than it would have been without the filter. This leads to ratio of rectification of almost unity due to RMS and DC values of the filtered current waveform to be almost the same and an improved transformer utilization factor.

Capacitor Filter

The filtering action of a capacitor connected across the output of the rectifier comes from the fact that it offers a low reactance to AC components. Figure 14.10(a) shows a capacitor filter connected across the output of a full-wave rectifier. The AC components are bypassed to ground through the capacitor and only the DC is allowed to go through to the load. The capacitor charges to the peak value of the voltage waveform during the first cycle and as the voltage in the rectified waveform is on the decrease, the capacitor voltage is not able to follow the change as it can discharge only at a rate determined by (CR_{L}) time constant. In the case of light loads (or high values of load resistance), the capacitor would discharge only a little before the voltage in the rectified waveform exceeds the capacitor voltage thus charging it again to the peak value [Figure 14.10(b)]. The ripple content is inversely proportional to C and R_{L}.

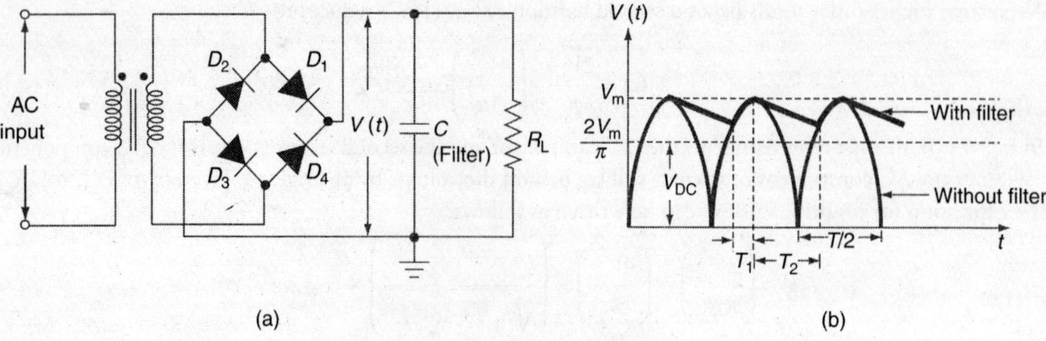

Figure 14.10 Capacitor filter.

Ripple can be reduced by increasing C for a given of R_L. For heavy loads when R_L is small, even a large capacitance value may not be able to provide ripple within acceptable limits. Ripple factor can be computed as follows.

Referring to the waveform of Figure 14.10(b), to a reasonable approximation, the ripple waveform can be considered to be a triangular one. The charge acquired by the filter capacitor during the time it is charging [T_1 in Figure 14.10(b)] equals the charge lost by it during the time it is discharging through load resistance R_L [T_2 in Figure 14.10(b)].

$$\text{Charge acquired} = V_r(\text{peak-to-peak}) \times C \tag{14.12}$$

$$\text{Charge lost} = I_{DC} \times T_2 \tag{14.13}$$

Equating the two, we get

$$V_r(\text{peak-to-peak}) \times C = I_{DC} \times T_2 \tag{14.14}$$

In the case of a large CR_L, time period T_2 equals $T/2$ where T is the time period of the AC input. This gives

$$V_r(\text{peak-to-peak}) \times C = \frac{I_{DC} \times T}{2} \tag{14.15}$$

$$V_r(\text{peak-to-peak}) = \frac{I_{DC} \times T}{2C} = \frac{I_{DC}}{2fC} \tag{14.16}$$

Assuming a triangular ripple waveform as outlined earlier, we get

$$\text{RMS value of the waveform} = \frac{V_r(\text{peak})}{\sqrt{3}}$$

Therefore,

$$V_r(\text{RMS}) = \frac{V_r(\text{peak-to-peak})}{2\sqrt{3}} = \frac{I_{DC} \times T}{4\sqrt{3}C} = \frac{I_{DC}}{4\sqrt{3}fC} \tag{14.17}$$

Also, $I_{DC} = V_{DC}/R_L$. Therefore,

$$V_r(\text{RMS}) = \frac{V_{DC}}{4\sqrt{3}fCR_L} \tag{14.18}$$

$$\text{Ripple factor, } r = \frac{V_r(\text{RMS})}{V_{DC}} = \frac{1}{4\sqrt{3}fCR_L} \tag{14.19}$$

Ripple factor (r) equals $2887/CR_L$ for power line frequency of 50 Hz and $2406/CR_L$ for a power line frequency of 60 Hz. Here C is in microfarads and R_L is in ohms. It may be mentioned here that the above expression for ripple factor holds good in the case of an ideal capacitor with a zero equivalent series resistance (ESR). In the case of practical capacitors, the ESR is easily of the order of several ohms or even a few tens of ohms for the large values of capacitance encountered in filter capacitors. In such cases, the ripple factor deteriorates from the value computed from Eq. (14.19). The ESR should also be considered while computing the repetitive peak current during the charging process and also the surge current that would flow when the power is initially is switched on and the filter capacitor is fully discharged.

LC Filter

We have seen that while an inductance filter is effective only at heavy load currents, a capacitor filter provides adequate filtering only for light loads. The performance of inductor and capacitor filters deteriorates fast as the load resistance is increased in the case of former or decreased in the case of the latter. Apparently, an appropriate combination of L and C could give us a filter that would provide adequate filtering over a wide range of load resistance R_L values.

Figure 14.11 shows an LC filter connected across the output of a full-wave rectifier. If the value of inductance (L) in the LC filter is small, the filter will predominantly be a capacitor filter and the capacitor will repetitively charge to the peak value and cut off the diodes. The current in this case is in the form of short pulses only. An increase in the value of inductance allows the current to flow for longer periods. If the inductance is further increased, we reach a stage where one diode or the other is always conducting with the result that the current and voltage to the input of LC filter are full-wave rectified waveforms. This is known as the critical value of inductance (L_C). If the inductance (L) is equal to or more than the critical inductance, the voltage applied to the filter can be approximated by Eq. (14.20).

$$V(t) = \frac{2V_m}{\pi} - \left(\frac{4V_m}{3\pi}\right)\cos 2\omega t \tag{14.20}$$

The ripple factor in the case of LC filter can now be computed as follows. For a properly designed LC filter, $X_C << R_L$ and $X_L >> X_C$ at a radian frequency of 2ω. X_L therefore primarily determines the AC component of ripple. Therefore,

$$I_r(\text{RMS}) = \frac{4V_m}{3\pi\sqrt{2}X_L} = \frac{\sqrt{2}}{3}\times\frac{V_{DC}}{X_L} \quad \text{as } V_{DC} = 2V_m/\pi \tag{14.21}$$

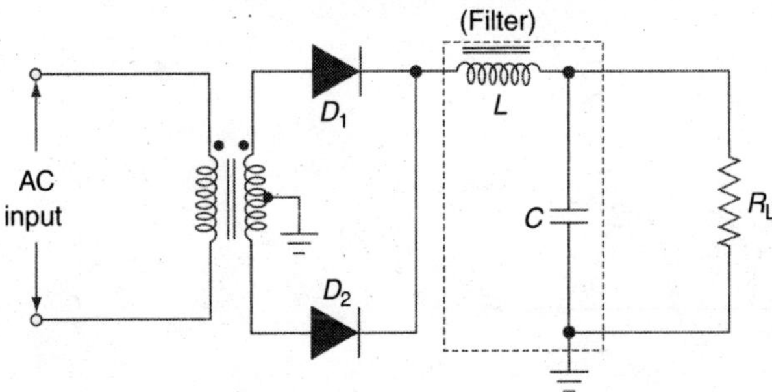

Figure 14.11 LC filter.

Also,

$$V_r(\text{RMS}) = I_r(\text{RMS}) \times X_C = \left(\frac{\sqrt{2}}{3}\right) \times V_{DC} \times \left(\frac{X_C}{X_L}\right) = \left(\frac{\sqrt{2}X_C}{3X_L}\right) \times V_{DC} \tag{14.22}$$

$$\text{Ripple factor, } r = \frac{\sqrt{2}X_C}{3X_L} = \left(\frac{\sqrt{2}}{3}\right) \times \left(\frac{1}{4\omega^2 LC}\right) = \left(\frac{\sqrt{2}}{12\omega^2}\right) \times \left(\frac{1}{LC}\right) \tag{14.23}$$

Remember that the full-wave rectified waveform input to the filter has a radian frequency of 2ω.

The above expression proves that the ripple factor in a choke input LC filter is independent of R_L. Equation (14.23) reduces to $1.2/LC$ for power line frequency of 50 Hz and $0.83/LC$ for a power line frequency of 60 Hz. In this expression, L is in henries and C is in microfarads.

The chosen value of inductance should be greater than or equal to the critical inductance. The value of critical inductance is such that the DC value of current is equal to or greater than the negative peak of the AC component to ensure a continuous flow of current. That is,

$$\frac{V_{DC}}{R_L} \geq \frac{4V_m}{3\pi X_L} \quad \text{or} \quad \frac{V_{DC}}{R_L} \geq \left(\frac{2}{3X_L}\right) \times V_{DC} \tag{14.24}$$

This gives,

$$X_L \geq \frac{2R_L}{3} \quad \text{or} \quad L \geq \frac{R_L}{3\omega} \tag{14.25}$$

Therefore,

$$\text{Critical inductance, } L_C = \frac{R_L}{3\omega} \tag{14.26}$$

L_C equals $R_L/942$ for a power line frequency of 50 Hz and $R_L/1131$ for a power line frequency of 60 Hz. Here, R is in ohms and L_C is in henries. In practice, L_C should be about 25% higher to take care of approximation made in writing expression for $V(t)$ as given in Eq. (14.20). This gives $L \geq R_L/754$ (for power line frequency of 50 Hz) and $\geq R_L/905$ (for power line frequency of 60 Hz).

Multiple LC sections can be used to further smoothen the output. Figure 14.12 shows one such filter using two LC sections. The filter can be analyzed in the same fashion as it was done in the case of a single section filter.

$$\text{Ripple factor, } r = \left(\frac{\sqrt{2}}{3}\right) \times \left(\frac{X_{C1}}{X_{L1}}\right) \times \left(\frac{X_{C2}}{X_{L2}}\right) \tag{14.27}$$

For $L_1 = L_2 = L$ and $C_1 = C_2 = C$,

$$r = \frac{\sqrt{2}}{48\omega^4 L^2 C^2} \tag{14.28}$$

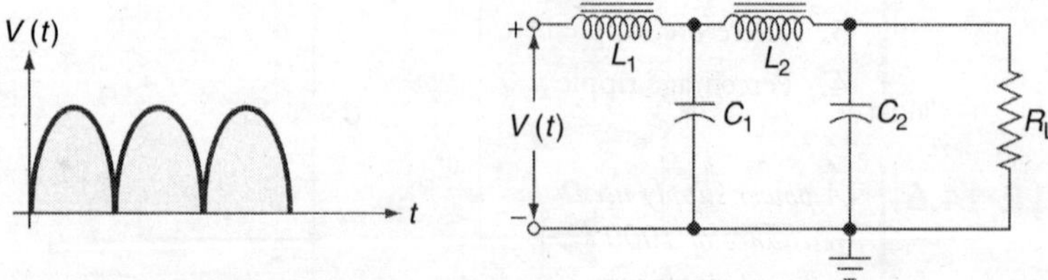

Figure 14.12 Two-section LC filter with full-wave rectified input.

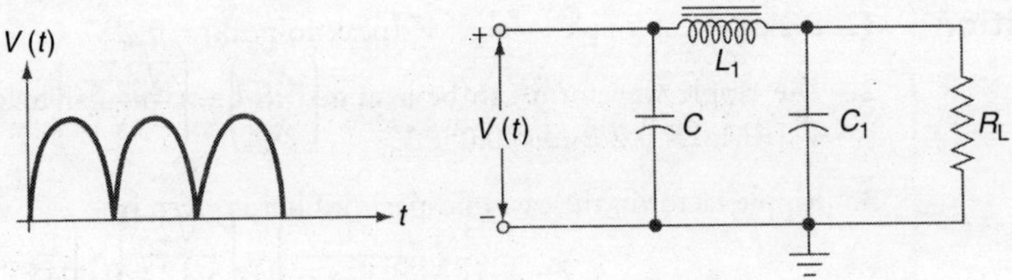

Figure 14.13 CLC or π-type filter.

Ripple factor equals $3/L^2C^2$ for power line frequency of 50 Hz and $1.45/L^2C^2$ for power line frequency of 60 Hz. Here, L is in henries and C in microfarads. The value of critical inductance is as it is in the case of single section filter.

CLC Filter (π-Filter)

Figure 14.13 shows the CLC filter, which is basically a capacitor filter followed by LC section. The ripple characteristics of this filter are similar to those of two-section LC filter and the expression for ripple factor can be written as

$$\text{Ripple factor, } r = \sqrt{2} \times \left(\frac{X_C}{R_L}\right) \times \left(\frac{X_{C1}}{X_{L1}}\right) \tag{14.29}$$

The circuit however suffers from the problem of high diode peak currents, poor regulation and a ripple that is dependent upon the value of load resistance. In the case of very small load current, one may replace the inductance (L) with a resistance equal in value to the inductive reactance at the ripple frequency of 2ω.

EXAMPLE 14.5 *Refer to the voltage waveform of Figure 14.14 observed across the load in the case of a power supply. Determine the ripple factor and percentage ripple content.*

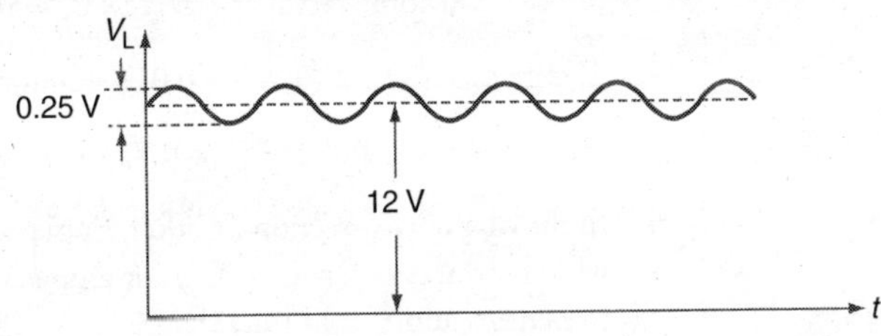

Figure 14.14 Example 14.5.

Solution

1. From Figure 14.14, $V_{DC} = 12$ V and V_r (peak-to-peak) = 0.25 V.
2. V_r (RMS) = $0.25/2\sqrt{2}$ = 0.088 V.
3. Therefore, ripple factor, $r = V_r\,(\text{RMS})/V_{DC} = 0.088/12 = 0.00737$.
4. Percentage ripple = 0.74%.

EXAMPLE 14.6 *A power supply uses a full-wave rectifier and a capacitor filter. The filter feeds a load resistance of 1000 Ω. If the DC voltage across the load is 12 V and the peak-to-peak value of ripple were not to exceed 0.2 V, determine the minimum capacitance value of the filter capacitor. Assume a power line frequency of 50 Hz.*

Solution

1. Peak-to-peak ripple voltage, V_r (peak-to-peak) = 0.2 V.
2. The ripple waveform can be assumed to be triangular in shape. Therefore, V_r (RMS) = $0.2/2\sqrt{3} = 0.058$ V.
3. Ripple factor in the case of capacitor filter is given by

$$r = V_r\,(\text{RMS})/V_{DC} = 0.058/12 = 0.0048$$

Therefore, $1/4\sqrt{3}fCR_L = 0.0048$.

4. Substituting the values of R_L and f, we get

$$C = 1/(4\sqrt{3} \times 50 \times 0.0048 \times 1000) = 601\ \mu\text{F}$$

EXAMPLE 14.7

An LC filter connected at the output of a full-wave rectifier operating at a power line frequency of 50 Hz is required to provide a ripple of 1 percent. It is recommended to have L/C ratio not to exceed 0.005 with L in henries and C in microfarads. Determine the required values of L and C. How would the ripple factor change if an identical LC section were connected in cascade to make it a two-section LC filter?

Solution

1. Ripple factor = $1.2/LC$ for a power line frequency of 50 Hz. In this expression, L is in henries and C is in microfarads.
2. $L/C = 0.005$ where L is in henries and C is in microfarads. This gives $L = 0.005C$.
3. Substituting the value of L in the expression for ripple factor, we get

$$\text{Ripple factor} = 1.2/(C \times 0.005C) = 1.2/0.005C^2 = 0.01$$

4. This gives, $C^2 = 1.2/(0.005 \times 0.01) = 24000$, which gives $C = \sqrt{24000} = 155\ \mu$F.
5. This gives $L = 0.005 \times 155 = 0.775$ henries.
6. In the case of two-section LC filter, ripple factor is given by $r = \sqrt{2}/(48\omega^4 L^2 C^2)$, which reduces to $r = (3/L^2C^2)$ for a power line frequency of 50 Hz. Here, L is in henries and C is in microfarads.
7. Substituting the values of L and C, we get

$$r = 3/[(0.775)^2 \times (155)^2] = 0.0002 = 0.02\%$$

EXAMPLE 14.8

A π-type CLC filter is connected across the output of a full-wave rectifier, which in turn is fed with a 50 Hz sine wave. The filter feeds a load resistance of 1000 Ω. If the desired ripple factor is 0.001 and the two capacitors are 100 μF each, determine the minimum value of inductance needed to get the desired ripple factor. Also determine the value of resistance required to replace the inductor and still produce the same ripple.

Solution

1. Ripple factor in the case of π-type CLC filter is given by

$$r = \sqrt{2} \times (X_C/R_L) \times (X_{C1}/X_{L1})$$

2. $X_C = 1/2\pi fC$ where $f = 100$ Hz because of full-wave rectification.
3. $X_C = 1/(2 \times 3.14 \times 100 \times 100 \times 10^{-6}) = 15.92\ \Omega = X_{C1}$.
4. $R_L = 1000\ \Omega$ and $X_{L1} = 2\pi fL = 628.3\ L$.
5. From the expression of ripple factor,

$$X_{L1} = \sqrt{2} \times (X_C/R_L) \times (X_{C1}/r) = 1.414 \times (15.92/1000) \times (15.92/0.001) = 358.4$$

Therefore, $L = 358.4/628.3 = 0.57$ henry.

6. Value of resistance required to replace the inductance and still provide the same ripple is equal to the inductive reactance.
7. Therefore, required value of resistance, $R = X_{L1} = 358.4\ \Omega$.

14.5 Linear Regulators

As outlined earlier, the regulator circuit in a power supply ensures that the load voltage (in the case of voltage regulated power supplies) or the load current (in the case of current regulated power supplies) is constant irrespective of variations in the line voltage or load resistance. In the present section are discussed different types of linear voltage regulator circuits. Three basic types of linear voltage regulator configurations include the emitter–follower regulator, series-pass regulator and shunt regulator. Each one of these is briefly described in the following sections.

Emitter–Follower Regulator

Figure 14.15 shows the basic positive output emitter–follower regulator. The emitter voltage, which is also the output voltage, remains constant as long as the base voltage is held constant. A Zener diode connected at the base ensures this. The regulated output voltage in this case is $(V_Z - 0.7)$ V. The emitter–base voltage of the transistor is assumed to be 0.7 V. Another way of explaining the regulation action provided by the

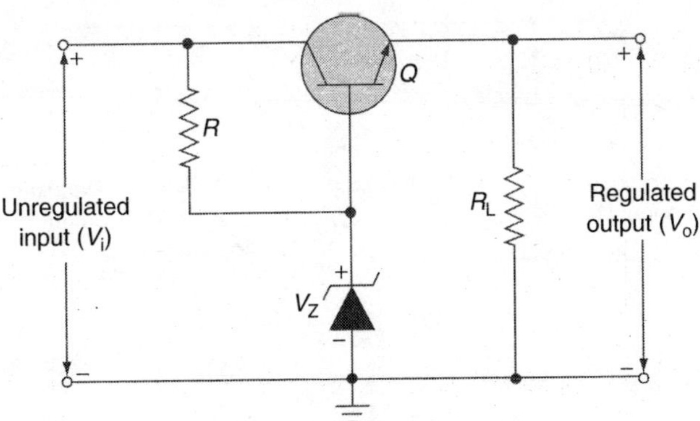

Figure 14.15 | Emitter–follower regulator for positive output voltages.

circuit is as follows. When the output voltage tends to increase, the emitter–base voltage of the series transistor decreases thus decreasing its conduction. This increases collector–emitter drop across the transistor to maintain a constant output voltage. When the output voltage tends to decrease, the emitter–base voltage increases thus increasing the conduction of the transistor. This decreases the collector–emitter drop across the transistor again maintaining a constant output voltage. Owing to high inherent current gain of the series-pass transistor, a low-power Zener diode can be used to regulate high value of load current. The base current in this case needs to be only $[1/(1 + h_{fe})]$ times the load current. Figure 14.16 shows the emitter–follower regulator circuit for negative output voltages. The regulated output voltage in this case is $-(V_Z - 0.7)$ V. If the load current is so large that it is beyond the capability of the Zener diode to provide the requisite base current, a Darlington combination can be used instead of a single transistor series-pass element (Figures 14.17 and 14.18). The regulated output voltages for the Darlington emitter–follower regulators of Figures 14.17 and 14.18 are $(V_Z - 1.4)$ and $-(V_Z - 1.4)$ V, respectively.

Series-Pass Regulator

The emitter–follower regulator circuit discussed in the previous section is also a type of series-pass regulator where the conduction of the series transistor decides the voltage drop across it and hence the output voltage. The Zener diode provides the reference voltage that controls the conduction of the transistor depending

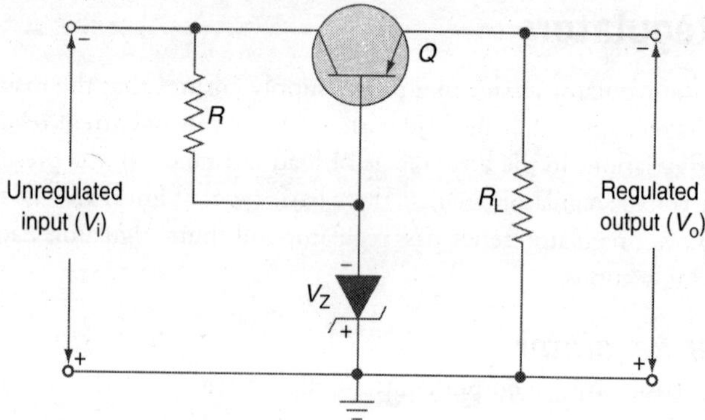

Figure 14.16 | Emitter–follower regulator for negative output voltage.

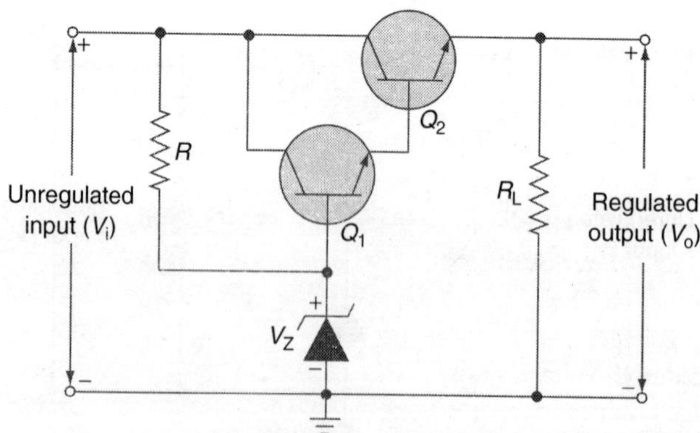

Figure 14.17 | Emitter–follower regulator using Darlington transistor pair (positive output).

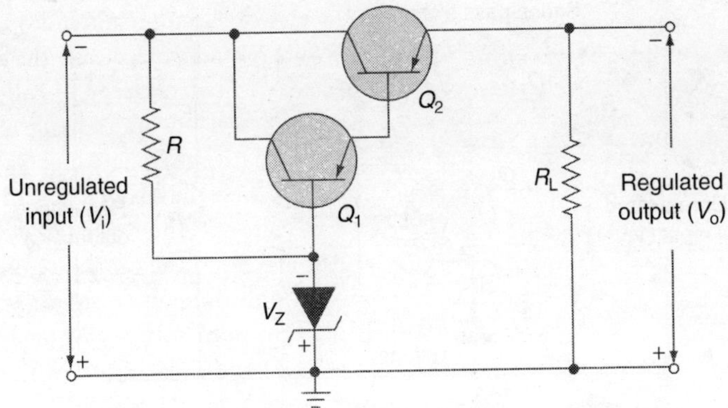

Figure 14.18 | Emitter–follower regulator using Darlington transistor pair (negative output).

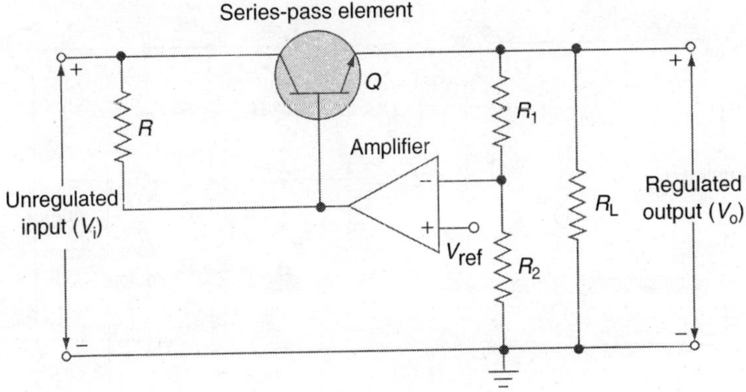

Figure 14.19 | Series-pass linear regulator.

upon the output voltage. Figure 14.19 shows the basic constituents of an improved series-pass-type linear regulator that is capable of providing much better regulation specifications. The series-pass element, a bipolar transistor in the circuit shown, again works like a variable resistance with the conduction of the transistor depending upon the base current. The regulator circuit functions as follows.

A small fraction of the output voltage is compared with a known reference DC voltage and their difference is amplified in a high-gain DC amplifier. The amplified error signal is then fed back to the base of the series-pass transistor to alter its conduction so as to maintain essentially a constant output voltage. The regulated output voltage in this case is given by $V_{ref} \times (R_1 + R_2)/R_2$.

As the output voltage tends to decrease due to decrease in input voltage or increase in load current, the error voltage produced as a result of this causes the base current to increase. The increased base current increases transistor conduction thus reducing its collector–emitter voltage drop, which compensates for the reduction in the output voltage.

Similarly, when the output voltage tends to increase due to increase in input voltage or decrease in load current, the error voltage produced as a consequence is of the opposite sense. It tends to decrease transistor conduction thus increasing its collector–emitter voltage drop again maintaining a constant output voltage. The regulation provided by this circuit depends upon the stability of the reference voltage and the gain of the DC amplifier. A typical series-pass regulator circuit using a bipolar transistor as the error amplifier is

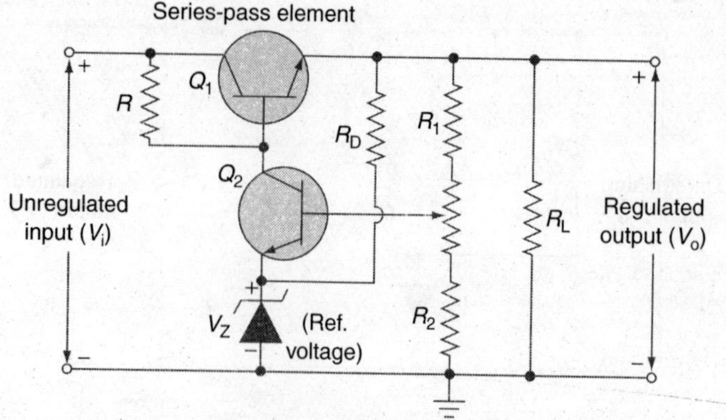

Figure 14.20 Series-pass linear regulator using bipolar transistor as error amplifier.

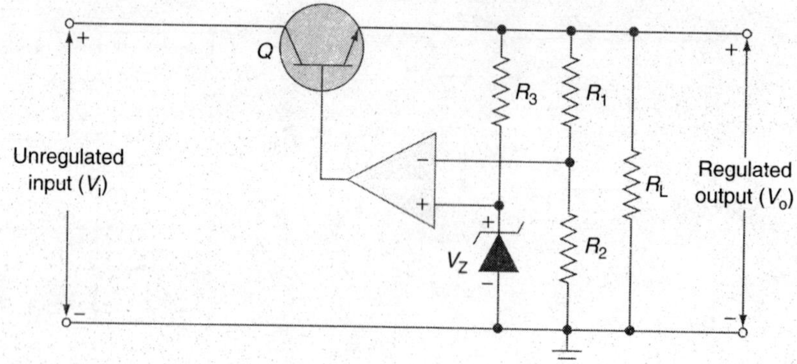

Figure 14.21 Series-pass linear regulator using opamp-based as error amplifier.

shown in Figure 14.20. Figure 14.21 shows another series-pass regulator circuit that uses an operational amplifier as the error amplifier. The operation of the circuit is similar to that of transistor-based one.

As compared to the emitter–follower type series-pass regulator, the one with an error amplifier in the feedback loop and discussed in this section provides better regulation due to the gain provided by the error amplifier. In this case, given change in output voltage causes a relatively much larger change in the base current of the series-pass element.

Current Limiting

The power dissipated in the series-pass transistor is the product of its collector–emitter voltage and the load current. As the load current increases within a certain range, the collector–emitter voltage decreases due to the feedback action keeping the output voltage as constant. The series-pass transistor is so chosen that it can safely dissipate the power under normal load conditions. If there is an overload condition due to some reason or the other, the transistor is likely to get damaged if such a condition is allowed to persist for long. In the worst case, if there were a short circuit on the output, the whole unregulated input would appear across the series-pass element increasing the power dissipation to prohibitively large magnitude eventually destroying the transistor. Even a series-connected fuse does not help in such a case, as the thermal time constant of the transistor is much smaller than that of the fuse. Thus it is always desirable to build overload protection or current limiting protection in the linearly regulated power supply design. One such configuration is shown in Figure 14.22.

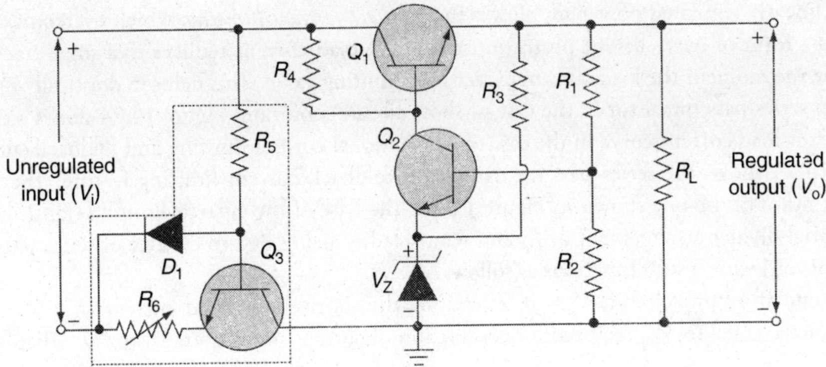

Figure 14.22 | Series-pass linear regulator with overload protection.

Under normal operating conditions, transistor Q_3 is in saturation. Thus, it offers very little resistance to the load current path. In the event of an overload or a short circuit, diode D_1 conducts thus reducing the base drive to transistor Q_3. Transistor Q_3 offers an increased resistance to the flow of load current. In the event of a short circuit, the whole of input voltage would appear across Q_3. Transistor Q_3 should be so chosen that it can safely dissipate power given by the product of worst-case unregulated input voltage and the limiting value of current. Diode D_1 and transistor Q_3 should preferably be mounted on the same heat sink so that emitter–base junction of Q_3 and P–N junction of D_1 are equally affected by temperature rise and the short circuit limiting current is as per the preset value. There can be other possible circuit configurations that can provide the desired protection function.

Figure 14.23 shows another circuit arrangement that provides current-limiting action and overload protection. When the load current is less than the limiting value, the circuit regulates the output voltage normally. Transistor (Q_3) is in cut-off state. As the load current reaches the limiting value, which is determined by resistor R_5, transistor Q_3 conducts and the major part of Q_1 base current gets routed through Q_3, substantially reducing its base drive.

The current-limiting feature described in the previous paragraphs has the advantage of protecting the series-pass transistor and rectifier diodes in the case of any accidental shorting of the output. However, the circuit suffers from the disadvantage of large power dissipation in the series-pass transistor in the event of an output short circuit. The power dissipated in this case is approximately equal to the product of the unregulated input voltage and the limiting value of the load current. A common form of current-limiting feature

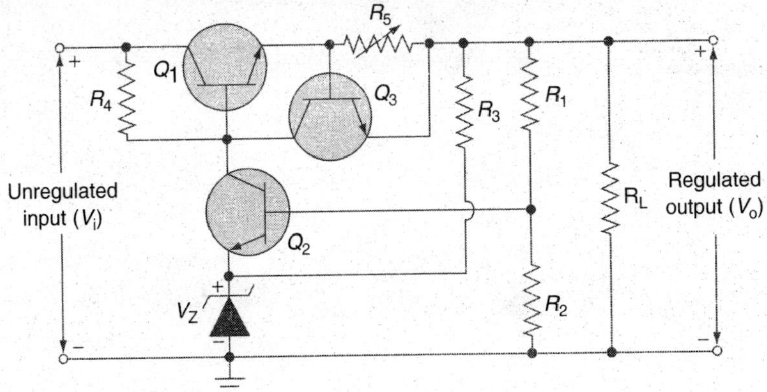

Figure 14.23 | Series-pass linear regulator with overload protection.

practiced in linearly regulated power supplies is the *foldback current limiting*, which overcomes this shortcoming. It is a form of over-current protection where the load current reduces to a small fraction of the limiting value the moment the load current exceeds the limiting value. This helps in drastically reducing the dissipation in series-pass transistor in the case of short circuit condition. Figure 14.24 shows a comparison of voltage versus load current curve in the case of conventional current limiting and foldback current limiting. Figure 14.25 shows the series-pass regulator with foldback current-limiting feature. The circuit is a slight modification of the one shown in Figure 14.23. The base of the current-limiting transistor Q_3 is fed from a potential divider arrangement of R_6 and R_7 instead of being tied to emitter of series-pass transistor Q_1. The circuit of Figure 14.25 functions as follows.

In the event of a short circuit, $V_o = 0$. Therefore, the short-circuit load current (I_{SL}) is the one that produces a voltage equal to V_{BE} required for conduction of current-limiting transistor Q_3. That is,

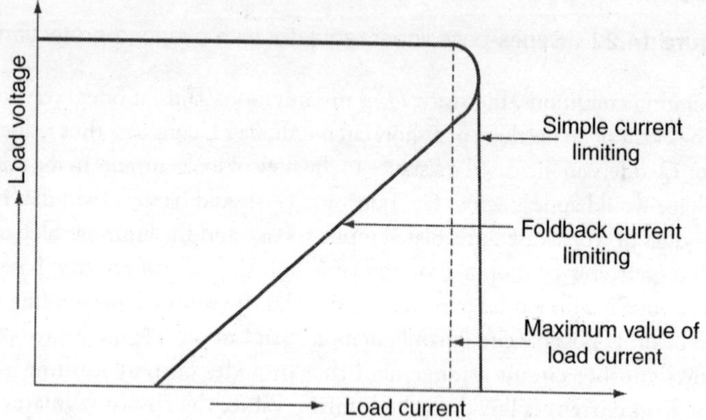

Figure 14.24 | Foldback current limiting.

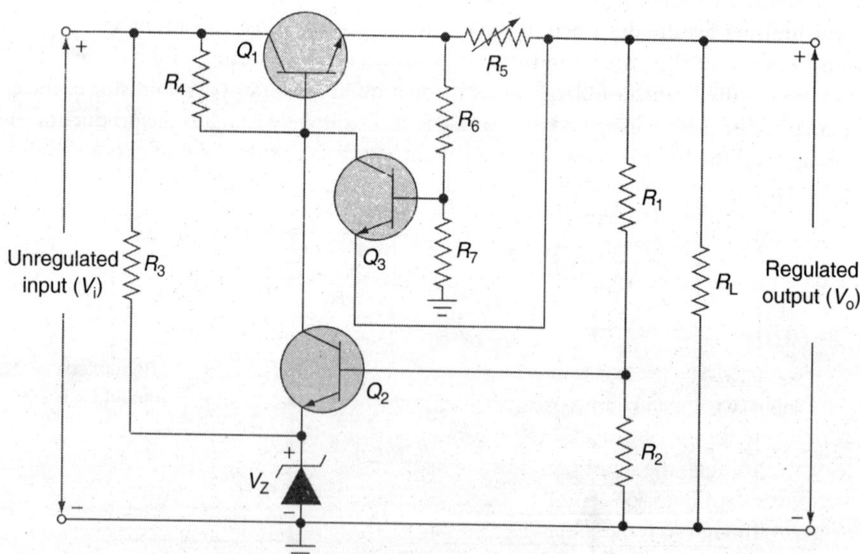

Figure 14.25 | Series regulator with foldback current limiting.

$$V_{BE} = (I_{SL} \times R_5) \times \frac{R_7}{R_6 + R_7} = K \times I_{SL} \times R_5$$

where $K = R_7/(R_6 + R_7)$. This gives

$$I_{SL} = \frac{V_{BE}}{K \times R_5} \tag{14.30}$$

When the output is not shorted, potential of Q_3 emitter terminal is V_o. Therefore, potential of its base terminal (V_{B3}) is given by

$$V_{B3} = V_o + V_{BE} = V_o + K \times I_{SL} \times R_5$$

Potential of the emitter terminal of Q_1 is given by

$$V_{E1} = \frac{V_o + K \times I_{SL} \times R_5}{K} \tag{14.31}$$

Therefore, maximum value of load current (I_{max}) under these conditions is given by

$$I_{max} = \left(\frac{1}{R_5}\right) \times \left[\left\{\frac{(V_o + K \times I_{SL} \times R_5)}{K}\right\} - V_o\right] \tag{14.32}$$

$$I_{max} = \frac{V_o + K \times I_{SL} \times R_5 - V_o \times K}{K \times R_5} \tag{14.33}$$

$$I_{max} = \frac{V_o \times (1 - K) + K \times I_{SL} \times R_5}{K \times R_5} \tag{14.34}$$

$$I_{max} = I_{SL} + \left(\frac{V_o \times (1 - K)}{K \times R_5}\right) \tag{14.35}$$

Equation (14.35) shows that the maximum load current or the limiting value of the load current is larger than the short-circuit current. Typical value of K is such that the maximum load current is about two to three times the short-circuit load current.

Other types of protection features that are usually built into power supplies include crowbaring and thermal shutdown. Crowbaring is a type of over voltage protection and thermal shutdown disconnects the input to the regulator circuit in the event of temperature of the active device(s) exceeding a certain upper limit. It may be mentioned here that the control and protection functions are usually provided by an integrated circuit (IC) in a modern power supply. A wide range of control ICs is available for both linear and switched mode power supplies.

Shunt Regulator

In a series-type linear regulator, the pass element is connected in series with the load and any decrease or increase in the output voltage is accompanied by a corresponding decrease or increase in the collector–emitter voltage of the series-pass transistor. In the case of a shunt-type linear regulator (Figure 14.26), regulation is provided by a change in the current through the shunt transistor to maintain a constant output voltage. The regulated output voltage in a shunt regulated linear power supply is the unregulated input voltage minus drop across the resistor R_1. Now, the current through R_1 is the sum of load current (I_L) and current through shunt transistor (I_S). As the output voltage tends to decrease, the base current through the transistor reduces with the result that its collector current (I_S) decreases too. This reduces drop across R_1 and the output voltage is restored to its nominal value.

Similarly, the tendency of the output voltage to increase is accompanied by an increase in current through the shunt transistor consequently increasing voltage drop across R_1, which in turn maintains a constant output voltage. A Darlington combination in place of shunt transistor enhances the current capability (Figure 14.27). The regulated output voltages in the case of shunt regulator circuits of Figures 14.26 and 14.27 are ($V_Z + V_{BE}$) and ($V_Z + 2V_{BE}$), respectively. Another shunt regulator configuration is shown in Figure 14.28. In this case, the base terminal of the shunt transistor is driven by the output of an opamp. A reference voltage and the sample of output voltage drive the two inputs of the opamp. If the two voltages differ, the output of opamp forces the shunt element to conduct more or less current through it, thus maintaining a constant output voltage.

Shunt regulator is not as efficient as a series regulator for the simple reason that the current through the series resistor in the case of shunt regulator is the sum of load current and shunt transistor current and it dissipates more power than the series-pass regulator with same unregulated input and regulated output specifications. In a shunt regulator, the shunt transistor also dissipates power in addition to the power dissipated in the series resistor. The only advantage with a shunt regulator is its simplicity and that it is inherently protected against overload conditions.

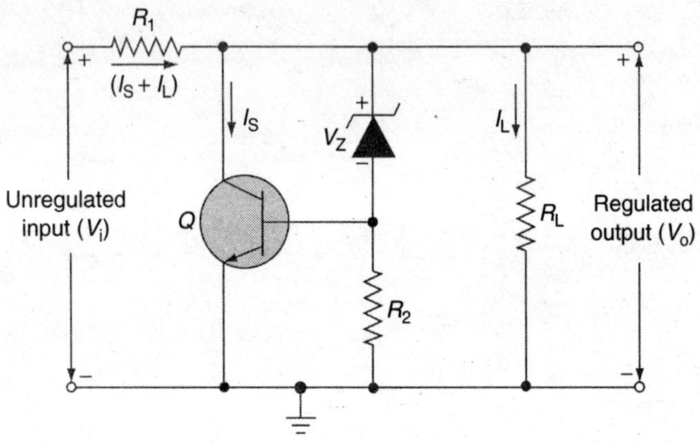

Figure 14.26 Shunt regulator.

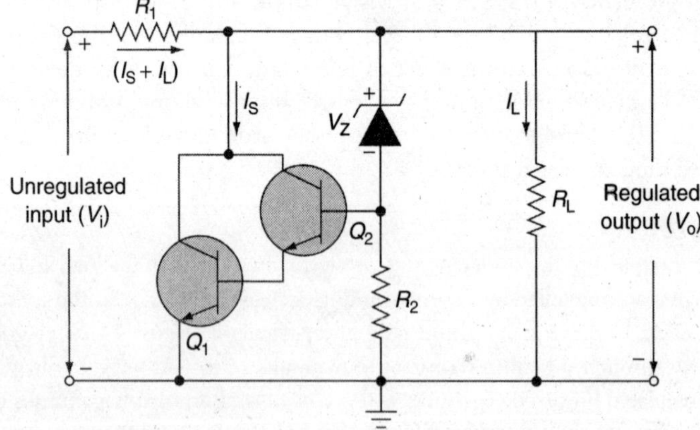

Figure 14.27 Shunt regulator with Darlington transistor pair.

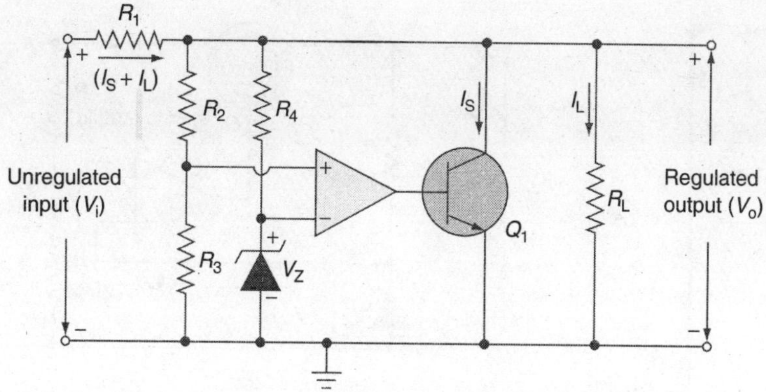

Figure 14.28 Opamp-based shunt regulator circuit.

EXAMPLE 14.9

Refer to the emitter–follower regulator circuit of Figure 14.29. Determine (a) regulated output voltage; (b) current through the Zener diode. Assume β of the transistor as 50, V_{BE} (Q) = 0.7 V, forward voltage drop of diode D_1 = 0.7 V, Zener diode voltage (V_Z) = 12 V.

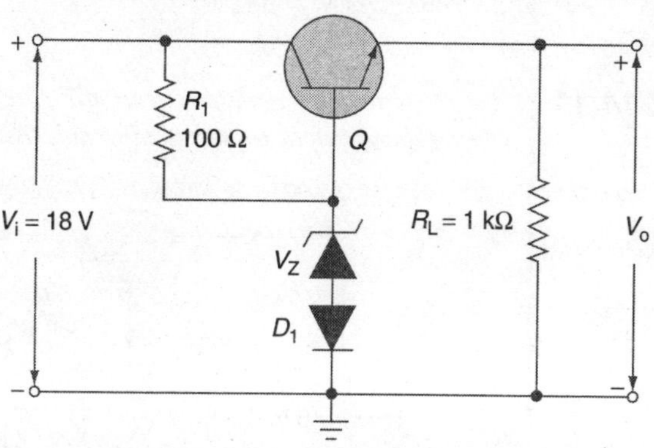

Figure 14.29 Example 14.9.

Solution

1. Regulated output voltage, $V_o = V_Z + V_{D1} - V_{BE}$ (Q) = 12 + 0.7 − 0.7 = 12 V.
2. Therefore, V_{CE} (Q) = 18 − 12 = 6 V.
3. Current through resistor R_1 = (18 − 12.7)/100 = 0.053 A = 53 mA. Part of this current flows towards the base terminal of Q and the rest flows through the series combination of the Zener diode and diode D_1.
4. Now, load current = 12/1000 = 0.012 A and β of transistor Q = 50.
5. Base current of transistor Q = 0.012/(1 + β) = 0.012/51 = 0.24 mA.
6. Therefore, current through Zener diode = $53 \times 10^{-3} - 0.24 \times 10^{-3}$ = 52.76 mA.

EXAMPLE 14.10

Refer to the opamp-based series-pass regulator circuit of Figure 14.30. Determine the regulated output voltage.

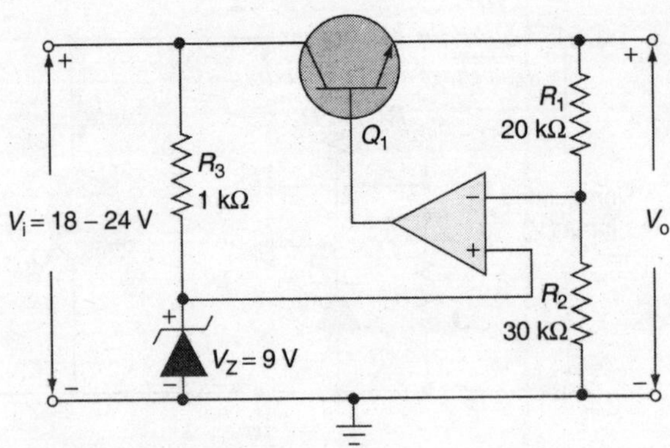

Figure 14.30 | Example 14.10.

Solution

1. The regulated output voltage is the one for which voltage at the inverting input of opamp equals the Zener voltage.
2. That is, $V_o \times 30 \times 10^3/(30 \times 10^3 + 20 \times 10^3) = 9$ or $0.6 \times V_o = 9$.
3. This gives $V_o = 9/0.6 = 15$ V.

EXAMPLE 14.11

For the series-pass regulator circuit of Figure 14.31, determine the range over which the regulated output voltage is adjustable. Assume V_{BE} $(Q_2) = 0.7$ V.

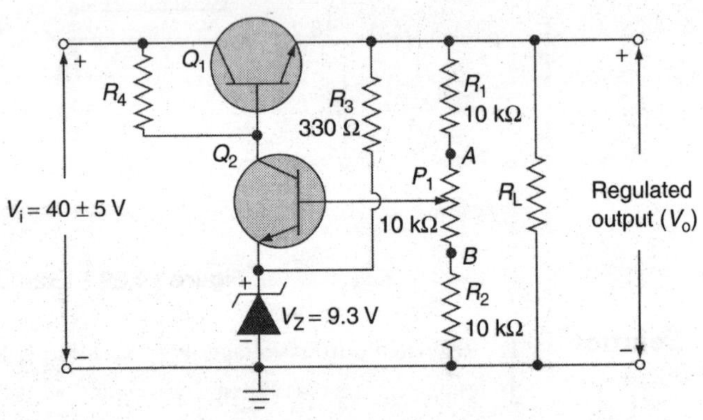

Figure 14.31 | Example 14.11.

Solution

1. Regulated output voltage when the potentiometer P_1 is at position A is given by

$$(9.3 + 0.7) \times [(10 \times 10^3 + 20 \times 10^3)/(20 \times 10^3)] = 15 \text{ V}$$

2. Regulated output voltage when the potentiometer P_1 is at position B is given by

$$(9.3 + 0.7) \times [(10 \times 10^3 + 20 \times 10^3)/(10 \times 10^3)] = 30 \text{ V}$$

3. Therefore, regulated output voltage is adjustable from 15 V to 30 V.

EXAMPLE 14.12 *For the basic shunt regulator circuit of Figure 14.32, determine (a) regulated output voltage and (b) maximum power dissipation in resistor R_S. Assume V_{BE} $(Q_1) = 0.7$ V.*

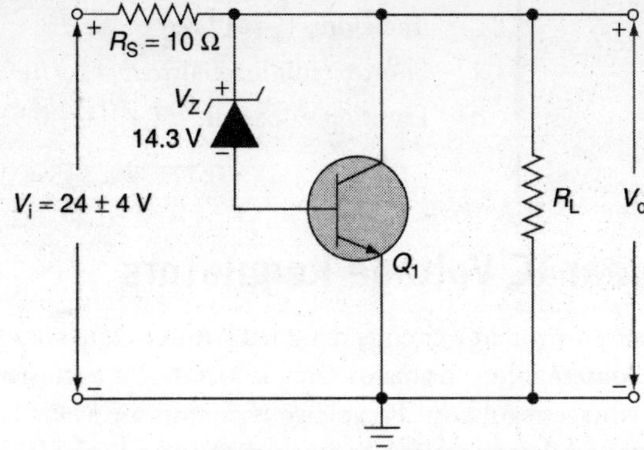

Figure 14.32 | Example 14.12.

Solution

1. Regulated output voltage, $V_o = V_Z + V_{BE}\ (Q_1) = 14.3 + 0.7 = 15$ V.
2. R_S dissipates maximum power when the unregulated input voltage has maximum value.
3. Now, maximum unregulated input voltage = 28 V.
4. Therefore, maximum power dissipation = $(28 - 15)^2/10 = 16.9$ W.

EXAMPLE 14.13 *Refer to the series-pass regulator circuit of Figure 14.33. The regulator circuit has foldback current-limiting feature. Determine (a) regulated output voltage, (b) limiting value of current in the case of short circuit. Assume V_{BE} $(Q_2) = 0.6$ V and V_{BE} $(Q_1) = V_{BE}$ $(Q_3) = 0.7$ V.*

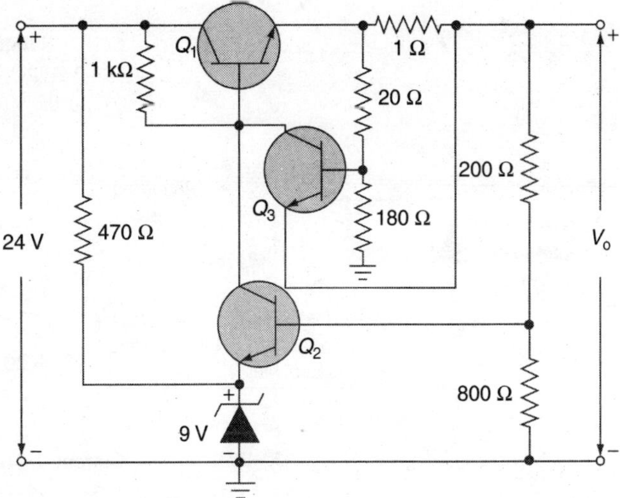

Figure 14.33 | Example 14.13.

Solution

1. Regulated output voltage V_o is given by

$$V_o \times 800/1000 = 9.6$$

Therefore, $V_o = 12$ V.

2. Short-circuit load current = 0.7/0.9 × 1 = 0.777 A.
3. Limiting value = 0.777 + [(1 – 0.9) × 12]/(0.9 × 1) = 0.777 + 1.2/0.9

$$= 0.777 + 1.333 = 2.11 \text{ A}$$

14.6 Linear IC Voltage Regulators

Series and shunt regulator circuits designed with discrete components were discussed in the preceding sections. Contemporary regulator circuits are almost exclusively configured around one or more ICs known as IC voltage regulators. IC voltage regulators are available to meet a wide range of requirements. Both fixed output voltage (positive and negative) and adjustable output voltage (positive and negative) IC regulators are commercially available in a wide range of voltage, current and regulation specifications. These have built-in protection features such as current limit, thermal shutdown and so on.

General-Purpose Precision Linear Voltage Regulator

IC 723 is one such general-purpose adjustable output voltage regulator that can be used in positive or negative output power supplies as series, shunt and switching regulator. The internal schematic arrangement of IC 723 resembles the typical circuit for a series-pass linear regulator and comprises a temperature compensated reference, an error amplifier, a series-pass transistor and a current limiter with access to remote shutdown (Figure 14.34).

Figures 14.35 and 14.36 show the basic circuits for building low positive output voltage (2 – 7 V) and high positive output voltage (7 – 37 V) regulator circuits. In the case of the circuit arrangement of Figure 14.35, the regulated output voltage is given by $V_{ref} \times [R_2/(R_1 + R_2)]$. In the case of the circuit arrangement of Figure 14.36, the output voltage is given by $V_{ref} \times [(R_1 + R_2)/R_2]$. In both cases, recommended value of R_3 is $(R_1 \times R_2)/(R_1 + R_2)]$ and $R_{SC} = 0.6/I_{SC}$, where I_{SC} is short-circuit limiting current value.

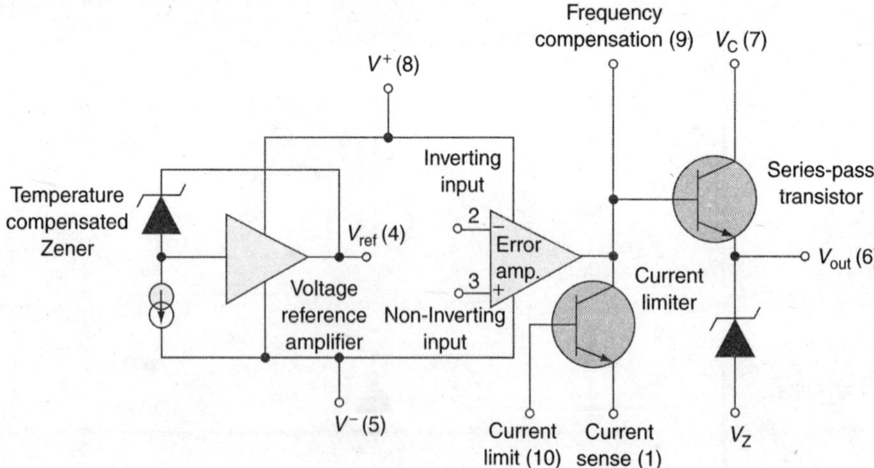

Figure 14.34 | Internal schematic arrangement of IC 723.

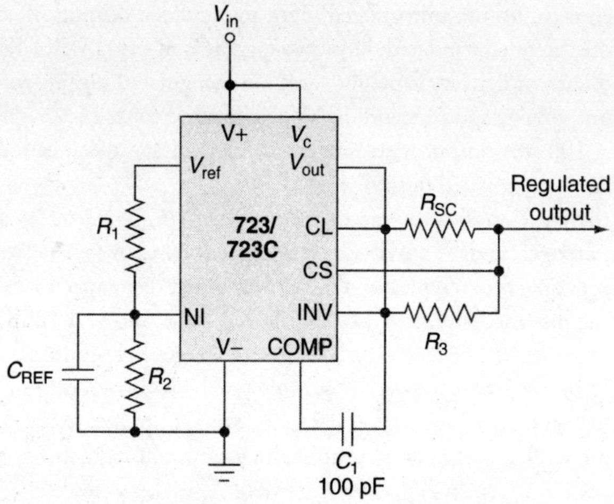

Figure 14.35 Low positive output voltage regulator using IC 723.

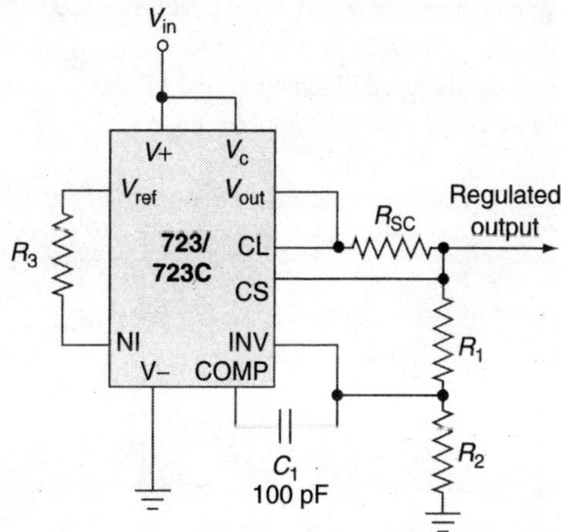

Figure 14.36 High positive output voltage regulator using IC 723.

Regulator circuits with enhanced load current capability can also be configured around regulator IC 723 with the help of external bipolar transistors. These and many more circuits can be found in application notes of IC 723.

Three-Terminal Regulators

In their basic operational mode, three-terminal regulators require virtually no external components. These are available in both fixed output voltage (positive and negative) as well as adjustable output voltage (positive and negative) types in current ratings of 100 mA, 500 mA, 1.5 A and 3.0 A. Popular fixed positive output voltage types include LM/MC 78XX-series and LM 140XX/340XX-series three-terminal regulators. LM 117/217/317 is a common adjustable positive output voltage regulator type number. Popular fixed negative output voltage types include LM/MC 79XX-series and LM 120XX/320XX-series three-terminal regulators. LM 137/237/337 is a common adjustable negative output voltage regulator type number. A two-digit number in place of "XX" indicates the regulated output voltage. An important specification of three-terminal regulators is the dropout voltage, which is minimum unregulated input to regulated output differential voltage required for the regulator to produce the intended regulated output voltage. It is in the range of 1.5 V to 3 V and is lower for regulators with lower load current delivery capability and lower regulated output voltage value. For example, a 5 V regulator has a dropout voltage specification of 2 V against 3 V for a 24 V regulator for the same current delivery capability. Also, a 100 mA output regulator has a drop voltage specification of 1.7 V against 3 V for 1500 mA regulator for the same regulated output voltage.

Figure 14.37 shows the basic application circuits using LM/MC 78XX-series and LM/MC 79XX-series three-terminal regulators. Here C_1 and C_2 are decoupling capacitors. C_1 is generally used when the regulator is located far from the power supply filter. Typically, a 0.22 μF ceramic disc capacitor is used for C_1. Capacitor C_2 is typically a 0.1 μF ceramic disc capacitor. LM 140XX/340XX-series and LM 120XX/320XX-series regulators are also used in the same manner. In the case of fixed output voltage three-terminal regulators, if the common terminal instead of being grounded were applied a DC voltage, the regulated output voltage in that case would be greater than the expected value by a quantum equal to the voltage applied to the common terminal.

Figure 14.38 shows the application of fixed output three-terminal regulator as a constant current source. The load current in this case is given by $V_{ref}/R + I_Q$, where I_Q is the quiescent current, typically 8 mA for 78XX-series regulators. For details on the features and facilities of three-terminal regulators and their application circuits, one can refer to data sheets and application notes provided by manufacturers of these devices.

LM 117/217/317 is an adjustable output three-terminal positive output voltage regulator and is available in current ratings of 500 mA, 1000 mA and 1500 mA. The output voltage is adjustable from 1.2 V to 37 V. In the high-voltage version of this series of regulators, designated as LM 117HV/217HV/317HV, the output voltage is adjustable from 1.2 V to 57 V. Figure 14.39 shows the application of LM 117/217/317 as an adjustable regulator.

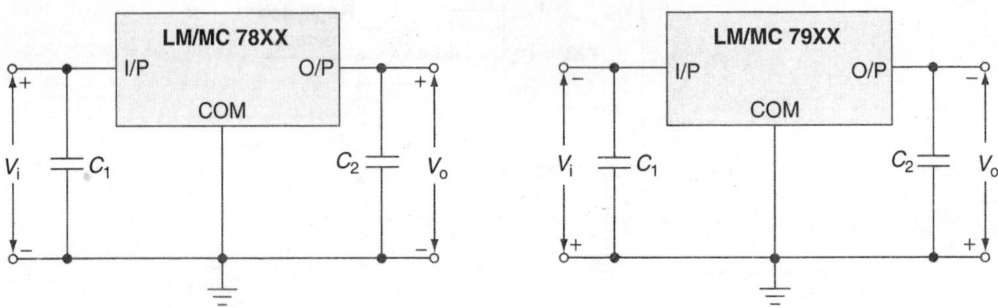

Figure 14.37 Basic application circuits using three-terminal regulators.

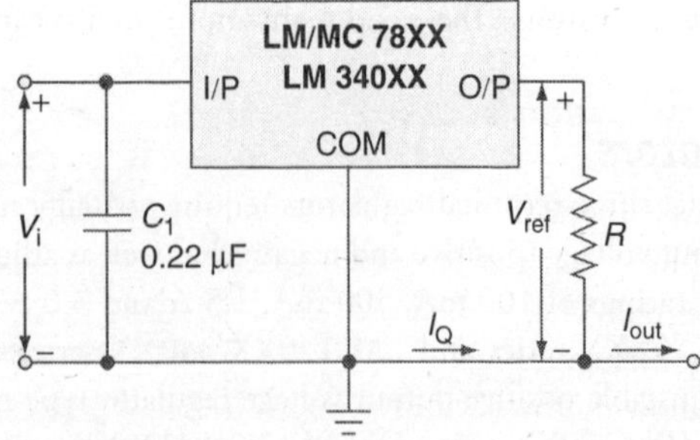

Figure 14.38 Three-terminal regulator as a constant current source.

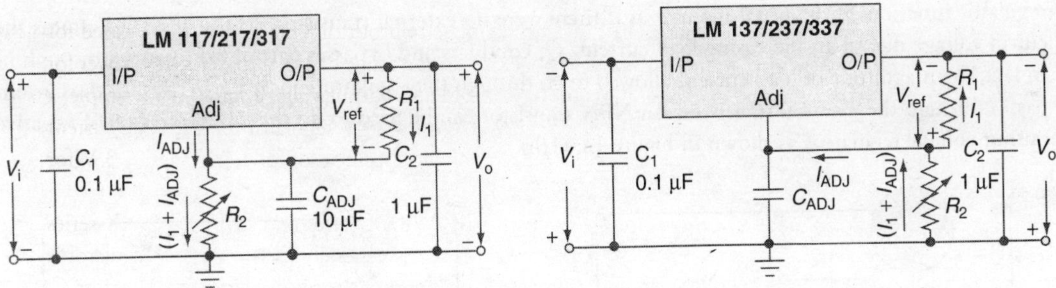

Figure 14.39 Basic application circuit using LM 117/217/317.

Figure 14.40 Basic application circuit using LM 137/237/337.

Here C_1 and C_2 are decoupling capacitors; C_{ADJ} provides ripple rejection. C_{ADJ} of 10 μF provides typically 80 dB rejection. The output voltage is given by Eq. (14.36):

$$V_o = V_{ref} + \left[\left(\frac{V_{ref}}{R_1}\right) + I_{ADJ}\right] \times R_2 \tag{14.36}$$

$$V_o = \left[\left\{V_{ref} \times \left(\frac{R_1 + R_2}{R_1}\right)\right\} + I_{ADJ} \times R_2\right] \tag{14.37}$$

V_{ref} and I_{ADJ} are typically 1.25 V and 100 µA, respectively.

LM 137/237/337 is an adjustable output three-terminal negative output voltage regulator and is available in current ratings of 500 mA, 1000 mA and 1500 mA. The output voltage is adjustable from −1.2 V to −37 V. In the high-voltage version of this series of regulators, designated as LM 117HV/217HV/317HV, the output voltage is adjustable from −1.2 V to −47 V. Figure 14.40 shows the application of LM 137/237/337 as an adjustable regulator. Here C_1 and C_2 are decoupling capacitors; C_{ADJ} provides ripple rejection. C_{ADJ} of 10 µF provides typically 80 dB rejection. The output voltage is given by

$$V_o = -\left[\left\{V_{ref} \times \left(\frac{R_1 + R_2}{R_1}\right)\right\} + I_{ADJ} \times R_2\right] \tag{14.38}$$

Here V_{ref} and I_{ADJ} are typically −1.25 V and 100 µA, respectively.

Boosting Current Delivery Capability

The load current delivery capability of three-terminal regulators can be increased to more than what they can deliver for a given unregulated input to regulated output voltage differential by using an external transistor. It may be mentioned here that the power dissipated in the regulator is the product of load current and input–output differential voltage. As the power dissipation increases beyond the rated value, the regulator usually goes to thermal shutdown mode. In this mode, the internal series-pass transistor becomes non-conducting, thus allowing the device to cool down.

Figure 14.41(a) shows the typical circuit where an external transistor is used to boost the load current delivery capability of the regulator. In this case, as long as V_{BE} (Q_1) remains below its cut-in voltage, the regulator functions in its usual manner as if there were no external transistor. As the V_{BE} (Q_1) attains the cut-in voltage due to an increasing load current, Q_1 conducts and bypasses part of load current through it. In fact, the magnitude of load current allowed to go through the regulator equals V_{BE}/R. Rest of the current passes through the external transistor. An NPN transistor can be used to do the job in the case of negative output voltage regulators as shown in Figure 14.41(b).

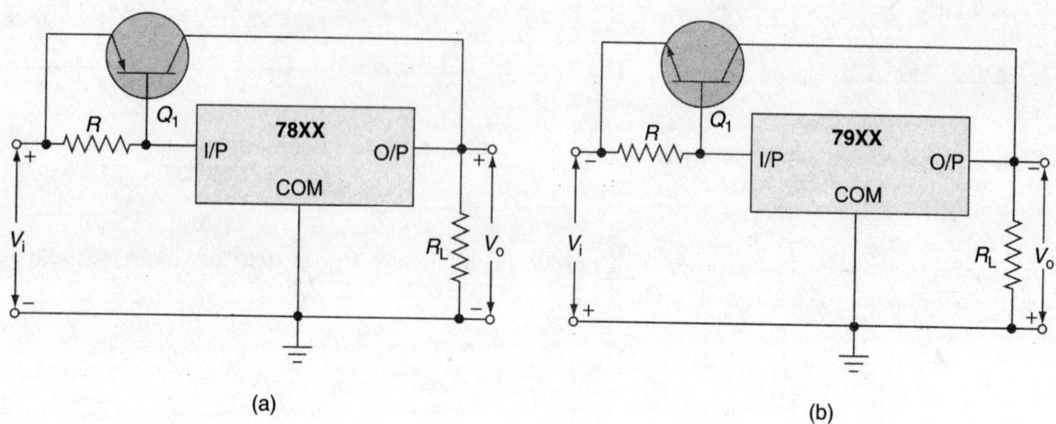

Figure 14.41 Use of external transistor to boost current delivery capability.

EXAMPLE 14.14 *Refer to the three-terminal regulator circuits of Figures 14.42(a) and (b). Determine the regulated output voltages in the two cases given that $V_Z = 3.3$ V and $V_{D1} = 0.7$ V.*

Solution

1. For the circuit of Figure 14.42(a)

$$V_o = 5 + V_Z + V_{D1} = 5 + 3.3 + 0.7 = 9\text{ V}$$

2. For the circuit of Figure 14.42(b)

$$V_o = -12 - V_{D1} = -(12 + 0.7) = -12.7\text{ V}$$

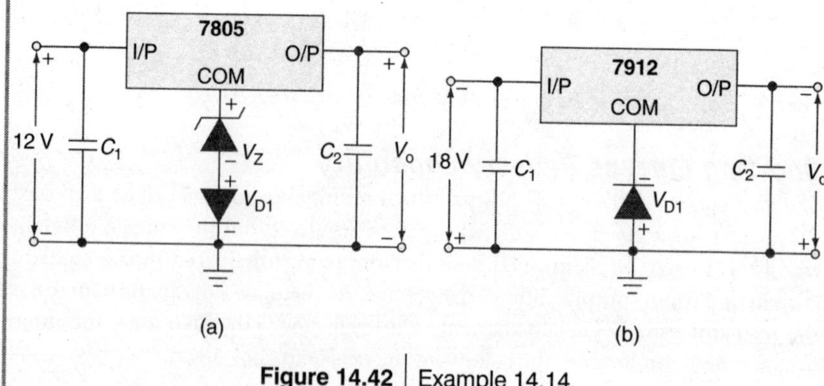

Figure 14.42 Example 14.14.

EXAMPLE 14.15 *Determine the regulated output voltage for the regulator circuit of Figure 14.43 given $V_{ref} = 1.25$ V.*

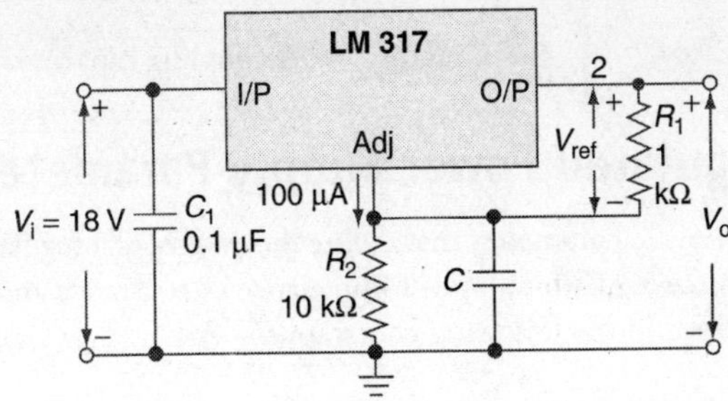

Figure 14.43 | Example 14.15.

Solution

1. The regulated output voltage is sum of voltages across resistors R_1 and R_2. It is given by

$$V_o = V_{ref} + \left[\left(\frac{V_{ref}}{R_1}\right) + I_{ADJ}\right] \times R_2$$

2. Substituting the values, we get

$$V_o = 1.25 + [(1.25/10^3) + 10^{-4}] \times 10 \times 10^3 = 14.75 \text{ V}$$

EXAMPLE 14.16 *Using IC voltage regulator-type number LM 7812, design a circuit that generates a variable output voltage adjustable from +15 V to +20 V from an unregulated input of +24 V. Assume quiescent current to be negligible.*

Solution

1. Figure 14.44 shows the basic circuit configuration. The output voltage V_o in this case is given by

$$V_o = 12 + [V_o \times R_2/(R_1 + R_2)]$$

$$V_o \times [1 - R_2/(R_1 + R_2)] = 12$$

$$V_o = 12 \times [1 + R_2/R_1]$$

2. V_o (min) = 15 = 12 × [1 + R_2/R_1], which gives R_2 (min) = $R_1/4$.

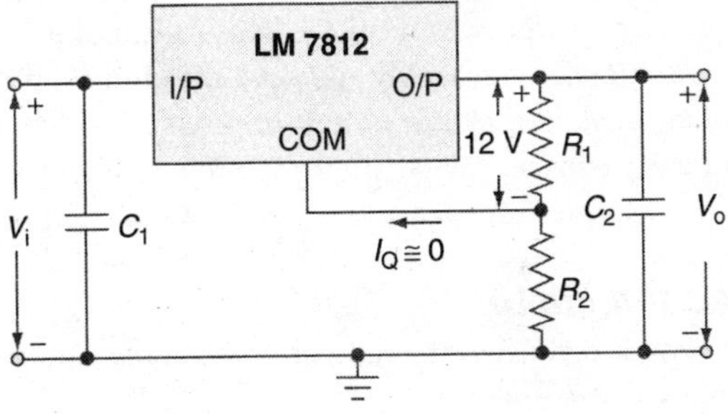

Figure 14.44 | Example 14.16.

3. V_o (max) = 20 = 12 × [1 + R_2/R_1], which gives R_2 (max) = $2R_1/3$.
4. Assuming R_1 = 47 kΩ, R_2 (min) = 11.75 kΩ and R_2 (max) = 31.3 kΩ.
5. C_1 and C_2 are decoupling capacitors and can be 0.1 μF ceramic disks each.

14.7 Regulated Power Supply Parameters

The characteristic parameters that define the quality of a regulated power supply include load regulation, line or source regulation, output impedance or resistance and ripple rejection factor. Each one of these is briefly described in the following paragraphs.

Load Regulation

Load regulation is defined as change in regulated output voltage of the power supply as the load current varies from zero (no-load condition) to maximum rated value (full-load condition). It is usually expressed as a percentage of full-load voltage. That is

$$\text{Percentage load regulation} = \left[\frac{V_{NL} - V_{FL}}{V_{FL}}\right] \times 100 \tag{14.39}$$

Since $V_{FL} \cong V_{NL}$, load regulation may be expressed as a percentage of no-load voltage.

Line Regulation

Line regulation is defined in terms of variation of regulated output voltage for a specified change in line voltage. It is usually expressed as percentage of nominal regulated output voltage. As an example, if the nominal regulated output voltage of 10 V varies by ±1% for a specified variation in line voltage, line regulation in that case would be (0.2/10) × 100 = 2%.

Output Impedance

Output impedance is an important parameter of a regulated power supply. It determines the load regulation of the power supply. The regulated power supply may be represented by a Thevenin's equivalent circuit comprising a voltage source equal to the open circuit voltage across power supply output terminals in series with impedance equal to the output impedance of the power supply. The voltage appearing across the load resistance is equal to the open circuit voltage minus drop across output impedance of the power supply. The voltage drop increases with increase in load current resulting in reduction of voltage across the load. Another way of explaining the same is that the output impedance of the power supply and the load resistance form a potential divider. The load voltage decreases with decrease in load resistance value. An ideal power supply has an output impedance of zero, which renders the output voltage independent of the load resistance value.

Practical power supplies very nearly approach the ideal condition because of emitter–follower nature of regulator circuit characterized by low output impedance, which is further reduced by a factor of (1 + loop gain) due to voltage feedback. Loop gain is the product of output voltage feedback factor and the gain of the error amplifier. Output impedance is typically of the order of few milli-ohms.

Ripple Rejection Factor

Ripple rejection factor is defined as the ratio of ripple in the regulated output voltage to the ripple present in unregulated input voltage. That is

$$\text{Ripple rejection factor} = \frac{V_{RIPPLE}\text{(output)}}{V_{RIPPLE}\text{(input)}} \tag{14.40}$$

When expressed in decibels, ripple rejection equals

$$20\log\left[\frac{V_{\text{RIPPLE}}(\text{output})}{V_{\text{RIPPLE}}(\text{input})}\right]\text{dB}$$

Ripple in unregulated input is nothing but a periodic variation in input voltage. It manifests at the output with a reduced value. Again, the factor by which ripple is reduced equals the de-sensitivity factor (1 + loop gain) due to negative feedback. That is

$$V_{\text{RIPPLE}}(\text{output}) = \frac{V_{\text{RIPPLE}}(\text{input})}{1+\text{Loop gain}}$$

EXAMPLE 14.17 *A regulated power supply operates from 220 ± 20 VAC. It produces a no-load regulated output voltage of 24 ± 0.5 VDC. Also, the regulated output voltage falls from 24 VDC to 23.8 VDC as the load changes from no-load to full-load condition for the nominal value of input voltage. Determine (a) line regulation and (b) load regulation.*

Solution

1. Line regulation = (24.5 – 23.5)/24 = 1/24 = 0.0417 = 4.17%
2. Load regulation = (24 – 23.8)/23.8 = 0.2/23.8 = 0.0084 = 0.84%

EXAMPLE 14.18 *A regulated power supply provides a ripple rejection of –80 dB. If the ripple voltage in the unregulated input were 2 V, determine the output ripple.*

Solution

1. Ripple rejection in dB is given by

$$20\log\left[\frac{\text{Output ripple}}{\text{Input ripple}}\right] = -80\text{ dB}$$

2. Therefore,

$$\log\left[\frac{\text{Output ripple}}{\text{Input ripple}}\right] = -4$$

$$\frac{\text{Output ripple}}{\text{Input ripple}} = 10^{-4}$$

3. Therefore, output ripple = 2×10^{-4} V = 0.2 mV.

EXAMPLE 14.19 *Figure 14.45 shows load voltage versus load current characteristics of a regulated power supply. Determine the output impedance of the power supply.*

Solution

1. Output impedance is given by ratio of change in output voltage for known change in load current.
2. From the given characteristic curve, output impedance = (24 – 23.5)/(10 – 0) = 0.5/10 = 0.05 Ω = 50 mΩ.

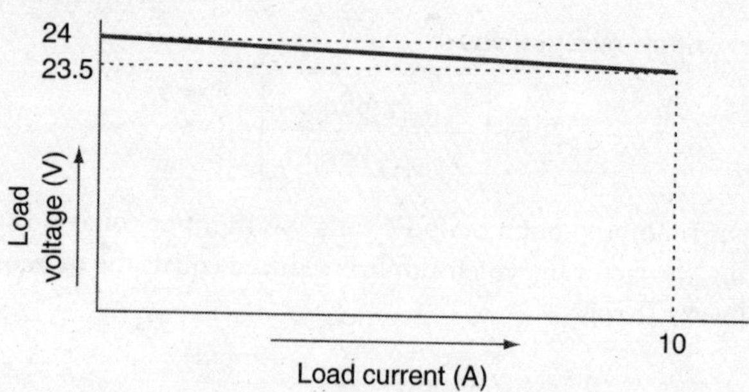

Figure 14.45 | Example 14.19.

EXAMPLE 14.20 *Refer to the three-terminal regulator circuit of Figure 14.46. Determine (a) load current; (b) current through LM 7812; (c) current through external transistor; (d) power dissipated in LM 7812. Take* $V_{BE}(Q_1) = 0.7$ *V.*

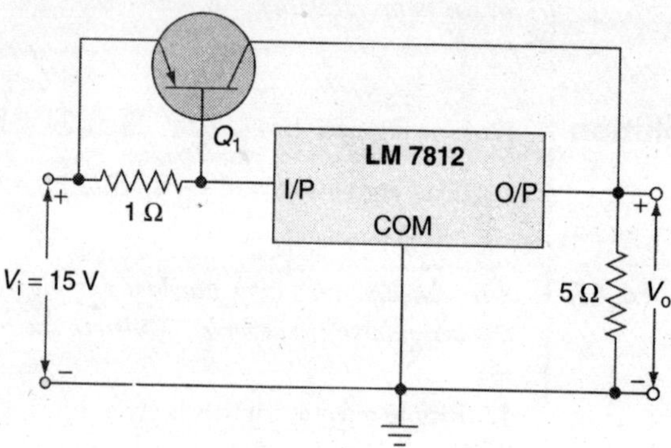

Figure 14.46 | Example 14.20.

Solution

1. Load current = 12/5 = 2.4 A.
2. Current through regulator = 0.7/1 = 0.7 A.
3. Current through external transistor = 2.4 – 0.7 = 1.7 A.
4. Voltage appearing at regulator input = 15 – 0.7 = 14.3 V.
5. Therefore power dissipated in the regulator = (14.3 – 12) × 0.7 = 1.61 W.

KEY TERMS

Emitter–follower regulator
Filter circuit
Line regulation
Load regulation
Output impedance
Peak inverse voltage
Ratio of rectification
Rectifier circuit
Regulator circuit
Ripple factor
Ripple frequency
Ripple rejection factor
Series-pass linear regulator
Shunt regulator
Three-terminal regulator
Transformer
Transformer utilization factor

OBJECTIVE-TYPE EXERCISES

Multiple-Choice Questions

1. The no load and rated load output voltages in a regulated power supply are the same. Its output impedance is therefore
   a. extremely small.
   b. zero.
   c. infinite.
   d. extremely large.

2. Which of the following filter types is suitable only for large values of load resistance?
   a. Capacitor filter
   b. Inductor filter
   c. Choke-input filter
   d. π-type CLC filter

3. Which of the following filter types is suitable only for small values of load resistance?
   a. Capacitor filter
   b. Inductor filter
   c. Choke-input filter
   d. π-type CLC filter

4. Identify the wrong expression.
   a. TUF = DC power delivered to load/AC rating of transformer secondary
   b. Load regulation = $[V_o$ (No load) – V_o (Full load)]/V_o (No load)
   c. Ratio of rectification = DC power delivered to load/AC power available across transformer secondary
   d. Ripple factor = RMS value of AC component/DC value of the rectified wave

5. If the transformer utilization factor for a particular rectifier configuration is small, it implies that
   a. for a given transformer rating, it would deliver a larger DC power to the load.
   b. for a given transformer rating, it would deliver lesser DC power to the load.
   c. the ratio of DC power delivered to the load to the AC power available at the input of rectifier circuit from transformer secondary is small.
   d. none of these.

6. Mark the rectifier circuit that has the least ripple.
   a. Half-wave rectifier
   b. Two-diode full-wave rectifier with center tapped secondary
   c. Bridge rectifier
   d. Both (b) and (c)

7. Which of the characteristic curves shown in Figure 14.47 is for linear power supply with foldback current limiting?
   a. Figure 14.47(a)
   b. Figure 14.47(b)
   c. Figure 14.47(c)
   d. Figure 14.47(d)

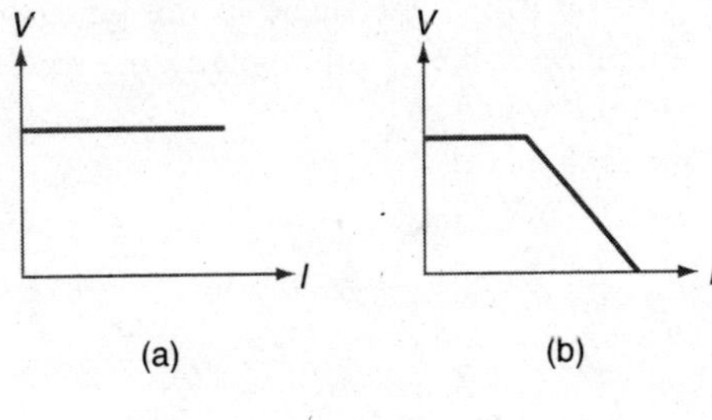

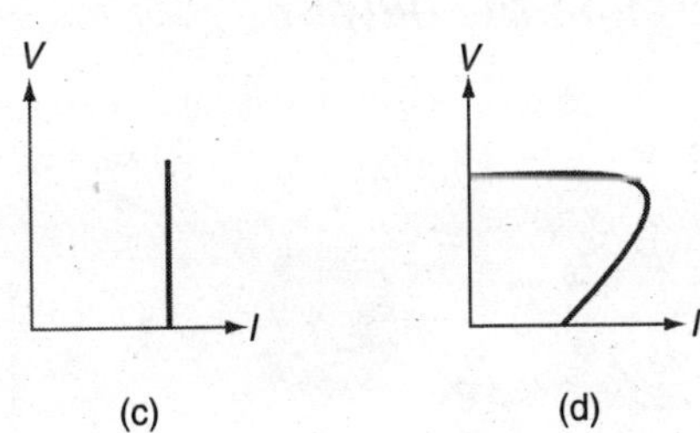

Figure 14.47 Multiple-choice question 7.

8. In a series-pass linear regulator, voltage drop across series-pass element
   a. is independent of changes in output voltage.
   b. changes directly with changes in output voltage.
   c. changes inversely with changes in output voltage
   d. none of these.

9. The type of linear voltage regulator that is inherently immune to overload condition is
   a. emitter–follower regulator.
   b. series-pass regulator with error amplifier in feedback loop.
   c. shunt regulator.
   d. none of these.

10. In a series-pass linearly regulated power supply, regulated output voltage is 12 V across a load resistance of 1.2 kΩ. The unregulated input is 18 ± 3 V. The worst case power dissipation in the series-pass element would be
    a. 0.09 W
    b. 0.9 W
    c. 0.05 W
    d. 0.21 W

11. A voltage regulator provides a ripple rejection of −60 dB. If the ripple in the unregulated input were 0.5 V, the ripple in the regulated output would be
    a. 0.5 mV
    b. 60 mV
    c. 1 mV
    d. 5 mV

12. Voltage regulators use
    a. positive feedback.
    b. negative feedback.
    c. either positive or negative feedback.
    d. no feedback.

13. IC 7912 produces a regulated output voltage of
    a. +12 V
    b. −12 V
    c. 0 to +12 V
    d. 0 to −12 V

14. Which of the following IC voltage regulators is an adjustable negative output voltage regulator.
    a. LM 317
    b. LM 117
    c. LM 217
    d. LM 237

15. In the case of foldback current limiting, the short circuit load current is
    a. less than the maximum possible load current.
    b. more than the maximum possible load current.
    c. equal to the maximum possible load current.
    d. zero.

Determine the Output

Refer to the regulator circuits of Figure 14.48(a)–(d). Determine the output voltage in each of the four circuits given that V_{BE} of transistors and the forward-biased diode voltage drop in different circuits is 0.7 V.

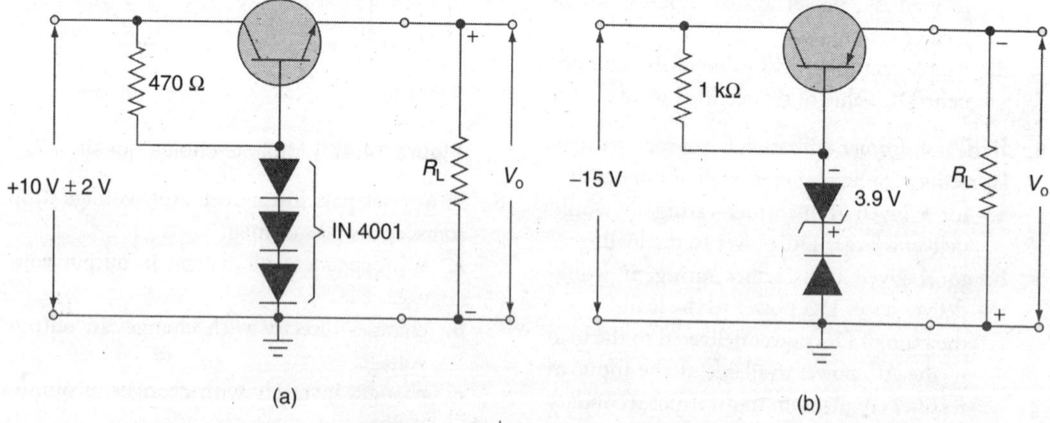

Figure 14.48 Regulator circuits.

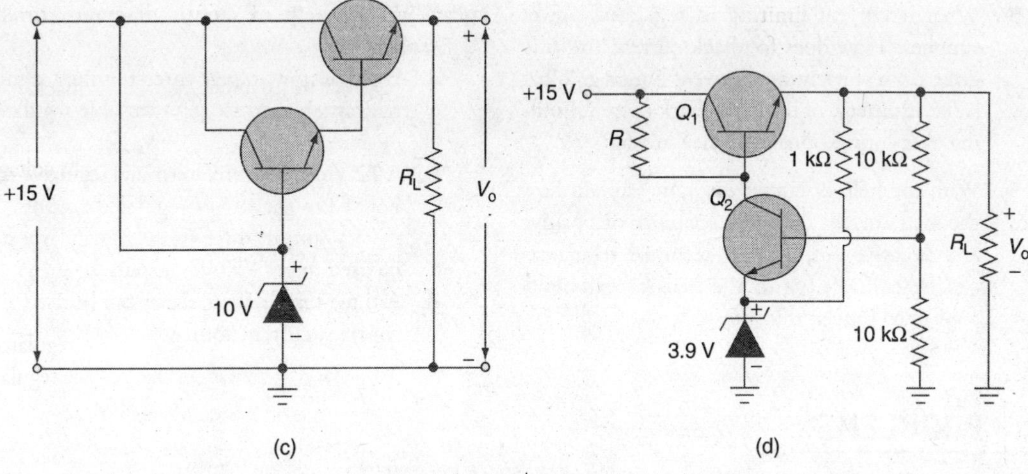

Figure 14.48 *Continued.*

REVIEW QUESTIONS

1. Name the constituent parts of a basic linearly regulated power supply. Briefly describe the function of each of the constituent parts.

2. Define the following parameters with reference to rectifier circuits. Also write expressions for these parameters in the case of half-wave, conventional full-wave with center-tapped secondary and bridge rectifier circuits.
   a. Ripple frequency
   b. Ratio of rectification
   c. Transformer utilization factor

3. Draw the basic circuit configurations in the case of following types of rectifier circuits.
   a. Conventional full-wave rectifier for negative output voltage
   b. Bridge rectifier for positive output voltage
   c. Half-wave rectifier for negative output voltage

   What is the minimum required peak inverse voltage rating of the diodes used in these rectifier circuits?

4. Give reasons for the following.
   a. Why inductor filter is suitable only for low values of load resistance?
   b. Why capacitor filter is suitable only for high values of load resistance?
   c. Why shunt regulator is not adversely affected by overload condition?
   d. Why is shunt regulator less efficient than a series-pass regulator?

5. Briefly describe the operational principle of an emitter–follower regulator. Draw the basic circuit configurations of positive output and negative output emitter–follower regulators.

6. With the help of basic circuit configuration, briefly describe the operational principle of a shunt regulator.

7. Define load regulation, line regulation, output impedance and ripple rejection factor with reference to regulated power supplies. What decides ripple rejection offered by a regulator circuit?

8. What is current limiting in regulated power supplies? How does foldback current limiting differ from conventional current limiting? What is the advantage of using foldback current limiting over conventional current limiting?

9. With the help of circuit diagram, explain how the load current delivery capability of positive and negative output three-terminal regulators can be enhanced with the help of externally connected bipolar transistors.

10. With the help of circuit diagrams, briefly explain how
    a. Fixed output voltage three-terminal regulator can be used to get a variable regulated output.
    b. A 12 V output three-terminal regulator can be used to get a 15 V regulated output.
    c. A −5 V output three-terminal regulator can be used to get −5.6 V output.
    d. A three-terminal regulator can be used as a constant current source.

PROBLEMS

1. Given that ripple factor in the case of a full-wave rectifier is 0.482, determine the ratio-of-rectification for the same.

2. Determine the transformer rating if it were to deliver a DC power of 1000 W to a resistive load using a bridge rectifier given that the transformer utilization factor in the case of bridge rectifier is 0.812.

3. If ripple factor and ratio-of-rectification are respectively designated as r and R, prove that $r = \sqrt{(1-R)/R}$.

4. A power supply uses a bridge rectifier and a capacitor filter. The filter feeds a load resistance of 500 Ω. If the DC voltage across the load is 12 V and the peak-to-peak value of ripple were not to exceed 0.1 V, determine the minimum capacitance value of the filter capacitor. Assume a power line frequency of 50 Hz.

5. A π-type CLC filter is connected across the output of a bridge rectifier, which in turn is fed with a 50 Hz sine wave. The filter feeds a load resistance of 1 kΩ. If the desired ripple factor is 0.002 and the two capacitors are 47 μF each, determine the minimum value of inductance needed to get the desired ripple factor. Also determine the value of resistance required to replace the inductor and still produce the same ripple.

6. Figure 14.49 shows the basic emitter–follower type of voltage regulator circuit. If the Zener diode is to be biased at least at 10 mA at all times, determine (a) regulated output voltage; (b) value of R given that transistor β is equal to 100 and $V_{BE} = 0.7$ V.

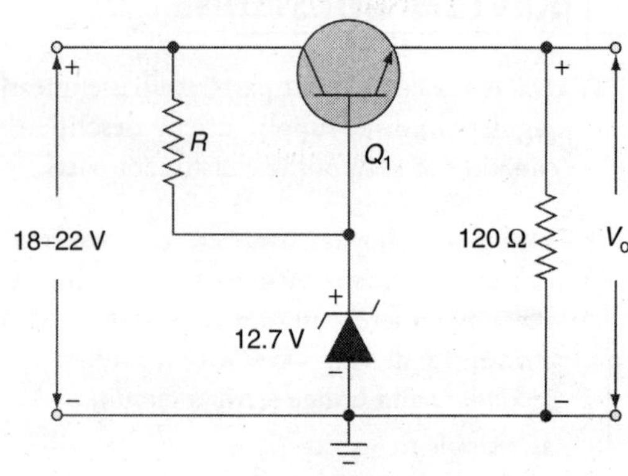

Figure 14.49 Problem 6.

7. Find the regulated output voltage (V_o) for the emitter–follower regulator circuit of Figure 14.50. Also determine the current (I_Z) if transistors Q_1 and Q_2 in the Darlington pair have β of 10 and 100, respectively. (Given that the forward voltage drop of diodes D_1 and D_2 is 0.6 V, V_{BE} (Q_1) = 0.6 V and V_{BE} (Q_2) = 0.6 V.

8. The output voltage of a regulated power supply drops by 1 V from no load to rated full load of 1 A. If the no load output voltage is 24 V, determine load regulation and output impedance of the power supply.

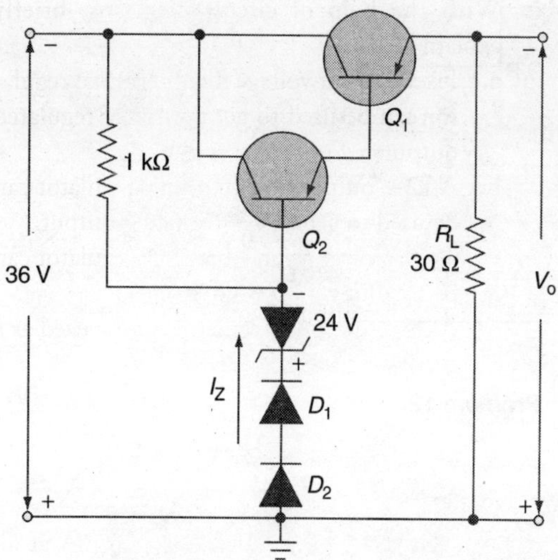

Figure 14.50 | Problem 7.

9. Refer to the series-pass regulator circuit of Figure 14.51. Determine the minimum and maximum possible regulated output voltages. Also determine the maximum power dissipated in transistor Q_1. Assume V_{BE} $(Q_1) = V_{BE}$ $(Q_2) = V_{BE}$ $(Q_3) = 0.6$ V.

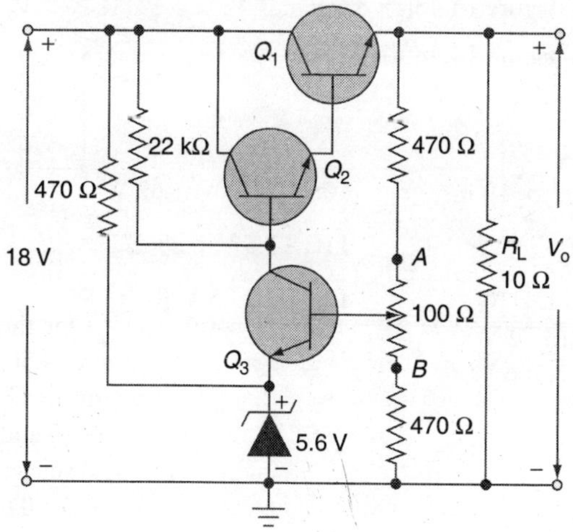

Figure 14.51 | Problem 9.

10. Refer to the three-terminal regulator circuit of Figure 14.52 using an external current boost transistor Q. Determine the power dissipated in regulator 7812. What is the power dissipated if the load resistance were reduced to 10 Ω? Assume V_{BE} $(Q) = 0.6$ V.

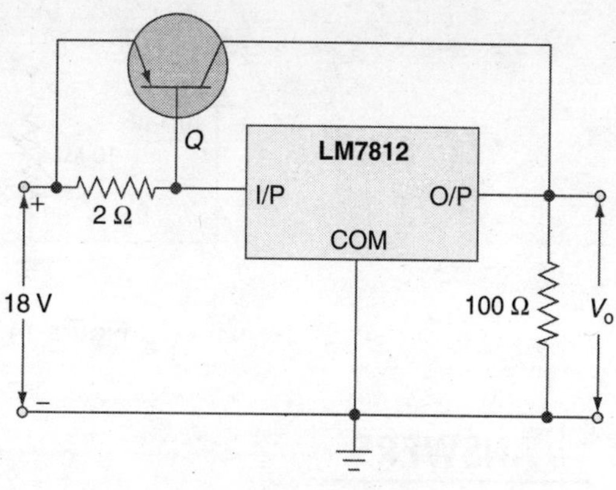

Figure 14.52 | Problem 10.

11. Refer to the three-terminal regulator circuit of Figure 14.53. Determine the regulated output voltage and power dissipated in the regulator.

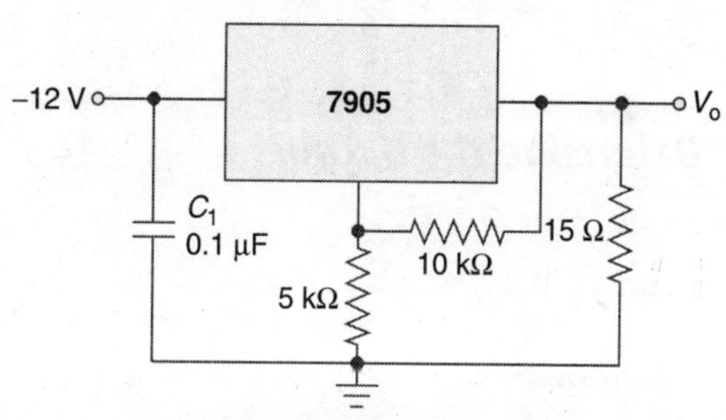

Figure 14.53 | Problem 11.

12. In the case of LM 317-based regulator circuit of Figure 14.54, determine (a) regulated output voltage with the variable resistance at its minimum value and voltage applied to the base terminal of transistor Q is 0 V; (b) regulated output voltage with the variable resistance at its maximum value and voltage applied to the base terminal of Q is 0 V; (c) regulated output voltage with the variable resistance at its minimum value and voltage applied to the base terminal of transistor Q is 5 V and (d) regulated output voltage with the variable resistance at its maximum value and voltage applied to the base terminal of transistor Q is 5 V. V_{ref} of LM 317 = 1.25 V.

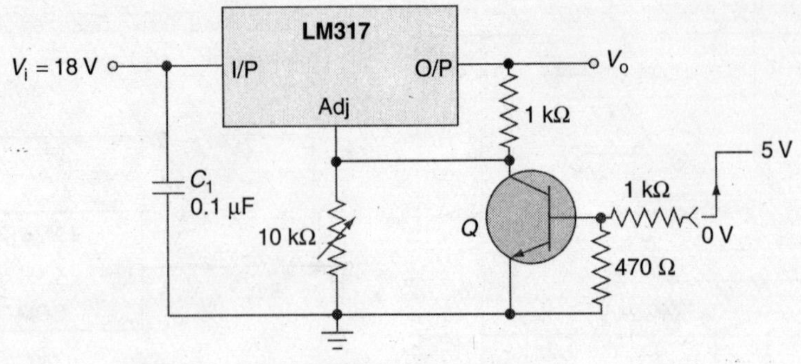

Figure 14.54 | Problem 12.

ANSWERS

Multiple-Choice Questions

1. (b)
2. (a)
3. (b)
4. (b)
5. (b)
6. (d)
7. (d)
8. (b)
9. (c)
10 (a)
11. (a)
12. (b)
13. (b)
14. (d)
15. (a)

Determine the Output

Figure 14.48(a): 1.4 V

Figure 14.48(b): −3.9 V

Figure 14.48(c): 8.6 V

Figure 14.48(d): 9.2 V

Problems

1. 0.812
2. 1233.7 W
4. 2400 μF
5. 0.645 henry, 405.3 Ω
6. (a) 12 V, (b) 524.75 Ω
7. $V_o = -24$ V, $I_Z = 10$ mA
8. 4.35%, 1 Ω
9. V_o (min) = 11.31 V, V_o (max) = 13.72 V, P_D (max) = 7.566 W
10. 0.691 W, 1.62 W
11. −7.5 V, 2.25 W
12. (a) 1.25 V, (b) 13.75 V, (c) 1.25 V, (d) 1.25 V

CHAPTER 15

Switched Mode Power Supplies

Learning Objectives

After completing this chapter, you will learn the following:

- Difference between a linearly regulated and switched mode power supply.
- Types of switched mode power supplies.
- Operational basics and design of flyback-type DC-to-DC converter.
- Operational basics of forward converter.
- Operational basics and design of push–pull converters.
- Types of switching regulators: Buck regulators, boost regulators, inverting regulators and three-terminal switching regulators.
- Connecting power converters in series and parallel.

Power supplies are often classified as linear power supplies or switched mode power supplies depending upon the nature of regulation circuit. Linear power supplies were discussed in Chapter 14. The focus in this chapter is on switched mode power supplies. In the case of switched mode power supplies, the unregulated DC input voltage is chopped at a high frequency with the help of an active device such as bipolar junction transistor, power MOSFET or insulated gate bipolar transistor (IGBT) and a transformer. The chopped waveform is then rectified and filtered to get the desired DC voltage. A sample of output voltage is used as a feedback signal to control some parameter of the drive waveform such as the duty cycle of the active device to achieve regulation. Switched mode power supply concept is the contemporary power supply design option for almost every conceivable requirement due to host of advantages it brings along with, which include high conversion efficiency, small size and weight and capability to generate any desired DC voltage from any available DC input. This chapter covers at length operational basics, design guidelines and role of integrated circuits in switched mode power supply design and other relevant topics. The text is supplemented by a large number of solved examples.

15.1 Switched Mode Power Supplies

As outlined earlier, based on the regulation concept, power supplies are classified as either linear or switched mode power supplies. Conventional AC/DC power supplies comprising a transformer, rectifier, filter and regulator (series or shunt type) constitute the linear power supply. The active device in the regulator circuit is always operated in the active or linear region of its output characteristics. Any change in the output voltage due to change in the input voltage or load current results in change in the voltage drop across the regulator transistor (in the case of a series regulator) or a change in the current through the regulator transistor (in the case of a shunt regulator) so as to maintain a constant output voltage across the load. Linearly regulated power supplies were discussed in Chapter 14.

DC-to-DC converters and DC-to-AC inverters belong to the category of switched mode power supplies (SMPS). Besides there are switching supplies operating from mains called off-line switching supplies. An off-line switching supply can be distinguished from a conventional AC–DC supply as in the case of the former the AC mains is rectified and filtered without using an input transformer, and the DC voltage so obtained is then used as an input to a switching type DC-to-DC converter.

In a SMPS, the active device that provides regulation is always operated in a switched mode, that is, it is operated either in cut-off or in saturation. The input DC is chopped at a high frequency (typically 10 kHz to 100 kHz) using an active device [bipolar junction transistor (BJT), metal oxide semiconductor field effect transistor (MOSFET), insulated gate bipolar transistor (IGBT) or silicon-controlled rectifier (SCR)] and the converter transformer. The transformed chopped waveform is rectified and filtered. A sample of the output voltage is used as feedback signal for the drive circuit for the switching transistor to achieve regulation.

Linear versus Switched Mode Power Supplies

Some of the salient features of linear and switched mode power supplies are presented in the following paragraphs for the purpose of comparison between the two:

1. Linear power supplies are well known for their extremely good line and load regulation, low output voltage ripple and almost negligible radio frequency interference (RFI)/electro magnetic interference (EMI).
2. Switching power supplies, on the other hand, have much higher efficiency (typically 80–90% against 50–60% in the case of linear supplies) and reduced size/weight for a given power-delivering capability.
3. Quite often, compactness and efficiency are two major selection criteria. An improved efficiency and reduced size/weight are particularly significant when designing a power supply for a portable system where there is a requirement of a number of different regulated output voltages.
4. Also, unlike linear supplies, efficiency in switching supplies does not suffer as the unregulated input to regulated output differential becomes large.
5. In portable systems operating from battery packs and requiring higher DC voltages for their operation, the switching supply is the only option. We cannot use a linear regulator to change a given unregulated input voltage to a higher regulated output voltage.

Different Types of SMPS

SMPS are designed in a variety of circuit configurations depending upon the intended application. Almost all switching supplies belong to one of the following three broad categories:

1. Flyback converters.
2. Forward converters.
3. Push–pull converters.

There are variations in the circuit configuration within each one of these categories of SMPS. For instance, in the category of flyback converters, we have *self-oscillating flyback converters* and the *externally driven flyback converters*. Again, in the externally driven flyback converters, there are isolation and non-isolation type configurations. Also, there are *DC-to-DC* and *off-line flyback converters*.

Similarly, there are different circuit configurations in the other two categories of switching supplies also. Although these configurations differ to an extent, the basic operational principle and the design criteria for different types belonging to one category remain more or less the same.

15.2 Flyback Converters

The self-oscillating flyback DC-to-DC converter is the most basic converter based on the flyback principle. The other type is the externally driven flyback DC-to-DC converter. The two types are described in the following sections.

Self-Oscillating Flyback DC-to-DC Converter

Figure 15.1 shows the circuit arrangement in a self-oscillating or ringing-choke flyback DC-to-DC converter. A switching transistor, a converter transformer, a fast recovery rectifier and an output filter capacitor make up a complete DC-to-DC converter. It is a constant output power converter as is evident from the operational principle of this type of configuration.

During the conduction time of the switching transistor, the current through the transformer primary starts ramping up linearly with a slope equal to V_{in}/L_P. Here L_P is the primary inductance. The voltages induced in the secondary and the feedback windings, respectively, make the fast recovery rectifier reverse-biased and hold the conducting transistor in the "ON"-state.

When the primary current reaches a peak value I_P, where the core begins to saturate, the current tends to rise very sharply. This sharp rise in current cannot be supported by the fixed base drive provided by the feedback winding. As a result, the switching transistor begins to come out of saturation.

This is a regenerative process that ends up in the transistor getting switched off. The magnetic field due to the current flowing in the primary winding collapses, thus reversing the polarities of the induced voltages. The fast recovery rectifier is forward-biased and the stored energy is transferred to the capacitor and the load through the secondary winding. Thus, energy is stored during the ON-time and transferred during the OFF-time.

Figure 15.2 shows the relevant waveforms, which include the waveforms for collector–emitter voltage (V_{ce}), emitter–base voltage (V_{be}), magnetic flux (ϕ) in the transformer core, primary current (I_p) and secondary current (I_s). The waveforms are self-explanatory. The collector–emitter voltage is initially equal to V_{in}. In the subsequent cycles, the collector–emitter voltage (V_{ce}) during the OFF-time equals $V_{in} + V_o/n$, where n is the transformer step-up ratio. Magnetic flux in the core rises from 0 to ϕ_{max} during the conduction period when the primary current rises from zero to its peak value. The flux decreases from ϕ_{max} to 0 during the OFF-time.

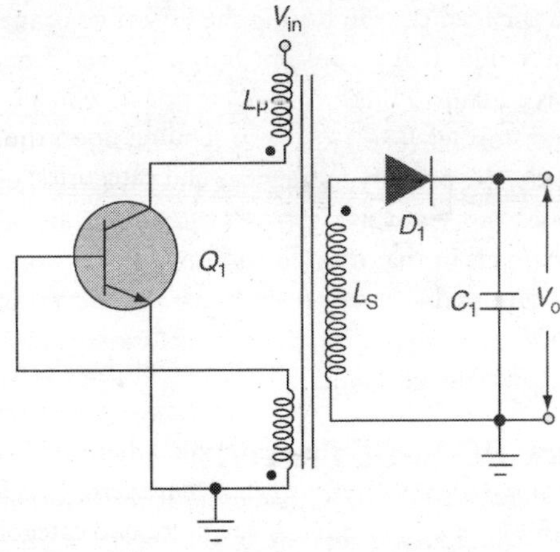

Figure 15.1 Self-oscillating flyback DC-to-DC converter.

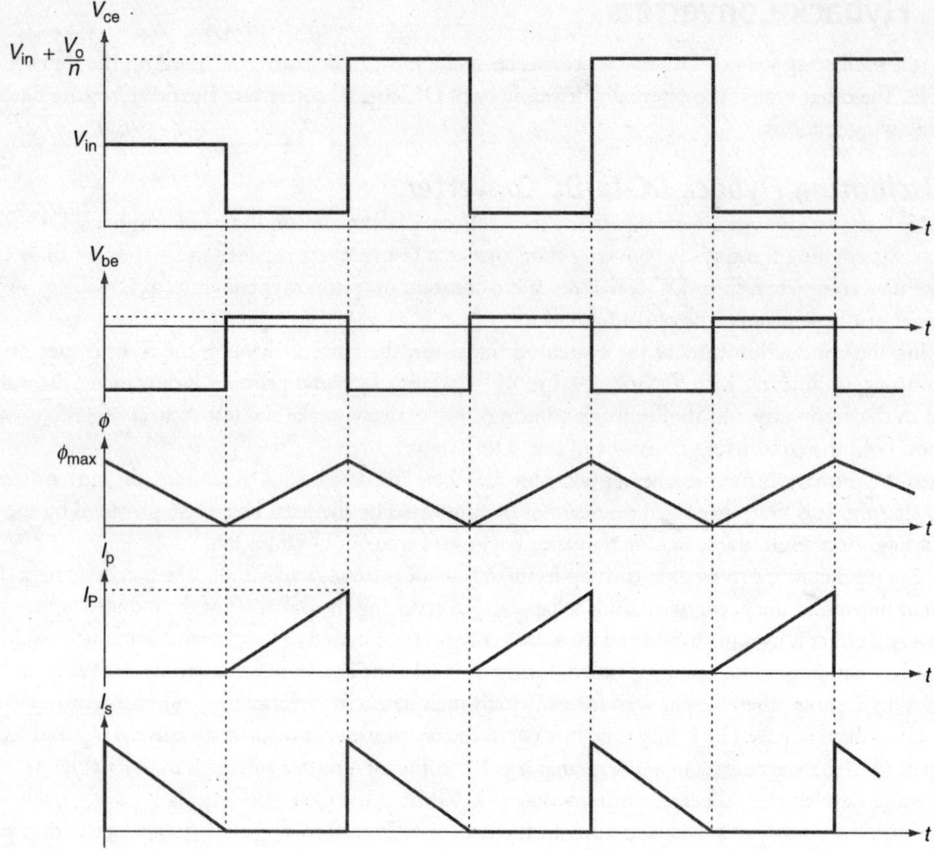

Figure 15.2 Relevant waveforms in the case of self-oscillating flyback DC-to-DC converter.

The output capacitor supplies the load current during the ON-time of the transistor when no energy is being transferred from the primary side. It is a constant output power converter and the power that the converter can deliver to the load is equal to $(1/2)\times L_P \times I_P^{\,2} \times f \times \eta$, which is the product of energy stored in the primary of the converter transformer $[(1/2)\times L_P \times I_P^2]$, switching frequency ($f$) and conversion efficiency (η). L_P and I_P are, respectively, the primary inductance and peak value of primary current. The output voltage reduces as the load increases and vice versa. Utmost care should be taken to ensure that the load is not accidentally taken off the converter. In that case, the output voltage would rise without limit until any of the converter components gets damaged. These converters are suitable for low output power applications due to their inherent nature of operation and may be used with advantage up to an output power of 150 W. They are characterized by high output voltage ripple.

Externally Driven Flyback DC-to-DC Converter

A variation of the self-oscillating flyback DC-to-DC converter is the externally driven flyback DC-to-DC converter (Figure 15.3). The basic principle remains the same. Energy is stored during turn-ON time and transferred during turn-OFF time of the active device. The feedback loop consisting of a comparator and the resistance divider provides the voltage sense as well as some degree of regulation.

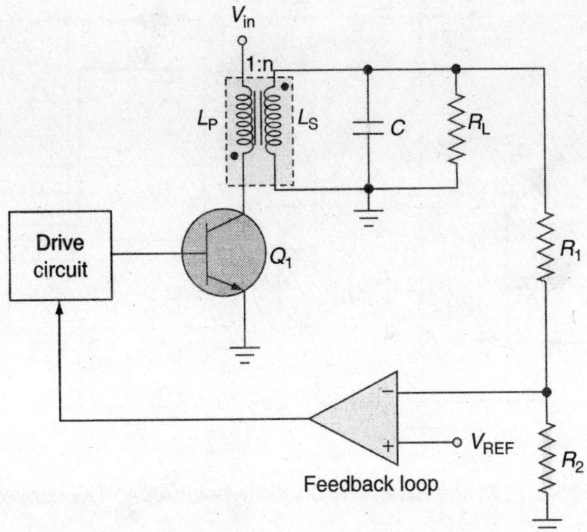

Figure 15.3 | Basic externally driven flyback DC-to-DC converter.

Extension of the converter circuit of Figure 15.3 is the externally driven flyback converter with pulse width modulation (PWM) control to achieve regulation. PWM is the most widely used control technique in conjunction with flyback converters. Figure 15.4 shows the circuit schematic. As the load current increases, the output voltage tends to fall. The PWM control senses the change and increases the turn-ON time so as to increase the power-delivering capability (increased turn-ON time means increased stored energy) and restores the output voltage. Similarly, an increase in the output voltage causes a reduction in the ON-time.

There are other control circuitries that provide regulation by changing the OFF-time rather than the ON-time. A reduced OFF-time increases the drive frequency and hence the power-delivering capability and vice versa.

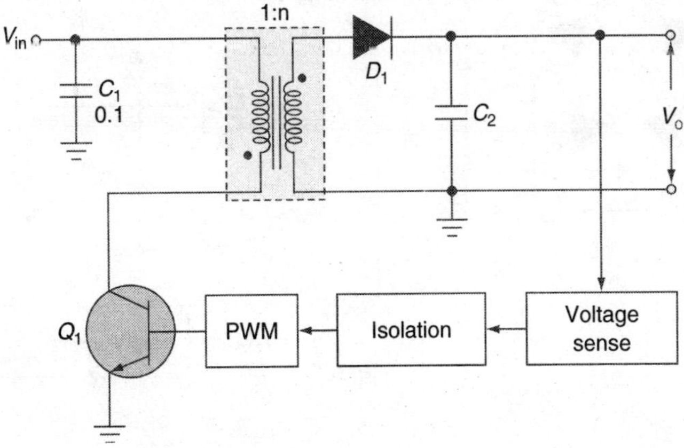

Figure 15.4 | Externally driven flyback DC-to-DC converter with PWM control.

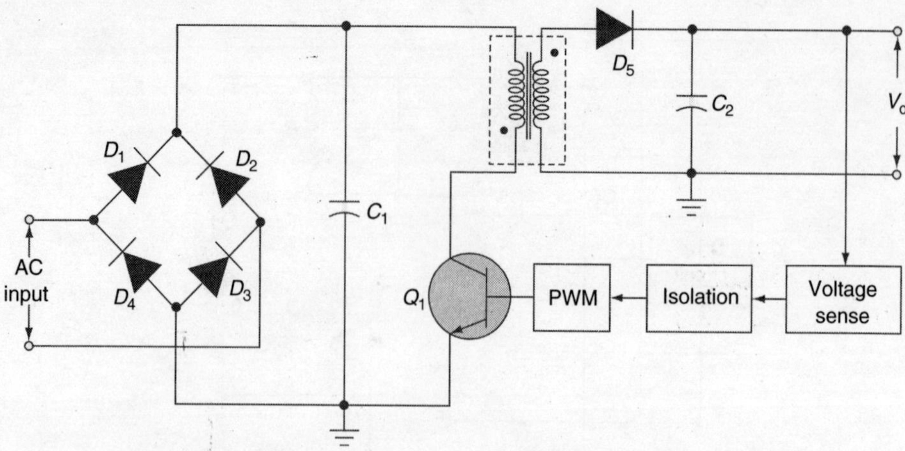

Figure 15.5 | Off-line externally driven flyback AC-to-DC converter.

A number of integrated circuits have been developed to provide drive and control functions for DC-to-DC converters. Some of these ICs provide PWM control while others offer constant ON-time and variable frequency operations. These ICs have built-in features like over-voltage protection, current limit and so on. Such ICs (TL497, TL494, TL594 and SG3524 to name a few) have considerably simplified the drive and control circuit design.

Most switching supplies used in consumer and industrial systems are off-line. Figure 15.5 shows an off-line externally driven flyback AC-to-DC converter. It is called off-line because the input voltage to the transistor switch is developed right from the AC line without first going through 50/60 Hz transformer. Bridge rectifier and the filter capacitor accomplish this in the circuit of Figure 15.5. The feedback loop in an off-line supply must have isolation so that the DC output is isolated from the AC line. A small transformer

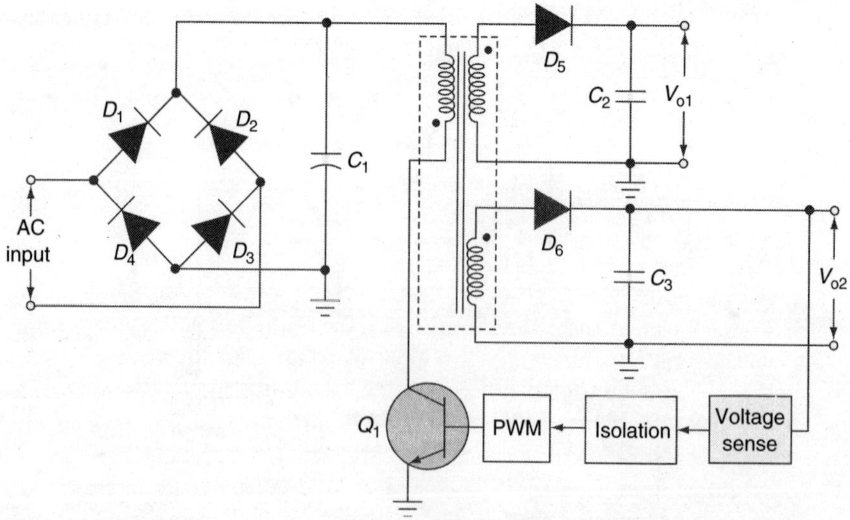

Figure 15.6 | Off-line flyback AC-to-DC converter with multiple outputs.

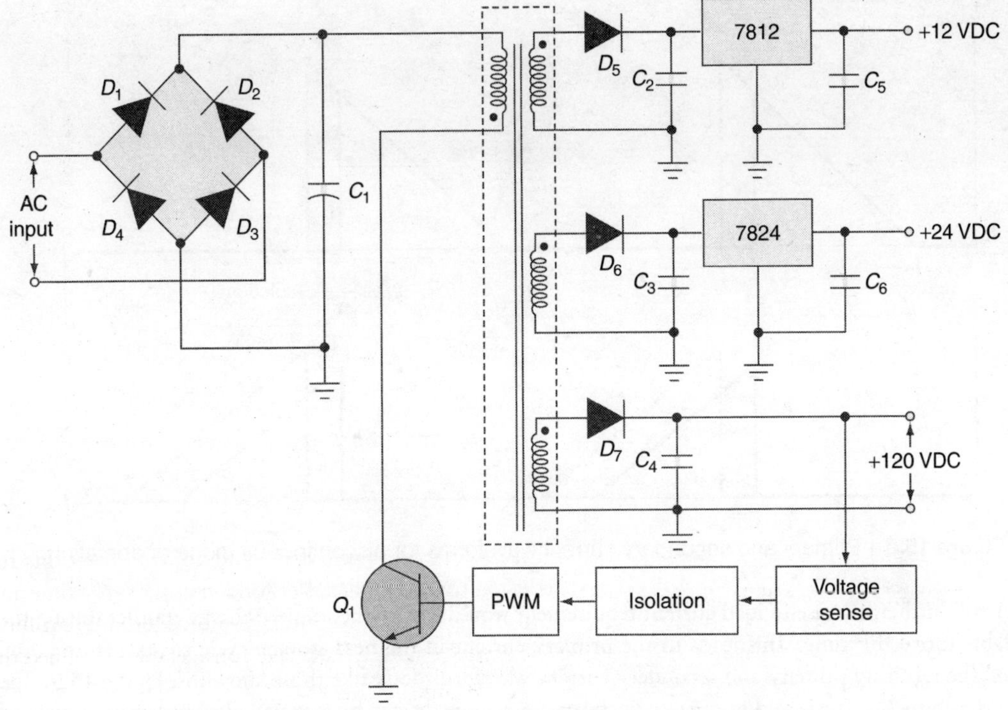

Figure 15.7 | Multi-output switching supply with post regulation.

or an opto-isolator usually accomplishes this. Most switching supplies are required to produce more than one regulated DC voltage. Figure 15.6 shows an off-line multiple output flyback DC-to-DC converter.

In case a more stringent regulation is required in respect of one or more outputs, linear post regulator can be used for the purpose as shown in Figure 15.7. Three-terminal IC regulators have been used here for the purpose.

Discontinuous and Continuous Operational Modes

There are two distinctly different operational modes of flyback converters. These are *discontinuous* mode and *continuous* mode. The circuit topology in the two cases is the same and it is the transformer's magnetizing inductance and the load current, which together decide the operational mode.

Figure 15.8 shows the primary and secondary current waveforms in the case of discontinuous mode of operation. The primary current starts from zero and ramps up to a peak value depending upon the magnetizing inductance, input DC voltage and turn-ON time of the switching device. As is evident from the waveforms, the energy stored during the turn-ON time of the switching device is completely transferred within the turn-OFF time. Increase in peak value of primary current due to increased turn-ON time necessitated by increased load current requirement produces an increased peak value of secondary current as shown by dotted lines. Consequently, the energy transfer time also increases. With further increase in load current requirement, a stage comes where the required energy transfer time equals the available turn-OFF time.

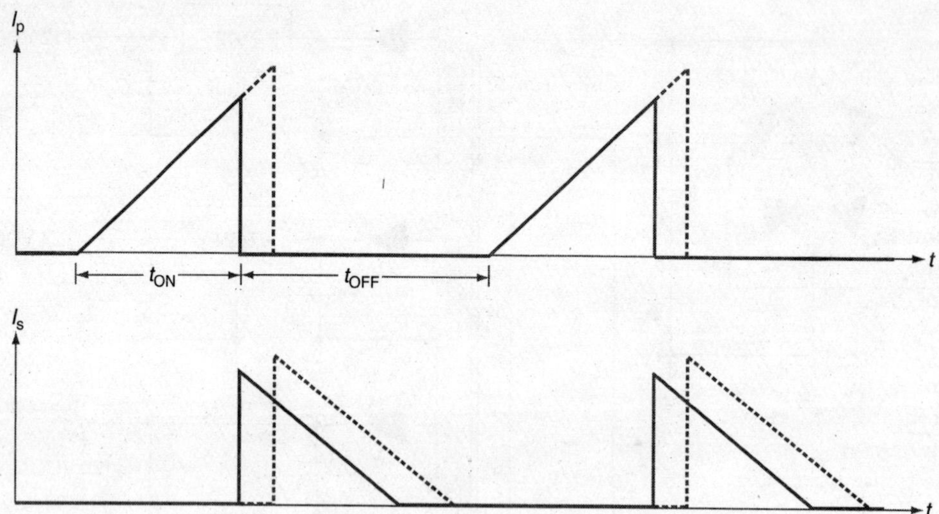

Figure 15.8 Primary and secondary current waveforms for discontinuous mode of operation.

A still further increase in load current requirement would lead to incomplete energy transfer during the available turn-OFF time. This leads to the primary current in the next storage cycle to start from a DC value. The resulting primary and secondary current waveforms look like those shown in Figure 15.9. The converter in such a case is said to operate in continuous mode. It may be mentioned here that in the case of continuous mode of operation, increase in load current requirement initially causes an increase in peak value of primary current, and thus the area of primary current trapezoid, and a decrease in the area of the secondary current trapezoid as shown; after a few switching cycles, the circuit finally relaxes to a state where volt-seconds across primary during turn-ON and turn-OFF periods are equal.

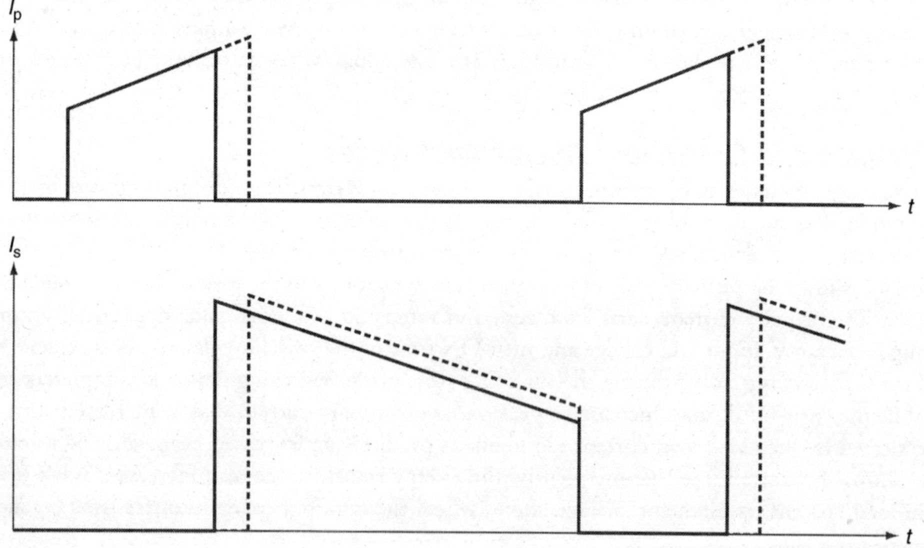

Figure 15.9 Primary and secondary current waveforms for continuous mode of operation.

The discontinuous mode is characterized by relatively much higher peak values of primary and secondary currents and a consequent lower magnetizing inductance as compared to continuous mode. Owing to lower magnetizing inductance, it responds more rapidly and with a lower transient output voltage spike to sudden changes in load current requirement. Without going into details, which would be beyond the scope of this text, in the case of continuous mode of operation, the feedback error amplifier bandwidth needs to be drastically reduced to have stable operation. Owing of these reasons, discontinuous mode is more widely used than the continuous mode despite the fact that the former has more severe radio frequency interference (RFI) problems. In the following section the basic design procedure for an externally driven flyback DC-to-DC converter operating in the discontinuous mode is discussed.

Design Procedure for Externally Driven Flyback DC-to-DC Converter

Design procedure for self-oscillating type and externally driven flyback DC-to-DC converters is the same except that in the case of the former, the switching transformer also has a feedback winding to generate the drive waveform for the switching transistor. In that case, one also needs to determine the number of turns for the feedback winding. Figure 15.10 shows the basic schematic arrangement of an externally driven flyback converter. Let

V_{in} = Input voltage in volts
V_o = Output voltage in volts
P_o = Output power to be delivered to load in watts
P_{in} = Power drawn from input source of power in watts
η = Expected conversion efficiency
t_{ON} = Conduction time in seconds
L_P = Primary inductance in Henries
I_P = Peak primary current in Amperes
I_S = Peak secondary current in Amperes
N_P = Primary turns
N_S = Secondary turns
B_{max} = Maximum flux density in the core in Tesla
ϕ = Magnetic flux in the core in Weber
A_C = Core cross-section in cm^2
W_A = Window area in cm^2
f = Switching frequency in Hz

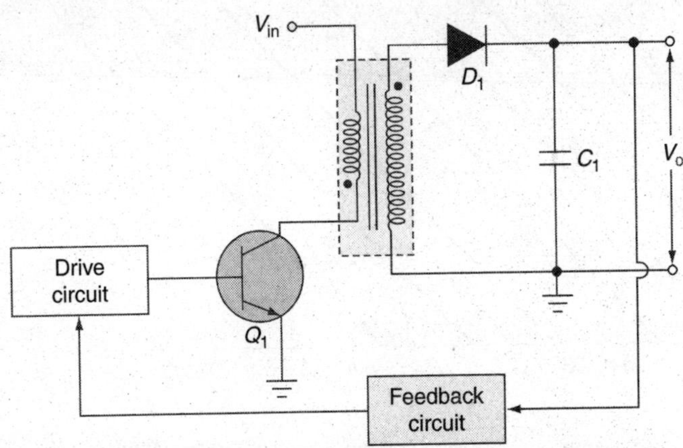

Figure 15.10 | Externally driven flyback converter.

The key component of the design exercise is the design of switching transformer. In the following paragraphs is presented step-by-step procedure for design of switching transformer for a flyback DC-to-DC converter.

The first step is to determine the size of the core in terms of the minimum area product required to deliver the desired amount of power to the load for the chosen values of operating frequency and maximum allowable temperature rise of the core. The area product is the product of winding window area and the cross-sectional area of the core. Manufacturers of transformer cores often provide nomograms indicating the power-handling capability of different types of cores manufactured by them as a function of operating frequency and given temperature rise. Designers can use these nomograms to choose suitable core for their application. These nomograms are, however, specific to the cores offered by the manufacturer. One such representative family of curves for toroidal ferrite cores is shown in Figure 15.11. Equation (15.1) gives a generalized expression to compute the required area product from known values of input power, operating frequency and maximum permissible flux density. Area product ($W_A A_C$) in cm^4 is given by

$$W_A A_C = \left[\frac{11 \times P_{in}}{K \times f \times B_{max}}\right]^{1.143} \tag{15.1}$$

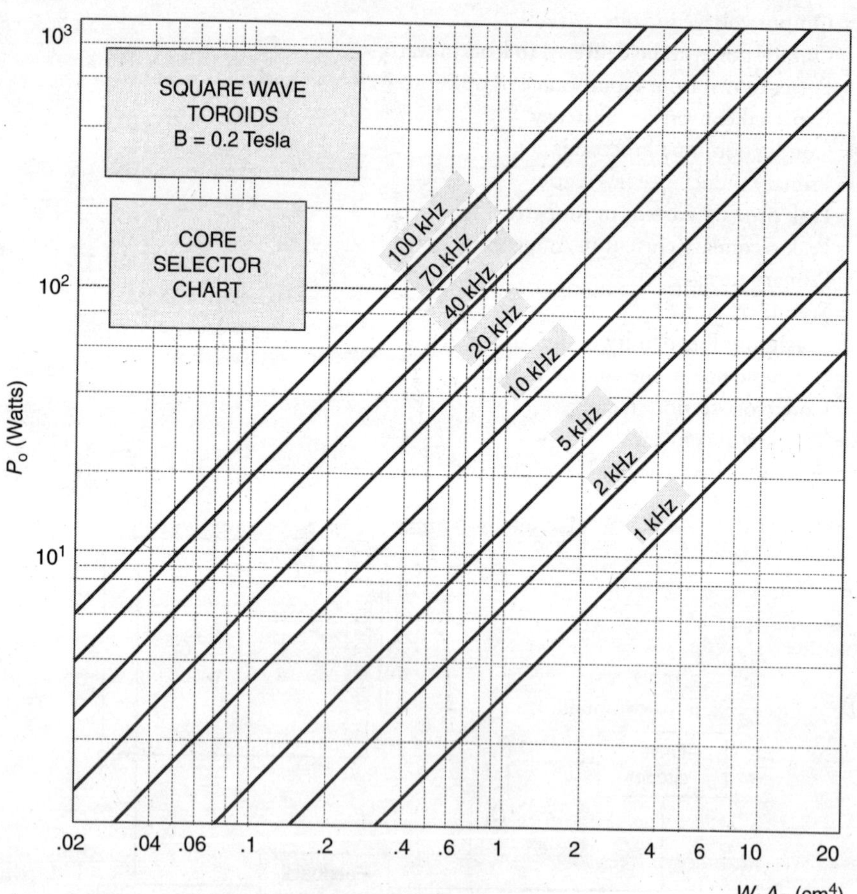

Figure 15.11 Power versus area product ($W_A A_C$) as function of switching frequency.

P_{in}, f and B_{max} are substituted, respectively, in W, Hz and T; K is the overall copper utilization factor and is the product of three factors, namely, primary area factor (ratio of effective primary area to the available window winding area), winding packing factor (typically 0.35–0.4) and RMS current factor (ratio of effective DC input current to RMS value of primary current). K is typically in the range of 0.1 to 0.2.

When the switching transistor is switched on for a time period equal to t_{ON}, then the peak primary current I_P can be computed from

$$V_{in} = \frac{L_P \times I_P}{t_{ON}} \tag{15.2}$$

$$V_{in} \times t_{ON} = L_P \times I_P$$

Also,

$$P_{in} = \frac{P_o}{\eta} \text{ and } P_{in} = \frac{L_P \times I_P^2 \times f}{2}$$

therefore

$$2P_o = \eta \times L_P \times I_P^2 \times f \tag{15.3}$$

Equations (15.2) and (15.3) can be solved simultaneously to get L_P and I_P as

$$I_P = \frac{2P_o}{V_{in} \times t_{ON} \times \eta \times f} \tag{15.4}$$

$$L_P = \frac{V_{in}^2 \times t_{ON}^2 \times \eta \times f}{2P_o} \tag{15.5}$$

The next step is to determine the number of primary turns that would not saturate the core. From first principles,

$$V_{in} = N_P \times \frac{d\phi}{dt}$$

$$= \frac{N_P \times B_{max} \times A_e}{t_{ON}}$$

$$N_P = \frac{V_{in} \times t_{ON}}{B_{max} \times A_e} \tag{15.6}$$

where A_e is the effective area of core cross-section. B_{max} to be substituted in the above expression should be a little less than the B_{max} rating of the chosen core material. Having determined primary turns, the next step is to determine the size of air gap that would give a primary inductance of L_P with N_P number of primary turns. Primary inductance can also be computed from

$$L_P = \frac{\mu_o \times \mu_r \times N_P^2 \times A_e}{l_e} \tag{15.7}$$

where μ_o is the permeability of free space = $4\pi \times 10^{-7}$ H/m; μ_r the initial relative permeability of the chosen core material; l_e the effective magnetic path length. Equation (15.7) is first used to determine the value of effective permeability μ_e that would make N_P turns of the primary winding give L_P Henries of primary inductance. Having determined the value of μ_e, the size of the air gap can then be found from

$$l_g = \frac{l_e}{\mu_e} \tag{15.8}$$

As the third step, the number of secondary turns can be determined from the known value of primary turns and the step-up ratio n. The step-up ratio is primarily decided by the $V_{CEO(max)}$ rating of the bipolar transistor or the $V_{DS(max)}$ rating of the MOSFET depending upon the switching device used in the circuit. In the case of bipolar transistor switch, during the turn-OFF time of the device, maximum voltage that appears across the collector–emitter terminals is given by $V_{in} + V_o/n$, where $n = N_S/N_P$. Therefore

$$V_{CEO(max)} = V_{in} + \frac{V_o}{n}$$

$$n = \frac{V_o}{V_{CEO(max)} - V_{in}}$$

This gives

$$N_S = \frac{N_P \times V_o}{V_{CEO(max)} - V_{in}} \tag{15.9}$$

Again, $V_{CEO(max)}$ to be substituted in Eq. (15.9) should be less than the $V_{CEO(max)}$ rating given in the transistor's data sheet. Drive circuit parameters can be determined from the required value of the base current I_B:

$$I_B = \frac{I_P}{h_{FE(min)}} \tag{15.10}$$

Primary and secondary wire sizes can be determined from calculated RMS values of primary and secondary currents.

Diode D_1 in Figure 15.10 should be a fast recovery rectifier. A fast recovery rectifier ensures that it is fully reverse-biased and there is no leakage of power during the conduction time of the transistor. The peak inverse voltage (PIV) rating of the rectifier should be more than twice the desired output voltage.

Capacitor C_1 should be such that time constant C_1R_L provides the desired output ripple specification. C_1R_L should be much larger than the turn-ON time of the switching device. It is chosen to be at least 10 times the turn-ON time (t_{ON}). That is

$$C_1 \times R_L = 10 \times t_{ON}$$

$$C_1 \times \left(\frac{V_o^2}{P_o}\right) = 10 \times t_{ON}$$

This gives

$$C_1 = \frac{10 \times t_{ON} \times P_o}{V_o^2} \tag{15.11}$$

In the case of self-oscillating flyback converter, one would also need to determine the number of turns N_B in the feedback winding. This is done on the basis of producing a voltage equal to $2V_{BE}$ across the base or feedback winding during the conduction time of the transistor. Out of $2V_{BE}$ voltage, V_{BE} is dropped across the resistance usually connected in series with base terminal and the remaining V_{BE} appears across the emitter–base junction. That is

$$N_B = N_P \times \left(\frac{2 \times V_{BE}}{V_{in}}\right) \tag{15.12}$$

EXAMPLE 15.1 *Figure 15.12 shows the basic ringing-choke flyback DC-to-DC converter along with the drive waveform across the feedback winding and the primary current waveform. From the data given in the circuit diagram, determine output voltage across the load resistance R_L if the conversion efficiency were 80%.*

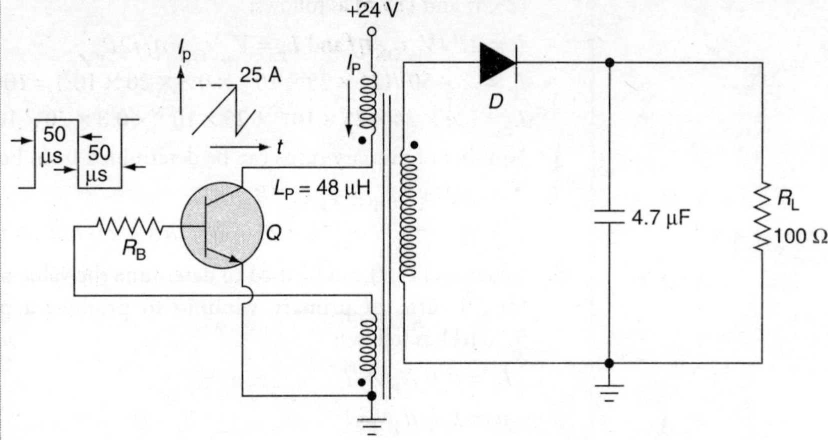

Figure 15.12 Example 15.1.

Solution

1. Power delivered by the converter of this type is given by the product of power stored in the primary of the switching transformer and the conversion efficiency. That is, power delivered = power stored × conversion efficiency.
2. Power stored in turn is equal to the product of energy stored and the switching frequency. That is, power stored = $(1/2)L_P I_P^2 f$.
3. $f = 1/(50 \times 10^{-6} + 50 \times 10^{-6})$ Hz = 10 kHz.
4. Therefore, power stored = $(1/2) \times 48 \times 10^{-6} \times 25 \times 25 \times 10 \times 10^3 = 150$ W.
5. Power delivered to load resistance $R_L = 150 \times 0.8 = 120$ W.
6. If V_o were the voltage across R_L, then
   $V_o^2/R_L = 120$, which gives $V_o = \sqrt{120 R_L} = \sqrt{120 \times 100} = 109.55$ W

Answer: Voltage across load resistance, R_L = 109.55 W.

EXAMPLE 15.2 *A flyback DC-to-DC converter operating in discontinuous mode is to deliver a power of 50 W to a load resistance of 5000 Ω. The converter operates from a regulated input of 24 VDC and produces 500 V across the load resistance. The toroidal core chosen for the purpose is capable of delivering the desired output power at a switching frequency of 20 kHz and flux density of 3000 gauss and has the following dimensional parameters.*

(a) Effective magnetic path length, l_e = 6.2 cm

(b) Effective cross-sectional area, A_e = 0.4 cm^2

Design the switching transformer assuming a conversion efficiency of 80% and the $V_{CEO(max)}$ rating of the switching transistor as 100 V.

Solution

1. $f = 20$ kHz. For a symmetrical drive waveform,

$$t_{ON} = t_{OFF} = 1/(2 \times 20 \times 10^3)\ \text{s} = 25\ \mu\text{s}$$

2. As a first step, we will find the required values of primary inductance and the corresponding peak primary current. These can be determined from Eqs. (15.4) and (15.5) as follows:

$$I_P = 2P_o/V_{in}t_{ON}\eta f \text{ and } L_P = V_{in}^2 t_{ON}^2 \eta f/2P_o$$

$$I_P = (2 \times 50)/(24 \times 25 \times 10^{-6} \times 0.8 \times 20 \times 10^3) = 100/9.6 = 10.4\ \text{A}$$

$$L_P = (24 \times 24 \times 25 \times 10^{-6} \times 25 \times 10^{-6} \times 0.8 \times 20 \times 10^3)/(2 \times 50) = 57.6\ \mu\text{H}$$

3. Number of primary turns can be determined from Eq. (15.6) as follows:

$$N_P = V_{in}t_{ON}/B_{max}A_e$$
$$= (24 \times 25 \times 10^{-6})/(0.3 \times 0.4 \times 10^{-4}) = 50$$

5. Equation (15.7) can be used to determine the value of permeability required for 50 turns of primary winding to produce a primary inductance of 57.6 μH as follows:

$$L_P = \mu_0 \mu_r N_P^2 A_e / l_e$$
$$\mu_r = L_P l_e / \mu_0 N_P^2 A_e$$
$$= (57.6 \times 10^{-6} \times 6.2 \times 10^{-2})/(4 \times 3.14 \times 10^{-7} \times 50 \times 50 \times 0.4 \times 10^{-4})$$
$$= (357.12 \times 10^{-8})/(1.256 \times 10^{-7}) = 28.43$$

6. Size of the air gap can be computed from Eq. (15.8) as follows:

$$l_g = 6.2/28.43\ \text{cm} = 2.2\ \text{mm}$$

7. Assuming permissible collector-to-emitter voltage at turn-OFF equal to 75% of the $V_{CEO(max)}$ rating of the switching transistor, the step-up ratio (n) can be computed as follows:

$$n = V_o/(V_{CEO(max)} - V_{in}) = 500/(75 - 24) = 500/51 = 9.8$$

Therefore, number of secondary turns, $N_S = 50 \times 9.8 = 490$.

8. Primary and secondary wire sizes can be determined from calculated RMS values of primary and secondary currents, respectively.

Answer: Primary inductance L_P = 57.6 μH, number of primary turns = 50, permeability μ_r = 28.43, size of the air gap = 2.2 mm, step-up ratio (n) = 9.8, number of secondary turns N_S = 490.

15.3 Forward Converter

Forward converter is another popular SMPS configuration. Figure 15.13 shows the basic circuit diagram of an off-line forward converter. There are some fundamental differences between a flyback converter and a forward converter. In the case of circuit diagram shown in Figure 15.13, when the transistor switch is turned ON, the polarities of the transformer windings (as indicated by the position of dots) are such that diode D_5 is forward-biased and diodes D_6 and D_7 are reverse-biased. Most of the energy in a forward converter is stored in the output inductor rather than the transformer primary used to store energy in a flyback converter. When the transistor switch is turned OFF, the magnetic field collapses. Diode D_5 is reverse-biased and diodes D_6 and D_7 are forward-biased. As the current through an inductance cannot

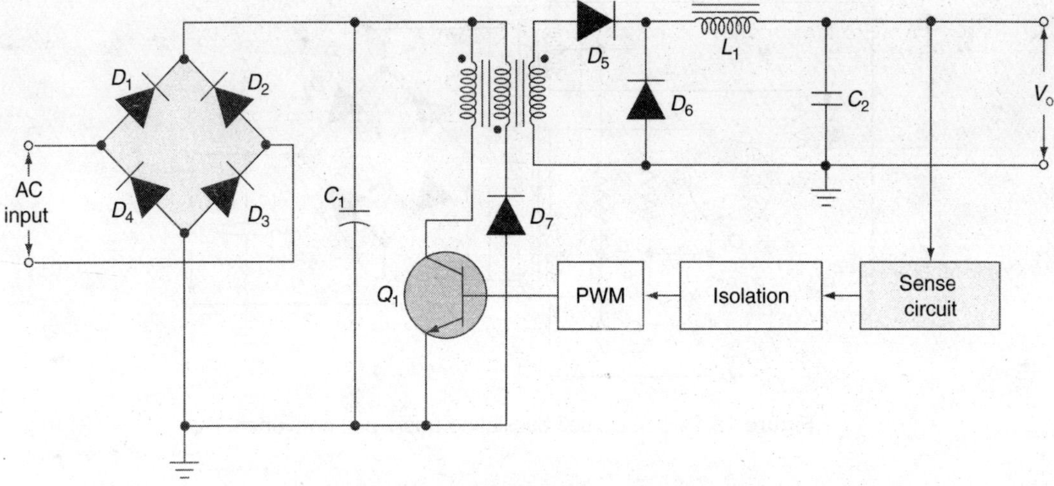

Figure 15.13 | Basic off-line forward converter.

change instantaneously, the output current continues to flow through the output and the forward-biased diode D_6 provides the current path.

Unlike a flyback converter, current in a forward converter flows from the energy storage element during both halves of the switching cycle. Thus for the same output power, a forward converter has much less output ripple than a flyback converter. Controlling the duty cycle of the transistor switch provides output regulation.

In the absence of the third winding and diode D_7, a good fraction of energy stored in the transformer primary is lost. This effect is more severe at higher switching frequencies. The third winding and the forward-biased diode D_7 return the energy, which would otherwise be lost and reset the transformer core after each operating cycle. This not only increases converter efficiency but also makes the converter transformer core immune to saturation problems.

15.4 Push–Pull Converter

Push–pull converter is the most widely used SMPS configuration belonging to the family of forward converters. There are several different circuit configurations within the push–pull converter sub-family. These circuits differ only in the mode in which the transformer primary is driven. These include the conventional two-transistor, one-transformer push–pull converter (both self-oscillating and extremely driven type); two-transistor, two-transformer push–pull converter; half-bridge converter and full-bridge converter.

Figure 15.14 shows the conventional self-oscillating two-transistor, one-transformer push–pull converter. Base resistors R_{B1} and R_{B2} are equal in magnitude. Its operation can be explained by considering it equivalent to two alternately operating self-oscillating flyback converters. When transistor Q_1 is in saturation, energy is stored in the upper half of the primary winding. When the linearly rising current reaches a value where the transformer core begins to saturate, the current tends to rise sharply, which is not supported by a more or less fixed base bias. The transistor Q_1 starts to come out of saturation. This is a regenerative process and ends up in switching off transistor Q_1 and switching on transistor Q_2. Thus transistors Q_1 and Q_2 switch ON and OFF alternately. When Q_1 is ON, energy is being stored in the upper half of the primary and the energy stored in the immediately preceding half cycle in the lower half of the primary winding (when transistor Q_2 was ON) is getting transferred. Thus energy is stored and transferred at the

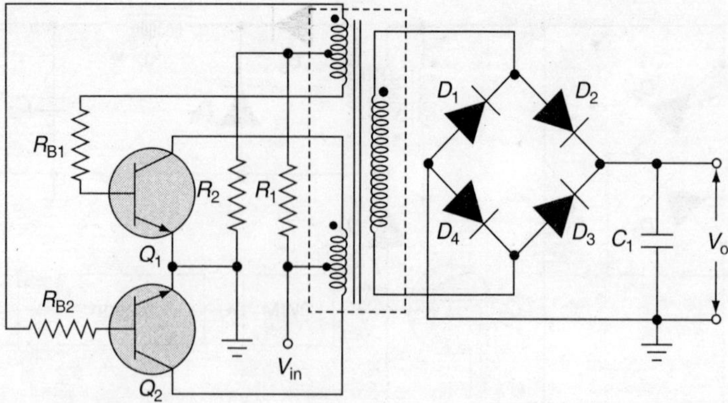

Figure 15.14 | Basic self-oscillating push–pull converter.

same time. The voltage across secondary is a symmetrical square waveform, which is then rectified and filtered to get the DC output.

As the primary is center-tapped, and only half of the primary winding is active at a time, the transformer is not utilized as well as it is in the case of other forms of push–pull converter, like half-bridge and full-bridge converters. Also, in this type of converter, switching transistors operate at collector stress voltages of at least twice the DC input voltage. As a result, a push–pull converter is not a highly recommended choice for off-line operation. A push–pull converter that has wider applications than its self-oscillating counterpart is the extremely driven push–pull converter (Figure 15.15). This has been possible due to availability of a variety of SMPS drive and control ICs.

Self-oscillating push–pull converters are frequently used along with a voltage multiplier chain to design a high-voltage, low-current power supply (Figure 15.16). This configuration is particularly useful for designing helium–neon laser power supplies. The basic push–pull converter converts the low DC input voltage to a stepped-up square waveform, which is then multiplied using a chain of diodes and capacitors.

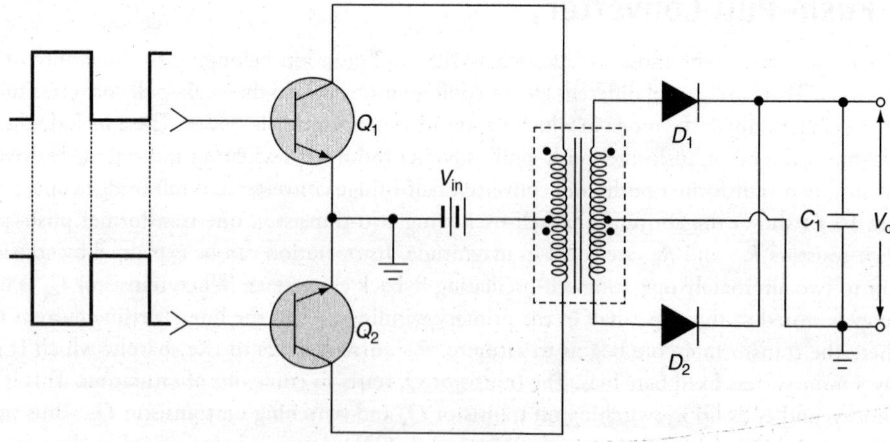

Figure 15.15 | Externally driven push–pull converter.

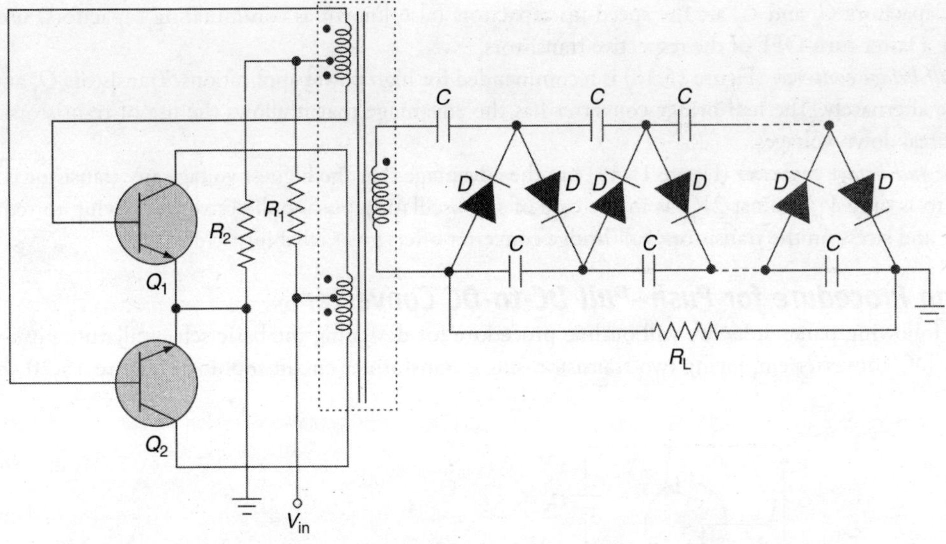

Figure 15.16 | Self-oscillating push–pull converter with voltage multiplier chain.

In the self-oscillating two-transistor, one-transformer push–pull converters, the transformer provides both power transformation as well as power switching. This circuit has some disadvantages. First, as the power switching is done at output power levels, the converter efficiency lowers quite a bit in the case of a high power converter. Second, the peak collector current depends upon the available base voltage, transistor gain and input characteristics and is dependent on load. As there is a wide variation in the characteristics from device to device, the circuit performance depends upon the particular device chosen. Also, the transformer core must be the expensive square loop material with a large maximum flux density rating.

These problems are overcome in the two-transformer, two-transistor push–pull converter (Figure 15.17). Power switching is done at base power level and the output transformer performs power transformation

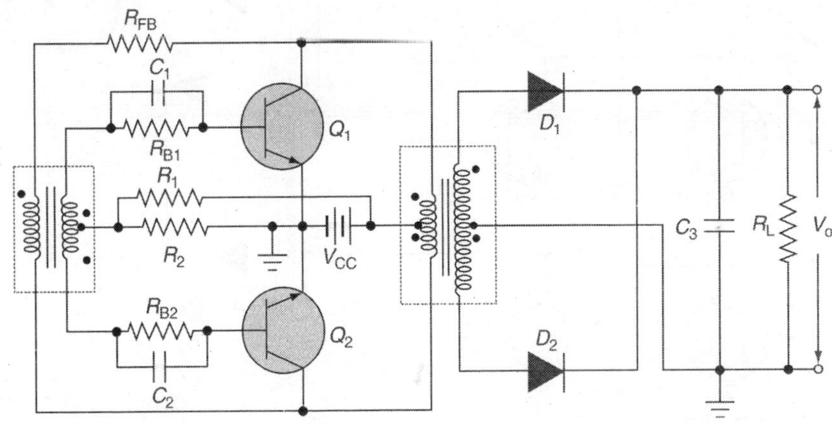

Figure 15.17 | Two-transformer, two-transistor push–pull converter.

only. Capacitors C_1 and C_2 are the speed-up capacitors (also known as commutating capacitors) used to achieve a faster turn-OFF of the respective transistors.

Half-bridge converter (Figure 15.18) is recommended for high power applications. Transistors Q_1 and Q_2 operate alternately. The half-bridge converter has the advantage that it allows the use of transistors with lower breakdown voltages.

The *full-bridge converter* (Figure 15.19) has the advantage that the highest voltage any transistor is subjected to is only V_{in} against $2V_{in}$ as in the case of self-oscillating push–pull converter. Owing to reduced voltage and stress on the transistors, full-bridge converter offers great reliability.

Design Procedure for Push–Pull DC-to-DC Converter

In the following paragraphs, we will outline procedure for designing the basic self-oscillating push–pull DC-to-DC converter employing two-transistor, single transformer circuit topology. Figure 15.20 shows

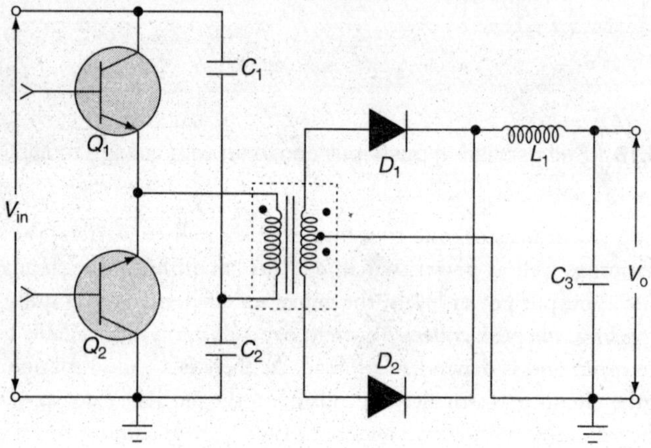

Figure 15.18 | Half-bridge converter.

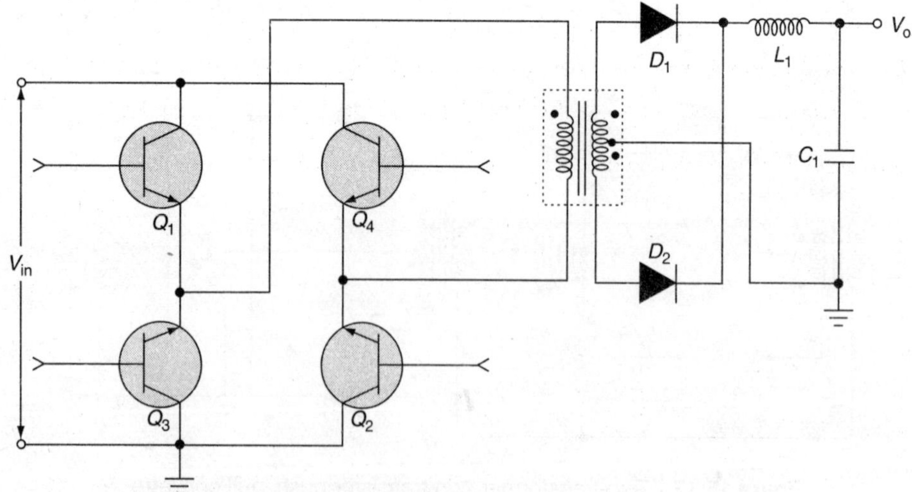

Figure 15.19 | Full-bridge converter.

the circuit diagram along with the relevant waveforms. The operational principle of this type of converter has already been described in the previous paragraphs. Step-by-step design procedure is outlined as follows.

The first step is to determine the size of the core in terms of the minimum area product required to deliver the desired amount of power to the load for the chosen values of operating frequency and maximum allowable temperature rise of the core. The selection of the core size is done either with the help of nomograms provided by the manufacturer or by using the generalized expression given by Eq. (15.1).
From the first principles,

$$V_{in} = N_P \times \frac{d\phi}{dt} \tag{15.13}$$

where N_P is the number of primary turns in the collector circuit of either of the two switching transistors and is equal to half of the primary turns.

It is evident from the waveforms that the magnetic flux varies from $-\phi_{max}$ to $+\phi_{max}$ or $+\phi_{max}$ to $-\phi_{max}$ when either of the two transistors is conducting. In both cases, change in magnetic flux equals $2\phi_{max}$. That is

$$d\phi = 2 \times \phi_{max}$$

Also, this change in flux occurs in a time period equal to half of the total time period. That is

$$dt = 0.5 \times T$$

where T is the time period of switching waveform, that is, $T = 1/f$, f being the switching frequency. Therefore,

$$dt = 1/(2 \times f)$$

Substituting for $d\phi$ and dt in Eq. (15.13), we get

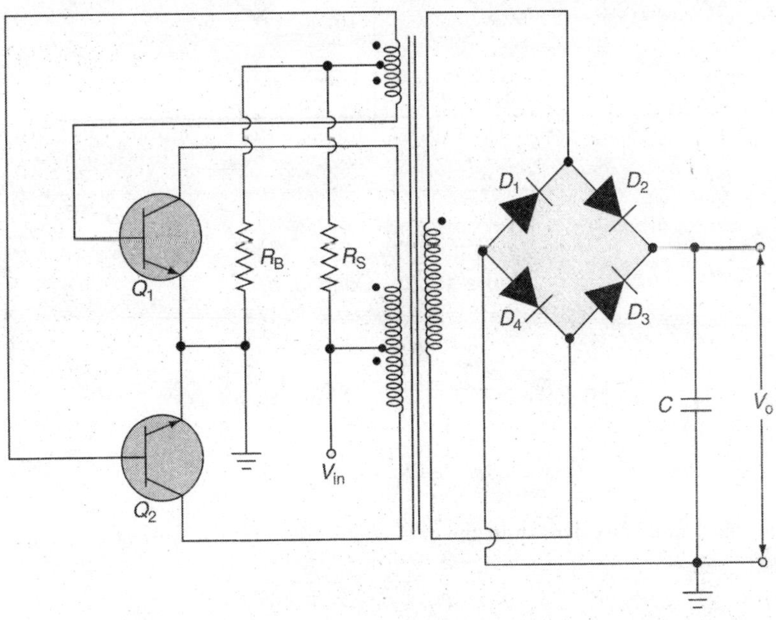

(a)

Figure 15.20 Self-oscillating push–pull converter: (a) Circuit diagram; (b) waveforms.

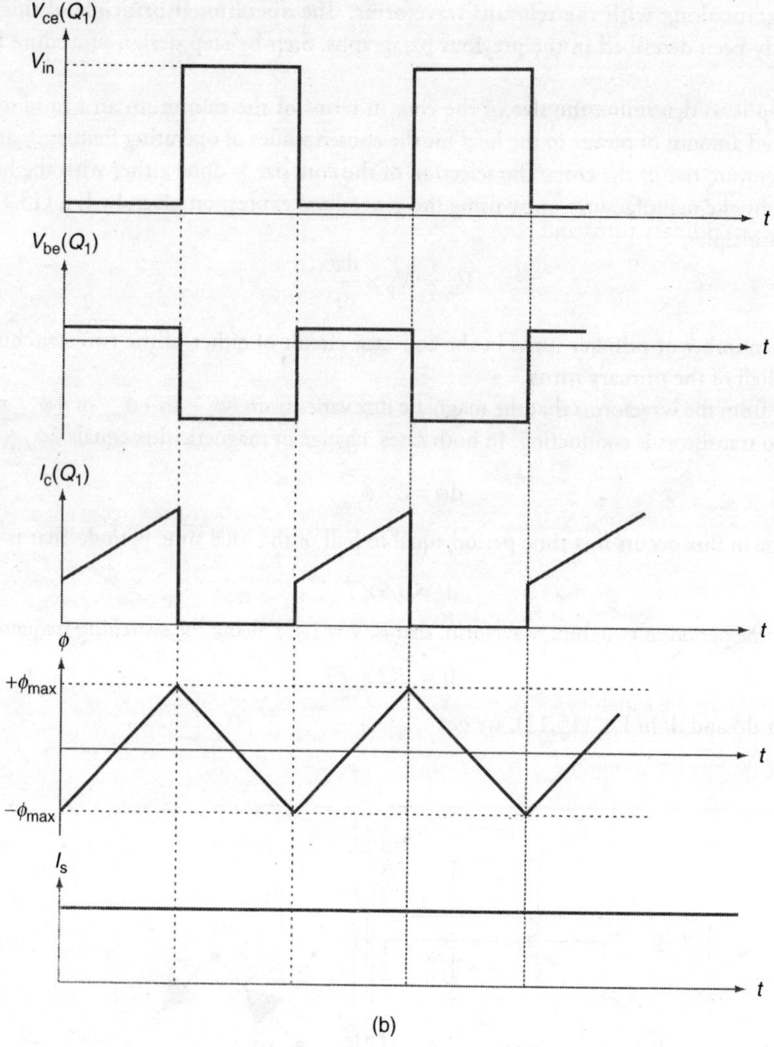

Figure 15.20 *Continued.*

$$V_{in} = N_P \times \frac{2 \times \phi_{max}}{1/(2 \times f)} = 4 \times N_P \times \phi_{max} \times f \quad (15.14)$$

Now

$$\phi_{max} = B_{max} \times A_e$$

where B_{max} is the maximum flux density in the core and A_e the effective area of core cross-section. This gives

$$V_{in} = 4 \times N_P \times B_{max} \times A_e \times f \quad (15.15)$$

Equation (15.15) can used to determine the number of primary turns:

$$N_P = \frac{V_{in}}{4 \times B_{max} \times A_e \times f} \tag{15.16}$$

Number of secondary turns N_S can be computed from the following equation:

$$N_S = N_P \times \left(\frac{V_o}{V_{in}}\right) \tag{15.17}$$

From the known values of primary turns and core parameters, primary inductance can be determined from

$$L_P = \frac{\mu_o \times \mu_r \times N_P^2 \times A_e}{l_e} \tag{15.18}$$

The primary inductance then determines the peak value of primary current, which can be computed as follows:

$$V_{in} = L_P \times \left(\frac{dI_P}{dt}\right) = \frac{2 \times L_P \times I_P}{0.5 \times T} = 4 \times L_P \times I_P \times f$$

Therefore,

$$I_P = \frac{V_{in}}{4 \times L_P \times f} \tag{15.19}$$

Maximum value of transistor's collector current is then given by

$$I_{C(max)} = I_P + I_{AV} = I_P + \frac{P_o}{\eta \times V_{in}} = \left(\frac{V_{in}}{4 \times L_P \times f}\right) + \left(\frac{P_o}{\eta \times V_{in}}\right) \tag{15.20}$$

The chosen transistors should be capable of handling collector current as given by Eq. (15.20). Maximum value of collector-to-emitter voltage appearing across each of the transistors equals [$2V_{in} + V_{BE}$ (winding)]. $V_{CEO(max)}$ of the chosen transistor should be about 25–30% higher than this value.

N_B can be determined in the same way as in the case of self-oscillating flyback converter. That is

$$N_B = N_P \times \left(\frac{2 \times V_{BE}}{V_{in}}\right) \tag{15.21}$$

R_B should be such that it produces a voltage of 0.6 V at the center tap of the feedback winding. That is

$$V_{in} \times \left(\frac{R_B}{R_B + R_S}\right) = 0.6$$

$$R_S = R_B \times \left[\frac{V_{in} - 0.6}{0.6}\right] \tag{15.22}$$

D_1–D_4 are rectifier diodes. These diodes should have the requisite peak inverse voltage (PIV) and forward current ratings. Again, capacitor C is chosen to meet the specified output ripple requirement. Capacitor C is usually chosen to make CR_L time constant much larger than (usually 100 times) the period T. That is

$$C \times R_L \geq 100 \times T$$

$$C \geq \frac{100}{R_L \times f}$$

Substituting $R_L = V_O^2/P_O$ in the expression for C, we get

$$C \geq \left(\frac{100 \times P_o}{V_o^2 \times f}\right) \tag{15.23}$$

EXAMPLE 15.3 *An externally driven push–pull DC-to-DC converter is to be designed to deliver a power of 100 W to a load resistance of 10 kΩ. The converter operates from a regulated input of 12 VDC and produces 1000 V across the load resistance. The toroidal core chosen for the purpose is capable of delivering the desired output power at a switching frequency of 20 kHz and flux density of 2000 gauss and has the following dimensional parameters.*

(a) Effective magnetic path length, $l_e = 8.3$ *cm*
(b) Effective cross-sectional area, $A_e = 0.57$ *cm*^{2}

Assuming core permeability and conversion efficiency to be 3000 and 80% respectively, design the transformer by determining primary and secondary number of turns and the relevant currents that would enable choose the right wire gauge for the primary and secondary windings. Assume two-transistor, single transformer topology and a symmetrical drive waveform.

Solution

1. As a first step, we will determine the number of primary turns, N_P.
$$N_P = V_{in}/(4B_{max}A_e f)$$
$$= 12/(4 \times 0.2 \times 0.57 \times 10^{-4} \times 20 \times 10^3) = 13.16$$
2. Primary winding can be taken as 14–0–14 center-tapped winding.
3. Number of secondary turns,
$$N_S = N_P(V_o/V_{in})$$
$$N_S = 14 \times 1000/12 = 1167$$
4. The primary current in each half of the primary winding flows for half of the period of the switching waveform and is equal to the sum of magnetizing current and a DC component. It is given by Eq. (15.20).

   Primary current $= (V_{in}/4L_P f) + (P_o/\eta V_{in})$

   $L_P = \mu_0 \mu_r N_P^2 A_e / l_e$

   $= 4 \times 3.14 \times 10^{-7} \times 3000 \times 14 \times 14 \times 0.57 \times 10^{-4}/8.3 \times 10^{-2} = 507\ \mu\text{H}$
5. Therefore maximum value of primary current for one-half of the period of switching waveform is given by

   $[12/(4 \times 507 \times 10^{-6} \times 20 \times 10^3)] + [100/(0.8 \times 12)] = 0.3 + 10.4 = 10.7$ A
6. RMS value of primary current can be determined from the maximum value of the current and the wave shape. In the present case, the waveform is almost a square waveform with a flat top and a duty cycle of 0.5 as the DC component is much larger than the magnetizing component. RMS value of such a waveform is given by

   RMS value of primary current $= 10.7 \times \sqrt{0.5} = 10.7 \times 0.707 = 7.56$ A
7. Secondary current is a DC given by V_o/R_L.
$$\text{Secondary current} = 1000/10000 = 0.1 \text{ A}$$
8. Primary and secondary wire sizes can be chosen for 7.56 A and 0.1 A, respectively.

15.5 Switching Regulators

Commonly used switching regulator configurations include *step-down* or *buck regulator, step-up* or *boost regulator* and *inverting regulator* also called *buck-boost regulator*. Each one of these configurations is briefly described in the following sections.

Buck Regulator

Figure 15.21 shows the basic buck regulator. It resembles the conventional forward converter discussed in Section 15.3 except for the fact that it does not use a transformer and there is no input–output isolation. Output voltage is always less than the input voltage and is given by $V_o = DV_{in}$, where D is the duty cycle ($= t_{ON}/T$) of the drive waveform to the transistor switch. Regulation is achieved by PWM of the drive waveform to the transistor switch. It is a very popular circuit configuration for fabrication of high-efficiency three-terminal switching regulators. The circuit operates as follows.

Transistor Q_1 acts like a single-pole, single-throw switch. When the transistor is turned ON, the voltage appearing at the emitter terminal of the transistor equals the input DC voltage assuming a zero drop across the collector–emitter terminals of the transistor. The current through the inductance L_1 ramps up to a value depending upon the input DC voltage, value of inductance and the turn-ON time. Diode D_1 during this time is reverse-biased. When the transistor is switched OFF, the polarity of voltage induced across the inductance reverses thus forward-biasing the diode D_1 called the free-wheeling diode. The diode clamps the voltage at emitter terminal of the transistor Q_1 to zero. Current through the inductance ramps down through the forward-biased free-wheeling diode during the time the transistor is switched OFF. Thus the voltage appearing across the input of LC filter is a waveform chopped between zero and the input DC voltage. The average value of this waveform is equal to ($V_{in} \times t_{ON}/T$). The LC filter transforms this chopped waveform into a ripple-free DC output voltage.

A sample of the output voltage is compared with a reference voltage in an error amplifier. The output of the error amplifier is fed to a pulse width modulator circuit. The pulse width modulator is typically a comparator circuit whose other input is fed with a sawtooth waveform of appropriate amplitude. The output of pulse width modulator circuit feeds the switching transistor. The phasing of the feedback circuit comprising error amplifier and pulse width modulator circuit is such that an increase or decrease in output voltage by a

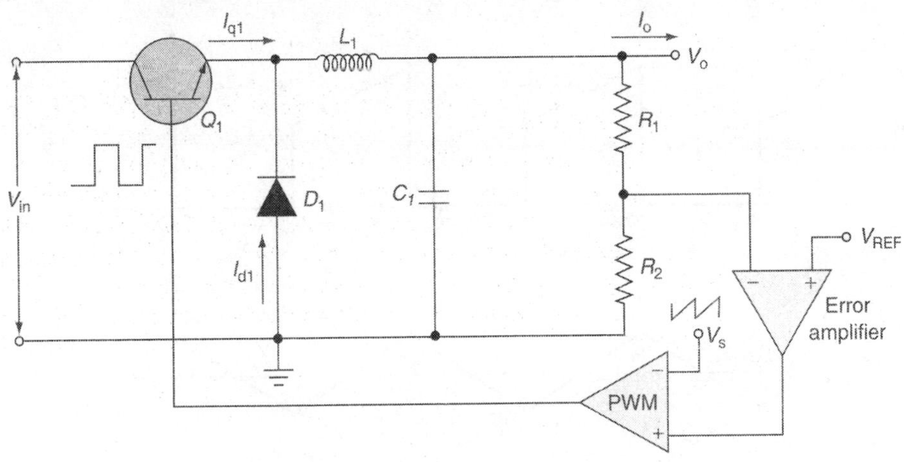

Figure 15.21 | Buck regulator.

certain percentage is accompanied by decrease or increase, respectively, in the ON-time of the switching transistor by the same percentage. The ON-time of the switching transistor Q_1 is so controlled as to make the sampled output voltage equal to the reference voltage applied to the error amplifier.

Figure 15.22 shows the relevant waveforms. These include the drive waveform to the base of transistor Q_1 [Figure 15.22(a)], voltage waveform appearing at the emitter terminal of the transistor Q_1 [Figure 15.22(b)], current waveform through the emitter terminal of Q_1 [Figure 15.22(c)], current waveform through free-wheeling diode D_1 [Figure 15.22(d)] and the output current I_o [Figure 15.22(e)]. The waveforms are self-explanatory.

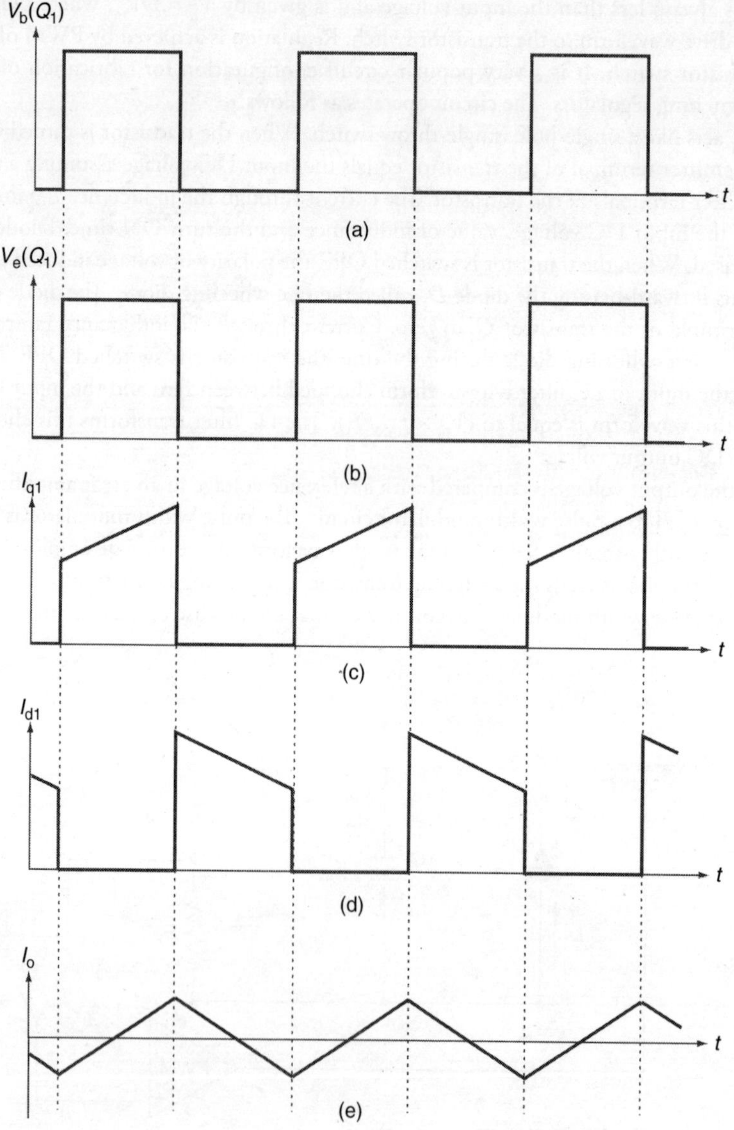

Figure 15.22 Relevant waveform for buck regulator of Figure 15.21.

Boost Regulator

The step-up switching regulator, also called the *boost regulator* (Figure 15.23), is based on the flyback principle. It resembles the basic flyback converter except that it is non-isolating type. The energy storage and transfer element in this case is an inductor rather than a transformer. When the switching transistor Q_1 conducts, the inductor stores energy in the form of magnetic field. Energy stored equals $(1/2) \times (L_1 I_P^2)$. As the diode D_1 is reverse-biased during conduction time of the switching transistor, the energy cannot be transferred to the output while it is being stored. When the switching transistor is driven to cut-off, diode D_1 gets forward-biased and the stored energy is delivered to the load along with the energy from DC input voltage. The voltage across the load equals the DC input voltage plus the voltage due to the energy stored in the inductor. The output voltage in this case is given by $V_o = V_{in}/(1 - D) = V_{in} \times (T/t_{OFF})$. Here D is the duty cycle and T is the total time period which is equal to $t_{ON} + t_{OFF}$.

The power output capability of this circuit is equal to the sum of the power stored in the inductor and the power delivered to the load during the turn-OFF time. The former component is given by $(1/2) \times (L_1 I_P^2 f)$, where f is the operating frequency. The second component results from the fact that the decaying current ramp through the inductance during turn-OFF time is flowing through the source of DC. This equals $V_{in} \times (I_P/2) \times (t_{OFF}/T)$ for a discontinuous mode of operation and decaying ramp time equal to t_{OFF}. The output power-delivery capability of the boost converter is therefore given by

$$P_o = \frac{1}{2} \times (L_1 \times I_P^2 \times f) + V_{in} \times \left(\frac{I_P}{2}\right) \times \left(\frac{t_{OFF}}{T}\right) \tag{15.24}$$

The feedback circuit is similar to the one described in the case of buck regulator. Again, a sample of the output voltage is compared with a reference voltage in an error amplifier, whose output feeds one of the inputs of a pulse width modulator circuit. The other input to the pulse width modulator circuit is a sawtooth waveform. The output of pulse width modulator circuit feeds the switching transistor. The phasing of the feedback circuit comprising the error amplifier and the pulse width modulator circuit is such that the pulse width of the drive waveform increases or decreases with decrease or increase in the output voltage to keep the output voltage as constant irrespective changes in input DC voltage and load current changes.

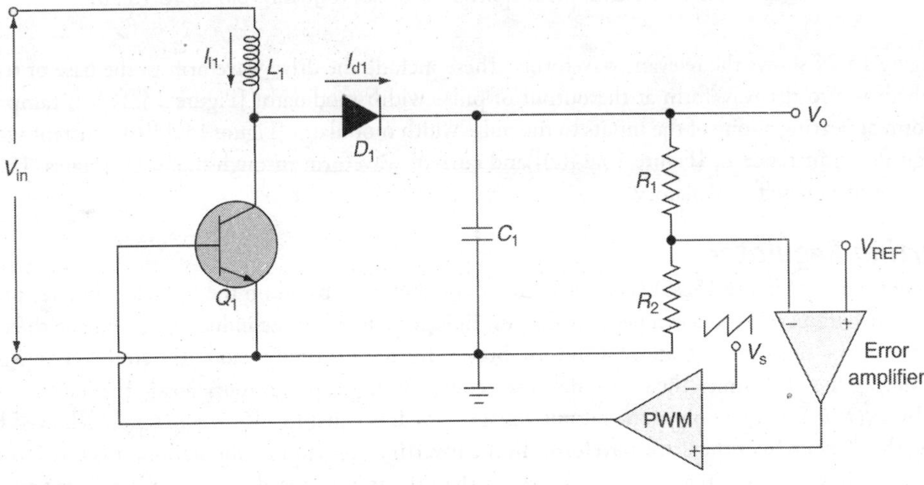

Figure 15.23 Boost regulator.

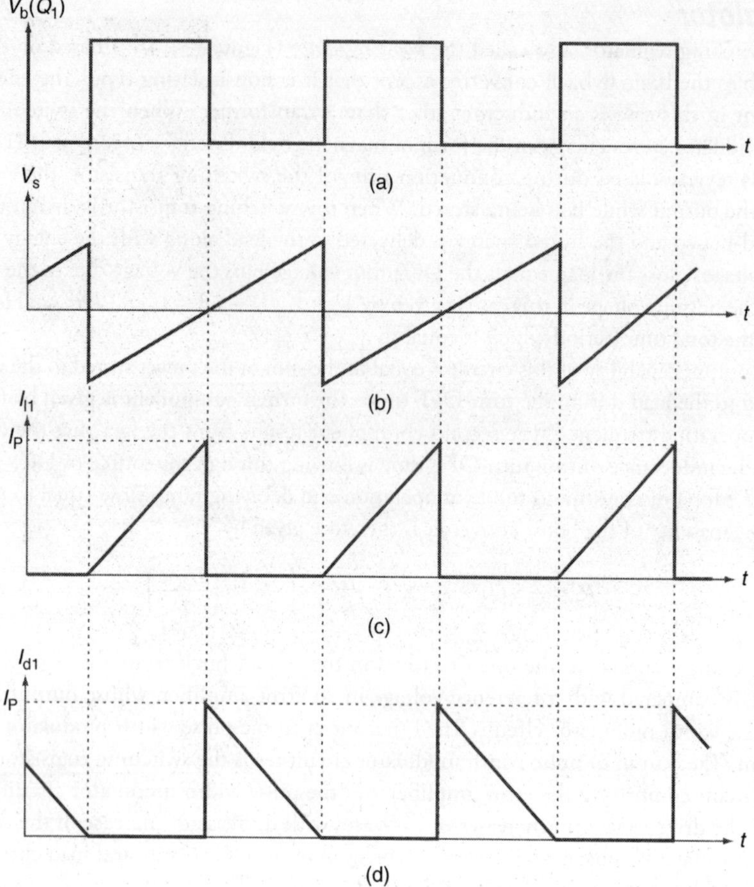

Figure 15.24 Relevant waveforms for boost regulator of Figure 15.23.

Figure 15.24 shows the relevant waveforms. These include the drive waveform to the base of transistor Q_1, which is also the waveform at the output of pulse width modulator [Figure 15.24(a)], ramp voltage waveform appearing at one of the inputs to the pulse width modulator [Figure 15.24(b)], current waveform through the inductance L_1 [Figure 15.24(c)] and current waveform through diode D_1 [Figure 15.24(d)]. The waveforms are self-explanatory.

Inverting Regulator

Inverting regulator (Figure 15.25) is another circuit configuration based on the flyback converter principle. For a positive input, it produces a negative output. Energy is stored in the inductor (L_1) during the conduction time of the transistor. Diode D_1 is reverse-biased during this time period. The stored energy is transferred during the OFF-time. The circuit delivers a constant output power to the load. The output voltage is given by $-\sqrt{(P_o R_L)}$. Regulation of the output voltage, which is equal to $-V_{in} \times t_{ON}/t_{OFF}$ is achieved by controlling the duty cycle of the drive waveform. In the inverting regulator configuration, it is possible to have an output voltage that is either less than or greater than the input. It is also sometimes referred to as *buck-boost* regulator. Unlike the boost regulator, during the turn-OFF time period, the decaying current ramp

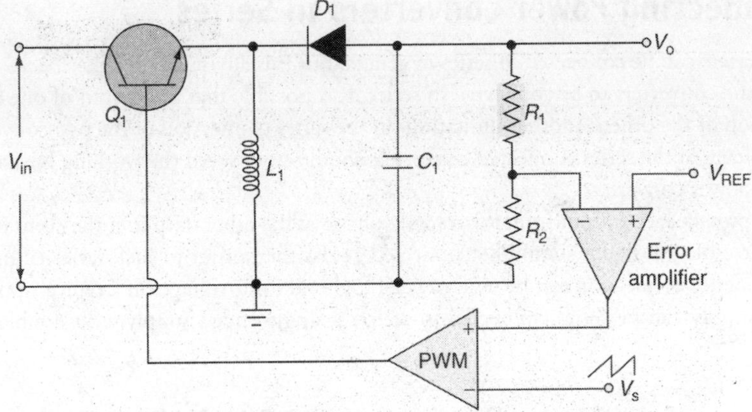

Figure 15.25 | Inverting regulator.

does not flow through the source of input DC. The output power-delivery capability of inverting regulator is therefore given by

$$P_o = \frac{1}{2} \times L_1 \times I_P^2 \times f \tag{15.25}$$

The waveforms are similar to those shown in the case of boost regulator.

Three-Terminal Switching Regulators

The basic buck regulator of Figure 15.21 has been widely exploited in the form of three-terminal switching regulators. Figure 15.26 shows the typical circuit configuration found inside such a regulator. Except for the switching transistor and the output inductor, all other component blocks have been integrated on the chip.

The output voltage is compared with a reference voltage and the difference is amplified to drive a pulse width modulator, which in turn operates the switch. The three-terminal regulator can be used to construct a step-down switching supply that works very well for a wide input voltage range (typically 4 to 1). Output power levels of 300 W are conveniently achievable.

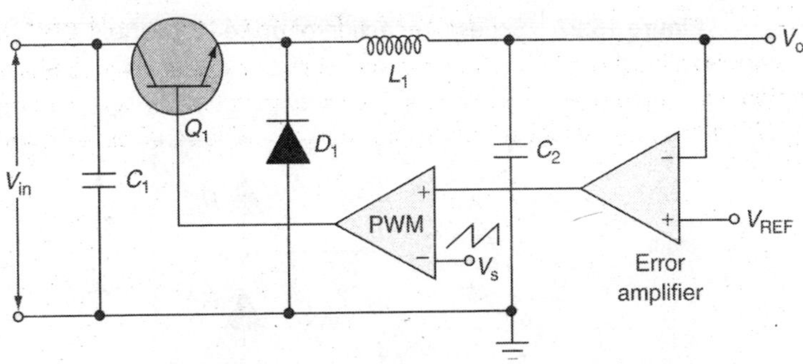

Figure 15.26 | Three-terminal switching regulator.

15.6 Connecting Power Converters in Series

Power converters can be connected in series in general but it is advisable to make checks with the specifications of the converters to be connected in series. It is possible that the output of one converter affects the feedback loop of the other. Another limitation on the series connection of the two converters is that the total output voltage of the series connected converters should not exceed the working breakdown voltage of any one of the power converters.

In order to protect each output from the reverse voltage of the other output in the event of a shorted-load condition, reverse-biased diodes should be connected across the output of each series-connected converter (Figure 15.27). Series connection can be used to get a higher output voltage. In a typical application, a dual-output power supply can be series connected to realize a single-ended supply with double output voltage (Figure 15.28).

15.7 Connecting Power Converters in Parallel

Power converters should be connected in parallel only when they have been specifically designed for the purpose or when the manufacturer recommends a parallel operation. The biggest problem in the parallel connection of the two converters arises from unequal load sharing. Unequal load sharing occurs primarily from the following reasons.

The output voltages of the converters are not precisely equal. The converter with greater output voltage will tend to provide the entire load current. Even if the output voltages are adjusted to be precisely equal, a difference in the output impedance and also its drift with time and temperature will cause the loads to become unbalanced.

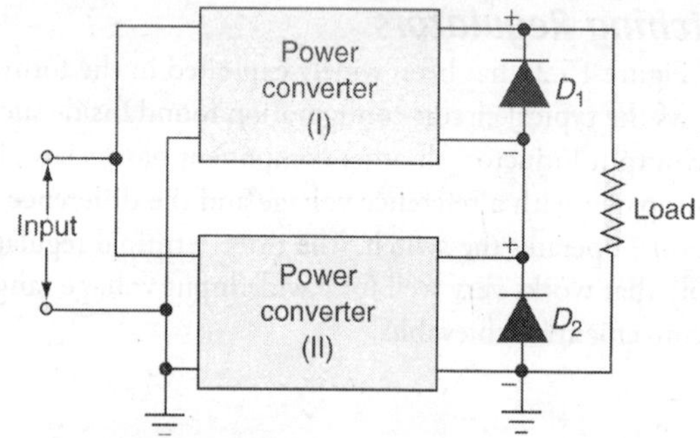

Figure 15.27 Series connection of power converters.

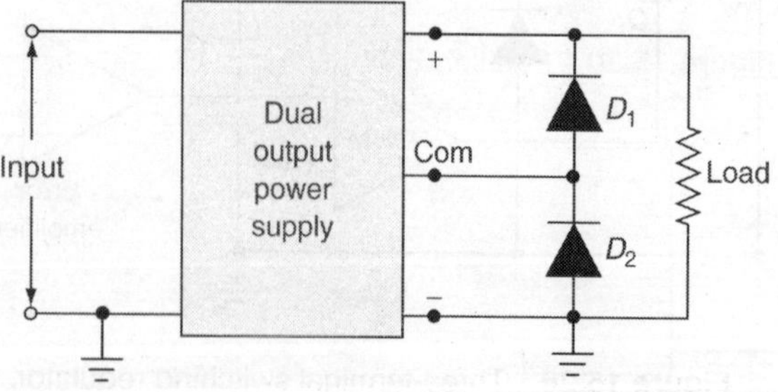

Figure 15.28 Series connection of dual-output power supply.

One method used to overcome this unequal load sharing is to use small individual series resistors (Figure 15.29). While this type of parallel connection could be useful in a few applications, it must be borne in mind that the series resistors degrade the output regulation seriously. Also, the circuit will always have current imbalance. If the two converters in Figure 15.29 had a nominal output voltage of 5 V, a 50 mV difference in the output voltages may cause a current imbalance of 25%. In such a case, each supply should not be capable of providing just 50% of the load current but 75% of it.

A good reason for parallel connection of power converters is to provide redundancy. The output may be connected in parallel through two diodes (Figure 15.30). For 100% redundancy, each power converter must be capable of supplying the total load current. In this case, it really does not matter whether the load is shared equally or not, though it is desirable that each output provides at least a part of the load current. The diodes permit one output to fail without affecting the other, which continues to supply the power to the load. Such a system is useful in applications where power supply failure is not tolerable, or where a high degree of reliability is required. If one of the power converters is replaced by a DC battery source of the same voltage, it becomes an uninterrupted DC power supply (Figure 15.31).

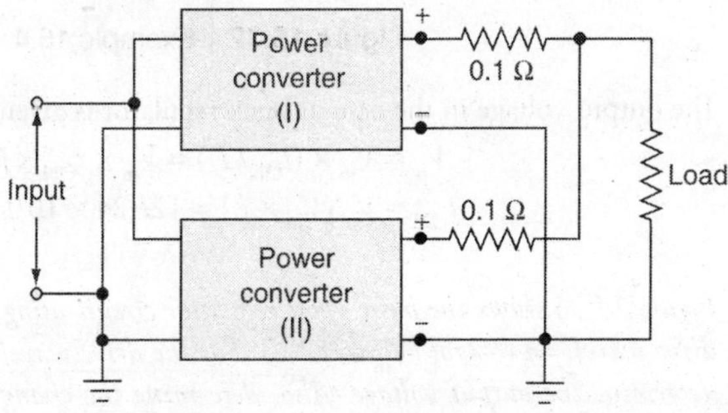

Figure 15.29 | Parallel connection of converters using series resistors.

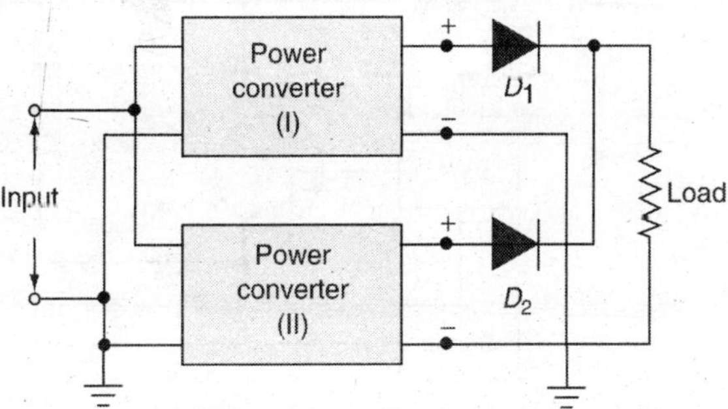

Figure 15.30 | Parallel connection of converters using diodes.

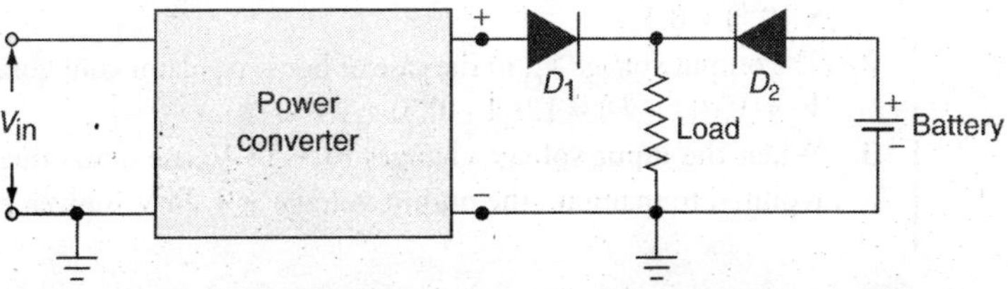

Figure 15.31 | Uninterrupted power supply.

EXAMPLE 15.4 *Figure 15.32 shows the basic buck regulator configuration. It produces a regulated output voltage of +12 V. If the unregulated input voltage at a certain time is +24 V, determine the ON-time of the drive waveform appearing at the base terminal of the switching transistor Q_1. Assume a switching frequency of 10 kHz.*

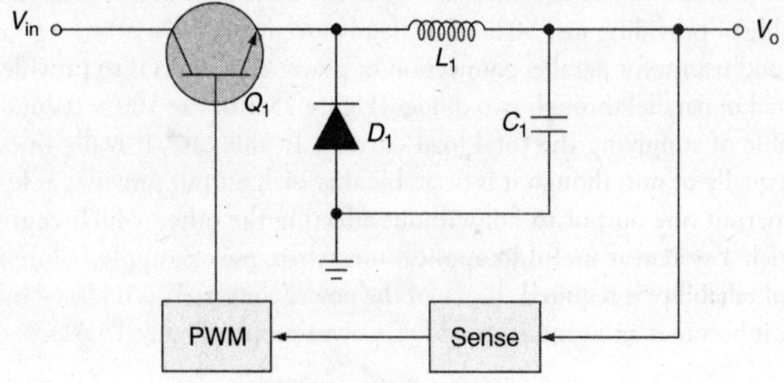

Figure 15.32 Example 15.4.

Solution The output voltage in the case of buck regulator is given by

$$V_o = V_{in} \times (t_{ON}/T) = V_{in} \times t_{ON} \times f$$

$$t_{ON} = V_o/(V_{in} \times f) = 12/(24 \times 10^4) = 50\ \mu s$$

EXAMPLE 15.5 *Figure 15.33 shows the basic boost regulator circuit using a pulse width modulated drive waveform control (V_{in} = 12 V). For the drive waveform shown in the circuit, determine the output voltage. Also, determine the changed ON-time of the drive waveform when the unregulated input voltage changes to +18 V.*

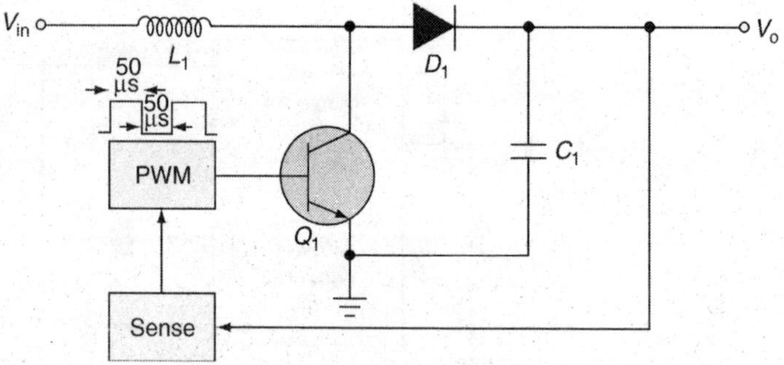

Figure 15.33 Example 15.5.

Solution

1. From the given drive waveform, duty cycle, $D = (50 \times 10^{-6})/(50 \times 10^{-6} + 50 \times 10^{-6}) = 0.5$.
2. The output voltage V_O in the case of boost regulator configuration is given by $V_o = V_{in}/(1 - D) = 12/(1 - 0.5) = 24$ V.
3. When the input voltage changes to + 18 V, the new value of duty cycle D required to maintain the output voltage at + 24 V is given by

$$24 = 18/(1 - D)$$
$$D = 1 - (18/24) = 0.25$$

4. Therefore, the changed value of on-time is given by $0.25 \times 100 \times 10^{-6} = 25$ μs.

EXAMPLE 15.6 *Figure 15.34 shows the basic inverting regulator circuit using a pulse width modulated drive control. Determine the output voltage if the switching frequency were 10 kHz.*

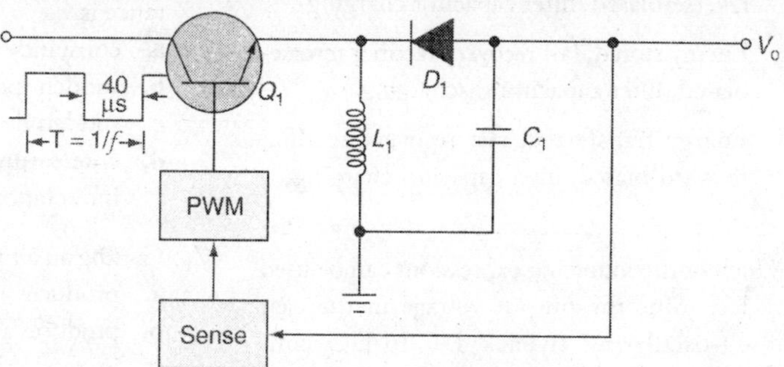

Figure 15.34 Example 15.6.

Solution

1. The output voltage is given by $V_o = -V_{in} \times (t_{ON}/t_{OFF})$.
2. From the given drive waveform, $t_{OFF} = 40$ μs, $f = 10$ kHz. This gives $T = 1/10^4$ s = 100 μs.
3. Therefore, $t_{ON} = 100 - 40 = 60$ μs.
4. This gives $V_o = -18 \times (60/40) = -27$ V.

KEY TERMS

Boost regulator
Buck-boost regulator
Buck regulator
Continuous mode
Discontinuous mode
Flyback converter
Forward converter
Full-bridge converter
Half-bridge converter
Inverting regulator
Push–pull converter
Switched mode power supplies

OBJECTIVE-TYPE EXERCISES

Multiple-Choice Questions

1. In a flyback DC-to-DC converter, the energy is stored in the primary winding of the switching transformer during
   a. turn-ON time of the switching device.
   b. turn-OFF time of the switching device.
   c. both turn-ON and turn-OFF times of the switching device.
   d. none of these.

2. Which of the following statements is true in the case of ringing-choke power converter during turn-ON time of the switching transistor?

   a. Energy stored, fast recovery rectifier forward-biased, filter capacitor charging
   b. Energy transferred, fast recovery rectifier reverse-biased, filter capacitor charging
   c. Energy stored, fast recovery rectifier reverse-biased, filter capacitor discharging
   d. Energy transferred, fast recovery rectifier forward-biased, filter capacitor charging

3. Which of the following expressions can be used to determine the output voltage in the case of self-oscillating flyback DC-to-DC converter?

   a. $V_o = \sqrt{P_o \times R_L}$
   b. $V_o = n \times V_{in}$ (n is the step-up ratio of the switching transformer)
   c. $V_o = \eta \times V_{in}$ (η is the conversion efficiency)
   d. $V_o = \sqrt{P_o / R_L}$

4. A DC-to-DC converter having a conversion efficiency of 80% is delivering a power of 16 W to the load. If the converter were producing an output voltage of 400 V from an input of 20 V, what would be the current drawn from the 20 V source?

   a. 1000 mA
   b. 500 mA
   c. 200 mA
   d. Cannot be determined from given data

5. Figure 15.35 shows the secondary current waveform in the case of

   a. forward-type DC-to-DC converter.
   b. flyback-type DC-to-DC converter.
   c. Buck-type switching regulator.
   d. none of these.

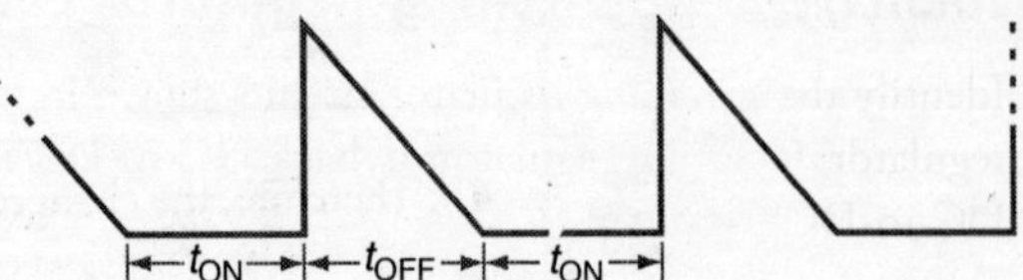

Figure 15.35 Multiple-choice question 5.

6. The effect of core saturation on primary inductance is

   a. constancy of primary inductance.
   b. sudden increase in primary inductance.
   c. sudden decrease in primary inductance.
   d. core saturation has no effect on primary inductance.

7. Cutting an air gap in the magnetic path of a core

   a. produces a relatively lower B for a given H.
   b. produces a relatively higher B for a given H.
   c. increases the core permeability.
   d. none of these.

8. Which component size is affected by frequency of operation of converter?

   a. Transformer and transistor
   b. Transformer and filter capacitor
   c. Switching transistor and filter capacitor
   d. Switching transistor, transformer, filter capacitor

9. The maximum value of primary current that can flow in a push–pull converter when either of the transistors is conducting is given by one of the following expressions.

   a. $(P_o/\eta V_{in}) + (V_{in}/4fL_P)$
   b. $P_o/\eta V_{in}$
   c. $V_{in}/4fL_P$
   d. None of these

10. An air gap of length equal to one-hundredth of the magnetic path length of a ferrite core with initial permeability of 3000 will reduce permeability to

   a. approximately 100.
   b. approximately 300.
   c. approximately 30.
   d. none of these.

Identify the Switching Regulator Configurations

Identify the switching regulator circuits shown in Figures 15.36(a)–(f). Choose from buck regulator, boost regulator, inverting regulator, flyback DC-to-DC converter, forward DC-to-DC converter and push–pull DC-to-DC converter.

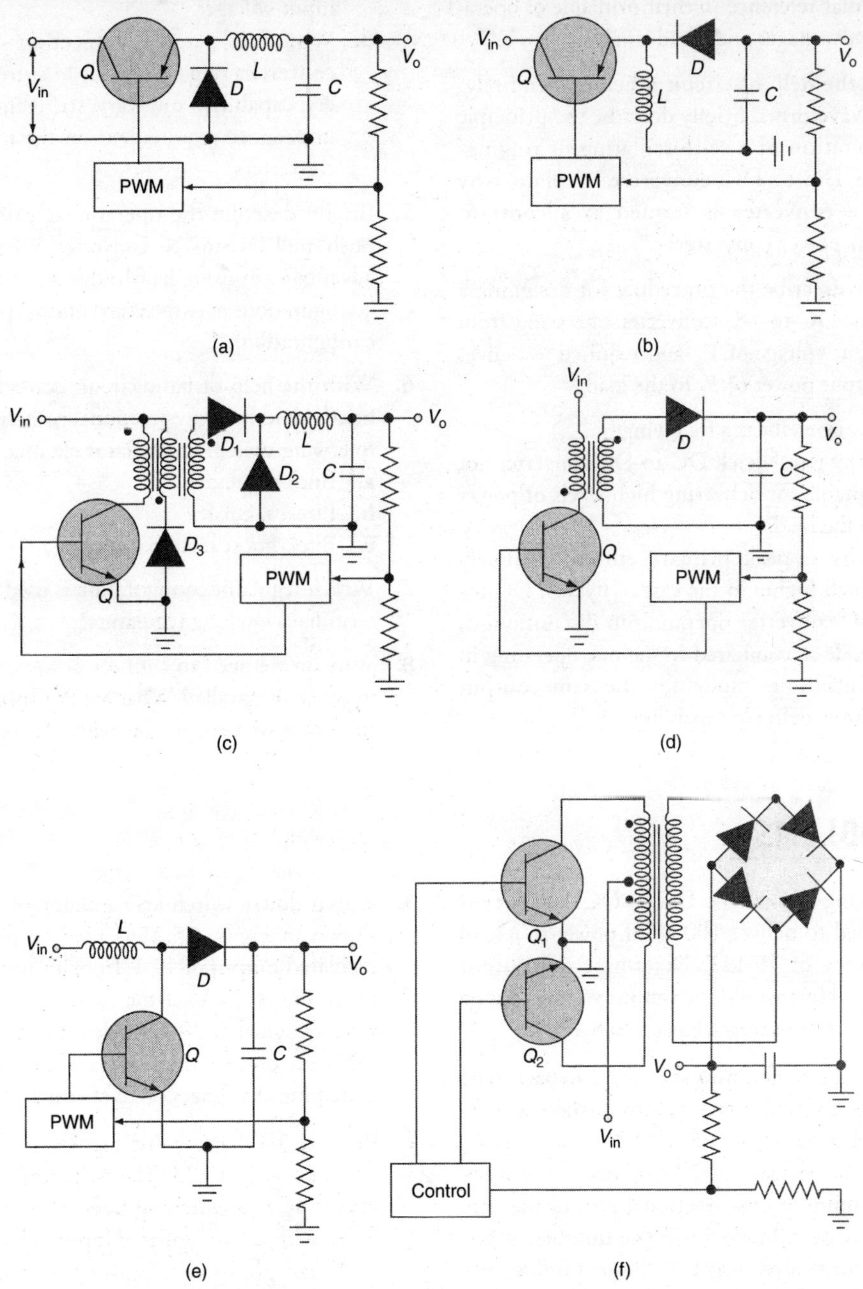

Figure 15.36 | Identify the switching regulator configurations.

REVIEW QUESTIONS

1. Distinguish between a linearly regulated power supply and a switched mode power supply with particular reference to their principle of operation, advantages and disadvantages.
2. With the help of circuit schematic and relevant waveforms, briefly describe the principle of operation of a self-oscillating or ringing-choke DC-to-DC converter. Explain why such a converter is termed as a constant output power converter?
3. Briefly describe the procedure for designing a flyback DC-to-DC converter operating from an input voltage of V_{in} and required to deliver an output power of P_o to the load.
4. Give reasons for the following:
   a. Why is a flyback DC-to-DC converter not suitable for delivering high levels of power to the load?
   b. Why is peak primary current relatively much higher in the case of flyback DC-to-DC converter operating in discontinuous mode as compared to the one operating in continuous mode for the same output power-delivery capability?
   c. Why can the boost regulator configuration not produce an output voltage less than the input voltage?
   d. Why does parallel connection of power converters to get higher load current delivery capability put very stringent output impedance requirement on the individual converters?
5. Briefly describe the operational principle of push–pull DC-to-DC converter. What are the advantages of using half-bridge and full-bridge configurations over the conventional push–pull configuration?
6. With the help of basic circuit configurations, briefly describe the operational principle of the following switching regulator circuits:
   a. Buck regulator
   b. Boost regulator
   c. Buck-boost regulator
7. Which regulator configuration is used in three-terminal switching regulators?
8. Why do we need to connect power converters in series or parallel? What are the special measures that we need to take while doing so?

PROBLEMS

1. A ringing-choke-type DC-to-DC converter is designed to deliver 100 W of power to a load resistance of 10 kΩ. Determine the output voltage. How would the output voltage change if the load resistance changes to 8.1 kΩ?
2. The switching transformer for a flyback-type DC-to-DC converter has to sustain a volt-second product of 6×10^{-4} V s and a maximum flux density of 2000 Gauss. Determine the minimum cross-sectional area of the core required to achieve this if the number of primary turns used to get the desired inductance were 50.
3. A step-down switching regulator of the type shown in Figure 15.21 is used to produce a regulated output of 12 V from an unregulated input of 18–24 V. If the switching transistor were switched at 20 kHz, determine the turn-ON time of the switching transistor for unregulated input voltages of 18 V and 24 V.
4. Refer to the basic boost regulator configuration of Figure 15.23. The switching regulator operating at a switching frequency of 10 kHz is fed with an unregulated input voltage of 9–15 V and produces a regulated output voltage of 24 V.

a. Determine the turn-ON time of the drive waveform at the time instant when the input voltage was measured to be 12 V.

b. Determine the input voltage at the time instant when the duty cycle of the drive waveform was measured to be 0.6.

5. Refer to the inverting regulator circuit of Figure 15.25. The regulator is switched at 20 kHz. The regulator produces a regulated output voltage of –12 V from an unregulated input of 9–15 V. Determine the turn-ON and turn-OFF times of the drive waveform for input voltages of (a) 9 V and (b) 15 V.

ANSWERS

Multiple-Choice Questions

1. (a)
2. (c)
3. (a)
4. (a)
5. (b)
6. (c)
7. (a)
8. (b)
9. (a)
10. (a)

Identify the Switching Regulator Configurations

Figure 15.36(a): Buck regulator
Figure 15.36(b): Inverting regulator
Figure 15.36(c): Forward converters
Figure 15.36(d): Flyback converter
Figure 15.36(e): Boost regulator
Figure 15.36(f): Push–pull converter

Problems

1. 1000 V, 900 V
2. 0.6 cm^2
3. 33.33 μs, 25 μs
4. (a) 50 μs; (b) 9.6 V
5. (a) t_{ON} = 28.6 μs, t_{OFF} = 21.4 μs; (b) t_{ON} = 22.2 μs, t_{OFF} = 27.8 μs

CHAPTER 16

Introduction to Operational Amplifiers

Learning Objectives

After completing this chapter, you will learn the following:

- Operational fundamentals of an opamp.
- Difference between an ideal opamp and a practical opamp.
- Internal architecture of a typical opamp.
- Major performance parameters of an opamp and their relevance to different application circuits configured around opamps.
- Selection criterion for choosing the right opamp for a given application.
- Types of opamps and their corresponding preferred application areas.

Amongst the general-purpose linear integrated circuits, the integrated circuit operational amplifier popularly known as opamp is undoubtedly the most widely used IC. Operational amplifier in essence is a high-gain differential amplifier capable of amplifying signals right down to DC due to use of direct coupling in the device's internal architecture. Owing to its high differential gain, high input impedance, low output impedance, large bandwidth and many other desirable features, operational amplifiers fit into almost every conceivable circuit application ranging from amplifiers to oscillators, computational building blocks to data conversion circuits, active filters to regulators and so on. This chapter gives an introduction to the fundamental topics relevant to operational amplifiers. The chapter begins with a brief description of the internal architecture of an operational amplifier. This is followed up by an introduction to different categories of operational amplifiers, selection criterion and definition and interpretation of major performance specifications. The text is amply illustrated by solved examples. Application circuits using operational amplifiers are discussed in the following chapter.

16.1 Operational Amplifier

An operational amplifier popularly known as an opamp is basically a high-gain differential amplifier capable of amplifying signals right down to DC. The capability of the opamp to amplify signals down to DC lies in the use of direct coupling mechanism in the internal architecture of the device. That is why it is also called a direct-coupled or a DC amplifier. The other main attributes of an opamp are very high input impedance, very low output impedance, very large bandwidth, extremely high value of open-loop gain and so on.

It is called an operational amplifier as it was originally conceived as an analog computation building block that could be used conveniently to perform mathematical functions like addition, subtraction, integration, differentiation and so on. Today opamps have unlimited applications. An opamp fits in any conceivable circuit application from analog computation to building amplifiers and oscillators, from active filters to phase shifters, from comparators to voltage regulators, from function generators to gyrators and so on and so forth. It is worthwhile mentioning here that an opamp becomes a true amplifier to perform all those above-listed circuit functions only when negative feedback is introduced around the opamp with the exception of oscillator, multivibrator and other similar building blocks which use positive feedback circuits. Figure 16.1 shows the circuit representation of an opamp. An opamp is usually a two input and one output device along with two power supply terminals one for positive supply and the other for negative supply with both having a common ground. The word "usually" is used here as there are opamps with differential outputs. There are also opamps with single power supply terminal.

The (+ve) input called non-inverting input gives a non-inverted amplified signal at the output. This means that with (–ve) input terminal grounded, the output signal is in phase with the input applied at the (+ve) input terminal. On the other hand, with (+ve) input terminal grounded, the output signal is inverted and amplified version of the signal applied at (–ve) input. That is why (–ve) input is also called inverting input.

The key parameters of an opamp like open-loop gain, input impedance, output impedance, common mode rejection ratio (CMRR), bandwidth and offsets should ideally be infinity, infinity, zero, infinity, infinity and zero, respectively. They do approach these values in the case of high performance opamps. These parameters, which often form the basis of selection criteria, are described in detail in Section 16.4. Not all key parameters are equally important while deciding the right type number for a given application. As an example, when the opamp is to be used as a comparator, the response time specification is perhaps the first priority and CMRR, a do not care one, whereas if we are building a differential amplifier with gain accuracy, CMRR and open-loop gain would be among the first few specifications to be paid more attention. Different categories of opamps are made with each category designed to suit a particular range of applications. Different types of opamps along with their salient features are described in detail in Section 16.5.

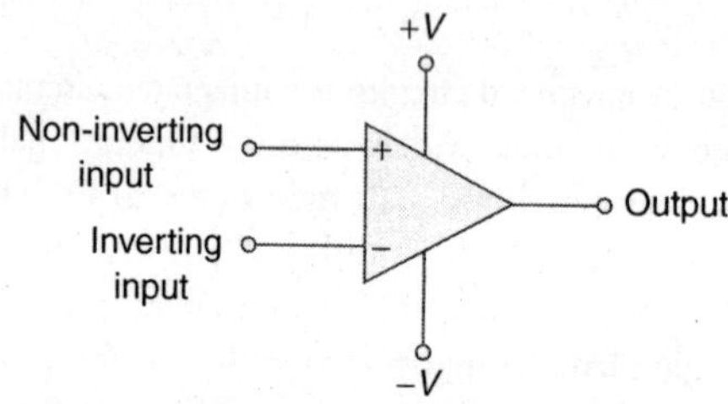

Figure 16.1 Circuit representation of an opamp.

16.2 Inside of the Opamp

The inside circuit of a typical opamp consists of a differential amplifier input stage that is followed by one or more differential amplifier gain stages. Generally, the differential amplifier input stage provides a differential output and the gain stages provide a single-ended output. The number of gain stages may be different for different opamps. The output of the final gain stage feeds the input of a class-B push–pull output stage. The output stage acts like a level translator and output driver. Figure 16.2 shows the block schematic arrangement of the internal circuit of a typical opamp with a differential input and a single-ended output. Now,

$$V_{out} = A_{OL} \times V_{in}$$

where A_{OL} is the open-loop voltage gain of the opamp, that is, voltage gain in the absence of any negative feedback. In the following sections, we will look at the basic circuits used to implement each of the building blocks of the operational amplifier.

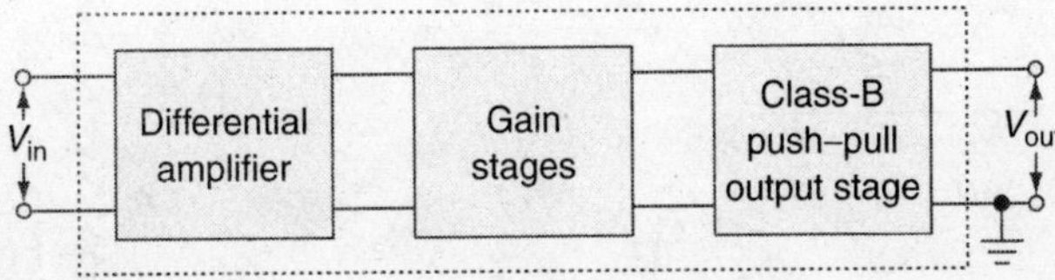

Figure 16.2 | Block schematic arrangement of a typical opamp.

Differential Amplifier Input Stage

Figure 16.3 shows the basic single-stage differential amplifier configuration. Note that the designers of IC amplifiers do not have the luxury of using coupling and bypass capacitors as it is not practical to fabricate large-value capacitors (larger than 50 pF) on the IC chip. This is one of the reasons that differential amplifier which requires no coupling and emitter bypass capacitors is the designers' preferred choice as the opamp input stage. Even large-value resistors are also not easy to fabricate in the IC form. Large-value resistances are simulated by using suitable transistor configurations.

The differential amplifier configuration is also sometimes called a long-tail pair as the two transistors share a common-emitter resistor. The current through this resistor is called the tail current. Figure 16.3 shows the configuration of a differential input–differential output differential amplifier. In the circuit of Figure 16.3, the base terminal of Q_1 is the non-inverting input and base terminal of transistor Q_2 is the inverting input. The output is in-phase with the signal applied at non-inverting input and out-of-phase with the signal applied at inverting input. This further implies that if two different input signals are applied to inverting and non-inverting inputs, the output is given by $A_d \times (V_1 - V_2)$.

For DC analysis, if we ignore the voltage drop across base–emitter junctions of the two transistors, the common emitter point for all practical purposes is at ground potential. That is, the tail current is given by V_{EE}/R_E, which is constant. The tail current is divided into two separate paths, one through Q_1 and the other through Q_2. As the two halves are symmetrical, total current sharing depends upon the voltages applied to the two inputs.

Figure 16.4 shows the circuit diagram and signal wave shapes at relevant points when the signal is applied to inverting and non-inverting inputs separately.

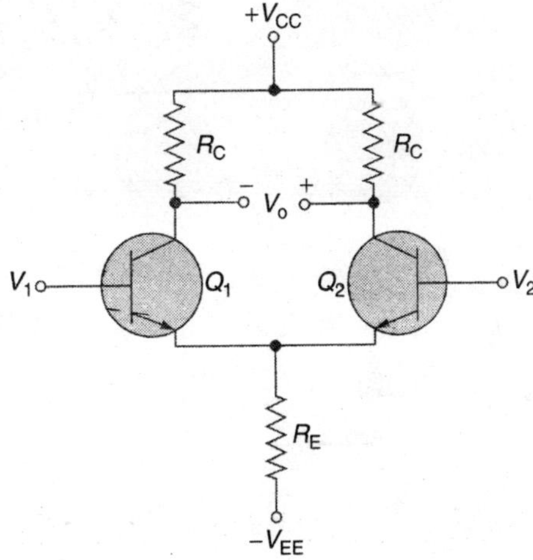

Figure 16.3 | Basic differential amplifier.

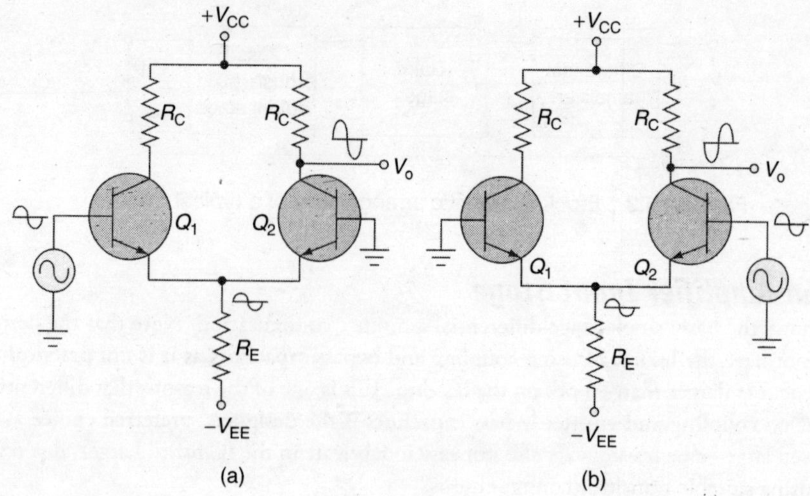

Figure 16.4 Differential amplifier with signal applied to (a) non-inverting input; (b) inverting input.

One of the key parameters of the differential amplifier is its ability to amplify differential input and its insensitivity to common mode input. This is expressed in terms of CMRR, which is nothing but ratio of differential gain to common mode gain. CMRR is described in detail Section 16.4 on opamp parameters. It can be verified that for the differential amplifier of Figure 16.3, differential gain is given by R_C/r_e' and the common mode gain is given by $R_C/2R_E$. CMRR therefore is given by $2R_E/r_e'$, where r_e' is the dynamic resistance of the base–emitter junctions of the two transistors.

It is evident from the expression for CMRR that the value of R_E should be as high as possible. That is why in practical opamp circuits, R_E is replaced by a constant current source. A current mirror configuration is also used to implement a constant current source. Figures 16.5 and 16.6, respectively, show differential

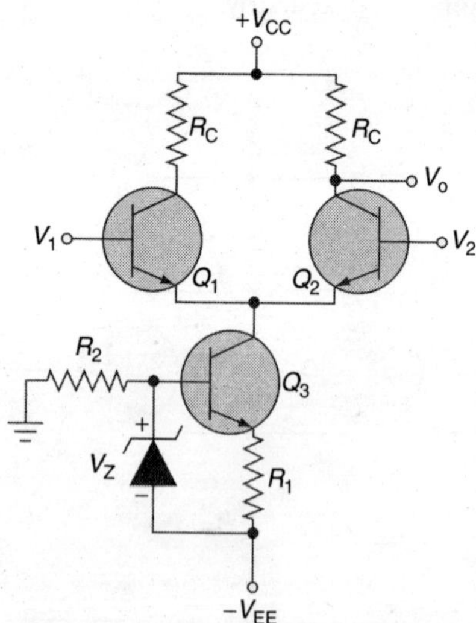

Figure 16.5 Differential amplifier with conventional constant current source in place of R_E.

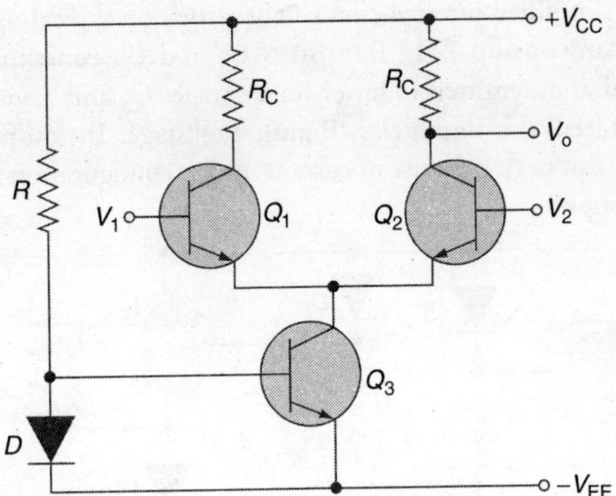

Figure 16.6 Differential amplifier with current mirror based constant current source in place of R_E.

amplifier circuits with a conventional constant current source and a current mirror configuration. We are familiar with the functioning of conventional constant current sources. The current mirror works as follows. If the diode connected across the base–emitter junction and the base–emitter junction diode of the transistor had matched current-voltage characteristics, the collector current of the transistor equals the current through resistor R. In other words, the collector current is a mirror image of the resistor current. As it is very easy to match the current-voltage characteristics of a diode and base–emitter junction diode of a transistor in ICs because of both being on same chip, current mirror configuration is commonly used as current source and active load in IC opamps. Figure 16.7 shows a differential amplifier stage with current mirrors being used instead of emitter resistor R_E and collector resistor R_C.

As outlined earlier, common-emitter amplifier and class-B push–pull amplifier constitute the second and final stages of the opamp, respectively. These have been described in detail in earlier chapters. Common-emitter amplifier stage or a cascade arrangement of more than one such stage provides most of the gain of the opamp. These stages when used inside an opamp will have active loads.

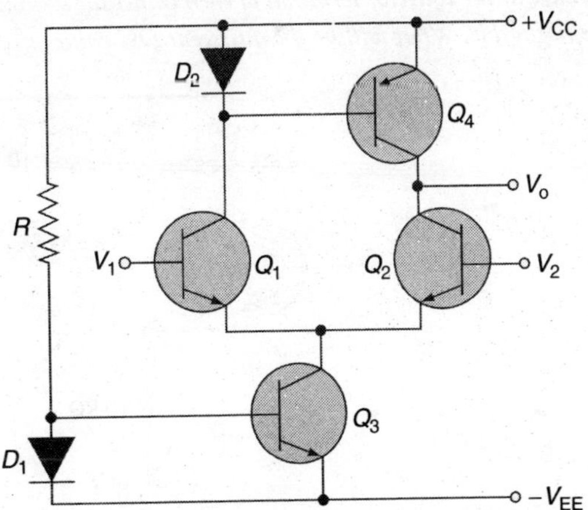

Figure 16.7 Differential amplifier with current mirrors used in place of emitter and collector resistors.

Figure 16.8 shows the simplified internal circuit schematic of a typical opamp. The diagram shown is that of the industry standard opamp 741. Transistors Q_1 and Q_2 constitute the differential amplifier. Transistor Q_6 is configured as an emitter–follower buffer stage. Q_5 and associated components make the common-emitter stage that feeds the output class-B push–pull stage. The output stage is configured around transistors Q_8 and Q_9. One can notice the use of current mirror configuration as active loads and also as the tail resistor of differential amplifier.

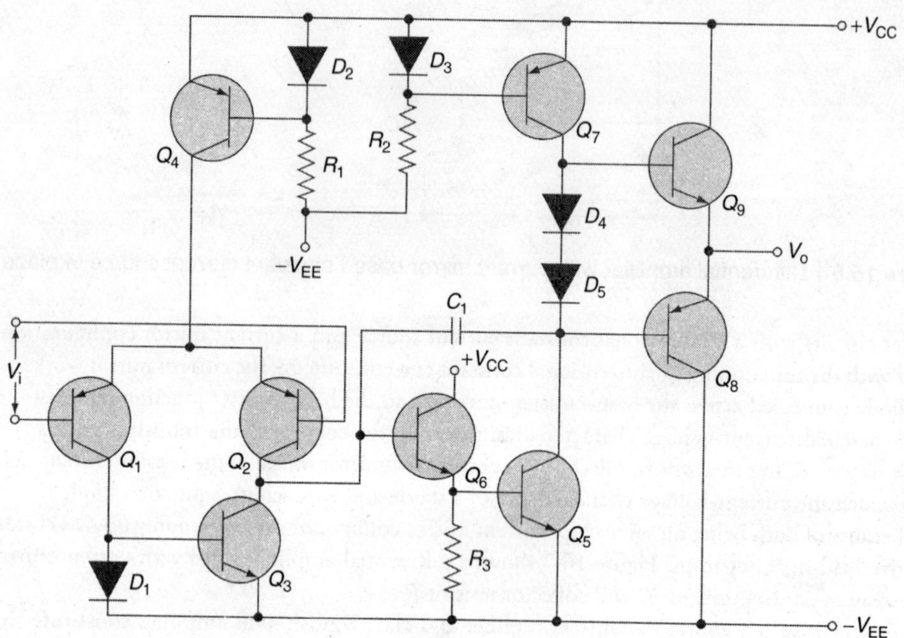

Figure 16.8 | Internal circuit diagram of a typical opamp.

EXAMPLE 16.1 *Refer to the differential amplifier circuit of Figure 16.9. Determine the quiescent DC voltage at the collector terminal of each transistor assuming V_{BE} of the two transistors to be negligible. What will be the quiescent DC values if V_{BE} is taken as 0.7 V?*

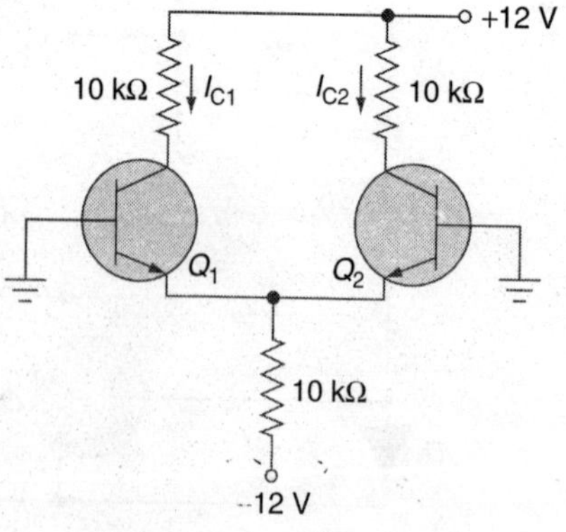

Figure 16.9 | Example 16.1.

Solution

1. Assuming V_{BE} to be negligible, the tail current $I_T = 12/10 \times 10^3 = 1.2$ mA.
2. Therefore emitter current of each transistor = $1.2 \times 10^{-3}/2 = 0.6$ mA.
3. Collector current of each transistor is approximately equal to its emitter current.
4. Therefore, collector current of each transistor = 0.6 mA.
5. Quiescent DC voltage at the collector of each transistor = $12 - 0.6 \times 10^{-3} \times 10 \times 10^3 = 6$ V.
6. If $V_{BE} = 0.7$ V, tail current = $(12 - 0.7)/(10 \times 10^3) = 1.13$ mA.
7. This gives emitter and hence collector current of each transistor as $(1.13 \times 10^{-3})/2 = 0.565$ mA.
8. Quiescent DC voltage at each collector in that case equals $12 - 0.565 \times 10^{-3} \times 10 \times 10^3 = 6.35$ V.

EXAMPLE 16.2

Refer to the differential amplifier circuit diagram of Figure 16.10. Determine the differential voltage gain, given that the transistors used in the circuit have $h_{ie} = 1$ kΩ and $h_{fe} = 40$.

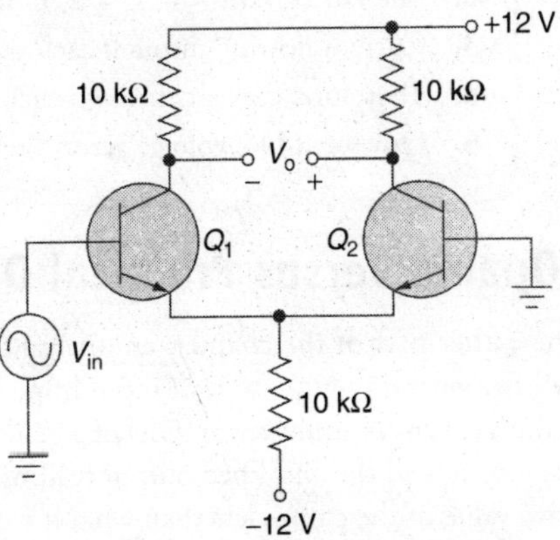

Figure 16.10 | Example 16.2.

Solution

1. Dynamic resistance r_e' of the base–emitter junction diode of the two transistors is given by h_{ie}/h_{fe}. Therefore, $r_e' = 1000/40 = 25$ Ω.
2. Differential voltage gain is given by $A_d = R_C/r_e'$.
3. Therefore, $A_d = 10{,}000/25 = 400$.

EXAMPLE 16.3

Refer to the differential amplifier circuit of Figure 16.11. Determine the tail current I_T and also the quiescent DC voltage across the output. Assume diode voltage drop to be 0.7 V.

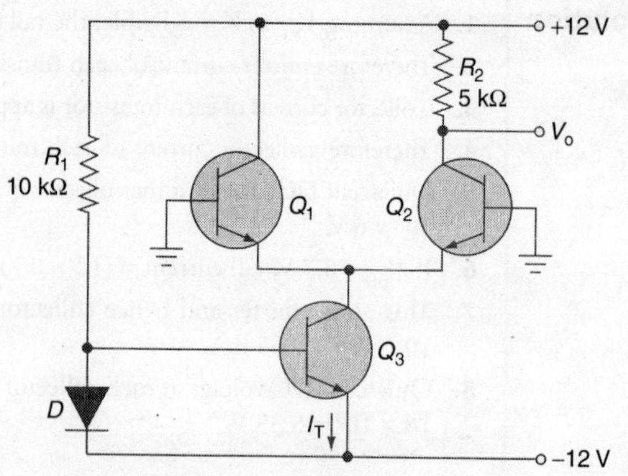

Figure 16.11 | Example 16.3.

Solution

1. Current I_R flowing through resistor R_1 is given by $I_R = (12 + 12 - 0.7)/(10 \times 10^3) = 23.3/(10 \times 10^3) = 2.33$ mA.
2. The tail current $I_T = I_R = 2.33$ mA.
3. Current flowing through each transistor is equal to half of the total tail current.
4. Therefore, current through each transistor = $2.33 \times 10^{-3}/2 = 1.165$ mA.
5. Quiescent DC voltage across output = $12 - 5 \times 10^3 \times 1.165 \times 10^{-3} = 6.175$ V.

16.3 Ideal Opamp versus Practical Opamp

As outlined in the earlier part of the chapter, an opamp is a direct-coupled high gain, high bandwidth differential amplifier with very high value of input impedance and very low value of output impedance. Figure 16.12 shows the Thevenin's equivalent model of a generalized amplifier fed at the input from a source having a source resistance R_s and the amplified output feeding a load resistance R_L. Owing to finite values of R_i and R_o, the effective value of the gain is less than what it would have been had R_i and R_o been infinite and zero, respectively.

Figure 16.13 shows the Thevenin's equivalent model of an opamp. V_I and V_{NI} are, respectively, inverting and non-inverting inputs and A_d is the open-loop differential voltage gain. This is the equivalent circuit model of a practical opamp. There are loading effects at the input and output ports due to finite values of

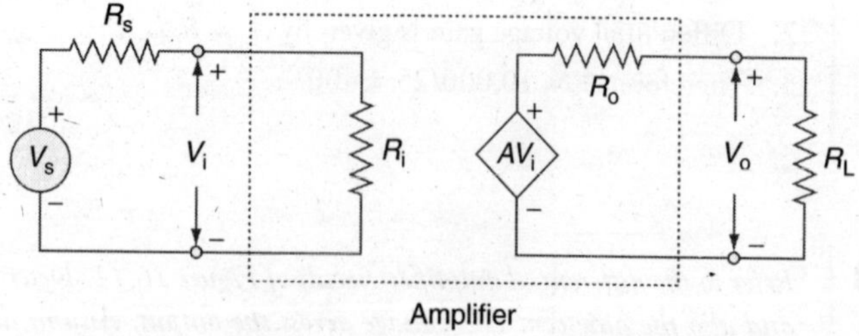

Figure 16.12 | Thevenin's equivalent model of generalized amplifier.

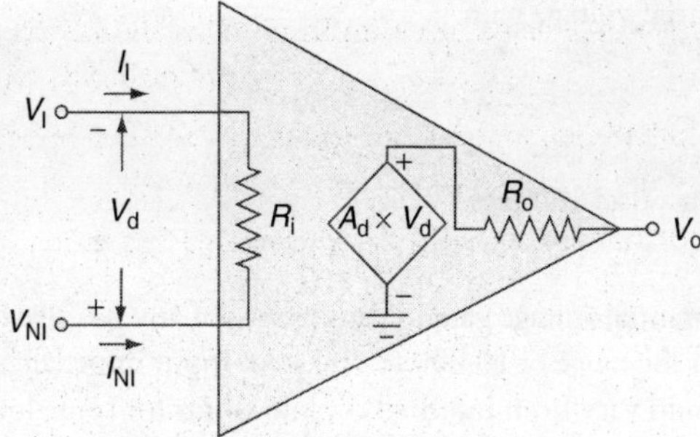

Figure 16.13 Thevenin's equivalent model of an opamp.

input and output resistances. The ideal opamp model was derived to simplify circuit calculations. The ideal opamp model makes three assumptions. These are as follows:

1. Input resistance, $R_i = \infty$
2. Output resistance, $R_o = 0$
3. Open-loop gain, $A_d = \infty$

From the three above-mentioned primary assumptions, other assumptions can be derived. These include the following:

1. Since $R_i = \infty$, $I_I = I_{NI} = 0$.
2. Since $R_o = 0$, $V_o = A_d \times V_d$
3. For linear mode of operation of opamp and a finite output voltage and infinite differential gain, $V_d = 0$.
4. Since output voltage depends only on differential input voltage, it rejects any voltage common to both inputs. Therefore, common mode gain = 0.
5. Bandwidth and slew rate are also infinite as no frequency dependencies are assumed.
6. Drift is also zero as there are no changes in performance over time, temperature, power supply variations and so on.

Figure 16.14 shows the Thevenin's equivalent model of an ideal opamp. To sum up, an ideal opamp is characterized by following basic properties. Knowledge of these properties is sufficient to design and analyze most of the circuits configured around opamps.

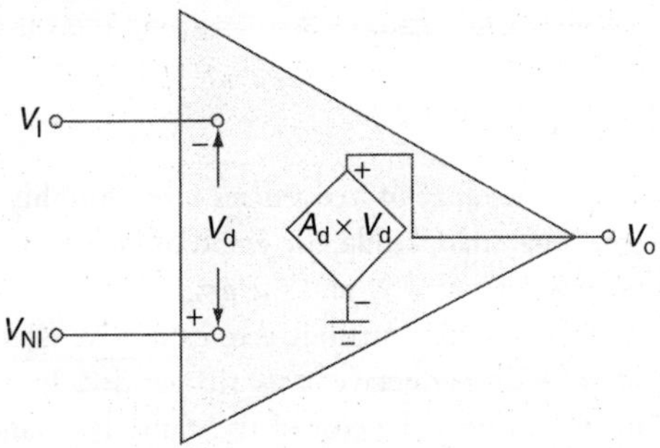

Figure 16.14 Thevenin's equivalent model of an ideal opamp.

1. Infinite open-loop differential voltage gain.
2. Infinite input impedance.
3. Zero output impedance.
4. Infinite bandwidth.
5. Zero DC input and output offset voltages.
6. Zero input differential voltage.

Open-loop gain is the differential voltage gain in the absence of any positive or negative feedback. Practical opamps have open-loop gain in the range of 10,000 to 100,000. Input impedance of an ideal opamp is infinite. In the case of real devices, it could vary from hundreds of kilo-ohms for some low-grade opamps to tera-ohms for high-grade opamps. An ideal opamp acts like a perfect voltage source with zero internal output impedance. For real devices, output impedance may be in the range of 10 to 100 Ω. The ideal opamp amplifies all signals from DC to highest AC frequencies. In the case of real devices, bandwidth is rather limited and is specified by gain-bandwidth product. An ideal opamp produces a zero output when both the inputs are grounded. In the case of real devices, there may be some finite DC output, referred to as output offset voltage, even when both the inputs are grounded. Output offset may vary from few nano-volts for ultra-low offset opamps to few milli-volts for general-purpose opamps. In the case of ideal opamps, voltage appearing at one input also appears at the other input for linear mode of operation. That is, differential inputs stick together.

16.4 Performance Parameters

Like any other component, the key parameters of an opamp too decide its suitability for a particular application. For instance, an opamp with a CMRR of 120 dB is much better suited for building a differential amplifier than another opamp having CMRR of 80 dB. Also, on the basis of slew rate or response time specifications, we cannot evaluate the performance of a precision opamp. A brief description of the key parameters of an opamp along with their practical implications is given in the following paragraphs. Key opamp parameters include the following:

1. Bandwidth
2. Slew rate
3. Open-loop gain
4. Common mode rejection ratio (CMRR)
5. Power supply rejection ratio (PSRR)
6. Input impedance
7. Output impedance
8. Settling time
9. Offsets and offset drifts

Bandwidth

Bandwidth of an opamp tells us about the range of frequencies it can amplify for a given amplifier gain. The frequency response curve of a typical opamp looks like the graph of Figure 16.15(a). It is nothing but the frequency response of the general-purpose opamp 741 and the graph has been reproduced from the data sheet of the said opamp. The high-frequency roll-off is attributed to capacitive effects appearing in shunt. Beyond cut-off, the frequency falls at a rate of 6 dB per octave or 20 dB per decade. When the opamp is used in the closed-loop mode, the bandwidth increases at the cost of the gain. The bandwidth is usually expressed in terms of the *unity gain crossover frequency* (also called gain-bandwidth product). It is 1 MHz in the case of opamp 741 as is evident from the graph. It could be as high as 1500 MHz in the case of high bandwidth

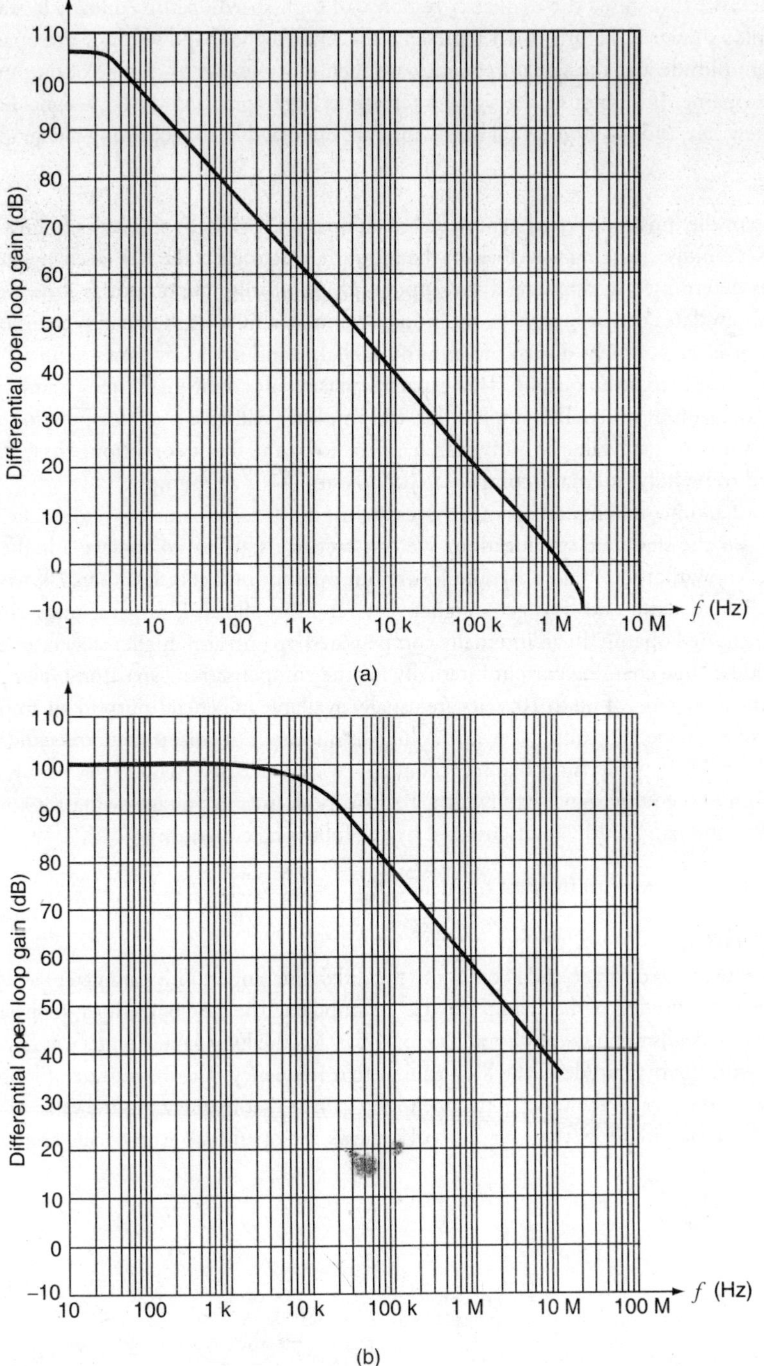

Figure 16.15 (a) Small signal bandwidth of general-purpose opamp 741; (b) small signal bandwidth of high-speed opamp AD829.

opamps. Figure 16.15(b) shows the frequency response of high-speed opamp AD829. It may be mentioned here that the plot shown in Figure 16.15 represents the small signal bandwidth of the opamp. That is, the output signal amplitude and the signal frequency are such that the rate of change of output is less than the slew rate of the opamp. If it is not so, the signal is termed as large signal and the large signal bandwidth is slew rate limited. Slew rate and the large signal bandwidth are discussed in the following paragraphs.

Slew Rate

Slew rate is one of the most important parameters of an opamp. It gives us an idea as to how well the opamp output follows a rapidly changing waveform at the input. It is defined as the rate of change of output voltage with time. It is determined by applying a step input and monitoring the output as shown in Figure 16.16. The step input simulates the large signal conditions. The incapability of the opamp to follow rapidly rising and falling input is, respectively, due to the minimum charge and discharge times required by an internally connected capacitor across the output. This capacitor has a value that guarantees stable operation of the opamp down to a gain of unity. This implies that the amplifier will give a stable operation and will not get into oscillations for any gain value as unity gain happens to be the worst condition. Now if it is so, then the amplifier is said to be fully internally compensated. Opamp 741 is an example.

In the case of an uncompensated opamp, this capacitor needs to be connected externally. In that case, we have a control on the slew rate specification. We can sacrifice stability to achieve a higher slew rate. For instance, if we know that we are never going to use our opamp for a gain less than 10, we could afford to connect a smaller capacitor and thus get a higher slew rate. But all this is possible only when we decide to use an uncompensated opamp. In an internally compensated opamp also, higher slew rate versions are available that provide a large charging current internally for the compensation capacitor. Opamp 741 has a slew rate of 0.5 V/μs. Slew rates of up to 10 V/μs are usually available in general-purpose opamps. In the case of some varieties of high-speed opamps, slew rate as high as hundreds of volts per microseconds is available. EL 2444 (high-speed quad opamp from Elantec) offers a slew rate of 325 V/μs.

Slew rate limits the large signal bandwidth. Peak-to-peak output voltage swing for a sinusoidal signal ($V_{\text{p-t-p}}$), slew rate and bandwidth are interrelated by the following equation:

$$\text{Bandwidth (highest frequency, } f_{\text{MAX}}) = \text{Slew rate}/(\pi \times V_{\text{p-t-p}}) \tag{16.1}$$

Open-Loop Gain

Open-loop gain is the ratio of single-ended output to the differential input. This parameter has a great bearing on the gain accuracy specification of the opamp wired as an amplifier. The ratio of the open-loop gain to the closed-loop gain (which depends upon the application circuit) is called the loop gain. Accuracy at any given frequency depends heavily on the magnitude of the loop gain at that frequency. The magnitude of loop gain at a given frequency depends directly on the value of the open-loop gain at that frequency as the value of closed-loop gain for a given application circuit is fixed. Figure 16.17 shows the open-loop gain versus frequency curve of an

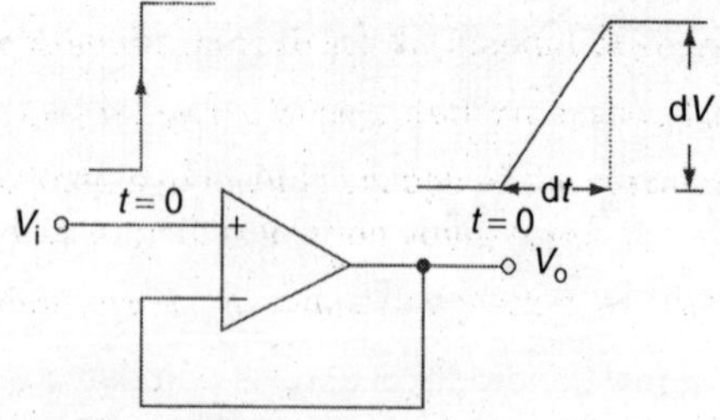

Figure 16.16 Response to step input.

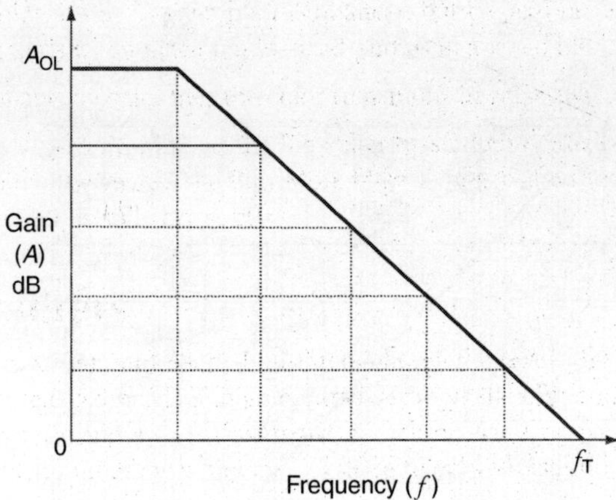

Figure 16.17 | Open-loop gain versus frequency.

opamp. As a thumb rule, the gain error at any given frequency is given by the ratio of the closed-loop gain to the open-loop gain. Thus a higher open-loop gain gives a smaller error for a given closed-loop gain.

Common Mode Rejection Ratio

Common mode rejection ratio (*CMRR*) is a measure of the ability of the opamp to suppress common mode signals. It is the ratio of the desired differential gain (A_d) to the undesired common mode gain (A_c). The ratio CMRR is usually expressed as CMR given by 20 log (A_d/A_c) dB. A lower CMRR or CMR reflects in terms of larger variation in the output of a differential amplifier due to variation in the common mode input when the differential input stays put. The common mode input is the average value of the two inputs. The common mode input affects the bias point of the input differential amplifier stage. Owing to lack of perfect symmetry in the two halves of the input differential amplifier stage, change in bias point changes the offset voltage. This in turn changes the output voltage. CMRR is also defined as the ratio of the change in the common mode input to the corresponding change in the output offset voltage.

CMRR is always specified for a given input voltage range. Exceeding the input voltage range would degrade the CMRR specification. In some opamps, the input voltage range is specified separately which implies that the given value of CMRR is guaranteed over the listed input voltage range. CMRR as published in data sheet is a DC parameter. CMRR when graphed versus frequency falls with increase in frequency as shown in Figure 16.18. The graph shown in the figure is taken from data sheet of opamp 741.

Power Supply Rejection Ratio

Power supply rejection ratio (*PSRR*) is defined as the ratio of change in the power supply voltage to corresponding change in the output voltage. The mechanism that produces PSRR is the same as that is responsible for CMRR. The power supply affects the bias point of the input differential amplifier stage of the opamp. Owing to inherent mismatch in the input circuitry, changes in bias point changes the offset voltage, which in turn changes the output voltage. PSRR is also defined as the ratio of change in one of the power supply voltage to the change in the input offset voltage with the other power supply voltage held constant.

PSRR like CMRR too is a DC parameter and its value falls with increase in frequency. The parameter is particularly significant as switched mode power supplies can have noise in the frequency range of 20 kHz to 200 kHz and even higher. PSRR is almost zero at these frequencies with the result that power supply noise appears as noise at the output of the opamp. Figure 16.19 shows PSRR versus frequency graph of opamp type AD 829.

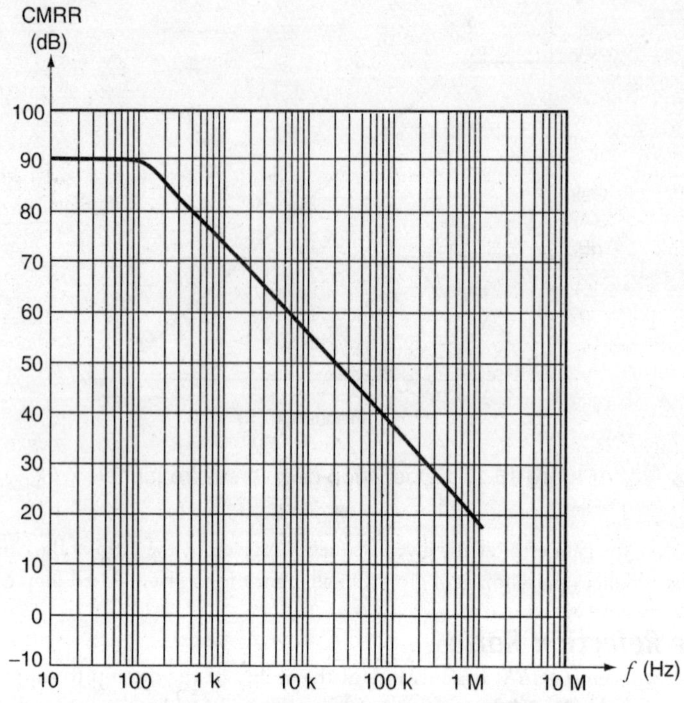

Figure 16.18 CMRR versus frequency.

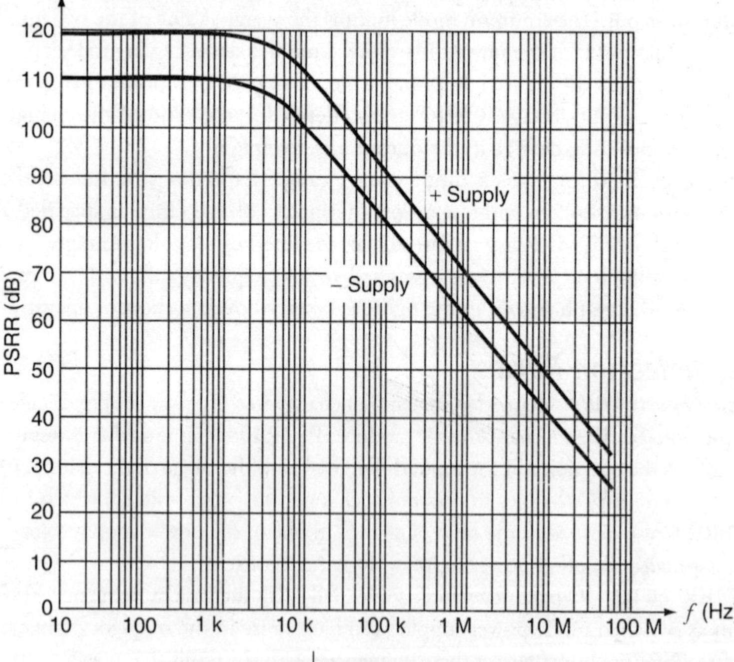

Figure 16.19 PSRR versus frequency.

Input Impedance

Input impedance is the impedance looking into the input terminals of the opamp and is mostly expressed in terms of resistance only. The effective input impedance is, however, different from what is specified in the data sheets when the opamp is used in the closed-loop mode. In the inverting amplifier configuration, the effective input impedance equals the input resistance connected externally from source of input signal to the inverting input terminal of the opamp. In the non-inverting amplifier configuration, it equals the product of loop gain and the specified opamp input impedance.

Output Impedance

Output impedance is defined as the impedance between the output terminal of the opamp and ground. Common-emitter (BJT) and common-source (FET) output stages used in rail-to-rail output opamps have higher output impedance than emitter–follower output stages. Output impedance becomes a critical parameter when using rail-to-rail output opamps to drive heavy loads. If the load were mainly resistive, it would decide how close the output can be to the rails. If the load were capacitive, the additional phase shift caused will erode the phase margin. Figure 16.20 shows the effect of output impedance on the output signal assuming that the output impedance is resistive in the case of a predominantly resistive load R_L [Figure 16.20(a)] and a capacitive load C_L [Figure 16.20(b)]. In the case of resistive load, Eq. (16.2) describes the output. Equation (16.3) gives the expression for the output in the case of capacitive load.

$$V_o = A_d \times V_d \times \left[\frac{R_L}{R_L + Z_o}\right] \tag{16.2}$$

$$V_o = A_d \times V_d \times \left[\frac{1}{j(f/f_o)+1}\right] \tag{16.3}$$

where $f_o = 1/2\pi Z_o C_L$ and Z_o is the output impedance of the opamp.

Settling Time

Settling time is a parameter specified in the case of high-speed opamps or the opamps with a high value of gain-bandwidth product. It gives the response of the opamp to large step inputs. It is expressed as the time taken by the opamp output to settle within a specified percentage of the final value (usually 0.1% or 0.01% of the final expected value) in response to a step at its input (Figure 16.21). The settling time is usually specified for opamp wired as a unity gain amplifier and it worsens for a closed-loop gain greater than 1.

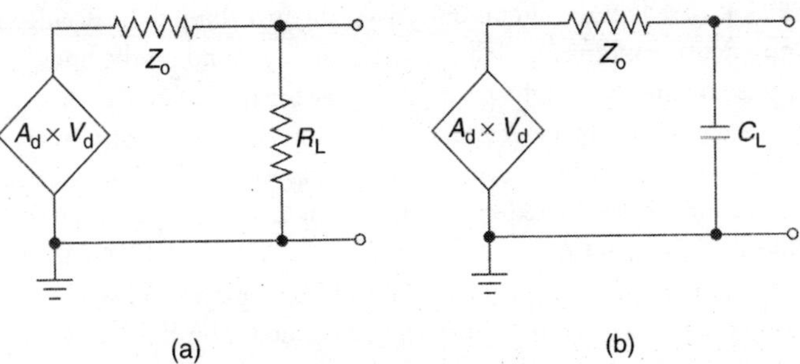

Figure 16.20 (a) Effect of resistive load R_L on output signal; (b) effect of capacitive load C_L on output signal.

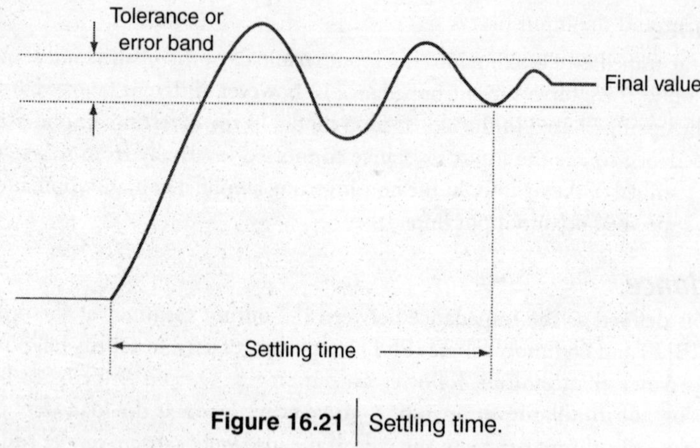

Figure 16.21 | Settling time.

Settling time is a design issue in data acquisition circuits when signals are changing rapidly. This parameter is very important when the opamp is being used as a sample-and-hold circuit at the input of an analog-to-digital converter or at the output of a high-speed digital-to-analog converter.

Offsets and Offset Drifts

Offset is a commonly used term with reference to opamps. An ideal opamp should produce a zero output for a zero differential input. But it is not so in the case of real opamps. It is observed that we need to apply a DC differential voltage externally to get a zero output. This externally applied input is referred to as the *input offset voltage*. This parameter may be as large as 5 mV in general-purpose opamps and as small as 200 μV in low offset opamps. The input offset voltage is often a function of power supply voltages. This variation is expressed in terms of PSRR. *Output offset voltage* is the voltage at the output with both the input terminals grounded. Another offset parameter is the *input offset current*. It is the difference between the two bias currents flowing towards the inputs of the opamp. Yet another important opamp parameter is the *input bias current*. It is defined as the average of the two bias currents flowing into the two input terminals of the opamp. The listed value of input and output offset voltages and input offset and bias currents tend to drift with temperature. This drift is also specified in the data sheets. Some general-purpose opamps (741 for instance) have a provision for externally nullifying the input offset voltage by usually connecting the fixed terminals of a potentiometer of a given resistance value across the designated terminals and connecting the center terminal to the negative supply voltage.

Having briefly described the key parameters in respect of different categories of opamps, the opamp selection should be no problem. Based on the circuit objectives, the first thing to be decided is the opamp category that would do the required job economically. Having made up our mind on the broad class of opamps, that is, we need a general-purpose opamp or a high-speed opamp or for that matter an instrumentation opamp, we can go through the specifications of the devices available in the chosen category to choose a device that suits our needs the best. We should give due attention to both AC as well as DC considerations. One of the major AC considerations for instance is the desired loop gain. As an example, if we wanted the opamp to yield an accuracy of 0.1% while amplifying an AC signal of 10 kHz by a gain of 10, then the opamp must have an open-loop gain of 10,000 at the operating frequency of 10 kHz. Opamp 741 will certainly not serve the purpose here. The open-loop gain for a given frequency can be verified from the gain versus frequency plot.

Similarly, slew rate must be high enough to follow the fastest changing input signal without causing distortion. It is always good as a thumb rule to choose an opamp that has a minimum slew rate of 25% larger than the fastest rate of change in the input signal.

Input offset voltage and the input bias current are the important DC considerations besides open-loop gain when it comes to choosing the right opamp in the precision category. Input bias current is particularly important when the source of input signal has relatively higher impedance. FET-input opamps or instrumentation amplifiers deserve an attention in such cases.

EXAMPLE 16.4 *Opamp LM 741 is specified to have a slew rate of 0.5 V/μs. If the opamp were used as an amplifier and the expected peak output voltage were 10 V, determine the highest sinusoidal frequency that would get satisfactorily amplified.*

Solution

1. Highest sinusoidal frequency f_{MAX} that would get satisfactorily amplified is given by f_{MAX} = Slew rate/$2\pi V_P$, where V_P is the expected peak output voltage.
2. In the present case, slew rate = 0.5 V/μs and $V_P = 10$ V.
3. Therefore, $f_{MAX} = (0.5 \times 10^6)/(2\pi \times 10) = 7.96$ kHz.

EXAMPLE 16.5 *The differential voltage gain and CMRR of an opamp when expressed in decibels are 110 dB and 100 dB, respectively. Determine the common mode gain expressed as a ratio.*

Solution

1. CMRR (in dB) = 20 log (A_d/A_{CM}) where A_d and A_{CM} are, respectively, the differential and common mode gain values.
2. CMRR (in dB) = 20 log A_d – 20 log A_{CM}.
3. That is, 20 log A_{CM} = 20 log A_d – CMRR = 110 – 100 = 10 dB.
4. This gives log A_{CM} = 10/20 = 0.5
5. Therefore, A_{CM} = Antilog 0.5 = 3.16

EXAMPLE 16.6 *In the case of a certain opamp, 0.5 V change in common mode input causes a DC output offset change of 5 μV. Determine CMRR in dB.*

Solution

1. CMRR = $\Delta V_{CM}/\Delta V_{OS} = 0.5/(5 \times 10^{-6}) = 10^5$.
2. CMRR in dB = 20 log 10^5 = 100 dB.

16.5 Types of Opamps

Opamps can be categorized on the basis of the performance specifications and consequently their application area and also on the basis of their internal structure as general-purpose opamps, high-speed and high-bandwidth opamps, precision opamps, power opamps, instrumentation opamps, Norton opamps (also known as current differencing opamps), opamp comparators and isolation opamps and so on and so forth.

General-Purpose Opamps

The term general-purpose opamp is generally used with reference to that category of opamps which has moderate or say reasonably good values for all the key parameters. In the case of general-purpose opamps, none of the major specifications as outlined earlier can be said to be exceptionally good or state-of-the-art and also none of the specifications is extremely poor. Within the broad category of general-purpose opamps, some type numbers may have slightly better overall performance specifications and thus called as high-performance general-purpose opamps. A general-purpose opamp of the type 741 may have an open-loop gain of typically 10^4–10^5, input impedance of 0.5–1 MΩ, output impedance of 50–100 Ω, CMRR of the order of 70–100 dB, output offset voltage of the order of a few milli-volts and an open-loop bandwidth in the range of 1 MHz. Those general-purpose opamps that have a JFET-based input differential amplifier stage have relatively much larger input impedance (typically 10^{12} Ω) and much better noise specifications. Hence, general-purpose opamps due to overall good performance specifications are used in a wide range of applications in low cost designs.

JEFT-input opamps are preferred in applications where high-input impedance and low noise are the main considerations.

High-Speed Opamps

High-speed opamps have high slew rate and bandwidth specifications. Today opamps with slew rate in hundreds of volts per microsecond and bandwidth in hundreds of MHz are commercially available. As an illustration, opamp type AD 829 from Analog Devices has slew rate and unity gain small-signal bandwidth specifications of 230 V/μs and 600 MHz, respectively. EL 2444 from Elantec is yet another high-speed opamp. It is a quad opamp with slew rate and unity gain small-signal bandwidth specifications of 325 V/μs and 60 MHz, respectively.

Precision Opamps

Precision opamps have extremely low offsets and a very high value of open-loop differential gain. The output offset voltage in such opamps may be of the order of several tens of microvolts. The open-loop gain approaches 120 dB.

Power Opamps

In power opamps, the power supply voltages and consequently the output voltage swing are no longer limited to ±18 V or so. These opamps have supply voltage rating of the order of several hundred volts and current delivering capability of the order of several amperes. However, these devices are very expensive and are manufactured by a few select manufacturers internationally.

Opamps Comparators

These are opamps specially designed for use in comparator applications. They have much faster response time (typically from a few nanoseconds to several tens of nanoseconds) than that of a conventional general purpose opamp (typically of the order of 1 μs). Comparator, in which one of the inputs is normally a reference voltage, switches between two states at the output depending upon whether the other input is higher or lower than the reference. In the case of general-purpose opamps being used as comparators, the output switches between two levels that are fixed and depends upon the supply voltages. These levels may not be compatible with the load requirement which in most of the applications is a logic circuit. In other words, the comparator output should be compatible to a certain logic family like TTL or CMOS. The response time and the output compatibility happen to be the two most important specifications in the case of opamp comparators. A comparator forms the basic building block in circuits like zero crossing detectors, level detectors, Schmitt triggers, square and triangle waveform generators.

Norton Opamps

A Norton opamp also known as the current differencing opamp differs from a conventional opamp in its internal circuit design. While in a conventional opamp, the input stage is a differential amplifier to achieve inverting and non-inverting input functions, in the case of a Norton opamp, the non-inverting input function is derived from the inverting input function by using a current mirror configuration. The non-inverting input current is derived from the one entering at the inverting input. While we talk about differential input voltage in the case of a conventional opamp, it is differential input current in the case of a Norton opamp. Single supply operation and the fact that most of the general-purpose opamp applications can be realized without significantly sacrificing performance characteristics coupled with low cost per opamp make Norton opamp a very attractive choice. A Norton opamp has a definite edge over a general-purpose opamp (of 741 types) in single supply operation. When a general-purpose opamp is used on a single supply, the minimum input voltage that can be applied while ensuring that the opamp responds to a differential input is limited by the minimum common mode input range (typically +2 V in general-purpose opamps). This is rather large. In addition, general-purpose opamps when used on single supply have poorer output voltage swing. Norton opamps have no such limitations. A Norton opamp is represented in a circuit by the circuit symbol of Figure 16.22(b). The conventional opamp is represented by the circuit symbol of Figure 16.22(a).

Instrumentation Opamps

An instrumentation opamp is a differential amplifier with a very high value of input impedance, very large CMRR and extremely low values of offsets and offset drifts. Like an opamp of the type described in the earlier paragraphs, it is differential input single-ended output gain block. Gain in an instrumentation opamp, if we so call it, is usually set with a single resistor whereas in a conventional opamp, the same in achieved with the help of two resistors. Instrumentation opamps are available in single IC packages. Figure 16.23 shows the circuit representation of an instrumentation opamp. Typical internal schematic of such a device is shown in Figure 16.24. As is clear from the schematic arrangement of Figure 16.24, it is a combination of three opamps. The output opamp has been wired as a differential amplifier with its non-inverting and inverting inputs fed from the outputs of the other two opamps wired as non-inverting amplifiers. The gain setting resistor (R_{gain}) is connected external to the device. Thus the two major problems in a conventional

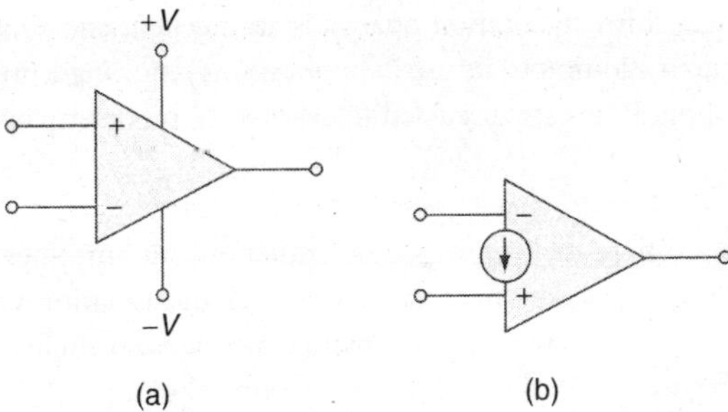

Figure 16.22 Circuit representation: (a) Conventional opamp; (b) Norton opamp.

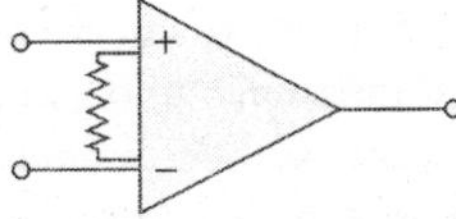

Figure 16.23 Circuit representation of an instrumentation opamp.

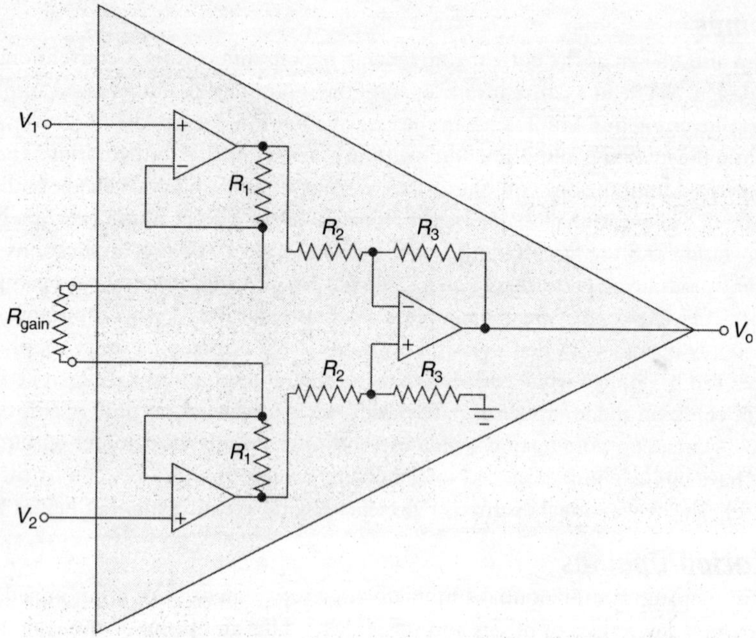

Figure 16.24 | Internal schematic of an instrumentation opamp.

opamp, namely, the low effective input impedance loading on to the signal source with comparatively high value of output impedance and the gain setting requiring simultaneous adjustment of two resistors leading to inaccuracies are overcome.

The essential characteristics of instrumentation opamps as outlined above make them very useful in amplifying low-level differential signals with high value of common mode content. Transducers such as thermocouples, biological probes, strain gauge bridges and current shunts produce small differential signals superimposed on common mode bias voltages. Instrumentation opamp is an excellent choice in such cases for meaningful acquisition and analysis of data in addition to its use in applications requiring a precision high quality differential amplifier. Some of these applications are discussed in chapter-17 on opamp application circuits.

Isolation Opamps

An isolation opamp is again a differential input, single-ended output amplifier with its output electrically isolated from the input. Isolation impedances as high as 10^{12} Ω and isolation voltages of about 1000 V are common. The differential amplifier in an isolation opamp may be an ordinary differential amplifier or an instrumentation amplifier. Figure 16.25 shows the circuit symbol of an isolation opamp. There are transformer-coupled isolation opamps [Figure 16.26(a)] mainly used in applications where linearity, gain accuracy, etc. are important and there optically coupled isolation opamps [Figure 16.26(b)] used in applications where speed and bandwidth are important.

Isolation opamps are used for those applications where electrical isolation between the source and the output is desirable. For instance, in medical instrumentation where the transducer or sensor is in physical contact with the patient, isolation opamp is an excellent interface between the transducer and the equipment (Figure 16.27). The isolation opamp provides a floating input for the signal source output and need for source ground connections is completely eliminated.

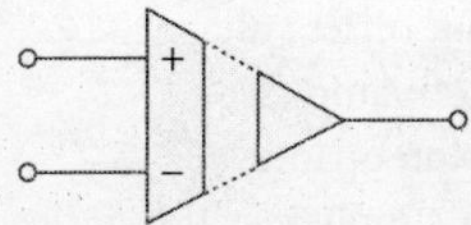

Figure 16.25 | Circuit symbol of an isolation opamp.

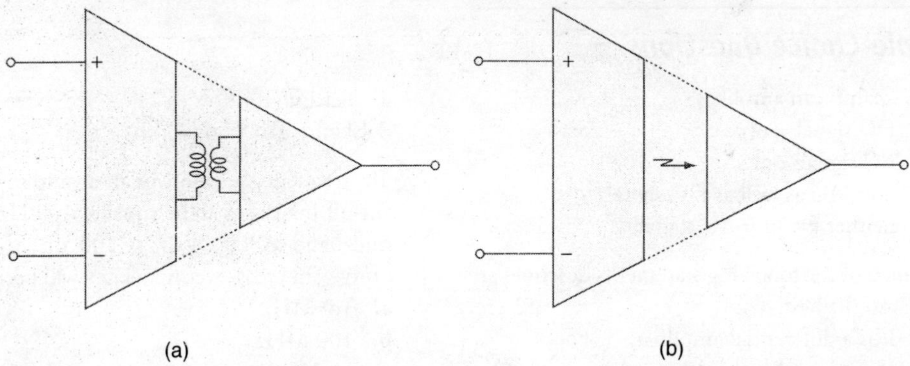

Figure 16.26 | (a) Transformer coupled isolation opamp; (b) optically coupled isolation opamp.

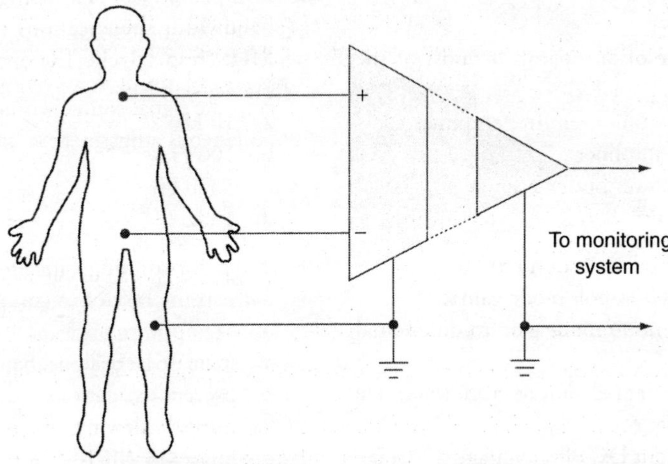

Figure 16.27 | Isolation opamp used in medical instrumentation.

KEY TERMS

Bandwidth
Common mode rejection ratio
Fully internally compensated opamp
General-purpose opamp
High-speed opamp
Ideal opamp
Input bias current
Input impedance
Input offset current
Input offset voltage
Instrumentation opamp
Isolation opamp
Loop gain
Norton opamp

Opamp
Opamp comparator
Open-loop gain
Output impedance
Output offset voltage
Power opamp
Precision opamp
Power supply rejection ratio
Settling time
Slew rate
Uncompensated opamp

OBJECTIVE-TYPE EXERCISES

Multiple-Choice Questions

1. An opamp can amplify
   a. DC signals only
   b. AC signals only
   c. both AC as well as DC signals
   d. neither DC nor AC signals

2. Which of the following statements describes an opamp the best?
   a. It is a differential amplifier.
   b. It is a large bandwidth amplifier.
   c. It is direct-coupled amplifier.
   d. It is a direct-coupled high-gain differential amplifier.

3. The input stage of an opamp in most of the cases is a
   a. high-gain common-emitter amplifier
   b. differential amplifier
   c. emitter–follower buffer
   d. none of these

4. The common mode rejection ratio is
   a. same as the common mode gain
   b. ratio of common mode gain to differential gain
   c. ratio of differential gain to common mode gain
   d. ratio of output DC offset voltage to change in common mode input

5. The input offset current is
   a. zero
   b. less than input bias current
   c. more than input bias current
   d. none of these

6. One of the following opamp parameters limits the large signal bandwidth.
   a. Slew rate
   b. CMRR
   c. Settling time
   d. Unity gain bandwidth

7. The frequency response of an opamp shows the cut-off frequency to be equal to 100 Hz. If the mid-band voltage gain is 100 dB, then the unity gain cross-over frequency will be
   a. 1.0 MHz
   b. 100 MHz
   c. 10 MHz
   d. indeterminate from given data

8. An opamp has open-loop gain and unity gain bandwidth specifications of 120 dB and 10 MHz, respectively. The open-loop cut-off frequency will be
   a. 10 Hz
   b. 100 Hz
   c. 1000 Hz
   d. 1 Hz

9. The compensating capacitor connected externally in the case of uncompensated opamps is to
   a. increase large signal bandwidth
   b. prevent oscillations
   c. improve slew rate
   d. increase CMRR

10. Identify the opamp type in which the output stage is designed to be compatible with some logic family.
    a. Opamp comparator
    b. High speed opamp
    c. Isolation opamp
    d. Instrumentation opamp

11. Which of the following opamp internally comprises three opamps out of which two are wired as buffers and the third is a difference amplifier?

a. Isolation opamp
b. Norton opamp
c. Instrumentation opamp
d. Opamp comparator

12. In which of the following opamp types, the input stage is not a conventional differential amplifier.
a. Norton opamp
b. Instrumentation opamp
c. Opamp comparator
d. Isolation opamp

13. Which of the following opamp types is ideally suited to single supply operation?
a. High bandwidth opamp
b. Instrumentation opamp
c. Norton opamp
d. General-purpose opamp

14. In the front-end differential amplifier inside an opamp, the tail resistor is usually replaced by
a. emitter–follower configuration
b. current mirror configuration
c. common-emitter amplifier configuration
d. a junction diode

15. In the internal circuit of an opamp, collector resistors are usually replaced by active loads to
a. increase differential gain
b. decrease common mode gain
c. increase bandwidth
d. increase efficiency

REVIEW QUESTIONS

1. What is an operational amplifier? How does it differ from common-emitter amplifier constructed using discrete components?

2. How would you characterize an ideal opamp? How does a practical opamp differ from an ideal opamp? Use Thevenin's equivalent circuit model to compare an ideal opamp with a practical opamp.

3. What is primarily responsible for giving an opamp the following characteristics?
a. High input impedance
b. Low output impedance
c. High open-loop gain
d. High common mode rejection ratio
e. Frequency response down to DC

4. Briefly describe the reasons for the following:
a. Why it is not possible to have an infinite CMRR?
b. Why internally compensated opamps have relatively lower slew rate?

5. Briefly describe the following opamp parameters with particular reference to their criticality for a given application circuit.
a. Slew rate
b. Open-loop gain
c. Settling time
d. Common mode rejection ratio

6. Briefly describe the following types of opamps with reference to major performance parameters.
a. High-speed opamps
b. Instrumentation opamps
c. Opamp comparators
d. General-purpose opamps

PROBLEMS

1. Refer to the differential amplifier circuit of Figure 16.28. Determine the quiescent DC voltage at the collector terminal of each transistor assuming V_{BE} of the two transistors to be equal to 0.7 V?

2. If the transistors used in the differential amplifier circuit of Figure 16.28 have $h_{ie} = 1\ k\Omega$ and $h_{fe} = 50$, determine the differential voltage gain.

3. Refer to the differential amplifier circuit of Figure 16.29. Determine the tail current I_T and also the quiescent DC voltage across the output. Assume V_{BE} of the transistors to be 0.7 V.

4. Opamp LF 356 is specified to have a slew rate of 5.0 V/μs. If the opamp were used as an amplifier and the expected peak output voltage were 12 V, determine the large signal bandwidth.

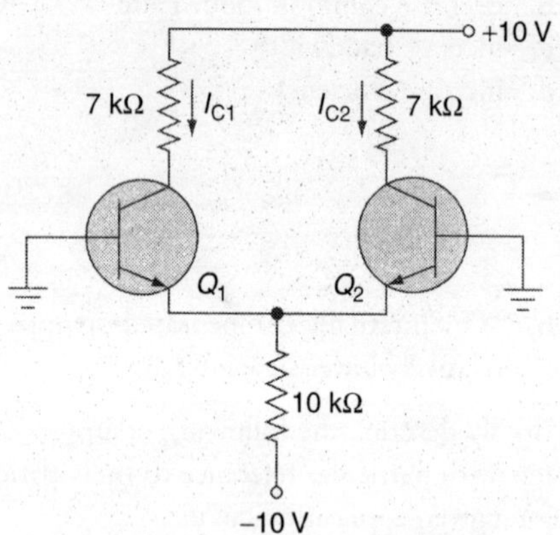

Figure 16.28 | Problem 1.

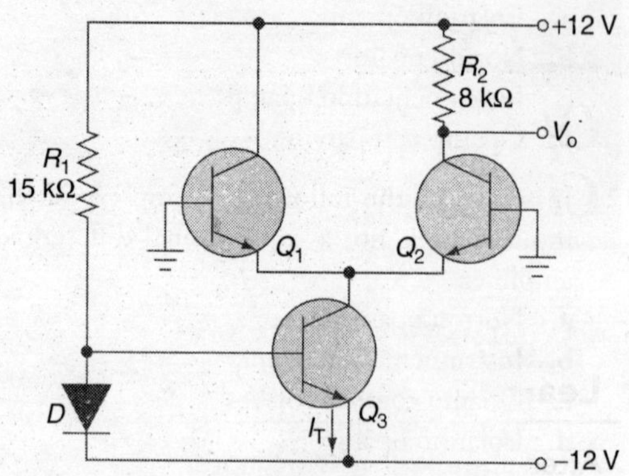

Figure 16.29 | Problem 3.

5. The differential voltage gain and CMRR of an opamp when expressed in decibels are 120 dB and 100 dB, respectively. Determine the common mode gain expressed as a ratio.

6. In the case of a certain opamp, 1.0 V change in common mode input causes a DC output offset change of 1.0 μV. Determine CMRR in dB.

7. The frequency response of an opamp shows the cut-off frequency to be equal to 10 Hz. If the mid-band voltage gain is 120 dB, determine the frequency at which the closed-loop gain will be unity.

ANSWERS

Multiple-Choice Questions

1. (c)
2. (d)
3. (b)
4. (c)
5. (b)
6. (a)
7. (c)
8. (a)
9. (b)
10. (a)
11. (c)
12. (a)
13. (c)
14. (b)
15. (a)

Problems

1. 6.745 V
2. 350
3. 1.55 mA, 5.8 V
4. 66.3 kHz
5. 10
6. 120 dB
7. 10 MHz

CHAPTER 17

Operational Amplifier Application Circuits

Learning Objectives

After completing this chapter, you will learn the following:

- Basic inverting and non-inverting amplifier configurations.
- Summing amplifier.
- Voltage follower circuit.
- Adder and subtractor circuits.
- Integrator and differentiator circuits.
- Rectifier circuits.
- Clipping and clamping circuits.
- Peak detector.
- Absolute value circuits.
- Comparator circuits.
- Active filters.
- Phase shifter circuits.
- Instrumentation amplifiers.
- Logarithmic amplifiers.
- Relaxation oscillators.
- Current-to-voltage and voltage-to-current converters.
- Sine wave oscillator circuits.

Fundamentals of operational amplifiers (opamps) in terms of internal architecture, characteristic parameters and types were discussed in detail in Chapter 16. The present chapter covers a large number of application circuits using opamps. As outlined in the previous chapter, an opamp fits into almost every conceivable circuit application due to its high differential gain, high input impedance, low output impedance, large bandwidth and many other desirable features. Application spectrum of opamps ranges from amplifiers to oscillators, computational building blocks (adder and subtractor circuits) to data conversion circuits (current-to-voltage, voltage-to-current, frequency-to-voltage, voltage-to-frequency, analog-to-digital and digital-to-analog converters), rectifiers to power supply regulators (linear and switching regulators), active filters, integrators and differentiators and so on. It is not possible to cover each and every conceivable circuit application in this chapter. However, almost all common applications of opamps are included in the chapter with particular emphasis on design equations governing different application circuits. Large number of solved examples are also included to illustrate the concepts discussed in the text.

17.1 Inverting Amplifier

An inverting amplifier is the one which in addition to changing the amplitude of the signal, changes the polarity of the input signal in the case of DC input and reverses the phase of the input signal in the case of AC input. Figure 17.1 shows the basic circuit diagram of an inverting amplifier configured around an opamp. It may be mentioned here that the power supply connections are not shown in the figures. It may be assumed that the opamps are given positive and negative supply connections as described in Chapter 16 unless otherwise stated. The circuit functions as follows. Assuming that the current flowing towards the negative opamp input terminal is zero, as would be the case for an ideal opamp, current flowing through input resistor R_1 is the same as the current flowing through the feedback resistor R_2. Owing to ground at (+ve) input, the R_1–R_2 junction is also at ground potential due to virtual earth phenomenon in opamps. Virtual earth with reference to opamps implies that there is a zero potential difference between the inverting and non-inverting input terminals. The concept of virtual earth has its origin in the infinite open-loop voltage gain of an ideal opamp, which further means that for a finite output, the differential input must be zero. Though virtual earth is valid for ideal opamps, the assumption yields very accurate results for opamps configured with heavy negative feedback. The expression for gain is derived as follows:

$$I = \frac{V_i}{R_1} = -\frac{V_o}{R_2} \tag{17.1}$$

So that

$$\frac{V_o}{V_i} = -\frac{R_2}{R_1} \tag{17.2}$$

Hence, closed-loop voltage gain (A_{CL}) is given by

$$A_{CL} = -\left(\frac{R_2}{R_1}\right) \tag{17.3}$$

Minus sign indicates that output is the phase-inverted version of input. By selecting proper values of R_1 and R_2 desired magnitude of gain can be achieved.

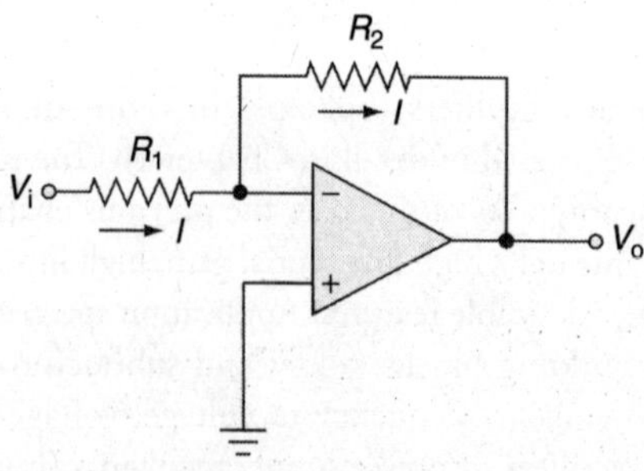

Figure 17.1 | Inverting amplifier.

Design Information

The inverting amplifier of Figure 17.1 has effective input impedance equal to R_1 as it comes in parallel with the high differential input impedance of the opamp. For a given value of closed-loop gain, higher the value of desired input impedance, higher is the value of resistor R_1, which in turn leads to a higher value of R_2. There is always an upper limit to the value of R_2 that can be connected for a given opamp. In fact, higher the input impedance of the opamp, larger is the maximum allowable value of R_2. In fact, the problem starts when the current flowing towards the negative input terminal of the opamp becomes comparable to the current (I). Things will be clearer if we look at the actual expression for gain that we would have arrived at if we had not made any assumptions.

The actual expression for the closed-loop gain A_{CL} for the amplifier circuit of Figure 17.1 is given by

$$A_{CL} = -\frac{A_{OL} R_2}{R_1 + R_2 + A_{OL} R_1} \cong -\frac{R_2}{R_1 + (R_2 / A_{OL})} \tag{17.4}$$

where A_{OL} is the open-loop gain of the opamp. This implies that when ratio R_2/A_{OL} is much smaller than R_1, the gain expression reduces to the expression of Eq. (17.3).

The input impedance of this circuit is same as the input resistance value, R_1. The output impedance of this circuit is approximated as

$$R_o = \left[\frac{R_1 + R_2}{R_1 A_{OL}}\right] R_{OL} \tag{17.5}$$

where R_{OL} is the open-loop output impedance of the opamp.

If the inverting amplifier of Figure 17.1 is needed to amplify AC signals only, the circuit may be modified to include coupling capacitors in series with input and output as shown in Figure 17.2. The frequency response of this amplifier does not extend down to zero. Coupling capacitors give a lower cut-off frequency depending upon the values of R_1 and C_1 on the input side and R_L and C_2 on the output side. R_L is the load resistance and is not shown in the figure. The lower cut-off frequency may be taken to be equal to higher of the two values. The two cut-off frequencies are given by Eqs. (17.6) and (17.7):

$$f_{CL1} = \frac{1}{2\pi R_1 C_1} \tag{17.6}$$

$$f_{CL2} = \frac{1}{2\pi R_L C_2} \tag{17.7}$$

Closed-loop bandwidth or upper cut-off frequency (f_{CU}) is given by Eq. (17.8).

$$f_{CU} = \text{Unity gain cross-over frequency of the opamp}/A_{CL} \tag{17.8}$$

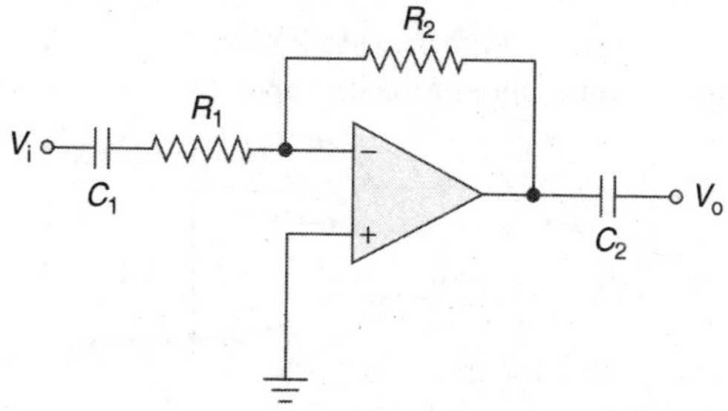

Figure 17.2 | Inverting amplifier for AC applications.

17.2 Non-Inverting Amplifier

Figure 17.3 shows an opamp-based non-inverting amplifier for DC applications. The expression for gain is derived as follows.

For the amplifier shown in Figure 17.3, due to virtual earth, the voltage of R_1–R_2 junction equals V_i. Also assuming that current flowing towards negative input terminal of the opamp is zero, we can write

$$I = \frac{V_i}{R_1} = \frac{V_o}{R_1 + R_2}$$

So that

$$\frac{V_o}{V_i} = \frac{R_1 + R_2}{R_1} = 1 + \frac{R_2}{R_1}$$

Hence, closed-loop voltage gain (A_{CL}) is

$$A_{CL} = 1 + \frac{R_2}{R_1} \tag{17.9}$$

Design Information

The actual gain expression in the case of an opamp-based non-inverting amplifier is given by

$$A_{CL} = \frac{A_{OL}(R_1 + R_2)}{R_1 + R_2 + A_{OL}R_1} \tag{17.10}$$

Equation (17.10) reduces to

$$\frac{R_1 + R_2}{R_1 + (R_2/A_{OL})}$$

for $A_{OL} >> 1$. Again if $R_2/A_{OL} << R_1$, the expression reduces to the expression of Eq. (17.9).

The input impedance (R_i) of this configuration is given by

$$R_i = R_{IL}A_{OL}\left(\frac{R_1}{R_1 + R_2}\right) \tag{17.11}$$

$$= R_{IL} \times \text{Loop gain}$$

where R_{IL} is the open-loop input impedance of the opamp; loop gain is given by the ratio of open-loop gain to the closed-loop gain (i.e., A_{OL}/A_{CL}).

The output impedance (R_o) can be computed from the following equation:

$$R_o = R_{OL}/\text{Loop gain} \tag{17.12}$$

where R_{OL} is the open-loop output impedance of the opamp.

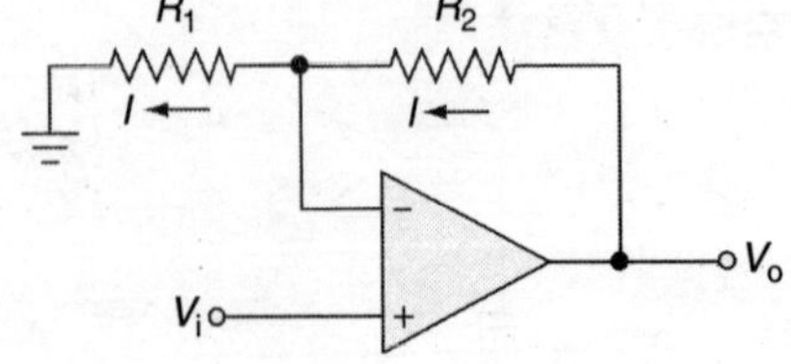

Figure 17.3 | Non-inverting amplifier.

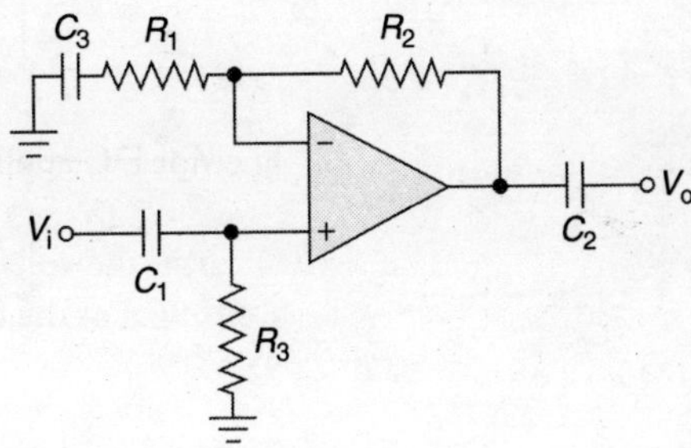

Figure 17.4 | Non-inverting amplifier for AC signals.

In case the non-inverting amplifier of Figure 17.3 is needed to amplify AC signals only, the circuit may be modified to include coupling capacitors C_1 and C_2 in series with input and output, respectively, and a bypass capacitor C_3 as shown in Figure 17.4. Coupling capacitors give a lower cut-off frequency depending upon the values of R_3 and C_1 on the input side and R_L and C_2 on the output side. R_L is the load resistance and is not shown in the figure. The two cut-off frequencies are given by the following equations:

$$f_{CL1} = \frac{1}{2\pi R_3 C_1} \tag{17.13}$$

$$f_{CL2} = \frac{1}{2\pi R_L C_2} \tag{17.14}$$

The bypass capacitor produces a lower cut-off frequency given by

$$f_{CL3} = \frac{1}{2\pi R_1 C_3} \tag{17.15}$$

The lower cut-off frequency may be taken as the highest of the three values. The upper cut-off frequency or the closed-loop bandwidth is given by the ratio of unity gain cross-over frequency of the opamp to the closed-loop gain.

17.3 Voltage Follower

Voltage follower is nothing but a non-inverting amplifier circuit with unity gain. Figure 17.5 shows the basic voltage-follower circuit. If we compare the voltage-follower circuit with the basic circuit arrangement of a non-inverting amplifier as shown in Figure 17.3, we find that $R_1 = \infty$ and $R_2 = 0$. Substituting these values in the expression for gain, we get $A_{CL} = 1$. In the circuit shown, there is 100% negative feedback from output to input. The negative feedback is of voltage-series type. This leads to increase in input impedance and decrease in output impedance by a large factor, approximately equal to open-loop gain A_{OL}.

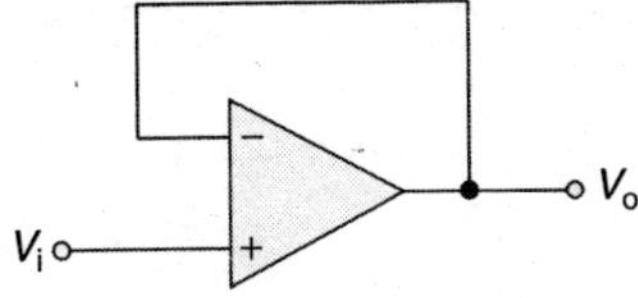

Figure 17.5 | DC voltage-follower circuit.

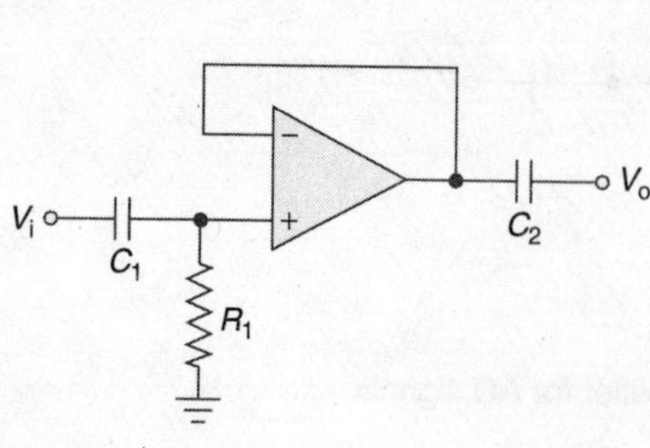

Figure 17.6 | Voltage follower for AC applications.

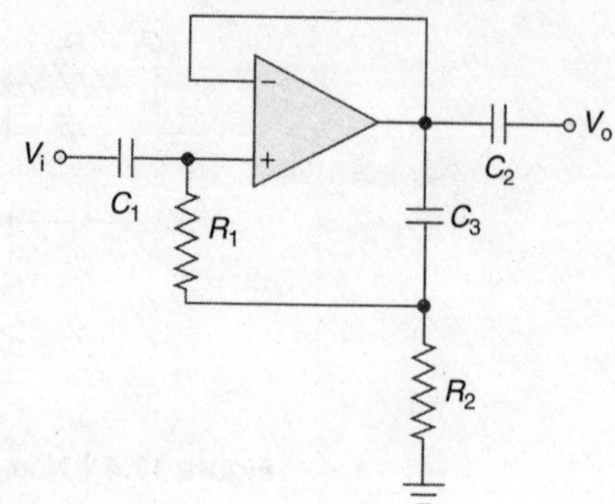

Figure 17.7 | Modified voltage follower for AC applications.

For AC applications, the input is applied through a capacitor C_1 and another capacitor C_2 is put in series with the output lead. These capacitors are meant for blocking the DC. The circuit is shown in Figure 17.6. Resistor R_1 provides a discharge path for capacitor C_1 and hence offers DC stability. The disadvantage of using resistor R_1 is that the input impedance of the voltage-follower configuration reduces practically to R_1, thus losing one of the key advantages of the voltage-follower configuration of high input impedance.

This is overcome in the circuit arrangement of Figure 17.7. For AC signals, capacitor C_3 is almost a short circuit. This means that signal amplitude on both ends of resistor R_1 is the same, resulting in practically zero current through it. This in turn implies very large input impedance due to near infinite effective value of R_1.

Voltage-follower circuit has many advantages. Owing to its extremely high input impedance, extremely low output impedance and unity gain; it acts as an ideal interface between a high impedance source and a low impedance load. Also, unity closed-loop gain leads to a very high closed-loop bandwidth equal to the unity gain cross-over frequency of the opamp. The output offset error is also very low because due to unity closed-loop gain, input errors are not amplified.

EXAMPLE 17.1 *Design an inverting amplifier using an opamp. The amplifier should have a voltage gain of 10 and an input impedance not less than 10 kΩ. If the input signal, which is a sinusoidal one, has a peak amplitude varying from 100 to 300 mV, determine the maximum possible input signal frequency that would be faithfully amplified. The chosen opamp has slew rate of 0.5 V/μs.*

Solution

1. Figure 17.8 shows the circuit diagram. The gain of this amplifier is $-(R_2/R_1)$ and its input impedance is approximately R_1.

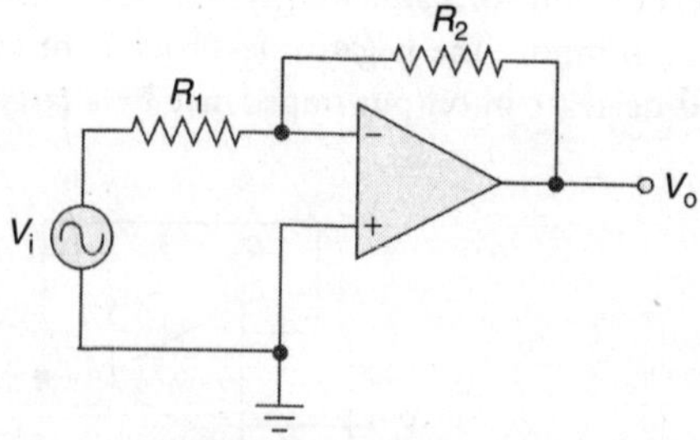

Figure 17.8 | Example 17.1.

2. Since the input impedance of the amplifier is not to be less than 10 kΩ, we can safely choose R_1 = 10 kΩ.
3. Therefore, $R_2 = 10 \times 10 \times 10^3$ = 100 kΩ.
4. The largest input signal amplitude = 300 mV.
5. Corresponding output signal = $300 \times 10^{-3} \times 10$ = 3000 mV = 3 V.
6. Highest sine wave frequency that would be faithfully amplified is given by f_{MAX} = Slew rate/$2\pi V_{o(max)}$.
7. Solving this equation, we get f_{MAX} = 26.5 kHz.

EXAMPLE 17.2

Design an opamp based non-inverting amplifier having a voltage gain of 11. Determine the input impedance of this amplifier if the chosen opamp has an open-loop gain of 100,000 and open-loop input impedance of 1 MΩ.

Solution

1. Figure 17.9 shows the basic non-inverting amplifier circuit.
2. Voltage gain of this amplifier is given by $[1 + (R_2/R_1)]$.
3. Therefore, $1 + R_2/R_1 = 11$. This gives $R_2/R_1 = 10$.
4. Let us choose R_1 = 10 kΩ. This gives R_2 = 100 kΩ.
5. Input impedance of this amplifier = Open-loop input impedance × Loop gain.
6. Loop gain = Open-loop gain/Closed-loop gain = 100,000/11 = 9090.91.
7. Therefore, input impedance = $1 \times 10^6 \times 9090.91$ = 9090.91 MΩ.

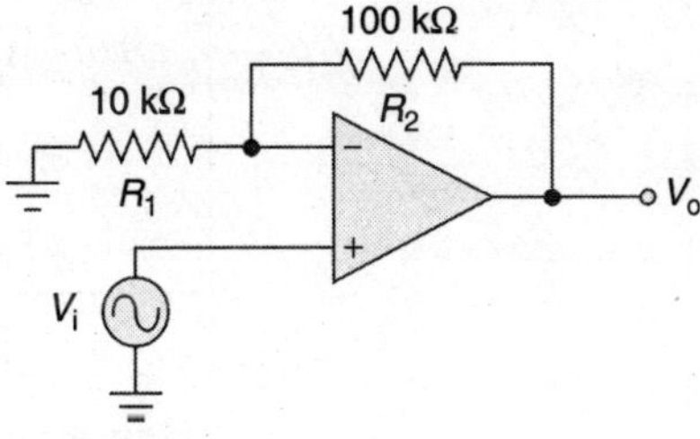

Figure 17.9 Example 17.2.

EXAMPLE 17.3

Refer to the inverting amplifier circuit of Figure 17.10. Determine the voltage gain of the circuit when the voltage applied to the gate of junction FET is (a) 0 V and (b) –5 V given that JFET has r_d = 500 Ω and $V_{GS(OFF)}$ = –5 V.

Solution

1. When V_{GS} = 0, JFET is conducting and its r_d = 500 Ω. Since the externally connected drain resistance is much larger than r_d, the non-inverting terminal is grounded for all practical purposes. Therefore, voltage gain = $(-100 \times 10^3)/(100 \times 10^3) = -1$.
2. When V_{GS} = –5 V, JFET is in cut-off state. The circuit in this case acts both like a non-inverting amplifier and an inverting amplifier simultaneously. Non-inverting voltage gain is $1 + (100 \times 10^3)/(100 \times 10^3) = 2$ and inverting voltage gain is $(-100 \times 10^3)/(100 \times 10^3) = -1$. This gives an overall voltage gain of 1.

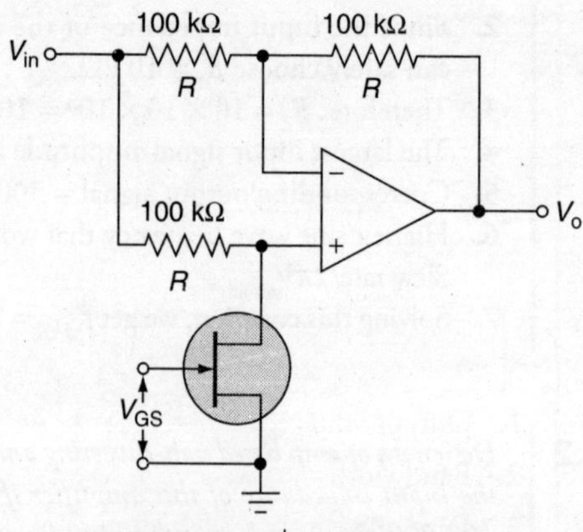

Figure 17.10 | Example 17.3.

EXAMPLE 17.4 *Refer to the amplifier circuit of Figure 17.11. Determine the voltage gain of the amplifier when the variable terminal of the potentiometer is at (a) point A and (b) point B.*

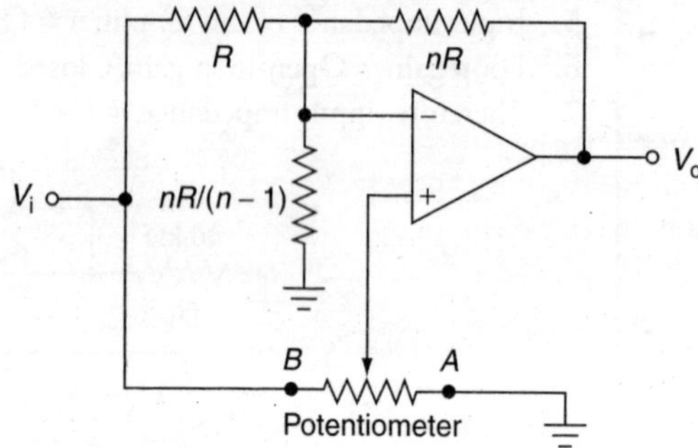

Figure 17.11 | Example 17.4.

Solution

1. When the variable terminal of the potentiometer is at A, the non-inverting terminal is grounded. The amplifier is a simple inverting amplifier with a voltage gain of $-(nR/R) = -n$.
2. When the variable terminal of the potentiometer is at B, the opamp acts both like a non-inverting and an inverting amplifier. Voltage gain in this condition is equal to a non-inverting voltage gain of

$$1+\frac{nR(2n-1)}{nR} = 2n$$

and an inverting voltage gain of $-nR/R = -n$. Net voltage gain in this condition is therefore equal to $2n - n = n$.

EXAMPLE 17.5 *Refer to the voltage-follower circuit of Figure 17.12. Determine (a) no load output voltage, (b) bandwidth and (c) closed-loop output impedance if the voltage observed across the load of 10 Ω were 99.5 mV. The opamp used has a unity gain cross-over frequency of 1 MHz.*

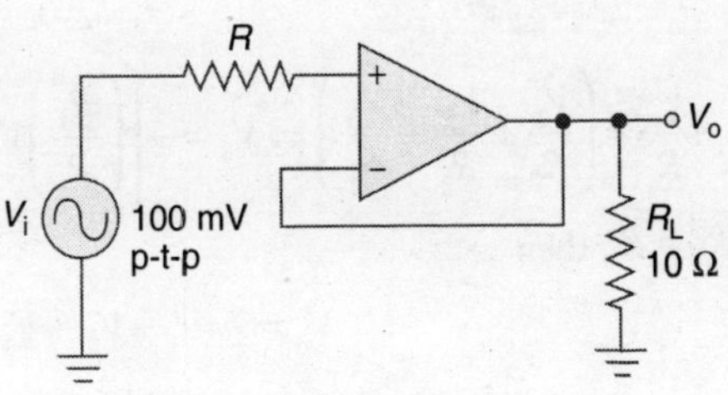

Figure 17.12 Example 17.5.

Solution

1. Output voltage = 100 mV as the voltage gain is unity.
2. Bandwidth = Unity gain cross-over frequency = 1 MHz.
3. Load current = $(99.5 \times 10^{-3})/10 = 9.95$ mA.
4. Therefore, closed-loop output impedance = $(100 \times 10^{-3} - 99.5 \times 10^{-3})/(9.95 \times 10^{-3}) = (0.5 \times 10^{-3})/(9.95 \times 10^{-3}) = 0.05\ \Omega$.

17.4 Summing Amplifier

Summing amplifier produces an output that is equal to the sum of input signals multiplied by their corresponding voltage gain values. In the case of voltage gain being unity for all input signals, the circuit becomes an adder circuit. Again, there are inverting and non-inverting varieties of summing amplifiers. In the case of voltage gain being unity, these behave as inverting and non-inverting adder circuits.

Figure 17.13 shows circuit diagram of three input inverting-type summing amplifier. The expression for output voltage is derived as follows.

$$I_1 = \frac{V_1}{R_1},\quad I_2 = \frac{V_2}{R_2},\quad I_3 = \frac{V_3}{R_3}$$

$$I = I_1 + I_2 + I_3 = \frac{V_1}{R_1} + \frac{V_2}{R_2} + \frac{V_3}{R_3}$$

Also

$$I = -\frac{V_o}{R_4}$$

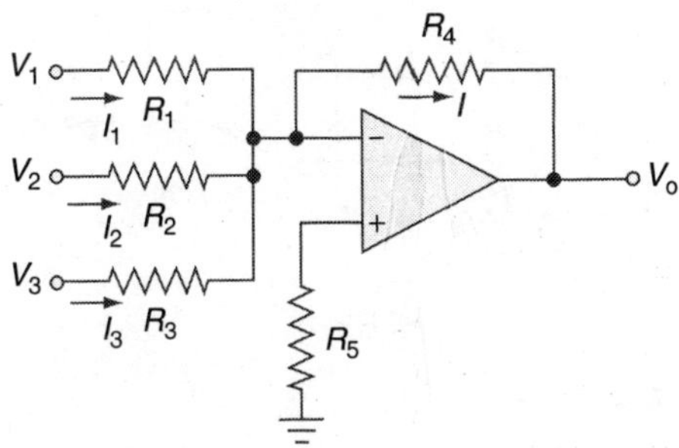

Figure 17.13 Inverting-type summing amplifier.

Therefore

$$-\frac{V_o}{R_4} = \left(\frac{V_1}{R_1} + \frac{V_2}{R_2} + \frac{V_3}{R_3}\right) \Rightarrow V_o = -\left[\left(\frac{R_4}{R_1}\right)V_1 + \left(\frac{R_4}{R_2}\right)V_2 + \left(\frac{R_4}{R_3}\right)V_3\right] \quad (17.16)$$

If $R_1 = R_2 = R_3 = R_4 = R$, then

$$V_o = -(V_1 + V_2 + V_3) \quad (17.17)$$

A non-inverting summing amplifier can be constructed from its inverting counterpart by cascading it with a unity gain inverting amplifier. The complete circuit is shown in Figure 17.14. If the values of resistors R_1, R_2, R_3 and R_4 are equal and values of resistors R_6 and R_7 are also equal, then the circuit in Figure 17.14 behaves as a non-inverting adder.

Assuming $R_1 = R_2 = R_3 = R_4 = R$ and $R_6 = R_7 = R'$, we have

$$V_{o1} = -(V_1 + V_2 + V_3) \quad (17.18)$$

$$V_{o2} = -V_{o1} = V_1 + V_2 + V_3 \quad (17.19)$$

An alternative non-inverting adder circuit, where the summing has been done at the non-inverting input, is shown in Figure 17.15. The given circuit behaves like a non-inverting amplifier with a gain of 1 to both the inputs as is evident from the following discussion.

In the case of circuit shown in Figure 17.15, with only V_1 present and V_2 grounded, voltage V_1' at non-inverting input is given by

$$V_1' = V_1 \times [(R/2)/\{R + (R/2)\}] = V_1/3 \quad (17.20)$$

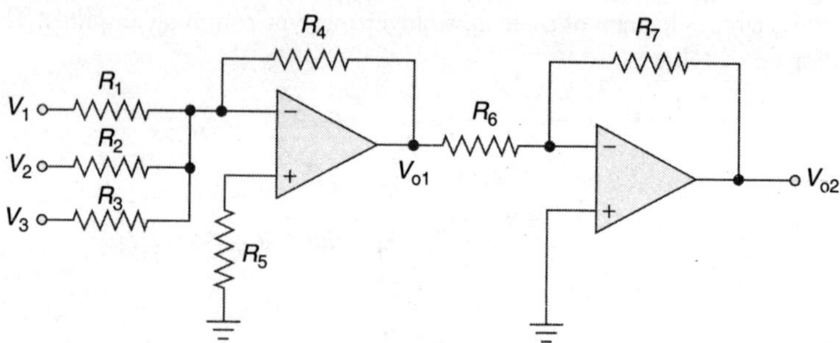

Figure 17.14 Non-inverting type summing amplifier.

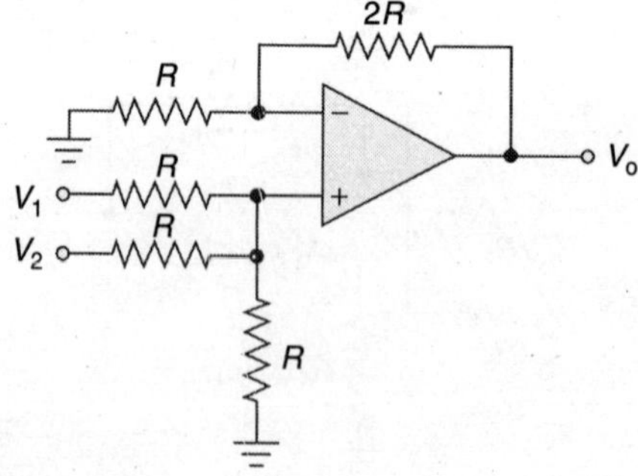

Figure 17.15 Non-inverting adder with single opamp.

This voltage gets amplified by a gain factor $(1 + 2R/R) = 3$ to produce V_1 at the output. Similarly, with V_1 grounded, V_2 also appears as V_2 at the output. When both inputs V_1 and V_2 are simultaneously present, output is $V_1 + V_2$, that is,

$$V_o = V_1 + V_2 \tag{17.21}$$

If the adder circuit of Figure 17.15 were to be used for adding n inputs, the feedback resistor value would be equal to nR.

17.5 Difference Amplifier

Difference amplifier produces an output that is equal to the difference of the two input signals multiplied by their corresponding voltage gain values. In the case of voltage gain being unity for the two input signals, the circuit becomes a subtractor circuit. Figure 17.16 shows the generalized form of a difference amplifier. Expression for the output is derived as follows.

With V_1 grounded, output V_{o2} due to V_2 alone is given by

$$V_{o2} = V_2 \times \left(\frac{R_4}{R_3 + R_4}\right) \times \left(1 + \frac{R_2}{R_1}\right) \tag{17.22}$$

With V_2 grounded, output V_{o1} due to V_1 alone is given by

$$V_{o1} = -V_1 \times \left(\frac{R_2}{R_1}\right) \tag{17.23}$$

When both inputs are present simultaneously, the output is equal to algebraic sum of the two. That is,

$$V_o = V_{o1} + V_{o2} = V_2 \times \left(\frac{R_4}{R_3 + R_4}\right) \times \left(1 + \frac{R_2}{R_1}\right) - V_1 \times \left(\frac{R_2}{R_1}\right) \tag{17.24}$$

For $R_1 = R_2 = R_3 = R_4 = R$, we get

$$V_{o1} = -V_1 \text{ and } V_{o2} = V_2$$

This gives

$$V_o = V_2 - V_1 \tag{17.25}$$

Figure 17.17 shows an alternative configuration for designing a subtractor circuit. With V_2 grounded, V_1 appears as $-V_1$ at the output of first opamp and as V_1 at the output of the second opamp. With V_1 grounded, V_2 appears as $-V_2$ at the output. When both inputs are simultaneously present, output is equal to $V_1 - V_2$.

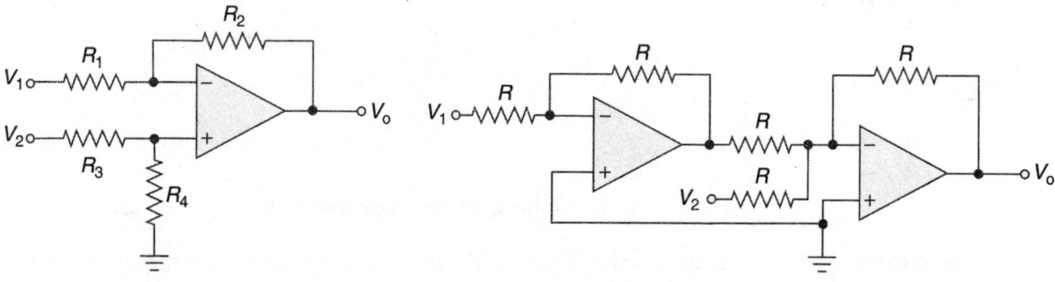

Figure 17.16 | Difference amplifier.

Figure 17.17 | Alternative form of subtractor circuit

17.6 Averager

An averager circuit produces an output that is equal to the average of the amplitudes of the applied input signals. Figure 17.18 shows the generalized form of an inverting averager circuit for n inputs. The circuit configuration is similar to that of an inverting-type summing amplifier. The circuit functions as follows. With only one input present at a time and all other inputs grounded, the gain value is $-1/n$. That is, each input is multiplied by a gain value equal to $-1/n$. When all the inputs are present simultaneously, the output is given by

$$V_o = -\left[\left(\frac{V_1}{n}\right)+\left(\frac{V_2}{n}\right)+\left(\frac{V_3}{n}\right)+\cdots+\left(\frac{V_n}{n}\right)\right] \tag{17.26}$$

$$V_o = -\left(\frac{V_1+V_2+V_3+\cdots+V_n}{n}\right) \tag{17.27}$$

A non-inverting averager may be built by connecting a unity gain inverting amplifier at the output of the circuit shown in Figure 17.18.

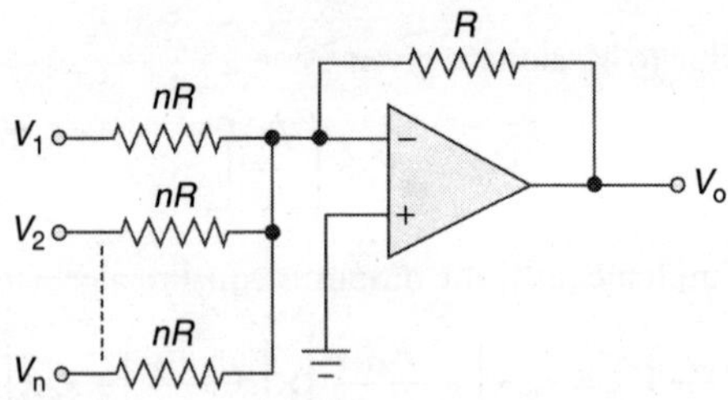

Figure 17.18 | Inverting-type averager circuit.

EXAMPLE 17.6 *Refer to the summing amplifier circuit of Figure 17.19. Derive the expression for output V_o.*

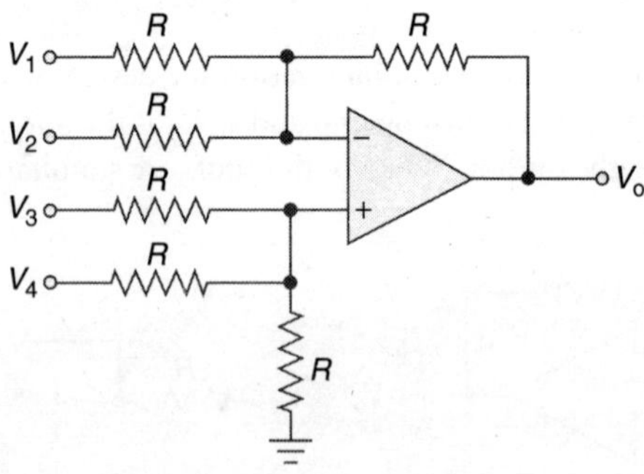

Figure 17.19 | Example 17.6.

Solution

1. Let us assume that V_{o1}, V_{o2}, V_{o3} and V_{o4} are the outputs, respectively, for V_1, V_2, V_3 and V_4 present one at a time with other inputs grounded.
2. With only V_1 present and all other inputs grounded, output $V_{o1} = -V_1$.

3. With only V_2 present and all other inputs grounded, output $V_{o2} = -V_2$.
4. With only V_3 present and all other inputs grounded, voltage appearing at non-inverting input is given by $(V_3 \times R/2)/[R + (R/2)] = V_3/3$. This gives output $V_{o3} = V_3/3 \times [1 + R/(R/2)] = V_3/3 \times 3 = V_3$.
5. Similarly, with only V_4 present and all other inputs grounded, output $V_{o4} = V_4$.
6. When all inputs are present simultaneously, output V_o equals algebraic sum of V_{o1}, V_{o2}, V_{o3} and V_{o4}.
7. That is, $V_o = V_3 + V_4 - V_2 - V_1$.

EXAMPLE 17.7 *Refer to the summing amplifier circuit of Figure 17.20. Derive the expression for the output V_o.*

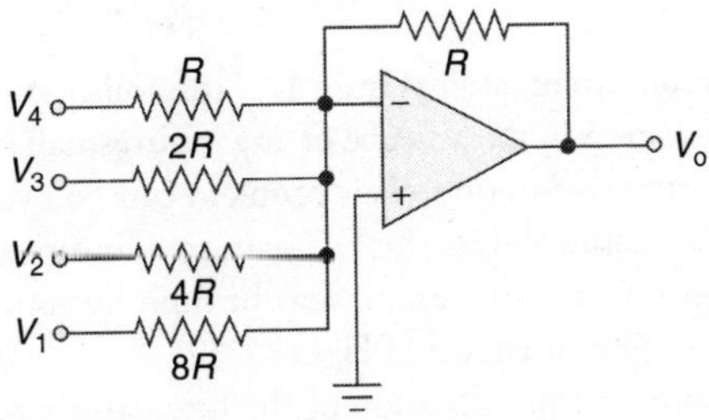

Figure 17.20 Example 17.7.

Solution

1. Let us assume that V_{o1}, V_{o2}, V_{o3} and V_{o4} are the outputs, respectively, for only V_1, V_2, V_3 and V_4 present one at a time with other inputs grounded.
2. $V_{o4} = -V_4 \times R/R = -V_4$.
3. $V_{o3} = -V_3 \times R/2R = -V_3/2$.
4. $V_{o2} = -V_2 \times R/4R = -V_2/4$.
5. $V_{o1} = -V_1 \times R/8R = -V_1/8$.
6. With all inputs present simultaneously, $V_o = -[V_4 + V_3/2 + V_2/4 + V_1/8]$.

17.7 Integrator

An integrator circuit is the one that produces an output proportional to the integral of the input. Figure 17.21 shows the circuit diagram of the basic opamp-based integrator. Since non-inverting input terminal has been grounded, *R-C* junction is also at ground potential due to virtual earth phenomenon in opamps. Thus, the voltage V_o effectively is the voltage across the capacitor *C*.

Assuming the opamp to be ideal, due to infinite impedance at the input terminals of the opamp, current flowing through resistor *R* flows through capacitor *C* too.

$$I = \frac{V_i}{R} = -\frac{C\mathrm{d}V_o}{\mathrm{d}t}$$

so that,

$$V_o = -\frac{1}{RC}\int V_i \mathrm{d}t = K\int V_i \mathrm{d}t$$

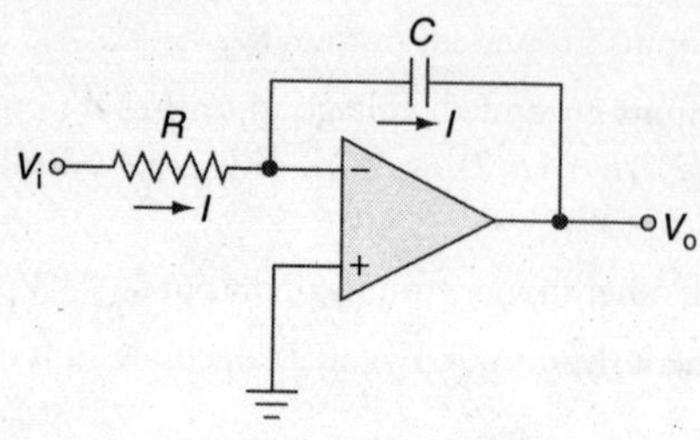

Figure 17.21 | Basic integrator.

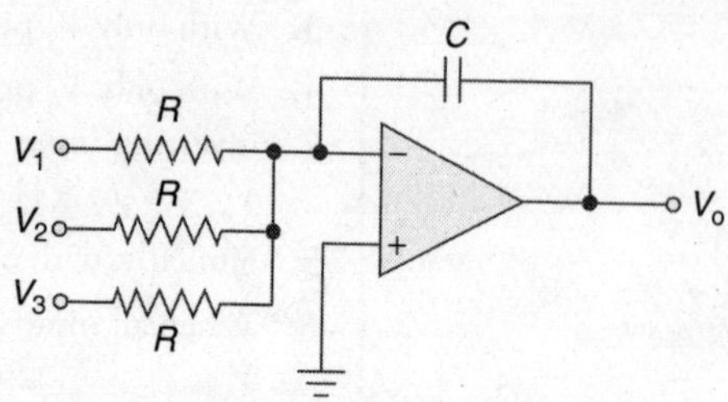

Figure 17.22 | Summing integrator.

Thus

$$V_o = K \int V_i \mathrm{d}t \tag{17.28}$$

where $K = -1/RC$.

The basic integrator circuit suffers from DC instability problems. The circuit offers a very high gain to DC which means that even in the absence of any input, small input offset voltage might cause the output to go to positive or negative saturation. This problem can be overcome by connecting a relatively large value resistor across *C*. This resistor limits the DC gain to a lower value and it may be chosen to be 10 times the input resistor *R*. Non-inverting integrator may be built by connecting a unity gain inverting amplifier at the output of inverting integrator circuit of Figure 17.21.

Figure 17.22 shows another variation of the integrator circuit. The circuit produces an output proportional to sum of integrals of multiple inputs. That is

$$V_o = K\left(\int V_1 \mathrm{d}t + \int V_2 \mathrm{d}t + \int V_3 \mathrm{d}t\right) \tag{17.29}$$

where $K = -1/RC$.

17.8 Differentiator

A differentiator circuit is the one that produces an output proportional to the differential of the input. Figure 17.23 shows the circuit diagram of the basic opamp-based differentiator. Since non-inverting input terminal has been grounded, *R-C* junction is also at ground potential due to virtual earth phenomenon in opamps. Thus, the voltage V_o effectively is the voltage across resistor *R*.

Assuming the opamp to be ideal, due to infinite impedance at the input terminals of the opamp, current flowing through resistance *R* flows through capacitor *C* too.

$$I = C\frac{\mathrm{d}V_i}{\mathrm{d}t} = -\frac{V_o}{R}$$

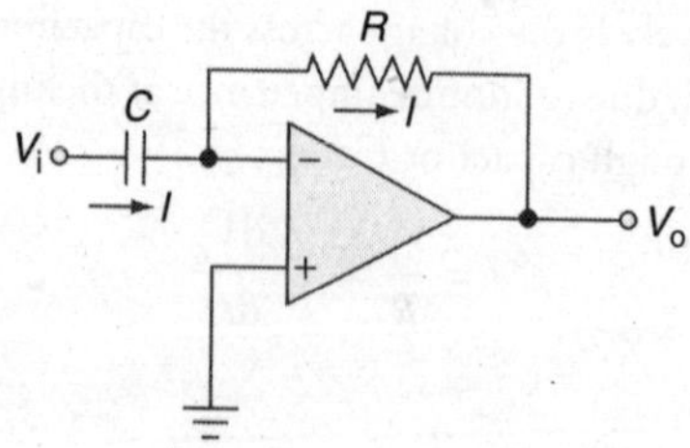

Figure 17.23 | Basic differentiator.

so that

$$V_o = -RC\frac{dV_i}{dt} \quad (17.30)$$

$$V_o = K\frac{dV_i}{dt}$$

where $K = -RC$. For $RC = 1$,

$$V_o = -\frac{dV_i}{dt}$$

Basic differentiator circuit has a tendency to go to oscillations at relatively higher frequencies. The problem can be overcome by connecting a resistor in series with the input capacitor. The resistor limits the gain at higher frequencies. The value of this resistor may be chosen to be in the range of one-tenth to one-hundredth of the feedback resistor. Non-inverting integrator may be built by connecting a unity gain inverting amplifier at the output of inverting differentiator circuit of Figure 17.23.

Figure 17.24 shows the schematic arrangement of a summing differentiator. Expression for output is derived as follows.

$$I_1 = C\frac{dV_1}{dt}, \quad I_2 = C\frac{dV_2}{dt}, \quad I_3 = C\frac{dV_3}{dt}$$

$$I = I_1 + I_2 + I_3 = C\left[\frac{dV_1}{dt} + \frac{dV_2}{dt} + \frac{dV_3}{dt}\right]$$

The current flowing towards inverting input terminal of the opamp is zero. This gives current through $R = I = (-V_o/R)$. This implies

$$-\frac{V_o}{R} = C\left[\frac{dV_1}{dt} + \frac{dV_2}{dt} + \frac{dV_3}{dt}\right] \quad (17.31)$$

$$V_o = -RC\left[\frac{dV_1}{dt} + \frac{dV_2}{dt} + \frac{dV_3}{dt}\right]$$

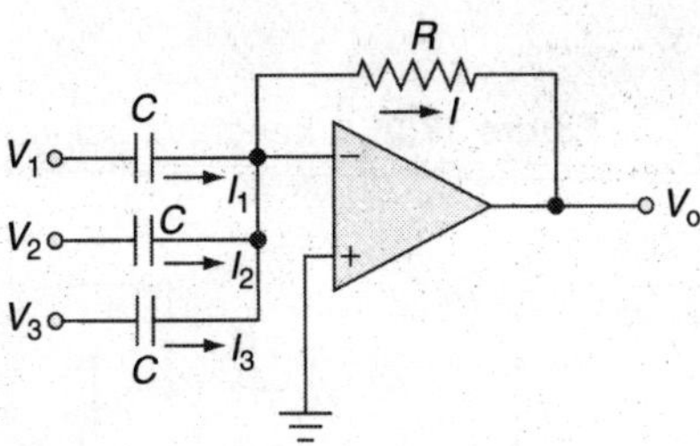

Figure 17.24 Summing differentiator.

EXAMPLE 17.8 *It is required to design an opamp-based circuit that generates an output $V_o = (\sin t - \cos t)$ from the available inputs $V_1 = \sin t$ and $V_2 = \cos t$. Design the circuit using (a) integrator configuration and (b) differentiator configuration.*

Solution

1. **Integrator configuration**
   - Summing integrator fed at its input by V_1 and V_2 and a unity gain inverting amplifier configuration connected at its output serves the purpose. Figure 17.25 shows the circuit diagram.
   - V_o' at the output of first opamp is given by $V_o' = -\int(V_1 + V_2)\mathrm{d}t$ provided that $R_1C = 1$ s.
   - Final output V_o is given by $-[-\int(V_1 + V_2)\mathrm{d}t] = \int(V_1 + V_2)\mathrm{d}t = \int(\sin t + \cos t)\mathrm{d}t = \sin t - \cos t$.
   - If R_1 is chosen to be equal to 10 kΩ, then for $R_1C = 1$ s, $C = 100$ μF.
   - R_2 may be taken as 10 times the value of R_1. That is, $R_2 = 100$ kΩ.
2. **Differentiator configuration**
   - Figure 17.26 shows the opamp-based differentiator circuit to implement the intended function.
   - $V_o = -\dfrac{\mathrm{d}(V_1 + V_2)}{\mathrm{d}t}$ provided that $R_1C = 1$ s.
   - $V_o = -\dfrac{\mathrm{d}(\sin t + \cos t)}{\mathrm{d}t} = \sin t - \cos t$.
   - If R_1 is chosen to be equal to 10 kΩ, then for $R_1C = 1$ s, $C = 100$ μF.
   - R_2 may be chosen to be equal to $0.01 \times R_1$. That is $R_2 = 100$ Ω.

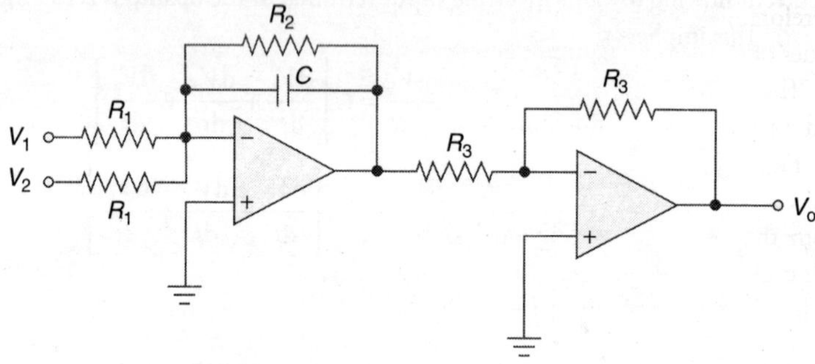

Figure 17.25 | Integrator solution for Example 17.8.

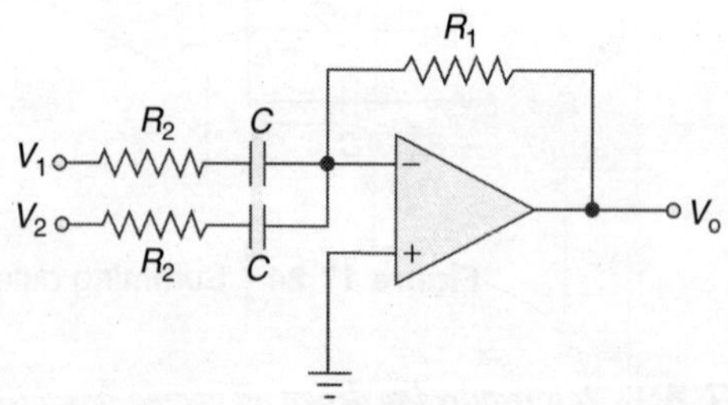

Figure 17.26 | Differentiator solution for Example 17.8.

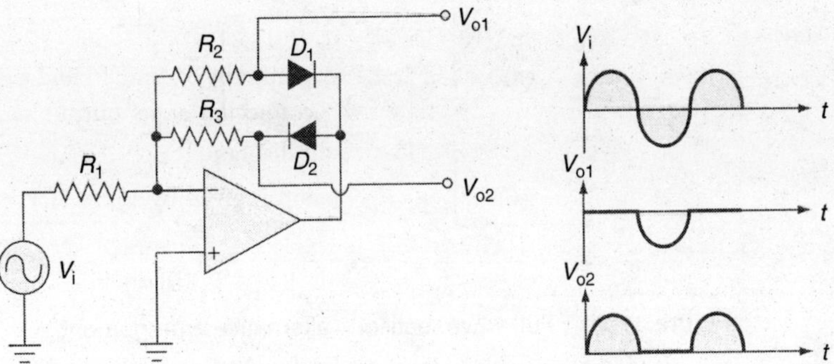

Figure 17.27 | Half-wave rectifier.

17.9 Rectifier Circuits

Conventional rectifier circuits do not produce an ideal rectified waveform at the output due to forward-biased voltage drop across the diode, which is 0.7 V in the case of silicon diodes. This problem is overcome in opamp-based rectifier circuits. Figure 17.27 shows the generalized half-wave rectifier circuit built around an opamp. The circuit functions as follows. Owing to non-inverting input of the opamp being at ground potential, during positive half cycles, diode (D_1) is forward-biased and the diode (D_2) is reverse-biased. The positive half cycles appear as negative half cycles due to phase inversion. Similarly, during negative half cycles, diode (D_1) is reverse-biased and diode (D_2) is forward-biased with the result that negative half cycles appear as positive half cycles again due to phase inversion. Remember that the moment input increases by a few milli-volts either in positive or in negative direction, the output tends to go to negative or positive saturation, respectively. It is therefore not necessary for the input to exceed the diode drop to produce the output. However, maximum values of peak positive output and peak negative output are (V_{SAT} – 0.7) and (–V_{SAT} + 0.7), respectively.

The two half-wave rectified outputs can be summed up in another opamp stage to get a full-wave rectified output as shown in Figure 17.28.

Figure 17.29 shows an alternative circuit arrangement for building a full-wave rectifier. During positive half cycle of the input signal, the diode is reverse-biased and therefore the feedback resistor is disconnected from the output of the opamp. The positive half cycles appear as such at the output. During negative half cycles, the diode is forward-biased. The negative half cycles get inverted and again appear as positive half cycles. Thus the output is a full-wave rectified signal.

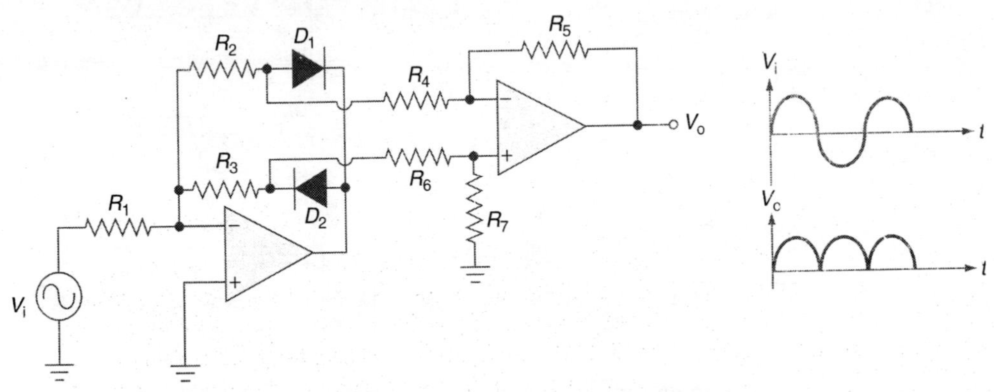

Figure 17.28 | Full-wave rectifier.

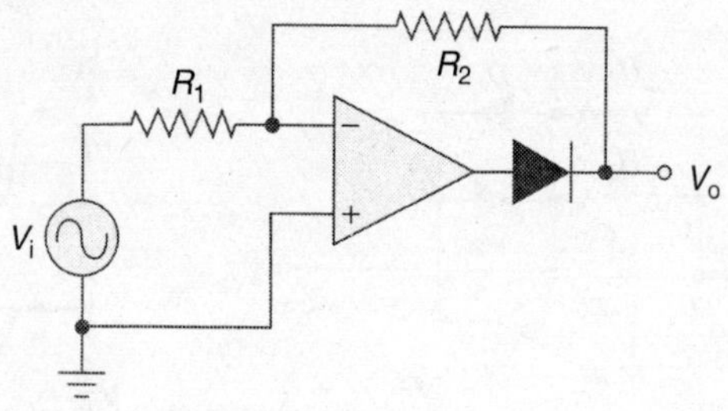

Figure 17.29 | Full-wave rectifier – alternative arrangement.

17.10 Clipper Circuits

Figure 17.30(a) shows a positive clipper circuit, a clipper circuit that clips positive half cycles above a certain reference voltage. The circuit functions as follows. During positive half cycles, for input voltages less than or equal to reference voltage (V_{REF}), the opamp output goes to positive saturation and diode (D_1) is reverse-biased with the result that the input appears as such at the output. The situation is the same during negative half cycles. When the input voltage exceeds the reference voltage (V_{REF}), the opamp output tends to go to negative saturation and the diode gets forward-biased. The output gets shorted to inverting input and the output is clamped to V_{REF}. The input and output waveforms are shown in Figure 17.30(b). If the polarity of the reference voltage is reversed in the clipper circuit of Figure 17.30(a), the clipping occurs below zero voltage as shown in Figure 17.30(b).

Figure 17.31(a) shows a negative clipper circuit. The circuit functions as follows. During positive half cycles and also for input voltages less negative or equal to $-V_{REF}$, diode D_1 is reverse-biased. The input appears as such at the output. For input voltages more negative than $-V_{REF}$, diode D_1 is forward-biased and the output gets clamped at the reference voltage. The input and output waveforms are shown in

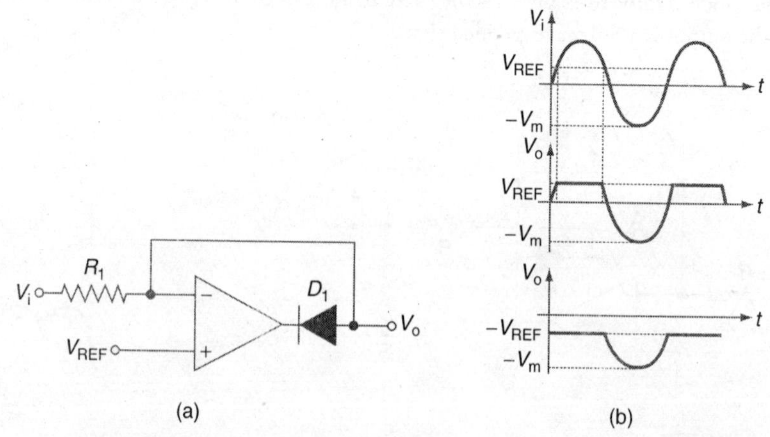

Figure 17.30 | Positive clipper circuit and relevant waveforms.

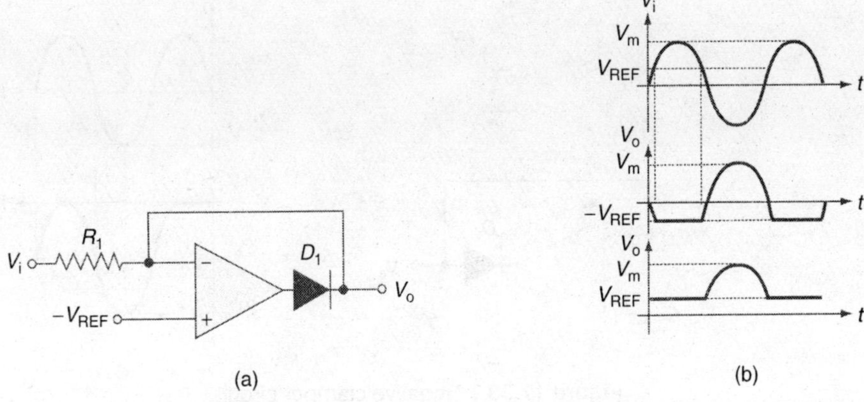

Figure 17.31 | Negative clipper circuit.

Figure 17.31(b). When the polarity of the reference voltage is reversed, clipping occurs above zero voltage. The output waveform in this case is also shown in Figure 17.31(b).

17.11 Clamper Circuits

Figure 17.32 shows the positive clamper circuit that clamps the negative peaks to zero. The circuit operates as follows. During the first negative half cycle, diode D_1 gets forward-biased and capacitor C charges through resistance R and the forward-biased diode to the peak of the negative half cycle voltage. During the positive cycle, the diode gets reverse-biased. There is no rapid discharge path for the capacitor and in this case, the output equals the input voltage plus the voltage across the capacitor. The negative peaks are thus clamped to zero voltage. If a reference voltage (V_{REF}), positive or negative, is applied to the non-inverting input terminal, the negative peaks are clamped at V_{REF} instead of zero. Figure 17.33 shows the negative clamper circuit that clamps positive peaks to zero.

The conventional clamper circuit cannot function as a clamper if the peak input signal is less than 0.7 V. The opamp-based clamper circuit has no such limitation. It functions as if the diode were ideal. This implies that the circuit can be used to clamp even milli-volt signals.

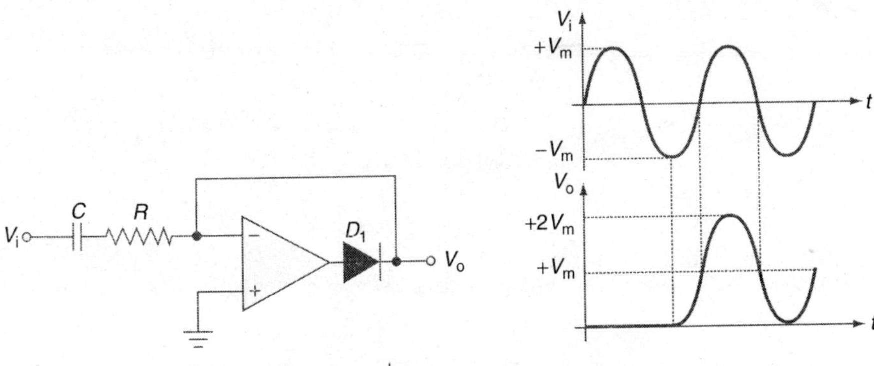

Figure 17.32 | Positive clamper circuit.

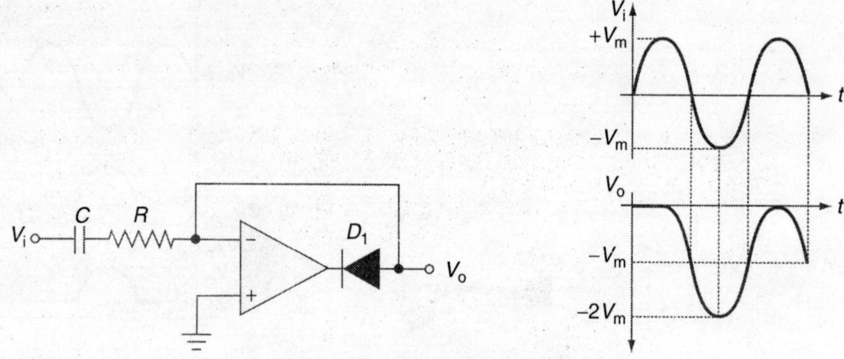

Figure 17.33 | Negative clamper circuit.

17.12 Peak Detector Circuit

Peak detector circuit produces a voltage at the output equal to peak amplitude (positive or negative) of the input signal. Figure 17.34 shows a positive peak detector circuit. As we can see, it is essentially a clipper circuit with a parallel resistor–capacitor connected at its output. The clipper here reproduces the positive half cycles. During this period, the diode D_1 is forward-biased. The capacitor rapidly charges to the positive peak from the output of the opamp through the ON resistance of the forward-biased diode. As the input starts decreasing beyond the peak, the diode gets reverse-biased, thus isolating the capacitor from the output of the opamp. The capacitor can now discharge only through the resistor (R) connected across it. The value of the resistor is much larger than the forward-biased diode's ON resistance. The purpose of this resistor is to allow a discharge path so that the output can respond to changing amplitudes of the signal peaks, decreasing amplitudes of the signal peaks to be more precise. The buffer circuit connected ahead of the capacitor prevents any discharge of the capacitor due to loading effects of the following circuit. The circuit can be made to respond to the negative peaks by reversing the polarity of the diode. Rest of the circuit is the same as in Figure 17.34.

The parallel R-C circuit time constant is typically 100 times the time period corresponding to the minimum frequency of operation. The R-C time constant also controls the response time. The response time is nothing but the time needed to respond to a decreasing peak amplitude of the input signal. Surely,

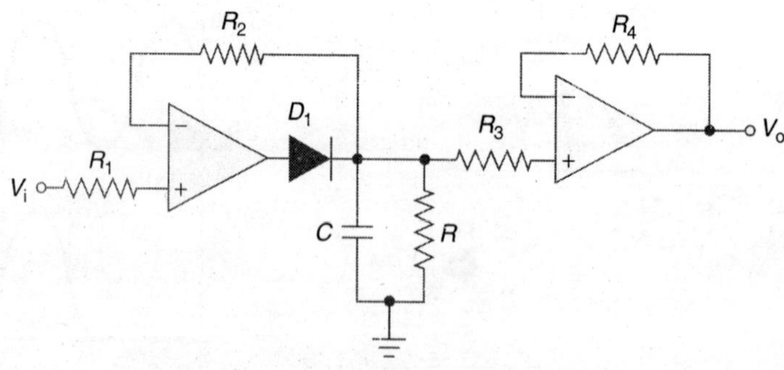

Figure 17.34 | Peak detector circuit.

a large time constant would make the response more sluggish. An attempt to reduce the time constant to improve the response time increases the output ripple. The chosen time constant is a compromise of the two conflicting requirements. Slew rate is the primary specification that needs to be looked into while choosing the right opamp for the clipper portion. The desired slew rate is such that the slew rate limited frequency, which is a function of peak-to-peak output swing and the slew rate, is at least equal to the highest frequency of operation. The peak-to-peak voltage swing at the output of the opamp is equal to $V_{pk} - (-V_{SAT}) = (V_{pk} + V_{SAT})$. Here V_{pk} is the maximum peak amplitude of the input signal and $-V_{SAT}$ is the maximum negative output voltage of the opamp.

17.13 Absolute Value Circuit

Figure 17.35 shows one possible opamp configuration that produces at its output a voltage equal to the absolute value of the input voltage. The circuit shown is a dual half-wave rectifier circuit discussed earlier followed by a difference amplifier. The circuit functions as follows.

When the applied input is of positive polarity (say $+V$), diode D_1 is forward-biased and diode D_2 is reverse-biased. The circuit reduces to what is shown in Figure 17.36. Simple mathematics shows that output (V_o) in this case is equal to $+V$. When the applied input is of negative polarity (say $-V$), diode D_1 is reverse-biased and diode D_2 is forward-biased. The equivalent circuit in this case is shown in Figure 17.37. By applying Kirchhoff's current law (KCL) at the inverting terminal of the first opamp, we can determine voltage (V_x) to be equal to $(2/3)V$. Also, V_x is related to V_o by $V_x = (2/3)V_o$. This implies that $V_o = V$. Thus the output always equals the absolute value of the input signal.

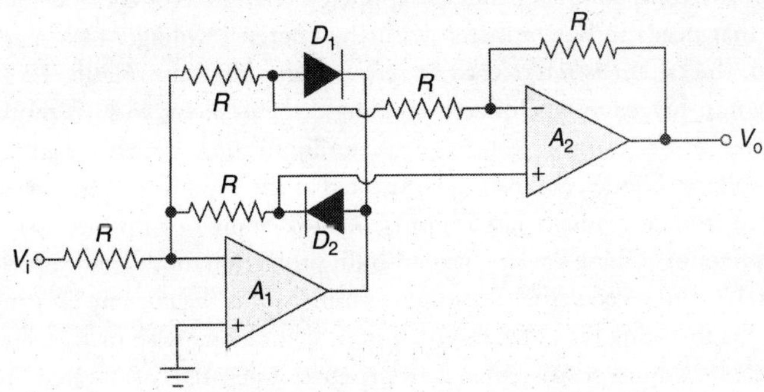

Figure 17.35 Absolute value circuit.

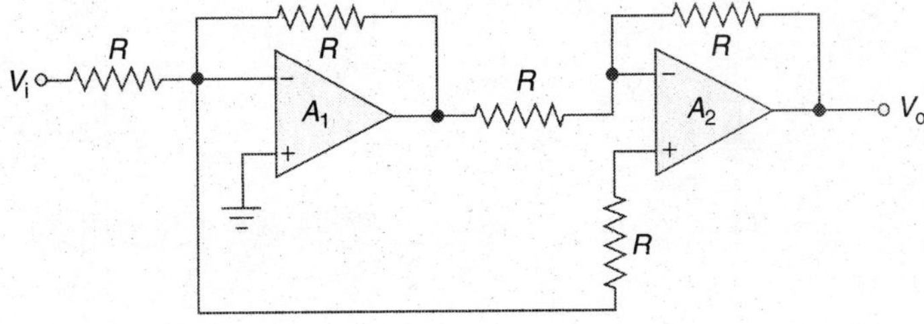

Figure 17.36 Equivalent absolute value circuit with positive input.

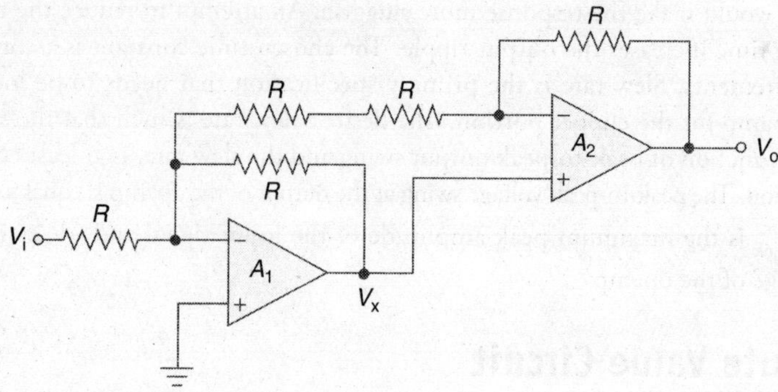

Figure 17.37 | Equivalent absolute value circuit for negative input.

17.14 Comparator

A comparator circuit is a two-input, one-output building block that produces a high or low output depending upon the relative magnitudes of the two inputs. An opamp can be very conveniently used as a comparator when used without negative feedback. Because of very large value of open-loop voltage gain, it produces either positively saturated or negatively saturated output voltage depending upon whether the amplitude of the voltage applied at the non-inverting input terminal is more or less positive than the voltage applied at the inverting input terminal.

One of the inputs of the comparator is generally applied a reference voltage and the other input is fed with the input voltage that needs to be compared with the reference voltage. In a special case where the reference voltage is zero, the circuit is referred to as zero-crossing detector. Figure 17.38 shows the basic circuit arrangement of a non-inverting type of zero-crossing detector along with its transfer characteristics. It is called a non-inverting zero-crossing detector because an input more positive than zero leads to a positively saturated output voltage. Diodes D_1 and D_2 connected at the input are to protect the sensitive input circuits inside the opamp from excessively large input voltages. Some opamps are specially designed and optimized for use as comparators. These devices have in-built protection diodes and therefore do not require external diode clamps to be connected across the input terminals. R is the current-limiting resistor.

Figure 17.39 shows the inverting type of zero-crossing detector along with its transfer characteristics. In this case, input voltage slightly more positive than zero produces a negatively saturated output voltage. One

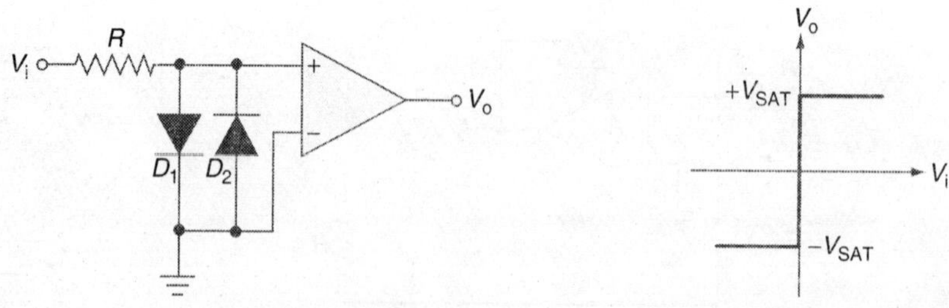

Figure 17.38 | Non-inverting zero-crossing detector.

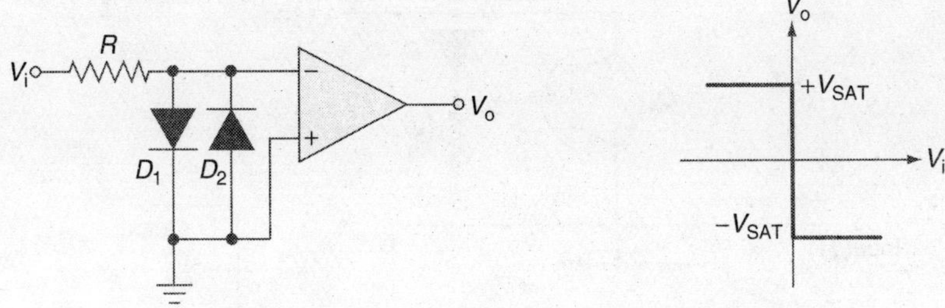

Figure 17.39 | Inverting zero-crossing detector.

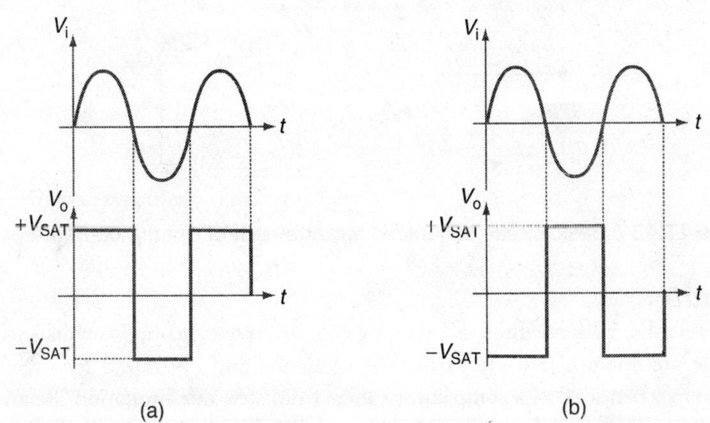

Figure 17.40 | Waveforms of (a) non-inverting zero-crossing detector; (b) inverting zero-crossing detector.

common application of zero-crossing detector is to convert sine wave signal to a square wave signal. Figures 17.40(a) and (b) respectively show relevant waveforms for non-inverting and inverting type of zero-crossing detector circuits.

In the generalized case, reference voltage may be a positive or a negative voltage. Figure 17.41 shows the circuit diagram of non-inverting comparator for a positive reference voltage. V_{REF} in this case is given by $+V_{CC} \times [R_2/(R_1 + R_2)]$. Figure 17.42 shows the circuit diagram of non-inverting comparator for a negative reference voltage. Reference voltage V_{REF} is given by $-V_{CC} \times [R_2/(R_1 + R_2)]$.

Inverting-type voltage comparators can similarly be built for positive and negative reference voltages.

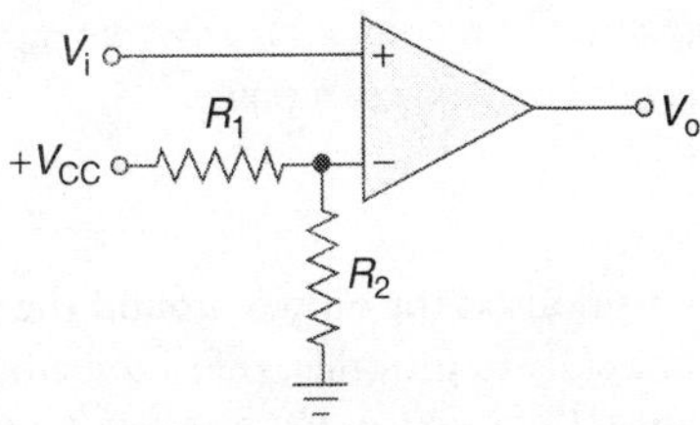

Figure 17.41 | Non-inverting comparator with positive reference.

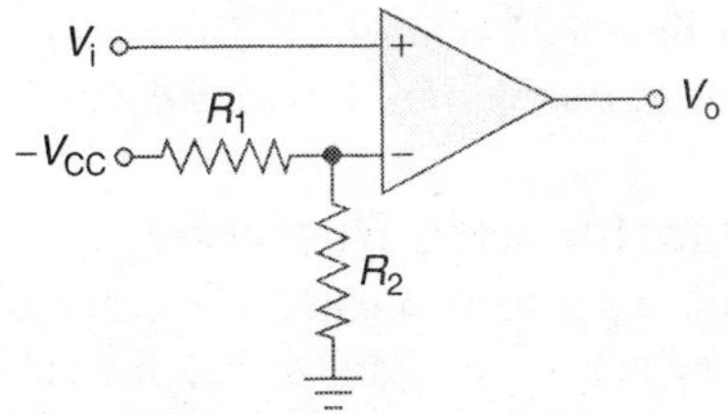

Figure 17.42 | Non-inverting comparator with negative reference.

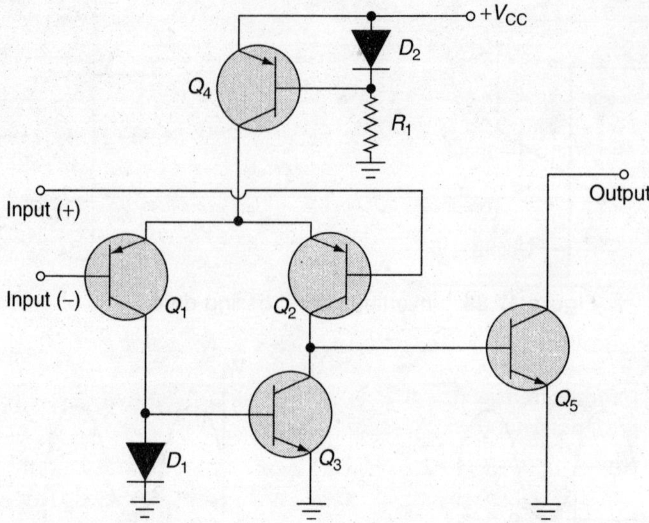

Figure 17.43 | Basic circuit schematic arrangement of opamp comparator.

Opamp Comparator

In the preceding paragraphs, we have discussed use of general-purpose opamps as voltage comparators. As outlined earlier, there are opamps that are particularly designed and optimized for use as comparators. General-purpose opamp when used as a comparator suffers from slew rate limitation. Relatively lower slew rate forces the transition time from one state to the other to be prohibitively large. Though this problem can be overcome by using a high-speed opamp with a higher slew rate specification, a better design approach to overcoming this limitation is by eliminating the compensation capacitor. It may be mentioned here that comparator works as a non-linear circuit element and therefore elimination of compensation capacitor has no derogatory effect on the performance. With compensation capacitor removed, the only capacitance remaining is the stray capacitance across the output. Thus, slew rates can be very high.

Another important parameter of a comparator is its ability to operate from a single supply and interface conveniently with popular logic families. Input circuit of opamp comparator is tailored to meet these two requirements. Figure 17.43 shows the simplified schematic diagram of opamp comparator. As seen in the figure, the output has an open-collector output stage. For the output stage to work properly, the output terminal needs to be connected to the positive supply voltage through an external resistor called pull-up resistor. It is called pull-up resistor as it pulls the output voltage to the supply voltage when the output transistor Q_5 (in Figure 17.43) is in cut-off state. Not all comparators have an open-collector output stage. In fact, pull-up resistor slows down the response time of the comparator. There are opamp comparators with active pull-up output stage that are capable of producing relatively much faster switching times. These comparators need dual power supplies.

Comparator with Hysteresis

When the input signal applied to the comparator contains noise, transitions at the output around the trip point tend to become highly erratic. Instead of being smooth from one state to the other, transition around the trip point is a cluster of pulses with randomly varying pulse width. The problem becomes particularly severe if the input signal were changing slowly. This phenomenon is demonstrated in Figure 17.44.

Figure 17.45(a) shows the circuit schematic of an inverting comparator with hysteresis along with its transfer characteristics. The circuit functions as follows. Let us assume that the output is in positive

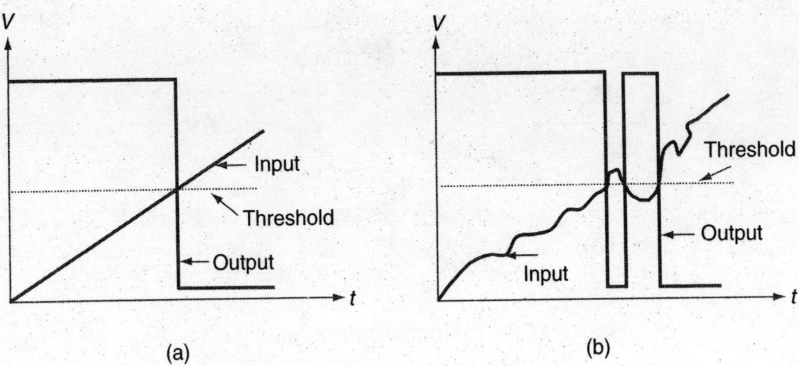

Figure 17.44 Erratic transitions caused by noisy input signal: (a) Ideal input signal; (b) noisy input signal.

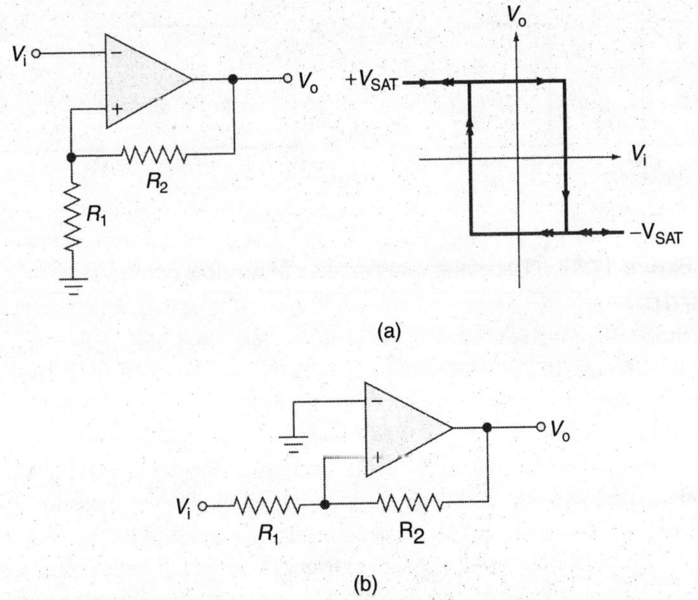

Figure 17.45 (a) Inverting comparator with hysteresis; (b) non-inverting comparator with hysteresis.

saturation ($+V_{SAT}$). Voltage at non-inverting input in this case is $V_{SAT} \times R_1/(R_1 + R_2)$. Due to this small positive voltage at the non-inverting input, the output is reinforced to stay in positive saturation. Now, the input signal needs to be more positive than this voltage for the output to go to negative saturation. Once the output goes to negative saturation ($-V_{SAT}$), voltage fed back to non-inverting input becomes $-V_{SAT} \times R_1/(R_1 + R_2)$. A negative voltage at the non-inverting input reinforces the output to stay in negative saturation. The input signal amplitude needs to become more negative than this for the output to go to positive saturation. In this manner, the circuit offers a hysteresis of $2V_{SAT} \times R_1/(R_1 + R_2)$.

Non-inverting comparator with hysteresis can be built by applying the input signal to the non-inverting input as shown in Figure 17.45(b). Operation of the circuit can be explained on lines similar to that of its inverting counterpart. Upper and lower trip points are, respectively, given by $+V_{SAT} \times R_1/R_2$ and $-V_{SAT} \times R_1/R_2$. Hysteresis in this case is equal to $2V_{SAT} \times R_1/R_2$.

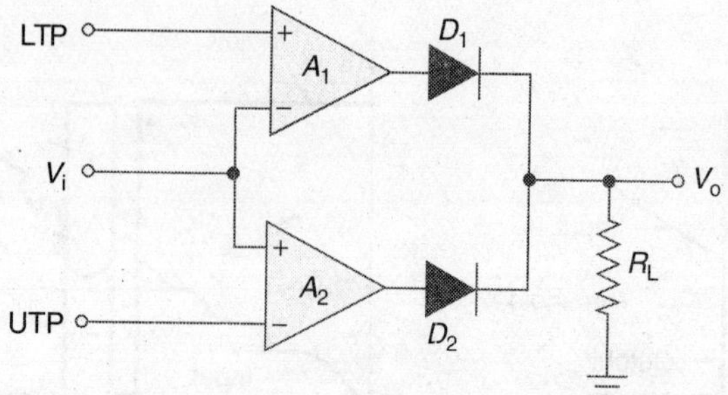

Figure 17.46 | Window comparator.

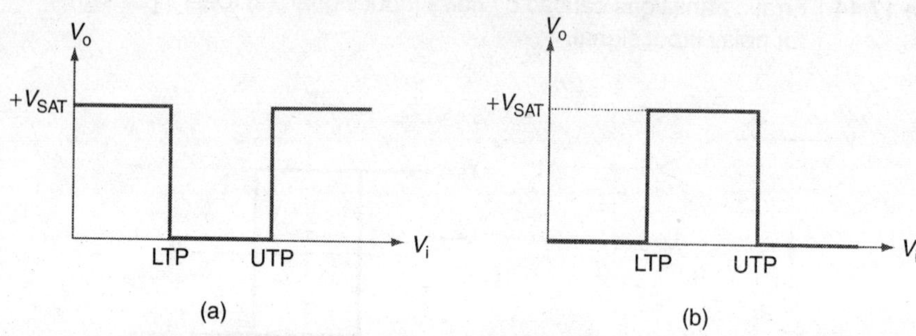

Figure 17.47 | Transfer characteristics of window comparator.

Window Comparator

In the case of a conventional comparator, the output changes state when the input voltage goes above or below the preset reference voltage. In a window comparator, there are two reference voltages called the lower and the upper trip points. Output is in one state when the input is inside the window created by the lower and upper trip points and in the other state when it is outside the window. Figure 17.46 shows the basic circuit diagram of one such window comparator. The circuit functions as follows. When the input voltage is less than the voltage reference corresponding to the lower trip point (LTP), output of opamp A_1 is at $+V_{SAT}$ and that of opamp A_2 is at $-V_{SAT}$. Diodes D_1 and D_2 are respectively forward- and reverse-biased. Consequently, output across R_L is at $+V_{SAT}$. When the input voltage is greater than the reference voltage corresponding to the upper trip point (UTP), the output of opamp A_1 is at $-V_{SAT}$ and that of opamp A_2 is at $+V_{SAT}$. Diodes D_1 and D_2 are respectively reverse- and forward-biased with the result that the output across R_L is again at $+V_{SAT}$. When the input voltage is greater than LTP voltage and lower than UTP voltage, the output of both opamps is at $-V_{SAT}$ with the result that both diodes D_1 and D_2 are reverse-biased and the output across R_L is zero.

Figure 17.47(a) shows the transfer characteristics of this window comparator. The transfer characteristics shown in Figure 17.47(b) can be obtained if we interchange the positions of LTPs and UTPs in Figure 17.46 and the comparators used are the ones with open-collector outputs. In this case a pull-up resistor will be connected from the cathode terminals of both diodes D_1 and D_2 to the supply terminal.

EXAMPLE 17.9 | *Refer to the clamping circuit of Figure 17.48. Determine the peak value of the clamped waveform at the output. Also determine the minimum recommended value of capacitance for the circuit to work as an efficient clamper. Assume the diode to be ideal.*

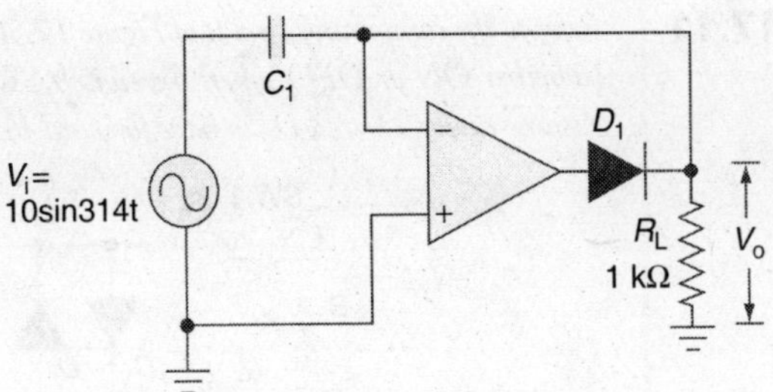

Figure 17.48 | Example 17.9.

Solution

1. The given circuit clamps negative peaks of the input waveform to zero.
2. Therefore peak value of the clamped waveform = 2 × 10 = 20 V.
3. Frequency of input waveform = $314/2\pi = 50$ Hz.
4. This gives time period T of the input waveform as 1/50 = 20 ms.
5. Recommended minimum value of C_1 is given by $R_L C_1 = 10T$.
6. That is, $C_1(\text{min}) = 10T/R_L = (10 \times 20 \times 10^{-3})/1000 = 200$ μF.

EXAMPLE 17.10 *Refer to the half-wave circuit of Figure 17.49 and the associated rectified output waveform. Determine V_1 and V_2 given that opamp has an open-loop gain of 100 dB and diode D_1 has a cut-in voltage of 0.7 V.*

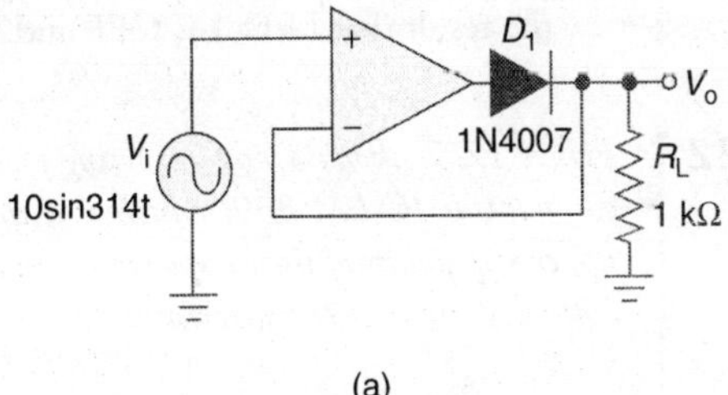

(a)

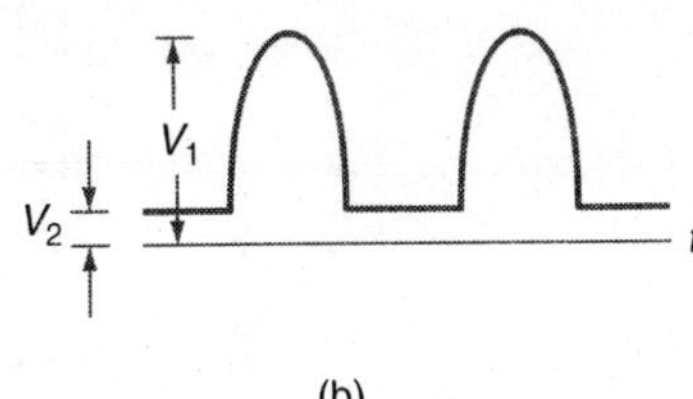

(b)

Figure 17.49 | Example 17.10.

Solution

1. $V_1 = 10$ V.
2. $V_2 = 0.7/A_{OL}$, where A_{OL} is the open-loop gain of opamp.
3. $A_{OL} = 100$ dB = 100,000.
4. Therefore, $V_2 = 0.7/100,000 = 7$ μV.

EXAMPLE 17.11

Refer to the comparator circuit of Figure 17.50. Determine the state of LED-1 and LED-2 (whether ON or OFF) when the switch SW-1 is in (a) position-A and (b) position-B. Assume diodes D_1 and D_2 to have forward-biased voltage drop equal to 0.7 V each.

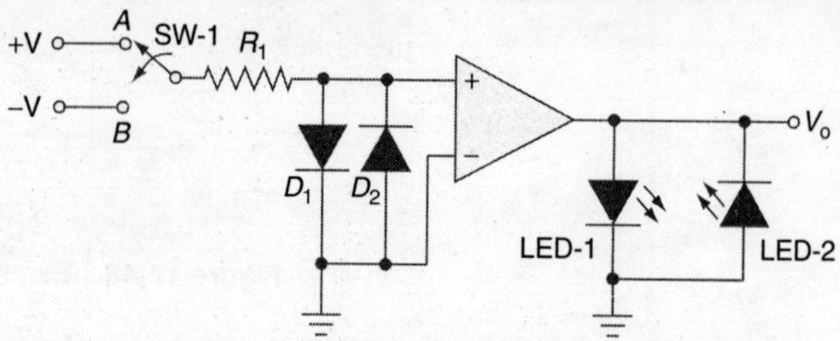

Figure 17.50 | Example 17.11.

Solution

1. When the switch SW-1 is in position-A, voltage appearing at non-inverting input is +0.7 V (equal to forward-biased voltage drop across D_1). That is, voltage at non-inverting input is more positive with respect to voltage at inverting input. Therefore, opamp output goes to positive saturation with the result that LED-1 is ON and LED-2 is OFF.
2. When the switch SW-1 is in position-B, voltage appearing at non-inverting input is −0.7 V (equal to forward-biased voltage drop across D_2). That is, voltage at non-inverting input is more negative with respect to voltage at inverting input. Therefore, opamp output goes to negative saturation with the result that LED-1 is OFF and LED-2 is ON.

EXAMPLE 17.12

Figure 17.51 shows a non-inverting type of window comparator configured around comparator IC LM 339, which is a quad comparator. Determine the lower and upper trip points of the comparator and also draw the output voltage V_o versus input voltage V_i transfer characteristics.

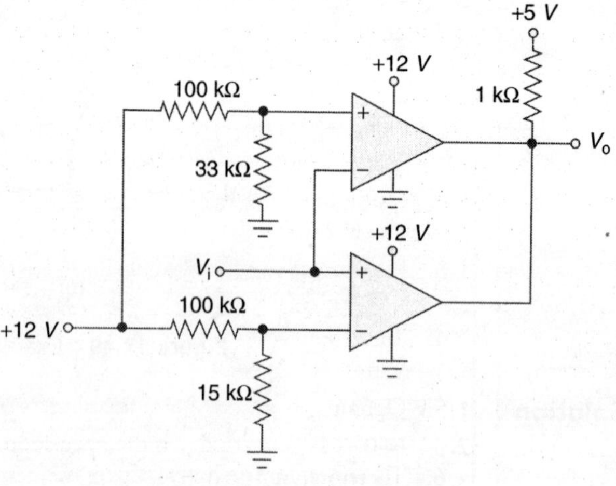

Figure 17.51 | Example 17.12.

Solution

1. Lower trip point (LTP) is given by $(12 \times 15 \times 10^3)/(115 \times 10^3) = 1.565$ V.
2. Upper trip point (UTP) is given by $(12 \times 33 \times 10^3)/(133 \times 10^3) = 2.977$ V.
3. Transfer characteristics are shown in Figure 17.52.

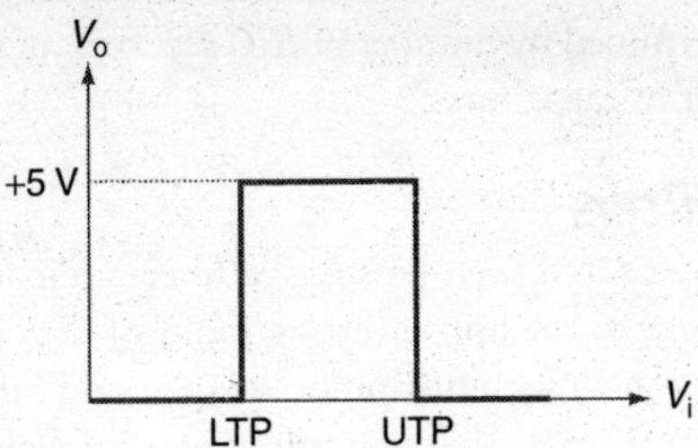

Figure 17.52 Solution to Example 17.12.

EXAMPLE 17.13 *Design an absolute value circuit using opamps to produce an output $V_o = |V_i|$ given that $-5\ V \leq V_i \leq +5\ V$ and the highest frequency likely to be encountered is 20 kHz. The circuit should have input impedance not less than 15 kΩ. Also give the desired values of slew rate and unity gain cross-over specifications of the opamp or opamps used in the circuit.*

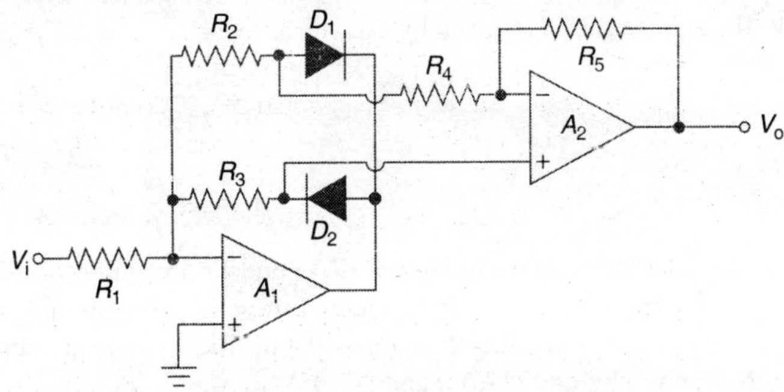

Figure 17.53 Example 17.13.

Solution

1. Figure 17.53 shows the circuit diagram. For this circuit to produce $V_o = |V_i|$, $R_1 = R_2 = R_3 = R_4 = R_5 = R$.
2. Input impedance of this circuit equals R_1, which equals R. Therefore, $R = 15$ kΩ.
3. Peak-to-peak value of input signal = 10 V. Highest expected signal frequency = 20 kHz.
4. Therefore, required slew rate $= \pi \times f_{MAX} \times 10 = 20 \times 10^3 \times 10\pi$ V/s = 0.628 V/μs.
5. Opamps A_1 and A_2 are operating at closed-loop gain values of 1 and 1.5, respectively.
6. Therefore, unity gain cross-over frequency specifications of A_1 and A_2 should be at least 20 kHz and 30 kHz, respectively.

17.15 Active Filters

In this section we will briefly describe opamp circuits used to build low-pass, high-pass, band-pass and band-reject active filters. We will confine our discussion to first- and second-order filters. Order of an active filter is determined by number of *R-C* sections (or poles) used in the filter, which for a few exceptions equals the number of capacitors.

First-Order Filters

The simplest low-pass and high-pass active filters are constructed by connecting lag and lead type of *R-C* sections, respectively, to the non-inverting input of the opamp wired as a voltage follower. Figures 17.54(a) and (b) respectively show such first-order low-pass and high-pass filter circuits. The cut-off frequency in both cases is given by Eq. (17.32). The circuits function as follows. In the case of low-pass circuit of Figure 17.54(a), at low frequencies, reactance offered by the capacitor is much larger than the resistance value and therefore applied input signal appears at the output mostly unattenuated. At high frequencies, the capacitive reactance becomes much smaller than the resistance value thus forcing the output to be near zero. The output is 0.707 times the input when the signal frequency is such as to make the capacitive reactance equal to the resistance value. This is called the upper cut-off frequency. The gain rolls off at a rate of 6 dB per octave or 20 dB per decade beyond the cut-off point. Roll-off rate beyond the cut-off point in the case of *n*-order filter is 6*n* dB per octave or 20*n* dB per decade. Operation of the high-pass circuit can also be explained on similar lines.

The filters shown in Figure 17.54 can also be configured so as to have the desired amplification of the input signal. Low-pass and high-pass filter circuits with gain are shown in Figures 17.55(a) and (b), respectively. The voltage gain A_v is given by Eq. (17.33).

$$f_C = \frac{1}{2\pi RC} \tag{17.32}$$

$$A_v = 1 + \frac{R_3}{R_2} \tag{17.33}$$

Single-order filters shown in Figures 17.54 and 17.55 employ non-inverting type of amplifier configuration. These filters could also be implemented using inverting amplifier configuration. Relevant circuits are shown in Figures 17.56. Cut-off frequency and mid-band gain values in the case of low-pass filter are, respectively, given by Eqs. (17.34) and (17.35).

$$f_C = \frac{1}{2\pi R_2 C_1} \tag{17.34}$$

$$A_v = -\frac{R_2}{R_1} \tag{17.35}$$

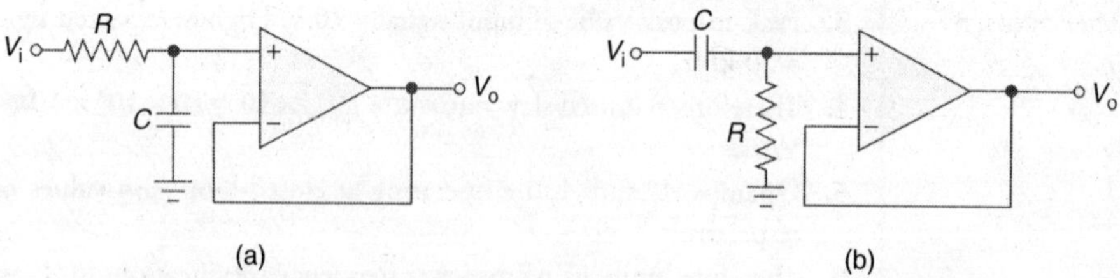

Figure 17.54 First-order active filters: (a) Low pass; (b) high pass.

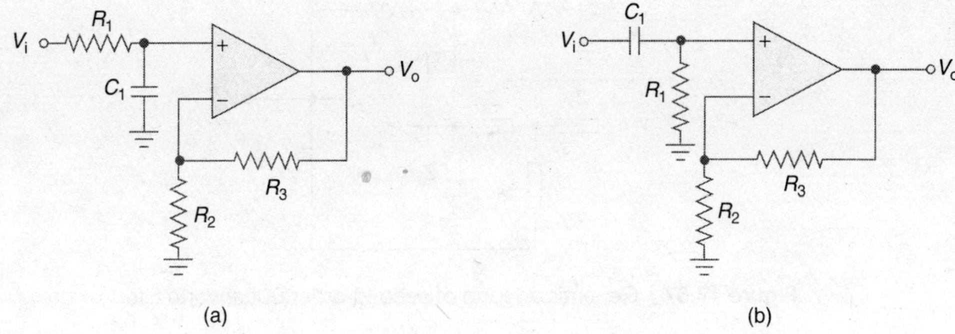

Figure 17.55 First-order filters with gain: (a) Low pass; (b) high pass.

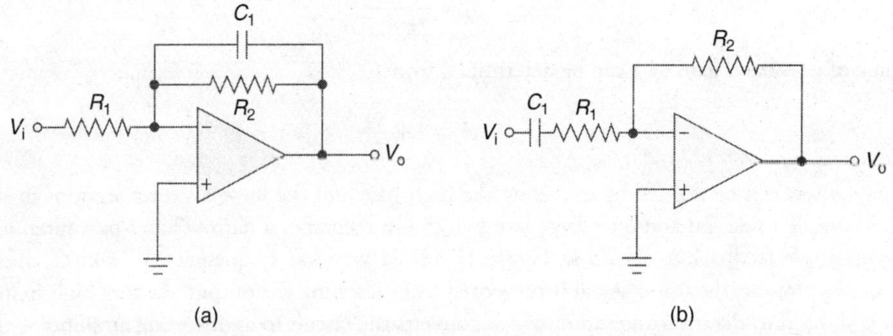

Figure 17.56 First-order filters using inverting configuration: (a) Low pass; (b) high pass.

The same in the case of high-pass filter are given by Eqs. (17.36) and (17.37).

$$f_C = \frac{1}{2\pi R_1 C_1} \tag{17.36}$$

$$A_v = -\frac{R_2}{R_1} \tag{17.37}$$

Second-Order Filters

Figure 17.57 shows the generalized form of a second-order Butterworth active filter. Butterworth filter, also called maximally flat filter, offers a relatively flat pass and stop band response but has the disadvantage of relatively sluggish roll-off. Other commonly used filters are the Chebychev and Cauer filters. Chebychev filters offer much faster roll-off but their pass band has ripple. Cauer filters have rippled pass and stop bands. There are other types of filters such as Bessel filters with their unique properties. Discussion on all these types is beyond the scope of the present text.

In the case of generalized form of second-order Butterworth filter, shown in Figure 17.57, we have the following:

1. If $Z_1 = Z_2 = R$ and $Z_3 = Z_4 = C$, we get a second-order low-pass filter.
2. If $Z_1 = Z_2 = C$ and $Z_3 = Z_4 = R$, we get a second-order high-pass filter.

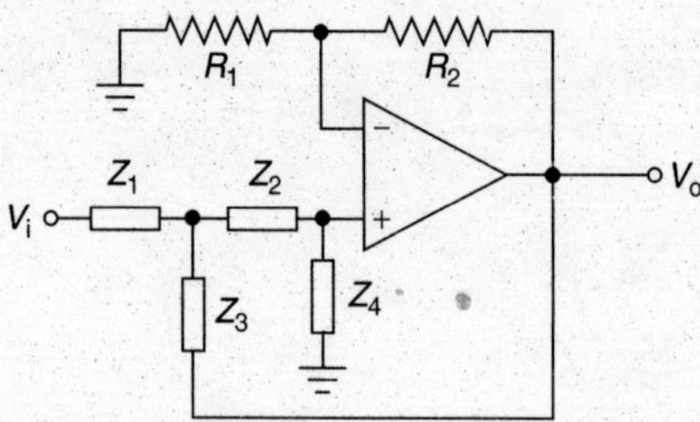

Figure 17.57 | Generalized form of second-order Butterworth filter.

The cut-off frequency is given by

$$f_C = \frac{1}{2\pi RC} \tag{17.38}$$

The value of pass band gain (A_v) can be determined from

$$A_v = 1 + \frac{R_2}{R_1} \tag{17.39}$$

Band-pass filters can be formed by cascading the high-pass and the low-pass filter sections in series. These filters are simple to design and offer large bandwidth. To construct a narrow band-pass filter, one needs to employ multiple feedback as shown in Figure 17.58. At very low frequencies, C_1 and C_2 offer very high reactance. As a result, the input signal is prevented from reaching the output. At very high frequencies, the output is shorted to the inverting input, which converts the circuit to an inverting amplifier with zero gain. Again, there is no output. Thus at both very low and very high frequencies, the output is zero. At some intermediate band of frequencies, the gain provided by the circuit offsets the loss due to the potential divider R_1–R_3. Mathematical expressions governing the design of the filter circuit are given in Eqs. (17.40)–(17.42):

Resonant frequency,

$$f_R = 2Q/2\pi R_2 C \tag{17.40}$$

where Q is the quality factor.

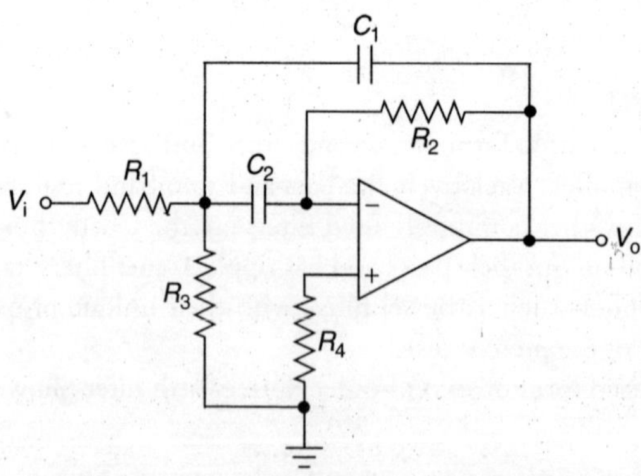

Figure 17.58 | Narrow band-pass filter.

For $C_1 = C_2 = C$, the quality factor is given by

$$Q = \left[R_1R_2/2R_3\right]^{1/2} \tag{17.41}$$

The voltage gain is

$$A_v = Q/2\pi R_1 f_R C \tag{17.42}$$

Band-reject filters can be implemented by summing together the outputs of the low-pass and high-pass filters. These filters are simple to design and have a broad reject frequency range.

Figure 17.59 shows the circuit diagram of second-order narrow band reject filter. It uses a twin-T network that is connected in series with the non-inverting input of the opamp. A twin-T network offers very high reactance at the resonance frequency and very low reactance at frequencies off-resonance. This phenomenon explains the behavior of the circuit. Another way of explaining the behavior of the circuit is as follows. Very low frequency signals find their way to the output via the low-pass filter formed by R_1–R_2–C_3. Very high frequency signals reach the output through the high-pass filter constituted by C_1–C_2–R_3. In an intermediate band of frequencies, both filters pass the signal to some extent but the negative phase shift introduced by low-pass filter is cancelled out by an identical positive phase shift by high-pass filter with the result that at any instant, the net signal reaching the non-inverting input and hence the output is zero. Component values of the twin-T network are chosen according to the following equations.

$$R_1 = R_2 = R,\ R_3 = R/2 \tag{17.43}$$

$$C_1 = C_2 = C,\ C_3 = 2C \tag{17.44}$$

$$0 \le R_4 \le (R_1 + R_2) \tag{17.45}$$

$$f_R = \frac{1}{2\pi RC} \tag{17.46}$$

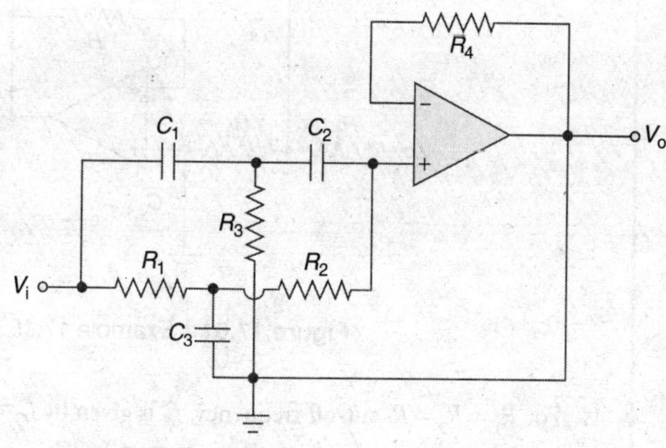

Figure 17.59 | Second-order band-reject filter.

EXAMPLE 17.14 *Refer to the first-order low-pass filter of Figure 17.60. Determine the cut-off frequency and the gain value at four times the cut-off frequency.*

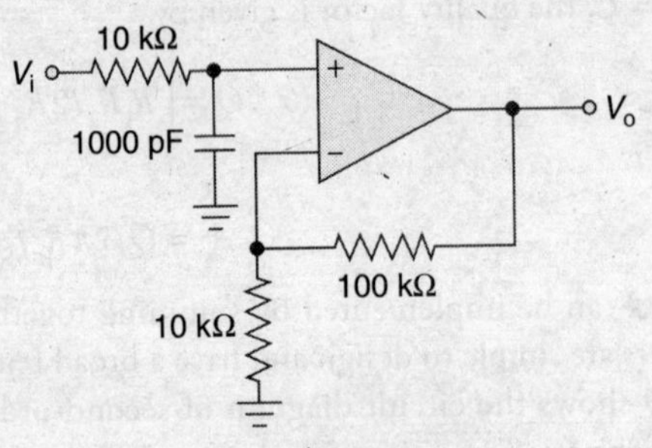

Figure 17.60 | Example 17.14.

Solution

1. Cut-off frequency,
$$f_C = 1/(2\pi \times 10 \times 10^3 \times 1000 \times 10^{-12}) = 10^5/2\pi \text{ Hz} = 15.915 \text{ kHz}$$
2. Gain, $A_v = (1 + 100 \times 10^3)/(10 \times 10^3) = 11 = 20.827$ dB.
3. Gain at cut-off point = 20.827 − 3 = 17.827 dB.
4. Gain at frequency four times the cut-off frequency will be 12 dB below the value of mid-band gain.
5. Therefore, gain at four times the cut-off frequency = 20.827 − 12 = 8.827 dB.

EXAMPLE 17.15

Figure 17.61 shows a second-order low-pass filter built around a single opamp. Calculate the values of R_1, R_2, C_1, C_2 and R_3 if the filter had a cut-off frequency of 10 kHz, Q-factor of 0.707 and input impedance not less than 10 kΩ.

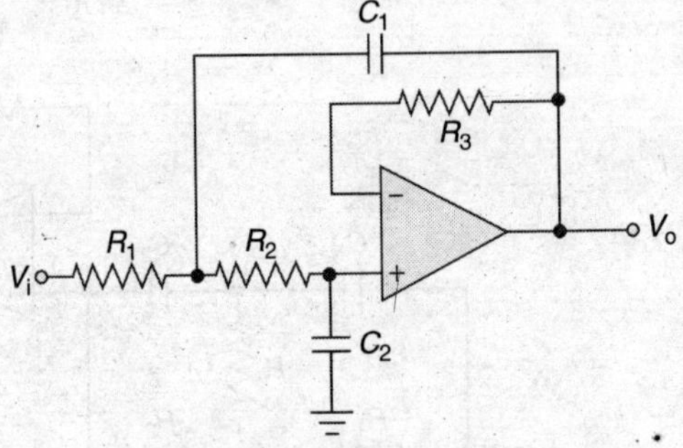

Figure 17.61 | Example 17.15.

Solution

1. For $R_1 = R_2 = R$, cut-off frequency, f_C is given by $f_C = 1/2\pi R\sqrt{C_1C_2}$.
2. Q-factor is given by $Q = (1/2) \times \sqrt{C_1/C_2}$.
3. For $Q = 0.707$, $C_1 = 2C_2$.
4. For input impedance of 10 kΩ, $R_1 = 10\text{ kΩ} = R_2$.
5. $f_C = 1/(2\pi \times 10 \times 10^3 \times C_2 \times \sqrt{2}) = 10 \times 10^3$.

6. This gives $C_2 = 0.0011$ μF.
7. $C_1 = 2C_2 = 0.0022$ μF.
8. R_3 is equal to $R_1 + R_2$ in order to have equal DC resistance between each opamp input and ground. Therefore, $R_3 = 20$ kΩ.

EXAMPLE 17.16 *Design an opamp-based twin-T band-reject filter having a notch frequency of 100 kHz. Specify the small-signal bandwidth of the chosen opamp if the highest expected frequency were 1 MHz.*

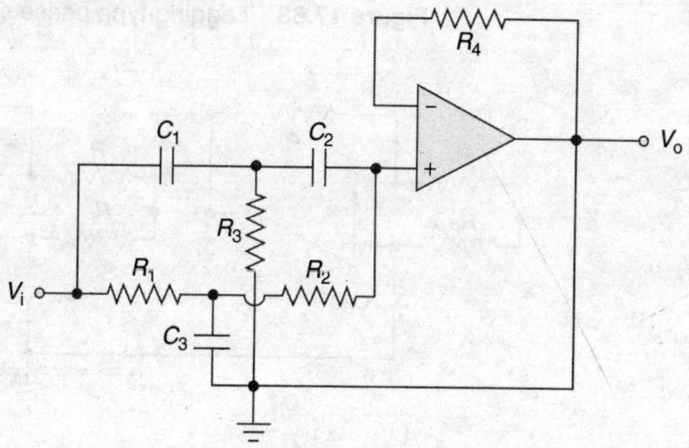

Figure 17.62 Example 17.16.

Solution

1. Figure 17.62 shows the circuit. The notch frequency is given by $f_R = 1/2\pi RC$ where $R_1 = R_2 = R$, $C_1 = C_2 = C$, $R_3 = R/2$ and $C_3 = 2C$.
2. Let $C_1 = 0.0001$ μF. This gives $R_1 = 1/2\pi \times 100 \times 10^3 \times 0.0001 \times 10^{-6} =$ 15.92 kΩ.
3. This gives $C_1 = C_2 = 0.0001$ μF and $C_3 = 0.0002$ μF.
4. $R_1 = R_2 = 15.92$ kΩ and $R_3 = 15.92 \times 10^3/2 = 7.96$ kΩ.
5. $R_4 = R_1 + R_2 = 15.92 \times 10^3 + 15.92 \times 10^3 = 31.84$ kΩ.

17.16 Phase Shifters

Figure 17.63 shows the circuit diagram of single opamp-based lagging-type phase shifter circuit. The output lags the input by an angle (θ) given by Eq. (17.47).

$$\theta \text{ (in degrees)} = -2 \tan^{-1} (\omega R_P C_P) \tag{17.47}$$

where $\omega = 2\pi f$, f being the frequency of the input signal.

The simple circuit shown in the figure can be used of shift the phase of the input signal over a wide range by varying R_P with 0° and –180° being the extremes. For $R_P << 1/\omega C_P$, the phase shift is near zero. (It will be 0° when $R_P = 0$ which is not practical). For $R_P >> 1/\omega C_P$, θ approaches –180° ($\theta = -180°$ only for $R_P =$ infinity which is again not feasible.) For $R_P = 1/\omega C_P$, $\theta = -90°$. Two such sections can be used in cascade to vary the phase shift over full 360°. Figure 17.64 shows the circuit diagram.

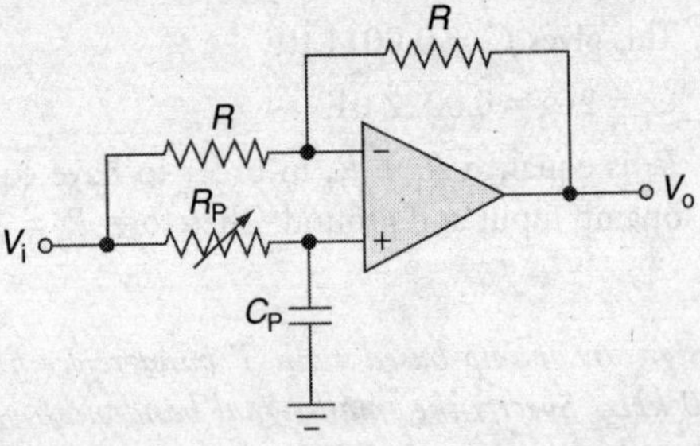

Figure 17.63 | Lagging-type phase shifter.

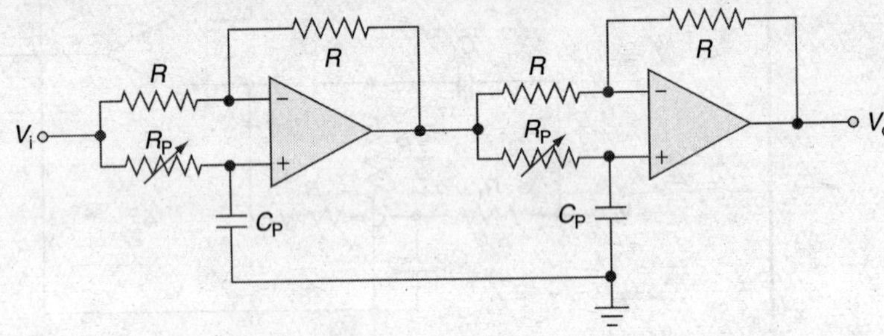

Figure 17.64 | Two-stage lagging-type phase shifter.

Figure 17.65 shows the circuit diagram of lead-type phase shifter. The circuit shown here is just the redrawn version of lagging-type phase shifter of Figure 17.63 with positions of R_P and C_P interchanged. The phase difference (θ) is given by

$$\theta \text{ (in degrees)} = 2 \tan^{-1} (\omega R_P C_P) \tag{17.48}$$

1. For $R_P = 1/\omega C_P$; $\theta = 90°$.
2. For $R_P >> 1/\omega C_P$; $\theta = 180°$.
3. For $R_P << 1/\omega C_P$; $\theta = 0°$.

Cascade arrangement of two lead-type phase shifter stages can be used for varying phase shift over full 360°.

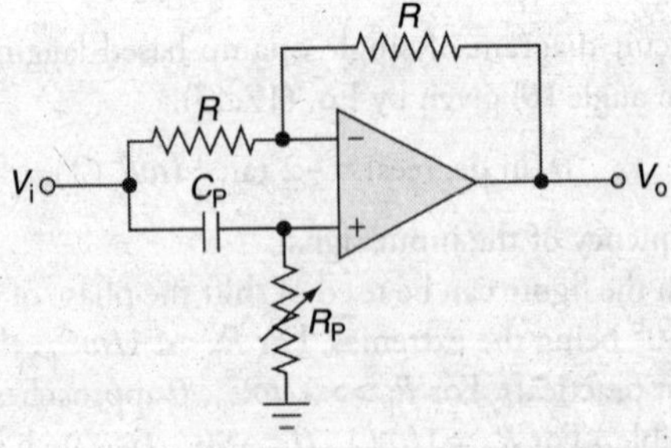

Figure 17.65 | Lead-type phase shifter.

EXAMPLE 17.17 *Design an opamp-based phase shifter to shift the phase of a sine wave signal by −60° with a gain of unity. If the input signal had a peak amplitude of 5 V and the highest input signal frequency were 50 kHz, determine the slew rate of the chosen opamp.*

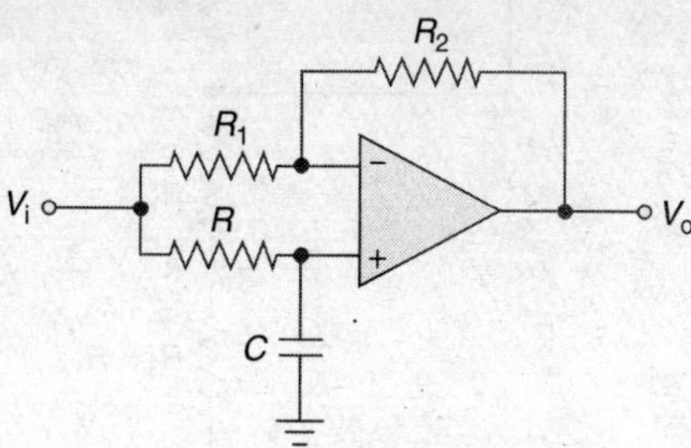

Figure 17.66 | Example 17.17.

Solution

1. Figure 17.66 shows the circuit diagram.
2. For unity gain, $R_1 = R_2$.
3. Lagging-type phase shift is given by $\theta = -2\tan^{-1}(2\pi fRC) = -60°$.
4. This gives $2\pi fRC = \tan 30° = 0.577$.
5. Solution of above equation gives $RC = 0.184 \times 10^{-5}$.
6. Let $C = 0.001$ μF. This gives $R = (0.184 \times 10^{-5})/(0.001 \times 10^{-6}) = 1.84$ kΩ.
7. Let $R_1 = R_2 = 10$ kΩ.
8. Peak amplitude of input signal = 5 V.
9. Slew rate can be determined from f_{MAX} = Slew rate/$2\pi V_p$.
10. This gives slew rate = $2\pi \times 5 \times 50 \times 10^3 = 157 \times 10^4$ V/s = 1.57 V/μs.

17.17 Instrumentation Amplifier

Instrumentation amplifier is nothing but a differential amplifier that has been optimized for DC performance to nearly approach the DC performance of an ideal opamp. As a result, instrumentation amplifier is characterized by a high differential gain, high CMRR, high input impedance and low input offsets and low temperature drifts.

Figure 17.67 shows the classical internal schematic arrangement of an instrumentation amplifier. The two input opamps are wired as non-inverting amplifiers to provide gain and very high input impedance and the output opamp is wired as difference amplifier with unity gain. The resistors used in the output stage are ultra-high precision, low temperature drift resistors. Precision resistors with tolerance specification in the range of ±0.01% to ±0.1% and temperature drift specification of 1 PPM/°C or better are commercially available.

We will now analyze the circuit shown in Figure 17.67 for common-mode and differential-input performance. The circuit can be divided into two distinct parts, namely, the pre-amplifier stage comprising opamps A_1 and A_2 and the difference amplifier configured around A_3. Let us assume that the common-mode input is $V_{in}(CM)$. Owing to same positive voltage applied to both the non-inverting inputs, voltages appearing at the output of opamps A_1 and A_2 and also at R_1–R_2 and R_3–R_4 junctions are equal. The result is

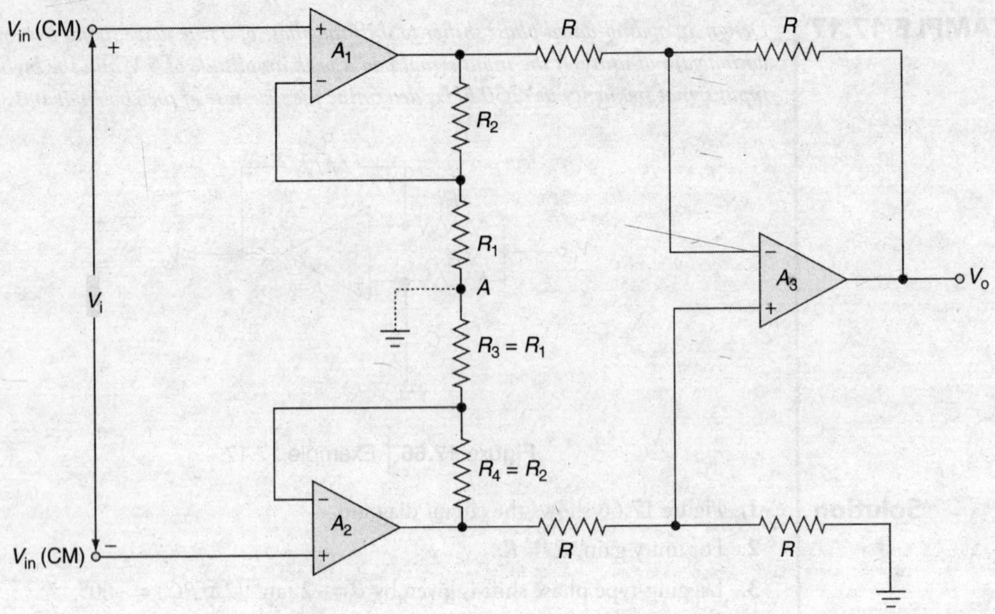

Figure 17.67 Instrumentation amplifier.

that point A is floating. This further implies that A_1 and A_2 act like voltage followers. In other words, common-mode gain A_{CM} of the preamplifier stage is unity. Tolerance specification of R_1 and R_2 has no effect on the common-mode gain of the pre-amplifier stage.

On the other hand, when a differential signal is applied to the input, signals appearing at two R_1–R_2 and R_3–R_4 junctions are equal and opposite creating a virtual ground at point A. The differential gain of this stage is therefore $1 + (R_2/R_1)$.

The difference amplifier stage has a common-mode gain equal to $\pm 2\Delta R/R$, where ΔR represents how closely the resistors are matched. Differential gain of this stage is unity. If we combine the results, we can say that the overall common-mode gain is equal to the common-mode gain of the difference amplifier stage and overall differential gain is equal to the differential gain of the pre-amplifier stage. That is, the differential gain is given by

$$A_v = 1 + \frac{R_2}{R_1}$$

Since point A is a virtual ground and not a mechanical ground, we can use a single resistor instead of two separate resistors. If this single resistor was R_G, then $R_1 = R_3 = R_G/2$.

Therefore,

$$A_v = 1 + \frac{2R_2}{R_G} \tag{17.49}$$

The overall common-mode gain is given by

$$A_{CM} = \pm 2\Delta R/R \tag{17.50}$$

In the integrated circuit instrumentation opamps, all the components except R_G are integrated on the chip. R_G is connected externally and is used to control the voltage gain.

EXAMPLE 17.18 *Refer to the instrumentation amplifier circuit of Figure 17.68. Resistors R_1 and R_2, respectively, have tolerance specifications of ±0.001% and ±0.05%. Determine the CMRR of this instrumentation amplifier in dB.*

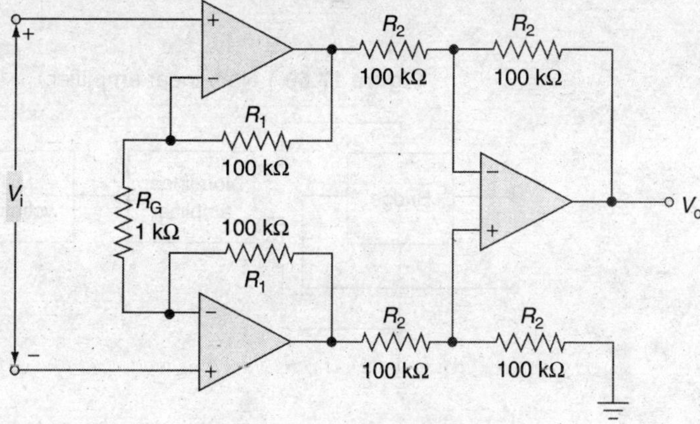

Figure 17.68 Example 17.18.

Solution

1. Differential gain, $A_v = 1 + 2R_1/R_G$. Therefore, $A_v = 1 + [(2 \times 100 \times 10^3)/(1 \times 10^3)] = 201$.
2. Common mode gain $= \pm 2\Delta R_2/R_2 = \pm 2 \times$ Tolerance of R_2.
3. Therefore common-mode gain $= 2 \times 0.0005 = 0.001$.
4. CMRR $= 201/0.001 = 201000$.
5. CMRR (in dB) $= 20 \log 201000 = 106.1$ dB.

17.18 Non-Linear Amplifier

In the case of a non-linear amplifier, the gain value is a non-linear function of the amplitude of the signal applied at the input. For example, the gain may be very large for weak input signals and very small for large input signals, which implies that for a very large change in the amplitude of input signal, resultant change in amplitude of output signal is very small. A simple method to achieve non-linear amplification is by connecting a non-linear device such as a PN junction diode in the feedback path (Figure 17.69). The amplifier shown in Figure 17.69 is a semi-log amplifier as the forward current through silicon diodes varies as log of the applied voltage.

For small values of input signal, diodes act as open circuit and the gain is high due to minimum feedback. When the amplitude of input signal is large, diodes offer very small resistance and thus gain is low. Such a circuit may typically cause output voltage to change in the ratio of 2:1 for an input change of 1000:1. Resistance R_1 decides the compression ratio. Higher the value of resistor R_1, lesser is the compression ratio.

A common application of such a non-linear amplifier is in AC bridge balance detectors. The output of bridge may vary over a wide range around its null point. In order to achieve null, the output is usually

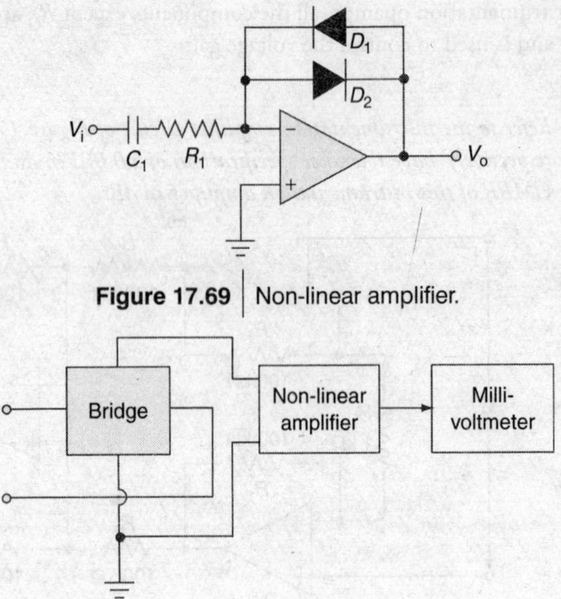

Figure 17.69 | Non-linear amplifier.

Figure 17.70 | Application of non-linear amplifier in AC bridge balance detectors.

applied to an AC milli-voltmeter whose sensitivity may have to be adjusted a number of times before a null is achieved. If the bridge output is applied to the non-linear amplifier of the type described in the preceding paragraphs (shown in Figure 17.70), the output of non-linear amplifier would vary only in a small range for a wide variation of bridge output. As an example, a variation of 10000:1 in the bridge output may cause a variation of only 6:1 in the amplifier output. This, when applied to the milli-voltmeter, enables the single range of milli-voltmeter to accommodate variations over a range of 10000:1.

17.19 Relaxation Oscillator

Relaxation oscillator is an oscillator circuit that produces a non-sinusoidal output whose time period is dependent on the charging time of a capacitor connected as a part of the oscillator circuit. Opamps adapt very well to construction of relaxation oscillator circuits that produce a rectangular output. Figure 17.71 shows the basic circuit arrangement of an opamp-based relaxation oscillator circuit.

The circuit functions as follows. Let us assume that the output is initially in positive saturation. As a result, voltage at non-inverting input of opamp is $+V_{SAT} \times R_1/(R_1 + R_2)$. This forces the output to stay in positive saturation as the capacitor C is initially in fully discharged state. Capacitor C starts charging towards $+V_{SAT}$ through R. The moment the capacitor voltage exceeds the voltage appearing at the non-inverting input, the output switches to $-V_{SAT}$. The voltage appearing at non-inverting input also changes to $-V_{SAT} \times R_1/(R_1 + R_2)$. The capacitor starts discharging and after reaching zero, it begins to discharge towards $-V_{SAT}$. Again, as soon as it becomes more negative than the negative threshold appearing at non-inverting input of the opamp, the output switches back to $+V_{SAT}$. The cycle repeats thereafter. The output is a rectangular wave. The expression for time period of output waveform can be derived from the exponential charging and discharging process and is given by

$$T = 2RC \ln\left(\frac{1+B}{1-B}\right) \tag{17.51}$$

where $B = R_1/(R_1 + R_2)$.

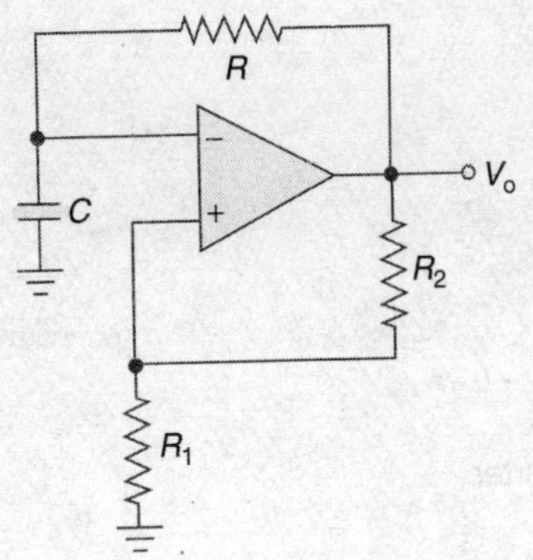

Figure 17.71 | Relaxation oscillator.

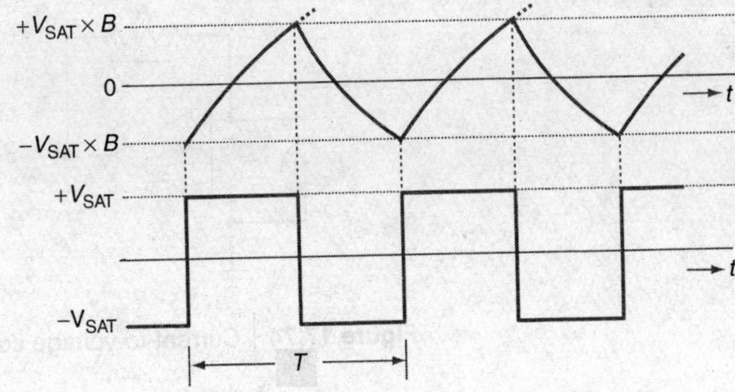

Figure 17.72 | Relevant waveforms of relaxation oscillator.

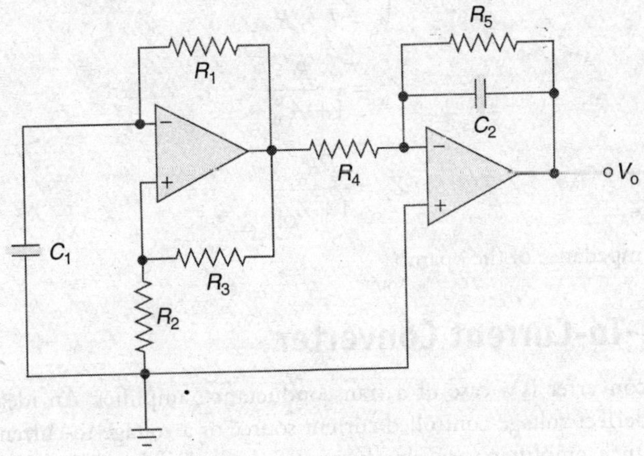

Figure 17.73 | Triangular waveform generator.

Figure 17.72 shows the relevant waveforms. The time period of output may be conveniently varied by varying the value of resistor R.

Relaxation oscillator forms the basis of waveform-generation circuits configured around opamps. For example, a triangular waveform generator may be built by cascading the relaxation oscillator block with an integrator block as shown in Figure 17.73.

17.20 Current-To-Voltage Converter

Current-to-voltage converter is nothing but a transimpedance amplifier. An ideal transimpedance amplifier makes a perfect current-to-voltage converter as it has zero input impedance and zero output impedance. Opamp wired as transimpedance amplifier very closely approaches a perfect current-to-voltage converter. Figure 17.74 shows the circuit arrangement. The circuit is characterized by voltage shunt feedback with a feedback factor of unity. This circuit has been discussed earlier in detail in Chapter 11 on *Negative Feedback Amplifiers*. The expressions for output voltage, closed-loop input and output impedances are given as follows.

$$V_o = I_i \times R \times \left(\frac{A_{OL}}{1 + A_{OL}} \right) \tag{17.52}$$

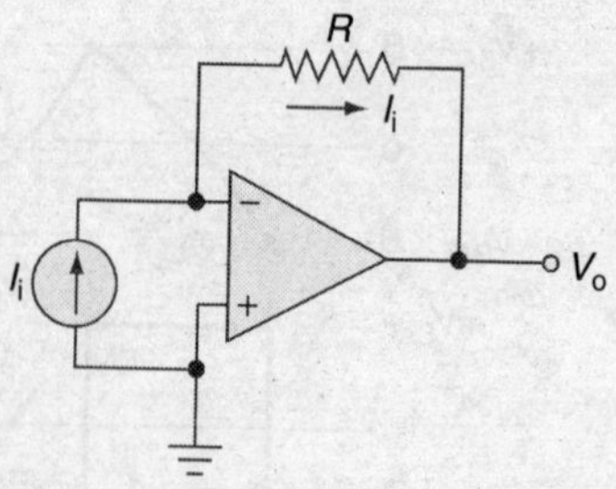

Figure 17.74 Current-to-voltage converter.

For $A_{OL} >> 1$, Eq. (17.52) simplifies to

$$V_o = I_i \times R \tag{17.53}$$

$$Z_{in} = \frac{R}{1 + A_{OL}} \tag{17.54}$$

$$Z_o = \frac{R_o}{1 + A_{OL}} \tag{17.55}$$

where R_o is the output impedance of the opamp.

17.21 Voltage-To-Current Converter

Voltage-to-current converter is a case of a transconductance amplifier. An ideal transconductance amplifier makes a perfect voltage-controlled current source or a voltage-to-current converter. Opamp wired as transconductance amplifier very closely approaches a perfect voltage-to-current converter. Figure 17.75 shows the basic circuit arrangement. The circuit is characterized by current series feedback. This circuit has been discussed earlier in detail in Chapter 11 on *Negative Feedback Amplifiers*. Expressions for output current, closed-loop input and output impedances are given as follows.

$$I_o = \frac{V_i}{R_1 + [(R_1 + R_2)/A_{OL}]} \tag{17.56}$$

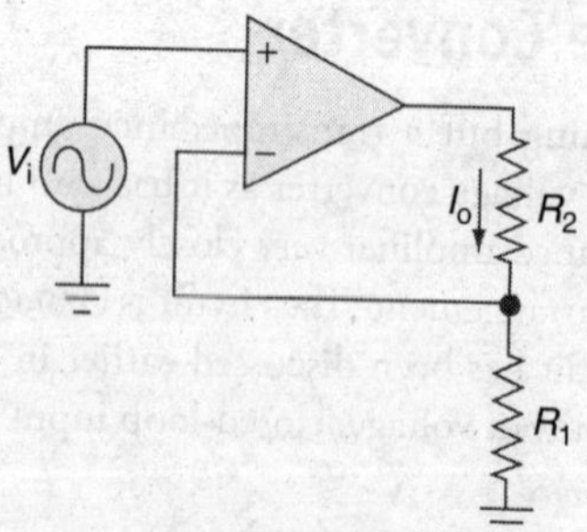

Figure 17.75 Voltage-to-current converter.

For $A_{OL} >> 1$, Eq. (17.56) simplifies to the following equation:

$$I_o = \frac{V_i}{R_1} \tag{17.57}$$

Closed-loop input impedance is given by

$$Z_{in} = R_i \times \left(1 + A_{OL} \times \frac{R_1}{R_1 + R_2}\right) \tag{17.58}$$

where R_i is the input impedance of the opamp.

Closed-loop output impedance is given by

$$Z_o = R_1 \times \left(1 + A_{OL} \times \frac{R_1}{R_1 + R_2}\right) \tag{17.59}$$

Voltage-to-current converter of Figure 17.75 operates with a floating load, which is not always convenient. Monolithic opamps specially designed as transconductance amplifiers to feed single-ended load resistances are commercially available.

EXAMPLE 17.19 *Refer to the relaxation oscillator circuit of Figure 17.76. Determine the peak-to-peak amplitude and frequency of the square wave output given that saturation output voltage of the opamp is ±12.5 V at power supply voltages of ±15 V.*

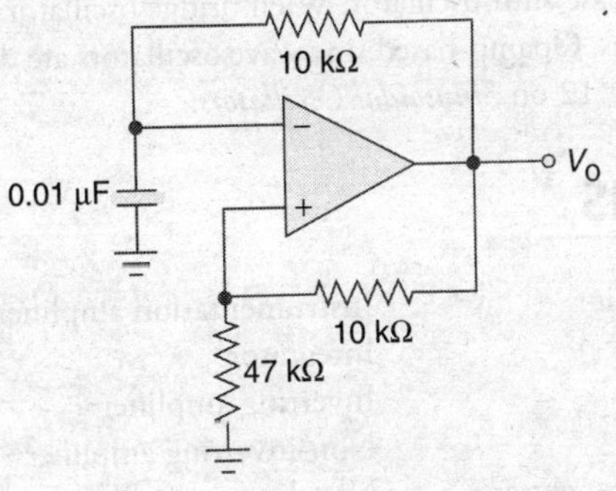

Figure 17.76 Example 17.19.

Solution

1. The feedback factor B is given by $(47 \times 10^3)/(47 \times 10^3 + 10 \times 10^3) = 0.825$.
2. Time period T of the output waveform is given by $T = 2RC \ln [(1 + B)/(1 - B)]$.
3. That is, $T = 2 \times 10 \times 10^3 \times 0.01 \times 10^{-6} \times \ln[(1 + 0.825)/(1 - 0.825)] = 0.469$ ms.
4. Therefore, $f = 1/\ 0.469$ kHz $= 2.13$ kHz.
5. Peak-to-peak amplitude of output $= 2V_{SAT} = 25$ V.

EXAMPLE 17.20 *For current-to-voltage converter circuit of Figure 17.77, determine output voltage, closed-loop input and output impedances given that chosen opamp has open-loop transimpedance gain of 100,000, input impedance of 1 MΩ and output impedance of 100 Ω.*

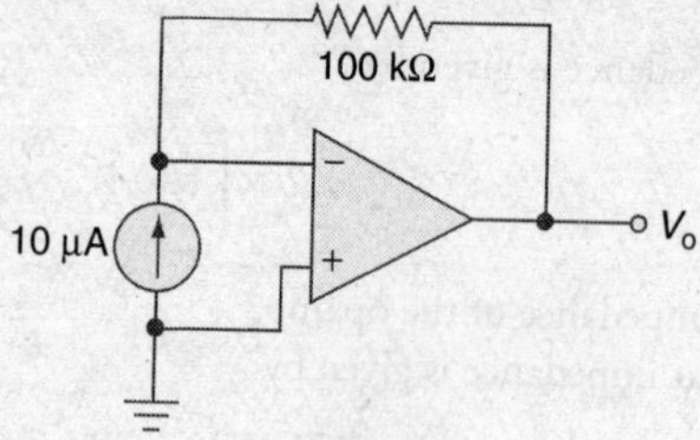

Figure 17.77 Example 17.20.

Solution

1. Output voltage = $10 \times 10^{-6} \times 100 \times 10^3 = 1$ V.
2. Closed-loop input impedance, $Z_{in} = R/(1 + A_{OL}) = 100 \times 10^3/(1 + 100{,}000) = 1\ \Omega$.
3. Closed-loop output impedance, $Z_o = R_o/(1 + A_{OL}) = 100/(1 + 100{,}000) = 0.001\ \Omega$.

17.22 Sine Wave Oscillators

Opamps adapt well to use in building sine wave oscillators, for example, in building RC oscillators – such as RC phase shift oscillator, Wien bridge oscillator and LC oscillators – such as Hartley, Colpitt and Clapp oscillators. Opamp-based sine wave oscillators are discussed in detail with large number of solved examples in Chapter 12 on *Sinusoidal Oscillators.*

KEY TERMS

Absolute value circuit
Active filter
Averager
Comparator
Current-to-voltage converter
Difference amplifier
Differentiator
Instrumentation amplifier
Integrator
Inverting amplifier
Non-inverting amplifier
Non-linear amplifier
Peak detector circuit
Phase shifter
Relaxation oscillator
Summing amplifier
Voltage follower
Voltage-to-current converter
Window comparator

OBJECTIVE-TYPE EXERCISES

Multiple-Choice Questions

1. Magnitude of closed-loop voltage gain of inverting amplifier is given by
   a. ratio of feedback resistance to input resistance.
   b. ratio of input resistance to feedback resistance.
   c. ratio of sum of input and feedback resistances to input resistance.

d. ratio of sum of input and feedback resistances to feedback resistance.

2. Magnitude of closed loop voltage gain of non-inverting amplifier is given by
   a. ratio of feedback resistance to the resistance connected from inverting input to ground.
   b. ratio of resistance connected from inverting input to ground to feedback resistance.
   c. ratio of sum of resistance connected from inverting input to ground and feedback resistance to resistance connected from inverting input to ground.
   d. none of these.

3. In a non-inverting amplifier, when the feedback resistance equals the resistance connected from inverting input to ground, the closed-loop gain is
   a. 1.
   b. 2.
   c. Infinity.
   d. less than 1.

4. In order to construct a voltage follower,
   a. input is applied to inverting input and the non-inverting input is shorted to output.
   b. input is applied to non-inverting input and inverting input is grounded.
   c. input is applied to inverting input and non-inverting input is grounded.
   d. input is applied to non-inverting input and the inverting input is shorted to output.

5. In an opamp circuit, "*N*" DC inputs are connected to the inverting input through individual resistances, which are of the same value. The feedback resistance connected from output to inverting input is of resistance value that is 1/*N*th of the input resistance value. Non-inverting input is grounded. The output in this case is
   a. indeterminate from given data.
   b. average of all inputs.
   c. sum of all inputs.
   d. none of these.

6. The roll-off rate in fourth order Butterworth low pass filter will be
   a. 80 dB per decade.
   b. 80 dB per octave.
   c. 24 dB per decade.
   d. 12 dB per octave.

7. If the input to an integrator were a rectangular pulse, the output would be
   a. sine wave.
   b. ramp.
   c. rectangular pulse.
   d. cosine wave.

8. Output of a relaxation oscillator circuit is a
   a. sine wave.
   b. cosine wave.
   c. square wave.
   d. triangular wave.

9. Cascade arrangement of relaxation oscillator and an integrator makes a
   a. triangular waveform generator.
   b. square waveform generator.
   c. sawtooth waveform generator.
   d. pulse generator.

10. Introduction of hysteresis in a comparator makes it
   a. prone to false triggering caused by noisy input signal.
   b. immune to false triggering caused by noisy input signal.
   c. a square waveform generator.
   d. none of these.

11. In an inverting summer circuit using opamp, DC voltages of +1 V, −2 V and +2 V are, respectively, applied to the input through 10 kΩ, 20 kΩ and 50 kΩ resistors. If the feedback resistance were 50 kΩ, the output voltage would then be
   a. +2 V
   b. −2 V
   c. −3 V
   d. +3 V

12. Figure 17.78 shows transfer characteristics of some opamp circuit. It could possibly be
   a. an inverting comparator.
   b. a non-inverting comparator.

c. an inverting amplifier with hysteresis.
d. a non-inverting amplifier with hysteresis.

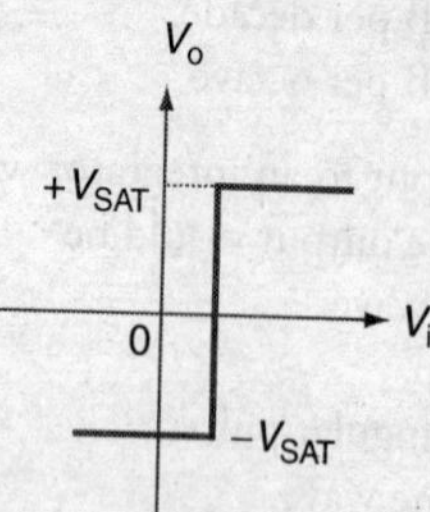

Figure 17.78 Question 12.

13. Refer to the transfer characteristics shown in Figure 17.79. Identify the circuit.

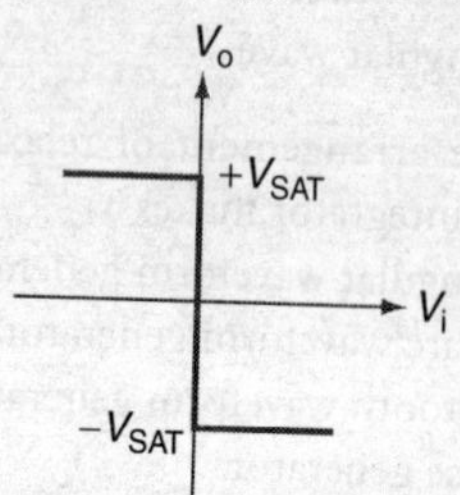

Figure 17.79 Question 13.

a. Inverting comparator
b. Non-inverting comparator
c. Inverting zero-crossing detector
d. Non-inverting zero-crossing detector

14. Figure 17.80 shows opamp-based integrator circuit. If this circuit were to integrate a symmetrical pulse waveform of 200 μs time period and if the DC gain of the integrator were to be limited to 100, what would be the values of C_1 and R_2?

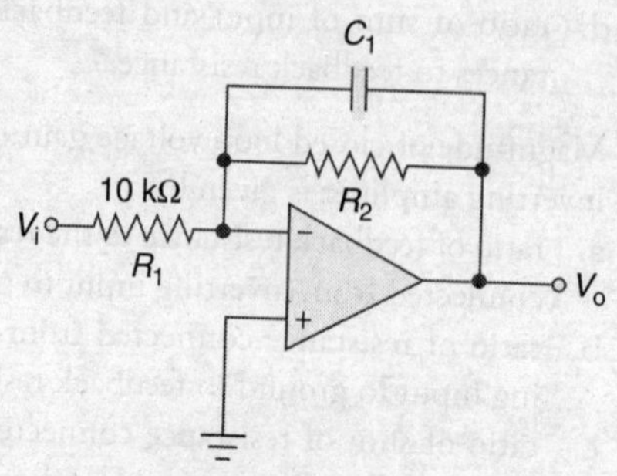

Figure 17.80 Question 14.

a. 0.1 μF, 1 MΩ
b. 0.01 μF, 1 MΩ
c. 0.1 μF, 100 kΩ
d. 0.01 μF, 100 kΩ

15. Refer to the opamp circuit of Figure 17.81. The circuit performs the function of which important building block.

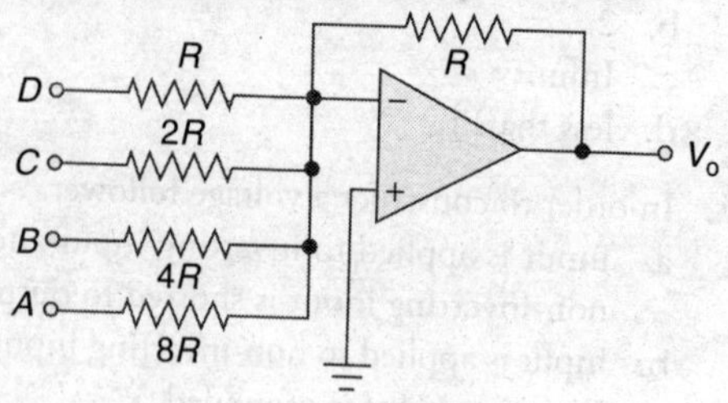

Figure 17.81 Question 15.

a. 4-input inverting summer
b. 4-input inverting averager
c. 4-bit D/A converter
d. Multiple input inverting amplifier

REVIEW QUESTIONS

1. With the help of circuit diagram, briefly describe the operation of an inverting amplifier. Derive expressions for voltage gain, input impedance and output impedance.
2. When an opamp is used in amplifier (inverting or non-inverting) configuration, what decides the maximum operational frequency for a given value of voltage gain? How is maximum operational frequency related to various relevant parameters in the case of a sine wave input signal?
3. On what parameters does the input impedance in the case of following opamp-based circuits depend upon:
   a. Inverting amplifier
   b. Non-inverting amplifier
   c. Current-to-voltage converter
   d. Voltage-to-current converter
   e. Instrumentation amplifier

4. Give a suitable circuit diagram that can be used to subtract two DC voltages. Derive an expression to prove that the output is difference of the two inputs.

5. Draw the circuit diagram of a voltage follower. What are its closed-loop voltage gain and bandwidth?

6. Draw the basic circuit schematic of a classical three-opamp instrumentation amplifier. Briefly describe its operational principle with particular reference to the role of the two opamps constituting the input stage and the output opamp wired as differential amplifier.

7. What is the main advantage of using an opamp-based rectifier over conventional rectifier? With the help of relevant circuit schematics, explain the functional principle of (a) half wave rectifier that clips positive half cycles and (b) peak detector.

8. What is an absolute value circuit? Draw the circuit schematic of one such circuit configured around opamp and briefly describe its functional principle.

9. Draw the circuit diagram of (a) phase shifter circuit that can introduce a phase shift in the range of 0° to −150° in a sine wave input signal and (b) phase shifter circuit that can introduce a phase shift of 0° to +150° in a sine wave input signal.

10. What is the main advantage of using a comparator with hysteresis over a conventional comparator? Explain with the help of relevant transfer characteristics.

11. With the help of relevant circuit schematic of a non-inverting comparator with hysteresis, briefly describe its operation and draw its transfer characteristics.

12. What is a window comparator? Draw the circuit diagram of a window comparator that produces a high output for input signal inside the window and a low output for input outside the window.

13. Draw the circuit schematic of a suitable opamp-based circuit that can be used to convert input sine wave signal into a symmetrical square wave output and briefly describe its operation.

14. Draw the circuit diagram of a current-to-voltage converter using opamp. What type of feedback is used in this circuit? What decides the maximum value of feedback resistance to be used in the circuit?

15. Give a suitable circuit schematic for building a triangular waveform generator using opamps. Briefly describe its operation.

PROBLEMS

1. You are asked to choose an appropriate opamp type number for your inverting amplifier configuration that has been designed for a voltage gain of 10. The input is a sinusoidal signal with peak-to-peak amplitude of 2 V. If the highest expected input signal frequency is 50 kHz, what should be the slew rate of the chosen opamp?

2. Design an opamp-based current to voltage converter having a transresistance gain of 100,000.

3. Design a non-inverting zero-crossing detector with a hysteresis of 100 mV. If the opamp had output saturation voltages of ±10 V, determine the highest input frequency that would yield output waveform transition time of not more than 10% of half of the time period of input signal. Chosen opamp has slew rate of 10 V/μs.

4. Refer to the comparator circuit of Figure 17.82. Determine the duty cycle of the output waveform.

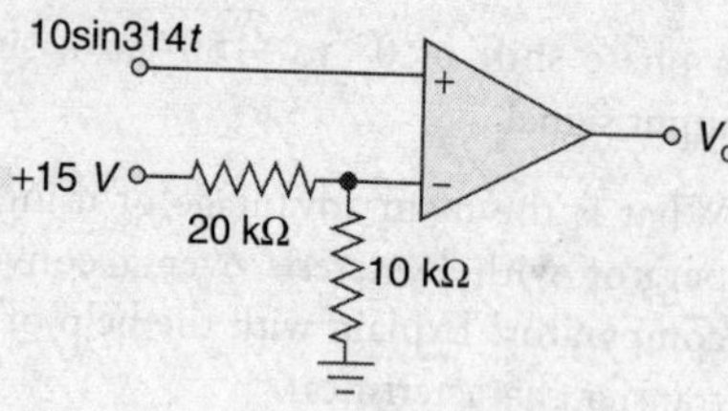

Figure 17.82 | Problem 4.

5. Figure 17.83 shows an inverting comparator with in-built hysteresis. Determine the peak-to-peak noise voltage that the comparator can withstand without false triggering given that LM 741 produces positive and negative saturation output of ±11 V for a power supply voltage of ±12 V.

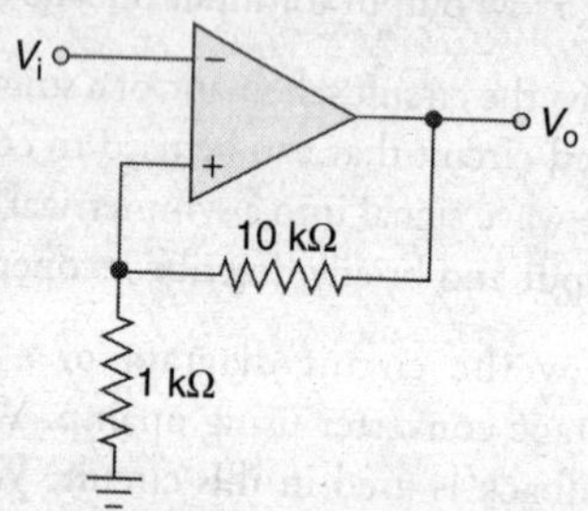

Figure 17.83 | Problem 5.

6. Refer to the opamp circuit of Figure 17.84. Identify the circuit and determine the output voltage.

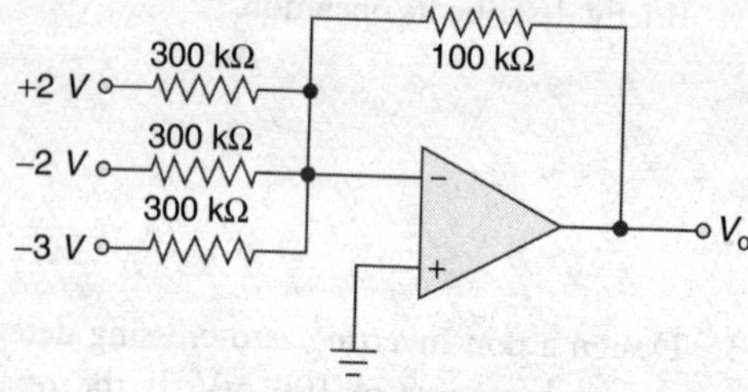

Figure 17.84 | Problem 6.

7. Determine the expression for the output voltage for the differentiator circuit of Figure 17.85.

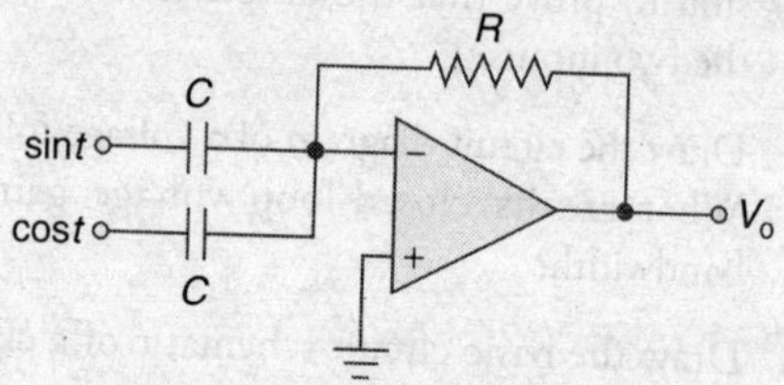

Figure 17.85 | Problem 7.

8. Identify the active filter circuit of Figure 17.86. Determine the cut-off frequency and voltage gain to DC.

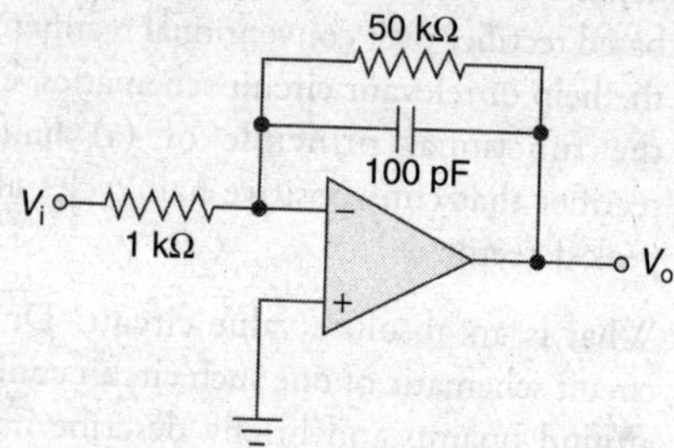

Figure 17.86 | Problem 8.

ANSWERS

Multiple-Choice Questions

1. (a)
2. (c)
3. (b)
4. (d)
5. (b)
6. (a)
7. (b)
8. (c)
9. (a)
10. (b)
11. (b)
12. (b)
13. (c)
14. (a)
15. (c)

Problems

1. 3.14 V/μs
2. Figure 17.87

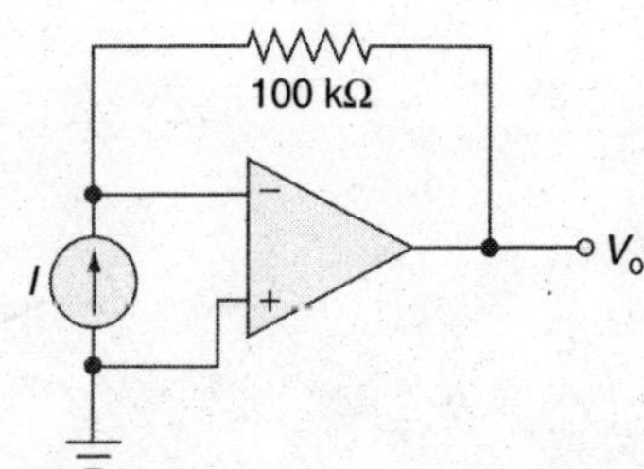

Figure 17.87 Solution to Problem 2.

3. Figure 17.88 with $R_2/R_1 = 199$, $f_{MAX} = 25$ kHz

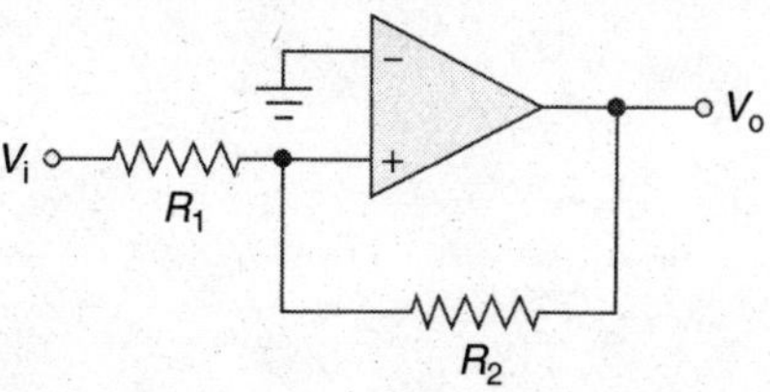

Figure 17.88 Solution to Problem 3.

4. 1/3
5. 2 V
6. Averager, 1 V
7. sin t − cos t
8. Low-pass filter, 31.84 kHz, 50

Index

α 77
α_{ac} 77
α cut-off frequency 364–365
β 80–81, 87
β_{ac} 81, 87
β cut-off frequency 363–364
γ 84–85
π-filter (see CLC filter)

1
1/f noise (see flicker noise)

7
74121 535
  Triggering circuits 535
74123 535, 536
  Triggering circuits 535, 536

A
Absolute value circuit 671–672
AC current gain (see β_{ac})
Acceptor atom (see trivalent atom)
Acceptor level 15
Active filter 680–685
  Band pass filter 682–683
  Band reject filter 683
  First-order filter 680–681
  Second-order filter 681–682
Active LCD display 288
  TFD display (see thin film diode display)
  TFT display (see thin film transistor display)
  Thin film diode display 288
  Thin film transistor display 288
Active region-BJT 71–73, 75–76, 80–81
  Common-base configuration 75–76
  Common-emitter configuration 80–81
A-GTO (see asymmetrical GTO thyristor)
Alloy-junction transistor 96, 97
Alpha (see α)
Ampere square seconds – diode 32
Ampere squared seconds – thyristor 231, 233
Amplification factor – FET 178,179
Amplifier bandwidth 303–304
Amplifier classification 423–425
  Current amplifier 423, 424
  Transconductance amplifier 423, 425
  Transresistance amplifier 423, 424, 425
  Voltage amplifier 423–424
Annular transistor 96, 98
Anode 25
APD (see avalanche photodiode)
Application circuits – photodiode 263–264, 265
Armstrong oscillator 479–481
  Basic configuration 480
  Series-fed configuration 481
  Shunt-fed configuration 480–481
Astable multivibrator 527, 531–534
  Schematic 532–533
  Timing waveforms 532–534
Asymmetrical GTO thyristor 241
Avalanche breakdown – transistor 88
Avalanche diode 49, 50
Avalanche multiplication 49
Avalanche photodiode 259, 261–262
Averager 662
Average AC resistance – diode 36

B
Band-pass filter 682–683
Band-reject filter 683
Bandwidth – amplifier 303–304
Bandwidth – opamp 636–638
Barkhausen criterion 458–459
Barrier potential 26
Base 70
Base current 72, 73
Base-spreading resistance 358–359
Base width modulation (see early effect)
Beta (see β)
Bias compensation 144–146
  Diode compensation 144–146
  Thermistor compensation 146
Bias stabilization 132–144
  Stability factor 133–144
Bipolar junction transistor 69–163
  BJT vs. Vacuum triode 70
  Configurations 73–85, 105–132
  Construction 70–71
  Bias compensation 144–146
  Bias stabilization 132–144
  Ebers-Moll model 86–87
  Fabrication techniques 96–98
  Lead identification 89–92
  Maximum rating 88, 89
  NPN transistor 70
  Operating point 103–105
  Operation 71–73
  Packages 89–92
  Phototransistor 94
  PNP transistor 70–71
  Power transistor 94–95
  Specifications 87–89

Switch 152–157
Testing 92–94
Thermal runway 146–152
Bipolar junction transistor – biasing 103
Bipolar junction transistor – configurations 73–85, 105–132
α 77
α_{ac} 77
β 80–81, 87
β_{ac} 81, 87
γ 84–85
Active region 71–73, 75–76, 80–81
Alpha (see α)
Base width modulation (see early effect)
Beta (see β)
Common-base configuration 73–78, 85, 128–130
Common-collector configuration 73, 83–85, 130–132
Common-emitter configuration 73, 78–83, 85, 105–128
Cut-off region 71, 76, 81
Early effect 74–75
Gamma (see γ)
Input characteristics 73–75, 78–79, 83, 84
Output characteristics 75–77, 79, 83, 84
Saturation region 76–77, 81
Bipolar junction transistor – fabrication techniques 96–98
Alloy-junction transistor 96, 97
Annular transistor 96, 98
Diffusion transistor 96, 97
Epitaxial transistor 96, 98
Grown-junction type transistor 96
Mesa transistor 97
Planar transistor 97
Point-contact transistor 96
Bipolar junction transistor – hybrid model 307–314
Graphical determination 312–314
Hybrid model for common-base configuration 308, 310
Hybrid model for common-collector configuration 308–309
Hybrid model for common-emitter configuration 307–308
Simplified hybrid model for common – base configuration 308, 310
Simplified hybrid model for common-collector configuration 308–309
Simplified hybrid model for common-emitter configuration 308
Bipolar junction transistor – specifications 87–89
β 87
β_{ac} 87
AC current gain (see β_{ac})
Breakdown voltage 88
DC current gain (see β)
Gain-bandwidth product 87, 88
h_{FE} (see β)
h_{fe} (see β_{ac})
Maximum ratings 88, 89
Power dissipation 88–89
Bipolar junction transistor – switch 152–157
Switching delays 153–154
Bipolar junction transistor – switching delays 153–154
Delay time 154
Fall time 154
Rise time 154
Storage time 154
Turn-ON time 154
Turn-OFF time 154
Bistable multivibrator 527–529
Schematic 527–529
Timing waveforms 527–529
BJT (see bipolar junction transistor)
Body resistance – diode 36
Bolometer 251, 252, 275, 276
Low temperature germanium bolometer 276
Metal bolometer 276
Thermistor bolometer 276
Boost regulator 613, 615–616
Circuit 615
Relevant waveforms 616
Break-over voltage – thyristor 231, 232
Breakdown diode 48–50
Avalanche diode 49, 50
Zener diode 49–50
Breakdown region – diode 29, 48
Bridge rectifier 550, 555–556
Brightness 278
Bubba oscillator 460, 467, 468
Buck regulator 613–614
Circuit 613
Relevant waveforms 614
Buck–boost regulator (see inverting regulator)
Buffered RC phase shift oscillator 465–466

C

Candela 252
Canonical form of amplifiers 458
Capacitor filter 559–561
Cascaded amplifier 333–338, 350–351, 378
BJT cascade amplifier 334–335
FET cascade amplifier 337
High-frequency response 378
Low-frequency response 350–351
Cascode amplifier 343–344
Cathode 25
Cathode ray tube display 279, 288–289
Advantages 289
Colored CRT display 288, 289
Disadvantages 289

Monochrome CRT display 288–289
CE short-circuit gain 362–366
β cut-off frequency 363–364
Short-circuit gain bandwidth product 363, 364
α cut-off frequency 364–365
Choke filter (see inductor filter)
Clamper 520–527, 669–670
Diode clamper 520–522
Negative clamper 520–521
Opamp-based clamper 669–670
Positive clamper 522
Clapp oscillator 479, 484–485
Class A amplifier 386, 393–405
Class A amplifier with direct coupled resistive load 393–397
Class A push–pull amplifier 393, 403–405
Transformer coupled class A amplifier 393, 397–403
Class A amplifier with direct coupled resistive load 393–397
Maximum efficiency 396
Output power 394–396
Class A push–pull amplifier 393, 403–405
Class AB amplifier 386, 387, 413
Class B amplifier 386–387, 405–413
Complementary-symmetry push–pull class B amplifier 405, 410, 411
Quasi-complementary push–pull class B amplifier 405, 410–412
Transformer-coupled push–pull amplifier 405, 406–410
Class C amplifier 386, 387, 388, 413–414
Tuned mode 414
Untuned mode 414
Class D amplifier 386, 388, 414–417
Full-bridge topology 416–417
Half-bridge topology 416–417
Class E amplifier 386, 388
Class F amplifier 386, 388
Class G amplifier 388
Class H amplifier 388
CLC filter 563
Clipper 514–520, 668–669
Diode clipper 514–515
Opamp-based clipper 668–669
CMOS devices 206–207
CMRR (see common mode rejection ratio)
Collector 70
Collector current 73
Collector-base junction 71
Collector-to-base bias configuration 105, 124–128
Advantages 126–127
DC analysis 124–126
Disadvantages 126–127
Load-line analysis 125–126
Colored CRT display 288, 289
Colpitt oscillator 479, 483–484
Colpitt oscillator configured around a BJT 483
Colpitt oscillator configured around an opamp 483
Common-base configuration 73–78, 85, 128–130
DC analysis 129
Load-line analysis 128–129
Common-collector configuration 73, 83–85, 130–132
Common-drain configuration 190–192
Common-emitter configuration 73, 78–83, 85, 105–128
Collector-to-base bias 105, 124–128
Emitter-bias 105, 110–115
Fixed-bias 105–110
Self-bias (see emitter-bias)
Voltage-divider bias with emitter-bias 105, 115–124
Common-gate configuration 192
Common mode rejection ratio 630, 636, 639, 640
Common-source configuration 183–190
Fixed-bias 183–185
Self-bias 183, 185–188
Voltage-divider 183, 188–190
Common mode gain 630, 639
Commutating capacitors 608
Comparator 643, 644, 672–676
Hysteresis 674–675
Window comparator 676
Zero-crossing detector 672–673
Complementary symmetry push–pull class B amplifier 405, 410–411
Conduction band 2
Conductivity 7
Conductor 1, 2, 3
Constant current source 630 631
Construction – bipolar junction transistor 70–71
Contact potential (see barrier potential)
Contact resistance – diode 36
Continuous mode-externally driven flyback converter 597–599
Contrast 278
Contrast ratio 278
Coupling coil 479
Critical rate of rise of OFF-state voltage – thyristor 231
Critical rate of rise of ON-state current – thyristor 231
Crossover distortion 409
Crowbar action 238–239, 571
CRT displays (see cathode ray tube displays)
Crystal oscillator 460, 488–493
Circuits 490–493
Frequency stability 490
Quartz crystal 489–490
Crystal oscillator circuits 490–493
Crystal-controlled Colpitt oscillator 491–492
Pierce oscillator 492–493

Current amplifier 423, 424
  Current gain 424
  Equivalent circuit 424
Current controllable device – thyristor 229–230
Current differencing opamp (see Norton opamp)
Current limiting 568–571
Current mirror 630–631
Current sampling 426, 427
Current-series feedback topology 434, 443–448
  Equivalent circuit 443, 444
  Gain 443–444
  Input resistance 444–445
  Output resistance 445
  Practical circuits 445–446
  Schematic arrangement 443, 444
Current-shunt feedback topology 434, 448–452
  Equivalent circuit 448, 449
  Gain 449
  Input resistance 449–450
  Output resistance 450
  Practical circuits 450–451
  Schematic arrangement 448, 449
Current-to-voltage converter 691–692
Cut-off region-BJT 71, 76, 81
  Common-base configuration 76
  Common-collector configuration 84
Cut-in voltage-diode 29

D

Dark current 56, 262
Darlington amplifier 338–343
DC current gain – transistor (see β)
Dee-star 252, 253
DE-MOSFET (see depletion MOSFET)
Depletion MOSFET 171–173, 192–194
  Biasing 192–194
  Characteristics curves 172, 173
  Construction 171
  N-channel depletion MOSFET 171–173
  Operation 172
  P-channel depletion MOSFET 171, 172
Depletion MOSFET – biasing configuration 192–194
Depletion region – diode 26
Desensitivity parameter 430
Detectivity 252, 253
DIAC 215, 229–230
Difference amplifier – opamp 661
Differential amplifier 629–634
Differential gain 630, 639
Differentiator 511, 513–514, 664–665
  Opamp-based differentiator 664–665
  RC differentiator circuit 511
  RL differentiator circuit 513–514
Diffusion capacitance – diode 37, 38
Diffusion current 20
Diffusion transistor 96, 97
  Mesa transistor 97
  Planar transistor 97
Digital IC-based monostable multivibrator 535, 536
  4098B 535
  74121 535
  74122 535
  74123 535, 536
  74221 535
Digital light processing technology 289, 290
Digital micromirror device 290
Diode 25–67
  Breakdown diode 48–50
  Capacitance 33, 37–38
  Dynamic V–I characteristics 45
  Equivalent circuits 38–43
  Forward bias 27
  Ideal diode 28
  Lead identification 58–59
  LED (see light-emitting diode)
  Light-emitting diode 54–55
  Load-line analysis 43–48
  P-junction 25–28
  Packages 58–59
  Parallel connection 57–58
  Photodiode 56, 57
  Point-contact diode 54
  Power diode 54
  Practical diode 29
  Resistance 33–37
  Reverse bias 27–28
  Schottky diode 53–54
  Series connection 56–57
  Specifications 31–33
  Testing 59–60
  Tunnel diode 51–53
  Varactor diode 50–51
  V–I characteristics 29–31
Diode capacitance 33, 37–38
  Diffusion capacitance 37, 38
  Space charge capacitance (see transition capacitance)
  Storage capacitance (see diffusion capacitance)
  Transition capacitance 37–38
Diode-equivalent circuits 38–43
  Ideal diode model 39–40
  Piecewise equivalent model 38–39
  Simplified equivalent model 39, 40
Diode ON resistance 29
Diode resistance 33–37
  Average AC resistance 36
  Dynamic resistance 33, 35–36

Static resistance 33, 34
Diode specifications 31–33
Ampere square seconds 32
Diode capacitance 33, 37–38
Diode resistance 33–37
Forward current 31
Forward recovery time 33
Forward voltage 31
Maximum average rectified current 32
Maximum junction temperature 32
Maximum power dissipation rating 32
Peak forward surge current 32
Peak inverse voltage (see reverse breakdown voltage)
Peak repetitive forward current 32
Power dissipation 32
Reverse breakdown voltage 29, 31, 32
Reverse current 32
Reverse recovery time 33
Reverse voltage 31
Diode – lead identification 58–59
Diode – packages 58–59
Diode – testing 59–60
Diodes – parallel connection 57–58
Diodes – series connection 56–57
Direct band gap semiconductor 6
Direct coupled amplifier 303, 304
Direct drive LCD display 285–286, 288
Discontinuous mode-externally driven flyback converter 597–599
Discrimination ratio 281
Display 249, 251, 278–290
Characteristics 278
Emerging technology 289–290
Types 278–290
Display characteristics 278
Brightness 278
Contrast 278
Contrast ratio 278
Legibility 278
Readability 278
Display types 278–290
Bar graph display 278, 279
Cathode ray tube display 279, 288–289
CRT (see cathode ray tube display)
Digital light processing technology 289, 290
DLP (see digital light processing technology)
Dot-matrix display 278–279
Electronic ink display 289, 290
FED (see field emission display)
Large displays 278, 279
LCD (see liquid crystal display)
LED (see light emitting diode)
Light-emitting diode 279–284
Liquid crystal display 279, 284–288
OLED (see organic light-emitting diode)
Organic light-emitting diode 289, 290
Plasma display 289, 290
Segmented display 278, 279
DLP (see digital light processing technology)
Donor energy level 11–12
Donor impurity atom (see pentavalent impurity atom)
Doping 10–12
Drain 166–167, 171, 172, 174
Drain resistance – FET 178
Dynamic drain resistance 178
Static drain resistance 178
Drain-source ON voltage 181
Drift current 20
Dual-gate MOSFET 204–205
Dynamic drain resistance-FET 178
Dynamic resistance-diode 33, 35–36
Dynamic V–I characteristics – diode 45

E

Early effect 74–75
Ebers-Moll model 86–87
Efficacy 250
Electron gun 288, 289
Electronic ink display 289, 290
Emitter 70
Emitter–base junction 71
Emitter-bias configuration 105, 110–115
Advantages 112–113
DC analysis 110–112
Disadvantages 112–113
Load-line analysis 112, 113
Emitter current 72, 73
Emitter-follower configuration (see common-collector configuration)
Emitter-follower regulator 548, 565–566, 567
Negative output 566
Positive output 565–566
Using Darlington amplifier (negative output) 566, 567
Using Darlington amplifier (positive output) 566
E-MOSFET (see enhancement MOSFET)
Energy band gap (see forbidden band gap)
Energy band diagram 2, 3, 4
Conductor 2, 3
Insulator 2
Semiconductor 4
Enhancement MOSFET 171, 173–178, 194–199
Biasing 194–199
Characteristic curves 174–176
Construction 173–174
N-channel enhancement MOSFET 173–176
Operation 173–174
P-channel enhancement MOSFET 173–174

Enhancement MOSFET-biasing configurations 194–199
Feedback biasing configuration 194–196
Voltage-divider biasing configuration 196–199
Epitaxial transistor 96, 98
Equivalent circuit – diode 38–43
Externally driven flyback converter 593, 594–604
Design procedure 599–602
Externally driven flyback DC-to-DC converter with pulse width modulation control 595
Off-line externally driven flyback AC-to-DC converter 596–597
Off-line multiplie output flyback DC-to-DC converter 596–597
Externally driven flyback DC-to-DC converter with pulse width modulation circuit 595
Externally driven push–pull converter 606
Extrinsic photoconductor 255
Extrinsic semiconductor 4, 10–18
N-type extrinsic semiconductor 10–14
P-type extrinsic semiconductor 14–18

F

FED (see field emission display)
Feedback amplifiers 423–456
Feedback network 426, 427, 428
Series connection 426, 427
Shunt connection 426, 428
Feedback topologies 434–452
Current-series feedback topology 434, 443–448
Current-shunt feedback topology 434, 448–452
Series-series feedback topology (see current-series feedback topology)
Series-shunt feedback topology (see voltage-series feedback topology)
Shunt-series feedback topology (see current-shunt feedback topology)
Shunt-shunt feedback topology (see voltage-shunt feedback topology)
Voltage-series feedback topology 434–439
Voltage-shunt feedback topology 434, 440–443
Fermi–Dirac probability function 8, 9, 13, 16–17
Intrinsic semiconductor 8, 9
N-type extrinsic semiconductor 13
P-type extrinsic semiconductor 16–17
Fermi level 8, 9, 13, 16–17
Intrinsic semiconductor 8, 9
N-type extrinsic semiconductor 13
P-type extrinsic semiconductor 16–17
Field effect transistor – applications 200–203
Amplifier 200
Analog switch 200
Current limiter 200, 201
Multiplexer 200
Oscillator 201
Voltage variable-resistor 200–201
Field effect transistor characteristic parameters 178–180
Amplification factor 178–179
Drain resistance 178
Transconductance 178–179
Field effect transistor – specifications 180–181
Drain source ON voltage 181
Forward transconductance 181
Gate leakage current 181
Input capacitance 181
ON-state drain current 181
Output capacitance 181
Output conductance 181
Pinch-off voltage 181
Power dissipation 180–181
Reverse gate-source breakdown voltage 180
Reverse transfer capacitance 181
Saturation drain current 181
Threshold voltage 181
Field effect transistor – testing 203–204
Field effect transistor – configurations 183–199
Junction field transistor configurations 183–192
Metal oxide semiconductor field effect transistor configuration 192–199
FET (see field effect transistor)
Field effect transistor 165–214
Applications 200–203
BJTs vs. FETs 165–166
Characteristic parameters 178–180
CMOS devices 206–207
Configurations 183–199
Dual-gate MOSFET 204–205
Insulated gate bipolar transistor 207–209
JFET (see junction field effect transistor)
Junction field effect transistor 166–171, 178–179, 180–182, 183–192, 203
Metal oxide semiconductor field effect transistor 171–183, 192–204
MOSFET (see metal oxide semiconductor field effect transistor)
Specifications 180–181
Testing 203–204
VMOS devices 205–206
Field emission display 289, 290
Filter 547, 548, 558–565
π-filter (see CLC filter)
Capacitor filter 559–561
Choke filter (see inductor filter)
CLC filter 563
Inductor filter 558–559
LC filter 561–563
First-order filter 680–681
High-pass filter 680–681

Low-pass filter 680–681
Fixed-bias configuration 105–110
Advantages 109
DC analysis 105–107
Disadvantages 109
Load-line analysis 107–109
Flicker noise 253, 254
Flux 250
Flyback converter 592, 593–604
Externally driven flyback converter 593, 594–604
Self-oscillating flyback converter 593–594
Flyback converter – operational modes 597–599
Continuous mode 597–599
Discontinuous mode 597–599
Foldback current limiting 569–571
Foot-candle 248
Forbidden bandgap 2
Forward bias – diode 27
Forward blocking state – PNPN diode 222
Forward converter 592, 604–605
Off-line forward converter 604–605
Forward current – diode 31
Forward recovery time – diode 33
Forward transconductance – FET 181
Forward voltage – diode 31
Fourth harmonic distortion component 392
Free electron 11
Frequency stability – oscillators 494–495
Full-bridge converter 608
Full-bridge topology – class D amplifier 416–417
Full-wave rectifier 550, 553–554, 556

G

Gain-bandwidth product – BJT 87, 88
Gain-bandwidth product – opamp 636
Gain stability – negative feedback 429, 430
Gamma (see γ)
Gate 166–167, 171, 172, 174
Gate leakage current 181
Gate turn-OFF thyristor 241
General-purpose opamp 643, 644
General-purpose precision linear voltage regulator 576–577
Generation-recombination noise 253, 254
Germanium 2–3
Germanium diode 29, 30
Giacoletto model (see hybrid-π model)
Grown-junction type transistor 96
GTO (see gate turn-OFF thyristor)

H

h-parameters 305–307
h_{11} 305, 306
h_{12} 305, 306
h_{21} 305, 306
h_{22} 305, 306–307
Open-circuit output admittance parameter (see h_{22})
Open-circuit reverse transfer voltage ratio parameter (see h_{12})
Short-circuit forward transfer current ratio parameter (see h_{21})
Short-circuit input impedance parameter (see h_{11})
h-parameters – BJT – graphical determination 312–314
h_{11} 305, 306
h_{12} 305, 306
h_{21} 305, 306
h_{22} 305, 306–307
Half-bridge converter 608
Half-bridge topology – class D amplifier 416–417
Half-wave rectifier 550, 552–553, 556
Hall coefficient 21
Hall effect 21–22
Hall voltage 21
Handling MOSFET 182–183
Harmonic distortion 389–393
Hartley oscillator 479, 481–482
Hartley oscillator configured using a BJT 481, 482
Hartley oscillator configured using an opamp 481, 482
Heat sink 95
h_f (see h_{21})
h_{fb} 308, 309, 310
h_{fc} 308, 309
h_{FE} (see β)
h_{fe} 81, 87, 307–308, 309, 313
h_i (see h_{11})
h_{ib} 308, 309, 310
h_{ic} 308, 309, 310
h_{ie} 307–308, 309, 312
High-frequency response of amplifiers 357–384
BJT amplifier 357–374
FET amplifier 374–378
Cascaded amplifier stages 378–380
High-frequency response of BJT amplifier 357–374
CC amplifier 371–374
CE amplifier 357–366
High-frequency response of cascaded amplifier stages 378–380
High-frequency response of common-collector transistor amplifier 371–374
High-frequency response of common-drain FET amplifier 377–378
High-frequency model for common-emitter transistor amplifier 357–366
CE short-circuit current gain 362–366
Hybrid-π conductances 358–361
Hybrid-π capacitances 361
Variation of hybrid-π parameters 361–362
High-frequency response of common-source FET amplifier 374–377
High-frequency response of FET amplifier 374–378
Common-drain amplifier 377–378
Common-source amplifier 374–377

High speed opamp 643, 644
h_o (see h_{22})
h_{ob} 308, 309, 310
h_{oc} 308, 309
ho_e 307–308, 309, 313–314
Holding current – PNPN diode 222, 223
Holding current – thyristor 231, 232
Holding voltage – PNPN diode 222, 223
Holding voltage – thyristor 231, 232
Hole 4
Hot-carrier diode (see Schottky diode)
h-parameter model 305–328
h_r (see h_{12})
h_{rb} 308, 309, 310
h_{rc} 308, 309
h_{re} 307–308, 309, 312–313
Hybrid model – bipolar junction transistor 307–314
  Common-base configuration 308, 310
  Common-collector configuration 308, 309
  Common-emitter configuration 307–308
  Graphical determination of h-parameters 312–314
  Relationship between h-parameters of different configurations 309
Hybrid model – bipolar junction transistor amplifier 314–319
  Current gain 315–316
  Input impedance 316
  Output admittance 317
  Voltage gain 316–317
Hybrid parameter model (see h-parameter model)
Hybrid parameters (see h-parameters)
Hybrid-π conductances 358–361
  Base-spreading resistance 358–359
  Conductance between terminals B′ and C (see feedback conductance)
  Conductance between terminals B′ and E (see input conductance)
  Conductance between terminals C and E 359–360
  Feedback conductance 359
  Input conductance 360
  Transconductance 361
Hybrid-π model 357–362
  Hybrid-π conductances 358–361
  Hybrid-π capacitances 361
  Variation of hybrid-π parameters 361–362
Hysteresis 530, 674–675

I

I^2t rating – diode (see ampere square seconds – diode)
I^2t rating – thyristor (ampere squared seconds – thyristor)
IC 723 576–577
  High positive output voltage regulator using IC 723 576–577
  Internal schematic 576
  Low positive output voltage regulator using IC 723 576–577
Ideal diode 28
Ideal diode model 39–40
Ideal opamp 635–636
IGBT (see insulated gate bipolar transistor)
Illuminance 252
Image intensifier 252, 273, 274
  Generation 0 device 274
  Generation 1 device 274
  Generation 2 device 274
  Generation 3 device 274
  Generation 4 device 274
Imaging sensor 252
Indirect band gap semiconductor 6
Inductor filter 558–559
Input bias current – opamp 642
Input capacitance – FET 181
Input characteristics – BJT 73–75, 78–79, 83, 84
  Common-base configuration 73–75
  Common-emitter configuration 78–79
  Common-collector configuration 83, 84
Input offset current – opamp 642
Input offset voltage – opamp 642
Input impedance – opamp 636, 641
Instrumentation opamp 643, 645–646, 687–689
Insulated gate bipolar transistor 207–209
Insulator 1–2
Integrated circuit multivibrator 535–542
  Digital IC-based monostable multivibrator 535, 536
  Timer IC-based multivibrator 535–540
Integrator 505–506, 512–513, 663–664
  RC integrator circuit 505–506
  RL integrator circuit 512–513
  Opamp-based integrator 663–664
Intensity 250
Internally compensated opamp 638
Intrinsic photoconductor 255
Intrinsic semiconductor 4–10
  Direct band gap semiconductor 6
  Intrinsic band gap semiconductor 6
Intrinsic stand-off ratio – UJT 216
Inverting amplifier – opamp 652–653
Inverting input – opamp 628
Inverting regulator 613, 616–617
Inverting zero-crossing detector 672–673
Isolation opamp 643, 646–647
  Optically coupled isolation opamp 646–647
  Transformer-coupled isolation opamp 646–647

J

JFET (see junction field effect transistor)
JFET – biasing configurations 183–192
  Common-drain configuration 190–192
  Common-gate configuration 192

Common-source configuration 183–190
JFET – characteristic curves 167–170
Ohmic region 168, 169
Pinch-off condition 168
Pinch-off voltage 168, 169
Saturation region 168, 169
Shockley's equation 169–170
Transfer characteristics 170
Voltage-controlled resistance region (see ohmic region)
JFET-parameters 178–179
Johnson noise 253–254
Junction field effect transistor 166–171, 178–179, 180–182, 183–192, 203
Biasing configurations 183–192
Characteristic curves 167–170
Characteristic parameters 178–180
Construction 166–167
Drain 166–167
Effect of temperature 170–171
Gate 166–167
JFET vs MOSFET 182
N-channel JFET 166–170
P-channel JFET 166–167, 170
Principle of operation 166–167
Source 166–167
Specifications 180–181
Testing 203

K

Knee voltage – diode (see cut-in voltage diode)

L

Lag-type RC phase shift oscillator 461–464
Lag-type T-network 470
Lagging-type phase shifter 685–686
Large signal amplifier 385–422
Characteristics 389–393
Class A amplifier 386, 393–405
Class AB amplifier 386, 387, 413
Class B amplifier 386–387, 405–413
Class C amplifier 386, 387, 388, 413–414
Class D amplifier 386, 388, 414–417
Class E amplifier 386, 388
Class F amplifier 386, 388
Class G amplifier 388
Class H amplifier 388
Classification 386–388, 393–417
Thermal management 417–418
Large signal amplifier – characteristics 389–393
Efficiency 389
Harmonic distortion 389–392
Large signal amplifier – classification 386–388, 393–417
Class A amplifier 386, 393–405
Class AB amplifier 386, 387, 413
Class B amplifier 386–387, 405–413
Class C amplifier 386, 387, 388, 413–414
Class D amplifier 386, 388, 414–417
Class E amplifier 386, 388
Class F amplifier 386, 388
Class G amplifier 388
Class H amplifier 388
Large signal bandwidth – opamp 638
Latching current – thyristor 231, 233
Latching optocoupler 291, 292
Law of mass action 18–19
LC filter 561–563
LC oscillator 460, 479–488
Armstrong oscillator 479–481
Clapp oscillator 479, 484–485
Colpitt oscillator 479, 483–484
Feedback coupling arrangements 479
Hartley oscillator 479, 481–482
LCD – response time 287
OFF time 287
ON time 287
LCD TFD display (see LCD thin film diode display)
LCD TFT display (see LCD thin film transistor display)
LCD thin film diode display 288
LCD thin film transistor display 279, 288
LCD (see liquid crystal display)
LDR (see photoconductor)
Lead identification – diode 58–59
Lead identification – BJT 89–92
Lead-type phase shifter 686
Lead-type RC phase shift oscillator 464–465
Lead-type T-network 466
LED (see light-emitting diode)
LED characteristic curves 280, 281
Directional characteristics 280, 281
Light output vs. Input current 280, 281
Spectral distribution curves 280, 281
V–I characteristics 280, 281
LED parameters 280–281
Candle power 280, 281
Forward voltage 280, 281
Peak spectral emission 280, 281
Radiant output power 280, 281
Spectral bandwidth 280, 281
Legibility 278
Light-dependent resistor (see photoconductor)
Light-emitting diode 54–55, 249, 251, 279–284
Characteristic curves 280, 281
Drive circuits 281–283
LEDs in parallel 282–283
LEDs in series 282–283
Parameters 280–281

Line regulation 582
Linear IC voltage regulator 576–582
 General-purpose precision linear voltage regulator 576–577
 Three-terminal regulator 577–582
Linear power supply 547–590
 Constituents 547–584
Linear power supply – constituents 547–584
 Filter 547, 548, 558–565
 Linear regulator 547, 548, 565–584
 Mains transformer 547, 548–550
 Rectifier 547, 548, 550–551
Linear regulator 547, 548, 565–584
 Linear current regulator 565
 Linear voltage regulator 548, 565–584
Linear voltage regulator 548, 565–584
 Emitter-follower regulator 548, 565–566, 567
 IC voltage regulator 576–582
 Series-pass regulator 548, 565, 566–571
 Shunt regulator 548, 565, 571–573
Liquid crystal 284
Liquid crystal display 279, 284–288
 Advantages 288
 Construction 284–285
 Disadvantages 288
 Driving a LCD 285–287
 Response time 287
 Types 285–288
Liquid crystal display – types 285–288
 Active LCD display 288
 Direct drive LCD 285–286, 288
 Multiplex drive LCD 285–287, 288
 Passive LCD display 288
 Reflective LCD display 287
 Transmissive LCD display 287, 288
 Transreflective LCD display 287, 288
LM 117/217/317 577–579
LM 120XX/320XX series 577
LM 137/237/337 577–579
LM 140XX/340XX-series 577
LM/MC 78XX-series 577–578
LM/MC 79XX-series 577–578
Load-line analysis – diode circuits 43–48
 AC applied voltage 44–46
 DC applied voltage 43–44
Load regulation 582
Long-tail pair 629
Loop gain 428, 429, 638
Low-frequency response – amplifier 304, 344–351
 BJT amplifier 345–347
 Cascaded amplifier 350–351
 FET amplifier 347–349
Low-frequency response – BJT amplifier 345–347
 Effect of bypass capacitor 345, 346–347
 Effect of input coupling capacitor 345
 Effect of output coupling capacitor 345, 346
Low-frequency response – cascaded amplifier 350–351
Low-frequency response – FET amplifier 347–349
 Effect of input coupling capacitor 347
 Effect of output coupling capacitor 347–348
 Effect of source capacitor 347–348
Low temperature germanium bolometer 276
Lower cut-off frequency 304
Lumen 250
Luminance 252
Luminous intensity (see photometric intensity)
Lux 252

M

Mains transformer 547, 548–550
 Design 548–549
 Primary current 549
 Secondary current 549
 Turns per volt 548
Majority carriers 12, 16
Maximum average rectified current – diode 32
Maximum junction temperature – diode 32
Maximum power dissipation rating – diode 32
Maximum power point 266
Maximum ratings – BJT 88, 89
MCP (see microchannel plate)
Meissner oscillator (see Armstrong oscillator)
Mesa transistor 97
Metal bolometers 276
Metal oxide semiconductor field effect transistor 171–183, 192–204
 Biasing configurations 192–199
 Characteristic parameters 178–180
 DE-MOSFET (see depletion MOSFET)
 Depletion MOSFET 171–173, 192–194
 E-MOSFET (see enhancement MOSFET)
 Enhancement MOSFET 171, 173–178, 194–199
 Handling 182–183
 JFET vs. MOSFET 182
 Specifications 180–181
 Testing 203–204
Microchannel plate 274
Miller's theorem 366–369
Minority carriers 12, 16
Monochrome CRT display 288–289
Monoshot (see monostable multivibrator)
Monostable multivibrator 527, 530–531, 532, 533, 535, 536, 537–540
 Digital IC-based monostable multivibrator 535, 536
 Quasi-stable state 531
 Retriggerable monostable multivibrator 531, 533
 Schematic 530–531

Timer IC 555 537–540
Timing waveforms 530–531, 532
MOSFET (see metal oxide semiconductor field effect transistor)
MOSFET-biasing configurations 192 – 199
Depletion MOSFET 192–194
Enhancement MOSFET 194–199
MPP (see maximum power point)
Multiplex drive LCD display 285–287, 288
Multistage amplifier (see cascaded amplifier)
Multivibrator 527–542
Astable multivibrator 527, 531–534
Bistable multivibrator 527–529
Integrated circuit multivibrator 535–542
Monostable multivibrator 527, 530–531, 532, 533, 535, 536, 537–540

N

N-channel depletion MOSFET 171–173
N-channel enhancement MOSFET 173–176
N-channel JFET 166–170
N-type extrinsic semiconductor 10–14
Narrow band-pass filter 682–683
Narrow band-rectifier filter 683
Negative clamper 520–521
Negative feedback 425–452
Advantages 429–431
Disadvantages 429, 432
Effect on gain 426–428, 429, 430
Feedback network 426, 427, 428
Feedback topologies 430–448
Negative feedback amplifiers 425–429
Sampling network 426, 427
Negative feedback – advantages 429–431
Bandwidth 429, 430–431
Gain stability 429, 430
Noise 429, 431
Non-linear distortion 429, 431
Negative feedback – disadvantages 429, 432
Gain 429
Input resistance 429, 432
Output resistance 429, 432
Negative feedback – topologies (see feedback topologies)
NEP (see noise equivalent power)
Night vision device 270
Noise photosensor (see photosensor noise)
Noise equivalent power 252, 253
Nomograms 600
Non-latching optocoupler 291, 292
Non-imaging sensor 252
Non-inverting amplifier – opamp 654–655
Non-inverting input – opamp 628
Non-inverting zero-crossing detector 672, 673
Non-linear amplifier – opamp 689–690
Non-linear distortion 431
Non-repetitive peak reserve voltage – diode 32
Non-repetitive peak reverse voltage – thyristor 230, 231
Non-sinusoidal oscillator 457–458
Norton opamp 643, 645
Notch filter 469
NPN transistor 69, 70, 71–73
Nyquist noise (see Johnson noise)

O

Off-line externally driven flyback AC-to-DC converter 596–597
Off-line forward converter 604–605
Opamp (see operational amplifier)
Offset drift – opamp 636, 642–643
Offset – opamp 636, 642–643
Input bias current 642
Input offset current 642
Input offset voltage 642
Output offset voltage 642
OLED (see organic light-emitting diode)
ON-state drain current 181
Opamp 627–699
Application circuits 651–699
Block diagram 628–634
Ideal opamp 635–636
Parameters 636–643
Practical opamp 634–635
Thenvenin's equivalent 634–636
Types 643–647
Opamp – application circuits 651–699
Absolute value circuit 671–672
Active filters 680–685
Averager 662
Clamper 669–670
Clipper 668–669
Comparator 672–676
Current-to-voltage converter 691–692
Difference amplifier 661
Differentiator 664–665
Instrumentation amplifier 687–689
Integrator 663–664
Inverting amplifier 652–653
Non-inverting amplifier 654–655
Non-linear amplifier 689–690
Peak detector 670–671
Phase shifter 685–687
Rectifier 667–668
Relaxation oscillator 690–691
Sine-wave oscillator 694
Summing amplifier 659–661
Voltage follower 655–656
Voltage-to-current converter 692–693

Opamp parameters 636–643
Bandwidth 636–638
CMRR (see common mode rejection ratio)
Common mode rejection ratio 636, 639, 640
Input impedance 636, 641
Offset drift 636, 642–643
Offset 636, 642–643
Open-loop gain 636, 638–639
Output impedance 636, 641
Power supply rejection ratio 636, 639–640
PSRR (see power supply rejection ratio)
Setting time 636, 641–642
Slew rate 636, 638
Opamp types 643–647
Current differencing opamp (see Norton opamp)
General-purpose opamp 643, 644
High speed opamp 643, 644
Instrumentation opamp 643, 645–646
Isolation opamp 643, 646–647
Norton opamp 643, 645
Comparator 643, 644
Power opamp 643, 644
Precision opamp 643, 644
Open circuit output admittance parameter (see h_{22})
Open circuit reverse transfer voltage ratio parameter (see h_{12})
Open loop gain – opamp 636, 638–639
Operating point (see quiescent point)
Operational amplifier (see opamp)
Optically coupled isolation opamp 646–647
Optocoupler 249, 250, 251, 291–297
Application circuits 293–294
Construction 291, 292
Parameters 291–293
Optocoupler parameters 291–293
Bandwidth 291, 293
CTR (see current transfer ratio)
Current transfer ratio 291
Forward optocoupling efficiency 291
Input current 291, 293
Isolation voltage 291
$V_{CE\ (max)}$ 293
Optoelectronic devices 249–301
Display 249, 251, 278–290
Optocoupler 249, 250, 251, 291–297
Photometric units 250–252
Photosensor 249, 250, 251, 252–277
Radiometric units 250–252
Optoelectronics 250
Optoisolator (see optocoupler)
Organic light-emitting diode 289, 290
Oscillator 457–501
Non-sinusoidal oscillator 457–458
Sinusoidal oscillator 457–501
Output capacitance-FET 181
Output characteristics-BJT 75–77, 79, 83, 84
Common-base configuration 75–77
Common-emitter configuration 79
Common-collector configuration 83, 84
Output conductance-FET 181
Output impedance – power supply 582
Output offset voltage 642
Output impedance – opamp 636, 641

P

P-channel depletion MOSFET 171, 172
P-channel enhancement MOSFET 173–174
P-channel JFET 166–167, 170
P-N junction 25–28
P-type extrinsic semiconductor 14–18
Packages – diode 58–59
Packages – BJT 89–92
Parallel connection – LEDs 282–283
Parallel connection – power converters 618–619
Parallel connection – thyristors 234–235
Parallel resonant frequency – crystal 489–490
Passive LCD display 288
PDP (see plasma display)
Peak detector – opamp 670–671
Peak forward surge current – diode 32
Peak inverse voltage – diode (see reverse breakdown voltage – diode)
Peak inverse voltage – rectifier 550, 551
Peak OFF-state voltage – thyristor (see break-over voltage – thyristor)
Peak point – UJT 217, 218
Peak repetitive forward current – diode 32
Peltier effect 418
Pentavalent impurity atom 11
Phase shifters 685–687
Lagging-type phase shifter 685–686
Lead-type phase shifter 686
Photoconductive mode 56, 262, 264, 265
Photoconductor 249, 251, 252, 255–259
Application circuits 255–258
Construction 255, 256
Extrinsic photoconductor 255
Intrinsic photoconductor 255
Material 255
Photodiode 56, 57, 249, 251, 252, 259–268
APD (see avalanche photodiode)
Application circuits 263–264, 265
Avalanche photodiode 259, 261–262
Modes 56, 262
Operation 262, 263–264, 265
Photoconductive mode 262, 264, 265
Photovoltaic mode 262, 263
PIN photodiode 259, 261
PN photodiode 259–260

Schottky photodiode 259, 261
Specifications 56
Spectral response 56, 259, 260
Types 259–262
V – I characteristics 262
Photodiode – operation 262, 263–264, 265
Photoconductive mode 262, 264, 265
Photovoltaic mode 262, 263
Photodiode types 259–262
APD (see avalanche photodiode)
Avalanche photodiode 259, 261–262
PIN photodiode 259, 261
PN photodiode 259–260
Schottky photodiode 259, 261
Photoelectric sensor 251, 252, 255–277
Image intensifiers 252, 273, 274
Imaging sensor 252
Non-imaging sensor 252
PhotoFET 249, 251, 252, 270, 271
Photo multiplier tube 248, 269–270
PhotoSCR 249, 251, 252, 270, 271–272
PhotoTRIAC 249, 251, 252, 270, 272
Photoconductor 249, 251, 252, 255–259
Photodiode 249, 251, 252, 259–268
Photoemissive sensor (see sensor with external photoeffect)
Phototransistor 249, 251, 252, 268–270
Photosensors with external photoeffect 251, 252, 273–277
Photosensors with internal photoeffect 251, 252, 255–273
Vacuum photodiode 252, 273
Photoemissive sensor (see photosensors with external photoeffect)
PhotoFET 249, 251, 252, 270, 271
Photometric flux 250
Photometric intensity 250–252
Photometric units 250–252
Photometry 250
Photomultiplier tube 252, 273–274
Photoresistor (see photoconductor)
PhotoSCR 249, 251, 252, 270, 271–272
Photosensor 249, 250, 251, 252–277
Characteristic parameters 252–254
Photoelectric sensor 251, 252, 255–277
Thermal sensor 251, 252, 275–277
Photosensor with external photoeffect 252, 273–277
Image Intensifier 252, 273, 274
Photomultiplier tube 252, 273–274
PMT (see photomultiplier tube)
Vacuum photodiode 252, 273
Photosensor – characteristic parameters 252–254
1/f noise (see flicker noise)
Dee-star 252, 253
Detectivity 252, 253
Flicker noise 253, 254
Generation-recombination noise 253, 254
Johnson noise 253–254
NEP (see noise equivalent power)
Noise 252, 253–254
Noise equivalent power 252, 253
Nyquist noise (see Johnson noise)
Quantum efficiency 252, 253
Quantum yield (see quantum efficiency)
Response time 252, 253
Responsivity 252, 253
Rise time 253
Sensitivity 252
Shot noise 253, 254
Spectral response 252, 254
Thermal noise (see Johnson noise)
Time constant 253
Photosensor – noise 252, 253–254
1/f noise (see flicker noise)
Flicker noise 253, 254
Generation-recombination noise 253, 254
Johnson noise 253–254
Nyquist noise (see Johnson noise)
Shot noise 253, 254
Thermal noise (see Johnson noise)
Phototransistor 94, 249, 251, 252, 268–270
Application circuits 269
PhotoTRIAC 249, 251, 252, 270, 272
Non-zero crossing photoTRIAC 272
Zero crossing photoTRIAC 272
Photovoltaic mode 58, 262, 263
Piecewise equivalent model – diode 38–39
Pierce oscillator 492–493
PIN photodiode 259, 261
Pinch-off voltage-JFET 168, 169
Pinch-off voltage-FET 181
Planar transistor 97
Plasma display 289, 290
PMT (see photomultiplier tube)
P-N junction 25–28
PN photodiode 259–260
PNP transistor 69, 70–71
PNPN diode 215, 220–227
Characteristics 222–223
Construction 220–221
Forward blocking state 222
Holding current 222, 223
Holding voltage 222, 223
Material 222
Operation 220–222
Rate effect 226–227
Relaxation oscillator 224–225
Saturation region 222
Transition region 222

Point-contact diode 54
Point-contact transistor 96
Polarizer 284
Positive clamper 522
Positive feedback 458, 459
Power amplifier (see large signal amplifier)
Power amplifier – thermal management 417–418
  Heat sink 418
  Thermoelectric coolers 418
Power converters – parallel connection 618–619
Power converters – series connection 618
Power derating curve – BJT 95, 147
Power diode 54
Power dissipation – BJT 88–89, 146–147
Power dissipation – diode 32
Power dissipation – FET 180–181
Power opamp 643, 644
Power supply rejection ratio – opamp 636, 639–640
Power transistor 94–95, 417
Practical diode 29
Practical opamp 634–635
Precision opamp 643, 644
Programmable unijunction transistor 241–242
  Construction 241–242
  V–I characteristics 242
PSRR (see power supply rejection ratio)
Punch-through effect (see Reach-through effect-BJT)
Push–pull amplifier 403
Push–pull converter 592, 605–612
  Design procedure 608–611
  Externally driven push–pull converter 606
  Full-bridge converter 608
  Half-bridge converter 608
  Self oscillating push–pull converter with voltage multiplier chain 606–607
  Self-oscillating two-transistor one transformer push–pull converter 605–606
  Self-oscillating two transistor, two transformer push–pull converter 607
Push–pull converter with voltage multiplier chain 606–607
Push–pull converter – design procedure 608–611
PUT (see programmable unijuntion transistor)
Pyroelectric sensor 251, 252, 275, 276–277
  Current mode pyroelectric sensor 277
  Voltage mode pyroelectric sensor 277

Q

Q-point (see operating point)
Quadrature oscillator 460, 468–469
Quantum efficiency 252, 253
Quantum of feedback 424
Quantum yield (see quantum efficiency)
Quartz crystal 489–486
  AC equivalent circuit 489
  Parallel resonant frequency 489–490
  Resonant frequencies 489–490
  Series resonant frequency 489–490
Quasi-complementary push–pull class B amplifier 405, 410 – 412
Quasi-stable state 531
Quiescent point 44, 103–105

R

Radiant incidence 252
Radiant – sterance 252
Radiometric flux 250
Radiometric intensity 250
Radiometric units 250–252
Radiometry 250
Rate effect – PNPN diode 226–227
Ratio of rectification 550, 551
RC-coupled amplifier 303–304
RC differentiator circuit 511
RC high pass filter 509–512
  As differentiator 511
  Frequency response 509–510
  Lower 3 dB cut-off frequency 509–510
  Response to pulse input 510
RC integrator circuit 505–506
RC low pass filter 503–509
  As integrator 505–506
  Frequency response 503–504
  Response to pulse input 505
  Response to step input 504–505
  Upper 3 dB cut-off frequency 504
RC oscillator 460, 461–475
  Bubba oscillator 460, 467–468
  Quadrature oscillator 460, 468–469
  RC phase shift oscillator 460, 461–466
  Twin-T oscillator 460, 469–471
  Wien bridge oscillator 460, 471–475
RC phase shift oscillator 460, 461–466
  Buffered RC phase shift oscillator 465–466
  Lag-type RC phase shift oscillator 461–464
  Lead-type RC phase shift oscillator 464–465
  Limitations 465
Reach-through effect – BJT 88
Readability 278
Rectifier 547, 548, 550–557, 667–668
  Bridge rectifier 550, 555–556
  Characteristic parameters 550–551
  Full-wave rectifier 550, 553–554, 556
  Half-wave rectifier 550, 552–553, 556
  Opamp-based rectifier 667–668
Rectifier – characteristic parameters 550–551
  Peak inverse voltage 550, 551
  PIV (see peak inverse voltage)

Ratio of rectification 550, 551
Ripple factor 550–551
Ripple frequency 550
Transformer utilization factor 550, 551
TUF (see transformer utilization factor)
Reflective LCD display 283
Regulated power supply 547–625
Linear power supply 547–590
Parameters 582–584
Switched mode power supply 591–625
Regulated power supply parameters 582–584
Line regulation 582
Load regulation 582
Output impedance 582
Ripple rejection factor 582–583
Relaxation oscillator – opamp 690–691
Relaxation oscillator-UJT 218–219
Repetitive peak OFF-state voltage – thyristor 231, 232
Repetitive peak inverse voltage – diode 32
Repetitive peak reverse voltage – thyristor 230, 231
Response time – photosensor 252, 253
Rise time 253
Time constant 253
Resonant frequency – crystal 489–490
Parallel resonant frequency 489–490
Series resonant frequency 489–490
Responsivity 252, 253
Retriggerable monostable multivibrator 531, 533
Reverse active region – BJT 71
Reverse bias – diode 27–28
Reverse breakdown voltage – diode 29, 31, 32
Non-repetitive peak inverse voltage 32
Repetitive peak inverse voltage 32
Reverse current – diode 32
Reverse gate-source breakdown voltage – FET 180
Reverse leakage current – diode (see reverse saturation current – diode)
Reverse recovery time – diode 33
Storage time 33
Transition time 33
Reverse saturation current – diode 27, 28, 29, 30, 31
Reverse transfer capacitance – FET 181
Reverse voltage – diode 31
Ringing choke-type flyback converter (see self-oscillating flyback converter)
Ripple factor 550–551
Ripple frequency 550
Ripple rejection factor 582–583
Rise time – amplifier 381
RL differentiator circuit 513–514
RL integrator circuit 512–513

S

Sag amplifier (see tilt amplifier)
Sampling network 426, 427
Current sampling 426, 427
Voltage sampling 426, 427
Saturation drain current – FET 181
Saturation region – BJT 71, 76–77, 81
Common-base configuration 76–77
Common-emitter configuration 81
Saturation region – PNPN diode 222
SBS (see silicon bilateral switch)
Schmitt trigger 529–530
Transfer characteristics 530
Schottky diode 53–54
Schottky photodiode 259, 261
SCR (see silicon controlled rectifier)
Second harmonic distortion 390, 392
Second-order filter 681–682
High pass filter 681
Low pass filter 681
Seeback effect 275
Self-bias configuration (see emitter-bias configuration)
Self-oscillating flyback converter 593–594
Self-oscillating push–pull converter with voltage multiplier chain 606–607
Self-oscillating two-transistor one-transformer push–pull converter 605–606
Self-oscillating two-transistor two transformer push–pull converter 607
Semiconductor 1, 2–20
Extrinsic semiconductor 4, 10–18
Intrinsic semiconductor 4–10
Semi-log amplifier 689, 690
Series connection – LEDs 282–283
Series connection – power converters 618
Series connection – thyristors 234
Series resonant frequency – crystal 489–490
Series-fed Armstrong oscillator 481
Series-pass regulator 548, 565, 566–571
Current limiting 568–571
Foldback current limiting 569–571
Series-pass regulator using BJT as error amplifier 567–568
Series-pass regulator using opamp as error amplifier 568
Series-pass regulator with foldback current limiting 570–571
Series-pass regulator with overload protection 568–569
Series-series feedback topology (see current-series feedback topology)
Series-shunt feedback topology (see voltage-series feedback topology)
Settling time – opamp 636, 641–642
S-GTO (see symmetrical GTO thyristor)
Shockley diode (see PNPN diode)
Shockley's diode equation 29
Shockley's equation – JFET 169–170
Short-circuit forward transfer current ratio parameter (see h_{21})

Short-circuit gain bandwidth product – BJT 363, 364
Short circuit input impedance parameter (see h_{11})
Shorted emitter construction – thyristors 232
Shot noise – photosensor 253, 254
Shunt regulator 548, 565, 571–573
  Opamp-based shunt regulator 572–573
  Shunt regulator with Darlington arrangement 572
Shunt-fed Armstrong oscillator 480–481
Shunt-series feedback topology (see current-shunt feedback topology)
Shunt-shunt feedback topology (see voltage-shunt feedback topology)
Silicon 2–3
Silicon bilateral switch 215, 229
Silicon controlled rectifier 215, 227–229, 235–240
  Applications 235–240
  Breakover voltage 227
  Construction 227
  Gate-triggering characteristics 228–229
  Operation 227
  V–I characteristics 228
Silicon diode 29, 30
Silicon unilateral switch 215, 220
Simplified hybrid model – bipolar junction transistor amplifier 320–328
  Common-base configuration 325–326
  Common-collector configuration 323–325
  Common-emitter configuration 320–323
Simplified equivalent model – diode 39, 40
Sine-wave oscillator (see sinusoidal oscillator)
Sinusoidal oscillator 457–501
  Barkhausen criterion 458–459
  Crystal oscillator 460, 488–493
  Frequency stability 494–495
  Initiation 459
  LC oscillator 460, 479–488
  RC oscillator 460, 461–475
  Types 460–461
  Voltage-controlled oscillator 493–494
Sinusoidal oscillator – types 460–494
  Crystal oscillator 460, 488–493
  LC oscillator 460, 479–488
  RC oscillator 460, 461–475
  Voltage-controlled oscillator 493–494
Slew rate 636, 638
Small signal analysis 305–355
Small signal analysis – BJT amplifiers 314–328
Small signal analysis – FET amplifiers 328–333
  Common-drain FET amplifier 330–331
  Common-source FET amplifier 329–330
Small signal bandwidth – opamp 636–638
SMPS (see switched mode power supply)
Solar cell 264–266
Solar cell efficiency 266
Source 166–167, 171, 172, 174
Space charge capacitance – diode (see transition capacitance – diode)
Stability factor 133–144
  $S_{I_{CO}}$ 133, 134–136, 140
  $S_{V_{BE}}$ 133, 136–138, 140
  S_{β} 133, 134, 138–140
State drive LCD (see direct drive LCD)
Static drain resistance – FET 178
Static resistance – diode 33, 34
Step-down regulator (see buck regulator)
Step-up regulator (see boost regulator)
Storage capacitance – diode (see diffusion capacitance-diode)
Summing amplifier – opamp 659–661
Summing differentiator – opamp 665
Summing integrator – opamp 664
Super beta amplifier (see Darlington amplifier)
SUS (see silicon unilateral switch)
Switched mode power supply 591–625
  Linear vs. Switched mode power supplies 592
  Parallel connection – power converters 618–619
  Series connection – power converters 618
  Switching regulators 613–617
  Types 592–612
Switched mode power supply – types 592–612
  Flyback converter 592, 593–604
  Forward converter 592, 604–605
  Push–pull converter 592, 605–612
Switching regulator 613–617
  Boost regulator 613, 615–616
  Buck regulator 613–614
  Buck-boost regulator (see inverting regulator)
  Inverting regulator 613, 616–617
  Step-down regulator (see buck regulator)
  Step-up regulator (see boost regulator)
  Three-terminal switching regulator 617
Switching time constant – diode 38
Symmetrical GTO thyristor 241

T

Tail current 629
Testing – BJT 92–94
TFD display (see thin film diode display)
TFT display (see thin film transistor display)
Thenvenin's equivalent of an amplifier 634
Thenvenin's equivalent of an ideal opamp 635–636
Thenvenin's equivalent of an opamp 634–635
Thermal noise (see Johnson noise)
Thermal management – large signal amplifiers 417–418
Thermal resistance – BJT 147
Thermal runway – BJT 146–152
Thermal sensor 251, 252, 275–277
  Bolometer 251, 252, 275, 276

Pyroelectric sensor 251, 252, 275, 276–277
Thermocouple 251, 252, 275–276
Thermopile 251, 252, 275–276
Thermal shutdown – linear power supply 571
Thermistor bolometer 276
Thermocouple 251, 252, 275–276
Thermoelectric cooler 418
Thermopile 251, 252, 275–276
Thin film diode display 288
Thin film transistor display 288
Third harmonic distortion 392
Three-terminal linear regulator 577–582
As constant current source 578
Boosting current delivery capability 579–580
LM 117/217/317 577–579
LM 120XX/320 XX-series 577
LM 140XX/340XX-series 577
LM/MC 78XX-series 577–578
LM/MC 79XX-series 577–578
LM137/237/337 577–579
Three-terminal switching regulator 617
Threshold voltage – diode (see cut-in voltage-diode)
Threshold voltage – FET 181
Thyristor 215, 220–241
Applications 235–240
Current controllable devices 233–234
DIAC 215, 229–230
Gate-turn-OFF thyristor 241
GTO thyristor (see gate-turn OFF thyristor)
Parallel connection 234–235
Parameters 230–233
PNPN diode 215, 220–227
SBS (see silicon bilateral switch)
SCR (see silicon controlled rectifier)
Series connection 234
Silicon bilateral switch 211, 225
Silicon controlled rectifier 215, 227–229, 235–240
Silicon unilateral switch 211, 216
SUS (see silicon unilateral switch)
TRIAC 215, 229–230
Thyristor – applications 235–240
AC power control 238
Bistable multivibrator 236
Crowbar protection 238–239
Full-wave controlled rectifier 236–237
Half-wave controlled rectifier 236, 237
Pulse generator 235
Thyristor – parameters 230–233
Ampere squared seconds rating 231, 233
Breakover voltage 231, 232
Critical rate of rise of OFF-state voltage 231, 232
Critical rate of rise of ON-state current 231, 232
Holding current 231, 232
Holding voltage 231, 232
I^2t rating (see ampere squared seconds rating)
Latching current 231, 233
Non-repetitive peak reverse voltage 230, 231
Peak OFF-state voltage (see break-over voltage)
Repetitive peak OFF-state voltage 231, 232
Repetitive peak reverse voltage 230, 231
Tickler coil 479
Tickler oscillator (see Armstrong oscillator)
Tilt amplifier 381–382
Timer IC 555 535–540
Astable multivibrator 537, 538
Internal construction 535–537
Monostable multivibrator 537–540
Total harmonic distortion 392
Transconductance amplifier 423, 425
Equivalent circuit 425
Gain parameter 425
Transconductance – BJT 361
Transconductance – FET 178–179
Transfer characteristics – JFET 170
Transformer coupled amplifier 303–304
Transformer coupled class A amplifier 393, 397–403
Advantages 397
Disadvantages 401
Efficiency 400
Output power 399–400
Variation of distortion with load 401
Variation of output-power with load 401
Transformer coupled isolation opamp 646–647
Transformer coupled push–pull class B amplifier 405, 406–410
Conversion efficiency 406–408
Crossover distortion 409
Harmonic distortion 409
Transformer utilization factor 550, 551
Transition capacitance – diode 37–38
Transition region – PNPN diode 222
Transmissive LCD display 287, 288
Transreflective LCD display 287, 288
Transresistance amplifier 423, 424, 425
Equivalent circuit 424, 425
Gain parameter 424
TRIAC 215, 229–230
Triangular waveform generator 691
Trivalent atom 11, 14–15
TUF (see transformer utilization factor)
Tunable diode (see varactor diode)
Tuned class C amplifier 414
Tunnel diode 51–53
Twin-T oscillator 460, 469–471
Magnitude response 470–471
Phase response 470–471

U

UJT (see unijunction transistor)
Uncompensated opamp 638
Unijunction transistor 215–220
  Construction 216
  Intrinsic stand-off ratio 216
  Operational principle 217–218
  Peak point 217, 218
  Relaxation oscillator 218–219
  Valley point 217, 218
  V – I characteristic curve 217–218
Unity gain crossover frequency – opamp (see gain bandwidth product – opamp)
Universal diode equation (see Shockley's diode equation)
Untuned class C amplifier 414
Upper cut-off frequency 304

V

Vacuum photodiode 252, 273
Vacuum triode 70
Valence band 2
Valence electron 1–2
Valley point – UJT 217, 218
Varactor diode 50–51
Variable voltage capacitance diode (see varactor diode)
Varicap (see varactor diode)
VCO (see voltage-controlled oscillator)
V – I characteristic – diode 29–31
  Temperature dependence 30–31
V – I characteristics – photodiode 262
Virtual earth 652
VMOS devices 205–206
Voltage amplifier 423–424
  Equivalent circuit 423–424
  Voltage gain 423–424
Voltage-controlled oscillator 493–494
  Hartley oscillator 493, 494
Voltage-follower 655–656
Voltage regulator 50, 547, 548, 565–584, 613–617
  Linear voltage regulator 548, 565–584
  Switching regulator 613–617
Voltage sampling 426, 427
Voltage-divider bias with emitter-bias configuration 105, 115–124
  Advantages 119
  DC analysis 116–118
  Disadvantages 119
Voltage-series feedback topology 434–439
  Equivalent circuit 434, 435
  Gain 434
  Input resistance 434–435
  Output resistance 435–436
  Practical circuits 436–437
  Schematic arrangement 434
Voltage-shunt feedback topology 434, 440–443
  Equivalent circuit 440
  Gain 440
  Input resistance 441
  Output resistance 441
  Practical circuits 441–442
  Schematic arrangement 440
Voltage-to-current converter 692–693

W

Watt 246
Wien bridge oscillator 460, 471–475
  Basic oscillator 471–473
  Distortion 473
  Wien bridge oscillator with automatic gain control 474–475
  Wien bridge oscillator with non-linear feedback 473
  Wien bridge oscillator with non-linear resistor 473–474
Window comparator 676

Z

Zener diode 49–50
Zero-crossing detector 672–673
  Inverting zero-crossing detector 672–673
  Non-inverting zero-crossing detector 672
Wave shaping circuit 503
  RC low-pass filter 503–509
  RC high-pass filter 509–512
  RL differentiator circuit 513–514
  RL differentiator circuit 512–513
  RL integrator circuit 512–513
  Diode clipper circuit 514–520
  Diode clamper circuit 520–527
  Multivibrators 527–542